Sentencing and Penal Policy in Canada

Cases, Materials, and Commentary

THIRD EDITION

ALLAN MANSON
Faculty of Law, Queen's University

PATRICK HEALY
Cour du Québec, Montréal

GARY TROTTER
Superior Court of Justice (Ontario)

JULIAN ROBERTS
Faculty of Law, Oxford University

DALE IVES
Public Prosecution Services Canada

emond

Toronto, Canada
2016

Emond Montgomery Publications Limited
60 Shaftesbury Avenue
Toronto ON M4T 1A3
http://www.emond.ca/lawschool

Printed in Canada.
Reprinted March 2020

We acknowledge the financial support of the Government of Canada. Canadä

Emond Montgomery Publications has no responsibility for the persistence or accuracy of URLs for external or third-party Internet websites referred to in this publication, and does not guarantee that any content on such websites is, or will remain, accurate or appropriate.

Vice president, publishing: Anthony Rezek
Publisher: Danann Hawes
Managing editor, development: Kelly Dickson
Senior editor, production: Jim Lyons
Production supervisor: Laura Bast
Copy editor: Nancy Ennis
Proofreaders: David Handelsman, Cindy Fujimoto
Permissions editor: Lisa Brant
Typesetters: Nancy Ennis, Tara Agnerian

Library and Archives Canada Cataloguing in Publication

Manson, Allan, author
    Sentencing and penal policy in Canada : cases, materials, and commentary / Allan Manson (Faculty of Law, Queen's University), Patrick Healy (Cour du Québec, Montréal), Gary Trotter (Superior Court of Justice (Ontario)), Julian Roberts (Faculty of Law, Oxford University), Dale Ives (Faculty of Law, University of Western Ontario). — Third edition.

Includes bibliographical references.
ISBN 978-1-55239-655-1 (hardback)

    1. Sentences (Criminal procedure)—Canada.   2. Sentences (Criminal procedure)—Canada—Cases.   3. Alternatives to imprisonment—Canada.   I. Healy, Patrick, author II. Roberts, Julian V., author   III. Trotter, Gary T., 1961-, author   IV. Ives, Dale, author   V. Title.

KE9355 M35 2017   345.71'0772   C2016-903526-3
KF9685 M35 2017

Acknowledgments

A book of this nature borrows heavily from other published material. We have attempted to request permission from, and to acknowledge in the text, all sources of such material. We wish to make specific references here to the authors, publishers, journals, and institutions that have generously given permission to reproduce in this text works already in print. If we have inadvertently overlooked an acknowledgment or failed to secure a permission, we offer our sincere apologies and undertake to rectify the omission in the next edition.

Cambridge University Press   RA Duff, *Trials and Punishments* (Cambridge: University of Cambridge Press, 1986). Copyright © 1986 Cambridge University Press. Reprinted with permission.

Department of Justice   *Victim Impact Statements at Sentencing: Judicial Experiences and Perceptions—A Survey of Three Jurisdictions*. <http://www.justice.gc.ca/eng/rp-pr/cj-jp/victim/rr06_vic3/rr06_vic3.pdf>. Department of Justice Canada, March 2006. Reproduced with the permission of the Minister of Public Works and Government Services Canada, 2016.

Library and Archives Canada   *Report on Aboriginal Peoples and Criminal Justice: Aboriginal Peoples and Criminal Justice* © Government of Canada. Reproduced with the permission of Library and Archives Canada (2016).

Manchester University Press   M Tonry, "Proportionality, Parsimony, and Interchangeability of Punishments" in RA Duff, S Marshall, RE Dobash & RP Dobash, eds, *Penal Theory and Practice: Tradition and Innovation in Criminal Justice* (Manchester: Manchester University Press, 1994). Reprinted with permission.

Minister of Public Works and Government Services Canada   "Recidivism Among Homicide Offenders" (1992) 4:2 Forum on Corrections Research 7. © Source: Correctional Service Canada, FORUM on Corrections Research, Volume 4, Number 2 (1992). Reproduced with the permission of the Minister of Public Works and Government Services Canada, 2016.

Oxford University Press   RA Duff, *Punishment, Communication, and Community* (Oxford: Oxford University Press, 2001). Reprinted with permission.

Oxford University Press   C Slobogin, *Risk Assessment* in J Petersilia & K Reitz, eds, *The Oxford Handbook of Sentencing and Corrections* (New York: Oxford University Press, 2012). Reprinted by permission of Oxford University Press.

Oxford University Press   CL Ten, *Crime, Guilt and Punishment* (Oxford: Clarendon Press, 1987). Reprinted by permission of Oxford University Press.

Oxford University Press   A von Hirsch, *Censure and Sanctions* (Oxford: Oxford University Press, 1996). Reprinted with permission.

Privy Council Office   Royal Commission on Aboriginal Peoples, *Bridging the Cultural Divide: A Report on Aboriginal People and Criminal Justice in Canada* (Ottawa: Supply and Services Canada, 1996). Permission granted by the Privy Council Office © Her Majesty the Queen in Right of Canada (2016).

Public Safety Canada   Public Safety Canada, *2014 Corrections and Conditional Release Statistical Overview* (Ottawa: Public Safety Canada, 2015). Reprinted with permission.

Queen's Printer for Ontario   *Report of the Attorney General's Advisory Committee on Charge Screening, Disclosure, and Resolution Discussions* (Honourable GA Martin, QC, Chair) (Toronto: Queen's Printer for Ontario, 1993). © Queen's Printer for Ontario, 2004. Reproduced with permission.

Stanford University Press   Carol Streiker, "Tempering or Tampering: Mercy and the Administration of Criminal Justice" in Austin Sarat and Nasser Hussain, eds, *Forgiveness, Mercy and Clemency* (Stanford, Cal: Stanford University Press, 2007). Copyright © 2007 by the Board of Trustees of the Leland Stanford Jr University. Reprinted with permission.

Taylor and Francis   N Lacey, *State Punishment: Political Principles and Community Values* (London: Routledge, 1988). Reproduced with permission of Taylor and Francis Books UK.

Thomson Reuters Canada Limited   Doob, Webster & Manson, "Zombie Parole: The Withering of Conditional Release in Canada" (2014) 61 Crim LQ 301. Reprinted with permission.

Thomson Reuters Canada Limited   JV Roberts, "Victim Impact Statements: Recent Developments and Research Findings" (2003) 47 Crim LQ 365. Reprinted with permission.

Thompson Reuters (Professional) UK Limited   E Erez, "Who's Afraid of the Big Bad Victim? Victim Impact Statements as Victim Empowerment *and* Enhancement of Justice" [1999] Crim L Rev 545. Reprinted with permission.

University of British Columbia Press   RG Green, *Justice in Aboriginal Communities: Sentencing Alternatives* (Saskatoon: Purich Publishing, 1998). Reprinted with permission of the Publisher from Justice in Aboriginal Communities by R.G. Green © University of British Columbia Press 1998. All rights reserved by the Publisher.

University of Chicago Press   Peter Scharff Smith, "The Effects of Solitary Confinement on Prison Inmates: A Brief History and Review of the Literature" (2006) 34 Crime & Justice Rev 441. Reprinted with permission.

University of Chicago Press A von Hirsch, "Proportionality in the Philosophy of Punishment" in M Tonry, ed, *Crime and Justice: A Review of Research*, vol 16 (Chicago: University of Chicago Press, 1992). Reprinted with permission.

University of Toronto Press A Doob, "Community Sanctions and Imprisonment: Hoping for a Miracle but Not Bothering Even to Pray for It" (1990) 32 Can J Corr 415. Reprinted with permission of University of Toronto Press.

Preface to the Third Edition

I was very pleased that for this project we were able to resurrect the old "sentencing gang": Patrick, Gary, Dale, and Julian. Given the extensive developments since the second edition and the consequential need for expertise, this edition would not have been possible without their insights and contributions. Their work has been invaluable and I thank them for it.

Since the second edition, we have seen numerous statutory changes to the sentencing regime in Canada. These include provisions that deal with pre-sentence custody, collateral orders, closing the window for conditional sentences, and dramatic changes to both the murder and dangerous offender regimes. As well, the Supreme Court of Canada has paid more attention to sentencing issues and continued with the evolution of Charter analysis. Combined, these developments necessitated substantial reconfiguration and updating of the book. You will notice that we have added a separate chapter called "The Charter and Sentencing." As well, the previous chapters on parole and imprisonment have been merged into a focused chapter called "Post-Appeal Sentence Issues." This was done in recognition of the complexity of parole and imprisonment issues and our inability in a book of this kind to do them justice. Part of me regrets this but we could not justify the number of pages it would require to do a comprehensive job. For those teachers with a special interest in this area, we hope that we have provided a sufficient background and that supplemental readings on an issue-by-issue basis will be easy to produce.

Throughout the various chapters, we are confident that you will find seminal cases, current cases, current statutory provisions, constructive commentary, and thoughtful criticism. It is our hope that this book will be pedagogically useful to law students and criminology students. Moreover, it should provide helpful background to practitioners and judges.

Personally, I completed my contributions while a Visiting Fellow at Wadham College, Oxford. I want to thank Wadham College, its staff, and Warden Ken Macdonald for their support. As well, for added sustenance, I need to thank the Prince of Wales pub in Iffley (Steve, Sue, and Richard) and the staff at the Magic Café (Jahan and Deki) on Magdalen Road.

Allan Manson
Oxford, 2016

Summary Table of Contents

Detailed Table of Contents

Table of Cases

A page number in boldface type indicates that the text of the case or a portion thereof is reproduced. A page number in lightface type indicates that the case is quoted briefly or discussed. Cases mentioned within excerpts are not listed.

An Introduction to Legal Punishment: Philosophy and Objectives

I. INTRODUCTION

This chapter introduces and explores the philosophical foundations of legal punishment. The body of literature concerning the philosophy of punishment is vast. The readings that follow provide a glimpse into this debate by illustrating some of the major theoretical themes.

The materials in this chapter consider why we have the institution of legal punishment. That is, from a philosophical perspective, how can the imposition of punishment by the state be justified? When the state intentionally inflicts an unwanted deprivation—that is, the imposition of physical and emotional pain or the loss of liberty—on its citizens, this is an act that demands a justification. A variety of philosophical justifications have been developed, but the two main philosophical traditions in this area are utilitarian and retributive.

Utilitarian or reductive theories of punishment are rooted in the work of British philosophers Jeremy Bentham and John Stuart Mill. Like utilitarianism as a general moral theory, the main premise of this approach to punishment is that the infliction of pain by the state is justified only insofar as it promotes favourable consequences. In this context, the desired favourable consequence is the reduction of crime through the "mechanisms" of deterrence, denunciation, incapacitation, and/or rehabilitation.

Retributive theories of punishment, which can be traced back to the works of Immanuel Kant and Georg Wilhelm Friedrich Hegel (and perhaps further back to biblical times), approach the problem from a completely different perspective. Punishment is imposed because it is *deserved* by an offender for the commission of an offence. When the state punishes an individual for the commission of an offence, the state is merely visiting on that person what he or she *deserves*.

The readings in this chapter provide context for the debate. Philosophies of punishment generally fall into two camps, the retributive and the utilitarian. A lively debate has arisen regarding the question of whether sentencing should simply punish the offender (retributivism) or whether it should attempt to prevent further offending by the offender or other potential offenders (utilitarianism). There are also hybrid theories of punishment that incorporate elements of both perspectives. In this first reading, R Antony Duff plots the contours or boundaries of this philosophical debate. Thereafter, separate sections are devoted to a consideration of the most influential utilitarian and retributive approaches to punishment.

R Antony Duff, *Trials and Punishments*
(Cambridge: Cambridge University Press, 1986) (footnotes omitted)

Philosophical discussions of the meaning and justification of criminal punishment tend to move along familiar and well-worn paths. It is agreed that a system of criminal punishment stands in need of some strenuous and persuasive justification: the briefest examination of our actual penal institutions confronts us forcibly with the question of how we can justifiably subject people to such treatment; and even a more abstract or idealised account of what punishment could or should be must recognise that any punitive practice will require powerful justification. But different moral perspectives generate different accounts of why it is that punishment needs justification—of what it is about punishment that makes it morally problematic: for some it is the fact that punishment inflicts, indeed is designed to inflict, pain or suffering that most forcibly raises the issue of justification; for others it is the coercive character of punishment—the fact that it is imposed on people against their express will, thus apparently infringing their freedom and autonomy—which is most disturbing. Such different perceptions of the problem of punishment are themselves related to quite different accounts of what does or could justify a system of criminal punishment.

Consequentialists, who have been for many years the predominant party in these discussions, insist that the point of a system of criminal punishment must lie in its beneficial effects (most obviously in the reduction of harmful modes of conduct by the deterrence, reform or incapacitation of those who do or might engage in them), and its justification in the extent to which these benefits outweigh the system's costs (the harm caused by punishment; the resources needed to identify and deal with those who are to be punished). Consequentialist accounts of punishment are as diverse as the ends which consequentialists may value and which punishment may serve: but I take it to be a common and defining feature of such accounts that they require punishment to be justified by reference to benefits to which it is *contingently* related as a means to a further end. Our initial specification of the ends which we are to pursue leaves open the question of the means by which they are to be pursued, since those ends, do not of their nature require any particular method of attaining them: so we must go on to ask which methods are in fact likely to be most economically efficacious. To justify a system of punishment it is therefore not enough to show that it pursues ends which are worth pursuing, nor indeed that its benefits outweigh its costs: we must also show, by an empirical inquiry into the likely effects of actual or possible social institutions, that this way of dealing with disvalued conduct is more economically effective than other possible methods of achieving our desired ends—than, for instance, a system of "social hygiene" which regards such conduct as symptomatic of a condition which needs curative treatment rather than as an instance of criminality requiring punishment.

This contingent relation between punishment and its justifying aims generates familiar objections to such consequentialist accounts. For the whole-hearted pursuit of such aims would surely sanction the imposition of manifestly unjust punishments: the punishment of innocent scapegoats; excessively harsh punishments for relatively trivial offences; a refusal to accept excusing-conditions which should in justice be accepted. It is at best a contingent truth that just punishments are consequentially efficient; and it may sometimes be true that unjust punishments are more efficient.

A consequentialist might respond to such objections by arguing that an adequately detailed consequentialist account, which attends to *all* the likely effects of particular kinds or systems of punishment, will not in fact have such disturbing implications; that it will come closer to an extensional equivalence which "ordinary moral views" than its critics may suppose. She may also try to provide a role for, and an explanation of, the principles of justice which her critics regard as morally significant; by arguing, for instance, that we have good consequentialist reasons to obey strict rules which forbid the punishment of the innocent or the unduly harsh punishment of the guilty. But she will still face some familiar objections; that she is relying on large and unsubstantiated empirical claims about the likely effects of different kinds of practice; that her reductive and instrumental account of the principles of justice fails to capture the sense and significance of those principles, or the role which they properly play in our moral thought; and that she "begs the institution" by assuming without adequate argument that a consequentialist concern to prevent harmful conduct will generate something like a system of criminal punishment, rather than some quite different system of social hygiene or behaviour-control. Some moral radical consequentialists have indeed taken this last route, and argued that a proper concern for the appropriate consequentialist ends should lead us to abandon punishment altogether.

An alternative response to these criticisms has been to insist that the positive justifying aims of punishment must indeed lie in its consequential benefits, but to allow that our pursuit of those aims is and should be limited by other considerations or side-constraints. Such limits may be set by our concern for ends other than, and conflicting with, those which provide the justifying aims of punishment; a concern to maximise the citizen's freedom in and control over his own life may set limits on who may be punished, and how, which are not dictated by the aim of preventing disvalued conduct: but they may also be set by an avowedly non-consequentialist concern for justice which forbids us to punish the innocent, and limits the kind or amount of punishment which may be attached to different offences. Punishment which efficiently serves its justifying aims may thus still be unjustified, if it fails to satisfy these further moral constraints—constraints which are independent of the consequential ends which punishment is to serve, and which focus on its intrinsic character.

It is here that retributivist ideas are allowed to play a part in an account of punishment. Traditional attempts to find the *positive* justification of punishment in its relation to a past offence are, their critics claim, unable to explain that justificatory relationship: insofar as they have any tolerably clear meaning they are seen to depend on an unargued and unarguable intuition that "the guilty deserve to suffer" (itself perhaps reflecting a desire for revenge which hardly deserves our moral respect); or on a covertly consequentialist appeal to some particular, and arbitrarily selected, kind of beneficial effect. But we need not therefore eliminate all notions of retribution: we can deal with them (and defuse them) by allowing that they do, once properly understood, have a role in an adequate account of punishment—though not the dominant role which their traditional proponents claimed for them. Ideas of retribution and desert are now to play an etiolated and negative role, setting constraints on our pursuit of the consequentialist goals which provide the positive justifying aim of punishment: they express independent principles of justice; or logical principles involved in the meaning of "punishment"; or subordinate principles within a Rule-Utilitarian system.

Retributivists, however, are unlikely to be satisfied with this subordinate role within a fundamentally consequentialist framework: and recent years have seen a revival of full-blooded retributivist attempts to locate the meaning of punishment, not in its contingent and instrumental contribution to some further end, but in its internal relationship to a past offence; and its justification in its intrinsic character as a response to that offence. This revival, involving both academic philosophers and more practically oriented legal theorists, has been motivated in part by the manifest failure of systems constructed or reformed along purportedly consequentialist lines to achieve their avowed ends, as well as by a more theoretical dissatisfaction with consequentialist accounts of punishment; and it has led to new attempts to explicate and defend the idea that punishment is justified as merited retribution for a past offence.

We can usefully talk of the common features, and the common logical structure, of consequentialist accounts of punishment: but can we usefully talk of retributivist accounts in this way; or has the label "retributivist" been applied to such a diversity of views and principles that it now lacks any unambiguous or unitary meaning? We must indeed distinguish retributivist accounts of the justifying purpose of punishment from those which seek only to set limits on our pursuit of consequentialist aims; and amongst the former we find a notable diversity of explanations of how it is that punishment is an appropriate response to crime. Some talk of the payment of a debt incurred by crime, or of the restoration of a balance disturbed by crime; others of the expiation, atonement, or annulment of crime; others of the denunciation of crime; and we cannot suppose that these are simply different ways of expressing the same idea. But such accounts do share what can usefully be called a retributivist perspective on punishment: for they all find the sense and the justification of punishment in its relation to a past offence.

A retributivist must explain the meaning of this justificatory relationship, and the values on which it depends. She must defend herself against the accusation that her account amounts at best to a distortion of logical or moral principles which have their proper and subordinate place within a consequentialist account of the justifying aims of punishment; and at worse to a piece of metaphysical mystery-mongering which conceals a desire for revenge or retaliation behind such opaque and unilluminating metaphors as "restoring the balance" or "annulling the crime." She must meet the claim that a coercive institution like punishment can be justified only by showing that it does some significant consequential good; and she may do this by arguing that the justification of punishment has, and need have, nothing to do with its consequences, and everything to do with its intrinsic character as a response to crime: the imposition of punishment on criminals is right independently of its consequences—even, perhaps, whatever its consequences.

The range of familiar accounts of punishment thus offers us three models for its justification. A consequentialist model justifies punishment by reference to further ends to which it is contingently and instrumentally related as a means; an intrinsicalist or retributivist model justifies it by reference to its intrinsic character as distinct form, and rather than, its consequences; and a "consequentialism with side-constraints" model seeks to combine these two modes of justification by insisting that a justified system of punishment must be an efficient method of pursuing the further ends which provide its justifying aims, whilst also satisfying the independent and intrinsicalist demands of justice.

II. UTILITARIAN THEORIES OF PUNISHMENT

As discussed in the introduction to this chapter, utilitarian or consequentialist theories of punishment justify the imposition of punishment in terms of the benefits that it achieves. The main benefit that consequentialist theories aspire to achieve is the reduction of crime. In *An Introduction to the Principles of Morals and Legislation* (1789), Jeremy Bentham wrote:

> Pain and pleasure are the great springs of human action. When a man perceives or supposes pain to be the consequences of an act, he is acted upon in such a manner as tends, with a certain force, to withdraw him, as it were, from the commission of that act. If the apparent magnitude of that pain be greater than the apparent magnitude of the pleasure or good he expects to be the consequence of the act, he will be absolutely prevented from performing it. The mischief which would have ensued from the act, if performed, will also by that means be prevented.
>
> With respect to a given individual, the recurrence of an offence may be provided against in three ways:
>
> 1. By taking from him the physical power of offending.
> 2. By taking away the desire of offending.
> 3. By making him afraid of offending.
>
> In the first case, the individual can no more commit the offence; in the second, he no longer desires to commit it; in the third, he may still wish to commit it, but he longer dares to do it. In the first case, there is a physical incapacity; in the second, a moral reformation; in the third, there is intimidation or terror of the law.

More traditionally, the language of these objectives is that punishment seeks to deter (either specifically or generally), incapacitate, or rehabilitate offenders. Moreover, punishment is said to have a denunciatory or expressive function, whereby the imposition of punishment is considered to be a symbolic reflection of society's abhorrence or abject disavowal of particular crimes.

As the readings below demonstrate, the utilitarian approach to punishment is vulnerable to attack on two levels. First, the goals that consequentialist theories seek to achieve are not met; that is, punishment is ineffective as a means of reforming offenders, deterring others, and generally reducing crime. This argument is rooted in a rather impressive body of empirical literature that bemoans the fact that social science has not been able to validate the efficacy of utilitarian claims. For a collection of a number of readings that address this issue, see Andrew von Hirsch, Andrew Ashworth & Julian Roberts, eds, *Principled Sentencing: Readings on Theory and Policy*, 3rd ed (Oxford: Hart, 2009).

The second level of attack is from a moral perspective. A theory of punishment that is founded on consequentialist notions has little regard for human dignity or autonomy in that it permits using individuals as a means to more collectivist ends. An example of this shortcoming that is popularized in the literature is the claim that a utilitarian theory of punishment authorizes the punishment of an innocent person if, in all of the circumstances, utility were to be maximized by such a practice. If this argument is valid, must we abandon our utilitarian notions *completely*, or can the point be dismissed as a fanciful complaint that occupies the most peripheral edges of an otherwise venerable philosophical tradition?

CL Ten, *Crime, Guilt and Punishment*
(Oxford: Clarendon Press, 1987) at 7, 36-37 (footnotes omitted)

2.1. The Effects of Punishment

The utilitarian theory justifies punishment solely in terms of the good consequences produced. There are disagreements among utilitarians about the nature of the good consequences which punishment is supposed to produce. Some utilitarians may even believe that the harm done by punishment outweighs the good, and hence punishment is not justified. But many utilitarians see the main beneficial effects of punishment in terms of the *reduction of crime*, and believe that punishing offenders will have at least some, if not all, of the following good effects. First, punishment acts as a deterrent to crime. The deterrent effects can be both individual and general. Punishment deters the offender who is punished from committing similar offences in future, and it also deters potential offenders. The offender who is punished is supposed to be deterred by his experience of punishment and the threat of being punished again if he re-offends and is convicted. This is the individual deterrent effect. The general deterrent effect of punishment on potential offenders works through the threat of their being subjected to the same kind of punishment that was meted out to the convicted offender.

Secondly, punishment is supposed to have reformative or rehabilitative effects. This is confined to the offender who is punished. He is reformed in the sense that the effect of punishment is to change his values so that he will not commit similar offences in future because he believes such offences to be wrong. But if he abstains from criminal acts simply because he is afraid of being caught and punished again, then he is deterred rather than reformed and rehabilitated by punishment. So the effects of individual deterrence and rehabilitation are the same. What distinguishes them is the difference in motivation.

The third good consequence of punishment is its incapacitative effect. When an offender is serving his sentence in prison, he is taken out of general social circulation and is therefore prevented from committing a variety of offences, even though he may neither be deterred nor reformed by punishment. Of course punishment would not have an overall incapacitative effect if the offender would not have re-offended even if he were free, or if his incarceration led someone else, who would not otherwise have done so, to engage in criminal activity, perhaps as his replacement in a gang. While in prison, the offender might still commit certain offences: he might assault a fellow prisoner or a prison guard. But his opportunities are generally reduced. In some cases, however, his contacts with other prisoners would create opportunities for further involvement in crime when he is released. The incapacitative effect, though perhaps most likely in the case of imprisonment, may also be present in other forms of punishment. For example, parole may have some incapacitative effect in that although the offender is free, the fact that he is under supervision may restrict his opportunities for criminal activities.

The empirical evidence of the effects of punishment is very complex, but a brief survey will be of some use.

It looks as if the present state of our knowledge provides no basis for claiming that punishment by imprisonment reforms or rehabilitates the criminal, or that it is an individual deterrent. The position is well summed up by the Report of the Panel of the National Research Council in the United States on Research on Deterrent and Incapacitative Effects, hereafter referred to as the Panel:

> The available research on the impact of various treatment strategies both in and out of prison seems to indicate that, after controlling for initial selection differences, there are generally no statistically significant differences between the subsequent recidivism of offenders, regardless of the form of "treatment." This suggests that neither rehabilitative nor criminogenic effects operate very strongly. Therefore, at an aggregate level, these confounding effects are probably safely ignored.

By "criminogenic effects" the Panel refers to the undesirable effects of imprisonment in either increasing the criminal's propensity to commit crimes or to extend the duration of his criminal career. Such effects are the opposite of the rehabilitative effects. So the present evidence seems to suggest that in general the effect of imprisonment, or of the various programmes for rehabilitation which accompany imprisonment, is neither to make the criminal a better nor a worse person with respect to the standards of behaviour set by the criminal law.

The evidence also suggests that in general punishment has no individual deterrent effect. Daniel Nagin points out that at the observational level it is difficult to distinguish between individual (or what he calls special) deterrence and rehabilitation. He concludes that, "The figures suggest that recidivism rates cannot be affected by varying the severity of the punishment, at least within acceptable limits." But Nagin cautiously adds that the evidence is only preliminary.

In a few specific cases there is indeed some evidence of the individual deterrent effect of punishment. Thus Johannes Andenaes draws attention to a study of amateur shoplifters which shows that detection and arrest, even without prosecution, produces serious shock. There is little or no recidivism among those who are apprehended and interrogated by the store police and then set free without being formally charged. A study of drunk driving in Sweden also shows that those drivers who had been arrested estimated the risk of being arrested as many times higher than other drivers.

There is disagreement about the general deterrent effects of punishment. Johannes Andenaes believes that, "In general terms it can only be stated that general deterrence works well in some fields and works poorly or not at all in other fields." But in 1974 Gordon Tullock published an article, "Does Punishment Deter Crime?" in which he surveyed the work done by economists and sociologists. Tullock points out that economists began their work under the impression that punishment would deter crime because demand curves slope downwards showing that if the cost of a good is increased then less of it will be consumed. So if the cost of committing crime is increased by more severe punishment, then there will be fewer crimes. Sociologists, on the other hand, started out with the intention of confirming what was then the accepted view in their discipline that punishment would not deter crime. But Tullock argues that, although their starting points and assumptions were radically different, both economists and sociologists, after analysing the evidence, came to the same conclusion that punishment did indeed deter crime. After surveying their studies Tullock himself is convinced that "the empirical evidence is clear," and he states his conclusions unequivocally: "Even granting the fact that most potential criminals have only a rough idea as to the frequency and severity of punishment, multiple regression studies show that increasing the frequency or severity of the punishment does reduce the likelihood that a given crime will be committed."

However, Tullock's confidence about the clarity of the empirical evidence is not shared by the Panel. The Panel argues that although the evidence consistently establishes a negative association between crime rates and sanctions (as measured by the risks of apprehension, conviction, or imprisonment), that is higher crime rates are associated with lower sanctions and vice versa, this does not necessarily show the general deterrent effect of sanctions. The negative association may be partly or wholly explained in terms of lower sanctions being the effect rather than the cause of higher crime rates. Higher crime rates may so overburden the resources of the criminal justice system that they reduce its ability to deal with new offenders. Overburdened judges and prosecutors may use their discretion to dismiss or reduce charges, or to offer attractive plea bargains. Overcrowding of prisons may lead to a reduction in the time served in prison as more prisoners are released early on parole. The sanctions imposed on certain crimes may be reduced. So unless one can separate out the effect of higher crime rates on sanctions from the deterrent effect of sanctions on crime, one cannot interpret the evidence as establishing the presence of the general deterrent effect of punishment. The Panel's cautious assessment of the evidence is summed up in its remark that "we cannot yet assert that the evidence warrants an affirmative conclusion regarding deterrence" but the Panel adds that "the evidence certainly favours a proposition supporting deterrence more than it favours one asserting that deterrence is absent." On the other hand, the Panel believes that the evidence does not even show a significant negative association between crime rates and the severity of punishment as measured by the time served in prison, but suggests that this may partly be accounted for in terms of various distortions.

Moving from the analysis of statistics to the experimental evidence, the Panel identifies three studies which are not methodologically flawed. Of these, two show that the level of crime decreased significantly with increases in the level of sanctions, while one showed that the removal of criminal sanctions for abortions in Hawaii did not affect the incidence of abortions. So it looks as if the present experimental evidence does not permit the drawing of general conclusions. But much of the experimental evidence is consistent with the operation of deterrence, as has been noted by Nigel Walker.

Finally, we turn to the incapacitative effect of punishment. In her review of the literature for the Panel, Jacqueline Cohen suggests that disagreements about the magnitude of that effect can be attributed almost entirely to the different estimates of the average crime rate of prisoners. The estimate of the increase in crime if current prison use were reduced or eliminated has been as low as five per cent. Estimating the incapacitative effect of present prison policies is one thing. There is also the different question as to what we can expect the incapacitative effect to be if present policies are changed. Here one estimate is of a five fold decrease in crime, but Cohen points out that this can only be achieved by increasing the prison population by between 355 per cent and 567 per cent. The incapacitative effect will not be the same for all crimes. Cohen points out that using the assumptions made by the available models, the increase in prison population required to reduce violent crimes is much less than the increases needed for similar reductions in other crimes. Violent crimes can be reduced by 10 per cent with less than 30 per cent increase in prison population. This kind of consideration has led to an increasing interest in the use of selective incapacitation in which the focus of imprisonment is on certain types of offenders who are identified as having a high rate of committing crimes.

We see that the evidence is perhaps more hospitable to the claim that punishment has some general deterrent effect and some incapacitative effect than it is to the claim that it has individual deterrent effect or that it rehabilitates offenders. This will no doubt be puzzling to some, but it provides a basis for caution in responding to a high rate of recidivism. Where there is such a high rate, it shows that punishment does not deter those who are punished. But it does not show that potential offenders are not in fact deterred by punishment, or that punishment does not incapacitate.

2.2. Punishing the Innocent

Let us now assume that the beneficial consequences of punishment outweigh the suffering that it inflicts on offenders. Critics of the utilitarian theory argue that if punishment is to be justified solely in terms of its good consequences, then punishment cannot be confined to offenders. There might be situations in which punishing an innocent person would produce better consequences that alternative courses of action. The utilitarian is therefore committed to punishing the innocent person. This objection has played an important role in the rejection of the utilitarian theory.

Let us consider an example made famous in the literature by H.J. McCloskey. Suppose that in a particular town with a mixed population a man from one racial group rapes a woman from the other group. Because of existing racial tensions the crime is likely to produce racial violence with many people being injured, unless the guilty man is apprehended quickly. Suppose further that the sheriff of the town can prevent the violence by framing an innocent man who was near the scene of the crime, and who will be accepted by the community as the guilty person. Surely, it is argued, the best consequences will be produced by the sheriff's fabrication of evidence against him which will result in his conviction and severe punishment. But the critics maintain that the sheriff's act and the subsequent punishment of the innocent man are both wrong.

There are many ways in which utilitarians, or those sympathetic to them, can respond to this objection, and I shall consider some of their main arguments. First, it is argued that "punishing the innocent" is a logical contradiction because punishment implies guilt. Secondly, the premises of the objection are challenged. It is suggested that punishing the innocent man will not in fact produce the best consequences if we take into account all the consequences of such punishment including the long-term and less obvious consequences. Thirdly, it is claimed that the only situations in which punishing the innocent is optimistic are hypothetical and "fantastic" situations rather than situations which arise, or are likely to occur, in the real world. It is then argued that for a variety of reasons, utilitarians should not be worried by what they are committed to in such fantastic situations. In discussing this third response, I shall also consider the views of those utilitarians who maintain that the punishment of the innocent would indeed be justified in situations where it produces the best consequences. If "commonsense morality" or our intuition disagree, so much the worse for them.

2.3. Punishment and Guilt

In his well-known paper, "On Punishment," Anthony Quinton argues that the notion of "punishment" implies guilt in the sense that "punishment" is defined in part as the infliction of suffering on the guilty. So when suffering is inflicted on innocent people, this cannot be properly described as punishment but as something else—judicial terrorism or social surgery. If we inflict suffering on an innocent man and try to pass it off as punishment, we are guilty of lying since we make a lying imputation that he is guilty and responsible for an offence. Part of Quinton's argument seems to rest on the importance of distinguishing between, for example, typhoid carriers and criminals even though both may sometimes be treated in rather similar ways. Thus a typhoid carrier, or a person with an infectious disease, will be quarantined. He will lose his freedom in much the same way that a criminal is deprived of his freedom when he is jailed. And yet we do not call quarantine a form of punishment precisely because the disease carrier is not guilty of an offence.

It is certainly true that in the typical cases of punishment it is inflicted on a person guilty of an offence. But the crucial issue is whether we can extend the notion of punishment to the infliction of suffering on the innocent without at the same time losing the distinction between punishment and various activities like the quarantine of disease carriers and certain kinds of medical or dental treatment which are painful.

In all these cases there is the infliction of some unpleasantness or suffering, but it is only in the case of punishment that the unpleasantness is essential to what is to be done. As Wasserstrom puts it "the point of the imposition of a deprivation when it is unmistakably a punishment is that it is being imposed because it is a deprivation, because the person upon whom it is being imposed should thereby be made to suffer and in that respect be worse off than before." On the other hand, the unpleasantness experienced by those who are quarantined, or by those undergoing medical treatment, is only incidental, and not essential to what needs to be done. Advances in medical technology may lead to the replacement of painful forms of treatment by pleasant, but still effective, treatment. Medical treatment does not have to be painful at all: a sweet pill is as much a medicine as a bitter pill. Similarly, quarantine implies a degree of isolation to prevent the spread of the infection, and that in itself will be unpleasant. But it can, if resources permit, be greatly outweighed by the pleasures of the surroundings in which one is put. But punishment implies at least an overall degree of unpleasantness. So we can distinguish between punishment and quarantine without falling back on the notion that the person who is punished must be guilty, or must at least be supposed to be guilty, of an offence.

However, the truth of the matter seems to be a bit more complex than we have so far acknowledged, and Quinton's argument, though mistaken, is interesting because it gestures towards that truth. Consider the difference between a monetary fine, which is a form of punishment, and a tax which is not. Arguably both are essentially unpleasant although both may be accepted or approved of as fully justified. What then is the difference between them? In *The Concept of Law* H.L.A. Hart points out that punishment involves "an offence or breach of duty in the form of violation of a rule set up to guide the conduct of ordinary citizens." When someone is punished, he has violated a standard of conduct to which he is supposed to conform. But when he pays a tax, he has not breached any such standard of conduct. The main purpose of taxes is to raise revenue and not to set up a standard of correct conduct. Indeed the revenue-raising function of a tax would be defeated if people generally reacted to income tax by not working, or to Value Added Tax by not eating in restaurants. On the other hand, the purpose of punishment is not defeated if, as a result of it, people cease to breach the relevant standard of conduct. On the contrary, the threat of punishment is most effective when it is unnecessary to carry it out. This important difference between punishment and a tax can be blurred, as Hart acknowledges, when, for example, those running a business simply assimilate the relatively small fines for breaches of rules into the costs of the goods they produce, and pass them on to their consumers. It is also blurred in the other direction when a government imposes a tax on luxury goods partly in order to discourage their use.

A related difference between punishment and other forms of deprivation or unpleasant treatment is that punishment expresses condemnation or disapproval of the conduct punished. The person punished is blamed for what he did, and this explains the peculiar unfairness of punishing the innocent who are of course blameless.

But now, if we accept the idea that punishment involves the breach of a standard of conduct, how is this different from Quinton's point that punishment is always for an offence? The element of truth in Quinton's position is that there must be some wrongdoing or some offence for there to be punishment. But this is not to say that the person punished must be the offender. An innocent person can be punished for an offence committed by someone else. This can happen not only when the legal authority makes a mistake and punishes the wrong person, but also when it deliberately frames an innocent person.

But suppose now that my arguments fail, and Quinton's analysis of the concept of punishment is correct. It certainly does not follow that it is wrong to imprison innocent people or even to execute them. What follows is merely that we cannot *describe* these acts as *punishing* the innocent. But the real issue is a moral issue as to whether we are justified in inflicting suffering on innocent persons. Admittedly this is not exactly the same issue as whether we should *punish* the innocent which raises the additional problem of whether we may unjustly blame the blameless, but none the less it is a serious moral issue. Quinton argues that "the suffering associated with punishment *may* not be inflicted on them, firstly, as brutal and secondly, if it is represented as punishment, as involving a lie." The second objection does not hold if we do not represent the infliction of suffering on the innocent as a form of punishment. And the first objection is not one of which utilitarians can avail themselves if the brutal treatment of the innocent will in fact produce the best consequences. So the argument against the utilitarian can now be reformulated as follows: why should we confine ourselves to punishment in those cases where the infliction of suffering on the innocent will produce the best consequences?

The objection to the utilitarian position is clearly moral, and hence it cannot be evaded by appealing even to a correct definition of the notion of punishment. A proper regard for the way in which terms are used will enable us to describe correctly the moral problem which confronts us, but it cannot solve that problem for us.

2.4. *The Disutility of Punishing the Innocent*

The second utilitarian response to the charge that utilitarians are committed to punishing the innocent draws our attention to the less obvious bad consequences of punishing innocent persons, and argues that on balance the punishment of the innocent will always produce worse consequences than the failure to do so. For example, it is claimed that the fact that an innocent man has been punished will soon leak out, and when that happens, there will be a loss of confidence in the sheriff and widespread fear among the population that any one of them might be the next innocent victim of the sheriff's attempt to prevent similar violence in future. Furthermore, the sheriff himself will have his sensibilities blunted once the barrier against framing and punishing the innocent has been removed. He is more likely to adopt a similar policy the next time he faces a problem of maintaining order, and on that occasion, there may be no strong utilitarian as for punishing an innocent person. It is also not certain that there will in fact be racial violence if an innocent person is not punished. On the other hand, the suffering of the innocent person who is punished is very real. The suffering of the innocent man is likely to be greater than that of the guilty. The punishment will come as a big shock to the innocent man, and he will be angered and distressed in a way that the guilty person will not be.

But at each point of this utilitarian response, the critic can counter by tightening up the description of the example under consideration. Thus the sheriff suffers from a sudden fatal illness soon after the punishment of the innocent man, and he makes no death-bed confessions. No one else knows about the fabrication of evidence and the secret is buried with the sheriff. The innocent man who is punished has no relatives or close friends, and he himself is well endowed with an unusual temperament which faces unexpected disaster with calm resignation. We must not forget the unconvicted real offender who is still free and conceivably could give the whole show away. So he dies unexpectedly when he is run over by a bus on his way to the sheriff's funeral. Now we are back where we started with an example in which the punishment of an innocent person produces the best consequences and so should be accepted by the utilitarian. ...

I have so far assumed, for the sake of argument, that it is only in fantastic situations that utilitarians are committed to punishing the innocent. But it is now time to say something about this assumption. Most utilitarians seem to make the assumption. Thus Hare writes: "The retributivists are right at the intuitive level, and the utilitarians at the critical level." But contrast this with David Richards's claim in *The Moral Criticism of Law* that the utilitarian theory of punishment "clearly seems to allow and even require the punishment of the innocent, since it is very plausible that a higher degree of criminal deterrence would be achieved by punishing the children or relatives or friends or lovers of criminals in addition to or even in place of the criminal. Primitive systems of law often do exactly this, ..." In the face of these conflicting claims, two remarks are appropriate. First, no one can claim with confidence that, on the balance of probabilities, there are no actual cases in which punishing the innocent will produce the best consequences. But secondly, the strength of our conviction, which is shared by many utilitarians, that punishing the innocent in the real world is unjustified, cannot be accounted for simply on the basis of utilitarian considerations. If we were guided by purely utilitarian considerations, we would not be entitled to be as confident as we in fact are that such punishment in the real world is wrong, and we should indeed be prepared to experiment with limited proposals for the punishment of the innocent.

Indeed we can go further and argue that in the present state of our knowledge, surveyed earlier, the evidence of the desirable effects of punishment is not always as firmly based as is often assumed, and this presents some difficulties for a purely utilitarian justification of punishment. From the utilitarian point of view punishing offenders produces bad consequences which are certain and not speculative, namely the suffering inflicted directly by punishment on offenders and indirectly on their friends and relatives. Against this, there is no equally firm evidence, in all cases where punishment is thought to be justified, of its countervailing good effects. There is some evidence of incapacitative effects although the extent of these effects varies with different types of offences, and the evidence is also consistent with there being some general deterrent effect. Again, there is good reason to think that the total abandonment of the practice of punishment would have unfortunate results. But there are specific crimes in which the utilitarian case for punishment, while not ruled out, is not particularly strong. It is then unclear what we should do in the present state of our knowledge if we were guided by purely utilitarian considerations. In fact our thinking on these matters is also guided by non-utilitarian considerations. Other things being equal, we think it better that the guilty should suffer through punishment than that there should be similar suffering by the innocent victims of crime. Again, given that the practice of punishment has some utilitarian justification, there will also be offenders who may justifiably be punished by appealing to non-utilitarian considerations. For example, if the punishment for some offences can be justified on utilitarian grounds in terms of the general deterrent effect and the incapacitative effect of such punishment, then it is unfair to allow those who have committed more serious offences to go unpunished even if in these latter cases the existing evidence is inadequate to show that punishment has similar good effects.

I do not believe that the practice of punishment would be justified if there were a decisive utilitarian case against it, or if it did not at least have some utilitarian support. But this is not to say that all desirable aspects of that practice can be justified in purely utilitarian terms.

NOTE

Another empirical problem that haunts the utilitarian tradition is the inefficacy of risk predictions concerning reoffending. Most jurisdictions around the world employ risk-of-reoffending scales. These scales—such as the Level of Service Inventory–Revised (LSI–R™)—take a number of factors into account to classify the offender as low, medium, or high risk of reoffending. The accuracy or validity of the scales has improved significantly in recent years. Nevertheless, the problem of overprediction remains. Many offenders predicted to reoffend, and therefore subject to a more punitive sanction, do not in fact commit further offences. In a recent survey of the literature, Christopher Slobogin draws the following conclusions.

Christopher Slobogin, "Risk Assessment"
in J Petersilia & K Reitz, eds, *The Oxford Handbook of Sentencing and Corrections* (New York: Oxford University Press, 2012) ch 8 at 209-10 (footnotes and references omitted)

Risk assessment in sentencing raises numerous concerns, which can be expressed in terms of one significant conundrum: risk assessment is only likely to be sufficiently and knowably accurate if it is based on actuarial instruments, but it is only likely to avoid constitutional, justice, and fairness objections if it relies on demonstrably less accurate unstructured clinical judgment that eschews use of demographic information and other immutable traits. Compromise approaches such as structured professional judgment and adjusted actuarial risk assessment can mitigate this tension but not eliminate it, while creating accuracy and efficacy problems of their own.

Given these difficulties, some commentators have suggested that risk assessment should only be used to divert an offender from prison or to mitigate a prison sentence. An additional reason for adopting this practice is that the relationship between recidivism and sentence length—short of a term that pushes the offender into old age—may well be a positive one. If so, then using risk assessment to enhance sentences will often not make sense from a public safety perspective.

Two other alternatives envision a somewhat larger sentencing role for risk assessment. One option, advanced by the Council of Europe, is to establish that "factors such as unemployment, cultural or social conditions of the offender should not influence the sentence to discriminate against the offender." This principle would prohibit increased restrictions on liberty based on an offender's employment, educational, or socioeconomic status, but would allow enhanced dispositions based on prior criminal acts. Another approach is to place limitations not on risk factors but on the dispositional consequences of a risk assessment. The revisions to the Model Penal Code's sentencing provisions permit "sufficiently reliable" risk assessment to inform both diversion and sentence enhancements, as long as the dispositions are within the range dictated by retributive principles. Of course, if only past crimes can enhance the sentence (as with the Council of Europe proposal), then important risk factors will not be acknowledged and prior criminal history—which is entirely static—may assume an exaggerated importance. If the risk assessment takes place at the front end and results in a determinate sentence (as occurs under the MPC's provisions), then the effects of aging and risk management will not be taken into account.

A final option is to eliminate risk assessment as a consideration at sentencing, and instead rely entirely on desert or deterrence theories within the criminal justice system. As other chapters in this book make clear, these latter approaches also have their drawbacks. In particular, desert-based punishment, like modern risk assessment, is usually focused on a very narrow subset of factors, despite the huge number of variables that might be related to culpability. Furthermore, these factors—consisting primarily of antisocial conduct and the accompanying mental states and circumstances—can result from the same status-like traits that inform risk assessment. Most importantly, assessments of blameworthiness are rife with uncertainty; a desert-based system of punishment makes large sentencing differentials dependent on provably unreliable decisions about whether a crime was premeditated, reckless, or negligent; a mistake was reasonable or unreasonable; or provocation was understandable. The case against risk assessment must also consider the case against other reasons to punish.

Finally, reviews of the deterrence research suggest that the impact of sentencing on aggregate crime rates is modest. Increasing the severity of punishments will have little impact on the overall crime rate or on recidivism rates. Advocates of harsher sentencing regimes (including mandatory sentences of imprisonment) often assert that more severe sentencing will deter offenders and thus lower crime rates. Scholars at the University of Cambridge reviewed research on the relationship between sentence severity and crime rates. They concluded by drawing the following conclusion:

The USA has had severer sentences than England in the last decade and a half, and US crime rates have generally been falling or steady while England's (at least, until recently) have been rising. But a closer analysis of the trends generally does not show substantial negative correlations between [severity] levels and crime rates. Such figures thus give scant support to recent claims that America's tougher penalties have shown demonstrably greater success in deterring crime.

See Andreas von Hirsch, Anthony E Bottoms, Elizabeth Burney & PO Wikstrom, *Criminal Deterrence and Sentence Severity* (Oxford: Hart, 1999).

III. RETRIBUTIVE THEORIES OF PUNISHMENT

The notion of retribution as a basis for punishment is rooted in the works of Kant and Hegel. This theory holds that punishment ought to be (or must be) imposed when it is deserved. In its purest form, retribution is reflected in the ancient *lex talionis*—that is, "an eye for an eye." The question whether any beneficial consequences will result from the imposition of punishment is irrelevant. Indeed, an uncompromising retributivist would argue that if punishment is in fact deserved, it ought to be imposed, notwithstanding the possibility of disastrous consequences.

In the excerpt that follows, Nicola Lacey explores the main features and criticisms of "classical" retributivism. Classical retributivism is criticized for being intuitive or transcendental at its base and dependent on metaphor for its explanation. Retributivists attempt to justify the imposition of punishment by asserting that punishment "restores the balance," "annuls the crime," or "repays a debt to society." Do these expressions lend any force to retributivism, or do they merely restate its elemental content—that is, that the guilty *deserve* to suffer? Retributive approaches to punishment are also criticized for being nothing more than institutional revenge. Are there meaningful differences between personal revenge and a system of state punishment predicated on retributive notions?

Retributive theories of punishment have seen a revival in recent decades. Some of the more positive features of retributivism have been resurrected under the banner of a "just-deserts" theory (or the "new retributivism," as it is sometimes called). Just-deserts theorists rely on retributive notions to justify proportionate sentencing. Just-deserts theorists, such as Andrew von Hirsch, have invoked retributive theory to construct a sentencing regime committed to the idea of proportionality. Variations of this regime found their way into the United States when a number of states adopted determinate sentencing guidelines. The excerpts from von Hirsch and Tonry debate the value of this retributive dimension of sentencing.

Nicola Lacey, *State Punishment: Political Principles and Community Values*
(London: Routledge, 1988) at 16-18, 21-27 (footnotes omitted)

Backward-Looking Justifications

The central case of an exclusively backward-looking justification is that of classical retributivism in its strong form. I take this theory to be making the claim that the state has both a right and a duty to punish, in the sense of inflicting unpleasant consequences upon an offender in response to her offence to the extent that, and by reason of that fact that, she deserves that punishment. Desert thus operates as both a necessary and a sufficient condition for justified punishment. Theories which present desert as a necessary but not a sufficient condition will be considered as mixed theories. Thus the key notion employed by backward-looking theories is that of desert. Some writers treat desert as an axiomatic or self-evident moral principle, assuming that it needs no further explanation. Others, however (the present writer included), whilst acknowledging the place of desert in our moral intuitions and reactive attitudes, find the concept puzzling when they attempt further to analyze its normative appeal, at least in the context of punishment. Indeed, it has been argued that the apparent irreducibility of the notion gives rise to suspicions that the claim that X ought to be punished because she deserves to be punished merely amounts to the claim that X ought to be punished because she ought to be punished. If the intuition is not shared, it seems impossible to push the argument further—so this is hardly a helpful contribution to the complex debate about the justifiability of punishment. Thus many writers have acknowledged the necessity of further unpacking the notion of desert, and we need to examine some of these attempts in order to fairly evaluate the adequacy of backward-looking justifications of punishment.

The Lex Talionis

Perhaps the crudest yet the most fundamental attempt is represented by the ancient lex talionis: an eye for any eye, a life for a life, and so on. This principle, if it merits the name, certainly has the attraction of simplicity: unfortunately this is all that can be said for it. Two devastating objections eliminate it from the list of possible candidates as adequate explications of the desert principle. Most obviously, in terms of the question of how much punishment is inflicted, it supplies clear practical guidance as to the proper measure only in a selective number of cases. The penalty for murder or mutilation may seem clear, but what punishment ought to be inflicted for fraud, perjury or blackmail? The indeterminancy of the principle in these cases ought to make us wary of the status of its apparent clarity in others. And any subtler reinterpretation, such as the argument that murderers simply lose their right not to be killed, or thieves not to be stolen from, hardly generates a morally adequate or even clear set of prescriptions for a criminal justice system. Secondly, and more importantly, this principle fails to capture one of the greatest strengths of the retributivist tradition: that is, its accommodation of a strong principle of responsibility generating limitations on who may properly be punished. It is generally claimed that no punishment is deserved unless the offence is committed by an agent who is responsible in the sense of having a certain degree of knowledge of relevant circumstances and capacity for control of her actions. [As for the] significance and meaning of the principle of responsibility ... for the moment it is sufficient to recall that our moral response appears to differ enormously according to whether a killing is intentional or accidental; a wounding deliberate or negligent. This commonly acknowledged moral distinction between responsibility based merely on causation—strict liability—and that based on "mental elements"—such as intent or recklessness—is ignored by the lex talionis, which directs the same response in each case. Added to the fact that the lex talionis offers no real arguments about why we should punish in the first place, these defects make it clear that we shall have to look further afield for an adequate explanation of the principle of desert central to the retributivist tradition.

The Culpability Principle

A more promising account explicates the idea of desert in terms of culpability, using this notion not only to identify the justifying reasons for punishment and those who may properly be punished, but also to fix the proper measure of punishment, in terms of a relationship of commensurability or proportionality between the offence and the punishment inflicted. Culpability is generally explained as a function of the gravity of the harm caused (such as death, injury or damage to property) combined with the degree of responsibility (intent, recklessness, negligence or mere inadvertence) of the actor. But the notion of culpability also enshrines, as indeed it must if it is to count as a justifying argument for punishment, a moral judgment about the wrongfulness of the behaviour in question. Culpability, in other words, is equated with blameworthiness, and blameworthiness is equated in turn with punishment-worthiness. This does seem to reflect an important aspect of our entrenched habits and attitudes of praising and blaming, and in a more accurate way than does the lex talionis. However, as a normative theory of punishment, this approach too has its difficulties. Some of these, which I shall call internal criticisms, take the form of problems thrown up by the argument from culpability on its own terms: if we were to accept the principle, what would its implications be? Others, which I shall call external criticisms, cast doubt more fundamentally on the adequacy of the principle itself: does it offer an adequate explication of the content and normative force of arguments from desert? Both kinds of difficulty will have to be addressed in order to give a fair appraisal of the culpability principle. ...

Finally, and most importantly, however, serious external criticisms can be made of the culpability principle's account of why it is that we should punish. For it is not clear that the move from a judgment of blameworthiness to one of punishment-worthiness should be made so lightly. Even though our desert-based reactive attitudes may be firmly held, surely we should reflect carefully and seek further reasons before we take the additional step of deliberately acting in a harmful way against a particular individual on the basis of them? A judgment that someone has behaved wrongly does not involve or justify the further judgment that they should be punished. Ultimately, the culpability principle seems to give us no explanation of why we should think it right to punish offenders merely by reason of their past culpable actions. By what means does such an argument, if argument it is, distinguish itself from a principle of vengeance? By what moral alchemy does the prima facie wrong of punishment following on the wrong of the offence create a morally preferable situation? Why should an offence alone generate a moral reason for punitive action? None of these issues is demystified by the culpability principle.

Forfeiture of Rights, Unfair Advantages and the Restoration of a Moral Equilibrium

Given what has been said of the failure of these first two models of desert theory to generate a satisfactory justification of punishment, it makes sense to attempt further to explicate the desert principle within the context of some wider, compatible, background political philosophy. Thus the other attempts I shall consider explore the links between the concept of desert and those of justice, fairness and equality. The concepts of justice and fairness have indeed been central to the desert tradition, and it is thus with these that I shall begin.

The first of the more sophisticated versions of the desert principle which I shall consider may conveniently be labeled the forfeiture of rights view. On this view, the meaning of the claim that an offender deserves to be punished is explained within the context of the existence of a legal system which generates reciprocal political obligations upon citizens to obey its norms. Thus by virtue of a voluntarily committed offence an individual violates here obligations not only to the state but also to all other citizens, and the state is justified in depriving her of her civil rights. The thesis can be put in an extreme and a moderate form. In its extreme form it claims that an offender forfeits all her civil rights by virtue of any voluntarily committed offence. This seems on the face of it to be an implausible claim, generating as it does no limit on the amount or type of justifiable punishment and thus abandoning the proportionality principle central to the retributive tradition. A more plausible version is that which argues that the offender only forfeits a set of rights equivalent to these which she has violated: once the proportionate set of rights has been forfeited, the offender can re-enter political society on fair terms with the law-abiding.

Thus on the moderate view a full set of political rights is due to a citizen so long as she meets her political and legal obligations. This argument does generate a clear principle identifying who may be punished, but doubts remain about just what the argument amounts to as a set of positive justifying reasons for punishment. *Why* should an offender forfeit any civil rights? What does the argument add to the blank, mysterious claim that she deserves it? A further refinement argues that a voluntary offence is taken to show that the offender in a sense chose or willed her own punishment, or at least consented to it, where she was responsible for the offence, aware of its normative consequences, and acting within a fair system of rules. The punishment therefore respects the autonomy of the agent, treating her as an end in herself rather than as a means to some diffused social good. Again, this argument has some appeal as a claim about who should be punished, but as an account of why they should be punished it is inadequate: it can hardly be claimed that offenders consent to their disadvantaging punitive treatment in anything like the strong sense of consent which we generally take to be necessary to justify harsh treatment of one person by another. We can easily imagine an offender who meets the conditions of the principle yet who states in committing her offence that she does not consent to any punishment: the only way in which such an offender can be brought within the ambit of the principle is through some form of social contract argument. I shall consider the difficulties with this approach in commenting on the second sophisticated version of the desert principle, which raises a similar issue. Before moving on, however, it is worth raising the question of whether in any case the consent argument for punishment could count as a genuinely desert-based principle. In attempting to unpack that idea, we seem to have moved a considerable distance from our unreconstructed starting point.

The second version may be called the unfair advantage view. Again, we are to imagine a background system of reciprocal political obligations, and we are invited to take the view that the essence of a voluntary offence is the taking by the offender of an unfair advantage: in failing to restrain herself, the offender has had the advantage of fulfilling choices forbidden to others. The purpose and justification of punishment is, in effect, to remove that unfair advantage and to restore the "moral equilibrium" or relationships of justice that existed prior to the offence. On one extreme version of the view, until punishment is inflicted, all members of society are in some way implicated in the moral disequilibrium created by the crime, which they have failed to redress. It is presumably this type of thought which prompts Kant to say that even on the dissolution of society all murderers held in the jails ought to be executed. There is perhaps a connection between such views about the value to be attached to the restoration of the oral equilibrium and the argument that punishment "reaffirms the right"—both in terms of the rightness of the standards breached by the offence and in terms of the pre-existing relationships of justice between the members of political society. Here at last we have not only an argument about who may properly be punished, but also a positive claim about the reasons for that punishment—although reasons which, as I shall argue, are at such a high level of abstraction that their contribution to de-mystification of the desert principle is limited.

These two versions of desert theory have the important advantage over those so far considered of locating principles of punishment in their proper context—that is, within a general set of political principles. Indeed, these views are probably best understood within the social contract tradition in political philosophy, which asks us to imagine some hypothetical initial agreement upon a certain system of rules and methods of enforcement which can and must then fairly be administered by means of imposition of the agreed sanctions. But these views are not without their practical and theoretical difficulties. In the first place, neither of them gives very clear practical guidance about the fair measure of punishment in particular cases. What actual punishment would forfeit a set of rights equivalent to those violated by a rapist, a petty thief, a reckless driver? What sanction would be sufficient to remove the unfair advantage gained by the provoked manslaughterer, the tax evader or the burglar? As in the case of the law of the talion and the culpability principle, resort to arguments from conventionality agreed, customary or consequence-based penalty scales seem hard to avoid. Secondly, real difficulties have been raised about the social contract tradition itself; in what sense can a *fictitious* agreement generate obligations for real people? This subject will have to be taken up in detail in later chapters. Furthermore, these views are dependent for their force, as we have already noted, on the existence of a fair set of rules. This is not fatal in itself, but the criteria which dictate that there is indeed a just equilibrium which can be restored are not generated by the forfeiture of rights or unfair advantage principles alone. The views do presuppose an independent account of what counts as an unfair advantage and a just equilibrium.

Finally, it seems legitimate to ask whether the metaphorical ideas of restoring relationships of justice or moral equilibria outweigh the obvious disvalues attached to the suffering and other costs of punishment. Do these theories really ignore such cost completely? If not, what weight do they accord them? In what real sense does punishment "restore the right"? Do these theories really remove the mystery attaching to the original, simple desert principle, or are they, too, a form of moral alchemy? Or, in trying to avoid the mystery, do they not collapse into versions of utilitarian or other consequentialist justification? Is the real reason for punishment underlying these theories the need to uphold a just and effective legal system, to prevent private vengeance, to remove feelings of unfairness on the parts of victims? Can any account of punishment which ignores these factors generate a satisfactory justification? And if so many questions crucial to the justification of punishment can only be answered by looking beyond the desert principle, how strong a claim can that principle make to constitute *the* justification of punishment?

Let us turn finally to a version of the desert principle which explores its links with a principle of equality. On this view, to punish someone who deserves punishment is to act in accordance with a principle of equal treatment: treat like cases alike, and different ones differently. Through her voluntary offence, the offender has singled herself out from other citizens: offenders and non-offenders ought to be treated differently. But this will not do as a theory of desert, let alone as a theory of punishment. First of all, it is too minimal: on this basis alone it might justify treating the offender better than the non-offender, so long as this was done consistently. In addition, the principle generates no answer to the question of how much we ought to punish. Finally, the principle tells us nothing about why an offence makes the offender relevantly different in a way which justifies punitive treatment. Not every type of voluntary differentiating action, even one affecting others, justifies a punitive response. Thus the principle of equal treatment cannot explain the principle of desert, although it may form an important part of that principle.

Retributive Theory

We are now in a position to evaluate the question of whether any of the arguments we have considered as possible explications of the idea of desert makes sense of the puzzle of the justification of punishment. This can best be done by means of a summary of the answers generated by those arguments to the three questions originally imposed. First of all, why should we punish? It is really in answering this fundamental question that the arguments associated with desert are at their most deficient. Even the more sophisticated versions barely rise above the level of metaphor, and leave us with the suspicion that the idea of desert cannot be distinguished from a principle of vengeance or the unappealing assertion that two wrongs somehow make a right. Within the context of a general set of political principles, arguments such as that from unfair tax advantage can answer this question, but when such a supplementation is made, it is no longer clear that what we have is a desert theory at all, rather than a consequence-based account. In addition, the possibility of a background system which is not universally just complicates the force of the claim that punishment aims to restore a moral equilibrium. Moreover, why should we necessarily give absolute priority to the demands of this narrow retributive conception of justice as opposed to those of mercy, forgiveness and humanity?

    Secondly, how much ought we to punish? This is the question to which the idea of desert promises us a clear and determinate answer, yet on analysis it fails to fulfill that promise. Without supplementation by either conventionally agreed scales of punishment or arguments from consequences, arguments from desert tell us very little about what punishments we ought to inflict. Thirdly, many of the arguments closely associated with the retributive tradition do generate a determinate answer to the question of whom we should punish: we should only punish those who have responsibly committed offences. It is perhaps in this area that the tradition really does encompass a principle which will be fundamental to the justification of punishment, and one which is indeed reflected in our differing response to the accidental, the negligent and the deliberate offence. Yet it is not clear why these arguments need employ the concept of desert: they can be developed perfectly adequately in terms of responsibility, fairness and other arguments from distributive as opposed to retributive justice, as we shall see. And in the absence of any adequate explanation of what the desert principle amounts to, let alone of a desert-based answer to the central question of why we should punish, the responsibility principle in any case only operates as a limiting one which would have to be combined with some other arguments to generate a justification of punishment. In addition, with respect to the broader aspect of the third question, that is, what kinds of actions ought to be punished, the principles we have considered have to be supplemented by a set of general, consistent yet independent political principles in order to give any complete guidance.

Negatively, then, the retributive tradition seems accurately to reflect our considered judgment about excuses, justifications and mitigating principles: it can tell us why not to punish certain categories of person; but it fails to tell us why we should punish any persons, and in what sorts of circumstances. In addition, consistent adherence to the main purported arguments from desert would issue in a criminal justice system in some respects radically more extensive, in others greatly less so, than those generally acknowledged to be acceptable. This last factor is of course not decisive, but we may use our intuitions where they are reflected in the shape of current systems as at least pointers to the need for modification of possible theories.

Andrew von Hirsch, "Proportionality in the Philosophy of Punishment"
in Michael Tonry, ed, *Crime and Justice: A Review of Research*, vol 16
(Chicago: University of Chicago Press, 1992) at 44-56, 79-94 (references omitted)

The last two decades have witnessed continuing debate over the rationales for allocating sanctions among convicted offenders. Various guiding theories or strategies have been put forward: "just deserts," "limiting retributivism," "selective incapacitation." The choice among them is sometimes treated as a matter of deciding allegiances: one adheres to "just deserts" or not, just as one decides to be a Democrat or a Red Sox fan or not. If one opts for just deserts, then one must worry about the scaling of penalties. If one does not, then perhaps one can disregard such issues.

Such a perspective is, I think, misleading. Sanctioning rationales differ from one another largely in the emphasis they give the principle of proportionality that is, the requirement that sanctions be proportionate in their severity to the seriousness of offenses. A desert rationale is one that gives the principle a dominant role. Other viewpoints permit proportionality to be trumped, to a greater or a lesser degree, by ulterior concerns such as those of crime control. ...

B. Desert Theories

Traditional retributive theories, such as Kant's, were sketchy. While contending that justice calls for deserved punishments, they seldom explored the grounds of penal desert claims: namely, *why* wrongdoers deserve punishment. Recently, philosophers have been looking for explanations. The two leading accounts today are, respectively, the "benefits and burdens" theory and "expressive" desert theories.

1. *Benefits and Burdens.* The benefits and burdens theory originated in the writings of two contemporary philosophers, Herbert Morris and Jeffrie Murphy. Both have recently questioned the theory, but a number of other philosophers continue to support it.

The theory offers a retrospectively oriented account of why offenders should be made to suffer punishment. The account focuses on the law as a jointly beneficial enterprise: it requires each person to desist from predatory conduct; by desisting, the person not only benefits others but is benefited by their reciprocal self-restraint. The person who victimizes others while still benefiting from their self-restraint thus obtains an unjust advantage. Punishment's function is to impose an offsetting disadvantage.

The theory has some attractions. It goes beyond fuzzy notions of "paying back" wrongdoing or "righting" the moral balance. It points to a particular unwarranted advantage the wrongdoer obtains: namely, that of benefiting from others' self-restraint while not reciprocally restraining himself. The rationale for the penalty is retrospective in focus, as a desert-oriented account should be: to offset, through punishment, the unjustly obtained benefit.

The theory has difficulties, however. One problem is that it requires a heroic belief in the justice of the underlying social arrangements. Unless it is true that our social and political systems succeed in providing mutual support for all members, including criminal offenders, then the offender has not necessarily benefited from others' law-abiding behavior.

The theory also becomes awkward when one uses it to try to decide the quantum of punishments. One difficulty is assessing benefits and burdens. The theory cannot focus on literal benefits the offender obtains as some of the worst assaultive crimes can be quite unprofitable whereas other (apparently less serious) theft crimes may provide the offender with a considerable profit. What thus must matter, instead, is the additional degree of freedom the offender has unfairly appropriated. But notions of degrees of freedom are unhelpful in making comparisons among crimes. It is one thing to say the armed robber or burglar permits himself actions that others refrain from taking and thereby unfairly obtains a liberty that others have relinquished in their (and his) mutual interest. It is different, and far more obscure, to say the robber deserves more punishment than the burglar because, somehow, he has arrogated to himself a greater degree of unwarranted freedom than the burglar has.

The theory would also seem to distort the way the gravity of crimes is assessed. R.A. Duff has pointed out the artificiality of treating victimizing crimes, such as armed robbery, in terms of the "freedom-of-action" advantage the robber gains over uninvolved third parties, rather than in terms of the intrusion into the interests or rights of actual or potential victims. Perhaps, tax evasion can be explained in terms of unjustified advantage: the tax evader refuses to pay his or her own tax, yet benefits from others' payments through the services he or she receives. Tax evasion, however, is scarcely the paradigm criminal offense, and it is straining to try to assess the heinousness of common offences such as robbery in similar fashion.

2. *"Expressive" Theories.* "Expressive" theories are those that base desert claims on the censuring aspects of punishment. Punishing someone consists of doing something painful or unpleasant to him, because he has committed a wrong, under circumstances and in a manner that conveys disapprobation of the offender for his wrong. Treating the offender as a wrongdoer, Richard Wasserstrom has pointed out, is central to the idea of punishment. The difference between a tax and a fine, for example, does not rest in the kind of material deprivation imposed: it is money, in both cases. It consists, rather, in the fact that with a fine the money is taken in a manner that conveys disapproval or censure; whereas with a tax no disapproval is implied.

A sanction that treats conduct as wrong that is, not a "neutral" sanction has two important moral functions that, arguably, are not reducible to crime prevention. One is to recognize the importance of the rights that have been infringed. Joel Feinberg has argued that the censure in punishment conveys to victims and potential victims that the state recognizes they are wronged by criminal conduct, that rights to which they are properly entitled have been infringed.

The other role of censure, discussed by R.A. Duff, is to address the wrongdoer as a moral agent, by appealing to his or her sense of right or wrong. This, Duff suggests, is not just a preventive strategy. While it is hoped that the actor will reconsider his actions and desist from wrongdoing in the future, the censure is not merely a means of changing his behavior otherwise, there would be no point in censuring actors who are repentant already (since they need no blame to make the effort to desist) or who are seemingly incorrigible (since they will not change despite the censure). Any human actor, the theory suggests, is a moral agent, capable (unless clearly incompetent) of evaluating others' assessment of their conduct. The repentant actor has his own assessment of the conduct confirmed through the disapproval of others; the defiant actor is made to understand and feel others' disapproval, even if he refuses to desist. Such communication of judgement and feeling, Duff argues, is what moral discourse among rational agents is about. What a purely "neutral" sanction not embodying blame would deny even if no less effective in preventing crime is precisely that essential status of the person as a moral agent. A neutral sanction would treat potential offenders much as beasts in a circus as beings that must be restrained, intimidated, or conditioned into submission because they are incapable of understanding that harmful conduct is wrong.

Such censure-oriented desert theories have some potential advantages. They are less dependent on the supposition that the underlying social system is wholly just: an actor with cause for complaint against the social system may still be to blame, for example, if he knowingly injures those who have done him no wrong. Moreover, the theory is more easily squared with notions of proportionality. If punishment is seen as an expression of blame for reprehensible conduct, then the quantum of punishment should depend on how reprehensible the conduct is. The punishment for typical victimizing crimes would depend on how much harm the conduct does, and how culpable the actor is for the harm and no longer on how much extra freedom of action the actor has arrogated to himself vis-à-vis third parties. …

V. The Desert Model

A desert model is a sentencing scheme that observes the proportionality principle: punishments are scaled according to the seriousness of crimes. While speaking of a "desert model" might suggest a unique scale, that is not the intent. A variety of scales of differing overall severity and differing sanctions might satisfy the requirements of this model. It is the core elements of a desert model that are sketched here. Fuller accounts of the model and its rationale are available elsewhere, as are discussions of the use of the model in scaling noncustodial sanctions.

A. Ordinal Proportionality

Ordinal proportionality is the requirement that penalties be scaled according to the comparative seriousness of crimes. Two main sub-requirements are involved. First, parity. The proportionality principle permits differences in severity of punishments only to the extent these differences reflect variations in the degree of blameworthiness of the conduct.

Accordingly, when offenders have been convicted of crimes of similar seriousness, they deserve punishment of similar severity unless special circumstances (i.e., of aggravation of mitigation) can be identified that render the offense, in the particular context, more or less deserving of blame than would normally be the case. Second, rank ordering. Punishing one crime more than another expresses more disapproval for the former crime, so that it is justified only if that crime is more serious. Punishments thus are to be ordered on a penalty scale so that their relative severity reflects the seriousness rankings of the crimes involved. This restricts the extent to which the arrangement of penalties on the scale can be varied internally for crime preventive purposes. Imposing exemplary penalties for a given type of offense to halt a recent upswing in its incidence, for example, would throw the ranking of offenses out of kilter unless other penalties are adjusted accordingly. …

B. Scale Anchoring and Cardinal Proportionality

Cardinal proportionality requires that a reasonable proportion be maintained between overall levels of punitiveness and the gravity of the criminal conduct. The scale should not, for example, be so inflated that even lesser criminal conduct is penalized with substantial deprivations.

Since cardinal proportionality places only broad and imprecise constraints on how much the penalty scale can be escalated or deflated, substantial leeway remains for locating the scale's anchoring points. What other factors would be relevant?

The penal traditions of the jurisdiction would be a starting point. Since the censure expressed through punishment is a convention, it, like any other convention, will be influenced by tradition. Normative considerations, however, may justify altering this convention. One such consideration is the goal of reducing the suffering visited on offenders.

Should crime prevention also be considered in setting the anchoring points? Certain preventive strategies would alter the comparative rankings of punishments and thus infringe ordinal proportionality. Selective incapacitation, for example, calls for the unequal punishment of offenders convicted of similar offenses on the basis of predictive criteria that do not reflect the seriousness of the criminal conduct.

Other preventive strategies, however, would not necessarily be open to this objection. Consider general deterrence. Were the penalties for particular offense categories to be set by reference to those penalties' expected deterrent effects, it would infringe ordinal proportionality, as it would no longer be the seriousness of crimes that determined the ordering of sanctions. Suppose, instead, that deterrence were used differently: penalties might be ordered according to the crimes' seriousness on the scale, with the scale's overall magnitude being decided (in part) by its expected net impact on crime. Were the requisite empirical knowledge available (which it is not today), it might be possible to compare the overall deterrent impacts of alternative scale magnitudes. That information could then be used to help anchor the scale, without disturbing the ordering of penalties. Moreover, this approach would not necessarily lead to increases in severity. Penalties might be cut back below their historical levels, on grounds that no significant loss of deterrence would occur.

• • •

A desert-based scheme is necessarily somewhat confining in its requirement that offense seriousness, and not a variety of possible other considerations, should decide comparative punishment. Its confining character makes it easier to scale penalties in a coherent fashion, but it also limits the possibilities of achieving various other goals or objectives. Moreover, the proportionality principle rests on a particular value that of equity. Other values of various sorts might be thought to override equity considerations, in at least some situations. Hence, we need to consider the "hybrid" models: those that, to a lesser or greater extent, allow departures from ordinal desert requirements in order to achieve other purposes. …

There is also the question of the degree of guidance a theory provides for the scaling of penalties. The proportionality principle, we have seen, offers no unique solutions, particularly because of the leeway it allows in the setting of a scale's anchoring points. However, the principle does offer considerable structure (although not unique solutions) for the comparative ordering of penalties. If proportionality is dislodged from this central, organizing role, it may not be easy to develop alternative (e.g., prevention-based) rationales that can provide much guidance. While a considerable body of theory exists concerning the principle of proportionality, lacunae remain. More thought needs to be given to the following topics, among others.

The Criteria for Gauging the Seriousness of Crimes, Particularly the Harm Dimension of Seriousness. A "living-standard" conception of harm may be a start, but it requires further scrutiny and elaboration.

Spacing. Proportionality calls not only for penalties ranked according to the gravity of crimes but also for spacing among penalties that reflects degrees of difference in crime seriousness. The spacing question, however, has received little attention.

Anchoring the Scale. If penalties are graded according to offense seriousness and the scale as a whole is not inflated or deflated unduly, the requirements of ordinal and cardinal proportionality have been satisfied, and one must look elsewhere for grounds for anchoring the scale. What these grounds might be remains largely to be explored.

There are also a number of practical issues needing further thought. One concerns back-up sanctions. Under any punishment theory emphasizing proportionality, non-custodial sanctions (rather than the severe penalty of imprisonment) should be employed for crimes other than serious ones. Using such sanctions raises the question of what should befall defendants if they violate the terms of the penalty or example, if they refuse to pay a fine or complete a stint of community service. How much added punitive bite may the back-up sanction legitimately entail?

Michael Tonry, "Proportionality, Parsimony, and Interchangeability of Punishments"
in R Antony Duff, Sandra Marshall, Rebecca E Dobash & Russell P Dobash, eds,
Penal Theory and Practice: Tradition and Innovation in Criminal Justice
(Manchester, UK: Manchester University Press, 1994) at 68-69, 74-75, 77-79
(references omitted)

Critique of Principle of Proportionality

Efforts to apply philosophers' distinctions to policy-makers' decisions necessarily raise different concerns than do disagreements among philosophers. Current initiatives to increase use of "non-custodial" penalties in the United Kingdom and "intermediate" sanctions in the United States necessarily require translation of theorists' distinctions into practitioners' realities.

It is at this point of translation that the case for strong proportionality conditions breaks down. There are at least five major difficulties. First, strong proportionality conditions require objectification of categories of offenders and offenses that are oversimplified and overinclusive. Second, proportionality arguments are often premised on objective legal measures of desert, typically current and past crimes, other than on the subjective degree of moral culpability expressed by the offender, under particular circumstances and conditions. Third, strong proportionality conditions run head-on into "just deserts in an unjust society." Fourth, strong proportionality conditions violate notions of parsimony by requiring imposition of unnecessarily severe punishments in individual cases in order to assure formal equivalence of suffering. Fifth, strong proportionality conditions presuppose that imposition of offenders' deserved punishments is an overriding moral imperative rather than one of several competing ethical considerations.

The Illusion of "Like-Situated Offenders"

If recent efforts in the United Kingdom and the United States to increase use of intermediate sanctions are to succeed, the appropriateness of different punishments for "like-situated offenders" must be recognised.

"Like-situated offender" is nested in quotation marks to express the artificiality of notions of like-situated offenders, comparable crimes, and generic punishments. A strong proportionality-in-punishment argument insists on equal treatment of like-situated offenders and proportionately different treatment of differently situated offenders. A fundamental difficulty is that this assumes that offenders can conveniently and justly be placed into a manageable number of more-or-less desert categories and that standard punishments can be prescribed for each category. Unfortunately, neither side of the desert–punishment equation lends itself to standardization.

Neither offenders nor punishments come in standard cases. The practice of dividing offenders and punishments into generic categories produces much unnecessary suffering and provides only illusory proportionality. A look at Minnesota's sentencing guidelines shows why. ...

Problems of objectification of crimes, offenders, and punishments are especially stark in a numerical guidelines system. In systems that feature written policy guidelines, they lurk beneath the surface. The Minnesota illustration is generally relevant to analysis of proportionality in punishment, however, because it makes real world implications of strong proportionality conditions starkly apparent. If proportionality is an, or the, overriding principle in the distribution of punishment in practice, then the imperfections of objectification that I describe are presumably regrettable but acceptable costs to be paid for a principled punishment system. If they appear unacceptable, the problem may be that the principle of proportionality offers less helpful guidance than its proponents urge.

Objective Measure of Responsibility

Von Hirsch's proportionality argument relies on objective measures of penal deservedness. This is curious. Desert theories, especially blaming theories, are premised on notions of individual blameworthiness, which seem inexorably linked to particularised judgments about moral responsibility. Objective measures of harm are seldom sufficient for conviction in the criminal law: that is why doctrines of competency, *mens rea*, and affirmative defense exist and why doctrines like strict liability and felony-murder are disfavored. If individualised moral judgments are germane to conviction, it is not obvious why they are not also germane to punishment.

If punishment is principally about blaming, surely it is relevant whether the offender was mentally impaired, socially disadvantaged, a reluctant participant, or moved by humane motives. Surely it is morally relevant, whatever the path to conviction, what the offender did, with what *mens rea*, and under what circumstances. Surely it is morally relevant whether a particular punishment will be more intensely experienced by one person than by another. In other words, the three subjective considerations that Minnesota's guidelines ignore—what did he really do, what will the conditions of his sanction really be, will he suffer more intensely than others—are relevant to moral judgments of blameworthiness and proportionate punishments. Nigel Walker expresses this when he observes: "Retributive reasoning would lead instead to a 'personal price list' which would take into account not only gradations of harm but offenders' culpability and sensibility."

The failure of von Hirsch's arguments to take account of individualised differences in culpability and individual effects of punishment looks strange when we recall that von Hirsch's is a retributive theory. Utilitarian theories reject interpersonal comparisons of utility, as Lionel Robbins' classic essay explains, either on measurement grounds (variable intensity of satisfactions, utility monsters, and so on), or on normative grounds (no individual's satisfactions *should* count for more). However, utilitarian theories are concerned with general policies and aggregate social measures and not with fine-tuned moral judgments.

An Unjust Society

Punishment schemes that attach high value to proportionality necessarily ignore the differing material conditions of life, including poverty, social disadvantage, and bias, in which human personalities and characters take form. The substantive criminal law rejects motive for intention and in the English-speaking countries allows no formal excusing or mitigating defense of social disadvantage. Yet in both the United Kingdom and the United States, most common law offenders are products of disadvantaged and deprived backgrounds and in both countries vastly disproportionate numbers of alleged, convicted, and imprisoned offenders are members of racial and ethnic minorities. The likelihood, for example, that a black American male is in prison today is eight times greater than that a white American male is in prison.

The problem of "just deserts in an unjust world" is a fundamental problem for a strong proportionality constraint. Whether retributive theories are rationalised in terms of benefits and burdens, or equilibrium, or blaming, or condemnation, or penance, they must presume equal opportunities for all to participate in society. when some are disabled from full participation by discrimination, disability, or exclusion, by denial of access to public goods, by the burdens of social and economic disadvantage, it is difficult to claim that they enjoy the benefits of autonomy that produce obligation. To take just one example, proponents of benefits and burdens theories are hard pressed to explain how a person who is denied society's benefits deserves to be burdened by social obligation. ...

Parsimony

Proponents of strong proportionality conditions necessarily prefer equality over minimization of suffering. For nearly two decades in the United States, Andrew von Hirsch and Norval Morris have been disagreeing over the role of parsimony in punishment. Von Hirsch has argued for strong desert limits on punishment and high priority to pursuit of equality and proportionality in punishment. Morris has argued that desert is a *limiting*, not a defining, principle of punishment and that policy should prescribe imposition of the least severe "not undeserved" sanction that meets legitimate policy ends. Within these outer bounds of "not undeserved" punishments Morris has consistently argued for observance of a principle of parsimony.

To some extent Morris and von Hirsch have argued past each other. Morris argues that a desert approach is unnecessarily harsh and von Hirsch responds by noting that he personally favors relatively modest punishments and, in any case, desert schemes are not inherently more severe than other schemes. In turn, von Hirsch argues that Morris's "not undeserved" proportionality constraints are vague, the breadth of allowable ranges of sentencing discretion is never specified, and Morris responds by noting that absolute measures of deserved punishment are unknowable and that his aim is to minimise imposition of penal suffering within bounds that any given community finds tolerable.

The problem is that they start from different major premises—von Hirsch's is the "principle of proportionality," Morris's the "principle of parsimony." The difference between them can be seen by imagining a comprehensive punishment scheme, perhaps resembling Minnesota's. Imagine that policy makers have conscientiously classified all offenders into ten categories and, using von Hirsch's ordinal/cardinal magnitude and anchoring points approach, have decided that all offenses at level VII deserve twenty-three-to twenty-five-month prison terms. Imagine further that reliable public opinion surveys have shown that 90 per cent of the general public would find a restrictive non-custodial punishment, "not unduly lenient" and a 36-month prison term "not unduly severe" for level VII offenses.

. . .

Sorting Out Principles

Disagreements about just punishments, like disagreements about the death penalty or abortion, are often in the end disagreements about powerful intuitions or deeply embedded values. It may be that differences in view between those who give primacy to proportionality and those who give primacy to parsimony cannot be bridged.

The burden of persuasion should rest, however, it seems to me on those who reject Isaiah Berlin's observations that "not all good things are compatible, still less all the ideals of mankind" and that "the necessity of choosing between absolute claims is then an inescapable characteristic of the human condition."

Punishment raises at least two important conflicts between ideals—between the principles of proportionality and parsimony, between the quests for criminal justice and social justice. ...

If we were single-mindedly devoted to equal opportunity, then, we should view equalization of life chances as an overriding goal of social policy. However, Fishkin argues, efforts to equalize life chances run head on into another powerful principle, that the value of autonomy in a private sphere of liberty encompasses a principle of family autonomy, of non-intrusion by the state into the family's sphere of private liberty.

In other words, equal opportunity and family autonomy conflict fundamentally. Full respect for equal opportunity would involve intrusion into the family that would widely be seen as objectionably intrusive. Full respect for family autonomy would widely be seen as cruel disregard for children's basic needs.

And so it may be with punishment. Principles of proportionality and parsimony may simply conflict, with resolutions between them necessarily partial and provisional.

IV. COMMUNICATIVE DIMENSIONS OF LEGAL PUNISHMENT

Two important theories of punishment emphasize the communicative nature of sentencing. In the first, Andrew von Hirsch elaborates on his censure-based account of legal punishment. In the second, an alternative perspective that is also communicative in nature is described by RA Duff. Duff's theory shares some commonalities with von Hirsch's theory, but it is also conceptually distinct. According to Duff, punishment should be understood as a kind of secular penance that seeks to communicate censure of the offender, but also (and here is where his theory differs from that of von Hirsch) to persuade the offender to repent, reform, and seek reconciliation with the victim and the community. From this description it can be seen that Duff's penitential theory is more ambitious than the communicative theory advocated by von Hirsch, according to which the expression of censure is sufficient (along with the prudential disincentive to reoffend).

Andrew von Hirsch, *Censure and Sanctions*
(Oxford: Oxford University Press, 1996) at 9–13 (footnotes omitted)

2. *Censure-Based Justifications for Punishment*

Reprobative accounts of the institution of the criminal sanction are those that focus on that institution's condemnatory features, that is, its role as conveying censure or blame. The penal sanction clearly does convey blame. Punishing someone consists of visiting a deprivation (hard treatment) on him, because he supposedly has committed a wrong, in a manner that expresses disapprobation of the person for his conduct. Treating the offender as a wrongdoer, Richard Wasserstrom has pointed out, is central to the idea of punishment. The difference between a tax and a fine does not rest in the kind of material deprivation (money in both cases). It consists, rather in the fact that the fine conveys disapproval or censure, whereas the tax does not.

An account of the criminal sanction which emphasizes its reprobative function has the attraction of being more comprehensible, for blaming is something we do in everyday moral judgements. A censure-based account is also easier to link to proportionality: if punishment conveys blame, it would seem logical that the quantum of punishment should bear a reasonable relation to the degree of blameworthiness of the criminal conduct.

Why the Censure?

That punishment conveys blame or reprobation is, as just mentioned, evident enough. But why *should* there be a reprobative response to the core conduct with which the criminal law deals? Without an answer to that question, legal punishment might arguably be replaced by some other institution that has no blaming implications—a response akin to a tax meant to discourage certain behaviour.

P.F. Strawson provides the most straightforward account. The capacity to respond to wrongdoing by reprobation or censure, he says, is simply part of a morality that holds people accountable for their conduct. When a person commits a misdeed, others judge him adversely, because his conduct was reprehensible. Censure consists of the expression of that judgement, plus its accompanying sentiment of disapproval. It is addressed to the actor because he or she is the person responsible. One would withhold the expression of blame only if there were special reasons for not confronting the actor: for example, doubts about one's standing to challenge him.

While Strawson's account seems correct as far as it goes—blaming *does* seem part of holding people accountable for their actions—it may be possible to go a bit further and specify some of the positive moral functions of blaming.

Censure addresses the victim. He or she has not only bee injured, but *wronged* through someone's culpable act. it thus would not suffice just to acknowledge that the injury has occurred or convey sympathy (as would be appropriate when someone has been hurt by a natural catastrophe). Censure, by directing disapprobation at the person responsible, acknowledges that the victim's hurt occurred through another's fault.

Censure also addresses the act's perpetrator. He is conveyed a certain message concerning his wrongful conduct, namely that he culpably as injured someone, and is disapproved of for having done so. Some kind of moral response is expected on his part—an expression of concern, and acknowledgement of wrongdoing, or an effort at better self-restraint. A reaction of indifference would, if the censure is justified, itself be grounds for criticizing him.

Censure gives the actor the opportunity for so responding, but it is not a technique for evoking specified sentiments. Were inducing penitent reflection the chief aim, as R.A. Duff has claimed, there would be no point in censuring actors who are either repentant or defiant. The repentant actor understands and regrets his wrongdoing already; the defiant actor will not accept the judgement of disapproval which the censure expresses. Yet we would not wish to exempt from blame either the repentant or the seemingly incorrigible actor. Both remain moral agents, capable of understanding others' assessment of their conduct—and censure conveys that assessment. The repentant actor finds his self-evaluation confirmed through the disapproval of others; the defiant actor is made to feel and understand the disapproval of others, whatever he himself may think of his conduct. Such communication of judgement and feeling is the essence of moral discourse among rational agents.

Were the primary aim that of producing actual changes in the actor's moral attitudes, moreover, the condemnor would ordinarily seek information about his personality and outlook, so as better to foster the requisite attitudinal changes. But blaming, in ordinary life as well as in more formal contexts, does not involve such enquiries. One ascribes wrongdoing to the actor and conveys the disapprobation—limiting enquiry about the actor to questions of his capacity for choice. The condemnor's role is not that of the mentor or priest.

The criminal law gives the censure it expresses yet another role: that of addressing third parties, and providing them with reason for desistence. Unlike blame in everyday contexts, the criminal sanction announces in advance that specified categories of conduct are punishable. Because the prescribed sanction is one which expresses blame, this conveys the message that the conduct is reprehensible, and should be eschewed. It is not necessarily a matter of inculcating that the conduct is wrong, for those addressed (or many of them) may well understand that already. Rather the censure embodied in the prescribed sanction serves to *appeal* to people's sense of the conduct's wrongfulness, as a reason for desistence.

This normative message expressed in penal statutes is not reducible, as penal utilitarians might suppose, to a mere inducement to compliance—one utilized because the citizenry could be more responsive to moral appeals than bare threats. If persons are called upon to desist because the conduct is wrong, there ought to be good reasons for supposing that it *is* wrong; and the message expressed through the penalty about its degree of wrongfulness ought to reflect how reprehensible the conduct indeed is. This point will be elaborated upon in the next chapter, where penal censure is contrasted with instrumentalist strategies of "shaming."

The foregoing account explains why predatory conduct should not be dealt with through neutral sanctions that convey no disapproval. Such sanctions—even if they were no less effective in discouraging the behaviour—deny the status of the person as an agent capable of moral understanding. A neutral sanction would treat offenders or potential offenders much as tigers might be treated in a circus, as beings that have to be restrained, intimidated, or conditioned into compliance because they are incapable of understanding why biting people (or other tigers) is wrong. A condemnatory sanction treats the actor as a *person* who is capable of such understanding.

A committed utilitarian might insist that treating the actor as a person in this fashion can only be warranted on instrumental grounds. Nigel Walker takes this view: if "... the message which expresses blame need have not utility," he asserts, "where lies the moral necessity?" This, however, is reductionist. Treating the actor as someone capable of choice, rather than as a tiger, is a matter of acknowledging his dignity as a human being. Is this acknowledgement warranted only if it leads to beneficial social consequences? Those consequences would not necessarily be those of crime prevention—for, as just noted, it might be possible to devise a "neutral" sanction (one designed to visit material deprivation but convey no blame) that prevents crime at least as well. Might society somehow have better cohesion if actors are treated as being responsible (and hence subject to censure) for their actions? Making such a claim would involve trying to reduce ethical judgments to difficult-to-confirm predictions about social structure. While one can have some confidence in the moral judgement that offenders should be treated as agents capable of choice, it will be difficult to verify that so treating them will lead to a more smoothly running society.

Why the Hard Treatment?

It is still necessary to address punishment's other constitutive element: deprivation or hard treatment. Some desert theorists (John Kleinig and Igor Primoratz, for example) assert that notions of censure can account also for the hard treatment. They argue that censure (at least in certain social contexts) cannot be expressed adequately in purely verbal or symbolic terms; that hard treatment is needed to show that the disapprobation is meant seriously. For example, an academic department does not show disapproval of a serious lapse by a colleague merely through a verbal admonition; to convey the requisite disapproval, some curtailment of privileges is called for. This justification has plausibility outside legal contexts, where the deprivations involved are modest enough to serve chiefly to underline the intended disapproval. However, I doubt that the argument sustains the criminal sanction.

The criminal law seems to have preventive features in its very design. When the State criminalizes conduct, it issues a legal threat; such conduct is proscribed, and violation will result in the imposition of specified sanctions. The threat appears to be explicitly aimed at discouraging the proscribed conduct. Criminal sanctions also seem too onerous to serve just to give credibility to the censure. Even were penalties substantially scaled down from what they are today, some of them still could involve significant deprivations of liberty or property. In the absence of a preventive purpose, it is hard to conceive of such intrusions as having the sole function of showing that the State's disapproval is seriously intended.

This reasoning led me to suggest, in a 1985 volume, a bifurcated account of punishment. The penal law, I said, performs two interlocking functions. By threatening unpleasant consequences, it seeks to discourage criminal behaviour. Through the censure expressed by such sanctions, the law registers disapprobation of the behaviour. Citizens are thus provided with moral and not just prudential reasons for desistence.

However, the two elements in my account, reprobation and prevention, remained uneasily matched. Whereas the censuring element appeals to the person's moral agency, does not the preventive element play merely on his fear of unpleasant consequences? If the person is capable of being moved by moral appeal, why the threat? If not capable and thus in need of the threat, it appears that he is being treated like a tiger. A clarification of the preventive function—and its relation to the censuring function—is needed.

The preventive function of the sanction should be seen, I think, as supplying a prudential reason that is tied to, and supplements, the normative reason conveyed by penal censure. The criminal law, through the censure embodied in its prescribed sanctions, conveys that the conduct is wrong, and a moral agent thus is given grounds for desistence. He may (given human fallibility) be tempted nevertheless. What the prudential disincentive can do is to provide him a further reason—a prudential one—for resisting the temptation. Indeed, an agent who has accepted the sanction's message that he ought not offend, and who recognizes his susceptibility to temptation, could favour the existence of such a prudential disincentive, as an aid to carrying out what he himself recognizes as the proper course of conduct.

A certain conception of human nature, of which I spoke in the previous chapter, underlies this idea of the preventive function as a supplementary prudential disincentive. Persons are assumed to be moral agents, capable of taking seriously the message conveyed through the sanction, that the conduct is reprehensible. They are fallible, nevertheless, and thus face temptation. The function of the disincentive is to provide a prudential reasons for resisting the temptation. The account would make no sense were human beings much better or worse; an angel would require no appeals to prudence, and a brute could not be appealed to through censure.

RA Duff, *Punishment, Communication, and Community*
(Oxford: Oxford University Press, 2001) at 129-30

On my account, criminal punishment should be conceived of as a communicative enterprise that aims to communicate to offenders the censure they deserve for their crimes, and thus to bring them to repent their crimes, to reform themselves, and to reconcile themselves with those they have wronged. This account, I claim, provides a morally plausible rationale for penal hard treatment as part of this communicative enterprise—as a secular penance, which itself serves the aims of repentance, reform, and reconciliation. It does justice to the central retributivist concern that punishment must focus on and be justified by its relationship to the crime for which it is imposed. It also does justice to the consequentialist concern that punishment must be justified by some good that it aims to achieve, and to the abolitionist concern that we should aim not to "deliver pain" to offenders but to achieve such goods as restoration, reparation, or reconciliation. But it does justice to such concerns by revising or reinterpreting them.

In relation to retributivism, it explains the meaning of the idea that the guilty deserve to suffer, but it does so partly by insisting that punishment cannot be purely backward-looking. It must also aim to achieve some future good. In relation to consequentialism, it identifies the goods that punishment should aim to achieve, but insists that punishment is not to be justified as a contingently efficient instrumental means to those ends. It is justified as a method that is intrinsically appropriate to those ends, once they are properly understood. From this it also follows that punishment can be justified as a proper attempt to pursue those ends even when we have good reason to believe that it will fail to achieve them.

In relation to abolitionism (and accounts of "restorative" justice, of mediation, and of probation that portray their aims as essentially non-punitive), it agrees that we should aim at such ends as restoration and reconciliation, but insists that in the kinds of cases that properly concern the criminal justice system, what makes these reparative aims necessary is the fact that a wrong has been committed and the restoration and reconciliation are then properly achieved precisely by punishment—understood not as mere pain delivery but as a secular penance.

Punishment as thus conceived is consistent with, indeed expressive of, the defining values of a liberal political community. It addresses offenders, not as outlaws who have forfeited their standing as citizens, but as full members of the normative political community; it is inclusionary rather than exclusionary. It treats them as citizens who are both bound and protected by the central liberal values of autonomy, freedom and privacy. It holds them answerable, as responsible moral agents, for the public wrongs they commit. But it also respects their own autonomy (since it seeks to persuade rather than merely coerce), their freedom (since it constitutes a legitimate response to their wrongdoing and leaves them free to remain unpersuaded), and their privacy (since it addresses only those aspects of their lives and actions that properly fall within the public sphere).

V. MOVING FROM PHILOSOPHY TO PRACTICE:
THE MODEL PENAL CODE PROJECT

A. Limiting Retributivism and the American Law Institute

Relying on the work of Norval Morris, *The Future of Imprisonment* (Chicago: University of Chicago Press, 1974), the sentencing discourse in the United States has spawned another approach, now known as "limiting retributivism." This takes some utilitarian concerns and caps them with proportionality. Limiting retributivists argue that a sentence cannot be imposed that is out of proportion to the particular offence and that attention must always be paid to what the sentence is intended to achieve. That is, restraint or "the principle of parsimony," as Morris called it, must operate to ensure that the least intrusive sentence is imposed. While this recognizes the importance of proportionality, it stands in stark contrast to von Hirsch and Ashworth, who argue that individual desert should determine the sentence, generally without regard to consequential effects. While Morris would agree (at 75) that it is unjust to impose "punishment in excess of what is felt by the community to be the maximum suffering justly related to the harm the criminal has inflicted," he would add that judges must be able to choose and pursue legitimate sentencing objectives within the limit of what the community finds acceptable.

Pragmatism has influenced the evolution of limiting retributivism, which now accepts that judicial discretion needs to be constrained to a greater extent than simply providing an upper limit. Recent accounts accept a greater role for proportionality and less room for judicial discretion. As a result, proportionality now also imposes a lower limit, thereby establishing a band or range of acceptable punishment.

In 2001, the American Law Institute (ALI) launched its Model Penal Code Sentencing Project. The Project has been developing a model set of provisions: see Model Penal Code: Sentencing, Discussion Draft No 11, 2015. This project will ultimately (probably in 2016) result in a draft code that will follow the general approach of limiting retributivism.

> One goal of a revised Model code is to encourage the introduction of generally applicable rules and principles to the sanctioning process to the extent such governance is feasible, reserving room for individualized discretion in cases where good reasons can be cited for a more qualitative mode of decision-making.

The ALI discussions and reports start with Norval Morris and limiting retributivism by acknowledging the importance of proportionality in sentencing, but also expressing concern that proportionality cannot provide sufficiently precise guidance. Despite its endorsement of limiting retributivism in general, the ALI's notion of penal parsimony is somewhat different from that advocated by Norval Morris. Section 1.02(2)(a)(i) of the latest (11th) ALI draft makes proportionality the first general principle of sentencing: "[T]o render sentences in all cases within a range of severity proportionate to the gravity of offenses; the harm done to victims, and the blameworthiness of offenders."

This is followed by the following reference to utilitarian considerations:

> [W]hen reasonably feasible, to achieve offender rehabilitation, general deterrence, incapacitation of dangerous offenders, restitution to crime victims, and reintegration of offenders into the law abiding community, provided these goals are pursued within the boundaries of proportionality in subsection (a)(i); and (iii) to render sentences no more severe than necessary to achieve the applicable purposes in subsections (a)(i) and (a)(ii).

In crafting its proposed model, the ALI makes a number of important choices, many of which reflect pragmatic considerations spawned by the American experience and developed by leading limiting retributivism advocates, particularly Michael Tonry. Essentially, among other related elements, the model decides that a sentencing system must:

- pursue the "elusive commodity" of a high degree of uniformity in sentences;
- apply its principles on a system-wide basis;
- include some power to provide, or at least address, resources;
- deal with "racial and ethnic over-representations"; and
- provide better information about itself and its effectiveness.

The ALI's latest draft leaves some important questions to judicial discretion. Section 1.02(2)(b)(i) states that a sentencing system should look "to preserve judicial discretion to individualize sentences within a framework of law." It defines a range of severity within which a sentence must fall, but permits judges to pursue specific objectives within that range (so long as they do so with restraint). As well, it encourages the use of intermediate sanctions. Significantly, the draft currently adds procedural and normative factors to the sentencing matrix, including individualization, the elimination of discrimination, the prevention of unjustified racial overrepresentation in sentenced groups, and the encouragement of intermediate punishments. This permits judges to impose proportional sentences while still maintaining judicial concern for the human aspects of the sentencing system and preserving the courts' ability to respond where warranted by the circumstances of the case. Perhaps the breadth of these considerations leaves the ALI's model provisions open to the criticism that Andrew Ashworth calls "cafeteria-style" sentencing—that is, as in Canada, judges are free to choose among principles, largely according to their own predilections.

As noted, much of the ALI approach is pragmatic. This may be attributable to recent American experiences, including the high and highly racialized jail population. As well, it needs to be remembered that the ALI wants to create a model that is likely to be adopted by the states. Hence, in many respects, its work represents not only pragmatism but also compromises. An important but controversial aspect of the ALI approach is its advocacy of the role of a "sentencing commission" to construct the guidelines that would be provided to judges. This is a response to a two-pronged argument: the judiciary needs guidance, but it lacks the institutional competence to do the empirical and policy analysis that fair and proportionate guidelines require. While some sentencing commissions in the United States— for example, Minnesota—have been applauded for their work, other schemes, including the federal one, have been heavily criticized for their rigidity and punitive nature. Recognizing the potential pitfalls, the ALI draft details the constitution, structure, mandate, and resources that an effective commission requires.

NOTE

The initial focus of this introductory chapter was on punishment and the traditional debate between retributivist and utilitarian justifications for punishment. When we moved into the more recent period, we observed how contemporary thinkers have wrestled with issues that go beyond any general justifications and attempt to provide theoretical explanations for how punishments ought to be allocated across a range of offences. In other words, the debate has shifted from punishment to the more pragmatic institution of sentencing and its distribution of punishments. The next chapter continues in this direction, but moves from theory to the set of concepts and methodologies that Canadian judges have used to decide which sentencing option should be used in a particular case.

FURTHER READING

Ashworth, Andrew. *Sentencing and Criminal Justice*, 6th ed (Cambridge: Cambridge University Press, 2015).

Brooks, Thom, ed. *Sentencing: Critical Essays in Legal Philosophy* (Farnham, UK: Ashgate, 2014).

Canadian Sentencing Commission, Honourable JR Omer Archambault, Chair. *Sentencing Reform: A Canadian Approach—Report of the Canadian Sentencing Commission* (Ottawa: Supply and Services Canada, 1987).

Frase, Richard S. *Just Sentencing* (New York: Oxford University Press, 2013).

Hart, Herbert. *Punishment and Responsibility: Essays in the Philosophy of Law* (Oxford: Oxford University Press, 2008).

Petersilia, Joan & Kevin R Reitz, eds. *The Oxford Handbook of Sentencing and Corrections* (New York: Oxford University Press, 2012).

Simmons, A John, Marshall Cohen, Joshua Cohen & Charles R Beitz, eds. *Punishment: A Philosophy and Public Affairs Reader* (Princeton, NJ: Princeton University Press, 1994).

Slobogin, Christopher. "Risk Assessment" in Joan Petersilia & Kevin R Reitz, eds, *The Oxford Handbook of Sentencing and Corrections* (New York: Oxford University Press, 2012) ch 8.

Tonry, Michael. *Why Punish? How Much?* (New York: Oxford University Press, 2011).

Tonry, Michael, ed. *Retributivism Has a Past. Has It a Future?* (New York: Oxford University Press, 2011).

Tonry, Michael & Richard S Frase, eds. *Sentencing and Sanctions in Western Countries* (New York: Oxford University Press, 2001).

von Hirsch, Andrew. *Censure and Sanctions* (Oxford: Oxford University Press, 1993).

von Hirsch, Andrew & Andrew Ashworth. *Proportionate Sentencing: Exploring the Principles* (Oxford: Oxford University Press, 2005).

von Hirsch, Andrew, Andrew Ashworth & Julian Roberts, eds. *Principled Sentencing*, 3rd ed (Oxford: Hart, 2009).

Webster, Cheryl Marie & Anthony N Doob. "Searching for Sasquatch: Deterrence of Crime Through Sentence Severity" in Joan Petersilia & Kevin R Reitz, eds, *The Oxford Handbook of Sentencing and Corrections* (New York: Oxford University Press, 2012) ch 7.

CHAPTER TWO

Judicial Methodology and the Legislative Context

I. INTRODUCTION

Chapter 1, An Introduction to Legal Punishment: Philosophy and Objectives, illustrates the historical divergence of philosophical views about the justifications for punishment. The vigorous debate is understandable given that it encompasses not only the controversial subject of punishment but also fundamental questions about the relationship between the state and its citizens. Punishment is, after all, the application of coercive force by the state. Of course, punishment and sentencing are not synonymous or congruent concepts given that sentencing involves considerations and objectives that are not purely punitive.

This chapter examines the positive law of sentencing as stated by Parliament and applied by the courts. It traces the evolution of judicial attitudes in Canada toward sentencing and the changing statutory framework, especially the reform in 1996 of Part XXIII of the *Criminal Code*, RSC 1985, c C-46, which, for the first time, legislated a statutory statement of the principles and purposes of sentencing. This is set out later in this chapter.

This chapter has three purposes. First, we try to identify the aims of sentencing as they are formally recognized in Canada. Second, we look at the methodological guidance that is provided to judges who must make sentencing decisions. We consider whether there is any more consistency or coherence in the Canadian law on sentencing than there is in debates concerning the philosophical dimensions of the subject. In practical terms, is there sufficient guidance to sentencing judges so that the function of sentencing can be considered a principled exercise that produces acceptable results?

The third purpose of this chapter relates to issues of sentencing efficacy. Aside from controversies about the premises of sentencing, there is also considerable debate about the effectiveness of particular sentences and sentencing objectives. While this subject takes up much space in the media, it is really the domain of modern criminology, which is concerned with not only theoretical aspects of sentencing but also empirical assessments of the administration of criminal justice. This chapter begins to explore the question of whether judges ought to be attuned to these questions and, if so, how current research can be integrated into judicial methodology.

II. THE ROLE OF JUDICIAL DISCRETION

The question of judicial discretion is at the heart of understanding sentencing in Canada. Until 1996, the *Criminal Code* provided no guidance as to the objectives of sentencing or its relevant principles. Judges filled in the conceptual blanks as part of a discretionary exercise. Over the years, many jurists have asserted that the chief aim of sentencing was the protection of society. However, even this simple statement has produced various interpretations, uncertainty, and contradiction, given the conflicting views about how protection is best achieved. More recently, we see that our Code designates the concept of proportionality as a "fundamental" principle of sentencing. Some suggest that it is *the* "fundamental" principle. If proportionality is clearly understood and consistently applied, it would indeed produce greater uniformity. But is uniformity the only goal of a sentencing system? What about utilitarian and restorative objectives? What about individualization? The scope for debate and disagreement has produced a degree of disparity in sentencing. Perhaps some degree of disparity is healthy. However, from a systemic perspective, there is a strong argument for principles that shape judicial discretion to ensure that examples of disparity are justifiable and clearly explained.

The problem for the judiciary starts with the recognition that phrases such as "a proper and just sentence," "a fit sentence," or "an appropriate sentence" do not lead inevitably to a specific result. Without providing a clear decision-making template, two reasonable people could reach different conclusions about what is a fit sentence in a given case with neither being self-evidently wrong. Moreover, if sentencing is an individualized exercise, as our Supreme Court has regularly pronounced, it requires flexibility to ensure a result that is fit for the offender and for the administration of criminal justice. In Canada, the historical record suggests that the best mechanism for ensuring this result is the trained use of judicial discretion. Parliament has rarely prescribed sentences that must be imposed following a finding of guilt. Recently, there is a trend in this direction that arises in certain visceral high-profile situations. As a result, one observes a growing number of situations in which Parliament has declared penalties that must be imposed, typically a mandatory minimum term of imprisonment. Still, the majority of offences, as set out in the *Criminal Code*, only stipulate a maximum term of imprisonment and allow for a range of alternatives to imprisonment.

Although the reform of 1996 (discussed later in this chapter) refined the debate, judicial discretion continues to play the central role in Canadian sentencing, and its importance is acknowledged in the *Criminal Code* in much the same form as it appeared in the 1892 legislation:

> 718.3(1) Where an enactment prescribes different degrees or kinds of punishment in respect of an offence, the *punishment to be imposed is, subject to the limitations prescribed in the enactment, in the discretion of the court that convicts a person who commits the offence.*
>
> (2) Where an enactment prescribes punishment in respect of an offence, the punishment to be imposed is, subject to the limitations prescribed in the enactment, in the discretion of the court that convicts a person who commits the offence, but no punishment is a minimum punishment unless it is declared to be a minimum punishment. [Emphasis added.]

The breadth of the discretion recognized in the law of sentencing should be immediately apparent. Judges not only are empowered to determine what is a fit sentence in the individual case but also have a discretion to determine the proper aims of sentencing decisions in the general run of cases. Wherever there is such discretion, there is also the possibility of disparity in approach and in result.

A. The Amalgam or "Wise Blending" of Values

Whether by design or default, Canadian courts historically adopted an approach that allowed judges to recognize and weigh various aims of sentencing, including rehabilitation, incapacitation, retribution, denunciation, and deterrence. In *R v Lyons*, [1987] 2 SCR 309, a dangerous offender case, La Forest J said:

> [26] In a rational system of sentencing, the respective importance of prevention, deterrence, retribution and rehabilitation will vary according to the nature of the crime and the circumstances of the offender.

This approach has made individualization the key perspective for judicial decision-making.

R v Willaert

[1953] OR 282, 105 CCC 172 (CA)

MacKAY JA:

The appellant was tried at Sarnia on September 16, 17, 18, 19 and 22, 1952, before Barlow J and a jury, on an indictment charging that he on May 2, 1952, committed rape on one Shirley Post, and was found guilty. The learned trial Judge sentenced the appellant to imprisonment for life. This application is taken for leave to appeal against the length of sentence.

By s. 299 of the *Cr. Code*, a person guilty of rape may be sentenced "to suffer death or to imprisonment for life, and to be whipped." ...

A useful statement of the policy of the law as administered in England is set forth in 9 Hals., 2nd ed., pp. 254-5, para. 362: "The policy of the law is, as regards most crimes, to fix a maximum penalty, which is intended only for the worst cases, and to leave to the discretion of the judge to determine to what extent in a particular case the punishment awarded should approach to or recede from the maximum limit. The exercise of this discretion is a matter of prudence and not of law."

There is little in the record itself to mitigate the gravity of the crime; nevertheless, in measuring sentence, every circumstance should be taken into consideration, and in the exercise of judicial discretion regard should be had to: the age of the prisoner; his past and present condition of life; the nature of the crime; whether the prisoner previously had a good character; whether it is a first offence; whether he has a family dependent upon him, the temptation; whether the crime was deliberate or committed on momentary impulse; the penalty provided by the Code or statute; whether the offence is one for which under the code the offender is liable to corporal punishment and, if so, whether corporal punishment should be imposed.

I am respectfully of opinion that there are three principles of criminal justice requiring earnest consideration in the determination of punishment, *viz.*, deterrence, reformation and retribution.

The governing principle of deterrence is, within reason and common sense, that the emotion of fear should be brought into play so that the offender may be made afraid to offend again and also so that others who may have contemplated offending will be restrained by the same controlling emotion. Society must be reasonably assured that the punishment meted out to one will not actually encourage others, and when some form of crime has become widespread the element of deterrence must look more to the restraining of others than to the actual offender before the Court.

Reformation is the most hopeful element in the question of punishment in most cases, and it is in that direction that the efforts of those concerned with criminal justice will be more and more directed. But reformation, too, has its distinct limitations. It has been found in England that many who have passed through all the stages of binding over to keep the peace, probation, approved school, Borstal institution, and prison, have yet become habitual criminals. They appear to be beyond all human reformative agencies.

The underlying and governing idea in the desire for retribution is in no way an eye for an eye or a tooth for a tooth, but rather that the community is anxious to express its repudiation of the crime committed and to establish and assert the welfare of the community against the evil in its midst. Thus, the infliction of punishment becomes a source of security to all and "is elevated to the first rank of benefits, when it is regarded not as an act of wrath or vengeance against a guilty or unfortunate individual who has given way to mischievous inclinations, but as an indispensable sacrifice to the common safety": See Bentham, Rationale of Punishment, p. 20, quoted at p. 255 of Halsbury *loc. cit.*

I am respectfully of opinion that the true function of criminal law in regard to punishment is in a wise blending of the deterrent and reformative, with retribution not entirely disregarded, and with a constant appreciation that the matter concerns not merely the Court and the offender but also the public and society as a going concern. Punishment is, therefore, an art—a very difficult art—essentially practical, and directly related to the existing needs of society. A punishment appropriate today might have been quite unacceptable 200 years ago and probably would be absurd 200 years hence. It is therefore impossible to lay down hard and fast and permanent rules.

· · ·

The tendency in recent years has been to impose more moderate sentences. At one time it was commonly assumed that the only purpose of punishment was to punish, but today its function is conceived in very different terms. It may be to try to reclaim the offender for society, to induce and stimulate habits of regularity and reliability even to compensate partially for an education that ended prematurely, and generally to try to awaken in the mind of the vicious and irresponsible a sense of the obligations of life and citizenship. Such moderation in sentence may not be warranted in the case of confirmed criminals but in that of the first offender an effort at reclamation is surely the part of wisdom and prudence in judicial discretion.

NOTE

The general principle stated in *Willaert* remains good law in the sense that it provides a fair explanation of the Canadian approach—a proper sentence requires a wise blending of penal aims to be "fit" for the offence and the offender. Some of the more specific claims made by MacKay JA have been eclipsed by later developments.

The characterization of sentencing and punishment as an art, however, seems astonishing. More recently, Australian courts have applied the phrase "intuitive synthesis" to describe the judicial function. Is this any more helpful? In what other area of law can one find resort to such an unprincipled explanation of the judicial role? Perhaps this was simply a reflection of an inability to provide a clearer explanation. Certainly it could not have been an assertion of some special talent bestowed on judges at the moment of their appointment. For many decades, *Willaert* was often cited as the leading example of the role of judicial discretion, which included not only the issue of specific options that might be considered but a determination of what are "fit" or appropriate aims of sentencing in a given case. The scope of discretion, in both senses, might be constrained by the guidance of appellate courts or, in some instances, by legislative directive. Indeed, the evolution of sentencing policy requires guidance on a number of fronts. The *Willaert* approach provided an open and flexible template for sentencing judges, leaving their discretion dramatically unconstrained.

One person's flexibility is another person's vagueness and lack of clarity. The "amalgam" or "wise blending" approach was discussed by David P Cole & Allan Manson, *Release from Imprisonment: The Law of Sentencing, Parole, and Judicial Review* (Toronto: Carswell, 1990) at 16-17:

> While this blending of penal objectives permeates the sentencing process and provides both systemic and individual justifications, it generates its own inevitable tensions due to the inherent contradictory nature of some objectives. At the same time, it hides the uncomfortable observation that precision and consistency may be unattainable goals.
>
> Added to this calculus we see judicial recognition of particular factors which highlight the influence of one or another of the principles of sentencing. Cases involving youthful offenders, mentally ill offenders or recidivists, and cases arising from violence against children, women or racial minorities have provoked judges to emphasize particular principles. Thus, notwithstanding the general acceptance of the amalgam approach, the existence of some distinctive features highlights the significance of protection of the public, rehabilitation, deterrence or denunciation in direct response to the category of case.

The amalgam approach allowed judges to determine sentences by referring to an array of different considerations, even different rationales. It asserts no priority among the aims of sentencing, although the courts of the various provinces have developed some rules of practice under the guidance of the Court of Appeal. The amalgam approach does not prevent the courts of different provinces from adopting different approaches, nor does it prevent judges within a single court from disagreeing. Andrew Ashworth has criticized this approach to judicial discretion as inimical to "rule of law" values by permitting sentencing decisions premised on different rationales:

> Both the element of public censure and the potential loss of fundamental rights render it imperative that the rule of law should apply to such decisions as far as possible: although the sentencing decision will always require an element of judgment, that judgment should be exercised within a framework of law, applying principles and standards set out in advance.

A Ashworth, *Sentencing and Criminal Justice*, 6th ed (Cambridge: Cambridge University Press, 2015) at 446. Does the Canadian amalgam approach violate the rule of law? Is it a healthy example of the common law in action, or is it a recipe for unjustified disparity?

III. STATUTORY STATEMENT OF PURPOSE, PRINCIPLES, AND OBJECTIVES

Following the Report of the Canadian Sentencing Commission, *Sentencing Reform: A Canadian Approach* (Ottawa: Minister of Supply and Services Canada, 1987), Parliament added the following, with some subsequent modifications, to the *Criminal Code* in 1996: see *An Act to amend the Criminal Code (sentencing) and other Acts in consequence thereof*, SC 1995, c 22 ("Bill C-41"):

> 718. The fundamental purpose of sentencing is to protect society and to contribute, along with crime prevention initiatives, to respect for the law and the maintenance of a just, peaceful and safe society by imposing just sanctions that have one or more of the following objectives:
>
> (a) to denounce unlawful conduct and the harm done to victims or to the community that is caused by unlawful conduct;
>
> (b) to deter the offender and other persons from committing offences;
>
> (c) to separate offenders from society, where necessary;
>
> (d) to assist in rehabilitating offenders;
>
> (e) to provide reparations for harm done to victims or to the community; and
>
> (f) to promote a sense of responsibility in offenders, and acknowledgment of the harm done to victims or to the community.
>
> • • •
>
> 718.1 A sentence must be proportionate to the gravity of the offence *and* the degree of responsibility of the offender.
>
> 718.2 A court that imposes a sentence shall also take into consideration the following principles:
>
> (a) a sentence should be increased or reduced to account for any relevant aggravating or mitigating circumstances relating to the offence or the offender, and, without limiting the generality of the foregoing,
>
> (i) evidence that the offence was motivated by bias, prejudice or hate based on race, national or ethnic origin, language, colour, religion, sex, age, mental or physical disability, sexual orientation, or any other similar factor,
>
> (ii) evidence that the offender, in committing the offence, abused the offender's spouse or common-law partner,
>
> (ii.1) evidence that the offender, in committing the offence, abused a person under the age of eighteen years,
>
> (iii) evidence that the offender, in committing the offence, abused a position of trust or authority in relation to the victim,
>
> (iii.1) evidence that the offence had a significant impact on the victim, considering their age and other personal circumstances, including their health and financial situation,

(iv) evidence that the offence was committed for the benefit of, at the direction of or in association with a criminal organization,

(v) evidence that the offence was a terrorism offence, or

(vi) evidence that the offence was committed while the offender was subject to a conditional sentence order made under section 742.1 or released on parole, statutory release or unescorted temporary absence under the *Corrections and Conditional Release Act* shall be deemed to be aggravating circumstances;

(b) a sentence should be similar to sentences imposed on similar offenders for similar offences committed in similar circumstances;

(c) where consecutive sentences are imposed, the combined sentence should not be unduly long or harsh;

(d) an offender should not be deprived of liberty, if less restrictive sanctions may be appropriate in the circumstances; and

(e) all available sanctions, other than imprisonment, that are reasonable in the circumstances and consistent with the harm done to victims or to the community should be considered for all offenders, with particular attention to the circumstances of Aboriginal offenders.

As well, since 1996, Parliament has directed courts to give "primary consideration to the objectives of denunciation and deterrence" in cases involving "the abuse of a person under the age of eighteen years": see s 718.01; cases involving assaults on a police officer: see s 718.02; and cases where someone "wilfully and without lawful excuse, kills, maims, wounds, poisons or injures a law enforcement animal": see s 718.03.

While it is clearly important and advantageous to have these principles and objectives entrenched in the *Criminal Code*, they lead to a number of questions. How will the judiciary interpret the provisions? How will judges develop methodologies for dealing with individual cases in light of the need to reconcile sometimes contradictory principles and objectives? Do the principles and objectives provide sufficient guidance to sentencing judges? We explore these questions in the rest of this chapter.

IV. JUDGES STRUGGLE TO DEVELOP A PRINCIPLED APPROACH

Over time, the amalgam approach has made protection of society, deterrence, denunciation, rehabilitation, and reparation the major objectives of sentencing. These objectives are sometimes referred to as the principles of sentencing, but that is an erroneous characterization. Principles are substantive rules that shape how judicial discretion is applied to choices between these objectives and to the various sentencing options that the *Criminal Code* provides. For many years, one could find no real discussion of principles and objectives by the Canadian judiciary. Although this was a byproduct of the amalgam approach, it must have struck many thoughtful and conscientious judges as unsatisfactory. Those who recognized that sentencing was a serious matter were left with little guidance from Parliament and little discussion of central tenets by their judicial colleagues.

Judicial attitudes toward sentencing objectives and the applicable principles have not always been consistent, and certainly have not been static. Currently, the most important principles are proportionality, parity, and restraint. By the late 1980s, judges began to struggle with hard sentencing questions dealing with the application of principles and the scope of sentencing objectives. The 1996 statement of principles, purpose, and objectives focused these inquiries, but the following cases show that the efforts by judges to grapple with undeveloped principles and conflicting objectives continues to be a difficult process.

When reading the cases below, try to assess whether the decision reflects a change in judicial attitude and, if so, consider what may have motivated it. Also take note of the variety of sources on which the decisions rely. The individual pronouncements may not be the last word on the subject but they are important elements in an evolutionary process.

A. Proportionality

In an early decision, *R v Priest* (1996), 30 OR (3d) 538 (CA), in which the Ontario Court of Appeal was required to consider and apply the concept of proportionality, the late Justice Marc Rosenberg made the following insightful comments:

> In the recently proclaimed s. 718.1, Parliament sets out the fundamental principle of sentencing:
>
> > 718.1 A sentence must be proportionate to the gravity of the offence and the degree of responsibility of the offender.
>
> Although only now codified, this principle is well established in this country. Chief Justice Lamer in *R. v. M. (C.A.)*, [1996] 1 S.C.R. 500 at p. 530, 105 C.C.C. (3d) 327 at p. 349, noted that this principle now has a constitutional dimension:
>
> > Within broader parameters, the principle of proportionality expresses itself as a constitutional obligation. As this court has recognized on numerous occasions, a legislative or judicial sentence that is grossly disproportionate, in the sense that it is so excessive as to outrage standards of decency, will violate the constitutional prohibition against cruel and unusual punishment under s. 12 of the Charter.
> >
> > The principle of proportionality is rooted in notions of fairness and justice. For the sentencing court to do justice to the particular offender, the sentence imposed must reflect the seriousness of the offence, the degree of culpability of the offender, and the harm occasioned by the offence. The court must have regard to the aggravating and mitigating factors in the particular case. Careful adherence to the proportionality principle ensures that this offender is not unjustly dealt with for the sake of the common good.

In *Arcand*, below, some of the dimensions of proportionality were addressed by a majority of the Alberta Court of Appeal (sitting with five judges) in a lengthy decision dealing with "starting points" (discussed in greater detail below in Section V.C, "Looking for Guidance").

R v Arcand
2010 ABCA 363 (footnotes and citations omitted)

FRASER CJA (Côté and Watson JJA concurring)

[45] We do not intend to explore in detail all the contours of the proportionality principle. However, since one of the Crown's main arguments is that the Reconsideration Cases failed to meet the proportionality principle, we find it necessary to address generally what this principle means and its relationship to the other sentencing principles under s. 718.2. We also touch on how the statutory sentencing principles relate to the objectives of just sanctions under s. 718.

[46] The roots of proportionality in sentencing run deep, dating back two centuries to the days of Blackstone. Its status as a guiding principle of long-standing in the common

law is well recognized. Nonetheless, it was not until the latter part of the 20th century that legislators statutorily embraced the concept of a proportionate or "deserved" sentence as the *governing* sentencing principle.

[47] When Parliament reformed sentencing in Canada in 1996, it deliberately chose to make the proportionality principle—otherwise known as the "just deserts" principle— the *only* governing sentencing principle under the *Code*. The proportionality principle in s. 718.1 requires that a sentence *must* be proportionate to the gravity of the offence and the degree of responsibility of the offender. This principle is fundamental to the integrity of the sentencing regime that Parliament has prescribed. Therefore, these are not just words to be uttered and then ignored in the sentencing process.

[48] Proportionality is based on a simple, yet compelling, premise. The severity of sanction for a crime should reflect the overall degree of moral blameworthiness, that is the seriousness, of the criminal conduct. And that is properly measured by two things: the gravity of the offence and the offender's degree of responsibility. Or to put it the way that Andrew von Hirsch and Andrew Ashworth have done:

> The principle of proportionality requires the *severity* of penalties to be determined by reference to the *seriousness* of crimes.

[49] In other words, sanctions should be scaled according to the seriousness of the criminal conduct. In assessing comparative degrees of seriousness, the principle of proportionality distinguishes between what has been described as *ordinal* and *cardinal* proportionality.

[50] Ordinal proportionality addresses how severely crimes should be sanctioned relative to each other. Ordinal proportionality has three requirements: parity; rank-ordering; and spacing of penalties. Parity calls for offenders convicted of criminal acts of *comparable blameworthiness* to receive sanctions of *like severity*. Rank-ordering involves deciding the relative seriousness of various crimes, that is, which is worse than another, and ranking them accordingly. Spacing of penalties involves determining the extent of the gap between the crimes once rank-ordered. For all these purposes, courts are able to draw on the penalties set by Parliament for various offences.

[51] Cardinal proportionality involves two steps. The first includes identifying a category or categories within an offence based on varying degrees of seriousness. The second is to determine the appropriate sentence to anchor the identified categories. With respect to this second step:

> Such Judgments require a starting point, however, and the issue of cardinal magnitude deals with finding that starting point.

[52] Why did Parliament choose proportionality as the governing principle? One answer is that it accords with principles of fundamental justice and with the purpose of sentencing—to maintain respect for the law and a safe society by imposing *just sanctions*. Further, just sanctions being the goal of sentencing, proportionality must be the overarching principle since a disproportionate sanction can never be a just sanction.

[53] In addition, without a governing principle to guide the exercise of sentencing discretion, there would be no common standard against which judges would impose sentence. Sentencing would then essentially be a free-for-all, with individual judges picking and choosing those facts and considerations that struck a particular chord with them,

and then selecting one principle after the fact to justify the result. Parliament did not choose this sentencing framework. Rather, Parliament made proportionality the fundamental—and dominant—principle of sentencing, not an ornamental decoration for the *Code*.

[54] Finally, proportionality is what makes the blunt tool of punishment a valid and itself morally acceptable element of social order. Without proportionality as the governing sentencing principle, sentencing would be either the arbitrary application of state power or an ineffective response to criminal conduct. It follows that in prescribing proportionality as the mandatory sentencing principle, Parliament was not attempting to constrain only disproportionately high sentences. As two academics have explained:

> There is little in the voluminous literature on desert theory, and less in ss. 718 to 718.2 of the Code to suggest that proportionality is a one-way street, designed only to inhibit excessive severity. A derisory penalty for a serious crime of violence can also be disproportionate, in the sense that the seriousness of the crime is not reflected in the severity of the sentence imposed.

[55] Nor do we accept that proportionality is of no use except to set both an upper and lower limit. On this thinking, proportionality limits, but does not help determine, sentence. However, the proportionality principle, properly understood, is intended to—and does—provide far more guidance than merely setting the outer limits, that is a maximum and a minimum, of a just sanction, though it most assuredly does that as well. Binding authority confirms that the proportionality principle is the dominant principle driving the determination of sentence: *R. v. Malmo-Levine*; *R. v. Proulx*; and *R. v. Nasogaluak*. Therefore, compliance with it is vital to preserving the integrity and credibility of the sentencing system that Parliament has prescribed.

2. What Is the Relationship Between the Proportionality Principle and the Secondary Sentencing Principles and Sentencing Objectives?

[56] Through the sentencing principles and objectives, Parliament has provided the courts with an integrated framework for determining sentences which comply with the proportionality principle. To explain how the proportionality principle works together with the secondary principles and sentencing objectives to form that framework, we must delve further into the meaning of its two components, "gravity of the offence" and "degree of responsibility of the offender."

[57] What is meant by "gravity of the offence"? This concept is directed to what the offender did wrong. It includes two components: (1) the harm or likely harm to the victim; and (2) the harm or likely harm to society and its values. What influences that analysis apart from the degree of injuriousness inherent in the crime itself? The answer lies in s. 718.2. Before exploring that section, though, we turn to the other half of the proportionality principle, the degree of responsibility of the offender, because it too leads to s. 718.2.

[58] The "degree of responsibility of the offender" as used in s. 718.1 certainly includes the *mens rea* level of intent, recklessness or wilful blindness associated with the *actus reus* of the crime committed. For this assessment, courts are able to draw extensively on criminal justice principles. The greater the harm intended or the greater the degree of recklessness or wilful blindness, the greater the moral culpability. However, the reference in s. 718.1 is not simply to the "*mens rea* degree of responsibility of the offender" at the time

of commission of the crime. Parliament evidently intended "degree of responsibility of the offender" to include other factors affecting culpability. These might relate, for example, to the offender's personal circumstances, mental capacity or motive for committing the crime. Where else does the *Code* provide for an offender's degree of responsibility generally to be taken into account? Here, too, the answer takes us to s. 718.2.

[59] Section 718.2 directs the sentencing judge to take into consideration a number of principles. All are either components of the proportionality principle or properly influence its interpretation and application. Either way, all are relevant in determining a just sanction that satisfies the proportionality principle.

Does this explanation of proportionality square with the following, more recent, decisions from the Supreme Court of Canada that address proportionality?

R v Ipeelee
2012 SCC 13, [2012] 1 SCR 433

[This case raised the issue of sentencing an Aboriginal offender for the offence of breaching the terms of a long-term offender supervision order (LTSO). It is discussed in greater detail in Chapter 16, Aboriginal Offenders.]

LeBEL J (McLachlin CJ and Binnie, Deschamps, Fish, and Abella JJ concurring):

[34] The central issue in these appeals is how to determine a fit sentence for a breach of an LTSO in the case of an Aboriginal offender. In particular, the Court must address whether, and how, the *Gladue* principles apply to these sentencing decisions. But first, it is important to review the principles that guide sentencing under Canadian law generally.

[35] In 1996, Parliament amended the *Criminal Code* to specifically codify the objectives and principles of sentencing (*An Act to amend the Criminal Code (sentencing) and other Acts in consequence thereof*, S.C. 1995 c. 22 (Bill C-41)). According to s. 718, the fundamental purpose of sentencing is to contribute to "respect for the law and the maintenance of a just, peaceful and safe society." This is accomplished by imposing "just sanctions" that reflect one or more of the traditional sentencing objectives: denunciation, general and specific deterrence, separation of offenders, rehabilitation, reparation to victims, and promoting a sense of responsibility in offenders and acknowledgement of the harm done to victims and to the community.

[36] The *Criminal Code* goes on to list a number of principles to guide sentencing judges. The fundamental principle of sentencing is that the sentence must be proportionate to both the gravity of the offence and the degree of responsibility of the offender. As this Court has previously indicated, this principle was not borne out of the 1996 amendments to the *Code* but, instead, has long been a central tenet of the sentencing process (see e.g. *R. v. Wilmott* (1966), 58 D.L.R. (2d) 33 (Ont. C.A.), and, more recently, *R. v. Solowan*, 2008 SCC 62, [2008] 3 S.C.R. 309, at para. 12, and *R. v. Nasogaluak*, 2010 SCC 6, [2010] 1 S.C.R. 206, at paras. 40-42). It also has a constitutional dimension, in that s. 12 of the *Canadian Charter of Rights and Freedoms* forbids the imposition of a grossly disproportionate sentence that would outrage society's standards of decency. In a similar

vein, proportionality in sentencing could aptly be described as a principle of fundamental justice under s. 7 of the *Charter*.

[37] The fundamental principle of sentencing (i.e., proportionality) is intimately tied to the fundamental purpose of sentencing—the maintenance of a just, peaceful and safe society through the imposition of just sanctions. Whatever weight a judge may wish to accord to the various objectives and other principles listed in the *Code*, the resulting sentence must respect the fundamental principle of proportionality. Proportionality is the *sine qua non* of a just sanction. First, the principle ensures that a sentence reflects the gravity of the offence. This is closely tied to the objective of denunciation. It promotes justice for victims and ensures public confidence in the justice system. As Wilson J. expressed in her concurring judgment in *Re B.C. Motor Vehicle Act*, [1985] 2 S.C.R. 486, at p. 533:

> It is basic to any theory of punishment that the sentence imposed bear some relationship to the offence; it must be a "fit" sentence proportionate to the seriousness of the offence. Only if this is so can the public be satisfied that the offender "deserved" the punishment he received and feel a confidence in the fairness and rationality of the system.

Second, the principle of proportionality ensures that a sentence does not exceed what is appropriate, given the moral blameworthiness of the offender. In this sense, the principle serves a limiting or restraining function and ensures justice for the offender. In the Canadian criminal justice system, a just sanction is one that reflects both perspectives on proportionality and does not elevate one at the expense of the other.

[38] Despite the constraints imposed by the principle of proportionality, trial judges enjoy a broad discretion in the sentencing process. The determination of a fit sentence is, subject to any specific statutory rules that have survived *Charter* scrutiny, a highly individualized process. Sentencing judges must have sufficient manoeuvrability to tailor sentences to the circumstances of the particular offence and the particular offender. Appellate courts have recognized the scope of this discretion and granted considerable deference to a judge's choice of sentence. ...

[39] There are limits, however, to the deference that will be afforded to a trial judge. Appellate courts have a duty to ensure that courts properly apply the legal principles governing sentencing. In every case, an appellate court must be satisfied that the sentence under review is proportionate to both the gravity of *the offence* and the degree of responsibility of *the offender*.

Following on the issue of deference by appellate courts to trial judges, the Supreme Court revisited and refined this question in its 2015 controversial decision in *R v Lacasse*. Wagner J, for the majority, explained proportionality as follows:

R v Lacasse
2015 SCC 64, [2015] 3 SCR 1089

WAGNER J (Abella, Moldaver, Karakatsanis, and Côté JJ concurring):

[12] In such cases, proportionality is the cardinal principle that must guide appellate courts in considering the fitness of a sentence imposed on an offender. The more serious

the crime and its consequences, or the greater the offender's degree of responsibility, the heavier the sentence will be. In other words, the severity of a sentence depends not only on the seriousness of the crime's consequences, but also on the moral blameworthiness of the offender. Determining a proportionate sentence is a delicate task. As I mentioned above, both sentences that are too lenient and sentences that are too harsh can undermine public confidence in the administration of justice. Moreover, if appellate courts intervene without deference to vary sentences that they consider too lenient or too harsh, their interventions could undermine the credibility of the system and the authority of trial courts. With respect, I am of the opinion that the Court of Appeal was wrong in this case to reduce the sentence imposed by the trial judge by basing its intervention on the fact that he had departed from the established sentencing range.

[In a lengthy dissent Gascon J addressed the role and meaning of proportionality in more detail.]

GASCON J (McLachlin CJ concurring) (dissenting):

[128] The principle of proportionality has a long history as a guiding principle in sentencing, and it has a constitutional dimension: *R. v. Nasogaluak*, 2010 SCC 6, [2010] 1 S.C.R. 206, at para. 41; *R. v. M. (C.A.)*, [1996] 1 S.C.R. 500, at p. 530. A person cannot be made to suffer a disproportionate punishment simply to send a message to discourage others from offending: *Nur*, at para. 45. … Although a court can, in pursuit of the objective of general deterrence, impose a harsher sentence in order to send a message with a view to deterring others, the offender must still deserve that sentence: *R. v. Paré*, 2011 QCCA 2047; G. Renaud, *The Sentencing Code of Canada: Principles and Objectives* (2009), at para. 3.13. If a judge fails to individualize a sentence and to consider the relevant mitigating factors while placing undue emphasis on the circumstances of the offence and the objectives of denunciation and deterrence, all that is done is to punish the crime: *R. v. R. (M.)*, 2010 QCCA 16, 73 C.R. (6th) 136. Proportionality requires that a sentence not exceed what is just and appropriate in light of the moral blameworthiness of the offender and the gravity of the offence. From this perspective, it serves as a limiting principle: *Nasogaluak*, at para. 42.

[129] My colleague states that the principle of proportionality means that the more serious the crime and its consequences, or the greater the offender's degree of responsibility, the heavier the sentence will be (para. 12). I would qualify this statement somewhat. In my view, an offender's degree of responsibility does not flow inevitably and solely from the gravity of the offence. The gravity of the offence and the moral blameworthiness of the offender are two separate factors, and the principle of proportionality requires that full consideration be given to each of them: *Proulx*, at para. 83. As s. 718.1 *Cr. C.* provides, "[a] sentence must be proportionate to the gravity of the offence *and* the degree of responsibility of the offender."

[130] Whereas the gravity of the offence concerns the harm caused by the offender to the victim as well as to society and its values, the other aspect of the principle of proportionality involves factors that relate to the offender's moral culpability:

> The "degree of responsibility of the offender" as used in s. 718.1 certainly includes the mens rea level of intent, recklessness or wilful blindness associated with the actus reus of the crime

committed. For this assessment, courts are able to draw extensively on criminal justice principles. The greater the harm intended or the greater the degree of recklessness or wilful blindness, the greater the moral culpability. However, the reference in s. 718.1 is not simply to the "mens rea degree of responsibility of the offender" at the time of commission of the crime. Parliament evidently intended "degree of responsibility of the offender" to include other factors affecting culpability. These might relate, for example, to the offender's personal circumstances, mental capacity or motive for committing the crime. Where else does the *Code* provide for an offender's degree of responsibility generally to be taken into account? Here, too, the answer takes us to s. 718.2.

Section 718.2 directs the sentencing judge to take into consideration a number of principles. All are either components of the proportionality principle or properly influence its interpretation and application. Either way, all are relevant in determining a just sanction that satisfies the proportionality principle. [Citation omitted.]

(*R. v. J.L.M.A.*, 2010 ABCA 363, 499 A.R. 1, at paras. 58-59; see also *Nasogaluak*, at para. 42; *M. (C.A.)*, at para. 40.)

[131] The application of the proportionality principle may therefore cause the two factors to conflict, particularly where the gravity of the offence points strongly to a sentence at one end of the range while the moral culpability of the offender points in the other direction: *R. v. Hamilton* (2004), 72 O.R. (3d) 1 (C.A.), at para. 93, quoted in C.C. Ruby , G.J. Chan and N.R. Hasan, *Sentencing* (8th ed. 2012), at pp. 26-27. In short, although it is true that the gravity of the crime is a relevant factor, it must nevertheless be considered in conjunction with the offender's degree of responsibility, a factor that is unrelated to the gravity of the offence.

When the Supreme Court of Canada considered the constitutionality of a mandatory minimum sentence for a firearms offence in *R v Nur*, 2015 SCC 15, [2015] 1 SCR 773, the majority made this comment about proportionality:

[44] Mandatory minimum sentences, by their very nature, have the potential to depart from the principle of proportionality in sentencing. They emphasize denunciation, general deterrence and retribution at the expense of what is a fit sentence for the gravity of the offence, the blameworthiness of the offender, and the harm caused by the crime. They function as a blunt instrument that may deprive courts of the ability to tailor proportionate sentences at the lower end of a sentencing range. They may, in extreme cases, impose unjust sentences, because they shift the focus from the offender during the sentencing process in a way that violates the principle of proportionality. They modify the general process of sentencing which relies on the review of all relevant factors in order to reach a proportionate result. They affect the outcome of the sentence by changing the normal judicial process of sentencing.

These cases emphasize the centrality of the severity of the offence to proportionality, incorporating questions of culpability (or blameworthiness), and the harm caused. In 1992, a while ago now, Wood JA expressed the following view of the relationship between culpability and harm in *R v Sweeney* (1992), 11 CR (4th) 1 (BCCA):

There is a prevailing belief that sentences should reflect, and be proportionate to, both "the gravity of the offence and the degree of responsibility of the offender." In my view, the gravity of the offence and the degree of responsibility of the offender are determined by the moral culpability of the offender's conduct.

As a society, we long ago opted for a system of criminal justice in which the moral culpability of an offence is determined by the state of mind which accompanies the offender's unlawful act. Thus the consequences of an unlawful act when either intended, or foreseen and recklessly disregarded, aggravate its moral culpability. But consequences which are neither intended nor foreseen and recklessly ignored cannot aggravate the moral culpability of an unlawful act, except and to the extent that Parliament so decrees.

As I noted earlier, for the same offence committed by the same offender, the moral culpability of the offence of impaired driving simpliciter is the same as that of impaired driving causing either death or bodily harm. That is because in both cases the mental element of the crime consists of the intention to drive with a reckless disregard for foreseeable consequences. The fact that death or bodily harm does or does not result when any such offence is committed is more likely to be due to chance than to any circumstance of foreseeability, for such consequences are always foreseeable whenever a person impaired by alcohol gets behind the wheel of a car and drives.

In light of the post-1996 cases included above, do these views have any current applicability?

B. Parity

Another principle of sentencing with long antecedents is parity, expressed now in s 718.2(b) of the *Criminal Code*:

> 718.2(b) a sentence should be similar to sentences imposed on similar offenders for similar offences committed in similar circumstances;

Although the principle of parity is subordinate to that of proportionality, it continues to have traction. The following cases are examples of how Canadian courts have interpreted and applied the principle of parity.

R v Lacasse
2015 SCC 64, [2015] 3 SCR 1089

[54] The determination of whether a sentence is fit also requires that the sentencing objectives set out in s. 718 of the *Criminal Code* and the other sentencing principles set out in s. 718.2 be taken into account. Once again, however, it is up to the trial judge to properly weigh these various principles and objectives, whose relative importance will necessarily vary with the nature of the crime and the circumstances in which it was committed. The principle of parity of sentences, on which the Court of Appeal relied, is secondary to the fundamental principle of proportionality. This Court explained this as follows in *M. (C.A.)*:

> It has been repeatedly stressed that there is no such thing as a uniform sentence for a particular crime. ... Sentencing is an inherently individualized process, and the search for a single appropriate sentence for a similar offender and a similar crime will frequently be a fruitless exercise of academic abstraction. [para. 92]

[55] This principle of parity of sentences also means that the deference owed to the sentencing judge must be shown except in the circumstances mentioned above. The Court said the following in this regard in *L.M.*:

> This exercise of ensuring that sentences are similar could not be given priority over the principle of deference to the trial judge's exercise of discretion, since the sentence was not vitiated by an error in principle and the trial judge had not imposed a sentence that was clearly unreasonable by failing to give adequate consideration to certain factors or by improperly assessing the evidence (*M. (C.A.)*, at para. 92, quoted in *McDonnell*, at para. 16; *W. (G.)*, at para. 19; see also Ferris, at p. 149, and Manson, at p. 93). [para. 35]

NOTE

Three important observations must be made. First, notwithstanding the long history of parity as a principle of sentencing, it is subordinate to proportionality. Second, parity can never be applied mechanistically, given the myriad circumstances in which offences are committed and the similarly various personal characteristics that offenders present to the sentencing court. Finally, parity encompasses comparisons with both sentences imposed in similar cases and sentences imposed in the same case on co-offenders. The next two cases are examples of both of the latter situations.

Atkinson v R
2015 NBCA 48

RICHARD JA (Bell and Green JJA concurring):

[1] After pleading guilty to charges of impaired driving causing death (s. 255(3) of the *Criminal Code of Canada*) and impaired driving causing bodily harm (s. 255(2)), both charges arising out of the same incident, recidivist Boyd Reginald Atkinson was sentenced to concurrent terms of imprisonment on November 21, 2013. On the first count, the Provincial Court judge sentenced him to imprisonment for ten years, but reduced the term to nine years and five months to account for the time Mr. Atkinson had spent remanded in custody. On the second count, the judge sentenced him to three years. The judge also prohibited Mr. Atkinson from operating a motor vehicle for the rest of his life. Mr. Atkinson seeks leave to appeal the sentence imposed for the s. 255(3) offence. He claims the sentence is clearly unreasonable and not in keeping with sentences customarily imposed for crimes of this kind. ...

• • •

[4] On April 17, 2013, Mr. Atkinson and Marc Landry purchased liquor and made their way to a pub in downtown Moncton. By evening, they were both extremely intoxicated. Mr. Landry, who owned a 2000 Pontiac Grand Am vehicle, was more intoxicated than Mr. Atkinson. The testing of samples taken following the collision that caused Ms. Horsman's death revealed that Mr. Atkinson had between 275 milligrams and 295 milligrams of alcohol in 100 milliliters of his blood, whereas Mr. Landry had approximately 339 mg. The limit beyond which operating a motor vehicle is a criminal offence is 80 mg.

[5] Although Mr. Atkinson's driving privilege was suspended, it was he who came to be driving the Pontiac Grand Am. It was he who maneuvered it at a high rate of speed across two solid yellow lines and caused it to collide with Ms. Horsman's vehicle.

[6] Before the collision, the Pontiac Grand Am was proceeding westbound on Killam Drive, which is the road leading past the Moncton Coliseum and then onto an overpass that crosses Wheeler Boulevard before the roadway turns into the Berry Mills Road. Mr. Atkinson's driving on Killam Drive was erratic. He was driving slowly, braking at inappropriate moments, and then accelerating frequently. The vehicle swerved on the roadway. At the intersection of the first entrance to the Coliseum, the vehicle almost stopped at the traffic light although the signal was green. It almost stopped again at the intersection of the second entrance to the Coliseum, but it accelerated again, and crossed over two solid yellow hash marked areas before returning to its own lane of travel. Mr. Atkinson then overtook other vehicles in a zone where passing was prohibited and barely missed colliding with the side of an oncoming truck. After overtaking one of the vehicles, the Pontiac Grand Am passed over a second solid yellow hash marked space and crossed all the way into the left eastbound lane, a full two lanes over from the westbound lane. It was at that moment that Mr. Atkinson collided with Ms. Horsman's vehicle as she slowed down and moved to her right, partly onto the shoulder of the road, evidently in an attempt to avoid the oncoming Grand Am.

[7] The Grand Am was equipped with a Sensing Diagnostic Module. The data retrieved after the collision indicates that, just prior to impact, Mr. Atkinson was driving at a speed of 136 km/h and was accelerating. He did not brake before impact. The speed limit in that area is 60 km/h.

[8] The force of the collision caused the front-end dash and tires of both vehicles to be pushed up such that they surrounded the bodies of the occupants. From the impact, Ms. Horsman suffered a broken leg and internal bleeding, which led to her death. The passenger in the Grand Am, Mr. Landry, suffered a fractured right ankle and multiple bruises. Mr. Atkinson was also injured in the collision.

[9] Following the laying of charges, Mr. Atkinson pled guilty to impaired driving causing the death of Ms. Horsman and impaired driving causing Mr. Landry bodily harm. The offences to which Mr. Atkinson pled guilty have maximum sentences of imprisonment for life, in the case of impaired driving causing death (s. 255(3)), and imprisonment for ten years in the case of impaired driving causing bodily harm (s. 255(2)).

[10] At the sentencing hearing, it was revealed that Mr. Atkinson had a number of related previous convictions: one in 1989 for refusing to provide a sample of his breath; one in 1992 for driving with a concentration of alcohol in his blood that exceeded 80 mg; and two similar offences in 2009. He was thus before the court to be sentenced for his fifth and sixth offences under related provisions of the *Criminal Code*. Mr. Atkinson's criminal record also revealed two convictions for uttering threats (ss. 264.1(a) and 264.1(b)) and one for failing to comply with an undertaking (s. 145(3)(b)), in 2008, and two violations of a probation order (s. 733.1(1)(b)) in 2009. A pre-sentence report revealed that, at the time of sentencing, Mr. Atkinson was 42 years old. He is the father of two teenagers, but neither resided with him at the time. Mr. Atkinson reported having struggled with alcohol consumption since the age of 18, and having successfully completed an Alcohol Recovery program in 2008, but admitted to a continued struggle with consumption even after completing the program.

• • •

[13] At the sentencing hearing, defence counsel focused his arguments on the principle contained in s. 718.2(b) of the *Criminal Code*, which states: "a sentence should be similar to sentences imposed on similar offenders for similar offences committed in

similar circumstances." He pointed to cases with similarities to the present one and argued the judge should impose concurrent sentences of imprisonment of four to six years for the offence under s. 253(3) and two to three years for the one under s. 255(2).

[14] As stated earlier, the Provincial Court judge sentenced Mr. Atkinson to concurrent terms of imprisonment of nine years and five months, and three years.

• • •

[32] The parity principle is but one of the many principles that must be taken into account when crafting a sentence in order to give effect to the purpose of sentencing. These are set out in s. 718 ... .

[33] Viewed this way, parity is not an imperative; it is but one factor. The reasoning of the majority of the Supreme Court in *R. v. L.M.*, 2008 SCC 31, [2008] 2 S.C.R. 163, per LeBel J., confirms this:

> Moreover, the majority of the Court of Appeal attached great importance to the principle that a sentence should be similar to sentences imposed on similar offenders for similar offences committed in similar circumstances (paras. 41 *et seq.*), which is one of the normative sentencing principles provided for in the *Criminal Code* (s. 718.2 *Cr. C.*). Although this principle permits an appellate court to temper the discretionary aspect of the sentencing process, it was applied incorrectly by the majority of the Court of Appeal.
>
> *This exercise of ensuring that sentences are similar could not be given priority over the principle of deference to the trial judge's exercise of discretion, since the sentence was not vitiated by an error in principle and the trial judge had not imposed a sentence that was clearly unreasonable* by failing to give adequate consideration to certain factors or by improperly assessing the evidence (*M. (C.A.)*, at para. 92, quoted in *McDonnell*, [1997] 1 S.C.R. 948 at para. 16; *W. (G.)*, at para. 19; see also Ferris, at p. 149, and Manson, at p. 93). This Court has clearly confirmed the "trial judge's traditionally broad sentencing discretion" (*M. (C.A.)*, [1996] 1 S.C.R. 500 at para. 56). Furthermore, this principle has been codified in s. 718.3 *Cr. C.*
>
> *Owing to the very nature of an individualized sentencing process, sentences imposed for offences of the same type will not always be identical. The principle of parity does not preclude disparity* where warranted by the circumstances, because of the principle of proportionality (see *Dadour*, at p. 18). As this Court noted in *M. (C.A.)*, at para. 92, "*there is no such thing as a uniform sentence for a particular crime.*" From this perspective, an appellate court is justified in intervening only if the sentence imposed by the trial judge "is in substantial and marked departure from the sentences customarily imposed for similar offenders committing similar crimes" (*M. (C.A.)*, at para. 92). [paras. 34-36] [Emphasis in original; underlining added]

• • •

[36] Admittedly, one finds a very broad range of sentences for impaired driving causing death in the jurisprudence. In *R. v. Ruizfuentes*, 2010 MBCA 90, [2010] M.J. No. 310 (QL), Chartier J.A. (as he then was) conveniently summarized many of these in an appendix to his decision. He first reviewed the sentences customarily imposed for first offenders, and then turned his attention to those for second or subsequent offenders. In the latter category, he includes the following:

> *R. v. Regnier (R.H.)*, 2002 SKCA 82, 219 Sask. R. 316: Six years of imprisonment and a nine-year driving prohibition for criminal negligence in the operation of a motor vehicle causing death. While impaired, and with two and one-half times the legal limit, he drove on the

wrong side of the road and was involved in a head-on collision. The accused had a lengthy record of alcohol-related driving offences.

R. v. Kaserbauer (P.), 2003 MBQB 28, 171 Man. R. (2d) 230: One year of imprisonment, plus 18 months of probation followed by a three-year driving prohibition for an accused who had a prior drinking and driving conviction.

R. v. Hall (2007), 83 O.R. (3d) 641 (C.A.): Four years' and ten months' imprisonment and a ten-year driving prohibition. As his breathalyzer tests were conducted more than two hours after the offence, his blood alcohol was estimated to be between 129 and 165 milligrams of alcohol in 100 millilitres of blood. He had a prior related record.

R. v. Rhyason (B.P.), 2007 ABCA 119, 404 A.R. 191: Three years of imprisonment for impaired driving causing death. This was an increase from the 18-month sentence he had received from the trial judge. He was 21 years old at the time of the offence and was remorseful. He registered low breathalyzer readings of .120 and .100. He had one previous drinking and driving conviction.

R. v. Bear (C.C.), 2008 SKCA 172, 320 Sask. R. 12: Six years of imprisonment and a lifetime driving prohibition for impaired driving causing death and impaired driving causing bodily harm. The accused was 31 years old and, amongst other prior offences, had three previous convictions for impaired driving. He drove through a stop sign while impaired. In his presentence report he was rated as a high risk to reoffend, based primarily on his numerous failure-to-comply offences and his alcohol abuse. The trial judge noted that the accused had not accepted responsibility for the offence and, to the contrary, had attempted to shift blame to the other driver.

R. v. Richard (A.L.), 2009 MBQB 181, 241 Man. R. (2d) 298: Six years of imprisonment and a 15-year driving prohibition. Although the 33-year-old accused had no prior drinking and driving convictions, he had a serious criminal record for violent crime and warrants were in existence at the time of the offence for his arrest for failure to appear in court and failure to report for bail supervision. His licence had been suspended and he was under recognizance to abstain from alcohol when he went to a party and drank to the point of impairment. He then got behind the wheel of a van he knew was stolen. He got into an accident resulting in the death of the victim. The Crown asked for six years; counsel for the accused submitted five years was appropriate.

R. v. Morneau, 2009 QCCA 1496: Six years of imprisonment and a 12-year driving prohibition for impaired driving causing death and impaired driving causing bodily harm for a 39-year-old accused who had breathalyzer readings of .247. He also had three prior drinking and driving convictions. Leave to appeal to S.C.C. refused, [2009] S.C.C.A. No. 408.

R. v. Niganobe (J.), 2010 ONCA 508, 95 M.V.R. (5th) 175: Five years of imprisonment and a 15-year driving prohibition for impaired driving causing death and impaired driving causing bodily harm. The accused had a prior criminal record including a conviction for impaired driving in 2003. She did not have a driver's licence and in fact had never been licensed to drive. The trial judge also found that the accused had not accepted responsibility for her conduct and therefore continued to pose a danger to the public.

• • •

[41] In *Kummer*, MacPherson J.A. notes that although the Court had recently upheld sentences of four and five years in cases where impaired driving had resulted in death (*R. v. Ramage*, 2010 ONCA 488, [2010] O.J. No. 2970 (QL), and *R. v. Junkert*, 2010 ONCA

549, [2010] O.J. No. 3387 (QL)), these sentences were not meant to "cap the sentences available for this kind of offence" (para. 19). He gives three reasons for this:

First, imposing such a cap would contradict the *Criminal Code* and defy the will of Parliament. The maximum sentence for the offence of impaired driving causing death is life imprisonment. It must remain within the realm of possibility that a life sentence could be imposed for this crime. Absent a determination that the maximum penalty is unconstitutional, this court is not entitled to lower the maximum penalty any more than it is entitled to raise it.

Second, in *Junkert* itself this court cautioned against thinking formulaically about sentence ranges in drinking and driving cases involving death. As expressed by O'Connor A.C.J.O. at para. 40:

I begin by noting that courts should be cautious in rigidly applying "a range" of sentences in cases such as this, involving impaired driving causing death. In *R. v. Heaslip* (2001), 10 M.V.R. (4th) 220, 49 W.C.B. (2d) 347 (Ont. C.A.), in dismissing a Crown appeal from a sentence for two counts of impaired driving causing bodily harm, this court said:

In *R. v. L.(J.)* [(2000), 147 C.C.C. (3d) 299 (Ont. C.A.)], this Court also recognized that cases involving drinking and driving did not demonstrate a particular range of sentencing but rather that the sentences were driven by the almost "infinite variety of circumstances in which this offence can be committed."

Third, there is precedent for the imposition of sentences more severe than those found in *Ramage* and *Junkert* in impaired driving causing death cases. In *R. v. Wood* (2005), 197 O.A.C. 43 (C.A.), the appellant, who had an extensive criminal record, was sentenced to nine years' imprisonment after killing three people and injuring one while driving without a license with a blood alcohol level nearly twice the legal limit. In *R. v. Mascarenhas* (2002), 60 O.R. (3d) 465 (C.A.), a nine-year sentence, [2000] O.J. No. 4707, was substituted by this court for one of twelve years. The appellant in that case struck and killed two pedestrians while driving with a blood alcohol level between .339 and .353. The appellant had three previous impaired driving convictions, and at the time of the offence was on bail for a drinking and driving offence, had a suspended license, and was on a recognizance that prohibited him from drinking and driving. [paras. 20-22]

[42] I agree with MacPherson J.A. and particularly with the statement of O'Connor A.C.J.O. that "cases involving drinking and driving did not demonstrate a particular range of sentencing but rather that the sentences were driven by the almost 'infinite variety of circumstances in which this offence can be committed.'"

[43] If anything, the range of appropriate sentences for impaired driving causing death is a very broad one, and remains so out of necessity in order to reflect the myriad of circumstances under which these offences can be committed. The range is defined by sentences at both ends that are not clearly unreasonable, in that they do not constitute a substantial and marked departure from those customarily imposed. Factors such as the degree of intoxication, the manner of driving and previous convictions are influential circumstances when imposing a sentence in the higher end of the range. In the present case, Mr. Atkinson was highly intoxicated, driving with callous disregard for other users of the roadway, driving while his privilege was suspended, and had been convicted of

related offences in four previous instances. These are very weighty factors. None of the mitigating factors have sufficient weight to offset the aggravating circumstances. Thus, in my view, it is beyond dispute that the sentencing judge was justified in imposing a term of imprisonment at the high end of what can be considered a reasonable sentence.

[44] The question then becomes what would constitute a substantial and marked departure from a reasonable sentence for an offence of this type, in similar circumstances, by an offender similar to Mr. Atkinson? A particular sentence will constitute a substantial and marked departure from sentences customarily imposed if the differences are considerable, and strikingly noticeable. However, in making this assessment, one has to consider that nothing compels a judge to impose identical sentences and that "[t]he principle of parity does not preclude disparity *where warranted by the circumstances*, because of the principle of proportionality": *L.M.* at para. 36. One must also recall that the objective severity of the offence is reflected by its maximum punishment of imprisonment for life, which contemplates there are cases where such a sentence could be imposed. In addition, among the myriad of circumstances that can vary from case to case, one might consider a particular need for deterrence in the community where the offence occurred. ...

[45] It cannot be said that a sentence of imprisonment for ten years is disproportionate to the gravity of the offence. Mr. Atkinson, after all, killed a young mother of two. He voluntarily became highly intoxicated and drove a motor vehicle on a busy roadway, in a wild and erratic manner, with total disregard for the safety of other motorists. To borrow from the trial judge, Mr. Atkinson gambled with Ms. Horsman's life. It is she who lost. This was a terrible, and entirely preventable, tragedy for which he is solely responsible. Thus, the fundamental principle contained in s. 718.1, that the sentence be proportional to the gravity of the offence and Mr. Atkinson's degree of responsibility, is in no way offended by a sentence of ten years.

[46] Admittedly, no one has identified any cases in New Brunswick where imprisonment for ten years has been imposed for an offence under s. 255(3). Nevertheless, research has revealed cases in other provinces where, as MacPherson J.A. noted in *Kummer*, nine years has been imposed for similar types of offences, albeit in somewhat different circumstances. In my view, a jump to ten years in the circumstances of the present case for this repeat offender is not one that a reasonable person would view as considerable or strikingly noticeable. It is still far removed from the maximum sentence endorsed by Parliament, yet it marks the courts' increasing need to properly denounce this type of behaviour and deter those who might otherwise continue to leave this "terrible trail of death, injury, heartbreak and destruction" of which the Supreme Court spoke in *Bernshaw*. Thus, I see no merit to the second ground of appeal.

R v Downes
2015 ONCA 674

STRATHY CJO (MacPherson JA and Speyer J concurring):

[9] The appellant was sentenced to six years imprisonment for his role in an enterprise to smuggle 2.1 kilograms of cocaine into Canada. The appellant concedes that that the appropriate range of sentence for a first time offender, absent exceptional circumstances,

is six to eight years. See *R. v. Cunningham*, [1996] O.J. No. 448 (Ont. C.A.) at para. 29. The appellant's complaint is that the sentence he received violates the principle of parity of sentencing. It is contended it does so because two other offenders involved in the same cocaine smuggling scheme were given conditional sentences following pleas of guilty. In each case, the sentence imposed followed a joint recommendation by crown and defence counsel.

[10] The parity principle is a principle of fairness. Its purpose is designed to ensure a sentence is similar to sentences imposed on similar offenders for similar offences committed in similar circumstances. However, as this court stated in *R. v. Courtney*, 2012 ONCA 478 at para. 4:

> The parity principle does not require that all co-accused be subject to the same sentence, or even that they be treated similarly for sentencing purposes. On the contrary, disparate sentences for different offenders, for the same offence, do not violate the parity principle so long as they are warranted by all the circumstances. See *R. v. Ipeelee*, [2012] S.C.J. No. 13, at paras. 78 to 79, per LeBel J.

[11] We are of the view that the sentence imposed on the appellant does not violate the parity principle. Indeed, the sentence imposed on the overseer of this drug smuggling enterprise was 10 years imprisonment for his role in the operation following a plea of guilty. The other two participants who received conditional sentences played a more subordinate role than the appellant in the criminal enterprise. In the case of the courier, Nicola Morgan, she co-operated with authorities, pled guilty, and testified as to the appellant's participation. Similarly, the second individual who received a conditional sentence played a more limited role with respect to the drug importation scheme.

[12] In assessing the appropriate sentence, the trial judge took into account the major role played by the appellant, the significant amount of cocaine imported and the detrimental impact of the importation of cocaine on society. We see no error in the sentence.

[13] The appeal from conviction and sentence is therefore dismissed.

C. Restraint

We can trace the concept of restraint back to Bentham and his utilitarian concern that, given the obvious pains of punishment, a sentence should be no more than absolutely necessary to achieve its objectives. Using a different name for the same principle, Norval Morris argued that all sentencing systems should be "parsimonious" in the imposition of sentence. Similarly, von Hirsch has included restraint in his conception of proportionality as the guiding principle of sentencing. In a similar vein, Lamer CJ in *R v M (CA)*, [1996] 1 SCR 500 noted:

> [78] The Canadian Sentencing Commission in its 1987 Report on Sentencing Reform also endorsed retribution as a legitimate and relevant consideration in the sentencing process. While the Commission noted that strict retributivist theory on its own fails to provide a general justification for the imposition of criminal sanctions, the Commission argued that retribution, in conjunction with other utilitarian justifications of punishment (i.e., deterrence and rehabilitation), contributes to a more coherent theory of punishment (… at 141-42, 143-45). More specifically, the Commission argued that a theory of retribution centred on "just deserts" or "just sanctions" provides a helpful organizing principle for the imposition of criminal sanctions (at

p. 143). Indeed, as the Commission noted, retribution frequently operates as a principle of restraint, as utilitarian principles alone may direct individualized punishments which unfairly exceed the culpability of the offender.

In Canada, since 1996, the principle of restraint is reflected in three *Criminal Code* provisions:

1. 718(c) to separate offenders from society, *where necessary*;
2. 718.2(d) an offender should not be deprived of liberty, *if less restrictive sanctions may be appropriate in the circumstances*; and
3. 718.2(e) *all available sanctions, other than imprisonment, that are reasonable in the circumstances and consistent with the harm done to victims or to the community should be considered for all offenders*, with particular attention to the circumstances of Aboriginal offenders. [Emphasis added.]

The following cases show how the Supreme Court has interpreted and applied restraint.

R v Gladue
[1999] 1 SCR 688

[Note that this case, as well as *Ipeelee*, which follows, is seminal in the evolution of the treatment of Aboriginal offenders by the Canadian criminal justice system. It is discussed in detail in Chapter 16. Here, we are looking only at its general comments on restraint.]

CORY and IACOBUCCI JJ:

[38] The wording of s. 718.2(e) on its face, then, requires both consideration of alternatives to the use of imprisonment as a penal sanction generally, which amounts to a restraint in the resort to imprisonment as a sentence, and recognition by the sentencing judge of the unique circumstances of aboriginal offenders. The respondent argued before this Court that this statutory wording does not truly effect a change in the law, as some courts have in the past taken the unique circumstances of an aboriginal offender into account in determining sentence. The respondent cited some of the recent jurisprudence dealing with sentencing circles, as well as the decision of the Court of Appeal for Ontario in *R. v. Fireman* (1971), 4 C.C.C. (2d) 82, in support of the view that s. 718.2(c) should be seen simply as a codification of the state of the case law regarding the sentencing of aboriginal offenders before Part XXIII came into force in 1996. In a similar vein, it was observed by Sherstobitoff J.A. in *McDonald*, *supra*, at pp. 463-64, that it has always been a principle of sentencing that courts should consider all available sanctions other than imprisonment that are reasonable in the circumstances. Thus the general principle of restraint expressed in s. 718.2(e) with respect to all offenders might equally be seen as a codification of existing law.

[39] With respect for the contrary view, we do not interpret s. 718.2(e) as expressing only a restatement of existing law, either with respect to the general principle of restraint in the use of prison or with respect to the specific direction regarding aboriginal offenders. One cannot interpret the words of s. 718.2(e) simply by looking to past cases to see if they contain similar statements of principle. The enactment of the new Part XXIII was a watershed, marking the first codification and significant reform of sentencing principles in the history of Canadian criminal law. Each of the provisions of Part XXIII, including

s. 718.2(e), must be interpreted in its total context, taking into account its surrounding provisions.

[40] It is true that there is ample jurisprudence supporting the principle that prison should be used as a sanction of last resort. It is equally true, though, that the sentencing amendments which came into force in 1996 as the new Part XXIII have changed the range of available penal sanctions in a significant way. The availability of the conditional sentence of imprisonment, in particular, alters the sentencing landscape in a manner which gives an entirely new meaning to the principle that imprisonment should be resorted to only where no other sentencing option is reasonable in the circumstances. The creation of the conditional sentence suggests, on its face, a desire to lessen the use of incarceration. The general principle expressed in s. 718.2(e) must be construed and applied in this light.

[41] Further support for the view that s. 718.2(e)'s expression of the principle of restraint in sentencing is remedial, rather than simply a codification, is provided by the articulation of the purpose of sentencing in s. 718.

R v Proulx
2000 SCC 5, [2000] 1 SCR 61

LAMER CJ (L'Heureux-Dubé, Gonthier, McLachlin, Iacobucci, Major, Bastarache, and Binnie JJ concurring):

[17] Parliament has sought to give increased prominence to the principle of restraint in the use of prison as a sanction through the enactment of s 718.2(d) and (e). Section 718.2(d) provides that "an offender should not be deprived of liberty, if less restrictive sanctions may be appropriate in the circumstances," while s. 718.2(e) provides that "all available sanctions other than imprisonment that are reasonable in the circumstances should be considered for all offenders, with particular attention to the circumstances of aboriginal offenders." Further evidence of Parliament's desire to lower the rate of incarceration comes from other provisions of Bill C-41: s. 718(c) qualifies the sentencing objective of separating offenders from society with the words "where necessary," thereby indicating that caution be exercised in sentencing offenders to prison; s. 734(2) imposes a duty on judges to undertake a means inquiry before imposing a fine, so as to decrease the number of offenders who are incarcerated for defaulting on payment of their fines; and of course, s. 742.1, which introduces the conditional sentence. In *Gladue*, at para. 40, the Court held that "[t]he creation of the conditional sentence suggests, on its face, a desire to lessen the use of incarceration."

• • •

[96] Both ss. 718.2(d) and 718.2(e) seek to vindicate the important objective of restraint in the use of incarceration. However, neither seeks to do so at all costs. Section 718.2(d) provides that "an offender should not be deprived of liberty, if less restrictive sanctions *may be appropriate in the circumstances*" (emphasis added). Section 718.2(e) provides that "all available sanctions other than imprisonment *that are reasonable in the circumstances* should be considered" (emphasis added). In my view, a determination of when less restrictive sanctions are "appropriate" and alternatives to incarceration "reasonable" in the circumstances requires a consideration of the other principles of sentencing set out in ss. 718 to 718.2

[97] In determining which principles favour of a conditional sentence and which favour incarceration, it is necessary to consider again the nature and purpose of the conditional sentence. Through an appreciation of Parliament's intention in enacting this new sanction and the mischief it seeks to redress, trial judges will be better able to make appropriate use of this innovative tool.

[98] The conditional sentence, as I have already noted, was introduced in the amendments to Part XXIII of the *Code*. Two of the main objectives underlying the reform of Part XXIII were to reduce the use of incarceration as a sanction and to give greater prominence to the principles of restorative justice in sentencing—the objectives of rehabilitation, reparation to the victim and the community, and the promotion of a sense of responsibility in the offender.

R v Lacasse
2015 SCC 64, [2015] 3 SCR 1089

GASCON J (McLachlin CJ concurring) (dissenting):

[132] I would also qualify my colleague's statement that the courts have "very few options other than imprisonment" (para. 6) for meeting the objectives of general or specific deterrence and denunciation in cases in which they must be emphasized. In my view, the courts should not automatically assume that imprisonment is always the preferred sanction for the purpose of meeting these objectives. To do so would be contrary to other sentencing principles. Rather, a court must consider "all available sanctions, other than imprisonment," that are reasonable in the circumstances: s. 718.2(e) *Cr. C.*; *Gladue*, at para. 36.

[133] The common law principle that even where a term of imprisonment is necessary, it should be the lightest possible sanction in the circumstances is codified in s. 718.2(d) *Cr. C.*: Ruby, Chan and Hasan, at p. 510. This Court has noted Parliament's desire to give increased prominence, for all offenders, to this principle of restraint in the use of prison as a sanction: *Proulx*, at para. 17. A court that emphasizes general deterrence must therefore always be mindful of both the principle of restraint and that of proportionality: Ruby, Chan and Hasan, at p. 15, citing *R. v. Hawkins*, 2011 NSCA 7, 298 N.S.R. (2d) 53, at paras. 42 and 47; see also *R. v. Wismayer* (1997), 33 O.R. (3d) 225 (C.A.); *R. v. Coffin*, 2006 QCCA 471, 210 C.C.C. (3d) 227; F. Dadour, *De la détermination de la peine: Principes et applications* (2007), at p. 8.

D. Denunciation

R v M (CA)
[1996] 1 SCR 500

LAMER CJ (La Forest, L'Heureux-Dubé, Sopinka, Gonthier, Cory, McLachlin, Iacobucci, and Major JJ concurring):

[81] Retribution, as well, should be conceptually distinguished from its legitimate sibling, denunciation. Retribution requires that a judicial sentence properly reflect the moral blameworthiness of that particular *offender*. The objective of denunciation mandates that

a sentence should also communicate society's condemnation of that particular offender's *conduct*. In short, a sentence with a denunciatory element represents a symbolic, collective statement that the offender's conduct should be punished for encroaching on our society's basic code of values as enshrined within our substantive criminal law. As Lord Justice Lawton stated in *R. v. Sargeant* (1974), 60 Cr. App. R. 74, at p. 77: "society, through the courts, must show its abhorrence of particular types of crime, and the only way in which the courts can show this is by the sentences they pass." The relevance of both retribution and denunciation as goals of sentencing underscores that our criminal justice system is not simply a vast system of negative penalties designed to prevent objectively harmful conduct by increasing the cost the offender must bear in committing an enumerated offence. Our criminal law is also a system of values. A sentence which expresses denunciation is simply the means by which these values are communicated. In short, in addition to attaching negative consequences to undesirable behaviour, judicial sentences should also be imposed in a manner which positively instills the basic set of communal values shared by all Canadians as expressed by the *Criminal Code*.

[82]   As a closing note to this discussion, it is important to stress that neither retribution nor denunciation alone provides an exhaustive justification for the imposition of criminal sanctions. Rather, in our system of justice, normative and utilitarian considerations operate in conjunction with one another to provide a coherent justification for criminal punishment. As Gonthier J. emphasized in *Goltz* ... [[1991] 3 SCR 485], at p. 502, the goals of the penal sanction are both "broad and varied." Accordingly, the meaning of retribution must be considered in conjunction with the other legitimate objectives of sentencing, which include (but are not limited to) deterrence, denunciation, rehabilitation and the protection of society. Indeed, it is difficult to perfectly separate these interrelated principles. And as La Forest J. emphasized in *Lyons*, the relative weight and importance of these multiple factors will frequently vary depending on the nature of the crime and the circumstances of the offender. In the final analysis, the overarching duty of a sentencing judge is to draw upon all the legitimate principles of sentencing to determine a "just and appropriate" sentence which reflects the gravity of the offence committed and the moral blameworthiness of the offender.

E. Rehabilitation

R v Preston
(1990), 47 BCLR (2d) 273, 79 CR (3d) 61 (CA)

WOOD JA (McEachern CJ and Lambert, Anderson, and Wallace JJA concurring):
The Crown applies for leave to appeal, and if leave is granted, appeals from the sentences imposed with respect to each of three convictions recorded against the respondent for possession of the narcotic diacetylmorphine (heroin). In each case the passing of sentence was suspended for a period of two years, and the respondent was ordered to be released on the terms and conditions contained in three separate probation orders.

• • •

II

The respondent is now 41 years old. She has been a heroin addict for over 20 years. In that time she has made a number of unsuccessful attempts to overcome her addiction. As a result of her lack of skills and education, her addiction, and poor health brought on by the self-abuse associated with that addiction, she has not worked for most of that time. She has been on social assistance continuously since 1974.

Up to the time of the matters now before the court, she has amassed at total record of 23 convictions, including eight for narcotics offences, four of which were for trafficking in heroin, five soliciting or other prostitution related convictions, and an assortment of escape, unlawfully at large, failing to appear and breach of probation convictions. Apart from concurrent sentences of two years less one day on three counts of trafficking in heroin, imposed in 1976, her longest sentences have been 18 months on a charge of confinement, also in 1976, and 18 months for another heroin trafficking conviction in 1985. All other sentences imposed upon her have been for 90 days or less.

• • •

While conceding that the prospect of full and complete rehabilitation was not assured, counsel for the respondent pointed out to the trial judge that whatever hope there was would be destroyed by a term of imprisonment. Counsel for the Crown, stressing the importance of deterrence and the protection of the public, submitted that in light of the nature of the offence and her previous criminal record the respondent ought to be sentenced to a term of imprisonment.

The trial judge gave lengthy reasons for making the orders he did. He was clearly aware of the many decisions of this court, which have either upheld or imposed substantial periods of imprisonment for similar offences committed by similar offenders. In the end he took the view that he ought to order a disposition of these charges which would encourage what he saw as a genuine motivation for rehabilitation on the part of the respondent.

• • •

There is no doubt that heroin addicts present as poor candidates for rehabilitation, if such is measured only in terms of the number who successfully overcome their addiction. Little in the way of reliable statistics is available, but what information there is suggests that it is unrealistic to talk of a "cure" for heroin addiction. Success is measured by the extent to which the addiction is controlled, often by substitute drugs which can be legally prescribed. Some of these substitutes, like methadone, are themselves highly addictive, but their pharmacological properties are such that the addict can, if willing, maintain a relatively normal and even useful lifestyle, free from the need to commit crimes to support the craving for heroin.

• • •

The role of incarceration in this cycle not only fails to achieve its ultimate goal which is the protection of society, but it also costs society a great deal of money, which might better be spent elsewhere. Statistics Canada reports that during the 1988/1989 fiscal year the cost of maintaining a prisoner in a custodial facility averaged $46,282 in a federal penitentiary and $36,708 in a provincial jail.

The object of the entire criminal justice system, of course, is the protection of society, and I say at once that if incarceration is the only way of protecting society from a particular offender then, transitory and expensive though it may be, that form of protection must be invoked. But where, as in this case, the danger to society results from the potential of the addict to commit offences to support her habit, and it appears to the court that there is a reasonable chance that she may succeed in an attempt to control her addiction, then it becomes necessary to consider the ultimate benefit to society if that chance becomes a reality.

• • •

With respect, that benefit seems obvious. If the chance for rehabilitation becomes a reality, society will be permanently protected from the danger which she otherwise presents in the fashion described above. As well, the cost associated with her frequent incarceration will be avoided.

• • •

What then is the proper approach for the court to take when sentencing in a case such as this? When the benefit to be derived to society as a whole, as a result of the successful rehabilitation of a heroin addict, is balanced against the ultimate futility of the short-term protection which the community enjoys from a sentence of incarceration, I believe it is right to conclude that the principle of deterrence should yield to any reasonable chance of rehabilitation which may show itself to the court imposing sentence. To give the offender a chance to successfully overcome his or her addiction, in such circumstances, is to risk little more than the possibility of failure, with the result that the cycle of addiction leading to crime leading to incarceration will resume, something that is inevitable, in any event, if the chance is not taken. On the other hand, as has already been pointed out, if the effort succeeds the result is fundamentally worthwhile to society as a whole.

I am not persuaded that the trial judge erred in principle in this case when he considered the rehabilitation of the respondent to be of greater importance than any deterrent value that a sentence of incarceration might have. Indeed, I am of the view that he was right in the approach that he took.

Underlying much of the argument of counsel for the Crown was the suggestion that to approve the disposition of the trial judge in this case would be to "decriminalize" heroin. Nothing could be further from the truth. A court would only be justified in giving more weight to the possibility of rehabilitation, rather than deterrence, where there is a reasonable basis for believing that the motivation for such change is genuine and there is a reasonable possibility that it will succeed. There will undoubtedly be many cases in which no such prospect exists, and in such cases it would be an error in principle to allow the factor of deterrence to be overshadowed by the illusion of rehabilitation. I have every confidence in the ability of the trial judges in this province to successfully separate fact from fiction in such matters.

• • •

To the extent that this goal must be considered by the court when imposing sentence, it may be, and often is, referred to as a "factor" of sentencing. In *R v. Pettigrew*, [1990] BCWLD 1260, BCCA, Vancouver No. CA011983, 12th April 1990 [now reported 56 CCC (3d) 390], Taylor JA referred to it, at p. 5 [394 (CCC)], as:

> ... the elusive "fifth factor" of the sentencing system—the imposition of punishment, so as [sic] to speak, "for its own sake," rather than for isolation of the offender, rehabilitation, deterrence of the offender or deterrence of others.

As Taylor JA pointed out, this factor has been given different labels over the years, as its role in the rationale of sentencing has undergone at least the perception, if not the reality, of change. Retribution was one of its earlier titles. This court rejected retribution per se as a legitimate goal of sentencing in *R v. Hinch*, 62 WWR 205, 2 CRNS 350, [1968] 3 CCC 39. Denunciation has been used as a descriptive term for this factor as well. This court has from time to time upheld or imposed sentences designed to express society's abhorrence of the crime committed. Another, more recent, perception is that the punishment imposed ought to represent "just deserts" for the crime committed, thus suggesting a proportionality between the moral blameworthiness of the offender and the sanction imposed.

· · ·

In light of everything that has been said so far about the benefit to society if the respondent succeeds in her efforts to control her addiction to heroin, I am of the view that a sentence of imprisonment could not be justified or imposed in this case on the basis of the so-called fifth factor of sentencing.

F. General Deterrence

The objective of general deterrence is included in s 718(b) of the *Criminal Code*. In sentencing cases, it is commonly twinned with denunciation to support a harsh, or at least harsher, sentence. However, general deterrence remains a controversial issue in light of numerous studies that question its efficacy. In *R v Nur*, 2015 SCC 15, [2015] 1 SCR 773, currently the leading case on s 12 Charter challenges to mandatory minimum sentences (discussed in detail in Chapter 17, The Charter and Sentencing), the majority of the Supreme Court addressed this controversy:

[112] The state bears the burden of showing that the mandatory minimum sentences of imprisonment found to violate s. 12 of the *Charter* are rationally connected to the goals of denunciation, deterrence, and retribution. To do so, the government must establish that there is a causal connection between the infringement and the benefit sought "on the basis of reason or logic": *RJR-MacDonald Inc. v. Canada (Attorney General)*, [1995] 3 S.C.R. 199, at para. 153. Viewed thus, are the means the law adopts a rational way for Parliament to pursue its objective?

[113] The government has not established that mandatory minimum terms of imprisonment act as a deterrent against gun-related crimes. Doubts concerning the effectiveness of incarceration as a deterrent have been longstanding. *Sentencing Reform: A Canadian Approach—Report of The Canadian Sentencing Commission* (1987), concludes as follows:

a) Even if there seems to be little empirical foundation to the deterrent efficacy of legal sanctions, the assertion that the presence of some level of legal sanctions has no deterrent effects whatsoever, has no justification. The weight of the evidence and the exercise of common sense favour the assertion that, taken together, legal sanctions have an overall deterrent effect which is difficult to evaluate precisely.

b) The proper level at which to express strong reservations about the deterrence efficacy of legal sanctions is in their usage to produce particular effects with regard to a specific offence. For instance, in a recent report on impaired driving published by the Department of Justice, Donelson asserts that "law-based, punitive measures alone cannot produce large, sustained reductions in the magnitude of the problem" (Donelson, 1985; 221-222). Similarly, it is extremely doubtful that an exemplary sentence imposed in a particular case can have any perceptible effect in deterring potential offenders.

c) The old principle that it is more the certainty than the severity of punishment which is likely to produce a deterrent effect has not been invalidated by empirical research. In his extensive review of studies on deterrence, Beyleveld (1980; 306) concluded that "recorded offence rates do not vary inversely with the severity of penalties (usually measured by the length of imprisonment)" and that "inverse relations between crime and severity (when found) are usually smaller than inverse crime-certainty relations." [Emphasis added; 136-37.]

[114] Empirical evidence suggests that mandatory minimum sentences do not, in fact, deter crimes: see, e.g., A. N. Doob and C. M. Webster, "Sentence Severity and Crime: Accepting the Null Hypothesis" (2003), 30 *Crime & Just.* 143; M. Tonry, "The Mostly Unintended Effects of Mandatory Penalties: Two Centuries of Consistent Findings" (2009), 38 *Crime & Just.* 65. The empirical evidence "is clear: mandatory minimum sentences do not deter more than less harsh, proportionate, sentences" (A. N. Doob and C. Cesaroni, "The Political Attractiveness of Mandatory Minimum Sentences" (2001), 39 Osgoode Hall L.J. 287, at p. 291).

[115] Despite the frailty of the connection between deterrence and mandatory minimum sentence provisions, a rational connection exists between mandatory minimum terms of imprisonment and the goals of denunciation and retribution. Therefore, this requirement of the s. 1 test is met.

V. METHODOLOGY, DISPARITY, AND UNIFORMITY OF APPROACH

Is uniformity of outcomes required in a sentencing system? Certainly the concept of parity as between similar offenders and similar offences has been around for a long time and seems to be a natural attribute of the rule of law. This is particularly so when one considers the effects of some crimes on their victims and the consequences in human terms of some punishments on those on whom they are inflicted. But in a principled system, it is not disparity but unjustified disparity that cannot be condoned. Offences are committed in myriad ways, by various offenders, producing an array of consequences. Canadian courts constantly remind us that sentencing is an individualized process. In *R v M (CA)*, Lamer CJ said:

[92] ... It has been repeatedly stressed that there is no such thing as a uniform sentence for a particular crime. ... Sentencing is an inherently individualized process, and the search for a single appropriate sentence for a similar offender and a similar crime will frequently be a fruitless exercise of academic abstraction. As well, sentences for a particular offence should be expected to vary to some degree across various communities and regions in this country, as the "just and appropriate" mix of accepted sentencing goals will depend on the needs and current conditions of and in the particular community where the crime occurred.

Still, parity should produce a high degree of consistency, but the Canadian Sentencing Commission in its 1987 report found "considerable unwarranted variation in sentencing" (at 77). However, without an overarching coherent theory with clearly articulated principles, uniformity may be difficult to produce. Without guidance, the scope of judicial discretion in sentencing matters places the sentencer in a difficult position. Clearly there are diverse views and controversies about issues as fundamental as the underlying philosophy of sentencing, the efficacy of various sentences, and the legitimacy of certain factors such as public opinion. One would hope that a principled approach could be developed so that the intrusive impact of sentences is not left entirely to the predilections of a particular judge or the extent to which a judge is able to rise above public uproar. But, so far, we have not been able to discern a clear and easily applicable set of principles with the unequivocal support of either philosophers or jurists.

R v Hamilton
(2004), 72 OR (3d) 1 (CA) (footnotes and some citations omitted)

DOHERTY JA (O'Connor ACJO and Gillese JA concurring):
[This important case dealing with drug mules, the sentencing judge's role, and the use of data is discussed in detail in Chapter 4, Facts of the Offence for Sentencing. Here we have included an excerpt in which Doherty JA, in his usual analytical style, provides a succinct explanation of the judicial methodology applied in Canada to incorporate the various principles and objectives of sentencing.]

[87] Sentencing is a very human process. Most attempts to describe the proper judicial approach to sentencing are as close to the actual process as a paint-by-numbers landscape is to the real thing. I begin by recognizing, as did the trial judge, that the fixing of a fit sentence is the product of the combined effects of the circumstances of the specific offence with the unique attributes of the specific offender: *R. v. Currie*, [1997] 2 S.C.R. 260 at pp. 278-80 S.C.R.; *R. v. Gladue*, [1999] 1 S.C.R. 688 at para. 80; *R. v. Proulx* ... , at 105-8; *R. v. Borde* (2003), 172 C.C.C. (3d) 225 at 238 (Ont. C.A.).

[88] The case-specific nature of the sentencing inquiry is reflected in the proportionality requirement, described as the fundamental principle of sentencing in s. 718.1 of the *Criminal Code*:

> A sentence must be proportionate to the gravity of the offence and the degree of responsibility of the offender.

[89] The proportionality requirement, long a touchstone of Canadian sentencing law (see *R. v. Wilmott*, [1967] 1 C.C.C. 171 at 178-79 (Ont. C.A.)), accepts the "just deserts" rationale for state-imposed punishment. Whatever other ends a sentence may hope to achieve, it must first and foremost fit the specific crime and the specific offender: Andrew Ashworth, *Sentencing and Criminal Justice*, 2nd ed. (London: Butterworths, 1995) at p. 70.

[90] The "gravity of the offence" refers to the seriousness of the offence in a generic sense as reflected by the potential penalty imposed by Parliament and any specific features of the commission of the crime which may tend to increase or decrease the harm or risk of harm to the community occasioned by the offence. For example, in drug importation cases, the nature and quantity of the drug involved will impact on the gravity of the offence. Some of the factors which increase the gravity of the offence are set out in s. 718.2(a).

[91] The "degree of responsibility of the offender" refers to the offender's culpability as reflected in the essential substantive elements of the offence—especially the fault component—and any specific aspects of the offender's conduct or background that tend to increase or decrease the offender's personal responsibility for the crime. In drug importation cases, the offender's role in the importation scheme will be an important consideration in assessing the offender's personal responsibility.

• • •

[93] Fixing a sentence that is consistent with s. 718.1 is particularly difficult where the gravity of the offence points strongly in one sentencing direction and the culpability of the individual offender points strongly in a very different sentencing direction. The sentencing judge must fashion a disposition from among the limited options available which take both sides of the proportionality inquiry into account. As indicated in

Priest ... , factors which may accentuate the gravity of the crime cannot blind the trial judge to factors mitigating personal responsibility. Equally, factors mitigating personal responsibility cannot justify a disposition that unduly minimizes the seriousness of the crime committed.

[94] In some circumstances, one side of the proportionality inquiry will figure more prominently in the ultimate disposition than the other. For example, where a young first offender is being sentenced for a number of relatively serious property offences, the sentence imposed will tend to emphasize the features which mitigate the offender's personal culpability rather than those which highlight the gravity of the crimes: *R. v. Priest* ... . If, however, that same young offender commits a crime involving serious personal injury to the victim, the "gravity of the offence" component of the proportionality inquiry will be given prominence in determining the ultimate disposition.

[95] Proportionality is the fundamental principle of sentencing, but it is not the only principle to be considered. Parity, totality, and restraint are also principles which must be engaged when determining the appropriate sentence: Criminal Code, ss. 718.2(b)-(e). The restraint principle is of particular importance where incarceration is a potential disposition. That principle is reflected in ss. 178.2(d) and (e):

> (d) an offender should not be deprived of liberty, if less restrictive sanctions may be appropriate in the circumstances; and
>
> (e) all available sanctions other than imprisonment that are reasonable in the circumstances should be considered for all offenders, with particular attention to the circumstances of aboriginal offenders.

[96] The express inclusion of restraint as a principle of sentencing is one of the most significant features of the 1996 Criminal Code amendments statutizing sentencing principles for the first time. As Professor Manson explains:

> Restraint means that prison is the sanction of last resort ... . Restraint also means that when considering other sanctions, the sentencing court should seek the least intrusive sentence and the least quantum which will achieve the overall purpose of being an appropriate and just sanction.

[97] Counsel on the appeal addressed at some length the potential application of s. 718.2(e) to groups, like blacks, who it is alleged have also been the victims of discrimination in the justice system and the community at large.

[98] There can be no doubt that s. 718.2(e) applies to all offenders. Imprisonment is appropriate only when there is no other reasonable sanction. The closing words of the section recognize that restraint in the use of imprisonment is a particularly important principle with respect to the sentencing of aboriginal offenders. The restraint principle takes on added importance because the historical mistreatment of aboriginals by the criminal justice system as reflected in the highly disproportionate number of aboriginals sentenced to imprisonment, taken with aboriginal cultural views as to the purpose of punishment, can combine to make imprisonment ineffective in achieving the purpose or objectives of sentencing where the offender is an aboriginal: *R. v. Wells* ... , at p. 385. The restraint principle is applied with particular force where the offender is an aboriginal not to somehow try to make up for historical mistreatment of aboriginals, but because imprisonment may be less effective than other dispositions in achieving the goals of sentencing where the offender is aboriginal.

[99] Parliament has chosen to identify aboriginals as a group with respect to whom the restraint principle applies with particular force. If it is shown that the historical mistreatment and cultural views of another group combine to make imprisonment ineffective in achieving the goals of sentencing, it has been suggested that a court may consider those factors in applying the restraint principle in sentencing individuals from that group: see *R. v. Borde, supra*, at p. 236. There was no evidence in the mass of material adduced in these proceedings to suggest that poor black women share a cultural perspective with respect to punishment that is akin to the aboriginal perspective.

[100] In any event, proportionality remains the fundamental principle of sentencing. Section 718.2(e) cannot justify a sentence which deprecates the seriousness of the offence. Where the offence is sufficiently serious, imprisonment will be the only reasonable response regardless of the ethnic or cultural background of the offender: *R. v. Wells* ... , at p. 386.

[101] In addition to complying with the principles of sentencing, sentences must promote one or more of the objectives identified in s. 718:

(a) to denounce unlawful conduct;
(b) to deter the offender and other persons from committing offences;
(c) to separate offenders from society, where necessary;
(d) to assist in rehabilitating offenders;
(e) to provide reparations for harm done to victims or to the community; and
(f) to promote a sense of responsibility in offenders, and acknowledgement of the harm done to victims and to the community.

[102] The relevance and relative importance of each of the objectives identified in s. 718 will vary according to the nature of the crime and the circumstances of the offender: *R. v. Lyons*, [1987] 2 S.C.R. 309 at 329; *R. v. Morrisey*, [2000] 2 S.C.R. 90 at pp. 116-18.

[103] If the offence is particularly serious in that it causes or threatens significant harm to an individual or segment of the community, the objectives of denunciation and general deterrence will usually dominate the other objectives identified in s. 718. Prior to the introduction of the conditional sentence, where the objectives of deterrence and denunciation dominated, imprisonment was almost inevitable.

. . .

[111] Fixing the range of sentences for a particular offence, of course, does not determine the sentence to be imposed on a particular offender. The range is in large measure a reflection of the "objective seriousness" of the crime: *R. v. H. (C.N.)* ... , at p. 266. Once the range is identified, the sentencing judge must consider specific aggravating and mitigating factors. The mitigating factors may be so significant as to take the case below the otherwise appropriate range. For example, in *R. v. H. (C.N.)*, the offender's cooperation with the authorities and his belief that he was importing marijuana and not cocaine, along with other more common mitigating factors, justified a sentence that was well below the range of sentence established for the importation of very substantial amounts of cocaine.

A. Individualization

The Supreme Court of Canada continually reminds us that sentencing in Canada is an "individualized" process. The following excerpts make this clear. There is no question that offences and offenders present a multiplicity of different circumstances, some mitigating and some aggravating. The attraction of "individualization" means that a measure of disparity is inherent. Many practitioners claim that this element of disparity is the strongest virtue of a system that seeks to ensure the protection of society through fit sentences. They argue that a sentence cannot be fit unless it can be justified as an appropriate response to the individual offence and the individual offender that acknowledges the unique character of each case. The prospect of disparity obviously undermines uniformity, but it can also affect certainty, predictability, and the appearance of fairness. Perhaps it is right that the priority of principles and objectives in sentencing should vary, or at least evolve, over time. It may also be right that the principles of sentencing in Canada should vary from place to place, or at least from jurisdiction to jurisdiction, given recognized differences. These are controversial questions.

R v Proulx

2000 SCC 5, [2000] 1 SCR 61

LAMER CJ (L'Heureux-Dubé, Gonthier, McLachlin, Iacobucci, Major, Bastarache, and Binnie JJ concurring):

[82] This Court has held on a number of occasions that sentencing is an individualized process, in which the trial judge has considerable discretion in fashioning a fit sentence. The rationale behind this approach stems from the principle of proportionality, the fundamental principle of sentencing, which provides that a sentence must be proportional to the gravity of the offence and the degree of responsibility of the offender. Proportionality requires an examination of the specific circumstances of both the offender and the offence so that the "punishment fits the crime." As a by-product of such an individualized approach, there will be inevitable variation in sentences imposed for particular crimes. In *M. (C.A.)* ... , I stated, at para. 92:

> It has been repeatedly stressed that there is no such thing as a uniform sentence for a particular crime. ... Sentencing is an inherently individualized process, and the search for a single appropriate sentence for a similar offender and a similar crime will frequently be a fruitless exercise of academic abstraction. As well, sentences for a particular offence should be expected to vary to some degree across various communities and regions in this country, as the "just and appropriate" mix of accepted sentencing goals will depend on the needs and current conditions of and in the particular community where the crime occurred.

B. Sentencing Ranges

R v Wright

(2006), 83 OR (3d) 427 (CA) (some citations omitted)

BLAIR JA (Goudge and Sharpe JJA concurring):

[16] Sentencing "ranges" are useful in promoting the "parity" principle because they provide guidelines to trial judges for the imposition of similar penalties for similar offences of a similar nature involving similar offenders: see *R. v. McDonnell*, [1997] 1 S.C.R. 948; and *R. v. Stone*, [1999] 2 S.C.R. 290. As Finch C.J.B.C. pointed out in *R. v.*

A.J.C. (2004), 186 C.C.C. (3d) 227 at para. 36, relying on *R. v. Bernier* (2003), 177 C.C.C. (3d) 137 (B.C.C.A.), they are nothing more than guidelines and are certainly not conclusive of the appropriate sentence in any given case. Each sentencing must be conducted as an individualized exercise. This point was underscored by Moldaver J.A. in *R. v. D. (D.)* (2002), 163 C.C.C. (3d) 471 at para. 33 (Ont. C.A.):

> Before going any further, I wish to emphasize that the ranges which I have identified are not meant to be fixed and inflexible. On the contrary, sentencing is not an exact science and trial judges must retain the flexibility needed to do justice in individual cases. The suggested ranges are merely guidelines designed to assist trial judges in their difficult task of fashioning fit and just sentences in similar cases.

R v Lacasse
2015 SCC 64, [2015] 3 SCR 1089

WAGNER J (Abella, Moldaver, Karakatsanis, and Côté JJ concurring):

[56] The principle of parity of sentences has sometimes resulted in the adoption of a system of sentencing ranges and categories. This concern for parity in sentencing did not originate with the codification of the principle in 1996. As early as the 19th century, "tariffs" were being used by the English courts: D.A. Thomas, *Principles of Sentencing* (2nd ed. 1979), at p. 29. The tariffs synthesized, as it were, the relevant principles applicable to each type of crime in order to standardize sentencing for it:

> While in certain contexts the Court articulates a principle, or series of principles, in a systematic manner, it is frequently necessary to identify the operative principles from the examination of a considerable number of cases, none of which specifically identifies the relevant criteria, but which, when viewed collectively, clearly conform substantially to a pattern which can be described. This is particularly true of what is conventionally known as "the tariff," the principles governing the lengths of sentences of imprisonment.

(Thomas, at p. 5)

[57] Tariffs differ from sentencing ranges in that tariff-based sentencing is theoretically the opposite of sentence individualization, which the ranges allow: Thomas, at p. 8. On the other hand, the principle underlying the two approaches is the same: ensuring that offenders who have committed similar crimes in similar circumstances are given similar sentences. The same is true of the starting-point approach, which is used mainly in Alberta but sometimes also in other Canadian provinces: *R. v. McDonnell*, [1997] 1 S.C.R. 948, at para. 69. Ultimately, whatever mechanism or terminology is used, the principle on which it is based remains the same. Where sentencing ranges are concerned, although they are used mainly to ensure the parity of sentences, they reflect all the principles and objectives of sentencing. Sentencing ranges are nothing more than summaries of the minimum and maximum sentences imposed in the past, which serve in any given case as guides for the application of all the relevant principles and objectives. However, they should not be considered "averages," let alone straitjackets, but should instead be seen as historical portraits for the use of sentencing judges, who must still exercise their discretion in each case:

> Even when an appellate court has established a range, it may be that a fact pattern will arise, which is sufficiently dissimilar to past decisions that the "range," as it were, must be expanded. The fundamental point is that a "range" is not a straitjacket to the exercise of discretion of a sentencing judge.

(*R. v. Keepness*, 2010 SKCA 69, 359 Sask. R. 34, at para. 24)

[58] There will always be situations that call for a sentence outside a particular range: although ensuring parity in sentencing is in itself a desirable objective, the fact that each crime is committed in unique circumstances by an offender with a unique profile cannot be disregarded. The determination of a just and appropriate sentence is a highly individualized exercise that goes beyond a purely mathematical calculation. It involves a variety of factors that are difficult to define with precision. This is why it may happen that a sentence that, on its face, falls outside a particular range, and that may never have been imposed in the past for a similar crime, is not demonstrably unfit. Once again, everything depends on the gravity of the offence, the offender's degree of responsibility and the specific circumstances of each case. LeBel J. commented as follows on this subject:

> A judge can order a sentence outside that range as long as it is in accordance with the principles and objectives of sentencing. Thus, a sentence falling outside the regular range of appropriate sentences is not necessarily unfit. Regard must be had to all the circumstances of the offence and the offender, and to the needs of the community in which the offence occurred.

(*Nasogaluak*, at para. 44)

[59] In *Brutus*, the Quebec Court of Appeal described the limits of the process of ensuring the similarity of sentences as follows:

> [TRANSLATION] There is no doubt that the sentence imposed in this case differs from certain sentences imposed in other cases for the same offence. However, as our colleague Rochon J.A. stated in *Ferland v. R.*, 2009 QCCA 1168, with respect to the principle of parity of sentences that is set out in section 718.2(b) *Cr. C.*, it "has some limits because of the individualized nature of the sentencing process" and cannot provide a basis for departing from the principle of deference to the trial judge's exercise of his or her sentencing discretion (*R. v. L.M.*, *supra*, at para. 35). [para. 12]

[60] In other words, sentencing ranges are primarily guidelines, and not hard and fast rules: *Nasogaluak*, at para. 44. As a result, a deviation from a sentencing range is not synonymous with an error of law or an error in principle. Sopinka J. stated this clearly in *McDonnell*, although he was referring in that case to categories of assault:

> ... [I]n my view it can never be an error in principle in itself to fail to place a particular offence within a judicially created category of assault for the purposes of sentencing. ... If the categories are defined narrowly, and deviations from the categorization are generally reversed, the discretion that should be left in the hands of the trial and sentencing judges is shifted considerably to the appellate courts. [para. 32]

[61] Any other conclusion would have the effect of authorizing appellate courts to create categories of offences with no real justification and accordingly intervene without deference to substitute a sentence on appeal. But the power to create categories of offences lies with Parliament, not the courts: *McDonnell*, at para. 33.

• • •

[65] The appellant correctly observes that Quebec is the only province in which the courts have subdivided the sentencing range into categories for the crime of impaired driving causing death. Other provinces have also adopted the range system, but without subdividing the ranges into categories. In those provinces, sentences vary from 18 months to two years in the least serious situations and from seven to eight years in the most serious: *R. v. Bear*, 2008 SKCA 172, 320 Sask. R. 12, at para. 59; *R. v. Berner*, 2013 BCCA 188, 297 C.C.C. (3d) 69, at para. 37; *R. v. Smith*, 2013 BCCA 173, 246 C.C.C. (3d) 386, at para. 60; *Stimson*, at para. 18; *Ruizfuentes*, at para. 22.

[66] The Ontario Court of Appeal has refused to define a sentencing range for the crime of impaired driving causing death, noting that the crime can be committed in an infinite variety of circumstances: *Junkert*, at para. 40; *R. v. Kummer*, 2011 ONCA 39, 103 O.R. (3d) 649. This is why there is so much variation in the ranges and why penitentiary sentences much longer than six and a half years have been reported almost everywhere in Canada.

[67] Like the range itself, the categories it comprises are tools whose purpose is in part to promote parity in sentencing. However, a deviation from such a range or category is not an error in principle and cannot in itself automatically justify appellate intervention unless the sentence that is imposed departs significantly and for no reason from the contemplated sentences. Absent an error in principle, an appellate court may not vary a sentence unless the sentence is demonstrably unfit.

[68] My colleague finds that the Court of Appeal's reasons, read as a whole, show that it did not intervene solely because of a deviation from the sentencing range (para. 144). With respect, I cannot agree with this interpretation. As can be seen from the Court of Appeal's reasons, it justified its intervention on the basis that it was not open to the trial judge to impose a sentence falling into the third category of the sentencing range, because personal factors unfavourable to the respondent, which would normally support such a sentence rather than one from the second category, were almost non-existent in this case. It is clear from the Court of Appeal's reasons that it based its intervention primarily on an erroneous determination of the applicable sentencing category by the trial judge.

[69] I believe that the Court of Appeal was wrong to apply the sentencing range rigidly. By saying that the sentence should have been in the second category rather than at the lower end of the sentences in the third category, the Court of Appeal substituted its own assessment for that of the trial judge without first determining that the sentence in question was demonstrably unfit. In doing so, the Court of Appeal erred in applying the sentencing range mechanism as if it were a straitjacket. The sentencing ranges must in all cases remain only one tool among others that are intended to aid trial judges in their work.

[70] In this case, even though the sentence fell outside one of the categories of sentences that have been established since *Comeau*, this did not mean that it was manifestly excessive. Terms of imprisonment of six years or more have in fact been imposed on people without criminal records who were convicted of impaired driving causing death. For example, in *Kummer*, the Ontario Court of Appeal upheld an eight-year prison sentence imposed on a driver with no criminal record who had caused the deaths of three people while driving under the influence of alcohol. In *R. v. Wood* (2005), 196 C.C.C. (3d) 155, the Ontario Court of Appeal upheld a nine-year sentence imposed on a person who had no criminal record for impaired driving but had caused the deaths of three people and caused permanent injuries to another. In *Morneau*, the Quebec Court of Appeal

upheld a six-year term of imprisonment on a charge of impaired driving causing the death of one person. Although the offender in that case already had a criminal record consisting of three convictions, the convictions all dated back more than ten years. In light of the foregoing, therefore, the sentence of six and a half years imposed in the instant case on an offender who caused the deaths of two young girls was not disproportionate.

C. Looking for Guidance

Andrew Ashworth has observed that there are three techniques available to avoid unjustified disparity: (1) legislating a clear statement of purpose and principles; (2) legislating sentencing guidelines for specific categories of offences; and (3) encouraging guideline judgments from appellate courts: see Andrew Ashworth, "Three Techniques for Reducing Sentence Disparity" in Andrew von Hirsch & Andrew Ashworth, eds, *Principled Sentencing* (Boston: Northeastern University Press, 1992) at 282. In 1996, Parliament responded with a statutory statement of purposes and principles of sentencing. Below, we consider whether this approach has been successful in providing a principled approach. Other jurisdictions have looked to sentencing commissions to provide stipulated prescriptive guidelines for sentencing judges with greater or lesser opportunities to deviate from the norm. Appellate courts have been delegated as the tool for inducing principled uniformity in some jurisdictions through the encouragement of guideline judgments. In *R v McLeod* (1993), 81 CCC (3d) 83 (Sask CA), Vancise JA argued that it is the role of the appellate courts to "develop and articulate guidelines."

Assuming that a strong argument for reduction of unjustified disparity can be made, which institution and which technique ought to be used to achieve it? In considering this issue, imagine a spectrum of approaches. At each end of that spectrum are positions that can, for convenience only, be described as "subjective" and "objective." The essential characteristic of "subjective" sentencing is the individualized decision, determined entirely at the discretion of the judge. As we move along the spectrum, we find a growing set of principles, each building on its predecessors, that are established by statute and the authoritative decisions of appellate courts. Finally, at the end of the spectrum is the truly "objective" approach to the sentencing decision, which eliminates or suppresses the exercise of judicial discretion by stipulating the appropriate penalty. This conceptual spectrum allows for various models of sentencing that lie somewhere between a purely subjective and purely objective model. The imperfections of purely subjective or purely objective models of sentencing are immediately apparent. Both would be unjust—the former because discretion would be unconstrained by principle and the latter because principle could not bend to ensure that justice is done in the individual case.

It can be argued that a natural and useful tendency of a system that emphasizes the need for individualized sentencing is to construct a range of sentencing options that are considered appropriate for the offence and the offender. Ideally, this range emerges over time. But how many cases are required before one can say what constitutes the "usual range"? Although the individualized approach to sentencing and the "wise blending" of principles have applied in Canada for a considerable time, the appellate courts of some provinces have attempted to introduce a greater measure of objectivity in sentencing decisions so as to enhance consistency and reduce disparity. The crux of these initiatives is to identify a "starting point" for sentences in a given class of offences.

In *R v Sandercock*, below, the Alberta Court of Appeal developed the "starting point" approach later followed in some provinces, at least with respect to sexual assault cases. The case involved what the court characterized as a "major sexual assault." Kerans JA offered the following explanation of the new approach.

R v Sandercock
1985 ABCA 218, 22 CCC (3d) 79

KERANS JA (Laycraft CJ and McDermid JA concurring):

[2] We first re-affirm the commitment of this court to the "starting-point approach" to sentencing. This approach, first expressed by this court in *R v. Johnas et al.* (1982), 2 CCC (3d) 490, 32 CR (3d) 1, 41 AR 183, has been criticized as a euphemism for a mandated minimal sentence. Also, Crown counsel often make that suggestion. These interpretations misunderstand that approach. On the contrary, it does not arbitrarily confine the discretion of the sentencing court. Rather, it offers a rational structure for its exercise, and a structure which is just because it guards against both disparity and inflexibility.

• • •

[4] On the other hand, the guidance offered should not be too rigid. A fixed guideline, or tariff (or, indeed, even an "approved range"), fails to take into account the immense variety of circumstances which can be found in different cases involving a conviction for the same offence. Even putting aside the offender's circumstances, those who advocate some form of fixed sentences fail to appreciate that the definitions of the crimes in the *Criminal Code* contain only certain key elements required for guilt. For example, the definition of robbery requires only the taking of the property of another accompanied by an act of violence. The elements for guilt are the same whether the offence involves an elaborate bank hold-up or, literally, taking candy from a baby. The category of "robbery" is simply too broad for any meaningful sentence regime. The manifest object of the *Criminal Code* is that the sentencing process will adjust for the other important factors, whether aggravating or mitigating. This is why the sentencing judge is given a wide scope of terms of possible sentences.

[5] The crime of sexual assault, like the crime of robbery, is so broadly defined that it encompasses all manner of crimes, some serious, some not so serious. A rational sentencing structure segregates them into meaningful categories. The minimal and maximal sentences permitted by law remain possible, although to be sure the former is unlikely for the serious categories and the latter for the less serious.

[6] The sentencing process now adopted by this court is to state atypical categories with precision, and to acknowledge at the same time that each actual case presents differences from the archetypical case. These differences might mitigate or aggravate. Nevertheless, the idea of a typical case affords a starting-point for sentencing because one can state a precise sentence for that precise category. An actual sentence in a real case will vary upwards or downwards from that depending upon the balance of the factors present in the actual case. Many archetypes already exist, of which "bank hold up" is a good example. What cannot always be found in the cases is a precise definition of such typical cases, and this imprecision can lead to confusion. Nor can a precise starting-point always be found.

[7] This, then, is the starting-point approach: first, a categorization of a crime into "typical cases," second, a starting sentence for each typical case, third, the refinement of the sentence to the very specific circumstances of the actual case.

NOTE

Subsequently, the Alberta Court of Appeal extended the starting-point or tariff approach to sentencing by applying it to a number of offences. In *R v S (WB)* (1992), 73 CCC (3d) 530 (Alta CA), the court established a starting point of four years for sexual offences against children in the context of a trust or "near-trust" relationship. Similarly, in *R v Brown* (1992), 73 CCC (3d) 242 (Alta CA), a starting point for interspousal assaults was established and subsequently confirmed in *R v Ollenberger*, 1994 ABCA 72, 29 CR (4th) 166. With respect to manslaughter, however, the variety of ways in which the offence can be committed persuaded the Alberta Court of Appeal that it was not amenable to the starting-point approach: see *R v Tallman*, 1989 ABCA 47, 68 CR (3d) 367. The Manitoba Court of Appeal has applied the starting-point analysis to this type of case. In *R v CD* (1991), 75 Man R (2d) 14 (CA) and *R v MFD* (1991), 75 Man R (2d) 21 (CA), the court established a four- to five-year starting point for sexual assaults perpetrated by family members where the victim is a young child and the sexual abuse extends over a period of time. The Nova Scotia Court of Appeal has also adopted the starting-point approach in a number of different types of cases: see *R v Owen* (1982), 50 NSR (2d) 696 (CA) and *R v Boutilier* (1985), 66 NSR (2d) 310 (CA).

The Court of Appeal for Ontario refused to follow the starting-point approach established in *Sandercock* and *R v Johnas*, 1982 ABCA 331. In *R v Glassford* (1988), 42 CCC (3d) 259 (Ont CA), a case involving a sexual assault on a woman, the court reiterated this position (at 265):

> As in the past, this court declines to follow and apply the judgment in *Sandercock*. A review of the other cases cited reveals that primarily each case must be decided on its own facts. Further, the cases reflect a trend in recent years towards longer sentences for offences of this character.

These sexual assault cases raise an important question: from a methodological perspective, is a "usual range" the same as a starting point? Is the starting-point approach radically different from or inconsistent with the idea of an appropriate range? Does it do more than define a starting point within a range and compel trial judges to have good reasons for departing from the starting point? See the approach to manslaughter sentencing in *R v Devaney* (2006), 213 CCC (3d) 264 (Ont CA).

Whether the starting-point approach provides an improvement in sentencing methodology is contentious. The appropriate starting point must be stated for a defined class of offences but, as the Alberta Court of Appeal makes clear, a "class of offences" is not a broad abstraction but a comparatively narrow category, such as break-and-enter committed by youthful offenders in an urban setting. In *Sandercock* and *Ollenberger*, the court noted that the classes of sexual assault and domestic assault, respectively, must be significantly subdivided before the court can determine a suitable starting point. Some of these subdivisions are concerned with characteristics pertaining to the mode of committing the offence while others are concerned with characteristics of offenders. These subdivisions assume that the Court of Appeal is competent to make decisions that distinguish not only in degree but in kind between different classes of offences. Unless it can be shown that the appellate courts have this experience and competence, it is far from evident that the starting-point approach is an improvement over the more flexible "range" approach.

The issue of institutional competence has a number of other dimensions. At present, appellate courts do not have resources to conduct empirical research and consultations. They may not, without help, have resources to critically assess research that exists. Still, starting points were a creative idea. It is difficult to know in retrospect whether the goal was to induce greater uniformity, provide a more clearly explicable methodology, or even to encourage a harsher sentencing regime.

In 1997, the Supreme Court of Canada heard an appeal in a starting-point case from Alberta, where the trial judge had imposed two sentences of 12 months each, to be served concurrently, for sexual assaults on a 16-year-old foster child and a 14-year-old babysitter. The Alberta Court of Appeal, applying *Sandercock*, held that the judge erred in not characterizing the offences as major sexual assaults and raised the sentences to 4 years and 1 year consecutive. On appeal to the Supreme Court of Canada, a majority of 5 to 4 reversed the Court of Appeal decision and restored the original sentence. When reading the following extracts, consider the controversy between legality and sentencing policy and between individualization and reducing disparity, and whether either judge takes into account issues of institutional competence.

R v McDonnell
[1997] 1 SCR 948, 6 CR (5th) 231

SOPINKA J (Lamer CJ, Cory, Iacobucci, and Major JJ concurring):

[17] … The respondent submitted that the sentencing judge in the present case failed to consider relevant factors and that the sentence was demonstrably unfit. Moreover, both the respondent and the Court of Appeal appear to have treated the failure of the sentencing judge to characterize the offence as a major sexual assault as an error in principle. I will discuss these contentions in turn.

B. Relevant Factors and Demonstrable Unfitness

[18] *Sandercock* … established in Alberta the notion of a "major sexual assault," which carried with it a presumptive sentence ("starting point") of three years. *Sandercock* stated at p. 84 that the key to a major sexual assault is the "evident blameworthiness of the offender" as reflected in the extent to which the offender's actions demonstrated a "contemptuous disregard for the feelings and personal integrity of the victim." The Court of Appeal held in the present case that the sentencing judge erred in failing to find that the first offence amounted to a major sexual assault.

[19] In concluding that the sentencing judge had mischaracterized the nature of the assault which was the subject of the first offence, the Court of Appeal relied on several factors. First, the court stated (at p. 173):

One salient fact cannot be overlooked. This was not, despite the defence suggestion, a case of "fondling." It was a case of penile penetration of the vagina. The fact that McDonnell only succeeded in partially penetrating the complainant's vagina with his penis because of the complainant's efforts to resist him does not make this any less a major sexual assault. Partial penetration will suffice. Accordingly, this assault falls squarely within what is described in *Sandercock* as one of the archetypical cases of major sexual assault.

Second, the court did not accept the submission of the defence, which the court stated (at p. 173) the "trial judge appears to have implicitly accepted," that the first offence could not constitute major sexual assault because of the absence of psychological harm. The court held that non-consensual intercourse leads to a very high likelihood of trauma, which likelihood is one of the indicia of a major sexual assault according to *Sandercock*. In any event, the court concluded based on viva voce evidence and the victim impact statement that the complainant in the first case did suffer psychological harm. On the basis of these factors, the court concluded that the first offence was a major sexual assault and that the sentence ordered by the sentencing judge was insufficient.

[20] In my view, the Court of Appeal fails to point to a relevant factor not considered by the sentencing judge that would give rise to appellate review of the sentence. The first factor emphasized by the Court of Appeal, partial penetration, was explicitly cited by the sentencing judge. She stated:

> The assault, while reprehensible, was an isolated one, *and it was a situation of far more than fondling as the accused attempted penetration.* However, in that case, there was no involvement of violence nor of threats. It did not involve oral sex nor anal intercourse, and *there was only partial penetration.* [Emphasis added.]

Clearly, the sentencing judge did consider penetration as a factor in reaching a sentence. Thus, consideration of this factor fails to give grounds to alter the sentence.

[21] The second factor alluded to by the Court of Appeal, psychological trauma, was also considered by the sentencing judge. The judge stated:

> It was a traumatic experience for the victim, but she was already 16 years old and was having other problems which may have contributed to her subsequent state of mind.

The judge later stated:

> In sentencing Terry McDonnell, I take into account his strong family support, the strong community support, his remorse and his desire to quit drinking, *but also the trauma suffered by the victim at a time when she was already troubled,* and the fact that FACS doesn't see counselling as being of any use to prevent re-offending, for Mr. McDonnell might simply re-offend if drunk again.

It is clear, in my view, that the sentencing judge did not fail to consider the trauma to the complainant in the first assault.

[22] Finally, the Court of Appeal stated (at p. 175) that it was "perverse" for the sentencing judge to treat the other personal problems the first complainant had been having around the time of the assault as a mitigating factor. I disagree with this characterization of the sentencing judge's views in the matter. It appears to me that in the first statement above the sentencing judge noted the problems the complainant had been having as a partial explanation of her personal problems after the assault; that is, not all her problems after the assault were attributable to the assault. The second statement by the sentencing judge indicates that while there were mitigating factors, the complainant's personal

problems actually made the assault more serious. The Court of Appeal did not interpret the judge correctly, in my view, in reaching its conclusion that the sentencing judge had misused the evidence of the problems that the first complainant had been having.

[23] The respondent's submission that the judge failed to consider relevant factors in my view cannot succeed with respect to the first offence. The respondent also submits that the sentence imposed was demonstrably unfit. The sentence originally imposed for the first offence was one year, whereas the Court of Appeal imposed a four-year sentence. The "starting point" as set out in *Sandercock* for a major sexual assault was three years. These differences in themselves provide me no basis to conclude that the judge's sentence originally passed was demonstrably unfit.

[24] *Sandercock* does not purport to create a rigid tariff. At pp. 82-83 the Alberta Court of Appeal stated:

> ... [T]he [sentencing] guidance offered should not be too rigid. A fixed guideline, or tariff (or, indeed, even an "approved range"), fails to take into account the immense variety of circumstances which can be found in different cases involving a conviction for the same offence. Even putting aside the offender's circumstances, those who advocate some form of fixed sentences fail to appreciate that the definitions of the crimes in the *Criminal Code* contain only certain key elements required for guilt. ... The manifest object of the *Criminal Code* is that the sentencing process will adjust for the other important factors, whether aggravating or mitigating. *This is why the sentencing judge is given a wide scope of terms of possible sentences.* [Emphasis added.]

Indeed, for reasons which follow, I conclude that it would be inappropriate to do so. Faithful to this instruction, the sentencing judge took into account all relevant mitigating and aggravating circumstances and arrived at what she considered was an appropriate sentence. Accordingly, the sentence's departure from the Court of Appeal's view of the appropriate starting point does not in itself imply that the sentence was demonstrably unfit.

[25] Moreover, I note that in a case not dissimilar to the present case, the Alberta Court of Appeal imposed a custodial sentence of one year. In *R v. A.B.C.* (1991), 120 AR 106, the accused had sexually assaulted his sedated 16-year-old daughter, fondling her breasts and vagina and possibly penetrating her vagina with his penis. The Court of Appeal vacated the two-year suspended sentence and imposed a custodial sentence of one year. The respondent submitted in oral argument, and my colleague McLachlin J appears to have accepted this submission, that *A.B.C.* was decided on the basis of procedural delays and other particular facts and should not affect the present analysis. On the contrary, to the extent that the particular facts in *A.B.C.* determined the sentence in that case, it may also be equally argued that the particular facts of the present case determined the one-year sentence meted out by the sentencing judge for a sexual assault similar in nature to that in *A.B.C.* It is difficult to conclude that a sentence of one year in the present case, given the similarities to *A.B.C.*, was demonstrably unfit. While this sentence is at the bottom of the scale, this does not make it demonstrably unfit. I note that in both *Shropshire* and *M. (C.A.)*, two recent, unanimous decisions, this Court refused on the basis of deference to reduce sentences that were clearly at the high end of the spectrum.

[26] In summary, with respect to the first assault, the trial judge did not fail to consider relevant factors, nor was the sentence demonstrably unfit.

[27] With respect to the second offence, the same conclusion applies: the judge did not ignore the factors raised by the Court of Appeal, nor is there any indication that the sentence was demonstrably unfit. The sentencing judge did, as the Court of Appeal acknowledged (at p. 176), consider the trauma to the complainant, stating:

> Regarding the charges of assault against [the second complainant], the victim in this case has been traumatized, but the acts of the accused were very much in the "less grave" category. Mr. McDonnell is a man of otherwise good character and is a strong member of his community. He has always maintained employment and supported his family. An additional lengthy consecutive custodial sentence to the custodial sentence imposed on the first charge would only seek to destroy the accused and his family and is not necessary to deter others from committing such an offence.
>
>   I will thus sentence him to six months in jail concurrent to the first sentence, plus probation for the same period of time.

Neither the Court of Appeal nor the respondent points out a factor ignored by the sentencing judge in reaching her conclusion of a sentence of six months for the second offence. Nor is there any reason given by either the respondent or the Court of Appeal to conclude that a six-month sentence was demonstrably unfit. The Court of Appeal simply disagreed with the sentence ordered and substituted its own opinion for that of the sentencing judge.

[28] My colleague McLachlin J disagrees with this analysis and states that the sentences imposed by the sentencing judge were outside the acceptable range. While the above analysis generally addresses her reasoning, I add here that I disagree with her conclusion that a variety of past cases reveals that the sentence in the present case was demonstrably unfit. McLachlin J provides at para. 110 a lengthy list of cases which she contends support the conclusion that a sentence under two years in the present case was inappropriate. While I will not review each case upon which she relies, I will note that, in my view, many of the cases provided are inappropriate cases to consider in the present context. For example, in *R v. S.G.O.R.* (1991), 113 AR 36 (CA), aside from other sexual offences involved in the case, the accused raped his daughter over 20 times from when she was four years old until she was 12. In *R v. S.(W.B.); R v. P.(M.)* (1992), 73 CCC (3d) 530 (Alta. CA), the accused S. engaged repeatedly in anal intercourse with his six-year-old stepdaughter and his stepson, who was initially in grade three, over a period of two years. The accused P. committed both anal and vaginal rape of a seven-year-old child, physically beating her head and body. *R v. Spence* (1992), 78 CCC (3d) 451 (Alta. CA), involved an accused raping his 15-year-old cousin and physically beating and threatening her. *R v. Nicholson* (1993), 145 AR 262 (CA), involved 20 to 30 acts of intercourse starting when the complainant was 12 years old; associated with this abuse, the accused, amongst other things, discharged a rifle in the direction of the complainant as she attempted to escape his residence. Other cases cited by McLachlin J involved children much younger than the complainants in the present case, such as *R v. Lapatak* (1995), 169 AR 385 (CA), which involved a three-year-old victim.

[29] In my view, many of the cases cited by McLachlin J involved offences considerably more serious than the present case. While any sexual offence is serious, particularly on young people, the violence of the offences, the repetition of the offences, and the extreme youth of the victims in the cases cited above clearly distinguish them from the present

case. Indeed, contrary to supporting McLachlin J's position, in my view the variable circumstances in the cases she cites highlight the importance of individualized sentencing. In any event, in my respectful view, the sentences in the cases she cites do not lead to the conclusion that the sentences in the present case were demonstrably unfit. The sentences in the present case, while low, were not demonstrably unfit.

C. Error in Principle

[30] While I have concluded that the sentencing judge did not ignore factors and that the sentences were not demonstrably unfit, according to *M.(C.A.)* and *Shropshire*, appellate review of a sentence is also appropriate if the sentencing judge committed an error in principle. Both the Court of Appeal and the respondent appear to treat the alleged departure from *Sandercock* as an error in principle. For example, the Court of Appeal found and the respondent submitted that the first assault was a "major sexual assault" in contradiction to the finding of the sentencing judge. The Court of Appeal stated (at pp. 172-73):

> We have concluded that the trial judge erred in finding that this was not a major sexual assault. This court made it clear in *R v. Sandercock* … , that the key to a major sexual assault is the "evident blameworthiness of the offender" as reflected in the extent to which the offender's actions demonstrated a "contemptuous disregard for the feelings and personal integrity of the victim." Here, McDonnell's actions in the first case clearly fall within the category of a major sexual assault.

The court then treated the error as one which justified alteration of the sentence, which implicitly treated the failure to find the major sexual assault as an error in principle. The Court of Appeal concluded that the sentencing judge wrongly declined to find a major sexual assault in part on the basis of what the court viewed as a misapprehension of the requirements for a major sexual assault. The court stated that the sentencing judge appeared to accept the argument of the defence that there was no significant psychological harm in the first case, and therefore there was no major sexual assault. The court stated (at p. 173) that while actual psychological harm may generally be presumed from non-consensual intercourse, it is not the actual harm, but the high likelihood of harm from the nature of the assault that gives rise to a major sexual assault.

[31] I disagree with the Court of Appeal that the sentencing judge accepted the argument of the defence that there was no psychological harm. As noted above, the sentencing judge specifically found psychological harm to the complainants in both cases. In my view, even if the sentencing judge required proof of such harm before finding a major sexual assault, the sentencing judge appeared to find such harm so any "error" in this regard did not affect the outcome.

[32] In any event, in my view it can never be an error in principle in itself to fail to place a particular offence within a judicially created category of assault for the purposes of sentencing. There are two main reasons for this conclusion. First, *Shropshire* and *M.(C.A.)*, two recent and unanimous decisions of this Court, clearly deference should be shown to a lower court's sentencing decision. If an appellate court could simply create reviewable principles by creating categories of offences, deference is diminished in a manner that is inconsistent with *Shropshire* and *M.(C.A.)*. In order to circumvent deference and to enable appellate review of a particular sentence, a court may simply create a

category of offence and a "starting point" for that offence, and treat as an error in principle any deviation in sentencing from the category so created. Indeed, that is what the Court of Appeal in Alberta has done in the present case. If the categories are defined narrowly, and deviations from the categorization are generally reversed, the discretion that should be left in the hands of the trial and sentencing judges is shifted considerably to the appellate courts.

[33] Second, there is no legal basis for the judicial creation of a category of offence within a statutory offence for the purposes of sentencing. As has been true since *Frey v. Fedoruk*, [1950] SCR 517, it is not for judges to create criminal offences, but rather for the legislature to enact such offences. By creating a species of sexual assault known as a "major sexual assault," and by basing sentencing decisions on such a categorization, the Alberta Court of Appeal has effectively created an offence, at least for the purposes of sentencing, contrary to the spirit if not the letter of Frey.

[34] The danger of courts encroaching into the realm of Parliament by creating offences is illustrated by the present case. The Court of Appeal appeared to base its conclusion that the first assault was a "major sexual assault" on the likelihood of psychological harm and indeed on the existence of actual harm. The court thus concluded that the sentence should be based on the existence of such harm. There is, however, a specific offence that deals with sexual assault causing bodily harm within the *Criminal Code*, namely s. 272(c). I note that *R v. McCraw*, [1991] 3 SCR 72, established that psychological harm from a sexual assault may be considered bodily harm. Given Parliament's intention to treat sexual assaults causing bodily harm under s. 272(c), it is particularly inappropriate to create a "major sexual assault," which is based at least in part on the existence of harm to the complainant pursuant to s. 271. While the Court of Appeal at times appeared to rely simply on the likelihood of harm in the present case, in *Sandercock* itself, actual harm was contemplated. *Sandercock* stated at p. 85, "[t]he other aspect which creates a major sexual assault is the effect on the victim." In my view, if the prosecution is to be based on the harm to the victim, the accused should be charged under the appropriate section, s. 272(c). It is not for the courts to establish a subset of offence within s. 271 that is based on harm.

[35] There is a further problem with the treatment of harm by the Court of Appeal in the present case in that it appeared at times to establish a presumption of psychological harm from a sexual assault. Admittedly, at other times the Court discussed the likelihood of psychological harm from an offence as illustrating the seriousness of the offence, rather than actual harm itself. To illustrate this ambiguity, consider the following passage (at p. 173):

> The first point we wish to make is that we cannot envision a situation where nonconsensual intercourse—vaginal, anal or oral—would not fall into the major sexual assault category. ...
> In addition, in each case, there also exists a very real likelihood of psychological harm. Therefore, what must be understood is that *it is not necessary that the Crown prove the existence of this kind of harm as a condition precedent to the courts classifying a sexual assault as a major one. Psychological harm is presumed in the absence of evidence to the contrary.*
> [Emphasis added.]

The court later stated (at p. 174):

> To put the matter another way, the offender is being sentenced on the basis of a major sexual assault, not because any specific psychological consequences have flowed from the attack

but rather because of the nature of the attack and the fact that it poses the very real *likelihood* of long-term emotional or psychological harm. The fact that no such harm may materialize, a fact one could not possibly know until the victim's life had been lived in its entirety, is not a mitigating factor. However, that said, this does not mean that the consequences of the sexual assault are irrelevant. The degree of seriousness of the actions may be measured against the likely long-term consequences of the prohibited act. In other words, where the psychological harm has been severe, that may well be an aggravating factor. Of course, where harm beyond that which would be normally presumed is claimed in a case, the Crown must lead evidence to substantiate it. [Emphasis in original.]

[36] These passages are somewhat unclear. At one point it appears that the court presumes that psychological harm would result from a sexual assault, while at another point it appears that the court is not presuming psychological harm, but rather is simply noting, correctly in my view, the *likelihood* of psychological harm resulting from the actions of the accused. *McCraw, supra*, established that a threat to commit sexual assault amounted to a threat to commit assault causing bodily harm because of the high likelihood of psychological harm resulting from a sexual assault, a likelihood recognized by the Court of Appeal in the present case. Such a likelihood does not, however, establish a legal presumption of harm in cases involving an actual assault, as opposed to a threat. If harm is an element of the offence, the Crown must prove its existence beyond a reasonable doubt.

[37] To the extent that the Court of Appeal held that the Crown need not prove psychological harm in some instances, but rather such harm may be presumed, it was in error. As stated above, if the Crown wishes to rely upon the existence of psychological harm, in my view the Crown should charge under the section set out in the Code that contemplates harm, s. 272(c), and prove the offence. If an element of the offence, bodily (psychological) harm, is presumed, the Crown is improperly relieved of part of the burden of proof, which is contrary to the presumption of innocence. Accepting that harm may be an aggravating factor under s. 271, *R v. Gardiner*, [1982] 2 SCR 368, held that each aggravating factor in a sentencing hearing must be proved beyond a reasonable doubt. Such an approach is confirmed by Parliament in the new s. 724(3)(e) of the *Criminal Code* (as amended by SC 1995, c. 22, s. 6). If psychological harm may be presumed, the burden of proving harm as an aggravating factor is improperly lifted from the Crown and shifted to the accused to disprove harm.

[38] In the present case, a presumption of harm is unnecessary. The sentencing judge found as a fact that each complainant in the present case was traumatized. The sentence was reached after considering the harm that resulted from the offences. Thus, the Court of Appeal's discussion of the presumption of harm was, in my view, both erroneous and unnecessary; harm existed and was considered in setting the sentence.

[39] The Court of Appeal appeared to make two other suggestions of errors in principle by the trial judge. I note that the respondent did not specifically raise these alleged errors in written argument before this Court, but raised them specifically only in oral argument. One error alleged by the Court of Appeal was that the trial judge improperly relied on *R v. R.P.T.* (1983), 7 CCC (3d) 109 (Alta. CA). The court stated that, notwithstanding that the principles it set out were revisited in *R v. S.(W.B.)*; *R v. P.(M.), supra*, *R.P.T.* was factually inapplicable because in the present case there was no family that might be restored. In my view, the court erred in finding that the trial judge relied on *R.P.T.* with

respect to the restoration of the family. *R.P.T.* held at p. 114 that even where there is a family to restore, if the sexual assault by a person in loco parentis on a family member were serious, "[t]he only solution, however imperfect ... must be to graft a rehabilitative sentence to a denunciatory sentence." If the assault were less serious and if there were a family to restore, a lesser sentence may be imposed; indeed, if the circumstances were "less significant" (p. 115), a suspended sentence may be appropriate.

[40]   In the present case, the sentencing judge stated that while she was cognizant of *R.P.T.*, "this is not a case where simple rehabilitation will suffice." She stated that a rehabilitative sentence must be grafted to a denunciatory sentence. She thus apparently relied on the aspect of *R.P.T.* which held that *despite* the existence of a family, both a denunciatory and a rehabilitative sentence are required where the assault is serious. Contrary to the position of the Court of Appeal, she did not rely on the aspect of *R.P.T.* which stated that restoration of the family should be a mitigating consideration in cases where the assault is less serious. Given that the sentencing judge did not follow *R.P.T.* to rely on family restoration to mitigate the sentence, the Court of Appeal failed to point out an error in principle by the sentencing judge with respect to *R.P.T.*

[41]   Another error suggested by the Court of Appeal was that the sentencing judge improperly relied upon the passage of time "between the first and second offence (and sentencing)" (p. 177). The sentencing judge did not in any way rely upon the passage of time between the first offence and the second offence. Neither did the sentencing judge rely upon the passage of time between the first offence and sentencing per se, but rather the judge stated that "the time elapsed since the offence has relevance in relation to the relative effect of this on both the accused and the victim." I presume that the sentencing judge was referring to effect of the actions on the accused since the offence, which included, for example, remorse and a desire to quit drinking, and to the effect of the actions on the victim since the offence, which included the psychological harm that the victim had displayed since the offence. These factors may be relevant considerations and the sentencing judge did not err in principle in referring to them.

[42]   I note that my colleague McLachlin J states that she agrees that failing to characterize the offence into a particular, judicially created category of assault is not an error in principle which would justify appellate review. However, I am concerned that while she *states* she does not view it as such an error, she effectively treats it, if not as an error in principle, then otherwise as an error giving rise to appellate review. She states at para. 109:

> As indicated earlier, the "starting point" is not a principle of law, but rather a tool to determine the proper range of sentence for a certain type of offence. Failure to allude to the appropriate starting point or range is not an error of principle as that term is used in *M.(C.A.)*, *supra*. If the trial judge fails to refer to the appropriate starting point or range but in the end imposes a sentence within the acceptable range of sentence for the offence as adjusted for the particular circumstances of the offender, a court of appeal should not interfere. On the other hand, if the sentence falls outside the appropriate range, the court of appeal must interfere: *Shropshire*, *supra*.

This statement, combined with her emphasis on starting points in her analysis of demonstrable unfitness in the present case, suggests to me that McLachlin J in effect treats the failure to characterize an assault properly as an error permitting appellate intervention on sentencing. That is, the failure to characterize the assault properly is not an error in principle, but if the sentence reached as a result of that error is not very similar or identical to the sentence that would have been reached had the mischaracterization not occurred, appellate courts may intervene. In my view, this effectively states that while appellate courts must permit sentencing judges to err in characterizing the offence, appellate courts may intervene, notwithstanding deference, if the trial judge's mischaracterization affected significantly the sentence ordered. Given that different views of the nature of the assault would almost inevitably lead to different sentences, in my view, mischaracterization is treated by McLachlin J as an error which will often lead to appellate intervention. In my view, as stated, mischaracterization of the offence according to judicially created categories is not an error in principle, nor should it be treated as one. In my respectful opinion, McLachlin J takes an overly permissive approach to appellate intervention that is inconsistent with both *Shropshire* and *M. (C.A.)*.

[43] I add that I do not disagree with McLachlin J that appellate courts may set out starting-point sentences as guides to lower courts. Moreover, the starting point may well be a factor to consider in determining whether a sentence is demonstrably unfit. If there is a wide disparity between the starting point for the offence and the sentence imposed, then, assuming that the Court of Appeal has set a reasonable starting point, the starting point certainly suggests, but is not determinative of, unfitness. In my view, however, the approach taken by McLachlin J in the present case places too great an emphasis on the effect of deviation from the starting point. Unless there otherwise is a reason under *Shropshire* or *M. (C.A.)* to interfere with the sentence, a sentence cannot be altered on appeal, notwithstanding deviation from a starting point. Deviation from a starting point may be a factor in considering demonstrable unfitness, but does not have the significance McLachlin J gives it.

• • •

McLACHLIN J dissenting (La Forest, L'Heureux-Dubé, and Gonthier JJ concurring):

• • •

[57] My difficulty with the position of the appellant and the reasons of Sopinka J stems mainly from a different understanding of the nature and effect of the "starting-point" approach to sentencing. It is therefore necessary to set out my conception of that approach at the outset.

[58] The starting-point approach to sentencing involves two steps. First, the judge determines the range of sentence for a typical case. Using that range as a starting point, a trial judge then adjusts the sentence upward or downward on the basis of factors relating to the particular offence and offender: *R v. Hessam* (1983), 43 AR 247 (CA), *R v. Sandercock* (1985), 22 CCC (3d) 79 (Alta. CA). This approach is distinguished from the tariff approach to sentencing which takes no account of the individual circumstances of the offender: C.C. Ruby, *Sentencing* (4th ed. 1994), at p. 479. The tariff approach looks only at the nature of the offence. In contrast, the starting-point approach mandates consideration of specific aggravating and mitigating factors directly relevant to the individual accused. In this way, the starting-point approach combines general considerations relating to the crime committed with personalized considerations relating to the particular offender and the unique circumstances of the assault.

[59] The first step on the starting-point approach consists of determining the appropriate range of sentence for an offence of this type in a typical case, assuming an offender of

good character with no criminal record. In the case of sexual assault, the judge looks at the manner in which the assault was committed (e.g., by violence or threats or trickery), the nature of the sexual activity, and, most importantly, whether or not this sort of offence is likely to cause lasting emotional or psychological injury. The "key ... to a major sexual assault is the evident blameworthiness of the offender," the "contemptuous disregard for the feelings and personal integrity of the victim": *Sandercock, supra*, at p. 84. The inquiry at this stage, to repeat, is generalized and objective. The task of the judge at this stage is to determine the blameworthiness of an offender who commits the type of offence at issue in a typical case. Because the inquiry at this point is general, it proceeds on certain assumptions. The issue, on harm, is not whether actual trauma occurred, but whether this sort of criminal act *would be likely* to cause lasting emotional or psychological trauma. As to the offender, it is assumed that the offender is of good character and has no criminal record. See *Sandercock, supra*.

[60] The exercise of choosing a starting point in this way resembles the long-standing practice of setting a range of sentence as a tool to arrive at a just and appropriate sentence that reflects both the crime and the individual circumstances of the offence and the offender. As Ruby, *supra*, at p. 482, notes, "[i]t certainly is not a new method of sentencing." The starting point may be viewed as the mid-point in the traditional range of sentences for a particular sort of crime.

[61] The choice of a starting point is only—as the phrase makes clear—a starting point. Based as it is on assumptions as to the harm likely to flow from a *typical* case of the type of criminal act and the good character of the accused, it could not in fairness or principle serve as a final indication of the appropriate sentence in a particular case. As noted in *Sandercock, supra*, every case has its own unique characteristics, and every offender his or her own unique history. The goals of sentencing—deterrence, retribution and rehabilitation—play out differently depending on the peculiar concatenation of circumstances presented in each case. In short, the sentence must be individualized to the particular crime and the particular offender before the court. Having determined a starting point, the judge must go on to consider these factors and their effect on the appropriate sentence. The factors peculiar to the particular case and offender before the court may mitigate, resulting in a lower sentence than the typical case reflected by the starting point. Or they may exacerbate, resulting in a higher sentence than would prevail in the typical case.

(2) Why Was the Starting-Point Approach Developed?

[62] The starting-point approach was developed as a way of incorporating into the sentencing process the dual perspectives of the seriousness of the offence and the need to consider the individual circumstances of the offender. It represents a restatement of the long-standing practice of sentencing judges of beginning by considering the range of sentence that has been posed for similar criminal acts followed by consideration of factors peculiar to the case and offender before them.

[63] Despite the common practice of first determining a range and then individualizing the sentence, the jurisprudence dealing with the proper approach to sentencing is not as clear as might be desired. Professor A. Young, *The Role of an Appellate Court in Developing Sentencing Guidelines* (1988), a report written for the Canadian Sentencing Commission, offers a useful history of sentencing theory in Canada and the failure of the

courts to adequately meet the challenge of devising a principled and consistent approach to sentencing.

[64] Appellate review of sentences was initiated only in 1921, explaining the absence of long-standing principles to guide trial judges. Prior to 1921, trial judges gave the sentence they saw fit and that was the end of the matter. Nor, in the years after 1921, were the courts instrumental "in designing relevant sentencing principles to assist lower-courts. ... Only in recent years have the appellate courts begun to express dissatisfaction with the impressionistic nature of sentencing decisions" (Young, *supra*, at p. 6). The maxim "Let the punishment fit the crime" might rule on Gilbert and Sullivan's stage, but in the courts the theme was "that the punishment should fit the offender" (Young, at p. 8). Precedents and theory played little part in the sentencing process. "In a sentencing model based upon the primacy of the individual there is little need for precedents that can extend beyond the characteristics of the offender in any given case" (Young, at p. 8). The Saskatchewan Court of Appeal (*R v. Natanson* (1927), 49 CCC 89) put the conventional wisdom this way (at p. 90):

> It would be impossible, and if possible it would be undesirable to lay down any general rule as to the punishment to be inflicted for any particular class of offence. Every case must be dealt with on its own facts and circumstance[s].

Similarly, in *R v. Connor and Hall* (1957), 118 CCC 237, the Ontario Court of Appeal opined (at p. 238):

> It serves little useful purpose and affords little assistance to the Court to know what sentences have been imposed in other countries or jurisdictions or by other Courts.

[65] The traditional notion that sentencing is primarily a matter of impression for the sentencing judge and only secondarily a matter of principle began to be questioned by the courts in the mid-60s. Behind the challenge lay increasing recognition that some measure of uniformity was essential in a sentencing process that not only was just, but was perceived to be just. In *R v. Baldhead*, [1966] 4 CCC 183 (Sask. CA), it was held that a sentence could be reviewed if it represented "a marked departure from the sentences customarily imposed in the same jurisdiction for the same or similar crimes" (p. 187).

[66] *Baldhead* did no more than confer judicial respectability on an emerging general consensus that the law should award similar sentences for similar crimes, subject to adjustment for factors peculiar to each case. Sentences may properly vary somewhat from case to case to reflect factors peculiar to the particular act and offender on trial. But it affronts common-sense notions of justice if people who have committed the same criminal act receive wildly disparate sentences. It is neither fair nor just that one person languish in prison years after another, who committed a similar act, is released to liberty. *Baldhead* expressed the growing view that a measure of uniformity, tempered but not obliterated by considerations particular to each case, must stand as a fundamental goal of sentencing law.

[67] Many courts since *Baldhead* have embraced the objective of uniformity as a factor to be considered in sentencing. However, the relationship between the goal of sentencing uniformity and the goal of reflecting in a sentence the circumstances of the particular case and offender remained largely ill-defined up until the jurisprudence advocating a starting-point approach. Alongside decisions advocating the need for a measure of uniformity, stand other decisions evincing reluctance to commit it to principle. As Young,

supra, puts it: "The courts have not wholly embraced the notion of uniformity for fear that broad, general principles will fail to take into account the unique characteristics of every offender" (pp. 9-10). By contrast, the starting-point approach represents an attempt to marry in one sentencing principle the values of uniformity and individualization.

[68] It was no accident that the starting-point approach was eventually applied in the context of the crime of sexual assault. The wide spectrum of conduct embraced by the crime of "sexual assault" and the disparate views different judges may take with respect to the gravity of particular types of sexual assaults give rise to wide variations in sentences for offences that seem quite similar. See P. Marshall, "Sexual Assault, The Charter and Sentencing Reform" (1988), 63 CR (3d) 216. Depending on where a particular judge placed a particular type of sexual assault on the spectrum of severity and the seriousness with which he or she regarded that assault, a sentence might be high or low or anywhere in between. The disparities between sentences threatened to go beyond the legitimate area of divergence represented by the individual circumstances of a particular offender and offence, to a more generalized divergence based on judicial views of the seriousness of the offence. This called for judicial action. As the Manitoba Court of Appeal put it in *R v. Jourdain and Kudyba* (1958), 121 CCC 82, at p. 87:

> It is the duty not only of this Court but of all the Courts of the Province and the Crown to do whatever is possible to bring about uniformity and equalization of sentences for crimes of the same or similar gravity.

The response of courts, charged as they were with maintaining reasonable uniformity of sentences, was to introduce the concept of the "starting point."

(3) In What Jurisdictions Has the Starting-Point Approach Been Adopted?

[69] The Courts of Appeal for Alberta, Nova Scotia (*R v. Zong* (1986), 173 APR 432), Manitoba (*R v. Muswagon* (1993), 88 Man. R (2d) 319), British Columbia (*R v. Post* (1996), 72 BCAC 312) and Saskatchewan (*R v. Jackson* (1993), 87 CCC (3d) 56) have applied the starting-point approach to sentencing to deal with marked disparities in sentences for certain crimes. The Ontario Court of Appeal in *R v. Glassford* (1988), 27 OAC 194 explicitly rejected the starting-point approach to sentencing articulated in *Sandercock*, *supra*. However, that same court has recently adopted the approach in narcotics cases. See *R v. Cunningham* (1996), 104 CCC (3d) 542.

[70] In addition to the Canadian examples, the English Court of Appeal also appears to have adopted this approach. In *R v. Edwards*; *R v. Brandy*, the English Court of Appeal, Criminal Division, suggested that "[a]n appropriate level of sentencing for serious dwelling house burglary where the house was unoccupied was three years on a conviction, with variations either way to reflect the particular circumstances of the case" (*The Times*, July 1, 1996). In fact, it appears that the starting-point concept is not of recent origin in England. Cross, *The English Sentencing System* (2nd ed. 1975), states at p. 148:

> The statement of 1900 is contained in a Memorandum produced by Lord Alveston (the then Lord Chief Justice) in an effort to get agreement among the Queen's Bench Judges about the normal punishment of offences. It was sent to the Home Office and no further action appears to have been taken on it; but it is now printed as Appendix 5 of *Enforcing the Law* by Professor Jackson of Cambridge. The Memorandum states that it is not possible to do more than

recommend "a range of punishments within certain limits" and throughout it speaks of periods such as three to five years penal servitude as the "correct range." When dealing with rape, for instance, the Memorandum mentions five to seven years penal servitude as giving:

> a reasonable range of punishment to be increased if there are accompanying circumstances of aggravation, such, for example, as rape by a gang or by a parent or master, or with brutal violence, and to be reduced if there are extenuating circumstances.

[71] The Australian courts appear to follow a similar approach. In *R v. Jabaltjari* (1989), 46 A Crim. R 47, the Court of Criminal Appeal (Northern Territory) did not interfere with the trial judge's approach described as follows: "Having fixed on the objective sentence his Honour then made appropriate adjustments downward to give effect to the mitigating circumstances personal to the respondent" (p. 64). Although the approach is referred to by the Court as the "tariff" approach, it seems to be identical to the starting-point approach.

NOTE

The practical result of the majority's decision in this case is to restore the concurrent sentences of 12 months' imprisonment. Do you think this is appropriate or "fit" for these offences? Does the majority decision signal the end of starting points, or does it merely reduce them to guides for sentencing judges? See the decision in *R v Waldner* (1998), 15 CR (5th) 159 (Alta CA) per Berger JA at 169.

In the recent Supreme Court decision in *Lacasse*, above at para 61, the majority relied on Sopinka J's decision when it criticized the Quebec Court of Appeal for adopting categories within offences, stating that "the power to create categories of offences lies with Parliament, not the courts."

After many years of struggling with the impact of *McDonnell*, the Alberta Court of Appeal issued a lengthy judgment in *R v Arcand*, below, which grappled with the issues of proportionality and the need for guidance. In that decision, it reasserted its attachment to the "starting point" approach, *McDonnell* notwithstanding.

R v Arcand
2010 ABCA 363 (footnotes omitted)

FRASER CJA (Côté and Watson JJA concurring):

[1] Without public confidence in the criminal justice system, respect for the rule of law is imperilled. This Crown sentence appeal raises a number of issues directly related to maintaining public confidence in the sentencing process.

[2] The approach to sentencing in Canada is a product of this country's experience and history, and of steps taken—and not taken—through the years. It took almost 130 years from Confederation before Parliament codified, through Bill C-41, the purpose and principles of sentencing that courts must follow in imposing sanctions on offenders. As part of these sentencing reforms which came into effect in 1996 (collectively the "1996 Sentencing Reforms"), Parliament underscored how vital public confidence is to the authority of law. It accomplished this by providing in s. 718 of the *Criminal Code* that the fundamental purpose of sentencing is "to contribute, along with crime prevention

initiatives, to respect for the law and the maintenance of a just, peaceful and safe society." How is that purpose to be achieved? The answer is also found in s. 718—"by imposing just sanctions" that have one or more of the objectives specified in the section.

[3] What is a just sanction? Again, Parliament has spoken. As part of the 1996 Sentencing Reforms, it mandated in s. 718.1 of the *Code* that a sentence *must* be proportionate to two things: the gravity of the offence and the degree of responsibility of the offender. Together, these determine the offender's overall culpability. That being so, the object of the sentencing exercise is to fashion a "just and appropriate" sentence that meets both aspects of the proportionality principle in s. 718.1. Other sentencing principles, including those in s. 718.2 (sometimes referred to as the "secondary principles"), are to be considered in determining a just and appropriate sentence which reflects the gravity of the offence committed and the moral blameworthiness of the offender.

[4] The narrow issue on this appeal is the fitness of the sentence imposed on the respondent, Jordan Leroy Miles Arcand, who sexually assaulted the complainant while she was passed out and sleeping in her family home. The Crown contends that the sentence imposed, 90 days in jail to be served intermittently plus three years probation, fails to comply with the proportionality principle. This calls into question what the proportionality principle means and its relationship to the secondary principles and sentencing objectives prescribed by Parliament.

· · ·

[8] We must face up to five sentencing truths. First, it is notorious amongst judges, of whom there are now approximately 2,100 in this country at three court levels, that one of the most controversial subjects, both in theory and practical application, is sentencing. That takes us to the second truth. The proposition that if judges knew the facts of a given case, they would all agree, or substantially agree on the result, is simply not so. The third truth. Judges are not the only ones who know truths one and two, and thus judge shopping is alive and well in Canada—and fighting hard to stay that way. All lead inescapably to the fourth truth. Without reasonable uniformity of approach to sentencing amongst trial and appellate judges in Canada, many of the sentencing objectives and principles prescribed in the *Code* are not attainable. This makes the search for just sanctions at best a lottery, and at worst a myth. Pretending otherwise obscures the need for Canadian courts to do what Parliament has asked: minimize unjustified disparity in sentencing while maintaining flexibility. The final truth. If the courts do not act to vindicate the promises of the law, and public confidence diminishes, then Parliament will.

· · ·

[25] The *Sentencing Commission Report* considered the significant problems it identified in sentencing to be reparable. While it still advocated relying on the judiciary, especially the appeal courts, it concluded that developing sentencing guidelines case by case was too slow and reactive. And that individual appeal courts had no capacity in any event to set national standards. For these reasons, it recommended that a permanent national sentencing commission be created to provide the courts with sentencing guidance. It also set out an elaborate scheme of presumptive guideline sentences. While it intended that these guidelines would be more than "purely advisory," they were to be less than "mandatory." As a result, it proposed that all sentences be subject to appeal, and that judges be required to give written reasons for departure from the guidelines. It also recommended that the *Code* explicitly grant appeal courts the power to establish policies

governing the application of sentencing guidelines and to amend, for compelling reasons, the presumptive custodial ranges set by the sentencing commission.

• • •

[35] When Parliament implemented the 1996 Sentencing Reforms, it determined, despite the recommendations of the *Sentencing Commission Report*, that the power to decide just sanctions would remain with the courts. However, it did not intend that sentencing discretion to be standardless. Rather, it moderated the discretion left with the courts in two critically important ways.

[36] First, as noted, Parliament confined the exercise of judicial discretion to statutorily prescribed sentencing principles and objectives. Certain principles and objectives might have more or less weight depending on the circumstances of the case before the court. But in the end, the sentencing court must fashion a just and appropriate sentence that meets the proportionality principle. Second, although Parliament left sentencing to the courts, it insisted, for the first time, on a crucial process requirement—that courts provide reasons for sentence. Section 726.2 of the *Code* provides:

> When imposing a sentence, a court shall state the terms of the sentence imposed, and the reasons for it, and enter those terms and reasons into the record of the proceedings.

[37] By imposing this duty, Parliament assumed that rational reasons for sentencing could be provided in each case—and insisted that they would be. Since Parliament does not legislate without purpose, the reasons provided should be "real." Mere "honourable mention" of the governing principles will not do.

• • •

[46] The roots of proportionality in sentencing run deep, dating back two centuries to the days of Blackstone. Its status as a guiding principle of long-standing in the common law is well recognized. Nonetheless, it was not until the latter part of the 20th century that legislators statutorily embraced the concept of a proportionate or "deserved" sentence as the *governing* sentencing principle.

[47] When Parliament reformed sentencing in Canada in 1996, it deliberately chose to make the proportionality principle—otherwise known as the "just deserts" principle—the *only* governing sentencing principle under the *Code*. The proportionality principle in s. 718.1 requires that a sentence must be proportionate to the gravity of the offence and the degree of responsibility of the offender. This principle is fundamental to the integrity of the sentencing regime that Parliament has prescribed. Therefore, these are not just words to be uttered and then ignored in the sentencing process.

• • •

[48] Proportionality is based on a simple, yet compelling, premise. The severity of sanction for a crime should reflect the overall degree of moral blameworthiness, that is the seriousness, of the criminal conduct. And that is properly measured by two things: the gravity of the offence and the offender's degree of responsibility. Or to put it the way that Andrew von Hirsch and Andrew Ashworth have done:

> The principle of proportionality requires the *severity* of penalties to be determined by reference to the *seriousness* of crimes.

[49] In other words, sanctions should be scaled according to the seriousness of the criminal conduct. In assessing comparative degrees of seriousness, the principle of

proportionality distinguishes between what has been described as *ordinal* and *cardinal* proportionality.

[50] Ordinal proportionality addresses how severely crimes should be sanctioned relative to each other. Ordinal proportionality has three requirements: parity; rank-ordering; and spacing of penalties. Parity calls for offenders convicted of criminal acts of *comparable blameworthiness* to receive sanctions of *like severity*. Rank-ordering involves deciding the relative seriousness of various crimes, that is, which is worse than another, and ranking them accordingly. Spacing of penalties involves determining the extent of the gap between the crimes once rank-ordered. For all these purposes, courts are able to draw on the penalties set by Parliament for various offences.

[51] Cardinal proportionality involves two steps. The first includes identifying a category or categories within an offence based on varying degrees of seriousness. The second is to determine the appropriate sentence to anchor the identified categories. With respect to this second step:

> Such Judgments require a starting point, however, and the issue of cardinal magnitude deals with finding that starting point.

[52] Why did Parliament choose proportionality as the governing principle? One answer is that it accords with principles of fundamental justice and with the purpose of sentencing—to maintain respect for the law and a safe society by imposing *just sanctions*. Further, just sanctions being the goal of sentencing, proportionality must be the overarching principle since a disproportionate sanction can never be a just sanction.

[53] In addition, without a governing principle to guide the exercise of sentencing discretion, there would be no common standard against which judges would impose sentence. Sentencing would then essentially be a free-for-all, with individual judges picking and choosing those facts and considerations that struck a particular chord with them, and then selecting one principle after the fact to justify the result. Parliament did not choose this sentencing framework. Rather, Parliament made proportionality the fundamental—and dominant—principle of sentencing, not an ornamental decoration for the *Code*.

[54] Finally, proportionality is what makes the blunt tool of punishment a valid and itself morally acceptable element of social order. Without proportionality as the governing sentencing principle, sentencing would be either the arbitrary application of state power or an ineffective response to criminal conduct. It follows that in prescribing proportionality as the mandatory sentencing principle, Parliament was not attempting to constrain only disproportionately high sentences. As two academics have explained:

> There is little in the voluminous literature on desert theory, and less in ss. 718 to 718.2 of the Code to suggest that proportionality is a one-way street, designed only to inhibit excessive severity. A derisory penalty for a serious crime of violence can also be disproportionate, in the sense that the seriousness of the crime is not reflected in the severity of the sentence imposed.

[55] Nor do we accept that proportionality is of no use except to set both an upper and lower limit. On this thinking, proportionality limits, but does not help determine, sentence. However, the proportionality principle, properly understood, is intended to—and does—provide far more guidance than merely setting the outer limits, that is a maximum and a minimum, of a just sanction, though it most assuredly does that as well. Binding authority confirms that the proportionality principle is the dominant principle

driving the determination of sentence: *R. v. Malmo-Levine*; *R. v. Proulx*; and *R. v. Nasoga-luak*. Therefore, compliance with it is vital to preserving the integrity and credibility of the sentencing system that Parliament has prescribed.

· · ·

[109] The Supreme Court has previously affirmed, in both *R. v. McDonnell* and *R. v. Stone*, the legitimacy and utility of starting point sentencing and the role of courts of appeal in ensuring its integrity. Nevertheless, it has been suggested that the Supreme Court's affirmation of starting point sentencing came with so many restrictions that its effective use in Canada has been substantially curtailed, if not ended.

[110] This argument appears to rest on the majority judgment of the Supreme Court in *McDonnell*. Some interpret that judgment to mean that starting points, while permitted, cannot constrain the exercise of a sentencing judge's discretion. In other words, starting points are acceptable in concept but meaningless in practice. In particular, it is asserted that a sentencing judge does not err in failing to recognize that an offence falls within a category for which an appeal court has set a starting point. Or fails to advert to a relevant starting point. However, both assertions, while correct as far as they go, capture one corner of the topic only. To understand why, we must explore the majority reasoning in *McDonnell* along with subsequent legislative and case developments.

[111] Admittedly, the majority judgment in *McDonnell* stated that it can never be an error in principle to fail to place a particular offence within a judicially created category of assault for purposes of sentencing. The majority gave two reasons for this conclusion. First, if a court could create a category and simply treat any deviation from it as an error in principle, that would unduly diminish the deference that should be shown to a lower court's sentencing decision. Second, only Parliament, not courts, can create categories of offences for sentencing purposes. Consequently, the majority criticized this Court's use of the term "major sexual assault" to describe the kinds of offences that would attract a three year starting point under *Sandercock*.

[112] Since *McDonnell*, the law has evolved. McDonnell was sentenced under the law as it existed prior to the 1996 Sentencing Reforms. With those Reforms, Parliament determined that the proportionality principle would be the governing sentencing principle. As explained earlier, the proportionality principle contemplates categorization of offences by the courts for sentencing purposes and the setting of starting points. So too does the parity principle prescribed by Parliament as part of the 1996 Sentencing Reforms. Parliament intended that the proportionality principle and other statutory sentencing principles would henceforth guide the exercise of discretion by sentencing judges. Thus, it is not for the courts to constrain the application of those sentencing principles by rejecting what is inherent in their application. In any event, starting point sentencing not only permits deviations from the starting point; those deviations are instrumental to this process.

[113] Further, in *Stone*, which followed the adoption of the 1996 Sentencing Reforms, the Supreme Court addressed the subject of categorization and starting points. It confirmed that provided there was a clear description of the category created for purpose of setting starting points, or for that matter sentencing ranges, then such categorization was permissible, indeed required. Bastarache J., speaking for the Court, referred to appellate courts setting starting points as guides for lower courts and said:

> ... [A] clarity requirement must be read into this appellate court authority because such guides would not be useful without a clear description of the category created and the logic

behind the starting point appropriate to it. The same need for clear direction applies to ranges set by appellate courts.

[114]　Hence the Supreme Court approved the notion of a category within an offence for the purposes of setting a starting point. This is entirely in keeping with the proper application of the proportionality principle. Where the offence does not involve a large range in possible sentence, there would be little use in a starting point. Disparity in sentencing practice would be minor given the limited scope of possible sentences. But where an offence covers a wide variety of criminal conduct, it is here that categorization for purposes of setting starting points is most useful. This point was implicitly recognized by Lamer C.J.C. in *Proulx* where he stated:

> Starting points are most useful in circumstances where there is the potential for a large disparity between sentences imposed for a particular crime because the range of sentence set out in the *Code* is particularly broad.

[115]　We acknowledge that in one sentence in *R. v. Wells*, the Supreme Court cited with approval a statement by the majority in *McDonnell* criticizing categorization. But this comment in *Wells* was clearly *obiter dictum* only. We prefer to rely on the Supreme Court's *ratio* on this point in *Stone*. We do so because the Supreme Court not only explicitly addressed and resolved the categorization issue in *Stone*, but also because the approach it sanctioned, approving categorization provided it is done with precision, preserves, rather than guts, starting point sentencing.

[116]　It is this simple. Either starting point sentencing has a meaningful function in Canada or it does not. In our view, it does, particularly given the developments in the law since *McDonnell*. This includes the obligation on the part of appeal courts to properly define categories within an offence for purposes of setting a starting point. Starting point sentencing also obliges appeal courts to assess the fitness of a sentence imposed in light of the relevant starting point and the reasons offered for the resulting sentence. In fact, even without a relevant starting point for an offence, it would be reviewable error for a sentencing judge to fail to give proper weight to the gravity of an offence by diminishing its seriousness.

[117]　That said, we concede that it is not an error in principle, *by itself*, for a sentencing judge to fail to expressly place an offence within a properly described category or to fail to expressly advert to a relevant starting point *provided that the resulting sentence is reasonable in the circumstances having regard to the relevant starting point as adjusted for that offence and that offender*. But if the resulting sentence is not, then that will constitute an error in principle that may warrant appellate intervention.

[118]　Continued attempts to render starting point sentencing practically useless reduce to this. Canadian courts, properly in our view, hold out to the Canadian public that starting points are used as one guideline sentencing tool to minimize unjustified disparity in sentencing. But if sentencing judges are free to disregard categories and associated starting points set by appeal courts without rational reasons for doing so, then starting point sentencing has no real value. This would be akin to saying: starting points are permissible; appellate courts can set them provided they are clear; and sentencing judges are free to disregard them with impunity. What then would be the purpose of starting points? If a sentencing judge need only pay lip service to a starting point, and not even that, then a starting point would provide a guide to no one and nowhere.

[119] This is not our understanding of the sentencing regime that Parliament adopted beginning with the 1996 Sentencing Reforms nor of the effect of Supreme Court decisions. However, if we are wrong; if starting point sentencing in Canada exists in name only despite the fact it is contemplated by the proper application of the proportionality principle, then Parliament may wish to consider its options. This may include determining what further steps might be taken to ensure that Canadian appeal courts are able to effectively set starting points in aid of the uniformity of approach Parliament intended when it made proportionality the governing sentencing principle.

· · ·

[121] Typically, ranges are viewed as guidelines only to give judges an idea of what final sentence is considered to be "in the range." As with starting points, the category to which a range is to be applied must be clearly defined. Therefore, the value of a range is directly linked to the degree to which the required sentencing rigour has been applied to defining the range and to the reasoning in the cases making up the range. Or, at a minimum, where unifying principles might be discerned from what otherwise appear to be a number of disparate results.

[122] As useful as ranges may be, they constitute the most rudimentary sentencing guideline. At the front end of the sentencing process, they are of limited value. Why? By definition, a range goes from a low to a high end. Since there may be considerable distance between the two, where is the judge to start the sentencing process? Throwing a mental dart at the range and starting with that assists neither consistency of approach nor confidence in its outcome.

[123] Further, the "research" that produces such putative ranges is often limited and parochial. Case data is frequently bereft of fact details or wanting in discussion of principle and policy. What purports to be a fair description of a "range" is too often a matter of counsel's hunting through a limited case collection in search of support for a particular viewpoint. For practical reasons, counsel's research may well be bent towards recency and locality. But sentencing is not a matter of trawling cases for a preferable comparator, and then simply adopting it. Worse, the public may suspect that some courts too simply sift the collection until they find a case that produces the result the judge is looking for.

[124] The sticking point is this. Without any proper assessment of proportionality, an appeal court's use of a range alone to determine fitness of a sentence is highly problematic. Since a range typically covers a wide spectrum, the mere fact a sentence falls within a range, or not significantly outside it, tells an appeal court little, if anything, about whether the actual sentence is fit. A sentence could be disproportionately low or high and still be somewhere in the "range." Consider a case where a mature offender with a recent prior related record is convicted of drugging and raping a woman in her own home. No mitigating factors exist. The offender receives a sentence at the bottom end of the range or even outside that bottom end, say one year imprisonment. Does this mean the sentence is fit simply because it does not fall significantly outside the range? Clearly not. This example points out the fallacy in using the mere fact a sentence falls somewhere in a customary range or not significantly outside it as the sole or even critical determinant for appellate review.

[125] These limitations of sentencing ranges are understandable. Ranges, which evolved out of the tariff approach, represent a compilation of some sentences imposed by some judges in some cases in some part of the past. Further, a sentencing range is not an essential component of the proportionality principle. A range develops as an *outcome* of

proportionality; it is not necessarily a *determinant* of it. Despite these restraints, ranges continue to have value, particularly as a verification check on outcomes as well as an influential factor in setting starting points. Nevertheless, as helpful as ranges may be, the sentencing regime Parliament has prescribed includes the use of more appropriate analytical methods to guide sentencing.

. . .

[129] This brief canvas of sentencing approaches in Canada and in England and Wales reveals five points about sentencing tools and just sanctions. First, appeal courts in Canada have adopted, albeit on an *ad hoc* basis and to different degrees, some or all of the three guideline sentencing tools currently used in England and Wales to provide guidance to sentencing judges: categorization, starting points and sentencing ranges. Second, the experience in England and Wales demonstrates that all three can be combined—and have been—as part of an integrated approach to sentencing. Third, to function properly, both starting points and ranges require appropriately defined categories. Fourth, this Court's adoption of starting points was born out of the leadership demonstrated by the Court of Appeal of England and Wales. Fifth, the methodologies some appeal courts use in Canada to provide guidance to trial courts may differ, but the motivating factor, a commitment to proportionality and fair and equal treatment for all, remains a constant throughout.

D. Structured Sentencing in Foreign Jurisdictions

Many countries—for example, South Africa, Australia, and India—have resisted calls to develop sentencing guidelines, and judges in these jurisdictions continue to sentence as they have for decades, enjoying wide discretion and guided only by appellate review: see Andrew von Hirsch, Andrew Ashworth & Julian Roberts, eds, *Principled Sentencing*, 3rd ed (Oxford: Hart, 2009) ch 6. Although Canada has also declined to introduce sentencing guidelines, a number of other jurisdictions have legislated a more structured approach to sentencing.

Sentencing guidelines of one kind or another now exist in several jurisdictions, including the United States, South Korea, Uganda, China, Scotland, and England and Wales. Other countries, such as Macedonia and New Zealand, have indicated an intention to introduce guidelines. There is clearly an international movement away from the traditional discretionary model in which courts of first instance are guided only by appellate review.

The oldest—and the most researched—are found in the United States, where guidelines originated in the 1970s. Many US states use two-dimensional sentencing grids. One dimension is the seriousness of the crime and the other the offender's criminal history. For any given offence, the guidelines specify a sentence-length range for each of a number of categories of criminal history. A sentencing court in a state like Minnesota must impose a sentence within a relatively narrow range. If it wishes to impose either a less or a more severe sentence, the court must find "substantial and compelling" reasons why the guideline sentence is not appropriate: see Richard S Frase, "Sentencing Under the Minnesota Guidelines" in Andrew von Hirsch, Andrew Ashworth & Julian Roberts, eds, *Principled Sentencing* (Oxford: Hart, 2009). The US-style guidelines have been rejected by other jurisdictions, principally because they appear too mechanistic and permit insufficient flexibility for a court to individualize the sentence.

In contrast to the US models, the guidelines in England and Wales structure sentencers' discretion, yet allow more flexibility than the US grid-based approach. Under the English approach, courts follow a step-by-step approach to determining sentence: Andrew Ashworth & Julian V Roberts, eds, *Sentencing Guidelines: Exploring the English Model* (Oxford: Oxford University Press, 2013). A definitive guideline exists for all principal offence categories. At sentencing in England and Wales, courts must first assign the case to one of several levels of seriousness. Each seriousness level carries its own sentence range, and courts then select a sentence within that range, taking into account all relevant mitigating and aggravating factors: Julian V Roberts & Anne Rafferty, "Sentencing Guidelines in England and Wales: Exploring the New Format" (2011) 9 Crim L Rev at 680-89; see also Sentencing Council, online: <https://www.sentencingcouncil.org.uk>. Courts must follow the relevant sentencing guideline, unless the court is satisfied that it would be contrary to the interests of justice to do so. Finally, other countries, such as Sweden and Israel, have developed what may be described as "guidance by words." These systems articulate principles with which to guide sentencers, but do not provide specific sentencing ranges.

FURTHER READING

Ashworth, Andrew. *Sentencing and Criminal Justice*, 6th ed (Cambridge: Cambridge University Press, 2015).

Ashworth, Andrew & Julian V Roberts, eds. *Sentencing Guidelines: Exploring the English Model* (Oxford: Oxford University Press, 2013).

Ashworth, Andrew. "Three Techniques for Reducing Sentence Disparity" in Andrew von Hirsch & Andrew Ashworth, eds, *Principled Sentencing* (Boston: Northeastern University Press, 1992).

Canadian Sentencing Commission, Honourable JR Omer Archambault, Chair. *Sentencing Reform: A Canadian Approach—Report of the Canadian Sentencing Commission* (Ottawa: Supply and Services Canada, 1987).

Cole, David P & Allan Manson. *Release from Imprisonment: The Law of Sentencing, Parole, and Judicial Review* (Toronto: Carswell, 1990).

Frase, Richard S. "Sentencing Under the Minnesota Guidelines" in Andrew von Hirsch, Andrew Ashworth & Julian Roberts, eds, *Principled Sentencing* (Oxford: Hart, 2009).

Roberts, Julian V & Anne Rafferty, "Sentencing Guidelines in England and Wales: Exploring the New Format" (2011) 9 Crim L Rev 680.

von Hirsch, Andrew & Andrew Ashworth, eds. *Principled Sentencing* (Boston: Northeastern University Press, 1992).

von Hirsch, Andrew, Andrew Ashworth & Julian Roberts, eds. *Principled Sentencing*, 3rd ed (Oxford: Hart, 2009) ch 6.

CHAPTER THREE

Aggravating and Mitigating Factors

I. INTRODUCTION

The Canadian approach to sentencing requires that judges impose a fit sentence that reflects the relevant objectives and principles, and the particular circumstances of the offence and offender.

Section 718.2(e) of the *Criminal Code*, RSC 1985, c C-46 requires that the judge consider all available reasonable sanctions. The statutory structure may point to a specific sanction or subset of available sanctions, or may suggest a quantum band for specific sanctions. The ultimate decision, however, is refined by factors that are more discriminating than the broadly conceived objectives and principles. Traditionally, judges have recognized sets of factors that affect the gravity of the offence and the court's perception of the offender's culpability and have then applied them to make the ultimate decisions about which sanction to impose and its quantum. Depending on the nature of the consequential effect, these are known as either mitigating or aggravating factors.

Section 718.2(a) now entrenches the common law by requiring judges to increase or reduce a sentence by taking into account aggravating or mitigating circumstances, relevant to the offence or the offender. The Code lists a few examples of aggravating circumstances, some of which were clearly encompassed by the common law and others that were being applied in some cases but were also, to some extent, controversial. There are no examples of mitigating factors in the Code. This asymmetry is puzzling, as is the selection of factors now placed on a statutory footing. Why did Parliament select these aggravating factors and not others? Was there a perception that courts were paying insufficient attention to these factors? No evidence was offered to justify the decision. Some of the codified aggravating factors are relatively obvious, in which case one wonders why the legislature believed it necessary to direct judges in this respect. Finally, it is unclear why Parliament declined to provide guidance about the role of previous convictions at sentencing, a factor that affects large numbers of sentencing decisions and that remains open to multiple interpretations.

Virtually every written or oral decision includes some characterization of the relevant aggravating and mitigating factors. Over the years, the common law has recognized dozens of factors that can have a mitigating or aggravating effect. Yet, these factors are rarely examined and courts seem to accept their aggravating or mitigating effect without much debate. Of course, some are self-evident, but others are not so clear. There can be legitimate controversies about their relation to the sentencing function.

Mitigating and aggravating factors represent a truly enigmatic aspect of the sentencing process in that they are always present, they are rarely discussed, and there is no coherent theory of mitigation and aggravation outside those cases that affect the gravity of an offence or the culpability of the offender. It would be worthwhile to pursue the issue of a principled approach to mitigation and aggravation for the following reasons:

- All aspects of sentencing decisions need to be principled to avoid arbitrariness.
- Only principled decisions can generate reasons that are essential to a legal decision-making process.
- Only principled decisions can be properly communicated to the offender and the public.
- Understanding the rationale for a mitigating or aggravating factor can lead to the recognition of other factors that, although seemingly distinct, strike the same sentencing chord.
- Principles will help determine the proper extent of mitigation and aggravation.

It is also important to use mitigating and aggravating factors in an appropriate way to ensure proportionality in sentencing. As noted in Chapters 1 and 2, the sentencing reforms of 1996 designated proportionality as the fundamental principle of sentencing. If a particular factor is given excessive weight at sentencing, or if an extralegal factor is incorporated into the sentencing decision, will this not undermine proportionality?

For the most part, the underlying premises that explain the applicability of an aggravating or mitigating factor seem to relate to one of three considerations:

1. The gravity of the offence as defined by the offender's culpability and the consequential harm that was caused.
2. The ways in which the offender's personal characteristics or circumstances relate to applicable objectives of sentencing.
3. Systemic exigencies that compel some consideration of mitigation.

The first category is self-evident, while the second is extremely elastic, often contentious, and devoid of a sound theoretical underpinning. It includes many aspects of character as well as the ever-expanding categories of pro-social and anti-social conduct that courts accept as being relevant to making sentencing choices. The third category, systemic exigencies, encompasses situations where the elements or needs of the criminal justice system have compelled some sentencing response.

II. THE MENU OF RELEVANT MITIGATING FACTORS

The case law dealing with aggravating and mitigating factors is vast. Many of the commonly accepted factors are discussed in Allan Manson, *The Law of Sentencing* (Toronto: Irwin, 2000) 131-48. Below is a list of many of the factors recognized by Canadian courts. Some are common; others arise uncommonly. When you are reviewing this non-exhaustive set of factors, consider whether and how they relate to the objectives of sentencing in s 718 of the *Criminal Code*.

1. *First offender:* The situation of an offender who has not previously been found guilty by the criminal process is mitigating because it generates a number of favourable inferences. From a rehabilitative perspective, it is assumed that the offender will respond positively to the deterrent effects of arrest, charging, finding of guilt, and imposition of sanction. This discounts any special need for individual deterrence and suggests that a lenient response is in order. Also, being a first offender is taken to demonstrate prior good character. Although first offender status is no guarantee of a non-custodial sentence, there is both a presumption against custody and a significant reducing effect if custody is mandated.

2. *Prior good character:* During the trial stage, good character evidence is usually limited to reputation in the community. For sentencing purposes, character is much broader and will often include opinions attributed to relatives, friends, associates, and acquaintances, as well as achievements that reflect on character. Usually, the goal is to show that the offence is out of character or that, by reason of good character, the offender is redeemable. This can extend beyond opinions and include conduct that shows positive social and personal values. For example, evidence of honesty or generosity will be relevant to a crime of dishonesty, while evidence of compassion will be relevant to a crime of violence.

Claims of prior good character are often confused with claims about standing in the community, which can have questionable bases as a mitigating factor and are often more relevant to reintegrative potential. For example, evidence of a person's volunteer work is not mitigating when the offence arises from those activities. In general, courts have found that good character claims are inappropriate when dealing with offences committed in the dark corners of people's lives. With respect to sexual offences, the Supreme Court has recognized that they are usually perpetrated in private, out of sight and knowledge of friends and associates. Accordingly, evidence of good community reputation has little probative value (see *R v Profit*, [1993] 3 SCR 637).

3. *Guilty plea and remorse:* Historically, a guilty plea was considered to be a mitigating factor because it implied remorse and an acknowledgment of responsibility. More recently, systemic justifications have prevailed partly due to pressures on justice system resources. The extent of the mitigating value is affected by the timing of the guilty plea—the earlier, the better. This is especially true if one intends to include consideration for the victims. Avoiding the need to have a victim testify is a legitimate factor, but its weight depends on when the guilty plea is entered.

Demonstrations of remorse, if sincere, are also worthy of mitigation. Apologies and other efforts at reparation can convey a stronger message than the guilty plea alone. Remorse can be indicated even after a trial. An accused's right to compel the Crown to prove its case does not remove the opportunity to show remorse, although it may diminish it.

4. *Evidence of impairment:* Impairment of judgment can be a mitigating circumstance depending on the offence in question. A sentence ought to be proportionate to culpability—that is, intended consequences are considered to be more grave than those caused by negligence. This is a principle of fundamental justice. Accordingly, evidence that an accused was suffering from impaired judgment can be significant at the sentencing stage.

However, voluntary intoxication has been the subject of variable and inconsistent treatment. In the early 20th century, it was accepted as a defence to a crime of specific intent. During the same period, it was accepted as a mitigating factor upon sentencing: see the comments of Kerans JA, below, in *R v Sandercock*, 1985 ABCA 218. It is important to distinguish between a planned offence and one generated spontaneously with little regard for consequences. Moreover, with respect to crimes of violence, where there is a history of drunken violence, intoxication is an aggravating circumstance.

Emotional, physical, and psychological impairment can mitigate culpability for other offences because they affect judgment. Deliberate choices are more culpable than those clouded by depression, medication, and extraordinary stress. One example, gambling addiction, has been recognized as a mitigating background with respect to consequential thefts and frauds. In *R v Horvath*, [1997] 8 WWR 357 (Sask CA), a former bank manager who was convicted of thefts totalling almost $200,000 from her employer and fraud in the amount of $35,000 from another financial institution was found to have been pathologically addicted to video lottery terminals. She lost money, incurred debts, and began stealing from her employer. After hearing expert evidence about her gambling addiction and her efforts to deal with it, the judge sentenced her to a conditional sentence of two years less a day in duration. The Crown appealed arguing that the amount stolen and the breach of trust required a custodial sentence. For the court, Bayda CJS dismissed the appeal:

> [41] Perhaps the factor that carries most weight in assessing the gravity of the offences in the particular case is the one that generated those offences. The offences were the products of a distorted mind—a mind seriously diseased by a disorder now recognized by the medical community as a mental disorder. The acts committed at the command of that mind were not acts of free choice in the same sense as are the acts of free choice of a normal mind. A pathological gambler does not have the same power of control over his or her acts as one who does not suffer from that complex disease. Accordingly, where those acts constitute criminal offences, the moral culpability—moral blameworthiness—and responsibility are not of the same order as they would be in those cases where the mind is not so affected.

This highlights the potential role of an addiction in reducing culpability sufficiently to warrant a conditional sentence even in a case aggravated by a breach of trust. However, in cases where there is a prior record, courts have not been so sympathetic to the gambling addiction factor. Still, some appellate courts have not followed *Horvath* and have held that a proven gambling addiction should not serve as an exceptional circumstance that warrants a conditional sentence. This view does not recognize that the gambling addiction is not offered as an excuse but rather as a factor that diminishes culpability if it has affected the offender to the point where there is little or no free will. Then, the offender's blameworthiness has been substantially reduced and this should be reflected in the sentence.

5. *Employment record:* A good employment record will always be considered a mitigating factor, although its impact may be diminished or even surpassed by the nature of the offence. Courts respond favourably to a good work record because it demonstrates responsibility and conformity to positive community norms that are the antithesis of crime. Consequently, the offender has more promising rehabilitative prospects, particularly if the work record is consistent over a long period of time. However, courts should be careful not to turn the absence of a good work record into an aggravating factor. Many offenders, especially those with little training and education and those who live in disadvantaged communities with high unemployment, have diminished opportunities for work. However, lawyers should consider finding out about potential surrogates for employment that also show diligence and responsibility—for example, volunteer work or even a pattern of assistance to family and friends.

6. *Collateral or indirect consequences:* The recognition of collateral consequences has been accepted by the Supreme Court of Canada in *R v Pham*, 2013 SCC 15, below, in the immigration context. However, the issue requires a nuanced interpretation depending on the varying nature of potential consequences:

- physical injury or even disability suffered by the offender resulting from the commission of the offence or flight afterward;
- loss of employment or even profession;
- loss of business and future opportunities; or
- loss of access to children

These, and other possible consequences, require an analysis of the offence in question to determine whether there ought to be a mitigating effect. Physical injury may be relevant for sentencing purposes, especially if there will be lasting effects. It may bear on a number of sentencing goals like individual and general deterrence and rehabilitation. Although the loss of employment or professional qualifications will often be raised as a collateral consequence, its relevance depends on the nexus, if any, between the offence and the job or practice of a profession. For example, there is a difference between a surgeon who is struck off the professional roll for criminal negligence causing death after performing surgery while intoxicated as compared to a physician who is convicted of fraud in the course of a non-medical business enterprise. The former warrants no sympathy for losing a profession that his conduct shows he was ill-suited to perform; the loss of livelihood for the latter is not directly related to professional qualities. Similarly, note the situation of a police officer convicted of assaulting a prisoner compared to an assault on a golf course.

7. *Post-offence rehabilitative efforts:* Progress in dealing with personal problems and efforts to improve or repair one's social situation are always given mitigating credit. There may be concerns that such efforts are self-serving, but they warrant credit because they show both recognition of personal difficulties and a commitment to remedying them. Of course, one needs to show sincerity and motivation, which can usually be done through material from a treatment program, job, family, or friends. At the sentencing stage, some credit will be given for rehabilitative plans, but it is always preferable if an offender is already a participant who is achieving some degree of progress rather than simply explaining a plan for the future. Regrettably, not all communities have available resources; moreover, not all treatment facilities are available at public expense. Accordingly, there is a real opportunity

for the privileged offender to gain an advantage over the non-privileged offender. This does not diminish the mitigating effect of an offender's sincere rehabilitative efforts. However, it means that courts should be sensitive to resource difficulties and give credit to the time and energy spent looking for appropriate resources and attempting to qualify for them because they equally reflect introspection and a commitment to change. In cases of drug and alcohol abuse, where the offence is closely linked to the addiction, courts should be cautious about imposing a sentence that can disrupt rehabilitative progress. More to the point, the absence of progress is not as critical as the fact that efforts at treatment show some interest in change. It is an accepted part of dealing with drug addiction that hard-core addicts will fail a number of times along the road to recovery.

8. *Unrelated meritorious conduct:* This is a subset of character, discussed in point 2, above. Courts have accepted the mitigating effect of acts of charity or bravery unrelated to the offence. The basis is that such conduct suggests positive aspects that should enhance reha-bilitative prospects. Also, this conduct is the kind of community involvement that one wants to encourage. It is sometimes referred to as "moral credit." Examples are saving a child from drowning or attempting to rescue people trapped in a fire.

9. *Acts of reparation or compensation:* Sections 718(e) and (f) are statutory recognition of the objectives of providing "reparations for harm done to victims or to the community" and promoting a "sense of responsibility in offenders, and acknowledgment of the harm done to victims and to the community." While a sentence may be directed to these ends, an offender is entitled to some mitigating credit for acts of reparation or compensation done prior to sentencing. Obviously, some harm is more easily rectified and some offenders are in a better position to take steps to repair damage. Still, these are steps that should be encouraged.

10. *Provocation and duress:* Provocation is discussed in the excerpt from *Sandercock*, 1985 ABCA 218, below. Any situations that reduce the degree of culpability or moral blame-worthiness present relevant mitigating circumstances. The defence of duress or compulsion is limited by s 17 of the Code and the common law, but there will be situations where there is some evidence of compulsion but no substantive defence to the charge. It should be consid-ered less blameworthy to act under threat than of one's own initiative. The common case is a drug courier who argues that a threat was made to encourage his or her participation. There may be no defence of duress, but there may still be facts that support its use for sen-tencing purposes.

Acts or words that provoke a violent response are in the same category. In cases of mur-der, provocation under s 232 of the Code reduces the offence to manslaughter in limited circumstances. For all other forms of assault, provocation is not a partial defence, but can provide mitigation upon sentencing. Punching someone is an assault, but it is a less blame-worthy assault if it was provoked by an insult, threat, violent gesture, or other form of offen-sive or wrongful conduct. However, a disproportionate response has less relevance. Conversely, the provocation may have been so severe and the retaliation so slight that the mitigating effect produces a discharge.

11. *Delay in prosecution:* Delay can be an appropriate mitigating factor because it extends the ordinary impact of the criminal process. However, there are two separate aspects: (1) delay by authorities, and (2) delay by victims in coming forward. Looking first at delay by authorities, there is also a Charter dimension. First, can delay at the sentencing lead to a stay?

The Supreme Court has concluded that s 11(b) includes the Charter right to be sentenced within a reasonable time. In *R v MacDougall*, [1998] 3 SCR 45, McLachlin J, as she then was, noted the potential adverse effects of living in "suspense" pending sentencing, and held:

> [33] … Delay in sentencing extends the time during which these constraints on an individual's liberty are imposed. While the sentencing judge may take these into account, there is no guarantee that this will occur. It follows that delay in sentencing may prejudice the accused's liberty interest.

For the purpose of Charter s 11(b), McLachlin J applied the usual tests and concluded that, in the absence of any indicia of prejudice, the bulk of the delay occasioned by judicial illness could not be considered unreasonable. Accordingly, stays were not warranted. What is significant, however, is the recognition that delay can be an appropriate mitigating factor because it extends the ordinary impact of a sentence. Regardless of a s 11(b) claim, one can argue that any delay that is deliberate, unnecessary, or unreasonable ought to be a mitigating factor.

With respect to delays by victims in coming forward, it is not uncommon to see an allegation that occurred decades before, usually a case involving physical or sexual abuse of the victim when the victim was a child. These are matters that are taken seriously today, often involving a breach of trust that is now recognized in the Code as an aggravating factor. A custodial sentence of some length is usually sought for denunciatory and deterrent purposes. By itself, the intervening delay does not mean much and will not be considered as a mitigating factor. However, delay may present corollaries that can be mitigating. For example, a lengthy intervening period with no repetition of offending can be an important mitigating factor. This, of course, will be enhanced to some extent by evidence of productive social integration in terms of employment and family life during that period. The extent of the mitigating factor's influence is affected by the gravity of the offence and is diminished by a lack of remorse or denial that the offence was a serious matter. The age of the offender may also play a role. The offender may have become elderly, which, by itself, is not mitigating but may be accompanied by ill health or infirmity, which ought to be considered because of the inherent hardships of incarceration. The capacity of the justice system to reach back into time for prosecutions may cause some dismay, but in Canada we do not have limitations on prosecutions and there is no automatic benefit that accrues to offenders because of the passage of time.

A related delay issue, albeit uncommon, relates to deliberate delay in commencing a prosecution when an offender is already serving a sentence of imprisonment. The need to resolve outstanding charges is pertinent to release plans. Some courts have recognized this kind of delay as mitigating because it is in everyone's interests, including the offender's, to proceed expeditiously to determine responsibility and impose a fair sanction. Moreover, from the offender's perspective, the authorities should not be able to arbitrarily postpone release by sitting on a warrant or evidence. Given the recognized interest in sentencing within a reasonable time, an example of deliberate or negligent delay that may prolong a term of imprisonment should generate mitigating consideration, including the possibility of a concurrent sentence even if otherwise not warranted.

12. *Gap in criminal record and the intermediate recidivist:* These related factors serve to place an offender's record into a context as it bears on rehabilitative prospects. A significant gap in criminal-history record indicates an ability to conform to legal norms for a substantial

period of time. The effect of the gap is relative, but it would be enhanced if it included a period of good employment or responsible domestic relations. How the mitigation is applied depends on the nature of the offence. Where it can legitimately be concluded that imprisonment is the only reasonable alternative, a significant gap should be an important argument against an automatic escalation of the duration of imprisonment.

The "intermediate recidivist" refers to a category identified by DA Thomas, *Principles of Sentencing*, 2nd ed (London: Heinemann, 1979) at 20-22. It includes an offender with a record of prior convictions but who has, arguably, reached a point in life where a corner can be turned. This can arise if there is a recent period of constructive employment with good prospects, a new domestic relationship, long-awaited success in dealing with an addiction or other personal difficulty, or a combination of these kinds of potentially reformative life events. Notwithstanding the record, and depending on the gravity of the offence, a court should give serious consideration to a non-custodial sanction that will enhance the prospect of rehabilitation rather than frustrate it. One vehicle that may be particularly well-suited to this category of offender is the conditional sentence, if available.

13. *Test case:* Legislative provisions that have novel or ambiguous dimensions can gener-ate good-faith attempts to test their scope. An effort to create a test case for adjudicative purposes can result in a mitigated sentence, especially for non-violent crimes. Given the costs, rigours, and uncertainties of protracted litigation, there can be a mitigating effect for an accused who decides to carry it forward even if this decision arose after the charge.

14. *Mistaken belief in the nature of a prohibited substance:* Substantive criminal law has produced some complicated and sometimes contradictory rulings about when a mistaken belief can exonerate. For sentencing purposes, culpability is measured by blameworthiness. Consequently, the offender's mental state should be the focus of sentencing attention. While the factual context cannot be ignored, a belief that a less serious offence was in pro-gress is a mitigating factor. This is consistent with the principle of fundamental justice that recognizes greater blameworthiness in intended consequences compared to those that are negligently produced. Some mitigating distinction should be drawn to reflect the mistaken belief. Even if it has no impact on criminal responsibility, it does reflect a reduced level of blameworthiness. In *R v Sagoe*, [1998] OJ No 4721 (QL) (CA), the Ontario Court of Appeal con-sidered a situation where the offender had been convicted of possession of heroin for the purposes of trafficking. The offender maintained that she did not know that the substance was heroin. The court, in reducing the sentence from two years to six months, commented:

> [6] … The trial judge appears to have thought that it was irrelevant that the appellant was wilfully blind to the nature of the narcotic involved, as opposed to having knowledge that it was heroin. This is not correct. Although the appellant had to be sentenced as being in possession of heroin for the purpose of trafficking, the fact that she did not know it was heroin was a miti-gating factor.

III. SYSTEMIC MITIGATION

Notwithstanding the view expressed above, that remorse was the original rationale for a guilty plea reduction, the better view is that the criminal process needs to encourage guilty pleas for systemic reasons and that, in most situations, some reduction is warranted for this reason alone. In England, the Sentencing Guidelines Council has issued a definitive guideline:

see <http://www.sentencingcouncil.org.uk/wp-content/uploads/Reduction_in_Sentence
_for_a_Guilty_Plea_-Revised_2007.pdf>.

This provides a sliding scale from a recommended one-third to lower reductions based on the timing of entering the pleas. It also provides for limited situations where a full reduction is not warranted. For example, the guideline states:

> 5.3 Where the prosecution case is overwhelming, it may not be appropriate to give the full reduction that would otherwise be given. Whilst there is a presumption in favour of the full reduction being given where a plea has been indicated at the first reasonable opportunity, the fact that the prosecution case is overwhelming without relying on admissions from the defendant may be a reason justifying departure from the guideline.

Another situation of systemic mitigation is giving assistance to police authorities. In the case of *R v NH (C)*, below, the late Rosenberg JA discussed what has come to be known as the "informer's discount."

R v NH (C)
(2002), 62 OR (3d) 564 (CA)

ROSENBERG JA:

[40] There is a division in the authorities as to when co-operation with the police should be considered a mitigating factor and, if so, the amount of the "discount" from the usual sentence that can be expected. The courts have found that co-operation with the police is a substantial mitigating factor where the accused has provided extensive information that has led to the prosecution of others for serious offences. For example, in *R. v. John Doe* (1999), 142 C.C.C. (3d) 330 (Ont. S.C.J.), Hill J. imposed a conditional sentence of two years less one day on a charge of importing 1.5 kg. of cocaine, a case that he acknowledged would ordinarily call for a sentence of four to five years.

[41] The appellant, relying on the *John Doe* case, submits that to be relevant to sentencing, the accused's information or assistance must be of practical use in the sense that it can be acted upon. The appellant refers to the following passage from p. 341 of that case:

> [I] am of the view that the mere providing of information which is already known to the police, or which fails to prove reliable in the sense of leading to arrests, seizures, or to the banking of useful intelligence information in the view of the authorities, is not worthy of sentencing credit.

[42] In my view, this is too narrow an expression of the circumstances in which credit should be given for assistance to the police. I prefer the somewhat broader view taken by the majority in *R. v. Cartwright* (1989), 17 N.S.W.L.R. 243 (C.C.A.) at 252-53:

> In order to ensure that such encouragement is given, the appropriate reward for providing assistance should be granted whatever the offender's motive may have been in giving it, be it genuine remorse (or contrition) or simply self-interest. What is to be encouraged is a full and frank co-operation on the part of the offender, whatever be his motive. The extent of the discount will depend to a large extent upon the willingness with which the disclosure is made. The offender will not receive any discount at all where he tailors his disclosure so as to reveal only the information which he knows is already in the possession of the authorities.

The discount will rarely be substantial unless the offender discloses everything which he knows. To this extent, the inquiry is into the subjective nature of the offender's co-operation. If, of course, the motive with which the information is given is one of genuine remorse or contrition on the part of the offender, that is a circumstance which may well warrant even greater leniency being extended to him, but that is because of normal sentencing principles and practice. The contrition is not a necessary ingredient which must be shown in order to obtain the discount for giving assistance to the authorities.

Again, in order to ensure that such encouragement is given, the reward for providing assistance should be granted if the offender has genuinely co-operated with the authorities whether or not the information supplied objectively turns out in fact to have been effective. The information which he gives must be such as could significantly assist the authorities. The information must, of course, be true; a false disclosure attracts no discount at all. What is relevant here is the potential of the information to assist the authorities, as comprehended by the offender himself ... .

[43] Many of the policy considerations for giving credit for assistance to the police apply whether or not the information turns out to be useful in fact. Hill J. listed those considerations in the *John Doe* case at pp. 339-340:

(1) The authorities can apprehend serious criminals including upper-level offenders in criminal organizations ...

(2) The police are able to seize contraband or to prevent the distribution of drugs ...

(3) The speedy proffering of information is encouraged by those who have it as part and parcel of their acceptance of responsibility for the matters with which they are charged ...

(4) The known availability of a sentence reduction for meaningful assistance to the police encourages other informers to come forward ...

(5) The spectre of substantial sentencing leniency for informer assistance encourages criminals to have less confidence in each other ...

(6) A sentence for an offender who has helped the police may be one of intense severity in prison on account of such matters as fear of reprisals or removal to a prison far from family ...

(7) Time spent in jail may, of necessity, have to be in solitary confinement or protective custody for the informer prisoner's protection ...

(8) In some cases, the accused/informer's family may be at risk of vengeance from the criminal element ...

(9) Where the informer's identity is known, as in the instance where he or she provides testimony against others, the risks to the informer and family may subsist after release ...

(10) Where an informer's identity is known, that person's days of living by crime are probably at an end.

IV. JUDICIAL COMMENTARY ON SOME SPECIFIC EXAMPLES

A. Drunkenness and Provocation

In the seminal "starting point" case of *R v Sandercock*, 1985 ABCA 218, Kerans JA made the following comments:

[26] We will conclude by reference to factors sometimes offered in mitigation but which are often suspect: those cases where the offender says he was drunk, or the victim of cultural conflict, or where the victim was allegedly negligent as to his or her own safety, or provoked the assault, or where the victim is of bad character.

[27] Drunkenness generally should not be a mitigating factor. Nevertheless, the fact that an assault is totally spontaneous can offer mitigation, and sometimes drunkenness is a factor in determining whether the attack is spontaneous or whether the likely consequences were fully appreciated.

[28] The circumstances in life of the victim, if known to the offender, can affect the assessment of the foreseeable pain to the victim: see, for example, *R v. Ricketts* (unreported, May 31, 1985, Calgary Appeal No. 17000) [since reported 61 AR 175]. Ricketts, in breach of his earlier agreement with a prostitute to pay her for an act of fellatio, suddenly demanded it free at knife-point. Her sense of outrage and fear should not be minimized, but I am sure that she would agree that the foreseeable risk of psychological shock to her was not as great as would be, say, a similar threat to somebody who had led a sheltered life: see *R v. Marsh* (unreported February 4, 1980, 12641). In this limited sense, the life-circumstances, or "character," of the victim might be relevant to sentencing. This is because these factors alter the level of reasonably foreseeable harm, which is the test, and not because grave consequences chanced to happen. In general terms, an accused is punished for blameworthiness and not for the actual consequences of the crime, although these are not to be disregarded: see *R v. Jacobs* (1982), 70 CCC (2d) 569, 16 MVR 15, 39 AR 391.

[29] Provocation of the offender by the victim is an obvious mitigating factor. More difficult to decide is whether, in a given case, there has been provocation. It is surely not provocation, for example, simply to be a woman, or to be attractive, or to be prettily attired. Sexual arousal is not the same thing as the arousal of a desire to seek sexual satisfaction by violence to another, and provocation of the first is not necessarily provocation of the second.

[30] Negligence of the victim as to his or her own safety is generally not relevant. The blameworthiness of the offender is not in the least diminished because the victim imprudently provides the offender with an opportunity for crime, nor does it necessarily follow that such imprudence lessens the likely pain, outrage and indignity which then visits the victim.

B. Collateral Consequences

As discussed above, there are many collateral consequences that flow from imposed sentences, some as a function of legislation; others as results of social, personal, or occupational implications of a conviction or term of incarceration; and some in the form of disqualification from benefits or activities. In the United States, a major focus of debate over collateral consequences relates to exclusions from voting in public elections. This is no longer an issue in Canada after the Supreme Court decision in *Sauvé v Canada (Chief Electoral Officer)*, 2002 SCC 68, [2002] 3 SCR 519, which held that a prohibition against voting by penitentiary prisoners violated s 3 of the Charter.

The general issue of collateral consequences was discussed by the Supreme Court of Canada in *R v Pham*, below, as well as the specific and common context of immigration consequences.

R v Pham
2013 SCC 15, [2013] 1 SCR 739

WAGNER J (LeBel, Fish, Abella, Rothstein, Moldaver, and Karakatsanis JJ concurring):

[1] The central issue in this appeal is whether a sentence otherwise falling within the range of fit sentences can be varied by an appellate court on the basis that the offender would face collateral consequences under the *Immigration and Refugee Protection Act*, S.C. 2001, c. 27 ("*IRPA*"), s. 64, that were not taken into account by the sentencing judge.

[2] Since the Crown conceded that, had it been aware of the collateral consequences at the time of the sentencing hearing, it would have agreed to a sentence of two years less a day, this Court decided at the conclusion of oral argument to allow the appeal and reduce the sentence from two years to two years less a day. The following are the reasons for that decision.

II. Background

[3] Hoang Anh Pham was convicted on charges of producing marihuana and possessing it for the purpose of trafficking contrary to ss. 7(1) and 5(2) of the *Controlled Drugs and Substances Act*, S.C. 1996, c. 19. In light of a joint submission by the Crown and counsel for the appellant, the Provincial Court of Alberta imposed a sentence of two years' imprisonment.

[4] Mr. Pham appealed the sentence, seeking to have it reduced by one day. He argued that the sentencing judge was not aware of and, for this reason, did not consider the collateral consequences of a sentence of two years' imprisonment on his immigration status. Under the *IRPA*, a non-citizen sentenced in Canada to a term of imprisonment of at least two years loses the right to appeal a removal order against him or her. Considering that a sentence of two years less a day, like the imposed sentence of two years, remained within the range of appropriate sentences, the Crown conceded that the sentence should be reduced by one day. It must be noted that neither the appellant's counsel nor the Crown had raised these issues before the sentencing judge, who apparently was not aware of the collateral consequences.

[5] Despite the Crown's concession, the majority of the Court of Appeal of Alberta refused to vary the appellant's sentence by one day, holding that, in the circumstances, allowing the appeal from a sentence situated within the range of otherwise fit sentences would inappropriately undermine the provisions of the *IRPA* (2012 ABCA 203, 533 A.R. 192, at paras. 24-25). The dissenting judge would have allowed the variation, noting that, had the appellant's counsel been aware of the collateral consequences of a two-year sentence in this case, a joint submission for a sentence of two years less a day would have been agreed upon (para. 33).

· · ·

[11] In light of these principles, the collateral consequences of a sentence are any consequences for the impact of the sentence on the particular offender. They may be taken into account in sentencing as personal circumstances of the offender. However, they are not, strictly speaking, aggravating or mitigating factors, since such factors are by definition related only to the gravity of the offence or to the degree of responsibility of the offender (s. 718.2(a) of the *Criminal Code*). Their relevance flows from the application of the

principles of individualization and parity. The relevance of collateral consequences may also flow from the sentencing objective of assisting in rehabilitating offenders (s. 718(d) of the *Criminal Code*). Thus, when two possible sentences are both appropriate as regards the gravity of the offence and the responsibility of the offenders, the most suitable one may be the one that better contributes to the offender's rehabilitation.

[12] However, the weight to be given to collateral consequences varies from case to case and should be determined having regard to the type and seriousness of the offence. ...

[13] Therefore, collateral consequences related to immigration may be relevant in tailoring the sentence, but their significance depends on and has to be determined in accordance with the facts of the particular case.

[14] The general rule continues to be that a sentence must be fit having regard to the particular crime and the particular offender. In other words, a sentencing judge may exercise his or her discretion to take collateral immigration consequences into account, provided that the sentence that is ultimately imposed is proportionate to the gravity of the offence and the degree of responsibility of the offender.

[15] The flexibility of our sentencing process should not be misused by imposing inappropriate and artificial sentences in order to avoid collateral consequences which may flow from a statutory scheme or from other legislation, thus circumventing Parliament's will.

[16] These consequences must not be allowed to dominate the exercise or skew the process either in favour of or against deportation. Moreover, it must not lead to a separate sentencing scheme with a *de facto* if not a *de jure* special range of sentencing options where deportation is a risk.

· · ·

[20] Accordingly, the sentencing judge is not compelled in all circumstances to adjust a sentence in order to avoid the impact of collateral immigration consequences on the offender. It remains open to the judge to conclude that even a minimal reduction, i.e. from two years' imprisonment to two years less a day, would render the sentence inappropriate for the particular offence and the particular offender. Collateral immigration consequences are but one relevant factor amongst many others related to the nature and the gravity of the offence, the degree of responsibility of the offender and the offender's personal circumstances.

[21] The reasons of Doyon J.A. in *R. v. Guzman*, 2011 QCCA 136, provide an illustration of this approach to the treatment of collateral immigration consequences in sentencing. In that case, the Quebec Court of Appeal was asked to grant a minimal variation of a sentence to ensure that the sentence would not have adverse consequences for the offender's immigration status. Doyon J.A. declined to acquiesce in this request, stating that, in light of the facts of the case, a reduction of the sentence, even a modest reduction of one day, would be both unfit and inconsistent with the principles of sentencing. He held as follows, at paras. 102-3:

> [TRANSLATION] In summary, the status of the appellants and the impact of the prison sentences on their right to appeal to the Immigration Appeal Division are relevant circumstances and must be taken into consideration. However, given the circumstances in which the offences were committed, their seriousness, the profile of the appellants, and the objectives and principles of sentencing set out in the *Criminal Code*, I am of the view that the

sentences inflicted on the appellants are fit even if they are not reduced by one day, as the appellants seek.

... [T]he near total lack of factors suggesting a real possibility of rehabilitation and change of behaviour on the part of the appellants *convinces me that, even if the judges had been aware of all of the relevant facts, they would not have imposed sentences of less than two years' imprisonment* solely to allow the appellants to preserve their right of appeal. [Emphasis added.]

[22] In sum, collateral immigration consequences may be just as relevant in sentencing as the collateral consequences of other legislation or of circumstances specific to the offender.

[23] Where the issue of immigration consequences is brought to the trial judge's attention and the trial judge applies the proper sentencing principles but nonetheless decides on a two-year sentence, then, absent fresh evidence, deference is owed to that decision. Where this issue has not been raised before the trial judge and the Crown does not give its consent, an affidavit or some other type of evidence should then be adduced for consideration by the Court of Appeal.

[24] An appellate court has the authority to intervene if the sentencing judge was not aware of the collateral immigration consequences of the sentence for the offender, or if counsel had failed to advise the judge on this issue. In such circumstances, the court's intervention is justified because the sentencing judge decided on the fitness of the sentence without considering a relevant factor: *M. (C.A.)*, at para. 90. As I explained above, however, the aim of such an intervention is to determine the appropriate sentence in light of the facts of the particular case while taking all the relevant factors into account. Although there will be cases in which it is appropriate to reduce the sentence to ensure that it does not have adverse consequences for the offender's immigration status, there will be other cases in which it is not appropriate to do so.

C. Cultural Factors

In terms of guilt, ignorance of the law is no excuse. Similarly, with respect to the partial defence of provocation, Canadian courts have rejected a role for cultural background in assessing the adequacy of a wrongful act or insult. In *R v Humaid* (2006), 81 OR (3d) 456 (CA), Doherty JA held:

[93] ... These beliefs are *antithetical to fundamental Canadian values*, including gender equality. It is arguable that as a matter of criminal law policy, the "ordinary person" cannot be fixed with beliefs that are irreconcilable with fundamental Canadian values. [Emphasis added.]

See also the Supreme Court decision in *R v Tran*, [1994] 2 SCR 951. But Canada is a multicultural country in which citizens, residents, and visitors come from diverse cultural backgrounds. Many continue to follow myriad cultural practices involving language, dress, cuisine, and other aspects of life. So the controversial question arises whether a cultural attitude can mitigate a sentence.

R v HE
2015 ONCA 531

BENOTTO JA (Hoy ACJO and Doherty JA concurring):

[1] The respondent lived with his wife for sixteen years—thirteen years in Iran and nearly three in Canada. During the entire time, he regularly assaulted her and their children.

[2] He was convicted of sexual assault and four counts of assault for the crimes that occurred in Canada.

[3] The sentencing judge imposed a total sentence of 18 months in a reformatory plus probation for one year. In doing so, he credited the respondent with an unspecified amount of time for his pre-trial house arrest and took into account the "cultural impact" of the move from Iran to Canada. The Crown seeks leave to appeal the sentence. For the reasons that follow, I would grant leave and allow the appeal.

• • •

[27] The respondent did not rely on cultural issues to justify or explain his behaviour. He did not testify, and his defence was a denial that the events took place. Yet, twice in his reasons, the sentencing judge referred to cultural issues.

[28] The first reference to a "significant cultural gap" was the sentencing judge's explanation for the wife's surprise at the sanctions for domestic violence. The second reference was to the "cultural impact" of moving from Iran to Canada. The sentencing judge said this was a "factor" in his deliberations, but "not a sentencing principle." He stated: "As far as I'm able to ascertain from the evidence those culture differences moved with them from Iran to Canada."

[29] The sentencing judge's reasons indicate that he considered the cultural impact in his determination of the appropriate sentence. Although his reasons are unclear, it appears as though he considered culture as a mitigating factor. This is an error for two reasons. First, the respondent never took the position that cultural differences impacted his conduct. On the contrary, in the pre-sentence report he expressly disavowed any suggestion that he felt culturally justified in assaulting his wife and children; his defence was denial of the events. The respondent's factum in this court took the same position.

[30] Second, and more importantly, cultural norms that condone or tolerate conduct contrary to Canadian criminal law must not be considered a mitigating factor on sentencing.

[31] The Alberta Court of Appeal commented on this issue in *R. v. Teclesenbet*, 2009 ABCA 389, 469 A.R. 193. In that case, the offender had immigrated to Canada five days before slapping his wife and beating her with a shoe. The wife was hospitalized, and the offender was convicted of assault causing bodily harm. The sentencing judge accepted as a mitigating factor the offender's claim that, in his home country of Sudan, his behaviour was commonplace. The offender received a conditional discharge and 12 months' probation. The Crown's appeal was allowed. McDonald J.A. wrote for the court, at para. 9:

> The law of Canada applies equally to all who are in Canada regardless of the length of time they have resided here. To suggest that it might be acceptable to beat one's wife with a stick elsewhere does not mitigate the seriousness of the offence and is contrary to the purpose of domestic violence laws.

[32] Earlier, in *R. v. Brown* (1992), 125 A.R. 150 (C.A.), the same court wrote, at para. 29:

> Even if there were before the court a more articulated submission based on social attitudes within a particular ethnic or religious community to which the accused belongs, the courts of this province and of this country should be alert to the risk of moderating sentencing policy in such a case where to do so would mean that some women in Canadian society would be afforded less protection than others.

[33] A cultural practice that is criminal in Canada does not mitigate the perpetrator's conduct for sentencing purposes. Cultural differences do not excuse or mitigate criminal conduct. To hold otherwise undermines the equality of all individuals before and under the law, a crucial *Charter* value. It would also create a second class of person in our society—those who fall victim to offenders who import such practices. This is of particular significance in the context of domestic violence. All women in Canada are entitled to the same level of protection from abusers. The need to strongly denounce domestic violence is in no way diminished when that conduct is the product of cultural beliefs that render women acceptable targets of male violence. If anything, cultural beliefs may be an aggravating factor enhancing the need for specific deterrence in cases where the sentencing judge is satisfied that the offender continues to maintain those views at the time of sentencing.

D. State Misconduct

R v Nasogaluak
2010 SCC 6, [2010] 1 SCR 206

[This case is discussed in a number of other chapters in this book. Here, the excerpt deals only with the issue of state misconduct. The case arose from an arrest for impaired driving during which the accused was punched numerous times by police officers resulting in broken ribs that punctured one of his lungs. The difficult issue of the relationship between Charter violations is discussed in Chapter 17.]

LeBEL J (McLachlin CJ and Binnie, Deschamps, Fish, Abella, Charron, Rothstein, and Cromwell JJ concurring):

[1] This is a sentencing appeal from the Court of Appeal of Alberta that raises important issues in respect of constitutional remedies. The respondent, Mr. Lyle Marcellus Nasogaluak, had his sentences for the offences of impaired driving and flight from police reduced to conditional discharges as a remedy for the breaches of the *Canadian Charter of Rights and Freedoms* that he endured at the time of his arrest and detention. The main issue is whether his sentences were lawfully reduced as a remedy for the excessive force used by police.

. . .

[3] As we shall see, the sentencing regime provides some scope for sentencing judges to consider not only the actions of the offender, but also those of state actors. Where the state misconduct in question relates to the circumstances of the offence or the offender, the sentencing judge may properly take the relevant facts into account in crafting a fit sentence, without having to resort to s. 24(1) of the *Charter*. Indeed, state misconduct

which does not amount to a *Charter* breach but which impacts the offender may also be a relevant factor in crafting a fit sentence.

• • •

[48] Indeed, the sentencing regime under Canadian law must be implemented within, and not apart from, the framework of the *Charter*. Sentencing decisions are always subject to constitutional scrutiny. A sentence cannot be "fit" if it does not respect the fundamental values enshrined in the *Charter*. Thus, incidents alleged to constitute a *Charter* violation can be considered in sentencing, provided that they bear the necessary connection to the sentencing exercise. As mitigating factors, the circumstances of the breach would have to align with the circumstances of the offence or the offender, as required by s. 718.2 of the *Code*. Naturally, the more egregious the breach, the more attention the court will likely pay to it in determining a fit sentence.

• • •

[53] It is important to note that a sentence can be reduced in light of state misconduct even when the incidents complained of do not rise to the level of a *Charter* breach. In *Pigeon*, the court did not need to determine whether the accused's s. 7 rights had been violated, as there was sufficient scope within the regular sentencing process to address the impropriety of the police officers' actions. Likewise, the Ontario Court of Appeal held in *R. v. Bosley* (1992), 18 C.R. (4th) 347, that the trial judge had properly considered excessive but not unconstitutional delay as a mitigating factor in his determination of a fit sentence (see also *R. v. Leaver* (1996), 3 C.R. (5th) 138 (Ont. C.A.)). And in *R. v. Pan-ousis*, 2002 ABQB 1109, 329 A.R. 47, the Alberta Court of Queen's Bench treated the delay in the proceedings as a relevant mitigating factor that led to a reduced sentence for the offence of trafficking in cocaine. Although the delay did not amount to a s. 11(b) violation, the court held that it had caused prejudice to the accused that was relevant and probative to the sentencing process. The majority of the Alberta Court of Appeal, in brief oral reasons (2004 ABCA 211 (CanLII)), reversed the trial judge's decision and imposed a sentence of incarceration of two years less a day and a heavy fine. The majority did not state whether it disagreed with the trial judge's finding that delay was a relevant mitigating circumstance, but it is notable that its final sentence went below the trial judge's apprecia-tion of the usual sentences for serious drug offences.

[54] To be certain, the concept of recognizing harm or prejudice caused to the offender as a mitigating circumstance upon sentencing did not originate with the *Charter*. In the pre-*Charter* case of *R. v. Kirzner* (1976), 14 O.R. (2d) 665, the Ontario Court of Appeal reduced a sentence for drug offences to reflect the police force's role in exposing the offender to the opportunity to commit the offences for which he was convicted. The RCMP had used the offender, who was addicted to heroin, as an informer to infiltrate and gain information about the drug trade in Montreal. The court found that, although the defence of entrapment was not available to the accused, the police were sufficiently implicated in the offender's actions to warrant a reduction of his sentence. Likewise, the Ontario Court of Appeal reduced a sentence in the pre-*Charter* context to mitigate the effects of an unlawful search of the accused's premises in *R. v. Steinberg*, [1967] 1 O.R. 733. Excessive delay attributable to the prosecution or police has also been considered a mitigating factor in a number of pre-*Charter* cases (*R. v. Cooper (No. 2)* (1977), 35 C.C.C. (2d) 35 (Ont. C.A.); *R. v. Simon* (1975), 25 C.C.C. (2d) 159 (Ont. C.A.)). Likewise, delay arising out of stra-tegically delayed charges in respect of contemporaneous offences has led to reduction of

the sentences (*R. v. Parisien* (1971), 3 C.C.C. (2d) 433 (B.C.C.A.); *R. v. Burke*, [1968] 2 C.C.C. 124 (Ont. C.A.); *R. v. Fairn* (1973), 12 C.C.C. (2d) 423 (N.S. Co. Ct.)).

[55] Thus, a sentencing judge may take into account police violence or other state misconduct while crafting a fit and proportionate sentence, without requiring the offender to prove that the incidents complained of amount to a *Charter* breach. Provided the interests at stake can properly be considered by the court while acting within the sentencing regime in the *Criminal Code*, there is simply no need to turn to the *Charter* for a remedy. However, if a *Charter* breach has already been alleged and established, a trial judge should not be prevented from reducing the sentence accordingly, so long as the incidents giving rise to the breach are relevant to the usual sentencing regime. Of course, as we shall see, as a general rule, a court cannot reduce a sentence below a mandatory minimum or order a reduced sentence that is not provided for by statute. That said, circumstances of a *Charter* breach or other instances of state misconduct, in exceptional circumstances, do allow a court to derogate from the usual rules to which its decisions are subject.

V. STATUTORY AGGRAVATING FACTORS

A. Criminal Code, Section 718.2

718.2 A court that imposes a sentence shall also take into consideration the following principles:

(a) a sentence should be increased or reduced to account for any relevant aggravating or mitigating circumstances relating to the offence or the offender, and, without limiting the generality of the foregoing,

(i) evidence that the offence was motivated by bias, prejudice or hate based on race, national or ethnic origin, language, colour, religion, sex, age, mental or physical disability, sexual orientation, or any other similar factor,

(ii) evidence that the offender, in committing the offence, abused the offender's spouse or common-law partner,

(ii.1) evidence that the offender, in committing the offence, abused a person under the age of eighteen years,

(iii) evidence that the offender, in committing the offence, abused a position of trust or authority in relation to the victim,

(iii.1) evidence that the offence had a significant impact on the victim, considering their age and other personal circumstances, including their health and financial situation,

(iv) evidence that the offence was committed for the benefit of, at the direction of or in association with a criminal organization,

(v) evidence that the offence was a terrorism offence, or

(vi) evidence that the offence was committed while the offender was subject to a conditional sentence order made under section 742.1 or released on parole, statutory release or unescorted temporary absence under the *Corrections and Conditional Release Act* shall be deemed to be aggravating circumstances.

NOTE

Clearly, ss 718.2(a)(i) to (iii) were recognized by the common law before statutory entrenchment. Their inclusion in the Code emphasizes the aggravating role that these factors play. Underlying these provisions are two unifying themes: the promotion of equality and the recognition of power imbalances as an aggravating context. The gravity of an offence is increased when it manifests a rejection of equal respect or an abuse of power against a vulnerable individual, or when it is motivated by a wrongful assertion of power. For an example of the role of s 718.2(a)(i), see *R v Miloszewski*, [1999] BCJ No 2710 (QL) (Prov Ct), where sentences of 12 to 15 years were imposed on relatively young offenders for manslaughter. A caretaker at a Sikh temple had been brutally beaten to death. This case demonstrates the potential of aggravating factors to increase the severity of the sentence. Sentences for manslaughter are typically in the range of 5 to 8 years.

As a result of an amendment in 2003, the Code now also provides the following factors, some aggravating and some potentially mitigating, which are applicable when sentencing an "organization":

> 718.21 A court that imposes a sentence on an organization shall also take into consideration the following factors:
>
> (a) any advantage realized by the organization as a result of the offence;
>
> (b) the degree of planning involved in carrying out the offence and the duration and complexity of the offence;
>
> (c) whether the organization has attempted to conceal its assets, or convert them, in order to show that it is not able to pay a fine or make restitution;
>
> (d) the impact that the sentence would have on the economic viability of the organization and the continued employment of its employees;
>
> (e) the cost to public authorities of the investigation and prosecution of the offence;
>
> (f) any regulatory penalty imposed on the organization or one of its representatives in respect of the conduct that formed the basis of the offence;
>
> (g) whether the organization was—or any of its representatives who were involved in the commission of the offence were—convicted of a similar offence or sanctioned by a regulatory body for similar conduct;
>
> (h) any penalty imposed by the organization on a representative for their role in the commission of the offence;
>
> (i) any restitution that the organization is ordered to make or any amount that the organization has paid to a victim of the offence; and
>
> (j) any measures that the organization has taken to reduce the likelihood of it committing a subsequent offence.

An organization is defined in s 2 as

> (a) a public body, body corporate, society, company, firm, partnership, trade union or municipality, or
>
> (b) an association of persons that
>
> (i) is created for a common purpose,
>
> (ii) has an operational structure, and
>
> (iii) holds itself out to the public as an association of persons.

B. Controlled Drugs and Substances Act

This statute, enacted in 1996 by SC 1996, c 19 to replace the *Narcotic Control Act*, contains its own statement of purpose and a list of applicable aggravating factors:

> 10(1) Without restricting the generality of the *Criminal Code*, the fundamental purpose of any sentence for an offence under this Part is to contribute to the respect for the law and the

maintenance of a just, peaceful and safe society while encouraging rehabilitation, and treatment in appropriate circumstances, of offenders and acknowledging the harm done to victims and to the community.

(2) If a person is convicted of a designated substance offence for which the court is not required to impose a minimum punishment, the court imposing sentence on the person shall consider any relevant aggravating factors including that the person

(a) in relation to the commission of the offence,

(i) carried, used or threatened to use a weapon,

(ii) used or threatened to use violence,

(iii) trafficked in a substance included in Schedule I, II, III or IV or possessed such a substance for the purpose of trafficking, in or near a school, on or near school grounds or in or near any other public place usually frequented by persons under the age of eighteen years, or

(iv) trafficked in a substance included in Schedule I, II, III or IV, or possessed such a substance for the purpose of trafficking, to a person under the age of eighteen years;

(b) was previously convicted of a designated substance offence; or

(c) used the services of a person under the age of eighteen years to commit, or involved such a person in the commission of, a designated substance offence.

(3) If, under subsection (1), the court is satisfied of the existence of one or more of the aggravating factors enumerated in paragraphs (2)(a) to (c), but decides not to sentence the person to imprisonment, the court shall give reasons for that decision.

NOTE

In 2012, to potentially ameliorate the impact of mandatory minimum sentences in cases of addiction, Parliament, in the *Safe Streets and Communities Act*, SC 2012, c 1, s 43(2), added the following to s 10:

10(4) A court sentencing a person who is convicted of an offence under this Part may delay sentencing to enable the offender

(a) to participate in a drug treatment court program approved by the Attorney General; or

(b) to attend a treatment program under subsection 720(2) of the *Criminal Code*.

(5) If the offender successfully completes a program under subsection (4), the court is not required to impose the minimum punishment for the offence for which the person was convicted.

VI. JUDICIALLY RECOGNIZED AGGRAVATING FACTORS

As with mitigating factors, there are numerous references in the case law to factors that are considered to be aggravating. Most of these bear on the gravity of the offence—for example, the extent of harm caused, number of victims, use of weapons, and infliction of brutal injury. These are, for the most part, self-evident. They describe characteristics that necessarily place an offence at the more serious end of the gravity spectrum. There is ample case law that accepts the following list of aggravating factors as being relevant to sentencing:

- previous convictions,
- actual or threatened violence or use of weapon,
- cruelty or brutality,
- substantial physical injuries or psychological harm,

- offence committed while subjected to judicially imposed conditions,
- multiple victims or multiple incidents,
- group or gang activity,
- impeding victim's access to the justice system,
- substantial economic loss,
- planning and organization,
- vulnerability of victim, and
- deliberate risk-taking.

Consider this list and try to explain exactly why the particular circumstance or characteristic should be aggravating. How does it increase culpability or make the offender more blameworthy? Should there be any limits on the applicability of any of these factors? Are there other factors that you would consider aggravating? If so, can you articulate why they warrant a more severe penalty? What about personal characteristics—are there any that you consider aggravating and, if so, why?

VII. FACTORS NOT TO BE TREATED AS AGGRAVATING

There are some factors that at first blush may appear relevant to sentencing, but on closer analysis cannot be logically or fairly linked to the proper set of considerations that should bear on the sentencing function. Courts of appeal have identified a small number of factors that sentencing judges should not consider to be aggravating. The fact that the offender pleaded not guilty should not be used to aggravate the sanction. Otherwise, an accused is being penalized for exercising the constitutional right to be presumed innocent until the Crown has proven the case beyond a reasonable doubt. Similarly, courts of appeal have held that the conduct of the defence at trial should not be held against an offender: see *R v Kozy* (1990), 74 OR (2d) 545 (CA).

A harder question to resolve concerns the absence of evidence of remorse. Although a guilty plea and other indicia of remorse are considered to be mitigating factors, does this mean that an absence of remorse is an aggravating factor? If it did, it would mean that anyone who did not accept guilt at the time of sentencing would be subjected to an increased sentence. Given that convictions are subject to appeal, and convicted persons are entitled to continue to deny guilt, should an absence of evidence of remorse be treated as a neutral factor? Of course, this does not include conduct that demonstrates callousness or actual absence of remorse. If every mitigating factor has a reciprocal aggravating factor, itself a contentious proposition, then callousness is the reciprocal of remorse.

A similar issue arises with respect to cooperation with authorities. Evidence of assistance is often considered to be mitigating. What about the converse—that is, a situation where the authorities want information and the offender refuses to assist? Remember that the law does not require confessions and it does not compel an accused person to divulge information about accomplices.

In *R v Wristen* (1999), 47 OR (3d) 66 (CA), a second-degree murder case, the Ontario Court of Appeal said:

> [73] The appellant was not legally obliged to assist the police. He was entitled to exercise his right to silence and require the prosecution to prove the case against him beyond a reasonable doubt. Exercising this right is not an aggravating consideration on sentence.

However, after accepting that principle, the court upheld the increase in parole eligibility to 17 years even though the trial judge was influenced by the convicted man's efforts to conceal the killing of his wife. It held that it was proper that the judge consider the efforts to hide the offence and the refusal to provide any information about the location of the body. The defence was that the woman had just disappeared and that the husband was not responsible for her death. This position was maintained throughout the appeal. Given the accused's denial of responsibility, can he be expected to disclose the location of the body? Is this different from a situation where the failure to cooperate with authorities can be characterized as callous disregard for the survivors or a victim, which is legitimately aggravating?

VIII. SPECIAL ISSUES

A. Assessing Relevant Factors in Cases of Sexual Abuse

One of the difficult areas of sentencing arises when there are convictions for sexual or physical abuse of children. Such cases often involve a panoply of aggravating factors—extensive harm, vulnerable victims, multiple victims, and abuse of position of trust. In 2012, Parliament added the following to the *Criminal Code*:

> 718.01 When a court imposes a sentence for an offence that involved the abuse of a person under the age of eighteen years, it shall give primary consideration to the objectives of denunciation and deterrence of such conduct.

Given the serious nature of the offences encompassed, as already judicially noted (see e.g. *R v M (G)* (1992), 11 OR (3d) 225 (CA), Abella JA, as she then was; *R v D (D)* (2002), 58 OR (3d) 788 (CA)), what role should s 718.01 play, if any?

Many cases, however, are the result of old offences. What is the impact of the passage of time? Does it produce a mitigating effect if there has been no repetition of offending? Does it mitigate only if conduct has been exemplary? What is the relevance of indicia of good character in business or civic circumstances?

R v HS
2014 ONCA 323

[1] B.H., the victim in this sexual assault case, spent most of her childhood in the care of the Catholic Children's Aid Society. During the period from 1976 to 1978, B.H. had been in 22 foster homes. In early 1978, when B.H. was placed in the care of the respondent and his wife, as foster parents, she was in a desperately fragile state.

[2] Starting in the late spring of 1978 and into mid-July of that year, when B.H. was barely 15 and the respondent was 24, the respondent engaged in unprotected vaginal intercourse with B.H. on a number of occasions. B.H. became pregnant. The Catholic Children's Aid Society ("CCAS") was advised and removed B.H. from the respondent's home. The CCAS placed B.H. in what was then known as a home for unwed mothers where she gave birth to a baby girl. B.H. raised her daughter initially on her own and then with the assistance of a partner.

[3] In April 2010, B.H. reported the matter to the police who, in turn, contacted the respondent. DNA testing proved that the respondent was the father of B.H.'s daughter.

[4] The respondent was charged with: (1) rape, contrary to s. 144 of the 1978 *Criminal Code of Canada* ("1978 Code"); (2) having sexual intercourse with a previously chaste female person who was not his wife over 14 and under 16 years of age, contrary to s. 146(2) of the 1978 Code; and (3) having illicit sexual intercourse with his foster daughter, contrary to s. 153(1)(a) of the 1978 Code. After the preliminary inquiry the Crown withdrew the rape charge. The respondent pleaded guilty to, and was convicted of, having sexual intercourse with a female person between 14 and 16 years of age and illicit sexual intercourse with his foster daughter.

[5] At the sentencing hearing, the Crown sought a custodial sentence of two to two and one-half years. The defence sought a conditional sentence of two years less a day. The sentencing judge accepted the defence position and imposed a conditional sentence of two years less one day to be served in the community with terms that amounted to a strict house arrest. The sentencing judge also imposed a three-year period of probation during which the respondent was required to perform 360 hours of community service. Accompanying SOIRA and DNA orders were made.

· · ·

[10] B.H. had attended court for the plea and for the sentencing hearing. The sentencing judge began her analysis by describing her observations of B.H. as follows: "To describe her appearance as that of a broken woman would be an understatement."

[11] The sentencing judge then made observations about the respondent. She commented on the extensive support provided by his friends and family and noted the difficulty they had reconciling the respondent's positive personality traits with the "monstrous error in judgment" he had made in committing the offences. The sentencing judge observed that the respondent had taken the witness stand and apologized to B.H. She concluded that the respondent, through his guilty plea, had taken responsibility for his actions.

[12] The sentencing judge identified denunciation and general deterrence as the primary sentencing principles.

[13] The sentencing judge then considered whether the circumstances called for a sentence to be served in the penitentiary, as argued by the Crown, or whether, as submitted by the defence, this was one of those "rare" cases in which a conditional sentence would satisfy the sentencing principles she had identified. After reviewing the authorities upon which each side relied, the sentencing judge concluded, at para. 28, that this was a "rare case" and that "the conditional sentence imposed will address both the punitive and rehabilitative aspects of sentencing."

· · ·

[34] Crown counsel submits that the sentencing judge erred by: (1) listing the respondent's health problems at the time of sentencing as a mitigating factor; (2) treating the stigma in the community arising from the criminal charges against the respondent and his convictions as having the same denunciatory effect as jail; and (3) minimizing the respondent's culpability by adopting the defence suggestion that the respondent's crimes reflected merely a "horrendous error in judgment."

[35] I make three observations.

[36] First, I would reject the Crown's contention that the sentencing judge minimized the respondent's culpability by characterizing his criminal conduct as merely an "error in judgment." In my view, when the reasons are read as a whole, they indicate that the

sentencing judge appreciated the seriousness of the crimes of which the respondent was convicted and their tragic—indeed, as she put it, their "heart wrenching"—impact on the complainant.

[37] However, I agree that the sentencing judge erred by treating various of the respondent's health problems (diabetes, pituitary gland issues and sleep apnea) as a mitigating factor on sentencing.

[38] The status of the offender's health may be a relevant consideration on sentencing, but in this case there was no evidence at the sentencing hearing that the respondent's medical conditions could not be properly treated while he was incarcerated. In these circumstances, no reduction in an otherwise fit sentence was warranted due to the respondent's health problems: *R. v. Aquino* (2002), 55 W.C.B. (2d) 314 (Ont. C.A.); *R. v. Malicia*, [2004] O.J. No. 2554 (C.A.); *R. v. R.L.*, 2013 ONCA 504.

[39] I also agree with the Crown that the sentencing judge erred by finding the stigma of the criminal proceedings and the respondent's convictions to be a mitigating circumstance. Absent evidence that the prosecution affected the respondent in a manner beyond what one would expect for any person facing criminal proceedings of this serious nature, this consideration was irrelevant: *R. v. R.W.D.* (2005), 198 C.C.C. (3d) 541, 199 O.A.C. 254 (Ont. C.A.), at para. 12. There was no such evidence in this case.

[40] These two errors adversely affected the sentencing judge's ability to properly assess the respondent's moral culpability.

[41] It is of paramount importance that children be protected from seducers and predators through sentences that emphasize the principles of denunciation and deterrence: *R. v. D.D.* (2002), 58 O.R. (3d) 788 (C.A.), at para. 34.

[42] Mid-to-upper single digit penitentiary sentences are appropriate where an adult in a position of trust sexually abuses a young child on a regular basis over a substantial period of time: See *D.D.*, at para. 44.

[43] In *R. v. S.H.*, 2011 ONCA 215, this court upheld a sentence of four years and three months on conviction for several historical sexual and domestic offences. When he was sentenced, the offender was 55 and had a serious medical condition. The court noted the offender's age and serious medical condition; that the offences had occurred years earlier; and that the offender had no criminal record. However, the court reinforced that "absent exceptional circumstances, adult offenders in a position of trust who sexually abuse children over a substantial period of time can expect to receive mid to upper single digit penitentiary terms."

[44] In my view, the sentence imposed, in the light of the circumstances of these offences and this offender, is manifestly unfit and an unjustifiable departure from the range.

• • •

[47] The respondent committed serious crimes with serious consequences. The aggravating factors are significant. The respondent occupied a unique position of trust in relation to B.H. As previously noted, B.H. was particularly vulnerable. In fact, she had been judicially declared to be a child in need of protection under the child welfare legislation in place at the time. After a period of unimaginable instability in her young life, B.H. found herself in the respondent's home. According to the agreed statement of facts, it was there that B.H. felt safe for the first time in her life, until the respondent violated her trust by subjecting her to repeated unprotected vaginal intercourse.

[48] The negative effect of crime on its victims is always an important consideration on sentencing. See *R. v. Drabinsky*, 2011 ONCA 582, 274 C.C.C. (3d) 289, at para. 179 (Ont. C.A.). B.H.'s account of how the sexual abuse impacted her life is tragic.

[49] The guilty plea and the respondent's lack of a prior criminal record, work history and otherwise good standing in the community are valid mitigating circumstances to take into account. However, their weight must be considered in the light of the fact that it is not unusual for individuals who commit this kind of offence to have jobs or to otherwise be individuals of apparent good character: See *R. v. M. (G.)* (1992), 11 O.R. (3d) 225 (C.A.), at p. 232.

[50] Here, as in all cases, the dominant sentencing principle is that the sentence must be commensurate with the gravity of the criminal conduct. As the sentencing judge correctly identified, the subordinate sentencing principles are general deterrence and denunciation. The application of these principles and the relevant jurisprudence supports the imposition of a lengthy custodial sentence.

[51] However, there are additional factors relevant to this court's determination of a fit sentence in the unique circumstances of the respondent before this court at this time.

[52] One such factor is the time lapse. The offences took place over 35 years ago. There is no evidence that the respondent has lead anything but an exemplary life since 1978. The man before the court today is not the same as the man who committed the crimes. The question is how much, if any, weight ought to be given to the lapse of time in crafting a fit sentence for the respondent.

[53] The leading case on the treatment of time lapse in sentencing is *R. v. Spence* (1992), 78 C.C.C. (3d) 451 (Alta. C.A.), adopted by Juriansz J.A. for this court in *R. v. W.W.M.* (2006), 205 C.C.C. (3d) 410 (Ont. C.A). In *Spence*, at pp. 454-456, the court held that:

> When a period of many years has elapsed between the commission of an offence of sexual assault and its discovery by the authorities, that circumstance dictates review of the degree to which the usual principles of sentencing are applicable in such circumstances.
>
> • • •
>
> The lapse of time does not in any way render inapplicable the principles of general deterrence and denunciation. The first of these requires a sentence which will intimidate those other than the offender who might be tempted to follow his example. The second requires a sentence by the imposition of which the court will reflect society's view of the wrongness of the conduct, and persuade those who might be confused about what is right and wrong. These two principles may overlap in their effect on the choice of sentence.
>
> The need for the sentence to reflect the community's desire to denounce offences of the kind with which we are concerned is not diminished by the passage of time. Conversely, if the court were to impose a lenient sentence because of the passage of time, some members of the community might regard the sentence as judicial condonation of the conduct in question. That would tend to lessen respect for the administration of justice. In the circumstances we are considering in these appeals, the lapse of considerable time, and (we assume, for the purpose of discussion) the intervening years of unblemished conduct, do not lessen the relevance of these two principles.
>
> • • •
>
> The only sentencing principles which may be affected by the lapse of time are those of individual deterrence and rehabilitation. By individual deterrence we mean that the sentence

should deter the accused from committing a similar offence in the future. By rehabilitation we mean that the sentence imposed should reflect the hope that somehow, while serving his or her sentence, the accused will be rehabilitated and at its end will resume his or her place in society as a useful and law-abiding citizen. These two principles overlap. In the case of a sexual offence against a child, when on occasion the child does not report the offence to the police or any other authority until many years after the event, should the sentence be less than what it would have been if the prosecution had occurred not long after the commission of the offence? If the accused, during the intervening years, has led an exemplary life in all respects, including non-repetition of sexual offences, and upon the matter ultimately being reported to the authorities and during the resulting investigation and prosecution he is remorseful, then the principles of individual deterrence and rehabilitation may arguably, by themselves, not justify a stern sentence of the kind which would have been obligatory many years earlier. It will be noted, however, that if, despite having led an exemplary life, the offender lacks remorse, any potential discount must be less than it otherwise would have been. Indeed, in cases of this sort, of sexual abuse of children by parents, one might well ask whether one could ever have both remorse and lengthy suppression of the facts.

[54] Given the respondent's circumstances, the principles of specific deterrence and rehabilitation have no relevance. As previously noted, the relevant sentencing principles in this case are denunciation and general deterrence. A fit sentence must reflect the need to respond to these principles. As made clear in the above passages from *Spence*, these particular sentencing principles are unaffected by the passage of time. See also: *W.W.M.* at paras. 21-25 and *R. v. S. (R.)*, [1997] A.J. No. 1136, 209 A.R. 231 (Alta. C.A.).

[55] I am therefore of the view that while a delay of over 35 years is a relevant consideration, its mitigating impact is reduced by its lack of relevance to the operative sentencing principles.

[56] Applying the principles mandated in s. 718 of the *Code* that are germane to the circumstances of this particular offender and these particular offences, I conclude that the objectives of general deterrence and denunciation, and the importance of ensuring parity with other sentences in similar circumstances, support a sentence of five years.

[57] However, there are other factors that must be taken into consideration in the unique circumstances of this case.

[58] First, while I have concluded that the principles of general deterrence and denunciation cannot be adequately served without incarceration, the fact that the respondent has spent the last two years in legal limbo uncertain as to whether he would be incarcerated and, if so, for how long, is a relevant factor to take into account: See *R. v. Hamilton* (2003), 172 C.C.C. (3d) 114 (Ont. S.C.), at paras. 216-219.

[59] Second, I am mindful of the fact that the Crown seeks a harsher sentence on appeal than that sought below. While there is no rule or principle that precludes the Crown from repudiating its position taken at trial, jurisprudence has established that it may only be done in exceptional circumstances—where it can be shown that the public interest in the orderly administration of justice is outweighed by the gravity of the crime and the gross insufficiency of the sentence: See *R. v. P.J.B.* (1999), 141 C.C.C. (3d) 290 (Nfld. C.A.); *R. v. Marks* (1994), 91 C.C.C. (3d) 421 (Nfld. C.A.); *Attorney General of Canada v. Roy* (1972), 18 C.R.N.S. 89 (Que. Q.B.).

[60] The public's interest in the orderly administration of justice requires a consideration of any potential unfairness to the offender resulting from the Crown's change of position as to sentence on appeal.

[61] Appellate courts have refused to intervene in a sentence where the record demonstrated that the offender acted in reliance upon the Crown's position below. Courts have been particularly reticent to give effect to increased Crown submissions on appeal where offenders have pleaded guilty after receiving sentencing assurances from the Crown, or where the parties have made a joint submission on sentence: See *R. v. Agozzino* (1969) 6 C.R.N.S. 147 (Ont. C.A.); *R. v. Wood* (1988), 43 C.C.C. (3d) 570, 29 O.A.C. 99 (Ont. C.A.); *R. v. Simoneau* (1978), 40 C.C.C. (2d) 307 (Man. C.A); *R. v. Dubien* (1982), 67 C.C.C. (2d) 341 (Ont. C.A.); *Attorney General of Canada v. Roy* (1972) 18 C.R.N.S. 89 (Que. Q.B.); *R. v. Edwards* (2001), 54 O.R. (3d) 737. In such cases, appellate courts have found that it would prejudice the offender to allow the Crown to repudiate its position on appeal. See also: *R. v. Fleury* (1971), 23 C.R.N.S. 164 (Que. C.A.); *R. v. Wood* (1975), 26 C.C.C. (2d) 100 (Alta. C.A.).

[62] The crimes the respondent committed are profoundly serious. For the reasons set out above, I have concluded that the sentence imposed is contrary to the governing jurisprudence and is patently unfit. Furthermore, the record discloses no evidence that the respondent conducted himself in a particular manner in reliance on the expectation that the trial Crown would propose a lenient sentence. Nor, in my view, does the record support a reasonable inference that the respondent relied upon the Crown's position below in any particular respect. As a result, unlike in the authorities cited above, it is not possible to identify any unfairness to the respondent in allowing the Crown to request a longer sentence on appeal.

[63] In my view, it follows that that this is one of the exceptional cases in which the public interest in the orderly administration of justice is outweighed by the gravity of the crime and the gross insufficiency of the sentence. There is therefore no reason why this court should not consider the sentence sought by the Crown on appeal even though it is greater than the sentence the Crown sought below.

[64] That said, this court, in fulfilling its ultimate responsibility to determine a fit sentence, pursuant to s. 687 of the *Code*, must take into account the Crown's position at trial and on appeal. I agree with the position espoused by Watt J.A. of this court in his dissent in *R. v. Peters*, 2010 ONCA 30, 250 C.C.C. (3d) 277, at para. 57 that, in the interest of fairness, the term of imprisonment imposed on appeal may be somewhat circumscribed by the position of Crown counsel at trial and on appeal.

[65] In the light of these additional factors and in the unique circumstances of this case, I would grant leave to appeal sentence, allow the appeal and set aside the sentence imposed by the sentencing judge. I would impose a sentence of three years. The respondent is entitled to a credit of one year for the year he has served of his conditional sentence. I would not impose any period of probation but maintain the remainder of the existing ancillary orders.

[66] In the result, I would impose a custodial sentence of two years, to commence on the day that the respondent surrenders. I would have the respondent surrender three days after the date of the release of these reasons, failing which a warrant should issue for his arrest.

In *R v RSH*, 2005 BCSC 927, Wedge J convicted a man who had no prior record of a series of sexual assaults by a person in a position of authority on a child who was aged seven and eight at the time of the assaults. The offences were described as follows:

> [15] At trial, the victim testified that the accused assaulted her on several occasions when her family was living in Houston. She also testified that he assaulted her when she and her family visited the accused in Kamloops, and when the accused visited her family … . From the child's evidence, I concluded that the accused used his hand and his penis in attempts to masturbate her. She described the accused rubbing her genital area "for a long, long, long, long, time" with his penis and his hand.

In the extract below, Wedge J offered the following opinion on sentences for sexual assaults of children.

R v RSH

2005 BCSC 927

WEDGE J:

[41] …

Adult sexual predators who would put the lives of innocent children at risk to satisfy their deviant sexual needs must know that they will pay a heavy price. In cases such as this, absent exceptional circumstances, the objectives of sentencing proclaimed by Parliament in s. 718(a), (b) and (c) of the *Criminal Code*, commonly referred to as denunciation, general and specific deterrence, and the need to separate offenders from society, must take precedence over the other recognized objectives of sentencing.

We as a society owe it to our children to protect them from the harm caused by offenders like the appellant. Our children are at once our most valued and our most vulnerable assets. Throughout their formative years, they are manifestly incapable of defending themselves against predators like the appellant and as such, they make easy prey. People like the appellant know this only too well and they exploit it to achieve their selfish ends, heedless of the dire consequences that can and often do follow.

In this respect, while there may have been a time, years ago, when offenders like the appellant could take refuge in the fact that little was known about the nature or extent of the damage caused by sexual abuse, that time has long since passed. Today, that excuse no long holds sway. The horrific consequences of child sexual abuse are only too well known.

Wedge J sentenced the accused to 20 months' imprisonment followed by two years' probation. This sentence was affirmed on appeal: see *R v Hall*, 2005 BCCA 566.

B. Social Disadvantage

There is little doubt that much crime can be traced back to histories of poverty, abuse, and family dysfunction. Some people can rise above the limiting and even crippling circumstances of their impoverished backgrounds; many cannot. In a wealthy country like Canada, young people are the products not only of their family environments but also of the community's schools and hospitals, and sometimes of other public entities like children's aid agencies and social institutions that intervene in the lives of dysfunctional families. Can a disadvantaged background be excluded from the sentencing matrix?

In *R v George* (1998), 126 CCC (3d) 384 (BCCA), a dangerous offender case, the BC Court of Appeal had to consider the "pattern of aggressive behaviour" test in s 753(a)(ii) of the *Criminal Code*. In doing so, it observed:

> [15] … The dangerous offender provisions may fall more heavily on the poor and disadvantaged members of our society if their childhood conduct is counted against them. This appellant had to face school as an aboriginal foster child living in a non-aboriginal culture with an IQ at or near the retarded level. It is understandable that any child with this background would get into a lot of trouble by lashing out aggressively when challenged by his or her environment.

In *R v Borde* (2003), 63 OR (3d) 417 (CA) Rosenberg JA said:

> [27] … The appellant's fundamental submission is that because of the similarity between the plight of Aboriginal Canadians and African-Canadians, the court should adopt a similar form of analysis for the purposes of sentencing. Further, he submits that the background of the appellant exhibits many of the same factors often found in the background of Aboriginal offenders including poverty, family dislocation, chaotic child rearing and alcoholism. I accept that there are some similarities and that the background and systemic factors facing African-Canadians, where they are shown to have played a part in the offence, might be taken into account in imposing sentence. However, for the following reasons, the evidence is not relevant in this case.

One can construct a number of arguments that support the recognition of social disadvantage as a mitigating factor:

1. *Sentencing as a moral exercise:* R.A. Duff, the Scottish legal philosopher from Stirling University, has argued that a community that has denied to some people full membership in that community loses its moral standing to sentence them. It therefore needs to take into account their social disadvantage when sentencing them: see RA Duff, *Punishment, Communication, and Community* (Oxford: Oxford University Press, 2001). This argument derives from Duff's earlier work, where he describes sentencing as a form of moral exercise that is communicative in nature where the sentence communicates censure to the offender and the community. Duff's view, along with other claims, was subjected to a careful critique in Andrew von Hirsch & Andrew Ashworth, *Proportionate Sentencing: Exploring the Principles* (Oxford: Oxford University Press, 2005) at 62-74. Hirsch & Ashworth's major concern seems to be that if one agrees with Duff then the factor goes beyond mere mitigation. If a community lacks standing to sentence, then it compels an exemption from sentencing rather than mitigation.

2. *Fairness:* A related argument concerns the pressures on socially disadvantaged defendants. Regardless of whether society is responsible for the disadvantage, it may be unfair to expect the same level of compliance with the law from people who are greatly disadvantaged. Compliance is much easier for well-placed individuals than for impoverished ones. Should a court mitigate punishment on these grounds?

3. *Substantive equality jurisprudence under s 15:* Charter equality jurisprudence has expounded the view that difference matters in the pursuit of equality. Accordingly, material differences need to be taken into account to achieve equal treatment. This means that in a

case like *R v Hamilton* (2004), 72 OR (3d) 1 (CA), discussed in Chapter 2, race and gender are relevant in respect of the offenders, but also in relation to the findings made by the trial judge about drug couriers and the city of Brampton. In that case, Hill J at trial (2003), 172 CCC (3d) 114 (Ont Sup Ct J) found:

> [180] On the evidentiary record, I am satisfied that in Brampton:
>
>> (1) black persons, men and women, are charged with cocaine importation in numbers disproportionate to their percentage in the general population;
>> (2) black women, more often than not single mothers, are charged and sentenced to penitentiary sentences for cocaine importation in numbers disproportionate to their percentage in the general population.

4. *Sentencing viewed from an instrumental or functional perspective:* Sentencing creates a traditional inquiry that produces individualized findings about the offender including matters like work record, school achievements, family support, and prior criminal record. For some people, because of a background of social disadvantage in respect of a particular family or community, this is an illusory inquiry. The court is then deprived of essential information in a way that also deprives the offender of a fair sentencing hearing. Accordingly, some accommodation must be made to bring the case within an acceptable framework that is at least comparable to the sentencing matrix available for other offenders. This bears some similarity to the "fairness" argument made above in point 2.

Do you find any of these arguments persuasive?

C. Mercy

The issue of mercy and its relation to sentencing is a difficult one. We have chosen to deal with it separately because it touches on many aspects of mitigation that can produce leniency, but it also generates arguments that, as a discrete concept, it ought to remain outside the judicial sentencing process. Most people would accept with little difficulty the claim that there must be some residual concept or principle that does not relate to a specific sentencing objective but that permits a compassionate response. However, aside from the hard questions about scope and applicability, there are harder fundamental questions. Does mercy operate outside the justice system, within the justice system, or a bit of both, depending on what you consider is encompassed by the rubric?

For some time, there has been a healthy philosophical debate about this issue. However, lawyers have tended to assume that there are some matters that speak solely to compassion and mercy, which judges can consider, and the post-sentence arena known as the pardon or clemency process can pick up what's left.

Austin Sarat and Nasser Hussain published an interesting array of articles on this topic: see Austin Sarat & Nasser Hussain, *Forgiveness, Mercy, and Clemency* (Stanford: Stanford University Press, 2007). From that collection, the following excerpt from Carol Steiker's thoughtful article "Tempering or Tampering: Mercy and the Administration of Criminal Justice" conveys the tone of the philosophical debate while also raising considerations that the sentencing system needs to consider (at 20):

> The first and openly normative question immediately implicates a host of related inquiries. What is the relationship between mercy and justice? Does justice require the imposition of

deserved punishment? Is mercy related or opposed or indifferent to the moral desert of an offender? Does mercy describe merely an act, or does it describe something about the state of mind of the mercy giver? Or something about the relationship between the mercy giver and receiver? What is the relationship between mercy and the constellation of emotions or attitudes we call pity, empathy, compassion and forgiveness. Is mercy opposed to reason? Can the exercise of mercy be evaluated? How, if at all, can whatever view of mercy we choose to embrace guide us to its proper application? In short, is mercy a good normative lens, among others, through which to judge the exercise of discretion within our sentencing system?

The second, more institutional question comes with its own host of corollaries. Is mercy appropriate for the public spheres at all? If so, is it possible to realize institutionally? Which institutional actors would be best suited to promote any particular vision of mercy? Should prosecutors think of themselves as open to appeals for mercy in the exercise of their charging discretion? What about juries? Should their power to render acquittals that are unreviewable be recognized as a proper locus for the power of mercy? Should sentencing judges consider appeals for mercy, or are such appeals more properly directed toward those with the powers of executive clemency and pardon? Can legislatures be merciful? Or is mercy necessarily individual, perhaps the province only of discrete victims of crime? Under this last view, should the legal system have any role in fostering conditions for reconciliation between victims and offenders? By attempting to carve out and protect a power of mercy within our criminal justice system, do we inevitably increase the problems of arbitrariness and bias beyond what we would endorse without such a commitment?

These extremely perceptive questions cover the landscape of contemporary sentencing issues. The answers that you might explore are affected dramatically by your own views on such controversial issues as the appropriate theoretical basis for sentencing, the proper role of judicial discretion and judges, the importance of forgiveness and redemption as aspects of human interrelationships, how reasons for sentencing decisions can satisfy the diverse range of audiences for whom they are intended, and whether a sentencing system should be self-conscious about the impact of its outcomes in racial, class, and gender terms.

Is there a difference between mercy and compassion? Assume that a jury has returned a verdict of guilty against a business person who allegedly defrauded the shareholders of a public company of millions of dollars. Four weeks prior to his sentencing, his entire family—his spouse and three teenaged children—are killed in a multi-vehicle highway collision. Surely, at the sentencing hearing, every defence counsel in the world would raise this tragic fact. Would any prosecutor object on the ground of relevance? But what is the relevance of the four deaths? Can the judge take them into account to mitigate the sentence? Notwithstanding the offender's suffering, this suffering was not imposed by the state nor did it flow from the offence or the prosecution. Would you respond differently if the offence had caused physical rather than financial harm? In that case, how important are the victims' views—that is, whether they speak of forgiveness or retribution?

It is not coincidental that the residual pardoning power in Commonwealth jurisdictions can be traced to what was known as the "Royal Prerogative of Mercy." Justice may have been administered by the courts but mercy came from the sovereign. Is this dichotomy too simplistic, too stark, and just anachronistic?

In driving offences resulting in death or serious harm, the victim is often a passenger in the offender's vehicle. Imagine that the offender is convicted of impaired driving causing death and the deceased victim is his son or best friend. The loss of this individual constitutes an "immanent" punishment, the severity of which far exceeds any legal sanction. Should the court take this circumstance into account at sentencing? A custodial sentence is the norm for this offence. Should a sentencing court impose a lesser, non-custodial sentence in such cases? Is the concept of proportionality blind to such considerations? Aside from the issue of proportional sentencing, counsel for the defendant may argue that, from a utilitarian perspective, a non-custodial sanction is justified. The fatal consequences of the crime are unlikely to leave the offender and this suggests that an individual deterrent sentence is unnecessary. Is this an appropriate application for the exercise of mercy on the ground of compassion? In *R v Ramage,* 2010 ONCA 488, Doherty JA made the following comment while dismissing an appeal from a four-year sentence:

> [77] … The letters filed on his behalf on sentencing are a tribute to a life well led by the appellant. He is a dedicated father and husband. The appellant's remorse is real and deep. He will probably never forgive himself for what has happened to his friend, Mr. Magnuson, although the Magnuson family has forgiven him and asked the trial judge to not incarcerate the appellant. The trial judge fully canvassed the "moving and rare" position taken by the Magnuson family and properly considered their request as one of the many factors that were relevant to his determination of an appropriate sentence.

PROBLEMS

Consider the following problems and identify the factors that you believe should be mitigating and those that are aggravating. Justify your selection by reference to the purpose and principles of sentencing, or to some consideration that may be considered external to the sentencing process, such as mercy.

1. Green was convicted of three counts of assault causing bodily harm that occurred in 1997 and 1998. In 1995, Green and his spouse adopted the two young daughters of Green's spouse's sister. The two girls, Helen and Doris, were five and seven at the time. Their parents had been killed in an automobile collision. For the next ten years, the girls led terrible lives within the Green household. Essentially, they were family slaves performing all the washing, cleaning, and meal preparation for the Greens and their three sons. Their days were marked with abuse. Helen was so damaged by the experience that it took her ten years to move from kindergarten to grade 6. She left school in grade 7 and ran away.

The offences consisted of (1) Helen being beaten with the cord from the iron; (2) Helen being struck with a broom handle; and (3) Doris being punched and kicked, resulting in a broken nose and bruises. While there was a suggestion that Green would often walk into the bathroom when the girls were naked, Green denied these events and any voyeuristic or other illicit purpose.

Green is now 63 years old. He owned a successful hardware store in a small town from 1994 to his retirement in 2014. He was a hockey coach, a member of the Rotary, and a supporter of local charities. In 2006 he was selected as Man of the Year for his work on the new hospital wing. Although it is not well known, Green has had an alcohol problem all his adult life. When Doris first advised Green in 2014 that she had talked to the police about these events, he sought psychiatric help and began attending AA. Green's counsel has advised the court that the beatings occurred when Green was drunk. He has a previous record of two common assaults, one in 1974 and one in 1976 for which he received a $25 and $50 fine, respectively. In 2008, he was convicted of impaired driving.

After the preliminary inquiry, Green wrote a lengthy letter of apology to both Helen and Doris. Doris does not want to see Green go to jail, but wants the community "to know Green for the cruel man he is." Helen, who has had a difficult life, has written that "Green should pay for the harm he has caused. Only a long jail term will be sufficient." Green pleaded guilty at trial.

2. Ferris has pleaded guilty to assaulting his estranged spouse. They had agreed to meet to discuss financial arrangements for their two children. While having a cup of coffee, his spouse told him she needed more money. Ferris said that he would talk to his lawyer but that business had been bad. (He was an electrician who had become an electrical contractor.) As they were leaving the coffee shop an altercation took place. According to Ferris, he removed his wallet to pay the bill and she grabbed for the wallet saying, "Do you still carry wads of money?" Her account was that she asked to see his wallet and did not make a grab for it. Ferris grabbed her by the shoulders and threw her down.

Ferris is 38 years old with no prior record. He was charged with assaulting an employee in 2007, but the charge was withdrawn when the employee did not attend for his trial.

He attempted to persuade his spouse not to proceed with the charges stemming from the assault, but she refused. He threatened to stop making his maintenance payments but, in fact, has continued them at an increased level. A few weeks ago, he jumped into a creek to rescue an infant who had fallen in. This kind of heroic behaviour is not new. He received a civic medal for rescuing a man from a burning car in 2006.

Although he and his wife are separated, he has continued his relationship with his children. He went to a psychologist for anger-management counselling once. Since the offence, he has been charged with another assault arising from an argument over a parking space. (It is alleged that he jumped from his truck and punched a driver who had taken a space that he was waiting for.)

3. Harry had a great time at university in the late 1960s. One "down" episode was when he was arrested for possessing an ounce of marijuana. At the time, some judges were participating in a mini-version of the war on drugs. As a result, he was sentenced in 1968 to 30 days in jail. While judicial attitudes toward possession of marijuana have ameliorated substantially, the same could not be said for trafficking. In 1972, Harry was convicted of possession for the purposes of trafficking when a parcel containing 2 kilograms of marijuana was seized after being delivered to his home. For this offence, he was sentenced to 12 months' imprisonment.

After his release from prison, Harry completed his BComm degree and obtained an MBA at a prestigious business school. He redirected his entrepreneurial skills and ambitions and started to work for a stock brokerage firm. By 1990, he had made a fortune. He and his wife decided to retire to the country. They purchased a large farm and built a new home on the property. It was a huge house on a hill with dozens of windows looking out over a lush valley. They kept horses, sheep, and llamas. They grew their own vegetables and even used a windmill to generate electricity.

In June 2012, the local RCMP drug squad executed a search warrant on an expensive downtown condominium apartment in Toronto. After seizing a few pounds of marijuana, the Mounties began interrogating the occupier of the premises trying to obtain information. The man named Harry as his source of supply. (Harry denies knowing this man or ever having met him.) Armed with a search warrant, the RCMP officers travelled to Harry's farm, where they found four huge underground rooms devoted entirely to growing marijuana. They contained hundreds of plants of all sizes, at various stages of development. Specialized areas were set aside for drying and packing. Sergeant Turnbull, a Mountie with 25 years' experience, said: "This is the most sophisticated grow operation I have ever seen." He estimated that the plants could be translated into a value of $400,000 on the street. Harry and his wife were charged with "production" contrary to s 7(2)(b) of the *Controlled Drugs and Substances Act*. It was agreed that Harry would plead guilty and the charge against his wife would be withdrawn.

Harry is now 69 years old. Other than a conviction for mischief to property ($500 fine) arising from a political demonstration in 1995, his record consists of the two drug convictions in 1968 and 1972. Harry has been self-supporting since his retirement. Along with his wife, Anne, he has been active in the life of their rural community. They were the prime movers in starting a food bank and are directors of the annual arts festival. Harry is an active volunteer with various environmental groups and has turned a large portion of his acreage to solar power collection so that he can do his bit to fight global warming. Harry and Anne have recently adopted two young orphans, three and eight years old, from a third-world country. At the moment, the children speak only French. Harry is bilingual, but Anne is a unilingual anglophone.

Harry's counsel submitted that a non-custodial sentence was an appropriate disposition, especially given his childcare obligations and his commitment to pro-social activities. The prosecutor submitted that a deterrent sentence was needed, especially given the planning, profit potential, and sheer size of the operation. He suggested two to three years' imprisonment. When asked pursuant to s 726 if he had anything to say prior to sentencing, Harry commented:

> Marijuana is a natural substance which is helpful to many sick and disabled people. Our goal was to ensure access to this beneficial plant. I stand before this court as a victim of narrow-minded and oppressive governmental policies. Thank you, Your Honour, for permitting me to express my views.

FURTHER READING

Ashworth, Andrew. "Re-evaluating the Justifications for Aggravation and Mitigation at Sentencing" in JV Roberts, ed, *Mitigation and Aggravation at Sentencing* (Cambridge: Cambridge University Press, 2011).

Cox, Edward. "Circumstances of Aggravation" and "Mitigation of Punishment" in *The Principles of Punishment: As Applied in the Administration of the Criminal Law, by Judges and Magistrates* (Miami: Hardpress Classics Series, 1877) ch 16 and 17.

Manson, Allan. "Aggravating and Mitigating Factors" in *The Law of Sentencing* (Toronto: Irwin Law, 2000) ch 7.

Renaud, Gilles. "Mitigating and Aggravating Principles and Circumstances" in *Speaking to Sentence* (Thomson: Carswell, 2004) ch 4.

Roberts, Julian V, ed. *Mitigation and Aggravation at Sentencing* (Cambridge: Cambridge University Press, 2011).

Warner, Kate. "Equality Before the Law: Racial and Social Background Factors as Sources of Mitigation at Sentencing" in Julian V Roberts, ed, *Mitigation and Aggravation at Sentencing* (Cambridge: Cambridge University Press, 2011).

CHAPTER FOUR

Facts of the Offence for Sentencing

I. INTRODUCTION

The sentencing hearing follows a finding of guilt. That finding might be the result of a trial in which the trier of fact has found that the guilt of the accused has been proved beyond a reasonable doubt. Alternatively, and this covers most cases, a finding of guilt is made after the accused enters a plea of guilty. In either case, once there is a finding of guilt, the trial judge must consider and pronounce sentence. But this cannot be done unless the judge has relevant factual information about the offender and the offence. This chapter considers the manner in which facts about the commission of an offence and the offender are put in evidence at the time of sentence, and more specifically the manner in which disputed facts are put in evidence at the sentencing hearing. With respect to fact-finding concerning the offender and the victim, see Chapter 5, Sources of Information Relating to the Offender.

Where a finding of guilt is made following a guilty plea, there has been no trial of the general issue. The plea is a formal admission of the averments in the information or indictment. (Guilty pleas are discussed in Chapter 7, Plea Discussions and Joint Submissions.) These averments typically disclose little more than the name of the offender, the offence, and the event to which it relates. Thus the court must inquire into the facts concerning the offence and the offender. Where there has been a trial, most relevant facts will have emerged in evidence already, although there might yet be information relevant to sentence that has not been adduced. Further difficulties can arise in cases of trial by jury. The trial judge is bound to impose a sentence that is consistent with the jury's verdict. The verdict typically leaves no doubt about the relevant findings, but there are cases where the findings underlying the verdict are ambiguous or unclear. Apart from facts essential to the verdict, there are often other facts disclosed by the evidence that will be material for purposes of sentencing. Whether a finding of guilt is made following a trial or a guilty plea, additional evidence of relevant facts may be adduced by the parties with respect to the determination of a fit sentence.

II. THE SENTENCING HEARING

A judge who is properly seized of jurisdiction to record a finding of guilt is compelled to pronounce sentence and until then there is no final judgment in the matter: see *Criminal Code*, RSC 1985, c C-46, s 720, reproduced below. Although this principle applies in all cases, sentencing hearings can take different forms. There are many high-volume courts where the disposition of cases, including sentencing hearings that follow guilty pleas, appears almost perfunctory. Pleas are recorded at speed; sentences are pronounced quickly and with a minimum of reflection. So, too, in straightforward cases, where the parties have nothing new to add following the production of evidence at trial, the judge will often proceed directly to sentence unless counsel seek a postponement in order to prepare submissions. In other cases, at the request of counsel or the judge, a future date might be set for a sentencing hearing in which the parties may present evidence and submissions that are relevant to an appropriate disposition.

A conviction is not perfected until and unless there has been both a recorded finding of guilt and the pronouncement of a lawful sentence. The Code provides basic principles of law and procedure, but sentencing practice also varies from jurisdiction to jurisdiction. The significance of this point is not merely formal or technical. A finding of guilt is a necessary condition for the imposition of a sentence but, excepting mandatory minimum sentences, the finding does not of itself determine a sentence, let alone a fit sentence, for the offence or the offender. The determination of a sentence is an integral but distinct aspect of judgment in criminal cases. In this aspect of adjudication the law requires judges to respond to the offender's wrongdoing in a manner that reflects accepted principles of sentencing.

III. THE FACTUAL BASIS OF SENTENCING

In *R v Gobin*, Huband JA summarized the standard procedure for submissions on sentence and noted that it is the same whether there has been a finding of guilt after trial or on a guilty plea.

R v Gobin
(1993), 85 CCC (3d) 481 (Man CA)

HUBAND JA:

[2] Usually Crown counsel and defence counsel will agree on the factual circumstances relating to the commission of the offence. Those will be outlined to the Court, and counsel will make their submissions on that factual foundation.

[3] Where there is no firm agreement, Crown counsel is entitled to put forth the prosecution's understanding of the facts. It is open to defence counsel to make a submission based upon a different and less aggravated version of facts, so long as it is consistent with the wording of the indictment to which the plea of guilty has been entered.

[4] If the Crown wishes to contest the accused's version, evidence must be tendered to support the more aggravated scenario. The accused can, of course, then elect to produce evidence to support his version.

[5] If the Crown does not call evidence to support the more aggravated circumstances, then the accused's description of events is to be accepted, unless there is some manifest reason why that interpretation of the facts is contrived or erroneous.

• • •

[7] The question raised on this appeal is whether those same principles hold when the accused is found guilty after a trial rather than by entering a plea.

• • •

[21] The fact that the Crown was put to the task of proving the case against the accused does not change the basic rules. If a plea of guilty had been entered, Crown counsel would have been in a position to recount the circumstances much as they were revealed in the testimony of witnesses, and defence counsel would have been entitled to make his submission.

To determine an appropriate sentence the court must have relevant information. If this is not found in the evidence at trial or in an agreed statement of facts by the parties, additional evidence must be produced. Such evidence will be produced by the parties if they wish, but the judge may also request that parties produce evidence for purposes of sentencing. There might be no dispute between the parties regarding the evidence, but often there is. While the evidence for sentencing cannot contradict the facts that support the finding of guilt, it will have a decisive effect on the nature and severity of the sentence.

R v Gardiner
[1982] 2 SCR 368

[Gardiner pleaded guilty to a charge of assault causing bodily harm to his wife. At the sentencing hearing, Gardiner's testimony conflicted with that of the victim as to the circumstances of the offence. The trial judge accepted the evidence of the victim and held that the standard of proof was that of a balance of probabilities.]

DICKSON J (Martland, Ritchie, and Chouinard JJ concurring):

The Burden of Proof

A. *Introduction*

The question now to be addressed is this: What burden of proof must the Crown sustain in advancing contested aggravating facts in a sentencing proceeding, for the purpose of supporting a lengthier sentence; is the standard that of the criminal law, proof beyond a reasonable doubt, or that of the civil law, proof on a balance of probabilities?

The Crown [appellant] argues for the acceptance of a lesser onus of proof at sentencing than the traditional criminal onus of beyond a reasonable doubt, which applies at trial to the determination of guilt.

Relying heavily on American authorities, the Crown suggests that there is a sharp demarcation between the trial process and the sentencing process. Once a plea or finding of guilty is entered, the presumption of innocence no longer operates and the necessity of the full panoply of procedural protection for the accused ceases. Sentencing is a discretionary and highly subjective exercise on the part of the trial judge. The primary concern at a sentencing hearing is the availability of accurate information upon which the trial judge can rely in determining an appropriate sentence in the particular circumstances of the offender. For this reason the strict rules on the admissibility of evidence are relaxed. The trial judge is no longer confined to the narrow issue of guilt but is engaged in the difficult task of fitting the punishment to the person convicted. To require that the Crown prove contested issues beyond a reasonable doubt would be to complicate and extend sentencing hearings and convert the sentencing process into a second trial, with a resultant loss of economy.

In the event that the essentially civil onus of preponderance of evidence is rejected, the Crown proposes, in the alternative, an "intermediate" standard of "clear and convincing" evidence to apply to sentencing hearings.

The respondent [accused], on the other hand, argues for the application of the reasonable doubt standard to sentencing hearings. The "bifurcation" between trial and sentencing, proposed by the Crown, the respondent finds artificial and against the authorities. From the offender's point of view, sentencing is the most critical part of the whole trial process, it is the "gist of the proceeding," and the standard of proof required with respect to controverted facts should not be relaxed at this point. To do so is prejudicial to the accused. Administrative efficiency is insufficient justification for so radical a departure from the traditional criminal onus of beyond a reasonable doubt.

[Dickson J then reviewed authorities in Canada, England, the United States, and elsewhere.]

F. The Principles

Sentencing is part of a fact-finding, decision-making process of the criminal law. Sir James Fitzjames Stephen, writing in 1863 [in "The Punishment of Convicts," *Cornhill Magazine* 189], said (quoted in Olah, "Sentencing: The Last Frontier of the Criminal Law" (1980), 16 CR (3d) 97, at p. 98) that: "the sentence is the gist of the proceeding. It is to the trial what the bullet is to the powder." The statement is equally true today.

One of the hardest tasks confronting a trial judge is sentencing. The stakes are high for society and for the individual. Sentencing is the critical stage of the criminal justice system, and it is manifest that the judge should not be denied an opportunity to obtain relevant information by the imposition of all the restrictive evidential rules common to a trial. Yet the obtaining and weighing of such evidence should be fair. A substantial liberty interest of the offender is involved and the information obtained should be accurate and reliable.

It is a commonplace that the strict rules which govern at trial do not apply at a sentencing hearing and it would be undesirable to have the formalities and technicalities characteristic of the normal adversary proceeding prevail. The hearsay rule does not govern the sentencing hearing. Hearsay evidence may be accepted where found to be credible and trustworthy. The judge traditionally has had wide latitude as to the sources and types of evidence upon which to base his sentence. He must have the fullest possible information concerning the background of the accused if he is to fit the sentence to the offender rather than to the crime.

It is well to recall in any discussion of sentencing procedures that the vast majority of offenders plead guilty. Canadian figures are not readily available but American statistics suggest that about 85 percent of the criminal defendants plead guilty or *nolo contendere*. The sentencing judge therefore must get his facts after plea. Sentencing is, in respect of most offenders, the only significant decision the criminal justice system is called upon to make.

It should also be recalled that a plea of guilty, in itself, carries with it an admission of the essential legal ingredients of the offence admitted by the plea, and no more. Beyond that, any facts relied upon by the Crown in aggravation must be established by the Crown. If undisputed, the procedure can be very informal. If the facts are contested, the issue should be resolved by ordinary legal principles governing criminal proceedings, including resolving relevant doubt in favour of the offender.

To my mind, the facts which justify the sanction are no less important than the facts which justify the conviction: both should be subject to the same burden of proof. Crime and punishment are inextricably linked. "It would appear well established that the sentencing process is merely a phase of the trial process.": Olah, at p. 107. Upon conviction the accused is not abruptly deprived of all procedural rights existing at trial: he has a right to counsel, a right to call evidence and cross-examine prosecution witnesses, a right to give evidence himself and to address the court.

· · ·

In my view, both the informality of the sentencing procedure as to the admissibility of evidence and the wide discretion given to the trial judge in imposing sentence are factors militating *in favour of* the retention of the criminal standard of proof beyond a reasonable doubt at sentencing. Olah at p. 121:

> [B]ecause the sentencing process poses the ultimate jeopardy to an individual enmeshed in the criminal process, it is just and reasonable that he be granted the protection of the reasonable doubt rule at this vital juncture of the process.

The rationale of the argument of the Crown for the acceptance of a lesser standard of proof is administrative efficiency. In my view, however, the administrative efficiency argument is not sufficient to overcome such a basic tenet suffusing our entire criminal justice system as the standard of proof beyond a reasonable doubt. I am by no means convinced that, if the standard of proof were lowered, conservation of judicial resources would be enhanced. In the event of a serious dispute as to facts, it would be in the interests of the accused to plead not guilty in order to benefit at trial from the higher standard of reasonable doubt. This would be not only destructive of judicial economy but at the same time prejudicial to whatever mitigating effect might have come from a guilty plea, as evidence of remorse.

[Dickson J then rejected a lesser standard than proof beyond a reasonable doubt in respect of aggravating facts.]

Appeal dismissed.

NOTE

Few sentencing cases involve a formal evidentiary hearing. More often, the trial judge will proceed informally to hear submissions on sentence once a finding of guilt has been made. The following case considers what should be done when conflicts arise as to the factual basis of a sentence and no evidence has been called on the points in dispute.

R v Poorman
(1991), 6 CR (4th) 364 (Sask CA)

VANCISE JA (Wakeling JA concurring):

The appellant was charged with assault causing bodily harm, entered a plea of guilty and was sentenced to 9 months consecutive to any sentence currently being served.

He appeals, contending that the sentence was excessive in the circumstances.

During the oral sentencing presentation by the Crown and defence, the trial Judge was presented with conflicting statements of the circumstances surrounding the offence: the circumstances alleged by the Crown which, if accepted, must be considered as aggravating; and the circumstances alleged by the defence which, if accepted, would be mitigating. No sentencing hearing was held to resolve this apparent conflict.

Thus, this Court is once again called upon to comment upon and set out the procedure to be followed by trial judges during oral informal sentencing submissions when confronted with conflicting submissions, material, or assertions surrounding the commission of the offence or the personal circumstances of the accused. The issue encompasses not only the procedures to follow but the power of the trial judge to resolve conflicting assertions and facts which do not go to guilt or innocence but which have or could have a critical effect on the length of the sentence.

Facts

Mr. Poorman and the victim, Mr. Elaschuk, were serving prisoners in the Regina Correctional Centre at the time of the offence. On the day in question, Mr. Poorman was in a common area of the Correctional Centre watching television when Mr. Elaschuk and some other inmates entered the area. The Crown prosecutor contends that Mr. Poorman got up from his chair, walked to where he, the victim, and his friends were seated, and for no reason and without any warning or provocation struck the victim in the face, breaking his glasses and inflicting a 1-inch-long wound which bled profusely. As noted, both counsel gave conflicting versions of the circumstances surrounding the events which took place. In order to appreciate the degree of conflict between the two versions, it is necessary to set out specifically the submissions made by both sides.

The Crown, after narrating the facts in the previous paragraph, stated that Mr. Elaschuk then asked the appellant why he hit him and continued with the following submission:

> What he describes following that is the Accused grabbing him and holding what the victim called a knife, a butter knife that they use in their eating routine, holding this thing into his back and forcing him from the common area into a cell, delivering to him a Kleenex, or having someone deliver Kleenex or toilet paper or something like that to him, telling him

"close up the bleeding and don't say anything of this to the guards or—" He threatened to stick him with the knife. And stated that, you know, that he had done this before and he'd be prepared to do it again.

There had been no communication between these persons even as acquainted residents in the unit, and the victim has testified that there was no oral or gesturing provocation whatever to this. There appears to have been no reason for this.

He submitted:

In sentencing, the Court is asked to consider the particular circumstances as between victim and Accused here being, in essence, strangers, the absence of anything provocative on the part of the victim orally or in gesture, the apparent absence of any reason for the—the assault, the potential danger that could have resulted from the location of the assault, the location of the injury from the assault. It's fortunate that he is not injured more so from the blow in the glasses that were worn. I believe the glasses were filed in exhibit at Preliminary Hearing and should be here at Court.

The Court is also asked to consider significant, very significant, the setting in which this occurs; at the correctional centre as—between inmates.

The appellant's counsel also made oral submissions. The relevant portion is as follows:

MS. MALONEY: First of all, My Lord, with respect to the circumstances of the offence I wish to emphasize that this assault is a single blow, minor injuries. There were no stitches or anything of that sort required, no effect on this person's eyesight or anything of that nature, and that Mr. Poorman was acting alone. He had not ganged upon this person, so to speak, by means of acting in concert with anyone else.

Mr. Poorman has maintained from the outset that there was never any knife involved, never any weapon of any sort involved. What he does indicate is that there is some background to this assault, to this single blow that he administered to the complainant in the area where they were all watching television.

My client indicates that there was some provocation, or at least some—

THE COURT: Now, whoa.

MS. MALONEY: … some situation that resulted in him being angry.

THE COURT: I'm wondering, then, whether—are you so questioning the facts given to me by the Crown that perhaps we should vacate the not guilty plea.

MS. MALONEY: No, My Lord.

THE COURT: Excuse me, the guilty plea.

MS. MALONEY: It's not my intention to dispute that Mr. Poorman is guilty of an assault causing bodily harm in this situation. There is some background, though, that should have some bearing. I would suggest, in terms of trying to afford the Court some understanding—

THE COURT: Okay.

MS. MALONEY: … of the context in which to place its sentencing.

My client indicates that the complainant had made an advance to him by touching him in a way that Mr. Poorman perceived as a sexual touching and as a result he flared up in anger and struck the person the single blow. It was impulsive and in some anger, certainly. But the situation was not prolonged. As I indicated it was a single striking motion.

The Crown replied to the issue of the knife and the provocation as follows:

If I may respond to some of my friend's comments, My Lord, before filing the record.

Concerning the knife, I don't think anything significant turns on the Crown's submission concerning the knife aspect of this, and my friend's response is that that is not the item for sentencing before the Court, that aspect is—was stayed this morning, *there is that dimension to the story, though, and it is in opposition. There is issue on the fact there.*

Concerning the item of provocation that my friend raises there is issue in that regard. The Crown represents there was nothing provocative said or done prior to this. If that causes the Court a distress in considering sentence the victim is present and prepared to testify, as is the Accused present and able to testify if he chooses. [Emphasis added]

The Crown prosecutor went on to state on issue of provocation:

I invite the Court to hear evidence on the issue of provocation (inaudible—not near microphone). If it is not a matter of distress to the Court in sentencing then certainly the Crown will not proffer the evidence.

There was an adjournment, and when the proceedings resumed, and before sentencing, the appellant, in response to an invitation from the trial Judge to speak, again raised the issue of provocation in these terms:

Yes, Your Honour. Yes, I do. This assault wasn't (inaudible—not near microphone) mention a few facts about what I told that evolved around the assault. (Inaudible—not near microphone) time the assault happened we were sitting around the TV area and the victim was sitting behind me talking to somebody and they were talking about the use of jails (inaudible—not near microphone) and I turned around and told them "You guys want to keep it down." And I got up and I walked away and then (inaudible—not near microphone) I was leaving he touched me. That's when I blew up, you know. And that's what—that's what provoked me.

Thus there is a clear contradiction on two issues: (a) the presence of a knife; and (b) provocation. The trial Judge was invited to order a hearing on the issue of provocation but declined. It is not clear from the transcript whether he declined because he had resolved the issue contrary to the interests of the appellant or whether he considered it was not relevant in the circumstances.

Disposition

There are two questions raised here: (1) the power of the trial judge to resolve conflicting oral submissions on informal sentencing presentations; and (2) the procedure to be followed in informal sentencing hearings. Dickson J (as he then was) considered the standard of proof which is applicable on a sentencing hearing in *R v. Gardiner*, [1982] 2 SCR 368, 30 CR (3d) 289, 140 DLR (3d) 612, 68 CCC (2d) 477, 43 NR 361. In that case, he was dealing with a formal sentencing hearing and considered the onus and standard of proof. ...

• • •

The Court was not required to consider the procedure where there is a conflict between the Crown and the defence version of facts which are not crucial for the determination of guilt or innocence in an informal sentencing hearing. Bayda CJS considered the issue at length in *Canada (Attorney General) v. Boulet (sub nom. R v. Boulet)* (1990), 78 CR (3d) 309, 58 CCC (3d) 178, 85 Sask. R 93 (CA) (in dissent on other issues). The other two members of the panel disagreed with the result reached by the Chief Justice respecting the fitness of the sentence under appeal and specifically stated that they found it unnecessary to consider the principles stated by him respecting the rules, power of the trial judge to resolve questions of dispute, and the procedure to be followed in a sentencing hearing. In this case, it is not necessary to consider the issue in as detailed a fashion as did the Chief Justice, but it is useful to refer to some of the cases and comments that he referred to. The Chief Justice referred to the English cases of *R v. Newton* (1982), 77 Cr. App. R 13; and *Williams v. R* (1984), 77 Cr. App. R 329 (Div. Ct.) which set out the law of England as it relates to the powers of a trial judge to resolve conflicting versions of fact made during an informal sentencing hearing.

In *Newton*, the Lord Chief Justice of England set out the choices available to a trial in similar circumstances. Two of the three choices he commented upon are relevant in Canada. He stated at p. 15:

> The second method which would be adopted by the judge in these circumstances is himself to hear the evidence on one side and another, and come to his own conclusion, acting so to speak as his own jury on the issue which is the root of the problem.

The third option he described as follows:

> The third possibility in these circumstances is for him to hear no evidence but to listen to the submissions of counsel and then come to a conclusion. But if he does that, then ... where there is a substantial conflict between the two sides, he must come down on the side of the defendant. In other words where there has been a substantial conflict, the version of the defendant must so far as possible be accepted.

Thus in this case, if the trial Judge was of the opinion that the matter should have been resolved, his choice was to "so far as possible accept" the version of the accused and sentence him on that version of the facts, or, if he was not of the opinion that he could resolve the matter on that basis, he would hear the sworn evidence, resolve the dispute, and then sentence the accused. In *Williams, supra*, the Crown made certain statements not proved by evidence nor admitted by the accused, and the accused declined an invitation to have the disputed issues tried. The Crown submitted that because the accused had failed to call evidence as was suggested by the Crown, the version of the Crown should be accepted. Lord Justice Goff, in dealing with the procedures suggested by the Crown, said the following:

> [I]n my judgment, following the principles stated by the Lord Chief Justice in *Newton* ... the Court had really only two courses open to it, assuming, as I do, that there has been a sharp divergence or substantial conflict: either to listen to submissions on both sides and proceed on the basis that the version the defendant should, as far as possible, be accepted or, if the court was not prepared to do that, then to hear evidence. It may be that such evidence, when called, will be very slight; it may be that it will be the subject of cross-examination and no evidence will be called in contradiction. But even so, given the sharp divergence or substantial

conflict and given the fact that the court is not prepared to proceed on the basis that the defendant's version is substantially correct, the Court must, it seems to me, hear the evidence before forming its own view in respect of the matter which is in dispute.

As did Bayda CJS, we adopt these principles and hold that where there is a divergence of opinion or conflict of evidence not proven, the trial judge must not accept the Crown's version of the unproven facts as related at an informal hearing. If there is substantial conflict he must either: (1) hold a formal sentencing hearing at which time the Crown must prove the facts alleged on the criminal standard of proof, that is, beyond a reasonable doubt; or, (2) "so far as possible," accept the accused's version of the facts stated at the informal hearing, at which there is no evidence.

In this case, there were two disputed issues surrounding the circumstances of the offence which do not bear on the guilt or innocence of the appellant but which could affect the length of the sentence: the possession of the knife by the appellant at the time of the commission of the offence and the threat to use it if the victim "ratted"; and, whether the appellant was provoked as a result of the overtures of a homosexual nature which he alleges were made by the victim before he, the appellant, smacked him in the face.

The trial Judge, in sentencing the appellant to 9 months imprisonment consecutive to any other sentence he is currently serving, did not accept the version of the facts of the appellant. In our view, in circumstances such as this he should have ordered a sentencing hearing, at which point the Crown could call evidence on the disputed facts and appellant could call evidence or at the very least cross-examine the witnesses proffered by the Crown.

The sentence of 9 months consecutive is therefore set aside and the matter is remitted to the trial Judge for the holding of a sentencing hearing to determine the proper sentence to be imposed.

NOTE

The courts have repeatedly stressed that the determination of a fit sentence requires the production of adequate information about the offender and the offence: see e.g. *Gardiner*, above; *R v Jones*, [1994] 2 SCR 229 at 398; *R v Lévesque*, 2000 SCC 47 at para 30, [2000] 2 SCR 487; and *R v Lacasse*, 2015 SCC 64, [2015] 3 SCR 1089. Part XXIII of the *Criminal Code* codifies in part the procedure that should be followed to establish the factual basis for sentencing. Sections 720 to 726.2 of the Code (as amended by SC 1995, c 22) read as follows:

720. A court shall, as soon as practicable after an offender has been found guilty, conduct proceedings to determine the appropriate sentence to be imposed.

• • •

723(1) Before determining the sentence, a court shall give the prosecutor and the offender an opportunity to make submissions with respect to any facts relevant to the sentence to be imposed.

(2) The court shall hear any relevant evidence presented by the prosecutor or the offender.

(3) The court may, on its own motion, after hearing argument from the prosecutor and the offender, require the production of evidence that would assist it in determining the appropriate sentence.

(4) Where it is necessary in the interests of justice, the court may, after consulting the parties, compel the appearance of any person who is a compellable witness to assist the court in determining the appropriate sentence.

(5) Hearsay evidence is admissible at sentencing proceedings, but the court may, if the court considers it to be in the interests of justice, compel a person to testify where the person

(a) has personal knowledge of the matter;

(b) is reasonably available; and

(c) is a compellable witness.

724(1) In determining a sentence, a court may accept as proved any information disclosed at the trial or at the sentencing proceedings and any facts agreed on by the prosecutor and the offender.

(2) Where the court is composed of a judge and jury, the court

(a) shall accept as proven all facts, express or implied, that are essential to the jury's verdict of guilty; and

(b) may find any other relevant fact that was disclosed by evidence at the trial to be proven, or hear evidence presented by either party with respect to that fact.

(3) Where there is a dispute with respect to any fact that is relevant to the determination of a sentence,

(a) the court shall request that evidence be adduced as to the existence of the fact unless the court is satisfied that sufficient evidence was adduced at the trial;

(b) the party wishing to rely on a relevant fact, including a fact contained in a presentence report, has the burden of proving it;

(c) either party may cross-examine any witness called by the other party;

(d) subject to paragraph (e), the court must be satisfied on a balance of probabilities of the existence of the disputed fact before relying on it in determining the sentence; and

(e) the prosecutor must establish, by proof beyond a reasonable doubt, the existence of any aggravating fact or any previous conviction by the offender.

• • •

726.1 In determining the sentence, a court shall consider any relevant information placed before it, including any representations or submissions made by or on behalf of the prosecutor or the offender.

726.2 When imposing a sentence, a court shall state the terms of the sentence imposed, and the reasons for it, and enter those terms and reasons into the record of the proceedings.

These provisions restate the conclusions of the Supreme Court in *Gardiner* in general terms. There are, however, some ambiguities in these provisions that merit attention. For example, what is meant by the requirement that disputed but non-aggravating facts need only be proved to a balance of probabilities? If it means that disputed mitigating facts must be proved by the offender on a balance of probabilities, does this not diminish the principle that underlies *Gardiner*? It may be argued that *Gardiner* was concerned specifically with aggravating factors but that the court's observations concerning the application of the higher criminal standard addressed all situations. Moreover, in *R v Pearson*, [1992] 3 SCR 665, Lamer CJ suggested that the Crown's obligation was a principle of fundamental justice within the meaning of s 7 of the *Canadian Charter of Rights and Freedoms*, Part I of the *Constitution Act, 1982*, being Schedule B to the *Canada Act 1982* (UK), 1982, c 11. Does this mean that the validity of s 724(3)(d) is open to challenge as being inconsistent with principles of fundamental justice? Also at the core of these considerations is a concern about the nature and scope of the presumption of innocence following a finding of guilt. While that finding establishes the offender's liability, the sentencing decision must reflect the offender's culpability in the commission of the offence.

As noted in *Gardiner*, the courts have long held that the strict rules of admissibility at trial do not apply in the sentencing hearing. There is some analogy therefore to principles that apply in bail hearings. Section 723(5) expressly allows the judge to receive and consider hearsay, thus relaxing an exclusionary principle that has greater force at trial. Moreover, pre-sentence reports are generally nothing but hearsay. Similarly, a written victim-impact state-ment, produced in the absence of the victim, cannot readily be reconciled with notions of admissibility applicable at trial. Section 726.1 allows the court to consider "any relevant information placed before it." Information in this context is a broader concept than evidence that is admissible under strict rules of admissibility at trial. Although the range of informa-tion that may be considered at the sentencing hearing is broad, it is not without constraint. (In *R v Hunter* (1997), 11 CR (5th) 156 (Alta QB), the court noted, too, that the power to compel the production of information in a sentencing hearing requires some "logical nexus" between what is ordered and issues that are properly before the sentencing judge.) A heightened degree of reliability and persuasiveness is necessary, obviously, where aggravat-ing factors are in dispute. Furthermore, no degree of reliability or persuasiveness would entitle a judge to consider information that tends only to support conclusions expressly rejected in determining the finding of guilt. Finally, the requirement to give reasons (s 726.2) will also force judges to note the factual considerations that are the basis for sentencing decisions. Indeed, this might be one of the most important effects of this requirement. There remain, however, questions concerning the degree of flexibility that is permissible in deter-mining relevant facts for the purpose of sentencing.

R v Kunicki
2014 MBCA 22

CAMERON JA (Hamilton and MacInnes JJA concurring):

[2] In September 2009, the accused was arrested by the Winnipeg Police Service in possession of seven bags of cocaine weighing approximately 23 grams each and one piece of crack cocaine weighing 11.46 grams, the overall amount totalling 6.136 ounces.

[3] In February 2013, the accused entered a guilty plea to a charge of possession for the purpose of trafficking. At the sentencing hearing, the Crown asked that the accused be sentenced to five years' incarceration. In support of its position, the Crown called an expert witness who testified that, in his opinion, the accused was a mid-level trafficker.

[4] The accused asked for a conditional sentence of two years less a day. Through submissions of counsel, he disputed that he was a mid-level trafficker. Rather, he said that all of the cocaine seized belonged to him and that he was a significant addict who used the cocaine, but would also "chip off and sell a bit" to support his addiction. While his counsel did not specifically state that the accused was a street-level trafficker, she said that he was "not even a mid-level courier."

[5] The accused said that his friend (the friend) allowed the accused to live with him following his arrest and had given the accused employment on the condition that the accused remain drug free, which the accused said he had managed to do. The accused provided the court with letters of support from the friend and the friend's common-law wife. The letter from the friend's common-law wife indicated that the accused had lived with them for "the past 3 years." The accused also filed a report from Dr. Somers indicating that, if the accused abstained from the use of drugs, he was at a lower risk to reoffend.

[6] The sentencing judge observed that it was for the Crown to prove beyond a reasonable doubt that the accused was a mid-level trafficker. He found it noteworthy that, at the time of his arrest, there was no other evidence found that put the accused in possession of any trafficking-related paraphernalia or money, and that there was no evidence that the accused ever trafficked at the ounce level. While he agreed that the amount of cocaine found on the accused was significant, he accepted the accused's explanation that he was a "heavily addicted user and sold cocaine at the street level to fund his habit."

[7] After finding that the accused was a street-level trafficker, the sentencing judge listed what, in his view, were the aggravating factors and, next, stated:

> The mitigating factors are: there was no question [that] when the accused was picked up in September of 2009 he was a youthful offender, only 23 years of age. At the point in time when he was arrested he had never been incarcerated before nor has he been incarcerated pursuant to a sentence of any court [to date]. He entered a guilty plea. *Since this incident in 2009 he has moved in with his employer,* he indicates and it's supported by his employer that he holds down permanent employment and he has overcome his addiction.
>
> *Since September of 2009 I have no evidence before me that he has become re-involved in any criminal offence while on judicial interim release,* no allegation that he has an affiliation to a gang and despite its shortcomings, as pointed out by the Crown, the report of Dr. Somers assesses [the accused] at a low risk to reoffend so long as he abstains from the use of drugs.
>
> I am satisfied that [the accused] has taken major steps in turning his life around and I am satisfied that he himself does not pose a danger to the safety of the community. I am also satisfied that the principles of sentencing can be addressed by a conditional sentence. He has entered a guilty plea; he has taken major steps to rehabilitate himself and to obtain employment. I do not wish to set back his rehabilitation by a sentence of real jail. He's an excellent prospect for rehabilitation [emphasis added].

[One of the central issues on appeal was whether the sentencing judge erred in finding that the accused was a street-level trafficker.]

[17] The finding that the accused was a street-level trafficker was a finding of fact made by the sentencing judge and is to be reviewed on the standard of palpable and overriding error. See *R. v. Thomas (R.T.)*, 2010 MBCA 91 at para. 51, 258 Man.R. (2d) 146.

[18] The contention that the accused was involved in the drug trade as a mid-level trafficker was an aggravating factor. Therefore, the Crown had the responsibility of proving it beyond a reasonable doubt. See *R. v. Ramos (Z.M.)*, 2007 MBCA 87 at paras. 13-15, 214 Man.R. (2d) 280; *R. v. Gardiner*, [1982] 2 S.C.R. 368; and s. 724(3) of the *Criminal Code* (the *Code*). The Crown relied on the expert testimony of Sgt. Atkins (Atkins), who testified that it was his opinion that the accused was a mid-level trafficker, based on the following factors: i) the amount of cocaine seized; ii) the manner in which it was packaged; iii) his experience that street-level traffickers were not trusted with such a large amount of cocaine; and, iv) the accused was not in possession of any paraphernalia that would indicate that he was a street-level trafficker. In cross-examination, Atkins agreed that it was possible for an addict to buy cocaine at the ounce level and sell some of it to support his or her addiction, but that he had no personal knowledge of such a situation.

[19] The accused, through his counsel's submissions, claimed that he was not a mid-level trafficker or a mid-level courier. He claimed that he sold cocaine to support his addiction. This submission was consistent with what the accused told Dr. Somers. In brief, the accused was relying on hearsay to support the contention that he was a street-level trafficker.

[20] The Crown contends that, because the issue of the accused's degree of involvement in the drug trade was contested, s. 724(3) of the *Code* required the accused to present evidence in answer to the evidence the Crown presented.

[The court reproduced s 724(3).]

[22] However, s. 724(3) must be read in conjunction with s. 723 of the *Code*, which sets out the procedure for receiving evidence at sentencing hearings.

[The court reproduced s 723(5).]

[23] As is apparent, the *Code* specifically allows for the presentation of hearsay evidence in a sentencing hearing. In *Gardiner*, Dickson J., writing for the majority of the Supreme Court of Canada, considered the role of hearsay in the sentencing hearing (at p. 414):

> It is a commonplace that the strict rules which govern at trial do not apply at a sentencing hearing and it would be undesirable to have the formalities and technicalities characteristic of the normal adversary proceeding prevail. The hearsay rule does not govern the sentencing hearing. Hearsay evidence may be accepted where found to be credible and trustworthy. The judge traditionally has had wide latitude as to the sources and types of evidence upon which to base his sentence. He must have the fullest possible information concerning the background of the accused if he is to fit the sentence to the offender rather than to the crime.

[24] Recently, in *R. v. Nguyen*, 2012 ONCA 534 (QL), the Ontario Court of Appeal summarily dealt with the issue of the role of hearsay in sentencing proceedings where the evidence is disputed, stating (at para. 1):

> *The trial judge is entitled to rely on hearsay to make findings of fact on sentence even if the facts are disputed*: s. 723(5). Of course, the party relying on the disputed fact carries the onus: s. 724(3)(b). *We see no legal impediment to a party discharging that burden with disputed hearsay evidence, although trial judges will, quite properly, often decline to rely on hearsay evidence to prove facts in dispute.* [emphasis added]

[25] I disagree with the Crown's position that, in the circumstances of this case, s. 724(3) of the *Code* operates to compel an accused person to produce evidence of such quality as would be admissible in a trial. To be clear, however, this does not mean that in every case the sentencing judge is compelled to accept an accused's explanation provided by way of submissions of counsel. See *R. v. Coss (T.A.)*, 2012 MBQB 272, 285 Man.R. (2d) 89. The determination as to whether to accept the hearsay evidence or not, and the weight to be placed on it, is one for the sentencing judge.

[26] The sentencing judge found that the accused's degree of responsibility was that of a street-level trafficker who sold cocaine to fuel a significant drug habit. Based on the accused's explanation, the sentencing judge had a reasonable doubt that this was, as the Crown attempted to prove, trafficking at a scale larger than individual doses. If that had

been proven, a sentence in line with that discussed in *Rocha* would have been appropriate given the amount of cocaine that was seized. The sentencing judge was entitled to receive the hearsay evidence of the accused's explanation as evidence and weigh it in light of the other evidence. The sentencing judge did not err in law in doing so. The sentencing judge also did not commit a palpable and overriding error of fact in having a reasonable doubt as to the accused's responsibility being anything more than a street-level trafficker. In that regard, he acknowledged that the finding was a close call, as is evidenced by his statement that he was making such a finding "perhaps naively." Nonetheless, it was a finding he was entitled to make.

The Code and the cases address distinctions that affect the factual basis for sentencing. Was the trial before a jury or before a judge alone? Are the facts for sentencing disputed and, if so, are the facts aggravating or mitigating?

R v Brown
[1991] 2 SCR 518

STEVENSON J (La Forest, L'Heureux-Dubé, Gonthier, and Cory JJ concurring):

The accused appeals, by leave, a sentence of 12 months' imprisonment for dangerous driving imposed at trial and affirmed on appeal by a divided Court of Appeal [reported (1990), 75 CR (3d) 76, 23 MVR (2d) 89, 53 CCC (3d) 521, 81 Sask R 295]. The issue is whether the trial Judge and the majority of the Court of Appeal erred in considering the consequences of death and bodily injury when the jury had acquitted the accused of dangerous driving causing death and bodily injury.

The accused was the driver of a motor vehicle involved in a collision with another motor vehicle. As a result of the collision, two passengers in the other vehicle died and two others were injured.

The accused was initially charged with two counts of causing death by criminal negligence. This was reduced by the preliminary inquiry Judge to dangerous driving causing death. Shortly before the trial, a new indictment was filed, adding two additional counts of dangerous driving causing bodily injury.

At the trial, the Crown argued that the accused was speeding and had driven through a red light, that this manner of driving was dangerous, and that the dangerous driving had caused the collision and resulted in death and injuries. The defence argued that the appellant was not exceeding the speed limit by an excessive amount, nor did he disobey the traffic light. Moreover, the defence urged that the manner of the appellant's driving was not causally connected to the collision or the deaths or the injuries.

The jury found the accused not guilty of causing death or bodily injury by dangerous driving but guilty of the included offences of dangerous driving, simpliciter.

On sentencing, the trial Judge noted that deterrence was the element that was most significant in this case and then turned to various relevant facts. The appellant's traffic infractions, he said, "do reflect some disregard for the rules to be obeyed in driving a vehicle." He then commented that:

Now in this case, under the jury, they found you guilty of dangerous driving alone. And it's probably fortunate for you that they did. But the facts still are that two people died as the result—or following that collision. And two others suffer injuries that they are still being treated for today.

Included in the case on appeal was a letter or report written by the trial Judge to the Court of Appeal, which contains the following statement:

Nothing is clearer than the death and injuries to the four victims arose directly from that collision. It was a flagrant example of dangerous driving taking all the circumstances into account.

Before the Court of Appeal, the accused argued that the sentence was excessive for dangerous driving, simpliciter. The majority of the Court of Appeal noted that, "If the [accused] is correct, the sentence here does not bear an acceptable comparison [to other cases]."

In the Court of Appeal, the majority upheld the trial Judge's sentence. In the course of his majority judgment Wakeling JA said:

The appellant suggests that the trial judge's right is restricted severely because if he goes too far he is basing the sentence on facts which must have been rejected by the jury, otherwise the lesser verdict of dangerous driving would not have been rendered. The Crown says the trial judge not only can but has a duty to consider all of the evidence in order to determine a proper sentence, which evidence includes the fact the accused is at least partly to blame for a serious accident which took two lives. If the appellant is correct, the sentence here does not bear an acceptable comparison to such cases. … If the Crown is correct, then the sentence is not exceptional when compared to cases in which the consequences are similar to those involved in this case.

In dissent, Tallis JA noted the Judge's obligation to respect the jury verdict, which expressly rejected any causal connection between the way he was driving and the deaths and injuries, and concluded the sentence should have been reduced to 6 months' imprisonment.

The majority referred to an apparent divergence between English and Australian courts on the position to be taken regarding findings of fact by a sentencer when the determination of guilt has been made by a jury. Clayton C. Ruby, *Sentencing*, 3d ed. (Toronto: Butterworths, 1987), at pp. 61-62; D.A. Thomas, *Principles of Sentencing*, 2d ed. (London: Heinemann, 1979), at p. 367; and *Tremblay v. R* (1969), 7 CRNS 315 (Que. CA), were cited.

The divergence to which the majority of the Court of Appeal referred centres on the question of whether the judge is bound to assume that the jury took the most lenient view of the facts which would support the verdict. That issue does not arise here because the only factual question relates to the consequences, and on that factual question the jury's decision is not in doubt. Thomas makes it clear that subject to the jury's express and implied factual findings, the judge must make the necessary sentencing findings. He or she must, of course, make those findings in keeping with the law relating to the finding of facts on sentencing set out in *R v. Gardiner*, [1982] 2 SCR 368, 30 CR (3d) 289, 140 DLR (3d) 612, 68 CCC (2d) 477, 43 NR 361, which establishes that while all credible and trustworthy evidence may be accepted, disputed facts relied upon by the Crown in aggravation must be established beyond a reasonable doubt.

In *Tremblay, supra*, the trial Judge, in sentencing for a manslaughter conviction, expressed his opinion that the accused was guilty of deliberate murder. The majority of the Court of Appeal decided not to interfere with the sentence on the basis that rid of references or expressions of opinion to give the accused's acts the character of murder, the acts were sufficiently grave to justify the sentence (a maximum). The dissenting Judge found that the sentence was not fit and that it was influenced by the conclusion that the acts were murder. The majority thus found the sentence was "fit," untainted by impermissible considerations.

Before us, the parties were agreed that there is no relevant difference between the English and Australian positions. In its factum filed here, the Crown set out the English position, again quoting Thomas from an article, "Establishing a Factual Basis for Sentencing" [1970] Crim. LR 80, at p. 82, where he says:

> [T]he Court of Appeal has developed the principle that where the factual implication of the jury's verdict is clear, the sentencer is bound to accept it and a sentence which is excessive in the light of the facts implied in the verdict will be reduced. ... This principle can only apply however where the factual implication of the jury's verdict is clear; where ... the factual implication is ambiguous, the court has held that the sentencer should not attempt to follow the logical process of the jury, but may come to his own independent determination of the relevant facts.

This statement reflects the correct principle, namely, that the sentencer is bound by the express and implied factual implications of the jury's verdict. There are other authorities to the same effect: *R v. Speid* (1985), 46 CR (3d) 22, 9 OAC 237, 20 CCC (3d) 534 (CA) at p. 47 [CR]; Kevin Boyle and M.J. Aiken, *Sentencing Law and Practice* (London: Sweet & Maxwell, 1985), at pp. 225, 227 and 229; Richard George Fox and Arie Freiberg, *Sentencing: State & Federal Law in Victoria* (Melbourne: Oxford University Press, 1985), at p. 48; Eric Stockdale and Keith Devlin, *Sentencing* (London: Waterloo, 1987), at p. 62.

The Crown, here, took a different position, namely, that the "narrow question" was whether the jury's verdict was ambiguous, leaving the sentencing Judge free to make an independent determination. The argument is that the Judge did not adequately describe the test for causation set out in *R v. Smithers*, [1978] 1 SCR 506, 40 CRNS 79, 15 NR 287, 34 CCC (2d) 427, 75 DLR (3d) 321; *R v. Pinske* (1988), 6 MVR (2d) 19, 30 BCLR (2d) 114 (CA), affirmed orally by this Court, [1989] 2 SCR 979, 18 MVR (2d) xxxiv, 100 NR 399, 40 BCLR (2d) 1515. Counsel for the Crown analyzed the jury charge and argued that questions that were asked by the jury indicated that it may not have been properly instructed or that it had misunderstood the law on causation. Those are arguments against the jury's acquittal on the more serious charges and, if correct, would found an appeal of the acquittal. The Crown did not appeal the acquittals for dangerous driving causing death and bodily injury and must accept the verdicts.

The findings of dangerous driving, simpliciter, in the face of the more serious charges leaves no room for speculation. The jury has negated the factor of causation. This verdict was unambiguous and the trial Judge was bound by it. So was the Court of Appeal.

Since Parliament has chosen to make dangerous driving a consequence-related crime, the consequence of death or bodily injury must be taken to be excluded under a determination of guilt of dangerous driving, simpliciter. The Crown, here, conceded that had the accused entered a guilty plea to dangerous driving, simpliciter, it could not argue a more serious sentence based upon these consequences: *R v. Doerksen* (1990), 19 MVR

(2d) 16, 62 Man. R (2d) 259, 53 CCC (3d) 509 (CA). There is, in my view, no valid distinction between the two situations.

It follows that the appeal must be allowed. The appellant invites us to substitute an appropriate sentence. The determination of a fit sentence for an offence is generally to be determined by the provincial appellate courts. In my view, Tallis JA has fully considered the matter and determined the fit sentence in Saskatchewan in the circumstances of this offence. I would adopt his conclusion and impose a sentence of 6 months' imprisonment and affirm the driving prohibition of 3 years imposed at trial.

Appeal allowed.

NOTE

At issue in *Brown* was whether the trial judge imposed sentence on an improper factual basis. The Supreme Court leaves no doubt that it is an error of law for the trial judge to take into consideration factors that were specifically rejected by the jury in reaching their verdict. But a more frequent issue in jury trials arises when the jury's findings cannot be identified precisely. In such circumstances, the trial judge must make his or her own findings of fact for the purpose of sentencing. A common and prudent factor is for the judge to state findings of fact arising from a jury trial before pronouncing sentence. These matters are now partly covered in s 724 of the *Criminal Code*.

R v Ferguson
2008 SCC 6, [2008] 1 SCR 96

McLACHLIN CJ (Bastarache, Binnie, LeBel, Deschamps, Fish, Abella, Charron, and Rothstein JJ concurring):

[3] This case arises out of the fatal shooting of Darren Varley by an RCMP officer, in the small town of Pincher Creek in southwestern Alberta, while he was being held in a cell at the RCMP detachment. The RCMP officer who shot Mr. Varley, Michael Esty Ferguson, was charged with second-degree murder but convicted by a jury of the lesser offence of manslaughter. The judge imposed a conditional sentence of two years less a day, notwithstanding the mandatory minimum sentence of four years imposed by s. 236(a) of the *Criminal Code* for manslaughter with a firearm ((2004), 39 Alta. L.R. (4th) 166, 2004 ABQB 928). The majority of the Alberta Court of Appeal overturned that sentence, and held that the mandatory minimum must be imposed ((2006), 65 Alta. L.R. (4th) 44, 2006 ABCA 261). Constable Ferguson appeals to this Court, contending that a four-year sentence in the circumstances would constitute cruel and unusual punishment contrary to s. 12 of the *Charter*, and that the trial judge was right to grant him a constitutional exemption from the four-year minimum sentence imposed by Parliament.

• • •

[15] The appropriateness of a sentence is a function of the purpose and principles of sentencing set out in ss. 718 to 718.2 of the *Criminal Code* as applied to the facts that led to the conviction. It follows that the appropriateness of the minimum sentence of four years that Parliament has prescribed for Constable Ferguson's offence depends on what the jury concluded about Constable Ferguson's conduct.

[16] This poses a difficulty in a case such as this, since, unlike a judge sitting alone, who has a duty to give reasons, the jury gives only its ultimate verdict. The sentencing judge therefore must do his or her best to determine the facts necessary for sentencing from the issues before the jury and from the jury's verdict. This may not require the sentencing judge to arrive at a complete theory of the facts; the sentencing judge is required to make only those factual determinations necessary for deciding the appropriate sentence in the case at hand.

[17] Two principles govern the sentencing judge in this endeavour. First, the sentencing judge "is bound by the express and implied factual implications of the jury's verdict": *R. v. Brown*, [1991] 2 S.C.R. 518, p. 523. The sentencing judge "shall accept as proven all facts, express or implied, that are essential to the jury's verdict of guilty" (*Criminal Code*, s. 724(2)(a)), and must not accept as fact any evidence consistent only with a verdict rejected by the jury: *Brown*; *R. v. Braun* (1995), 95 C.C.C. (3d) 443 (Man. C.A.).

[18] Second, when the factual implications of the jury's verdict are ambiguous, the sentencing judge should not attempt to follow the logical process of the jury, but should come to his or her own independent determination of the relevant facts: *Brown*; *R. v. Fiqia* (1994), 162 A.R. 117 (C.A.). In so doing, the sentencing judge "may find any other relevant fact that was disclosed by evidence at the trial to be proven" (s. 724(2)(b)). To rely upon an aggravating fact or previous conviction, the sentencing judge must be convinced of the existence of that fact or conviction beyond a reasonable doubt; to rely upon any other relevant fact, the sentencing judge must be persuaded on a balance of probabilities: ss. 724(3)(d) and 724(3)(e); see also *R. v. Gardiner*, [1982] 2 S.C.R. 368; *R. v. Lawrence* (1987), 58 C.R. (3d) 71 (Ont. H.C.). It follows from the purpose of the exercise that the sentencing judge should find only those facts necessary to permit the proper sentence to be imposed in the case at hand. The judge should first ask what the issues on sentencing are, and then find such facts as are necessary to deal with those issues.

[19] Following these principles, the trial judge in this case was required to find facts, consistent with the jury's manslaughter verdict, to the extent that this was necessary to enable him to sentence Constable Ferguson. The sentencing inquiry was shaped by s. 236(a)'s prescription of a four-year mandatory minimum sentence. The only issues were whether the sentence should be more than four years, as the Crown contended, and whether the facts of the case were such that a four-year sentence would be grossly disproportionate, as Constable Ferguson contended.

[20] The trial judge correctly turned his mind to the basis on which he had instructed the jury it could reach a verdict of manslaughter. The trial judge had instructed the jury that if it rejected both self-defence and intent for murder (intent to cause death or bodily harm likely to cause death), it must reach a verdict of manslaughter. The trial judge did not leave any other basis for a manslaughter verdict with the jury. Hence the trial judge correctly concluded that on the basis of the jury's verdict, he must find facts consistent with the jury's rejection of both self-defence and intent for murder. On the basis of the jury's rejection of intent for murder, the trial judge properly concluded that the jury had found that when he fired the second shot, Constable Ferguson neither intended to cause death nor bodily harm that he knew was likely to cause death.

[21] However, the trial judge did not stop with these conclusions. He went on to make detailed findings of fact on Constable Ferguson's conduct. It was open to him under s. 724(2)(b) of the *Criminal Code* to supplement the jury's findings insofar as this was

necessary for sentencing purposes. However, it was not open to him to go beyond what was required to deal with the sentencing issues before him, or to attempt to reconstruct the logical process of the jury: *Brown*; *Fiqia*. Nor was it open to him to find facts inconsistent with the jury's verdict or the evidence; a trial judge must never do this. The trial judge in the case at bar committed both these errors.

[22]   First, the trial judge erred in attempting to reconstruct the logical reasoning of the jury. The law holds that the trial judge must not do this, and for good reason. Jurors may arrive at a unanimous verdict for different reasons and on different theories of the case: *R. v. Thatcher*, [1987] 1 S.C.R. 652. It is speculative and artificial to attribute a single set of factual findings to the jury, unless it is clear that the jury must unanimously have found those facts. Where any ambiguity on this exists, the trial judge should consider the evidence and make his or her own findings of fact consistent with the evidence and the jury's findings.

[23]   Here the trial judge, having properly concluded that the jury must have rejected self-defence and intent for murder, went on to attempt to reconstruct further facts that may or may not reflect what was in the mind of the jurors. First, he found that the jury must have concluded that the first shot had been fired in self-defence. Although there is evidence capable of supporting such a finding, this finding was not required by the jury's verdict. The jury's verdict does not unequivocally indicate a particular characterization of the two shots. Indeed, the jury was not asked to make a finding one way or the other about the first shot. The Crown based its case on the second shot, presumably because the evidence was that the second shot caused death, and the first shot did not. The trial judge should have considered all the evidence in order to make his own findings of fact consistent with the jury's verdict to the extent they were relevant to the two issues before him.

[24]   Second, and more critically, the trial judge went on to develop a theory to support the jury's verdict which was not only speculative, but contrary to the evidence. This theory was that Constable Ferguson's second shot was instantaneous and instinctive, the virtually automatic result of his police training. The theory rests on the premise that Constable Ferguson was following training that made the second shot following on a first self-defence shot a matter of instinctive reaction rather than conscious decision. Based on this theory, the trial judge found as a fact that Constable Ferguson was not acting in anger when he fired the second shot, but in response to his training. This finding was critical to the trial judge's conclusion that the minimum sentence of four years prescribed by s. 236(a) of the *Criminal Code* constituted cruel and unusual punishment, violating s. 12 of the *Charter*.

[25]   There are two problems with this crucial finding. First, it is inconsistent with the trial judge's other conclusions as well as with the jury's verdict. As the Court of Appeal noted, the instantaneous and instinctive shot theory contradicts the trial judge's conclusion that the first shot was fired in self-defence and the second was not, a conclusion that requires that the two shots be regarded as two separate transactions to be evaluated individually according to the criteria for self-defence in *Criminal Code*, s. 34(2). The instantaneous and instinctive theory, on the other hand, rests on the premise that the second shot was a virtual continuation of the first shot, motivated by the same mental state, namely self-defence. Had the trial judge found that the second shot was instantaneous and instinctive, he should have considered the two shots together as a single transaction, and would have been required by the jury's verdict to hold that this transaction, in its entirety, did not constitute self-defence.

[26] Second, the instantaneous and instinctive explanation for the second and fatal shot does not sit comfortably with uncontradicted evidence relating to the circumstances of the shooting. The booking officer estimated the time between the two shots at up to three seconds, as did the inmate in the next cell, Herman No Chief. While the length of the interval between the two shots may be difficult to determine with precision, it seems clear that there was an interval. This was not a case of immediately successive shots. This is supported by the fact that Constable Ferguson's firearm did not permit rapid, automatic second shots.

[27] The finding that Constable Ferguson's second shot was not a matter of anger or judgment, but simply a matter of training, is a vital component of the trial judge's conclusion that Constable Ferguson was at the very low end of the spectrum of moral blameworthiness, such that four years' imprisonment would be grossly disproportionate and intolerable to an informed public, and so would violate s. 12 of the *Charter*. It follows that his conclusion that the four-year minimum sentence was unconstitutional in this case is fatally flawed.

R v Grandine
2015 ONSC 18 (footnotes omitted)

CLARK J:

[1] On October 17, 2011, Karissa Grandine drowned in the bathtub of her Scarborough home. Her husband, Philip Grandine, was tried by this court, sitting with a jury, on an indictment charging that he drowned her and did thereby commit first degree murder. He was found guilty of the lesser offence of manslaughter and is now before the court to be sentenced.

Position of the Crown

[2] The Crown proposes a range of sentence of 15 to 18 years' imprisonment. Counsel bases this submission on what she argues are a host of aggravating factors that make this case one that is near murder.

Position of the Offender

[3] Counsel for the accused contends that the range the Crown suggests is grossly excessive and, further, that many of the proposed facts upon which the Crown relies in support of this range are, as a consequence of the jury's verdict, unavailable to the court.

[4] Counsel suggests that an appropriate range of sentence is six months to two years less a day. This range is, of course, predicated on a very different factual underpinning than that which the Crown urges upon the court.

The Fact-Finding Process

[5] Both sides acknowledge that the cause of death was drowning. What was in dispute before the jury is how the deceased came to drown. That question is still very much in dispute in terms of the factual basis upon which the parties argue this Court should impose sentence.

[6] Blood taken from the deceased at autopsy was found to contain a significant level of lorazepam, a drug belonging to the benzodiazepine family of pharmaceuticals, marketed in Canada under the trade name "Ativan." Amongst other side effects, lorazepam is known to have a significant sedative effect.

[7] The Crown contended before the jury that, unbeknownst to Karissa Grandine, the accused, with the intent to kill her, gave her lorazepam in a sufficient amount that he knew its sedative properties would debilitate her, both physically and mentally. The Crown asked the jury to conclude that, once he had drugged her, he persuaded her to get into the bath or, alternatively, physically put her in the tub. Once in the tub, the Crown asked the jury to conclude that the accused either waited for the inevitable to occur or, again in the alternative, he took an active role in drowning his wife. In her submissions on sentence, Ms. Kellway continues to assert that the accused administered lorazepam to his wife, although she acknowledges that the jury's verdict estops the court from finding that, in so doing, he intended to kill his wife.

[8] The defence contended before the jury, and continues to maintain, that, in all likelihood, the deceased took the lorazepam herself, with no involvement or participation on the part of the accused. On the defence theory, the deceased either took the lorazepam to assist herself in committing suicide or, in the alternative, having taken the drug, she simply fell, hit her head, lost consciousness and drowned. Indeed, on the latter theory, it is possible, counsel contends, that the lorazepam played no role whatsoever in what was simply a tragic accident.

[9] These competing theories inform the dramatically different positions advanced by the parties in their respective submissions.

[10] Quite apart, however, from the disparate versions of the facts they urge upon the court, the parties fundamentally disagree as to the nature and scope of the fact-finding process upon which the court must now embark. More specifically, there is dispute concerning the extent to which, as a consequence of the jury's verdict, the court is constrained as to the facts it can find. There is also dispute concerning whether, in the event of disagreement on the facts, the court is obliged to adopt the version most favourable to the defence. Therefore, before proceeding to set out the facts I have found, I propose to first delineate the legal principles I have considered and applied in making those findings.

[11] To begin, finding the facts can be more difficult for the sentencing court in manslaughter cases than with other types of offences. As McEachern C.J.B.C. noted in *R. v. Gauthier* (No. 2), [1996] 78 B.C.A.C. 85, 108 C.C.C. (3d) 231, at para. 41, "guilty verdicts in manslaughter ... cases ... are necessarily ambiguous descriptions of how the offence was committed."

[12] The court is, of course, "bound by the express and implied factual implications of the jury's verdict": *R. v. Brown*, [1991] 2 S.C.R. 518, at page 523; *Criminal Code*, R.S.C. 1985, c. C.46, ss. 724(2)(a). That said, for a sentencing court to be bound in this way, the fact must be "essential to the jury's verdict": s. 724(2)(a). Beyond that, the court "may find any other relevant fact that was disclosed by the evidence at the trial ...": s. 724(2)(b).

[13] Where there is dispute respecting a fact that is relevant to the determination of a fit sentence, the court is statutorily obliged to "request that evidence be adduced as to the existence of the fact unless the court is satisfied that sufficient evidence was adduced at the trial": s. 724(3)(a). In this case, no one sought to call further evidence concerning the facts upon which the court should impose sentence and I am satisfied that sufficient

evidence was adduced at trial to render it unnecessary to hear further evidence to make the factual findings I have made.

[14] Respecting facts to be considered on sentence, both the onus and quantum of proof are well established. The party alleging a fact bears the burden of proving it (s. 724(3)(b)) on a balance of probabilities (s. 724(3)(d)), except where the Crown alleges that the disputed fact amounts to an aggravating factor, in which case the prosecutor must establish the fact beyond a reasonable doubt: s. 724(3)(e).

[15] Citing *R. v. Poorman*, [1991] S.J. No. 274, 66 C.C.C. (3d) 82 (C.A.), defence counsel asserts that, where the facts are in dispute, the court is obliged to give the accused the benefit of the doubt by finding the facts most favourable to him. With respect, *Poorman* does not stand for that proposition.

[16] Contrary to Mr. Thakore's position, however, it is well established that "the trial judge is entitled to make up his own mind on disputed questions of fact which are relevant to sentence": *R. v. Tuckey*, [1985] O.J. No. 142, 20 C.C.C. (3d) 502 (C.A.); *R. v. Tempelaar*, [1993] O.J. No. 3409; 95 O.A.C. 235; aff'd [1993] S.C.C.A. No. 541, 203 N.R. 7.

[17] More recently, in *Gauthier*, at para. 49, Southin J.A. stated that "a trial judge is under no obligation, as a matter of law, when sentencing after the verdict of a jury, to give an accused the benefit of that view of the evidence which is most favourable to the accused."

[18] Ryan J.A., who wrote the principal opinion in *Gauthier*, stated, at para. 21:

> In *R. v. Brown*, [1991] 2 S.C.R. 518, the Supreme Court of Canada approved (at p. 523) the following passage from the article "Establishing a Factual Basis for Sentencing" found in [1970] Crim. L.R. 80 at p. 82, where the author, D.A. Thomas, says:
>
> > ... the Court of Appeal has developed the principle that where the factual implication of the jury's verdict is clear, the sentencer is bound to accept it and a sentence which is excessive in the light of the facts implied in the verdict will be reduced ... . This principle can only apply however where the factual implication of the jury's verdict is clear; *where ... the factual implication is ambiguous, the court has held that the sentencer should not attempt to follow the logical process of the jury, but may come to his own independent determination of the relevant facts.*
>
> > This statement reflects the correct principle, namely that the sentencer is bound by the express and implied factual implications of the jury's verdict. There are other authorities to the same effect: *R. v. Speid* (1985), 46 C.R. (3d) 22, at p. 47; Boyle and Allen, *Sentencing Law and Practice* (1985), at pp. 225, 227 and 229; Fox and Freiberg, *Sentencing: State and Federal Law in Victoria* (1985), at p. 48; Stockdale and Devlin, *Stockdale and Devlin on Sentencing* (1987), at p. 62. [Emphasis added by Ryan J.A.]

R v Roncaioli
2011 ONCA 378

[The accused was a physician charged with manslaughter in the death of his wife by injection of lethal quantities of anaesthetics. The case for the defence was that the accused had injected his wife with therapeutic doses of anaesthetics but that she had administered to herself the fatal doses. The prosecution advanced theories of manslaughter by criminal negligence and by means of an unlawful act. The accused was sentenced to prison for seven years. The appeal against sentence focused on the degree of culpability, which turned on the characterization of the offence by the sentencing judge as manslaughter by means of aggravated assault rather than criminal negligence.]

LASKIN JA (Armstrong and LaForme JJA concurring):

[56] The trial judge gave lengthy and thorough reasons for the seven-year sentence that she imposed. She set out her factual findings, and then listed both the mitigating and aggravating consideration she weighed in her assessment of the appropriate sentence. She concluded that "a substantial penitentiary sentence is necessary to meet the needs of denunciation and deterrence and to reflect Dr. Roncaioli's moral blameworthiness."

[57] Central to the trial judge's conclusion was her finding that Dr. Roncaioli intentionally injected his wife with the two anaesthetics, and that those injections constituted an aggravated assault. Indeed, the trial judge also found that the aggravated assault was planned, and that "the manslaughter in this case more resembles murder than an accidental killing."

[58] The appellant submits that the trial judge erred in principle in sentencing him on the basis of unlawful act manslaughter. He argues that, as the basis for the jury's verdict was unclear, he was entitled to the benefit of the doubt and to be sentenced for manslaughter by criminal negligence, which he contends is not as morally blameworthy as unlawful act manslaughter. In making this submission, the appellant relies on the decisions of this court in *R. v. Cooney* (1995), 98 C.C.C. (3d) 196 (Ont. C.A.) and *R. v. Craig* (2003), 177 C.C.C. (3d) 321 (Ont. C.A.), which I wrote. In *Cooney* at 204, the court said "the sentencing judge is obliged to give to the convicted accused the benefit of the doubt regarding the basis on which he was convicted by the jury." In *Craig* I followed this principle.

[59] I do not accept the appellant's submission. On reflection, I have concluded that the principle set out in *Cooney* and *Craig* is inconsistent with several Supreme Court of Canada cases: see *R. v. Brown*, [1991] 2 S.C.R. 518, *R. v. Tempelaar*, [1995] 1 S.C.R. 760, and more recently *R. v. Ferguson*, [2008] 1 S.C.R. 96. Where the basis of the jury's verdict is unclear, the correct principle is that the sentencing judge should make his or her own independent determination of the facts, consistent with the jury's verdict.

[60] In the case before us, the trial judge recognized that the basis of the jury's verdict was unclear, and applied this principle. She made ten factual findings, which she listed, consistent with the jury's verdict and with the evidence. For the purposes of sentencing, it was open to the trial judge to then determine that the appellant had committed unlawful act manslaughter and she did not err in doing so.

IV. SELF-INCRIMINATION AND SILENCE AT
THE SENTENCING HEARING

Does the fact that the sentencing process begins only after a finding of guilt has been registered mean that the presumption of innocence no longer applies? We have seen that with respect to factors raised to aggravate the sentence, the Crown must prove them beyond a reasonable doubt if they are contested. (This is subject to the judge's ability in a jury trial to make findings of fact so long as they are consistent with the verdict.) Accordingly, allegations are not sufficient; there must be a satisfactory factual foundation for the sentencing process even though the accused has been found guilty. What about silence? It is clear that for purposes of determining criminal responsibility, the accused's silence cannot be considered. Can the absence of an explanation for the conduct that comprises the offence be considered and used as an aggravating factor?

R v Shropshire
[1995] 4 SCR 227

[The accused pleaded guilty to second-degree murder after shooting the deceased in the chest three times. He offered no explanation for the killing. The trial judge sentenced him to life imprisonment and set the parole ineligibility period at 12 years. On appeal, the BC Court of Appeal reduced the period to 10 years on the basis that, *inter alia*, there were no unusual circumstances to warrant an increase beyond the minimum of 10 years. The Supreme Court of Canada reversed and restored the 12-year period.]

IACOBUCCI J (Lamer CJ and La Forest, L'Heureux-Dubé, Sopinka, Gonthier, Cory, McLachlin, and Major JJ concurring):

[35] ... I do not see any error on the part of the trial judge. He adverted to the fact that the respondent had pleaded guilty and was only 23 years old. He recognized that the Crown was not seeking a period of parole ineligibility beyond the minimum. Nevertheless, in a legitimate exercise of his discretionary power, and after correctly reviewing the factors set out in s. 744, he imposed a 12-year period of parole ineligibility. He referred to the following factors as specifically justifying the 12-year period of parole ineligibility:

(a)   [T]he circumstances of the killing were strange in that they provided no real answer to why it took place, and the respondent was unwilling or unable to explain his actions;

· · ·

[37] Factor (a), however, presents some difficulty. The respondent raises the question whether the trial judge erred in interpreting the respondent's silence in such a manner as to justify extending the period of parole ineligibility.

[38] In response, I would affirm the analysis of Goldie JA in the court below and would hold that this silence is readily assimilable within the "circumstances surrounding the offence" criterion. The crux of Goldie JA's comments is that, in the absence of any explanation for a random and seemingly senseless killing, the trial judge was correct in sentencing the respondent in light of his refusal to offer an explanation. It was found that his refusal was deliberate and in and of itself unusual. After all, the respondent, a drug dealer with previous convictions for robbery and armed robbery, shot the victim Buffam in cold blood without provocation of any kind.

[39] It is not for the trial judge to speculate what the respondent might have said to mitigate the severity of the offence. I quite agree with Goldie JA that the right to silence, which is fully operative in the investigative and prosecutorial stages of the criminal process, wanes in importance in the post-conviction phase when sentencing is at issue. However, in so agreeing, I emphasize that the respondent pleaded guilty; I leave for future

consideration the question of drawing a negative inference from the silence of the accused when he or she has pleaded not guilty and wishes to appeal the conviction. In the case at bar, the trial judge even went so far as to invite the accused to suggest why he may have committed the offence, but no response was forthcoming. As held by Goldie JA, the respondent "cannot expect to be rewarded for remaining silent in the circumstances." The court and the public clearly have an interest in knowing why a human life was taken by an offender.

[40]   Goldie JA's comments and the decision of the trial judge on the "silence" issue are fully consonant with the position taken by the Ontario Court of Appeal. In *R v. Able* [(1993), 65 OAC 37 (CA)], the Court of Appeal increased two co-accused's periods of parole ineligibility. At p. 39 it was held:

> No explanation has been forthcoming from either of the appellants with respect to the reason for the killing ... [which] can be best described as a callous, brutal, pointless, execution-style killing of a helpless victim.

I conclude that in certain circumstances, such as those presented in this case, it is proper to take into account the absence of an explanation of attenuating factors.

[41]   The respondent suggests that Goldie JA's comments and the decision of the trial judge contravene the pronouncements of this court in *R v. Gardiner*, [1982] 2 SCR 368. I recognize that, in *Gardiner*, this court extended certain procedural rights to sentencing proceedings. However, these were limited to the right to counsel, the right to call evidence, the right to cross-examine and the right to address the court. There is no mention made of the creation in its identical form of a substantive right such as the right to silence.

[42]   At the sentencing stage, the Crown has already proved beyond a reasonable doubt that the accused has committed the crime for which he or she stood charged or, as in this appeal, the accused has pleaded guilty to the offence; if the accused then seeks to receive the least severe sentence commensurate with his or her conviction (*i.e.* for second degree murder, life imprisonment with eligibility for parole after 10 years have elapsed) it is incumbent upon the accused to play a somewhat active role in the process. I note that the right to silence is a manifestation of the presumption of innocence: *R v. Broyles*, [1991] 3 SCR 595; *R v. Hebert*, [1990] 2 SCR 151; *R v. Chambers*, [1990] 2 SCR 1293. The presumption of innocence flows to those "charged with an offence" or suspected of having committed one; once an individual has been convicted of an offence he or she is no longer simply "charged."

Appeal allowed; parole ineligibility set at twelve years.

NOTE

Is the court converting an absence of evidence into an aggravating factor? Such a conclusion would be difficult to reconcile with *Gardiner* and the principles examined in this chapter. The observations in *Shropshire* must be qualified by the overriding principle that the sentence must be consistent with the evidence before the court and not coloured by speculative aggravating factors that might (or might not) be consistent with the absence of evidence.

Once there is a finding of guilt, it is true that the presumption of innocence is spent to the extent that the prosecution is relieved of further obligation to prove the offence beyond a reasonable doubt. If the burden and standard of proof are all that is meant by the presumption of innocence, it would seem to follow that there is no scope for its application in the sentencing hearing. But this might be an unduly hasty conclusion because there is a meaningful way in which the presumption of innocence can apply in sentencing. It is clear that the prosecutor must prove disputed facts beyond a reasonable doubt if those facts are aggravating. Thus the higher standard of proof is required to establish heightened culpability. The rationale for this standard might not flow directly from the presumption of innocence, but it serves a purpose that is entirely consistent with that principle: see *R v Pearson*, [1992] 3 SCR 665 at 54-55, Lamer CJ. Similarly, the conclusion in *Brown*, above, can be explained in an analogous fashion. The court concluded that the accused could not properly be sentenced with reference to elements of culpability that were rejected by the jury. What is this at the sentencing stage if not some vestigial protection of the presumption of innocence and the principle against self-incrimination?

For discussion of *Shropshire*, see Gary T Trotter, "Murder, Sentencing, and the Supreme Court of Canada" (1996), 43 CR (4th) 288, and J Norris, "Sentencing for Second-Degree Murder" (1996) 1 Can Crim L Rev 199.

V. FACTS RELATING TO OTHER OFFENCES

Another issue addressed by the Code, at least in part, concerns the extent to which the sentencing judge may take into account facts relating to the commission of another offence by the accused, whether charged or not. The matter is of great importance, obviously, because a fit sentence can only be one that is fit for the offence of which the offender was found guilty. In *R v Edwards* (2001), 54 OR (3d) 737 (CA), after a careful review of the jurisprudence, Rosenberg JA concluded that apart from the provisions of s 725 the sentencing judge has a discretion to admit and consider evidence of previous uncharged conduct by the accused in the assessment of his background and character. The interpretation of s 725 and the views expressed in *Edwards* have been considered by the Supreme Court of Canada.

R v Larche
2006 SCC 56, [2006] 2 SCR 762

FISH J:

I

[1] Offenders are punished in Canada only in respect of crimes for which they have been specifically charged and of which they have been validly convicted.

[2] To this general rule, there is only one true exception: In sentencing an offender, the judge may consider any uncharged offences *that form part of the circumstances of the offence.*

[3] The trial judge in this case applied s. 725(1)(c) of the *Criminal Code*, R.S.C. 1985, c. C-46, over the objections of Crown counsel, and the decisive question is whether he was entitled to do so. I agree with the courts below that he was.

• • •

II

[6] The respondent Jean-Paul Larche participated in a criminal operation that exported cannabis from the Eastern Townships of Quebec across the American border and repatriated the proceeds to Canada. For that, Mr. Larche and others were arrested and charged in Canada in June 2002. Less than one month later, they were indicted in the United States in connection with the same operation.

[7] Mr. Larche was indicted in Canada on two counts, the first for having conspired to produce, possess, and traffic in cannabis, and to possess the proceeds; the second for having committed drug-related offences under the direction of a criminal organization or for its profit.

[8] Both counts were drafted as if the underlying criminal enterprise, which was plainly transnational in scope, ended right at the US–Canadian border.

[This was done to facilitate an anticipated extradition request from the United States government for conspiracy to distribute marijuana, during essentially the same period, in that country.]

[10] Mr. Larche pleaded guilty to both counts … .

• • •

[12] Defence counsel … urged the trial judge—over the Crown's objections—to apply s. 725(1)(c) of the *Criminal Code* in determining the sentence. The Crown's own submissions on sentence, he argued, established that the prerequisites of that provision were satisfied. Mr. Larche had participated in the Cusson gang's operations both in Canada and in the United States. His participation in these crimes constituted "facts forming part of the circumstances of the offence[s]" for which he was to be sentenced, within the meaning of s. 725(1)(c). And, again in the words of s. 725(1)(c), these facts "could constitute the basis for a separate charge."

[13] Sansfaçon JCQ agreed and, applying s. 725(2) of the *Criminal Code*, he noted three "facts"—or uncharged offences—on the indictment:

1. [TRANSLATION] Between December 2001 and July 2002, Jean-Paul Larche participated on 3 (three) occasions in the exportation of marihuana from Quebec to Massachusetts on behalf of the criminal organization headed by Marc-André Cusson.
2. Between December 2001 and July 2002, Jean-Paul Larche on several occasions brought back from the United States money derived from the sale of marihuana, in total between $500,000 and $600,000 in US currency, on behalf of the criminal organization headed by Marc-André Cusson.
3. On May 31, 2002, in the state of Vermont, Jean-Paul Larche had in his possession $110,000 in US currency (Yankee Barn Home incident in New Hampshire) derived from the sale of marihuana on behalf of the criminal organization headed by Marc-André Cusson.

[14] The first two notes describe what might reasonably be characterized as the missing half of the single criminal enterprise that was the true substratum of the indictment. As earlier explained, it had been "carved out" of the offences charged to accommodate an anticipated request for Mr. Larche's extradition to the United States. Both notes relate to

facts over which Canadian courts have jurisdiction and I agree with the Court of Appeal that Sansfaçon JCQ was entitled to consider those facts in determining the sentence. He was then required by s. 725(2) to enter them on the indictment, as he in fact did.

[15] Like the Court of Appeal, however, I believe s. 725(1)(c) only applies to uncharged offences over which Canadian courts have territorial jurisdiction. The third note, by its plain terms, does not satisfy this requirement. It concerns an event that occurred entirely in Vermont. This alone is sufficient to dismiss Mr. Larche's cross-appeal, which seeks to revive that note.

III

. . .

[18] The Crown contends that s. 725 is a codification of pre-existing common law principles, particularly those set out in *R v. Garcia*, [1970] 3 C.C.C. 124 (Ont. C.A.). This is true of s. 725(1)(a) and (b), and to some extent of para. (b.1). But the rest of s. 725—including s. 725(1)(c) and s. 725(2), which concern us here—is new law.

[19] Under *Garcia*, facts capable of supporting separate charges could be considered in determining the sentence *only if they were covered by other pending charges*. *R v. Robinson* (1979), 49 C.C.C. (2d) 464 (Ont. C.A.), also cited by the Crown, is to the same effect. Section 725(1)(b) and, albeit in a more structured way, para. (b.1) thus express in statutory form the practice recognized by *Garcia* and *Robinson*. See *R v. Howlett* (2002), 163 O.A.C. 48 (C.A.), at para. 13.

[20] Section 725(1)(c), on the other hand, allows the court to take into consideration facts that *could* constitute the basis for a separate charge that *has not*—or at least not yet—been laid.

[21] As Cory and Iacobucci JJ emphasized in *R v. Gladue*, [1999] 1 S.C.R. 688, at para. 39:

> One cannot interpret the words of s. 718.2(e) simply by looking to past cases to see if they contain similar statements of principle. The enactment of the new Part XXIII was a water shed, marking the first codification and significant reform of sentencing principles in the history of Canadian criminal law. Each of the provisions of Part XXIII, including s. 718.2(e), must be interpreted in its total context, taking into account its surrounding provisions.

[22] This cautionary injunction applies here. ... Section 725(1)(c) and s. 725(2) are best understood not by looking to past cases but by considering their plain terms, their evident purpose, and their relationship not only to the rest of s. 725 but also to other provisions of Part XXIII of the *Criminal Code* and to the scheme of the *Criminal Code* as a whole.

[23] I mentioned earlier that the decisive question on this appeal is whether s. 725(1)(c) can be applied without the Crown's consent, as in this case. To that question, the plain words of s. 725 command an affirmative answer. Parliament has provided that trial judges cannot apply paras. (b) and (b.1) without the consent of both the Crown and the offender. No such requirement appears in para. (c). This could not have been a legislative oversight. Had Parliament intended to require the consent of either the Crown or the accused in order for trial judges to apply s. 725(1)(c), it would have said so, as it did in the two immediately preceding paragraphs of the same subsection of the *Code*.

[24] This view of the matter is entirely consistent with the purpose of the provision. Read together, s. 725(1)(c) and s. 725(2) serve two main purposes.

[25] First, s. 725(1)(c) dispels any uncertainty whether a sentencing judge can take into account as aggravating factors other uncharged offences that satisfy its requirements.

[26] Second, s. 725(2) then protects the accused from being punished twice for the same offence: incrementally, as an aggravating circumstance in relation to the offence charged, and then for a second time should a separate charge subsequently be laid in respect of the same facts. This protection is essential, since the usual safeguards would not apply: The accused, if later charged with offences considered by the trial judge under s. 725(1)(c), could neither plead *autrefois convict* nor, unless charged with what is found to be "the same delict," invoke the rule against multiple convictions set out in *Kienapple v. The Queen*, [1975] 1 S.C.R. 729.

[27] I stated at the outset that s. 725(1)(c) was the only true exception to the rule that offenders are punished in Canada only in respect of crimes for which they have been specifically charged and of which they have been validly convicted. I do not consider subs. (1)(b) and (b.1) to be true exceptions to that rule because they both relate to *separately charged offences* for which offenders may be punished only (1) *with their consent* and (2) if they *agree to plead guilty* (para. (b)) or, "*agre[e] with the facts asserted*" and "*acknowledg[e] having committed the offence*" (para. (b.1)).

[28] As we have seen, s. 725(1)(c) permits a court, in determining the sentence, to consider any fact that forms part of the circumstances of the offence even if it could form the basis for a separate charge. These uncharged but proven offences, if they are considered at all, will invariably be treated as "aggravating circumstances" within the meaning of s. 718.2(a) and related provisions of the *Criminal Code*. It is true, of course, that not all aggravating circumstances, or factors, are crimes in themselves. The offender's previous convictions, for example, and the vulnerability of the victim due to infirmity or age, are not offences in themselves. But, like uncharged offences that may be considered under s. 725(1)(c), they are aggravating as opposed to mitigating circumstances because they warrant *more severe*—not *more lenient*—sentences.

[29] This typical effect of s. 725(1)(c) is well illustrated by the Crown's position in this case: The Crown urged the trial judge to sentence Mr. Larche to six years' imprisonment, less time served, *if he applied s. 725(1)(c)*, or three to four years' imprisonment *if he did not*.

[30] On appeal, the three-year sentence imposed by the trial judge was increased to six years due to the requirement in s. 467.14 of the *Criminal Code* that sentences for crimes committed under the direction or for the benefit of criminal organizations be served consecutively. Consistent with its position that s. 725 should not apply and with its submissions at trial, the Crown recommended in the Court of Appeal a total sentence of three years in all—two years on the first count, and one year, consecutive, on the second. That recommendation was reiterated in this Court.

[31] The Crown's position in this regard should not be mistaken for compassion or leniency. It was driven by the Crown's attempt to ensure that Mr. Larche could later be extradited to the United States to face trial there for the corresponding half of his crimes committed in that country. That would expose Mr. Larche, upon conviction, to a mandatory minimum sentence of five years' and a maximum of forty years' imprisonment. The Crown's suggestion that a total sentence of three years be imposed on the Canadian charges, if s. 725(1)(c) were not applied, must be understood in that light.

IV

[32] As appears from the plain wording of both provisions, s. 725(1)(c) and s. 725(2), read together, are at once discretionary and mandatory. Discretionary, because courts *may*—not *must*—consider the facts that could support other charges; mandatory, because if they do, they *must*—not *may*—note on the record that they have done so.

[33] In my view, the discretion afforded judges by s. 725(1)(c) is not trumped by s. 718.2, which enumerates principles of sentencing that courts "shall ... take into consideration." One of these principles, set out in s. 718.2(a), is that "a sentence should be increased or reduced to account for any relevant aggravating or mitigating circumstances." Though framed in mandatory terms—"shall" and "should"—s. 718.2 must be read in its entire context and in its grammatical and ordinary sense harmoniously with the scheme of the Act, the object of the Act, and the intention of Parliament: see *65302 British Columbia Ltd. v. Canada*, [1999] 3 S.C.R. 804, at para. 50.

[34] I turn first to the context of s. 718.2. It is part of a detailed, intricate and comprehensive sentencing scheme introduced by Parliament, as I have already mentioned, in 1995. The "Fundamental purpose of sentencing" and its objectives are set out in s. 718. Under the heading "Fundamental principle," s. 718.1 then provides that "[a] sentence must be proportionate to the gravity of the offence and the degree of responsibility of the offender." In this context and under the heading "Other sentencing principles," s. 718.2 then states:

> 718.2 A court that imposes a sentence shall also take into consideration the following principles:
>> (a) a sentence should be increased or reduced to account for any relevant aggravating or mitigating circumstances relating to the offence or the offender, and, without limiting the generality of the foregoing ... .

Taking this principle into consideration does not require the court to apply it without regard to the other principles of sentencing set out in the *Code* or in binding decisions of the courts. Nor does it override s. 725.

V

[36] It was argued before us that there is an implicit requirement of consent of either the accused, or the Crown—or both—before s. 725(1)(c) can apply.

[37] The Crown submits that it would be [translation] "absurd" and would violate prosecutorial discretion to hold that s. 725(1)(c) allows the accused to [translation] "unilaterally" avoid extradition or escape a more severe sentence resulting from the Crown's decision to segment charges. It follows, says the Crown, that s. 725(1)(c) cannot be applied without the Crown's consent.

[38] This submission fails because s. 725(1)(c) is not subject to "unilateral" application by *either* of the parties. Its application remains at all times subject to the sentencing judge's discretion.

[39] It is true that prosecutorial discretion in the laying of charges will not lightly be interfered with by the courts. But proceedings cannot be delayed abusively to increase punishment: *R v. Parisien* (1971), 3 C.C.C. (2d) 433 (B.C.C.A.), particularly at p. 437. Nor can offences be artificially fractioned in the pursuit of a like objective.

[40] In the present case, the Court of Appeal held that s. 725(1)(c) can only be applied with the consent of the accused. Applying its previous decision in *R v. Pearson*, [2001] R.J.Q. 69, the court stated:

> [TRANSLATION] If s. 725(1)(c) can be applied only with the consent of the accused, it must therefore be because this provision permits the court to consider facts *extrinsic* to the offence to which *the accused has pleaded guilty*. Given the right of every accused person to be presumed innocent, it cannot be that the provision permits the court to consider facts not strictly within the framework of the offence for which the accused is to be punished unless the accused has been tried for [the other] offence. [Emphasis in original; para. 25.]

[41] This position flows from a legitimate concern that an accused's conviction or plea of guilt on one charge could be hijacked for the purpose of punishing that accused for unanticipated accusations of wrongdoing. An indictment must be sufficiently precise factually for the accused to grasp the reproached circumstances or "transaction," and sufficiently precise legally to permit the accused to know which charge he or she must answer among the various charges that might characterize the act: *R v. G.R.*, [2005] 2 S.C.R. 371, 2005 SCC 45.

[42] However, with respect for the contrary view, this concern does not justify reading in the requirement of the accused's consent where the legislator has declined to provide for it. On the contrary, in s. 724(3)(e), the legislator has specifically provided a procedure for considering aggravating facts over the accused's objection.

[43] Section 724(3)(e) provides that "[w]here there is a dispute with respect to any fact that is relevant to the determination of a sentence, ... the prosecutor must establish, by proof beyond a reasonable doubt, the existence of any aggravating fact." As I have already said, the facts relevant to the determination of a sentence in accordance with s. 725(1)(c) would normally be aggravating facts. A dispute arises when the accused refuses to recognize the veracity of such facts, or, to put it another way, does not consent to the application of s. 725(1)(c). This procedure appears to me to contemplate the application of s. 725(1)(c) without the accused's consent.

[44] The requirement in s. 724 of proof beyond a reasonable doubt is imperative in light of the presumption of innocence, which applies to *all* alleged offences. The finality of s. 725(1)(c) is to increase punishment on the basis of an uncharged offence. Where the offender disputes his guilt of that offence, the presumption of innocence applies.

[45] In addition to the requirement of proof beyond a reasonable doubt, the legislator has provided two other safeguards in s. 725(1)(c). Applied with vigour, these three safeguards are together adequate to address the important concerns expressed by the Quebec Court of Appeal in *Pearson* and again in the present case.

[46] First, as Rosenberg JA observed in *R v. Edwards* (2001), 54 O.R. (3d) 737 (C.A.), "the occasions on which [s. 725(1)(c)] may be invoked are carefully circumscribed by the requirement that the facts form part of the circumstances of the predicate offence" (para. 35). Unrelated offences, which the offender would not expect to be confronted with, are excluded. Second, judges can be relied on, in the exercise of their discretion under s. 725(1)(c), to decline to consider uncharged offences if this would result in unfairness to the accused—or for that matter, to the Crown, for example in taking the Crown by surprise so as to foreclose prematurely the laying of additional charges.

[47] Section 725(1)(c) has three components, which may be broken down this way: "In determining the sentence, a court … [1] may consider any facts [2] forming part of the circumstances of the offence [3] that could constitute the basis for a separate charge." The use of the word "may" signifies that the provision is discretionary, as I have already mentioned. The requirements of "forming part of the circumstances of the offence" and the necessity that these facts be capable of constituting "the basis for a separate charge" are two necessary preconditions for the exercise of that discretion.

[48] I begin by considering the requirement that the facts form part of the circumstances of the offence. Parliament has made plain the need to establish a nexus or "connexity" between the uncharged criminal conduct and the offence for which the offender has been convicted.

[49] Care must also be taken, in applying s. 725 over the accused's objection, to ensure that the sentencing hearing is not transformed into a "trial within a trial." This is relevant to a court's exercise of discretion, once the threshold requirements of s. 725(1)(c) have been met, especially given the need for the accused to anticipate the extent of their jeopardy and the right to jury trial for certain offences. But the need to avoid a series of "spin-off" trials at the sentencing stage is, at best, of marginal value in determining whether an uncharged offence forms part of the circumstances of the offence for which the accused must be sentenced.

[50] In my view, whether facts form part of the circumstances of the offence must ultimately be resolved on a case-by-case basis. Broadly speaking, however, there do appear to me to be two general categories of cases where a sufficient connection may be said to exist. These two categories, as we shall see, are not hermetic or mutually exclusive, and will often overlap.

[51] The first would be connexity either in time or place, or both. This flows from the ideal animating s. 725(1)(c): In principle, a single transaction should be subject to a single determination of guilt and a single sentence that takes into account all of the circumstances. In its application, this principle is subject, of course, to the constraints fixed by Parliament in the governing provisions of the *Criminal Code*, including, notably, s. 725.

[52] In *Edwards*, Rosenberg JA refers to the concept of *res gestae* as applied in *R v. Gourgon* (1981), 58 C.C.C. (2d) 193 (B.C.C.A.). The notion of *res gestae*—or "things done" (*Black's Law Dictionary* (8th ed. 2004), at p. 1335)—relates to a close spatial and temporal connection, and may therefore be helpful in this context.

[53] In *R v. Paré*, [1987] 2 S.C.R. 618, this Court considered whether culpable homicide perpetrated "while committing" an indecent assault had to be "exactly coincidental" with the underlying assault, or merely form part of the same sequence of events or transaction. Wilson J, for a unanimous court, adopted the transactional definition (see pp. 632 and 634).

[54] Both *res gestae* and the phrase "while committing" are narrower than the expression "facts forming part of the circumstances of the offence" employed in s. 725(1)(c). The "circumstances" of an offence are more than the immediate transaction in the course of which it transpires. Thus, in addition to encompassing the facts of a single transaction, s. 725(1)(c) also applies, in my view, to the broader category of related facts that inform the court about the "circumstances" of the offence more generally.

[55] "Facts" (or uncharged offences) of this sort that have occurred in various locations or at different times cannot properly be said to form part of the transaction covered by

the charge for which the offender is to be sentenced. Recourse to s. 725(1)(c) may nevertheless be had where the facts in question bear so close a connection to the offence charged that they form part of the circumstances surrounding its commission. In determining whether they satisfy this requirement of connexity, the court should give appropriate weight to their proximity in time and to their probative worth as evidence of system or of an unbroken pattern of criminal conduct.

[56] In this case, Sansfaçon JCQ made plain in his reasons that it was of the very essence of the enterprise that cannabis would be exported and sold in the United States and that the proceeds would be repatriated to Canada. From the perspective of both object and *modus operandi*, this enterprise did not stop at the border. Its constituent elements were seamlessly connected and, considered globally, the offences charged were in fact committed partly north and partly south of the border. Accordingly, I am satisfied that the facts set out in all three notes "form[ed] part of the circumstances of the offence" and therefore met the requirement of connexity.

[57] The second requirement of s. 725(1)(c) is that the facts "could constitute the basis for a separate charge." The question is whether that means a separate charge *in Canada*. I believe that it does. To hold otherwise would permit Canadian courts, through the indirect mechanism of s. 725, to punish for crimes *entirely* committed abroad and thus to arrogate unto themselves an extraterritorial jurisdiction not vested in them by Parliament.

[58] This jurisdictional requirement is particularly relevant to the third note entered by the trial judge. It relates to an uncharged offence that was committed entirely in the United States and, in particular, to an incident that occurred in Vermont on May 31, 2002. Acting on information provided by the RCMP, the American Drug Enforcement Administration ("DEA") began on that day to follow Mr. Larche as he headed towards the Canadian border with US$110,000 in cash. Mr. Larche sensed that he was under police surveillance. In the apparent hope of later recuperating the money, he deposited it precipitously as a down payment on a "Yankee Barn" home. The DEA, however, was by then not far behind—and "beat him to the draw."

[59] The test for territorial jurisdiction according to *Libman v. The Queen*, [1985] 2 S.C.R. 178, is a "real and substantial connection" to Canada (*United States of America v. Lépine*, [1994] 1 S.C.R. 286). Facts that form "part of the circumstances of the offence" may *often*—but will not *always*—have a real and substantial connection to Canada. The two phrases are neither synonymous nor co-extensive, though the inquiries they mandate may sometimes overlap. Thus, my earlier conclusion that the third note forms part of the circumstances of the offence does not necessarily mean that it also has the required "real and substantial connection" to Canada.

[60] A real and substantial connection has been found to be absent in more compelling cases than this one. For example, in *R v. B.(O.)* (1997), 116 C.C.C. (3d) 189 (Ont. C.A.), a Canadian trucker sexually assaulted his 13-year-old Canadian granddaughter in his Canadian registered vehicle while travelling through the US en route back to Canada. It was held that Canadian courts did not have jurisdiction.

[61] While on the day of the "Yankee Barn" home incident Mr. Larche intended to operate in the same fashion as usual, fate intervened and he never made it back to Canada with the money. The event took place entirely in the United States. I agree with the Court of Appeal that Canadian courts therefore have no jurisdiction over it, and I would dismiss the cross-appeal formed by Mr. Larche in that regard.

[62] On the facts of this case, considering the criminal enterprise as a whole, a real and substantial connection to Canada *did* exist, however, for the facts contained in the first two notes. These facts are analogous to the foreign component of a transnational fraud headquartered in Canada, over which Canadian courts have jurisdiction according to *Libman*.

• • •

Appeal and cross-appeal dismissed.

R v Angelillo
2006 SCC 55, [2006] 2 SCR 728

CHARRON J (McLachlin CJ and Bastarache, LeBel, and Deschamps JJ concurring):

1. Introduction

[1] During sentencing, is it appropriate for the court to consider evidence of facts tending to establish the commission of another offence in respect of which the offender has been charged but not convicted? If such evidence is admissible in principle, is it in the interests of justice in the instant case to allow the Crown to introduce this fresh evidence on appeal?

[2] After pleading guilty to a charge of theft, Gennaro Angelillo was sentenced to a term of imprisonment of two years less a day to be served in the community, subject to his complying with certain conditions that are not in issue in this appeal. At the time of sentencing, Crown counsel was unaware that Mr. Angelillo was under police investigation once again for incidents that had occurred after his guilty plea and that later led to new charges. Relying on that evidence, the Crown introduced three motions in the Quebec Court of Appeal in which it sought leave to introduce fresh evidence, leave to appeal the sentence and a stay of sentence. The Court of Appeal dismissed the motion to introduce fresh evidence, because in its view [translation] "[t]his evidence is not relevant" and because "[t]o accept what the prosecution is proposing would mean accepting that the respondent can be punished more severely for committing an offence of which he might be found not guilty" ([2004] QJ No. 11670 (QL), at paras. 6 and 14). The court also dismissed the other two motions. The Crown has appealed to this Court.

• • •

[4] The Crown submits that the Court of Appeal erred in holding that evidence of facts tending to establish the commission of another offence is irrelevant to the determination of the appropriate sentence, regardless of the purpose being pursued, unless the offence in question resulted in a conviction. The Crown wishes to produce this fresh evidence not to prove that the other offence was committed, but for the sole purpose of establishing Mr. Angelillo's character—a distinction that was accepted by the Ontario Court of Appeal in *R v. Edwards* (2001), 155 C.C.C. (3d) 473, but rejected by the Court of Appeal in the case at bar. In light of the sentencing submissions, and more particularly of the pre-sentence report, according to which Mr. Angelillo [translation] "has done some soul-searching, which seems to be sincere, about his inappropriate behaviour" and his

"time in court [has] had a major deterrent effect," the Crown contends that the fresh evidence easily meets the requirement of relevance.

[5]   Although I have concluded that the fresh evidence is relevant and I recognize that, in principle, evidence of facts tending to establish the commission of another offence of which the offender has not been convicted can in certain cases be admitted to enable the court to determine a just and appropriate sentence, I would, for the reasons that follow, dismiss the appeal. Since the fresh evidence constitutes the basis for outstanding charges against Mr. Angelillo for which he has not yet stood trial, it can be admitted only in the context of the procedure provided for in s. 725(1)(b) or (b.1) *Cr. C.* The conditions for that procedure include a requirement that the offender's consent be obtained. Furthermore, I feel that the Crown has not shown due diligence. Accordingly, the Court of Appeal's decision not to admit the fresh evidence is affirmed and the appeal is dismissed.

• • •

[17]   ... I feel that it may be helpful to make a few general comments regarding the relevance of evidence of acts that have resulted neither in charges nor in convictions, since the Court of Appeal seems to have rejected out of hand the reasoning of Rosenberg JA of the Ontario Court of Appeal in *Edwards*. The court stated in particular that it did not see the distinction Rosenberg JA had drawn in saying that evidence of such acts cannot be adduced for the purpose of obtaining a disproportionate sentence against the offender for the offence in question or of punishing the offender for an offence of which he or she has not been convicted, but that such evidence can be adduced to shed light on the offender's background and character. In my view, Rosenberg JA was correct in drawing that distinction, and it is an important one. I will therefore begin by discussing certain general principles relating to the admissibility of extrinsic evidence for sentencing purposes before commenting on the relevance of the evidence the Crown wished to adduce in the case at bar.

3.2 Presumption of Innocence and Sentencing

[18]   Every accused person has the right to be presumed innocent. This fundamental right is not only set out in s. 6 *Cr. C*, but is also guaranteed by s. 11(d) of the *Canadian Charter of Rights and Freedoms*. However, the presumption of innocence is not irrebuttable. At the sentencing stage, it has obviously been rebutted with respect to the offence of which the accused has been convicted. There is therefore no question that, in determining the just and appropriate sentence, the judge can consider the underlying facts of the offence that has been proved. Moreover, sentencing is an individualized process in which the court must take into account not only the circumstances of the offence, but also the specific circumstances of the offender. I would like to note at the outset that the requirements for admissibility and the standard of proof to be applied in establishing all the relevant circumstances for sentencing purposes are issues that have already been considered by this Court, and that they are not in any way new principles.

• • •

3.3 Sentencing Principles

[22]   The principles of sentencing are now codified in ss. 718 to 718.2 *Cr. C.* These provisions confirm that sentencing is an individualized process in which the court must take into account not only the circumstances of the offence, but also the specific circumstances

of the offender (see *Gladue*; *Proulx*, at para. 82). Thus, the objectives of sentencing cannot be fully achieved unless the information needed to assess the circumstances, character and reputation of the accused is before the court. The court must therefore consider facts extrinsic to the offence, and the proof of those facts often requires the admission of additional evidence.

[23] Since the offender must be punished only for the offence in issue, the court will generally not admit evidence of other offences that have not been proved. In the present case, the Court of Appeal rightly referred to the following comment by LeBel JA in *R v. Pelletier* (1989), 52 C.C.C. (3d) 340, at p. 346:

> [TRANSLATION] While the accused's character may be shown, and his previous criminal record established, the sentencing process must not become the occasion for indirectly punishing the accused for offences which have not been established by the normal means of proof and procedure, or that one did not wish to bring.

[24] There are many provisions of the *Criminal Code* under which evidence that is, by nature, capable of showing that the offender has committed another offence can be admitted at the sentencing hearing. First, evidence of any prior convictions may be adduced. The admissibility of such extrinsic evidence does not generally pose any problems. For example, s. 721(3)(b) provides that, unless otherwise specified by the court, any pre-sentence report must contain the history of prior convictions. There is no doubt that the court may take prior convictions into account in determining the appropriate sentence. In taking them into account, however, the court must not punish the offender again. The fundamental principle of proportionality requires that the sentence be proportionate to the gravity of the offence and the degree of responsibility of the offender; a prior conviction cannot, therefore, justify a disproportionate sentence. This principle, which is set out in s. 718.1 *Cr. C.*, assures repeat offenders the right not to be "punished ... again," as guaranteed in s. 11(h) of the *Charter*. The sentence imposed on a repeat offender may well be more severe, but this is not contrary to the offender's right not to be punished again. From the standpoint of proportionality, the sentence imposed in such a case is merely a reflection of the individualized sentencing process.

· · ·

[26] Since the fresh evidence in the present case has resulted in new charges against Mr. Angelillo, s. 725(1)(b) or (b.1) could have been invoked in respect of those charges, but neither of these provisions could be applied without Mr. Angelillo's consent. On the other hand, s. 725(1)(c)—under which a court may consider facts forming part of the circumstances of the offence that have not resulted in charges—does not require the offender's consent. The scope of that provision is discussed in *R v. Larche*, 2006 SCC 56, [2006] 2 SCR 762. I will simply note, for the purposes of my analysis, that s. 725(1)(c) would have been inapplicable even if new charges had not been laid against Mr. Angelillo, because the facts alleged in the fresh evidence did not "[form] part of the circumstances of the offence" within the meaning of that provision. When the conditions set out in s. 725 are met, the consideration of other offences does not violate the offender's rights. In such cases, as specified by Parliament, the court must note on the information or indictment any charges or facts considered in determining the sentence, and s. 725(2) provides that "no further proceedings may be taken with respect to any offence described in those charges or disclosed by those facts."

[27] Third, if none of the paragraphs of s. 725(1) are applicable, the evidence in the instant case may be the type of extrinsic evidence that was in issue in *Edwards*. As Rosenberg JA recognized, there may be situations in which evidence that relates to one of the sentencing objectives or principles set out in the *Criminal Code* shows that the offender has committed another offence but *never been charged with or convicted of it*. Such facts may nevertheless be relevant and must not automatically be excluded in every case. As is often the case, the admissibility of the evidence will depend on the purpose for which its admission is sought. For example, let us assume that—as happens too often, unfortunately—a man is convicted of assaulting his spouse. The fact that he abused his spouse in committing the offence is an aggravating circumstance under s. 718.2(a)(ii). Section 718 requires the court to determine the appropriate sentence that will, among other things, denounce unlawful conduct, deter the offender from re-offending, separate the offender from society where necessary, and promote a sense of responsibility in the offender and acknowledgment of the harm he or she has done. It is therefore important for the court to obtain all relevant information. This is why several provisions of the *Criminal Code* authorize the admission of evidence at the sentencing hearing.

• • •

[30] I now return to my example of the man who has assaulted his spouse. The extrinsic evidence could establish that this was an isolated incident for which the offender has expressed remorse and that the offender has demonstrated an ability to change his behaviour to prevent any risk of re-offending. However, the evidence could also show, on the contrary, that it was a common occurrence in the couple's relationship and one that could well occur each time the offender is intoxicated or frustrated. In the latter case, the offender would not be able to argue that facts extrinsic to the offence that demonstrate his violent character are irrelevant, on the basis that this evidence may show that he has committed other assaults in respect of which he has been neither charged nor convicted. These facts are relevant and, in my opinion, are admissible in principle because they relate to the sentencing objectives and principles that are expressly set out in the *Criminal Code*. The offender cannot invoke the presumption of innocence to *exclude* character evidence, since that presumption has in fact been rebutted with respect to the offence of which he has been convicted.

[31] I cannot agree with Fish J, who would admit no evidence of acts tending to establish the commission of another offence in respect of which the offender has not been charged, except in the context of s. 725(1)(c). Under that provision, as is explained in *Larche*, the court may consider any facts *forming part of the circumstances of the offence* that could constitute the basis for a separate charge. I concede that there may be cases in which such facts are also relevant to the offender's character or reputation. But it is not always easy to tie evidence of reputation or character to a separate offence. Nor does such evidence always form part of the circumstances of the offence—sometimes it only forms part of the circumstances of the offender. With respect, if Fish J were right, a pre-sentence report setting out facts demonstrating that the offender has a violent character, is a drug addict, has no respect for the court's authority or has not learned his or her lesson could violate the presumption of innocence, since such facts could very well tend to establish the commission of various offences, including assault, possession of narcotics and breach of recognizance. I do not believe this to be the effect of the presumption of innocence. The presumption does not constitute a general exclusionary rule of evidence that precludes the admission of all

extrinsic evidence relevant to sentencing for the offence in issue on the basis that it might establish the commission of another offence. This does not mean that the offender has no procedural protection where extrinsic evidence is concerned. There are a number of other principles that assure the offender's right to a fair trial. I will explain this.

[32] If the extrinsic evidence is contested, the prosecution must prove it. Since the facts in question will doubtless be aggravating facts, they must be proved beyond a reasonable doubt (s. 724(3)(e)). The court can sentence the offender only for the offence of which he or she has been convicted, and the sentence must be proportionate to the gravity of that offence. In addition, the judge can and must exclude otherwise relevant evidence if its prejudicial effect outweighs its probative value such that the offender's right to a fair trial is jeopardized. Finally, the court must draw a distinction between considering facts establishing the commission of an uncharged offence for the purpose of punishing the accused *for that other offence*, and considering them to establish the offender's character and reputation or risk of re-offending for the purpose of determining the appropriate sentence for *the offence of which he or she has been convicted*. In my example, the sentence imposed on a violent offender may well be more restrictive than the sentence imposed on an offender who has committed an isolated act, but this is in no way contrary to the presumption of innocence. The sentence may also be more restrictive in the case of a repeat offender if the Crown presents evidence of the offender's criminal record, but this does not violate the offender's right, guaranteed by s. 11(h) of the *Charter*, not to be "punished ... again." In both cases, again from the standpoint of proportionality, the more severe sentence is merely a reflection of the individualized sentencing process.

[33] Finally, Fish J fears that the Crown could easily, and even in good faith, avoid the application of s. 725 by withdrawing or postponing a new charge for the sole purpose of introducing evidence of subsequent acts as aggravating facts in order to obtain a more severe sentence (para. 59). In my view, there is no real danger that this would happen. It must be recalled, as Fish J himself mentions in *Larche*, at para. 39, that "proceedings cannot be delayed abusively to increase punishment: *R v. Parisien* (1971), 3 C.C.C. (2d) 433 (B.C.C.A.)." In *Parisien*, the Court of Appeal reduced the sentence because of the Crown's actions.

· · ·

[38] For these reasons, the Court of Appeal's decision not to admit the fresh evidence is affirmed and the appeal is dismissed.

FISH J (Binnie J concurring):

I

[39] I agree with Justice Charron that the appeal should be dismissed. I agree as well with the reasons on which her conclusion rests.

[40] With respect, however, I do not share my colleague's view that sentencing courts may consider uncharged *and unrelated* offences. Parliament has addressed the issue in s. 725(1)(c) of the *Criminal Code*, R.S.C. 1985, and c. C-46. In virtue of that provision, sentencing courts may consider uncharged offences only if they are related to the offence charged—that is to say, only if they consist in "facts forming part of the circumstances [of the crime for which the accused is to be sentenced]." And Parliament has taken care

to protect offenders from being twice punished in this regard: Offences considered by the sentencing court pursuant to s. 725(1)(c) cannot form the basis of further proceedings against the offender.

[41] Justice Charron would permit sentencing courts to consider uncharged offences even if they are unrelated, and she would remove for these unrelated offences the protection that Parliament has expressly provided for related offences. Moreover, as we shall see, this proposal rests on the doubtful proposition that evidence of an aggravating factor—other offences—is not introduced for purposes of punishment although it will almost invariably have that effect.

· · ·

III

[46] Parliament put in place barely a decade ago a comprehensive set of statutory provisions on sentencing. As Justice Charron mentions, these provisions together form "a true penological code" (para. 21). And as part of that "code," Parliament has set out in s. 725 the requirements for considering, in the determination of a sentence, other offences for which the offender has been neither tried nor convicted.

[47] *Charged* but untried offences, as in this case, cannot be considered unless they meet the requirements of s. 725(1)(b) or (b.1). As my colleague explains, those conditions have not been met and it is for that reason that they could not be considered in determining Mr. Angelillo's sentence—even if the Crown had proceeded with diligence.

[48] The facts underlying these charged offences are no less relevant to Mr. Angelillo's "background and character" than they would be if charges had not been laid. My colleague nonetheless finds, and I agree of course, that evidence of those facts could not be admitted because it failed to satisfy the requirements for its admission established by Parliament in s. 725(1)(b) and (b.1) of the *Criminal Code*. Yet she would admit that evidence if the charges had not—or not yet—been laid. As mentioned at the outset I do not share that view.

[49] In any event, Parliament has provided in s. 725(1)(c) that *uncharged* offences may only be considered if they are based on "facts forming part of the circumstances of the offence" for which the offender is to be sentenced. For the sake of brevity, I refer to these offences as "connected" or "related" offences.

[50] In *R v. Larche*, 2006 SCC 56, [2006] 2 S.C.R. 762, released concurrently, I have dealt in some detail with this requirement of connexity. The criteria set out there should in large measure allay the understandable concerns mentioned by Justice Charron with respect to cases of domestic abuse, where a history of similar incidents that have never given rise to charges would nonetheless form "part of the circumstances of the offence" within the meaning of s. 725(1)(c): *Larche*, at paras. 54-55.

[51] Parliament has decided that not all evidence relevant to the background and character of the offender may be considered by the sentencing judge. The rule proposed by Justice Charron would give a court the discretionary power to consider uncharged offences that do *not* form part of the circumstances of the offence. This would in practice override the inherent restriction of s. 725(1)(c) and render it entirely superfluous.

[52] The rule proposed by Justice Charron would also lack the statutory procedural safeguards that Parliament has provided with regard to s. 725 of the *Criminal Code*. Section 725(2) prohibits the subsequent prosecution of uncharged offences considered by a

court in determining the sentence under s. 725(1)(c). These uncharged offences, once considered, must be noted on the information or indictment. This protects the accused from double punishment, unless the conviction for the offence of which the offender has been found guilty is set aside or quashed on appeal.

[53] It is true, as my colleague mentions, that previous convictions may properly be taken into account in determining the sentence for a subsequent offence. Here, however, the question was whether the sentencing court could consider *subsequent offences* for which the respondent *had not been convicted*. My colleague would answer that question in the affirmative, but for the fact that charges had already been laid. In her view, a sentencing court may consider unrelated and uncharged offences, previous or subsequent, under the rubric "background and character"—or, more accurately perhaps in this case, "*future* background and character." With respect, I do not agree.

[54] In the case of previous convictions, the book has been closed—no further proceedings may be instituted. In the present case, proceedings not only can be, but in fact *were*, instituted.

[55] My colleague's proposal would permit subsequent prosecution of uncharged offences that have already led to a stiffer penalty for a charged offence. And, where the uncharged offence relates to facts that occurred after those for which the offender has been charged and convicted, a "feedback loop" would almost invariably operate. The offender would then be more severely punished on the first offence because he or she later committed a second offence. Once that second offence has been made the subject of a charge, the offender would likely be punished more severely on this new charge *because of the earlier offence for which the offender has already received a stiffer sentence on account of the second offence which was not yet then charged.*

[56] In this context, I note in passing that *R v. Edwards* (2001), 155 C.C.C. (3d) 473 (Ont. C.A.), and *Lees v. The Queen*, [1979] 2 S.C.R. 749, upon which my colleague relies, are both readily distinguishable from the present matter. In *Edwards*, the contentious facts related in part to an offence that was said to have been committed 18 years earlier in Jamaica and no charge could therefore be laid in Canada. The other contentious facts related to evidence of a "pattern of violence," a matter I have already considered above (para. 50). In *Lees*, no charge had been laid either, and it was "even doubtful whether there was a possible offence" (McIntyre J, at p. 754).

· · ·

[58] Justice Charron disagrees only with respect to *uncharged* offences, which are in her view admissible if they go to "background and character," whether or not they comply with s. 725(1)(c) of the *Criminal Code*. In her opinion, as I understand it, if the uncharged offences go to background and character *and comply* with s. 725(1)(c), they cannot form the basis of further proceedings; but if they go to background and character *and do not comply* with s. 725(1)(c), the offender may subsequently be charged and punished for those previously considered offences. In short, as mentioned earlier, Justice Charron would permit sentencing courts to consider uncharged offences even if they are unrelated, and she would remove for these unrelated offences the protection that Parliament has expressly provided for related offences.

· · ·

[64] In this light, I am unable to agree that evidence of uncharged offences, an acknowledged aggravating factor, can be admitted on the ground that it goes to "background and

character" *but not to punishment.* Offenders whose sentences are increased on account of this aggravating factor—uncharged offences—will be forgiven for thinking that it has caused them to be more severely punished.

[65] H.L.A. Hart put this aspect of the matter admirably almost a half-century ago. Dealing then with the putative distinction between considerations of "background and character" and "punishment" in the determination of sentences—in the context of what had since at least 1908 been characterized in central Europe as "double-track" penology—Professor Hart stated:

> [T]he "double-track" system has been elaborated in ways which may seem to us somewhat metaphysical: punishment which is to be "guilt-adequate," i.e. orientated towards the criminal act, is carefully distinguished from mere "measures" orientated to the criminal's character and the needs of society. The recent German Penal Code preserves this distinction though it is regretted as artificial by many. Certainly the prisoner who after serving a three-year sentence is told that his punishment is over but that a seven-year period of preventive detention awaits him and that this is a "measure" of social protection, not a punishment, might think he was being tormented by a barren piece of conceptualism—though he might not express himself in that way.

(*Punishment and the Elimination of Responsibility* (1962), at p. 12.)

Nor would the prisoner be much moved by my colleague's explanation that a more severe sentence for a charged offence is not punishment for the uncharged offence that is the reason for its increased severity.

• • •

IV

[69] It is not my position, as my colleague suggests (at para. 31), that offenders can invoke the presumption of innocence to exclude evidence of unrelated and uncharged offences. Nor is there any need for them to do so: In my respectful view, that evidence is inadmissible for the reasons set out above. I think it nonetheless useful to add a brief word on Justice Charron's suggestion that the offender cannot invoke the presumption of innocence to exclude the evidence of untried offences because "that presumption has in fact been rebutted *with respect to the offence of which he has been convicted*" (para. 30 (emphasis added)).

[70] It is true of course, as Justice Charron mentions, that the presumption of innocence is overcome by a conviction—but only by a conviction *for the offence charged.* A finding of guilt on charges that have been tried has no bearing on the offender's presumed innocence regarding offences that were never charged or admitted.

The court was unanimous in *Larche*, and unanimous in the result in *Angelillo*, but there remain divided views on the extent to which the judge may consider evidence of other conduct when deciding on sentence. One division relates to the admissibility—for any purpose—of evidence of conduct that is unrelated to the offence for sentence. Another point is whether territorial jurisdiction is a constraining factor. A related issue concerns the discretion to exclude evidence for purposes of sentencing.

R v PM
2012 ONCA 162

ROSENBERG JA (MacPherson and Epstein JJA concurring):

[The accused was charged with several sexual offences against his daughter. He was also charged with offences of production and possession of child pornography. Some items of pornography involved his daughter; many did not. The trial judge refused to view some of the images.]

[22] The Crown's principal submission on this appeal was that the trial judge erred in refusing to view the disc containing the child pornography and the videos of the appellant sexually assaulting the victim. Crown counsel argued that, having admitted the disc as an exhibit, the trial judge was bound to view that exhibit as he would any other piece of real evidence. Alternatively, if the trial judge did not admit the disc as an exhibit then he erred in failing to do so.

[23] An issue arose at the hearing of the appeal as to whether the trial judge had in fact admitted the disc as an exhibit. In my view, he marked the disc for identification but did not admit the disc as evidence. Just prior to the excerpts from the trial judge's reasons set out in paragraph 17 of this decision, the trial judge said the following: "I will file it and give it an exhibit number for identification, should it become important at a later date in another court. I do not intend to view it." Then, in his reasons the trial judge indicated that he found that the prejudicial effect of admitting the evidence outweighed its probative value. This is the language of exclusion of evidence.

[24] Since the trial judge refused to admit the disc as evidence, the Crown appeal raises two questions. First, whether the trial judge has the discretion to refuse to admit relevant evidence at a sentence hearing; and second, if the judge does have such discretion, whether it was properly exercised in this case.

[25] Section 723 of the *Criminal Code* provides that before determining the sentence, the court "shall" give the prosecutor and the offender the opportunity to make submissions with respect to any facts relevant to the sentence imposed, and "shall" hear any relevant evidence presented by the prosecutor and the offender. Further, s. 726.1 provides that in determining the sentence, a court "shall" consider any relevant evidence placed before it. Nevertheless, in my view, a trial judge at sentencing should exclude otherwise relevant evidence proffered by the Crown where the prejudicial effect of the evidence outweighs its probative value.

[26] In *R. v. Angelillo*, 2006 SCC 55, [2006] 2 S.C.R. 728 at para. 32, Charron J., speaking for the majority of the court, had to consider the admissibility at the sentence hearing of evidence showing the commission of other offences than those for which the offender was being sentenced. After referring to several sections of the *Criminal Code*, including ss. 723 and 726.1, Charron J. confirmed that at the sentence hearing the trial judge "can and must exclude otherwise relevant evidence if its prejudicial effect outweighs its probative value such that the offender's right to a fair trial is jeopardized."

[27] In deciding whether the prejudicial effect of the prosecution evidence outweighs its probative value the judge must consider any number of relevant factors. The weight to be accorded the various factors is primarily a matter for the sentence judge and thus the

judge's decision is entitled to deference. This deference is part of the broader deference owed to trial judges in managing the sentence hearing and determining the sentence. The Supreme Court of Canada has repeatedly recognized that appellate courts owe considerable deference to the trial judge's decision as to the quantum and type of sentence. For example, in *R. v. Shropshire*, [1995] 4 S.C.R. 227 at para. 46:

> An appellate court should not be given free rein to modify a sentencing order simply because it feels that a different order ought to have been made. The formulation of a sentencing order is a profoundly subjective process; the trial judge has the advantage of having seen and heard all of the witnesses whereas the appellate court can only base itself upon a written record. A variation in the sentence should only be made if the court of appeal is convinced it is not fit. That is to say, that it has found the sentence to be clearly unreasonable.

[28] In *R. v. M. (C.A.)*, [1996] 1 S.C.R. 500, Lamer C.J. explained the functional justification for this deference, even where there has not been a full trial because the offender has pled guilty. In particular he noted, at para. 91, that:

> A sentencing judge still enjoys a position of advantage over an appellate judge in being able to directly assess the sentencing submissions of both the Crown and the offender. A sentencing judge also possesses the unique qualifications of experience and judgment from having served on the front lines of our criminal justice system.

[29] In my view, this functional justification applies as much to the conduct of the hearing, including the decision as to whether the prejudicial effect of the proposed evidence outweighs its probative value, as it does to the ultimate decision of quantum. The trial judge, by reason of "experience and judgment from having served on the front lines of our criminal justice system," is in the best position to decide what evidence is required to determine a fit sentence and to decide how, and in what manner, the evidence should be received. It is hardly for this court to decide how the trial judge presiding over a busy trial court should manage sentence hearings. Provided the judge exercises the discretion reasonably and gives the parties the opportunity to fully present their positions, this court ought not interfere.

• • •

EPSTEIN JA (dissenting in part concerning the trial judge's refusal to view the images):

• • •

[69] The explanation in *Mohan* of the weighing of probative value against any prejudicial effect was in the context of expert evidence proffered at trial. The concern was that such evidence would be improperly used by the trier of fact, perhaps by the jury's being unduly impressed by the expert's credentials. It is primarily in the trial context where impermissible reasoning may lead to unfairness that the probative value and prejudicial effect test is used.

[70] As I will explain, sentencing hearings are different. In my view, the differences call for a modification of the general exclusionary rule such that, if relevant to the admissibility analysis at all, the potential prejudice of the evidence in issue should be given less weight.

[71] As my colleague notes, the Supreme Court, in *R. v. Angelillo*, [2006] 2 S.C.R. 728, does refer to the discretion to exclude evidence on the basis that its prejudicial effect

outweighs its probative value in a sentencing hearing. However, it is important to recognize that in *Angelillo* the court was considering the particular issue of whether extrinsic evidence of other offences (uncharged or unproven) allegedly committed by the offender is admissible against him in a sentencing proceeding. Writing for the majority of the court, and responding to the minority's view that such extrinsic evidence would not ordinarily be admissible, Charron J., in *obiter*, was emphasizing the procedural protections offenders have in a sentencing hearing (at paras. 31-32):

> There are a number of other principles that assure the *offender's* right to a fair trial. I will explain this.
>
> If the extrinsic evidence is contested, the prosecution must prove it. Since the facts in question will doubtless be aggravating facts, they must be proved beyond a reasonable doubt (s. 724(3)(e)). The court can sentence the offender only for the offence of which he or she has been convicted, and the sentence must be proportionate to the gravity of that offence. *In addition, the judge can and must exclude otherwise relevant evidence if its prejudicial effect outweighs its probative value such that the offender's right to a fair trial is jeopardized.* [Emphasis added.]

[72] I make three observations concerning the import of *Angelillo*. First, Charron J.'s reference to the general exclusionary rule was in the context of the particular circumstances present in *that case* where extrinsic evidence of as yet unproven unrelated offences is tendered against the offender. Second, it is clear that the focus was on prejudice *to the offender*, and more specifically, to the offender's right to a fair sentencing proceeding. Third, at para. 21, Charron J. emphasized that all prior case law must be read in the light of the sentencing provisions contained in Part XXIII of the *Criminal Code*. This, in my view, includes the legislated focus on relevance in ss. 723 and 726.1 of the *Code*, which specifically address the treatment of evidence in the context of a sentencing hearing. Section 723 provides that before determining a sentence, the court "shall hear any *relevant* evidence presented by the prosecutor or offender," and s. 726.1 directs that "[i]n determining a fit sentence, a court shall consider any *relevant* information placed before it" [Emphases added].

[73] This wording of these provisions demonstrates that at a sentencing hearing, the emphasis is on the relevance of proffered evidence, a point Charron J. appreciated in *Angelillo* at para. 28, where she said:

> Section 723 *requires* the court to give the prosecutor and the defence an opportunity to make submissions with respect to any facts relevant to the sentence to be imposed *and to hear any evidence they see fit to submit*. Section 726.1 clearly states that all this information *must* be considered in determining the sentence. [Emphasis added].

These legislative provisions support the proposition that for the purposes of admitting evidence during a sentencing hearing, the dominant factor is the *relevance* of the evidence.

[74] Parliament's specific focus in this respect is consistent with the unique context of sentencing. The dominant concern addressed by the weighing of prejudice against probative value for the purposes of determining admissibility during the trial itself is that the evidence in issue may lead to impermissible reasoning, either as a result of the evidence being used for an improper purpose or having the potential to inflame the trier of fact— either of which has the potential of rendering the accused's trial unfair. At the sentencing

stage, the trier of fact is always a judge and the issue is no longer guilt but the determination of a fit sentence—a determination for which the trial judge should have as much relevant information as possible; see *R. v. Lévesque*, [2000] 2 S.C.R. 487, at para. 30.

[Leave granted; appeal dismissed.]

R v Virani
2012 ABCA 155

[The accused was convicted of disqualified driving. It was his tenth conviction for this offence. He was sentenced to 12 months in prison, probation for two years, and a driving prohibition of three years.]

THE COURT (Watson, Bielby, and O'Ferrall JJA):

[4] The Crown's first procedural complaint was that the trial judge refused to consider admissible evidence offered by the Crown. The evidence in question consisted of a pre-sentence report and an associated forensic assessment which were prepared concerning the respondent earlier in the history of these proceedings, originally at the request of the defence following the respondent having entered a guilty plea. The guilty plea was struck and the respondent was tried and then found guilty. In the course of the sentencing which followed, the trial judge summarily agreed with defence counsel's objection to the Crown making reference to these items without hearing from Crown counsel or for that matter giving the respondent's counsel much of a chance to bolster his submission [SAB 123/25]. Thereafter both counsel took the ruling as it was.

• • •

[11] There is some merit in the Crown's first procedural objection. It is not open to a trial judge to summarily exclude from consideration evidence which is relevant to sentencing and which is offered by either the Crown or the Defence: see s. 723(2) and s. 726.1 of the *Code*. As reflected by the decisions of *R v Angelillo*, 2006 SCC 55, [2006] 2 S.C.R. 728, and *R v McIvor*, 2008 SCC 11, [2008] 1 S.C.R. 285, the *Code* provides in a rather inclusionary manner for the admission of relevant evidence as to sentence. Nonetheless, as with all evidence, the cases remind us that courts must be attentive to issues of admissibility and to the balance of probative force and prejudice. See also *R v Hunt*, 2002 ABCA 155, 166 C.C.C. (3d) 392 at para. 16.

[12] We note the view expressed by Epstein JA dissenting in *R v M (P)*, 2012 ONCA 162, [2012] O.J. No. 1148 (QL) as to the proper interpretation of *Angelillo*. We agree with her observation at para. 84 in *M (P)* that, if a trial judge is able to dismiss evidence out of hand without looking at it, "the determination of the admissibility of otherwise relevant evidence could be affected by who the trial judge is and the nature of his or her experience adding considerable uncertainty to counsel's preparation for the sentencing hearing." It should be remembered that the proposed evidence here was identified as including a formal pre-sentence report which was prepared by Court direction pursuant to s. 722 of the *Code* and a formal forensic assessment. On that description, it is difficult to see any basis for objection to admissibility. Nor did the trial judge furnish reasons identifying

any. The rationale offered by trial counsel for the respondent was simply that it was prepared prior to the guilty plea. Perhaps if counsel had the opportunity to elaborate on his
objection there might have been more to it, but, quite properly, counsel on appeal does
not attempt to invent something unsaid.

[13] The trial judge erred in law at least in not considering this evidence so that he
could then, if necessary, entertain submissions on admissibility of any parts of it. It is a
classic part of the role of trial judges that they are gatekeepers as to admissibility. Decisions
as to admissibility in the criminal law are nowadays routinely made in light of the trial
judge receiving the evidence first, and then making a decision about it. Indeed, it is hard
to reckon how a trial judge could weigh probative force against prejudice without actually
considering the evidence. The law entrusts trial judges with the ability to then disabuse
themselves of evidence which they recognize and hold to be inadmissible or … more
prejudicial than probative. There is no facial forensic logic to determining cogency or
admissibility without regard to the subject matter.

[14] Conceivably, there may be unusual cases where on the face of things the irrelevance
or inadmissibility of proposed evidence is so plain, or its great prejudicial effect and pale
probative value is so obvious, that a court might hesitate before examining the evidence
and might then require submissions before taking that step. But even then there would
be no presumption that the court could not disabuse itself of the evidence if need be.

[Appeal allowed in part.]

VI. JUDICIAL NOTICE OF RELEVANT FACTS

To what extent may a judge take judicial notice of facts relevant to sentencing? This question
arose incidentally in *Gladue* and has also been posed in several other cases. It is a question
that affects fact-finding not only in relation to the particular offender but also in relation to
the nature and incidence of the offence. At least part of the answer would seem to be
obvious. If the facts in question are in dispute between the parties, they must be proved by
affirmative evidence. If there is no direct dispute on the facts between the parties, might it
be argued nonetheless that the principle of judicial notice is inapplicable to facts that are
contentious in themselves—that is, facts that are a matter of dispute?

R v Gladue
[1999] 1 SCR 688

[This case is considered more fully in Chapter 16, Aboriginal Offenders. The Supreme
Court of Canada considered a wide range of issues relevant to the determination of a fit
sentence for an Aboriginal offender. Reference to judicial notice was made toward the
end of the opinion of Cory and Iacobucci JJ.]

CORY and IACOBUCCI JJ:

[82] The foregoing discussion of guidelines for the sentencing judge has spoken of
that which a judge must do when sentencing an aboriginal offender. This element of duty

is a critical component of s. 718.2(e). The provision expressly provides that a court that imposes a sentence *should* consider all available sanctions other than imprisonment that are reasonable in the circumstances, and *should* pay particular attention to the circumstances of aboriginal offenders. There is no discretion as to whether to consider the unique situation of the aboriginal offender; the only discretion concerns the determination of a just and appropriate sentence.

[83] How then is the consideration of s. 718.2(e) to proceed in the daily functioning of the courts? The manner in which the sentencing judge will carry out his or her statutory duty may vary from case to case. In all instances it will be necessary for the judge to take judicial notice of the systemic or background factors and the approach to sentencing which is relevant to aboriginal offenders. However, for each particular offence and offender it may be that some evidence will be required in order to assist the sentencing judge in arriving at a fit sentence. Where a particular offender does not wish such evidence to be adduced, the right to have particular attention paid to his or her circumstances as an aboriginal offender may be waived. Where there is no such waiver, it will be extremely helpful to the sentencing judge for counsel on both sides to adduce relevant evidence. Indeed, it is to be expected that counsel will fulfil their role and assist the sentencing judge in this way.

[84] However, even where counsel do not adduce this evidence, where for example the offender is unrepresented, it is incumbent upon the sentencing judge to attempt to acquire information regarding the circumstances of the offender as an aboriginal person. Whether the offender resides in a rural area, on a reserve or in an urban centre the sentencing judge must be made aware of alternatives to incarceration that exist whether inside or outside the aboriginal community of the particular offender. The alternatives existing in metropolitan areas must, as a matter of course, also be explored. Clearly the presence of an aboriginal offender will require special attention in pre-sentence reports. Beyond the use of the pre-sentence report, the sentencing judge may and should in appropriate circumstances and where practicable request that witnesses be called who may testify as to reasonable alternatives.

[85] Similarly, where a sentencing judge at the trial level has not engaged in the duty imposed by s. 718.2(e) as fully as required, it is incumbent upon a court of appeal in considering an appeal against sentence on this basis to consider any fresh evidence which is relevant and admissible on sentencing. In the same vein, it should be noted that, although s. 718.2(e) does not impose a statutory duty upon the sentencing judge to provide reasons, it will be much easier for a reviewing court to determine whether and how attention was paid to the circumstances of the offender as an aboriginal person if at least brief reasons are given.

NOTE

The allusion to judicial notice is not developed further in *Gladue*. In this context, it means clearly that judges should take judicial notice of facts relating to systemic and background characteristics of Aboriginal communities. It obviously does not mean that the sentencing of Aboriginal offenders alone would raise this concern about judicial notice because there might be many other sentencing contexts in which systemic or background factors would be material. The extent to which judicial notice should be permitted with respect to such issues is a matter that requires caution. Is it possible, for example, for a judge to take judicial notice of the incidence or prevalence of a certain type of offence within a community? For these purposes, what are the differences among evidence, notice, and mere anecdote or hearsay?

R v Laliberte
2000 SKCA 27 (footnotes omitted)

[The accused, an Aboriginal woman, pleaded guilty to two counts of trafficking in a controlled substance and two counts of possession of the proceeds of trafficking. She was sentenced to a conditional sentence of 12 months' imprisonment, including 4 months of electronically monitored house arrest, two years' probation, and restitution in the amount of $120. The Crown sought leave to appeal. It was granted, and the appeal was dismissed. In the course of his judgment, Vancise JA refers to the question of judicial notice.]

VANCISE JA:

[60] The sentencing judge must also be provided with general information concerning systemic poverty, alcohol and substance abuse, cultural and racial bias in the community at large. As well, the sentencing judge must receive information concerning the particular circumstances surrounding the offence.

[61] The Supreme Court suggested [in *Gladue*] that to accomplish the sentencing task, it would be necessary for the sentencing judge to "take judicial notice of the systemic or background factors and the approach to sentencing which is relevant to aboriginal offenders." [[1999] 1 SCR 688, 731-32 (para 83).] This raises an evidentiary issue which is problematic. Surely in the context of this judgment Justices Cory and Iacobucci are not suggesting that the systemic or background factors are so "notorious" in general as to be capable of proof without evidence or that they can be verified by resort to reports of indisputable accuracy and applied to the particular facts.

[62] The systemic cultural and background factors to which Justices Cory and Iacobucci refer are set out in great detail in *Gladue*. All the factors described are conclusions of fact taken from texts, articles, studies, or commissions of inquiry on aboriginal problems, including the *Report of the Aboriginal Justice Inquiry of Manitoba*, and *The Justice System and Aboriginal People*. Those factors were described as:

> Years of dislocation and economic development have translated, for many aboriginal peoples, into low incomes, high unemployment, lack of opportunities and options, lack or irrelevance of education, substance abuse, loneliness, and community fragmentation. These and other factors contribute to a higher incidence of crime and incarceration.

It will be necessary for the sentencing judge to take into account those factors which have been demonstrated as having caused or contributed to the aboriginal offender being before the court.

[63] The issue of how to deal with discrimination of aboriginal peoples was examined by the Supreme Court in *R v. Williams* [[1998] 1 SCR 1128] in the context of a challenge for cause, where the issue was widespread bias or prejudice in the community which had the potential to impact on the impartiality of a jury. McLachlin J concluded *on the evidence* of that case that there was widespread bias against aboriginal peoples in Canada and there

is evidence that this widespread racism has translated into systemic discrimination in the criminal justice system [at para 58]. McLachlin J did not take judicial notice of that fact.

[64] In *Williams*, the accused called witnesses and tendered evidence to establish widespread prejudice and bias in the community against aboriginal people. This evidence demonstrated there was a reasonable possibility of bias or a realistic potential of racial bias or prejudice on the part of jurors in the context of challenge for cause in the selection of a jury. McLachlin J stated it might not be necessary to duplicate that effort in future cases to establish racial prejudice in the community because the potential for racial prejudice could be demonstrated either by evidence or by judicial notice or by proving facts capable of immediate and accurate verification.

[65] In *R v. Fleury* [[1999] 3 WWR 62 (Sask QB)] Barclay J considered whether widespread bias or prejudice existed in Saskatchewan which might impact on the impartiality of a jury in the context of a challenge for cause. Again, after hearing evidence from an expert in the field and examining reports of commissions of inquiries, he concluded on the evidence that there was systemic racism sufficient to permit the accused to challenge jurors for cause.

[66] Klebuc J in *R v. Carratt* [[1999] SJ No 626 (QB)] refused to take judicial notice of racial bias in the context of a sentencing hearing held to determine whether to impose a conditional sentence on an aboriginal offender. He was unwilling to accept the finding made by Barclay J in *Fleury* that systemic racism exists in Saskatchewan. He found he could not make such a finding in the absence of evidence on that issue in the particular community where the offence occurred. He was unable to determine on the evidence before him whether anti-aboriginal racism existed and had materially affected the particular offender's ability to obtain employment for example, and was the cause of the offender being before the Court.

[67] Klebuc J was satisfied on the evidence of Professor Quigley of the Faculty of Law of the University of Saskatchewan, that aboriginal peoples suffered from poverty, substance abuse and racism and were overrepresented in the prison population. At the end of the day, however, he was unable to find that those factors were the cause of the particular aboriginal offender's criminal conduct and he refused to impose a community-based sentence. I agree generally with the approach he used in attempting to comply with the directives in *Gladue*.

[68] The evidentiary question is thus reduced to: are the systemic or background matters so "notorious" that a sentencing judge can take judicial notice of them without further evidence when deciding whether to apply a restorative approach to sentencing so as to make the system more relevant to aboriginal peoples?

[69] Justices Cory and Iacobucci seem to have provided at least a partial answer to that evidentiary question by stating, immediately after their comments on judicial notice, that it will probably be necessary for some evidence to be adduced to assist the sentencing judge to decide these issues. In my opinion, evidence will be required on the "*Gladue* sentencing hearing" to establish the systemic factors referred to by the Supreme Court as well as to demonstrate how those factors have contributed to the offender being before the court and how those factors should influence the type of sentence to be imposed on the particular aboriginal offender. No operation of the principle of judicial notice will provide enough specific relevant evidence about the particular systemic or background factors which exist in the offender's community. Nor will it provide specific evidence as to

how those factors have affected the particular aboriginal offender and whether they resulted in him being before the Court. It will be necessary for the accused to call some evidence to assist the sentencing judge in determining whether, in the particular community where the offender resides, there are systemic or other background factors which have had an influence on how this particular offender came before the court with the result that there will be a different approach to sentencing and the kind of sentence to be imposed.

If the Supreme Court in *Gladue* intended to approve the use of official reports or social science data as sources of information, further clarification will be required on this point because, as Vancise JA observes in *Laliberte*, the statement by Cory and Iacobucci JJ concerning judicial notice is broad and problematic. For example, what about the personal experience of the judge, a matter that raised controversy when it was considered (in another context) in *R v S (RD)*, [1997] 3 SCR 484? No one expects a judge to dissociate herself from her entire experience as a citizen, a lawyer, or a judge, but personal experience is not always reliable—and might be positively unreliable—as a basis for making decisions on sentence. A judge should be able to rely on her knowledge of local sentencing practices or treatment options, but this should also be expressed in open court and put on the record so that the parties know the basis of the decision. The statutory requirement that the sentencing judge provide reasons for her decision is consistent with this.

Judicial notice dispenses with the need for proof of relevant facts, and it is problematic, to say the least, where those facts are complex and contentious. The personal experience of the judge as a source of relevant factual information is also problematic, either because it might be unreliable or because it might induce the judge to ignore relevant evidence. Some issues require a firm evidentiary foundation before they can affect a sentencing decision. One way of accomplishing this is to produce expert evidence, as was done in *Laliberte*. An issue that illustrates the need for firm evidence is the prevalence or incidence of an offence in the local community. Reliance on such information for stronger sentences is controversial because It Is a form of exemplary justice. Nonetheless, a marked increase in the incidence of an offence or the recognition of a substantial rate of occurrence has been accepted by the courts as a relevant aggravating factor. But a judge cannot rely on her personal experience or observations concerning the court's recent cases as a basis for this decision: see e.g. *R v Priest* (1996), 30 OR (3d) 538, 110 CCC (3d) 289 at 293 (CA). Moreover, courts have demanded solid evidence and not just anecdotal accounts from local police officers: see e.g. *R v Petrovic* (1984), 47 OR (2d) 97 (CA) and *R v Edwards* (1996), 28 OR (3d) 54 (CA).

In *R v Spence*, 2005 SCC 71, [2005] 3 SCR 458, the Supreme Court held that the permissible scope of judicial notice may vary according to the nature of the issue in question and that stricter standards should be applied where the fact in issue is determinative of an issue before the court. This decision signalled a caution against expansive use of judicial notice and provides another good reason to be wary of judicial notice in sentencing decisions. For other comments, see William J Vancise & Patrick Healy, "Judicial Notice in Sentencing" (2002) 65 Sask L Rev 97.

An expansive view of judicial notice in sentencing appears to be favoured in *Lacasse*.

R v Lacasse
2015 SCC 64, [2015] 3 SCR 1089

[The trial judge imposed a sentence of 6.5 years following guilty pleas to two charges of impaired driving causing death. In doing so he took notice of the high incidence of offences of impaired driving in the local district.]

WAGNER J (Abella, Moldaver, Karakatsanis, and Côté JJ concurring):

[87]   In conducting his sentencing analysis, the trial judge also referred to the [TRANS-LATION] "local situation" factor (para. 73) and stressed the need to convey a strong message of general deterrence and denunciation. The Court of Appeal completely over-looked this in its decision. With all due respect, I find that in so doing, the Court of Appeal made another error.

[88]   I note in this regard that the respondent submits that the trial judge erred in considering the particular situation in the Beauce region with regard to impaired driving offences. In my view, the respondent is wrong.

[89]   Even though the *Criminal Code* applies everywhere in the country, local charac-teristics in a given region may explain certain differences in the sentences imposed on offenders by the courts. The frequency of a type of offence in a particular region can certainly be a relevant factor for a sentencing judge. In *M. (C.A.)*, Lamer C.J. stated the following:

> The determination of a just and appropriate sentence is a delicate art which attempts to balance carefully the societal goals of sentencing against the moral blameworthiness of the offender and the circumstances of the offence, *while at all times taking into account the needs and current conditions of and in the community.* [Emphasis added; para. 91.]

He then added the following in the next paragraph:

> As well, sentences for a particular offence should be expected to vary to some degree across various communities and regions in this country, as the "just and appropriate" mix of accepted sentencing goals will depend on the needs and current conditions of and in the particular community where the crime occurred. [para. 92]

[90]   Although the fact that a type of crime occurs frequently in a particular region is not in itself an aggravating factor, there may be circumstances in which a judge might nonetheless consider such a fact in balancing the various sentencing objectives, including the need to denounce the unlawful conduct in question in that place and at the same time to deter anyone else from doing the same thing. It goes without saying, however, that the consideration of this factor must not lead to a sentence that is demonstrably unfit.

[91]   The Quebec Court of Appeal has played an important role in the development of the Canadian case law on this subject. For example, in *R. v. Valiquette*, 2004 CanLII 20126, at paras. 48-50, it affirmed the decision of the trial judge, who had considered an upsurge in crimes involving the production of drugs in the Joliette district in order to emphasize the objectives of denunciation and general deterrence in the determination of a just and reasonable sentence.

[92]   Similarly, the Quebec Court of Appeal found in *R. v. Nguyen*, 2007 QCCA 1500, at para. 7 (CanLII), that, in determining the sentence, the trial judge had been right to take into account the fact that there had been a large number of offences involving the

cultivation of cannabis in certain parts of the Basses-Laurentides region, as well as the existence of a well-developed narcotics trafficking network there. In the Court of Appeal's view, the trial judge had not therefore been wrong to impose a sentence that would be harsh enough to deter individuals who might be tempted by the lure of gain to commit such offences.

[93] Other Canadian courts of appeal have also referred to the principle that the local situation may be one of the relevant factors to consider in determining a just and appropriate sentence: *R. v. Morrissette* (1970), 1 C.C.C. (2d) 307 (Sask. C.A.), at p. 310; *R. v. Laurila*, 2010 BCCA 535, 296 B.C.A.C. 139, at para. 6; *R. v. Woghiren*, 2004 CanLII 46649 (Ont. C.A.), at para. 3.

[94] It is true that considerations of procedural fairness will generally require that a judge who intends to attach weight to the local reality and to the frequency of a crime in a given region offer the parties an opportunity to make representations on the subject. However, this was not an issue in the case at bar, given that the local reality was not in dispute. The record shows that the point about the local reality was raised by the appellant in argument in a timely fashion and that the respondent therefore had all the information he needed in deciding to say nothing in this regard: transcript from September 14, 2013, A.R., vol. II, at p. 91.

[95] In any event, I am of the view that it was open to Judge Couture to take judicial notice of the evil represented by the large number of offences related to drinking and driving that are committed in the Beauce district. Judge Couture was the resident judge in that district. He was therefore in a position to observe and assess the magnitude of the problem in his region, especially given that it is well established in our law that judges can take judicial notice of the contexts in which they perform the duties of their offices: *R. v. Z.Z.*, 2013 QCCA 1498, at para. 68 (CanLII); *R. v. Hernandez*, 2009 BCCA 546, 277 B.C.A.C. 120, at para. 29. This Court stated in *R. v. MacDougall*, [1998] 3 S.C.R. 45, at para. 63, per McLachlin C.J., that trial judges and provincial courts of appeal are in the best position to know the particular circumstances in their jurisdictions. In the case at bar, the frequency of impaired driving offences is something that can be determined objectively by consulting the court rolls. In short, it is public information that is known and uncontroversial, and the local reality was not in dispute in the instant case.

[96] In the circumstances, requiring the preparation and filing of additional evidence to establish that prosecutions for impaired driving offences were regularly on the penal or criminal roll in the Beauce district is in my opinion pointless. It is the trial judge who is in the best position to know the nature of the cases before his or her court.

[97] My colleague agrees that, in the circumstances, Judge Couture cannot be criticized for the comments he made on the situation in his region in referring (at para. 72) to [TRANSLATION] "this scourge" in his district. Having said this, my colleague states that Judge Couture was not in a position to take judicial notice of the fact that impaired driving is trivialized in the Beauce region more than elsewhere in Quebec. Yet that is not what Judge Couture did. Rather, he merely asked out loud whether, given the large number of criminal charges involving impaired driving that have been laid in the Beauce district, driving in such a state is trivialized there more than elsewhere.

[98] In any case, it would have been open to the trial judge, as the resident judge in the Beauce district and one who was required to sit in other judicial districts, to compare the hearing rolls in the Beauce district with the rolls of other districts had he in fact done

so. In *R. v. Dumais*, 2010 QCCA 1030, at para. 7 (CanLII), the Quebec Court of Appeal affirmed the sentence that had been imposed by the trial judge, which was based, in part, on his having taken judicial notice of a scourge of drug trafficking in the Baie-Comeau area. Even though the trial judge did not reside in Baie-Comeau, he was familiar with the community, where he sat regularly and where he had previously presided over a trial concerning a major drug trafficking network that had taken several weeks to complete.

[99]   At any rate, I am of the opinion that the mere fact that the trial judge found that impaired driving is a scourge in the Beauce district was in itself sufficient for him to consider this factor in determining what would be a just and appropriate sentence.

[100]   The case law of the Quebec Court of Appeal supports this conclusion. For example, in *Valiquette*, that court found that it had been open to the trial judge to consider an upsurge in crimes involving the production of narcotics in the Joliette district as a relevant factor in the sentencing process. It did not require the trial judge to compare the local situation with the situation elsewhere before emphasizing the objectives of general deterrence and denunciation, as it merely stated that [TRANSLATION] "the judge [had] not err[ed] in taking the local situation and the upsurge in this type of crime in the Joliette area into account": *Valiquette*, at para. 48.

[101]   And in a recent case, *R. v. St-Germain*, 2015 QCCA 1108, at paras. 38 and 47 (CanLII), the Quebec Court of Appeal affirmed a decision in which the trial judge had emphasized the objectives of deterrence and denunciation because of the upsurge in crimes involving the production of drugs in the Joliette district. No comparative analysis was necessary, nor was one required by the Court of Appeal, in support of that conclusion.

[102]   Moreover, the fact that trial judges normally preside in or near the communities that have borne the consequences of the crimes in question is one of the factors in support of deferring to their sentencing decisions, and it is not necessary for them to have knowledge of the situations in other judicial districts. They are accordingly aware of the frequency of various offences in their communities, and for that reason in particular, they are in the best position to determine what weight to attach to this and [TRANSLATION] "to properly assess the particular combination of sentencing objectives that is just and appropriate for the protection of [the] community": *R. v. Pelletier*, 2008 QCCA 1616, at para. 3 (CanLII).

[103]   For the reasons set out above, I am of the opinion that Judge Couture did not make an error in principle by referring in his decision to the particular situation in the Beauce region as one of the relevant factors to consider in imposing an exemplary or deterrent sentence.

[104]   For the same reasons, I respectfully find that the Court of Appeal erred in principle by failing to consider the local situation factor in its decision despite the fact that it had previously found this factor to be legitimate in other cases. Given that Judge Couture had stressed the relevance of the local situation in the circumstances of this case, it was inappropriate for the Court of Appeal to disregard this factor in assessing the fitness of the sentence, as that meant that its analysis was incomplete.

[105]   In conclusion, it is my opinion that the sentence of six years and six months' imprisonment imposed by Judge Couture, although severe, falls within the overall range of sentences normally imposed in Quebec and elsewhere in the country and is not demonstrably unfit. It must therefore be restored.

GASCON J (McLachlin CJ concurring) (dissenting):

[155] Second, the views expressed by the authors and the courts also do not seem to me to be so uniform on the question whether it is appropriate for a judge to take judicial notice of the frequency of a crime in his or her community during sentencing.

[156] This Court considered the application of the doctrine of judicial notice in *R. v. Spence*, 2005 SCC 71, [2005] 3 S.C.R. 458. Ultimately, the permissible scope of judicial notice should vary according to the nature of the issue under consideration: *Spence*, at para. 60. Thus, the closer a fact approaches the dispositive issue, the more stringent is the test for its admissibility: *Spence*, at paras. 60-61; P. Béliveau and M. Vauclair, *Traité général de preuve et de procédure pénales* (22nd ed. 2015), at para. 2366. When a fact falls between an adjudicative fact (one that is at the centre of the controversy between the parties) and a background fact (one that is only at the periphery of the controversy, and that the court will assume to be uncontroversial), the court must ask itself

> whether such "fact" would be accepted by reasonable people who have taken the trouble to inform themselves on the topic as not being the subject of reasonable dispute *for the particular purpose for which it is to be used*, keeping in mind that the need for reliability and trustworthiness increases directly with the centrality of the "fact" to the disposition of the controversy. [Emphasis in original.]

(*Spence*, at para. 65) This is why a court may take judicial notice of a "fact" in one case but decline to do so in another case in which the issue is dispositive: *Spence*, at para. 65.

[157] My colleague refers to some cases in support of the proposition that judges can take judicial notice of the conditions that exist in a region. In only one of those cases did the sentencing judge take judicial notice of the local situation: *R. v. Valiquette*, 2004 CanLII 20126 (Que. C.A.), at paras. 48-50. In the other cases, the courts of appeal did note that a trial judge could consider the local situation when imposing a sentence, but there was no indication that they agreed that judicial notice could be taken of such evidence.

[158] In the case at bar, the trial judge referred to the situation in his district, but he also suggested that impaired driving is trivialized there more than elsewhere (para. 72). However, the judicial notice that judges can take of their communities is not without limits. In my view, caution must be exercised in establishing its scope. According to my colleague, judicial notice in this regard is not limited to the magnitude of the problem observed by the judge in his region, but can also be extended to a comparison of the local situation with situations in other places as well as to information gathered from the hearing rolls of courts (paras. 95 and 98). This seems to me to go much farther than judicial notice of the fact that a city has a francophone majority or of recent unlawful conduct in a particular community, to which reference was made in the cases cited by my colleague in support of his remarks (para. 97; *R. v. Z.Z.*, 2013 QCCA 1498, at para. 68 (CanLII); *R. v. Hernandez*, 2009 BCCA 546, 277 B.C.A.C. 120, at para. 29). Being familiar with the local situation in one's region is one thing, but claiming to compare that situation with what happens elsewhere in order to draw conclusions or inferences from it is something else.

The differences between the majority and minority views in *Lacasse* will attract further debate about the scope of judicial notice in sentencing. A question that arises from these divergent views concerns who is qualified to take notice of what. There is no obvious reason to suppose that judicial notice in sentencing can be restricted to cases involving indigenous persons, as in *Gladue*, or to the incidence of crime in a local district, as in *Lacasse*. It might seem self-evident that the more a fact is material to the outcome of a decision, and the more it is open to debate or uncertainty, the less appropriate it will be to take judicial notice of that fact. This is particularly apparent when the fact in issue is taken to increase the severity of a sentence. Further, what experience qualifies a particular judge in a particular court to take judicial notice?

VII. LIMITS OF FACT-FINDING

There is a distinction between evidence and argument but, taken together, these are the materials that constitute the record of the case before adjudication. There are principles governing the presentation of acceptable evidence and argument. Related to these principles are others concerned with the respective roles of parties, advocates, and judges.

The distinction between evidence and argument is sometimes obscure. For example, suppose a research report is published in a peer-reviewed journal by a criminologist. The publication includes empirical data and an analysis of that data, and concludes that a legislated increase in the sentencing regime for a specific offence produced a significant reduction in the subsequent occurrence of that offence. In other words, the new article tends to show that deterrence works. Relying on this article, a prosecutor argues that, in the face of increasing prevalence of the same offence, the sentencing judge should raise the "usual range" substantially to pursue the goals of protection and crime reduction through deterrence.

If the criminologist is not called, qualified, and examined, any assertion in the essay that is offered for the truth of its contents would appear to be a farrago of expert opinion and hearsay. What if the article is not cited by a party at all but is raised by the trial judge? What if the essay is not cited by anyone at trial but appears for the first time in an appellate factum? What if it is not argued on appeal by the parties but is cited by the appellate court in its judgment?

The criminologist's essay, including the empirical data and the conclusions, is only one example in an array of matter between evidence and argument that could variously be characterized as hearsay, opinion, literature, or anecdote. Some of this might well be credible and trustworthy, but much of the time it does not easily fit with the orthodox views on evidence and argument. Moreover, it can be extremely dangerous and open to exaggeration and manipulation. Academic views, data, and interpretation can be refuted. See the wonderful controversy involving a challenge to a position on crime reduction taken by Steven Levitt (of *Freakonomics* fame), "The Case of Critics Who Missed the Point: A Reply to Webster et al." (2006) 5:3 Criminol & Pub Pol'y 449; Cheryl Marie Webster, Anthony N Doob & Franklin E Zimring, "Proposition 8 and Crime Rates in California: The Case of the Disappearing Deterrent" (2006) Criminol & Pub Pol'y 417; and other related commentary in (2006) Criminol & Pub Pol'y 413-78.

In the interests of having the fullest range of information relevant to sentence, perhaps there should be some relaxation of orthodox views. But it is terrain that is fraught with difficulty, as the next case illustrates.

R v Hamilton

(2004), 72 OR (3d) 1 (CA)

DOHERTY JA (O'Connor ACJO and Gillese JA concurring):

I

[1] The imposition of a fit sentence can be as difficult a task as any faced by a trial judge. That task is particularly difficult where otherwise decent, law-abiding persons commit very serious crimes in circumstances that justifiably attract understanding and empathy. These two cases fall within that category of cases.

[2] As difficult as the determination of a fit sentence can be, that process has a narrow focus. It aims at imposing a sentence that reflects the circumstances of the *specific* offence and the attributes of the *specific* offender. Sentencing is not based on group characteristics, but on the facts relating to the *specific* offence and *specific* offender as revealed by the evidence adduced in the proceedings. A sentencing proceeding is also not the forum in which to right perceived societal wrongs, allocate responsibility for criminal conduct as between the offender and society, or "make up" for perceived social injustices by the imposition of sentences that do not reflect the seriousness of the crime.

[3] In the two sentences under appeal, the trial judge lost that narrow focus. He expanded the sentencing proceedings to include broad societal issues that were not raised by the parties. A proceeding that was intended to determine fit sentences for two *specific* offenders who committed two *specific* crimes became an inquiry by the trial judge into much broader and more complex issues. In conducting this inquiry, the trial judge stepped outside of the proper role of a judge on sentencing and ultimately imposed sentences that were inconsistent with the statutory principles of sentencing and binding authorities from this court.

II

Overview

[4] The respondents were caught trying to smuggle cocaine they had swallowed into Canada from Jamaica. Each pleaded guilty to one count of importing cocaine. The charges were unrelated, but as the respondents proposed to rely on the same expert evidence, the charges proceeded by way of a joint sentencing hearing.

[5] At trial, counsel for the respondents indicated they would seek conditional sentences relying on Dr. Doob's expert opinion evidence to the effect that general deterrence had little or no value in sentencing offenders like the respondents, and on the respondents' positive antecedents. The Crown, relying on cases from this court to the effect that cocaine importers—even if they are classified as couriers—should usually receive substantial jail terms, sought sentences of between two and three years.

[6] After a lengthy hearing, the trial judge, in thoughtful and detailed reasons, concluded that the respondents should receive conditional sentences. He rested his conclusion that conditional sentences were appropriate primarily on his finding that the respondents, because of their race, gender, and poverty, were particularly vulnerable targets to those who sought out individuals to act as cocaine couriers. He made these findings based on

material he had produced during the hearing and his own experiences as a judge. Ms. Hamilton received a conditional sentence of twenty months on terms that provided for partial house arrest in the first year of the sentence and a curfew for the remainder of the sentence. Ms. Mason received a conditional sentence of two years less a day on terms that provided for partial house arrest in the first fifteen months of the sentence and a curfew for the rest of the sentence.

[7] The Crown appealed. I agree with Crown counsel's submission that the trial judge effectively took over the sentencing proceedings, and in doing so went beyond the role assigned to a trial judge in such proceedings. I am also satisfied that the sentences imposed reflect errors in principle. While I would not hold that sentences of less than two years were inappropriate in all of the circumstances, I would hold that the trial judge fell into reversible error in imposing conditional sentences. On a proper application of the relevant principles of sentencing and the authorities of this court, these offences merited substantial prison terms, despite the mitigating effect of the respondents' personal circumstances.

· · ·

IV

The Reasons for Sentence

[26] As will be discussed in more detail below, the sentencing proceedings evolved over several months into an inquiry into a variety of issues, most of which were introduced and pursued by the trial judge. Although all of the issues canvassed during the proceedings were dealt with in the reasons for judgment, not all were ultimately germane to the sentences imposed by the trial judge. For example, the trial judge concluded that Dr. Doob's evidence could play no role in his determination of the appropriate sentence (paras. 165-69). I do not propose to review those parts of the reasons that do not figure in the ultimate dispositions.

[27] The trial judge's decision to impose conditional sentences can be traced through four stages. First, he held (paras. 178, 220) that the sentencing guidelines set down in *R. v. Madden* (1996), 27 O.R. (3d) 640, 104 C.C.C. (3d) 548 (C.A.) and *R. v. Cunningham* (1996), 27 O.R. (3d) 786, 104 C.C.C. (3d) 542 (C.A.) providing for sentences in the range of three to five years for the importation of cocaine in amounts of "one kilogram more or less," did not have direct application since the amounts of cocaine imported by the respondents were significantly less than one kilogram. ...

[28] Second, the trial judge held, based on materials he had produced and his own experience presiding in a court that dealt with many cases involving cocaine importation from Jamaica, that the respondents were the victims of systemic racial and gender bias. These biases contributed to the respondents' impoverished circumstances and made them particularly vulnerable to those who sought out persons to courier cocaine to Canada from Jamaica. The trial judge concluded that the systemic racial and gender bias played a role in the commission of the offences and should mitigate the sentence imposed. He said at para. 224:

> Since cocaine importation by a courier is not a violent and serious offence, as that expression is used in the *Wells* and *Borde* cases, the question naturally arises as to whether systemic and background factors relating to the commission of this offence can more generously serve to

mitigate the sentence to be imposed. *In my view, systemic and background factors, identified in this case ... should logically be relevant to mitigate the penal consequences for cocaine importers conscripted as couriers.* [Emphasis added.]

[29] Third, after considering the systemic and background factors and other mitigating factors relevant to each respondent, the trial judge concluded that sentences in the upper reformatory range were appropriate (para. 231).

[30] Fourth, in deciding that the respondents should receive conditional sentences under s. 742.1, the trial judge again said at para. 234:

> Neither Pre-sentence report rejected community supervision as a potential aspect of any sentence imposed. Systemic and background factors relating to the offender's involvement in these crimes militate toward serious consideration of imprisonment to be served conditionally. In all of the circumstances, the sanction of a conditional term of imprisonment does not violate the principles of sections 718 to 718.2 of the *Criminal Code*.

[31] The trial judge justified the imposition of conditional sentences on an alternative basis. After observing that the case law could be read as limiting the availability of conditional sentences for convicted cocaine importers to "exceptional circumstances," the trial judge held that such circumstances existed in these cases, indicating at para. 234:

> [I]n the highly unusual circumstances of the excessive delay between plea and sentencing and the test case features of these cases, the terms of imprisonment ought to be served conditionally.

• • •

V

The Arguments on Appeal

[32] The Crown challenges the manner in which the sentencing proceedings were conducted and the fitness of the sentences imposed.

[33] Crown counsel acknowledges that the trial judge has a broad discretion in the conduct of sentencing proceedings. He alleges, however, that the trial judge lost his appearance of impartiality by raising various issues on his own initiative, directing the Crown to locate and produce evidence on those issues, producing his own evidence on some of those issues, and eventually imposing sentences based in large measure on findings that were the product of the material produced by the trial judge and his personal experiences. It is the Crown's contention that, while no doubt well-intentioned, the trial judge effectively took on the combined role of advocate, witness, and judge, thereby losing the appearance of a neutral arbiter.

[34] Insofar as the fitness of the sentences is concerned, the Crown submits that stripped to the essentials, the respondents received conditional sentences because they were poor, black, and female. He submits that none of these factors diminish the seriousness of the offence or justify a conditional sentence. Counsel further argues that the imposition of conditional sentences based on the race and gender of the respondents will only reinforce the prevailing wisdom among drug overlords that young black women make ideal drug couriers, thereby perpetuating and exacerbating the vulnerability of the very group the trial judge sought to assist.

[35] Crown counsel advances several specific alleged errors in principle in support of his submission that the sentences are unfit. He contends that:

- the trial judge made findings of fact pertaining to the respondents' involvement in the crimes that had no basis in the evidence;
- there was no evidence to support the finding that systemic racism or gender bias played a role in the commission of the offence;
- the trial judge improperly used evidence of systemic racial and gender bias to lower the respondents' sentences below sentences which could properly reflect the seriousness of the offences;

. . .

[36] The respondents submit that there was nothing wrong with the way in which the trial judge conducted the sentencing hearing. They contend that a trial judge's obligation to impose a fit sentence may require the judge to go beyond the case as presented by counsel. The respondents submit that through the trial judge's initiative, several important issues, all of which were relevant to the imposition of a fit sentence, were raised and addressed in the course of these proceedings. They rely on s. 723(3) of the *Criminal Code*, which specifically permits a trial judge to raise matters on his or her own initiative at sentencing.

[37] The respondents further contend that the trial judge took pains to raise the issues in a way that would ensure that all parties had a full and fair opportunity to respond to those issues. Counsel argue that it was much better for the trial judge to make counsel aware of the relevant material available to him before using that material, rather than simply relying on it without giving counsel any chance to address its merits. The respondents submit that there is nothing in the conduct of the proceedings or in the nature of the material produced by the trial judge that suggests he had formed firm, unalterable views on the issues he raised with counsel.

[38] The respondents also observe, accurately, that the Crown did not object to the manner in which the proceedings were conducted, but instead fully participated in those proceedings. They strongly contend that as the Crown did not object at trial, it cannot raise these objections on appeal.

[39] With respect to the fitness of sentence, the respondents begin with a submission that the length of the sentences imposed by the trial judge—slightly less than two years—is within the appropriate range having regard to the amounts of cocaine imported by Ms. Mason and Ms. Hamilton. The respondents next argue that the trial judge properly took into consideration the personal mitigating factors. The respondents further submit that the trial judge was obliged to factor his own experience into the assessment of the evidence before him and to place that evidence in its proper social context. In these circumstances, the systemic racial and gender bias suffered by the respondents was properly viewed as a relevant mitigating circumstance. The respondents further submit that if they are correct in arguing that sentences of less than two years were within the appropriate range, the circumstances of these offenders fully justify conditional sentences. Counsel quite properly remind this court that the trial judge's weighing of the various relevant factors must be accorded deference in this court unless it can be said to be unreasonable.

. . .

VI

The Conduct of the Proceedings

(a) How the Proceedings Unfolded

[45] Ms. Hamilton and Ms. Mason entered guilty pleas on March 6 and April 16, 2002, respectively. The proceedings were adjourned for the preparation of pre-sentence reports and to allow the respondents to obtain expert evidence directed at the efficacy of general deterrence as a principle of sentencing in cases like these.

[46] The defence retained Dr. Doob, a respected criminologist. His report was provided to the Crown shortly before July 29, 2002. On July 29th, the Crown requested a brief adjournment to consider its position in light of Dr. Doob's report. On that same day, the trial judge, purporting to act under s. 723(3) of the *Criminal Code*, advised the Crown that he wanted the Crown to produce evidence on what the trial judge referred to as the "certainty of detection." In exchanges with Crown counsel, it became clear that the trial judge was concerned about a number of issues. These included:

- the steps, if any, taken by the Government of Canada to reduce the incidence of drug smuggling from Jamaica;
- the extent to which the Government of Canada used its power to regulate and license air carriers to encourage those carriers to take steps to curtail illicit drug importation;
- Canada's treaty obligations and any protocol obligations applicable to the interdiction of drug smuggling; and
- steps taken at airports in Jamaica and Pearson International Airport to combat drug importation.

[47] During his dialogue with Crown counsel, the trial judge said:

> I'm not at all clear, in my mind, what, if anything, Canada has done to the licensing and regulatory scheme for landing rights for airplanes, international flights, in order to make the point with air carriers that we do have illicit narcotic laws that exist and we expect partnership and enforcement.

[48] The trial judge also expressed concern that the airlines could be seen as being "wilfully blind" to the importation of cocaine from Jamaica.

[49] The trial judge candidly acknowledged that his inquiry into the "certainty of detection" issues as part of the sentencing process was "admittedly a new way of looking at the world."

• • •

[51] Some time before November 12th, the Crown produced material in response to the "certainty of detection" issues raised by the trial judge.

[52] A few days before November 12th, the proceedings took a dramatic turn. The trial judge, through his secretary, sent counsel about 700 pages of material garnered from his own researches. The material consisted of reports from various governmental agencies in different countries, statistical information relating to the Canadian population at large and the prison population, law reform material from various countries, and newspaper articles. The material related to [four] broad areas:

- the extent of cocaine use and the harm caused by its use;
- the "certainty of detection" issues earlier identified by the trial judge and, in particular, "high tech" steps taken in other jurisdictions to combat drug importation through international airports;
- statistical information and various reports relating to rates of imprisonment generally, rates of imprisonment broken down by gender and race, and rates of imprisonment for drug-related offences; and
- reports relating to racial and gender discrimination in and out of jail.

[53] On November 12th, the trial judge advised counsel that he had decided to produce this material when it became apparent to him that information of the kind contained in his material was "not coming from either side." There had been no suggestion by any party to the proceedings that race or gender had any relevance to the determination of fit sentences for the respondents before the trial judge distributed his material.

[54] The trial judge invited submissions on the admissibility of the material he had produced. Crown counsel indicated that he was "a bit surprised" when he received the material as, in his view, it substantially broadened the scope of the sentencing hearing. Crown counsel observed that the material introduced "a racial issue" into the sentencing proceedings for the first time.

[55] A lengthy discussion ensued between the Crown and the trial judge. After acknowledging that the defence had not raised race, the trial judge said:

> But clearly as a trial judge in this port of entry, Brampton, responsible for the Pearson International Airport, I think it is fair to say that having done this for almost nine years, that I have been struck by the number of single mothers, black women who have appeared before me over that time period. *And it leads me to wonder whether this is a group that is targeted for courier conscription by the overseers, whether in fact, compared to other narcotics offences or other offences generally, females, female blacks, form a disproportionate group within the population of people sentenced for cocaine importing.* Where that takes me I'm not sure, but we should know in sentencing, it seems to me, whether there is a disproportionate effect on any particular group by a sentencing policy. [Emphasis added.]

[56] The trial judge made it clear that he was not suggesting that the respondents' arrests or prosecutions were racially motivated or otherwise tainted by racial or gender bias. The trial judge was, however, concerned that the substantial jail sentences routinely imposed for cocaine importation had a disproportionate effect on a disadvantaged group, namely poor black single mothers, because drug overseers selected their couriers from that disadvantaged group. The trial judge referred to race and gender as part of the "contextual perspective" he was obliged to take on sentencing.

[57] Ultimately, Crown counsel indicated that he wished some time to consider his position on the issue of race as raised by the trial judge. Counsel added:

> I'm not suggesting that it is not appropriate for a court to consider that, it's just that I didn't direct my mind to it and it may significantly add to the amount of time I require to re-focus my attention on that issue. ...

[58] The sentencing proceedings continued on November 12th, 13th, and 14th. Dr. Doob testified on November 12th and November 13th. On November 14th, the Crown called three witnesses, one from Air Canada and two from Canada Customs, to address

some of the "certainty of detection" issues raised by the trial judge. Two of these witnesses were questioned at length by the trial judge.

[59] The sentencing proceedings recommenced on December 19, 2002, and continued on January 20 and January 22, 2003. During these proceedings, the trial judge produced approximately 300 additional pages of material relating to the issues he had raised during the sentencing proceedings. The Crown called one more witness to address some of the "certainty of detection" issues and also filed certain material dealing with those issues as well as the race/gender issues raised by the trial judge. Throughout this part of the proceedings, the trial judge continued to request additional information from the Crown and the Crown continued to attempt to respond to those requests. In the end, the Crown was unable to produce all of the statistical information that the trial judge had requested.

[60] At no stage of the proceedings did the Crown object to the trial judge raising the issues that he raised, or object to the trial judge taking into account the material the trial judge had produced.

[61] The trial judge rendered judgment on February 20, 2003. His reasons made extensive reference to the material he produced and tracked the concerns he expressed when he introduced the issues of race and gender bias into the proceedings.

(b) Did the Trial Judge Go Too Far?

[62] I will first address the respondents' argument that this court should not reach the merits of this ground of appeal. …

[63] … Crown counsel contends that the trial judge, in overstepping his role, fundamentally altered the nature of the proceedings. Counsel contends that the trial judge turned the proceedings from one designed to determine a fit sentence for individual offenders, to one designed to enquire into a variety of societal problems which, the trial judge, through his experience, had come to associate with the sentencing of black women who courier drugs into Canada from Jamaica. Crown counsel contends that this fundamental alteration of the essential purpose of the proceeding in and of itself invalidates the result.

[64] … I think there is merit to … the Crown's submission. The nature of the proceedings was fundamentally changed and this change contributed to the errors in principle reflected in the sentences imposed.

[65] Having read and reread the transcripts, I must conclude that the trial judge does appear to have assumed the combined role of advocate, witness, and judge. No doubt, the trial judge's extensive experience in sentencing cocaine couriers had left him with genuine and legitimate concerns about the effectiveness and fairness of sentencing practices as applied to single poor black women who couriered cocaine into Canada for relatively little gain. The trial judge unilaterally decided to use these proceedings to raise, explore, and address various issues which he believed negatively impacted on the effectiveness and fairness of current sentencing practices as they related to some cocaine importers. Through his personal experience and personal research, the trial judge became the prime source of information in respect of those issues. The trial judge also became the driving force pursuing those issues during the proceedings.

[66] No one suggests that a trial judge is obliged to remain passive during the sentencing phase of the criminal process. Trial judges can, and sometimes must, assume an active role in the course of a sentencing proceeding. Section 723(3) of the *Criminal Code* provides

that a court may, on its own motion, require the production of evidence that "would assist in the determination of the appropriate sentence." Quite apart from that statutory power, the case law has long recognized that where a trial judge is required by law to consider a factor in determining the appropriate sentence and counsel has not provided the information necessary to properly consider that factor, the court can, on its own initiative, make the necessary inquiries and obtain the necessary evidence: *R v. Wells*, [2000] 1 S.C.R. 207, 141 C.C.C. (3d) 368, at pp. 233-35 S.C.R., pp. 390-91 C.C.C.; *R v. Gladue*, [1999] 1 S.C.R. 688, 133 C.C.C. (3d) 385, at paras. 84-85.

[67] Recognition that a trial judge can go beyond the issues and evidence produced by the parties on sentencing where necessary to ensure the imposition of a fit sentence does not mean that the trial judge's power is without limits or that it will be routinely exercised. In considering both the limits of the power and the limits of the exercise of the power, it is wise to bear in mind that the criminal process, including the sentencing phase, is basically adversarial. Usually, the parties are the active participants in the process and the judge serves as a neutral, passive arbiter. Generally speaking, it is left to the parties to choose the issues, stake out their positions, and decide what evidence to present in support of those positions. The trial judge's role is to listen, clarify where necessary, and ultimately evaluate the merits of the competing cases presented by the parties.

[68] The trial judge's role as the arbiter of the respective merits of competing positions developed and put before the trial judge by the parties best ensures judicial impartiality and the appearance of judicial impartiality. Human nature is such that it is always easier to objectively assess the merits of someone else's argument. The relatively passive role assigned to the trial judge also recognizes that judges, by virtue of their very neutrality, are not in a position to make informed decisions as to which issues should be raised, or the evidence that should be led. Judicial intrusion into counsel's role can cause unwarranted delay and bring unnecessary prolixity to the proceedings.

[69] Judges must be very careful before introducing issues into the sentencing proceeding. Where an issue may or may not be germane to the determination of the appropriate sentence, the trial judge should not inject that issue into the proceedings without first determining from counsel their positions as to the relevance of that issue. If counsel takes the position that the issue is relevant, then it should be left to counsel to produce whatever evidence or material he or she deems appropriate, although the trial judge may certainly make counsel aware of materials known to the trial judge which are germane to the issue. If counsel takes the position that the issue raised by the trial judge is not relevant on sentencing, it will be a rare case where the trial judge will pursue that issue.

[70] It is also important that the trial judge limit the scope of his or her intervention into the role traditionally left to counsel. The trial judge should frame any issue that he or she introduces as precisely as possible and relate it to the case before the court. This will avoid turning the sentencing hearing into a de facto commission of inquiry.

[71] The manner in which the proceedings were conducted created at least four problems. First, by assuming the multi-faceted role of advocate, witness, and judge, the trial judge put the appearance of impartiality at risk, if not actually compromising that appearance. For example, the trial judge introduced the issues of race and gender bias into the proceedings, and then, through the material he produced and the questions he addressed to Crown counsel, the trial judge appeared to drive the inquiry into those matters towards certain results. Those results are reflected in his reasons. Looking at the

entirety of the proceedings, there is a risk that a reasonable observer could conclude that the trial judge's findings as to the significance of race and gender bias in fixing the appropriate sentences had been made before he directed an inquiry into those issues. At the very least, the conduct of the proceedings produced a dynamic in which the trial judge became the Crown's adversary on the issues introduced by the trial judge.

[72] Although the appearance of impartiality was put at risk by the conduct of these proceedings, the trial judge did take steps to try and preserve the appearance of fairness. He gave counsel clear indications of his concerns and any tentative opinions he had formed. He also provided the material to counsel to which he planned to refer in considering the issues he had raised. This procedure was much fairer to the parties and much more likely to produce an accurate result than had the trial judge simply referred to the material without giving counsel any notice: *R v. Paul* (1998), 124 C.C.C. (3d) 1, 158 D.L.R. (4th) 231 (N.B.C.A.); *Cronk v. Canadian General Insurance Co.* (1995), 25 O.R. (3d) 50, [1995] O.J. No. 2751 (C.A.) at p. 518 (O.R.); Ian Binnie, "Judicial Notice: How Much Is Too Much?" in *Law Society of Upper Canada, Special Lectures 2003: The Law of Evidence* (Toronto: Irwin Law, 2004) 543 at 564-65. Much of the material produced by the trial judge was not suggestive of any particular answer to the questions raised by the trial judge in the course of the proceedings. The scrupulous fairness with which the trial judge conducted the proceedings went some way towards overcoming the potentially adverse effects of the extraordinary role he assumed in the conduct of the proceedings.

[73] The second problem arising from the trial judge's approach is that it produced a fundamental disconnect between the case on sentencing presented by counsel for the respondents and the case of the paradigmatic cocaine courier constructed by the trial judge. From the time he first introduced race and gender into the proceedings, the trial judge spoke in terms of poor black single women who were "targeted" and "conscripted" by drug overseers to act as couriers. The trial judge referred to these couriers as "virtue-tested" by drug overseers and as living "in the despair of poverty." The trial judge also described these couriers as using the small compensation they received from the drug overseers to pay rent, feed children, and support a subsistence-level existence.

[74] Counsel for the respondents chose to provide next to no information about the respondents' involvement in these crimes. Ms. Hamilton indicated she acted out of financial need. Ms. Mason offered no explanation. There was no evidence that these respondents were conscripted, virtue-tested, or paid minimal compensation, nor was there evidence that such compensation was used to pay for the necessaries of life. The reasons for sentence indicate to me that the trial judge based his sentences more on his concept of the typical drug courier than on the evidence pertaining to these two individuals.

[75] A third problem with the trial judge's conduct of the proceedings is that it created a real risk of inaccurate fact-finding. The trial judge introduced a veritable blizzard of raw statistical information. He also produced various forms of opinion on a wide variety of topics. None of this material was analyzed or tested in any way.

[76] It is difficult to know what to make of the statistical data without the assistance of evidence from a properly qualified witness. For example, the trial judge made extensive reference to statistics dealing with the incarceration of black women in Canadian penitentiaries. As I understand his analysis, he concluded that since the percentage of black women in the penitentiary was approximately three times higher than the percentage of black women in the general population, black women were over-represented in the prison

population. He inferred from that conclusion support for his further conclusion that sentencing practices as applied to those who imported cocaine from Jamaica reflected systemic social, racial, and gender bias against poor black women.

[77] It is not clear to me what connection, if any, there is between the number of black women in the penitentiary and the relevance, if any, of race or gender to sentencing principles as applied to the crime of cocaine importation. Furthermore, it is not apparent to me that any inference can be drawn from a single statistic indicating that black women make up six per cent of the female penitentiary population and only about two per cent of the general population. That statistic would have to be considered in the context of other statistical information indicating that the percentage of black women in the penitentiary has dropped dramatically over the last eight years (by almost a third), as has the actual number of black women in the penitentiary system. These decreases have occurred despite significant increases in the general black population and significant increases in the overall female penitentiary population. These statistical trends could suggest that current sentencing practices are well on their way to eliminating any over-representation of black females in the penitentiary.

[78] Even the one statistical feature highlighted by the trial judge is of questionable value. The population giving rise to the trial judge's conclusion that black females are over-represented in the penitentiary population is a very small one. As of January 2003, there were twenty-five black women in the penitentiary out of a total population of almost 350,000 black women in Canada. That means that .007 per cent of the female black population in Canada is in the penitentiary. The validity of any inferences drawn from such small numbers must be open to question.

[79] Similarly, the trial judge compared the number of black women appearing before him charged with cocaine importation with the number of black women he saw in his local shopping mall to support his conclusion that black women were over-represented in the population of persons charged with cocaine importation. Absent some expert evidence, I do not think the trial judge could make any informed decision as to the significance of that personal observation in determining the relevance, if any, of race or gender to sentencing practices as applied to cocaine importation.

[80] The trial judge acknowledged that there were other reasons which could explain the over-representation of black women among couriers bringing cocaine into Canada from Jamaica. The population of Jamaica is largely a black population. It seems sensible that those seeking couriers would seek out individuals with some connection to Jamaica and some "innocent" explanation to offer to the authorities for travel to and from Jamaica. Absent any evidence, the trial judge could not make an informed choice from among the various possible explanations for this over-representation.

[81] I do not think the meaning of the statistics introduced by the trial judge or the inferences that could be properly drawn from them is self-evident. There were real risks that these statistics could be misunderstood and misused absent proper expert evidence. Instead of being treated with the caution that all statistics deserve, these statistics—probably because they were introduced by the trial judge—took on a strong aura of reliability and were treated as if they were self-explanatory.

[82] A fourth difficulty with the way the trial judge conducted these proceedings is evident from his introduction of the "certainty of detection" issues. These issues consumed a good deal of time and effort. In the end, quite properly, they played virtually no role in

determining the appropriate sentence. The trial judge summarized the evidence at length (paras. 27-51), but then made only two brief references to it. He referred to the evidence when rejecting the respondents' argument that general deterrence should be discounted as a principle of sentencing (paras. 154-56) and he referred to it in rejecting the Crown's argument that a conditional sentence would deprecate the gravity of the offence of importing cocaine (para. 228). With respect, I see no connection between the "certainty of detection" issues and the question of whether a conditional sentence would deprecate the gravity of the offence.

[83] In the end, the inquiry into the "certainty of detection" issues produced little, if anything, of assistance in the determination of the appropriate sentences. This is not surprising. The complexity of those issues could not be properly identified and explored in a sentencing hearing. A sentencing hearing is not the appropriate forum in which to inquire into Canada's compliance with various treaty obligations. The inquiry into the "certainty of detection" issues did, however, lengthen and complicate the proceedings. The inquiry into these issues also contributed to the impression that the trial judge had decided to conduct an inquiry into matters that concerned him rather than conduct a sentencing hearing to determine the appropriate sentence for these two respondents.

· · ·

(c) The Errors in Principle

(i) The Findings of Fact

[114] The trial judge concluded that conditional sentences were appropriate largely because the personal responsibility of the respondents for their crimes was significantly diminished by the effects of systemic racial and gender bias. In the trial judge's view, society had to take its share of the responsibility for the respondents' crimes (paras. 188, 221). On the trial judge's approach, society assumed its share of responsibility for the respondents' conduct through a mitigation of the penalty imposed on the respondents.

[115] The trial judge made several findings of fact which were specific to the respondents' involvement in their offences. He relied on these findings to support his conclusion that their personal culpability was significantly reduced. He found as a fact that:

- the respondents were "conscripted" by the "drug distribution hierarchy" to participate in their crimes (para. 198);
- the involvement of the respondents was the result of "virtue-testing" by "drug operation overseers" (para. 195);
- the respondents were paid relatively minimal amounts and used those amounts to provide the bare necessities for their families (para. 191); and
- the respondents' children would be "effectively orphaned" if the respondents were incarcerated (para. 198).

[116] Although the rules of evidence are substantially broadened on the sentencing inquiry, factual findings that are germane to the determination of the appropriate sentence and are not properly the subject of judicial notice must be supported by the evidence. There was no evidence to support the findings of fact outlined immediately above.

[117] The respondents chose not to offer any explanation for, or description of, their involvement in the crimes, apart from Ms. Hamilton's indication that she acted out of

financial need. The trial judge had no information as to how the respondents came to be involved in this scheme, what their prior association or relationship was with the individuals who may have hired them, when or where the importation plans were formed, what amount of compensation was paid to the respondents, or how the respondents proposed to use that compensation. He also had no information concerning the care of the children if the respondents went to jail. All of this information was uniquely within the knowledge of the respondents. If the respondents were conscripted—that is, compelled to engage in this activity—they could have said so. If they agreed to be involved in the crimes only after repeated requests, they could have said so, just as they could have provided other details concerning their involvement in the scheme and the compensation they received. Similarly, if the effect of the respondents' imprisonment on the children was as drastic as the trial judge held it to be, I would have expected the respondents to have led evidence to that effect.

[118] The Crown's concession that the respondents were couriers did not constitute an admission that they possessed every characteristic that the trial judge ascribed to couriers. Nor do I accept the contention that requiring the respondents to lead the kind of evidence described above works any hardship on them. This kind of evidence has been given in other cases: *e.g.* see *R v. Bennett, supra.* Safety concerns arising out of implicating others in the scheme can be addressed if and when they arise. In any event, concerns about the potential safety of the offender should he or she provide certain evidence, do not justify assumptions that have no basis in the evidence.

[119] The trial judge did not purport to base the findings of fact outlined above on any material that actually related to these respondents. Instead, he relied on his experiences in sentencing other individuals who couriered cocaine from Jamaica. He applied those generalizations to these respondents (paras. 179-83, 191-98). In doing so, he relied on *R v. S. (R.D.)*, [1997] 3 S.C.R. 484, 118 C.C.C. (3d) 353. I read that authority as prohibiting the very kind of fact-finding made by the trial judge.

• • •

[126] *R v. S. (R.D.)* draws a distinction between findings of fact based exclusively on personal judicial experience and judicial perceptions of applicable social context, and findings of fact based on evidence viewed through the lens of personal judicial experience and social context. The latter is proper; the former is not.

[127] The proper use of personal experience and social context can be demonstrated by reference to Ms. Hamilton's evidence concerning the motive for her crime. She testified that she acted out of dire financial need. The fact that a crime was committed for financial gain can, in some circumstances, mitigate personal responsibility, and, in different circumstances, it can increase personal responsibility. The trial judge was required to determine what weight should be given on sentencing to Ms. Hamilton's admitted financial motive for committing the crime. In making that assessment, he was entitled to put her statement as to her motive in its proper context by recognizing, based on his experiences and the operative social context, that individuals in the circumstances of Ms. Hamilton often find themselves in very real financial need for reasons that include societal factors, like racial and gender bias, over which those individuals have no control. Used in this way, the tools of personal judicial experience and social context help illuminate the evidence. This use can be contrasted with the trial judge's use of his experience in other cases to make the specific finding of fact that these respondents were conscripted—that is, compelled by

drug overseers to engage in this criminal activity—when there was no evidence as to how the respondents came to be involved.

[128] The limits on judicial fact-finding based on prior judicial experience and social context are necessary for at least two reasons. First, fact-finding based on a judge's personal experience can interfere with the effective operation of the adversary process. It is difficult, if not impossible, to know, much less explore or challenge, a trial judge's perceptions based on prior judicial experiences or his or her appreciation of the social issues which form part of the context of the proceedings. Second, fact-finding based on generalities developed out of personal past experience can amount to fact-finding based on stereotyping. That risk is evident in this case. The trial judge appears to have viewed all poor black single women who import cocaine into Canada from Jamaica as essentially sharing the same characteristics. These characteristics describe individuals who, because of their difficult circumstances, have virtually no control over their own lives and turn to crime because they are unable to otherwise provide for their children. While this may be an apt description of some of the individuals who turn to cocaine importing, it is stereotyping to assume that all single black women who import cocaine into Canada fit this description.

(ii) The Relevance of Systemic Racial and Gender Bias

[129] The trial judge took findings of fact for which I have found there was no evidence and combined them with what he described as the "systemic and background factors" of the respondents to mitigate the length of their sentences (para. 224) and to justify conditional sentences (para. 234). The phrase "systemic and background factors" referred to the trial judge's findings that the respondents were the subjects of societal racial and gender bias. The combined impact of the trial judge's specific findings of fact and his use of racial and gender bias is evident in para. 224:

> In my view, systemic and background factors, identified in this case … should logically be relevant to mitigate the penal consequences for cocaine importers conscripted as couriers.

[130] In making his findings with respect to the "systemic and background factors," the trial judge relied on his personal observations in sentencing cocaine couriers and conclusions drawn from the material he produced during the sentencing inquiry. He reasoned that institutional racism and gender bias contributed to the respondents' poverty and their inability to escape that poverty through legitimate means. He further held that those circumstances made the respondents ideal targets for those seeking individuals willing to take the risk of bringing cocaine into Canada for relatively minimal compensation. Finally, the trial judge held that single black women were over-represented among those who acted as cocaine couriers. This line of reasoning led him to hold at para. 193:

> The cocaine importation proscription has a differential impact on African Canadians in large measure because of social and economic inequalities.

[131] I can accept the trial judge's observation that in his jurisdiction black women make up a higher percentage of the population charged with cocaine importation from Jamaica than do black women in the general Canadian population. At trial, Crown counsel conceded this kind of over-representation. I also have no difficulty accepting the self-evident observation that individuals in difficult economic circumstances with few prospects

for improvement make ideal targets for criminals seeking individuals willing to bring cocaine into Canada from Jamaica for relatively little compensation. Nor do I think that anyone can take issue with the general assertion that racial and gender bias can contribute to the economic plight of individuals like the respondents. That is, of course, not to say that racial and gender bias must be taken as accounting for the poverty of all single black women who find themselves in the same position as the respondents. Each case must be assessed individually on the basis of the material placed before the sentencing court.

[132] However, it is the criminal drug overseer who chooses couriers from among those whose economic condition makes them possible candidates. To the extent that economic circumstances makes one a potential courier, the pool of potential couriers is obviously large and not limited to blacks or women. If black women are over-represented among those who courier drugs into Canada from Jamaica, it must be because the criminal drug overseers choose individuals fitting that description in a disproportionate number. There was no suggestion in the material adduced before the trial judge that black females are over-represented among those hired to courier drugs from places other than Jamaica, or among those hired to smuggle other forms of contraband into Canada. This suggests to me that the obvious explanation for the over-representation of black females among cocaine couriers is the correct explanation. Jamaica is a predominantly black country. Presumably, those selecting couriers are more likely to select individuals with some connection to Jamaica and some plausible, innocent explanation to offer for their trip to Jamaica because experience tells them that these individuals have a better chance of avoiding detection than would other individuals whose economic circumstances would make them equally willing to take the chance. The direct cause of over-representation of black women among drug couriers is found in the selection processes of those who hire them.

[133] The fact that an offender is a member of a group that has historically been subject to systemic racial and gender bias does not in and of itself justify any mitigation of sentence. Lower sentences predicated on nothing more than membership in a disadvantaged group further neither the principles of sentencing, nor the goals of equality.

[134] A sentencing judge is, however, required to take into account all factors that are germane to the gravity of the offence and the personal culpability of the offender. That inquiry can encompass systemic racial and gender bias. As the court explained in *R v. Borde, supra*, at p. 236:

> However, the principles that are generally applicable to all offenders, including African-Canadians, are sufficiently broad and flexible to enable a sentencing court in appropriate cases to consider both the systemic and background factors that may have played a role in the commission of the offence. …

[135] Reference to factors that may "have played a role in the commission of the offence" encompasses a broad range of potential considerations. Those factors include any explanation for the offender's commission of the crime. If racial and gender bias suffered by the offender helps explain why the offender committed the crime, then those factors can be said to have "played a role in the commission of the offence."

[136] It is explicit in the case of Ms. Hamilton and implicit in the case of Ms. Mason that their impoverished circumstances and poor economic prospects played an important role in their decision to commit these crimes. The reason for their desperate financial

circumstances was relevant on sentencing. On the evidence, the respondents were not poor because they did not want to work, were irresponsible or because they had led a lifestyle beyond their means. The respondents were in dire economic circumstances for two main reasons. First, they assumed the responsibilities of parenthood at a very early age thereby substantially limiting their economic and educational prospects. Second, at an almost equally young age, they were burdened with the full responsibility for raising young children when the fathers of their children abandoned them.

[137] The respondents did not try to forge any evidentiary connection between institutional racial and gender inequality and their particular circumstances. There was no attempt to bring the generalizations set out in the material relied on by the trial judge home to the lives of these respondents. Absent that kind of evidence, the trial judge could not find that the respondents' difficult economic circumstances were the direct result of systemic racial and gender bias. In any event, I do not think it is particularly helpful or necessary to try to attribute the respondents' economic circumstances to systemic societal racial or gender bias. What is important for the purpose of sentencing is that the respondents' very difficult economic circumstances, the underlying causes of their crimes, are very real and are to a large extent the product of circumstances that are either beyond their control, or for which they cannot be faulted.

[138] As indicated earlier, an offender's explanation for a crime committed for money can enhance or mitigate personal culpability. The respondents' explanation for their crimes, heard by a judicial ear attuned to the realities of the lives of persons like the respondents, warranted some mitigation of the respondents' personal culpability.

[139] How should the respondents' dire economic circumstances be taken into consideration? Clearly, they do not affect the seriousness of the offence. The crime of importing cocaine is no less serious because the importer did it for reasons which attract empathy and mitigate personal culpability. Because factors which go to explain the reason for the offender's commission of the crime do not reduce the seriousness of the crime, those factors must be given less weight in cases like these where the seriousness of the offence is the pre-eminent consideration on sentencing. The same factors could be given more weight in cases involving less serious crimes where the personal responsibility of the offender takes on more significance.

[140] Even where the crime committed is very serious, however, factors going to personal culpability for the crime must still be considered. For the reasons outlined above, the circumstances which led the respondents to commit these crimes entitle them to some mitigation. It must, however, be stressed that consideration of the circumstances which led an offender to commit a crime is only part of the overall assessment that must be made in determining personal culpability for the purposes of imposing a sentence which complies with the proportionality principle. Our criminal law rejects a determinist theory of crime. The respondents had a choice to make and they made that choice knowing full well the harm that the choice could cause to the community. The economic circumstances of the respondents made their choice more understandable than it would have been in other circumstances, but it remains an informed choice to commit a very serious crime. The blunt fact is that a wide variety of societal ills—including, in some cases, racial and gender bias—are part of the causal soup that leads some individuals to commit crimes. If those ills are given prominence in assessing personal culpability, an individual's responsibility for his or her own actions will be lost.

[141] There is nothing unique or new in the approach to sentencing outlined above. Trial judges have always entertained submissions to the effect that an offender is basically a good person whose crime is the product of a combination of circumstances, some of which are beyond the offender's control or responsibility. Put in the language of proportionality, these arguments are directed at lessening the personal culpability of the individual offender. If the trial judge accepts such arguments, the sentence imposed will be less onerous than it would have been but for those arguments. As Durno J put it in *R v. Bennett, supra*, a case very much like these cases, at pp. 14-15:

> The offender's background is always a relevant factor on sentencing. A sentence must be appropriate for both the offence and the offender. A person with a disadvantaged background, who has been subjected to systemic prejudices or racism, or was exposed to physical, sexual or emotional abuse, may receive a lower sentence than someone from a stable and peaceful background, where the offence is in some way linked to the background or systemic factors. The relevant factors in one person's background will be case specific. A single factor will rarely be determinative.

[142] Evidence of the respondents' economic circumstances and the causes of those circumstances were potentially relevant to sentencing in a second way. One of the purposes of sentencing is to get at the root causes of the criminal activity and where possible eliminate that cause. If the cause of criminal activity can be addressed in probation terms relating to things such as job training, the fact that the offender's economic circumstances are the result of factors beyond his or her control would offer support for the claim that the sentence should be tailored to include probationary terms which address the underlying causes of the criminal activity. In cases involving serious crimes like this one, those terms would usually follow some period of imprisonment. Counsel for Ms. Hamilton suggested the kind of probation terms I have outlined above. None were imposed.

[143] For the reasons set out above, the trial judge erred in holding that systemic racial and gender bias justified conditional sentences. Those factors provided part of the context for the respondents' explanation for their commission of the crimes. That explanation could not detract from the seriousness of the crimes, the principal reason the proportionality principle usually requires incarceration of drug importers.

[144] The trial judge's imposition of conditional sentences is also inconsistent with existing jurisprudence, holding that conditional sentences will seldom be available for drug importation. If the trial judge accurately identified the prototypical drug courier, then on his analysis conditional sentences must become the norm for those caught couriering cocaine into Canada from Jamaica. That approach undermines the seriousness of the crimes and the harm done by those crimes to Canadian society, and it is in direct conflict with decisions from this court that were binding on the trial judge.

· · ·

VIII

The Appropriate Sentence

[164] Where a trial judge commits an error in principle, the sentence imposed is no longer entitled to deference and it falls to the appellate court to impose the sentence it thinks fit: *R v. Rezaie* (1996), 31 O.R. (3d) 713, 112 C.C.C. (3d) 97 (C.A.) at pp. 712-20

O.R., p. 103 C.C.C. Applying the analysis described earlier in these reasons, and bearing in mind the gravity of these offences and the circumstances tending to mitigate the personal culpability of the respondents, I think a term of imprisonment of twenty months would have been an appropriate sentence for Ms. Hamilton and a term of imprisonment of two years less a day would have been an appropriate sentence for Ms. Mason.

• • •

[167] I would grant leave to appeal and dismiss the appeals.

PROBLEMS

1. The accused has been found guilty of five counts of fraud on the government, including fraud on the scheme for social assistance and fraud on a program for the creation of jobs. The facts disclose that these fraudulent activities occurred over a period of seven years and the amounts gained, in total, exceeded $85,000. At trial, the accused raised a defence of necessity that was based on the theory that there was no other source of income for the accused and the accused's child. The defence was expressly rejected by the judge, who said that even if the accused was experiencing extremely hard times, there could still be no defence of necessity in law.

At the sentencing hearing, the accused intends to again raise the issue of necessitous circumstances—that is, having no source of income.

The prosecution intends to adduce evidence of a previous conviction of trafficking in marijuana that was recorded some 15 years ago. It intends to show the existence of an outstanding support order that the accused has done nothing to enforce. The prosecution also wishes to put in evidence the fact that the accused faces a pending charge of possession of stolen goods. Finally, the prosecution seeks to prove that despite the absence of a regular and legitimate income, the accused's standard of living is relatively high, not least because she lives with others who have been charged with unrelated, but similar, offences of fraud.

What difference would it make if the finding of guilt were based on a plea of guilty?

2. Small was charged with two counts of sexual assault, both allegedly committed during the summer of 1988 when he was the manager of a resort hotel in Muskoka. The Crown's disclosure indicates that the two victims will say:

Count 1: V was a 17-year-old maid at the hotel. One morning, Small walked into a room where she was cleaning. He spoke with her for a while and offered her a better job if she was "friendlier" to him. She quickly left the room. The next day, he followed her into a room and locked the door. He began talking about how difficult it was to get employment that summer and what a shame it would be if she lost her job. He started rubbing her arm and then grabbed her toward him. She fought with him and he threatened her if she didn't "shut up." After the rape, he avoided her and never spoke to her again.

Count 2: B was a 15-year-old babysitter hired to look after Small's young son while he and his wife worked. He returned to his apartment one day when his son was asleep. He and B had a cup of tea together. After the tea, Small began asking questions about B's boyfriends and the level of sexual activity among her peers. B was uncomfortable with the conversation and started to leave. Small grabbed her shoulders and threw her onto a sofa. He pinned her down and tried to remove her shirt, but she screamed. This woke up his son and Small ran out of the apartment.

a. Assume that the Crown elects to proceed summarily, and Small enters guilty pleas. When the facts, as above, are read in, Small's counsel says:

The essential elements of the offence of sexual assault are admitted with respect to both counts. However, the accused does not admit that the interaction in count one included sexual intercourse. Also, the involvement in count two did not extend beyond touching.

b. Assume that the Crown elects to proceed by indictment and Small elects trial by judge and jury. At his trial, V and B testify as above. On the witness stand, Small denies count one. He says that he and V had a consensual sexual relationship that continued all summer. With respect to B and count two, he testified that one day she sat beside him on a sofa when his son was asleep. She started asking him about V and made some suggestive comments to him. He interpreted these as a "come-on," and he touched her breast. When she backed away, he jumped from the sofa. He never went close to her again. The jury found him guilty on both counts.

How should the judge determine the factual basis for sentencing in (a) and (b)?

FURTHER READING

Reitz, Kevin. "Proof of Aggravating and Mitigating Factors at Sentencing" in Julian V Roberts, ed, *Mitigation and Aggravation at Sentencing* (Cambridge: Cambridge University Press, 2011).

CHAPTER FIVE

Sources of Information Relating to the Offender

I. INTRODUCTION

Because of the relaxed rules of evidence at a sentencing hearing, an offender may partici-pate in the process in a number of ways. Witnesses, such as family members, friends, or employers, may be called to give evidence about the offender's character and employment record. The offender's counsel may submit expert evidence from a physician, psychiatrist, or psychologist to offer an explanation for the offender's conduct or place it in a behavioural context. Information from these latter sources is usually tendered by way of written reports or letters.

There are codified aspects of the sentencing hearing that bear directly on the offender's participation. Section 726 of the *Criminal Code* gives the offender the right to speak person-ally at the hearing. Section 721 empowers the court to order a pre-sentence report (PSR). These provisions are discussed below, along with ss 723, 724, and 726.1, which provide both the prosecutor and counsel for the offender with the right to make submissions to a sentenc-ing judge to present "any other relevant information" in relation to the offence (discussed in Chapter 4, Facts of the Offence for Sentencing) and the offender (the focus of this chapter).

II. THE RIGHT TO SPEAK TO SENTENCE

By virtue of s 726 of the *Criminal Code*, the offender must be provided with an opportunity to address the judge before sentence is imposed. This section provides as follows:

> 726. Before determining the sentence to be imposed, the court shall ask whether the offender, if present, has anything to say.

This section was placed in the Code in 1996. The predecessor provision, s 668, provided as follows:

> 668. Where a jury finds an accused guilty ... the judge presiding at the trial shall ask the accused whether he has anything to say before sentence is passed on him, but an omission to comply with this section does not affect the validity of the proceedings.

For an interesting discussion of the history of the predecessor provision and the importance of the right that it preserves, see Allan Manson, *The Law of Sentencing* (Toronto: Irwin Law, 2001) at 190-94. Note that the current Code provision does not include the caution that an omission does not affect validity. Different views were expressed on the consequences of this saving provision. In *R v Schofield* (1976), 36 CRNS 135 (NBCA), Bugold JA concluded that it was a denial of the right to a fair trial to impose sentence without giving the offender an opportunity to make submissions as to sentence and therefore the sentence could not stand. In contrast, in *R v Dennison* (1990), 109 NBR (2d) 388 (CA), the majority agreed that the failure to give an offender the opportunity to speak was a denial of the right to a fair trial, but adopted a narrower view of the effect of the provision. The majority distinguished between deliberate and inadvertent denials of the opportunity to speak and concluded that the saving provision applied to inadvertent denials, which could be remedied by giving the offender the opportunity to speak on appeal. In contrast, deliberate denials violated the offender's s 7 Charter rights, and therefore justified a Charter remedy in the form of a meaningful yet proportionate reduction in sentence. In dissent, Hoyt JA held that neither type of omission constituted a Charter breach and that both types of omissions could be remedied by allowing the offender to speak to sentence on the appeal. Moreover, where counsel had spoken to sentence on the offender's behalf, there was no violation of s 7 of the Charter.

The courts continue to grapple with the same issue under s 726. The following case was one of the earliest cases decided under the current legislation. Does the Manitoba Court of Appeal (particularly Philp JA in his concurring reasons) go too far in limiting the right contained in s 726?

R v Senek
(1998), 130 CCC (3d) 473 (Man CA)

LYON JA (Monnin JA concurring):

[2] The appellant pled guilty to a count of break, enter and theft of commercial premises and was sentenced by Swail PJ to nine months in jail. He appeals from this sentence on the principal ground that the trial judge erred in failing, before passing sentence, to ask the appellant if he had anything to say on his own behalf pursuant to s. 726 of the *Criminal Code* (the Code).

· · ·

[5] At trial, counsel for the Crown, after relating the facts of the charge, suggested a sentence of 9 to 12 months in jail. Thereafter Mr. Sawchuk, counsel for the accused, made a lengthy submission (9½ pages in the 20-page transcript of the proceedings) urging the court that any sentence imposed be a conditional one.

[6] At the conclusion of counsel's address, the trial judge proceeded immediately to thank counsel and to deal with the question of [the appropriate] sentence ... . He did not ask the offender if he had anything to say as required by s. 726 of the Code ... .

· · ·

[9] Defence counsel submits that the sentencing hearing was invalidated by this error and asks this Court to vacate the trial judge's sentence and substitute for it a 9-month sentence to be served conditionally. Counsel relies primarily on *R v. Dennison* (1990), 80 CR (3d) 78 (NBCA). *Dennison* was decided under the predecessor of this section (formerly

s. 668) which contained a proviso that the failure to give the accused an opportunity to make a statement before sentencing did not affect the validity of the proceedings. That proviso was removed by amendment in 1995.

[10] In *Dennison*, both Crown and defence counsel addressed the court with respect to sentence following the appellant's conviction by a jury on a charge of attempted murder. Ryan JA, for the majority, said (at p. 84) that the trial judge made "... a conscious decision ... to take away this right of the accused to be heard ... ." It was not a matter of inadvertence but was a (at pp. 84-85):

> ... [D]eliberate act of denial of a codified right relating to imprisonment. ...
>
> It is not enough, in the case of an advertent act by the judge, to give an accused an automatic leave to appeal and ask him what he would have or might have said. ... The consequences of inadvertence and advertence should not be identical.

[11] In the result, the majority of the court reduced the sentence from 12 years to 9 years. It is to be noted, of course, that *Dennison* is clearly distinguishable from the case at bar in that the trial judge here merely proceeded inadvertently to pass sentence after an extended plea by defence counsel for a conditional sentence.

[12] Significantly in *Dennison*, Hoyt JA (as he then was) in his dissenting opinion noted that Ryan JA in his reasons had indicated that the majority was following a practice which had developed in the New Brunswick court of granting leave and reducing the original sentence. Hoyt JA submitted that the New Brunswick practice differed from that adopted in other provinces and in the Supreme Court, citing authorities where the courts had fashioned a remedy for failure to permit an accused to speak before sentence. He also stated (at p. 80), in support of his dissent, "... that omission, whether accidental or deliberate, does not amount to a violation of the accused's Canadian Charter of Rights and Freedoms rights."

• • •

[18] In the case at bar, it is worthwhile to note that no objection was made by defence counsel to the trial judge's failure to ask the accused if he had anything to say. Indeed the record discloses that there was no comment or objection before or after sentencing about this oversight on the part of the trial judge. Similarly, on the hearing of the appeal, counsel for the accused admitted that the 9-month sentence was within the appropriate range but should have been a conditional one. The only error the trial judge made was his failure to ask the accused if he had anything to say, a matter that was not raised until the notice of appeal was filed.

[19] In summary, on the hearing of the appeal, no affidavit evidence was submitted on behalf of the accused, nor was there any indication by the accused or his counsel that he had anything to say either to the trial court or to the appellate court beyond what his counsel had said *in extenso* at trial and on appeal. Practice indicates that an accused sometimes wishes to correct the record given by the Crown or to supplement or correct his counsel's submissions. There was no indication of such a desire by the appellant either at trial or on appeal. The appellant was well represented by counsel both at trial and on appeal who, on both occasions, set forth his argument thoroughly and at length ... .

[20] This pure, inadvertent oversight by the trial judge resulted in no disadvantage or unfairness to the accused, nor did the trial judge's error constitute a substantial wrong or miscarriage of justice. In my opinion, it was simply a procedural oversight which had no

bearing either on the trial judge's sentence or on our determination of the fitness of that sentence on appeal. At best, this ground of appeal could aptly be described as an after-thought advanced in support of an appeal which otherwise was without merit.

[21] Accordingly, I would dismiss the appeal.

PHILP JA:

[22] I am in complete agreement with the analysis and disposition of this appeal by my colleague, Justice Lyon. The accused was represented by counsel at his sentencing hearing and on his appeal in this Court. Complete and thorough submissions were made on his behalf in mitigation of his sentence. The omission of the sentencing judge to ask the accused whether he had anything to say had no effect on the validity of the proceedings.

[23] In my view, s. 726 of the *Criminal Code* should not be interpreted so as to accord to a convicted person the right to address the court personally at his sentencing hearing when his counsel has made a submission on his behalf in mitigation of sentence.

[24] The legislative history of s. 726 suggests that the origins of the provision have long since been obscured and forgotten. Originally, the provision applied only to jury trials. It had no application to offenders who were tried for indictable offences without a jury.

[25] And until the 1953-54 re-enactment of the *Criminal Code*, SC 1953-54, c. 51, the provision was directed to whether the accused had "anything to say why sentence should not be passed upon him according to law." The provision had nothing to do with the mitigation of the sentence that was to be passed.

[26] The provision may well be a vestige of the "benefit of clergy" privilege that existed into the 19th century and which "operated greatly to mitigate the extreme rigor of the criminal laws." (See *Black's Law Dictionary* (6th ed. 1990), at pp. 158-59.) The privilege did not mitigate the sentence to be imposed, but rather, its application exempted the person claiming the privilege after his conviction from the punishment of death.

Appeal dismissed.

NOTE

Philp JA might be right that the "origins of the provision have long since been obscured and forgotten" in Canada, but this is not the case in the United States. The right to speak to one's sentencer, historically known as the right of allocution, has been traced back to the period in England when capital penalties were common and an accused person had no ability to give evidence: see *Green v United States*, 365 US 301 (1961) and P Barrett, "Allocution" (1944) 9 Mo L Rev 115. Not surprisingly, the issue has been given new life south of the border with the proliferation of capital punishment and the use of juries within the capital phase of sentencing. It has been argued that the ancient right of allocution permits the prisoner to seek leniency by speaking directly to the jury without cross-examination. Some circuit courts of appeal have held allocution to be a constitutional right: see e.g. *Badman v Estelle*, 957 F (2d) 1253 (9th Cir 1992) and *United States v Moree*, 928 F (2d) 654 (5th Cir 1991). The US Supreme Court has not yet directly addressed this issue. In *Green v United States*, 365 US 301 (1961), a case that did not deal with capital punishment, the Supreme Court was unanimous in accepting the proposition that an offender should be entitled to speak to the sentencing judge even if represented by counsel who has made a sentencing submission. Frankfurter J noted that even "the most persuasive counsel may not be able to speak for a defendant as the defendant might, with halting eloquence, speak for himself." However, in *Hill v United States*, 368 US 424 (1962) at 428, the Supreme Court concluded that the sentencing judge's failure to give an offender who was represented by counsel the opportunity to speak on his own behalf was "neither a jurisdictional nor constitutional" error, and therefore the denial of the right could not be collaterally attacked through a *habeas corpus* application.

In the following case, the offender was sentenced to six months' imprisonment after pleading guilty to robbery. The Crown appealed sentence. The defence sought to adduce fresh evidence, resiling from the admission of facts on the guilty plea.

R v Gouthro

2010 ABCA 188

THE COURT (Côté, Picard, and Bielby JJA):

· · ·

[30] Defence counsel suggested to us that he had a right to adduce his new evidence for a second reason. The trial judge did not address the accused directly before passing sentence, when he asked what more was to be said. Section 726 of the Criminal Code requires that he address the accused expressly with that question. ...

[31] Nor need we decide what may be the result after a deliberate decision by a sentencing judge not to ask the accused to speak. It is admitted that the omission was inadvertent here.

[32] We have found no case giving an accidental failure to invite the accused to speak any effect on appeal. And a number of decisions decline to give it any effect: *R. v. Dumesnil* (1995) 67 Q.A.C. 233; *R. v. Senek* (1998) 131 Man. R. (2d) 50 (C.A.); *R. v. Bouchard* (1998) 117 B.C.A.C. 155; *R. v. Holub* (1992) 155 O.A.C. 278 (C.A.); *R. v. Haug* (2002) 219 Sask. R. 276 (C.A.); *R. v. Amin*, 2010 MBCA 41; *R. v. Korte*, 2008 ABCA 286.

[33] In our view, a Court of Appeal may well have power to receive now, weigh, and give effect to, a statement or submission by an accused respondent which he or she should have been asked for by the trial judge under s. 726. Whether or not that is correct generally, it is true when the trial judge made errors of principle in sentencing, and so the Court of Appeal must sentence afresh. ... After all, a Court of Appeal has no power to send the matter back to the trial court to re-sentence.

· · ·

[38] What if the courts were to hold that every time that a sentencing judge forgot to ask for comments from the accused (as he is told to by s. 726) agreed facts could be discarded? That would simply mean that no agreed facts bind an accused. That would contravene a great deal of law, including s. 724. One cannot read one vague section (726) as repealing another clear one (s. 724).

[39] Furthermore, s. 726 is not a call for further evidence. Its question to the accused is put after argument, just before passing sentence. The opening words of the section confirm that: "Before determining the sentence to be imposed." The judge would not do that until after argument. Indeed s. 723(1) requires such argument before sentence. And argument always comes in all court proceedings after evidence (or agreed facts). (See s. 723(2).)

[40] Therefore, what s. 726 calls for is more argument, not evidence. And maybe an expression of remorse or intention, or an apology.

[41] To the extent that the accused wished … or might have wished, to give such argument or state his feelings, he has that chance now on appeal. His counsel has even filed a "respondent's statement pursuant to s. 726 of the *Criminal Code*." And his affidavit covers apology, remorse, and agreement to probation and its proposed terms. The Crown does not object to these latter items. We see no prejudice to the respondent accused from receiving argument or such personal statements of remorse or intent at this later stage rather than at the earlier stage. That is especially so because the Crown alleges reversible error and asks us to sentence afresh. If we do so, it will clearly not be too late for new argument. That is sufficient relief. If there was a wrong, that cures it. We must recall that on a sentence appeal neither the Code, nor the case law, allows a new hearing in the original trial court. …

Do you agree with the court's description of what an offender is permitted to address when given the opportunity under s 726? Is it the intent of the provision to permit further "argument" by an offender? Does the answer to this question turn on the issue of whether the offender is represented by counsel?

If s 726 creates an entitlement, is there a meaningful difference between an inadvertent failure to ask whether the offender has anything to say and a deliberate refusal to hear from an offender, as occurred in *Dennison*, above?

What is defence counsel's role in safeguarding the offender's entitlement to speak? See Smith JA in *R v MacMillan*, 2003 BCCA 372:

[12] … The appellant was represented at the trial by experienced counsel who … did [not] advise the trial judge that the appellant wished to address the Court. After hearing submissions on sentence, the trial judge reserved overnight and pronounced sentence the next day. Nothing was said at that time … about any desire on the part of the appellant to make a statement. If the appellant had something to say to the trial judge, his counsel would have or should have so advised the judge.

Another issue that arises when an offender chooses to speak is whether the remarks must be given under oath and the accused can be cross-examined. This proposal, of course, is inconsistent with the right of allocution. But if the offender's comments are given informally, is there any limit on the subject matter? Surely, the offender cannot attempt to relitigate guilt or rebut factual evidence adduced in the usual manner, but must restrict the comments to personal attitudes, beliefs, or commitments that have some bearing on the sentencing: see *R v Braun* (1995), 95 CCC (3d) 443 (Man CA); see also *R v Izzard* (1999), 175 NSR (2d) 288, [1999] NSJ No 18 (QL) (CA) for an example of the difficulties that a judge can get into if the conversation with an offender moves into factual issues about the offence.

III. PRE-SENTENCE REPORTS

Pre-sentence reports are provided for in s 721 of the *Criminal Code* as follows:

721(1) Subject to regulations made under subsection (2), where an accused, other than an organization, pleads guilty to or is found guilty of an offence, a probation officer shall, if required to do so by a court, prepare and file with the court a report in writing relating to the accused for the purpose of assisting the court in imposing a sentence or in determining whether the accused should be discharged pursuant to section 730.

(2) The lieutenant governor in council of a province may make regulations respecting the types of offences for which a court may require a report, and respecting the content and form of the report.

(3) Unless otherwise specified by the court, the report must, wherever possible, contain information on the following matters:

(a) the offender's age, maturity, character, behaviour, attitude and willingness to make amends;

(b) subject to section 119(2) of the *Youth Criminal Justice Act*, the history of previous dispositions under the *Young Offenders Act*, chapter Y-1 of the Revised Statutes of Canada, 1985, the history of previous sentences under the *Youth Criminal Justice Act*, and of previous findings of guilt under this Act and any other Act of Parliament;

(c) the history of any alternative measures used to deal with the offender, and the offender's response to those measures; and

(d) any matter required, by any regulation made under subsection (2), to be included in the report.

(4) The report must also contain information on any other matter required by the court, after hearing argument from the prosecutor and the offender, to be included in the report, subject to any contrary regulation made under subsection (2).

(5) The clerk of the court shall provide a copy of the report, as soon as practicable after filing, to the offender or counsel for the offender, as directed by the court, and to the prosecutor.

Some of the cases that follow were decided under the predecessor provisions, which did not include any indication of what a PSR should contain. However, they illustrate what the courts considered appropriate in terms of the content of a PSR and are still valuable today.

It is important to realize that although counsel may make submissions to the sentencing judge on the issue of whether a PSR ought to be prepared, it is a matter that falls within the (unreviewable) discretion of the sentencing judge. Accordingly, in some circumstances, ordering a PSR coerces the offender and his or her family to participate in the sentencing process. This is why it is important to ensure that only appropriate information finds its way into these reports.

The first group of cases illustrates the problem of unnecessary and prejudicial information appearing in a PSR. Cases excerpted later in this chapter involve problems with PSRs that contain information from the offender that is inconsistent with findings made or evidence given at the trial.

R v Dolbec
[1963] 2 CCC 87 (BCCA)

BIRD JA:

Dolbec and one Olson were involved in the theft of a motor car over the value of $50 on July 29, 1962, for which offence Dolbec was charged and convicted on July 30, 1962, on a plea of guilty entered before Magistrate J.J. Lye at Port Coquitlam, British Columbia. He was then remanded for sentence to August 7, 1962.

Meantime a pre-sentence report required by the learned Magistrate was prepared by an officer of the Provincial Probation Branch which was considered by the Magistrate prior to the imposition of the sentence.

It is apparent … that the learned Magistrate in imposing a sentence of nine months' imprisonment on this 19-year-old youth, whose record showed no prior convictions, was strongly influenced in determining sentence by the information furnished in the pre-sentence report.

Regrettably that report was not furnished to the appellant before sentence was imposed, nor was he given any information relative to the contents of the report which was highly prejudicial to the appellant. Dolbec was not represented by counsel either at the time of his conviction or sentence.

It is evident from examination of the report that the Probation Officer had formed a poor opinion of the appellant based to a substantial degree upon information received from other persons, none of whom are named therein, nor does the report otherwise disclose the source of any such information or the grounds for the officer's belief in its validity. The Probation Officer closes the report with the following comment and recommendation:

Comment

Subject is a 19 year old single male presently facing sentence on a charge of car theft. He is intelligent and seeks to blame his accomplice. Although chronologically he is 19, emotionally he is much less—he has never grown up, shows a marked degree of immaturity and irre-sponsibility. Locally he is described as a smart alec, lippy punk who frequents all the ques-tionable cafes and hangouts. His earnings come from the pool cue and part time work at Fraser Mills (he has lost the latter source of income). Exacerbating the above is his love of alcohol and it is suggested that has a greater hold on him than he is prepared to admit.

This is the first criminal offence on his record but he is certainly heading for serious trouble. An extremely doubtful candidate for probation because of his irresponsibility and also that placing him on Probation would bring pressures to bear that he probably couldn't stand thereby forcing him into a worse situation than at present. He has been getting away with so much for so long that Probation to him would probably mean he had once again "beat the rap." The strong point in this whole situation is the family rallying to keep closer tabs on him but unfortunately there seems no motivation from within himself to lead a different life. Institutionalization would assist him in forming definite living habits and may exercise a stabilizing influence on a lad who has been drifting from some time.

On the hearing of the appeal counsel for the appellant filed affidavits of Dolbec, as well as of the principal of the High School attended by him in 1961, and of his parish priest.

• • •

In my judgment this appeal from sentence must be allowed for the following reasons:

1. The appellant was seriously prejudiced by the fact that the Magistrate took into account when sentence was imposed the contents of the probation report, no part of which was communicated to the appellant and of which he had no knowledge and, con-sequently, no opportunity to refute factual statements contained therein which he now says were untrue.

• • •

2. The prejudicial comments contained in the probation report as to the character and conduct of the appellant are so greatly at variance with the depositions made by the

appellant's high school principal in 1961, and by his parish priest, as to arouse a doubt of the validity of the information obtained by the Probation Officer.

R v Junkert
2010 ONCA 549

O'CONNOR ACJO (Armstrong and Watt JJA concurring):

[1] The car being driven by the appellant struck and killed a woman who was jogging in a residential neighbourhood. The appellant's ability to drive was impaired by alcohol.

[2] The trial judge convicted the appellant of impaired driving causing death and dangerous driving causing death. He sentenced the appellant to five years' imprisonment on the first charge and three years concurrent on the second. In addition, the trial judge imposed a 10-year driving prohibition.

[3] The appellant appeals his convictions and sentence. I would dismiss the appeals.

• • •

[51] In dismissing the [sentence] appeal, I do not want to be taken as in any way adopting or approving the pre-sentence report that was filed with the court at the time of sentencing.

[52] Prior to imposing sentence, the trial judge ordered a pre-sentence report. In his report, the probation officer painted a very negative picture of the appellant. He portrayed the appellant as a person who lacked remorse for what he had done, had a poor attitude towards work, had not pursued needed counselling and had "contempt for court orders."

[53] Fortunately, Mr. Herman, the appellant's counsel at trial, cross-examined the probation officer to great effect. As to the appellant's remorse, the cross-examination showed that the probation officer relied almost entirely on the superficial observations of a single police officer whom the probation officer erroneously believed was the arresting officer. The probation officer did not speak to two other police officers who had more contact with the appellant and who testified at trial that the appellant was remorseful.

[54] The cross-examination also disclosed that the appellant had provided the probation officer with a report from a counsellor who had seen the appellant on several occasions after the accident. In his report, the counsellor indicated that "it was clear that remorse and regret and guilt very much occupied [the appellant's] mindset and contributed to the host of depressive symptoms." The probation officer made no reference to this part of the counsellor's report in the pre-sentence report.

[55] The probation officer also did not speak about the appellant's remorse to any of the individuals whose names the appellant provided to him. All of those people would have said that the appellant was remorseful. In short, the pre-sentence report presented a misleading and unfair picture about the issue of the appellant's remorse.

[56] The pre-sentence report was also deficient in other respects. For example, the report painted an incomplete picture of the appellant's work record. The report also implied unfairly that the appellant was somehow at fault for not continuing counselling after the accident.

[57] As I said above, it was fortunate that Mr. Herman's cross-examination exposed the deficiencies in the report. The trial judge recognized those deficiencies. ...

[58] Given the trial judge's approach to the pre-sentence report, it is understandable that the appellant did not raise the inadequacy of the report as a ground of appeal. I see no basis to interfere with the sentence on the basis of the report.

[59] That said, I raise the issue of the pre-sentence report here for two purposes. First, I think it is important to note the problems that became apparent with the pre-sentence report in this case so that hopefully similar problems do not arise in the future. A pre-sentence report is intended to be an accurate, independent and balanced assessment of an offender, his background and his prospects for the future. When preparing pre-sentence reports, probation officers must be thorough and fair and should canvass the relevant information before commenting on a particular issue.

[60] Clearly, it is an acceptable practice for probation officers to speak to arresting police officers and other police officers who may provide useful information about an offence and the offender. However, a pre-sentence report is intended to be more than a mere report of what the police think about the offence or the offender. Probation officers are professionals. They have an obligation to the court and the parties to canvass all of the relevant information and to provide a professional assessment that the court can rely upon.

[61] The second reason that I have raised the issue of the pre-sentence report is out of fairness to the appellant. The report painted the appellant as a person lacking genuine remorse when there is significant evidence to the contrary. I am concerned that the Parole Board, when considering the issue of the appellant's release, not be misled by the inaccuracies in the pre-sentence report. The Parole Board should look at the full record which includes the testimony of all of the police officers at trial, the counsellor's report and the letters filed by the appellant at the time of sentencing which were not challenged by the Crown.

Consider the following case in which the offender was being sentenced for one count of importing cocaine into Canada. He had no prior criminal record. The PSR contained the usual material relating to the offender's background and other matters.

R v Carrera-Vega
2015 ONSC 4958

FAIRBURN J:

[17] The PSR also attributes certain comments to Constable Jeff Smith, the officer-in-charge of the investigation. He is said to have expressed the view that, while Mr. Carrera-Vega does not have a criminal record, this was not likely his first time smuggling drugs into Canada. Officer Smith is purported to have said that he believed Mr. Carrera-Vega was a drug courier and that he was attempting to make "quick and easy money."

[18] The PSR concludes by saying that the offence appears to have been "motivated by greed and an opportunity to make easy money." The PSR addresses the general societal harm done by drugs and the issues associated with drug trafficking, including guns, gangs and organized crime. The PSR refers to the author's "belief" that the offence "would have further contributed to this problem and affected society as a whole had the subject not been arrested."

[19] Counsel says that I should only give effect to the parts of the PSR that outline the personal and education history of the accused. Counsel argues that I should give no weight to the parts of the PSR referring to the officer-in-charge's suspicions about drug importing from Argentina, the nature of the offence, and the Dr. Alexander information [concerning the offender's potential to reoffend]. The Crown accepts that the author may have stepped over the line when it came to the information from the officer-in-charge.

[20] PSR's are intended to provide the court with a context against which the principles of sentencing can be more accurately applied. Section 721 of the *Criminal Code* governs what should be included in a PSR. Among other things, s. 721(3) requires that a report contain information on the following matters: "the offender's age, maturity, character, behavior, attitude and willingness to make amends." PSR's should address the offender's background and the author's views about the offender's future. PSR's are intended to provide an "accurate, independent and balanced assessment of the offender, his background and his prospects for the future": *R v Junkert*, 2010 ONCA 549 [*Junkert*].

[21] In striving to reach this goal, probation officers who author these reports must be guided by principles of fairness and endeavor to be as thorough as possible. This can be accomplished by canvassing all relevant information, including speaking with police officers involved in the matter before the court who may provide relevant information about the offence and the offender: *Junkert,* at para. 60.

[22] Reports cross the line when they focus on an officer's views of an offence or offender, to the exclusion of other information. They also cross the line where an investigator's "impressions of the facts relating to the offence charged" are related: *R v Rudyk*, [1975] N.S.J. No. 33 (C.A.) at paras. 17-18; *R. v. Green,* 2006 ONCJ 364 at paras. 13-14.

[23] While there was nothing wrong with Officer Smith providing information to the probation officer, his views as to whether the accused had imported drugs prior to this offence find no proper place in the report. This is a matter for which the accused has never been convicted, let alone charged. It is an unsubstantiated view held by the officer and I disregard it in arriving at a fit disposition.

[24] … I also disregard the information provided by Dr. Alexander about reoffending.

R v McPherson
2013 ONSC 1635

BALTMAN J:

[1] Mr. McPherson was found guilty by a jury of two prostitution-related offences under s. 212 of the *Criminal Code*, both involving the complainant K.H. The convictions were for a) procuring a person to become a prostitute (212(1)(d)) and b) controlling her movements with a view to aiding or compelling her to engage in prostitution, for gain (212(1)(h)).

[2] In addition, Mr. McPherson has pled guilty to one charge of uttering threats against another female complainant, A.A., under s. 264.1(1)(a) of the *Code*. This offence occurred after the offences related to K.H.

[3] He is now before me for sentencing.

. . .

[10]   A pre-sentence report was submitted to the court. Unfortunately, most of it was useless, if not improper, because the probation officer who authored the report included extensive commentary on the offence and the offender's role in it. In particular, she went on at length about what she viewed as the aggravating features of the crime and the offender's denial of responsibility for what befell the complainant. Essentially she maligned him for maintaining his innocence, a factor which should be irrelevant given his plea of "not guilty."

[11]   Moreover, at numerous points the author made disparaging remarks about the offender's behaviour toward the complainant and the justice system, e.g.:

- He drew the complainant "away" from her family and friends, thereby making her "vulnerable and dependent" on him;
- He used "verbal, physical and psychological violence" against her;
- He blames his conviction on a "corrupt justice system";
- He maintains the complainant "invented the whole story" to get back at him for breaking up with her; and
- He perceives that he is the true "victim" in this case.

[12]   The content of a pre-sentence report is stipulated by s. 721(3) of the *Code*. Unless otherwise specified by the court, the report is to contain information on the offender's "age, maturity, character, behaviour, attitude and willingness to make amends." The purpose of the report is to help the judge arrive at a sentence that both reflects the relevant circumstances of the offender and accords with the principles and objectives of sentencing. Its goal is not to serve as a forum for the author's personal views of the offender's role in the offences: see *R. v. Green*, [2006] O.J. No. 3925, paras. 12-16 (Trotter J.).

The following two cases present a different problem. In these cases, exculpatory information from the offenders found its way into their PSRs. What use should sentencing judges make of this type of information? Should it make any difference if the offender testified at trial?

R v Rudyk
(1975), 1 CR (3d) 26 (NSCA)

MacKEIGAN CJNS:

The Crown has appealed herein from the sentences imposed on the respondent by His Honour Judge P.J.T. O'Hearn in the County Court Judge's Criminal Court District No. 1 at Halifax following conviction of the respondent on two charges [of unlawfully stealing money while armed with an offensive weapon, a knife, contrary to s 343 of the *Criminal Code*.]

• • •

The learned trial judge sentenced the respondent to 14 days' imprisonment to be served intermittently and, in addition, to pay a $500 fine (or 60 days in default of payment), together with a period of probation of one year.

• • •

The respondent Rudyk was originally charged with both offences jointly with one Nelson Michael Lawlor. Following a preliminary inquiry in May 1974, both were committed for trial. On 10th October 1974 Lawlor pleaded guilty to both offences before O'Hearn Co. Ct. J who, on 25th October 1974, sentenced him to four years' imprisonment on each count, to run concurrently.

Rudyk was tried on both charges jointly before O'Hearn Co. Ct. J. After most of the Crown's case had been presented Rudyk changed his plea to guilty and, after an adjournment for a pre-sentence report, was sentenced by O'Hearn Co. Ct. J on 25th January 1975.

The facts disclosed by the Crown evidence are as follows. At about 11:40 p.m. on 30th April 1974 Rudyk, accompanied by Lawlor, parked his car in front of Richard's Grocery, a small corner shop in south-end Halifax. Lawlor entered the shop and, at knife-point, robbed the female clerk of over $200. Rudyk meanwhile got out of the car, stood near the trunk and glanced several times at a witness who was parked across the street. Lawlor ran from the shop and shouted, "Let's go!" Both men jumped in the car and drove away.

Driving directly to the scene of the second crime, a small shop in north-end Halifax, Rudyk stopped and Lawlor entered the shop at about 11:55 p.m. Holding a knife to the shopkeeper's stomach, he robbed him of about $93. Afterward Rudyk's car, a bright yellow Toyota, was seen driving away.

Only a few minutes later the car containing the pair was stopped on the approaches to the Angus L. Macdonald Bridge. Rudyk, the driver, had about $240 of the stolen money in his jacket. Lawlor, in the passenger's seat, had the rest of the money in his possession.

Neither Lawlor nor Rudyk gave evidence. Rudyk also did not testify at the time of sentencing.

The pre-sentence report, however, contained a version of the events quite different from that recounted above, one which, if true, would make one wonder why Rudyk pleaded guilty. I set it forth in full:

> He had been drinking with a friend, his girlfriend, and the friend's wife. His friend suggested the two of them go for a drive. Along the way, the friend told the accused to stop the car, whereupon he entered a store and came running back to the car and stuffed something into the accused's pockets. The accused drove on and was again asked to stop for cigarettes at another store. The friend entered this store, and re-entering the car, told the accused to get moving. Shortly afterward, they were apprehended by the police.
>
> The accused stated that it was the police who had informed him that a knife had been used in the robberies, and that when he later searched for the knife in the glove compartment of his car, it was missing. He stated that ordinarily when he drinks, he gives his car keys to a reliable person, or else takes a taxi home. He described his condition as one of inebriation for he had few recollections of the offence, apart from what the co-accused and the police had informed him.

The probation officer who prepared the report stated that the Halifax police inspector who had investigated the crimes said that "although the accused had been drinking, he was fully aware of what he was doing at the time."

The respondent was 24 years old at the time of the offence. He has a good family and employment background and no criminal record. He has been employed in the navy for over five years. All his superior officers spoke very well of him. He had performed his work satisfactorily and had never been in trouble.

The learned trial judge in imposing sentence said:

… I am not satisfied that it was your initiative, but I think that at some point in the thing you understood what was going on and went along with it, through, probably through weakness more than anything else and possibly because of intoxication. In other words, I don't accept the theory that you were the initiator of it, or the prime mover and I don't necessarily accept the theory that you knew how it was being done … So, I am giving you the benefit of considerable amount of doubt.

In this report to this court, he said:

On the day fixed for sentencing I heard counsel for the Crown and for the accused and did not accept the theory of the prosecution that the accused was more aware of the offences than he pretended to be because of the evidence I had heard and *because of the contents of the pre-sentence report*. (The italics are mine.)

He said further that he imposed the sentence he did:

As there appeared to be a very real prospect of public benefit from the rehabilitation of the accused in this case and as his participation appeared to be relatively minor.

I respectfully think that the learned judge should not have been influenced, as he obviously was, by the story that Rudyk told the probation officer. That self-serving story was not given to the court by Rudyk himself, when he could have been cross-examined by the Crown. It was inconsistent with the guilty plea. It strains one's credulity. It is quite conceivable that Rudyk had no prior knowledge that Lawlor was going to rob the first store. But how could he, after having $200 placed in his jacket following Lawlor's hasty departure from the first store, have believed that Lawlor's visit to the second store was an innocent search for cigarettes?

I would here urge that a pre-sentence report be confined to its very necessary and salutary role of portraying the background, character and circumstances of the person convicted. It should not, however, contain the investigator's impressions of the facts relating to the offence charged, whether based on information received from the accused, the police or other witnesses, and whether favourable or unfavourable to the accused. And if the report contains such information the trial judge should disregard it in considering sentence.

In the present case, putting aside the pre-sentence report, I can find nothing in the evidence before the learned trial judge to support the theory that the respondent did not know what was going on and was thus an innocent dupe who was, at worst, party after the fact.

• • •

These facts make it impossible to reconcile the sentence imposed on the respondent with the four years' imprisonment meted out to his companion Lawlor.

• • •

Having regard to all the circumstances, and giving the respondent the benefit of all doubts that the evidence permits, I would allow the Crown's appeal and vary the sentence imposed on the respondent to one of two years' imprisonment in a federal institution on each charge, to run concurrently, without probation.

R v Urbanovich and Brown
(1985), 19 CCC (3d) 43 (Man CA)

MATAS JA:

Tracie Marie Urbanovich and Robin Harold Brown have appealed from conviction and sentence on a joint charge of causing the death by criminal negligence of Lee Anna Brown, between March 1st and May 29, 1981 (*Criminal Code*, s. 203). Each appellant was sentenced to seven years' incarceration. (I will refer to the parties as the appellants or the accused.)

The appellants had been living together for some time prior to January, 1981, and continued their relationship during the material time. The victim was the appellants' four-month-old daughter.

· · ·

The trial was held before Lockwood Co. Ct. J (as he then was) sitting without a jury. The appellants were separately represented. They did not testify but their lengthy voluntary statements were admitted in evidence.

· · ·

Lockwood Co. Ct. J reviewed the evidence of … [the doctors and nurses who treated the child at the Children's Hospital, and Mr. Brown's sister]. He mentioned the evidence of [Ms. Urbanovich's] mother and said that [at 171] "In the light of the medical evidence little weight should be attached" to her evidence.

Lockwood Co. Ct. J relied on the definition of criminal negligence in s. 202 of the *Code* and the provisions of s. 197 prescribing the duty to provide necessaries of life, which would include medical treatment: *R v. Popen* (1981), 60 CCC (2d) 232 at p. 240 (Ont. CA). Lockwood Co. Ct. J found that the infant sustained a series of serious injuries caused by the acts of Mr. Brown and that the inference to be drawn from all the evidence is that the child was a victim of deliberately applied trauma. … [He] held as well that Mr. Brown was liable for depriving the child of the opportunity of receiving proper medical treatment.

Lockwood Co. Ct. J held that Ms. Urbanovich was not directly responsible for the injuries to the infant but that she failed to take reasonable steps to protect the infant from the violence which caused the injuries. … [He also] held Ms. Urbanovich had deprived the infant of necessary medical attention. …

The proceedings were adjourned to September 28, 1983, for submissions on sentence. In the meantime, separate pre-sentence reports for each appellant were prepared and a psychiatric assessment was prepared in respect of Mr. Brown by Dr. I.J. Kowalchuk. The learned trial judge made extensive references to the pre-sentence reports in giving his reasons for imposition of the sentence. At the conclusion of his remarks, Lockwood Co. Ct. J said [24 Man R (2d) 189 at 191-92]:

> At trial I drew the inference from the evidence that "the child was a victim of deliberately applied trauma." However, the new evidence introduced at the sentencing hearing, by way of pre-sentence reports, bears out what Dr. Ferguson said [at the trial] about the acts not being "committed." He testified:
>
>> I have never stated that I felt that these were committed acts, but I nevertheless feel that the onus on individuals as parents is grave to protect children and to admit to a string of events of this nature resulting in a child's death, to me, is a very serious matter.

It now seems clear from this further evidence that the acts of the accused Brown were probably not consciously deliberate, but rather took place when his mind was besotted by the effects of the consumption of alcohol, or drugs, or both. Seen in this light, the acts were not any less criminal. They do however, fall into a different category for the purposes of determining sentence. Deliberate acts of violence over a period of time resulting in death, in my view, should attract a higher range of sentence than acts which are not deliberate in the strict sense of the word.

In my view, Lockwood Co. Ct. J was right in convicting the appellants. The evidence at the trial amply supported the convictions. But, in my opinion, Lockwood Co. Ct. J erred in the way he treated the material presented at the sentencing hearing.

• • •

Pre-Sentence Reports

• • •

In the pre-sentence report with respect to Mr. Brown, the author of the report began by saying: "In view of the evidence presented at this trial, the circumstances of this offence will not be mentioned here." However, under the heading of "Attitude Towards This Offence," Mr. Brown is quoted as referring to the "accidents" and to his criticism of the medical authorities for not being diligent enough in their examination, observation and treatment. Mr. Brown also denied any assaults. Later in the report, under the heading "Children," Mr. Brown is quoted extensively on his consumption of drugs and alcohol and on a description of several incidents involving the infant.

With respect to Ms. Urbanovich, the author of the pre-sentence report also said that since evidence was presented to the court on the circumstances of the offence it would not be presented in the report. Under the heading "Attitude Toward Offence," Ms. Urbanovich is quoted as maintaining innocence and as being critical of the pediatrician. She also referred to the consumption of alcohol and/or marijuana and referred to having been present on at least "four accidents that Brown had with the baby." Ms. Urbanovich is quoted as repeating her innocence. Throughout the report references are found to the kind of care the infant was receiving by the parents.

In my respectful opinion, none of this evidence was admissible in so far as the conviction was concerned and should have been disregarded by the learned trial judge.

• • •

I agree that a trial judge is not *functus officio* until the completion of the sentencing process and that it would have been open to Lockwood Co. Ct. J, had he felt it necessary, to permit the reopening of the trial for the calling of further evidence by the defence. What was not open to him was to consider self-serving statements by the accused as affecting the conclusions he arrived at after hearing the evidence called by the Crown and the submissions of counsel on conviction.

I think we would be opening the door to a very difficult procedure if we were to permit persons accused of crime to await the conclusion of all the evidence, decide not to give evidence as it is their right to do, and to provide information helpful to themselves, with respect to the conviction, through the medium of a pre-sentence report.

On the issue of how to handle matters that come to light at the sentencing stage that may have an impact on the findings at trial, see *R v Drysdale*, 2011 ONSC 5451 and *R v Griffith*, 2013 ONCA 510.

R v Hildebrandt elaborates further on the proper content of a PSR by examining the treatment of disputed facts in the report, the use (and abuse) of risk assessments, and the relevance of general victim-impact information.

R v Hildebrandt
2005 SKPC 35

WHELAN PROV CT J:

Introduction and Issues

[1] Mr. Hildebrandt plead[ed] guilty to charges … [of possession of child pornography contrary to s 163.1 of the *Criminal Code*].

[2] The Crown sought a conditional sentence of 18 months duration and defence counsel asked the court to impose a conditional sentence followed by probation. This sentencing became protracted for a variety of reasons, including; a dispute over the facts, the content of the pre-sentence report and a request for a psychological assessment. I undertook to provide my reasons for sentence subsequent to imposition of sentence on April 7, 2005.

[3] These reasons address the following issues:

1. Having regard to the content of the pre-sentence report:

   a. How should the author of a pre-sentence report address disputed facts?
   b. What weight, if any, should be given to the risk assessments contained in the pre-sentence report and the opinion of the probation officer concerning risk?
   c. What, if any, general information pertaining to victim impact is appropriately contained in the pre-sentence report?

· · ·

Facts Surrounding the Offences

[4] The defendant took his computer in for repairs. A technician found pornographic images and text involving children under 12 years of age. Shortly after this discovery, the defendant called the technician to tell him not to look at the CD as the contents were private. The defendant initially admitted to the police that he knew the images and text were on his computer but maintained that he didn't know they were illegal. He subsequently gave a written statement admitting that he possessed the material which formed the basis of the counts for which he was sentenced.

[5] The defendant insisted that he didn't intend to download images involving children. He believed that he was downloading adult pornography involving adult females. He observed pictures of nude female children whom he believed to be under age 10. He said that once he appreciated the nature of the pictures, he knew that he should get rid of them and in the course of doing so, his computer crashed.

[6] The defendant offered several reasons for his belief that the downloaded written material was not illegal, including that they were fiction and were obtained on the internet. He said that he believed that stories which involved children who were 14 years of age or older were legal. He also said he believed that as the stories were fictional, they were legal. He knew that he had 30 to 40 such stories stored on his computer. There were two stories in particular, "Teens for free" and "Asians for free," according to counsel, that formed the basis of the second charge. The court was advised that he attempted to write a story that offended s. 163.1.

[7] He admitted to being aroused by stories involving sex between fathers and teenage daughters and brothers and teenage sisters. He used these stories as masturbatory fantasies. He spoke of being aroused by teens, aged 14 years and up. The pornographic material was for Mr. Hildebrandt's own use. There was no evidence of distribution.

[8] The Crown filed with the court 20 of the images seized from the defendant's computer, with a view to illustrating the behaviour complained of. Of these, all but 1 were nude poses. There was some doubt in my mind about the age of some of the persons featured and indeed whether they offended the Code section as there was no apparent sexual activity, but clearly there were several images of pre-pubescent children. There were many images in which genitalia were depicted. Two of the images were very explicit; one included a male partner in a pose of what appeared to be partial penetration of a young girl. There were no signs of distress in any of the images.

Background Information

Pre-Sentence Report

[9] Mr. Hildebrandt is single. He had no prior criminal record. He is a long-term resident of the city and has maintained his current residence for 10 years. His longest intimate relationship lasted about one year and ended in 1982. His father was described as an evangelical Mennonite minister and a staunch disciplinarian who meted out punishment which was abusive in nature.

[10] He has been fairly open about these offences with his pastor, who offered some insight into the defendant's personality. He described him as an unusual fellow whom others may find difficult to interact with and understand. He lacks social skills and this impacts upon his ability to form and maintain relationships and contributes to his social isolation. His faith has been a source of grounding. The pastor expressed concern about the defendant's idleness but believed him capable of personal change.

[11] The defendant obtained grade 12 and a bachelors degree … from Briarcrest Bible College. He was in the military for seven years and for a time was stationed overseas. Since 1993 he has been dependent upon social assistance and has been designated as unemployable due to medical issues.

[12] He was assessed as a suitable candidate for supervision and sexual offender programming in the community.

Psychological Assessment

[13] Mr. Hildebrandt was referred by the Court for a psychological risk assessment pertaining to suitability for treatment and risk for re-offending.

[14] Dr. D. Helmer assessed the defendant. He reported that Mr. Hildebrandt suffered a stroke in November 2004. He wrote:

Formulation

Mr. Hildebrandt does not show significant cognitive or motor deterioration from his stroke of November 2004. He presents with schizoid personality features and is likely to remain fairly isolated socially. He has no criminal history. Mr. Hildebrandt is somewhat vague about what he finds stimulating sexually. Since he doesn't have any significant cognitive deficits, he would likely benefit from community programming, assuming his level of affective involvement is sufficient. This profile suggests that Mr. Hildebrandt is likely a low risk to the community and can be managed through community programming.

Recommendations
1. Mr. Hildebrandt has not suffered cognitively to any significant extent as a result of his stroke. Cognitively, he is functional enough to benefit from community programming.
2. Because of the distancing and avoidance of affect, one key issue for psychological intervention will be to generate sufficient affect to make the intervention viable.
3. Phallometric testing may be an option to pursue pertaining to ascertaining what Mr. Hildebrandt finds sexually stimulating.
4. As long as he doesn't personally own a computer the chances of relapse are likely low in this case.

· · ·

Reasoning

· · ·

1. Having Regard to the Content of the Pre-Sentence Report

a. How Should the Author of a Pre-Sentence Report Address Disputed Facts?

[19] Disputed facts should ideally be resolved by counsel, preferably before the plea is recorded and in any event before the sentencing hearing. As a matter of experience, factual disputes often first make their appearance in the pre-sentence report.

[20] In this case a factual dispute was addressed by the author of the pre-sentence report. This is an excerpt from the report under Criminal Involvement:

… Daniel denies he intended to download images of child abuse and claims he believed he was downloading pornography involving adult females, which he had done numerous times before. He admits he observed pictures of nude female children, whom he estimated to be under the age of ten, but that once he realized the content of these pictures he knew he had to get rid of them. … As he was doing so he states his computer crashed. Daniel could not recall where he downloaded these pictures from but maintains he was seeking adult pornography at the time.

… Daniel possesses a variety of cognitive distortions that he used to justify his behavior. While he denies intending to download images of child abuse, his position is discredited and contradicted by the content of the pornographic stories he admits to downloading (emphasis added).

· · ·

[24] The difficulty with the information contained in the pre-sentence report is that the probation officer presented the defendant's version in such a way that it suggested a denial of responsibility, disputed the defendant's version, and presented argument in so doing. While having regard to the decision of Bayda CJA in *R v. Boulet, supra*, it may be appropriate, even helpful, to outline a version of the facts that differs from that of the Crown, especially where it is a denial of responsibility. By presenting argument, the probation officer entered into the realm of advocacy; this function must remain reserved for counsel. The approach taken by the probation officer was not in keeping with the *Format and guide for the preparation of pre-sentence reports*, excerpted above, at 1.2 and 1.3, which provides that the probation officer is to be impartial and is not to reinvestigate the facts. Further, pursuant to 2.2 the probation officer is directed to ensure that the report is objective and free of bias.

[25] On an instructive note, it is important, when facts contained in the pre-sentence report are challenged, that the record be corrected. In their article, Using Pre-Sentence Reports to Evaluate and Respond to Risk, Vol 47 *Criminal Law Quarterly* 302, Justice David P. Cole and Glenn Angus discussed the potential for misleading and inaccurate information in a pre-sentence report to be conveyed to the authorities who deal with the offender post-sentence and wrote at page 350:

> **7. Post-Sentence Uses of the PSR**
>
> If no objection is taken to the facts contained in the PSR, or if any factual disputes are resolved in favour of what has been written in it, obviously future users—the probation service, penal and parole authorities—may rely on it as valid. However, where the sentencer accepts as accurate some other version of any of the facts relevant to the sentence contained in the PSR, there are several points that need to be considered about whether or when these officials will obtain this information so that they will be in a position to make informed decisions about how to address the offender's potential for future offending.

[26] It is my view, based on the foregoing, that the author of a pre-sentence report may, in the event of a guilty plea, outline the accused's account of the offence. … However, this should not be done after a trial where the trial judge will have made findings of fact. While the offender's attitude may be relevant, there is no purpose in providing an account which has the potential to conflict with the trial judge's findings. It is the responsibility of the author of the report to inform him/herself about whether or not the offender pled guilty or was found guilty after a trial. Where the probation officer reports the offender's version of the facts after a guilty plea, he or she must refrain from being argumentative about the facts and must maintain a position of neutrality.

b. What Weight if Any Should Be Given to the Risk Assessments Contained in the Pre-Sentence Report and the Opinion of the Probation Officer Concerning Risk?

[27] The author of the pre-sentence report apparently administered three separate risk assessments: the Offender Risk Assessment Management System (ORAMS), the Static 99, and the Stable 2000 Risk Assessment.

[28] The ORAMS was described as an "actuarial based assessment with a primary scale for predicting general recidivism and a secondary scale for sexual offending." The latter scale has not been validated by research. With respect to the general recidivism

scale, Mr. Hildebrandt was assessed as a low risk to re-offend. The author did not report the results of the secondary scale.

[29] The Static 99 was described as an instrument "designed to assist in the prediction of sexual recidivism for sexual offenders." Mr. Hildebrandt's score placed him in the moderate-low risk category for sexual recidivism. No information regarding validation was provided. With respect to this score the probation officer stated: "It is concluded that this Static 99 score under represents Daniel's risk at this time." This statement was not elaborated upon.

• • •

[31] In their article, Using Pre-Sentence Reports to Evaluate and Respond to Risk, Vol 47 *Criminal Law Quarterly* 302, Justice David P. Cole and Glenn Angus discussed the use of risk assessment tools in the sentencing process in the context of the validity and reliability of the tools and the *Mohan* test (*R v. Mohan* (1994), 29 CR (4th) 243, 89 CCC (3d) 402, [1994] 2 SCR 9). At page 314:

> Although the case law will no doubt continue to emerge, it seems reasonably safe to assume that the validity and reliability of some of the major offender assessment tools either have or very soon will pass the *R v. Mohan* test. Thus, it becomes important for criminal justice professionals to understand the circumstances and the context in which these instruments are already being used in the PSR process.

The authors discussed three dangers regarding the use of the risk assessment tools, including the practice of probation officers providing their personal opinions in what amounts to a risk assessment override. They state beginning at page 315:

> All of the literature on assessment tools emphasizes that the assessor must have "seasoned judgment [to arrive at] a balanced decision-making model." If the assessment tool is used as a file organizer in concert with other verified file information, and if it is completed by a properly trained person, we would suggest that it may be an appropriate diagnostic instrument. However there are at least three dangers.
>
> The first is that the instrument may be completed by an insufficiently trained person, without complete and accurate background documentation. In the present context, we question whether a probation officer, however well motivated, can be said to have been appropriately trained to use these complex tools properly, on the basis of a brief in-service training. Most psychologists, for example, advocate for tools to be used as part of measures or batteries that are culture-fair and updated for norms and statistical properties.
>
> A second problem that is beginning to emerge is that results achieved on one or more assessment instruments are sometimes "overridden" by Minister policy … . In *R v. Clarke*, … the writer of the PSR administered a risk assessment instrument being used by correctional and probation authorities in that province. She concluded as follows:
>
>> Utilizing the Primary Risk Assessment, Mr. Clarke presents as a low-medium risk to reoffend. However, given the serious nature of the assault, the risk would be overridden and the defendant would be supervised as a high risk offender. The factors which would impact upon the risk include two prior convictions, his age and sex. As well, Mr. Clarke's attitude is such that he is not receptive to assistance and not motivated to change because he maintains the incident was one of self-defence … . He expresses no empathy for his victim in this case.

• • •

Finally, as discussed in section 6 of this article, there can be little doubt that probation officers sometimes try to affect the sentence imposed through what is—or is not—included in the PSR. Consciously or not, any assessor can affect the outcome of the assessment by the manner in which the "fields" are completed. This points up the need for ongoing checks of what is referred to in the literature as "inter-rater reliability"—trying to ensure that responses are properly and consistently recorded.

... [Footnotes omitted].

[32] I was not content to accept the information and opinion in the pre-sentence report with respect to risk to re-offend and ordered a psychological assessment with a view to receiving a qualified assessment of risk for sexual offending and cognitive ability.

• • •

c. What if Any General Information Pertaining to Victim Impact Is Appropriately Contained in the Pre-Sentence Report?

[34] The report included information taken from the internet which has been reproduced in part:

Victim Impact
Renold and Creighton (2003) observed that this was an under-researched and neglected area. Such information as is available is from small scale clinical and survivor studies. The impact of a child's involvement in child pornography is difficult to distinguish from that of the other forms of sexual exploitation they were undergoing when the pictures were taken. Studies have looked at children involved in sex rings, prostitution and intra and extra-familial sexual and ritual abuse. Whilst many of the short- and long-term symptoms are similar to those associated with other forms of sexual exploitation some seem to be exacerbated by involvement in child pornography. Feelings of powerlessness, shame and fear of disclosure were heightened (Silbert, 1989; Itzin, 1996; Hunt & Baird, 1990).

• • •

[36] Whether or not expert evidence regarding the impact of child pornography upon the victim will be introduced is best left to counsel in an advocacy setting. The author of the pre-sentence report was not presented as an expert witness, nor was the author of the article that was referred to in the report. There was no suggestion by counsel that such information met the criteria of necessity. Rather, counsel provided me with several reported decisions which discuss the impact of child pornography on the children featured ... [citations omitted].

[37] The information provided did not come within the framework of a victim impact statement; it did not pertain to impact on an individual victim. While the author was likely motivated by a genuine desire to inform the court, it was not appropriate that the pre-sentence report reproduce such information. It was not in keeping with the requirement that the pre-sentence report be impartial and objective and did not meet the *Mohan* test for the admission of expert evidence, most particularly the requirement of necessity. Even having regard to the more flexible approach regarding the reception of information for sentencing, the admission of expert evidence should be determined by the court upon application by counsel, after argument. The sentencing hearing has great potential in its impact upon the defendant and the court must be careful that information filed with the

court be scrutinized for relevance, necessity, and reliability or that the source meets with appropriate qualifications. Further, it is important that pre-sentence reports not present information, under the authority of a court order, which would not otherwise be accepted in sentencing submissions, without the exercise of judicial consideration.

[38] I do not know whether the author of the pre-sentence report was following policy set by the Department of Corrections and Public Safety with respect to the risk assessment material included in the report. I obtained and referred to general policy information regarding the preparation of pre-sentence reports. My comments are not intended to be personally critical of the author, whom I know to have considerable experience as a proba-tion officer. I do not question his personal integrity or commitment to his work. However, I felt that the issues that arose were of sufficient importance that I should elaborate upon my comments expressed in open court. On one occasion, the probation officer attended court and offered to give testimony about the report. Unfortunately the matter had been adjourned to an exceptionally busy docket and the expectation was that we were dealing with a routine adjournment at that time. It was suggested that he return on the adjourned date but he did not and hence the court did not have the benefit of his remarks, nor did he have the benefit of the court's reasoning.

[39] Before leaving this discussion about the content of the pre-sentence report, I might add that I considered a number of options, including; rejecting the report entirely, amending or deleting those portions that were offensive, and reordering the report. I resolved rather to provide my written reasons following sentence in the interests of a more expedient approach to time and resources. I felt that it would not be possible to amend or delete some offending portions of the report, given the presentation of background information in the context of the risk assessments. I did not wish to reject the report outright and order a new pre-sentence report as I felt that there was some useful infor-mation in the report and I saw no use in ordering a new one. In *R v. Purchase*, [1992] NSJ No. 582 (QL), 22 WCB (2d) 479 (NSSC), the court considered a rather extreme example of an unsuitable report. It was rejected and a new pre-sentence report was ordered.

IV. OTHER SOURCES OF INFORMATION

As mentioned at the beginning of this chapter, there are innumerable types of information that may be presented at a sentencing hearing to shed light on the offender. As discussed in Chapter 4, ss 723, 724, and 726.1 provide a broad framework for the receipt of information about an offender. For example, character references (letters and testimony), employment letters, and medical reports are routinely received and considered by sentencing judges, as are offenders' criminal records. In run-of-the-mill cases, these documents are admitted with-out objection. When matters become controversial, cross-examination is often permitted.

Sometimes the offender does not have, or does not wish to adduce, a psychiatric report or assessment. Does s 723(3), which allows a court to "require the production of evidence that would assist it in determining the appropriate sentence," enable a court to order a psychiatric report? Courts are divided on this issue.

When Parliament amended the mental health provisions of the *Criminal Code* in 1991 (see SC 1991, c 43, s 4, s 672.11, which deals with court-ordered assessments), it expressly omitted sentencing as one of the potential purposes. This was not an oversight. However, in some provinces, judges have utilized provincial legislation to find the power to order psychiatric reports for sentencing purposes.

In *R v Lenart* (1998), 39 OR (3d) 55 (CA), the court held that it was appropriate for the sentencing judge to utilize the *Mental Health Act*, RSO 1990, c M.7 and remand the offender for a psychiatric assessment. Responding to a division of powers constitutional challenge, Finlayson JA said:

> This case can be disposed of on the basis that the provisions in question are in pith and substance provincial legislation, but touch upon or affect federal matters. The legislation in question provides a mechanism to furnish the court with information that may assist with sentencing, and is consistent with co-operation with respect to mental health and criminal matters, as reflected in the reasoning of Cartwright J. in [*Fawcett v Attorney General (Ontario)*, [1964] 2 OR 399 (CA)]. Moreover, as the case-law suggests, remand provisions have been held to be constitutional in other circumstances. The introduction in this case of a challenge to psychiatric remand for sentencing purposes may raise a distinction without a difference, as the applicable psychiatric remand provisions in all circumstances provide information to assist a tribunal in its criminal justice decision-making process and have been approved by other courts, albeit generally not for sentencing purposes.

In dissent, Goudge JA questioned the use of a provincial power in the circumstances.

In *R v Blackwell*, 2007 BCSC 1468, 227 CCC (3d) 275, the sentencing judge considered whether it had power to order a psychiatric assessment through a combination of ss 723(3) and 721(4) and have the author of the pre-sentence report make the appropriate arrangements. As Smith J held:

> [35] The exercise of the court's discretion in determining an appropriate sentence requires the court to balance all of the principles of sentencing as they apply to a specific offender. Those include denunciation, specific and general deterrence, separation from society where necessary, rehabilitation and providing reparations for and acknowledging the harm done by the offender to victims and the community. With a youthful first offender, the principle of rehabilitation is significant. Additional principles of sentence further require the court to increase or decrease a sentence to account for any relevant aggravating or mitigating circumstances relating to the offence or the offender, including evidence that the offences were motivated by mental disability. The overarching principle is that a sentence must be proportionate to the gravity of the offence and the degree of responsibility of the offender.
>
> • • •
>
> [38] The very broad discretion given a sentencing judge requires him or her to receive all the potentially relevant information regarding the offences and the offender. In my view, a psychiatric assessment of Mr. Blackwell, in the circumstances of these offences, would be helpful in crafting an appropriate sentence.
>
> [39] In the result, I find the court has jurisdiction to order a psychiatric assessment for sentencing purposes pursuant to ss. 721(4) and 723(3) of the *Code* in order to fulfill its obligation under ss. 718, 718.1 and 718.2 of the *Code*. I am also satisfied that in the circumstances of this case, such an assessment is warranted and would assist the Court in crafting an appropriate sentence.
>
> [40] Accordingly, the probation officer assigned to complete the PSR is also directed to arrange for Mr. Blackwell's attendance with a qualified professional for the purposes of completing a psychiatric assessment to be included as part of the PSR.

See also *R v MB*, 2014 ABQB 683, in which the court ordered psychiatric reports, but crafted conditions on the implementation of the order and subsequent use of the report. Does this serve to highlight the problem rather than solve it?

See *R v Gettliffe-Grant*, 2006 BCSC 1943, in which the sentencing judge reached the opposite conclusion. As Koenigsberg J concluded:

[9] When one considers the profound invasion of privacy engaged by a non-consensual psychiatric assessment, the very limited and circumscribed circumstances in which a court may order one pursuant to the *Criminal Code* is not surprising. To underscore my conclusion that neither s. 721 nor s. 723 purport to confer jurisdiction to allow such an invasion of privacy, one need only compare the specificity of the provisions allowing an assessment in s. 672.11 and thereafter, with the general, broad, and non-specific provisions relied upon by the Crown.

Relying on *R v Hamilton* (2004), 72 OR (3d) 1 (CA) and *R v Hunter* (1997), 11 CR (5th) 156 (Alta QB), the court held at para 11 that ss 721(4) and 723(3) are limited to "investigation and non-conscriptive evidence."

Without the consent of the offender, and in the absence of a specific power in the *Criminal Code*, should sentencing judges be permitted to compel an offender to undergo a psychiatric assessment for the purposes of sentencing? What about if the sentencing judge has concerns about the offender's fitness at the sentencing stage? See Allan Manson, "Fitness to Be Sentenced: An Historical, Comparative and Practical Review" (2006) 29 Intl J L & Psychiatry 262. In what came to be known as the "VIA Rail terrorist case," see the decision of the sentencing judge in ordering a fitness assessment of one of the offenders: *R v Jaser*, 2015 ONSC 4729.

In a related decision, *R v Esseghaier*, 2015 ONSC 5855, one of the offenders produced his own psychological report. The offender did not testify at trial. The assessment suggested (at para 42) that the offender had a "debilitating addiction to a wide variety of drugs" and during the commission of the offences was "chronically high and intoxicated." The sentencing judge, Code J, applied some of the cases discussed above (*Rudyk* and *Urbanovich*) and held that the psychological report was inadmissible as an attempt to controvert the jury's verdict. The psychologist in that case was cross-examined extensively on his opinion.

PROBLEM

Bill Carver has been charged with theft over $5,000 and ten counts of fraud under $5,000. In a separate prosecution, he was charged with possession of cocaine, which was found in his home when he was arrested on the other charges. The federal Crown proceeded with the cocaine charge, but it was dismissed when the certificate of analysis proved defective (the reference number did not correspond to the reference on the seized substance). Carver entered guilty pleas to the theft and fraud counts.

Carver is a 38-year-old man, self-employed in the insurance and financial services business. The charges arise from events that occurred over a two-month period. First, Carver did not remit approximately $6,800 in premiums to the Mutual of Yamaha Insurance Company but converted it to his own use. Second, he offered ten customers the opportunity to buy investment units in a fictitious dot.com company for $3,000 each and obtained a total of $30,000 from the ten victims. None of the money has been recovered. Other than these offences, he has a record consisting of a single fraud conviction that dates back to 1984.

Carver's counsel has described him as a hard-working family man who suffers from a compulsive gambling addiction. His addiction overcame him and, in a period of weakness, he committed the offences. Counsel advises that he has started going to Gambler's Anonymous meetings. He submitted that a conditional sentence with house arrest and compulsory treatment was an appropriate response.

Crown counsel disputes this characterization. She submits that Carver used the money for gambling and cocaine, but that he suffers from no psychiatric disorder. He just lives an exorbitant life that includes trips to Las Vegas, high-stakes poker, and cocaine. (The evidence of cocaine use comes from the drugs seized upon arrest and the PSR, below.) She submits that a six-month jail sentence is appropriate.

The trial judge obtained a PSR, which contains the following comments:

I have spoken with the fraud victims who were all either business clients or acquaintances of Carver. One of the victims advised that she works in a bar that Carver frequents and that it is common knowledge that he is a heavy cocaine user. Another victim, a 74-year-old retired factory worker who lives on a pension, said that the money taken from him was his only savings. Almost all of the victims feel betrayed and asked me to advise the court that a period of incarceration is required. The author agrees with this view. I have taken the file information and applied the IJMIU risk assessment scale to Carver. (A brochure describing the IJMIU and its validity prepared by its developers is attached.) He got a score of 75+, which puts him in the category of moderate to high risk to reoffend.

On the date of the sentencing, one of the victims, Colin Collins, comes to court. Crown counsel advises that

Mr. Collins wants to make an oral victim impact statement. He has not prepared anything in writing, but wants to explain to the judge exactly how he felt when he learned that his trusted financial adviser had defrauded him. He also wants to describe the effect of the loss of the money.

1. Are there any problems with the PSR?
2. What is the consequence of the dispute over whether Carver suffers from a disorder? Can the court order a psychiatric assessment to resolve the dispute and, if so, what is the authority for it?
3. Can the court consider the cocaine use?
4. Should the court hear from Mr. Collins?
5. How should the court handle the victim impact information in the report?

FURTHER READING

Bonta, James et al. *Presentence Reports in Canada* (Ottawa: Ministry of Public Safety, 2005).

Cole, David P & Glen Angus. "Using Pre-sentence Reports to Evaluate and Respond to Risk" (2003) 47 Crim LQ 302.

Manson, Allan. *The Law of Sentencing* (Toronto: Irwin Law, 2000) ch 8.

Proband, Stan. "Probation and Community Penalties" in M Tonry, ed, *The Oxford Handbook of Crime and Criminal Justice* (New York: Oxford University Press, 2011).

CHAPTER SIX

Victim Participation in the Sentencing Process

I. INTRODUCTION AND BACKGROUND

The role of the victim in the sentencing process has always been controversial and, until recently, somewhat uncertain. Controversy and uncertainty still characterize the role of the victim at other critical junctures of the criminal process as victims' rights continue to crystallize: see generally Kent Roach, *Due Process and Victims' Rights: The New Law and Politics of Criminal Justice* (Toronto: University of Toronto Press, 1999). The sentencing process is the only juncture in the criminal prosecution where the participation of victims is formalized. Section 722 of the *Criminal Code*, RSC 1985, c C-46 allows for the introduction of victim impact statements (VISs) at the sentencing hearing. Victim impact statement regimes now exist in almost all common law jurisdictions, and VISs have been the subject of a considerable volume of scholarship and commentary.

This chapter addresses the modern approach to victim participation in the sentencing process in Anglo-Canadian law. However, it is necessary to step back and consider historical developments in this area. The participatory rights of victims in the sentencing process have not always been so accommodating. Criminal prosecutions evolved from a system of "blood feuds" in which wrongful acts that we now characterize as "criminal" were considered merely "tortious." This gave considerable power to the aggrieved person (and his or her family) to control the process that brought redress. Apparently, this "golden age" of the victim lasted into medieval times: Alan Young, "Two Scales of Justice: A Reply" (1993) 35 Crim LQ 355 at 364. In the 13th century, when certain wrongs were considered a breach of or an affront to the King's Peace, the victim started to fade from the forefront of the legal process. The law relating to the redress of criminal wrongs was arrogated by the state. (Sociologist Nils Christie argues that the historical record of criminal prosecutions is an example of the state "stealing the conflict" from the real parties—that is, the wronged and the wrongdoer: see Nils Christie, "Conflicts as Property" (1975) 17 Brit J Crim 1.)

Until recently, the criminal justice system was reluctant to afford the victim any formal rights of participation in the sentencing process. *R v Antler* (1982), 29 CR (3d) 283 (BCSC) and *R v Robinson* (1983), 38 CR (3d) 255 (Ont H Ct J) exemplify the early judicial approach to VISs in Canada. In *Antler*, McLachlin J (as she then was) held that it was for Parliament, not the courts, to grant victims the right to make representations at an offender's sentencing. In *Robinson*, the court concluded that the views of the victim were not relevant to establishing a fair and just sentence. Research suggested that victims of crime were "revictimized" because they were disempowered by the criminal process: see the *Canadian Federal–Provincial Task Force on Justice for Victims of Crime Report* (Ottawa: Solicitor General, 1983) at 60. As a result, victims felt alienated from the criminal justice system. This alienation sometimes manifested itself in the victim's lack of confidence in the process and his or her withdrawal of coopera- tion with criminal justice officials: see Alan Young, "Two Scales of Justice: A Reply," above at 375; see also Edna Erez, "Victim Participation in Sentencing: Rhetoric and Reality" (1990) 18 J Crim Justice 19.

The organization of the so-called victims' rights movement and the use made of this movement by law-and-order crime-control politics have generated a renewed interest in the role of victims in the criminal process: see generally Kent Roach, *Due Process and Victims' Rights: The New Law and Politics of Criminal Justice* (Toronto: University of Toronto Press, 1999); see also Leslie Sebba, *Third Parties: Victims and the Criminal Justice System* (Columbus, Ohio: Ohio State University Press, 1996), who reminds us that the study of social movements like the victims' rights movement is complex. Nevertheless, Sebba notes (at 2-10) seven sociolegal/ historical developments that are relevant to the renewed interest in victims: (1) the rise of victimology as a subdiscipline of criminology; (2) the results of victimization surveys in many countries; (3) the rise of "law-and-order" politics; (4) the role of feminist and other grassroots movements; (5) the alignment of the victim movement with political and social radicalism; (6) the resurgence of just-deserts theory in the current dialogue on the philosophy of punish- ment; and (7) the development of "informalist" approaches to punishment that attempt to reconcile the victim with the offender. The enactment of legislation permitting the introduc- tion of VISs is one concrete reform in this area. The enactment of various victims' bills of rights (mentioned in Section III, "Looking to the Future," below) is another result of this movement.

The chapter begins with three extracts, each dealing with the role of the victim at sen- tencing. In the first extract, Edna Erez provides a context for the discussion of the use of VISs in Canada. The next two extracts deal with research into the VIS regime in Canada and the perceptions and experiences of judges in four provinces. Further information on the use of VISs in Canada and other common law jurisdictions can be found in the selected readings provided at the end of the chapter.

Edna Erez, "Who's Afraid of the Big Bad Victim? Victim Impact Statements as Victim Empowerment *and* Enhancement of Justice"
[1999] Crim L Rev 545 at 545-55 (footnotes omitted)

Victim-oriented reforms have been adopted in numerous countries with different legal systems. Many jurisdictions have passed legislation providing for restitution from the offender, compensation from the state and various services to victims who have been impacted by a crime. Whereas most of these reforms have been accepted and welcomed, the reform providing victims with a voice, most commonly in the form of victim impact statements (VIS), has been very controversial. As recently as last summer, Andrew Ashworth, in a conference on "Integrating the Victim Perspective in Criminal Justice," warned against two dangers inherent in current practices of victim integration in criminal justice: "victims in the service of severity" and "victims in the service of offenders." According to Ashworth, the movement to incorporate victim perspectives has sometimes coincided with the movement toward greater penal severity. Ashworth echoes concerns, raised previously by others, that the use of victim impact statements in criminal justice decision making may cause increases in sentence severity. He further claims that submission of victim impact statements (VIS) to the court may be detrimental to procedural and substantive justice, as well as to the victims who provide input. Using victims to accomplish the goal of harsher sentences, according to Ashworth, amounts to "victim prostitution."

This line of thinking is a continuation and expansion of Ashworth's earlier article on victim impact statements ["Victim Impact Statements and Sentencing," [1993] Crim LR 498] in which he offered several legally based arguments against the use of victim impact statements in court. In this earlier article, Ashworth also examined the available social science evidence on the effect of VIS on criminal procedure, sentencing, and victims, and concluded, for a variety of reasons discussed below, that VIS is not a desirable practice to adopt.

This article is a response to the objections to the use of VIS in criminal justice and to concerns about the presumed detrimental effects of incorporating victim perspectives as expressed in Ashworth's earlier and more recent writing. It examines the arguments against the use of VIS in court and presents recent research findings on the effects of VIS on substantive and procedural justice, and on victims. The article then discusses the policy implications of recent research for victims' perspectives in adversarial legal systems, and concludes with a call for reconsidering the usefulness of VIS for criminal justice.

Definition and Practices of Victim Input

Victim impact statements address the effects of the crime on the victim, in terms of the victim's perceptions and expressions of the emotional, physical or economic harm he or she sustained as a result of the crime. The information for the VIS is collected, depending on the country, by justice agents such as the police (in Canada, Australia and New Zealand), or by probation officers, victim assistance or prosecution staff (in the USA). There is an agreement that the preparation of VIS should preferably be conducted by an agency that is not associated with offenders' information, such as a probation department. In a minority of jurisdictions victims prepare the statements themselves, without the assistance of any agency assigned to the task.

There is also a consensus that victim statements should ideally be contemporaneous, that is, describe the physical and emotional status of the victim at the time of sentencing. VIS, therefore, need to be updated prior to sentencing, usually by the agency responsible for the initial preparation of the VIS.

Cynicism and Research: The Use of VIS in Sentencing

The major arguments raised by Ashworth against the use of victim impact statements in sentencing revolve around three distinct issues: preservation of defendants' rights, or guarding against the erosion of the adversarial legal system, the question of sentencing for unforeseen results, and the difficulties of raising expectations. A separate issue (relevant only for those endorsing the VIS as a tool designed to better inform the court about victim harm) is whether the VIS should be read only by the prosecutor when he or she prepares the case for prosecution, or whether the VIS should be tendered to the court and available to the judge.

Procedural Issues, Sentencing Aims, and Defendant Rights

Most commentators and practitioners view the provision of victim impact information as important and generally consider victim input on the harm they suffered a step toward improving criminal justice procedures and goals. However, some observers are concerned about the potential of VIS negatively to affect defendant rights in adversarial legal systems. They also highlight the presumed incongruence between the concept of VIS, which implies a restitutive model of justice, and the conventional approach to justice. Under the restitutive model, calls for punishment that satisfies or restores the victim are inconsistent with conventional visions of justice, which view crime as a violation against the State, not a specific victim. Critics also view VIS as undermining consistent and "proportionate" treatment of offenders, and the penological system which views the "public interest" as the only justification for increased severity of penalties. Lastly, the practice of victim input could provide victims with an opportunity to subject offenders to "unfounded or excessive allegations, made from the relative security of VIS."

Research suggests that the concerns expressed by opponents of the VIS concerning possible erosion of adversarial criminal justice principles, rights of defendants and imposition of harsher sentences have not materialised. Studies conducted in the USA and in Australia comparing sentencing outcomes of cases with and without VIS, and research in Australia on sentencing trends and comparison of sentence outcomes before and after the VIS reform, suggest that sentence severity has not increased following the passage of VIS legislation. Nor has the VIS affected sentencing patterns or outcomes in the majority of the cases. The findings of qualitative research shed a better light on these "no difference" aggregate patterns. For instance, based on in-depth interview data of legal professionals in Australia, judges and prosecutors (and some defence lawyers) recognised that the information available from the VIS shed new light in a few cases, and assisted in imposing a more commensurate sentence. Although they stated that VIS were sometimes redundant or the harm was inferentially available from other documents in the file, they also described in detail a few cases they tried in which the content of VIS caused them to rethink the penalty they had in mind prior to reading the VIS. In this minority of cases in which VIS made a difference, the data revealed that the sentence was as likely to be more lenient as it was to be more severe than initially thought. For example, if the offence was perpetrated in an unusually cruel manner, or with disregard to special vulnerability of the victim, then the sentence was likely to be higher. The practitioners likewise provided instances of cases they tried where the VIS led to the imposition of a more lenient sentence than would have been indicated. For example, cases in which the victim's statement disclosed that the victim had made a complete recovery or in circumstances where certain injury had been mistakenly attributed to the crime. These kinds of qualitative findings provide a more textured account of the apparent pattern of "no difference" findings in quantitative studies of sentencing outcomes: some changes in outcomes do occur, but they are hidden as in the aggregate they offset each other. Without victim input, sentences might well have been too high or too low. In other words, contrary to the suggestions of Ashworth and others, it seems that VIS make an important contribution to proportionality rather than to severity of sentencing.

The concern that victims would use the VIS as an opportunity to subject offenders to unfounded accusations has also not materialised. In most jurisdictions currently practising VIS, victims do not prepare their own statement but it is filtered or "edited" by the specific agency responsible for the preparation of VIS. Moreover, "retelling" victims' stories often "sterilizes" them to such an extent that judges noted that the VIS was mild compared to what would have been expected in the light of the offence involved. VIS therefore turns out to be an understatement rather than an overstatement of the harm sustained in the particular offence. The recent pilot project in England confirms that victim statements tend to understate the impact of offences, and that the VIS scheme does not encourage exaggeration, inflammatory input or vindictiveness.

Concern that defendants would challenge the content of VIS thereby subjecting victims to unpleasant cross-examination on their statements has also not materialised. Legal professionals have stated that challenges to VIS in court are quite rare. According to these professionals, there are strategic disincentives militating against calling victims to the witness stand and cross-examining them on the content of their statements. There was an agreement among the legal professionals that a good defence attorney would not challenge the VIS directly and would not call victims to be cross-examined because of the adverse effects it may have on the sentence. Decision makers who hear and observe victims testifying about the impact of the crime on them may be affected by the testimony and therefore more inclined, according to the legal professionals, to impose a harsher sentence. In this respect, the concern about protecting victims from unnecessary and possibly degrading questioning regarding the content of their VIS (as distinguished from cross-examining victims about their testimony in the trial) seems to be unwarranted.

The Optimal Procedure for Bringing the VIS to the Court's Attention

There is a disagreement about whether VIS should be presented directly to the court. Some suggest that VIS should only assist prosecutors in the preparation of the case, and should not be available for the court to read. The rationale is that prosecutors represent both the victim and "the public interest," and they are charged with preparing and presenting the case. The recent report by JUSTICE, as well as a position paper by Victim Support, recommend that victims only provide details of the relevant harm they suffered to the prosecution, for preparation of the case. Prosecutors then will present the harm to the court, using their discretion as to what and how it should be presented.

This strategy, however, warrants closer examination in the light of the research on the effects of "retelling" on the content of the resulting story. This "construction of stories" or "retelling" of facts for legal consumption is often affected by various resource considerations and by the priorities of the collecting agency. When information is mediated through justice agents, there is a higher likelihood of loss or distortion of critical details. Also, research suggests that stories are often constructed to suit the goals and objectives of the mediating agency.

The Effects of VIS on Victims

Another argument against the use of VIS in sentencing is that it has harmful effects on victims. Some argued that VIS subject victims to pressures, and that victims may feel burdened by the responsibility for deciding the penalty.

This argument is empirically inaccurate, and does not represent the majority of victims who get involved in criminal justice proceedings. The cumulative knowledge acquired from research in various jurisdictions, in countries with different legal systems, suggests that victims often benefit from participation and input. With proper safeguards, the overall experience of providing input can be positive and empowering. Research conducted in the United States and Australia on victims of various crimes, where a VIS is relevant (i.e. a personal harm or loss was suffered by a specific victim), suggests that victims are interested in having a voice. These studies indicate that by and large victims do not feel burdened by being heard, nor do they feel pressured by knowing that their input has been conveyed to decision makers. The English victim statements pilot project confirms this finding. In fact, victims in continental legal systems who served as a party to the prosecution (as continental legal procedures allow) were highly satisfied with this role in the proceedings, and their level of satisfaction with justice was positively correlated with the amount of their participation. The literature on procedural justice provides theoretical explanations for these findings. According to procedural justice theories, litigants' satisfaction with justice and sense of fairness of the outcome is more affected by the procedures in which decisions were made rather than by the outcomes. Proceedings which provide victims with a voice or "process control" enhance their satisfaction with justice and sense of fair treatment.

Research in adversarial legal systems also suggests that the majority of victims of personal crimes wished to participate and provide input, even when they thought their input was ignored or did not affect the outcome of their case. Victims have multiple motives for providing input, and having a voice serves several functions for them. For some, input restores the unequal balance between themselves and the offender, particularly in cases in which the victim did not have an opportunity to testify or be heard because they were resolved by a plea. Others wanted "to communicate the impact of the offense to the offender." For the majority of the victims, filling out a VIS was a forum to formally express the crime impact on them, a civil duty they considered important for reaching a just sentence.

Providing input for VIS also helps victims to cope with the victimisation and the criminal justice experience. Many victims who filled out VIS claimed that they felt relieved or satisfied after providing the information. The recent English pilot project found that for the majority of the victims filing the statement was a worthwhile therapeutic experience, and the cathartic effect of recording the impact of the offence had been an end in itself. In-depth interviews of rape victims in the United States about their reasons for participation in criminal justice provide textured insights into the psychological, internally oriented benefits for victims' voices. Over half of the victims felt that input will assist with achieving substantive justice, and almost three quarters sought procedural justice. Through participation and input, victims wanted to engage the criminal justice process and, in the words of Nils Christie, to assert "ownership of the conflict" which they felt was misappropriated from them in the name of the state. Others wanted to reduce the power imbalance they felt with the defendant, resolve the emotional aspects of the rape, achieve emotional recovery, or achieve formal closure. This was particularly true for victims who never had the chance to be involved in the justice process because of a plea. Many victims also wanted to remind judges of the fact that behind the crime is a real person who is a victim.

The literature in the growing field of therapeutic jurisprudence provides support to the proposition that having a voice may improve victims' mental condition and welfare. Scholars in this area have discussed in length the therapeutic advantages of having a voice, and the harmful effects that feeling silenced and external to the process may have on victims.

Research further suggests that the overwhelming majority of the victims want their VIS to be used in sentencing, and many of them seek to influence the sentence imposed on the offender via the input. Although some of those who thought their input was ignored showed a lower level of satisfaction with justice because of raised expectations, this issue need not be used as an argument against the proposition that VIS can increase victim satisfaction with justice. First, the potential problem of heightening victim expectations can be resolved by explaining to victims that the VIS is only *one* of the factors judges use to determine the type and severity of penalties. As Ashworth recognises, research has shown that victims who receive explanations of the proceedings throughout the process tend to be satisfied with the outcome. Further, explanations may enhance victim satisfaction even when the outcome does not reflect victims' conception of a deserved sentence. There is no reason to suspect that explanations about the multiple factors that affect sentencing decisions will not be effective in preventing heightened expectations. One of the major aims of the victim movement, and the driving force behind it, was to help victims overcome their sense of powerlessness and reduce their feelings that the system is uncaring. Properly administered VIS schemes may be an effective way of achieving this objective, as well as creating realistic expectations.

Victims can also receive indirect benefits from providing input. A major source of satisfaction for victims is when judges pay attention to their input by citing victims' own phrases from impact statements in judicial sentencing comments. Victims feel gratified when their sense of harm is validated in judges' remarks. Victim advocates in Australia as well as in the United States indicate that victims who have heard or read sentencing comments in which judges quote their impact statements in sentencing remarks often say, "I could not believe the judge has actually listened to what I had to say."

Research also confirms that judges are sometimes unaware of victim suffering and injuries resulting from crime, because the information did not find its way into the file, either intentionally (due to bargaining considerations, or because of priorities of agencies charged with receiving the information and preparing the statements) or accidentally (due to agents underestimating the importance of the information, lack of resources to do the job, or mere incompetence or laziness). In the past, judges and other legal professionals had little opportunity to receive direct detailed input from victims and become acquainted with short and long-term effects of various crimes. Research shows that legal professionals who have been exposed to VIS have commented on how uninformed they were about the extent, variety and longevity of various victimisations, and how much they have learned from VIS about the impact of crime on victims from properly prepared VIS.

Sentencing, Unforeseen Results, and the "Normal" Victim

One of the major challenges in criminal justice sentencing is forming a fair and accurate picture of crime and its consequences to guide decision makers in their difficult task. As

I have argued elsewhere, being regularly exposed to victim input may provide a more balanced notion of the "normal" victim and the boundaries of harm and injury in criminal victimisation. The prosecution has its priorities and constraints in addressing the task of prosecuting offenders. More often than not, its organisational interests are in opposition to those of the victim, and they may not be interested in disclosing the full scope of the crime impact. Research also suggests that judges employ several justifications in discarding victim input, including its subjective or emotional nature, or its alleged unreliability due to victims' motives to lie or exaggerate. To resist victims' input because, for instance, it is subjective (the most common reason judges offer for objecting to VIS) is to suggest that there is an objective way to measure harm, or to experience loss, damage and injury. Yet, harm is perceived and experienced differently, according to victims' demographic and personal attributes as well as their prior experiences. Research about the relativity of harm questions the notion of the "normal" victim, and highlights legal professionals' resistance to consider victim input which differs from their own assessment of "appropriate" level of suffering and hence a "believable VIS." As feminists have shown in the context of rape and sexual harassment, the subjectivity of harm (or for that matter any personal experience) cannot be transformed to, or be judged by, "objective" measures without doing injustice to the experience and the person reporting it. Many recent legislative acts include what has been defined in the past as "merely" subjective experience. Research has also documented that harm descriptions which legal professionals have considered exaggerated or unbelievable are indeed common experiences which those acquainted with crime's impact on victims view as within the range of "normal" reactions to victimisation.

Conclusion

The purpose of instituting VIS was to provide victims a voice, not to restructure sentencing priorities. The legislation concerning victim input was not intended to substitute harm for culpability, nor to consider harm as the overriding criterion in sentencing. Providing victims with a voice has not only many therapeutic advantages and related fairness considerations, it also ensures that sentencing judges become aware of the extent of harm suffered by victims. Incorporation of victim statements also enhances sentence proportionality rather than harshness. Although it might be argued that the number of cases in which VIS make a difference in the outcome (i.e. result in either lower or higher penalty) is relatively low, to the individuals involved, and to the justice system as it whole, this makes all the difference.

To institute a meaningful reform in the area of victim participation, it is important to win the co-operation of all parties involved: prosecutors, judges and defence attorneys. These players have various professional and organisational incentives to oppose the introduction of victim input in proceedings. To date, legal professionals have had ample substantive and procedural reasons to excuse or justify their reluctance to comply with the VIS reform. The purpose of this paper was to expose these unsubstantiated justifications, and to oppose the use of research findings, which are taken out of context, to buttress what is essentially a political stand against victim integration in criminal justice.

In the light of recent evidence which challenges the traditional legal arguments against the VIS, it is time to re-evaluate the legal profession's approach to the concept and practice of victim input. Researchers in this area have pointed out that the problem of VIS has not been the instrument itself or its effect on proceedings, defendants and victims, but rather the hostile environment in which VIS has been implemented. Comparativists encourage us to increase appropriate legal transplants and decrease inappropriate ones. There is sufficient evidence at this point to suggest that VIS (among other victim-oriented reforms) is an appropriate transplant. VIS can hardly be considered a form of "victim prostitution" which "ought to be exposed and opposed." Rather, it needs to be redefined and viewed as a useful vehicle to enhance justice in adversarial criminal justice systems while it simultaneously helps and empowers victims. To approach victims in a paternalistic manner, and ignore victims' wishes to be heard, is to continue past approaches to victims as the "forgotten persons" of the system, and perpetuate the time-honoured tradition of treating victims as invisible. The social science evidence clearly suggests that we have no reason to fear, and every reason to include, victims in the criminal justice process.

Julian V Roberts, "Victim Impact Statements:
Recent Developments and Research Findings"
(2003) 47 Crim LQ 365 at 371-75, 376-83, 386-89 (edited; footnotes omitted)

Purposes Ascribed to Victim Impact Statements at Sentencing

Almost every scholarly article and research report begins with some discussion of the purpose that a victim impact statement is designed to serve. Many consist of anodyne statements that lack clarity while others fail to do full justice to the concept of victim impact, or reflect a deep mistrust of the whole notion of victim involvement in sentencing. VIS have been described as a "sop" to victims, a political reform designed to placate victims without actually influencing the sentencing process, and a form of therapy for victims: the system provides the victim with an opportunity to ventilate their feelings, and then business of the courts carries on.

The following purposes and benefits have been ascribed to Victim Impact Statements:

- to provide crown counsel with information about the offence;
- to provide sentencing judges with information about the seriousness of the crime, and, to a lesser extent, the culpability of the offender. This should help the court impose a sentence which is consistent with the principles of sentencing;
- to provide the court with a direct source of information about the victim's needs which may assist in the determination of more appropriate reparative sanctions;
- to provide the court with information about the appropriate conditions which might be imposed on the offender;
- to provide the victim with a public forum in which to make a statement reflecting their suffering;
- to provide the court with an opportunity to recognize the wrong committed against an individual victim;
- to provide the victim with the opportunity to communicate the effects of the crime to the offender;
- to allow victims to participate in sentencing, albeit in a non-determinative fashion; [and]

- to promote the idea that although crimes are committed against the state, and the judicial process involves a bipartite proceeding, crimes are committed against individual citizens.

From these primary purposes, proponents of the use of VIS hope:

- to increase victim satisfaction with the judicial process, in particular sentencing, and conversely to decrease the sense of alienation felt by many victims as they pass through the criminal justice system;
- to increase awareness among offenders of the harm they cause;
- to increase awareness among criminal justice professionals of the effects of criminal victimization;
- to increase public confidence in the administration of justice, particularly with respect to sentencing;
- to promote the possibility of reconciliation between the offender and the victim by encouraging offender empathy; [and]
- to provide victims with some sense of closure with respect to the crime, and thereby facilitate psychological healing.

Victim Impact Statements and the Codified Purpose and Principles of Sentencing

The link between many of the traditional sentencing purposes such as rehabilitation and deterrence and victim impact statements is certainly tenuous or non-existent; knowing more about the impact of the crime will not help the court devise a more effective deterrent sentence. However, retributive theories of sentencing are concerned with the limited input of victims at sentencing, at least with regard to the seriousness of the offence. Crime seriousness is the primary (but not exclusive) determinant of sentence severity under a desert-based rationale. Some commentators argue that the danger with the use of VIS is that they carry the potential to render the sentencing process more punitive. Thus Kent Roach describes them as a "symbolic and punitive reform." There has been apprehension that, nursing personal animus as a result of the crime, and adhering to unrealistic expectations of the sentencing process, victims may demand sentences well outside the normal range. When these demands remain unfulfilled, disappointment and resentment of the criminal justice system will surely follow.

Codified Purpose of Sentencing

Section 718 of the *Code* describes the purpose of sentencing, and contains two clear references to the role of the victim. This section articulates the fundamental purpose of sentencing, and identifies a number of sentencing objectives, including deterrence, denunciation, incapacitation and rehabilitation. These include most of the traditional goals of sentencing. However, the last two sentencing objectives in section 718 make specific reference to crime victims. One of these objectives relates to reparation, and the second has a particular significance for victim impact. According to section 718(f), one of the statutory sentencing objectives is: "*to promote a sense of responsibility in offenders, and acknowledgment of harm done to victims and to the community.*"

A clear way of acknowledging the harm to the victim is for the judge to cite the victim impact information communicated to the court by means of a VIS, or through submissions from the Crown. And further, promoting a sense of responsibility in offenders may well begin by sensitising them to the harm that they have inflicted, and the VIS may prove a useful conduit for this information. While judges may not cite victim impact in the absence of the victim, it is worth recalling that the offender is always present.

Codified Principles of Sentencing

Sections 718-718.2 of the *Code* identify a fundamental purpose of sentencing, a fundamental principle, as well as a series of subordinate principles. Section 718.1 articulates the "fundamental" principle in sentencing, namely proportionality. This principle is derived from retributive theories of punishment, specifically the just deserts version articulated by von Hirsch. Desert-based theories are essentially communicative theories of sentencing. A message of disapprobation is conveyed to the offender, and the severity of the sentence represents the measure of legal censure. But the communication is not restricted to a single message conveyed by a legal authority to an offender.

The sentence also carries a communication for the victim of the crime. The imposition of a sanction constitutes official recognition that this individual has been wronged. By permitting a victim to submit a statement of impact, the sentencing process introduces another possible communication: between the victim and the offender. The VIS thus plays a central role within communicative sentencing. Duff makes this point in his recent monograph on the subject: "criminal punishment ... is a mode of communication ... . It seeks to induce remorse in the offender." Remorse is more likely to emerge during a sentencing hearing in which the victim addresses the impact of the crime, rather than a prosecutor. No relationship exists between the prosecution and the offender. However, one has been established between the offender and the victim. In addition, for many crimes of violence, a relationship between the two parties will have pre-dated the commission of the crime.

The VIS provides the most appropriate vehicle by which to convey information about the impact of the crime. Indeed, a number of judgments have acknowledged as much. Crown submissions on the seriousness of the crime made prior to sentencing deprive the victim of the direct communication to the court, and the offender. This results in an interpretation being filtered through a professional's experience, one that may not always correspond with the view of the victim.

The VIS therefore represents a means by which to communicate a message to the offender. Confronting the offender with the consequences of his or her actions, and accompanying the message by the censure of the court (the sentence) is essential if the sentencing process is to achieve its codified goals. In fact, the VIS is a communication directed at two audiences: the sentencing judge and the offender. To date, almost all the emphasis in the scholarly literature has been upon the former. The case law to date as well as much of the research has represented VIS almost exclusively as a source of information for the court. In *Gabriel* for example, Hill J identifies four principal purposes of VIS. Three of these relate to the sentencing judge while the fourth relates to promoting the image of the administration of justice. None of these purposes involves communication between the parties giving rise to the criminal proceeding in the first place: victim and offender. The VIS offers a vehicle for communication from the victim to the offender, and from the judge to the victim and the offender.

Encouraging these forms of communication should not transform the sentencing hearing into a tripartite proceeding, nor should it undermine the central assumption of the adversarial system that a crime is committed against the state and not a private party. One of the few judgments that relate the VIS to the offender is written by Bagnall J in *R v. Redhead* where the judgment notes that: "the words of the victim of a crime might well serve to educate the offender as to the effects of his or her criminal behaviour."

The importance of the message to the offender should not be under-estimated. Hearing from the victim involves a completely different communicative dynamic from hearing about the impact of the crime through the sentencing submissions of the prosecutor. The adversarial system creates an antagonistic dynamic between the accused or offender and the prosecutor; this dynamic may well undermine the effectiveness of the communication. Hearing from the victim may also serve as a salutary reminder to the offender of the consequences of his actions. This should not be interpreted as a means of humiliating the offender, or an attempt at public debasement. Nor is it a message of intimidation associated with a deterrent sentence. Rather, it is a message of *sensitization*; an appeal from one individual to another: the victim sensitizes the offender to the effects of his or her conduct on other people.

At this point I review research relating to a series of questions arising from the use of victim impact statements.

How Often Are VIS Submitted?

Several commentators have noted that a major problem with VIS programs is that few victims actually submit an impact statement. This may be the case, but it is unclear what an appropriate or acceptable participation rate would be. It is unrealistic to expect all crime victims to submit an impact statement. It is the prerogative of the victim to decide whether or not to submit a statement, and many victims may have sound reasons for not participating in the sentencing process in this way. Evaluating whether the participation rate is high or low inevitably leads to a consideration of the reasons why many victims elect not to submit a statement. If a victim decides not to submit a VIS for personal reasons unrelated to the crime, or because they have sufficient faith that the prosecutor will faithfully represent the impact of the crime, it is hard to consider their "non-participation" a failure of the criminal justice system. On the other hand, if victims decide not to submit an impact statement because they have little faith that it will be used, because they have been warned that it will not be considered by the judge, or because they fear that submission of a VIS will have a negative impact on them personally, then remedial action is necessary.

The completion rates in the Department of Justice VIS research conducted in the 1980s generated an overall completion rate of 23%. It would be wrong to infer that the remainder of the samples of victims refused to participate, as the failure to contact the victim was twice as likely to be the cause of non-completion than refusal on the part of the victim. This research was conducted over a decade ago, and it is probable that participation rates are higher now, as a result of the legislative amendments and the existence of provincial victim assistance programs. Nevertheless, the inescapable conclusion is that for one reason or another, only a minority of crime victims elect to submit a statement of impact, and far fewer are actually present in court at the sentencing hearing. This result is consistent with research in other jurisdictions. Alexander and Lord cite a participation rate of one victim in four, and rates appear to be lower still in Australia and England and Wales.

Which Factors Influence the Victim's Decision to Submit an Impact Statement?

The Canadian research identified three principal reasons cited by victims for submitting a statement: (a) to ensure that justice was done; (b) because it "seemed like a good idea and was their civic duty," and (c) to "communicate the impact of the crime to the offender." It is also clear that part of the low rate of participation arises from the fact that many victims of property crimes see little benefit, and no need, to submit an impact statement. This explains the fact that the refusal rate with respect to submitting a VIS was twice as high for property crimes as personal injury offences in one of the site studies conducted by the Department of Justice in 1990. In her study of VIS, Muir reports that the most common reason given by victims for not submitting were (i) they did not perceive the VIS to be important, (ii) the incident was too trivial to justify a VIS, and (iii) the victims had forgotten about the VIS. She adds that: "The notion that revenge or desire to bring about harsher sentences is the main motivating factor for victim participation was not supported by the data." Campbell Research Associates found that the most frequently cited reason for completing a VIS was to influence sentencing.

Findings with respect to this issue vary across jurisdictions. Hoyle et al. found that the majority of the victims in their study in England and Wales explained that they had submitted a VIS for expressive reasons (i.e., to communicate a message of impact). Slightly over half cited an instrumental reason, namely the desire to influence the outcome of the sentencing hearing. In the survey of crime victims in South Australia, Erez, Roeger and Morgan report that the main reason that victims cited for providing information for a VIS was to ensure that justice was done (cited by over two-thirds of the respondents). The other reasons cited included communicating the impact of the crime to the offender, and in order to discharge a civic duty.

Many victims who submit a VIS, it would appear, expect the VIS to have an impact on sentencing outcomes. This suggests that even if they do not overtly seek to influence judges, victims expect their statement to have some effect. Either way, disappointment may arise if the victim perceives the statement to have had no impact on the sentence imposed. Since in both jurisdictions the victim's statement is incorporated in the same way, namely to inform the court but not to influence the sentence, the discrepancy in victims' expectations may be explained by the nature of information provided by criminal justice professionals.

Do VIS Influence Sentencing Practices?

Much of the research in the area has addressed the question of whether the introduction of victim impact statements changes sentencing practices. The answer is critical to advocates and critics alike: many of the former argue that if VIS do not affect sentencing practices, victims will become disillusioned by the process. Critics respond that if sentencing practices do change as a result of the introduction of VIS, the principle of parity in sentencing will be undermined. Indeed, apprehension of the effect of VIS on sentencing patterns drives much of the opposition toward the role of the victim in sentencing. VIS are therefore criticized from both directions: if they affect the sentence of the court, they will be criticized for undermining equity in sentencing; if they have no impact, they will be faulted for having raised (and then subsequently dashed) victims' expectations.

Tests of the "impact" hypothesis have been conducted in many jurisdictions, and these have generally found little effect on sentencing patterns. Erez, Roeger and Morgan report the results of an analysis of aggregate sentencing patterns in South Australia before and after the introduction of victim impact statements (in 1989). The results are crystal clear: sentencing patterns did not become more severe in the post-reform phase. The researchers also concluded that the introduction of the VIS did not have any significant impact on the length of sentences of imprisonment. Fears that the arrival of victim impact statements would result in harsher sentencing were therefore groundless. The same pattern has emerged from Canadian research. Muir examined the impact of VIS on sentencing outcomes on her study in Calgary and summarizes the results in the following way: "It must be concluded from this [analysis] that the availability of victim impact statements did not have any important or noticeable impact on sentences handed down by the courts." A similar pattern of findings emerged from other sites in this research. The finding of no impact on sentencing patterns has been replicated in many other studies.

Interviews with legal professionals confirm the findings from empirical research. Erez, Roeger and Morgan note that there is agreement among the legal professionals in South Australia that victim input has not increased sentence severity. This conclusion also applies to surveys of criminal justice professionals in other jurisdictions. Finally, with respect to the question of impact on sentencing patterns, it is perhaps not surprising that there is little evidence of change, in light of the fact that in Canada (as elsewhere), there is no specific direction to judges; they are simply asked to "consider" the victim's statement, which could mean anything, and is probably interpreted by judges in a protean fashion.

Other factors also militate against victim impact statements having the kind of impact on sentencing outcomes that can be detected by an aggregate analysis. First, most sentencing hearings follow a guilty plea. Often the plea is itself the result of negotiations between counsel, and these discussions may well have resulted in agreement to place a joint submission before the court. Plea negotiations of this kind impair the ability of the system in at least two ways. First, the case is most likely to proceed expeditiously to a sentencing hearing. Second, the Crown will not have the time or the resources to contact the victim. It is unclear, at present, what effect the statutory requirement that the court solicit the Crown with respect to whether the victim has been apprised of her right to submit a VIS has had in cases such as these.

How Well Do Victims Understand the Role of VIS in Sentencing?

A near universal issue concerns the gap between what victims expect, and the use actually made of VIS at sentencing. Many victims expect the content of their statements to influence the nature and severity of the sanction imposed. It is perhaps not an unreasonable expectation in light of the wording in s. 722, which, it will be recalled, states that: "For the purpose of *determining the sentence* to be imposed on an offender or whether the offender should be discharged pursuant to section 730 in respect of any offence, *the court shall consider* any statement that may have been prepared in accordance with subsection (2) of a victim of the offence judges" (emphasis added). A report on focus groups conducted with victims in Toronto makes the point clearly: "When the concept of [VIS] was first presented to victims, they all believed that it would affect the sentence given." This result is consistent with the findings from the Department of Justice research conducted shortly after the 1988 legislation was proclaimed.

Once again, some VIS forms may contribute to confusion among victims. The Victim Impact Statement information guide used in Ontario states that "[t]he Victim Impact

Statement *may* be used during the sentencing hearing" (emphasis added), and, more curiously, "[t]he judge will decide whether or not to consider the victim impact statement when determining the sentence." Small wonder, then, that in the research on victims conducted by Meredith and Paquette "participants were unclear as to whether or not judges are required to actually read the statements that they had prepared at all."

In addition to holding misperceptions about the true purpose of a VIS, many victims are simply confused: Campbell Research Associates report that approximately one-quarter of the victims in their study did not know the purpose of the statements. This study was conducted in 1989, but it is unlikely that victims have a much clearer perception of the purpose of VIS in 2002. The fact that many victims want to influence sentencing is hardly surprising; indeed it is a natural reaction, reflecting widespread public confusion over the role of the victim in the sentencing process, and indeed the true nature of a criminal proceeding under the adversarial system. But victims may well accept the role currently assigned to them if it is explained thoroughly, with sensitivity, and by the right authority.

A clear danger associated with VIS concerns the problem of unfulfilled expectations. If victims expect their statement to affect sentence outcome, and then perceive (correctly, in light of the research findings described earlier) that their input had no discernible impact, what is their reaction likely to be? This question has been addressed in a number of studies, and the result is predictable. Erez and Tontodonato for example, report that victims who expected to influence the outcome but who thought their input had not affected the sentence were less satisfied. It is also worth noting that this negative reaction generalized to the criminal justice system as a whole; victims who had expected their statement to affect sentencing held more negative opinions of the system. Herein lies the danger of arousing, and then failing to fulfill, expectations among crime victims. In this way, a reform designed to promote victim satisfaction may actually result in lower levels of satisfaction. This finding points to the importance of clarifying for victims the true nature and purpose of a VIS.

Do VIS Improve Victim Satisfaction with the Sentencing Process?

If submitting a VIS has no positive, or even a negative effect on victim satisfaction levels, one of the principal justifications for encouraging victims to submit a statement vanishes. Researchers have accordingly attempted to ascertain whether submitting a VIS increases victim satisfaction. In the early Canadian work there were no significant differences in satisfaction levels of victims who had submitted or had not submitted a VIS. Unfortunately, that research had an important design flaw: there is no way of knowing about the influence of other pre-court differences between the groups (in addition to whether they submitted a VIS). What is needed is a pre-post design of people who choose to submit a statement.

Research in other jurisdictions that has avoided this methodological problem has generally found little increase in satisfaction levels of victims who have submitted a VIS. Davis and Smith conducted an experiment in which participants were assigned at random to either participate or not participate in a victim impact program. The results revealed that the victim impact statements had no effects on a number of different measures. The use of random assignment permits clear causal inferences to be drawn. Davis and Smith concluded that victim impact statements constituted an "unfulfilled promise" to crime victims.

Recent empirical research on victim impact statements in Canada consisted of focus groups involving victims. The findings suggest that completing a victim impact statement was perceived to have some benefits for the victim. Perhaps the best measure of whether victims perceive any utility to the VIS lies in their response to the question "Would you complete this form again in the future, knowing what you know now?" Most respondents in the focus group research reported that they would go through the process again. This finding is consistent with the research conducted in the 1980s. Thus Campbell Research Associates report that almost all the victims who had completed a VIS would be willing to submit a statement if they were victimized again. There is clearly variation with respect to this issue, however. Respondents participating in the Toronto focus group in this research took a very negative view, responding that they would not participate again. They cited the lack of impact on sentencing patterns, and the experience of being cross-examined as the factors responsible for their resolve to not participate in the future. This outcome underlines the fact that local variation exists with respect to the nature of victims' experiences.

Julian V Roberts & Allen Edgar, *Victim Impact Statements at Sentencing:*
Judicial Experiences and Perceptions—A Survey of Three Jurisdictions
(Ottawa: Department of Justice Canada, 2006) (edited)

Since their introduction in 1988, victim impact statements (VIS) have generated considerable controversy. This is true in Canada as well as other jurisdictions. To this point however, there has been an almost complete absence of information about the attitudes and experiences of the most important criminal justice professional with respect to sentencing: judges. The present research explored judicial perceptions and experiences in four provinces: Ontario, British Columbia, Alberta and Manitoba.

Most Judges Sentence a Large Number of Offenders Every Month

The caseload in Canada's criminal courts creates a large number of sentencing hearings. Respondents were asked how many sentencing hearings they conducted each month, and the averages were: BC: 55; Alberta: 33; Manitoba: 38. The aggregate average for the three jurisdictions was 42 sentencing hearings per month, considerably lower than the average number reported by judges in Ontario (71). These statistics have important implications for the sentencing process, and in particular for the question of victim input: judges are under great pressure to get through a large number of cases.

Victim Impact Statements (VIS) Are Submitted in Only a Small Percentage of Cases

One of the problems identified in the research literature is confirmed in this survey of judges: victim impact statements appear in only a small percentage of cases being sentenced. In BC, judges reported that a VIS had been submitted in 8% of cases, compared to 11% in Manitoba and 13% in Alberta. These statistics are comparable to the responses from Ontario in 2002 when on average judges reported seeing a VIS in 11% of cases.

Many Judges Report an Increase in the Number of VIS Submitted

Judges in all four jurisdictions reported an increase in the number of VIS submitted in recent years. This is particularly true in Manitoba where 41% of the respondents reported seeing a moderate or significant increase in the number of VIS.

Judges Report Having Difficulty in Determining Whether the Victim Has Been Apprised of His or Her Right to Submit an Impact Statement

It is sometimes challenging for a judge to know whether a victim impact statement has been submitted. Respondents were asked about this particular issue. Almost half (42%) the respondents in all jurisdictions stated that it was "difficult in most cases." This pattern of responses suggests that it is frequently difficult to ascertain whether the victim has been provided with the opportunity to submit a victim impact statement.

Judges Often Have to Proceed to Sentencing Without Knowing Whether the Victim Has Been Apprised of the Right to Submit a VIS

Judges often have to proceed to sentence the offender without knowing whether a victim impact statement has been prepared. The results of the survey revealed considerable variability regarding whether judges have to proceed to sentence the offender without knowing the status of the victim impact statement. The percentage that responded that they often proceeded without this information varied from 35% in Manitoba to 70% in British Columbia. Across the three 2006 surveys almost two-thirds of judges stated that they often had to proceed without knowing the status of the victim impact statement.

Only Rarely Do Victims Elect to Make an Oral Presentation of the Impact Statement

How often do victims elect to make an oral presentation of their victim impact statement? It seems to be a quite rare occurrence in all jurisdictions. The most frequent response across all jurisdictions was "very occasionally." Approximately three-quarters of respondents held this view. In British Columbia 24% of the sample stated that the victim had never expressed an interest in delivering the statement orally whereas in Alberta only 5% gave this response.

Most Judges Report No Change in the Number of Victims Wishing to Make an Oral Presentation of Their Victim Impact Statements

Judges were asked whether they had perceived any increase since 1999 in the number of victims who expressed a desire to deliver their statements orally. Considerable variation emerged across jurisdictions. Thus in British Columbia 69% of respondents reported no change in the number of victims expressing a desire to deliver statements orally whereas in Manitoba fewer than one quarter held this view. Manitoba judges were significantly more likely to report seeing an increase in requests for an oral delivery of the statement.

Victims Seldom Cross-Examined on Contents of Their Victim Impact Statements

Some victims have been cross-examined on the contents of their victim impact statements. This can be stressful for the victim, as several victims have affirmed. It is unclear how often this practice occurs. Responses to the survey suggest that it is a relatively rare occurrence: 97% stated that it never or almost never took place. This is consistent with findings from the survey conducted in Ontario, where 84% of respondents stated that cross-examination of the victim never or almost never took place.

*Most Judges Perceive Victim Impact Statements to Contain Information That Is
in General Useful, as well as Relevant, to Sentencing*

Judges were asked: "*In general, are victim impact statements useful?*" The response options
were that the statements were useful "in all cases," "in most cases," "in some cases" and
"in just a few cases." Consistent with the responses from Ontario, judges in the three other
jurisdictions clearly found victim impact statements to be useful. Combining the first two
response categories it can be seen that 62% of judges in British Columbia reported that
VIS were useful in most or all cases. The percentage was slightly lower in Manitoba (59%)
and lowest in Alberta (35%). Over all three jurisdictions 50% of judges held this view.
Only 19% of judges believed that VIS are useful in "just a few cases." This pattern of results
suggests that contrary to some commentators, judges do in fact find victim impact statements useful.

The second question relating to this issue asked judges whether they found VIS useful
in terms of providing information relevant to the principles of sentencing. Again, the
general reaction was affirmative although there was considerable inter-jurisdictional
variability. The response was particularly positive in Manitoba where almost half (47%)
of judges stated that they found VIS to contain information relevant to sentencing principles often, almost always or always. This response was made by fewer judges in British
Columbia (36%) and far fewer in Alberta (12%). Over the three jurisdictions, approximately three quarters of judges reported finding relevant information; only one-quarter
of the total sample stated that VIS never contained information relevant to the principles
of sentencing.

Perceptions of Judges Consistent with Those of Crown Counsel

It is worth noting that a similar trend emerged from the survey of Crown counsel conducted in Ontario. In that survey, approximately one-third of respondents indicated that
in most cases, or almost every case, the VIS contained new or different information relevant to sentencing (see Cole, 2003). Similarly, when asked whether victim impact statements were useful to the court, approximately two-thirds of the Crown counsel responded,
"yes, in most cases." No respondents in that survey indicated that victim impact statements
were never or almost never useful to the court at sentencing.

VIS Constitute a Unique Source of Information Relevant to Sentencing

It may be argued that the information contained in the victim impact statement is useful,
but redundant, in the sense that it has already emerged at trial or from the Crown submissions at sentencing. To address this question the survey posed the following question:
"*How often do victim impact statements contain information relevant to sentencing that
did not emerge during the trial or in the Crown's sentencing submissions?*" As with a number
of other questions, the most positive response came from the Manitoba judges where 29%
stated that VIS often represented a unique source of information. In British Columbia
only 17% held this view, and not one respondent in Alberta held it. The aggregated
response was more positive than negative. Across the three jurisdictions 47% stated that
VIS often or sometimes contained useful information unavailable from other sources;
only 21% responded that VIS almost never contained such information. These trends

parallel those emerging from the survey of Ontario judges. Taken together the responses to these inter-related questions suggest that from the judicial perspective—which is surely the most important—the victim impact statement represents a useful source of information relevant to sentencing.

The VIS Often Contains the Victim's Recommendations Regarding Sentence

The survey asked judges how often, in their experience, victim impact statements contain the victims' wishes regarding the sentence that should be imposed. The pattern of responses varied according to the respondent's jurisdiction. Only 12% of judges in Manitoba stated that the victim's wishes regarding sentencing were often, always or almost always present. The proportion of judges responding in this way was significantly somewhat higher in Alberta (19%), and much higher in British Columbia (37%). It was highest of all in Ontario where almost half the sample (43%) in 2002 reported seeing victim "submissions" on sentencing often, almost always or always. Across the three new jurisdictions 24% stated that sentence recommendations were often, almost always or always present. Only one quarter (25%) stated that victim sentence recommendations were never or almost never present. These responses demonstrate the need to better inform victims about the true purpose of the victim impact statements, and to guide them regarding the kinds of information that should not be included in their statement.

Judges Often Refer to the Victim Impact Statement or Its Contents

Consistent with the trend for judges to be sensitive to the issue, we found that most judges reported that they almost always or often referred to the victim impact statements in their reasons for sentence. This trend was most noticeable in British Columbia where over half (53%) almost always referred to VIS or victim impact in reasons for sentence. The percentages reporting this were considerably lower in Manitoba (35%) and Alberta (29%). Across the three jurisdictions, 39% of respondents almost always referred to victim impact when giving reasons for sentence. Overall, only 5% stated that they never referred to victim impact statements.

If the Victim Is Present at Sentencing Judges Often Address Him or Her Directly

Most sentencing hearings take place in the absence of the victim. However, when they are present, it is clearly of assistance to be addressed by the court. The last question on the survey was the following: "*Do you ever address the victim directly in delivering oral reasons for sentence?*" Results indicated that judges are certainly alive to this issue: almost two-thirds (63%) of all respondents stated that they sometimes or often addressed the victim directly. Sixteen percent never or almost never addressed the victim, and 21% stated that they did so "only occasionally."

Many Judges Believe That VIS Increase Victim Satisfaction

One purpose of the VIS is to promote victim satisfaction with the sentencing process. Respondents were next asked whether in their experience victims who submitted an impact statement appeared more satisfied. Before reviewing the findings it is worth noting that a substantial proportion of respondents expressed the view that they were unable to respond to the question. The trends were consistent across jurisdictions: judges were more likely to hold the view that submitting a victim impact statement promoted victim satisfaction.

Overall, in the three jurisdictions approximately one third of respondents (32%) held the view that victims who submitted a statement were often or always more satisfied. Alberta judges held the most positive views. Thus, 39% of respondents in that province believed that victims who submitted a statement often or always seemed more satisfied. In the other two provinces the proportions of respondents holding this view were slightly lower (26% and 27%).

Conclusion

As a result of the surveys conducted in four jurisdictions we now have a much more informed view of the utility of victim impact statements. It was encouraging to note that while variability emerged across the jurisdictions in response to some questions, there was generally considerable consensus—particularly regarding the most important issues concerning the victim impact statement regime. We would end this report on the perceptions of judges in four jurisdictions by concluding that despite a number of criticisms victim impact statements perform a useful function in the sentencing process in Canada.

NOTE

VISs were introduced over 30 years ago in the United States. Since then, almost all common law jurisdictions have introduced victim impact statement regimes: see Julian V Roberts, "Crime Victims, Sentencing, and Release from Prison" in Joan Petersilia & Kevin R Reitz, eds, *The Oxford Handbook of Sentencing and Corrections* (New York: Oxford University Press, 2012). The crucial difference between the VIS regimes in Canada and the United States is that victims in most American states have the right to make sentence recommendations as part of their impact statement. As discussed below, except in certain circumstances, "submissions" on sentence by the victim are currently prohibited in Canada and in all other common law jurisdictions. As the above readings illustrate, the use of victim impact statements and victim input at sentencing remains controversial, and a number of scholars have opposed their use. Nevertheless, the now substantial research literature on VISs suggests that many of the adverse effects have not emerged: see e.g. James Chalmers, Peter Duff & Fiona Leverick, "Victim Impact Statements: Can Work, Do Work (For Those Who Bother to Make Them)" (2007) Crim L Rev 360. In addition, although VISs still appear in only a small proportion of all sentencing decisions, sentencers seem to find their presence beneficial to determining an appropriate sentence. Although, for a variety of reasons, only a minority of crime victims elect to depose a VIS at sentencing, those who do report benefiting from the experience. A telling statistic is that of all victims who deposed a VIS, approximately four out of five express an intention to do so again in the event of future victimization. For a recent academic exchange of views on the subject of the role of victim impact evidence, see the articles and notes in (2010-2011) 15 Can Crim L Rev 1 and following.

II. THE CURRENT LEGAL FRAMEWORK

The first formal statutory provision for the admission of VISs was enacted by *An Act to Amend the Criminal Code (Victims of Crime)*, RSC 1985, c 23 (4th Supp), s 7 (passed in 1988). This provision has been amended from time to time and now appears as s 722 of the *Criminal Code*, set out below. (The section was re-enacted in Bill C-41, *An Act to Amend the Criminal Code (Sentencing)*, SC 1995, c 22 and amended by *An Act to Amend the Criminal Code (Victims of Crime)*, SC 1999, c 25, ss 17 and 18, and the *Modernization of Benefits and Obligations Act*, SC 2000, c 12, s 95(d). These Acts made changes throughout the *Criminal Code* to recognize victims explicitly and to extend various Code provisions to common law partners. An example of these types of changes is seen in the bail provisions. Victims may also provide impact statements for disposition hearings for individuals found not criminally responsible for an offence and for parole hearings for convicted offenders: see *Criminal Code*, ss 672.5(14) to (16) and s 745.63. Most recently, the various provisions relating to victims' input into sentencing have been amended by the *Canadian Victims Bill of Rights*, SC 2015, c 13, s 2 (Bill C-32, in force 23 July 2015), amending ss 718, 718.2, and 722 of the *Criminal Code*. This legislation also enacted a general "community impact statement" provision.) It is important that s 722 be read and interpreted in its proper statutory context in conjunction with the purposes and principles of sentencing in ss 718 to 718.2 of the *Criminal Code*. In particular, "to provide reparations for harm done to victims or to the community" (s 718(e)) and "to promote a sense of responsibility in offenders, and acknowledgment of the harm done to victims or to the community" (s 718(f)) are identified as objectives of the sentencing function: see the discussion of these issues in Chapter 2, Judicial Methodology and the Legislative Context; note also that s 718.2 identifies certain victim features or characteristics that are relevant for sentencing purposes.

The current version of s 722 of the *Criminal Code* provides as follows:

722(1) When determining the sentence to be imposed on an offender or whether the offender should be discharged under section 730 in respect of any offence, the court shall consider any statement of a victim prepared in accordance with this section and filed with the court describing the physical or emotional harm, property damage or economic loss suffered by the victim as a result of the commission of the offence and the impact of the offence on the victim.

(2) As soon as feasible after a finding of guilt and in any event before imposing sentence, the court shall inquire of the prosecutor if reasonable steps have been taken to provide the victim with an opportunity to prepare a statement referred to in subsection (1).

(3) On application of the prosecutor or a victim or on its own motion, the court may adjourn the proceedings to permit the victim to prepare a statement referred to in subsection (1) or to present evidence in accordance with subsection (9), if the court is satisfied that the adjournment would not interfere with the proper administration of justice.

(4) The statement must be prepared in writing, using Form 34.2 in Part XXVIII, in accordance with the procedures established by a program designated for that purpose by the lieutenant governor in council of the province in which the court is exercising its jurisdiction.

(5) The court shall, on the request of a victim, permit the victim to present the statement by

(a) reading it;

(b) reading it in the presence and close proximity of any support person of the victim's choice;

(c) reading it outside the court room or behind a screen or other device that would allow the victim not to see the offender; or

(d) presenting it in any other manner that the court considers appropriate.

(6) During the presentation

(a) the victim may have with them a photograph of themselves taken before the commission of the offence if it would not, in the opinion of the court, disrupt the proceedings; or

(b) if the statement is presented by someone acting on the victim's behalf, that individual may have with them a photograph of the victim taken before the commission of the offence if it would not, in the opinion of the court, disrupt the proceedings.

(7) The victim shall not present the statement outside the court room unless arrangements are made for the offender and the judge or justice to watch the presentation by means of closed-circuit television or otherwise and the offender is permitted to communicate with counsel while watching the presentation.

(8) In considering the statement, the court shall take into account the portions of the statement that it considers relevant to the determination referred to in subsection (1) and disregard any other portion.

(9) Whether or not a statement has been prepared and filed in accordance with this section, the court may consider any other evidence concerning any victim of the offence for the purpose of determining the sentence to be imposed on the offender or whether the offender should be discharged under section 730.

722.1 The clerk of the court shall provide a copy of a statement referred to in subsection 722(1), as soon as practicable after a finding of guilt, to the offender or counsel for the offender, and to the prosecutor.

NOTE

Section 722.2 requires a sentencing court to also consider any "community impact statement" (CIS) that is filed with the court. A CIS is a "statement made by an individual on a community's behalf ... describing the harm or loss suffered by the community as a result of the commission of the offence and the impact of the offence on the community." As with a VIS, the statement is to be in writing using the prescribed form, and may be presented in the same manner as the VIS: see e.g. *R v Nicholls*, 2015 ONSC 8136.

A. Definition of "Victim"

Following the enactment of this legislation, the courts grappled with the question of who is a victim within the meaning of the provision. As originally enacted, the provision referred to "*the* person to whom harm is done or who suffers physical or emotional loss as a result of the commission of the offence." A restrictive approach to the role of victims based in part on this language is perpetuated in *R v Curtis* (1992), 69 CCC (3d) 385 (NBCA). In *Curtis*, the offender pleaded guilty to assault causing bodily harm to another man who had formed a friendship with his estranged wife by punching and kicking the man a number of times, causing serious injuries that required hospitalization and surgery. The assault took place in front of his estranged wife and his daughter. At issue on appeal was whether the sentencing court had erred in accepting a VIS from the estranged wife on behalf of herself and her daughter relating to the assault and its effect on her and her daughter and her future relationship with the victim's mother. In finding that her statement was not admissible, the court stated:

> It is to be observed that the definition of "victim" contained in s. 735(1.4)(a) refers to "*the* person" to whom harm is done or who suffers loss. In my opinion, the use of the definite article in the definition section restricts the meaning of the word "victim" to the "direct" victim of the offence.

In addition to the use of the definite article in para. (a) of s. 735(1.4), support for a restricted meaning of the word "victim" can be found in para. (b) of s. 735(1.4) which permits certain other persons to submit a victim impact statement where "the person" referred to in para. (a) is dead, ill or otherwise incapable of making a statement. From this it would seem to follow that if the direct victim is not dead, ill or otherwise incapable, these other persons would not be allowed to submit a victim impact statement. Moreover, one of these other persons is a victim's spouse. If it was intended to allow anybody affected by an offence to submit a victim impact statement, surely one such person would be the spouse of the direct victim. Yet it appears that she or he is excluded unless the "victim" is incapacitated.

• • •

While an argument can perhaps be made that the definition of "victim" in s. 735(1.4)(a) could be read to include not only the direct victim of an offence but also a person who suffers physical or emotional loss as the result of the commission of an offence, I am not persuaded that this would be a proper reading of the legislative intent as expressed in the definition. In this respect, it is to be noted that prior to the amendment of s. 735, the Code did not allow for the introduction of victim impact statements. If Parliament had intended to permit courts to receive statements from anyone other than a direct victim, it is my opinion it could more clearly have made provision for the reception into evidence of multiple victim impact statements. [Emphasis added.]

R v Phillips (1995), 26 OR (3d) 522 (Gen Div) addressed the same issue raised in *Curtis*, but reached a different conclusion. Phillips was convicted of second-degree murder in the killing of a police officer. The Crown tendered victim impact statements from the deceased's fiancée, his partner on the force, and a representative of a local police–community association. The latter statement spoke of the impact that the death had on the small community where the officer lived and served. In finding these statements admissible, the court stated:

With the greatest of respect to the New Brunswick Court of Appeal [in *Curtis*], I am unable to accept this interpretation which I find would unreasonably limit the ambit of this provision in the *Criminal Code*. I do so for two reasons. They both relate to the application of the *Interpretation Act*, RSC 1985, c. I-21.

First, s. 33(2) of that Act states that words in the singular include the plural. Accordingly, there is no reason to restrict the definition of "victim" in s. 735(1.4)(a) to the singular. I find nothing in para. (b) thereof to lead me to the conclusion that it was in any way intended to, or in fact, has the effect of limiting the definition of "victim" in para. (a). This proposition would appear to be directly contrary to the legislative intent of the amendment which was adopted by the House of Commons Legislative Committee prior to the third reading of Bill C-89. See "Two Scales of Justice: The Victim as Adversary" (1993), 35 *CLQ* 334, an article by Mr. Steven Skurka, at p. 344 (footnote 27). ... My second concern related to the *Interpretation Act* involves s. 12 thereof which [deems every enactment to be remedial and requires that it be given "such fair, large and liberal construction and interpretation as best ensures the attainment of its object"].

• • •

Applying [this broad and liberal] approach to the issue at bar, I have to consider the policy that motivated Parliament to permit consideration of a VIS and then apply those principles to the definition of "victim" in s. 735(1.4). In *R v. Nelson*, Stuart TCJ of the Yukon Territorial Court ... outlined the purpose of this 1988 amendment ... :

The victim impact statement accords the victim an opportunity to ensure that their concerns are incorporated in the sentencing process without being exposed to the trauma of testifying ... Sentencing, among its many objectives, aspires to impose a sentence that the victim will regard as just. Ensuring that their concerns are heard creates the basis for victims to accept and believe in the fairness of the process ... . Finally, without the victim's impact, the seriousness of the crime cannot be fully appreciated. What may be viewed from the bench as trivial, may in fact be serious, and conversely what may be generally regarded as a serious crime may not be if the full story was before the court … Victim impact statements can help offenders appreciate the ramifications of their conduct on others and thereby add an awareness essential to promote and sustain genuine contrition and the will to change their behaviour.

· · ·

[T]hese comments reflect the virtual flood of victims' rights initiatives that have been undertaken in the common law jurisdictions in the last decade … . As well, they confirm the fact that retribution continues to be a valid consideration in the sentencing process … .

· · ·

… My experience has not been that victims wish to monopolize the sentencing process; they merely want to be able to participate in it in a meaningful way.

The provision of the three contested VIS herein will assist me in lifting the character of P.C. Nystedt from the status of a "faceless human cipher." I see no potential for them to distort the sentencing hearing into an exclusive process to rectify the purely private interests of their authors. They will merely provide a balance to the anticipated evidence that will be advanced on behalf of the offender in mitigation of sentence. Accordingly, both sides will be afforded a hearing that reflects the principles of fundamental justice … . I am persuaded that the definition of "victim" in s. 735(1.4) should be given a broad and liberal interpretation.

The approach in *Phillips* is now reflected in the legislation. First, in 1999, Parliament amended the definition of victim by changing "*the* person" to "*a* person": see SC 1999, c 25, s 17(3), which contemplates a much wider class of persons being affected by a crime than just the direct victim. For further discussion on the scope of "victim" under the 1999 provisions, see *R v Hames*, [2000] AJ No 1538 (QL) (QB) and *R v McDonough* (2006), 209 CCC (3d) 547 (Ont Sup Ct J). In 2015, Parliament confirmed this broad notion of "victim" and also extended the definition to specifically encompass other types of loss and harms, as set out in ss 2 and 2.2 of the Code:

2. In this Act,

· · ·

victim means a person against whom an offence has been committed, or is alleged to have been committed, who has suffered, or is alleged to have suffered, physical or emotional harm, property damage or economic loss as the result of the commission or alleged commission of the offence and includes, for the purposes of sections 672.5, 722 and 745.63, a person who has suffered physical or emotional harm, property damage or economic loss as the result of the commission of an offence against any other person.

· · ·

2.2(1) For the purposes of sections 606, 672.5, 722, 737.1 and 745.63, any of the following individuals may act on the victim's behalf if the victim is dead or incapable of acting on their own behalf:

(a) the victim's spouse, or if the victim is dead, their spouse at the time of death;

(b) the victim's common-law partner, or if the victim is dead, their common-law partner at the time of death;

(c) a relative or dependant of the victim;

(d) an individual who has in law or fact custody, or is responsible for the care or support, of the victim; and

(e) an individual who has in law or fact custody, or is responsible for the care or support, of a dependant of the victim.

(2) An individual is not entitled to act on a victim's behalf if the individual is an accused in relation to the offence or alleged offence that resulted in the victim suffering harm or loss or is an individual who is found guilty of that offence or who is found not criminally responsible on account of mental disorder or unfit to stand trial in respect of that offence.

NOTE

The definition of "victim" now includes "a person who has suffered physical or emotional harm, property damage or economic loss *as the result of the commission of an offence against any other person*" (emphasis added). Given the inclusion of this phrase, exactly how broad is the definition of "victim"? Does it include anyone who observed or reacted to the crime?

B. The Content of the Victim Impact Statement and the Method of Presentation

Initially, the provision was largely silent on the content of a VIS and the method of presentation. The provision merely specified that a VIS should be in writing, describe "the harm done" or "loss suffered" by the victim, and be "in accordance with the procedures established by a program designated for that purpose" by the province. This required each province and territory to develop its own form and procedures for introducing such statements in court. In 1999, the provision was amended to require the court, "on the request of a victim," to read his or her statement or present the statement "in any other manner that the court considers appropriate": see SC 1999, c 25, s 17(1). Most recently, in 2015, the provision was further amended by including, for the first time, a prescribed form for a VIS and, second, setting out differing manners of presentation for VISs: see SC 2015, c 13, s 26. Before considering the new form and methods of presentation, it is useful to briefly examine the guidelines set out by the courts prior to the enactment of the 2015 amendments. When reviewing the following cases, consider how the content of VISs relate to the aims and principles of sentencing in ss 718 to 718.2 of the Code; what should and should not be included in a VIS and why; how VISs are to be placed before the court; and the relationship between the various sections of the Code regulating proof of facts for sentencing, including the extent to which counsel may cross-examine a victim on his or her statement.

R v Berner
2013 BCCA 188

[Berner was convicted of dangerous driving causing death, dangerous driving causing bodily harm, impaired driving causing death, and impaired driving causing bodily harm. She was driving at almost twice the speed limit on a familiar road when she hit some speed bumps, lost control of her car, and struck a woman and her child. The woman was seriously injured and the child died as a result of the collision. Berner had been drinking before the accident and, on the basis of her manner of driving, the court found her ability to drive was impaired by alcohol. In this excerpt, we focus on one ground of appeal raised—namely, that the sentencing judge erred in allowing the Crown to present victim impact statements that included photographs of the child and a video of the child's performance with several other children at a Christmas concert.]

THE COURT (Ryan, Hinkson, and MacKenzie JJA):

a) *The Victim Impact Statements*

[9] The purpose of sentencing is to protect the public through sanctions a court imposes upon a person found guilty of committing an offence. Each codified objective of sentencing is designed to further the protection of the community. ...

[10] In addition, s. 718.1 of the *Criminal Code* states that it is a fundamental principle that a sentence be proportionate to the gravity of the offence and the degree of responsibility of the offender.

[11] Broadly speaking, a sentencing judge looks to the conduct and culpability of the offender and punishes the offender for that conduct through the application of the principles and objectives of deterrence, rehabilitation, denunciation and proportionality.

[12] Victim impact statements play an important role in the sentencing process. They were formally introduced into sentencing proceedings by legislation in 1988. While there was some inconsistency among the courts as to the admissibility of such evidence prior to codification, the general trend was toward acceptance. The issue was resolved in *R. v. Swietlinski*, [1994] 3 S.C.R. 481 at 503, where Chief Justice Lamer observed: "It is well known that the victim's testimony is admissible at a hearing on sentencing." The current statutory scheme, enacted in 1995, is set out in s. 722 of the *Criminal Code*. That section provides:

> 722(1) For the purpose of determining the sentence to be imposed on an offender or whether the offender should be discharged pursuant to section 730 in respect of any offence, the court shall consider any statement that may have been prepared in accordance with subsection (2) of a victim of the offence *describing the harm done to, or loss suffered by, the victim arising from the commission of the offence.*
>
> (2) A statement referred to in subsection (1) must be
>
>   (a) prepared in writing in the form and in accordance with the procedures established by a program designated for that purpose by the lieutenant governor in council of the province in which the court is exercising its jurisdiction; and
>
>   (b) filed with the court.
>
> (2.1) The court shall, on the request of a victim, permit the victim to read a statement prepared and filed in accordance with subsection (2), or to present the statement in any other manner that the court considers appropriate.
>
> (3) Whether or not a statement has been prepared and filed in accordance with subsection (2), the court may consider any other evidence concerning any victim of the offence for the purpose of determining the sentence to be imposed on the offender or whether the offender should be discharged under section 730.
>
> *Definition of "victim"*
>
> (4) For the purposes of this section and section 722.2, "victim," in relation to an offence,
>
>   (a) means a person to whom harm was done or who suffered physical or emotional loss as a result of the commission of the offence; and
>
>   (b) where the person described in paragraph (a) is dead, ill or otherwise incapable of making a statement referred to in subsection (1), includes the spouse or common-law partner or any relative of that person, anyone who has in law or fact the custody of that person or is responsible for the care or support of that person or any dependant of that person. [Emphasis added.]

[13] Section 722(2) requires a sentencing judge to consider a victim impact statement "for the purpose of sentencing." The content of the statement is restricted to a description of "the harm done to, or loss suffered by, the victim arising from the commission of the offence." Section 722(3) also allows a sentencing judge to consider "any other evidence concerning any victim of the offence for the purpose of determining the sentence to be imposed on the offender." We will return to this subsection later in these reasons.

[14] Two things flow from the admission of victim impact statements. First, on the reading of the victim impact statement in court the consequences of the offender's actions are brought home palpably to the offender. Second, the trial judge is made aware of the damage the commission of the criminal offence has caused the victim(s) and thus, indirectly, the community in general. In this way the victim impact statement addresses the objective of sentencing set out s. 718(f), which we have earlier reproduced.

[15] It is important then, that the victim impact statement should not contain material which distracts the court from its proper consideration.

[16] In *R. v. Bremner*, 2000 BCCA 345, this Court approved of the view expressed in the Ontario case of *R. v. Gabriel* (1999), 137 C.C.C. (3d) 1, 26 C.R. (5th) 364 (Ont. S.C.). Speaking for the Court Madam Justice Proudfoot said this:

> [26] In the case of *R. v. Gabriel* ... Mr. Justice Hill, in a very comprehensive judgment dealing with all aspects of Victim Impact Statement under s. 722 ... said the following (at para. 22):
>
>> Without, in any fashion, diminishing the significant contribution of victim impact statements to providing victims a voice in the criminal process, it must be remembered that a criminal trial, including the sentencing phase, is not a tripartite proceeding. A convicted offender has committed a crime—an act against society as a whole. It is the public interest, not a private interest, which is to be served in sentencing.
>
> I agree with that general statement by Mr. Justice Hill that sentencing hearings are not tripartite proceedings, rather they are a proceeding between society, as represented by the Crown, and a convicted person.
>
> [27] In *Gabriel*, Mr. Justice Hill set out what should be presented to the court when victim impact statements are submitted. I reproduce them here as I think they are extremely useful (at paras. 29-33):
>
>> Impact statements should describe "the harm done to, or loss suffered by, the victim arising from the commission of the offence." The statements should not contain criticisms of the offender, assertions as to the facts of the offence, or recommendations as to the severity of punishment.
>>
>> Criticism of the offender tilts the adversary system and risks the appearance of revenge motivation.
>>
>> Attempts to state, or presumably to restate, the facts of the offence usurps the role of the prosecutor and risks inconsistency with, or expansion of, prior trial testimony, or facts read in, and agreed to, on the guilty plea appearance. Such was the case in *R. v. McAnespie* (1993), 82 C.C.C. (3d) 527 (Ont. C.A.) (reversed (1993), 86 C.C.C. (3d) 191 (S.C.C.)) where additional disclosure by the complainant, relating to the offence, was made by the complainant in her victim impact statement.
>>
>> The Attorney General represents the public interest in the prosecution of crime.

Recommendations as to penalty must be avoided, absent exceptional circumstances, i.e., a court-authorized request, an aboriginal sentencing circle, or as an aspect of a prosecutorial submission that the victim seeks leniency for the offender which might not otherwise reasonably be expected in the circumstances. The freedom to call for extraordinary sentences, beyond the limits of appellate tolerance, unjustifiably raises victim expectations, promotes an appearance of court-acceptance of vengeful submissions, and propels the system away from necessary restraint in punishing by loss of liberty (s. 718.2(d) of the *Code*; *R. v. Gladue*, *supra* at paras. 40, 41, 57, 93). It has been suggested that frequently the victim's limited knowledge of available sentencing options may lead the victim to rely on more severe options: H.C. Rubel, *Victim Participation in Sentencing Proceedings* (1985-86), 28 C.L.Q. 226 at 240-241. The independent neutrality of the judiciary requires that the court not react to public opinion as to the severity of sentences: *R. v. Porter* (1976), 33 C.C.C. (2d) 215 (Ont. C.A.) at 220 *per* Arnup J.A. [Footnotes omitted.]

[17]   We would add to the comments of Mr. Justice Hill that victim impact statements should not contain material which appears to be an appeal to the sentencing judge to place a value on the life of the victim, or to compensate grief through the imposition of a harsh sentence.

[18]   In the case before us, the appellant opposed the introduction into evidence through the father's victim impact statement at her sentencing hearing of photographs of the child who died as a result of injuries from the accident, and a video of the child singing Christmas carols with other children. The sentencing judge ruled that both were admissible. We were advised by counsel that the length of the video was 1 minute and 42 seconds. The sentencing judge gave his reasons for admitting the video evidence in unreported reasons for judgment delivered approximately two weeks before he heard submissions as to sentence: *R. v. Berner* (27 October 2010), Surrey 171252-1 (B.C.P.C.).

[19]   In doing so the sentencing judge correctly accepted that the intention in allowing victim impact statements into evidence was to bring information to the court about the impact of the crime for which the offender is to be sentenced and not to permit victims to take an adversarial position to either the Crown or the offender. Insofar as the video evidence was concerned, the sentencing judge said at paras. 7-9 of his reasons:

In this case I am told that the girl's father will be reading in a victim impact statement which the Crown, I assume, will review and make sure that it does not contain any of the questionable material referred to in the cases the Crown gave me. But in my view, what is the video doing? Certainly I would agree with Mr. Tarnow, if this was becoming an attempt to take away the sentencing process from an objective inquiry into what a fit sentence should be, hearing submissions and evidence necessarily from counsel, from either side, if it was taking away from that process and turning it into a condemnation and a persecution of the accused and a long tribute to the life of this young girl, that would of course be completely wrong and I would forbid it.

However, as I hear from Ms. Wendel, this video will merely supplement the written impact statement of the father, who will be reading it out. And often something as emotional as a child being killed, and I don't think I am wrong here, that either as counsel or as a judge there is nothing more emotionally upsetting, creating more turmoil than a case where a child has been killed. It is a human reaction to that, and you can't help it.

The victim in this case, the father may not be able to articulate with the force he wants the impact that this crime has had on him, and the video may well assist him in appropriately identifying that impact. That strikes me that that's the intent of this particular video being played.

[20] With respect, we are unable to accept this reasoning. We accept that a sentencing judge has discretion to admit, for example, a photograph of the victim under s. 722(3) of the *Criminal Code*, but we are unable to accept that the volume and nature of the additional evidence was an acceptable adjunct to the victim impact statement.

[21] In *R. v. Jackson* (2002), 163 C.C.C. (3d) 451, the Ontario Court of Appeal dealt with a victim impact statement filed by a police officer who was the victim of a shooting. His statement gave evidence regarding the causes and incidence of crime, the use of firearms and the like. In holding that the statement exceeded the limits of what is permitted in a victim impact statement Mr. Justice Sharpe, speaking for the court, said at paras. 53-56:

> I do not accept the [Crown's] submission that a statement of this kind falls within the contemplation of the *Criminal Code* provisions relating to victim impact statements. At the time of sentencing, s. 722(3) provided as follows:
>
> > A statement of a victim of an offence prepared and filed in accordance with subsection (2) *does not prevent the court from considering any other evidence concerning any victim of the offence for the purpose of determining the sentence to be imposed on the offender* or whether the offender should be discharged pursuant to section 730.
>
> The [Crown] also relies on s. 723(2), which required the court to hear "any relevant evidence" on sentencing, and on s. 723(3), which provided as follows:
>
> > The court may, on its own motion, *after hearing argument from the prosecutor and the offender, require the production of evidence that would assist it in determining the appropriate sentence.*
>
> In my view, these provisions do not assist [the Crown]. I do not read s. 722(3) as giving the prosecution or the victim the option of either providing a victim impact statement or making a statement to the court immediately before a sentence is passed. The references to filing a victim impact statement in accordance with s. 722(2) and to "any other evidence" indicate to me that s. 722(3) is subsidiary to s. 722(2) and that it merely supplements the normal procedure with respect to victim impact statements. Section 722(3) does not allow for an alternate method of placing victim impact evidence before the court. With respect to s. 723(2), I do not read this provision as requiring a court to consider evidence tendered in a manner that fails to respect directly applicable *Criminal Code* provisions governing its admissibility. Finally, I fail to see how s. 723(3) has any relevance to the present case as the court clearly did not require the production of further evidence on its own motion.
>
> By enacting the victim impact provisions as part of the sentencing process, Parliament has indicated the importance of giving due regard to the views and concerns of victims and to the need to treat victims with courtesy, dignity and respect. I can certainly understand why [the victim] felt as strongly as he did about this serious crime, which had endangered his life. However, it is important that the procedures contemplated by the *Criminal Code* for victim impact evidence be followed. In my view, the *Criminal Code* does not allow a victim, especially one who has not given a victim impact statement, to make his own plea for a stiff

sentence after all of the evidence has been called and after both counsel have made their submissions. By asking the court to follow this unusual procedure, Crown counsel and [the victim] brought about a situation that created an appearance of unfairness at one of the most critical moments in the process. [Underline emphasis added.]

[22] We agree with this interpretation of s. 722 by the Ontario Court of Appeal.

[23] In the case before us the child's father read his statement and showed ten photographs and a video of his daughter over a large video screen mounted in the courtroom so that those in the audience could view the presentation. The father's loss was and is overwhelming. It is understandable that through this presentation he wanted to show what he could not describe in words.

[24] Counsel for both the appellant and the Crown acknowledged on this appeal that the day in provincial court was already a sombre and difficult one. Watching the presentation that accompanied the father's victim impact statement would have been a profoundly emotional experience for all who saw it. But it is the heightening of those emotions, in a courtroom, which carries the risk of unjust consequences. One of the harms which could result from permitting victims to pay tribute to their loved ones in the public forum of the courtroom is that their expectations may be raised and their belief that the tribute will influence the length of a sentence may be encouraged.

[25] There are other dangers. While a sentencing judge must try to understand a victim's experience, he or she must do more than that. He or she must craft a fit sentence by taking into consideration all relevant legal principles, and the circumstances of the offence and the offender. In emotionally charged cases such as this, a sentencing judge must keep in mind his or her position of impartial decision maker. The sentencing judge must be wary of the risk of valuing victims, based on the strength of feelings expressed in the victim impact statement. In our view, this risk was intensified by the video material and ten photographs placed before the sentencing judge in this case. The personal characteristics of the victim should play no part in crafting a fit sentence, however tragic the circumstances. It is in the public interest to deter and denounce all unlawful deaths.

[26] As we noted earlier, s. 722 of the *Criminal Code* holds that victim impact statements are admissible "for the purpose of determining the sentence to be imposed on an offender." Where there is some question as to the admissibility of an impact statement, a sentencing judge should consider whether the statement, or a component thereof, furthers this purpose, keeping in mind the statutory scheme as a whole and in particular the principles of sentencing in s. 718 of the *Criminal Code*.

[27] Before moving on, we wish to stress that victims and their families are not expected to appreciate these distinctions. It is the responsibility of Crown counsel to communicate with victims and their families about the appropriate content of victim impact statements, vet the materials once received, and not seek to admit victim impact statements which go beyond these parameters.

NOTE

Despite the error in admitting the additional material, the court concluded it had no impact on the ultimate sentence imposed, quoting the judge's comment at para 20 that "a judge cannot allow any feeling of sympathy or compassion for the offender to compromise his or her duty to objectively assess the offender's moral blameworthiness; nor can he or she allow any sense of anger or outrage at the offender's conduct to compromise his or her duty to exercise restraint in imposing a sentence."

R v W (V)
2008 ONCA 55, 229 CCC (3d) 344

[A young offender was convicted of three robberies. The Crown sought serious violent offence (SVO) designations under the *Youth Criminal Justice Act* (YCJA) and relied on victim impact statements from two of the victims to prove they had suffered psychological harm amounting to "serious bodily harm." The court found that an SVO designation was part of the sentencing process and therefore the VISs were admissible for the purpose of determining whether the designation should be made. The remaining issue, which we focus on here, was whether the offender had the right to cross-examine the victim on his or her statement.]

SHARPE JA (Laskin and MacPherson JJA concurring):

Admissibility of Victim Impact Statements as Evidence of an SVO

[14] Victim impact statements may be used "[f]or the purpose of determining the sentence to be imposed on an offender or whether the offender should be discharged pursuant to s. 730 in respect of any offence" and to describe "the harm done to, or loss suffered by, the victim arising from the commission of the offence." The *Criminal Code* provisions relating to victim impact statements apply to youth justice proceedings by virtue of s. 50(1) of the YCJA.

. . .

The Right to Cross-Examine

[22] I turn to the appellant's principal submission, namely the contention that he had the right to cross-examine the victims on their victim impact statements.

[23] Section 42(9) of the YCJA provides a summary procedural code for SVO designations and stipulates four elements:

- the Crown must apply for such a designation
- the parties must be given an opportunity to be heard
- the youth justice court must hold a hearing
- the youth justice court judge must make a judicial determination that the offence is an SVO.

[24] These requirements make it clear that an SVO designation is a discrete process that entails a judicial determination based on the evidence following a hearing at which the offender must be accorded procedural fairness.

[25] In *R. v. Gardiner* ... , Dickson J. held that "facts which justify the sanction are no less important than the facts which justify the conviction" and that "[c]rime and punishment are inextricably linked." This means that at the sentencing stage, "the accused is not

abruptly deprived of all procedural rights existing at trial: he has a right to counsel, a right to call evidence and cross-examine prosecution witnesses, a right to give evidence himself and to address the court."

[26] The *Criminal Code*, s. 724(3), codifies the *Gardiner* analysis and makes the following provision with respect to disputed facts on a sentencing hearing:

724(3) Where there is a dispute with respect to any fact that is relevant to the determination of a sentence,

(a) the court shall request that evidence be adduced as to the existence of the fact unless the court is satisfied that sufficient evidence was adduced at the trial;

(b) the party wishing to rely on a relevant fact, including a fact contained in a presentence report, has the burden of proving it;

(c) either party may cross-examine any witness called by the other party;

(d) subject to paragraph (e), the court must be satisfied on a balance of probabilities of the existence of the disputed fact before relying on it in determining the sentence; and

(e) the prosecutor must establish, by proof beyond a reasonable doubt, the existence of any aggravating fact or any previous conviction by the offender.

[27] Although victim impact statements are not specifically mentioned, I can see no principled reason for excluding them from the reach of the general rule articulated by Dickson J. in *Gardiner* or these procedural protections listed in s. 724(3). I conclude, therefore, that victim impact statements are admissible, pursuant to s. 722(1), but that their use is subject to the general provisions of s. 724(3). The Crown bears the burden of proving any disputed fact and the offender has the right to cross-examine on the evidence the Crown leads.

[28] However, I do not read either *Gardiner* or s. 724(3) as meaning that an offender has an automatic or open-ended right to insist that victims attend for cross-examination any time the Crown wishes to use a victim impact statement in a sentencing hearing. Nor do I agree that s. 7 of the Charter mandates such a right. Conferring an automatic or unconstrained right to cross-examine would risk undermining the very purpose of victim impact statements, namely, to give victims a voice in the criminal justice process, to provide a way for victims to confront offenders with the harm they have caused, and to ensure that courts are informed of the full consequences of the crime. Conferring an open-ended right to cross-examine might discourage victims from offering such statements and re-victimize those who do. On the other hand, an absolute bar on cross-examination would unduly interfere with offenders' procedural rights.

[29] It seems to me that the way to reconcile the use of victim impact statements with the procedural rights conferred by s. 7 of the Charter, s. 42(9) of the YCJA and s. 724(3) of the *Criminal Code* is to impose a threshold "air of reality" burden on the offender to satisfy the sentencing judge that a fact or facts contained in the victim impact statement are disputable and that the request to cross-examine is not "specious or empty": see Allan Manson, *The Law of Sentencing* (Toronto: Irwin Law, 2001) at 198. If there is no factual dispute that meets this low threshold, the protections accorded by s. 724(3) are not triggered and I fail to see how there could be any violation of the appellant's s. 7 Charter rights.

[30] This analysis suggests that there is a discretion on the part of the sentencing judge to assess the offender's request in the light of the facts that have been proved and the

evidence that has been led, whether at the trial or on the sentencing hearing, with a view to achieving a just reconciliation between respecting the procedural rights of the offender and respecting the legitimate role of the victim in the sentencing process. The sentencing judge's duty to ensure that the offender's procedural rights are protected entails a discretion to permit cross-examination when satisfied that there is an air of reality to the claim that the facts are in dispute and that the offender's request to cross-examine is not specious or empty.

[31] Although there is little jurisprudence and commentary discussing cross-examination on victim impact statements, the case law and commentary that does exist supports the conclusion that cross-examination may be allowed, but only at the judge's discretion.

[32] In *R. v. Lafleche*, 2001 ABCA 292 (CanLII), [2001] A.J. No. 1504, 293 A.R. 285 (C.A.), the Alberta Court of Appeal decided that the sentencing judge had erred in accepting the complainant's testimony at the sentencing hearing "under the guise of a victim impact statement": para. 22. The court held, "we find that [the sentencing judge's] denial of a right to cross-examine the complainant on the new factual assertions on the guise of it simply being a victim impact statement was also an error at law and in principle": para. 23.

[33] In *R. v. Shaban*, [2004] A.J. No. 1310, 2004 ABQB 558, at para. 20, the Alberta Court of Queen's Bench supported the notion that a trial judge retains discretion to permit or deny cross-examination. The court suggested, "To permit cross-examination on a Victim Impact Statement without permission of the Court would fly in the face of s. 722 and would have a chilling effect on victims who are given the right to have their statements considered at the time of sentencing."

[34] Allan Manson, *The Law of Sentencing, supra*, supports a qualified right to cross-examine. Kent Roach [in] "The Role of Crime Victims Under the Youth Criminal Justice Act" (2003) 40 Alta. L. Rev. 965 at 987, states, "Victims may be subject to adversarial cross-examination on their statement."

[35] Finally, a Department of Justice survey of judges suggests that cross-examination on victim impact statements does occur, but that judges maintain control over it. Ten percent of the 110 judges surveyed had presided over a case in which a victim was cross-examined at sentencing on the victim impact statement. The courts exercised discretion: "Judges cited the inclusion of contradictory facts or facts not in evidence as some of the few instances where they would allow cross-examination on a victim impact statement": Policy Centre for Victim Issues/Department of Justice, Multi-Site Survey of Victims of Crime and Criminal Justice Professionals Across Canada: Summary of Judiciary Respondents (Ottawa: Department of Justice Research and Statistics Division, 2005) at 13.

Application to the Facts of This Case

[36] Unfortunately, neither *Gardiner* nor s. 724(3) appears to have been drawn to the attention of the youth justice court judge. He was asked to deal with the issue as a possible breach of s. 7 of the Charter. As I have already noted, he ruled that it was only "in the clearest of cases" that denying the right to cross-examine would constitute a Charter breach and that he was not satisfied that these were the "clearest of cases." While I do not wish to be taken as endorsing the view that a s. 7 Charter breach is only made out "in the

clearest of cases," I do say that the youth justice court judge erred by applying a more stringent test than mandated by s. 724(3), namely, whether there was a "dispute with respect to any fact that is relevant to the determination of a sentence."

[37] However, the youth court judge also found that the likelihood of cross-examination changing or affecting the substance of the victim impact statements was "remote." I agree with that assessment. In my view, had the judge applied the "air of reality" test, in view of the evidence led at trial as to the manner in which these offences were committed, he necessarily would have come to the conclusion that the request to cross-examine the victims was specious or empty. The appellant pointed what appeared to be a handgun while masked in a dark location, an act obviously intended to instil intimidation and fear in the victim. To make an SVO designation, the judge need not find that the offender actually caused serious bodily harm: the designation can also be based on a finding that the offender attempted to cause serious bodily harm. In my view, any challenge to the allegations of trauma in the victim impact statements lacked an air of reality and there was no prospect that through cross-examination on the victim impact statements the appellant could have avoided a finding of harm or attempted harm sufficient to support an SVO finding.

[38] Accordingly, I would grant leave to appeal, but dismiss the appeal.

NOTE

Not all courts have agreed that victims can be cross-examined on their statements: see e.g. *R v WM*, 2010 BCCA 370. Further, as discussed in Roberts and Edgar, extracted above, even in those jurisdictions where cross-examination is permitted, it is exceedingly rare. For further discussion on the applicable test for cross-examination of a victim on his or her VIS, see *R v BT*, 2013 ONCA 535.

Cook c R
2009 QCCA 2423 (footnotes omitted)

[Cook was convicted of manslaughter. The only testimony heard at the sentencing hearing was the sworn presentation of a written VIS prepared by the deceased's daughter in which she described the consequences for her and her family of the sudden and brutal death of her mother. Relying on the VIS, the trial judge found as an aggravating factor on sentencing that Cook had taken the life of someone who was loved and well-respected by her family and others in her entourage. Cook appealed arguing that the trial judge erred in his use of the VIS and finding this to be an aggravating factor on sentencing.]

HILTON JA (Forget and Léger JJA concurring):

[58] As this ground of appeal relates to the manner in which the trial judge treated the written victim impact statement prepared by Mme Frenière's daughter Nataly Dupuis and her subsequent sworn testimony during which she read the statement, I believe it is useful to first review the provisions in the *Criminal Code* that relate to such statements.

[59] It is not disputed that since Mme Dupuis was the daughter of Mme Frenière, she was a "victim" for the purpose of delivering a statement pursuant to subsection 722(4)(b) *Cr. C.*

[60] In this instance, the statement was not in accordance with the form prescribed and the procedures contemplated by subsection 722(2)(a) *Cr. C.*, but the trial judge was nevertheless able to make use of the written statement and testimony pursuant to subsection 722(3) *Cr. C.*

[61] A victim whose written statement satisfies the criteria in subsection 722(1) *Cr. C.* is entitled to read her statement, in open court, as subsection 722(2.1) *Cr. C.* provides. The obligation imposed on a court to permit a victim impact statement to be read in such circumstances is cast in mandatory terms, which suggests that a trial judge has no discretion to refuse a victim the right to read a statement as long as it conforms to the requirements of subsection 722(2) *Cr. C.*

[62] It is also interesting to note that before imposing sentence on an accused, pursuant to subsection 722.2(1) *Cr. C.*:

> … the court *shall inquire of the prosecutor or a victim of the offence, or any person representing a victim of the offence*, whether the victim or victims have been advised of the opportunity to prepare a statement referred to in subsection 722(1). [Emphasis added]

[63] Crown prosecutors therefore have an equally specific obligation to have informed themselves of the answer to the question a trial judge must ask them in accordance with that provision, especially if none of the victims of the offence are present at the sentencing hearing.

[64] Finally, subsection 722(1) *Cr. C.* describes the treatment a court must ascribe to a victim impact statement, which again it will be seen is cast in mandatory terms:

> 722(1) For the purpose of determining the sentence to be imposed on an offender or whether the offender should be discharged pursuant to section 730 in respect of any offence, *the court shall consider* any statement that may have been prepared in accordance with subsection (2) of a victim of the offence describing the harm done to, or loss suffered by, the victim arising from the commission of the offence. [Emphasis added]

[65] Therefore, in my opinion it is clear that Parliament intended that however a victim impact statement may be prepared or delivered, a trial judge engaged in the sentencing process must consider it. To the extent any such statement may stray into areas beyond its purpose, such as by proposing a sentence, seeking to achieve personal revenge, speaking to the character of the accused, or stating facts relating to the offence that are not in the record, trial judges are accustomed to taking no account of whatever is irrelevant.

[66] Moreover, the value of such statements to a judge involved in the difficult process of sentencing should not be underestimated, as the comments of an experience trial judge such as Martin J. in *R. v. Dadgar* illustrate:

> [2] While I've often wondered whether the provisions of the *Code* which allow for "victim impact statements" advance things very much, the testimony of Mrs. Seleta has certainly given me a very clear understanding of what the consequences of this act have been. It is an understanding which I could only otherwise imagine had I not had the opportunity to hear from her.

[67] It is easy to see from the circumstances of this case, as well as those mentioned by Martin J. in the extract that I have just quoted, that the actual presence of a victim and his or her subsequent testimony is more likely to make an impression than the mere

completion of the form prescribed by the Lieutenant Governor in Council in accordance with subsection 722(2) *Cr. C.* In Quebec, that form certainly elicits appropriate information relating to physical, psychological and economic consequences of the commission of an offence, but it leaves little scope for the kind of eloquent commentary given by Mme Dupuis on which the trial judge relied.

[68] I see no reason in principle why a victim impact statement, however it may be prepared or delivered, cannot be used by a trial judge in assessing whether any of its contents can constitute aggravating or mitigating factors. As Prof. Julian Roberts, a recognized scholar in the field of sentencing has recently written, there is no statistical data that suggests that doing so increases the severity of sentences.

[69] The author also notes that it is generally preferable that the offenders hear of the consequences of their conduct directly from those who were affected by it rather than from a prosecutor, since this has the effect of enhancing the possibility of the offender expressing remorse. In such circumstances, a sentencing judge is likely to consider the expression of remorse as a mitigating factor, thus showing that victim impact statements should not be regarded exclusively as a device designed to increase sentences. In that respect, they also contribute to the attainment of one of the objectives of sentencing described in subsection 718(f) *Cr. C.*, namely, the promotion of "a sense of responsibility in offenders, and acknowledgment of the harm done to victims and to the community."

[70] As I mentioned in paragraph [26], the trial judge considered it appropriate to take into account the impact of Mme Frenière's death on those who were close to her. Her statement did not stray into inappropriate subject matters.

[71] That being said, the manner in which the trial judge expressed the aggravating factor—that Mr. Cook took the life of someone who was loved and well-respected by her family and others in her entourage—leads Mr. Cook to argue that there is no hierarchy of persons whose lives are considered more valuable than others for sentencing purposes. In that respect Mr. Cook is correct. Every human life is valuable, and the precipitous termination of life by homicide is no more or less egregious depending on the personal characteristics of the deceased, whatever they maybe.

[72] I nevertheless believe that the trial judge did not intend the effect Mr. Cook ascribes to his description of the aggravating factor. Rather, consistent with his preface to the introduction of the extracts from Mme Dupuis' victim impact statement, I think it is far more likely the trial judge was referencing the effect on Mme Dupuis and other members of her family, including her unborn child, of the sudden death of her mother. That becomes all the more apparent when the extracts from the victim impact statement that the trial judge cited ... are examined.

[73] Viewed in that light, and considering the mandatory legislative scheme surrounding victim impact statements that Parliament has established, the trial judge committed no error in making use of Mme Dupuis' statement to reach a conclusion that the devastating effect of Mme Frenière's death on her immediate family constituted an aggravating factor.

As noted, the 2015 amendments to the provision included a prescribed form for the VIS that sets out guidelines on what victims may and may not include in their VIS. This form is reproduced below. When reviewing this form and the notes that follow, consider to what extent the newly amended provisions and forms conform to or differ from the pre-existing law, and whether any changes made respond adequately to the various concerns expressed over time about the content and use of VISs. For some early views on the impact of the new provision, see *R v BP*, 2015 NSPC 34.

Form 34.2
Victims Bill of Rights Act, SC 2015, c 13, s 722(4)

Victim Impact Statement

This form may be used to provide a description of the physical or emotional harm, property damage or economic loss suffered by you as the result of the commission of an offence, as well as a description of the impact of the offence on you. You may attach additional pages if you need more space.

Your statement must not include

- any statement about the offence or the offender that is not relevant to the harm or loss you suffered;
- any unproven allegations;
- any comments about any offence for which the offender was not convicted;
- any complaint about any individual, other than the offender, who was involved in the investigation or prosecution of the offence; or
- except with the court's approval, an opinion or recommendation about the sentence.

You may present a detailed account of the impact the offence has had on your life. The following sections are examples of information you may wish to include in your statement. You are not required to include all of this information.

Emotional Impact

Describe how the offence has affected you emotionally. For example, think of

- your lifestyle and activities;
- your relationships with others such as your spouse, family and friends;
- your ability to work, attend school or study; and
- your feelings, emotions and reactions as they relate to the offence.

_____

_____

_____

_____

Physical Impact

Describe how the offence has affected you physically. For example, think of

- ongoing physical pain, discomfort, illness, scarring, disfigurement or physical limitation;

- hospitalization or surgery you have had because of the offence;
- treatment, physiotherapy or medication you have been prescribed;
- the need for any further treatment or the expectation that you will receive further treatment; and
- any permanent or long-term disability.

_____
_____
_____
_____

Economic Impact

Describe how the offence has affected you financially. For example, think of

- the value of any property that was lost or damaged and the cost of repairs or replacement;
- any financial loss due to missed time from work;
- the cost of any medical expenses, therapy or counselling;
- any costs or losses that are not covered by insurance.

Please note that this is not an application for compensation or restitution.

_____
_____
_____
_____

Fears for Security

Describe any fears you have for your security or that of your family and friends. For example, think of

- concerns with respect to contact with the offender; and
- concerns with respect to contact between the offender and members of your family or close friends.

_____
_____
_____
_____

Drawing, Poem or Letter

You may use this space to draw a picture or write a poem or letter if it will help you express the impact that the offence has had on you.

☐ I would like to present my statement in court.

To the best of my knowledge, the information contained in this statement is true.

Dated this .... day of ...... 20..., at ....

Signature of declarant

If you completed this statement on behalf of the victim, please indicate the reasons why you did so and the nature of your relationship with the victim.

_____

_____

Dated this .... day of ...... 20..., at ....

Signature of declarant

NOTES

1. Clearly, a VIS must be relevant to issues that are properly before the court and should not cross into extraneous areas. This includes limiting the statement to the offence actually before the sentencing court: see *R v Talbot*, [1995] OJ No 4304 (QL) (Gen Div). However, the demarcation lines are not easy to draw and maintain given the personal nature of the victim's input, particularly in cases where there is a prior relationship of some sort between the victim and offender. There can be particular problems related to the oral presentation of a VIS. Although the contents of a prepared written statement can be vetted in advance, must the victim be warned not to stray beyond its wording? What if the victim engages in impromptu additions? How should the judge intervene? For an example of the personal and visceral kinds of comments that victims may deliver when given an opportunity to make an oral statement, see *R v KL*, [1999] OJ No 5085 (QL) (Sup Ct J), Kurisko J, where one of the victims launched into a personal attack on the offender.

2. In *R v Gabriel* (1999), 137 CCC (3d) 1, 26 CR (5th) 364 (Ont SC), discussed in *Berner*, above, Hill J suggested that the 1999 amendments, specifically the inclusion of the word "shall" in s 722(2.1), would "remove the court's ability to prevent a victim reading an impact statement." The 2015 amendments adopt the same language used in the earlier amendment: see now s 722(5)). Is Hill J correct? Certainly, the amendments are directed at giving victims a greater role in the decisions about whether and how to present a VIS. But do they have the effect of entirely precluding the judge's discretion to rule that a written statement is the proper manner of presentation? Hill J identified some reasons why a victim should, in specific cases, present a written rather than an oral VIS. Principally, the reasons relate to the health and stability of the victim and the need to ensure security in the courtroom. The 2015 amendments allow victims to include a poem or drawing or letter if this would assist them in describing the impact that the offence had on them. Does this method of presentation have the potential to unduly influence judges? Can a judge no longer respond to these concerns by requiring that a VIS be in writing only? Has the language of the provision elevated the victim's status to almost that of a party? Surely, all Code provisions must be interpreted in the manner that best preserves the integrity and fairness of the judicial process. For a response to these

issues in relation to the 1999 amendments, see *R v Sparks* (2007), 251 NSR (2d) 181 (Prov Ct); *Berner*, above; and *Cook*, above.

3. In *Gabriel*, Hill J held that VISs should not contain sentence recommendations "absent exceptional circumstances—that is, a court-authorized request, an Aboriginal sentencing circle, or as an aspect of a prosecutorial submission that the victim seeks leniency for the offender which might not otherwise reasonably be expected in the circumstances." In *R v Proulx*, 2000 SCC 5 at para 113, [2000] 1 SCR 61, the Supreme Court of Canada held that "[i]n determining whether restorative objectives can be satisfied ... , the judge should consider ... the victim's wishes as revealed by the victim impact statement." In what other circumstances might a court seek a victim's views on the sentence? Is it appropriate to consider a victim's plea for leniency? See *R v Tkachuk*, 2001 ABCA 243; *R v RG*, 2003 NLCA 73. For a recent restatement of the general prohibition, see *R v Dunford*, 2015 SKQB 386 at para 20, where the court stated, "While victims of an offence are not permitted to have a role in suggesting the type or length of sentence to be imposed, victim impact statements are useful and important in describing to a court the loss experienced by all victims." In Form 34.2, victims are advised that their statement should not contain *"except with the court's approval*, an opinion or recommendation about the sentence (emphasis added)." Does this have the potential to encourage more victims to ask to be allowed to express their views on sentence and thus to broaden the circumstances in which victims will be allowed to express an opinion or recommendation about the sentence? When a victim is allowed to express an opinion or recommendation on sentence, what role should this play in determining the offender's sentence? Since most victims have no legal training, can courts be expected to give such recommendations much, if any, weight? Does it make a difference if the recommendation is for leniency? If the provision is simply for expressive purposes, does the provision risk creating unrealistic expectations on the part of victims? See Marie Manikis, "Victim Impact Statements at Sentencing: Towards a Clearer Understanding of Their Aims" (2015) 65 UTLJ 85.

4. In *Gabriel*, Hill J indicated that 20 VISs were far too many. What is the danger in accepting a multiplicity of statements? How many VISs should a court accept? If too many statements are filed, how does a sentencing judge select which statements to consider? See *R v Roberts*, 2001 ABQB 520, 289 AR 127; *R v McDonough*, above.

5. What happens if a sentencing judge imposes a sentence without inquiring whether a victim has been advised of the opportunity to make a VIS, and therefore fails to comply with s 722(2)? See *R v Tellier*, 2000 ABCA 219 for a discussion of this issue under the 1999 amendments.

6. In *R v Geddes* (2006), 201 Man R (2d) 34 (CA), the Manitoba Court of Appeal rejected a victim's application for intervenor status in a sentence appeal. The court noted both the lack of jurisprudence granting such a right to private individuals and Crown counsel's role as representative of the public interest.

7. In *R v Jackson* (2002), 58 OR (3d) 593, 163 CCC (3d) 451 (CA), discussed in *Berner*, above, the Ontario Court of Appeal indicated that the Crown is responsible for ensuring that a VIS complies with the Code requirements. Other appellate courts have expressed similar views: see *R v Labrash*, 2006 BCCA 357. Ideally, the Crown should review the statement before it is submitted to the court, delete any inadmissible content, and explain to the victim why that information is being excluded. If this is not possible because of the late preparation or delivery of the statement, Crown counsel should request that the court disregard or ignore the improper information. For a discussion of these issues, see *R v McDonough*, above, and *R v IDU*,

2007 SKPC 4. Equally, however, there is some obligation on defence counsel to object to inadmissible content because the failure to do so may be taken into account on appeal: see e.g. *R v Revet*, 2010 SKCA 71; *R v KG*, 2010 ONCA 177; see also s 722(8), which directs courts to "take into account the portions of the statement that it considers relevant to the determination referred to in subsection (1) and disregard any other portion."

8. In *Cook*, the Court of Appeal for Quebec concluded that sentencing judges could use a VIS to assess whether any of its contents could constitute aggravating or mitigating factors. A similar view was expressed in *R v AG*, 2015 ONCA 159 at para 73, where the court found it was "not an error in principle for a sentencing judge to determine that the impact of the crime on a victim, as described in a victim impact statement, is an aggravating factor. If it were otherwise, victim impact statements would have limited utility and the mandate to consider them as part of the sentencing process found in s. 722 of the *Criminal Code* would be rendered meaningless." For contrary views see *R v WM*, 2010 BCCA 370 at para 16; *R v Deer*, 2014 ABCA 88 at para 21.

III. LOOKING TO THE FUTURE

As noted at the beginning of the chapter, the sentencing process is the only juncture in the criminal process where the role of victims has been articulated. The preceding case excerpts demonstrate that the courts still adhere to the traditional dualistic models of criminal justice that do not afford a great role for victims. Nevertheless, beginning in 1995, Parliament sought to amplify the voices of victims by amending s 722 to permit greater knowledge of the rights victims have in the process. It seems likely that the next locus of debate will revolve around the extent to which the 2015 amendments will encourage courts to allow victims to make sentencing recommendations as part of their impact statement.

In addition to amending s 722, the 2015 legislation also enacted the *Canadian Victims Bill of Rights*, SC 2015, c 13, s 2. Like the provincial and territorial victim bills of rights that were enacted earlier, this legislation is largely declaratory and informational. It contains the following preamble:

> Whereas crime has a harmful impact on victims and on society;
>
> Whereas victims of crime and their families deserve to be treated with courtesy, compassion and respect, including respect for their dignity;
>
> Whereas it is important that victims' rights be considered throughout the criminal justice system;
>
> Whereas victims of crime have rights that are guaranteed by the *Canadian Charter of Rights and Freedoms*;
>
> Whereas consideration of the rights of victims of crime is in the interest of the proper administration of justice;
>
> Whereas the federal, provincial and territorial governments share responsibility for criminal justice;
>
> Whereas, in 1988, the federal, provincial and territorial governments endorsed the *Canadian Statement of Basic Principles of Justice for Victims of Crime* and, in 2003, the *Canadian Statement of Basic Principles of Justice for Victims of Crime, 2003*.

The legislation confers on victims various "rights" in relation to the investigation and prosecution of offences, the corrections and conditional release process, and proceedings of courts and review boards in relation to persons found not criminally responsible on

account of mental disorder or unfit to stand trial. These include the right to certain information about the criminal justice system and the case, the right to protection from intimidation
and retaliation, the right to participate by providing their views about decisions that affect
their rights and by providing a VIS, and the right to request restitution. However, these rights
are to be exercised through the mechanisms provided by law (s 19(1)) and are to be interpreted and applied in a manner that does not interfere with the proper administration of
justice (s 20). Further, while the legislation requires federal departments, agencies, and bodies involved in the criminal justice system to have an administrative complaints mechanism
for victims (s 25), there is no cause of action or right to damages arising from a breach of any
of these rights (s 28), and no decision or order can be appealed solely on the basis of a
breach or denial of such rights (s 29). Finally, the legislation expressly does not confer party,
intervenor, or observer status on a victim in any proceeding (s 27).

As noted already, not all reforms in the name of victims' rights have come from Parliament. Provincial and territorial bills of rights also entitle victims to information from police
and prosecutors at each stage of the criminal process. However, as with the recent federal
legislation, there is no formal mechanism by which these rights may be enforced against
those who fail to measure up to the requirements of the statute: see e.g. the limiting provisions in Ontario's *Victims' Bill of Rights, 1995*, SO 1995, c 6—s 2(1) establishes the basic rights
of victims; s 2(2) provides that the principles set out in s 2(1) are "subject to the availability of
resources and information, what is reasonable in the circumstances of the case, what is consistent with the law and the public interest and what is necessary to ensure that the resolution of criminal proceedings is not delayed"; s 2(5) provides that "[no] new cause of action,
right of appeal, claim or other remedy exists in law because of this section or anything done
or omitted to be done under this section"; see also *Vanscoy v Ontario*, [1999] OJ No 1661 (QL)
(Sup Ct J). These bills also contain provisions that are relevant to civil litigation. Because they
are provincial and territorial enactments, these bills have no *direct* bearing on the participatory rights of victims in criminal proceedings. However, they provide a rich context of victim
empowerment in which s 722 must be interpreted. The newly enacted federal bill of rights
adds to this context. Thus, these types of enactments and other societal recognition of victims' rights may eventually come to have considerable *indirect* impact on the criminal process.
Indeed, they may lend legitimacy to the evolution of criminal justice models from dualistic
paradigms (accused versus the state) to more encompassing models that recognize broader
victims' interests. For a discussion of the scope and limitations of the various bills, see Marie
Manikis, "Imagining the Future of Victims' Rights in Canada: A Comparative Perspective"
(2015) 13 Ohio St J Crim L 163.

The legitimate needs of victims who have suffered physical injury, personal loss, or financial loss likely extend beyond the criminal justice system, which has a narrower focus and
limited resources and is circumscribed by the limits of federal jurisdiction. The practical
operation of schemes for the compensation, counselling, and rehabilitation of victims is best
dealt with by agencies designed specifically for those purposes. These agencies are often
under provincial and territorial jurisdiction. Provincial and territorial statutes that address the
role of victims are typically drafted in broad terms that, at least symbolically, champion the
rights of victims. The preamble to the *Canadian Victims Bill of Rights*, reproduced above, is a
good example of this approach. However, it is important to ask what resources and/or concrete ameliorative steps, if any, accompany the grand claims made by provincial and territorial legislation bearing on victims' rights.

IV. FURTHER READING ON VICTIM IMPACT STATEMENTS

Ashworth, Andrew. "Victim Impact Statements and Sentencing" (1988) Crim L Rev 498.

Campbell, Kathryn M. "Judicial Attitudes Regarding Victim Impact Statements: Perspectives from Québec" (2015) 19 Can Crim L Rev 341.

Erez, Edna & Julian V Roberts. "Victim Participation in the Criminal Justice System" in Randy J Davis, Arthur J Lurigio & Susan Herman, eds, *Victims of Crime* (Beverly Hills, Cal: Sage, 2012).

Manikis, Marie. "Recognizing Victims' Role and Rights During Plea Bargaining: A Fair Deal for Victims of Crime" (2012) 58 Crim LQ 411.

Manikis, Marie. "Victim Impact Statements at Sentencing: Towards a Clearer Understanding of Their Aims" (2015) 65 UTLJ 85.

Manikis, Marie & Julian V Roberts. "Victim Impact Statements at Sentencing: Developments in Caselaw" (2012) 5 Victims of Crime Research Digest 2.

Meredith, Colin & Chantal Paquette. *Victims of Crime Research Series: Summary Report on Victim Impact Statement Focus Groups* (Ottawa: Policy Centre for Victim Issues, Department of Justice Canada, 2001).

Roach, Kent. "Crime Victims and Sentencing" in Don Stuart, Ron Delisle & Allan Manson, eds, *Towards a Clear and Just Criminal Law: A Criminal Reports Forum* (Toronto: Carswell, 1999).

Roberts, Julian V. "Victim Impact Statements and the Sentencing Process: Enhancing Communication in the Courtroom" (2003) 47 Crim LQ 365.

Roberts, Julian V. "Victim Impact Statements at Sentencing: Lessons Learned and Future Priorities" (2008) 1 Victims of Crime Research Digest 3.

Roberts, Julian V & Allen Edgar. *Victim Impact Statements at Sentencing: Judicial Experiences and Perceptions—A Survey of Three Jurisdictions* (Ottawa: Department of Justice Canada, 2006).

Roberts, Julian V & Marie Manikis. "Victim Impact Statements at Sentencing: Exploring the Relevance of Ancillary Harm" (2010) 15 Can Crim L Rev 1.

Roberts, Julian V & Marie Manikis. "Victim Personal Statements: Latest (and Last) Trends from the Witness and Victim Experience Survey in England and Wales" (2012) 13 Criminol & Crim Justice 245.

CHAPTER SEVEN

Plea Discussions and Joint Submissions

I. INTRODUCTION

The preceding chapters on procedure and evidence portray the sentencing process as primarily adversarial in nature. Indeed, it is when matters are in dispute in the criminal justice process that the parties must resort to the rules of evidence and procedure. However, at the sentencing stage, there may be little dispute between the prosecutor and the offender. Although estimates vary, it is beyond dispute that the overwhelming majority of cases are resolved by a guilty plea: see Report of the Canadian Sentencing Commission, *Sentencing Reform: A Canadian Approach* (Ottawa: The Commission, 1987) at 406 (Report of the Canadian Sentencing Commission). Often, guilty pleas follow discussion between the prosecutor and defence counsel about what sentence ought to be imposed. This same process can occur when sentencing follows a finding of guilt at trial.

The practice of plea bargaining continues to be the subject of great controversy both in the legal profession and in the public at large: see Stanley A Cohen & Anthony N Doob, "Public Attitudes to Plea Bargaining" (1989) 32 Crim LQ 85. Every aspect of the practice was considered in the Honourable G Arthur Martin, Chair, *Report of the Attorney General's Advisory Committee on Charge Screening, Disclosure, and Resolution Discussions* (Toronto: Queen's Printer for Ontario, 1993) ("the Martin Report"). This chapter does not retrace the contours of this elaborate debate. Instead, we take as our starting point the Martin Report's statement in recommendation 46 (at 281):

> 46. The Committee is of the opinion that resolution discussions are an essential part of the criminal justice system in Ontario, and, when properly conducted, benefit not only the accused, but also victims, witnesses, counsel, and the administration of justice.

This chapter focuses on the extent to which prior arrangements made by counsel can constrain the discretion of the sentencing judge in his or her approach to the sentencing function. As we shall see, the boundaries of these constraints are often elucidated in situations where the sentencing judge rejects the arrangements presented by counsel. It then falls to the appellate courts to unravel what happened and decide whether the judge should have imposed the sentence agreed on by counsel.

II. THE JOINT SUBMISSION

A. Definitions

Discussions surrounding joint submissions are often encumbered by problems of nomenclature. It is therefore important to define relevant terms.

Plea bargains may take many forms. A joint submission is really just one method of plea bargaining: see Simon Verdun-Jones & Alison Hatch, *Plea Bargaining and Sentencing Guidelines* (Ottawa: Canadian Sentencing Commission, 1985) at 3, where the authors list 13 forms of plea bargaining. These are reproduced in the Report of the Canadian Sentencing Commission, above at 404-5. The Canadian Sentencing Commission defines (at 404) a plea bargain as "any agreement by the accused to plead guilty in return for the promise of some benefit." A plea bargain or plea arrangement may take the form of the Crown's withdrawal of one or more charges in exchange for the accused's guilty plea to one or more charges. (The plea of guilty may be taken into account as a mitigating factor: see *R v Johnston and Tremayne*, [1970] 4 CCC 64 (Ont CA); see also *R v Fegan* (1993), 80 CCC (3d) 356 (Ont CA), where Finlayson JA (at 8), in discussing the guilty plea, made the following statement: "It is considered by the sentencing judge as an expression of remorse. By expressing finality to the conviction process, it invites leniency in the sentencing portion of the trial." This is not always the case, however: see the Martin Report at 310, which emphasizes that the earlier the guilty plea is entered, the greater the mitigation that may be enjoyed. This principle is exemplified in *R v Pitkeathly* (1994), 29 CR (4th) 182 (Ont CA); *R v Stang*, 2002 ABCA 15; and *R v Smith*, 2009 MBQB 54; see also Allan Manson, *The Law of Sentencing* (Toronto: Irwin Law, 2001) at 133. There need be no further agreement about the type or quantum of punishment that ought to follow. Similarly, a plea bargain may involve a plea of not guilty to the charge as laid, but a plea of guilty to a lesser and included offence. A good example of this type of arrangement is when an accused person who is charged with murder enters a plea of guilty to the lesser and included offence of manslaughter.

These two aspects of the plea-bargaining process are engaged largely without the sentencing judge's input—that is, these types of arrangements are conceived of and driven by counsel, and do not depend on the assent of the sentencing judge: see s 606(4) of the *Criminal Code*, RSC 1985, c C-46. It is recognized that the trial judge is granted the discretion to reject a plea to a lesser offence if the facts do not support such a reduction, although the Ontario Court of Appeal in *R v Naraindeen* (1990), 80 CR (3d) 66 (Ont CA) suggests that some deference ought to be afforded to prosecutorial discretion in this context. The potential for a clash between judicial and prosecutorial discretion may be avoided if, instead of relying on s 606(4) to facilitate a plea to a lesser offence, the prosecutor has a new information laid (or a new indictment drafted) to charge the specific offence for which the guilty plea is offered. There is little that a sentencing judge can do to upset this type of "charge-bargaining" arrangement. This is not to say, however, that these types of arrangements ought to be shrouded in secrecy. On the contrary, the public interest is better served by the public disclosure of any agreement in open court: see the Martin Report at 315-17, where the virtues of openness and accountability of this aspect of the process are discussed. This view is also shared by the Canadian Sentencing Commission, above at 422-23. Of course, there will be exceptions to openness where the exigencies of unique circumstances dictate.

The joint submission may be a subset of the broader category of plea bargains or may follow a finding of guilt. There is no magic in the term "joint submission." It simply reflects a process whereby both counsel advocate the same disposition for the offender. Such an arrangement may be attached to other arrangements like those discussed above, or it may be the only aspect of the case on which counsel agree. However, it is unique in that it takes effect only upon the assent of the sentencing judge. The following discussion of joint submissions focuses mainly on the judicial role. When reviewing the material in this chapter, consider the following issues: What is the test for rejecting a joint submission? How much must the sentencing judge know about the basis for the joint submission? If a sentencing judge is considering rejecting a joint submission, what procedure should be followed? If the sentencing judge decides to reject a joint submission, what, if any, are the offender's options?

B. The Treatment of the Joint Submission: Sentencing Judge Not Bound

The practice of Canadian courts has been somewhat inconsistent in dealing with the treatment of joint submissions. On the one hand, the courts have recognized the value of plea arrangements and demonstrated concern for the consequences that would accrue if judges were to give them little consideration. On the other hand, it is vital to preserve judicial independence and integrity by allowing sentencing judges to refuse to accede to a joint submission when circumstances dictate.

Appeal courts have therefore held that while sentencing judges are not bound by a joint submission, they should depart from them only in specific circumstances. However, appeal courts have used different terminology in setting down the exact test that sentencing judges must apply in deciding whether to reject a joint submission. The following case considers whether this differing terminology reflects different standards or merely different ways of expressing the same standard.

R v Douglas

(2002), 162 CCC (3d) 37 (Qc CA)

FISH JA:

We are concerned in this case with a plea agreement negotiated by experienced Crown counsel in consultation with the police officers in charge of the investigation.

The main elements of the agreement—manifestly interdependent—were joint submissions on sentence in exchange for pleas of guilty in two related files.

Pursuant to the agreement, the appellant pleaded guilty, in the first file, to armed robbery and illegal confinement, and the parties jointly recommended concurrent sentences of four years' imprisonment on each count. The trial judge found that four years was "unreasonable" and imposed five instead.

In the second file, the appellant pleaded guilty to conspiracy and, as agreed, Crown counsel suggested a concurrent one-year sentence. The trial judge imposed a one-year consecutive term, or the equivalent of six-years concurrent.

With commendable integrity and candour, Crown counsel now urges us to allow the prisoner's appeal.

For the reasons that follow, I would do so.

· · ·

III

Canadian appellate courts have expressed in different ways the standard for determining when trial judges may properly reject joint submissions on sentence accompanied by negotiated admissions of guilt.

Whatever the language used, the standard is meant to be an exacting one. Appellate courts, increasingly in recent years, have stated time and again that trial judges should not reject jointly proposed sentences unless they are "unreasonable," "contrary to the public interest," "unfit," or "would bring the administration of justice into disrepute."

The Ontario Court of Appeal has enunciated the applicable standard in terms proposed by ... [the Martin Report].

The policy purposes underlying the Court's approach and its choice of terminology are well explained in the Martin Report. These are the particularly relevant passages:

· · ·

The Committee recognizes that an important, sometimes the most important, factor in counsel's ability to conclude resolution agreements, thereby deriving the benefits that such agreements bring, is that of certainty. Accused persons are ... prepared to waive their right to a trial far more readily if the outcome of such a waiver is certain, than they are for the purely speculative possibility that the outcome will bear some resemblance to what counsel have agreed to. And likewise, from the perspective of Crown counsel, agreed upon resolutions that have a stronger, rather than weaker sense of certainty to them are more desirable because there is less risk that what Crown counsel concludes is an appropriate resolution of the case in the public interest will be undercut.

· · ·

While the presiding judge cannot have his or her sentencing discretion removed by the fact of there being a joint submission, it is none the less appropriate ... for the sentencing judge to have regard to the interest of certainty in resolution discussions when faced with a joint submission. Accordingly, where there is no reason in the public interest or in the need to preserve the repute of the administration of justice to depart from a joint submission, a sentencing judge should ... give effect to the need for certainty in agreed upon resolutions by accepting the joint submission of counsel.

· · ·

These considerations are reflected in *Cerasuolo* [(2001), 151 CCC (3d) 445 (Ont CA)], where Finlayson JA, speaking for a unanimous Court, observed:

This court has repeatedly held that trial judges should not reject joint submissions unless the joint submission is contrary to the public interest and the sentence would bring the administration of justice into disrepute: e.g. *R v. Dorsey* (1999), 123 OAC 342 at 345. This is a high threshold and is intended to foster confidence in an accused, who has given up his right to a trial, that the joint submission he obtained in return for a plea of guilty will be respected by the sentencing judge.

The Crown and the defence bar have cooperated in fostering an atmosphere where the parties are encouraged to discuss the issues in a criminal trial with a view to shortening the trial process. This includes bringing issues to a final resolution through plea bargaining. This laudable initiative cannot succeed unless the accused has some assurance that the trial judge will in most instances honour agreements entered into by the Crown. While we cannot overemphasize that these agreements are not to fetter the independent evaluation of sentences proposed, there is no interference with the judicial independence of the sentencing judge in requiring him or her to explain in what way a particular joint submission is contrary to the public interest and would bring the administration of justice into disrepute.

Commenting on these observations and likewise speaking for the Court, Prowse JA, of the British Columbia Court of Appeal, stated in *Bezdan* [[2001] BCJ No 808 (QL) (CA)]:

I am in general agreement with the sentiments expressed in the second paragraph of the passage quoted. It is apparent that the administration of criminal justice requires cooperation between counsel and that the court should not be too quick to look behind a plea-bargain struck between competent counsel unless there is good reason to do so. In those instances in which the sentencing judge is not prepared to give effect to the proposal, I also agree that it would be appropriate for that judge to give his or her reasons for departing from the "bargain." I would not go so far as to say that a sentencing judge can only depart from the sentence suggested in the joint submission if he or she is satisfied that the proposal is contrary to the public interest, or that the sentence proposed would bring the administration of justice into disrepute. It is not clear to me that these two circumstances cover all situations in which a sentencing judge might conclude that the sentence proposed was "unfit."

A similar threshold appears to have been established in Alberta. Speaking for a unanimous court in *C. (G. W.)* [(2000), 150 CCC (3d) 513 (Alta CA)], Berger JA explained:

The obligation of a trial judge to give serious consideration to a joint sentencing submission stems from an attempt to maintain a proper balance between respect for the plea bargain and the sentencing court's role in the administration of justice. The certainty that is required to induce accused persons to waive their rights to a trial can only be achieved in an atmosphere where the courts do not lightly interfere with a negotiated disposition that falls within or is very close to the appropriate range for a given offence. "The bargaining process is undermined if the resulting compromise recommendation is too readily rejected by the sentencing judge." *R v. Pashe* (1995), 100 Man. R (2d) 61 (Man. CA) at para. 11.

Joint submissions, however, should be accepted by the trial judge unless they are unfit: *R v. Sinclair*, [1996] AJ No. 464 (QL) (Alta. CA) at para. 4 ... ; or unreasonable: *R v. Hudson*, [1995] AJ No. 797 (QL) (Alta. CA) at para. 1, online: QL (AJ). In *R v. Dorsey* (1999), 123 OAC 342, the Ontario Court of Appeal held at p. 345 that "a joint submission should be departed from only where the trial judge considers the joint submission to be contrary to the public interest and ... if accepted, would bring the administration of justice into disrepute." That view accords with the position of the Manitoba Court of Appeal in *R v. Pashe*, *supra*, at para. 12, that "while a sentencing judge has an overriding discretion to reject a joint recommendation, *there must be good reason to do so*, particularly ... where the joint recommendation is made by experienced counsel." [Emphasis added by Berger JA.]

The approach adopted by the Manitoba Court of Appeal in *Pashe*, cited with approval in *C. (G. W.)*, was again implemented by that Court in *Chartrand* [(1998), 131 CCC (3d) 122 (Man CA)], where Kroft JA, delivering the unanimous judgment, put the matter this way:

> A sentencing judge is not bound to accept the recommendation, but it should not be rejected unless there is good cause for so doing. This case does not fall into that category.
>
> Notwithstanding the discretion of the trial judge, and even though the sentence imposed might not be so high as to be declared unreasonable, where a joint submission has been made between competent counsel which is not so unfit that it demands rejection, then that recommendation should not be ignored.
>
> • • •

Finally, in *Dubuc* [(1998), 131 CCC (3d) 250 (Qc CA)], again a unanimous judgment, this Court, too, cited and applied *Pashe, supra*.

In my view, a reasonable joint submission cannot be said to "bring the administration of justice into disrepute." An unreasonable joint submission, on the other hand, is surely "contrary to the public interest." Accordingly, though it is purposively framed in striking and evocative terms, I do not believe that the Ontario standard departs substantially from the test of reasonableness articulated by other courts, including our own. Their shared conceptual foundation is that the interests of justice are well served by the acceptance of a joint submission on sentence accompanied by a negotiated plea of guilty—provided, of course, that the sentence jointly proposed falls within the acceptable range and the plea is warranted by the facts admitted.

• • •

In the present case, the Crown and the defence jointly urged the trial judge to impose carefully negotiated sentences of four years' imprisonment in one file and one year, concurrent, in the other. The trial judge considered that the four year sentence was "unreasonable," in part because that was the minimum sentence permitted by law and did not adequately take into account the aggravating factors present in this case. Instead, the judge imposed a sentence of five years.

With respect, moreover, I find it difficult to conclude, as the trial judge did, that a five-year sentence was reasonable, but the proposed four-year sentence was not.

Appellate courts in the other provinces and territories have used the same or similar terms in articulating the standard for rejecting a joint submission: see e.g. *R v Guignard*, 2005 NBCA 35, 195 CCC (3d) 145; *R v Druken*, 2006 NLCA 67, 215 CCC (3d) 394; and *R v Cromwell*, 2005 NSCA 137, 202 CCC (3d) 310.

What factors should a sentencing judge consider in deciding whether to reject a joint submission? How much information should counsel present to the sentencing judge when putting forward a joint submission? What procedure should sentencing judges follow if they are considering rejecting a joint submission? The following two cases address these issues.

R v Sinclair
2004 MBCA 48, 185 CCC (3d) 569

STEEL JA:

This case raises once more the difficult question of when it is appropriate for a court to deviate from a joint recommendation as to sentence.

The accused pled guilty to a charge of assault causing bodily harm. The assault was completely unprovoked. There was a joint submission by counsel that since the accused had already spent an equivalent of between 10 and 12 months in custody (assuming double credit), he should now be released with a sentence of time served. In addition, a period of probation with conditions was suggested. The sentencing judge was clearly troubled by the unprovoked nature of the assault. He asked the accused for some sort of reason given the fact that the victim was unknown to him and had said nothing to him as he was passing. The accused had no explanation.

After considering the matter and the fact that he had been presented with a joint recommendation from experienced counsel, he declined to follow that submission. Instead, considering the accused's criminal record, including several convictions for violent offences, the completely unprovoked nature of the assault and the need for specific and general deterrence, he sentenced the accused to an additional three months in custody, which, taking pre-sentencing detention into account, constituted an effective sentence of 15 months, with no order of probation. This court dismissed the accused's appeal as to sentence, with reasons to follow. These are those reasons.

• • •

When deciding whether to depart from a joint recommendation, a court should consider the following factors.

There is a continuum in the spectrum of plea bargaining and joint submissions as to sentence. In some cases, the Crown's case has some flaw or weakness and the accused agrees to give up his or her right to a trial and to plead guilty in exchange for some consideration. This consideration may take the form of a reduction in the original charge, withdrawal of other charges or an agreement to jointly recommend a more lenient sentence than would be likely after a guilty verdict at trial. Evidence always varies in strength and there is always uncertainty in the trial process. In other cases, plea negotiations have become accepted as a means to expedite the administration of criminal justice. That is the case here, where the accused's decision to forego his right to a trial must be considered within the context of a backlog in trial dates and the months already spent in pre-trial detention. The clearer the *quid pro quo*, the more weight should be given an appropriate joint submission by the sentencing judge. See *R v. Broekaert (D.D.)* (2003), 170 Man. R (2d) 229, 2003 MBCA 10, at para. 29, and *Booh* [2003 MBCA 16, 170 Man R (2d) 249], at para. 11.

Recognizing that cases fall at various places in the continuum, the essence of the plea bargain or joint submission should be placed on the record in open court. The judge must have a solid factual basis on which to make an independent, reasoned decision. If a trial judge is not given or fails to inquire into the circumstances underlying a joint sentencing submission, then he or she will be hard pressed to determine whether there is good cause to reject that joint submission.

• • •

If the joint submission is as a result of, for example, an evidentiary gap in the Crown's case or the absence of an essential witness, this is information that should be provided to the court by counsel, and particularly Crown counsel.

· · ·

In this case, Crown counsel indicated he was recommending a sentence of time served since the "Crown's recommendation is still that the time having spent in custody is appropriate in the circumstances considering the nature of the offence, considering any exigencies in, in the Crown's case. And I make reference to that only in respect of having spoken to the complainant this morning." Defence counsel, in his submission, elaborated on that point by adding that the police were not able to identify the accused and the complainant told the Crown attorney something different than in his statement given to police on the day in question.

The sentencing judge did give serious consideration to the joint submission. However, he also considered several other factors upon which he placed considerable weight in his reasons. The "exigencies" of the case referred to by both counsel when speaking in favour of the joint submission were mitigated by the fact that the accused had made, what the judge considered, a clear admission of guilt to the police. The offender had a record of prior involvement that included elements of violence. He had ended up in custody as a result of continued involvement. The accused had initially been released after six days in custody, but was arrested again as a result of a breach of recognizance. He spent another 26 days in custody, was released again, breached again and then remained in custody until his sentencing since his bail was revoked. Perhaps most troubling to the judge was the fact that the offence was totally unprovoked, and when questioned, the accused showed "a complete lack of care, a complete lack of concern, a total disinterest."

Consequently, the sentencing judge concluded that the proposed sentence was unreasonably low and that to send the proper "message to those in the community" for purposes of denunciation and deterrence, the circumstances required more than a sentence of time served. In so rejecting the joint submission, he articulated clear and cogent reasons. There should be deference to the exercise of the sentencing judge's discretion in these circumstances.

R v C (GW)
2000 ABCA 333, 150 CCC (3d) 513

BERGER JA (Picard and Costigan JJA concurring):

[1] The Appellant is a 32 year old aboriginal male. On November 15, 1999, he pleaded guilty to two counts of sexual assault in connection with events which took place between January 1983 and December 1985 when he was between the ages of 14 and 17. The offences, which included numerous incidents of sexual impropriety, were visited upon two children aged 6 to 9 and 9 to 12 respectively, who were in the care of the Appellant in his parents' home.

[2] The learned sentencing judge received a joint submission urging a period of probation subject to strict conditions. That submission was rejected for reasons set out below. The Appellant was sentenced to one year of closed custody plus 18 months probation on each count to be served concurrently.

[3] In rejecting the joint submission, the learned sentencing judge reasoned as follows:

> With the greatest of respect to two lawyers, whom I both respect, the sentence that is proposed, or the disposition that is proposed does not take into account adequately the principles of general deterrence, individual deterrence, the principles enunciated in Section 718 of the *Criminal Code*, the need for rehabilitation of this accused, and more importantly, the interests of the victims.
>
> • • •
>
> I am mindful of the [Saddle Lake Youth Justice Committee's] recommendations insofar as the best interests of this accused, that a probation period of two years would be appropriate. I am also mindful of the other side of the coin, being the position of the victims, that general deterrence—or deterrence, both general and individual, is of primary consideration here.
>
> • • •

[19] This Court has made clear on more than one occasion that a joint submission need not be followed as long as it is given "serious consideration," particularly where there is a guilty plea. *R v. Wood* (1989), 43 CCC (3d) 570 (Ont. CA). Where a trial judge "demonstrated a thorough appreciation of the relevant facts, their significance, and of the proper sentencing principles" appellate intervention on the basis of reviewable error in rejection of a joint sentencing submission will not likely be warranted. *R v. Beaulieu* (1997), 118 Man. R (2d) 148 (Man. CA) at para. 8, and *R v. L.(S.M.)*, [1998] AJ No. 1442, 40 WCB 449 (Alta. QB).

[20] But "serious consideration" cannot occur in a factual vacuum. In my opinion, no "thorough appreciation of the relevant facts" can occur in the absence of a careful and diligent inquiry of counsel as to the circumstances underlying a joint sentencing submission. Given the high level of deference afforded to sentencing judges in the exercise of their discretion to reject joint submissions, the need for a thorough inquiry takes on even greater significance. Yet, in the case at bar, the learned trial judge did not inquire into the circumstances which formed the basis of the joint sentencing submission.

[21] In *R v. Morissette*, [1996] OJ No. 3071 (Ont. CA) at para. 1, the trial judge had rejected a joint submission as to sentence without giving reasons for doing so, and had imposed a higher sentence than that recommended jointly by counsel. The majority of the Court were of the view "that without hearing the basis upon which the joint submission was made, it cannot be said that there were compelling reasons to reject it. In the absence of such reasons, it should have been accepted." More recently, in *R v. Quinn*, [1999] OJ No. 2706 (Ont. CA), Doherty JA, speaking for the Court, held that "the trial judge erred in principle in departing from a joint submission without calling upon the Crown to explain the basis upon which the final submission was arrived at." In neither case did the Ontario Court of Appeal expand upon the articulated principle.

[22] The Manitoba Court of Appeal also appears to have touched upon the issue in *R v. Sherlock* (1998), 131 Man. R (2d) 143 (CA), Kroft JA made the following observations regarding plea bargaining and joint submissions (at para. 32):

> I fully accept that the efficient administration of justice requires that there be an element of negotiation between counsel for the Crown and counsel for the accused relating to the entry of pleas and the recommendation of sentence. The negotiations, or bargaining, will often go on over a substantial period of time. On other occasions, legitimate pragmatism will require that arrangements be made at the courtroom door. *In either case, it is important to trial judges*

*and courts of appeal that the nature of the bargain be clearly presented on the record. Without
that assistance, no court can adequately assess the extent to which it should be constrained by
the joint recommendation of counsel.* [Emphasis added]

[23] In the past, Courts have been inclined to acknowledge that, in the face of a joint
submission, they must be mindful that the prosecution possesses a much more intimate
understanding of the case at bar than the Court itself. In *R v. Maheu*, [1992] AQ No. 21
(Que. CA), the Quebec Court of Appeal commented as follows:

> But, it is also clear that serious consideration should be given by the court to recommenda-
> tions of Crown counsel, particularly where the facts outlined, following a guilty plea, are
> sparse. The Court then has to recognize that Crown counsel is more familiar than itself with
> the extenuating or aggravating circumstances of the offence which may not be fully disclosed
> in the summary of facts: see *R v. Fleury* (1971), 23 CRNS 164 (Que. CA).

[24] With respect, no one should have a more intimate understanding of the case at bar
than the Court itself. The facts that guide the sentence disposition ought not to be "sparse."
Crown counsel, at the end of the day, ought not to be more familiar with the extenuating
or aggravating circumstances of the offence than the sentencing judge. The facts of the
case ought to be fully disclosed. Those facts must surely include the circumstances underlying the joint sentencing submission (subject, of course, to any claim of privilege).

[25] Joint submissions are often the result of [what is] commonly referred to as a "plea
bargain." The plea bargain may have been struck because of an evidentiary gap in the
Crown's case. The absence of Crown witnesses may have influenced the plea bargain and
the resulting joint submission. On the other hand, the plea bargain may well have been
the result of an appreciation by the accused of the futility of running a trial. The inevitability of a finding of guilt may well have resonated. If the latter consideration motivated the
plea bargain, the credit for the guilty plea would, surely, not be as great as if the guilty
plea truly represented an acknowledgement of wrong doing and an expression of remorse.
It is essential that the sentencing judge determine what facts or factors motivated the plea
and gave rise to the joint submission. The sentencing disposition may vary accordingly.
It follows that the failure to so inquire prior to rejecting a joint submission may well
constitute reversible error.

[26] In addition to the foregoing, the procedure followed by the sentencing judge in
rejecting the joint submission in this case is a matter of concern. Once a sentencing judge
concludes that he might not accede to a joint submission, fundamental fairness dictates
that an opportunity be afforded to counsel to make further submissions in an attempt to
address the sentencing judge's concerns before the sentence is imposed. In this case,
lengthy submissions were made by both counsel in support of a probationary term which
evoked no expressions of concern by the sentencing judge. He then retired to consider
the disposition of the case. It was only upon his return to the courtroom, and in the course
of giving reasons for rejecting the joint submission, that counsel had any indication of
concern on his part. As a result, they were afforded no opportunity to address that concern. Indeed, had the sentencing judge made his concern known to counsel in a timely
fashion, the foundation upon which the joint submission rested might well have been
laid. I do not suggest that any particular procedure is de rigueur; I say only that the
principle of *audi alteram partem* should be followed.

Conclusion

[27] For all of these reasons, the appeal must be allowed.

[28] ... [T]his Court, like the trial judge, has no information as to the factual foundation that gave rise to the joint submission. Accordingly, counsel are directed to provide the Court, within 21 days of the release of this judgment, with advice in writing (letter form will do) as to the facts or factors underlying the joint submission. The Court will then be in a position to impose an appropriate sentence in accordance with s. 687(1)(a) of the *Criminal Code*.

NOTE

For further guidance on the information to be provided to the sentencing judge, see *R v Tkachuk*, 2001 ABCA 243, 159 CCC (3d) 434, which indicates that counsel (1) should fully disclose the facts of the case, including the aggravating and mitigating factors; (2) should, if the proposed sentence is not obviously within the accepted range of sentence for that offence, explain to the court the reasons for departing from a sentence within that range; and (3) normally need not and should not disclose their negotiating positions and the substance of their discussions leading to the agreement as these are private.

Section 726.2 of the *Criminal Code* requires sentencing judges to provide reasons for sentence. When sentencing judges reject a joint submission, must they explain their reasons for rejecting it or is it sufficient to simply explain the reasons for the sentence that is ultimately imposed on the offender? This issue is considered in the following case.

R v Haufe
2007 ONCA 515

THE COURT (Doherty, Feldman, and MacPherson JJA):

[1] The appellant, Oliver Haufe, seeks leave to appeal the sentence imposed by Justice B.J. Frazer following the appellant's guilty plea for robbery. The sentence imposed was 18 months in custody (in addition to credit given for 48 days spent in pre-trial detention) followed by two years probation.

[2] The robbery occurred on December 29, 1995. It was a home robbery in which two intruders were surprised by the returning home owner. An altercation followed and the home owner was beaten, injured and taken to hospital. A fingerprint left at the scene led to the arrest of the appellant more than ten years later on April 1, 2006.

[3] The appellant's principal ground of appeal is that the trial judge erred by rejecting the joint submission for sentence of counsel (namely, six months in custody) and imposing a sentence that tripled the proposed sentence (18 months).

[4] The sentencing judge did warn defence counsel that he was considering the imposition of a sentence higher than the joint submission. He also afforded defence counsel an opportunity to make further submissions after he issued his warning. However, in our view, the sentencing judge did not comply with the legal principles that apply to the

rejection of a joint submission relating to sentence. In the leading case, *R.v. Cerasuolo* (2001), 151 CCC (3d) 445 at 447-8 (Ont. CA), Finlayson JA stated:

> This court has repeatedly held that trial judges should not reject joint submissions *unless the joint submission is contrary to the public interest and the sentence would bring the administration of justice into disrepute*: e.g. R v. Dorsey (1999), 123 OAC 342 at 345. *This is a high threshold and is intended to foster confidence in an accused, who has given up his right to a trial, that the joint submission he obtained in return for a plea of guilty will be respected by the sentencing judge.*
>
> The Crown and the defence bar have cooperated in fostering an atmosphere where the parties are encouraged to discuss the issues in a criminal trial with a view to shortening the trial process. This includes bringing issues to a final resolution through plea bargaining. *This laudable initiative cannot succeed unless the accused has some assurance that the trial judge will in most instances honour agreements entered into by the Crown.* While we cannot over-emphasize that these agreements are not to fetter the independent evaluation of the sentences proposed, *there is no interference with the judicial independence of the sentencing judge in requiring him or her to explain in what way a particular joint submission is contrary to the public interest and would bring the administration of justice into disrepute.* [Emphasis added.]

[5] With respect, the sentencing judge's reasons in this case do not meet the requirements of *Cerasuolo*. The sentencing judge said nothing about the joint submission that counsel placed before him. This was particularly regrettable given that the Crown position on sentence had been the subject of a litigation conference in the Crown office which led to a formal letter to defence counsel setting out the Crown position. In these circumstances, the sentencing judge's silence about the joint submission does not "explain in what way a particular joint submission is contrary to the public interest and would bring the administration of justice into disrepute."

[6] Finally, in our view, it cannot be said that the sentence proposed in the joint submission (six months) was so clearly unreasonable as to make the imposition of an 18 month sentence more or less self-evident. The sentencing judge himself identified several factors—the fact that the offence was committed in 1995, the guilty plea, and the appellant's good conduct including employment, overcoming addiction, and non-commission of crimes in the two years before being sentenced for the 1995 robbery. In our view, these factors called out for an explanation of why the sentencing judge rejected the joint submission and imposed a custodial sentence three times higher than the joint submission.

[7] Leave to appeal sentence is granted, the appeal is allowed and a custodial sentence of six months is imposed.

NOTES

1. Can offenders withdraw their guilty plea if it becomes apparent during the presentation of submissions that the sentencing judge will not accede to a joint submission? See *R v Rubenstein* (1987), 41 CCC (3d) 91 (Ont CA):

> The power of the trial Judge to impose a sentence cannot be limited to a joint submission, and the joint submission cannot be the basis upon which to escape the sentencing judge when it appears that he chooses to reject the joint submission. As Judge Draper observed, an accused who could thus withdraw his plea could simply keep doing so until he found a trial judge who

would accept a joint submission. A plea of guilty in the same way as a finding of guilt after trial exposes an accused to a proper sentence to be determined by the trial judge. ... To permit an accused to withdraw his plea when the sentence does not suit him puts the court in the unseemly position of bargaining with the accused.

2. In the light of the ability of sentencing judges to reject joint submissions, is there an obligation on defence counsel before entering a guilty plea to inform the accused that the court is not bound to accept a joint submission? What if the accused is unrepresented? See *R v Grimsson* (1997), 100 BCAC 253 (CA); *R v Samms* (1993), 107 Nfld & PEIR 172 (Nfld CA).

3. How important is the contingency of a guilty plea in determining whether a joint submission is enforceable on appeal? Is there a qualitative difference between a joint submission that essentially induces a guilty plea and one that does not? Is one entitled to more deference than the other? In addition to the cases excerpted above, see *R v Dubuc* (1998), 131 CCC (3d) 250 (Qc CA); *R v Neale*, 2000 BCCA 157; *R v AN*, 2011 NSC 21, 269 CCC (3d) 106; *R v Knockwood*, 2009 NSCA 98; *R v Sinclair*, above.

4. When co-accused are being sentenced in separate proceedings, what weight, if any, should the sentencing judge give to the sentence imposed on another co-accused if that sentence was the result of a joint submission? See *R v Christie*, 2004 ABCA 287, 189 CCC (3d) 274.

5. Joint submissions usually occur in the context of a guilty plea, but sometimes Crown and defence counsel may make a joint submission as to the appropriate sentence after a contested trial. In such circumstances, does a sentencing judge have broader latitude to reject the submission?

6. If a joint submission is "obviously" unfit, is a sentencing judge still required to give reasons for rejecting the joint submission? On an appeal, what are the consequences, if any, of failing to do so?

7. Apart entirely from joint submissions, appellate courts have indicated that sentencing judges should not normally depart from the proposed range sought by counsel (and, in particular, should not exceed the position of the Crown because that may have influenced the decision to plead guilty) without giving counsel notice and the opportunity to make further submissions. However, a failure to provide notice is not necessarily a reversible error on appeal, particularly if there were no negotiations between counsel as to the range of sentence to be proposed. Even if there were discussions, an appeal court may remedy the procedural deficiency by allowing further submissions to determine whether a variation in sentence is required. Ultimately, the question remains whether in all the circumstances the sentence imposed is fit: see *R v Noel*, [2006] OJ No 3183 (QL) (CA); *R v Burback*, 2012 ABCA 30; *R v RRB*, 2013 BCCA 224; *Gabriel c R*, 2015 QCCA 1391.

III. SENTENCE APPEALS AND JOINT SUBMISSIONS

Appellate review of sentencing decisions is a complex aspect of the law. Although it has inspired a great deal of activity over the past number of years, we leave the nuances of this area to Chapter 17, Appeals: see generally Allan Manson, "The Supreme Court Intervenes in Sentencing" (1996), 43 CR (4th) 306; Gary Trotter, "Appellate Review of Sentencing Decisions" in Julian V Roberts & David P Cole, eds, *Making Sense of Sentencing* (Toronto: University of Toronto Press, 1999). For now, we examine only the impact of joint submissions in the appellate sphere. As discussed in previous chapters, the sentencing judge at first instance is granted substantial discretion in determining an appropriate sentence. The power of the courts of appeal to review sentencing decisions is found in s 687 of the *Criminal Code*. This section provides as follows:

> 687(1) Where an appeal is taken against sentence, the court of appeal shall, unless the sentence is one fixed by law, consider the fitness of the sentence appealed against, and may on such evidence, if any, as it thinks fit to require or to receive,
>
> (a) vary the sentence within the limits prescribed by law for the offence of which the accused was convicted; or
>
> (b) dismiss the appeal.

Although this appellate power appears to be quite broad on its face, recent cases from the Supreme Court of Canada have narrowed the scope of review considerably. The Supreme Court has sent a clear message that the decisions of sentencing judges must be approached with great deference. Today, courts of appeal may intervene only if there was an error in principle or if the sentence imposed at first instance was "demonstrably unfit" or "clearly unreasonable": see *R v Shropshire*, [1995] 4 SCR 227, 102 CCC (3d) 193; *R v M (CA)*, [1996] 1 SCR 500, 46 CR (4th) 269; *R v McDonnell*, [1997] 1 SCR 948, 114 CCC (3d) 436; *R v Nasogaluak*, 2010 SCC 6, [2010] 1 SCR 206; *R v Lacasse*, 2015 SCC 64, [2015] 3 SCR 1089.

A. Appeals by the Offender

The appropriateness of a joint submission can arise in two situations when the offender launches an appeal. First, the offender may appeal on the basis that the sentencing judge erred in failing to abide by a joint submission. The principles that apply to this situation are set out in the first part of this chapter: see e.g. *R v Druken*, 2006 NLCA 67, 215 CCC (3d) 394 (defence appeal allowed when sentencing judge rejected joint submission); *R v Oake* (2010), 252 CCC (3d) 498 (Nfld CA) (defence appeal allowed when sentencing judge rejected joint submission); *R v N (A)*, above (defence appeal dismissed when sentencing judge rejected joint submission); *R v Steeves*, 2010 NBCA 57, 258 CCC (3d) 506 (defence appeal allowed when sentencing judge rejected joint submission); and *R v Douglas*, above.

The other, and less common, situation is where the sentencing judge imposes a sentence in accordance with the joint submission, but, on appeal, the offender disavows the joint submission and contends that the sentence is unfit. In the cases that follow, consider whether the approach of the appeal court respects the interests that are said to be recognized by joint submissions.

R v Wood

(1988), 43 CCC (3d) 570 (Ont CA)

LACOURCIÈRE JA:

Following the committal of the accused for trial for first degree murder, Crown counsel ... indicated that a plea of guilty to manslaughter would be acceptable if a joint submission for a sentence of 14 years was agreed upon. At trial, counsel for the appellant, who had considerable experience in criminal matters, participated in this joint submission. [The trial judge accepted the joint submission. However, he also made a recommendation that the appellant not be released on parole until at least one-half of his sentence had been served. The appellant appealed.]

· · ·

While the Crown generally will not be a allowed to repudiate a position taken at trial where the accused has relied on his position before entering a guilty plea, Crown counsel has no authority to bind the Attorney-General in the exercise of his discretion to appeal. The ultimate responsibility to determine the fitness of sentence is on the Court of Appeal … . Certainly the accused is given greater latitude than the Crown on an appeal of this kind in that he is generally not bound to the same extent by the submissions of his counsel as to sentence.

· · ·

In the present case, the learned trial judge indicated his awareness of the case-law with respect to joint submissions and, in agreeing with the joint submission, he said:

> The problem for any trial judge in sentencing is to decide on the fitness of the sentence to be imposed and I am always prepared to consider the recommendations of counsel as to their views on the range of sentence, particularly when their observations fall within the range which is normally imposed for offences of this kind, but there is a duty on the judge to ignore such recommendations if, in his view, they are improper, because a sentence is a matter of public interest and should be consistent with the gravity of the offence and the relevant facts and all the cogent surrounding circumstances. I may say that I am in accord with the sentence proposed of 14 years. I think it falls within the reasonable range for a crime of this nature and the circumstances under which it was committed.

However, in analyzing the competing principles to be considered in determining the fitness of sentence, we believe that the learned trial judge over-emphasized the incidence of violent crimes in the community and the need for general deterrence for the protection of society. In doing so, in our view, he failed to give sufficient weight to the appellant's obvious remorse and to his incipient rehabilitation. In addition, no reference was made on the available record, or in the reasons for sentence, to the 16-month period of pre-trial incarceration.

The facts disclose a spontaneous stabbing following a family quarrel in circumstances where both the appellant and the victim had ingested alcohol and drugs. There was room for doubt as to the requisite intent for murder. In our view, it was appropriate for Crown counsel to consent to the plea of manslaughter. But, in our view, the Crown overreached in attaching a condition of a joint submission to a sentence which was far in excess of the usual range of sentences for manslaughter in the circumstances of the present case. The condition placed the accused, as well as experienced defence counsel, in a difficult position and to some extent may have hampered the trial judge. It would have been preferable to submit an appropriate range of sentence and to let the trial judge determine the sentence.

· · ·

Having regard to the gravity of the offence, the mitigating circumstances, the appellant's pre-trial custody, his sincere remorse and his exemplary institutional record and notwithstanding the joint submission at trial, we think an appropriate and fit sentence would be eight years. The trial judge's recommendation to the Parole Board should be disregarded, but the s. 98 order for a period of 10 years will stand.

R v Sriskantharajah
(1994), 90 CCC (3d) 559 (Ont CA)

FINLAYSON JA (Carthy and Austin JJA concurring):

The appellant pleaded not guilty to an indictment containing two counts of murder in the first degree of her two young daughters. After the trial commenced, she changed her plea to guilty of manslaughter on both counts. [In accordance with a joint submission], [t]he trial judge ... sentenced her to six years on each count to be served concurrently. [The appellant appealed.]

There are very strong mitigating circumstances in favour of the appellant, as found by the trial judge. [The offender was severely and chronically depressed, virtually abandoned by her husband (who otherwise abused her), and left to raise her two young children (one of whom had been brain damaged) in a country where she did not speak the language of the dominant culture.]

It was conceded that there is no danger of the appellant re-offending and she is not a risk to society. As counsel for the Crown put it, she is a greater risk to herself than to anyone else.

The court received fresh evidence which supports counsel for the appellant's submission that the cultural and linguistic isolation of the appellant, a Tamil from Sri Lanka, would be alleviated to some extent if she could be incarcerated in Toronto where she would be in contact with Parkdale Community Legal Services, the South Asian Women's Centre, and the Elizabeth Fry Society of Toronto, all of which have agreed to co-operate in a program directed to teaching her English and assisting her in re-integrating into the community. These facilities are not available to the same extent in the Kingston Prison for Women.

This court has stated repeatedly that it will not lightly interfere with a sentence imposed following a joint recommendation, but I do not agree with the submission of the Crown that the burden rests upon the appellant to demonstrate that the sentence imposed would bring the administration of justice into disrepute. In this case, it is worth noting that the sentence imposed amounts really to 10 years, which was reduced by the trial judge to six years in order to give the appellant credit for two years of pre-trial custody. I note also that the trial judge stated that in ordinary circumstances he would have considered the recommend range of sentence (10 to 12 years) to be markedly excessive.

In support of her contention that this court must be satisfied that the sentence imposed by the trial judge would bring the administration of justice into disrepute, counsel for the Crown referred the court to ... [the Martin Report] and particularly to p. 329 where it is stated:

> The sentencing judge will not ... have committed any error in principle in accepting a joint submission ... provided he or she arrives at the independent conclusion, based upon an adequate record, that the sentence proposed does not bring the administration of justice into disrepute and is otherwise not contrary to the public interest. Indeed, this recommendation embodies the essence of the sentencing judge's obligations in passing sentence. In so recommending, the Committee has endeavoured to define the discretion of the sentencing judge in sufficiently broad terms to ensure that the sentence imposed is ultimately just, but at the same time accorded the parties as much assurance as can be had that their agreed-upon resolutions will find favour with the Court. In this way, it is hoped that the justice system

and the community as a whole can profit to the greatest extent possible from the benefits of resolution discussions.

• • •

I acknowledge the appropriateness of this recommendation, especially as an admonition against imposing sentences that are too lenient, but, as stated in the excerpt, the sentence must be in the public interest, embracing a variety of concerns. Certainly, there can be no suggestion that review of these arrangements by this court is not to be exercised in an appropriate case. Deference to this court in these matters appears to be accepted by the Martin Report (at p. 332):

> Appellate review is essential to ensure that sentences imposed following resolution discussions are, at all times, within an appropriate range. Permitting Crown counsel in the appellate courts to take a position that need not necessarily accord with the position taken by the Crown at trial, permits the Crown to assist the appellate courts as fully as possible in discharging their duty to ensure that the trial courts have resolved cases in a manner that is fit and just.

The Committee notes that the rule permitting Crown appeals from joint submissions is complemented by a similar rule benefitting an accused. Indeed, the Ontario Court of Appeal has stated in *R v. Wood* that:

> Certainly the accused is given greater latitude than the Crown on an appeal of this kind in that he is generally not bound to the same extent by the submissions of his counsel as to sentence.

The Court went on to observe that, ultimately, the fitness of the sentence imposed, not the positions of the parties, is the dominant consideration.

This case is exceptional. The appellant was diagnosed at the Clarke Institute of Psychiatry as suffering from a major depression combined with a mixed personality disorder. This depression significantly impacted upon the appellant's judgment. Her perception of life, its reality and future prospects were negatively or fatalistically skewed by this depression. Suicide became the only logical solution to her problems. In the circumstances of this crime and this particular accused, a plea bargain made eminent sense and was in the best interest of justice. However, the sentence recommended in the joint submission was simply too long.

A non-penitentiary sentence is justified where, as here, the case demonstrates that the offence arose from the compulsion of mental illness, the offender poses little or no risk to the community, there is no significant risk of re-offence and an appropriate treatment and rehabilitation is available.

• • •

Accordingly, leave to appeal is granted, the appeal is allowed and the sentence is reduced to a reformatory term of two years less one day to be followed by a period of probation for three years.

NOTES

1. In *Wood*, was it fair for Lacourcière JA to conclude that the joint submission "may have hampered" the trial judge? Should the Court of Appeal have so easily disregarded the opinion (reflected in the agreement to the joint submission) of experienced defence counsel as to Wood's chances of being convicted of second-degree murder?

2. In *Sriskantharajah*, what was the precise basis on which the Court of Appeal intervened in this case? Given the more deferential standard of review signalled by the Supreme Court of Canada in the *Shropshire* line of cases, would *Sriskantharajah* be decided differently today? See *R v Ranger*, [2006] OJ No 1271 (QL) (Sup Ct J).

3. It is fair to say that the overwhelming majority of joint submissions are accepted by sentencing judges and left undisturbed by courts of appeal. The decisions reproduced in this chapter are therefore atypical. Still, these are the cases that find their way into the law reports and attract considerable attention. What effect do cases like those discussed above have on plea bargaining in general?

4. Another issue that sometimes arises in appeals against sentence by the offender (where the trial judge imposes a sentence in excess of the joint submission) is whether the Crown is duty-bound to maintain the "agreement" on appeal. The range of possible answers to this question is apparent in the discussion of the limits on the Crown in the next section.

B. Appeals by the Crown

Cases involving joint submissions may sometimes result in an appeal by the Crown. Similar to appeals from an offender, there are two situations in which the Crown might appeal. The first situation occurs when the sentencing judge disregards a joint submission and imposes a more *lenient* sentence.

R v DeSousa
2012 ONCA 254, 286 CCC (3d) 252

DOHERTY JA (MacPherson and Sharpe JJA concurring):

[14] ... What standard should a trial judge apply in determining whether it is appropriate to impose a sentence that is more lenient than a sentence proposed by way of a joint submission?

[The court quoted from the Martin Report ("the most important examination of the criminal process in Ontario in the last 40 years") and noted that it did not distinguish between "jumping" and "undercutting" a joint submission.]

[21] The Martin Report recognizes that certainty of result plays a valuable role in the criminal justice system. The report also recognizes that certainty serves not only the interests of the accused, but those of the Crown as representative of the public interest. To the extent that judges reject joint submissions, certainty suffers. This is true whether the judge "jumps" or "undercuts" the joint submission.

[22] Certainty of result is, of course, not the ultimate goal of the sentencing process. Certainty must yield where the harm caused by accepting the joint submission is beyond the value gained by promoting certainty of result. The standard described in both *Cerasuolo* and the Martin Report—that is, whether the proposed sentence would bring the administration of justice into disrepute or would otherwise not be in the public interest—draws the line where certainty of result must give way to other criminal justice interests. I think

the standard is applicable regardless of whether a trial judge is inclined to go above or below the sentence proposed in the joint submission.

[23] In holding that a trial judge should apply the same test when deciding whether to depart from a joint submission, upward or downward, I do not suggest that the factors relevant to the application of that standard will be identical in both situations. If a trial judge is considering imposing a higher sentence than the sentence agreed upon, concerns about the fairness to an accused who has given up a right to a trial in anticipation of a certain sentence will figure largely in the trial judge's determination of whether the agreed-upon sentence in the joint submission is so low as to bring the administration of justice into disrepute or is otherwise not in the public interest. Obviously, concerns about the accused's fair trial rights are not in play if the trial judge is considering imposing a sentence that is lower than the agreed-upon sentence.

[24] As alluded to in the extract from the Martin Report ... , where a judge is considering "undercutting" a joint submission, he or she must have regard to the community's reasonable expectations that the court will impose a sentence in accordance with that agreed upon in the joint submission. Confidence in the operation of the justice system will suffer where an accused enjoys the benefits of a plea bargain, perhaps, for example, escaping prosecution on other more serious charges, but is not required to serve the sentence agreed upon as part of that bargain. In deciding whether to reject a joint submission, trial judges must be alive to the potential negative impact on the administration of justice. The consideration of that potential impact finds expression in the standard articulated in *Cerasuolo* and the Martin Report.

[25] For these reasons, the trial judge erred in principle.

The following case is another example of the Crown appealing from a sentence that was the product of a joint submission, but with a slight twist.

R v Dubien
(1982), 67 CCC (2d) 341 (Ont CA)

MacKINNON ACJO:

This is an application by the Crown for leave to appeal and, if leave be granted, an appeal from a sentence imposed of five years after a plea of guilty to a charge of rape.

The application for leave to appeal is strenuously opposed on the ground that the Crown is "estopped" from appealing as, it is argued, the respondent relied on the position taken by Crown counsel at the trial and changed his plea to guilty on the basis of that "position."

The parties presented an agreed statement of facts to this court as to what was discussed between counsel at the trial and in the trial judge's chambers. These facts are as follows.

[Dubien was charged with raping a 14-year-old girl. During the trial, a discussion about a possible plea occurred in chambers between defence counsel, the Crown, and the trial judge. The defence offered to plead guilty to attempted rape because the Crown had stated that if the accused was found guilty of rape at the conclusion of trial, it would seek to have the accused declared a dangerous offender. The trial judge indicated that he would sentence the accused to four to five years in prison on a guilty plea to attempted rape. The Crown would not accept a plea to attempted rape, but indicated that if the accused pleaded guilty to rape and acknowledged a need for psychiatric assistance, the Crown would abandon the dangerous offender application and seek a sentence of seven to ten years. The trial judge indicated that given the slight degree of penetration an appropriate sentence for a guilty plea to either rape or attempted rape was five years. Crown counsel maintained his position. However, he also indicated that a term of five years was not so lenient as likely to be appealed; if it was imposed he would not recommend an appeal to the Crown law office and, in his view, absent such a recommendation, no appeal would be brought. At the same time, Crown counsel stated, and the accused understood, that he had no power to bind the attorney general on matters of appeal and that it was ultimately for the attorney general to decide whether to appeal. After discussion with the accused, defence counsel indicated that the accused would plead guilty to rape in the expectation of a sentence of five years and a recommendation that the sentence would be served in a psychiatric hospital.]

When the matter resumed before the trial judge, Crown counsel argued that the sentence for the offence to which the respondent had now pleaded guilty should be a penitentiary term of from seven to ten years. When the trial judge imposed a five-year penitentiary term, Crown counsel did not recommend an appeal nor had he, of course, proceeded with an application to have the respondent declared a dangerous offender. [The matter, however, came to the attention of the office of the Attorney General independently and the application for leave to appeal resulted.]

Counsel for the respondent argues that the whole system of "plea bargaining" will collapse if leave to appeal is given. It was an *in terrorem* submission that has little relevance to the facts of this case. The Attorney General's hands cannot be tied because counsel for the respondent failed to give his client a complete exposition of the Crown's position, namely, that Crown counsel could not and was not purporting to bind the Attorney General's exercise of his authority to decide whether an appeal should or should not be taken from the sentence imposed in the instant case.

On reviewing the material filed on the appeal one cannot help feeling that even if counsel had fully explained to the respondent the Crown's position as to the rights and duties of the Attorney General, it would have made no difference to his decision to plead guilty. He had succeeded in having the threat of an application to have him declared a dangerous offender withdrawn and he knew that he was going to receive a five year sentence whether he pleaded guilty to rape or attempted rape and he knew that counsel for the Crown would not recommend an appeal no matter how upset he was at that sentence. When the trial was completed with the sentencing there was no repudiation by Crown counsel of any of his "undertakings" to which he attached the caveat already noted.

Counsel for the respondent submitted that to grant the Attorney General leave to appeal would bring the whole administration of justice into question and destroy the necessary trust which must exist between the Crown and defence counsel. I do not agree. Of course discussions between counsel can be appropriate and helpful in certain cases and I can think of many situations where there is an "understanding," based on many relevant factors and experience, between counsel, which the Attorney General would not seek to repudiate. But that is not this case. Counsel for the Crown made it quite clear that the

Attorney General could still exercise his discretion in the matter of an appeal, and that he (Crown counsel) was "upset" (to use the terminology of the respondent in his affidavit) about the proposed sentence of five years, even though he would not recommend an appeal if such a sentence were imposed. Even if he had not "conditioned" his understanding, counsel for the Crown could not take away the discretion vested in the Attorney General to determine whether an appeal should or should not be taken or the obligation imposed on this court to consider the fitness of the sentence when the matter is before us.

With great deference to the very experienced and able trial judge, I am of the view that it is not advisable for a judge to take any active part in discussions as to sentence before a plea has been taken, nor to encourage indirectly a plea of guilty by indicating what his sentence will be. It was apparent in the instant case that the sentence was going to be the same whether the respondent changed his plea or not, and there was no suggestion or implication so far as the trial judge was concerned, that the sentence would be lighter if the respondent changed his plea to guilty. A trial judge can only determine what a just sentence should be after he has heard all relevant evidence in open court on that subject and listened to the submissions of counsel.

One would expect that if there was essential agreement between counsel in their submissions as to the "usual" sentence, that would carry weight, and the Crown's position at trial would be a circumstance for an appeal court to consider in considering the fitness of the sentence appealed against: *R v. Wood* (1975), 26 CCC (2d) 100 (Alta. CA). In *R v. Turner*, [1970] 2 QB 321 at p. 327, Lord Parker CJ stated that the only exception to the rule that the judge should never indicate the sentence he has in mind to impose is where it may be helpful to indicate, "whether the accused pleads guilty or not guilty, the sentence will or will not take a particular form, e.g., a probation order or a fine, or a custodial sentence."

It seems to me that the failure of the Attorney General to raise the question of the fitness of the sentence under the circumstances of this case would be more likely to bring the administration of justice into disrepute than otherwise. There was an error, in my view, in the sentence imposed of such a nature as to require the Attorney General, in the discharge of his duty, to appeal that sentence to ensure that the administration of justice is fairly and properly carried out. The appeal, as I have stated, is not a repudiation of the Crown's qualified position at trial. I would grant leave to appeal.

In *Dubien*, the Court of Appeal allowed the appeal and substituted a sentence of nine years' imprisonment. Is the court's conclusion that the appeal did not amount to a "repudiation" of the position of the Crown at trial convincing? Had Crown counsel in *Dubien* recommended an appeal to the attorney general, how might this have altered the court's response? Is it a relevant consideration that the position of Crown counsel at trial "induced" or "encouraged" a plea of guilty? If it did not, should a court of appeal feel less constrained to assess the fitness of sentence? See *R v Agozzino*, [1970] 1 CCC 380 (Ont CA); *Attorney General of Canada v Roy* (1972), 18 CRNS 89 (Qc QB); and *R v Cusack* (1978), 41 CCC (2d) 289 (NSCA).

Consider whether the position expressed in the following excerpt from the Martin Report strikes a fair balance in this area.

Honourable GA Arthur Martin, QC, Chair, *Report of the Attorney*
General's Advisory Committee on Charge Screening, Disclosure,
and Resolution Discussions
(Toronto: Queen's Printer for Ontario, 1993)
at 281, 330, 332-34 (footnotes omitted)

46. The Committee is of the opinion that resolution discussions are an essential part of
the criminal justice system in Ontario, and, when properly conducted, benefit not only the
accused, but also victims, witnesses, counsel, and the administration of justice generally.

• • •

59. The Committee observes that Crown counsel at trial cannot bind the Attorney
General's discretion to appeal. The Committee recommends that where Crown counsel at
trial agrees to a joint submission which the sentencing judge accepts, the Attorney General
should appeal only where the sentence is so wrong as to bring the administration of justice
into disrepute.

• • •

While it is clear therefore that neither Crown nor defence counsel on appeal is bound in
law by the position of the Crown at trial, the Committee recognizes that such a rule has
great potential to undermine the finality of resolution agreements. This in turn may reduce
the tendency for resolution agreements to be pursued, thereby diminishing the advantages
which they offer, as discussed above. There is an important need for certainty in resolution
agreement outcomes that appellate counsel must respect, in the same manner as a sentencing judge should respect the need for certainty when imposing sentence following a joint
submission. Accordingly, the Committee has recommended that where Crown counsel
at trial has agreed to a joint submission which the sentencing judge has accepted, that
sentence should be appealed by the Crown only where the sentence is so wrong as to bring
the administration of justice into disrepute. Much like the balance struck in the Committee's recommendation with respect to sentencing on a joint submission at the trial level,
the Committee is of the view that this recommendation strikes the appropriate balance
at the appellate level between ensuring resolution agreement outcomes are final, and
preserving the role of the Attorney General's appellate counsel in ensuring the due
administration of criminal justice. The Committee also observes that it may be undesirable
for an accused person to appeal as a matter of course from a sentence imposed that is in
accordance with a joint submission.

It is important to note that, while the present recommendation is similar in some
respects to the recommendation concerning sentencing on a joint submission at trial, it
does have a significant difference. The Committee has recommended that the sentencing
judge may depart from a joint submission if the sentence proposed would bring the
administration of justice into disrepute or if the sentence is not in the public interest.
However, the Committee has recommended that the Crown should appeal from an
accepted joint submission only if the sentence imposed would bring the administration
of justice into disrepute. Thus, in the Committee's view, the circumstances in which it is
appropriate for the Crown to appeal against a joint submission sentence are more limited
than the circumstances in which it is appropriate for the sentencing judge to depart from
a joint submission. The Crown's right to appeal from a joint submission sentence should
not be exercised simply to seek minor adjustments or refinements to a sentence. Rather,

the Crown should appeal only where the sentence imposed pursuant to a joint submission represents an error so grave as to bring the administration of justice into disrepute.

There are few common law jurisdictions that accord the Crown rights of appeal as broad as those found in the *Criminal Code*. The Committee's recommendation with respect to launching Crown appeals following a sentence imposed in accordance with a joint submission is therefore consistent with traditional notions of restraint which should invariably accompany the exercise of the Crown's right of appeal. Such restraint recognizes the importance for preserving, to the greatest extent possible, the finality of resolution agreements entered into by the Crown. It also recognizes that both the joint submission itself and the fact that it was accepted by the sentencing judge as not being contrary to the public interest, must be accorded due weight by appellate Crown counsel considering an appeal.

IV. CONCLUSION

This chapter has addressed several aspects of plea discussions in the sentencing process. There are, however, many other aspects of plea discussions worthy of examination, especially those that are practical in nature. Some issues that have not been addressed relate to matters such as the trial judge's role in resolution discussions, the prospect of counsel approaching trial judges in chambers to discuss a proposed resolution, and a lawyer's duty to another lawyer when disavowing a plea bargain entered into by previous counsel. Local plea-discussion practices vary so significantly that it is not possible to fully canvass these issues here, nor does the case law reflect the range of practices that exist across and within jurisdictions.

The Martin Report is a good place to start any assessment of the procedural aspects of plea discussions and joint submissions. For cases dealing with judicial involvement in plea and resolution discussions, see *R v Wood* (1975), 26 CCC (2d) 100 (Alta CA); *R v Dubien*, above; *R v White* (1982), 39 Nfld & PEIR 196 (Nfld CA); and *R v O'Quinn* (2002), 59 OR (3d) 321 (CA).

For a thorough consideration of Crown discretion and circumstances in which it is entitled to repudiate a plea agreement, see *R v Nixon*, 2011 SCC 34, [2011] 2 SCR 566. The court held that negotiating or repudiating a plea agreement is an act of prosecutorial discretion and is subject to judicial review only through the abuse of process doctrine. As Charron J wrote:

> [68] … In the absence of any prosecutorial misconduct, improper motive or bad faith in the approach, circumstances, or ultimate decision to repudiate, the decision to proceed with the prosecution is the Crown's alone to make. Reasonable counsel may indeed, and often do, differ on whether a particular disposition is in the public interest in the circumstances of the case. The ADM, in good faith, determined that Crown counsel's assessment of the strength of the evidence was erroneous and, on that basis, having regard to the seriousness of the offences, concluded that it would not be in the public interest to terminate the prosecution on the criminal charges. This can hardly be regarded as evidence of misconduct.
>
> [69] This does not mean that plea agreements can be overturned on a whim. The method by which the decision was reached can itself reveal misconduct of a sufficient degree to amount to abuse of process. But that is not what occurred here. The act of repudiation was indeed a rare and exceptional occurrence. The evidence revealed that there have been only two prior occurrences in Alberta, "one in the 1980s and one within the year prior to the trial in this matter" … . There was also no evidence of abusive conduct in the process leading to the decision to repudiate.

Finally, it is important to consider plea discussions and joint submissions in a broader context. Plea negotiations may induce or encourage a guilty plea. Depending on the offender's potential jeopardy and the extent to which it is attenuated by a proposed joint submission, it may induce an invalid guilty plea, thereby giving rise to a miscarriage of justice. Plea comprehension inquiries, now prescribed by s 606(1.1) of the *Criminal Code*, are meant to guard against this consequence; however, the procedure is not foolproof.

R v Hanemaayer, 2008 ONCA 580, 234 CCC (3d) 3 is an example of this danger. Writing for the court, Rosenberg JA characterized the appeal as "an important cautionary tale for the administration of criminal justice." The accused was charged with break and enter and other offences. The case turned on weak identification evidence. Fearing the worst—that is, a lengthy penitentiary term—Hanemaayer changed his plea in the middle of trial and was sentenced in accordance with a joint submission for two years less a day. Twenty years later, he was able to set aside his plea and clear his name. In allowing the appeal, Rosenberg JA observed that there was no doubt that Paul Bernardo was the person who committed the offences to which Hanemaayer pled guilty. As he held at 8: "The justice system held out to the appellant a powerful inducement that by pleading guilty he would not receive a penitentiary sentence": see *R v Shepherd*, 2016 ONCA 188, which also involved a miscarriage of justice resulting from a guilty plea. More generally, see the discussion in Joan Brockman, "An Offer You Can't Refuse: Pleading Guilty When Innocent" (2010) 56 Crim LQ 116.

FURTHER READING

Brook, Carol A et al. "A Comparative Look at Plea Bargaining in Australia, Canada, England, New Zealand, and the United States" (2016) 57 Wm & Mary L Rev 1147.

Di Luca, J. "Expedient McJustice or Principled Alternate Dispute Resolution? A Review of Plea Bargaining in Canada" (2005) 50 Crim LQ 14.

Ireland, David. "Bargaining for Expedience? The Overuse of Joint Recommendations on Sentence" (2015) 38 Man LJ 273.

Lippke, Richard. *The Ethics of Plea Bargaining* (New York: Oxford University Press, 2011).

Wright, Ron. "Charging and Plea Bargaining as Forms of Sentencing Discretion" in Joan Petersilia & Kevin Reitz, eds, *The Oxford Handbook of Sentencing and Corrections* (New York: Oxford University Press, 2012).

Verdun-Jones, Simon. "Plea Bargaining" in *Criminal Justice in Canada: A Reader* (Toronto: Nelson, 2016) ch 14.

CHAPTER EIGHT

Absolute and Conditional Discharges

I. INTRODUCTION

The sentencing options that are available to a judge are set out in Part XXIII of the *Criminal Code*, RSC 1985, c C-46, as amended. They range from a discharge, which is considered to be the least intrusive option, to imprisonment, the most serious and restrictive sanction available under Canadian law. This chapter and subsequent chapters discuss the various options that a court may impose as a sanction for wrongdoing.

Typically, the imposition of a sentencing option or sanction is dependent on a conviction being entered against an offender. However, in certain circumstances, the *Criminal Code* permits a judge to provide relief against the full opprobrium of a criminal conviction by allowing for an absolute or a conditional discharge. These sanctions are best understood by considering the registration of a conviction as a two-stage process. Although a conviction is generally considered to be synonymous with the finding of guilt by a judge or jury, it is more accurate to say that a conviction is perfected when a finding of guilt and sentence are formally recorded: see *R v McInnis* (1973), 23 CRNS 152 at 156-63 (Ont CA); *R v Senior* (1996), 181 AR 1 (CA), aff'd [1997] 2 SCR 288; and *R v Pearson*, [1998] 3 SCR 620. It is only *after* a finding of guilt that the judge considers whether a *conviction* (as opposed to a discharge) ought to be imposed. In other words, in appropriate circumstances, it is open to a judge to sanction an offender with a discharge, whether absolute or conditional, and not record a conviction. As illustrated below, a conditional (but not absolute) discharge involves a term of probation.

The immediate effect of a discharge, whether it is absolute and immediate in its effect or conditional and thus delayed during the probationary term, is that there is no criminal record of conviction and sentence against the accused under the *Criminal Records Act*, RSC 1985, c C-47, as amended. This is a matter of great importance to the offender because there are disabilities that may follow the recording of a criminal conviction, including difficulties with employment, travel, immigration, or other significant personal matters. Nevertheless, before an offender's non-conviction record is sealed, even a discharge can create difficulties for the offender. Further, while a discharged offender's record under the *Criminal Records Act* will be sealed once the appropriate period has passed, the federal legislation does not govern the use of local or provincial police records and offenders must therefore independently apply for the destruction of these records. As will be seen below, a discharge may be granted in the discretion of the court only if this disposition is in the best interests of the offender and is not contrary to the public interest.

II. THE STATUTORY CRITERIA

There are certain restrictions on when a discharge is available, some of which are fixed. For example, a discharge cannot be imposed on an organization. Discharges are not available if the offence is punishable by a minimum penalty or carries a maximum penalty of 14 years or more. In all other cases, the availability of a discharge is determined by a balancing of the best interests of the offender and the public, as required by s 730 of the Code, which provides as follows:

> 730(1) Where an accused, other than an organization, pleads guilty to or is found guilty of an offence, other than an offence for which a minimum punishment is prescribed by law or an offence punishable by imprisonment for fourteen years or for life, the court before which the accused appears may, if it considers it to be in the best interests of the accused and not contrary to the public interest, instead of convicting the accused, by order direct that the accused be discharged absolutely or on the conditions prescribed in a probation order made under subsection 731(2).

> • • •

> (3) Where a court directs under subsection (1) that an offender be discharged of an offence, the offender shall be deemed not to have been convicted of the offence except that
> (a) the offender may appeal from the determination of guilt as if it were a conviction in respect of the offence;
> (b) the Attorney General and, in the case of summary conviction proceedings, the informant or the informant's agent may appeal from the decision of the court not to convict the offender of the offence as if that decision were a judgment or verdict of acquittal of the offender or a dismissal of the information against the offender; and
> (c) the offender may plead *autrefois convict* in respect of any subsequent charge relating to the offence.
> (4) Where an offender who is bound by the conditions of a probation order made at a time when the offender was directed to be discharged under this section is convicted of an offence, including an offence under section 733.1, the court that made the probation order may, in addition to or in lieu of exercising its authority under subsection 732.2(5), at any time when it may take action under that subsection, revoke the discharge, convict the offender of the offence to which the discharge relates and impose any sentence that could have been imposed if the offender had been convicted at the time of discharge, and no appeal lies from a conviction under this subsection where an appeal was taken from the order directing that the offender be discharged.

III. APPLYING THE CRITERIA

The following cases illustrate how the courts determine whether to grant a discharge. A discharge must be either absolute or conditional, not some combination of the two. As the cases below illustrate, the decision is largely discretionary in nature, constrained only by the balancing of the best interests of the accused and the public interest. There is no guidance in s 730, or in the relevant cases, on the issue of when it is appropriate to grant an absolute discharge instead of a conditional discharge, which involves a period of probation. As a practical matter, the determination often turns on whether the offender is able to convince the court that he or she has already addressed the concerns that might otherwise make a term of probation appropriate by, for example, engaging proactively in counselling or other forms of treatment or volunteer work: see e.g. *R v Olatona*, 2015 ABPC 222. In some cases, regardless of an offender's efforts, probation may be ordered simply to ensure that appropriate victim safeguards—for example, non-contact, communication, or association provisions—are in place for a period of time. It is clear that certain conditions of probation are improper in this context. The Code does not authorize the payment of a fine as one of the conditions of a conditional discharge. Nor can a charitable donation be mandated: see *R v Choi (JW)*, 2013 MBCA 75 at paras 50-54. However, a restitution order may be imposed along with a discharge, whether it is absolute or conditional. As discussed in Chapter 10, Monetary Sanctions: Fines, Restitution, and the Victim Surcharge, a fine may be imposed only after the entering of a conviction (see s 734.1), whereas a restitution order may be imposed when the offender is convicted or discharged under s 730 (see s 737.1). As well, discharged offenders must pay the victim surcharge: see s 737(1).

R v Fallofield
(1973), 13 CCC (2d) 450 (BCCA)

FARRIS CJBC:

The two questions in this appeal are:

1. Did the Provincial Court Judge err in refusing to grant an absolute or a conditional discharge; and
2. If the answer is yes, has this Court the power to make such an order?

In my opinion, the answer to both questions is yes.

The appellant pleaded guilty to a charge of being in unlawful possession of some pieces of carpet of a total value of less than $200, knowing the same to have been obtained by theft. The appellant is a corporal in the Canadian Armed Forces, aged 26, married, and with no previous record. He and his two co-accused were employed by the Fairfield Moving & Storage Company in Victoria. Apparently the appellant was supplementing his income by what is commonly known as "moonlighting."

In September last, the three men were delivering refrigerators to a new apartment building and took from the premises some left-over pieces of carpeting. The accused had five pieces of carpeting of a value of $33.07. The co-accused likewise had small quantities of carpet.

The police officer who investigated the matter said that, when he attended at the residence of the accused, the accused turned over the five pieces of carpet and stated that he thought they were scraps. The officer also testified that he found the accused to be friendly and co-operative and would agree that "rather than being a thief, was more simply a foolish individual, getting involved in something slightly more serious than a foolish prank but not really a thief at nature."

A warrant officer from the Canadian Armed Forces was called and testified that "Corporal Fallofield is one of the best men we have. He is a very good worker—a very conscientious man." He further testified that this conviction "could very possibly affect his future career in the Navy."

At the hearing in the Court below, counsel for the appellant applied under the *Criminal Code*, RSC 1970, c. C-34, s. 662.1(1) [en 1972, c 13, s 57] for a conditional discharge. ... The trial judge declined to grant the discharge, convicted the appellant, and sentenced him to a fine of $100, or in default, 30 days in prison. It is from this disposition of the matter that the present appeal is brought.

The basis of the trial Judge's refusal to grant the discharge was that he did not think that "this was a case of strict liability or that it is a case where the offence being committed was entirely completely unintentional or unavoidable." ...

In my respectful opinion, the trial Judge proceeded upon a wrong principle. There is nothing in the language of the section that so limits its application. ...

• • •

From this review of the authorities and my own view of the meaning of s. 662.1, I draw the following conclusions; subject, of course, to what I have said above as to the exercise of discretion.

(1) The section may be used in respect of *any* offence other than an offence for which a minimum punishment is prescribed by law or the offence is punishable by imprisonment for 14 years or for life or by death.

(2) The section contemplates the commission of an offence. There is nothing in the language that limits it to a technical or trivial violation.

(3) Of the two conditions precedent to the exercise of the jurisdiction, the first is that the court must consider that it is in the best interests of the accused that he should be discharged either absolutely or upon condition. If it is not in the best interests of the accused, that, of course, is the end of the matter. If it is decided that it is in the best interests of the accused, then that brings the next consideration into operation.

(4) The second condition precedent is that the court must consider that a grant of discharge is not contrary to the public interest.

(5) Generally, the first condition would presuppose that the accused is a person of good character, without previous conviction, that it is not necessary to enter a conviction against him in order to deter him from future offences or to rehabilitate him, and that the entry of a conviction against him may have significant adverse repercussions.

(6) In the context of the second condition the public interest in the deterrence of others, while it must be given due weight, does not preclude the judicious use of the discharge provisions.

(7) The powers given by s. 662.1 should not be exercised as an alternative to probation or suspended sentence.

(8) Section 662.1 should not be applied routinely to any particular offence. This may result in an apparent lack of uniformity in the application of the discharge provisions. This lack will be more apparent than real and will stem from the differences in the circumstances of cases.

Applying these conclusions, this is a case where it is appropriate to grant an absolute discharge. It is clear that it is in the best interests of the accused that such a discharge be granted. I cannot see that such a grant is contrary to the public interest. I find it difficult to believe that the deterrence of others will be in any way diminished by the failure to render a conviction against this accused.

Accordingly, if this Court has the power so to do I would grant a discharge and I see no point in imposing conditions.

R v Bram
1982 ABCA 256, 30 CR (3d) 398

LAYCRAFT JA (Harradence and Pruvis JJA concurring):

[1] In this case the accused was convicted after trial of the offence of offering money to an employee of Edmonton Telephones to release to him the addresses and telephone numbers of persons with silent numbers. He was employed as a "skip tracer," that is, one whose job it is to trace persons who have changed their addresses for the purposes of avoiding payment of sums due on credit accounts. The accused was granted an absolute discharge and the Crown now appeals that disposition. The Crown does not seek incarceration or, indeed, any other particular sentence. It merely argues that on his conviction for this offence the accused should be left with a criminal record.

[2] The accused is a survivor of the holocaust of World War II, in which many millions of his co-religionists were murdered. He is the only member of a family of 12 persons who survived the European death camps. At some time after World War II he arrived in Canada, where he married and raised a family. He has been an exemplary citizen and at 58 years of age has never been convicted of any offence other than the present one. In the material filed with us a wide range of citizens speak highly of him. He is described as an upright man and a citizen of exceptional quality. It is apparent that he did not for a time realize that he was doing wrong in the commission of this offence. He seemed to feel that in tracing persons who deliberately avoid obligations such conduct is permissible, though he now does realize that he was doing wrong.

[3] S. 662.1 of the *Criminal Code* of Canada authorizes an absolute discharge when, in the words of the section, the Court

considers it to be in the best interest of the accused and not contrary to the public interest.

[4] The tests for the application of this section were extensively reviewed by this Court in *R. v. MacFarlane* (1976) 3 Alta. L.R. 341 in which a number of factors were listed particularizing the general words of the section. The case points out that, apart from those cases in which there is need to deter the accused himself from further offences, the absolute discharge will in almost every case be in the interests of the accused. There is no such need in the present case, and the contest is therefore whether an absolute discharge would or would not be in the public interest.

[5] *R. v. MacFarlane* states that the jurisdiction to grant an absolute discharge should be used sparingly in the interests of preserving the general deterrence principle of criminal sentencing. Nevertheless that is not to say that it is only in the case of trivial or unintentional offences that absolute discharges should be granted. This point is expressed in Nadin-Davis on *Sentencing in Canada* at p. 479 in these terms:

While frugality is in order in the application of discharges, the Courts have repeatedly emphasized the wide range of possible candidates and offences. In *Fallofield*, 13 C.C.C. (2d) 450 it was held that s. 662.1 is not limited in application to cases of strict liability, or cases where the offence was completely unintentional or unavoidable. Extending this principle, the Ontario court in *Vicente* 18 C.R.LQ 292 has added that the granting of discharges should not be confined to trivial matters. In appropriate circumstances, a discharge may be granted in a case which is not trivial.

[6] The author also notes that the seriousness of the offence is naturally a pertinent consideration, and cites the *MacFarlane* decision, *supra*, for this proposition.

[7] In this case, applying the principles enunciated in *R v. MacFarlane*, we conclude that we will not interfere with the absolute discharge granted by the learned trial judge. The offence is not prevalent in the community, as the Crown readily conceded. The accused had little to gain directly from it, since his income was determined on an hourly basis and not as a percentage of recovery of unpaid accounts. For this accused in relation to this offence we see no need for deterrence, nor do we perceive that the public interest requires that persons dealing with him in the future be able to determine that the offence was committed. He has been an excellent citizen of his adopted country, of whom it may be said with a high degree of confidence that he will not offend again. That conclusion was apparently reached also by the learned trial judge, who observed him giving evidence for upwards of 1½ hours. No adequate grounds have been shown to us to interfere with the disposition by the trial judge. Accordingly the Crown is refused leave to appeal.

Leave to appeal refused.

NOTE

Initially there was some dispute about exactly when an appellate court could discharge an offender who had been convicted by the judge at first instance. *Cf* e.g. *R v Stafrace* (1972), 10 CCC (2d) 181 (Ont CA); *R v Sanchez-Pino* (1973), 11 CCC (2d) 53 (Ont CA); *R v Christman* (1973), 11 CCC (2d) 245 (Alta CA); and *R v McInnis* (1973), 23 CRNS 152 (Ont CA). It is accepted today that appellate courts can discharge offenders convicted at first instance if the court is satisfied that there is a basis to interfere with the conviction imposed below: see ss 673 (definition of "sentence") and 675(1)(b); see also *R v MacDonald*, 2013 ONCA 295.

As the cases above suggest, a discharge is often in an offender's best interest because of the impact of a conviction on, for example, the offender's employment, education, immigration status, and ability to travel. In *R v Pham*, 2013 SCC 15, [2013] 1 SCR 739, the Supreme Court of Canada held that the collateral consequences of a sentence can be considered in deciding on a fit sentence, but that such consequences cannot be used to justify what would otherwise be an inappropriate sentence.

R v Pham
2013 SCC 15, [2013] 1 SCR 739

WAGNER J (LeBel, Fish, Abella, Rothstein, Moldaver, and Karakatsanis JJ concurring):

[11] ... [T]he collateral consequences of a sentence are any consequences for the impact of the sentence on the particular offender. They may be taken into account in sentencing as personal circumstances of the offender. However, they are not, strictly speaking, aggravating or mitigating factors, since such factors are by definition related only to the gravity of the offence or to the degree of responsibility of the offender (s. 718.2(a) of the *Criminal Code*). Their relevance flows from the application of the principles of individualization and parity. The relevance of collateral consequences may also flow from the sentencing objective of assisting in rehabilitating offenders (s. 718(d) of the *Criminal Code*). Thus, when two possible sentences are both appropriate as regards the gravity of the offence and the responsibility of the offenders, the most suitable one may be the one that better contributes to the offender's rehabilitation.

[12] However, the weight to be given to collateral consequences varies from case to case and should be determined having regard to the type and seriousness of the offence. Professor Manson explains this as follows:

> As a result of the commission of an offence, the offender may suffer physical, emotional, social, or financial consequences. While not punishment in the true sense of pains or burdens imposed by the state after a finding of guilt, they are often considered in mitigation. ...
>
> • • •
>
> The mitigating effect of indirect consequences must be considered in relation both to future re-integration and to the nature of the offence. Burdens and hardships flowing from a conviction are relevant if they make the rehabilitative path harder to travel. Here, one can include loss of financial or social support. People lose jobs; families are disrupted; sources of assistance disappear. Notwithstanding a need for denunciation, indirect consequences which arise from stigmatization cannot be isolated from the sentencing matrix if they will have bearing on the offender's ability to live productively in the community. *The mitigation will depend on weighing these obstacles against the degree of denunciation appropriate to the offence.* [Emphasis added.]

(*The Law of Sentencing* (2001), at pp. 136-37)

• • •

[14] The general rule continues to be that a sentence must be fit having regard to the particular crime and the particular offender. In other words, a sentencing judge may exercise his or her discretion to take collateral ... consequences into account, provided that the sentence that is ultimately imposed is proportionate to the gravity of the offence and the degree of responsibility of the offender.

[15] The flexibility of our sentencing process should not be misused by imposing inappropriate and artificial sentences in order to avoid collateral consequences which may flow from a statutory scheme or from other legislation, thus circumventing Parliament's will.

One collateral consequence is the possibility of deportation. The immigration status of an offender is regularly offered in support of a discharge, rather than conviction. Sometimes, a conviction, as opposed to a mere finding of guilt, is said to have dramatic consequences for the purpose of immigration. As currently enacted, the *Immigration and Refugee Protection Act*, SC 2001, c 27 provides:

36(1) A permanent resident or a foreign national is inadmissible on grounds of serious criminality for

(a) having been convicted in Canada of an offence under an Act of Parliament punishable by a maximum term of imprisonment of at least 10 years, or of an offence under an Act of Parliament for which a term of imprisonment of more than six months has been imposed;

(b) having been convicted of an offence outside Canada that, if committed in Canada, would constitute an offence under an Act of Parliament punishable by a maximum term of imprisonment of at least 10 years; or

(c) committing an act outside Canada that is an offence in the place where it was committed and that, if committed in Canada, would constitute an offence under an Act of Parliament punishable by a maximum term of imprisonment of at least 10 years.

(2) A foreign national is inadmissible on grounds of criminality for

(a) having been convicted in Canada of an offence under an Act of Parliament punishable by way of indictment, or of two offences under any Act of Parliament not arising out of a single occurrence;

(b) having been convicted outside Canada of an offence that, if committed in Canada, would constitute an indictable offence under an Act of Parliament, or of two offences not arising out of a single occurrence that, if committed in Canada, would constitute offences under an Act of Parliament;

(c) committing an act outside Canada that is an offence in the place where it was committed and that, if committed in Canada, would constitute an indictable offence under an Act of Parliament; or

(d) committing, on entering Canada, an offence under an Act of Parliament prescribed by regulations.

(3) The following provisions govern subsections (1) and (2):

(a) an offence that may be prosecuted either summarily or by way of indictment is deemed to be an indictable offence, even if it has been prosecuted summarily;

(b) inadmissibility under subsections (1) and (2) may not be based on a conviction in respect of which a record suspension has been ordered and has not been revoked or ceased to have effect under the *Criminal Records Act*, or in respect of which there has been a final determination of an acquittal;

(c) the matters referred to in paragraphs (1)(b) and (c) and (2)(b) and (c) do not constitute inadmissibility in respect of a permanent resident or foreign national who, after the prescribed period, satisfies the Minister that they have been rehabilitated or who is a member of a prescribed class that is deemed to have been rehabilitated;

(d) a determination of whether a permanent resident has committed an act described in paragraph (1)(c) must be based on a balance of probabilities; and

(e) inadmissibility under subsections (1) and (2) may not be based on an offence

(i) designated as a contravention under the *Contraventions Act*,

(ii) for which the permanent resident or foreign national is found guilty under the *Young Offenders Act*, chapter Y-1 of the Revised Statutes of Canada, 1985, or

(iii) for which the permanent resident or foreign national received a youth sentence under the *Youth Criminal Justice Act*.

Because a discharge is not a criminal conviction, an offender who is discharged either conditionally or absolutely is not rendered inadmissible under the *Immigration and Refugee Protection Act*. A discharge is therefore invariably in the offender's best interests; the more difficult question is whether, in the overall circumstances of the case, a discharge is "not contrary to the public interest."

This question is usually the main focus of the sentencing court, regardless of the type of collateral consequence in issue. (There is *no* requirement that a discharge *be in the public interest*; all that is required is that it not be *contrary* to the public interest. As recognized by Heeney J in *R v May*, 2012 ONSC 6797 at para 16, "[t]he distinction is subtle, but potentially important. As framed by the sentencing judge, a higher standard is imposed, which would require the conclusion that the public interest would be positively advanced by granting a discharge. The Code, on the other hand, merely requires that the public interest not be negatively impacted in some way.") Often, the answer to whether a discharge is "not contrary to the public interest" depends on whether the court believes that there is a need to denounce and deter the conduct in question. The following cases deal with offender requests for discharges based on the impact a conviction would have on matters such as the offender's employment, education, and ability to immigrate. The recurring theme in these requests is the argument that a criminal conviction would place the offender in a position of disproportionate adversity or difficulty. When considering the decisions, try to identify types of offences, offender characteristics, or circumstances that tend to support or undermine an offender's request for a discharge. Why does a focus on denunciation and deterrence tend to undermine an offender's request for a discharge? Does the fact that the offender was found guilty after a trial disentitle him or her to a discharge? What if the offender has already received a discharge?

Whalen v R
2015 NBCA 67

RICHARD JA (Baird and French JJA concurring):

[1] Jessica Danielle Whalen appeals her conviction on two counts of harassment ... , and seeks leave to appeal the suspended sentence with accompanying probation order imposed following her conviction. The conduct for which she was found guilty followed the termination of her relationship with one of the complainants. Between October 26, 2012, and some time in 2013, Ms. Whalen repeatedly emailed her former boyfriend. Eventually, Ms. Whalen began communicating with a woman who had since become involved with the former boyfriend. The trial judge described the communications as hostile, coarse, vulgar, degrading and demeaning. In or about April 2013, Ms. Whalen ended the repeated communications of her own accord. There were a few subsequent communications but, for the most part, these appear to have had some measure of legitimacy. Nevertheless, eight months later, in December 2013, Ms. Whalen was charged with harassment.

• • •

[7] At the sentencing hearing, Crown counsel argued in favour of a conditional sentence followed by probation. On the other hand, defence counsel urged the Provincial Court judge to consider a conditional discharge. There are precedents supporting both positions.

[8] The judge settled on a "suspended sentence for a period of eighteen months" to run concurrently on each count, with supervised probation … .

[9] The judge had the benefit of a pre-sentence report she considered was "generally positive." The report revealed Ms. Whalen was a 27-year-old first offender who had been in a relationship with one [of] the two complainants for about six years, and had remained friends with him for some time afterward. It also disclosed that Ms. Whalen suffered from illnesses related to anxiety and depression for which she was under psychiatric care. Ms. Whalen felt she herself was victimized by the two people she was alleged to have harassed. She stated to the author of the pre-sentence report that she had maintained her innocence because she wanted an opportunity to express at trial what she felt they had put her through.

[10] Considering all the circumstances, the sentencing judge concluded a term of incarceration, even in the community, would not be a fit sentence. The judge was of the view, and I agree, that in the present case the applicable sentencing objectives could be addressed by a lengthy term of probation. According to the judge, the real question was whether a discharge should be ordered in the event of a successful probationary period. In the end, the judge decided against a conditional discharge. She explained that the question of a discharge took on "a new dimension given the fact that, at some point, … Ms. Whalen was offered a peace bond as a means to resolve this file, [an] offer which she refused" and that "[s]he was also offered a discharge if she acknowledged responsibility by pleading guilty, [an] offer she also refused." The judge acknowledged the Court could not force anyone to plead guilty, but stated that a peace bond did not imply an acknowledgement of guilt. In the end, the judge held it would not be in the public interest to grant Ms. Whalen a discharge because "the inescapable conclusion is that an individual cannot hijack the judicial process for purely personal reasons without expecting consequences to flow from such choices." The judge also held, without explanation, that Ms. Whalen had "not even demonstrated that the discharge would be in her own best interest."

[11] … In my view, the sentence in this case is the product of an error in principle. Thus, deference is not owed to the sentencing judge and "the court of appeal bears the burden of prescribing the punishment that it considers fit in the circumstances" … .

[12] While a guilty plea can be considered a mitigating factor in the sentencing process, there is ample authority for the proposition that an offender should not receive a more severe sentence because he or she pleaded not guilty. …

[13] With respect, I find the sentencing judge disregarded the principle that an offender cannot be punished for exercising his or her right to force a matter to trial. The judge's statements that sentencing took on a "new dimension" because Ms. Whalen refused offers of a peace bond, and later a discharge contingent on a guilty plea, together with the comment that, in the judge's view, "an individual cannot hijack the judicial process for purely personal reasons without expecting consequences to flow from such choice," referring to Ms. Whalen's reasons for proceeding to trial rather than pleading guilty, are clear indications of an error in principle. The judge denied a conditional discharge, not because a conviction was necessary to effect rehabilitation or deter Ms. Whalen from further harassing conduct, but rather to punish her for having insisted on her right to a full trial.

[14] Having concluded the sentence is a product of an error in principle, I turn now to the sentence I consider fit in the circumstances. In most cases where deterrence and denunciation are key sentencing principles a discharge is not suitable. However, in my

view, this case falls into an exceptional category. First, the evidence clearly indicates that Ms. Whalen suffers from mental health issues, for which she is now receiving treatment and follow-up. This, in and of itself, illustrates Ms. Whalen is committed to her rehabilitation. Secondly, this is not a case of harassing conduct continuing until the offender was apprehended. Rather, this is a case where the harassing conduct ended of Ms. Whalen's own accord months before she was arrested and charged. In my view, this is relevant for sentencing purposes, in that it significantly lessens the need for specific deterrence.

[15] The judge was of the view that the sentencing objectives could be met with a period of probation. I agree with that assessment. Where I differ with the sentencing judge is with respect to her conclusion that, because Ms. Whalen pleaded not guilty and forced a full trial, a conditional discharge was not appropriate. In my view, once it was determined that the relevant sentencing objectives would be met by a probation order, it is difficult to find that a conditional discharge would not be in Ms. Whalen's best interest. Ms. Whalen is a youthful first offender who, but for the conduct that formed the subject matter of these charges, has led a productive life. If the conditions of the probation order are sufficient to ensure Ms. Whalen's rehabilitation, and to deter her from further offensive conduct, nothing suggests that a conviction at the end of the probationary period will add anything to the mix. As for the public interest, the particular circumstances that make this case exceptional, i.e. the mental illness now under treatment, coupled with the offending conduct having ended months before the charges were brought, sufficiently distinguish this case from others in which non-discharge sentences were imposed for similar offences. I am not convinced that, in the particular circumstances of this case, it would be contrary to the public interest to order that Ms. Whalen be discharged on the conditions prescribed in a probation order.

[16] For these reasons, I would dismiss the appeal against conviction, and allow both the application for leave to appeal and the appeal against sentence. I would vary the concurrent sentences to conditional discharges for the same term and on the same conditions prescribed by the probation order issued by the sentencing judge.

R v Sharma
2015 ONSC 5950

CAMPBELL J:

[1] The appellant, Puneet Sharma, eventually pled guilty, mid-trial, to assaulting his wife with a weapon, namely, a stove element. In admitting his commission of the offence, the appellant agreed that, on June 4, 2012, he became very angry with his wife as a result of some incident of perceived disrespect on her part toward him. The appellant grabbed his wife by her shirt and pushed her over to the stove in the kitchen and held her in place over one of the heating elements. Members of the complainant's family who were present at the time tried to intervene, but the appellant physically resisted their efforts, maintaining his hold on his wife. The complainant received a small burn to the bottom of her chin, some small blisters on each hand, and some of the hair on the left side of her head was singed by the heat from the stove element. Ultimately, the other family members were able to successfully intervene in the incident to prevent any further injury.

[2] The appellant and the complainant were married in India in 2011, and his wife sponsored him to come to Canada in January of 2012. Their marriage now appears to be over as a result of this violent incident.

[3] At trial, the 30-year-old appellant sought the imposition of a conditional discharge. He had served four days of pre-trial detention and, following his release, had voluntarily performed some community service and had successfully completed anger management courses. Further, the appellant is university educated, with a degree in engineering and computer science, and has worked productively full-time in Canada as a computer consultant. He has no prior criminal record. The appellant sought the imposition of a conditional discharge as he feared that a conviction would ultimately result in his deportation. This potential immigration consequence of a conviction was a topic of much discussion at the sentencing hearing in this case.

[4] ... [T]he trial judge ... refused the appellant's request for a conditional discharge. Instead, the trial judge entered a conviction, suspended the passing of sentence and placed the appellant on probation for one year. In his reasons for sentence, the trial judge called the offence "appalling," noting that it "significantly endangered" the victim and amounted to an attempt by the appellant to "discipline" his wife. He described the appellant's degree of "moral blameworthiness" as "very high." The trial judge concluded that it would be a "significant error in principle" for him to grant the conditional discharge sought by the appellant.

[5] The appellant now appeals against his sentence. The fresh evidence tendered on the appeal reveals that, on February 23, 2015, the immigration proceedings against the appellant resulted in him being declared inadmissible, and he was ordered deported. That order has not yet been executed. ...

[6] ... [E]ven reviewing the sentence imposed by the trial judge without the deference normally accorded such decisions, and considering the matter anew, I have concluded that the appeal must be dismissed, as the trial judge correctly concluded that a conditional discharge was not a fit and appropriate sentencing disposition in all of the circumstances of this case.

[7] According to s. 730(1) of the *Criminal Code*, R.S.C. 1985, c. C-46, a conditional discharge may be imposed where such a disposition is in the "best interests of the accused" and is "not contrary to the public interest." There is no doubt that a conditional discharge would be in the best interests of the appellant. Most obviously, such a disposition would immediately avert his pending deportation. However, as the trial judge accurately noted during the sentencing hearing, the critical sentencing issue is whether the requested conditional discharge is "contrary to the public interest" given the recognized need to denounce and deter crimes of domestic violence. See *R. v. Outram*, 2015 ONSC 1934, [2015] O.J. No. 1454, at paras. 31-34 (and the authorities cited therein).

[8] In my view, [the trial judge] correctly determined that a conditional discharge would be contrary to the public interest. This was a serious and dangerous act of domestic violence on the part of the appellant, which could easily have resulted in even greater physical injuries to the victim. Notwithstanding the various mitigating features of this case, as highlighted by defence counsel at trial and on appeal, a conditional discharge would simply not proportionally reflect the "gravity of the offence and the degree of responsibility of the offender" as required by s. 718.1 of the *Criminal Code*. Nor would such a disposition sufficiently deter and denounce the commission of these types of serious violent crimes.

[9] While the adverse immigration consequences for the appellant are certainly an important factor to be taken into account in the imposition of sentence, such immigration consequences cannot justify the imposition of a sentence that is inconsistent with the fundamental purpose and principles of sentencing articulated in the *Criminal Code*. ...

[10] As I have indicated, in my view, the granting of a conditional discharge in all of the circumstances of this case would be inconsistent with the fundamental purpose of sentencing and the principles of sentencing outlined in the *Criminal Code*. In the result, the appeal against sentence must be dismissed. An order shall issue accordingly.

R v Foianesi
2011 MBCA 33, 277 CCC (3d) 366

CHARTIER JA (Hamilton and Freedman JJA concurring):

Introduction and Issues

[1] This is a sentence appeal. The accused pled guilty to one count of keeping a common gaming house contrary to s. 201(1) of the *Criminal Code* (the *Code*). The Crown acknowledges that this is the first prosecution for this type of offence in a very long time. The accused points out that the last reported case in this province dates back over 50 years (*R. v. Zedd* (1959), 126 C.C.C. 238 (C.A.)).

[2] At the sentencing hearing, the accused asked for a conditional discharge, while the Crown sought a significant fine and forfeiture of monies found on the accused's person. The sentencing judge determined that general deterrence was the primary principle of sentencing for these types of offences. He rejected the discharge sentencing option, finding that it would be contrary to the public interest because it did not address general deterrence concerns. He imposed a fine in the amount of $14,000, inclusive of surcharge and costs, and ordered forfeiture of part of the cash found on the accused at the time of arrest. The amount forfeited totalled $2,364.02.

[3] The principal issue on this appeal is whether the sentencing judge erred in his finding that general deterrence was the primary principle of sentencing for these types of offences.

• • •

The Facts

[5] In 2006, the Winnipeg Police Service started an investigation into illegal "Texas Hold 'Em Poker" games which were taking place at various establishments in the city. ...

[6] Although the accused was not a target of the original investigation, the police were drawn to him as a result of advertisements he posted on the Internet that there were regular cash Texas Hold 'Em Poker games at a location called "The Players Club." ...

[7] At the time of his arrest, the accused had $14,940 on his person. The profit he realized from the poker games over the 11-week period was estimated to be between $8,250 and $12,375.

• • •

Analysis

[9] ... [T]he sentencing judge found it would be contrary to the public interest to impose a conditional discharge because general deterrence was the primary principle of sentencing. ...

[10] I agree with the general proposition that discharges should not be available when general deterrence is the paramount sentencing principle. The reason is simple. General deterrence always causes a sentence to be harsher than what it would normally be if it was not a factor. See *R. v. B.W.P.; R. v. B.V.N.*, 2006 SCC 27, [2006] 1 S.C.R. 941 (at para. 36):

> Unlike some other factors in sentencing, general deterrence has a unilateral effect on the sentence. When it is applied as a factor in sentencing, it will always serve to increase the penalty or make it harsher; its effect is never mitigating. ...

As a result, and as was stated by Clayton C. Ruby *et al.*, *Sentencing*, 7th ed. (Markham: LexisNexis Canada Inc., 2008) at para. 9.17, "[a] need for general deterrence is inconsistent with a discharge." Since the discharge is the most lenient sentence in the *Code*, any increase in penalty brought about by general deterrence will necessarily take away the discharge provisions as a possible sentencing option. When general deterrence is the paramount sentencing consideration, the discharge will not be a sentencing option. When it is not the primary concern, there may be circumstances where the mitigating factors negate any increase in sentence, thereby leaving the discharge available.

[11] The question remains: Did the sentencing judge err when he found that general deterrence was the primary principle of sentencing in this case? If he did not err, then, in my view, his finding on appellate review would be unassailable. If he did err on this question, it would be an error in principle and this court would be able to substitute its own view of the appropriate sentence in the circumstances.

[12] The theory that underlies the sentencing principle of general deterrence is that the punishment given will serve as an example to discourage others from engaging in that particular criminal activity (see *B.W.P.*, at para. 2). Typically, general deterrence will be brought to the forefront of the sentencing principles in two situations. The first arises when the sentencing judge is dealing with a crime which is particularly heinous (murder, home invasions, crimes involving children or the vulnerable, etc.). Such crimes must always be deterred.

[13] The second arises when general deterrence can become a paramount consideration when sentencing an accused for a crime which, although not as serious as the ones stated above, is so prevalent in the community that it must be deterred in order to bring it under control. It has long been recognized that the prevalence of a particular crime in the community, or its absence, can be a relevant sentencing factor (see *R. v. Marsden (D.G.)*, 2004 MBCA 121, 187 Man. R. (2d) 298 at para. 44; *R. v. Priest* (1996), 110 C.C.C. (3d) 289 at 293 (Ont. C.A); and *R. v. C.D.* (1991), 75 Man. R. (2d) 14 (C.A.)). Moreover, the frequency or prevalence of a particular offence will bring general deterrence into play when it might not otherwise have been an important consideration. See *R. v. Sanchez-Pino* (1973), 11 C.C.C. (2d) 53 (Ont. C.A.), and *R. v. Sears* (1978), 39 C.C.C. (2d) 199 (Ont. C.A.) ... .

[14] So, what is the basis for the sentencing judge's finding that "general deterrence is the primary principle of sentencing for the court to consider in these types of cases"

(at para. 130)? Although the judge described the offence in this case as a "serious matter" (at para. 126), it cannot be seriously contended that the accused's conduct falls anywhere near the "heinous" type of criminal activity that usually brings general deterrence to the forefront. I say this for two reasons. First, unlike those offences which carry maximum sentences ranging from ten years to life imprisonment, this one carries a two-year maximum. Second, the accused's illegal conduct morphs into a lawful activity when it is conducted under the auspices of government control.

[15] Neither can it be said that the offence in question has become prevalent in this jurisdiction. It is hard to accept that general deterrence should be the primary principle of sentencing when the last reported case in this province dates back over 50 years.

[16] Finally, the basis for the sentencing judge's emphasis on general deterrence cannot have arisen from the jurisprudence. A number of the cases submitted from other jurisdictions show that conditional discharges were granted for these types of offences (see *R. v. Iaconetti (R.) et al.*, 2002 ABQB 776, 324 A.R. 87, and *R. v. Bateman*, 2007 BCPC 413). More importantly, none of them expressed the view that general deterrence should be the paramount consideration in such cases ... .

[The court noted one case where a court indicated deterrence was the primary consideration, but noted that this case was distinguishable because the offender was a corporation and therefore not even eligible for a discharge: see *R v ARC Amusements Ltd* (1989), 93 NSR (2d) 86 (SC (AD)).]

[18] For these reasons, although general deterrence is a relevant consideration when deciding whether to grant a discharge for this offence, I am respectfully of the view that the sentencing judge erred when he found that general deterrence was the "primary principle of sentencing" (at para. 130) in this case. He overemphasized general deterrence, which, in turn, caused him to rule out the discharge provisions. This was an error in principle and allows this court to substitute its own view of the appropriate sentence in the circumstances.

[19] As the sentencing judge stated in his reasons, the critical issue was whether a conditional discharge was an appropriate disposition. A conditional discharge may only be granted if the sentencing judge considers it to be in the best interests of the accused and not contrary to the public interest (s. 730(1) of the *Code*). I adopt the sentencing judge's reasons with respect to his finding that the granting of a discharge would be in the accused's best interests.

[20] This leaves the remaining consideration: Would the granting of the discharge be contrary to the public interest for the offence committed by this offender in the circumstances under which it was committed? For the reasons that follow, I am of the view that it would not.

[21] When considering the "contrary to the public interest" factor, a few propositions are matters of common sense and of general application. The more serious the offence, the less likely a discharge should be granted (see *Sanchez-Pino*). The more serious the offence, the greater the need for mitigating circumstances to be present before granting a discharge (see *R. v. Tschirhart*, unreported (14 January 1975) (Ont. C.A.)). Other considerations, which are more specific to the case at hand, include whether the resulting conviction will

impact the accused's occupation (see *R. v. Etienne* (1989), 49 C.C.C. (3d) 572 (B.C.C.A.)) and whether the accused was under a "reasonable mistake in belief as to the law" (see *R. v. Campbell and Mlynarchuk* (1972), 10 C.C.C. (2d) 26 at 35 (Alta. Dist. Ct.)).

[22] Let me first examine the mitigating circumstances. The accused was 42 years of age at the time of sentencing and had no prior criminal record. He has a university education. He owns and operates a successful retail chain known as Brewers Direct. He also has other commercial interests in income ventures and properties. Prior to his arrest, he was very much involved in the community. Over 20 letters of reference were filed at the sentencing hearing showing that he was dedicated to his family and the community and donated time and money to charitable causes and youth sports.

[23] In addition, the accused took responsibility for his actions by pleading guilty to this offence. He cooperated with the police throughout. His remorse is unmistakable. Because of the media attention given to the accused's arrest, he has been publicly disgraced. There is no reason to think he will ever again become involved in such activities. His prospects for rehabilitation are excellent. Finally, although this offence was organized and calculated, there was nothing surreptitious or underhanded in its organization. He advertised openly, operated in a public location and the doors to the club were open to all who wanted to play. There were no complaints of cheating, unfairness or rowdiness arising from the club's operation.

[24] There are aggravating circumstances. The accused played a leading role in the organization of the gaming house. This offence was profit-driven and occurred weekly over a period of two and one-half months. It was not a momentary lapse of judgment.

[25] This conviction has greatly impacted the accused. In addition to the public disgrace, the conviction limits the accused's business opportunities in the United States as well as his out-of-country travel ability as it relates to his business ventures and coaching responsibilities.

[26] The accused submitted he was under a misapprehension as to the state of the law and that he was not trying to flout the gambling laws. When the "Texas Hold 'Em Poker" games gained in popularity on television and over the Internet, he decided to start the club for people who shared his love of the game. His interest in the game is genuine. Indeed, he is an accomplished poker player who has travelled to the United States and Europe to play the game. The accused's misapprehension on the law rings true. As stated above, there was nothing clandestine about the operation. Although ignorance of the law is no excuse and provides no defence as to guilt, it can be used to gauge his level of moral blameworthiness when considering the fundamental principle of proportionality in s. 718.1 of the *Code*.

[27] Given the significant mitigating circumstances, the resulting impact on the accused's occupation and his lowered degree of blameworthiness, I am of the view that it would not be contrary to the public interest, in the particular circumstances of this case, to grant a conditional discharge.

[28] I now turn to the term of that discharge sentence. Had it been imposed at the time of the sentencing hearing, I would have made the discharge for a two-year term. However, the reasons for sentence were delivered more than one and one-half years later. During this time, this charge was hanging over the accused's head and he was subject to bail restrictions. In light of the inordinately lengthy period of time that has elapsed since his guilty plea, I would fix the term at one year. ...

[29] In addition to the $2,364 order of forfeiture made by the sentencing judge, which was not appealed, I would order a victim surcharge in the amount of $2,000, to be paid within six months of this order (see s. 737(3) of the *Code*). I believe that, in the circumstances, this unusually high victim surcharge is appropriate given this offence, the personal situation of the accused and his stated willingness to pay it or make any charitable donation as ordered by this court. In light of this court's comments in *R. v. Wisniewski (R.)*, 2002 MBCA 93, 166 Man.R. (2d) 73 at paras. 29-32, the issue of charitable donations is best left for another day.

[30] The accused's arrest and the subsequent publicity surrounding this matter appear to have conveyed the message to the community that this type of conduct will lead to criminal charges. This court has been told that, since the accused's arrest, there has not been a single prosecution for common gaming house related offences. However, two things must be said. First, it has long been a criminal offence to operate a gaming house and it is still against the law. Second, it must be understood that the precedential value of this decision is limited to these circumstances and this offender and must be viewed particularly in light of the fact that there had not been a single reported case of this offence in over 50 years. Should this type of offence begin to re-emerge, sentences may have to be harsher in order to address its increasing prevalence.

R v Samson
2015 YKCA 7

BAUMAN CJ (Neilson and Savage JJA concurring):

[1] The Crown applies for leave to appeal and, if leave is granted, appeals from the sentence imposed on Ms. Samson for theft over $5,000 contrary to s. 362(a) of the *Criminal Code*, R.S.C. 1985, c. C-46. The sentencing judge granted Ms. Samson a conditional discharge with one year's probation.

[2] The sentencing judge began his reasons for sentence by describing the circumstances of the offence. Ms. Samson was employed from 2008 to 2012 by a non-profit ambulance service in Mayo, Yukon, a small village approximately 400 kilometres north of Whitehorse. Between February 2011 and September 2012, Ms. Samson stole $8,380.78 from her employer.

[3] The judge then turned to Ms. Samson's personal circumstances. He noted that she is a member of the Na-cho Nyak Dun First Nation. She was employed by the Na-cho Nyak Dun from 2007 until she was dismissed in 2010. This took a heavy toll on her and she began to self-medicate with illicit drugs. She attributes her criminality to this breakdown. Ms. Samson has no prior criminal record.

[4] After her employer discovered the theft, Ms. Samson immediately accepted responsibility for what she had done. Less than one week later, she repaid $1,600. She cooperated with the police investigation and pleaded guilty.

[5] While awaiting sentencing, Ms. Samson was diagnosed with depression and prescribed certain medication she describes as helpful. She enrolled in a four-year First Nations Governance degree program at Yukon College, in which she has been successful.

She gained employment in the Housing and Wellness Departments of the Na-cho Nyak Dun and has expressed interest in running for its council.

[6] By the time of sentencing Ms. Samson had repaid, at considerable personal hardship, all the money she had stolen. She had been clean of illicit drugs for 18 months and had rarely consumed alcohol.

[7] The judge noted that Ms. Samson was "clearly remorseful" and recognized "it will take a lot to rebuild the trust of others" (at para. 25). He found that she was at a very low risk of reoffending.

[8] The judge then reviewed the purposes and principles of sentencing. He referred to s. 718.2(a)(iii) of the *Criminal Code*, which provides that a sentencing judge must consider it to be aggravating if "the offender, in committing the offence, abused a position of trust or authority in relation to the victim." He stated that Ms. Samson's breach of her employer's trust was an aggravating factor.

[9] The judge found the mitigating factors to include her guilty plea, her remorse and the fact that the offence occurred while she was in a period of personal turmoil and illicit drug use. He noted that she had taken steps to address her personal issues and had been clean of drugs for 18 months; she had repaid the money; and she is engaged in the Na-cho Nyak Dun First Nation and interested in pursuing a leadership role.

[10] The judge observed that it is "not at all unusual, in fact, more the norm, that this type of theft results in a jail sentence, even for first offenders" (at para. 33). However, he considered that this was "one of those rare and exceptional cases involving a breach of trust theft where a discharge is the appropriate disposition" (at para. 62).

• • •

[12] The judge had "no difficulty" concluding a discharge would be in Ms. Samson's interest. He noted that the Na-cho Nyak Dun is self-governing and its *Elections Act* precludes a person with a criminal record for theft from running for council. A discharge would allow Ms. Samson to run for council. Moreover, specific deterrence was not necessary.

[13] The judge also found a discharge to be not contrary to the public interest. In this regard he highlighted several factors a fair-minded member of the public would consider (at para. 66):

- Ms. Samson has no prior criminal history and appears to be of previous good character;
- She has pled guilty and accepted responsibility for this offence;
- She committed this offence, which involved numerous transactions and was not a minor offence, while in a period of personal turmoil and increased illicit drug use, while suffering from undiagnosed depression;
- She has taken significant steps to address her depression and underlying grief issues and her illicit drug use, and has been drug-free for 18 months with respect to illicit drugs;
- She has repaid all the monies, something that placed an increased financial burden on her and her family;
- There is no indication that the [employer] suffered any hardship or was deprived of any necessary equipment or other items, and I say this only to distinguish it from the cases which noted, as an aggravating factor, such hardship or deprivation suffered by the victim;

- She is an active and contributing member of her community;
- She has experienced considerable shame for her actions, with such shame being highlighted by the small size of her community.

[14] The judge took judicial notice of the systemic factors affecting Aboriginal persons generally and observed that a discharge would allow Ms. Samson the greatest opportunity to contribute to the Na-cho Nyak Dun community. By way of conclusion, he indicated he was "mindful of the need for denunciation and general deterrence" and stressed that Ms. Samson "wears her offence every day before her community" (at para. 71).

[15] The Crown applies for leave to appeal and submits the sentence is unfit. The Crown concedes the judge did not err in principle but says the sentencing range established by the jurisprudence entails that a term of imprisonment or conditional sentence order (a "CSO") was required.

[16] It is trite law that, "absent an error in principle, ... a court of appeal should only intervene to vary a sentence imposed at trial if the sentence is demonstrably unfit" (*R. v. C.A.M.*, [1996] 1 S.C.R. 500 at para. 92, *per* Chief Justice Lamer). As no error in principle is alleged, the question is whether a conditional discharge in this case is demonstrably unfit.

[17] Sentencing ranges are the practical application of the concept of parity enshrined in the *Criminal Code*: a sentence "should be similar to sentences imposed on similar offenders for similar offences committed in similar circumstances" (s. 718.2(b)). However, the *Criminal Code* also provides that a sentence "*must* be proportionate to the gravity of the offence and the degree of responsibility of the offender" (s. 718.1, emphasis added). The sentencing judge is best placed to assess these individualized factors. Accordingly, courts of appeal should show deference even when reviewing a sentence for parity .... .

[18] In other words, "while the range of sentences emerging from earlier cases provides guidance, it is not conclusive of an appropriate sentence in a given case" (*R. v. Peynado*, 2011 BCCA 524 at para. 27, *per* Madam Justice Neilson). "Only substantial disparity that cannot be justified by reference to differences in offenders and the circumstances of their offences will lead to appellate intervention" (*R. v. Payne*, 2007 BCCA 541 at para. 25, *per* Mr. Justice Smith).

[19] For its sentencing range the Crown relies upon *R. v. Hanifan*, 2001 YKSC 27; *R. v. Zenovitch*, 2001 YKSC 52; *R. v. Everitt*, 2010 YKSC 91; *R. v. Kohlhauser*, 2008 YKTC 68; *R. v. Reid*, 2004 YKCA 4; *R. v. Curtis*, [1995] Y.J. No. 125; *R. v. Smith*, [1991] Y.J. No. 224; *R. v. Walker*, [1989] Y.J. No. 135; and *R. v. Trerice*, [1988] Y.J. No. 89.

• • •

[25] Though not cited by the Crown, there have been decisions in which a conditional discharge was granted to an offender who stole from his or her employer.

• • •

[28] Thus, the established sentencing range for theft from the offender's employer does extend to conditional discharges.

[29] The question before this Court is whether, having regard to the circumstances of each of these decisions, Ms. Samson's conditional discharge is a "substantial and marked departure" from the established range. In my opinion, it is not.

[30] Ms. Samson's circumstances differ significantly from those of Ms. Zenovitch and Ms. Reid. Ms. Samson immediately took responsibility for her actions, quickly repaid the

money she had stolen and expressed remorse that the sentencing judge found to be genuine. Specific deterrence is simply not an issue. The breach of trust was much worse in *Zenovitch* and the sum of money was 25 times greater in *Reid*. Ms. Reid's theft also took place over a longer period of time, three years compared with one year and a half. Thus, none of the factors enumerated by Mr. Justice Hall in *Reid* obtain in respect of Ms. Samson.

[31] Ms. Samson is closer to Ms. Smith and Ms. Curtis, but here too there are distinguishing features. Unlike Ms. Smith and Ms. Curtis, Ms. Samson repaid the entire sum before sentencing, at considerable hardship. She committed her offence while in a time of personal turmoil and illicit drug use, but the sentencing judge found she had addressed her personal difficulties and was clean of illicit drugs.

[32] Ms. Samson's circumstances are closest to Ms. Carnelly's. I note that the amount of money involved here was greater ($8,400 compared with $1,600). However, in my opinion this difference alone did not require the sentencing judge to impose a more onerous sentence on Ms. Samson than was imposed on Ms. Carnelly. A conditional discharge was well within the margin of deference afforded by this Court and does not represent a "substantial and marked departure" from the established range.

[33] I have reached this conclusion without reference to the fact that, under the Na-cho Nyak Dun *Elections Act*, Ms. Samson would be disqualified for running for council if she had a criminal record for theft. (As noted, a conditional discharge entails a finding of guilt but does not give rise to criminal record.) However, I note that I do not agree with the Crown's submission that it was improper for the sentencing judge to consider this fact. Collateral consequences can be taken into account when crafting a sentence (*R. v. Pham*, 2013 SCC 15 at para. 11).

[34] The Crown also says "the sentencing judge has circumvented the Na-cho Nyak Dun *Elections Act*, and denied the First Nation the ability to control their election process." I disagree. The *Elections Act* refers only to a person who has a criminal record for theft. On its plain language, the Na-cho Nyak Dun did not intend to prevent from running for council a person who has been found guilty, but does not have a criminal record. If the Na-cho Nyak Dun was unaware of the distinction between findings of guilt and criminal records, it is of course at liberty, as a self-governing nation, to amend its *Elections Act*.

[35] The Crown further submits that, even if a conditional discharge is within the acceptable sentencing range, Ms. Samson cannot meet the "personal interest" criterion for a discharge. As noted above, a discharge is available only if the sentencing judge considers it "to be *in the interests of the accused* and not contrary to the public interest" (s. 730(1), emphasis added).

[36] Citing *R. v. Shortt*, 2002 NWTSC 47, the Crown submits that this criterion requires that, if the discharge is not granted, the accused will suffer a negative consequence beyond those incurred by every person convicted of the offence. The Crown submits that *Shortt* mandates a finding that disproportionate consequences *will* result from a criminal conviction. Mere possibility is insufficient.

· · ·

[38] The Crown submits that notwithstanding Ms. Samson's pursuit of a degree in First Nation's governance and her announced desire to possibly run for a position on the Na-cho Nyak Dun council, it is purely speculative to conclude that she will indeed suffer disproportionate consequences if she is convicted of this offence.

[39] I do not read *Shortt* as requiring a finding, effectively on a balance of probabilities, that Ms. Samson will suffer disproportionate consequences.

· · ·

[44] In the case of Ms. Samson, the sentencing judge was convinced that the entry of a conviction against her may have significant adverse repercussions in light of the possibility of her running for a position on her First Nation's council. That possibility was sufficiently real in the circumstances to satisfy the first condition for a discharge. I would not accede to this ground of appeal.

[45] In conclusion, the Crown has not shown that Ms. Samson's sentence is demonstrably unfit. It has not shown that a conditional discharge represents a substantial and marked departure from the sentencing range established by previous decisions. It has not demonstrated that Ms. Samson cannot otherwise bring herself within s. 730(1) of the *Criminal Code*. For these reasons, I would grant leave to appeal but dismiss the appeal from sentence.

Certain types of offences generally require a focus on denunciation and deterrence. One such area is crimes of domestic violence. However, in domestic violence offences at the lower end of the scale, the victim and the offender may wish to reconcile. In such cases, a conviction might create hardship for not only the offender but also the victim. Moreover, it is often in society's interest to foster reconciliation provided that the causes of the violence have been addressed. For these and other reasons, conditional discharges for lower-level domestic violence offences are not uncommon. Many jurisdictions also have specific programs or interventions directed toward domestic violence. In jurisdictions where these programs exist, lower-level domestic violence matters (which can include offences such as assault, criminal harassment, and mischief) may be resolved by way of a conditional discharge or a peace bond *provided that* the offender/accused successfully completes a program of counselling.

The general approach in *Fallofield*, extracted above, has been followed in subsequent cases, but the specific criteria for granting a discharge, whether conditional or absolute, cannot easily be enumerated. It is clear that in the absence of a prescribed minimum or maximum of 14 years or more, a discharge is a viable option for all offences. The courts have said repeatedly that discharges should neither be routinely granted nor routinely refused for any class of offence or offender. For example, although discharges in cases of drug trafficking and importation where the maximum sentence is less than 14 years are uncommon, they may still be granted: cf *R v Collier*, 2006 NBCA 92, 212 CCC (3d) 1, in which discharges imposed by the trial judge were overturned on appeal on two counts of trafficking in small amounts of marijuana, and *R v DeSousa*, 2012 ONCA 254, in which an absolute discharge for importing 34 kilograms of khat was upheld. As well, although sexual assault offences generally do not result in discharges (see *R v Peterson*, 2012 NBCA 67), discharges are not precluded (see *R v Moreau* (1992), 76 CCC (3d) 181 (Qc CA); and *R v Ingrey*, 2003 SKQB 300; and *R v AB*, 2015 ONCA 803).

Courts have held that an offender who has previously been discharged or even convicted of an offence is not, for this reason alone, ineligible for a discharge on a subsequent offence; however, the fact and timing of the prior discharge or conviction will be relevant in deciding whether a further discharge should be granted: see *R v ACKT*, 2015 ONSC 1169; *R v Barilko*, 2014 ONSC 1145; *R v Hayes*, [1999] OJ No 938 (QL) (Gen Div); *R v Elsharawy* (1997), 119 CCC (3d) 565 (Nfld CA); *R v Jones*, [1994] BCJ No 1248 (QL) (Prov Ct); *R v Tan* (1974), 74 CCC (2d) 184 (BCCA); and *R v Drew* (1978), 45 CCC (2d) 212 (BCCA).

With respect to employment, there are instances in which the nature of the offence, because of the offender's area of employment, militates against a discharge. One such area is where police, court, or corrections officers are involved. In *R v Carson* (2004), 185 CCC (3d) 541 (Ont CA), the accused, a police officer, assaulted a police officer with whom he was involved in a relationship. The Court of Appeal allowed his appeal against sentence and imposed a conditional discharge, partly because the offence was unrelated to the accused's professional duties and partly because of the time served before sentencing. However, the situation may be different when the offending act has a meaningful connection to the officer's professional duties. In *R v Blackburn* (2004), 186 CCC (3d) 51 (Ont CA), the accused was an off-duty police officer who was convicted of dangerous driving arising out of a "road rage" incident. During this incident, the officer intimidated the complainant by flashing his police badge. The Court of Appeal held that a discharge was inappropriate, partly because the accused's use of his badge constituted a "clear abuse of [his] position of authority and trust as a police officer": see also *R v LeBlanc*, 2003 NBCA 75, 180 CCC (3d) 265, in which a discharge was overturned in a case where a police officer committed theft during an investigation of a residential fire; *R v Byrne*, 2009 ONCA 134, 242 CCC (3d) 201, where, in the course of restoring a custodial sentence, the court commented that "[t]o the extent that some trial judges may have taken the approach that a custodial sentence is not appropriate where a court officer assaults a prisoner, that approach is erroneous"; and *R v Pickering*, 2015 ONSC 6695, in which the court upheld a 30-day conditional sentence against a court officer convicted of assault causing bodily harm against a prisoner. Nonetheless, a discharge remains an option even in cases where the offence is related to employment: see *R v Rice*, 2015 ONCA 478, where the court granted a conditional discharge to a police officer who used excessive force to effect an arrest. In these types of cases, is the question for the judge whether the consequence can be characterized as unfair or disproportionate to culpability, particularly if the offence is not directly related to the officer's duties?

NOTE

The *Criminal Records Act*, RSC 1985, c C-47, deals with the duration of the record of the discharge. Section 6.1(1) provides that "[n]o record of a discharge" shall be disclosed to any person, nor shall the existence of the record or the fact of the discharge be disclosed to any person if more than one year has passed since the offender was discharged absolutely or more than three years have passed "since the offender was discharged on the conditions prescribed in a probation order." Moreover, pursuant to s 6.1(2), the commissioner of the Royal Canadian Mounted Police, who is responsible for the custody of criminal records kept in an automated retrieval system known as CPIC (Canadian Police Information Centre), must purge the record of a discharge from the system after the relevant period has expired. However, the *Criminal Records Act* does not govern records kept by local or provincial police forces. These police forces set their own policies and guidelines for the destruction of the local records, and persons who receive discharges (or other non-conviction outcomes) must therefore apply directly to them if they wish to have the local record destroyed: see

Tadros v Peel (Police Service), 2009 ONCA 442, 97 OR (3d) 212; for a discussion of the issues and problems arising from the retention and disclosure of information in local police record systems, see also Canadian Civil Liberties Association, *The Case for Reframing Employment and Volunteer Police Record Check Practices in Canada* (May 2014); and Canadian Civil Liberties Association, *Presumption of Guilt? The Disclosure of Non-Conviction Records in Police Background Checks* (May 2012).

FURTHER READING

Manson, Allan. *The Law of Sentencing* (Toronto: Irwin Law, 2000) ch 9.

Monkman, Eric. "A New Approach to the Consideration of Collateral Consequences in Criminal Sentencing" (2014) 72:2 UT Fac L Rev 38.

Ruby, Clayton S, Gerald J Chan & Nader R Hassan. "Discharges" in *Sentencing*, 8th ed (Markham, Ont: LexisNexis Canada, 2012) 413.

Wilkins, James L. "Absolute and Conditional Discharge" (1976-1977) 19 Crim LQ 454.

CHAPTER NINE

Probation

I. INTRODUCTION

Community-based sanctions occupy a crucial position in the Canadian sentencing scheme. Unless they receive an absolute discharge, many offenders can realistically expect to receive a sentence that includes probation. In 2013-14, for example, 43 percent of all offenders who pleaded guilty received a sentence that included probation, with the median length of probation being one year: see Statistics Canada, "Adult Criminal Court Statistics in Canada, 2013/2014," by Ashley Maxwell, in *Juristat* 35:1, Catalogue No 85-002-X (Ottawa: Statistics Canada, 2015) at 9. Traditionally, the view has been that probation may be imposed on its own or in combination with a term of imprisonment (real or conditional) or a fine, but not both. Recently, it has been argued that all three sanctions can be imposed where appropriate to do so: see the discussion in Chapter 10, Monetary Sanctions: Fines, Restitution, and the Victim Surcharge. Probation is a sanction that is restorative and rehabilitative in focus, as emphasized by the Supreme Court of Canada in *R v Proulx*, 2000 SCC 5, [2000] 1 SCR 61: see the discussion in Chapter 12, Conditional Sentence of Imprisonment. However, as discussed below, this does not mean that courts cannot include terms or conditions that appear, on their face, to be punitive.

When probation was first introduced into Canadian law (*The Act to Permit the Conditional Release of First Offenders*, SC 1889, c 44), it was restricted to young first offenders and relatively minor offences. Moreover, it required the offender to enter into a recognizance, sometimes with sureties. Initially, there was no supervision or reporting but simply a requirement to keep the peace and be of good behaviour. In 1921, the *Criminal Code* was amended to permit forms of supervision that led eventually to an official probation service for adults. Legislation authorizing the appointment of probation officers was enacted in Ontario in

1922 and in British Columbia in 1946: see K Hamai et al, eds, *Probation Around the World: A Comparative Study* (London: Routledge, 1995) at 36. Stuart K Jaffary, "Probation for the Adult Offender" (1969) 27 Can Bar Rev 1020 at 1036 speculated that there were fewer than 20 probation officers in Canada at that time and that their qualifications fell far below those recommended by the Archambault Commission (the Royal Commission Report on Penal Reform in Canada) in 1938.

After major revision of the *Criminal Code* in 1955, two basic kinds of probation were available to sentencing judges. First, a court was allowed to order an offender to enter into a recognizance for up to two years, with or without sureties, and "to keep the peace and be of good behaviour." Such an order could be made in addition to a sentence for an indictable offence or "in addition to or in lieu of sentence" in summary conviction matters. The underlying intention seemed to be that sureties might be useful to encourage lawful behaviour: see the notes following s 637 in *Martin's Criminal Code*, 1955, which include a quotation from *Greaves' Consolidated Acts* explaining the English predecessor legislation. The second form of probation empowered a court to suspend the passing of sentence and order the accused to enter into a recognizance that could include reporting conditions, conditions requiring restitution or reparation, or "such further conditions as [the court] considers desirable." Here, the person responsible for supervision could return the offender to court and, in cases of breach, the offender could be re-sentenced.

These were the provisions applicable at the time of the review conducted by the Canadian Committee on Corrections. In the committee's 1969 report, *Toward Unity: Criminal Justice and Corrections*, known commonly as the Ouimet Report, an entire chapter was dedicated to probation. In general, the committee supported expanded use of community sanctions. It described probation as providing

> [o]ne of the most effective means of giving expression to one of the fundamental principles on which this report is based—that, whenever feasible, efforts to rehabilitate an offender should take place in the community.

The report was critical because the only remedy for non-compliance was for the Crown to apply for forfeiture of the indebtedness created by the recognizance. Moreover, it questioned the utility of attaching probation to a sentence of imprisonment because of the degree of prediction involved. However, the report noted a "substantial rate of success" with probation and advocated expanded use of it. The committee recommended using probation orders rather than recognizances with mandatory conditions that the offender keep the peace and be of good behaviour, appear in court when required, be under the supervision of a probation officer, and report periodically to that officer. It also recommended that the Code be amended to permit discretionary conditions "to fit the needs of the individual case." The report added the following comment:

> Conditions in a probation order should be kept to a minimum. Particularly, conditions that interfere with aspects of a probationer's life that have nothing to do with his offence should be avoided.

It can readily be seen that the committee viewed probation as a rehabilitative tool that ought not to be encumbered by extraneous prohibitions.

Not all of the Ouimet Report recommendations dealing with probation were adopted by Parliament. Probation continued to be available in addition to terms of imprisonment so long as the term did not exceed two years. Parliament did replace the recognizance with a probation order and a list of mandatory and discretionary conditions: see *Criminal Law Amendment Act*, SC 1968-69, c 38, s 75. It also created a separate offence for breach of probation.

For further discussion of probation, see Clayton C Ruby, Gerald J Chan & Nader R Hasan, *Sentencing*, 8th ed (Markham, Ont: LexisNexis, 2012) ch 10; Allan Manson, *The Law of Sentencing* (Toronto: Irwin, 2001) at 219-45; and CC Barnett, "Probation Orders Under the Criminal Code" (1977), 38 CR (NS) 165; see also the Report of the Canadian Sentencing Commission, *Sentencing Reform* (1987) ch 12, and the Report of the Standing Committee of the House of Commons on Justice and the Solicitor General, *Taking Responsibility* (1988) ("Daubney Report") ch 7.

When thinking about the role of probation, consider Professor Doob's views on alternatives to imprisonment in the following excerpt.

Anthony N Doob, "Community Sanctions and Imprisonment: Hoping for a Miracle but Not Bothering Even to Pray for It"
(1990) 32 Can J Crim 415 at 424-26 (footnotes omitted)

Imprisonment Is the "Standard" Sanction: Others Are Alternatives

Our thinking and sometimes our laws reflect a presumption in favour of imprisonment. Our penalty structure for criminal offences is uniformly stated in terms of the maximum sentence of imprisonment that can be imposed. Other sanctions, then, become "alternatives." This is not true of the *Young Offenders Act* where a number of different dispositions are listed (in s. 20(1) of the Act), the final one being custody. The problem is that even our language tends to encourage us to think first of imprisonment, and then of "alternatives."

It was in part for these reasons that the Canadian Sentencing Commission, in its 1987 report, used the term "community sanctions" instead of the more common terms such as "non-custodial" or "non-carceral" sanctions or "alternatives" to imprisonment. The Commission wanted to get away from the dichotomy between custody and all other sanctions, and wished to emphasize that it does not view imprisonment as the pivotal sanction with all other possible sentences being measured against it.

The linguistic distinction between the term "alternatives" and some term like "community sanctions" which emphasizes the independent status of the sanction is important beyond the symbolic point that it makes. It leads one to ask the obvious and critical question: if we have "community sanctions," when should they be imposed?

This in turn forces us to ask a series of other questions including the following:

- How should sentences—community sanctions included—be allocated?
- What purpose or purposes should sentencing serve?
- What principles should govern the determination of sentences?
- What kinds of offenders convicted of what kinds of offences should normally receive community sanctions?

An Example of an Attempt to Increase the Use of Community Sanctions: The Report of the Canadian Sentencing Commission

The formal Declaration of Purpose and Principles of Sentencing proposed by the Canadian Sentencing Commission need not be reproduced here (See Canada 1987: 152-155). For the purposes of this paper, it is sufficient to consider the following aspects of it:

a) The paramount principle determining the sentence is that the sanction be proportionate to the gravity of the offence and the degree of responsibility of the offender for the offence.
b) There is a presumption in favour of the least onerous sanction.
c) Imprisonment is to be imposed only for specific purposes.

The implications of this policy are important. First of all, since the severity of the sentence is supposed to be proportionate to the seriousness of the offence, it follows that the less serious offences—in particular the very common but less serious property offences—should predominately receive less severe sentences. Given that the Commission also endorsed the principle of restraint in the use of imprisonment, this statement could be operationalized as meaning that there should be an increased use of community sanctions.

But a statement of purpose and principles is not enough. It may tell judges what principles to follow and may give judges a fairly good idea for a particular case of the appropriate levels of sanction *in relation to* other cases. But on its own, such a statement does not tell the judge explicitly what kinds of sanctions should be imposed for particular kinds of cases. Thus a "proportionality" model such as that recommended by the Canadian Sentencing Commission is neither harsh nor lenient on its own: without further elaboration, it does not imply either an increased use of community sanctions nor an increased use of imprisonment. Principles are necessary, but they do not provide sufficient guidelines for the sentencing judge.

The Canadian Sentencing Commission went one step further in suggesting that explicit policy be made. It recommended that guidelines—created by a Commission, but assented to by Parliament—be made part of our sentencing law. Guidelines, under its recommendations, could consist of two separate parts. For all offences, there would be an explicit presumption of custody or community sanction. If the presumptive disposition were a sentence of imprisonment, the guidelines would indicate the presumptive range. If it were not, then, a community sanction would be imposed. Furthermore, the Commission recommended that specific guidance—presumably in the form of guidelines—be developed for the use of community sanctions. As von Hirsch, Wasik, and Greene (1989) have noted, explicit guidance for community sanction can be given that is consistent with an over-riding sentencing rationale.

Conclusion

In the context of the theme of this paper, then, community sanctions should not be "alternatives," but should become sanctions in their own right. More importantly, they should be sanctions that would be described in appropriate legislation as appropriate for certain kinds of cases. In other words, they wouldn't be add-ons to the system, but would be, presumptively, the correct sanction for many offences.

According to the Canadian Sentencing Commission, community sanctions should often be used instead of imprisonment and should be designated as the appropriate sentence for many common offences. Many very common property offences (for which a sizable number of offenders are currently imprisoned) would have, as the presumptive sentence, a community sanction. It is expected that, if the Canadian Sentencing Commission recommendations were implemented, the number of people incarcerated would drop because of the increased use of community sanctions.

Clearly, however, there can be no guarantee of success. There is a good deal of evidence that the criminal justice system is quite resistant to change. Changes cannot be made at one level of the system—in this case in the law governing sentencing—with an assurance that the changes would be implemented exactly as intended. It was for that reason, among others, that the Canadian Sentencing Commission recommended that a permanent sentencing commission be created. It could have as one of its major responsibilities the monitoring of sentencing to ensure that desired changes occurred. It would be able to recommend—and implement—changes quickly to eliminate unanticipated problems should they occur.

In Canada it would appear that a number of conditions must be met to be confident that there will be increased use of community sanctions, or "alternatives." These would include:

- The presence of well-run community sanctions;
- A policy that endorses the use of them;
- Legal and administrative procedures that put community sanctions on an equal footing with imprisonment as sentencing choices;
- Guidance to decision makers on the appropriate use of community sanctions.

Obviously it is possible to have successful "alternatives" without the policy changes I have suggested just as it might happen, to use the analogy I made earlier, that adding a third type of wine to a menu will shift customers away from the wines in short supply. However, if we want to ensure success, we probably have to work a little harder to achieve the changes we want. Those who believe in the effectiveness of prayer might try that. But Parliamentary action would seem to be a more sure bet.

II. THE STATUTORY FRAMEWORK

The statutory provisions governing probation are reproduced below, immediately after the *Juristat* extract. When reading these provisions, consider the following questions:

1. When *must* and when *may* a sentencing judge impose a probation order?
2. Can a probation order be combined with other sentencing options and, if so, which ones?
3. Do the existing mandatory and optional conditions and the case law considering them reflect the Ouimet Report's view that probation orders should include only the minimum conditions required and that conditions unrelated to the offence should not be imposed?

In reflecting on these questions, consider as well the following extract relating to offences against the administration of justice, the second-most common of which is breach of probation:

Statistics Canada, "Trends in Offences Against the Administration of Justice"
by Christopher Munch & Marta Burczycka, in *Juristat* 35:1,
Catalogue No 85-002-X (Ottawa: Statistics Canada, 2015) at 16

Offences against the administration of justice are most often the result of an offender's earlier criminal behavior and prior interactions with the justice system, and in this way are sometimes seen as a "revolving door" of crime. Understanding the volume and nature of this type of crime is important to understanding the pressures that may be affecting the justice system as a whole. For Canada's policing community, administration of justice offences represent about one tenth of all police-reported crime, and involve a relatively large proportion of individuals against whom charges are laid by police. The rate of persons formally charged with administration of justice offences is growing, especially among women, at a time when overall rates of persons charged with other kinds of crime continue to decline. The rate of persons charged with administration of justice offences was higher in 2014 than a decade ago, despite the decline in the actual rate of police-reported incidents of this type of crime. Canada's adult criminal courts must also devote resources to processing administration of justice cases. Over a third of all completed cases in 2013/2014 involved at least one administration of justice offence, and the proportion of cases that include this offence type has increased in comparison to 2005/2006. Findings of guilt are more common in cases involving administration of justice offences, and custody is more often the type of sentence imposed, suggesting further impacts on those elements of the justice system involved in corrections.

[In 2013-14, there were 328,524 completed cases that involved offences against the administration of justice. Of these, 109,822 related to breach of probation and 164,612 related to breaches of the conditions of release: see Table 8.]

Criminal Code
RSC 1985, c C-46, as amended

731(1) Where a person is convicted of an offence, a court may, having regard to the age and character of the offender, the nature of the offence and the circumstances surrounding its commission,

(a) if no minimum punishment is prescribed by law, suspend the passing of sentence and direct that the offender be released on the conditions prescribed in a probation order; or

(b) in addition to fining or sentencing the offender to imprisonment for a term not exceeding two years, direct that the offender comply with the conditions prescribed in a probation order.

(2) A court may also make a probation order where it discharges an accused under subsection 730(1).

731.1(1) Before making a probation order, the court shall consider whether section 109 or 110 is applicable.

(2) For greater certainty, a condition of a probation order referred to in paragraph 732.1(3)(d) does not affect the operation of section 109 or 110.

· · ·

732.1(2) The court shall prescribe, as conditions of a probation order, that the offender do all of the following:

(a) keep the peace and be of good behaviour;

(a.1) abstain from communicating, directly or indirectly, with any victim, witness or other person identified in the order, or refrain from going to any place specified in the order, except in accordance with the conditions specified in the order that the court considers necessary, unless

(i) the victim, witness or other person gives their consent or, if the victim, witness or other person is a minor, the parent or guardian, or any other person who has the lawful care or charge of them, gives their consent, or

(ii) the court decides that, because of exceptional circumstances, it is not appropriate to impose the condition;

(b) appear before the court when required to do so by the court; and

(c) notify the court or the probation officer in advance of any change of name or address, and promptly notify the court or the probation officer of any change of employment or occupation.

(2.1) For the purposes of subparagraph (2)(a.1)(i), the consent is valid only if it is given in writing or in the manner specified in the order.

(2.2) If the court makes the decision described in subparagraph (2)(a.1)(ii), it shall state the reasons for the decision in the record.

(3) The court may prescribe, as additional conditions of a probation order, that the offender do one or more of the following:

(a) report to a probation officer

(i) within two working days, or such longer period as the court directs, after the making of the probation order, and

(ii) thereafter, when required by the probation officer and in the manner directed by the probation officer;

(b) remain within the jurisdiction of the court unless written permission to go outside that jurisdiction is obtained from the court or the probation officer;

(c) abstain from the consumption of drugs except in accordance with a medical prescription, of alcohol or of any other intoxicating substance;

(c.1) provide, for the purpose of analysis, a sample of a bodily substance prescribed by regulation on the demand of a peace officer, a probation officer or someone designated under subsection (9) to make a demand, at the place and time and on the day specified by the person making the demand, if that person has reasonable grounds to believe that the offender has breached a condition of the order that requires them to abstain from the consumption of drugs, alcohol or any other intoxicating substance;

(c.2) provide, for the purpose of analysis, a sample of a bodily substance prescribed by regulation at regular intervals that are specified by a probation officer in a notice in Form 51 served on the offender, if a condition of the order requires the offender to abstain from the consumption of drugs, alcohol or any other intoxicating substance;

(d) abstain from owning, possessing or carrying a weapon;

(e) provide for the support or care of dependants;

(f) perform up to 240 hours of community service over a period not exceeding eighteen months;

(g) if the offender agrees, and subject to the program director's acceptance of the offender, participate actively in a treatment program approved by the province;

(g.1) where the lieutenant governor in council of the province in which the probation order is made has established a program for curative treatment in relation to the consumption of alcohol or drugs, attend at a treatment facility, designated by the lieutenant governor in council of the province, for assessment and curative treatment in relation to the consumption by the offender of alcohol or drugs that is recommended pursuant to the program;

(g.2) where the lieutenant governor in council of the province in which the probation order is made has established a program governing the use of an alcohol ignition interlock device by an offender and if the offender agrees to participate in the program, comply with the program; and

(h) comply with such other reasonable conditions as the court considers desirable, subject to any regulations made under subsection 738(2), for protecting society and for facilitating the offender's successful reintegration into the community.

(3.1) The court may prescribe, as additional conditions of a probation order made in respect of an organization, that the offender do one or more of the following:

(a) make restitution to a person for any loss or damage that they suffered as a result of the offence;

(b) establish policies, standards and procedures to reduce the likelihood of the organization committing a further offence;

(c) communicate those policies, standards and procedures to its representatives;

(d) report to the court on the implementation of those policies, standards and procedures;

(e) identify the senior officer who is responsible for compliance with those policies, standards and procedures;

(f) provide, in the manner specified by the court, the following information to the public, namely,

(i) the offence with which the organization was convicted;

(ii) the sentence imposed by the court, and

(iii) any measures that the organization is taking—including any policies, standards and procedures established under paragraph (b)—to reduce the likelihood of it committing a subsequent offence; and

(g) comply with any other reasonable conditions that the court considers desirable to prevent the organization from committing subsequent offences or to remedy the harm caused by the offence.

(3.2) Before making an order under paragraph (3.1)(b), a court shall consider whether it would be more appropriate for another regulatory body to supervise the development and implementation of the policies, standards and procedures referred to in that paragraph.

(4) A probation order may be in Form 46, and the court that makes the probation order shall specify therein the period for which it is to remain in force.

(5) The court that makes a probation order shall

(a) cause a copy of the order to be given to the offender and, on request, to the victim;

(b) explain the conditions of the order set under subsections (2) to (3.3) and the substance of section 733.1 to the offender, and

(c) cause an explanation to be given to the offender of the procedure for applying under subsection 732.2(3) for a change to the optional conditions and of the substance of subsections 732.2(3) and (5); and

(d) take reasonable measures to ensure that the offender understands the order and the explanations.

(6) For greater certainty, a failure to comply with subsection (5) does not affect the validity of the probation order.

. . .

732.2(1) A probation order comes into force

(a) on the date on which the order is made;

(b) where the offender is sentenced to imprisonment under paragraph 731(1)(b) or was previously sentenced to imprisonment for another offence, as soon as the offender is released from prison or, if released from prison on conditional release, at the expiration of the sentence of imprisonment; or

(c) where the offender is under a conditional sentence order, at the expiration of the conditional sentence order.

(2) Subject to subsection (5),

(a) where an offender who is bound by a probation order is convicted of an offence, including an offence under section 733.1, or is imprisoned under paragraph 731(1)(b) in default of payment of a fine, the order continues in force except in so far as the sentence renders it impossible for the offender for the time being to comply with the order; and

(b) no probation order shall continue in force for more than three years after the date on which the order came into force.

(3) A court that makes a probation order may at any time, on application by the offender, the probation officer or the prosecutor, require the offender to appear before it and, after hearing the offender and one or both of the probation officer and the prosecutor,

(a) make any changes to the optional conditions that in the opinion of the court are rendered desirable by a change in the circumstances since those conditions were prescribed,

(b) relieve the offender, either absolutely or on such terms or for such period as the court deems desirable, of compliance with any optional condition, or

(c) decrease the period for which the probation order is to remain in force,

and the court shall thereupon endorse the probation order accordingly and, if it changes the optional conditions, inform the offender of its action and give the offender a copy of the order so endorsed.

(4) All the functions of the court under subsection (3) may be exercised in chambers.

(5) Where an offender who is bound by a probation order is convicted of an offence, including an offence under section 733.1, and

(a) the time within which an appeal may be taken against that conviction has expired and the offender has not taken an appeal,

(b) the offender has taken an appeal against that conviction and the appeal has been dismissed, or

(c) the offender has given written notice to the court that convicted the offender that the offender elects not to appeal the conviction or has abandoned the appeal, as the case may be,

in addition to any punishment that may be imposed for that offence, the court that made the probation order may, on application by the prosecutor, require the offender to appear before it and, after hearing the prosecutor and the offender,

(d) where the probation order was made under paragraph 731(1)(a), revoke the order and impose any sentence that could have been imposed if the passing of sentence had not been suspended, or

(e) make such changes to the optional conditions as the court deems desirable, or extend the period for which the order is to remain in force for such period, not exceeding one year, as the court deems desirable,

and the court shall thereupon endorse the probation order accordingly and, if it changes the optional conditions or extends the period for which the order is to remain in force, inform the offender of its action and give the offender a copy of the order so endorsed.

(6) The provisions of Parts XVI and XVIII with respect to compelling the appearance of an accused before a justice apply, with such modifications as the circumstances require, to proceedings under subsections (3) and (5).

. . .

733.1(1) An offender who is bound by a probation order and who, without reasonable excuse, fails or refuses to comply with that order is guilty of

(a) an indictable offence and is liable to imprisonment for a term of not more than four years; or

(b) an offence punishable on summary conviction and is liable to imprisonment for a term of not more than 18 months, or to a fine of not more than $5000, or to both.

III. A TERM NOT EXCEEDING TWO YEARS

A probation order cannot be added to a term of imprisonment that exceeds two years (see Code s 731(1)(b)). Over the years, this has proven to be a complicated issue. It has given rise to the following questions: Does this include a sentence arising only from the current proceedings? Does it apply when the offender is serving a term made up of more than one element that exceeds two years in the aggregate? Is the amount of time an accused person spends in pre-trial custody included in the calculation?

What if the offender is serving a "remanet" from a previous sentence as a result of the revocation of parole or statutory release? What if the offender receives a probation order in addition to a sentence of less than two years, but subsequently receives another sentence that brings the aggregate above the two-year limit? In *R v Knott*, 2012 SCC 42, the Supreme Court of Canada reviewed earlier case law and settled many of the controversies in this area.

Knott involved an appeal by two offenders. The first had initially been sentenced to two years' imprisonment and three years' probation, and was then sentenced on a different matter to further periods of imprisonment, some of which were concurrent to the original sentence and others that were consecutive to that sentence, along with further periods of probation. The second was initially sentenced to two years less a day conditional sentence and two years' probation. Following a breach of the second accused's conditional sentence, his initial sentence remaining was converted to a custodial term. On the same day, he also was sentenced to a penitentiary term for a different offence. Both offenders, therefore, ultimately ended up with sentences exceeding two years, but the courts did not invalidate their existing probation orders. Both offenders appealed, arguing that because they had now received, cumulatively, more than two years' imprisonment on their sentences, the probation orders imposed on earlier dates contravened s 731(1)(b) of the *Criminal Code* and were therefore invalid.

In reviewing the court's decision, consider what factors led the court to reject what had been previously known as the "two-year rule." What other options did the court identify to address the historical concern about the utility of probation when an offender is subject to a lengthy period of imprisonment? Do these options provide an adequate response to this concern?

R v Knott

2012 SCC 42, [2012] 2 SCR 470

FISH J (McLachlin CJ and Deschamps, Abella, Rothstein, Moldaver, and Karakatsanis JJ concurring):

I

. . .

[4] The sole issue is whether the probation orders attacked by the appellants contravene s. 731(1)(b) of the *Criminal Code*. In virtue of that provision, a court that sentences an offender to imprisonment for "a term not exceeding two years [may] direct that the offender comply with the conditions prescribed in a probation order."

[5] None of the courts that made the probation orders in issue here sentenced either appellant to a term of imprisonment exceeding two years. And they were not "merged" by law, for the purposes of s. 731(1)(b), with other sentences the appellants were then serving or subsequently received.

[6] Earlier case law to the contrary has been overtaken by this Court's decisions in *R. v. Mathieu*, 2008 SCC 21, [2008] 1 S.C.R. 723, and *R. v. Middleton*, 2009 SCC 21, [2009] 1 S.C.R. 674. I refer here to prior decisions in some provinces (including British Columbia) that struck down a probation order because the accompanying prison sentence—*in combination with other sentences imposed against the same offender on other occasions*—exceeded two years. This was known as the "two-year rule."

[7] In the present matter, a five-member panel of the British Columbia Court of Appeal recognized that *Mathieu* and *Middleton* had exposed latent—and irreparable—cracks in the foundation of the "two-year rule." The Court of Appeal therefore felt bound to undertake a "new analysis" (2010 BCCA 386, 291 B.C.A.C. 236, at para. 68). In this fresh light, the Court of Appeal upheld all of the probation orders made against both appellants.

[8] We are now urged by the appellants to set aside the judgment of the Court of Appeal and quash the probation orders of which they were the beneficiaries when the orders were made: They would both have otherwise received longer terms of imprisonment.

[9] Their joined appeals should both be dismissed, not because the appellants are "sore winners," but because any other result would be unwarranted by the relevant provisions of the *Criminal Code*. And it would be contrary to society's interest in ensuring its own protection by preserving a sentencing option that favours the rehabilitation of offenders.

. . .

II

. . .

[17] Sentencing courts may impose separate but concurrent probation orders, attached to different counts. This may be done to add supplementary conditions appropriate in the

circumstances of different offences, or to ensure that the offender will remain subject to probation if one of the probation orders is later set aside or rendered inoperative.

[18]   While multiple probation orders may be made in this manner, no probation order may continue for more than three years from the date on which it came into force (*Criminal Code*, s. 732.2(2)(b)), subject to the exception involving subsequent convictions once a probation order has already come into force (s. 732.2(5)).

· · ·

IV

[25]   The British Columbia Court of Appeal was not the first court to question or reject the two-year rule previously applied (see *R. v. Pickell*, 2007 CanLII 25672 (Ont. S.C.J.)). It did nonetheless chart new territory in this case. The court had previously decided that an intervening sentence *could* invalidate a once lawful probation order (*R. v. Amyotte*, 2005 BCCA 12, 192 C.C.C. (3d) 412; *R. v. Pawlak*, 2005 BCCA 500, 217 B.C.A.C. 146; *R. v. McKinnon*, 2008 BCCA 416, 237 C.C.C. (3d) 345). So, too, had other provincial courts of appeal (*R. v. Miller* (1987), 36 C.C.C. (3d) 100 (Ont. C.A.); *R. v. Lucas*, 2009 NLCA 56, 293 Nfld & P.E.I.R. 90).

[26]   It had also been previously held, both in British Columbia and in Ontario, that probation cannot be ordered where the offender is subject to multiple sentences that, if aggregated, would exceed two years (*R. v. Pauls*, 2008 BCCA 322 (CanLII); *R. v. K. (K.)*, 2009 ONCA 254, 244 C.C.C. (3d) 124).

[27]   While the case law on this latter point was divided, the disagreement generally related to *how*, not *whether*, sentences were to be aggregated for the purposes of s. 731(1)(b). Some decisions calculated the "aggregate sentence" from the date the first sentence was imposed to the date the final sentence would expire (*R. v. Hendrix*, [1999] N.J. No. 181, 137 C.C.C. (3d) 445 (Nfld. C.A.); *R. v. Renouf*, 2001 NFCA 56, 160 C.C.C. (3d) 173; *R. v. Weir*, 2004 BCCA 529 (CanLII)). Others added the subsequent sentence to the remanet of previously imposed sentences (*R. v. Currie* (1982), 65 C.C.C. (2d) 415 (Ont. C.A.)).

[28]   For the most part, these decisions relied implicitly, if not explicitly, on the sentence merger provisions in s. 139 of the *Corrections and Conditional Release Act*, S.C. 1992, c. 20 ("*CCRA*") and its predecessors. This is no longer possible in light of *Middleton*, where the majority held that s. 139 was enacted for administrative purposes relating to parole and remission, and had no substantive impact on an offender's eligibility for an otherwise lawful sentence.

[29]   In my respectful view, s. 139 of the *CCRA* is therefore of no assistance in determining the legality of a probation order.

[30]   The remaining question, to which I now turn, is whether s. 731(1)(b)—in itself— prohibits the making of the probation orders that concerns us here.

V

· · ·

[32]   The Crown submits that the phrase "imprisonment for a term not exceeding two years" in s. 731(1)(b) relates only to the actual term of imprisonment imposed by a sentencing court at a single sitting. The appellants argue that "term" of imprisonment referred

to in that provision is the aggregate of the custodial term imposed by the sentencing court and all other sentences then being served or later imposed on the offender. In my view, the Crown's submission is correct and the appellants' submission fails.

[33] The ordinary meaning of s. 731(1)(b) is perfectly clear: A probation order may not be made where the *sentencing court* imposes a term of imprisonment exceeding two years. In determining whether two years has been exceeded, one looks at the term of imprisonment ordered by *the sentencing court on that occasion*—not at *other* sentences imposed by *other* courts on *other* occasions for *other* matters.

[34] Section 731(1)(b) admits of no ambiguity in this regard. The opening words of s. 731(1) read: "Where a person is convicted of an offence, a court may." The provision authorizes *that court* to make a probation order, "in addition to fining or sentencing the offender to imprisonment for a term not exceeding two years." On a plain reading of this provision, the phrase "imprisonment for a term not exceeding two years" refers to the sentence imposed by the court empowered by s. 731(1) to make the probation order.

[35] Had Parliament intended unexpired sentences from other occasions to be included in the phrase "imprisonment for a term ... exceeding two years," it would have said so. The language was close at hand. Section 743.1 of the *Criminal Code*, for example, expressly provides for the aggregation of sentences in determining whether an offender is to be sent to the penitentiary.

[36] The appellants submit that the two-year limitation in s. 731(1)(b) reflects Parliament's intention that probation orders not be imposed on offenders subject, even for reasons unrelated to the sentence accompanied by the probation order, to more than two years' imprisonment. There is some support for this view in *Miller*, where the Ontario Court of Appeal held that:

> ... the principle governing s. 663(1)(b) [now s. 731(1)(b)] of the *Code* is that Parliament intended that a probation order would not come into effect more than two years from the time of sentencing and that an accused would not be made subject to a probation order, if required to serve a sentence of more than two years. [p. 104]

[37] With respect, this articulation of Parliament's intent is consistent with neither the language of s. 731(1)(b), nor its statutory context.

[38] Section 731(1)(b) *does not address the coming into force of a probation order*. The provision empowers the sentencing court to *make* a probation order as part of the sentence. The availability of this non-custodial sentencing option is restricted where the required custodial portion of the sentence exceeds two years. But the *coming into force* of the order is not dealt with at all in s. 731(1)(b).

[39] For that, one must look to s. 732.2 of the *Criminal Code*.

[40] Nowhere does s. 732.2—or any other provision of the *Criminal Code*—provide that a probation order must come into force within two years of it being made.

[41] My interpretation of s. 731(1)(b) is supported as well by the purposive approach outlined in *Mathieu*. As I stated at the outset, the policy considerations underpinning probation orders are best promoted by an interpretation that preserves their availability to trial judges.

[42] It is well established that probation orders are intended to facilitate an offender's rehabilitation (*Mathieu*, at para. 20; *Proulx*, at para. 32). An interpretation of the phrase "imprisonment for a term not exceeding two years" that includes all outstanding sentences

would have the undesirable consequence of making probation orders unavailable to offenders who might well benefit from them (*Mathieu*, at para. 22).

[43] The sentencing objectives set out by Parliament in ss. 718 to 718.2 of the *Criminal Code* are best achieved by preserving—not curtailing—a sentencing court's arsenal of non-custodial sentencing options. Probation orders, where available and appropriate, serve that purpose well: They afford sentencing judges the flexibility to opt for shorter prison terms followed by community supervision, rather than the longer prison terms that they would have otherwise unnecessarily imposed to achieve the same ends.

[44] The appellants' interpretation of s. 731(1)(b), rejected in *Mathieu* (at para. 22), would have the undesirable consequence of increasing the custodial portion of an offender's sentences without any countervailing correctional advantage or benefit to society.

[45] Not infrequently, the offender and society will both benefit from a probation order that comes into force following imprisonment for an aggregate period of more than two years (*Mathieu*, at para. 20). The offender has the benefit of a shorter sentence of imprisonment, and society benefits from constraints aimed at facilitating rehabilitation and protecting society (*Shoker* [2006 SCC 44, [2006] 2 SCR 399], at para. 10).

[46] There will, of course, be situations in which a probation order may not serve a useful purpose when it follows a lengthy term of imprisonment. Parliament has anticipated this possibility by including both preventive and curative antidotes in the sentencing provisions of the *Code*.

[47] I take care not to be understood to have expressed here a decided view on sentencing issues that are not now but may one day confront the Court. Subject to that reservation, I think it fair to say that the purpose and principles of sentencing set out in the *Criminal Code* are meant to take into account the correctional imperative of sentence individualization. Consistent with this approach and subject to the conditions set out in s. 731(1)(b) of the *Code*, questions related to the fitness of probation orders in particular cases—as opposed to their availability in principle—are best left to be dealt with by the courts on a case-by-case basis as a matter of fitness.

[48] Before returning to the *Code*'s remedies against probation orders that render a sentence unfit when it is imposed, I acknowledge that neither Cartesian logic nor textual exegesis can satisfactorily resolve every perceived anomaly.

[49] For example, it may appear anomalous to cause the validity of a probation order to depend on whether the relevant sentences were imposed at a single session or on different occasions. I have already explained why the availability of a probation order depends on the "term of imprisonment" imposed when the order is made.

[50] How, then, do we deal with probation orders attached to sentences that, likewise, do not exceed two years' imprisonment—but do result in continuous custody for more than two years in combination with other sentences imposed on the same offender by the same sentencing court *at the same session*?

[51] It has consistently been held by courts across the country that probation orders of this sort contravene s. 731(1)(b): See, for example: *R. v. Young* (1980), 27 C.R. (3d) 85 (B.C.C.A.); *R. v. Hennigar* (1983), 58 N.S.R. (2d) 110 (C.A.); *R. v. McPhee* (1993), 128 N.S.R. (2d) 79 (C.A.); *R. v. Amaralik* (1984), 16 C.C.C. (3d) 22 (N.W.T.C.A.); *R. v. Hackett* (1986), 30 C.C.C. (3d) 159 (B.C.C.A.); *R. v. Gill* (1994), 162 A.R. 163 (C.A.); and *R. v. H.J.P.* (1995), 133 Nfld. & P.E.I.R. 20 (Nfld. C.A.).

[52] While some of these cases invoked s. 139 of the *CCRA* and its predecessors, I believe they were nonetheless correctly decided pursuant to s. 731(1) alone, bearing in mind the "totality" principle that remains unchallenged on this appeal.

[53] The appellants argue in this regard that the interpretation of s. 731(1)(b) adopted by the Court of Appeal is problematic in that it treats similarly situated offenders differently depending on the *timing* of a sentence. For example, an offender who is sentenced on different days to two years' imprisonment for one offence and one year consecutive for another may be subject to probation, while an offender who receives identical terms of imprisonment at the same hearing would not.

[54] This apparent anomaly, or inconsistency, must yield to Parliament's intent, and the best indication of Parliament's intent is the provisions it has enacted.

[55] I need hardly add that it would be a reviewable error for a sentencing court to exploit this difference for the sole purpose of circumventing the two-year rule in s. 731(1)(b). For example, in a proceeding involving multiple counts, indictments, or informations, the sentencing court must not adjourn the sentencing on some of the offences in order to make a probation order that would otherwise contravene s. 731(1)(b).

[56] Moreover, sentencing and appellate courts are empowered to ensure that probation orders are made and applied in an even-handed and appropriate manner. Judicial discretion—and the checks placed upon it—are sufficient to ensure that this scheme is fairly applied.

VI

[57] In light of the foregoing, I agree with the Court of Appeal that s. 731(1)(b) does not invalidate probation orders imposed on prior occasions.

[58] With respect, however, I take a somewhat different view of fresh probation orders. Like the Ontario Court of Appeal in *Currie* (at para. 4), the British Columbia Court of Appeal held in this case that, "[w]hen the sentence is imposed on a remanet, and the total of the new sentence and the remanet exceeds two years, probation should not be ordered" (para. 74).

[59] And, again as in *Currie*, the Court of Appeal held here that the sentencing court has the jurisdiction to impose a fresh probation order in such circumstances—but it would generally be an error in principle to do so (para. 73). This conclusion was based on the view that s. 731(1)(b) "makes it clear that the intention of Parliament was to limit probation orders to situations where the sentence to be served does not exceed two years" (*ibid.*).

[60] If it is an error in principle to make a probation order that follows an aggregate sentence of more than two years, the principle does not arise from s. 731. As I earlier explained, s. 731(1)(b) does not reflect any sort of Parliamentary intention that probation orders be limited to situations where the sentence to be served does not exceed two years.

[61] But probation orders permitted by s. 731(1)(b) are, like other elements of a sentence, subject to review for their fitness. Courts are precluded by the relevant sentencing principles from making a probation order that is clearly unreasonable in the circumstances: *R. v. Shropshire*, [1995] 4 S.C.R. 227. Put differently, a probation order that is manifestly inappropriate in itself or that renders unfit the sentence of which it is a part will be set aside on appeal.

[62] In considering whether a fresh probation order is appropriate, the sentencing court must thus take into account the particular circumstances of the offence, the character and needs of the offender, and the purpose and relevant principles of sentencing: *R. v. Nasogaluak*, 2010 SCC 6, [2010] 1 S.C.R. 206, at para. 43.

[63] In short, unexpired prior sentences remain an important consideration, though not necessarily decisive, in determining whether a probation order is appropriate.

VII

[64] A probation order that was appropriate when made may well be rendered inappropriate by a lengthy intervening term of imprisonment.

[65] For example, where a probation order will not come into force for many years after its imposition, or where the total period of incarceration is extended to the point that the offender will be subject to a lengthy period of community supervision while on parole or statutory release, a probation order will generally lack a meaningful rehabilitative purpose.

[66] Existing probation orders are not automatically invalidated in these situations, but this does not mean that subsequent sentencing courts may disregard them. Quite the contrary. Sentencing judges must take into consideration a probation order that, pursuant to s. 732.2 of the *Code*, will come into force following any additional terms of imprisonment imposed by that court.

[67] Sentencing judges should also ensure that offenders understand that probation orders previously imposed are not automatically invalidated by the imposition of additional terms of imprisonment.

[68] Moreover, where a fresh sentence may be thought to strip an existing probation order of its rehabilitative purpose, the sentencing judge should explain the substance of s. 732.2(3) of the *Criminal Code* to the offender. Pursuant to that provision, an offender, probation officer or prosecutor may apply at any time to the court that made the probation order to have the probationary period decreased or in effect terminated.

[69] The court that made the original probation order would have already caused an explanation of this provision to be given to the offender: s. 732.1(5). However, as the procedure contemplated by s. 732.2(3) is properly applied where an additional sentence overtakes a probation order, it is appropriate to remind the offender of his or her rights in this regard at the time of the subsequent sentencing.

[70] Finally, provided that the statutory and procedural requirements are met, the offender or the Crown may apply to the sentencing court *itself* under s. 732.2(3) to have an outstanding probation order varied or decreased.

VIII

[71] For the reasons given, all of the probation orders attacked by the appellants were valid when made and no prior or subsequent sentences imposed on either appellant had, or could have had, the effect of invalidating any of their probation orders, either prospectively or retrospectively.

[72] Accordingly, as mentioned at the outset, I would affirm the judgment of the British Columbia Court of Appeal and dismiss the appeals of Mr. Knott and D.A.P. to this Court.

Appeals dismissed.

IV. WHEN DOES THE PROBATION PERIOD BEGIN?

When probation is part of a suspended sentence, it usually starts immediately. However, if the period of probation follows a term of imprisonment, when does it begin? This is tricky because federal prisoners can be released on parole or statutory release subject to conditions, supervision, and the possibility of recommitment if revoked. But a provincial prisoner who is released due to earned remission is released free and clear. Before the 1996 amendments, this was a real controversy: see *R v Constant* (1978), 40 CCC (2d) 329 (Man CA). Now, s 732.2(1)(b) distinguishes between the two kinds of confinement and provides that the period of probation begins "as soon as the offender is released from prison or, if released from prison on conditional release, at the expiration of the sentence of imprisonment." Parole, whether provincial or federal, and statutory release all qualify as conditional release.

V. OPTIONAL CONDITIONS

What kinds of conditions can be attached to a probation order? Some of the optional conditions are clear; others are vague. Sometimes the vagueness relates to how an order should be structured or monitored. Appellate courts have occasionally struck out or reworded conditions as being too vague: see *R v Timmins*, 2006 BCCA 354, 211 CCC (3d) 333; *R v Kirton*, 2007 MBCA 38, 219 CCC (3d) 485; and *R v Bourque*, 2013 BCCA 447. Vagueness also pervades the kinds of sanctions that may be encompassed. For example, there is a residual subcategory, s 732.1(3)(h), that is now defined as "such other reasonable conditions as the court considers desirable ... for protecting society and for facilitating the offender's successful reintegration into the community."

In this section, we explore some of the more contentious optional conditions. The following cases deal with the definitions of available conditions as they were worded before 1996. Some of the controversies raised in these cases have now been overtaken by legislative amendments that specifically provide for the condition that previously had to be included, if at all, under the residual category. However, these cases provide insights into the interpretive issues that arise from the optional condition categories. In evaluating the propriety of these conditions in general, and as applied, remember that conditions that are imposed need not be related to the offences that were committed by the offender so long as they are otherwise linked to the needs of the offender: see *R v Shoker*, 2006 SCC 44 at para 13, [2006] 2 SCR 399.

A. Driving Prohibitions

R v Ziatas
(1973), 13 CCC (2d) 287 (Ont CA)

MARTIN JA:

This is an application for leave to appeal and an appeal by the accused from the sentence imposed upon him by Provincial Judge Foster upon conviction of the accused on his plea of guilty to a charge of assault with intent to resist arrest contrary to s. 246(2)(b) of the *Criminal Code*.

The Provincial Judge imposed a fine of $150 and placed the appellant on probation for a term of one year. One of the conditions of the probation order was that the appellant should not operate a motor vehicle for the period of one year. Counsel for the appellant contended that, since s. 238 [am 1972, c 13, s 18] of the *Criminal Code* expressly empowers a Court that convicts an offender of any of the offences enumerated in the section, to prohibit the offender from driving a motor vehicle for the period specified in the section, and since the offence of which the appellant was convicted is not one of the enumerated offences, the Court had no power to require as a condition of the probation order that the accused not operate a motor vehicle during the period of probation. Without deciding whether or not the Provincial Judge had jurisdiction to impose this condition as a term of the probation order, we are all of the view that he proceeded upon a wrong principle, inasmuch as he imposed this term of the probation order as an additional punishment to be imposed upon the accused, whereas his only power, if he had any jurisdiction to impose the condition under s. 663(2) of the *Criminal Code*, was to impose such reasonable conditions as he considered desirable for securing the good conduct of the accused and for preventing the repetition by him of the same offence or the commission of other offences.

In the circumstances the appeal is allowed and the condition that the accused not operate a motor vehicle during his term of probation is struck out of the probation order and the appeal is allowed to give effect to this variation.

Appeal allowed.

The ruling in *Ziatas* with respect to the residual subcategory has been followed in a number of cases and was approved of by the Supreme Court of Canada in *R v Shoker*, 2006 SCC 44 at para 13, [2006] 2 SCR 399, discussed below.

B. Random Drug Testing

The following decision addresses the propriety of random drug testing as a means of enforcing compliance with a probation order. The accused was convicted of breaking and entering with intent to commit sexual assault. A psychological assessment of the accused revealed that drug use was a problem and recommended that the accused be subject to random urinalysis. Although the Crown did not request such a condition, and the accused did not consent, the trial judge included a condition that required the accused to submit to urinalysis, blood test, or breathalyzer test on the demand of a police officer or a probation officer. The condition specified that a positive reading would constitute a breach of the condition. In *R v Shoker*, the Court of Appeal (2004 BCCA 643, 192 CCC (3d) 176) deleted the part of the condition that provided that a positive test amounted to a breach of probation. A majority of the court found that there was legal authority for the testing requirement under s 732.1(3)(h), the residual clause, as a means to enforce the abstinence condition, but that it violated s 8 of the Charter in the circumstances. A majority of the Supreme Court of Canada disagreed that the existing provisions authorized the testing and therefore did not have to address Charter considerations. In considering whether the testing requirement was authorized, the court also commented generally on the purpose and scope of, and interaction between, the optional conditions and residual clause.

R v Shoker
2006 SCC 44, [2006] 2 SCR 399

CHARRON J (McLachlin CJ, Binnie, Fish, and Abella JJ concurring):

[1] This appeal raises the question whether a sentencing judge may require a probationer to provide, on demand by the probation officer, samples of breath, urine or blood for analysis to determine compliance with an abstention term of the probation order. ...

[2] The Crown appeals to this Court and seeks to reinstate the enforcement condition. At issue is whether ss. 732.1(3)(c) and 732.1(3)(h) of the *Criminal Code*, RSC 1985, c. C-46, authorize the enforcement condition and, if permissible, whether the condition must be predicated by reasonable and probable grounds to suspect a violation of an abstention condition.

[3] For the reasons that follow, I would dismiss the appeal. A sentencing judge has a broad jurisdiction in determining appropriate conditions of probation. However, there is no authority under the *Criminal Code* to authorize a search and seizure of bodily substances as part of a probation order. In light of the fact that the impugned condition must be quashed for lack of jurisdiction, it is neither necessary nor advisable for this Court to answer the constitutional question. It is Parliament's role to determine appropriate standards and safeguards governing the collection of bodily samples for enforcement purposes.

2. The Facts and Proceedings Below

. . .

[6] The trial judge sentenced Mr. Shoker to 20 months' incarceration to be followed by a two-year period of probation subject to a number of conditions. The Crown did not ask that the order of probation include any condition for treatment or testing of bodily substances and the offender did not consent to those conditions. ...

. . .

3. Analysis

. . .

[10] ... Probation has traditionally been viewed as a rehabilitative sentencing tool: *R v. Proulx*, [2000] 1 SCR 61, 2000 SCC 5, at paras. 31-33. The probationer remains free to live in the community but certain restraints on his freedom are imposed for the purpose of facilitating his rehabilitation and protecting society. An offender who is bound by a probation order and who, without reasonable excuse, fails or refuses to comply with that order is guilty of an offence under s. 733.1 punishable by up to two years' imprisonment.

. . .

[13] Before discussing the issue that arises in this case, I wish to make a few general comments about the power to impose optional conditions under s. 732.1(3). The residual power under s. 732.1(3)(h) speaks of "other reasonable conditions" imposed "for protecting society and for facilitating the offender's successful reintegration into the community." Such language is instructive, not only in respect of conditions crafted under this residual power, but in respect of the optional conditions listed under s. 732.1(3): before a condition can be imposed, it must be "reasonable" in the circumstances and must be ordered for the purpose of protecting society and facilitating the particular offender's successful

reintegration into the community. Reasonable conditions will generally be linked to the particular offence but need not be. What is required is a nexus between the offender, the protection of the community and his reintegration into the community. See, for example, *R v. Kootenay* (2000), 150 CCC (3d) 311 (Alta. CA), and *R v. Traverse* (2006), 205 CCC (3d) 33 (Man. CA), where appellate courts have upheld conditions requiring abstinence from alcohol or drugs even though these played no part in the commission of the offence for which the offender was sentenced. On the other hand, conditions of probation imposed to punish rather than rehabilitate the offender have been struck out: *R v. Ziatas* (1973), 13 CCC (2d) 287 (Ont. CA); *R v. Caja* (1977), 36 CCC (2d) 401 (Ont. CA); *R v. Lavender* (1981), 59 CCC (2d) 551 (BCCA); *R v. L.* (1986), 50 C.R. (3d) 398 (Alta. CA). In contrast, punitive conditions may be imposed pursuant to s. 742.3(2)(f) as part of a conditional sentence: *Proulx*, at para. 34.

[14] The residual power to craft individualized conditions of probation is very broad. It constitutes an important sentencing tool. The purpose and principles of sentencing set out in ss. 718 to 718.2 of the *Criminal Code* make it clear that sentencing is an individualized process that must take into account both the circumstances of the offence and of the offender. It would be impossible for Parliament to spell out every possible condition of probation that can meet these sentence objectives. The sentencing judge is well placed to craft conditions that are tailored to the particular offender to assist in his rehabilitation and protect society. However, the residual power to impose individualized conditions is not unlimited. The sentencing judge cannot impose conditions that would contravene federal or provincial legislation or the *Charter*. Further, inasmuch as the wording of the residual provision can inform the sentencing judge's exercise of discretion in imposing one of the listed optional conditions as I have described, the listed conditions in turn can assist in interpreting the scope of "other reasonable conditions" that can be crafted under s. 732.1(3)(h). As we shall see, none of the listed conditions is aimed at facilitating the investigation of suspected breaches of probation. I will come back to this point later.

[15] The underlying purpose for imposing conditions of probation also serves to define the role of the probation officer. The intervener the Attorney General of Canada aptly describes the probation officer's functions in its factum (at para. 21):

> It is in the nature of a probation officer's duties to act as an officer of the court, to assist the probationer in his rehabilitation, and to monitor compliance with the conditions of probation imposed by the sentencing court. The supervising probation officer simultaneously performs two distinct functions, rehabilitation and enforcement. The twin goals of probation—rehabilitation of the offender and protection of society—require and justify supervision in order to ensure that the probationer in fact observes his conditions. This supervised control is a restraint on the probationer's freedom.
>
> The supervisory function of the probation officer in ensuring compliance with the conditions and the manner in which this function must be performed becomes of central importance in this case when we consider the full implications of enforcing an abstention order by requiring bodily samples. The determinative question is whether the supervisory power to demand samples of bodily substances for enforcement purposes may be conferred upon the probation officer by the court as a discretionary exercise of discretion or whether it must be authorized by statute.

3.2 The Impugned Condition

[16] For ease of reference, I repeat the terms of Condition 9:

CONDITION 9: Abstain absolutely from the consumption and possession of alcohol and non prescription narcotics and *to submit to a urinalysis, blood test or breathalyzer test upon the demand/request of a Peace Officer or Probation Officer to determine compliance with this condition. Any positive reading will be a breach of this condition.* [Emphasis added.]

[17] As indicated earlier, the sentencing judge did not have the jurisdiction to predetermine that any positive reading would constitute a breach of probation. Therefore, the last sentence of Condition 9 was properly deleted by the Court of Appeal. The first part of the condition is also not in issue. The abstention condition is expressly authorized under s. 732.1(3)(c) and, given Mr. Shoker's particular circumstances, it is entirely reasonable to impose this condition to facilitate his rehabilitation and to protect society. The prohibition against the possession of alcohol and non-prescription drugs, imposed pursuant to the s. 732.1(3)(h) residual power, is also not in dispute. What remains at issue is the requirement that bodily samples be provided on demand.

[18] The impugned condition is challenged essentially on *Charter* grounds. In reviewing a sentencing judge's exercise of discretion on *Charter* grounds, an appellate court should first consider whether the sentencing judge acted within his statutory jurisdiction. If a sentence is illegal on the basis that it is unauthorized under the governing legislation, it must be struck down and the constitutional issue does not arise. I will therefore consider whether the requirement to provide bodily samples as a condition of probation falls within the scope of s. 732.1.

3.3 Requiring Bodily Samples and Section 732.1 of the Criminal Code

[19] The Crown submits that s. 732.1(3)(c) abstention conditions are highly desirable for the rehabilitation of the offender and the protection of the public and that the sentencing objectives of such abstention terms can only be achieved if there is also an effective mechanism to enforce them. Therefore, the Crown argues that ss. 732.1(3)(c) and 732.1(3)(h), read together, authorize the imposition of random sampling of an offender's bodily substances to ensure compliance with the abstention condition. Mr. Shoker argues that the power to impose enforcement terms to the abstention condition neither flows implicitly from s. 732.1(3)(c) nor does it fall within the scope of s. 732.1(3)(h) "reasonable conditions." If Parliament had intended to authorize the seizure of bodily samples, he argues, it would have expressly so stated as it has done in other existing legislative schemes.

[20] I will deal firstly with s.732.1(3)(c). With respect to Hall JA's opinion to the contrary, the jurisdiction to impose enforcement terms cannot simply flow from the power to impose an abstention condition. The effect of including a s. 732.1(3)(c) abstention condition in a probation order is to define a criminal offence, the commission of which is punishable under s. 733.1. Enforcement powers are not implicit from the simple creation of an offence. For example, it cannot reasonably be contended that the prohibition against impaired driving under s. 253 implicitly includes the enforcement scheme for demanding bodily samples contained in ss. 254 to 258. Yet, in essence, that is the argument here. The Crown submits that the enforcement scheme should be implied as necessary to give effect

to a s. 732.1(3)(c) abstention condition. I do not accept this argument. Breach of probation is a criminal offence under the *Criminal Code* and, as such, it is subject to the usual investigatory techniques and manner of proof as any other offence. Hence, the probationer who is found consuming alcohol with his friends in a drinking establishment can be prosecuted based on the evidence of witnesses to the event. Likewise, the probationer who exhibits signs of alcohol or drug impairment can be prosecuted and the offence can be proven by testimonial evidence much in the same way as an offence for impaired driving. The power to demand bodily samples and the resulting analyses would undoubtedly assist in the enforcement of a s. 732.1(3)(c) condition, but it cannot on that basis simply be implied.

[21] The authority to impose enforcement terms, if any, must be found rather in the residual clause. As indicated earlier, s. 732.1(3)(h) gives the sentencing judge a broad power to craft other reasonable conditions designed to protect society and facilitate the offender's successful reintegration into the community. Hall JA was of the view that the authority could not be found under s. 732.1(3)(h) because Parliament has specifically addressed alcohol and drugs in s. 732.1(3)(c). The fact that Parliament has specifically addressed alcohol and drugs under s. 732.1(3)(c)—and also in ss. 732.1(3)(g.1) and 732.1(3)(g.2)—is certainly a relevant factor but, in my respectful view, it does not preclude the imposition of "other" alcohol and drug-related "reasonable conditions" under the residual clause. Any number of additional conditions aimed at ensuring that the probationer comply with the abstention condition can be imposed. Indeed, the prescription against the possession of alcohol and drug found in Condition 9 is one example. Similarly, a sentencing judge could prescribe that the offender not enter any premises where alcohol is sold or served; that he not associate with his favourite drinking buddies; or that he obey a curfew. All these conditions could be imposed to ensure better compliance with the abstention condition and thereby facilitate the offender's rehabilitation and protect society. Absent peculiar circumstances, it could not seriously be contended that any such condition would be unreasonable. ...

[22] On the face of it, s. 732.1(3)(h) therefore appears wide enough to permit enforcement terms such as the one imposed in this case since, it is argued, submitting to testing would also ensure better compliance with the abstention condition. However, the residual provision must be read in context. Since it provides for "other" reasonable conditions, the listed conditions under ss. 732.1(3)(a) to 732.1(3)(g.2) can assist in delineating the scope of the residual provision. It is noteworthy that the fulfilment of any of the listed conditions can have no incriminating consequence for the probationer. In addition, when the condition may pose a risk, such as participating in a treatment program, the consent of the offender is required before the condition can be imposed. Section 732.1(3)(h) speaks of "other reasonable conditions." It is reasonable to infer that additional conditions imposed under the residual power would be of the same kind as the listed conditions. However, conditions intended to facilitate the gathering of evidence for enforcement purposes do not simply monitor the probationer's behaviour and, as such, are of a different kind and, because of their potential effect, absent the probationer's consent to such conditions, raise constitutional concerns. For example, could Mr. Shoker be compelled, as a condition of his probation, to make his home available for inspection on demand to better monitor the prescription against the possession of alcohol or drugs? Such a condition in effect would subject him to a different standard than that provided by Parliament for the issuance of a search warrant. In my view, it could not reasonably be argued that the sentencing

judge would have the jurisdiction to override this scheme under the authority of the open-ended language of s. 732.1(3)(h). It would be up to Parliament, if it saw fit, to enact any such scheme.

[23] The sentencing judge's jurisdiction can be no greater in respect of the seizure of bodily samples. The seizure of bodily samples is highly intrusive and, as this Court has often reaffirmed, it is subject to stringent standards and safeguards to meet constitutional requirements. Significantly, in *R v. Borden*, [1994] 3 SCR 145, this Court held that where there is no statutory authorization for the seizure of bodily samples, consent must be obtained if the seizure is to be lawful. … In the various circumstances where Parliament has chosen to authorize the collection of bodily samples, it has not only used clear language; it has also included in the legislation, or through regulations, a number of standards and safeguards … .

. . .

[25] The establishment of these standards and safeguards cannot be left to the discretion of the sentencing judge in individual cases. There is no question that a probationer has a lowered expectation of privacy. However, it is up to Parliament, not the courts, to balance the probationers' *Charter* rights as against society's interest in effectively monitoring their conduct. Since the purpose of s. 8 is preventative, the following principle in *Hunter v. Southam Inc.*, [1984] 2 SCR 145, at p. 169, is particularly apposite here:

> While the courts are guardians of the Constitution and of individuals' rights under it, it is the legislature's responsibility to enact legislation that embodies appropriate safeguards to comply with the Constitution's requirements. It should not fall to the courts to fill in the details that will render legislative lacunae constitutional.

In this case, the Crown argues that reasonable and probable grounds are not required for the search and seizure of bodily substances from probationers and that the seizure of blood samples is also reasonable. Hall JA disagreed. He would have deleted the requirement to provide blood samples as too intrusive and conditioned the requirement to provide urine and breath samples upon the establishment of reasonable and probable grounds. Those are precisely the kinds of policy decisions for Parliament to make having regard to the limitations contained in the *Charter*. Parliament has specifically addressed the issue of alcohol and intoxicating substances in ss. 732.1(3)(c), 732.1(3)(g.1) and 732.1(3)(g.2) but it has not provided for a scheme for the collection of bodily samples as it has done in respect of parolees. Such a scheme cannot be judicially enacted on the ground that the court may find it desirable in an individual case. In addition to the constitutional concerns raised by the collection of bodily samples, the establishment of such a scheme requires the expenditure of resources and usually the cooperation of the provinces. This reality is exemplified in this case where the funding for urinalysis has been discontinued in British Columbia rendering the probation condition moot. This is yet another reason why the matter is one for Parliament.

[26] For these reasons, I would conclude that there is no statutory authority for requiring Mr. Shoker to submit bodily samples. In the absence of a legislative scheme authorizing the seizure of bodily samples, the enforcement of abstention conditions must be done in accordance with existing investigatory tools. The majority of the Court of Appeal was therefore correct in deleting that part of Condition 9 following the words "non prescription narcotics." I would dismiss the appeal.

LeBEL J (Bastarache J concurring):

[27] I have read the reasons of my colleague Charron J Although I agree with her that the appeal should be dismissed, I reach this result on a different basis. In my opinion, there is statutory authority for the kind of order made by the sentencing judge. But the terms of the order were open to review under s. 8 of the *Canadian Charter of Rights and Freedoms*. As they did not meet the requirements of s. 8, the appeal should fail.

· · ·

[36] With respect for those who hold other views, under very well-established rules of statutory interpretation, the *Criminal Code* grants the sentencing judge the authority to include monitoring procedures in probation orders. To hold otherwise might well cause unforeseen and undesirable effects, as the inflexibility of such an interpretative approach would likely require Parliament to attempt to foresee a wide range of individual situations and to address them in minute detail. A drafting technique such as this would hardly be consistent with the canons of sound legal drafting, even if it were feasible.

[37] Moreover, a narrow interpretation of the residual clause would cast doubt on a number of useful monitoring methods, which sentencing judges appear to be resorting to with increasing frequency. ...

[38] The range of possible conditions is broad. The purpose of such conditions is often to control aspects of the lifestyle of an accused to ensure that the goals of probation—protection of society and reintegration into the community—are achieved.

[39] We should not assume that such a discretion would be abused by sentencing judges or exercised in an unconstitutional manner in the absence of a detailed statutory framework. ...

[40] Any challenge in the instant case should have related to the reasonableness of the order under s. 8 of the *Charter*. The authority to impose the monitoring conditions exists. It remains to be seen whether the conditions meet the standards of the *Charter* (see Ruby, at para. 10.63).

[41] Before I move on to some brief comments on the application of s. 8 in the context of the case at bar, I must add that I agree with Charron J that the part of the order that would, in essence, turn a positive test into a breach of the conditions set out in the order is contrary to the principles of criminal law. Guilt must be proved in the usual manner, that is, beyond a reasonable doubt, and the accused is entitled to the protection of the law of criminal evidence and criminal procedure.

III. Application of Section 8

[42] Section 8 raises difficulties in respect of parts of the order. I agree that the part compelling the accused to undergo blood tests would be far too intrusive and would breach s. 8 absent a statutory framework consistent with the standards of the *Charter*.

[43] Although it may very well be a more efficient way to monitor compliance, random drug testing at the probation officer's discretion could become highly arbitrary. Courts would have difficulty defining a proper framework to supplement the silence of the Code. This is a situation where Parliament would be in a better position to address the issue. Its solution would then be open to review by the courts under s. 8 and s. 1 of the *Charter*.

[44] For these reasons, I agree with my colleague that the appeal should be dismissed.

Appeal dismissed.

NOTE

Parliament responded to the Supreme Court of Canada's decision in *R v Shoker* by adding ss 732.1(3)(c.1) and (c.2) to Code s 732.1(3) to authorize courts to include terms to enforce abstinence clauses in probation orders by requiring the offender to provide bodily samples either on demand where grounds exist to believe the clause has been breached or on a regular basis as specified by the offender's probation officer. Sections 732.1(7) to (12) set out the statutory conditions, subject to the regulations, governing how such samples and the records relating to them are to be taken, analyzed, stored, handled, and destroyed: see *Response to the Supreme Court of Canada Decision in R v Shoker Act*, SC 2011, c 7, brought into force 31 March 2015. Consider whether, in light of the court's comments in *R v Shoker*, these provisions will withstand constitutional scrutiny.

C. Community Service

Probation orders often include a term that offenders devote a certain amount of time to "community service." Until 1996, there was no specific provision authorizing judges to impose this important term. Courts used the residual subcategory as the authorization for community-service orders. Today, s 732.1(3)(f) specifically allows the court to impose up to 240 hours of community service to be completed within a period of 18 months. Consider these decisions in light of the Supreme Court of Canada's general comments in *R v Shoker*.

R v Tanner

(1983), 36 CR (3d) 64 (Man Prov Ct)

ALLEN PROV J:

The information in this case charges that:

Dennis Nelson Tanner, at the City of Winnipeg (in Manitoba) between the 16th day of December AD 1981 and the 28th day of August in the year of Our Lord one thousand nine hundred and eighty-two, while bound by a probation order made by Judge H. Collerman on the 25th day of June 1981, in Provincial Judges Court (Criminal Division), Public Safety Building, Winnipeg, did unlawfully and wilfully fail to comply with such order to wit: to carry out ninety-six hours of community work free of charge, terms, location and type of work to be arranged by Manitoba Probation Services, and failing to carry out ninety-six hours of community work as arranged by Manitoba Probation Service.

• • •

From the information quoted above, it can be seen that the learned trial judge specified that the accused perform 96 hours of community service work free of charge but left the terms, location, and type of work to be arranged by the Manitoba Probation Service. This, it is argued, is an unauthorized delegation by the learned trial judge of his judicial function; therefore, the order is void *ab initio*, and there is no basis for the present charge against the accused.

• • •

On the authorities cited herein and referred to by other courts, I believe my opening comment relative to the power to delegate one's judicial function is well founded. Equally, since the decision of the Supreme Court of Canada in *R v. Sterner*, [1982] 1 SCR 173, 64 CCC (2d) 160, 14 Sask. R 79, 40 NR 423, it is established that judges can delegate administrative functions.

The task in each case is to determine whether the delegation is of a judicial or administrative function. In determining that, regard must be had to the object of the legislation under which we act, what we wish to achieve, and the practicalities of the situation. Parliament has not legislated in a vacuum and programs providing for supervised probation, community service, and other means of punishing, rehabilitating, and deterring an accused person were created under a perceived need and after much study and consideration. The purpose of probation, community service and programs of like nature is to avoid, in appropriate cases, the imposition of terms of incarceration on those who, with assistance of whatever type may be necessary, may be rehabilitated and adequately punished without incarceration. The effort is made, through the type of programs described, to solve and alleviate anti-social behaviour, upgrade skills and education, and appraise and treat a variety of problems such as drug abuse, alcoholism and even a lack of social skills. The need for such programs can be, and under our laws must be, discovered by the court, with the assistance of persons and agencies available for that purpose, and it is the court that must prescribe the nature of the program to be followed by an accused person who is placed on probation in order to achieve the desired result. That I see as part of the judicial function.

But I cannot see that the day-to-day supervision of probationers is to be considered part of the judicial function. While as judges we may be able to identify the need for a program, few, if any of us, have the training or experience to oversee such programs on a day-to-day basis; we are dependent more and more on those who are probation officers, representatives of the Alcoholism Foundation, Alcoholics Anonymous, X-Kalay, the Salvation Army, and many other groups dedicated to assisting those who require these skills. It is the workers in these fields who have the necessary knowledge, skill and training to adapt the program of rehabilitation to the needs of the subject. The programs may require revision from time to time during the period of probation to adapt to the progress, or lack of it, by the subject. Efforts at first considered appropriate may have to give way to other methods that prove more appropriate. To have to specify in detail how a particular program should be carried out may be impossible for a judge at the time of sentencing.

At the risk of being over-zealous in making my point, let me give an example. Assume, as is often the case, that the accused is one who requires counselling. To assure that counselling, he is placed on probation with directions to report to the probation officer. Must we specify the time, place, frequency and method of reporting? If we do so, the result could be that the accused does not get the counselling required and the probation officer is unable to fulfil his assigned task properly. In another instance, the accused may respond rapidly and the need for counselling diminishes and eventually disappears well before the time of the expiration of the probation. Should the requirement to report be such that the already busy time of our social workers be utilized unnecessarily? Should the accused be imposed upon to comply with the conditions which, in this case, are no longer necessary or appropriate? The answer to these rhetorical questions is, in my opinion, no. I say this not only because I think it is the only workable answer (need and convenience do not change the law), but because, once the objective is recognized and prescribed by the court, surely the day-to-day application of the court order is administrative. Once a court has ordered, say, counselling, the manner, place, time and frequency of such counselling is surely a manner of carrying out, i.e., administering, the court's order.

This approach is, in my opinion, recognized by the legislation. So far as probation officers are concerned, they are, by virtue of s. 4(1)(a) of the *Manitoba Corrections Act*, CCSM, c. C230, officers of the court. The *Criminal Code* has, at least by implication, recognized probation officers and others as necessary adjuncts of the court: see ss. 662 [re-en 1972, c 13, s 57] and 663(2) of the Code. I repeat, Parliament was not acting in a vacuum but, in providing for probation and conditions of probation, recognized the need of the court for the assistance of those usually more fitted to carry out the administrative part of probation.

I realize that community service is somewhat different from other conditions of probation in that there is an element of punishment involved. It is a program designed to impress upon offenders that they must pay to an extent for their transgressions; it also recognizes that imprisonment is not necessary. The difficulty in a judge dictating the details of such service at the time of sentencing, particularly where the period of probation is lengthy, is mind-boggling. I repeat, difficulty is not the determining factor, but surely, once the need for community service is recognized by the court, the details of the nature of that work and time and place of performance are but administrative details.

. . .

Under the circumstances, I am of the view that the order of Collerman Prov. J is a valid order.

R v Richards
(1979), 11 CR (3d) 193 (Ont CA)

HOWLAND CJO:

The Attorney General of Canada applies for leave to appeal and, if leave be granted, appeals from the sentence imposed upon the respondent by Graburn Co. Ct. J on 24th October 1978, following a conviction entered the previous day on the respondent's plea of guilty to the offence of possession of diacetylmorphine (heroin), contrary to s. 3(1) of the *Narcotic Control Act*, RSC 1970, c. N-1. ...

The learned trial judge suspended the passing of sentence and released the respondent on the following statutory and special conditions contained in a probation order to be in force for one year, namely:

. . .

(5) within the first six months of the probation, after making the necessary arrangements through the probation officer and with officials of the Canadian National Institute for the Blind ("CNIB") here in Toronto, either personally or with a group of musicians of choice, to the blind young people associated with the Canadian National Institute for the Blind.

This probation order was subsequently varied by Graburn Co. Ct. J on 23rd April 1979 ... .

The variation which was made … provided for two benefit performances at the Oshawa Civic Centre, Oshawa, instead of the one performance at the CNIB Bayview Auditorium, Toronto.

The facts leading to the charge, so far as material, are these. On 27th February 1977 officers of the Ontario Provincial Police and the RCMP went to the Harbour Castle Hotel in Toronto to execute a warrant for the arrest of Anita Pallenberg, described as the "common law wife" of the respondent. In the course of the search of a bedroom in which the respondent was sleeping the officers found paraphernalia suitable for the administration of heroin. These items contained traces of heroin. The officers also found in the top drawer of a dresser a leather pouch, inside of which was a clear plastic bag containing a white powder; which on analysis proved to be 22 grams of heroin of 32 per cent purity.

• • •

The respondent is a musician and is a leading member of the Rolling Stones, a well-known "rock and roll" band. The respondent gave a statement to the police in which he admitted that the heroin was his. He indicated to the police that he had been a heavy user for four years and that he had purchased a large quantity of the drug to satisfy his habit for the five to six weeks that he was going to be in Canada. (It was conceded by the Crown that the heroin was purchased in Canada.) He also told the police that he had tried to "kick" the habit several times, but that he was on tour and did not have time to complete his treatment programmes.

• • •

The following facts derived from the submission of counsel, and the reports filed with the consent of both counsel on the proceedings with respect to sentence are not in dispute. The respondent is a British citizen and at the time of the imposition of sentence was 34 years of age. He received his early education at Dartford, Kent. He then attended an art school, where he studied graphic design and while there learned to play the guitar. The group known as the Rolling Stones was formed in 1962, and has been giving performances and making recordings since that time. In 1967 the respondent began to use drugs, and in 1969 he commenced to inject himself with heroin subcutaneously. Counsel for the respondent at trial attributed the respondent's experimentation with drugs to exhaustion following a grueling schedule. Be that as it may, the respondent's use of drugs developed to the point where he was using large amounts of heroin daily. The respondent, prior to his arrest on the present charge, had made several attempts to cure his addiction. …

The respondent, following his arrest on the present charge, again sought treatment … . The reports disclosed that the respondent … had made remarkable progress; and that he was strongly motivated to overcome his addiction. Regular laboratory tests showed that he was free from drugs and, in particular, free from heroin. …

On the hearing of the appeal, we received additional material, including a post-sentence report dated 12th June 1979 … . The post-sentence report verifies that the respondent has complied with the terms of the probation order with respect to treatment, that he has remained free from drugs and that he has continued to be strongly motivated to rid himself of his previous drug dependency.

The two concerts provided for in the amended probation order were held in April 1979. 2700 blind persons and their escorts attended the concerts and were admitted without charge. Tickets were sold to the general public. The respondent and the supporting musicians received no payment for their services. In addition, the respondent and Mick Jagger, the lead singer of the group, paid their own expenses. The CNIB received a net amount of $39,000 after the payment of all its expenses in connection with the concerts.

· · ·

We wish to make it clear that the appeal was pursued and brought on as expeditiously as the circumstances permitted, and no blame attaches to anyone in that respect. We are nonetheless of the view that at this stage of the proceedings, when the terms of the probation order with respect to treatment have been virtually completed and the prescribed community service has been performed, we ought not to vary the sentence unless we are satisfied that it is so manifestly wrong that we are required in the interest of justice to intervene.

We have not been so satisfied. To impose a custodial sentence now would impose a hardship greatly in excess of that which would have resulted from a custodial sentence in the first instance: see *R v. Bartkow* (1978), 1 CR (3d) S-36 (NSCA): and *R v. Binder*, Ont. CA, 3rd May 1979 (not yet reported).

· · ·

Mr. Scollin also contended that the type of community service directed to be performed was wholly inappropriate—that the giving of a concert by the respondent is not seen as punishment. With respect to the desirability, in general, of imposing a requirement in a probation order that an offender perform community services, we reiterate the views of this court expressed by Dubin JA in *R v. Shaw, supra*. He said at p. 362:

> During the appeal some concern was expressed as to the validity of that term in each probation order which required both of the respondents to perform community services. The trial judge was anxious that both these two young men make amends in a positive way for the damage that they had done, not only to society, but to their own peer groups. In my opinion s. 663(2)(h) of the *Criminal Code* authorizes the imposition of such a term ... .
>
>   Not only do I think that the provisions in the probation orders relating to this matter are valid, but in appropriate cases should be more extensively used.

In general, it is appropriate to require an offender to perform community services of the type that he is fitted to perform. In the present case, the service performed by the respondent benefitted substantially the CNIB. In the case of another offender not possessing the advantages of the respondent, a lesser service within the abilities of the offender may count as an equivalent.

Although we are strongly of the view that the probation order should also have contained a term that, in addition to performing the concerts, the respondent should engage in a programme to point out the disastrous consequences that the drug addict faces and actively to discourage the use of drugs, we do not consider it would now be appropriate or practical to impose new terms.

Appeal dismissed.

D. Treatment

Psychiatric treatment as a condition of probation has been controversial, especially since the *Canadian Charter of Rights and Freedoms*, Part I of the *Constitution Act, 1982*, being Schedule B to the *Canada Act 1982* (UK), 1982, c 11 came into force. Consider the following decision and approach it adopts. To what extent does this approach address the concerns of courts, offenders, and the public? Today s 732.1(3)(g) of the Code allows the court, with the agreement of the offender and the program director, to order the offender to actively participate in a treatment program approved of by the province. Does this provision fully address the issues that arise in this area?

R v Rogers
(1990), 61 CCC (3d) 481 (BCCA)

ANDERSON JA (McEachern CJ, Taggart, Legg, and Hollinrake JJA concurring):

This is an appeal from a sentence imposed on May 22, 1990, by McGivern Prov. Ct. J, wherein he ordered that the appellant be placed on probation for a period of 15 months [after having pleaded guilty to the offence of possession of a concealed weapon—namely, a knife]. The probation order reads, in part, as follows:

• • •

Now, therefore, the said offender shall, for the period of fifteen (15) months … comply with the following conditions … and, in addition,

1. You will report today to a Probation Officer at 275 E Cordova St., Vancouver, BC and then report to the Inter Ministerial Project at 219 Main St., Vancouver, BC. After that you will have to go back to the Inter Ministerial Project Office whenever they tell you to, at least once a month.
2. *You will, under their direction, seek and take whatever psychiatric assessment or treatment that can be arranged for you, and you shall do that as you are directed by the Inter Ministerial Project Office.*
3. As directed by the Inter Ministerial Project Office you shall report to the Forensic Psychiatric Outpatient Clinic on West Broadway, Vancouver, BC.
4. You will not have any knives in your pocket; on your possession in a public place, except while eating in a restaurant. (emphasis added)

• • •

The circumstances of the offence were described by counsel for the Crown as follows:

Your Honour, the circumstances here, it was April 9th, 1990, at approximately three twenty in the afternoon. A witness sees the accused cross Hornby and approaches a woman who's standing on the corner. Apparently there's quite a few people standing on the corner.

He is holding what appears to be a kitchen knife in his right hand. He is described as poking it, one of the people, one of these women who was standing there. The woman moves. There's no contact. The light changes and people start crossing the street. The accused then picks the knife up, puts it over his head and does really nothing with it. He then puts the knife back into his pocket.

• • •

The appellant appeared in court on April 11, 1990, and was remanded at that time for 30 days in order that a psychiatric assessment be obtained.

• • •

From the above assessment, the following facts may be gleaned:

(1) The appellant has been suffering from a chronic mental illness, schizophrenia, since 1982 or earlier.

(2) Since his admission to hospital, the appellant has received medication and his mental condition has greatly improved.

(3) Prior to his discharge from hospital, Dr. Levy discussed with the appellant the possibility of a "long acting," intramuscular injection but this was refused.

(4) The appellant has a past history of non-compliance with medication programs and, therefore, his future prognosis is poor.

We were informed by counsel for the appellant that he is now under the care of a private physician and that he is now, by consent, taking medication as prescribed by his physician.

The order made by McGivern Prov. Ct. J was made pursuant to s. 737(2)(h) of the *Criminal Code* reading as follows:

> (h) comply with such other reasonable conditions as the court considers desirable for securing the good conduct of the accused and for preventing a repetition by him of the same offence or the commission of other offences.

Counsel for the appellant submits that, in the circumstances of this case, a probation order compelling an accused person to "seek and take whatever psychiatric assessment or treatment that can be arranged for you" is contrary to s. 7 of the *Canadian Charter of Rights and Freedoms*.

He made reference to several reports of the Law Reform Commission of Canada in his factum as follows:

> The Law Reform Commission of Canada has considered the issue of treatment in relation to the criminal law in a number of publications. As far back as 1975, the Law Reform Commission in its working Paper number 14, "THE CRIMINAL PROCESS AND MENTAL DISORDER" [1975], indicated that probation orders which contained conditions of psychiatric treatment should only be made where the offender consents. See page 45 of the aforesaid report:

>> Probation orders with conditions of psychiatric treatment should be made only where: (1) the offender understands the kind of program to be followed, (2) he consents to the program and, (3) the psychiatric or counselling services have agreed to accept the offender for treatment.

> See also Working Paper 26, "MEDICAL TREATMENT AND CRIMINAL LAW" [1980], p. 73, where the following recommendations are contained:

>> (10) that the right of a competent adult to refuse treatment be specifically recognized by the *Criminal Code*;

>> (11) that treatment shall not be administered against an individual's refusal, unless there is a finding of incompetence or an exception recognized in law.

He also relied upon the judgment of the Supreme Court of Canada in *Reference re s. 94(2) of Motor Vehicle Act* (1985), 23 CCC (3d) 289.

I agree with the submissions made by counsel for the appellant. In my opinion, a probation order which compels an accused person to take psychiatric treatment or medication is an unreasonable restraint upon the liberty and security of the accused person. It is contrary to the fundamental principles of justice and, save in exceptional circumstances, cannot be saved by s. 1 of the Charter. Exceptional circumstances are not present here.

While, as counsel for the Crown has stated, it is unlikely that an accused person would be subjected to unusual or dangerous medication or treatment, that risk always exists. In my opinion, it is the protection of the public which is the principal support for an order compelling the compulsory taking of treatment or medication. That is insufficient to save the order under s. 1 of the Charter. Other less drastic means are available to accomplish that purpose.

The fact that the probation order in this case is invalid, as being contrary to the Charter, does not solve the problem confronting the court. While the rehabilitation of the appellant is important, the court must consider the risks involved in permitting the appellant to be at liberty on probation. In other cases, where the trial judge finds as a fact that an accused person is suffering from schizophrenia or a like illness and refuses to consent to prescribed treatment or medication, it might very well be that the trial judge would not consider probation. The risk to society might be too great and only incarceration may afford the necessary protection.

I do not think it is possible to say that a particular form of probation order will be appropriate for all cases. The sentence to be imposed on each offender must be based on the general principles of sentencing which include a consideration of the circumstances of the offence and of the offender. The result is that different conditions may be imposed in probation orders depending on the circumstances of each case. To the extent possible, the conditions should be designed to ensure the protection of the public. However, they should not compel an offender to undergo medical treatment including the compulsory taking of medication. It is with those considerations in mind that now consider the conditions numbered one to four in the probation order in the case at bar.

In this case the appellant has a history of non-compliance with prescribed treatment and medication. However, he has now consented to, and is taking, treatment and medication under the care of a private physician. If he continues to take the advice of his physician and takes medication as prescribed, the risk of unlawful behaviour on the part of the appellant will be greatly reduced.

Having regard to the above, I would supplant conditions numbered one to four in the probation order with the following provisions:

1. You will take reasonable steps to maintain yourself in such condition that:
   (a) your chronic schizophrenia will not likely cause you to conduct yourself in a manner dangerous to yourself or anyone else; and
   (b) it is not likely you will commit further offences.
2. You will forthwith report to a Probation Officer at 275 E Cordova St., Vancouver, BC and thereafter, if directed to do so, you will forthwith report to the Inter Ministerial project at 219 Main St., Vancouver, BC.
3. You will thereafter attend as directed from time to time at the Inter Ministerial project for the purpose of receiving such medical counselling and treatment as may be recommended except that you shall not be required to submit to any treatment or medication to which you do not consent.
4. If you do not consent to the form of medical treatment or medication which is prescribed or recommended, you shall forthwith report to your Probation Officer

and thereafter report daily to your Probation Officer. If directed to do so by your Probation Officer, you shall report to the Inter Ministerial Project at 219 Main Street, Vancouver, BC for the purpose of being monitored with respect to a possible breach of Condition 1 above.

5. You shall provide your treating physician with a copy of this order and the name, address and telephone number of your Probation Officer. You shall instruct your treating physician that if you fail to take medication as prescribed by him or fail to keep any appointments made with him, he is to advise your Probation Officer immediately of any such failures.

6. Except when eating in a restaurant you will not have any knife in your possession.

Appeal allowed.

For a similar ruling, see *R v Kieling* (1991), 64 CCC (3d) 124 (Sask CA), where the court deleted a term of probation that required the offender to "take prescribed medication." The offender had a long history of persistently harassing entertainer Anne Murray and her family: see also *R v L (JJ)*, 2001 MBCA 21 at paras 4-6, 152 CCC (3d) 572; *R v RT*, 2011 ONSC 1042 at paras 51-62; *R v Burgar*, 2014 BCSC 331 at paras 108-112; *R v TW*, 2015 ONSC 2167 at para 57.

E. Electronic Monitoring

The use of electronic monitoring technology is sometimes considered as a mechanism to achieve compliance with conditions imposed as part of bail, a probation order, or most commonly a conditional sentence. It is usually associated with the objective of effecting the "house arrest" of the offender or monitoring compliance with other conditions, such as curfews. In this respect, it has become an important aspect of the imposition of a conditional sentence because suitability for electronic monitoring is often a condition of this type of sentence: see Suzanne Wallace-Caprettal & Julian Roberts, "The Evolution of Electronic Monitoring in Canada: From Corrections to Sentencing and Beyond" in Mike Nellis, Kristel Beyens & Dan Kaminski, *Electronically Monitored Punishment* (London: Routledge, 2013) ch 2, who note (at 55) that "the vast majority of electronically monitored cases involve offenders serving a conditional sentence of imprisonment in the community." The use of electronic monitoring as an aspect of probation has been and remains controversial. With the recent restrictions on the availability of conditional sentences, the use of electronic monitoring as an element of probation has become even more controversial. The following cases address the concerns that arise in this area. The first case, *Erdmann*, pre-dates the creation of conditional sentences of imprisonment and discusses the general concerns over the use of electronic monitoring. The latter two cases, *Bankay* and *Shoker*, discuss the suitability of electronic monitoring and probation in cases where conditional sentences are no longer available.

R v Erdmann
(1991), 64 CCC (3d) 188 (Sask CA)

WAKELING JA (Gerwing and Sherstobitoff JJA concurring):

[1] The respondent pleaded guilty to two charges of trafficking in *cannabis* resin (hashish), and one charge of possession of hashish for the purpose of trafficking. It is not a case of an isolated incident, but rather a situation where the appellant acknowledges she is a user and has been trafficking for some time but thought it was safe to do so if she restricted her customers to her circle of friends and fellow users. The possession charge did not relate to a relatively trifling quantity, rather, it amounted to one-half pound, for which a price of $2,000 was being considered.

[2] The respondent is 22 years of age and has one child which she has placed with her mother for care and upbringing. She lives common law with a man who is also a user. At the time of the offence, she was employed part time at Sears, working approximately 30 hours per week.

[3] The trial judge felt a sentence of nine months was justified, applying the reasoning of such cases as *R v. McGinn* (1989), 49 CCC (3d) 137, 75 Sask. R 161, 7 WCB (2d) 338, emanating from this court. He, however, concluded that this was a suitable occasion to utilize an electronic monitoring device and therefore ordered a suspended sentence with six months of electronic monitoring and probation for one year.

[4] The principal issue on this appeal was whether the use of an electronic monitoring device was appropriate in this case.

[5] A Crown employee was present in court to answer questions regarding that program and she indicated the electronic monitoring device was being used effectively in a number of cases. When questioned about the criteria which was employed to determine which of the many convicted persons should serve their sentence in this fashion, she responded that it largely depended on the temperamental suitability of the party. In this case, Erdmann was considered a suitable candidate and this had been largely confirmed by reason of the fact she had been successfully monitored for approximately three months.

[6] A program summary was provided and that document described the target group in this way:

> Though a wide range of offenders are eligible for consideration of this sanction, the project's primary emphasis will be on native and female offenders as well as those individuals that normally would receive a sentence of incarceration with probation to follow.
>
> The selection of cases must be done on an individualized basis and will require careful screening of the offenders. In identifying these cases, Corrections will be looking for people that rate at the very high end of the offenders classification system and are clearly candidates for incarceration.

[7] This same issue regarding the use of an electronic monitoring device came before this court fairly recently when on a conviction for dangerous driving the trial judge imposed a sentence of 18 months' probation plus the application of the electronic monitoring program for approximately five months: *R v. Pearman*, delivered November 5, 1990 [since reported 26 MVR (2d) 1, 11 WCB (2d) 430].

[8] In *Pearman*, it was decided that the monitoring device did not provide a suitable penalty and a term of six months should have been imposed. The concern was expressed by the court in the following manner [at 3-4 (MVR)]:

> We note at the outset that the respondent was charged with dangerous driving, a serious offence which resulted in serious injury and damage to the victim. In our opinion, a suspended sentence and imposition of terms under the intensive probation supervision/electronic monitoring program was inappropriate in the circumstances of the case. The sentence failed to take into account the factor of deterrence and public confidence in the administration of justice. This Court recently stated in *R v. Powell* (1989), 19 MVR (2d) 36, 52 CCC (3d) 403, 81 Sask. R 301 [at 43 (MVR)]:
>
> > [I]n a crime of this nature, the factor of deterrence must be given adequate consideration. If the sentence adequately emphasizes community disapproval of such conduct by branding it reprehensible, one can hope that it will have a moral and educative effect on the attitude of the public. Not only will the offender refrain from repeating such conduct, but perhaps some other members of the public will appreciate the seriousness of such conduct.
>
> In our opinion, a sentence of 6 months' imprisonment is the minimum imprisonment that should have been imposed in these circumstances.

[9] We are obviously proceeding through the early stages of the electronic monitoring program. It is impossible to say how effective it may become and the extent of its application. It would be unfortunate for this court to set firm and absolute standards for the application of the program in its developmental stage, but at the same time it is quite appropriate to be somewhat cautious in our approach to its implementation. This is particularly so when others have incurred the penalty of institutional incarceration and no special circumstances have been shown to exist for the application of the program in this case, other than the fact the respondent is a temperamentally suitable candidate.

[10] This court has shown its concern about the harmful social consequences of the drug trade and the need to have special concern for the concept of general deterrence in order that everyone may be aware there is no easy way to experiment with the profits available from the sale of drugs. It is not sufficiently clear that the use of this program, in circumstances such as exist here, will adequately continue that message. This concern is consistent with that expressed in *R v. Pearman*.

[11] In the circumstances, this appeal is allowed. A sentence of nine months would ordinarily have been the minimum we would have imposed, but as a period of three months has already been spent with the program, the sentence is set at six months. The question of equivalency was discussed, and Crown counsel seemed generally to accept that it was reasonable to allow a month for a month, and we see no reason in this case to provide otherwise.

[12] The above represents, in a general way, the oral judgment delivered after the hearing. However, upon further reflection, the panel expresses its concern that if the courts are to play the dominant role in determining when this form of punishment is to be adopted, as may well be necessary and appropriate, then more help must be provided to the courts to enable the formulation of appropriate general criteria and the application

of that criteria. A decision as to the suitability of this form of punishment cannot be adequately made without some form of report, such as a pre-sentence report, outlining the basis upon which the recommendation is being made. Obviously, only a small percentage of those convicted of an offence are offered the opportunity of participating in this program. That selection must therefore, in fairness, be carefully made and should not be the result of a haphazard process. On the basis of what was before us, we cannot be assured of much more than the temperamental suitability of the respondent.

Appeal allowed.

R v Bankay
2010 ONCA 799

WINKLER CJO (Sharpe and Karakatsanis JJA concurring):

[1] This is a Crown appeal relating to sentence. The respondent pleaded guilty to aggravated assault. She had a history of conflict with the victim and bit off part of the victim's finger during a fight on school grounds.

[2] We agree with the appellant that the trial judge erred by imposing what amounted to a disguised conditional sentence. After indicating that she intended to impose a conditional sentence, the trial judge was informed by counsel that a conditional sentence was excluded as this was a serious personal injury offence. The trial judge then made a probation order with a term that imposed to 6 months of house arrest. It was an error of law to impose a sentence that circumvented Parliament's decision to exclude conditional sentences for this offence.

[3] A custodial term was required in the circumstances. In arriving at an appropriate sentence, we must take into account that we are dealing with a youthful first offender who has served 5 months and one week of house arrest. In the circumstances, we impose a sentence of 21 days custody to be served intermittently to allow her to continue with her studies. We maintain the other terms of probation order imposed by the trial judge.

[4] Leave to appeal sentence is granted and the sentence is varied accordingly.

In *R v Shoker*, 2006 SCC 44, [2006] 2 SCR 399, discussed above, LeBel J (Bastarache J concurring), in his dissenting discussion, discussed the potential utility and permissibility of various monitoring methods under the residual clause, commenting:

[37] [A] narrow interpretation of the residual clause would cast doubt on a number of useful monitoring methods, which sentencing judges appear to be resorting to with increasing frequency. For example, it might prevent the use of electronic monitoring, which allows probation officers or public authorities to make sure that conditions relating to house arrest or curfews are complied with. I note that a number of judges have found such conditions to be valid:

The conclusion is that section 732.1(3)(h) allows orders which restrict a defendant's lifestyle, such as curfews, orders that he or she not frequent specified places, or associate with specified persons, *or orders that a defendant be confined on electronic monitoring.*

• • •

The terms of probation can control the defendant's lifestyle. For example, *a defendant might be ... ordered to wear an electronic monitoring device ... .*

• • •

Thus, *curfews, house arrest (with or without electronic monitoring), bed checks ... etc., can all be appropriate "other conditions." It does not matter whether one sees them as reha-bilitative measures, control measures, or punishment.* What counts is not the label but an intent that the condition should further public protection or the acceptance of the defendant in the community, and some reasonable grounds for belief that it will have a tendency to effect those purposes. [Emphasis added.]

(T.W. Ferris, *Sentencing: Practical Approaches* (2005), at pp. 79, 116 and 216–17)

Ferris reports that the courts in the following cases held that electronic monitoring is lawful under s. 732.1(3)(h) : *R v. Carlson* (1996), 141 Sask. R 168 (CA); *R v. Curtis* (1996), 144 Sask. R 156 (CA); *R v. McLeod* (1992), 109 Sask. R 8 (CA).

Do you agree? Is the use of electronic monitoring or home confinement as a term of proba-tion consistent with the general restriction on the scope of optional conditions (to exclude conditions imposed for punitive purposes)? Does the inclusion of these types of terms in probation orders effectively convert such orders into conditional sentences or circumvent the new restrictions on the availability of conditional sentences for certain offences? For a dis-cussion of these issues, see *R v DESM* (1993), 80 CCC (3d) 371 (BCCA); *R v Bankay*, 2010 ONCA 799; and *R v Myette*, 2013 ABCA 371, 561 AR 321. See also the court's decision in *R v Voong*, 2015 BCCA 285, 325 CCC (3d) 267, in Chapter 12, Conditional Sentence of Imprisonment.

F. Banishment

R v Rowe
(2006), 212 CCC (3d) 254 (Ont CA)

SHARPE JA:

[1] The appellant was convicted of one count of criminal harassment of his former common-law partner contrary to s. 264(2)(b) of the *Criminal Code*. This was his third offence involving the same victim. He was sentenced to thirty days concurrent to an existing sentence. He was also sentenced to three years probation, also concurrent with an existing probation order. The sentencing judge imposed the following probation condi-tion: "Forthwith or in any event within two weeks of release leave the province of Ontario immediately."

[2] The appellant appeals both conviction and sentence. I see no merit in the convic-tion appeal. In my view, the reasons of the trial judge provide an adequate explanation of the basis for rejecting the appellant's evidence and for entering a conviction.

[3] The appellant submits that the trial judge erred in law by imposing a term of probation that amounts to banishment. In his reasons for sentence, the sentencing judge stated that he did not consider this "to be an injudicious exile" because the appellant had stated that he wanted to end his relationship with the victim and that upon release he intended to leave the jurisdiction and return to the Maritimes. The sentencing judge added that this was a serious offence and that the appellant's "continuation within a community such as Napanee/ Kingston area, in Ontario, will cause [the victim and her children] to be constantly in fear

of his presence." The sentencing judge added that it would be open to the appellant to apply to vary the condition if he received employment in some other part of Ontario.

[4] The appellant submits that banishment from Ontario cannot be justified as a condition of the probation order under s. 732.1(3) (h) ... .

[5] As the *Criminal Code* specifies that conditions of probation should facilitate "the offender's successful reintegration into the community," banishment remains the exception rather than the rule. It has been said on more than one occasion that banishment orders "should not be encouraged": see *R v. Malboeuf* (1982), 68 CCC (2d) 544 (Sask. CA) at 547; *R v. Williams*, [1997] BCJ No. 2101 (QL) at para. 9, 36 WCB (2d) 79 (BCCA). As a member of the Manitoba Court of Appeal, Dickson JA frowned on the practice of banishment in *R v. Fuller*, [1969] 3 CCC 348 at 351:

> In Canada communities are interdependent and relations between them should be marked by mutual respect and understanding. A practice whereby one community seeks to rid itself of undesirables by foisting them off on other communities violates this basic concept of consideration for the rights of others and should not be tolerated.

[6] On the other hand, orders banishing an offender from a specific community have been made against estranged spouses with a view to protecting the victim or to assisting with the offender's rehabilitation: see e.g. *R v. Stack*, [1998] BCJ No. 1492 (QL), 39 WCB (2d) 79 (BCCA); *R v. Peyton*, [1996] N.J. No. 120 (QL), 30 WCB (2d) 561 (Nfld. SC).

[7] Plainly, the larger the ambit of the banishment, the more difficult the order will be to justify. In *R v. Brooks*, [2005] OJ No. 105 (QL), this court upheld a probation term excluding the appellant from Muskoka, but, at para. 1, the court stated that it did so "given the appellant's avowed intention to leave that area as a step in his rehabilitative process." Banishment from an entire province is an extreme measure that could be justified only in exceptional circumstances, even in cases of domestic violence. The only case I have been able to uncover that upholds banishment from a province is *R v. Banks*, [1991] BCJ No. 424 (QL), 12 WCB (2d) 279, where the British Columbia Court of Appeal upheld such an order specifically on the ground that the appellant had proposed and consented to the condition. On the other hand, in a case similar to the one at bar, *R v. Stulac* (1983), 63 N.S.R. (2d) 357, at para. 5, the Nova Scotia Court of Appeal struck down a condition requiring an offender who had committed an offence against his domestic partner to leave the province for the term of his probation as "unnecessary to accomplish the purpose of keeping the appellant away from the victim."

[8] In my view, the probation term requiring the appellant to leave Ontario upon his release from prison cannot be justified as a reasonable measure for the protection of society. Moreover, banishment from the province far exceeds what is required to protect the victim. I note that the offence in the present case involved communications by telephone and mail. Banishment to another province will not effectively protect the victim from repetitions of that conduct and less drastic restrictions will protect the victim from other forms of harassment. Banishment from the province would be contrary to the second factor mentioned in s. 732.1(3)(h), "facilitating the offender's successful reintegration into the community." As neither of the factors specified in s. 732.1(3)(h) are present, the term cannot be justified as a reasonable condition and must be set aside.

[9] As this issue can be decided on the wording of s. 732.1(3)(h), it is not necessary for me to consider whether the order also constituted a violation of the appellant's mobility

rights under s. 6(2) of the *Canadian Charter of Rights and Freedoms* and I leave that question for another day.

. . .

Conviction appeal dismissed; sentence appeal allowed.

Although the court analyzed the propriety of the banishment condition solely on the basis of s 732.1(3)(h) of the *Criminal Code*, are there other narrower conditions that might be applicable in the circumstances and achieve the same effect? What types of conditions amount to "banishment" as discussed by the court? For further discussion of this type of probationary condition, see Allan Manson, *The Law of Sentencing* (Toronto: Irwin, 2001) at 234-39; *R v White*, 2015 BCSC 2383; and *R v Corby*, 2016 ONCA 40. For discussion on whether banishment infringes the Charter, see *R v Adam*, 2014 BCSC 1943.

VI. BREACH OF PROBATION

Some attention has been paid to the meaning of breaching the peace for the purposes of a probation order. In *R v Grey* (1993), 19 CR (4th) 363 (Ont Prov Div), it was held that a failure to keep the peace required at least an apprehended breach of municipal, provincial, or federal law and not some lesser standard of disruption. This was also the view of the Newfoundland Court of Appeal in *R v R (D)* (1999), 138 CCC (3d) 405 (Nfld CA); see also *R v Griffin*, 2013 ONCJ 811 at paras 33-52, reviewing the more recent case law and concluding that "a failure to be of good behaviour must involve a breach of a legal obligation created in legislation." In *R v Greco* (2001), 159 CCC (3d) 146 (Ont CA), the court upheld a ruling that an offender who breaches the peace abroad can still be tried for breach of probation in Canada. The court rejected the suggestion that keeping the peace was restricted to the Queen's peace in Canada. For comparison of procedures on breach of probation and breach of a conditional sentence, see Chapter 12.

When probation accompanies a suspended sentence, theoretically it is the passing of sentence that is suspended. Accordingly, s 732.2(5) of the Code provides a framework for dealing with a prisoner who, while bound by a probation order, is convicted of another offence, including the offence of non-compliance with a probation order. This can include imposing "any sentence that could have been imposed if the passing of sentence had not been suspended." Courts sometimes refer to the possibility of revocation and sentencing for the original offence as the "sword of Damocles" because it hangs over the offender until the completion of probation and thus provides some deterrent effect on the offender and others: see e.g. *R v Voong*, 2015 BCCA 285 at paras 37-43. However, as a practical reality, this procedure is rarely used in most jurisdictions. The usual response in cases of probation breach or new offences is to commence a prosecution under s 733.1. This is a hybrid offence, which, upon indictment, can lead to a sentence of up to two years or a maximum of 18 months upon summary conviction. (For cases where revocation was sought and granted, see *R v Blanchard*, 2009 YKCA 15; and *R v Patrick*, 2013 BCCA 321.) The revocation procedure in s 732.2(5) of the Code is also skeletal in the sense that it is triggered "on application of the prosecutor." Although decided under the predecessor legislation, as discussed below, fairness requires more.

R v Tuckey
(1977), 34 CCC (2d) 572 (Ont CA)

DUBIN JA:

On June 26, 1974, the appellant was given a suspended sentence and placed on probation for a period of three years by His Honour Judge Street, after pleading guilty to a charge of theft. On February 12, 1976, while in custody with respect to other matters, he was brought before the trial Judge. He was given no notice as to the nature of the proceedings which were to be held on that day.

• • •

Although the present *Criminal Code* does not require the formalities of an information and is silent as to procedure, I am satisfied that the basic principles of natural justice must prevail; one of which principles relevant here is that no man shall be condemned unless he has been given prior notice of the allegations against him and a fair opportunity to make full answer and defence.

In a proceeding under s. 664(4), although there is no longer a requirement for an information on oath, the minimum requirement surely must be that the accused before being brought before the tribunal should be given reasonable notice in writing of the Crown's intention to take such proceedings, which notice should clearly articulate the nature of the proceedings, the grounds upon which the Crown intends to rely in support of its application, the nature of the order sought, and the hearing date. Section 664(5) provides for the procedure which may be followed in bringing the accused before the Court.

In the instant case no such notice was given. The appellant had no opportunity to defend himself. Section 664(4) gives the Court that made the probation order a broad discretion as to the appropriate order to be made on an application brought pursuant to that section. The inquiry is not limited to proof of the violation of any condition in the probation order. It follows that the trial Judge had no right in the circumstances of this case to refuse the appellant his request for an adjournment to obtain counsel. It is to be noted that the appellant's ultimate acquiescence that the proceedings should continue was given *in terrorem*.

• • •

The appellant had pleaded guilty to a charge of theft. He had a prior criminal record, but the trial Judge originally thought it appropriate to suspend the passing of sentence and make an order for three years' probation. The appellant breached his probation, and an application under s. 664(4) was in order. By his conduct the appellant had forfeited his right to leniency. The function of the trial Judge was then to impose a sentence proportionate to the offence which the appellant had committed. The sentence of 30 months was not proportionate to that offence, even when it was imposed upon a person who was not entitled to leniency.

Appeal allowed.

NOTE

If a court revokes a probation order because the offender has committed another offence while on probation, can the court order that any sentence of imprisonment imposed on the original offence be served consecutive to the sentence imposed on the offence that resulted in the revocation of the probation? See *R v Clermont* (1986), 30 CCC (3d) 571 (Qc CA), aff'd [1988] 2 SCR 171.

FURTHER READING

Mair, George. *What Works in Probation* (Cullompton, Devon, UK: Willan, 2004).

Manson, Allan. "Sentencing Options" in *The Law of Sentencing* (Toronto: Irwin Law, 2000) ch 9.

Middlecoat, Karen. "The Probation Officer's Report" in *Criminal Justice in Canada: A Reader* (Toronto: Nelson, 2016) ch 8.

Roberts, Julian V & Suzanne Wallace-Capretta. "Electronic Monitoring and Community Custody in Canada" in R Bas et al, eds, *Electronically Monitored Punishment: Critical Perspectives* (Cullompton, Devon, UK: Willan, 2011).

Taxman, Faye. "Probation, Intermediate Sanctions, and Community-Based Corrections" in J Petersilia & K Reitz, eds, *The Oxford Handbook of Sentencing and Corrections* (New York: Oxford University Press, 2012).

CHAPTER TEN

Monetary Sanctions: Fines, Restitution, and the Victim Surcharge

I. INTRODUCTION

This chapter considers sanctions that involve orders to pay money. A fine is a sanction that uses a monetary burden as a punitive measure. Fines are paid to the state. A fine can be imposed alone or in conjunction with other sanctions. Although the imposition of a fine raises important procedural issues, it also raises fundamental questions about quantum. The amount of the monetary burden imposed depends on the financial resources and income-earning abilities of the offender.

Restitution refers to a monetary order intended to compensate for certain kinds of loss occasioned by the offence. These amounts are paid to the victims. Restitution orders are typically imposed in addition to other sanctions. As with the imposition of fines, the courts are often concerned with ensuring that any restitution order made does not exceed the offender's financial capabilities.

Finally, in addition to any other punishment imposed, all offenders are required to pay a victim surcharge. These amounts are intended to be used by provincial and territorial governments to fund programs to assist victims of crime. Unlike a fine or restitution order, the victim surcharge is mandatory, and there is a minimum amount payable regardless of an offender's financial circumstances. As discussed below, the recent removal of any discretion in relation to the imposition of the victim surcharge has created controversy.

In reviewing the cases and materials in this chapter, consider the different penological aims of these provisions. In determining whether a fine or restitution should be imposed, and the amount that is appropriate, have the courts properly distinguished between fines and restitution orders? Do ss 718 to 718.3 of the *Criminal Code*, RSC 1985, c C-46, as amended, lend any assistance to this analysis? What role, if any, does the mandatory victim surcharge play in determining the appropriateness of imposing a fine or restitution order, or the amount of such an order? What is the exact nature of the victim surcharge? How does it relate to other sentencing provisions and, in particular, to the traditional view that a fine can be coupled with probation or imprisonment, but not with both? Should Parliament give back to sentencing judges the discretion to waive in appropriate cases the imposition of the victim surcharge?

II. THE FINE

A. The Public Attitude to Fines

Fines are a common form of sentence, particularly for less serious offences. In 2013-14, for example, a fine was imposed in 30 percent of adult criminal court cases involving a guilty plea, with the median fine being $600: see Statistics Canada, "Adult Criminal Court Statistics in Canada, 2013/2014," by Ashley Maxwell, in *Juristat* 35:1, Catalogue No 85-002-X (Ottawa: Statistics Canada, 2015) at 10. This comprised 67,555 cases out of the total of 228,328 cases. The range of fines imposed in 2013-14 was as follows:

Amount of Fine	Number of Cases
$1 to $100	9,196
$101 to $300	14,133
$301 to $500	7,745
$501 to $1,000	14,908
$1,001 to $50,000,000	17,077
Amount Unknown	4,496
Total Cases	67,555

See CANSIM Table 252-0062, "Adult Criminal Courts, Guilty Cases by Amount of Fine, Annual (Number)" (accessed 7 February 2016).

Although a common form of sanction, historically at least, most Canadians do not believe a monetary penalty is "punishment." Before examining the relevant statutory provisions, it is therefore useful to consider how the Canadian public views fines as a sanction. Does this view correspond to the principles of sentencing set out in *Criminal Code* s 718.2 and, in particular, the principle of restraint set out in ss 718.2(d) and (e)?

Anthony N Doob & Voula Marinos, "Reconceptualizing Punishment:
Understanding the Limitations on the Use of Intermediate Sanctions"
(1995) 2 U Chicago L Sch Roundtable 413 at 429-33 (footnotes omitted)

B. The Limits on the Use of the Fine:
A Case Study of the Limits on Interchangeability

Canada makes heavy use of fines. In fact, fines are the most heavily used disposition in Canadian criminal courts. The Canadian Sentencing Commission ... recommended increased use of fines and suggested that a day or unit fine system be developed. Interestingly, however, the Canadian Sentencing Commission never addressed itself to the purposes that fines might or might not be able to serve *at* sentencing. In particular, ... it did not explore directly the limits on the use of intermediate punishments generally or the fine in particular. ... [It] saw all punishments as more or less qualitatively similar. This view of the simplicity of punishments was consistent with some very specific Canadian data on the community service order that had been carried out a few years earlier.

In a national public opinion poll, Canadian adults were asked what they thought the most appropriate sentence was for a first-time offender convicted of breaking and entering a private home and stealing property worth $250. They were given various traditional choices: probation, fines, imprisonment, or some combination. Twenty-nine percent chose imprisonment. When these respondents were asked whether instead of imprisonment, they would favor a community service order, almost everyone (90 percent) indicated they would favor it at least sometimes. Forty-one percent would prefer the community service order in all or most cases. An additional 36 percent would want it for "some" cases, with 14 percent favoring it "only in very rare cases."

We and others interpreted these findings to mean that Canadians, in general, support the use of intermediate punishments instead of imprisonment. Perhaps we were partially correct. However, it may simply be wrong that one can automatically substitute any convenient intermediate punishment such as a fine or community service for imprisonment when looking for a way to avoid using prison. Even if true, presumably there are limits: the size of the penalty has to be appropriate, and of course, ... the penalty must be imposed, and not just pronounced.

Some data recently collected by one of the authors of this Article suggest that the world is not so simple. In this study, a heterogeneous sample of people in Toronto answered a series of questions about fines. A number of conceptually separate sub-studies were embedded in the survey questionnaire. First, respondents were asked to think about a sentence handed down for a minor shoplifting charge. The sentence was described, for different groups of respondents, as being either a fine of two hundred dollars or four hundred dollars, or a prison sentence of four or eight days. The respondents viewed imprisonment as considerably more effective than fines in "expressing society's disapproval for the harm that was caused." At least as interesting is that the size of the penalty (within the rather constrained limits used in this experiment) did not make any difference in the perceived denunciatory value of the penalty. However, for both fines and imprisonment, those who had the sentence described to them as involving the higher penalty rated this penalty as being more severe. The results, then, do not appear to be a product of simple differences in perceived severity; if they had been, the results of the denunciatory value of the punishment would be parallel to those of the severity of the punishment.

In the experiment, harsher penalties were seen as being more severe, but imprisonment was seen as having a greater denunciatory value than fines. There appears to be something "special" about imprisonment that fines do not possess. Nevertheless, most of the respondents favored the use of a fine as a punishment for the offense. About 19 percent of the respondents saw a fine or imprisonment as being equally appropriate; about two-thirds of those who differentiated between fines and imprisonment favored the fine. Although the two types of penalties have different denunciatory values in the eyes of the respondents, denunciation cannot be too important, since respondents favor the use of the punishment that is not as able to "express society's disapproval for the harm that was caused."

Respondents were additionally asked whether they thought that "first time offenders who have committed the following offenses [should be given] a fine instead of imprisonment." If they thought that a fine was appropriate, they were to indicate the dollar value of the fine that they would recommend. Respondents could set the fine, then, at any amount they thought appropriate. In terms of severity, the sky was the limit.

The data ... demonstrate the limited acceptability of the fine. Even when respondents could set a fine of any size, they were generally unwilling to substitute a fine for imprisonment for minor violent offenses. They were, however, willing to suggest a fine as a substitute for imprisonment for most property offenses, even when the value of the property taken is relatively high. Imprisonment can, of course, be used to incapacitate an offender. Hence it is theoretically possible that respondents may have preferred imprisonment for those convicted of violent offenses in order to accomplish this goal. ...

· · ·

There is a final piece of evidence showing that fines had a meaning different from imprisonment. Respondents answered a series of questions in which they were asked to imagine that a particular sentence of imprisonment (expressed in months) was appropriate. They were asked whether they would find a fine of so many months of take-home income as an appropriate substitute. Half of the respondents were told what the cost of imprisonment would be. The critical issue here was whether respondents were affected in their decision by having the cost of imprisonment made salient. It turns out, once again, that the results were offense-specific. For the theft that was described, but not for minor assaults, mentioning the cost of imprisonment led the respondent to favor a fine. Despite being presented with the cost of imprisonment, fines were still viewed as being more appropriate for minor property offenses rather than minor instances of violence.

B. Criminal Code, Sections 734 to 736

The following sections of the *Criminal Code* are concerned with the applicability and enforceability of fines, including the use of imprisonment in default of payment. In 1996, substantial amendments were made to the fine provisions. These amendments authorized the use of a fine for any offence, either in addition to or in lieu of any punishment other than a minimum term of imprisonment: see s 734(1), and required courts to inquire into an offender's ability to pay before imposing a fine other than a minimum fine: see s 734(2) and the earlier decision in *R v Snider* (1977), 37 CCC (2d) 189 (Ont CA), adopting this approach before it was legislatively required.

Although s 734, the main section relating to fines, is straightforward, the ability to impose a fine in addition to another type of punishment has historically been understood to be limited by s 731(1)(b), relating to the making of probation orders: see discussion below. In addition, the fine provisions become complex in their response to defaults after an offender has been ordered to pay a fine. As currently enacted the fine provisions read as follows:

Power of court to impose fine

734(1) Subject to subsection (2), a court that convicts a person, other than an organization, of an offence may fine the offender by making an order under section 734.1

(a) if the punishment for the offence does not include a minimum term of imprisonment, in addition to or in lieu of any other sanction that the court is authorized to impose; or

(b) if the punishment for the offence includes a minimum term of imprisonment, in addition to any other sanction that the court is required or authorized to impose.

(2) Except when the punishment for an offence includes a minimum fine or a fine is imposed in lieu of a forfeiture order, a court may fine an offender under this section only if the court is satisfied that the offender is able to pay the fine or discharge it under section 736.

(3) For the purposes of this section and sections 734.1 to 737, a person is in default of payment of a fine if the fine has not been paid in full by the time set out in the order made under section 734.1.

(4) Where an offender is fined under this section, a term of imprisonment, determined in accordance with subsection (5), shall be deemed to be imposed in default of payment of the fine.

(5) The term of imprisonment referred to in subsection (4) is the lesser of

(a) the number of days that corresponds to a fraction, rounded down to the nearest whole number, of which

(i) the numerator is the unpaid amount of the fine plus the costs and charges of committing and conveying the defaulter to prison, calculated in accordance with regulations made under subsection (7), and

(ii) the denominator is equal to eight times the provincial minimum hourly wage, at the time of default, in the province in which the fine was imposed, and

(b) the maximum term of imprisonment that the court could itself impose on conviction or, if the punishment for the offence does not include a term of imprisonment, five years in the case of an indictable offence or six months in the case of a summary conviction offence.

(6) All or any part of a fine imposed under this section may be taken out of moneys found in the possession of the offender at the time of the arrest of the offender if the court making the order, on being satisfied that ownership of or right to possession of those moneys is not disputed by claimants other than the offender, so directs.

(7) The lieutenant governor in council of a province may make regulations respecting the calculation of the costs and charges referred to in subparagraph (5)(a)(i) and in paragraph 734.8(1)(b).

(8) This section and sections 734.1 to 734.8 and 736 apply to a fine imposed under any Act of Parliament, except that subsections (4) and (5) do not apply if the term of imprisonment in default of payment of the fine provided for in that Act or regulations is

(a) calculated by a different method; or

(b) specified, either as a minimum or a maximum.

Terms of order imposing fine

734.1 A court that fines an offender under section 734 shall do so by making an order that clearly sets out

(a) the amount of the fine;

(b) the manner in which the fine is to be paid;

(c) the time or times by which the fine, or any portion thereof, must be paid; and

(d) such other terms respecting the payment of the fine as the court deems appropriate.

Obligations of court

734.2(1) A court that makes an order under section 734.1 shall

(a) cause a copy of the order to be given to the offender;

(b) explain the substance of sections 734 to 734.8 and 736 to the offender;

(c) cause an explanation to be given to the offender of the procedure for applying under section 734.3 for a change to the optional conditions and of any available fine option programs referred to in section 736 as well as the procedure to apply for admission to them; and

(d) take reasonable measures to ensure that the offender understands the order and the explanations.

(2) For greater certainty, a failure to comply with subsection (1) does not affect the validity of the order.

Change in terms of order

734.3 A court that makes an order under section 734.1, or a person designated either by name or by title of office by that court, may, on application by or on behalf of the offender, subject to any rules made by the court under section 482 or 482.1, change any term of the order except the amount of the fine, and any reference in this section and sections 734, 734.1, 734.2 and 734.6 to an order shall be read as including a reference to the order as changed under this section.

· · ·

Licences, permits, etc.

734.5 If an offender is in default of payment of a fine,

(a) where the proceeds of the fine belong to Her Majesty in right of a province by virtue of subsection 734.4(1), the person responsible, by or under an Act of the legislature of the province, for issuing, renewing or suspending a licence, permit or other similar instrument in relation to the offender may refuse to issue or renew or may suspend the licence, permit or other instrument until the fine is paid in full, proof of which lies on the offender; or

(b) where the proceeds of the fine belong to Her Majesty in right of Canada by virtue of subsection 734.4(2), the person responsible, by or under an Act of Parliament, for issuing or renewing a licence, permit or other similar instrument in relation to the offender may refuse to issue or renew or may suspend the licence, permit or other instrument until the fine is paid in full, proof of which lies on the offender.

Civil enforcement of fines, forfeiture

734.6(1) Where

(a) an offender is in default of payment of a fine, or

(b) a forfeiture imposed by law is not paid as required by the order imposing it,

then, in addition to any other method provided by law for recovering the fine or forfeiture,

(c) the Attorney General of the province to whom the proceeds of the fine or forfeiture belong, or

(d) the Attorney General of Canada, where the proceeds of the fine or forfeiture belong to Her Majesty in right of Canada,

may, by filing the order, enter as a judgment the amount of the fine or forfeiture, and costs, if any, in any civil court in Canada that has jurisdiction to enter a judgment for that amount.

(2) An order that is entered as a judgment under this section is enforceable in the same manner as if it were a judgment obtained by the Attorney General of the province or the Attorney General of Canada, as the case may be, in civil proceedings.

Warrant of committal

734.7(1) Where time has been allowed for payment of a fine, the court shall not issue a warrant of committal in default of payment of the fine

(a) until the expiration of the time allowed for payment of the fine in full; and

(b) unless the court is satisfied

(i) that the mechanisms provided by sections 734.5 and 734.6 are not appropriate in the circumstances, or

(ii) that the offender has, without reasonable excuse, refused to pay the fine or discharge it under section 736.

(2) Where no time has been allowed for payment of a fine and a warrant committing the offender to prison for default of payment of the fine is issued, the court shall state in the warrant the reason for immediate committal.

(2.1) The period of imprisonment in default of payment of the fine shall be specified in a warrant of committal referred to in subsection (1) or (2).

. . .

(4) The imprisonment of an offender for default of payment of a fine terminates the operation of sections 734.5 and 734.6 in relation to that fine.

. . .

Fines on organizations

735(1) An organization that is convicted of an offence is liable, in lieu of any imprisonment that is prescribed as punishment for that offence, to be fined in an amount, except where otherwise provided by law,

(a) that is in the discretion of the court, where the offence is an indictable offence; or

(b) not exceeding one hundred thousand dollars, where the offence is a summary conviction offence.

(1.1) A court that imposes a fine under subsection (1) or under any other Act of Parliament shall make an order that clearly sets out

(a) the amount of the fine;

(b) the manner in which the fine is to be paid;

(c) the time or times by which the fine, or any portion of it, must be paid; and

(d) any other terms respecting the payment of the fine that the court deems appropriate.

(2) Section 734.6 applies, with any modifications that are required, when an organization fails to pay the fine in accordance with the terms of the order.

Fine option program

736(1) An offender who is fined under section 734 may, whether or not the offender is serving a term of imprisonment imposed in default of payment of the fine, discharge the fine in whole or in part by earning credits for work performed during a period not greater than two years in a program established for that purpose by the lieutenant governor in council

(a) of the province in which the fine was imposed, or

(b) of the province in which the offender resides, where an appropriate agreement is in effect between the government of that province and the government of the province in which the fine was imposed,

if the offender is admissible to such a program.

(2) A program referred to in subsection (1) shall determine the rate at which credits are earned and may provide for the manner of crediting any amounts earned against the fine and any other matters necessary for or incidental to carrying out the program.

(3) Credits earned for work performed as provided by subsection (1) shall, for the purposes of this Act, be deemed to be payment in respect of a fine.

(4) Where, by virtue of subsection 734.4(2), the proceeds of a fine belong to Her Majesty in right of Canada, an offender may discharge the fine in whole or in part in a fine option program of a province pursuant to subsection (1), where an appropriate agreement is in effect between the government of the province and the Government of Canada.

C. The Ability to Impose a Fine

As already noted, the current provisions address a number of situations that presented problems in the past. One anachronism required that a fine could be imposed for a sentence punishable by more than five years' imprisonment *only* if it was imposed *in addition to* a term of imprisonment. To satisfy this peculiar requirement, the courts were forced to impose ludicrous one-day prison sentences. This charade saw the offender enter into custody, only to be released moments later. Section 734(1) now authorizes the use of a fine for any offence, either in addition to or in lieu of another punishment (other than a mandatory sentence of imprisonment).

An issue that has not been resolved, at least as yet, is whether a court may impose a fine in addition to *both* imprisonment and probation. Traditionally the predominant view, based in part on the language of s 731(1)(b), but also on the principle of restraint, was that a sentencing court could impose a fine and *either* imprisonment or probation, but not both: see e.g. *R v St James* (1981), 20 CR (3d) 389 (Qc CA); *R v Kelly* (1995), 104 CCC (3d) 95 (Nfld CA); *R v Biron* (1991), 65 CCC (3d) 221 (Qc CA); *R v Wright* (1982), 8 WCB 120 (BCCA); *R v Blacquière* (1975), 24 CCC (2d) 168 (Ont CA); *R v Lindsay* (1986), 76 NSR (2d) 361 (CA); but see *R v Cartier* (1990), 57 CCC (3d) 569 (Qc CA); see also TW Ferris, "The Legality of Imposing a Fine, Imprisonment and Probation at the Same Time" (1996) 38 Crim LQ 277. This issue is now being revisited, largely because of amendments that removed all discretion from the courts in relation to the imposition of the victim surcharge. Most recently, in *R c Cloud*, 2016 QCCA 567, the court concluded that there is no impediment in principle to the joinder of probation, imprisonment, and a fine, provided that the sentence as a whole is consistent with the totality principle and is not in the result disproportionate. The ability of a court to impose a fine, imprisonment, and probation is considered in more detail in Section E, "Victim Surcharge," below.

D. The Ability to Pay a Fine

An issue that has been resolved by the current provisions is the obligation of sentencing courts, other than in cases that require the imposition of a minimum fine, to inquire into an offender's ability to pay: see s 734(2). The importance of considering the financial means of the offender is apparent in the light of enforcement provisions. Fines that are beyond the means of an offender may turn into de facto prison terms because of the enforcement mechanism of imprisonment in default. It is therefore critical that, at the "front end" of the process when the fine is actually imposed, it does not exceed the means of the offender. Even small fines may be beyond the means of some people. Although s 736 provides for the creation of "fine option programs" that allow offenders to discharge their fines by earning credits for work performed while in the program, such programs do not exist in Ontario, British Columbia, or Newfoundland and Labrador. As well, each program has its own eligibility criteria and the program may not be available in all parts of a province or territory: see Donna Calverley & Karen Beattie, *Community Corrections in Canada, 2004*, Catalogue No 85-567-XIE (Ottawa: Statistics Canada, 2005) at 9-10. The risk of imprisonment in default of payment thus raises the anachronistic spectre of "debtor's prison." Yet, surely, incarceration should be a response to the offender's criminal conduct, not to his or her financial status.

The 1996 amendments dramatically changed the mechanism for dealing with fine defaults. First, s 734(5) provides a formula for calculating the extent of imprisonment in default that, pursuant to s 734(4), is "deemed to be imposed." Does this mean that a judge has no discretion to refuse to add default time? Second, pursuant to s 734.7(1), a court cannot issue a warrant for committal unless it is satisfied that the alternative collection steps provided for in the Code are not appropriate or the offender has, "without reasonable excuse," refused to pay the fine or participate in a fine option program. Do these sections allow an offender who simply cannot afford to pay a fine to be imprisoned for default of payment?

In *R v Wu*, the Supreme Court of Canada considered these issues in the context of deciding whether a conditional sentence could be imposed on an impecunious offender in default of payment of a mandatory minimum fine. We consider conditional sentences in detail in Chapter 12, Conditional Sentence of Imprisonment. Here, we focus on the court's reasons for rejecting the use of a conditional sentence in such circumstances and its comments on the process that must be followed before a court can order an offender imprisoned for default of payment of a fine.

R v Wu
2003 SCC 73, [2003] 3 SCR 530

BINNIE J (McLachlin CJ and Gonthier, Iacobucci, Major, Bastarache, Arbour, and LeBel JJ concurring):

[1] In this appeal we are asked to consider whether a conditional sentence was validly imposed on the respondent offender for possession of contraband cigarettes. The offender might otherwise have been sent to jail for 30 days for non-payment of a mandatory $9,600 fine. In the trial judge's view, jail was not appropriate for this offender. On the other hand, the offender simply had no means to pay the fine. The trial judge thought a conditional sentence to be served by the offender in his home offered a way to avoid jail. I agree with the trial judge's initial conclusion that this was not an appropriate case for jail. I disagree with his sentencing solution. The *Criminal Code*, RSC 1985, c. C-46, properly interpreted, offered the sentencing judge a range of alternative solutions for this offender but a conditional sentence was not amongst them.

[2] Debtors' prison for impoverished people is a Dickensian concept that in civilized countries has largely been abolished. Imprisonment for civil debt was abolished in Ontario by the end of the 19th century. In its 1996 sentencing reforms, Parliament decreed that jail should be reserved for those whose conduct deserves to put them there. Here, the trial judge thought a fit sentence would be a suspended sentence with probation, but this was not possible under the Act. Yet debtors' prison "in the community," which is what a conditional sentence amounts to, is repugnant in the case of an individual who is undeserving of jail yet who simply cannot pay.

[3] ... [T]he purpose of imposing imprisonment in default of payment is to give serious encouragement to offenders with the means to pay a fine to make payment. Genuine inability to pay a fine is not a proper basis for imprisonment. A conditional sentence is a form of imprisonment. Therefore, a conditional sentence is not an appropriate sentence to impose on an offender simply because he or she has no means to pay a fine. Nothing in the Code authorises a conditional sentence to be used for collection purposes. Unless, in the terms of s. 734.7(1), the Crown can establish that a defaulter has "without reasonable excuse, refused to pay," a warrant of committal should not be issued.

[4] The conditions precedent to the imposition of a conditional sentence were accordingly not met. The sentencing judge commented that "hard cases make bad law and this is a hard case." In my view, with respect, it also made bad law. I would allow the appeal.

I. Facts

[5] The respondent, Yu Wu, was convicted of possession of 300 cartons of contraband cigarettes. The *Excise Act*, RSC 1985, c. E-14, s. 240(1.1)(a)(i), carried a minimum penalty of $0.16 per cigarette, which amounted to $9,600. ...

• • •

III. Analysis

[16] The principles of sentencing include Parliament's direction that "an offender should not be deprived of liberty, if less restrictive sanctions may be appropriate in the circumstances," and "all available sanctions *other than imprisonment* that are reasonable in the circumstances should be considered for all offenders" (s. 718.2(d) and (e) of the Code (emphasis added)).

[17] Applying these principles, the trial judge concluded very firmly that the respondent should not go to jail for what was seen as a relatively minor role in this cigarette smuggling operation. The respondent did not bring the goods across the border. He had no previous record for such an offence. He was no danger to the community. He was the sole support for his teenage daughter. Yet, in default of payment of a mandatory minimum $9,600 fine, which the judge believed the respondent had no ability to pay, he felt obliged to consider a significant period of incarceration. ... The judge found he retained a discretion [as to the length of the default period] and would have sentenced the respondent to 30 days in jail in default of payment were a conditional sentence not an available option.

[The statutory formula in s 734(5) of the Code for calculating default periods of imprisonment does not apply to the *Excise Act*. Under that formula, the period of default would have been 174 days.]

[18] That said, the trial judge concluded that a conditional sentence *was* available. ...

[The trial judge therefore fined the accused $9,600 without time to pay and in default of payment immediately sentenced the accused to a conditional sentence of 75 days to be served in the community.]

[19] ... [T]he Crown argues that the trial judge made an error of law in concluding that a conditional sentence was an available option. I agree.

[20] The Crown has a very practical interest in the subject matter of this appeal. Imprisonment terminates the Crown's power to pursue civil enforcement remedies to collect the money (s. 734.7(4) of the Code). Some individuals with savings in the bank might prefer spending 75 days under house arrest rather than paying $9,600. In this case, however, the evidence is that the respondent's poverty left him with no choice in the matter.

A. *The Mandatory Minimum Fine*

[21] Parliament is quite specific about the range of penalties in s. 240 of the *Excise Act* ... .

[Namely, in relation to an offence punishable on summary conviction, a fine not less than the mandatory minimum required *or* both that fine and imprisonment for two years or less].

[22] The trial judge could, in a proper case, have concluded that a fit sentence would include both the mandatory minimum fine *and* a period of imprisonment. He emphatically decided that imprisonment was not a fit punishment. Indeed, as stated, his preference would have been to impose no more than a suspended sentence with probation. ...

[23] A mandatory minimum fine of $9,600 imposed irrespective of the offender's means to pay is a legislated exception to the usual sentencing principles. Even before the 1996 sentencing reforms, the correct rule was that a fine should be assessed having regard to "the offender's ability to pay" (*R v. Snider* (1977), 37 CCC (2d) 189 (Ont. CA), at p. 190). It was quite open to Parliament to impose a minimum fine, but Parliament's amendments did not require that inability to pay should necessarily land the offender in jail. Indeed, the 1996 amendments show that Parliament did not intend to send the impoverished to jail by reason only of their inability to pay.

B. *Availability of Conditional Sentences*

· · ·

[26] The trial judge's explicit finding that this was a proper case for a suspended sentence and probation, and that imprisonment was *not* warranted, puts this case outside the scope of a conditional sentence. As stated in *Proulx*, at para. 37: "Sentencing judges should always be mindful of the fact that conditional sentences are only to be imposed on offenders who would otherwise have been sent to jail" for the offence that gave rise to the conviction. ...

[27] The statutory conditions precedent to a conditional sentence were not met in two important respects:

  (i) The trial judge, with the best of intentions, stood the *Proulx* reasoning on its head. He was searching for a mechanism to deal with an offence that in his view did *not* warrant imprisonment at all. He thought justice would be served by keeping the respondent, if at all possible, *out* of jail entirely. But the conditional sentencing regime is predicated on a finding in a particular case that jail for less than two years would be a fit sentence. The effect of the trial judge's approach would be to widen the net of the conditional sentencing regime to imprison in their homes offenders under punitive conditions purely on the basis of their inability to pay a fine. ...

  (ii) Conditional sentences are ... a sentencing option, if the conditions precedent are met, for the *original* offence ... . The distinction between sentencing provisions and enforcement of sentences is of long standing: *Regimbald v. Chong Chow* (1925), 38 Que. KB 440, at p. 445. Section 240 of the *Excise Act* permits the sentencing judge to send an offender to jail on summary conviction for up to two years. The trial judge rejected jail as a fit punishment for this offence. Jail only entered his calculation as a default provision for non-payment. As such, jail was triggered by the default, not the offence. No default, no jail. The decision of the judge to collapse the sentencing hearing into a default of payment hearing was done for administrative convenience, apparently, but it did not eliminate the fact that legally there was a shifting of gears from sentence to default to consideration of the appropriate sentence for default to committal. The conditional sentence is a creature of statute and nowhere in s. 742.1 or elsewhere in the Code is it suggested that conditional sentences are available to enforce unpaid fines.

C. The Trial Judge's Dilemma

[28] The trial judge's dilemma was that he was required by the *Excise Act* to impose a *minimum* fine of $9,600, rising to a *maximum* of $14,400 based on a mechanical formula applied to the quantity of contraband cigarettes found in the offender's possession. The trial judge did not dispute the logic of the minimum mandatory fine because in his view contraband is a serious problem in the community. His concern was the perceived inevitability of incarceration that would arise from enforcement action consequent on the respondent's inability to pay.

[29] The error in the trial judge's approach, with respect, was his conclusion that, in the case of this respondent, the only alternative to a conditional sentence was actual jail time.

[30] As a matter of law, there was nothing inevitable about incarceration in the event the respondent was simply unable to pay the $9,600 fine by reason of his poverty.

D. No Time Given for Payment

[31] As stated, the trial judge gave the respondent no time to pay. This was in accordance with a request from the defence, which sought to lay the basis for a conditional sentence. But it was an error. If it is clear that the offender does not have the means to pay immediately, he or she should be given time to pay: see *R v. Andrews*, [1974] 2 WWR 481 (BCSC), and *R v. Brooks*, [1988] NSJ No. 94 (QL) (CA). The time should be what is reasonable in all the circumstances: *R v. Beaton* (1984), 49 Nfld. & PEIR 15 (PEICA), and *R v. Tessier* (1957), 21 WWR 331 (Man. Co. Ct.). In *Attorney General of Canada v. Radigan* (1976), 33 CRNS 358, the Quebec Court of Appeal allowed the offender to pay a fine of $5,000 through semi-annual instalments of $625. The courts have considerable flexibility to respond to the particular facts of an offender's situation. It is wrong to assume, as was done in this case, that the circumstances of the offender at the date of the sentencing will necessarily continue into the future.

[32] Here, the trial judge issued a committal order forthwith. The Code provides that "[w]here no time has been allowed for payment of a fine and a warrant committing the offender to prison for default of payment of the fine is issued, the court shall state in the warrant the reason for immediate committal" (s. 734.7(2)). This language suggests that only in exceptional circumstances that call for judicial explanation should an immediate committal order be made. Here there were no exceptional circumstances. The reason given was simply that the respondent was on welfare and lacked the ability to pay.

[33] An offender's inability to pay is precisely the reason why time is allowed, not a reason why it should be altogether denied: *R v. Natrall* (1972), 9 CCC (2d) 390 (BCCA), at p. 397; *R v. Zink* (1992), 13 BCAC 241. It is true that the fine could not have been paid immediately, and perhaps never in full, but the mandatory minimum fine scheme imposed by Parliament was effectively nullified by immediately shifting the penalty from the respondent's financial interest to his liberty interest. Parliament clearly intended that an economic punishment be imposed for an economic offence. … As noted, committal of an offender for default of payment terminated the operation of all other enforcement mechanisms to collect the fine (s. 734.7(4)). It is often difficult to predict with certainty whether an offender will in future acquire the means to pay the fine, whether through his or her own labour, or perhaps a windfall.

E. Imprisonment for Debt

[34] The trial judge of course put his finger on a serious problem. Debtors' prison, a dreadful institution excoriated by Charles Dickens in *Little Dorrit*, is no longer with us. But according to the most recent report from Statistics Canada, 17 percent of all people in custody in provincial or territorial institutions in 2000-2001 were jailed for default on unpaid fines, i.e., at least one of the causes for their committal arose from a fine default: see Canadian Centre for Justice Statistics, *Adult Correctional Services in Canada, 2000-2001* (2002), at Table 7. The numbers are fairly steady, if in slight decline, from 20 percent in 1998-1999 to 19 percent in 1999-2000.

[The court reviewed other statistics that painted the same picture.]

[36] It is curious that, while a force behind the 1996 sentencing reforms to the Code was a reaction to the overuse of prison as a sanction (*R v. Gladue*, [1999] 1 S.C.R. 688, at para. 57), prison as an enforcement mechanism for unpaid fines remains at such a high level. In its 1987 report, the Canadian Sentencing Commission had observed that "[t]he imposition of a 'semi-automatic' prison term for fine default has been the subject of relentless criticism in the sentencing literature. There is statistical evidence to support the conclusion that the imprisonment of fine defaulters without reference to their ability to pay discriminates against impoverished offenders": *Sentencing Reform: A Canadian Approach—Report of the Canadian Sentencing Commission* (1987), at p. 380. The Commission recommended that "a quasi-automatic prison term not be imposed for fine default and that offenders only be incarcerated for *wilful* breach of a community sanction" (p. 381), meaning probation or fines (p. 347). In its 1996 sentencing reforms, Parliament took these views into account.

[37] I do not overlook the corollary problem that poverty should not become a shield against any punishment at all. Otherwise, smugglers will simply be encouraged to redouble their efforts to recruit impoverished people as runners. Nor is it suggested that jail is never a fit sentence for people in the respondent's position. In this case, however, we are confronted with a specific finding by the sentencing judge, not unreasonable in the circumstances, that jail was not a fit sentence for *this* offender.

• • •

F. Encouragement to Pay

[39] The appellant Crown states in its factum on the present appeal, "[t]he purpose of a term of imprisonment in default is to encourage fine payment; it is not punishment for an offence." "Encouragement" presupposes the offender has the wherewithal to somehow organize payment. If, as the collection lawyers say, you cannot get blood from a stone, no amount of "encouragement" is going to cause the stone to bleed.

[40] The Crown's submission finds an echo in late 18th century England. A leading scholarly study of the King's Bench debtors' prison points out that what creditors wanted

> was, above all, the power to *threaten* imprisonment. A debtor who was brought to court, even if he could put up bail, received a forceful reminder of his perilous situation. Court appearance might well induce a debtor with resources to re-order his priorities and settle outstanding claims. Even a debtor without resources might find himself able, under the shadow of the law, to dredge up sufficient funds from friends and relatives. [Emphasis in original.]

(J. Innes, "The King's Bench Prison in the Later Eighteenth Century: Law, Authority and Order in a London Debtors' Prison," in J. Brewer and J. Styles, eds., *An Ungovernable People: The English and Their Law in the Seventeenth and Eighteenth Centuries* ([London: Hutchinson's,] 1980), 250, at p. 254)

[41] Debtors' prison was used to enforce civil debts. In this case, we are dealing with debts owed to the Crown. One of the ideas underlying the 1996 sentencing reforms is that it was no more appropriate to use jail as a general collection agency for debts owed to the Crown than it is for debts owed to ordinary citizens.

[42] It is true, of course, that some of those serving jail time in default of payment even today are doing so for reasons of personal preference, a matter of choice, as documented in a recent study for the British Home Office: R. Elliott and J. Airs, *New Measures for Fine Defaulters, Persistent Petty Offenders and Others: The Reports of the Crime (Sentence) Act 1997 Pilots* (2000), at pp. 32-35, 44 and 68-69.

[43] However, the illusory nature of the "choice" between fine or imprisonment in many situations was noted by Kelly J in *R v. Hebb* (1989), 69 CR (3d) 1 (NSSC (TD)), at p. 13:

> It is irrefutable that it is irrational to imprison an offender who does not have the capacity to pay on the basis that imprisonment will force him or her to pay. If the sentencing court chooses a fine as the appropriate sentence, it is obviously discarding imprisonment as being unnecessary under the particular circumstances. However, default provisions may be appropriate in circumstances where the offender may *choose* not to pay, presumably on principle, and would elect to spend time incarcerated rather than make a payment to the state. For the impecunious offenders, however, imprisonment in default of payment of a fine is not an alternative punishment—*he or she does not have any real choice in the matter.* At least this is the situation until fine option programs or related programs are in place. In effect, imprisonment of the poor in default of payment of a fine becomes a punishment that would not otherwise be imposed except for the economic limitations of the convicted person. [[Emphasis] added.]

[44] It was to address some of these weaknesses in the sentencing options that the Minister of Justice subsequently introduced Bill C-41, proclaimed in force on September 3, 1996.

· · ·

H. *The 1996 Sentencing Reforms*

[46] The 1996 amendments made a number of important clarifications in this area of the law.

[47] Firstly, Parliament rejected in general the notion that a fine should be set without regard to an offender's ability to pay. A means inquiry is now a condition precedent to the imposition of a fine except where otherwise provided by law. ... In this case, of course, Parliament did impose a minimum fine which, in his present circumstances, the respondent was unable to pay.

[48] Secondly, in s. 734(2), Parliament cross-referenced s. 736 which introduced into the Code recognition of provincial "fine option programs" in which, assuming such a plan exists and the offender is eligible for it, the fine may be discharged "in whole or in part by earning credits for work performed during a period not greater than two years."

[49] Thirdly, Parliament provided that a defaulting offender should not be sent to jail unless he or she has "without reasonable excuse, refused to pay the fine or discharge it under s. 736" (see s. 734.7(1) of the Code).

[50] The Court of Appeal expressed concern that a fine that is not backed up with the threat of jail might be seen as a "hollow" sentence. The 1996 amendments make it clear, however, that while impoverished offenders are not to be jailed simply because of an inability to pay, they are nevertheless subject to available collection methods short of jail, including an obligation to work off their debts where a fine option program is in place. Moreover, the sentencing judge can certainly impose a fine plus a period of jail in default of payment to encourage payment. The problem here was that the sentencing judge moved directly from imposition to committal without passing through the intermediate stages of default and a s. 734.7(1) committal hearing.

[51] If no "fine option program" is in place and the offender defaults, the Crown has a number of civil remedies, including refusal to "issue or renew or may suspend [any] licence, permit or other instrument until the fine is paid in full" (s. 734.5 of the Code), or the criminal court order may be filed as a judgment in a court of civil jurisdiction, with all the usual civil law collection remedies (s. 734.6). A third option is committal to jail for default, but, as will be seen, this option is fenced in with important restrictions.

(i) *The Lack of a Functioning Fine Option Program in Ontario*

[52] The trial judge in this case made it clear that if a fine option program had been available in Ontario, he would have enrolled the respondent to work off the debt over a period of time through community service. "[I]f there was a regime in this province permitting offenders to work off the fines," he said, "this entire discussion would be obviated."

[53] All provinces and territories have a fine option program in place except for British Columbia, Newfoundland and Labrador, Nunavut and Ontario.

• • •

(ii) *Licence Suspension and Revocation*

[55] Enforcement options available to the Crown include the suspension or revocation of licences and permits held by the respondent. In the present case, the fine was imposed

under the federal *Excise Act*. There is no evidence of what federal permits or licences, if any, were held by the respondent. It is possible that he possessed a Canadian passport.

[56] In most cases, revocation or suspension of permits is a potent collection tool, especially where the fine is owed to the provincial Crown. Anyone who has tried to renew a driving licence despite an unpaid fine is familiar with the procedure. While suspension or revocation do not themselves produce payment of the fine, they put pressure on the offender to find the money. This remedy is frequently resorted to. It appears that in 2002 there were 95,909 driving permits in Ontario suspended as a result of default in the payment of fines: Ontario, Ministry of Transportation, *Driver Control Statistics* (2003). Apart from driving licences, suspension or revocation would be available provincially in respect of registration of vehicles, taxicab licences, hunting permits, work permits, timber cutting permits, mineral exploration licences, building permits and the full range of activities touched by the apparatus of the regulatory state.

[57] It may be that suspension of federal permits and licences would not have produced any significant payment in the respondent's case, but nevertheless, where applicable, it would be a punishment less restrictive of his liberty than house arrest.

(iii) Civil Enforcement

[58] Governments use collection agencies. If there is money to be found, these people are nothing if not persistent.

[59] Under s. 734.6, the Crown can register the unpaid sentence as a civil judgment. Providing the civil judgment is renewed at appropriate intervals, it carries on indefinitely. The fact the respondent was impoverished on the day of his sentencing does not mean he will be ever thus.

(iv) Committal Proceedings

[60] Under the Code, a fine default is not punishable by committal *unless* the other statutory remedies, including licence suspensions and civil proceedings, are "not appropriate in the circumstances," or "the offender has, *without reasonable excuse, refused* to pay the fine or discharge it under section 736 [fine options program]" (emphasis added). Section 734.7(1) of the Code provides:

> 734.7(1) [Warrant of committal] Where time has been allowed for payment of a fine, the court shall not issue a warrant of committal in default of payment of the fine
>   (a) until the expiration of the time allowed for payment of the fine in full; and
>   (b) unless the court is satisfied
>   (i) that the mechanisms provided by sections 734.5 and 734.6 are not appropriate in the circumstances, or
>   (ii) that the offender has, without reasonable excuse, refused to pay the fine or discharge it under section 736.

[61] Where the offender's "reasonable excuse" under subpara. (ii) for failure to pay a fine is poverty, the question is whether it is nevertheless open to a court to jail him or her under subpara. (i) because the self-same poverty makes it "not appropriate," i.e., futile, to resort to civil collection methods or permit suspensions. In my view, such a reading of s. 734.7, despite the drafter's use of the word "or" at the end of s. 734.7(1)(b)(i), would be absurd.

[62] Courts have not infrequently read "or" as "and" where the legislative context so requires: *Clergue v. H.H. Vivian and Co.* (1909), 41 SCR 607, *Re International Woodworkers of America, Local 2-306 and Miramichi Forest Products Ltd.* (1971), 21 DLR (3d) 239 (NBCA), and *Sullivan and Driedger on the Construction of Statutes* (4th ed. 2002), at pp. 66-69. See also, on this specific point, A. Manson, *The Law of Sentencing* (2001), at p. 249.

[63] If poverty were to be upheld as a stand-alone justification for a committal court to find collection methods other than jail "not appropriate," then the "without reasonable excuse" limitation in s. 734.7(1)(b)(ii) would afford poor people no protection at all. Yet it was the concern about overuse of jail for poor people for unpaid fines that was an important impetus behind the 1996 sentencing reforms.

[64] Use of the word "refused" in s. 734.7(1)(b)(ii) indicates a parliamentary expectation that the offender's particular circumstances allow him or her a choice. In this case, at least at the date of the sentencing, the respondent had no choice.

[65] The Crown, in its factum, fully accepted that committal proceedings are governed by the principle in s. 734.7(1)(b)(ii) that "the offender has, *without reasonable excuse, refused* to pay the fine or discharge [the debt]" (emphasis added). For example, the Crown argues:

> By operation of the warrant of committal provisions in s. 734.7 of the *Criminal Code*, there must be a judicial determination that an offender has "without reasonable excuse, refused to pay the fine" before he or she is ordered into custody.
>
> • • •
>
> While the "slamming of the jail door" is the incentive to make offenders with means pay their fines, *no one will go to jail for their genuine inability to pay.*
>
> • • •
>
> However, as will be discussed below, where a sentencing judge chooses to impose a default term of imprisonment, the warrant of committal provision in s. 734.7 of the *Criminal Code* operates to ensure that only those who *wilfully* evade payment will be incarcerated.
>
> • • •
>
> If the judge was satisfied that the Respondent was not *wilfully* evading the payment of the fine, there would be no basis for issuing a warrant of committal and the Respondent would not go to jail. [Emphasis in original.]

[66] Parliament has imposed a mandatory minimum fine in s. 240 of the *Excise Act*, but it has with equal authority provided in s. 734.7(1) of the *Code* that the offender should not go to jail for failure to pay it unless it is shown that he or she has "without reasonable excuse, refused to pay." That was not the position of the respondent when he was sentenced. He ought not to have been sentenced to serve a "term of imprisonment" in an institution *or* in the community.

III. The Proper Order

[67] In my view, the trial judge ought to have proceeded with his initial instinct to impose the mandatory minimum fine of $9,600 plus a reasonable time to pay and 30 days in default. If, as the trial judge expected, the respondent went into default despite the Crown's resort to available remedies short of committal, the Crown would then have had the choice whether to proceed further or not.

[68] If, as the trial judge anticipated, the respondent had continued simply to be unable to pay, the Crown, on its own acknowledgement to this Court, would not have sought such a committal.

[69] If, on the other hand, the respondent had come into money to pay all or part of the debt, he should quite properly have been required to do so.

IV. Disposition

[70] The appeal is allowed. As the respondent has served his conditional sentence, which would bar all further collection procedures under s. 734.7(4) of the *Code*, the Crown ought not to take any further collection procedures as a result of the conditional sentence's being set aside. A stay is therefore entered against any further collection procedures. As the appeal was brought by the Crown as a test case, the respondent should have his costs in this Court.

[Deschamps J dissented. Applying a "purposive sentencing approach," she concluded that because a court could impose a period of imprisonment in default of payment of the mandatory minimum fine, it could equally impose a conditional sentence in default of payment of that fine.]

In *Wu*, the offender was being sentenced under the *Excise Act*, which gives courts a discretion to impose a period of imprisonment in default of payment of a fine. Does such discretion exist under the *Criminal Code*? See ss 734(4) and (5). If not, what impact does this have on the court's analysis? For a discussion of this point, see Tim Quigley, "Annotation: *R v. Wu*" (2003), 16 CR (6th) 291.

For further consideration of the use of imprisonment in default of payment of a fine, see Andrew J MacDougall, "Hebb: Imprisonment in Default of Fine Payment and Section 7 of the Charter" (1989), 69 CR (3d) 23; Keith Jobson & Andrew Atkins, "Imprisonment in Default and Fundamental Justice" (1986) 28 Crim LQ 251; and Roy E Kimball, "In the Matter of Judicial Discretion and the Imposition of Default Orders" (1990) 32 Crim LQ 467.

For additional discussion on the issues of ability and time to pay a fine, see *R v Topp*, 2011 SCC 43, [2011] 3 SCR 119 and *R v Mahmood*, 2016 ONCA 75.

E. Victim Surcharge

The victim surcharge in the *Criminal Code* is a mechanism to fund services for victims of crimes. It must be imposed on a convicted or discharged offender. Until recently courts could waive the victim surcharge if imposing it would cause undue hardship to the offender or the offender's dependants. As a practical matter, courts often did so without much inquiry if the offender was being sentenced to a term of imprisonment or was on some form of social assistance. In response, Parliament removed all discretion and made the victim surcharge mandatory in all cases. The current provision, set out in the *Criminal Code*, s 737, reads:

> 737(1) An offender who is convicted, or discharged under section 730, of an offence under this Act or the *Controlled Drugs and Substances Act* shall pay a victim surcharge, in addition to any other punishment imposed on the offender.

(2) Subject to subsection (3), the amount of the victim surcharge in respect of an offence is

    (a) 30 per cent of any fine that is imposed on the offender for the offence; or

    (b) if no fine is imposed on the offender for the offence,

        (i) $100 in the case of an offence punishable by summary conviction, and

        (ii) $200 in the case of an offence punishable by indictment.

(3) The court may order an offender to pay a victim surcharge in an amount exceeding that set out in subsection (2) if the court considers it appropriate in the circumstances and is satisfied that the offender is able to pay the higher amount.

(4) The victim surcharge imposed in respect of an offence is payable within the time established by the lieutenant governor in council of the province in which the surcharge is imposed. If no time has been so established, the surcharge is payable within a reasonable time after its imposition.

• • •

(7) A victim surcharge imposed under subsection (1) shall be applied for the purposes of providing such assistance to victims of offences as the lieutenant governor in council of the province in which the surcharge is imposed may direct from time to time.

(8) The court shall cause to be given to the offender a written notice setting out

    (a) the amount of the victim surcharge;

    (b) the manner in which the victim surcharge is to be paid;

    (c) the time by which the victim surcharge must be paid; and

    (d) the procedure for applying for a change in any terms referred to in paragraphs (b) and (c) in accordance with section 734.3.

(9) Subsections 734(3) to (7) and sections 734.3, 734.5, 734.7, 734.8 and 736 apply, with any modifications that the circumstances require, in respect of a victim surcharge imposed under subsection (1) and, in particular,

    (a) a reference in any of those provisions to "fine," other than in subsection 734.8(5), must be read as if it were a reference to a "victim surcharge"; and

    (b) the notice provided under subsection (8) is deemed to be an order made under section 734.1.

The mandatory victim surcharge provision has been controversial. A number of questions have arisen. Is the victim surcharge a proper exercise of Parliament's criminal law power? What exactly is the victim surcharge? Is it an additional punishment, a general kind of restitution, or something else entirely? Is the surcharge properly characterized as a fine? What role, if any, does the mandatory nature of the surcharge play in determining the appropriate sentence for an offender? Should minimal fines be imposed in order to reduce the amount of the surcharge?

R c Cloud

2014 QCCQ 464, 8 CR (7th) 364 (footnotes omitted)

[Mr. Cloud was an Aboriginal offender. He was unemployed, destitute, alcoholic, and alone. He had no permanent address and had lost contact with his family, his community, and his people. Not surprisingly, he therefore had no ability to pay the mandatory $400 victim surcharge that would have applied had the court simply accepted the joint submission for concurrent terms of imprisonment and probation following his pleas of guilty to two indictable offences. The court agreed that the joint submission was appropriate *except* for the victim surcharge, which in this offender's circumstances rendered the overall sentence disproportionate and unreasonable. Because no constitutional challenge had been raised, the court accepted that it had to apply s 737 but determined that this first required the court to interpret the provision and related legislation to determine whether it could impose a more proportionate sentence by combining imprisonment, probation, *and* fines for the offences. Although the court was dealing with an Aboriginal offender, it indicated that this was not determinative and its analysis applied to all similarly situated offenders.]

HEALY JQC:

I Introduction

[1] This case concerns the application of the surcharge and requires consideration of the relation among principles of sentencing. These include the fundamental principle of proportionality and other principles, purposes and objectives in sentencing, individualisation of decision-making, consideration of aboriginal offenders, parity, restraint, and totality.

. . .

VII Surcharge

[16] The surcharge was first enacted in 1988. Until 1996 it was called the "victim fine surcharge" and has since been called simply the "victim surcharge." In its original formulation the calculus of the surcharge was expressed as follows:

> ... [T]he court imposing sentence on or discharging the offender shall, in addition to any other punishment imposed on the offender, order the offender to pay a victim fine surcharge in an amount not exceeding
>
> (a)   fifteen per cent of any fine that is imposed on the offender for that offence or, where no fine is imposed on the offender for that offence, ten thousand dollars, or
> (b)   such lesser amount as may be prescribed by, or calculated in the manner prescribed by, regulations made by the Governor in Council,
>
> subject to such terms and conditions as may be prescribed by regulations made by the Governor in Council.

The calculus of the surcharge later took its current form but with a lower tariff. The tariff was fifteen *per cent* (15%) of any fine imposed in the sentence or, if no fine was imposed, fifty dollars ($50.00) for each summary-conviction count and one hundred dollars ($100.00) for each indictable count. Before the amendments of 2013 the surcharge was a mandatory order imposed upon a finding of guilt according to the tariff set out in paragraph 737(1)(b). This tariff was applicable even in cases where a discharge was ordered but it was mitigated by a judicial discretion in any case to waive its imposition if there were a request to this effect and a concrete basis for believing that there would be undue hardship. As a matter of practice, however, this rule was relaxed in many jurisdictions. Evidence of hardship was not routinely required and judges would sometimes waive the surcharge without an express request or without extensive reasons. It might be noted that the surcharge was introduced into the Code before the sentencing reform that enacted a new Part XXIII in the Code with effect from 1996. This is noteworthy because the discretion to waive the surcharge complements the requirement in section 734(2) that a judge inquire into the means of an offender before imposing a fine. The amendments of 2013 doubled the tariff imposed by paragraph 737(1)(b) so that the surcharge is now thirty *per cent* (30%) of any fine imposed or, where no fine is imposed, one hundred dollars ($100.00) for each summary-conviction count and two hundred dollars ($200.00) for each indictable count. The surcharge continues to apply where a discharge is ordered but there is no longer a discretion to waive it for undue hardship or any other reason. It applies to all offences (from murder to shoplifting) and to all offenders (from the richest to the poorest), including aboriginal offenders, without distinction.

[17] A preliminary point concerning the calculus in the surcharge and related costs is useful before entering into a discussion of relevant legal issues. A case involving ten counts of failing to appear for an intermittent sentence would imply a surcharge of one thousand dollars ($1000.00). A case involving four counts of breach of conditions for (1) drinking alcohol, (2) in a bar, (3) after curfew, and (4) in the company of a person named in a no-contact order would attract a surcharge of four hundred dollars ($400.00). A case involving three counts of shoplifting pork chops would attract a surcharge of three hundred dollars ($300.00). Default on payment of the surcharge, if community service is not viable, would be discharged by imprisonment calculated in Quebec at approximately $81.00 *per diem*. Thus an unpaid surcharge of four hundred dollars ($400.00) would imply imprisonment for five (5) days. A conservative estimate of the daily cost of imprisonment to the state might be two hundred dollars ($200.00). To recover an unpaid surcharge of four hundred (400) dollars would therefore cost the public purse one thousand dollars ($1000.00) to imprison the defaulter for five (5) days. The costs of recovery are thus more than double the amount of the surcharge. And this is for the enforcement of amendments enacted in a statute entitled *Increasing Offenders' Accountability to Victims Act*. In the examples just given there is no calculus that would permit the conclusion that the surcharge is consistent with the fundamental principle of proportionality in section 718.1 of the Code.

VIII No Constitutional Question

[18] No constitutional question has been raised in this matter and for this reason I will not answer such a question. To do so requires notice to the Attorney General of Quebec and the Attorney General of Canada in order to afford a proper opportunity for written and oral submissions. Such a question might be posed on the premise that the surcharge violates section 12 of the Charter because it is grossly disproportionate in this case or in a reasonable hypothetical case. It might also be posed on the premise that individualisation and proportionality in sentencing are principles of fundamental justice under section 7 of the Charter that are incompatible with the surcharge as amended in 2013. Further, it might be argued that the surcharge raises concerns about equality as it is applied to aboriginal offenders. I repeat that no such questions are before the court today. The Charter need not be invoked, however, to support the following conclusion: as applied to Mr. Cloud, and as applicable to many other offenders, the surcharge imposed by section 737 would disturb reasonable and informed people because it is disproportionate—having regard to the *quantum*, the inflexibility of its terms and the inherent arbitrariness in

distinguishing between cases where a fine is or is not imposed or cases that proceed by summary-conviction procedure or indictment. It is a blunt instrument that is far too blunt to achieve any valid penal purpose and it will not, to quote Binnie J. in *Wu*, "cause the stone to bleed." But can the surcharge as adopted by Parliament be interpreted in a manner that avoids these effects?

IX Caution

[19] Before proceeding further, it is imperative to note that any concerns with the surcharge are not concerns with the policy that animates its existence. It is beyond question that the establishment and maintenance of a public fund, administered by the provinces and territories for the indemnification of victims of crime, is not only defensible but desirable. In principle there can be no objection to the contribution of offenders to such a fund and if such contributions will enhance their accountability for offending that is an additional benefit. There appears to be no empirical evidence that an increase in accountability actually is one of the effects of the surcharge but the absence or dearth of such evidence does not diminish the soundness of a policy to establish and maintain a fund. The question is whether the surcharge now in force can be reconciled with principles and objectives of sentencing in Canadian law.

X Principles

[20] The parties agree that the surcharge imposed by section 737, as amended, is applicable here. I agree with them. I have already reviewed the evolution of the surcharge since 1988. To address the central question in this matter, before considering the merits of the issue, I must examine the manner in which it should be characterised in law. For analytical purposes, as will be seen below in detail, a pivotal determination is whether the surcharge is an integral element of a sentence and, if it is, what kind of sentencing instrument it is. If the surcharge is an integral element of a sentence, the joint submission of the parties is not for a sentence comprising two elements but for a sentence comprising three elements: imprisonment, probation and the surcharge. Following the second day of hearing, the prosecution delivered supplementary submissions in writing. These make three principal assertions: that the surcharge is not a fine, that even if the surcharge were a fine the jurisprudence prohibits the imposition of a fine in addition to imprisonment and probation, and that the surcharge is a form of restitution. I cannot accept these propositions for the reasons developed below.

[21] I turn now to the principles that I adopt to determine a just, fit and appropriate sentence in Mr. Cloud's case. There are six.

[22] *First, the surcharge is a mandatory order that must be imposed in every case with the sentence, without consideration of the circumstances of the offence or the offender, and without regard for the offender's ability to discharge this debt.* This is the effect of the amendment of section 737 in 2013. It applies in this case and there is no basis in law on which I can waive its imposition on Mr. Cloud. The discretion to waive the surcharge was repealed in those amendments and that too is clear. The consequences of these amendments are awkward, however, even if they are clear in the manner I have described. For example, suppose a case of two indictable counts in which a fine of four hundred dollars ($400.00) is suggested in submissions on sentence. The judge is still obliged to consider

whether the offender has the means to pay that fine and may reject the option of a fine if the offender lacks the means to pay. If it is rejected, the judge must then determine a just, fit and proportionate sentence that satisfies the principles of sentencing justified by the Code and the jurisprudence. At the same time and in the same case, however, if no fine is imposed the judge must nevertheless impose a surcharge of two hundred dollars ($200.00) on each count for a total of four hundred dollars ($400.00). If the judge has determined that a fine of four hundred dollars ($400.00) is unreasonable, the same conclusion must ineluctably apply to the surcharge but the amendments deprive the judge of any discretionary power to remedy the imposition of that disproportionate and unreasonable burden.

[23] If the surcharge is not an element of a sentence, what could it be? Several possibilities might be considered. One is that the surcharge is a tax on criminality that is imposed as an administrative charge to alleviate a burden that would otherwise be borne by the state in the administration of criminal justice. A second might be that the surcharge is an order for costs against the accused, again to alleviate in part the state's burden of administering criminal justice at the expense of those who necessitate its existence and operation. A third possibility is that the surcharge is an oblique or indirect restitution order in which the offender is ordered to pay into a general fund dedicated to the indemnification of victims of crime and more generally of society at large. These three views overlap and each allows at least a foothold for an argument that the surcharge is not an element of a sentence but distinct from the sentence. The jurisprudence does not definitively approve of any one or more of these views. A more compelling explanation lies in the Code itself.

[24] *Second, the surcharge is an integral element of a sentence. It is not extraneous to the sentence.* Either the surcharge is an element of the sentence or it is not an element of the sentence. At the hearing the prosecution plainly submitted that the surcharge is not an element of the sentence but "something parallel." In section 673 and section 785 the Code provides that a sentence "includes" an order for an enhanced surcharge and before the amendments of 2013 included an order to waive the surcharge under what was section 737(5). This inclusive definition does not purport to be exhaustive. If a sentence could include an enhanced surcharge, or an order to waive the surcharge, it must include the surcharge itself as provided in section 737(2). In section 673 and section 785 the inclusion of the enhanced surcharge or the waiver was designed to allow for appellate jurisdiction to review either of these orders. No such inclusion was required for the surcharge itself under section 737(2) if the sentencing judge did nothing more than to apply the tariff set out in that provision. In such a case there could be no appeal but that in no way implies that the surcharge is not an integral element of the sentence imposed. In passing I note that in *Pham* the Supreme Court accepted that the sentencing judge may consider the collateral consequences of a sentence, such as deportation, while ensuring fidelity to the principle of proportionality in the terms of the sentence itself. The surcharge is not a collateral consequence but an essential and integral element of the sentence.

[25] Although the surcharge was originally introduced in 1988, before the reform of sentencing in 1996, its continuation after that reform was made subject to the application of the principle of proportionality and all of the other principles and objectives that were adopted in those amendments. Those principles and objectives continue to apply today throughout Part XXIII except to the extent that they have been expressly modified or

repealed. It follows that the amendments to the surcharge remain subject [to] those principles and objectives with the exception that the discretion to waive it has been repealed. Thus in principle the surcharge remains governed by the principle of proportionality and the individualisation of sentences, not only as applicable to all offenders but notably to aboriginal offenders. The repeal of the discretion to waive the surcharge does not sit comfortably with these principles and objectives, among others, because they are put further out of reach by the intent and effect of the amendments of 2013.

[26] *Third, the surcharge is not only an integral part of a sentence. It is properly described as a mandatory minimum sentence because it allows no exceptions.* It applies to every offence and every offender and is subject to variation in only two ways. It is applied as thirty *per cent* (30%) of any fine imposed or, if no fine is imposed, as a fixed amount of one hundred dollars ($100.00) for every summary-conviction count or two hundred dollars ($200.00) for every indictable count. The surcharge is thus contingent on the presence or absence of a fine or on the classification of offences. This would appear to be arbitrary as a measure of the quotient of accountability of offenders. It is not apparent that a reliable and proportionate quotient of accountability can be derived from a percentage of a fine. Even less is it apparent that one-half, or double, the quotient of accountability can be assured by the classification of offences. This is obvious in the case of hybrid offences that require an election by the prosecution, as is the case with the two counts to which Mr. Cloud pleaded guilty. More to the point, however, the surcharge is properly described as a mandatory minimum sentence because it must be applied even when the offender is given an absolute or conditional discharge, again without regard to the circumstances of the offence or the offender. And, again, Mr. Cloud's status as an aboriginal person is irrelevant according to the amendments of 2013.

[27] To repeat, if the surcharge is properly construed as a fine that is an element of punishment—indeed an *additional* element of punishment—there are ramifications. The most obvious is that it is not only part of a sentence but a mandatory minimum sentence. It applies to all offences and all offenders without regard for means or any distinguishing feature such as aboriginal status. As an element of a sentence, it follows that to the extent possible the surcharge must be subject to the principle of proportionality and to other principles and objectives of sentencing. The surcharge, before and after the amendments does not oust or override those principles and objectives but must be interpreted, to the extent permitted within the terms of the legislation, in a manner that is congruent and compatible with them.

[28] There is no need to rehearse the importance that the Code and the jurisprudence accord to the fundamental principle of proportionality and to the related principle of the individualisation of sentencing. Proportionality is most directly concerned with the gravity of the offence and the degree of responsibility in the offender. But it is more broadly concerned with protection against excessive leniency or excessive harshness in a sentence, having regard as well to the profile of the offender before the court. The individualisation of sentencing constrains a court, within the constraints otherwise imposed by law, to determine a fit sentence with regard to all relevant factors concerning the offence and the offender. This principle is reinforced by the constraining effects of the totality principle, which again imposes a limit on excess. As a mandatory minimum element of a sentence that does not discriminate between offences or offenders, the surcharge does not sit easily with the principles of proportionality or individualisation.

[29] The only distinction in section 737 is twofold. First, it distinguishes between cases where a fine is imposed and cases where no fine is imposed. Second, it distinguishes between summary-conviction offences and indictable offences. As with the law as it stood before the amendment in 2013, these grounds of distinction are seemingly arbitrary but the fixed tariff now imposed certainly calls for renewed attention. With respect to the provisions enacted by the amendments, it is appropriate to recall that they are adopted in an enactment entitled the *Increasing Offenders' Accountability to Victims Act*. The tariff is apparently designed to advance this objective but the empirical premise for doing so by this mechanism is not clear. To be precise, it is not clear how the grounds of distinction embedded within section 737 will enhance the accountability of offenders to victims.

[30] As the surcharge is a mandatory and additional element of a sentence, it enhances and aggravates the severity of the sentence. Perhaps in this context "accountability" has nothing to do with rehabilitation and increasing the offender's sense of personal responsibility to specific victims or to society in general. This is most apparent in French. The reform of 1996 identified this among the purposes of sentencing:

> susciter la conscience de leurs responsabilités chez les délinquants, notamment par le tort qu'ils ont causé aux victimes et à la collectivité.

The short title of the amending act in 2013 is this:

> *Loi sur la responsabilisation des contrevenants à l'égard des victimes.*

If a surcharge is disproportionate, having regard to the offence or the offender, it is inconceivable that its imposition could augment the accountability of the offender.

[31] The distinction between an offence for which a fine is imposed and an offence for which no fine is imposed might be explained as an attempt to control the severity of a financial penalty. Although the percentage is high, the option of a fine would require a judge to inquire into the offender's means to pay the fine and, as a corollary, the surcharge. The distinction between the tariff imposed for summary-conviction ($100.00 per count) and indictable offences ($200.00 per count) is more difficult, not least where the offence in question is hybrid. It can scarcely be expected that the tariff for a summary-conviction offence will yield half the quotient of accountability that can be expected for an indictable offence. It is inconceivable that the tariff for an indictable offence will yield double the quotient of accountability as for a summary-conviction offence. The arbitrariness in this calculus is even more troubling if the quotient of accountability in a hybrid offence is a by-product of prosecutorial election to proceed one way or the other.

[32] As an element of a sentence, the surcharge might stand alone in the case of a discharge but typically it must be cumulated with other elements of a sentence and combined together with them in conformity with the principles of sentencing, including proportionality and totality. This is so whatever the other elements of a sentence might be. Where a sentence contains elements of imprisonment and probation, for example, there will not be just these two elements because a third—the surcharge—must be added to them. This will always be true of every sentence because the Code now permits no exemption or waiver of the surcharge.

[33] *Fourth, the surcharge is an integral element of a sentence that is properly defined as a fine.* As already noted, this is evident in the inclusion of orders for enhancement or waiver of the surcharge under sections 737(3) and 737(5) respectively for purposes of

appeal. It is clearer in the definition of a fine in section 716: "'fine' includes a pecuniary penalty or other sum of money, but does not include restitution." For reasons that appear below I have concluded that the surcharge is not a form of restitution as legally defined in Canadian criminal law. If that is correct, I also conclude that by any use of language the surcharge is a pecuniary penalty or a sum of money. It is a fine imposed with the hope of increasing the accountability of offenders to victims of crime. This is a purpose that falls among the objectives of sentencing and for this reason alone I do not hesitate to conclude that the surcharge is a fine. As originally introduced in the Code, the surcharge was sometimes called a "victim fine surcharge." This can be translated as an additional fine or as a fine upon a fine but the sleight of words cannot alter its substance as a fine. Apart from sophistry, the mechanisms for enforcement of the surcharge confirm that it is properly defined as a fine. In the reform of 1996 the removal of the word "fine" from the phrase "victim fine surcharge" does not change its nature. As section 716 provides, it is a pecuniary penalty and a sum of money that is distinguishable from restitution. The surcharge is a penalty imposed in a sentence upon a finding of guilt that is a judgment debt payable to the state. This is the essence of any fine.

[34] These conclusions are reinforced by the language of section 737 itself. Before and after the amendments of 2013 section 737 requires the imposition of the surcharge "in addition to any other punishment imposed on the offender." This phrase can leave little doubt that the surcharge is an integral element of the sentence imposed. It could not be otherwise if it is imposed in addition to any other punishment. Its description as part of that punishment does not allow it to be separated from any other parts of a sentence. Further, this phrase confirms that the surcharge is properly construed as a fine within the meaning of section 716. A fine is a form of punishment; if the surcharge is applied in addition to any other punishment, it too is a fine.

[35] On this point the prosecution delivered written submissions to the effect that the surcharge is not an element of a sentence but something else. I reproduce an extract from these submissions, which includes extracts from *Crowell*:

> Pursuant to a contextual definition [of a fine], we submit that the victim surcharge is not a fine. Rather, it is a form of restitution, expressly excluded by the definition of "fine" in s. 716.
>
> To that effect, we believe the following analysis by the Nova Scotia Court of Appeal in *R. v. Crowell* is apposite:
>
>> The addition of a victim fine surcharge skews the result, not primarily to punish the offender but to raise money for a program administered by the province.
>>
>> • • •
>>
>> *Restitution or compensation, like incarceration, fines and probation, is one of the judicial instruments used for the protection of the public. Its role as such is increasing;* it is a deterrent that deprives the offender of the fruits of his crime and aids in the reformation of the sincerely repentant. In some circumstances it is the best possible protection for specific victims.
>>
>> • • •
>>
>> *The victim fine surcharge is a new concept in restitution: general rather than specific restitution made by an offender not to his or her own victim but to victims of crime generally by creating a fund to provide them with certain services.* It is a statutorily

imposed deterrent with perhaps a secondary relevance to reformation; its role as a deterrent is incidental to its fund-raising purpose.

• • •

The victim fine surcharge is like a tax for the purpose of raising a revenue, but unlike a tax in that it is also a further expression of public reprobation at the time of sentencing.

In an important aspect it is penal in its application and its consequences. In its fund raising aspect it represents an effort to rectify the harm done by criminal activity; a public purpose wholly related to the field of criminal law. Its identification with criminal law interests is so strong I would characterize it as a valid exercise of the federal criminal law making power even if it were strictly indistinguishable from a tax. The purpose will govern.

• • •

The victim fine surcharge is therefore neither a true tax nor a true fine, but rather a unique penalty in the nature of a general kind of restitution. As such it is penal in its pith and substance and therefore constitutional as a proper matter for parliamentary legislation under s. 92(27) of the Constitution Act, 1867. It must be taken into account by criminal court judges in crafting the sentences they impose.

This passage merits brief comment.

[36] *Crowell* was decided before the reform of Part XXIII by Bill C-41 in 1995. More specifically, it was decided before that reform enacted a statutory declaration of the principles and objectives of sentencing. It is apparent in the passage from *Crowell* that the Court describes the surcharge in language that is congruent with language used to describe the principles, objectives and instruments of sentencing as they have existed since 1996. The Court assimilates the surcharge to a form of restitution and to other instruments of sentencing such as incarceration, fines and probation—all forms of sentencing. It describes the surcharge as a deterrent (three times) and notes that it might have some relevance to reformation. It says that it bears some resemblance to a tax but distinguishes it as a tax because it is an expression of public "reprobation at the time of sentencing. In an important aspect it is penal in its application and its consequences." And the Court says that it is a "unique penalty in the nature of a general kind of restitution. … It must be taken into account by criminal court judges in crafting the sentences they impose."

[37] I repeat that the language of the Court in *Crowell* is the language of sentencing. It is consistent in this respect with Part XXIII after the reform of 1996. More to the point is the conclusion of the Court that the surcharge reflects a lawful exercise of Parliament's exclusive legislative authority over matters of criminal law. Even if much of the passage submitted is *obiter dicta*, it gains coherence and strength under current law (including section 716 and the terms of section 737(1)) as an assertion that the surcharge is an integral element of a sentence and that it is properly defined as a fine.

[38] To repeat, the surcharge meets the definition of a "fine" in section 716. This definition applies with equal clarity to a fine or a surcharge. It is a sum of money that can only be characterised as a pecuniary penalty. It would be an abuse of language to suggest otherwise. This view is reinforced by the language of section 737 itself. It says that the surcharge shall be imposed "in addition to any other punishment imposed." This section

not only assimilates the surcharge to a fine for purposes of collection and enforcement. It explicitly identifies the surcharge as a punishment among any other elements of punishment. This, to repeat, is also consistent with the definition of the surcharge as a fine.

[39] *Crowell*, far from being apposite in this case, and having been considered before the reform of 1996, is entirely consistent with a definition of the surcharge as a mandatory element of a sentence that is not only a punishment but a fine. Further, the only question in that decision was whether the surcharge is properly an instrument of the criminal law within Parliament's legislative authority. That question is not in issue here and the affirmative answer provided in *Crowell* is, again, consistent with the conclusion that the surcharge is a penal element of a sentence that is indistinguishable from a fine. Given the precise reasons in *Crowell*, this conclusion is reinforced by the removal in 2013 of a discretion to waive the surcharge.

[40] *Fifth, the surcharge is not a form of restitution formally recognised in Canadian criminal law.* It cannot be such a form of restitution simply because the money realised in the assessment of surcharges is dedicated to a fund to assist victims of crime. This is a loose and informal use of the word "restitution" to signify a process and a mechanism by which offenders may be compelled to contribute to a fund for the benefit of victims of crime. But this is not what restitution means in Canadian law. The surcharge is not compensation for actual loss to an identified person or entity and it has nothing to do with any notion of *restitutio in integrum* as that concept is legally understood. Section 738 provides that restitution may be ordered, under specific conditions, "in addition to any other *measure* imposed on the offender." Unlike the surcharge it is not imposed "in addition to any other *punishment* imposed on the offender." The surcharge may be ordered as a payment by the offender only to an ascertainable victim of his or her crime and only for a readily ascertainable amount. It is a specific order for compensation of a fixed loss by a direct victim. Only this is restitution. Both the Code in section 673 and section 785, as well as the jurisprudence, make plain that an order for restitution is an integral part of a sentence and that it is, within a sentence, a form of punishment. Only section 716 distinguishes restitution from a fine. But the surcharge is not restitution within the meaning of section 738 of the Code. The attribution of a surcharge to a fund for victims does not bring the surcharge within the section and it does not, for the reasons given earlier, take it out of the definition of a fine. It is not without interest that even if the surcharge were construed loosely as a form of restitution, having regard only to its purpose, the Code and jurisprudence make clear that the court should take into consideration the offender's ability to discharge the debt. Further, if the alternative to non-payment of the surcharge is participation in a fine-option programme or (where there is no such programme) imprisonment, it is nonsense to describe these mechanisms as a function of restitution within the meaning given by section 738.

[41] *Sixth, the surcharge is a fine that allows in a single sentence, subject to conditions, the imposition of a term of imprisonment, a term of probation and a fine.* In its written submissions the prosecution takes the position that a sentence cannot combine elements of imprisonment and probation with a fine. The textual basis for this view is the use of the word "or" in paragraph 737(1)(b). The prosecution takes the position that this section authorises a term of probation with imprisonment (less than two years) *or* a fine but not both, even if the total of both does not exceed two years. To reinforce this submission the prosecution cites several cases, including some from Quebec, in which it is affirmed that

a sentence cannot include elements of imprisonment, probation *and* a fine—even if the total duration does not exceed two years. The prosecution, it might be noted, did not refer to *Cartier*, rendered in 1990, where the Court of Appeal decided that a fine could be cumulated with an intermittent term of imprisonment and probation.

[42] The question of statutory interpretation has never been settled by the Supreme Court and before 1996 it was the subject of some debate and some dispute in the jurisprudence. The cases that prohibited the combination of jail, probation and a fine proceeded on a textual construction and, it appears, an argument of principle. The textual argument was that the word "or" in section 737(1)(b) must be read disjunctively. The argument of principle was that this construction would avoid excess in the terms of a sentence. These two points were not accepted everywhere, however, and in some cases it was held that a proper construction of the provision would allow for all three elements to be combined, provided that the net result was otherwise just, fit and proportionate. The counter-argument has been that the use of the word "or" does not necessarily mean that a fine can only be cumulated with one or the other of imprisonment or probation. It is equally consistent with the view that if one or the other or both of these elements are found within the terms of a sentence, a fine may be added if the totality principle and the proportionality principle are respected in the net result.

[43] Although the matter was never previously settled, this compulsory element of a surcharge that must be added to any other elements in a sentence puts an end to the question whether a fine can be cumulated with elements of imprisonment and probation. The surcharge *is* a fine and thus Parliament itself has concluded not only that a fine may be cumulated with other elements but that in all cases, including absolute discharges, the surcharge must be cumulated with other elements. In short, Parliament has defined the surcharge as a fine that is a necessary element of a sentence that must be combined with any other elements and thus subject, to the degree possible, to proportionality, individualisation, totality and other general principles of sentencing.

[44] For other reasons too I propose to follow the counter-argument just identified and I therefore decline to follow the jurisprudence that forbids the combination of imprisonment, probation and a fine. I do this for cogent legal reasons and not as disobedience to authority. One reason is textual. Section 737(1)(b) states when a probation order may be imposed and says that this is permissible when the sentence otherwise imposes a term of imprisonment or a fine. It allows for probation when the elements of the sentence includes imprisonment or a fine but there is no compelling reason to conclude that probation can be cumulated with only one or the other of these two options. The rationale for the word "or" is apparent if the word "and" is substituted. It would lead to the absurd conclusion that probation could be imposed only if the sentence also contained *both* elements of imprisonment and a fine. To use the word "or" allows the sensible interpretation that probation may be imposed if the other elements of the sentence include imprisonment or a fine, or both.

[45] As noted, the cases deciding that a sentence comprising jail, probation and a fine (if the first two elements did not exceed two years) was improper were decided long before the reform of 1996. Thus the interpretation of paragraph 737(1)(b) was not constrained by the principle of proportionality and the other principles and objectives since found in Part XXIII. Since that reform occurred it is entirely possible that a sentence comprising jail, probation and a fine could be just, fit appropriate and proportionate having regard

to the offence and the offender. This is the controlling point of principle. And this principle is not diminished if the sentence includes a fine that is cumulated with imprisonment or probation, or both, provided that the first two do not exceed two years in total.

[46] It must also be noted that the cases forbidding the cumulation of imprisonment, probation and a fine predate the enactment (in the reform of 1996) of section 734(1)(a), which provides as follows:

> Subject to subsection (2), a court that convicts a person, other than an organization, of an offence may fine the offender by making an order under section 734.1
>
> (a) if the punishment for the offence does not include a minimum term of imprisonment, *in addition to or in lieu of any other sanctions* that the court is authorized to impose.
>
> • • •
>
> Except where the punishment for an offence includes a minimum fine or a fine is imposed in lieu of a forfeiture order, a court may fine an offender under this section only if the court is satisfied that the offender is able to pay the fine or discharge it under section 736.

This paragraph explicitly allows a fine to be cumulated with any other sentencing options that are available, including therefore imprisonment and probation, subject only to compliance with the principles and objectives of sentencing stated in the Code. In short, the cases relied upon by the prosecution have been overtaken by legislative amendments. Not only is this manifest in section 734(1)(a). Once again, if the surcharge is properly characterised as a fine that forms an integral element of a sentence, Parliament itself contradicts the outdated jurisprudence upon which the prosecution relies by compelling a fine, and thus a combination of three elements, in any case where imprisonment and probation are imposed in a sentence.

[47] There is some irony here. The jurisprudence relied upon by the prosecution sought to ensure reasonableness and proportionality by imposing a formal and somewhat artificial limitation. After the amendments of 2013 the surcharge leaves open the manifest possibility of disproportionality in a mandatory fine—the surcharge—imposed upon any other punishment in the elements of a sentence. The imposition of a fine in addition to a term of imprisonment and probation (again, not more than two years) allows for a higher degree of proportionality by mitigating the effects of this mandatory minimum element. There is a further irony. The imposition of a mandatory fine in the form of a surcharge is a plain demonstration that Parliament itself not only allows a combination of imprisonment, probation and a fine but actually *requires* it wherever imprisonment and probation are included among the elements of a sentence. In the absence of a discretion to waive the surcharge, only the additional imposition of a fine will preclude a disproportionate result. Indeed, the rationale of avoiding excess is now entirely consistent with a combination of the three elements. Where jail and probation are proposed the addition of a modest fine allows for a mitigation of the surcharge. This additional element thus provides a basis to ensure, not to defeat, the proportionality of the sentence and the individualisation of its elements as appropriate for the offence and the offender.

• • •

[50] Within the measure allowed by law, the surcharge must be applied with due regard for proportionality, individualisation of sentencing and all of the principles and objectives of sentencing recognised in the Code and the jurisprudence. The absence of a discretionary waiver of the surcharge imposes a severe limit on decision-making in this

regard. But the imposition of an additional fine—with imprisonment and probation of less than two years—allows some margin in which to reach a proportionate and just result. The jurisprudence of the Supreme Court has been consistent in declaring that the principles and objectives of sentencing, most emphatically proportionality and the individualisation of sentences, must prevail.

[51] The surcharge now enforced by section 737 of the Code, allows no waiver or modulation to account for the offence or the offender. There is no basis on which to believe that the calculus it imposes will yield a higher quotient of accountability among offenders. There are many grounds on which to believe the opposite. I am bound, however, by the oath and dignity of my office. I cannot disobey the law now found in section 737. But, even in the absence of a constitutional question, I can interpret that law in a manner that best conforms in law, principle and policy to the whole of Part XXIII and the jurisprudence of the courts. This is what I will do by imposing a sentence composed of a term of imprisonment, a term of probation and a fine. The fine will diminish the applicable surcharge that would otherwise result in a disproportionate, unfit and unjust sentence.

The court therefore accepted the joint submission as originally stated (90 days imprisonment and two years probation, concurrent on each charge), but added a nominal fine of $5 on each count, thus reducing the victim surcharge from $200 on each count to $1.50 for each count, or $3 in total.

The prosecution appealed the decision in *Cloud* and the conclusions of the Court of Appeal (2016 QCCA 567) may be summarized briefly:

1. The surcharge is an element of a sentence.
   Paragraphs 57-59, 62, 68, 71.
2. A sentence can combine imprisonment, probation, and a fine; it must include the surcharge as prescribed by Parliament.
   Paragraphs 38-43, 53, 70.
3. The surcharge is not a fine, but a unique financial penalty that forms an integral and mandatory element of a sentence.
   Paragraphs 47, 55-56.
4. The principle of proportionality applies to all elements of a sentence, including the surcharge.
   Paragraphs 67-68.
5. If, after taking all elements of a sentence into consideration, the surcharge causes a disproportionate result, the remedy is not a nominal fine but a modification of the other elements to ensure a fit and proportionate sentence (totality principle).
   Paragraphs 72-73, 75, 77.

The Court of Appeal thus affirmed the decision at first instance but for two points. First, it held that the surcharge is not a fine, but a unique financial penalty that is distinguishable from a fine. Second, it concluded that if the applicable surcharge would lead to a disproportionate sentence the remedy should lie not in a reduction of the mandatory surcharge but in a reduction of the other elements of the sentence. The ramifications of the court's decision remain to be determined but note that there is now a discrepancy on two points between the law in Quebec and the law in other provinces and territories. The first is whether the surcharge is properly characterized as a fine, and the second is whether it is permissible to impose a sentence comprising imprisonment, probation, and a fine. There is also a challenge raised by the final conclusion of the court's decision. How can a sentencing court compensate for disproportionality due to the surcharge if the other elements of the sentence are mandatory? In the absence of a claim of gross disproportionality under s 12 of the Charter, it appears that a disproportionate result is inevitable. Further, even when the other elements are discretionary, by what calculus can there be a reduction of them? If the financial burden imposed by the surcharge would lead to a disproportionate sentence, how can this financial burden be offset in a reduction of jail time or some other element of a sentence? See the case excerpted in Section II.F, below, for further views on these issues.

F. Constitutionality of the Victim Surcharge

Does the mandatory victim surcharge offend s 7, 12, or 15 of the Charter? If so, can the provision be saved under s 1 of the Charter? When reviewing the excerpts below, consider the extent to which the differing characterizations of the surcharge and its relationship to the "sentence" imposed, as well as the possible components of that sentence, impact on the constitutional analysis undertaken by the court. What approach is most compelling? If there is a violation of s 7, 12, or 15 of the Charter that is not saved by s 1, what is the appropriate remedy?

We first consider the court's decision in *R v Michael*. Mr. Michael was an Inuit offender with alcohol and drug addictions. He had a severely disadvantaged background, limited family supports, was unemployed, and on social assistance. He was being sentenced on nine offences involving minor assaults or damage to property and breaches of court orders. The offences were committed while he was grossly intoxicated. The Crown proceeded summarily, and thus Mr. Michael was subject to a victim surcharge of $900, in addition to his sentence of four months and two years' probation. Mr. Michael had no current ability to pay the surcharges, and in the court's view he was unlikely in any reasonable period to have the ability to pay them. He challenged the victim surcharge on the basis that it violated ss 7 and 12 of the Charter, and could not be saved by s 1. In the extract below we focus on three questions raised by the court: (1) whether the victim surcharge is a punishment; (2) whether the victim surcharge was grossly disproportionate so as to violate s 12 of the Charter; and (3) whether the court could also impose a nominal fine to avoid or ameliorate the gross disproportionality. In assessing the second question, the court noted that the traditional structure of analysis for s 12 claims was not optimal given that the challenge was to a mandatory surcharge that applied to all offences and all offenders, but nonetheless utilized this structure because it captured the relevant considerations.

R v Michael

2014 ONCJ 360, 12 CR (7th) 44 (citations omitted)

PACIOCCO J:

II. The Section 12 Challenge

[2] Section 12 of the *Charter* assures everyone that they have "the right not to be subjected to cruel and unusual treatment or punishment." ... The place to begin is by

determining whether the victim surcharge is a "punishment" within the meaning of section 12 of the *Charter*.

A. Is Section 737 a "Punishment"?

• • •

[5] In my view this issue of substance can be resolved quite simply. Incarceration and fines are the two paradigmatic forms of punishment … . In *Canada (Attorney General) v. Whaling* … the Supreme Court of Canada reasoned without more that given this, a provision that increases the period of incarceration to be served is necessarily a punishment. The same holds true, in my view, for a provision like section 737, which enhances the amount of any fine that must be paid. How can a fine be a paradigmatic example of punishment, yet a provision adding 30% to the amount of a fine, not be a punishment? It does not matter what an enactment names the provision. If it increases the amount of a penalty by way of fine, it is, in my view, a punishment.

• • •

[7] [E]ven if the more laborious analysis invited by *R. v. Rodgers* … is applied, the outcome is the same. The two-part test identified in that case at para. 63 holds that "as a general rule, … the consequence will constitute a punishment when it forms part of the arsenal of sanctions to which an accused may be liable in respect of the particular offence and the sanction is one imposed in furtherance of the purpose and principles of sentencing." …

[8] I will deal with this second point first because it is simpler. I agree that the funds raised by the victim surcharge are to be used for the laudable purpose of providing important victim services. Section 737(7) says as much. Equally central if not more central to the purpose of the provision, however, is how this is to be done—by holding offenders accountable for those costs. This is self-evident from the text of the provision, which instructs that only offenders pay the victim surcharge and that they do so as part of the sentencing process. … [A]ll extrinsic sources confirm that the victim surcharge was enacted to make offenders pay for their crimes. … This proclaimed purpose, holding offenders to account, falls squarely within the purposes of sentencing contemplated in *Rogers*, and found in section 718. Those purposes include, most notably, "providing reparations for harm done to victims or to the community," and "promoting a sense of responsibility in offenders, and acknowledgement of the harm done to victims and to the community." Section 737 is intended to further these goals by making offenders pay. This is why section 737 was passed and then amended, and it is what section 737 purports to do. Section 737 meets the second leg of the *Rodgers* test.

[9] The first part of the *Rodgers* test, "that it forms part of the arsenal of sanctions to which an accused may be liable in respect of the particular offence" is also manifestly satisfied. Section 737 is not a self-standing provision distinct from the arsenal of sanctions surrounding it in Part XXIII of the *Criminal Code*, as the Crown contends. The indications to the contrary are too compelling to sustain this contention.

[10] First, although I am mindful not to exaggerate the impact of titles, the victim surcharge provision is found in the "Fines and Forfeiture" section of the *Criminal Code*. More importantly, section 737(1) begins by noting that it is to be imposed "in addition to any other punishment imposed on the offender." By inserting the word "other" Parliament was being direct, in my view, that it was creating an additional punishment. The

Crown counters that section 737 must not be a "fine" otherwise why would Parliament need to incorporate some of the fine provisions by reference through section 737(9)? There is some mileage in this submission, but there are two cogent responses. First, the fact that the victim surcharge is integrated in this way with other punishment mechanisms plays against the inference that section 737 stands as an island, distinct from the punishment provisions that surround it. Second, there are opposing, compelling indicators that the victim surcharge is in fact a fine.

[11] A most persuasive indication that the victim surcharge is a fine is the very definition of fine, found in section 716. That provision defines a "fine" as including "a pecuniary penalty or other sum of money, but does not include restitution." The victim surcharge, a sum of money, is not easily described as "restitution."

[12] First, the *Criminal Code* uses "restitution" as a term of art. It is found in the heading to sections 738.1-738.2, and throughout those provisions. Meanwhile the word restitution appears nowhere in section 737. Second, section 716 was enacted in 1999 four years after victim fine surcharges were legislated. Obviously, if Parliament intended the "restitution" exception to include victim fine surcharges, it would have either described the surcharge as "restitution" or used a clear term in the exception part of the fine definition that would encompass the victim fine surcharge.

[13] The reason Parliament did not take steps to describe the victim surcharge as "restitution," and therefore exempted from the status of a "fine," strikes me as obvious. A victim surcharge shares none of the characteristics of "restitution." … The hallmarks of restitution are that it involves payment to the victim equivalent to the loss caused in order to return to the status quo: *R. v. Cloud* … . The victim surcharge does no such thing. It requires the payment of money to the State, to be spent at the discretion of the State, to assist victims in a range of ways. There is no relationship between the payment an offender makes and the provision of benefits to their victim, if there even is a victim.

• • •

[16] In the end it does not matter to the instant analysis whether section 737 is a fine *per se*. However it is styled, it functions in substance like a fine. It is a sanction imposed on offenders for having committed offences by depriving them of *their* funds. Moreover, the amount of the surcharge is directly tied to the value of any fine imposed pursuant to section 734(1), and can be increased pursuant to section 737(3) if the sentencing judge decides, enhancing the sentencing experience. And much of the administrative structure developed for fines is incorporated by reference into section 737. … Even if this makes the victim surcharge a *sui generis* tool such that it is not a true fine, it is clear to me that section 737 is "part of the arsenal of sanctions to which an accused may be liable in respect of the particular offence."

[17] The victim surcharge therefore qualifies, in my view, as "punishment." This is so even though the victim surcharge does not behave like familiar punishments because it applies universally, it is impervious to many of the ordinary principles of sentencing, it is incongruous to apply a punishment other than probation to discharges, it does not sit well with the conventional interpretation of section 731(1)(b) which prohibits a "fine" from being used if both probation and jail are imposed, and the ability to pay is not required as it is for fines levied under section 734. The ill-fit of the victim surcharge with the familiar principles of sentencing and other sentencing provisions is not a reason to disregard what it, in substance, does. …

B. Does Section 737 Require "Cruel and Unusual" Punishment?

[18] Before a punishment contravenes section 12 it must be "more than merely excessive." The punishment must be "so beyond what would be proper or proportionate punishment as to be grossly disproportionate." It must, in degree, be "so excessive as to outrage standards of decency" ... . This is a halting standard, intended to reflect deference to Parliament's legislative authority.

[19] "A claim that a mandatory minimum sentence constitutes cruel and unusual punishment is tested in two ways. First a court must decide whether the punishment is grossly disproportionate as applied to the accused before the court. This particularized inquiry asks whether the mandatory minimum is grossly disproportionate punishment for the particular accused in the particular circumstances. If the sentence survives this particularized inquiry, the court goes on to decide whether the sentence is grossly disproportionate when applied to reasonable hypotheticals." ...

[The court undertook a detailed analysis of the gravity of each of the categories of offences committed by Mr. Michael, the particular circumstances of each offence, the personal background of Mr. Michael including his addiction issues and criminal history, and the kinds of sentences imposed for similar or related offences. Having undertaken this analysis, the court concluded that the appropriate range of sentence for the offences was in the area of four months followed by probation for two years. In relation to the surcharge, the court concluded that the minimum penalty at stake was the total victim surcharge, or $900, as the issue was the proportionality of Mr. Michael's sentence and the principle of totality therefore had to be applied to ensure the cumulative effect of the surcharges was not disproportionate. The court then addressed whether the addition of the victim surcharge rendered the overall sentence disproportionate.]

(c) Would Mr. Michael's Sentence Become Grossly Disproportionate if the Surcharge Were to Be Added?

• • •

The Actual Effect of the Punishment on the Individual

[58] A good deal of the argument before me focused on the effect of the impugned victim surcharge on Mr. Michael. ...

• • •

[68] The place to begin ... is with the Crown contention that there is "no actual impact on an offender who is and remains unable to pay." The Crown thesis is based first, on the adage that "you cannot get blood from a stone." If the person cannot pay, then payment will not occur. The Crown argues that where this is so it has no alternative recourse under the legislation. The "victim fine option" program contemplated by the *Criminal Code* is not an option for Mr. Michael as there is no program in place in Ontario, and Mr. Mack contends that, in any event, programs provided for under section 736 are at the option of the offender, as that provision says "an offender ... may ... discharge the fine, in whole or in part by earning credits for work." He argues that where it applies the fine option program is an offer to escape the threat of incarceration, not a form of community service

order. Meanwhile the sanction of incarceration in lieu of payment is not legally possible if the accused is, by reason of poverty, truly unable to pay. This is because, as the Supreme Court of Canada affirmed in *R. v. Wu, supra* at 60-66, the mechanism for incarcerating for non-payment, a warrant of committal available under section 734.7 of the *Criminal Code*, can be granted by a judge only if other collection mechanisms provided by law are not appropriate, and even then, only where the "offender has without reasonable excuse, refused to pay the fine." Someone who is too poor to pay is not refusing. They simply cannot pay: *R. v. Wu, supra* at paras 60-66. ...

[69]   In my view the Crown puts things too highly by equating limitations on the ability to collect with the absence of any actual impact on the offender, even assuming that an offender is and will remain unable to pay the levied amount.

[70]   First, as a matter of law an offender ordered to pay a victim surcharge is under a legal obligation to pay the victim surcharge. They are under sentence and this consequence in and of itself cannot be disregarded.

[71]   Moreover, the purpose of the victim surcharge order is to achieve payment. Even though Mr. Michael is in seriously straitened circumstances, unable to discharge his $900 obligation, I cannot assume that nothing will be recovered from him, and if there is even partial recovery, the victim surcharge will have had an effect.

[72]   In this regard there is evidence before me provided by the Crown showing that the Ministry of the Attorney General has a Service Agreement with the Management Board Secretariat "For the Collection of Outstanding Fines Accounts." Collection is handed over to private collection agencies. There is nothing in the law that I am aware of that requires these collection agents to hold off attempted recovery from the poor because it will cause hardship or they cannot realistic pay the whole amount. The assignment of collection agents is to get the money and they may ultimately secure some funds from Mr. Michael.

[73]   Even if collection efforts are not undertaken, or fail entirely, Mr. Michael, who will be under an order to pay, could feel obliged to use some of his meager funds in an attempt to satisfy the sentence, even if this causes significant hardship, and even though the Crown has no meaningful way to enforce payment. Simply put, I cannot proceed on the assumption that a legislated, solemnly imposed order made at the time of a criminal sentencing to pay funds will result in no payment being made.

[74]   Even if it does prove to be the case that money is never collected—a prospect that is not at all unrealistic—prolonged or indefinite delay in repayment has its own price. ... A person told that they could be incarcerated for not paying can be expected to find that threat stressful. They are apt to find it stressful even if told this will not happen if they are truly unable to pay. It cannot be disputed that the factual/legal question of when someone is sufficiently poor that a failure to pay will qualify as an innocent inability to pay rather than committable "refusal to pay" comes with no clear definition. Anyone on the margin who owes outstanding criminal levies and who attends to their obligations will be left to wonder whenever spending any money on themselves or their families whether that expenditure was necessitous enough to justify, or whether spending that money in this way could bring them to jail. In my view, I cannot ignore the effects of the risk of jail, when the sanction of jail has been established by the legislation precisely to intimidate individuals into paying. That is a stressor that must be taken to affect everyone who owes an unpaid victim surcharge.

[75] Exposing those who are poor such as Mr. Michael to perpetual, unsatisfied, sentencing obligations also deprives them of the ability to repay their debt to society. Because they do not have the means to repay, they lose the opportunity to be restored. I do accept that many offenders lack the sophistication to delve into deep questions of legal philosophy and moral responsibility, and that is probably true of Mr. Michael. Still, the notion of just punishment has long carried the promise that after the eye is given for the eye, the offender has discharged their debt and reconciliation can begin. The whole idea of restorative justice legislatively endorsed in the *Criminal Code* and recognized to be of cultural significance to aboriginal offenders such as Mr. Michael, depends on reconciliation. Indeed, some legal philosophers have justified punishment on the basis that it is a kindness to offenders to punish them since it permits them to heal. Whether this is persuasive or not, the flip side is. It is a cruelty in some measure to tell an offender that they must discharge an impossible sentence before their debt is expunged. Reducing all of this to a less ethereal plane, the point is that so long as Mr. Michael fails to pay the victim surcharge he remains indebted and criminalised. He has not paid the price for his crime and remains unrequited because he is poor. It is worth noting in my view that when it comes to the sentence of discretionary fines the law avoids this consequence by prohibiting fines from being used to punish offenders who cannot pay. In the case of victim surcharges, imposing unpayable monetary penalties is a legislatively accepted consequence. If it proves to be true that Mr. Michael never gets out from under the debt the impugned legislative scheme seeks to impose, it is a consequence that would befall him. He will remain indebted to society with all of the stigma and stress that imposes.

[76] As indicated, Mr. Konyer identified still other collateral consequences that would occur from overlong or perpetual poverty-caused non-payment by Mr. Michael, even if he is never actually deprived of the money. The Crown urges that many of these concerns are unrealistic in his case. The Crown urges that so long as Mr. Michael is unable to pay the victim surcharge, for example, it is unrealistic to imagine him undertaking licenced activities, and so he will not be affected by the collection strategy available under *Criminal Code* section 734.5 of refusing to give or renew licences and permits to him until a victim surcharge debt is discharged. The Crown also points out that it will not be victim surcharge that impairs his credit rating. I agree with these base observations, and as I pointed out during argument, the same point can be made in the case of a record suspension. The application for a record suspension costs $631. If Mr. Michael can pay that sum he can pay the victim surcharge.

[77] Having said all of this I cannot help but observe that the Crown argument entails recognition that Mr. Michael is so poor there is no realistic expectation that he will be able to engage in licenced activities, or ever seek credit, or ever afford to seek the modified forgiveness a record suspension entails, yet he is still expected under the impugned legislation to pay a $900 victim surcharge. I also find it to be material in evaluating the impact on Mr. Michael of the victim surcharge that, even if he gets on his feet, Mr. Michael's waiting time to apply for a record suspension will not begin to run until he has paid the victim surcharge. If Mr. Michael cannot pay that victim surcharge because of his poverty, the effect is that he will be perpetually disqualified from applying for full reintegration and formal forgiveness.

[78] As indicated, the Crown seeks to neutralize one of the key concerns mentioned above—that even if Mr. Michael does end up paying the $900 victim surcharge in whole

or in part—it will be oppressive for him to have to do so, because he can be given time to pay.

[79] The law that governs time to pay is expressed in *Criminal Code* section 737(4). In Ontario an Order in Council, 2173/99, was passed on 8 December 1999, as contemplated by section 737(4). It establishes a time to pay of 30 days for victim surcharges arising from summary conviction offences, and 60 days for indictable offences. Extensions of time to pay are permitted on application pursuant to *Criminal Code* section 737(8)(d), which incorporates section 734.3 by reference. That provision, section 734.3, permits a judge to vary the terms of a fine other than the amount. It has been interpreted to permit extensions of the default period to furnish a reasonable time to pay.

[80] The first observation I would make of the Crown's position is that while an "extension" can indeed be granted in the unlikely event that a substance abusing street person such as Mr. Michael has the wherewithal to prepare a written application, to serve it on the Crown, to file it and put it before a judge for consideration—all without the assistance of state-funded legal assistance—any extension that may be granted will not change the fact that he will still owe what is an otherworldly sum for him of $900.

[81] I also wonder about how realistic a solution extending time to pay is in Mr. Michael's case. How much of his $250 monthly income can he really be asked to contribute? The extraction of any amount from that paltry sum would cause unfair hardship, given his destitution. It strikes me that a "time to pay" order is just that, a direction to pay by the end of the prescribed period. If there is no realistic expectation that payment can be made within that period, it is more of a "hiatus order" than a "time to pay" order. Is the palliative for the economic hardship of a section 737 really the granting of what could easily become serial extensions? In my view, extending time to pay for someone who will not be able to pay in the foreseeable future is nothing more than a promise of ongoing legal obligation, with all of the stress and risks that this implies, only that stress is compounded by the imposition of impending deadlines that are apt to be unrealistic from the start.

[82] In spite of this the Crown urges that under the principles in *R. v. Wu*, 2003 SCC 73, the only appropriate response available for those like Mr. Michael who cannot pay now, is an extension of time. Those principles, the Crown argued, prevent an inability to pay from frustrating the operation of legislation, and I am legally bound to treat the extension of time as a sufficient constitutional palliative to the concerns Mr. Michael has raised.

[83] It is true that the Supreme Court of Canada did say in *R. v. Wu* ... "[a]n offender's inability to pay is precisely the reason why time is allotted, not a reason why it should be altogether denied," and in *R. v. Lavigne* ... the Court subsequently applied the *Wu* principle to a "fine in lieu of forfeiture" after holding that an inability to pay is not a factor that can influence whether the order should be made. In my view, however, these comments cannot be interpreted to have a bearing on either the evaluation of the impact of the victim surcharge on Mr. Michael, or on my assessment of its compliance with section 12.

[84] First, *R. v. Wu, supra*, and *R. v. Lavigne, supra*, involved payments that were very different in nature from the victim surcharge. Specifically, the victim surcharge is a pure levy unconnected to the particular offence or to any enrichment of the offender. In contrast, the sums owed in *Wu* and *Lavigne* are intended to require offenders to forfeit or lose any economic benefits gained by their offences. ... The actual correlation between the crimes and the sums imposed in these cases makes disregard of the ability to pay

understandable. This reasoning does not, however, transfer easily to victim surcharges which bear no economic relationship to the offence and apply whether the offence entails economic gain or not, or even whether there is a victim or not. Given the very different nature of the levies in issue, I cannot read the direction in *R. v. Wu* and *R. v. Lavigne* that "the proper response to inability to pay is time to pay" as an admonition to dismiss Mr. Michael's impact complaint by holding that the only recourse is to invite him to apply for an extension of time to pay.

[85] Second, and more decisively, the *Wu* and *Lavigne* cases did not involve *Charter* challenges. … In the absence of *Charter* challenge those judges had to apply the law as it was given to them, without more. The only proper response the law provided in the face of these presumptively valid statutory payment obligations was to grant an extension. … These decisions cannot be taken to hold that so long as time to pay is available, the *Charter* will have nothing to say about the fact of or amount of mandatory fines.

[86] As indicated, in my view granting Mr. Michael time to pay is impractical at present, and will do little to ameliorate the hardship that the victim surcharge imposes, and will add to the stress by imposing what could be a series of artificial deadlines for repayment. While there is no doubt that extensions of time to pay can reduce the harshness of a monetary repayment order for those who can manage to pay with difficulty, on the evidence before me repayment will remain an oppressive obligation even if time to pay is granted.

[87] In examining the impact of the minimum sentence on Mr. Michael there is another important feature that I believe I am required to consider, even if time to pay is granted, since it is a corollary of the minimum sentence. Even if Mr. Michael begins to find his feet, expecting someone as poor as he is to retire a $900 debt while he is recovering is more likely to inhibit than enhance the principles of sentencing that are rationally to be featured in his case. He will be beginning his rehabilitation in a deep financial hole. If he is forced to begin to make payments before he is financially secure it will cause stress and economic pressure. Enforcing this sentence while he gains his feet is more apt, in my view, to contribute to the kind of despondency and frustration that feeds this aboriginal offender's addiction and his misbehaviour than it is to aid in his rehabilitation or promote in him a sense of responsibility. Simply put, an impact of the imposition of the victim surcharge on Mr. Michael is that it is apt actually to impede both his ability to reintegrate and his achievement of a sense of accountability.

• • •

(d) Is the Victim Surcharge "Grossly Disproportionate" as Applied to Mr. Michael?

• • •

[90] As indicated, the penological goal as expressed by the Government and representative members of Parliament is "accountability" to victims. I also accept that although it is not a goal of penology *per se*, another penological goal is to raise funds for crime victims by having offenders augment the financial burdens that crime creates. There is also hope, no doubt, that this process will assist offender reconciliation and rehabilitation through the contribution that is required to the provision of victim services.

[91] With respect to the sentencing principles reflected in the "challenged minimum," I honestly can find none. At bottom the *Charter* complaint is that the victim surcharge rejects "cardinal proportionality" as expressed in section 718.1, disqualifies consideration

of aggravating and mitigating circumstances contrary to section 718.2(a), prevents consideration of the offender and therefore override the principle of sentencing equality or "ordinal proportionality" in section 718(b), and displaces principles that are central to the sentencing of aboriginal offenders.

[92] In terms of "the purpose animating Parliament's decision to use a mandatory minimum penalty" I accept the Crown position that the victim surcharge was made mandatory because sentencing judges were often not imposing it, waving it without proof of "undue hardship" and without providing reasons. There was evidence before me that in some jurisdictions, if an offender was sentenced to jail the victim surcharge was automatically waved on the predicate that it must be unduly difficult for someone in custody to pay. Parliament decided to make the victim surcharge mandatory to put an end to this. Indeed, to punctuate its point that this response was necessary and to illustrate the extent of the need, the Crown before me included, in its materials, cases where judges have avoided or evaded the victim surcharge even since it has become mandatory.

[93] There is a further issue relating to the purpose of the mandatory victim surcharge that remains, namely whether Parliament intended to ensure universal application of the victim surcharge even on those who cannot pay, or whether universality was simply a means to the end of preventing unmeritorious waivers. A review of the legislation does not answer this because the fact that the victim surcharge is to be applied universally is capable of reflecting either option.

[94] Hansard excerpts support the view that universality is a goal in its own right, and not a means to achieve a goal. [The court then reviewed the relevant extracts.]

• • •

[95] … Out of an abundance of caution because I do not want to understate Parliament's purpose, however, I will proceed on the basis that universal application may have been more than a means to achieve the purpose of preventing unmeritorious exclusions from the victim surcharge. I will treat universal enforcement by holding all offenders accountable through the provision of funds or community service as part of the purpose of the legislation in its own right.

[96] Parliament is, of course, entitled within constitutional limits to select the means it chooses to achieve its legislative goals. As indicated, *R. v. Nur* nonetheless requires me to consider whether there are "valid effective alternatives to the mandatory minimum." There are no "valid effective alternatives to the mandatory minimum" if universal application to ensure that every offender is held accountable for the costs of providing victim services is indeed a goal in its own right. …

[97] If the purpose of the mandatory minimum is stated more modestly, as done by the Crown in this case as preventing abuse by judges of the "undue hardship" exemption, there is an obvious "valid effective alternative to the mandatory minimum." An effective solution that has been available all along when a judge fails to apply the law properly is to use appeals or judicial review to overturn inappropriate decisions. … Judges will not misapply a law when given clear appellate direction on how to apply it, and if they do, they can easily be corrected.

[98] If Parliament wanted to constrain the discretionary decision of judges in this regard it could have made the "undue hardship" exemption more specific, by permitting exemption only for those who are unable to pay. It could go further and address its concern about the routine use by some judges of "jail" as an omnipresent form of "undue

hardship." This occurs because the statutory times to pay are so short that most incarcerated offenders will still be in custody when the victim surcharge falls due. The force in "undue hardship by jail" could be removed by providing that the statutory default time to pay the surcharge begins to run when the accused person is released from a sentence of incarceration. This would, in my view, remove judicial disquiet about imposing a victim surcharge knowing that it cannot be paid within the time set by law.

[99] It is no doubt obvious from the foregoing that I am persuaded, applying to the best of my ability objective legal standards, that a reasonable person, properly informed, would find that imposing $900 in surcharges on an addicted, impoverished and troubled Mr. Michael, in which each $100 component represents 40% of his monthly income and in which there is no adjustment allowed for his ability to pay, a sum that he is unlikely to be able to pay in the foreseeable future and that will result in an overlong if not perpetual delay in repayment of his debt to society for the modestly serious offences he committed, is "more than merely excessive." This remains so notwithstanding the penological goals and purposes animating this mandatory minimum penalty. While it creates these hardships for Mr. Michael the legislation fails to achieve universal accountability in the case of offenders who cannot pay, perhaps including Mr. Michael, and if its purpose is the more modest one of preventing judicial abuse of the "undue hardship" exemption, that could have been remedied in a less obtrusive fashion. I find that a reasonable person, properly informed, would be troubled by a provision that pursues its goals this ineffectively, and without reflecting core principles of sentencing. In my best judgment those persons would find Mr. Michael's punishment to be "so beyond what would be proper or proportionate punishment as to be grossly disproportionate" and "so excessive as to outrage standards of decency." ...

[100] This assessment does not, however, end matters. I still have to address the Crown's third theme before coming to a conclusion, that the gross disproportion that I have described as grounding the section 12 complaint, can simply be avoided by judges by applying the principles of sentencing.

(e) Can Gross Disproportion Be Avoided?

[101] Mr. Lalande, for the Crown, argued that if section 737 is part of the sentence, it can and must be applied consistently with the general principles of sentencing, including the principles of proportionality, totality and equality. It therefore does not require disproportionate results, let alone the grossly disproportionate punishment I have described. He said there are two ways that this can be achieved, (1) by taking the effects of the victim surcharge in section 737 into account when evaluating the overall sentence that needs to be imposed, or (2) by utilizing nominal fines to reduce the victim surcharge, calibrated at 30% of a fine imposed. Under the current legislation, if a fine is levied, this formula takes precedence over the $100 and $200 flat fees. If the fine is nominal, this reduces the victim surcharge to tolerable levels.

[102] In support of his position Mr. Lalande referenced an oral decision of my own, *R. v. Van Nguyen* (unreported), (7 April 2014), (Ont. C.J.), which I delivered in a busy plea court offering abridged reasons. In that case I imposed a nominal fine of $1 and the equivalent of 45 days in jail on an offender for two alcohol thefts from the LCBO. I explained that I imposed the nominal fine because I concluded that in all the circumstances

of the case, the time in jail coupled with $200 in surcharges would be disproportionate given his personal circumstances. By imposing two $1 fines, the surcharge would apply but at a modest rate of 60 cents, 30% of each fine, which would not add to the punitive impact of the overall sentence. I have done this in a handful of cases. Other judges have done the same, including Justice Healy in *R. v. Cloud, supra.*

[103] There is, in my view, a persuasive case to be made that this technique is appropriate and I believe it to be appropriate. Specifically, there is authority supporting the general proposition that mandatory minimum provisions must be applied consistently with the principles of sentencing, to the extent this can be done while still applying the mandatory minimum sentence. ...

• • •

[106] The case for adding nominal fines to each sentence to reduce the victim surcharge to ensure proportionality is premised on the notion that it is an example of this same technique—using available sentencing tools to ensure that the victim surcharge does not produce disproportion. Although nominal fines can appear to be a contrivance, it is not uncommon for courts to use them to achieve just outcomes. ...

[107] [Defence counsel] suggested ... that using nominal fines to achieve proportionality is unprincipled. He urged that I should not permit the mandatory impact of this sentencing tool to be masked in this way and thereby save a defective provision.

[108] ... It is entirely possible that appellate courts could take a similar view, and find that reducing the victim surcharge to mere cents by using nominal fines frustrates the clear intent of Parliament to ensure meaningful accountability.

[109] [However, there] is a difference, in my mind, between structuring a sentence to evade a binding rule as these judges admitted to, which is clearly impermissible, and structuring a sentence to ensure that when the minimum sentence imposed by law is applied, other binding rules of sentencing are respected to the extent possible. This includes using legal tools to structure an overall sentence that respects the principle of proportionality, which, after all, is a principle of fundamental justice that trial judges are constitutionally obliged to respect ... . The victim surcharge provisions hold that where a fine is imposed, the 30% rule is to be used. Nowhere do they say that a minimum fine amount is required for this to be a valid victim surcharge. Using nominal fines to protect sentencing principles, and then applying the victim surcharge according to the statutory formula in place, is, in my view, entirely appropriate.

[110] This technique for achieving proportionality in sentencing impoverished offenders in the face of victim fine surcharges is not available in all cases. First, the victim surcharge applies to discharges but the law does not permit a fine, nominal or otherwise, to be added to a "discharge." A sentencing judge imposing a discharge therefore has no choice but to impose a set victim surcharge of $100 or $200 per charge, regardless of its impact on sentence proportionality. Second, section 731(1)(b), as currently interpreted by binding authority in Ontario, including *R. v. Blacquiere* ... prohibits judges from imposing fines, nominal or otherwise, for charges that are being sentenced by a combination of incarceration and probation. In spite of the persuasive analysis in *R. v. Cloud, supra,* I am bound by that decision as are other courts in Ontario. As presently instructed, *Criminal Code* section 731(1)(b) prevents a nominal fine from being used where a fine and probation are combined for an offence, thereby precluding the use of nominal fines to ameliorate the disproportion that the victim surcharge can cause.

[111] In this case, however, my instant task is the particularized inquiry involving Mr. Michael. I did not impose nominal fines on Mr. Michael because, given the *Charter* challenge, it was not clear that this would be needed to remove the disproportion caused by the victim surcharge. By happenstance, and even though I felt it necessary to impose incarceration and probation for a number of the offences, I could in fact have added that fine without violating the prohibition in section 731(1)(b). When I sentenced Mr. Michael for the first two sets of offences I did not have to sentence him to jail because he had already served sufficient time in custody, pre-sentence. There was therefore no legal impediment to adding nominal fines for those charges to the probationary sentences I imposed. With respect to the third set of offences, I had only a few weeks before put Mr. Michael on the necessary rehabilitative terms of probation for a 2-year period. A new probation order would have been redundant, again leaving it open to me to have imposed nominal fines for those offences to ameliorate the disproportionate hardship of the victim surcharge, along with the jail sentences I imposed.

[112] My ability to have used nominal fines in his case drives me to the following conclusion with respect to the particularized inquiry. Simply put, I cannot find Mr. Michael's sentence to be grossly disproportionate because I could have used nominal fines to alleviate the burden of the victim surcharge that I have just described, and I believe I still can since I am still seized with his sentence. It is therefore not the law that has caused a grossly disproportionate sentence in his case that I have described. It is the fact that I have not yet exercised my discretion to have done so.

C. The Reasonable Hypothetical

[113] I am obliged, however, to go on and consider whether section 737 could produce gross disproportionality in the case of a reasonable hypothetical case. The Crown has cautioned that in fashioning a reasonable hypothetical case I must contemplate a hypothetical that bears resemblance to the case before me and that the reasonable hypothetical case must be one that must "focus on imaginable circumstances which could commonly arise in day-to-day life." ... In my view, this can easily be achieved by starting with Mr. Michael's case. The facts of his case not only commonly arise, they are the stock in trade of the Ontario Court of Justice "guilty plea" court in Ottawa. All that need be done with Mr. Michael's case is to imagine that, by chance, he had not already served the appropriate time in jail before he pled guilty before me on the first two set of charges, and that all three sets of charges were before me simultaneously. I would have been duty bound as a judge to sentence Mr. Michael to jail on those charges as the principles of sentencing required it, and I would have been duty bound to seek his rehabilitation through a probation order. Having done so, I would have then been prevented from adding a nominal fine to those charges for which jail and probation were ordered because it is illegal to sentence someone to jail, probation and a fine on the same charge. I would therefore have had no choice but to impose the victim surcharge on him using the $100 per offence tariff required by law. In view this reasonable hypothetical would cause gross disproportion in the fashion I have described above, thereby violating section 12.

[114] I am mindful in arriving at this position that in *R. v. Nur, supra* at para. 142 the Court directed that ordinarily in constructing reasonable hypotheticals, courts must look at the "conduct that includes all of the elements of the offence that triggers the mandatory

minimum, but no more. Characteristics of individual offenders, whether they aggravate or mitigate, are not part of the reasonable hypothetical." In this case, however, I am not conjuring up a mythical character to enhance the impact of the sentence, which is what I understand this direction to be preventing. I am using the very offender bringing the challenge. Moreover, that admonition does not appear to fit the case of a mandatory victim surcharge because the mandatory victim surcharge has no "elements of the offence." It is a roving punishment and must be evaluated as such. I am therefore of the view that I am permitted to look at the proportionality of the sentence realistically, by testing the proportionality of the sentence using the entire concept of cardinal proportionality and not just the "seriousness of the offence."

[115] Section 737 fails the reasonable hypothetical test and thereby *prima facie* violates section 12.

D. Is Section 737 Justified Under Section 1?

[116] ... In my view, it is not only difficult to justify a section 12 breach using section 1. It is impossible. I say this because the *Oakes* test requires that before a law is constitutionally valid it must be proportionate. How can a grossly disproportionate law satisfy the proportionality test? It cannot. Section 1 does not save section 737.

• • •

IV. Holding

[118] The victim surcharge provided for by section 737 violates section 12 of the *Charter* and is not saved by section 1. I therefore declare it to be of no force or effect. I also want to make clear that if I am wrong about the availability of the nominal fine to achieve proportionality, I would have struck section 737 down under the particularized inquiry.

Not all courts have agreed that the victim surcharge is a fine (or in essence a fine) and thus a form of punishment. As discussed in the cases above, the victim surcharge was originally characterized as a "general form of restitution." In *Cloud*, the Quebec Court of Appeal concluded that it was a unique financial penalty that is distinguishable from a fine. Although not adopting this characterization, the court in *R v Tinker*, below, concluded that the victim surcharge was not a penalty at all, but simply a consequence that flowed from conviction, rather like a DNA order. As a result, the court also found that the provision did not violate the Charter. The excerpts below focus on these issues.

R v Tinker, Judge, Bondoc & Mead
2015 ONSC 2284, 20 CR (7th) 174

GLASS J:

[1] The Respondents were charged separately for various charges pursuant to the *Criminal Code* of Canada. The trial judge raised the constitutional question about the validity of the Victim Surcharge provisions of the Code.

[2] Each Defendant entered guilty pleas at different days.

. . .

[11] The Crown proceeded by way of summary conviction for all charges for the Defendants.

. . .

[13] Each of the Defendants was a person of limited financial resources. The bottom line is that they do not have excess funds. One might reasonably anticipate that they would have to request extensions of time to pay victim surcharges even though the minimum here would be $100 for each of the offences.

. . .

Issues

[15] Was the victim surcharge in the nature of a fine?

[16] If not, what is a surcharge?

[17] If a surcharge is not a fine, is it a punishment or sanction for criminal behaviour?

[18] If there is a s. 7 Charter breach, what is the remedy?

[19] Although s. 1 had been raised, at the appeal the Crown advised that it was not relying on s. 1 of the Charter.

. . .

Analysis

[25] If a person breaks any criminal law in Canada, the individual will be subject to a victim surcharge which might range from 30% of any fine imposed or if no fine is created, then subject to a surcharge of $100 for each charge proceeded by way of summary conviction or $200 for each charge proceeded by way of indictment.

[26] [Section] 737(4) of the *Criminal Code* provides that any time to pay a surcharge is established by the province in which the Defendant lives. In Ontario, there is an order in council providing that a person is allowed 30 days to pay a surcharge for a summary conviction matter and 60 days for an indictable matter. That is covered by order in council 2173-99 for Ontario.

[27] [Section] 737(8)(d) of the *Criminal Code* provides that a person subject to a victim surcharge may apply for a change in terms for the surcharge to address being in default of paying by a given date.

[28] Mr. Kelneck has stated that the Crown will consent to an extension of time for payment of the surcharges for 2 years.

Is a Victim Surcharge a Fine, Punishment or Criminal Sanction?

[29] I do not read a surcharge to be a fine. It is not in the form of a penalty. It flows from a conviction for a crime, but it is not a sanction in its own right. Rather, it is quite simply what the Crown has described it to be, which is a sum of money established to be a consequence of breaking the law. That is different from a sanction because it is not in the same category as a fine, a tax, or a penalty. Rather, the surcharge is a sum of money that goes into a pool of resources to help victims of crime. Just as there are requirements for providing DNA samples upon conviction of offences and they are not sanctions, so do victim surcharges become requirements without being penalties.

Is a Victim Surcharge a Grossly Disproportionate Imposition?

[30] The Defendants submit that whether surcharges are sanctions or penalties or another form of required results flowing from conviction does not matter because however one might cut the cheese, the end result is grossly disproportionate for the individuals and should not be enforced. I disagree with this point.

[31] The Defendants go to the extent of saying that one should apply gross disproportionality to everyone when analyzing minimum victim surcharges. For example, minimum gun penalties have been found to be over the top of acceptance in Canada as in *R. v. Nur*, 2013 ONCA 677 and therefore a grossly disproportionate punishment. ...

[32] In *Nur*, Doherty J.A. analyzed first whether the law in question is grossly disproportionate to the accused person before the court and secondly whether the sentence is grossly disproportionate when it is applied to reasonable hypotheticals. He considered in paragraph 78 these factors:

- the gravity of the offence;
- the personal characteristics of the offender;
- the particular circumstances of the case;
- the actual effect of the punishment on the individual;
- the penological goals and sentencing principles reflected in the challenged minimum;
- the existence of valid effective alternatives to the mandatory minimum; and
- a comparison of punishments imposed for similar cases.

[33] The case before me is a far cry from being grossly disproportionate for the persons involved and further when applied to reasonable hypotheticals. With each Defendant, the conviction is made on summary conviction leading to a consideration of a surcharge of $100 each. The persons involved are not well-to-do persons. They have an economic life style that is very humble. However, there is a means of granting them significant time to pay the surcharges. The Crown has indicated a willingness to allow 2 years for payment. I might add that if there were some of the surcharges still outstanding at the end of 2 years, the person could apply for another extension. The same reasoning for the individual Defendants would apply to others in general in our society. I shall set out further analysis below.

Is the Victim Surcharge in Breach of s. 7 of the Charter?

[34] Justice Beninger noted that in *Canada (Attorney General) v. Bedford*, 2013 SCC 72 at paragraph 96, McLachlin C.J.C. emphasized that a s. 7 analysis focuses on inherently bad laws, meaning laws that remove life, liberty, or security of people in ways that run over basic values of people in Canada. She added that the principles of fundamental justice are an attempt to capture those values. Then, at paragraph 123, the Chief Justice wrote that the s. 7 question is whether anyone's life, liberty or security of the person has been denied by a law that is inherently bad. A law that has a grossly disproportionate, overbroad or arbitrary impact on one's person will be sufficient to establish a breach of s. 7.

[35] The victim surcharge set out in s. 737 of the *Criminal Code* of Canada does not fall into the category of bad law. As I state in these reasons, the surcharge is not grossly disproportionate. Nor is a surcharge too broad a sweep against persons. For the reasons that follow, the surcharge is valid legislation and is not contrary to s. 7 of the Charter.

[36] In *R. v. Wu*, 2003 SCC 73, the Supreme Court of Canada ruled that the trial judge should have imposed a minimum fine of $9600 as provided for a contraband cigarette case and then should have granted time to pay the minimum fine. If there continued to be payment less than full payment, the Crown might have to consider how far they might go with collection or simply not pursuing it any more. Further, if the financial resources of the person changed whereby the person might be able to pay, the individual could do so. The minimum fine worked out to $0.16 per cigarette. There were 300 cartons of contraband cigarettes.

[37] The *Wu* decision was not a Charter case, but it dealt with minimum fines, time to pay, and considerations of gross disproportionality.

[38] I think each of the Defendants here in the case before me is in a similar position to that of Wu.

[39] The trial judge in the case before me analyzed the case as one of grossly disproportionate criminal sanctions, but with the greatest of respect to the trial judge I find that his analysis is erroneous. The surcharge cannot be considered to be a fine-like sanction in the quiver of criminal sanction arrows because it only flows from the actions of the Defendants in a similar way to a DNA order. It is not in the form of punishment as one might sentence a person.

[40] I would reach the same conclusion taking the suggestion of the Defence that it does not matter whether or not a surcharge is a punishment like a fine because the imposition of a surcharge is not grossly disproportionate. Under s. 737, all calculations of a surcharge, be it following a fine or as a minimum when no fine is imposed, are not grossly disproportionate on their face. If a fine was imposed and 30% of that figure was calculated as a surcharge, it would be appropriate if the person apparently had the financial means to pay. If the individual was not well-resourced financially to do so, the quantum would be a ground of appeal of the amount of the fine which would then affect the surcharge calculation. If the appeal determined that there ought not to have been a fine, then the non-fine minimum would be present for the appeal court to impose. If the minimum figure were used, I do not find that $100 per charge for summary conviction matters or $200 per charge for indictable matters is grossly disproportionate. With a time to pay ability under s. 737(8)(d) of the *Criminal Code*, a Defendant of modest means can pay small amounts at a time or save small amounts to pay in one or more than one payment. In the case before me, with 2 years allowance to pay the surcharge sums, three Defendants have 2 charges each and one has 3 charges. At 3 charges with $300 in surcharge calculations, the person would be paying $2.88 per week. At 2 charges in such calculations, the person would be paying $1.92 per week. Even a person of very modest means can achieve such payments.

[41] If a person does not choose to set aside money or pay in instalments when given very reasonable time to pay, the individual becomes the author of their own misfortune when they come to the end of the period given to pay the surcharge.

[42] From that perspective, this is not grossly disproportionate for any of the 4 Defendants in the case before me nor for anyone in general.

Conclusion

[43] The minimum victim surcharge is not a fine or criminal punishment.

[44] Even if the surcharge were a form of criminal punishment, it is not grossly disproportionate to the Defendants involved nor is it grossly disproportionate for anyone facing such a surcharge.

[45] The victim surcharge in s. 737 of the *Criminal Code* of Canada is determined to be valid. It is not in contravention of s. 7 of the Charter.

[46] The victim surcharge will be imposed for each of the 4 Defendants in the sum of $100 per charge. Each Defendant is granted 2 years to pay the surcharge for each charge concurrent to each other. That means that each has 2 years to pay. If they have not completed payment within the 2 years, they still have an opportunity to apply for additional time to pay what is left owing. I use the 2 year period for payment taking into account that the Crown on the appeal advised that the Crown would consent to a 2 year period to pay the victim surcharges.

R v Eckstein
2015 ONCJ 222

PACIOCCO J:

[1] The case of Garrett Eckstein involves a challenge that has been brought to the victim surcharge, pursuant to s. 12 of the *Canadian Charter of Rights and Freedoms*.

• • •

[3] The challenge brought before me is based on the reasonable hypothetical situation generated in the decision of *R. v. Michael*. The claim that the imposition of the victim surcharge in Mr. Eckstein's case would be cruel and unusual treatment or punishment is based not so much on the implications for Mr. Eckstein, although there was allusion to the significant impact a $600 fine would have on a 19-year-old who is not working, but rather on the reasonable hypothetical that had inspired the decision in *R. v. Michael*.

[4] In order for Mr. Eckstein to have succeeded in his constitutional challenge it would not be necessary for the victim surcharge to have constituted cruel or unusual treatment or punishment in his case. The Supreme Court of Canada decision of *R. v. Ferguson*, 2008 SCC 6 (S.C.C.), made it clear that if a statute is unconstitutional the proper remedy under s. 52 is to declare it of no force or effect in all cases, rather than attempt to provide case-by-case discretionary decisions.

• • •

[10] In the circumstances before me, the defence has argued that the Ontario Superior Court decision in *R. v. Tinker* is not binding on me. That decision dealt with a constitutional challenge under s. 7 of the Charter. The court was clear that it was not adjudicating the constitutional validity of the provision based on s. 12, the cruel and unusual treatment or punishment section.

[11] In the course of the summary conviction appeal decision, however, the court made two findings relating to key issues in the reasoning that impelled me to find the provision unconstitutional in *R. v. Michael*. The first of those rulings in the case of *R. v. Tinker* is that the victim surcharge is not a punishment. In *R. v. Michael* I found the victim surcharge to be a punishment, and on that basis invoked s. 12 of the Charter.

[12] In addition, the *R. v. Tinker* decision held that the victim surcharge does not lead to grossly disproportionate results. The essence of the decision in *R. v. Michael* is the victim fine surcharge indeed leads to grossly disproportionate results.

[13] Mr. Brown for Mr. Eckstein urged that I am not bound by this decision because, as indicated, the presiding judge at the summary conviction appeal level made the decision based solely on s. 7, and made it clear that he was not ruling on s. 12.

[14] In addition, Mr. Brown argued that the reasoning of the court in the *Tinker* decision is not binding on me, because the reasoning supporting the decision is obiter. Specifically, s. 7 of the Charter provides relief in cases where the principles of fundamental justice are not observed, and the impact of that is to compromise the life, liberty, or security of the person of the Charter complainant.

[15] This requires a determination of the impact of the provision in question on life, liberty, or security of the person. It does not require a determination to be made as to whether or not the outcome of that provision constitutes a punishment. The argument, therefore, is that finding that the section in question of the victim surcharge is not a punishment is not central to the decision, and therefore not binding on me.

[16] The defence also argued that the gross disproportionality conclusion arrived at in *Tinker* was achieved without any consideration of any hypotheticals, notwithstanding the requirements that reasonable hypotheticals be taken into account. The submission is that the judge simply declared that the provision was not grossly disproportionate, because time to pay can be granted, and that this would remove gross disproportion not only for the offenders before him, but for any conceivable offender.

[17] As a result of these criticisms mounted of the *Tinker* decision, and other factors, if the *Tinker* decision had been offered to me as a persuasive precedent I would not be persuaded by it. Its determination that the victim surcharge is not a penalty does not disclose consideration of the textual and contextual factors that, in my view, require consideration, and which I addressed in detail in *R. v. Michael*.

[18] There is no discussion, for example, of the definition of "fine" in the *Criminal Code*, of the location of the victim surcharge provision in the "fine" section of the Code, or in its enforcement as a fine under the provisions of that statute. Nor is there any discussion of the objective of Parliament expressed consistently to use the victim surcharge as a way of making offenders accountable.

[19] Whether my decision in *Michael* on this issue is correct in law or not is for other courts to determine. However, I can say that based on the facial reasons expressed in *Tinker*, I would not have found them persuasive on that question.

[20] The decision that the legislation is not grossly disproportionate is based on the Crown's concession that two years is sufficient time to pay, and reduces the sting of the victim surcharge.

[21] The Order in Council that exists in Ontario pursuant to the delegated authority of the *Criminal Code* provides that payment of victim surcharges must be within 30 days. The extension of time to pay is discretionary, depending upon the decision of a judge. There is therefore no secure way to ensure that the victim surcharge will not be collected or sought to be collected in a quick rather than a protracted period.

[22] The decision in *Tinker* does not address the accused offenders who routinely appear before the provincial court. Many offenders who appear in these courts are addicted or mentally ill. They are often Aboriginal offenders who have often accumulated numerous convictions for minor offences, and quickly accumulate victim surcharges in the thousands of dollars, rather than in the more modest $100 summary conviction victim surcharge reflected for each of the counts in the decision before the court in *Tinker*.

[23] The decision in *Tinker* does not address the impact that it might have to have a sentence hanging over one's head indefinitely when an individual is not able to pay. It does not address the inability to expunge the debt to society, and a requirement that an individual remain under sentence because they are too poor to discharge their obligation.

[24] The decision does not address the inhibiting effects that accumulated victim surcharges can have on the ability of individuals who are attempting to rehabilitate themselves after serving their sentence. It does not look at the relative impact of victim surcharges on those who are poor, as opposed to those who are not, notwithstanding the principles of sentencing that require consideration of all relevant circumstances relating to all offenders.

[25] It does not consider the fact that individuals who do not pay their victim surcharges are ineligible for many licences, and ineligible to apply for parole (*sic*—pardon). Had this decision, therefore, been presented to me as a persuasive authority, I would not follow it, for the reasons expressed by me in *Michael*, whether those reasons are correct or not.

[26] The issue before me is therefore simpler. Is the decision binding on me? I am mindful that *Tinker* is a s. 7 case, and the arguments before me were presented under s. 12, and I agree with the submission of Mr. Brown that the punishment analysis is not binding on me, given that it is not one of the essential dispositions necessary to support the s. 7 finding.

[27] In any event, even if it was binding on me, I would have to go on and consider whether the victim surcharge is a treatment within the meaning of s. 12 before dispensing of any s. 12 challenge on the basis of the decision in *Tinker*.

[28] What is binding on me, however, is the finding that there is no gross disproportionality arising out of the victim surcharge. It is clear from the decision in *Tinker*, although the case law is not cited, that the decision is based on the principle of fundamental justice, requiring proportionality in the treatment of individuals whose life, liberty and security of the person is in peril.

[29] The Supreme Court of Canada, in *R. v. Malmo-Levine*, [2003] 3 S.C.R. 571 (S.C.C.), indicated that it would not be appropriate for courts to interpret the concept of proportionality differently under s. 7 than it is interpreted under s. 12. The Ontario Court of Appeal in the recent decision of *R. v. Safarzadeh-Markhali*, [2014] O.J. No. 4194 (Ont. C.A.), held that when a sentence, as opposed to the process by which a sentence is arrived at, is being challenged under s. 7, the appropriate principle of fundamental justice requires gross disproportionality.

[30] In my view, the finding with respect to s. 7 predicated upon the principle of fundamental justice of gross disproportionality in the *Tinker* case is inconsistent fundamentally with an essential component of the reasoning of this court in *R. v. Michael*, The *Tinker* decision and the *Michael* decision cannot live together, and the *Tinker* decision does not exist without its finding on a key component of the *Michael* holding.

[31] I am therefore of the view that unless and until a summary conviction appeal court or the Ontario Court of Appeal rules to the contrary, after considering all of the issues that require consideration, the *Tinker* decision does settle the question, and I am obliged to follow it.

[32] I am therefore rejecting the constitutional challenge that has been brought by Mr. Eckstein, and I will be imposing the victim surcharge.

R v Madeley
2016 ONCJ 108 (footnotes omitted)

[In *Madeley*, the court considered whether the surcharge violates the right to equality in s 15 of the Charter. Healy J raised this question hypothetically in *Cloud* with respect to indigenous offenders. Here it is considered with respect to offenders with mental disabilities.]

PACIOCCO J:

[1] On December 1, 2014, 36 year old Sunshine Madeley shoplifted makeup and then offered a threatening gesture to a store clerk who had detected her. As a result of her conduct that day she was arrested and ultimately brought before me. She pled guilty to the offence of threatening to cause death contrary to Criminal Code section 264.1(1)(a), and to breach of probation contrary to section 733.1(1)(b) by not keeping the peace and being of good behaviour.

[2] These are not Ms. Madeley's first offences. She is an unemployed, drug-addicted 36 year old woman with a history of mental illness and homelessness and a long criminal record for prostitution related offences, thefts and breaches of court orders. She is obviously poor. She is supported by the "Ontario Disability Support Program," ("ODSP").

• • •

[6] … [S]he urges that the mandatory victim surcharge provision contravenes equality rights assured under section 15 of the Charter. She complains that saddling individuals with debt obligations to hold them criminally accountable by requiring financial contributions to a fund for victim services has a disproportionate and discriminatory effect on those who cannot discharge their debt because they are disabled, in the sense defined by the *Ontario Disability Support Act*, 1997, c. 25.

• • •

[14] In this case, Ms. Madeley's complaints are primarily poverty-based, including her section 15 claim, which is predicated on the impact of the mandatory victim surcharge on the mentally disabled, a group that, disproportionately, is poor.

• • •

[25] I am persuaded that the victim surcharge has an adverse impact on the mentally disabled because of the class characteristic that mentally disabled persons are disproportionately poor. This makes the victim surcharge more onerous for the mentally disabled than it is for most other offenders, and leaves mentally disabled persons who cannot pay promptly because of their poverty, including Ms. Madeley, subjected to overlong exposure to the law's enforcement measures, and to the continued stigma and pressure of their undischarged criminal sentence.

[26] I am also persuaded that the effect of the victim surcharge discriminates against the mentally disabled. It exacerbates the historical economic disadvantage of many mentally disabled offenders and it leaves many of them under ongoing, if not perpetual, undischarged criminal sanction. In my view, through no fault of the offender, their lingering criminal debt can only feed the stereotypical link between mental disorder and criminality. Meanwhile, the enforcement mechanisms available to be used contribute to

marginalization of mentally disabled persons, and exacerbate their exclusion from full participation in society. In short, when applied to poor, mentally disabled individuals, section 737 enhances the perception of prejudice and the experience of displacement.

[27] This is so, in my view, even though other sentencing provisions that have a disproportionate impact on enumerated or analogous groups are not generally discriminatory. Typically, sentencing provisions are not "discriminatory," even when affecting a protected group disproportionately, because discrimination is to be measured through the eyes of a reasonable person standing in the position of the claimant, and who is deemed to be fully informed, including about the nature of the law that is being applied. A reasonable person in the position of an over-represented aboriginal or black offender, for example, would understand when they are being sentenced that they are not being sentenced because they are aboriginal or black, and that their sentence is not an affront to the group. Instead, they would appreciate that they are being sentenced as individuals because they deserve the punishment imposed. Even a reasonable person sentenced to a minimum fine for impaired driving, including a characteristically poor aboriginal offender, or a poor mentally disordered offender, would not feel discriminated against by the fixed financial penalty. They would be deemed to know that this fine is tailored to their specific conduct, and is imposed as an individual penalty because it is deserved.

[28] In contrast, the victim surcharge is not an individual consequence imposed on particular offenders based on what they have done, in light of their personal circumstance. Instead, the victim surcharge is a general consequence imposed on all offenders regardless of what they have done, and regardless of their personal circumstances. Simply put, there is no ameliorative explanation for the victim surcharge that can remove the reasonable perception that its disproportionate adverse effect has a discriminatory impact on the group at large.

[29] Put more specifically, a reasonable mentally disordered offender, too poor to pay the victim surcharge promptly, or at all, would know that they are being subjected to the ongoing enforcement effects and pressures of a sanction that is untethered to proportionality, moral fault, or notions of just desert, simply because of their class-related poverty. That reasonable person would also understand that, unlike those who can afford to pay, they have not yet been held fully accountable in law for their offence, and that their debt to society lingers, simply because of their class-related poverty. In my view, as laudable as the goal of raising funds for victim's services is, a reasonable person in this situation can only conclude that the law has an unfair and discriminatory effect on characteristically poor, mentally disabled offenders.

• • •

[58] Counsel for Ms. Madeley contends that the relevant personal characteristic for the purpose of the analysis is that Ms. Madeley is "an offender with a disability as defined by the *Ontario Disability Support Act*." The Crown is correct in stating that "ODSP offenders" is not an enumerated or analogous class. Protected classes under section 15 are not created by statutory eligibility requirements. They are recognized, instead, based on personal characteristics linked to historical disadvantage. I have no basis for concluding that persons receiving "ODSP" are, by virtue of that specific class membership, historically disadvantaged as the result of prejudice or stereotyping.

[59] On its face, this may appear to dispose of the section 15 Charter claim because I am to rule on the Charter application before me. To summarily dismiss this application

on that basis, however, would be churlish. In spite of how counsel articulated the relevant class, it is evident both from the written application and oral submissions received that Ms. Madeley's complaint is that she suffers from a mental disability, and that the victim surcharge levy is more burdensome and discriminatory for her because of her mental disabilities. In other words, her claim is based on "mental disability," a specifically enumerated class that unlike other enumerated classes includes personal circumstances that "may be, but [are] not necessarily immutable": *Granovsky v. Canada (Minister of Employment and Immigration)* [2000] S.C.J. No. 29 at para 28.

[60] The Crown disagrees with this characterization. It contends that even if Ms. Madeley is "mentally disabled," a claim that is not conceded, Ms. Madeley's complaint is, in substance, about the impact of the victim surcharge on the poor, and "[i]t is well established that income level is not a personal characteristic": *Guillemette v Canada* [1997] T.C.J. No. 589 at para 21(Tax Court of Canada); *Re Affordable Energy Coalition* 2009 NSCA 17; *R. v. Banks* (2007), 216 C.C.C. (3d) 19 (Ont. C.A.)

[61] It is true that "poor people" are not an enumerated or analogous class. This is because "the term [poor people] signifies an amorphous group" of persons whose poverty can arise in numerous ways and for various reasons: *R. v. Banks, supra* at para 104. Had Ms. Madeley said "I am bringing my claim on behalf of poor people," the Crown argument would prevail. But that is not what she is doing. As indicated, she is bringing this claim on behalf of mentally disabled persons, on the footing that poverty is a class characteristic that results in discriminatory effects against disabled persons if the victim surcharge is applied indiscriminately. In substance, then, the Crown's challenge to the integrity of the class is based on the theory that if the essence of a complaint made by a member of an enumerated group relates to the poverty or the income level of members of the group, it is not a tenable section 15 Charter claim.

[62] In spite of the able argument presented, this cannot be right. It would mean that gender-based equality claims grounded in the feminization of poverty, or equal pay for work of equal value complaints, could not be advanced under section 15 because they are, in substance, complaints about income level. Yet in … [*Quebec (Attorney General) v A*, 2013 SCC 5, [2013] 1 SCR 61], the majority of the Supreme Court of Canada found a *prima facie* section 15 breach based on the differential treatment of economic remedies on relationship break-up between married and non-married partners, and in *Newfoundland (Treasury Board) v. N.A.P.E.* [2004] 3 S.C.R. 381 the Supreme Court of Canada agreed with the courts below that legislation abolishing equal pay protection violated section 15 of the Charter. In both cases the legislation was saved only under section 1.

• • •

[79] So, does Ms. Madeley suffer from a mental disorder that has the effect of materially impeding her proper functioning, including her ability to function in the community? Mr. Phillips argues that Ms. Madeley must have a "mental disability" because she receives "ODSP," which is paid only to those who are disabled. I cannot act on this submission. In law, Ms. Madeley's receipt of ODSP, at best, represents a hearsay opinion held by someone who has not testified before me that she is disabled. I must therefore look at other available evidence.

[80] I will begin with evidence of her mental disorder. Ms. Madeley testified that she suffers from severe anxiety, depression, and post-traumatic stress disorder from the many years she has spent on the streets. She testified that she has recently been diagnosed with

bipolar disorder. She has been prescribed and takes Seroquel and Celexa for these conditions. The Crown did not challenge this evidence during cross-examination. Indeed, presentence report documentation from as long ago as 2004, secured by the Crown, verifies that Ms. Madeley had once been taken to a hospital under the *Mental Health Act* for suicidal ideation, and that she suffers from ADHD, and was recommended by the probation officer to consult a family doctor for issues of depression. She has also had a Canadian Mental Health Association worker for some time.

[81] The evidence before me also shows that Ms. Madeley struggles to participate effectively in society. She has lived long periods of her life on the streets, and has not had legitimate employment for many years. She has lost two children to child welfare agencies, and is a chronic recidivist. She has had only sporadic success with her rehabilitative efforts. Indeed, she was unable to organize herself adequately to complete a full presentence report in preparation of her sentencing before me, and the Probation and Parole Services Report of June 23, 2015 confirms that she has struggled to "get her act together."

[82] The Crown nonetheless challenged the claim that Ms. Madeley is disabled by urging that she is capable of working either now, or will be in the near future. Reliance was placed upon Ms. Madeley's testimony that she has worked in the past, is planning on taking a stabilization program offered by the Canadian Mental Health Association to learn life skills, and is hopeful that she will be able to find work. In my view, Ms. Madeley's condition cannot be measured either by her distant past, or by her current hopes. I am satisfied on the evidence before me, to the constitutional standard that applies—the balance of probabilities—that she is incapable of maintaining gainful employment and will remain dependent on social assistance in the foreseeable future.

[83] The Crown also challenged the correlation between Ms. Madeley's mental disorder and any disability she might have. Ms. Tansey contended that, on the evidence, Ms. Madeley's inability to participate in society may be related to her criminal record which Ms. Madelely herself focused on as her employment obstacle, or on Ms. Madeley's drug addiction, instead of any mental illness she may have.

[84] To be sure, it would have been prudent for Ms. Madeley's counsel to have provided medical evidence verifying the relationship between Ms. Madeley's mental illnesses and the challenges she has had in coping. Without attempting to resolve the "chicken and egg" relationship between Ms. Madeley's addictions and criminal record, and her mental illness, however, the fact that other pressures may also impede her proper functioning does not negate a "mental disability" finding. There is no question that if her mental health woes have not caused her to become an addicted criminal, her mental health has played a material role.

[85] This is not a matter of conjecture but of history. As described, mental health services have played a large role in assisting Ms. Madeley to try to cope in society. Her probation officer, responsible for her rehabilitation, suggested that she receive help with her depression, she is provided with CMHA assistance in the community, and as the Crown pointed out in argument, Ms. Madeley's rehabilitation aspirations rest with a mental health stabilization program offered by the CMHA.

[86] Given this and the conditions she describes, I am satisfied on the balance of probabilities that Ms. Madeley's mental illness contributes materially to her disability. She therefore has a mental disability within the meaning of section 15, and the standing to bring this challenge.

· · ·

[95] I must therefore determine without the benefit of a guiding decision whether the victim surcharge "has a disproportionately negative impact on a group or individual that can be identified by factors relating to enumerated or analogous grounds." More precisely, I have to resolve whether the victim surcharge has a disproportionately negative effect on Ms. Madeley and other mentally disabled persons, because of factors relating to their mental disability.

[96] Ms. Madeley did not provide statistical or expert evidence confirming the impact of the mandatory imposition of the victim surcharge on the mentally disabled. The "distinction-based" proposition being offered, however, is straightforward. It is that poverty is an historical or sociological disadvantage that makes it more difficult for many members of the group to pay the victim surcharge and avoid its enforcement strategies, the way that others who are not similarly situated can generally do.

. . .

[172] I am therefore finding that section 737 is in *prima facie* violation of section 15 of the Charter, the provision charged with "ameliorating the position of groups within Canadian society who have suffered disadvantage by exclusion from mainstream society as has been the case with disabled persons:" *Eaton v. Brant County Board of Education*, [1997] 1 S.C.R. 241 at para 66.

For further consideration of the constitutionality of the victim surcharge, see *R c Malouin*, 2015 QCCQ 14118; *R v Barinecutt*, 2015 BCPC 189; *R v Laroque*, 2015 ONSC 5407; and *R v Novielli*, 2015 ONCJ 192.

NOTE

1. Following the decision of the Court of Appeal in *Cloud*, in what ways and by what means could a sentencing court compensate for disproportionality attributable to the imposition of the surcharge?

2. Can a sentencing court order that the victim surcharge be paid out of funds seized from the offender that would otherwise be forfeited to the Crown in order to ensure that the surcharge is paid? See *R v Shearer*, 2015 ONCA 355 at paras 6-7.

3. The victim surcharge provisions allow the various jurisdictions to pass regulations setting the time to pay the surcharge and, if no regulation is passed, reasonable time to pay may be granted. Do regulations made prior to the recent amendments to the provisions continue to apply? See *R v Shaddon*, 2014 SKPC 70, 443 Sask R 53. If no regulation is passed, what constitutes reasonable time to pay? In *Tinker* and *Eckstein*, above, the Crown accepted that two years to pay was reasonable. What about even longer periods, especially if the offender is not being sentenced to a period of imprisonment? Must the court allow an offender time to pay? See *R v Bateman*, 2015 BCSC 2071 and *R v Chaussé*, 2014 QCCQ 5234, aff'd 2016 QCCA 568.

4. On the basis of *R v Madeley*, are there other grounds on which the surcharge might be considered inconsistent with s 15 of the Charter?

III. RESTITUTION

Before the 1996 amendments, the *Criminal Code* addressed the issue of making an offender reimburse his or her victims through two mechanisms. First, the Code contained a provision that permitted sentencing judges to make "compensation orders" in favour of named victims that could be enforced against the offender in the same way as a civil judgment. Second, the Code authorized the inclusion of "restitution orders" as a term of probation, which were enforceable, like any other term of probation, with the threat of a criminal charge under s 733.1.

In *R v Zelensky*, [1978] 2 SCR 940, the Supreme Court of Canada considered and upheld the compensation and restitution provisions as a valid exercise of Parliament's criminal law power. In the court's view, they reflected (at 949) "a scheme of criminal law administration under which property, taken or destroyed or damaged in the commission of a crime, is brought into account following the disposition of culpability, and may be ordered by the criminal court to be returned to the victimized owner if it is under the control of the court and its ownership is not in dispute or that reparation be made by the offender, either in whole or in part out of money found in his possession when arrested if it is indisputably his and otherwise under an order for compensation, where the property has been destroyed or damaged."

In 1996, a discrete form of restitution order replaced the earlier provisions. In 2015, further amendments were made to the restitution provisions that codified many of the principles developed by the courts. The current scheme is set out in ss 737.1 to 741.2 of the *Criminal Code*. These provisions answer a number of the technical issues that plagued the earlier scheme. Many cases dealing with the prior mechanisms of compensation and restitution therefore have little relevance today except to show the legislative history and explain why some provisions have been enacted. The current scheme also broadens the situations in which restitution may be ordered. What impact, if any, does this have on the constitutionality of the provisions? In considering the current sections and the applicable cases, keep in mind the following two purposes of sentencing as stated in s 718 of the Code:

   (e) to provide reparations for harm done to victims or to the community; and

   (f) to promote a sense of responsibility in offenders, and acknowledgement of the harm done to victims or to the community.

See *R v Yates*, 2002 BCCA 583, 169 CCC (3d) 506.

A. Criminal Code, Sections 737.1 to 741.2

Court to consider restitution order

   737.1(1) If an offender is convicted or discharged under section 730 of an offence, the court that sentences or discharges the offender, in addition to any other measure imposed on the offender, shall consider making a restitution order under section 738 or 739.

   (2) As soon as feasible after a finding of guilt and in any event before imposing the sentence, the court shall inquire of the prosecutor if reasonable steps have been taken to provide the victims with an opportunity to indicate whether they are seeking restitution for their losses and damages, the amount of which must be readily ascertainable.

   (3) On application of the prosecutor or on its own motion, the court may adjourn the proceedings to permit the victims to indicate whether they are seeking restitution or to establish

their losses and damages, if the court is satisfied that the adjournment would not interfere with the proper administration of justice.

· · ·

(5) If a victim seeks restitution and the court does not make a restitution order, it shall include in the record a statement of the court's reasons for not doing so.

Restitution to victims of offences

738(1) Where an offender is convicted or discharged under section 730 of an offence, the court imposing sentence on or discharging the offender may, on application of the Attorney General or on its own motion, in addition to any other measure imposed on the offender, order that the offender make restitution to another person as follows:

(a) in the case of damage to, or the loss or destruction of, the property of any person as a result of the commission of the offence or the arrest or attempted arrest of the offender, by paying to the person an amount not exceeding the replacement value of the property as of the date the order is imposed, less the value of any part of the property that is returned to that person as of the date it is returned, where the amount is readily ascertainable;

(b) in the case of bodily or psychological harm to any person as a result of the commission of the offence or the arrest or attempted arrest of the offender, by paying to the person an amount not exceeding all pecuniary damages incurred as a result of the harm, including loss of income or support, if the amount is readily ascertainable; and

(c) in the case of bodily harm or threat of bodily harm to the offender's spouse or common-law partner or child, or any other person, as a result of the commission of the offence or the arrest or attempted arrest of the offender, where the spouse or common-law partner, child or other person was a member of the offender's household at the relevant time, by paying to the person in question, independently of any amount ordered to be paid under paragraphs (a) and (b), an amount not exceeding actual and reasonable expenses incurred by that person, as a result of moving out of the offender's household, for temporary housing, food, child care and transportation, where the amount is readily ascertainable.

(d) in the case of an offence under section 402.2 or 403, by paying to a person who, as a result of the offence, incurs expenses to reestablish their identity, including expenses to replace their identity documents and to correct their credit history and credit rating, an amount that is not more than the amount of thoses expenses, to the extent that they are reasonable, if the amount is readily ascertainable; and

(e) in the case of an offence under subsection 162.1(1), by paying to a person who, as a result of the offence, incurs expenses to remove the intimate image from the Internet or other digital network, an amount that is not more that then the amount of those expenses, to the extent that they are reasonable, if the amount is readily ascertainable.

(2) The lieutenant governor in council of a province may make regulations precluding the inclusion of provisions on enforcement of restitution orders as an optional condition of a probation order or of a conditional sentence order.

Restitution to persons acting in good faith

739. Where an offender is convicted or discharged under section 730 of an offence and

(a) any property obtained as a result of the commission of the offence has been conveyed or transferred for valuable consideration to a person acting in good faith and without notice, or

(b) the offender has borrowed money on the security of that property from a person acting in good faith and without notice,

the court may, where that property has been returned to the lawful owner or the person who had lawful possession of that property at the time the offence was committed, order the offender to pay as restitution to the person referred to in paragraph (a) or (b) an amount not exceeding the amount of consideration for that property or the total amount outstanding in respect of the loan, as the case may be.

Ability to pay

739.1 The offender's financial means or ability to pay does not prevent the court from making an order under section 738 or 739.

Payment under order

739.2 In making an order under section 738 or 739, the court shall require the offender to pay the full amount specified in the order by the day specified in the order, unless the court is of the opinion that the amount should be paid in installments, in which case the court shall set out a periodic payment scheme in the order.

More than one person

739.3 An order under section 738 or 739 may be made in respect of more than one person, in which case the order must specify the amount that is payable to each person. The order may also specify the order of priority in which those persons are to be paid.

Public authority

739.4(1) On the request of a person in whose favour an order under section 738 or 739 would be made, the court may make the order in favour of a public authority, designated by the regulations, who is to be responsible for enforcing the order and remitting to the person making the request all amounts received under it.

(2) The lieutenant governor in council of a province may, by order, designate any person or body as a public authority for the purpose of subsection (1).

Priority to restitution

740. Where the court finds it applicable and appropriate in the circumstances of a case to make, in relation to an offender, an order of restitution under section 738 or 739, and

(a) an order of forfeiture under this or any other Act of Parliament may be made in respect of property that is the same as property in respect of which the order of restitution may be made, or

(b) the court is considering ordering the offender to pay a fine and it appears to the court that the offender would not have the means or ability to comply with both the order of restitution and the order to pay the fine,

the court shall first make the order of restitution and shall then consider whether and to what extent an order of forfeiture or an order to pay a fine is appropriate in the circumstances.

Enforcing restitution order

741(1) An offender who fails to pay all of the amount that is ordered to be paid under section 732.1, 738, 739 or 742.3 by the day specified in the order or who fails to make a periodic payment required under the order is in default of the order and the person to whom the amount, or the periodic payment, as the case may be, was to be made may, by filing the order, enter as a judgment any amount ordered to be paid that remains unpaid under the order in any civil court in Canada that has jurisdiction to enter a judgment for that amount, and that judgment is enforceable against the offender in the same manner as if it were a judgment rendered against the offender in that court in civil proceedings.

(2) All or any part of an amount that is ordered to be paid under section 738 or 739 may be taken out of moneys found in the possession of the offender at the time of the arrest of the offender if the court making the order, on being satisfied that ownership of or right to possession of those moneys is not disputed by claimants other than the offender, so directs.

Notice of orders of restitution

741.1 If a court makes an order of restitution under section 738 or 739, it shall cause notice of the content of the order, or a copy of the order, to be given to the person to whom the restitution is ordered to be paid, and if it is to be paid to a public authority designated by regulations made under subsection 739.4(2), to the public authority and the person to whom the public authority is to remit amounts received under the order.

Civil remedy not affected

741.2 A civil remedy for an act or omission is not affected by reason only that an order for restitution under section 738 or 739 has been made in respect of that act or omission.

The following case of *R v Castro* outlines the considerations that a sentencing court should take into account in deciding whether to make a restitution order against an offender. While reading this decision, consider the following questions: How does restitution factor into the overall sentence to be imposed? What must be shown in order to make a restitution order against an offender? Who bears the burden of proof? What is the relevance, if any, of related civil proceedings? To what extent, if any, must the court consider the offender's ability to pay? How is ability to pay to be assessed? Must the court allow time to pay? How is a restitution order enforced against an offender?

R v Castro
2010 ONCA 718, 261 CCC (3d) 304 (footnotes omitted)

KM WEILER JA (MacPherson and Armstrong JJA concurring):

[1] Should the order obliging the appellant, Carlos Castro, to make restitution in the amount of $141,752 to the victims of his thefts be upheld? For the reasons that follow, I would answer "yes" and dismiss this appeal.

Facts

1. Background

[2] The appellant was born in Peru on February 28, 1959, and immigrated to Canada in 1991. In 2000, he opened a paralegal firm with his brother, Manuel. The firm specialized in assisting victims of motor vehicle accidents in reaching personal injury settlements with insurance companies. The appellant's clients were new immigrants to Canada whose first language, like his, was Spanish. Many were unemployed and on social assistance or disability pensions.

[3] In April of 2001, the appellant began to steal from some of his clients. The appellant deposited the settlement cheques from the accidents in his trust account and then converted that money to his own use. The banking records show that he used the funds to buy money orders for an unknown purpose. When questioned by the clients as to where the money was, the appellant lied about not having reached a settlement or not having received the settlement cheque. In addition, the appellant was found guilty of forging the signature of one client, Ms. Blanca Benitez, on a release document that finalized a settlement agreement. He then used the document to defraud State Farm Insurance.

[4] Acting on complaints, the Financial Services Commission suspended the appellant's insurance licence in December 2004. By April 2005 the firm had stopped operating and was evicted by the landlord.

[5] Following a trial, the appellant was found guilty on May 27, 2008, of six counts of theft relating to the settlement money of six clients, two counts of forgery, and one count of fraud ... .

. . .

[8] The appellant was sentenced to 23 months' imprisonment plus 2 years' probation, and ordered to make restitution pursuant to s. 738(1) of the *Criminal Code*, R.S.C. 1985, c. C-46. He has served the custodial portion of his sentence. The appellant seeks to have the restitution portion of his sentence set aside or to have the amount reduced.

[9] Manuel Castro, who had also been charged, was acquitted. He had no signing authority on the firm's bank accounts and the trial judge found he was not directly involved in the transfer or conversion of funds.

. . .

The Issues on Appeal

[20] The appellant submits that in making the restitution order, the trial judge committed three errors: (1) he did not consider restitution alongside the sentence of incarceration, and ordered it as a "mechanical afterthought"; (2) he did not consider the appellant's ability to pay; and (3) he did not exercise caution and restraint in making the restitution order.

Analysis

[21] Section 738(1)(a) governs the making of restitution orders when money has been taken. It gives the court discretion to order the offender to make restitution by paying the victim "an amount not exceeding the replacement value of the property as of the date the order is imposed, less the value of any part of the property that is returned ... where the amount is readily ascertainable."

[22] A restitution order forms part of a sentence. In accordance with general sentencing principles, a restitution order is entitled to deference and an appellate court will only interfere with the sentencing judge's exercise of discretion on the basis of error in principle or if the order is excessive or inadequate: see *R. v. Devgan* (1999), ... 136 C.C.C. (3d) 238 (Ont. C.A.), at para. 28.

[23] A restitution order should not be made as a mechanical afterthought to a sentence of imprisonment: *R. v. Siemens* (1999), ... 136 C.C.C. (3d) 353 ([Man.] C.A.), at para. 10. Care must be taken not to simply add a restitution order to a sentence of imprisonment which, in itself, is a fit punishment for the crime, as this can amount to excessive punishment and offend the totality principle.

[24] The starting point for any discussion of the objectives and factors that inform a judge's exercise of discretion in making a restitution order is the Supreme Court of Canada's decision in *R. v. Zelensky*, [1978] 2 S.C.R. 940 ... . While the decision deals with predecessor legislation, the decision of Laskin C.J.C. nevertheless serves as a blueprint for the considerations to be taken into account in making a restitution order under

s. 738(1). These considerations were summarized by Labrosse J.A. in *Devgan* at para. 26 as part of a non-exhaustive list:

> In *Zelensky*, Laskin C.J. identified certain objectives and factors that relate to the application of s. 725(1). These considerations have been expanded upon in subsequent cases. Below, I have consolidated these objectives and factors, all of which are relevant to the issue of what constitutes a proper exercise of discretion for the purpose of s. 725(1).
>
> 1. An order for compensation should be made with restraint and caution;
> 2. The concept of compensation is essential to the sentencing process:
>   (i) it emphasizes the sanction imposed upon the offender;
>   (ii) it makes the accused responsible for making restitution to the victim;
>   (iii) it prevents the accused from profiting from crime; and
>   (iv) it provides a convenient, rapid and inexpensive means of recovery for the victim;
> 3. A sentencing judge should consider:
>   (i) the purpose of the aggrieved person in invoking s. 725(1);
>   (ii) whether civil proceedings have been initiated and are being pursued; and
>   (iii) the means of the offender.
> 4. A compensation order should not be used as a substitute for civil proceedings. Parliament did not intend that compensation orders would displace the civil remedies necessary to ensure full compensation to victims.
> 5. A compensation order is not the appropriate mechanism to unravel involved commercial transactions;
> 6. A compensation order should not be granted when it would require the criminal court to interpret written documents to determine the amount of money sought through the order. The loss should be capable of ready calculation.
> 7. A compensation order should not be granted if the effect of provincial legislation would have to be considered in order to determine what order should be made;
> 8. Any serious contest on legal or factual issues should signal a denial of recourse to an order;
> 9. Double recovery can be prevented by the jurisdiction of the civil courts to require proper accounting of all sums recovered; and
> 10. A compensation order may be appropriate where a related civil judgment has been rendered unenforceable as a result of bankruptcy.

* * *

[26] In general, the omission of a judge to give consideration to a relevant factor gives rise to reviewable error. Thus, the omission of a sentencing judge to give any consideration to the relevant factor of the offender's ability to repay the amount of money taken is an error. A restitution order is not intended to undermine the prospects for rehabilitation of the offender. See e.g. *R. v. Ali* ... (1997), 98 B.C.A.C. 239; *R. v. Biegus* ... (1999), 141 C.C.C. (3d) 245 (Ont. C.A.), at paras. 15 and 22; and *R. c. Ford* ... (2002), 2 C.R. (6th) 348 (C.Q. crim. & pn.).

[27] Reviewing courts have, however, consistently held that no single factor is itself determinative of whether a compensation order should be granted and that the weight to be given to individual considerations will depend on the circumstances of each case.

Those circumstances include two considerations I wish to emphasize: the nature of the offence and, when money has been taken, what has happened to the money.

[28] Insofar as the nature of the offence is concerned, in cases involving breach of trust, the paramount consideration is the claims of the victims: *Fitzgibbon* at pp. 1014-15. Ability to pay is not the predominant factor. Indeed, where the circumstances of the offence are particularly egregious, such as where a breach of trust is involved, a restitution order may be made even where there does not appear to be any likelihood of repayment: *R. v. Yates* ... (2002), 169 C.C.C. (3d) 506 (B.C.C.A.), at paras. 12 and 17.

[29] The decisions in *Ali*, *Biegus* and *Ford* do not involve a breach of trust. By contrast, *Fitzgibbon* involved an undischarged bankrupt lawyer who acknowledged the amounts he owed. He was ordered to pay compensation to the Law Society of Upper Canada's Compensation Fund and to reimburse a client for the amount by which the client's losses exceeded the maximum allowable claim from the Compensation Fund. Cory J., writing on behalf of the court, stated at pp. 1014-15 S.C.R.:

> [The appellant] used his position to defraud the very persons who had every reason to trust and rely upon him. The fraudulent acts of a lawyer directed against his own clients warranted the imposition of a compensation order even though the lawyer's means at the time of sentencing were minimal. *The claims of the victims of the fraudulent acts should be paramount.* (Emphasis added)

[30] In imposing a sentence where the offender has used his or her position to commit a breach of trust, the *primary* considerations are the protection of the public, general deterrence and the repudiation of the conduct of which the offender was found guilty. Relevant factors include the length of time over which the conduct took place, whether the offence was a sophisticated and well-planned scheme, the amount involved, and, most importantly, the impact of the offender's conduct on the victims. The *secondary* considerations are specific deterrence, rehabilitation and any mitigating circumstances such as a plea of guilty or co-operation with the authorities (in tracing the funds): *Scherer*, per Martin J.A. at para. 34.

[31] In *Sherer*, some of the victims had lost most or all of their life savings as a result of the offender's breach of trust. While Martin J.A. reduced the sentence of imprisonment from nine years to seven years, he upheld the compensation order in the amount of $2,173,164.21 to the persons aggrieved. Restitution in that case recognized the victims' needs and at the same time underlined the larger social interest in the imposition of a sanction related to the crime.

[32] Whether or not a breach of trust has occurred, the impact of the crime on the victim is an important factor. In *Biegus*, the appellant was one of several co-accused convicted of bank theft. The ringleader, Hornett, worked for Intercon Security and as a result had access to the combinations of ATM machines in various Royal Bank branches. Biegus was brought in by Hornett and participated with him in seven thefts. After Biegus pleaded guilty, he co-operated fully with the police and returned $14,000 of the cash. He received a sentence of two years less a day in jail and was ordered to make restitution of the remaining amount stolen in the seven thefts with Hornett, namely $638,534. The sentencing judge recognized that Biegus did not have the ability to pay this amount but did not say why this fact was irrelevant in imposing the order for restitution. On appeal, the court held that the sentencing judge erred in not addressing this factor and also erred

by failing to take into account the potentially unfair effect to Biegus of the restitution orders already made against two other co-accused. The court did not say that Biegus engaged in any breach of trust. The restitution order was excessive and prevented Biegus's rehabilitation. The court noted that the bank's insurer had already repaid the bank $453,387.70. Furthermore, the bank could be in a position to recover a portion of its losses from Hornett. Therefore, the court reduced the amount of restitution to $264,000, the amount Biegus acknowledged he received from the robbery. Where the victim is a large institution, or is likely to have insurance for the amount of the loss, the impact on the victim will obviously be much less than in situations where disabled or elderly persons have lost their ability to earn income and to replace the money taken.

[33] This brings me to a discussion of the second consideration I wish to emphasize, namely evidence as to what has happened to the money that was taken illegally, and how this evidence factors into a determination of the ability to pay.

[34] Ability to pay must take into consideration what disclosure has been made respecting where the money is or has gone. Depriving the offender of the fruits of his crime is one of the overarching goals of making a restitution order: see Working Paper 5: Restitution of the Law Reform Commission of Canada (Ottawa: Information Canada, October 1974), cited with approval by Laskin C.J.C. in *Zelensky*, at pp. 952-53. In cases of theft, robbery, fraud, breach of trust or the like, I see no reason why the court should accept an offender's bald assertion that he or she has no ability to make restitution because the money "is gone" when no evidence is proffered in support of this assertion. When the victims can clearly establish that "the replacement value of the property" under s. 738(1)(a) is the amount of money taken, surely it is the offender asserting that he or she has no ability to make restitution who is in the best position to provide transparency concerning what has happened to that money. A bald assertion that the money is gone should be given no weight. Similarly, when the location of the money illegally obtained by the offender is unknown, the sentencing judge is entitled to take that fact into account with respect to ability to pay in making a restitution order: see e.g. *R. v. Williams*, ... 2007 CanLII 13949 (S.C.J.), per Hill J. at para. 41.

[35] To summarize, a restitution order is simply part of the determination of an overall fit sentence, and general sentencing principles apply. While consideration of the offender's ability to pay and the impact of a restitution order on an offender's rehabilitation are factors to be considered, the weight to be given to these factors will vary depending on the nature of the offence and the circumstances of the offender. When the offence involves a breach of trust, a primary consideration is the effect on the victim; rehabilitation is a secondary consideration. Furthermore, consideration of the ability to pay includes the ability to make payment from the money taken as a source of restitution.

[36] I now apply these principles to this appeal.

1. Restitution in Addition to Imprisonment

[37] The appellant submits that the trial judge did not consider restitution alongside other aspects of the appellant's punishment. I disagree. The judge's sentencing decision must be read in context and as a whole. The judge determined that the appellant's case was similar to, but more serious than, four cases involving breach of trust where full restitution was ordered in addition to imprisonment of between 14 and 18 months: *R. v.*

McEachern ... (1978), 42 C.C.C. (2d) 189 (C.A.); *R. v. Smith* ... (2004), 191 O.A.C. 1 (C.A.); *R. v. Collalti*, [2003] O.J. No. 5353 (S.C.J.); and *Williams*. In the present case, although the trial judge did not explicitly say so, it is clear from his sentencing reasons that he considered the entirety of the sentence when making the restitution order.

2. Ability to Pay

[38] The appellant submits that the trial judge erred by not considering his ability to pay the full amount of the order. The appellant is currently unemployed and his only source of income is a monthly disability payment of $990. The restitution order in the full amount will negatively impact his post-incarceration rehabilitation. He submits that although this is a case where there has been an abuse of trust, in *Scherer* this court stated, "It may be that in some cases it would be inappropriate and undesirable to make a compensation order in an amount that is unrealistic to think the accused could ever discharge."

[39] The appellant's submission focuses on his present ability to pay. The trial judge's comment, at the conclusion of his reasons, that the appellant was only 49 years old and had many years of productive life ahead of him, is indicative that the trial judge was considering the appellant's future prospects in imposing the restitution order he did. The trial judge had before him evidence that the appellant hoped to open his own business restoring furniture and had a standing offer of employment with a cleaning company. The trial judge imposed a free-standing restitution order as opposed to making restitution a term of probation, which would have required payment within a relatively short time frame.

[40] In addition, the trial judge was entitled to note, as he did, that little or no restitution had been made. It is not clear to me whether Carlos Castro was present when Manuel Castro made his comment to Mr. Cristales about the money being "in a place where no one can get at it," nor were Carlos and Manuel Castro co-venturers. Thus, for the purposes of this appeal, I will assume that the comment is not admissible against the appellant. However, there was no evidence proffered as to what the appellant did with the money once he withdrew it from his trust account. The trial judge rightly rejected counsel's bald submission that the money had been used to buy drugs for his brother's cocaine habit. The lack of evidence as to what happened to the money obtained by the appellant's conduct was a fact open to the trial judge to consider regarding ability to pay.

[41] I therefore find that the trial judge did not fail to take into consideration the appellant's ability to pay.

3. Restraint and Caution in Making a Restitution Order

[42] In oral submissions before this court, the appellant submitted that the restitution order is a prejudice to him because he cannot apply for a pardon for his crimes until he has made restitution to his victims. Without a pardon, it is unlikely that the appellant will be able to obtain certain types of employment. Where fraud is involved, a restitution order survives bankruptcy. The victims are also free to pursue civil remedies. The appellant submits that in making a restitution order for the full amount owed, [the] trial judge did not exercise restraint and caution. The restitution order should be reduced.

[43] The comment that a restitution order should be made with restraint and caution is sometimes taken out of context as a free-standing brake on the making of a

compensation order. The comment by Laskin C.J.C. in *Zelensky* regarding restraint and caution was made in the context of a broader statement that the purpose of a compensation order should not be to enforce a civil obligation, particularly where the amount taken is unclear; rather, the purpose of a compensation order is as part of the sentence. See *Zelensky* at pp. 961-62 S.C.R. The fact that a restitution order provides a convenient, rapid and inexpensive means of recovery for the victim, especially a vulnerable victim, is one of the considerations in favour of the making of such an order.

[44] In this case, the court was advised that some of the victims initiated civil proceedings against the appellant, and at least one victim, Mr. Fausto Romero, has obtained a civil judgment that remains unsatisfied. Thus, the trial judge's purpose in ordering restitution was not to circumvent the civil process respecting a disputed amount. There was no dispute at trial as to the amount the appellant had stolen. The victims tended to understate the amounts they were owed. The trial judge determined the amount of restitution based on the victims' estimates and thus the amount ordered already represents a reduction.

[45] The civil judgment obtained remains unsatisfied. It appears that the appellant's paralegal firm, Castro and Associates, has gone bankrupt. The record is silent as to whether the appellant has personally declared bankruptcy. While the appellant points out that an order for the repayment of money obtained by fraud survives bankruptcy, there was only one allegation of fraud respecting forgery of Ms. Benitez's signature and no damage flowed from that. The other amounts were stolen. Inasmuch as a restitution order survives bankruptcy, it is possibly the only means of preserving the victims' claims against the appellant.

Conclusion

[46] The imposition of the restitution order was a proper exercise of the trial judge's discretion and he gave effect to the requisite factors. The appellant used his position as a paralegal to engage in a breach of trust vis-à-vis vulnerable disabled persons. He has some future prospects, and the disposition of the money obtained by his conduct is unknown. The restitution order may be the only means of preserving the victims' claims against the appellant. Accordingly, I would dismiss the appeal and uphold the restitution order.

[47] The court is indebted to counsel for a very thorough and well argued appeal.

NOTE

In a footnote to *Castro*, Weiler JA added the following to her comments on how to assess an offender's ability to pay a restitution order:

The sentencing judge should take into consideration more than present income. The offender's future ability to earn will be at least as important, if not more so, than his or her present means to pay: *R. v. Hoyt* … [(1992), 77 CCC (3d) 289 (BCCA)], at p. 299. The person who has striven to succeed in the past may well do so in the future and be able to make payment: *R. v. Moscone*, [1985] B.C.J. No. 1755 (C.A.). Consideration of the offender's ability to pay must also take into consideration any assets owned or controlled by the offender, such as equity in a home: *R. v. Rizzetto* … (2002), 210 N.S.R. (2d) 67 (C.A.), at para. 16; *Yates* at paras. 28-33.

Additional difficulties arise when restitution orders are sought in cases with multiple victims with different claims to restitution or where multiple offenders were involved in the commission of the offence. The following case illustrates some of the complexities that arise in cases involving more than one offender. The appellant and her father were charged with running a Ponzi scheme in which the appellant's father induced investors to contribute funds with a promise of high returns. When the Saskatchewan Financial Services Commission ordered the company to stop soliciting and accepting funds, the scheme collapsed. The appellant's father pleaded guilty to several offences and was sentenced to seven years imprisonment and restitution in the amount of $16,742,441.12. The appellant was convicted after trial and sentenced to 30 months jail and restitution in the amount of $1 million. On appeal, the court reduced the restitution order to $250,000. What factors prompted the court to make such a reduction?

R v Fast-Carlson
2015 SKCA 86, [2015] 11 WWR 673

WHITMORE JA (Richards CJ and Herauf JA concurring):

III. Issues

[9] The following issues arise based on the submissions of the parties:
   (a) Is the appellant's sentence with respect to the $1 million restitution order demonstrably unfit?
   (b) Is the restitution order imposed by the sentencing judge in error, as there is a theoretical possibility that the victims of the fraud may be over-compensated by the appellant and her father?

IV. Analysis

A. Is the Appellant's Sentence with Respect to the $1 Million Restitution Order Demonstrably Unfit?

• • •

[11] There are two leading cases that summarize the principles applicable to restitution orders. The first is *R v Siemens* (1999), 138 Man R (2d) 90 (CA). Huband J.A., writing for the Manitoba Court of Appeal, summarized the relevant principles as follows:

> [8] From the wording of s. 738(1)(a) and its predecessor, the old s. 725(1), it is obvious that it is discretionary as to whether the court orders restitution or not. There is case law concerning both the old s. 725(1) and the present s. 738(1)(a) which forms a useful guide as to how that discretion should be exercised.
>
> (1) The constitutional justification for a provision in the Code permitting restitution orders is that restitution is a part of the punishment. Where punishment is exacted in the form of a restitution order, there should be a corresponding reduction in other forms of punishment which might be imposed. In some cases, a restitution order will be a significant factor, while in others it will be trivial, depending on the circumstances, but it must be included as a factor in the totality of the punishment imposed.

(2) The means of the offender are to be considered as an important factor in determining whether restitution should be ordered. That factor was specifically mentioned by Laskin C.J.C., who wrote for the majority of the Supreme Court of Canada, in *R. v. Zelensky*, [1978] 2 S.C.R. 940, 41 C.C.C. (2d) 97. At p. 961, Laskin C.J.C. stated that the various factors, including the means of the offender, came down to this:

> … an order for compensation should only be made with restraint and with caution.

In the subsequent decision of the Ontario Court of Appeal in *R. v. Scherer* (1984), 16 C.C.C. (3d) 30, Martin J.A., speaking for the appeal panel, agreed that the means of the offender is a factor to be considered, but that it is not a controlling factor in every case. Martin J.A. went on to note at pp. 37-38:

> It may be that in some cases it would be inappropriate and undesirable to make a compensation order in an amount that it is unrealistic to think the accused could ever discharge.

(3) The impact of a restitution order upon the chances of rehabilitation of the accused, either pro or con, is a factor to be considered. In *R. v. Spellacy (R.A.)* (1995), 131 Nfld. & P.E.I.R. 127, at para. 79, the Court of Appeal of Newfoundland approbated a passage from *Sentencing in Canada* (1982), by R. Paul Nadin-Davis, which contained the following passage at p. 497:

> A compensation order which would ruin the accused financially, thus impairing his chances of rehabilitation, should not be imposed … .

(4) The shorter the sentence, the more likely it will be that a restitution order will be appropriate. Where the amount is manageable, there is every reason to impose an order of restitution when a sentence either does not involve imprisonment or is so short that it does not affect the offender's employment or the sentence can be served conditionally. Conversely, as an incarceratory sentence becomes longer, the futility of an order of restitution will become increasingly apparent.

(5) An order of restitution need not be for the full amount of the loss. As an example, in *R. v. Ali (K.N.M.)* (1997), 98 B.C.A.C. 239, a restitution order of $42,500 was reduced by the British Columbia Court of Appeal to $10,000 to better reflect the accused's capacity to meet the obligation which the order imposed.

(6) Difficulties in determining the amount of the victim's loss will militate against a restitution order since it would be unwise for a criminal court to become involved in the determination of damages. In *Spellacy*, O'Neill J.A. wrote at para. 75:

> The law is clear that an order ought not be made by a judge if it requires the court to make extensive inquiries and examine witnesses and evidence generally in an attempt to reach a conclusion.

[9] Similar complications will arise where, as in this case, there are multiple victims, some with large claims and some with small, each entitled to a proportionate share of whatever monies are paid by way of restitution.

[10] To these factors which have been delineated in previous judicial decisions I would add the following:

(1) Where there is a plea bargain, and restitution is not part of it, the court should be slow to make an order of restitution unless it is for a very modest sum.

(2) Even in a case where the discretion of the sentencing judge is not constrained by a joint recommendation, an order of restitution must not be made as a mechanical afterthought to an incarceratory sentence.

(3) The fact that there were multiple participants in the crimes, as there were in these break and enters, is a factor which militates against a restitution order enforceable against one accused, but not against the others.

[12] The second case is *R v Devgan* (1999), 121 OAC 265 (CA) [*Devgan*] from the Ontario Court of Appeal. Labrosse J.A., writing for the Court, summarized the factors that "are relevant to the issue of what constitutes a proper exercise of discretion" (para. 26) in deciding whether to make a restitution order:

[26] ... I have consolidated these objectives and factors, all of which are relevant to the issue of what constitutes a proper exercise of discretion for the purpose of s. 725(1).

1. An order for compensation should be made with restraint and caution;
2. The concept of compensation is essential to the sentencing process;
   (i) it emphasizes the sanction imposed upon the offender;
   (ii) it makes the accused responsible for making restitution to the victim;
   (iii) it prevents the accused from profiting from the crime; and
   (iv) it provides a convenient, rapid and inexpensive means of recovery for the victim;
3. A sentencing judge should consider;
   (i) the purpose of the aggrieved person in invoking s. 725(1);
   (ii) whether civil proceedings have been initiated and are being pursued; and
   (iii) the means of the offender;
4. A compensation order should not be used as a substitute for civil proceedings. Parliament did not intend that compensation orders would displace the civil remedies necessary to ensure full compensation to victims.
5. A compensation order is not the appropriate mechanism to unravel involved commercial transactions;
6. A compensation order should not be granted when it would require the criminal court to interpret written documents to determine the amount of money sought through the order. The loss should be capable of ready calculation.
7. A compensation order should not be granted if the effect of provincial legislation would have to be considered in order to determine what order should be made;
8. Any serious contest on legal or factual issues should signal a denial of recourse to an order;
9. Double recovery can be prevented by the jurisdiction of the civil courts to require proper accounting of all sums recovered; and
10. A compensation order may be appropriate where a related civil judgment has been rendered unenforceable as a result of bankruptcy.

[13] In *Sentencing*, 8th ed (Markham: LexisNexis, 2012), Clayton C. Ruby, Gerald Chan, and Nader R. Hason stated, "[t]he court must take any restitution order into account in

determining the appropriate sentence, as the totality principle applies to the whole of the sentence, including the order of restitution" (p. 62).

[14] As Laskin C.J.C. held in *The Queen v Zelensky*, [1978] 2 SCR 940 [*Zelensky*], the offender's capacity to pay is a relevant factor that a sentencing judge should take into account when deciding whether to order restitution:

> The Court's power to make a concurrent order for compensation as part of the sentencing process is discretionary. I am of the view that in exercising that discretion the Court should have regard to whether the aggrieved person is invoking s. 653 [the predecessor to s. 738] to emphasize the sanctions against the offender as well as to benefit himself. A relevant consideration would be whether civil proceedings have been taken and, if so, whether they are being pursued. *There are other factors that enter into the exercise of the discretion, such as the means of the offender, and whether the criminal court will be involved in a long process of assessment of the loss, although I do not read s. 653 as requiring exact measurement.* (Emphasis added, p. 961)

[15] The view in *Zelensky*, in which the ability to pay is simply one factor amongst many, is confirmed by the Ontario Court of Appeal in *R v Scherer* (1984), 5 OAC 297 (CA), leave to appeal ref'd, [1984] SCCA No 29 (QL). Writing for the Court, Martin J.A. held the following:

> [19] … I do not read the Chief Justice's judgment, however, as indicating that the means of the offender is, in every case, controlling. It may be that in some cases it would be inappropriate and undesirable to make a compensation order in an amount that it is unrealistic to think the accused could ever discharge

[16] In other situations, however, the Supreme Court has recognized that the offender's inability to pay should not dissuade a court from making a restitution order, particularly where the offender committed a breach of trust: see *R v Fitzgibbon*, [1990] 1 SCR 1005; see also *R v Griffiths*, 2005 ABCA 131 at para 4.

[17] In *R v Castro*, 2010 ONCA 718, 102 OR (3d) 609 [*Castro*]—a case involving a breach of trust—the offender appealed the restitution order, placing heavy emphasis on his inability to pay. However, the sentencing judge had commented that Mr. Castro was relatively young "and had many years of productive life ahead of him" (para. 39). The Ontario Court of Appeal upheld the restitution order. In so doing, the Court relied on the sentencing judge's comment about Mr. Castro's youth and concomitant future ability to pay:

> [39] The appellant's submission focuses on his present ability to pay. The trial judge's comment, at the conclusion of his reasons, that the appellant was only 49 years old and had many years of productive life ahead of him, is indicative that the trial judge was considering the appellant's future prospects in imposing the restitution order he did. The trial judge had before him evidence that the appellant hoped to open his own business restoring furniture and had a standing offer of employment with a cleaning company. The trial judge imposed a free standing restitution order as opposed to making restitution a term of probation, which would have required payment within a relatively short time frame.

[18] A current inability to pay is therefore not determinative of whether a restitution order should be made when the offender has committed a breach of trust.

[19] In *R v Melnychuk*, 2006 SKCA 4, 275 Sask R 319 [*Melnychuk*], this Court suggested that a court should take into account both the offender's short-term ability to pay and weigh it against the offender's long-term potential for gainful employment, which will in turn make restitution payments more likely. Weighing these competing considerations together, this Court held that the sentencing judge erred by only taking into account the offender's short-term inability to pay; the sentencing judge should not have ignored the fact that the offender was "young and has shown an ability to obtain remunerative employment in the past" (*Melnychuk*, para. 8). A restitution order was consequently appropriate because of the long-term possibility that the offender would earn sufficient means to make payments on the restitution order (notwithstanding her short-term inability to pay), and because the offender's fraud was a breach of trust (see para. 9).

[20] As this Court observed in *Melnychuk*, and which clearly informed the Ontario Court of Appeal's reasons in *Castro*, a breach of trust is an important factor in deciding whether to make a restitution order, notwithstanding current inability to pay. In *R v Nanos*, 2013 BCCA 339, 342 BCAC 22 [*Nanos*], the British Columbia Court of Appeal stated the following:

> [17] The case law is uniform on the consideration of restitution orders when the offences involve a breach of trust or theft-related cases when the stolen money is unaccounted for or not accounted for adequately. *In such a case, the fact that an offender has little or even no ability to pay the restitution order will be given little weight, as one of the principles behind the legislation is that an accused should be deprived of "the fruits of his crime."* (Emphasis added)

[21] As the Ontario Court of Appeal said in *Castro*, "in cases involving breach of trust, the paramount consideration is the claims of the victims … . Ability to pay is not a predominant factor" (para. 28). The Alberta Court of Appeal came to a similar conclusion in *R v Johnson*, 2010 ABCA 392, 493 AR 74: "an offender's means have limited import in cases of fraud" (para. 29). Put simply, reprehensible conduct or a breach of trust will weigh very heavily in favour of a restitution order, irrespective of the offender's inability to pay. Where an offender does not profit from the index offence, on the other hand, or there is no breach of trust, his inability to pay a restitution order becomes more important and merits more weight (see *Nanos*, para. 19).

• • •

[24] As the trial judge stated, this is one of the largest, if not the largest, fraud in the history of Saskatchewan. There were over 200 investors who lost in excess of $16 million in the scheme. The trial judge limited the fraud during the appellant's tenure at Marathon to a maximum of $6 million and ordered restitution of $1 million.

[25] The sentencing judge found that Ms. Fast-Carlson's culpability was less than that of her father: she was a facilitator as opposed to the planner of the fraud. Further, she was in far less of a position of trust and had direct dealings with fewer investors.

[26] In addition, the scheme did not constitute a "joint venture" as contemplated in *R v Perciballi* (2001), 146 OAC 1 (CA) (aff'd 2002 SCC 51, [2002] 2 SCR 761) [*Perciballi*]. The appellant was not a partner with her father in the fraud and did not profit from the fraud. She received only a wage that was not an inordinately high sum for the actual work done. It is clear that there is no need to deprive the appellant of the "fruits of her crime." As the trial judge found, she was used by her father for his purposes. There is no suggestion

that the proceeds of the fraud might have been hidden away so as to be available to the appellant and no suggestion that the appellant lives or has lived an extravagant lifestyle or has personal assets of any consequence.

[27] In *Zelensky* at p. 941, Laskin C.J.C. stated that "an order for compensation should only be made with restraint and with caution." In my view, when one considers that the appellant did not profit from the fraud, that she was not the architect of the fraud but was used by her father to facilitate the fraud and was in a significantly lesser position of trust, the restitution order of $1 million showed neither restraint nor caution. Not only does the amount of the order exceed the appellant's ability to pay at this time, such an order may well never be repaid and will hang over the appellant's head for her lifetime. It is, in essence, a fiscal life sentence. In such circumstances it is demonstrably unfit. Nevertheless, to absolve her of any and all responsibility for restitution would deprive the victims of any realistic opportunity of receiving any compensation for the fraudulent breach of trust. (Due to her father's health and other circumstances, it does not appear that he will be able to repay any amounts.) The appellant acknowledged that she had some ability to pay some of the principal back to investors and the sentencing judge found the appellant could still practice accounting after her release from prison.

[28] In my view, while a restitution order is appropriate, an order in the amount of $250,000 is an amount that is achievable, is within the means of the appellant to pay in the future, is not a disincentive for her to seek employment in the future, and affords some compensation, albeit nominal, for the victims.

B. Is the Restitution Order Imposed by the Sentencing Judge in Error, as There Is a Theoretical Possibility That the Victims of the Fraud May Be Over-Compensated by the Appellant and Her Father?

[29] It is clear from s. 738 of the *Criminal Code* (cited above) that the total restitution to which a victim is entitled, pursuant to a restitution order, shall not exceed the amount lost. The sentencing judge imposed a restitution order upon the appellant's father in the amount of $16,742,441.12, being the total amount the victims lost and also ordered the appellant to pay the sum of $1 million as a restitution order.

[30] The question thus becomes whether the *Criminal Code* permits a sentencing judge to make restitution orders against more than one offender that exceed in total the value of the loss by the victims.

[31] The Ontario Court of Appeal in *Devgan* said, "[d]ouble recovery can be prevented by the jurisdiction of the civil courts to require proper accounting of all sums recovered" (para. 26). Thus, where restitution orders are made against more than one offender, and the total value of those orders exceeds the total value of the property lost, the court itself can ensure that the total value of restitution paid by more than one offender does not exceed the total amount of the property lost.

[32] In *R v Biegus* (1999), 127 OAC 239 (CA), the Ontario Court of Appeal found "where there are multiple perpetrators, the order must ensure not only the proper recovery for the victim, but also not work an unfairness as between the perpetrators that would not result if the matter had been left to the civil courts" (para. 27). The Court went on to clarify that there is, however, "no bar which prevents a court from making an order against each co-accused for the full amount of the victim's loss if the circumstances justify such

an order" (para. 28), but did not clarify when the circumstances would justify such an order against each accused.

[33] The Ontario Court of Appeal found in *Perciballi* that it is appropriate to assign the full value of the loss to both appellants jointly and severally where the loss results from a joint venture. In that case, while both accused were ordered to pay the full amount of the money lost, the Court protected against double compensation by making the accused jointly and severally liable.

[34] It is arguably permissible for a court to make restitution orders against multiple offenders that exceed the total value of the property, provided the orders are constructed in such a way as to prevent any potential for over-compensation to the victims and inequity among perpetrators by making the offenders jointly and severally liable. This is difficult to do in this case as the trial judge imposed restitution orders of differing amounts upon each offender.

[35] Thus, while the sentencing judge considered the factors involved in a restitution order, and appropriately made the appellant the subject of a restitution order, in my view, and notwithstanding that the civil courts can prevent over-recovery, he erred in imposing a restitution order that exceeded the value of the property by the victims in the absence of a provision to prevent over-recovery. Therefore, to correct this in a manner that will not deprive the victims of even the largely theoretical possibility of any recovery, I would amend the restitution order with respect to Ms. Fast-Carlson such that Ms. Fast-Carlson shall be ordered to pay up to $250,000 restitution less any amounts paid by Mr. Fast in excess of $16,492,441.12 (being $250,000 less than the total amount of the fraud).

NOTES

1. Section 741.2 specifically states that the fact that a restitution order has been made under the *Criminal Code* does not itself affect the victim's ability to obtain a civil judgment for the harm caused and losses suffered as a result of the offence. What about the converse situation? That is, if the victim has already obtained a civil judgment against the offender, does the doctrine of *res judicata* apply to bar an order for restitution under the *Criminal Code*? In *R v Devgan* (1999), 136 CCC (3d) 238 (Ont CA), which was decided under the prior legislation, the Ontario Court of Appeal concluded that it did not:

> The position of the appellant cannot succeed ... . Just as s. 725 does not purport to interfere with any right of civil recourse, neither can a civil judgment purport to usurp the power given to a sentencing judge under s. 725(1). Compensation orders are discretionary, both as to whether an order should be made and as to amount. At most, the existence of a civil judgment is but a factor for the sentencing judge to consider in exercising this discretion.

If a restitution order is made in such a situation, can it include legal fees and disbursements incurred by the complainant in obtaining the civil judgment? What about prejudgment interest? See *Devgan*, above. Where both restitution orders and civil judgments are in place, civil courts have the ability to prevent double recovery by requiring a proper accounting of all sums recovered from the offender.

2. In *Devgan*, the Ontario Court of Appeal emphasized that restitution orders are not the appropriate mechanism to unravel complicated commercial transactions and they should therefore be granted only when the loss is readily calculable. A court should not make a

restitution order if this would require the court to interpret written documents or consider the effect of provincial legislation in order to determine the amount of money to be paid or if there is a serious contest on legal or factual issues. In short, restitutions orders are not a substitute for civil proceedings.

3. In *R v Fitzgibbon*, [1990] 1 SCR 1005, which involved fraud by a lawyer, the court held under the prior legislation that the Law Society of Upper Canada qualified as an aggrieved person because its compensation fund had made payments to the clients who had been defrauded. Could an order in favour of the Law Society still be made under the current provisions? What about an order in favour of a deceased victim's estate when the offender is the residual beneficiary under the will? See *R v Hooyer*, 2016 ONCA 44.

4. Although it seems self-evident that the means of the offender ought to be relevant to the *quantum* of a fine imposed on an offender, should it be relevant to the application of the restitution provisions? If the amount of the restitution order is easily quantifiable, why should a court refrain from making a restitution order if the offender demonstrates that he is unable to pay? Inability to pay is no answer to a civil action for damages. Why should it be relevant in the criminal law sphere? In *R v Biegus* (1999), 141 CCC (3d) 245, 127 OAC 239 (CA), the court offered the following rationale for taking ability to pay into account:

> [15] … A restitution order made by a sentencing court survives any bankruptcy of the accused: *Bankruptcy and Insolvency Act*, R.S.C. 1985, c. B-3, s. 178(1)(a). Therefore, it is there for life. It is not intended to be such a burden that it may affect the prospects for rehabilitation of the accused. That is why ability to pay is one of the factors which the court must consider.

5. Before the 1996 amendments, the probation provisions contained a discrete optional condition dealing with restitution that was commonly used to sequence payments over time. This provision was repealed and not replaced with one that deals expressly with sequenced payments. For discussion of this issue, see Allan Manson, *The Law of Sentencing* (Toronto: Irwin Law, 2001) at 254-55.

FURTHER READING

Ferris, TW. "The Legality of Imposing a Fine, Imprisonment and Probation at the Same Time" (1995-1996) 38 Crim LQ 277.

Lawrence, Michelle S. "Looking the Gift Horse in the Mouth: An Examination of the Canadian Approach to Criminal Restitution in Cases of Sexual Violence" (2016) 20 Can Crim L Rev 209.

Manson, Allan. "Sentencing Options" in *The Law of Sentencing* (Toronto: Irwin Law, 2000) ch 9.

Ruby, Clayton, Gerald J Chan & Nader R Hassan. "The Fine" in *Sentencing*, 8th ed (Markham, Ont: LexisNexis Canada, 2012) 465.

Imprisonment

I. INTRODUCTION

Imprisonment is available as a penalty for all offences. The *Criminal Code*, RSC 1985, c C-46, as amended, stipulates the maximum period of imprisonment that may be imposed. In some cases, expanded during the era of the Harper government, it provides for minimum penalties: see the discussion of minimum penalties in Section VI, below. Sentences of less than two years are served in provincial or territorial institutions: see s 743.1(3), while sentences that extend for two years or more, either by themselves or in the aggregate with other sentences, are served in federal penitentiaries: see ss 743.1(1) and (5). The structure and decision-making processes of the federal penitentiary system are determined by the *Corrections and Conditional Release Act*, SC 1992, c 20, which replaced both the *Penitentiary Act* and the *Parole Act*. Each province and territory has its own enabling legislation. In Chapter 19, Post-Appeal Sentence Issues, we discuss judicial review of internal prison and parole decisions.

The use of incarceration in Canada is striking. The Supreme Court has concluded that it is overused as a sentencing option. In *R v Gladue*, [1999] 1 SCR 688, the court said:

> [57] Thus, it may be seen that although imprisonment is intended to serve the traditional sentencing goals of separation, deterrence, denunciation, and rehabilitation, there is widespread consensus that imprisonment has not been successful in achieving some of these goals. Over-incarceration is a long-standing problem that has been many times publicly acknowledged but never addressed in a systematic manner by Parliament. In recent years, compared to other countries, sentences of imprisonment in Canada have increased at an alarming rate. The 1996 sentencing reforms embodied in Part XXIII, and s. 718.2(e) in particular, must be understood as a reaction to the overuse of prison as a sanction, and must accordingly be given appropriate force as remedial provisions.

This statement, however, cannot be viewed in the abstract. It needs to be put in context. How does one understand a concept like "over-incarceration" without some yardsticks with which to measure the use of incarceration?

We begin by providing the latest sentencing statistics available from Statistics Canada. These are derived from the Adult Criminal Court Survey (ACCS), which Statistics Canada conducts annually. As of March 2016, the latest data available from Statistics Canada derive from fiscal year 2013-14. (All statistics presented in this chapter derive from Statistics Canada, data release 28 September 2015, and ancillary CANSIM (Canadian Socio-Economic Information Management System) tables, available at Statistics Canada. For further information, see Statistics Canada, "Adult Criminal Court Statistics in Canada, 2013/2014," by Ashley Maxwell, in *Juristat* 35:1, Catalogue No 85-002-X (Canada: Minister of Industry, 2015).) Table 11.1 summarizes the relative use of the principal sanctions over the five-year period from 2009-10 to 2013-14. Note that many cases attract multiple sentences. Table 11.1 summarizes trends for the most severe sentence imposed. The consequence is that the most frequently imposed sentence—a term of probation—is underreported. (In 43 percent of all cases, probation was imposed either alone or in addition to another sentence.) Over this period, the total volume of sentenced cases declined by 14 percent.

The use of different disposals remained relatively constant over the years. It is noteworthy that the percentage of cases attracting a custodial term (because a custodial sentence is the most severe, the adult criminal court statistics capture all the cases receiving this sentence) increased from 33 percent to 36 percent, although the total number of committals to custody declined by 7 percent (from 88,982 to 82,764 cases). The proportion of all convictions resulting in a term of custody (excluding conditional sentences of imprisonment) has been quite stable over the past few decades, generally accounting for approximately one-third of cases. For example, in 1995-96, a prison sentence was imposed in 33 percent of all convicted cases: see Statistics Canada, "Adult Criminal Court Statistics, 1995-96," by Craig Grimes, *Juristat* 17:6, Catalogue No 85-002-XPE (Canada: Minister of Industry, 1997). Conditional sentences continue to account for only a small percentage of all cases, only 4 percent in 2013-14. Probation and fines were the most severe sentences imposed in approximately one-quarter of all cases over this period. With respect to sentence length, in 2013-14, the average sentence was 113 days, down from 124 in 2009-10. The median sentence (the number that divides the distribution in half; a more stable way of summarizing the distribution of sentences because it is less sensitive than the average, or mean, to a small number of more exceptional cases) remained at 30 days throughout the five-year period. In 2013-14, almost nine out of ten sentences of imprisonment were for six months or less; only 3 percent of custodial terms were two years or longer.

A. Remand Custody

A matter of great concern in Canada is the dramatic rise in the number of remand, as opposed to sentenced, prisoners. In 2013-14, on an average day, there were 11,493 adults in remand—that is, in custody awaiting trial or sentencing—and 9,889 in sentenced custody in the 12 provinces and territories that provide data to Statistics Canada through the adult correctional survey. In fact, the remand population has consistently exceeded the sentenced population in Canada. In the most recent year for which there is data (2013-14), adult prisoners in remand accounted for 54 percent of the total custodial population: see Correctional

Table 11.1   Volume and Distribution of Sentences, Canada, 2013-2014

Most serious sentence	2009-10	2010-11	2011-12	2012-13	2013-14
Custody	33%	34%	35%	36%	36%
	88,982	87,770	89,032	89,763	82,764
Conditional sentence of imprisonment	4%	5%	5%	4%	4%
	11,798	11,970	11,746	10,953	9,777
Probation	29%	29%	28%	26%	26%
	78,410	75,013	70,476	65,845	60,102
Fine	26%	27%	25%	26%	25%
	69,644	69,748	63,462	63,809	57,667
Other sentences	7%	6%	7%	8%	8%
	17,596	16,824	16,887	18,782	18,018
Total number of cases	266,430	261,325	251,603	249,152	228,328

Note: Adapted from Statistics Canada, Table 252-0057, Adult Criminal Courts, Guilty Cases by Most Severe Sentence. For complete notes, including missing data, see the original table (percentages rounded).

Services Program, *Adult Correctional Statistics in Canada, 2013/2014*, Chart 1, online: <http://www.statcan.gc.ca/pub/85-002-x/2015001/article/14163-eng.htm>. One conclusion to be drawn from these statistics is that Canada's traditionally high incarceration rate is in large measure driven by the increased remand population.

B. International Comparisons

Statistical agencies often make comparisons across jurisdictions, usually in terms of the rate of incarceration per 100,000 population. International imprisonment statistics can be deceiving, and comparisons should be made carefully. First, it is important to ensure that similar data are compared. Admissions—the number of people received in custody during a period—should not be confused with an average count—the average population over a period. Second, when looking at count or population data, it is essential to segregate sentenced offenders from the total population, which, in many systems, will include remand prisoners awaiting trial.

The most recent report of the Adult Correctional Services survey (see Correctional Services Program, *Adult Correctional Statistics in Canada, 2013/2014*, online: <http://www.statcan.gc.ca/pub/85-002-x/2015001/article/14163-eng.htm>) reveals that in 2013-14, on average, there were 37,864 offenders, both adult and youth combined, in custody in Canada. This total converts to an overall incarceration rate of 118 persons in custody per 100,000 population. The Statistics Canada report also notes that, among the countries of the OECD (Organisation for Economic Co-operation and Development), Canada's incarceration rate ranks in the middle of the distribution: see Figure 11.1. It is significantly higher than many European jurisdictions, but well below the United States, which had the highest incarceration rate (at 707 persons in custody per 100,000 population).

Figure 11.1   International Incarceration Rates, Organisation for Economic Co-operation and Development Countries

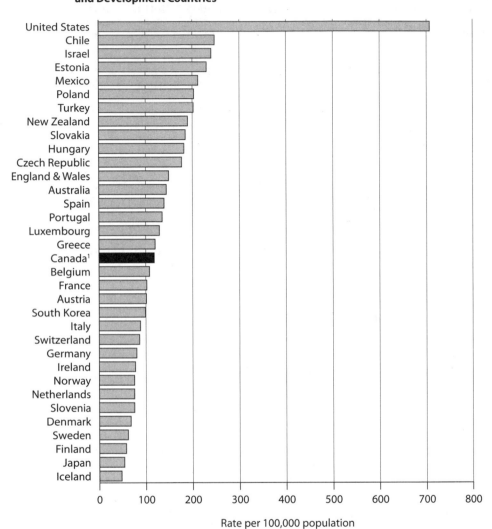

Rate per 100,000 population

1 For jurisdictions that could not provide 2013-2014 data, an estimate was used to produce the overall incarceration rate for Canada.

Note: Excludes young offenders 12 to 17 years of age in Quebec due to the unavailability of data for the period covered. The methodology used for counting sentenced inmates can vary among countries. These counts represent data accessed on January 26, 2015 from the International Centre for Prison Studies (www.prisonstudies.org/world-prison-brief), with the exception of data from Canada. The reference year can be different from the year indicated for Canada. For this reason, data are presented for information only (including those in remand), both youth and adults, and are calculated using the total population. The Organisation for Economic Co-operation and Development (OECD) has 34 member countries whose mission it is to promote policies to improve the socio-economic well-being of people throughout the world.

Source: H Fair & R Walmsley. *World Prison Brief (January 2015)*, International Centre for Prison Studies; Statistics Canada, Canadian Centre for Justice Statistics, Corrections Key Indicator Report, 2013/2014.

II. THE EFFECTS OF INCARCERATION:
ON PRISONERS AND CRIME RATES

The literature in this area is complex and vast. Imprisonment serves the twin purposes of incapacitation and separation. Certainly, incarceration provides a dramatic restriction in liberty during the period of incarceration, but whether this promotes any other anticipated goals of sentencing is controversial. Imprisonment not only separates the prisoner from the community but also places control over the environment and the daily routines of his or her life into the hands of the correctional system. Thus the impact of imprisonment must be measured both in terms of its duration and its personal effects. Supporters of imprisonment assume that its rigours will produce deterrence. It is also expected that there may be some degree of rehabilitation. This, of course, is a function of the extent to which the system provides programming directed at education, vocational training, or problems like substance abuse.

It cannot be assumed without confirming evidence that any system or institution in which a particular prisoner will eventually be confined actually provides relevant programming. There are, of course, intrinsic negative consequences associated with imprisonment. Communities, families, and employment opportunities change over time and a prisoner does not simply return to fill the place that he or she previously vacated. The mere separation of the offender from his or her family and friends is often the source of both economic and emotional repercussions, particularly for the family. Recent research has documented these effects, especially on the children of incarcerated parents. Moreover, depending on the quality of the correctional system and the way in which it is manifested in a particular institution, imprisonment can produce serious negative effects: see the discussion of health risks, violence, mental health, institutionalization, and other negative effects in Nigel Walker & Nicola Padfield, *Sentencing: Theory, Law and Practice*, 2nd ed (London: Butterworths, 1996) at 153-63; see also Craig Haney, "The Psychological Effects of Imprisonment" in Joan Petersilia & Kevin R Reitz, eds, *The Oxford Handbook of Sentencing and Corrections* (New York: Oxford University Press, 2012) 584.

One Canadian study dealing with violence in prisons concluded that a male prisoner runs a 14 times greater risk of being a victim of homicide in prison than does a man of comparable age living in the community: see Frank J Porporino & Phyllis Doherty, *An Historical Analysis of Victims of Homicide in Canadian Penitentiaries* (Ottawa: Solicitor General Canada, 1985); see also Anthony E Bottoms, "Interpersonal Violence and Social Order in Prisons" (1999) 26 Crime & Justice Rev 205; and Alison Liebling, "Suicide and Prison Coping" (1999) 26 Crime & Justice Rev 283.

There is an ongoing debate about the potential consequences of long-term confinement. This debate is especially significant given the growing number of prisoners serving life sentences as a result of both the aggregate of people with long periods of parole ineligibility and an apparent lengthening of sentences for some offences. Combined with the claim that imprisonment is ineffective in achieving sentencing objectives, this body of literature ought to be significant from a law reform perspective. However, substantive debate has too often been replaced by the politics of law and order. In earlier editions, we included excerpts from James Bonta & Paul Gendreau, "Re-examining the Cruel and Unusual Punishment of Prison Life" (1990) 14 L & Human Behavior 347, which concluded that "long-term imprisonment and specific conditions of confinement such as solitary, under limiting and humane conditions, fail to show any sort of profound detrimental effects." That article was juxtaposed with

Julian V Roberts & Michael Jackson, "Boats Against the Current: A Note on the Effects of Imprisonment" (1991) 15 L & Human Behavior 557, which was critical of both the Bonta & Gendreau methodology and the conclusion of the research review. Specifically with respect to solitary confinement, Roberts & Jackson concluded that the authors "seriously overstate what their kind of empirical research can tell us about the effects of solitary confinement."

For a more recent review of studies dealing specifically with solitary confinement, see Peter Scharff Smith, "The Effects of Solitary Confinement on Prison Inmates: A Brief History and Review of the Literature" (2006) 34 Crime & Justice Rev 441 at 487. This article surveyed the international research and came down on the side of Roberts & Jackson:

> All the studies just mentioned report significant adverse effects experienced during solitary confinement, and some go a long way toward identifying these as a product of isolation. Most earlier reviews dealing broadly with the literature on solitary confinement have also concluded that isolation of prisoners can be a very harmful practice (Bonta and Gendreau's [1990] study is the most obvious exception). In 1986, for example, psychiatrist Stuart Grassian and psychologist Nancy Friedman concluded that "late nineteenth and early twentieth-century German clinicians ... contributed altogether thousands of descriptions of psychosis associated with solitary confinement" while the "more recent literature on this subject has also nearly uniformly described or speculated that solitary confinement has serious psychopathological consequences" (Grassian and Friedman 1986, p. 53).
>
> Three years earlier in another review of the literature concerning the effects of solitary confinement, Reto Volkart concluded that ... [TRANSLATION] "[r]esearchers widely agree that massive effects of solitary confinement can set in very quickly—during the initial days or hours. But particular effects are also attributed to very long periods of solitary confinement." (Volkart 1983, pp. 18–19).
>
> In 2003 psychologist Craig Haney concluded that "empirical research on solitary and supermax-like confinement has consistently and unequivocally documented the harmful consequences of living in these kinds of environments" (2003, p. 130).
>
> In 2004 psychiatrist Henrik Steen Andersen concluded in a review that solitary confinement of remand prisoners "imposes additional strain and increases the risk of development of psychiatric morbidity," and furthermore noted that when "differences between SC [solitary confinement] and non-SC have been found in studies of sentenced prisoners the trend disfavours SC." Finally Andersen concluded that sensory deprivation "may contribute to the pathogenesis of incident disorders in SC" (2004, p. 40).

Aside from its effects on the prisoner, imprisonment is designed to have influence on crime rates too. Specifically, prison is designed to reduce reoffending by prisoners. One of the most researched questions in criminology concerns this crime-preventive effect. Researchers in many countries have compared the reoffending rates of offenders sent to prison with those of offenders punished in the community. Comparisons between the two groups must take into account the fact that, as a group, prisoners represent a higher risk of reoffending than probationers—they generally have longer criminal records and have been convicted of more serious crimes. However, careful multivariate research that isolates the effect of sentence (whether prison or probation) on subsequent reoffending has demonstrated that imprisonment is associated with higher, not lower, rates of reoffending. One of the most careful of such studies was published by the UK Ministry of Justice in 2015: Aidan Mews, Joseph Hillier, Michael McHugh & Cris Coxon, *The Impact of Short Custodial Sentences, Community Orders and Suspended Sentences on Re-offending* (London: Ministry of Justice Analytical Series, 2015). This research found that after controlling for all relevant background variables, short-term custody was associated with a higher recidivism rate than community penalties. Because most sentences of custody in the United Kingdom and Canada are short, this finding may be generalized to Canada. It is consistent with research in other countries and earlier work in Canada: see Paul Gendreau & Claire Goggin et al, *The Effects of Prison Sentences on Recidivism: User Report*, 1999-24 (Ottawa: Solicitor General Canada, 1999).

Research in the United States also questions the effect of incarceration on reoffending. Using a sample of 6,515 offenders in Pennsylvania, Nagin & Snodgrass explored the use of incarceration in relation to re-arrest over one year, two years, and ten years. They concluded:

> On the whole, the results provide no indication of whether the experience of incarceration increases or decreases reoffending rate. This holds whether we observe re-arrest during a very short window (one year) or a long window (ten years). The result holds across all six counties and persists even after pooling data to increase power. This result is quite consistent with an emerging body of work that uses randomization as the basis for concluding that incarceration has no clear impact on recidivism.

Drawing on the international literature, Nagin & Snodgrass note that there "is little persuasive evidence that incarceration reduces future criminality": Daniel S Nagin & G Matthew Snodgrass, "The Effect of Incarceration on Re-offending: Evidence from a Natural Experiment in Pennsylvania" (2013) 29 J Quantitative Criminology 601; see also Paul Nieuwbeerta, Arjan Blokland & Daniel S Nagin, "The Relationship Between First Imprisonment and Criminal Career Development: A Matched Samples Comparison" (2009) 25 J Quantitative Criminology 227. Similarly, a major review of the use of imprisonment by an expert panel in the United Kingdom concluded that the research evidence "does not suggest that imprisonment for many types of offence is more effective in deterring offending than non-custodial modes of punishment": *A Presumption Against Imprisonment: Social Order and Social Values* (London: British Academy, 2014) at 65.

III. CRIMINAL CODE, SECTIONS 718.3, 719, AND 743.1

There are a number of technical issues that relate to where and how terms of imprisonment are served. For the most part, these are determined by the *Criminal Code*.

A. Consecutive Sentences

The ability to impose a consecutive sentence arises from s 718.3(4):

Cumulative punishments
   718.3(4)   The court that sentences an accused shall consider directing
      (a) that the term of imprisonment that it imposes be served consecutively to a sentence of imprisonment to which the accused is subject at the time of sentencing; and
      (b) that the terms of imprisonment that it imposes at the same time for more than one offence be served consecutively, including when
         (i) the offences do not arise out of the same event or series of events,
         (ii) one of the offences was committed while the accused was on judicial interim release, including pending the determination of an appeal, or
         (iii) one of the offences was committed while the accused was fleeing from a peace officer.

Otherwise, a sentence commences when imposed: see s 719(1).

Some unusual consecutive sentence problems arise in relation to parole eligibility. For a useful tool, see "Multiple Sentences" in *Sentence Calculation: A Handbook for Judges, Lawyers, and Correctional Officials*, 3rd ed (Ottawa: Public Works and Government Services Canada, 2005), the public safety and emergency preparedness publication. One particular problem arises when a prisoner serving a sentence receives an additional consecutive sentence. This triggers the complicated operation of s 120.1 of the *Corrections and Conditional Release Act*, SC 1992, c 20:

> 120.1(1) A person who is not serving a sentence and who receives more than one sentence on the same day is not eligible for full parole until the day on which they have served a period equal to the total of
>> (a) the period of ineligibility in respect of any portion of the sentence constituted under subsection 139(1) that is subject to an order under section 743.6 of the *Criminal Code* or section 226.2 of the *National Defence Act*, and
>> (b) the period of ineligibility in respect of any other portion of that sentence.
> (2) If an offender who is serving a sentence, or is serving a sentence that was constituted under subsection 139(1), receives an additional sentence that is to be served consecutively to the sentence they are serving when the additional sentence is imposed—or receives, on the same day, two or more additional sentences to be served consecutively and the additional sentences are to be served consecutively to the sentence they are serving when the additional sentences are imposed—the offender is not eligible for full parole until the day on which they have served, from the day on which the additional sentence is or sentences are imposed, the total of the following periods:
>> (a) any remaining period of ineligibility in respect of the sentence they are serving when the additional sentence is or sentences are imposed, and
>> (b) the period of ineligibility in respect of the additional sentence or, in the case of two or more additional sentences, a period equal to the total of the periods of ineligibility in respect of all of the additional sentences.
> (3) Despite subsection (2), if an offender who is serving a sentence or a sentence that was constituted under subsection 139(1) receives an additional sentence or two or more sentences that are to be served consecutively to a portion of the sentence they are serving when the additional sentence is imposed—or receives, on the same day, two or more additional sentences including a sentence to be served concurrently with the sentence being served and one or more sentences to be served consecutively to the additional concurrent sentence—they are not eligible for full parole until the day on which they have served, from the day on which the additional sentence is or sentences are imposed, any remaining period of ineligibility to which they are subject and the longer of the following periods:
>> (a) one third of the period that equals the difference between the length of the sentence that was constituted under subsection 139(1), including the additional sentence or sentences, and the length of the sentence that they are serving when the additional sentence is or sentences are imposed; or
>> (b) the period of ineligibility of the additional sentence that is or sentences that are ordered to be served consecutively.

B. Locus of Confinement

The locus of confinement depends on the length of the sentence either by itself or as an aggregate with other sentences the prisoner must serve. This is prescribed by s 743.1:

Imprisonment for life or more than two years

743.1(1) Except where otherwise provided, a person who is sentenced to imprisonment for

(a) life,

(b) a term of two years or more, or

(c) two or more terms of less than two years each that are to be served one after the other and that, in the aggregate, amount to two years or more,

shall be sentenced to imprisonment in a penitentiary.

(2) Where a person who is sentenced to imprisonment in a penitentiary is, before the expiration of that sentence, sentenced to imprisonment for a term of less than two years, the person shall serve that term in a penitentiary, but if the previous sentence of imprisonment in a penitentiary is set aside, that person shall serve that term in accordance with subsection (3).

(3) A person who is sentenced to imprisonment and who is not required to be sentenced as provided in subsection (1) or (2) shall, unless a special prison is prescribed by law, be sentenced to imprisonment in a prison or other place of confinement, other than a penitentiary, within the province in which the person is convicted, in which the sentence of imprisonment may be lawfully executed.

(3.1) Despite subsection (3), an offender who is subject to long-term supervision under Part XXIV and is sentenced for another offence during the period of the supervision shall be sentenced to imprisonment in a penitentiary.

(4) Where a person is sentenced to imprisonment in a penitentiary while the person is lawfully imprisoned in a place other than a penitentiary, that person shall, except where otherwise provided, be sent immediately to the penitentiary, and shall serve in the penitentiary the unexpired portion of the term of imprisonment that that person was serving when sentenced to the penitentiary as well as the term of imprisonment for which that person was sentenced to the penitentiary.

(5) Where, at any time, a person who is imprisoned in a prison or place of confinement other than a penitentiary is subject to two or more terms of imprisonment, each of which is for less than two years, that are to be served one after the other, and the aggregate of the unexpired portions of those terms at that time amounts to two years or more, the person shall be transferred to a penitentiary to serve those terms, but if any one or more of such terms is set aside or reduced and the unexpired portions of the remaining term or terms on the day on which that person was transferred under this section amounted to less than two years, that person shall serve that term or terms in accordance with subsection (3).

IV. INTERMITTENT SENTENCES

A court may mitigate the full effect of a custodial sentence by ordering that it be served intermittently—that is, not continuously. This usually, but not always, means on weekends. This is made possible by s 732 of the *Criminal Code*, which provides:

732(1) Where the court imposes a sentence of imprisonment of ninety days or less on an offender convicted of an offence, whether in default of payment of a fine or otherwise, the court may, having regard to the age and character of the offender, the nature of the offence and the circumstances surrounding its commission, and the availability of appropriate accommodation to ensure compliance with the sentence, order

(a) that the sentence be served intermittently at such times as are specified in the order; and

(b) that the offender comply with the conditions prescribed in a probation order when not in confinement during the period that the sentence is being served and, if the court so orders, on release from prison after completing the intermittent sentence.

(2) An offender who is ordered to serve a sentence of imprisonment intermittently may, on giving notice to the prosecutor, apply to the court that imposed the sentence to allow it to be served on consecutive days.

(3) Where a court imposes a sentence of imprisonment on a person who is subject to an intermittent sentence in respect of another offence, the unexpired portion of the intermittent sentence shall be served on consecutive days unless the court otherwise orders.

The original intermittent sentence provisions were enacted by SC 1972, c 13, s 58, along with a set of other new and revised provisions described under the subheading "Absolute and Conditional Discharge, Suspended Sentence, Intermittent Sentence and Probation." These provisions were the result of recommendations in the Ouimet Report (*Report of the Canadian Committee on Corrections*, 1969), which discussed the utility of both weekend and nightly detention and found evidence of beneficial applications of such alternatives in European countries. It recommended that courts "be empowered to impose a sentence of imprisonment to be served intermittently, the total period of imprisonment not to exceed six months." Obviously, Parliament agreed with the Ouimet Report, except that it put a 90-day cap on intermittent sentences.

In *R v Parisian* (1993), 81 CCC (3d) 351 (Man CA), the offender appealed against a three-month sentence for possessing cannabis resin for the purposes of trafficking. The appellant sought only to serve the sentence intermittently. For the court, Twaddle JA said:

Ordinarily the decision to allow or not to allow a convicted person to serve time intermittently is one to be made by the sentencing judge. This court will only interfere if the decision is made on a wrong principle or is clearly wrong.

In the present case, the offence involved a relatively small quantity of narcotic; the accused was a small player; the sale which the accused intended to make were to persons who frequent a beverage room. Her circumstances are such that a sentence of three months if not served intermittently will cause some hardship because she has two children whom it would be difficult to place for care if she serves her sentence other than intermittently. Additionally, she has the opportunity to take a course of education to upgrade herself if she is free to take it from Monday to Friday. The accused has no prior record.

The learned sentencing judge imposed a sentence which is within the range for this particular offence and this offender, but we think she was wrong to characterize it as one at the lower end of that range. Additionally, she placed undue emphasis on the fact that the accused was unemployed and did not need an intermittent sentence to save her job. The need for the accused to educate herself and make arrangements for her children are equally valid reasons for an intermittent sentence.

In the circumstances, we are of the view that the judge's decision not to allow the sentence to be served intermittently was clearly wrong. Accordingly, we allow the appeal, set aside the sentence of three months imprisonment and substitute one of 90 days to be served intermittently.

Since 1972, the intermittent sentence has become an important element of a fair and rational sentencing scheme that includes both statutorily mandated minimum sentences of imprisonment and judge-made presumptions of incarceration. The most common role for the intermittent sentence is with respect to impaired driving offenders. When Parliament addressed the range of penalties applicable to this kind of offence in 1985 and created new offences with substantially higher maxima when bodily harm or death had occurred, it also tailored the impaired driving simpliciter sentences to integrate them with the availability of intermittent sentences. Previously, the mandated penalty for a third conviction was three months, outside the range of an intermittent sentence. However, the 1985 amendments (SC 1985, c 19, s 36) reduced this threshold to 90 days. Obviously, while Parliament was concerned with enhancing the penalties for this category, especially when the consequences are death or bodily harm, it was also concerned with instilling fairness in the system by permitting a judge to consider the appropriateness of an intermittent sentence. The potential scope of this consideration can be appreciated by noting the latest trends from Statistics Canada. In 2013-14, 2,636 sentences of imprisonment were imposed for an impaired driving conviction. The median sentence was 33 days (see CANSIM Table 252-0059, "Adult Criminal Courts, Guilty Cases by Mean and Median Length of Custody, Annual").

The most common use of an intermittent sentence is to respond to a case where a brief period of incarceration is mandated by either the Code or a presumption of incarceration but imprisonment for a continuous period will risk the offender's job, schooling, or family. Without an intermittent sentence, some offenders will not be able to maintain their careers, profession, or employment. It is the lowest people on the employment ladder—those with the least marketable skills and the least vocational resources—who will be replaced first. Thus it is likely that the working poor offender will become even more impoverished, while the middle-class offender will keep his or her job. Similarly, a parent from a traditional family has a spouse to care for children during a brief period of confinement. A single parent, if not able to find a willing relative, risks losing a child to the local Children's Aid Society, even over a 14-day sentence. Students struggling to succeed in an increasingly challenging world risk losing a school term as a consequence of a brief period of incarceration. Again, the more financially able the student is, the easier it is to overcome this obstacle, whether through extra tutoring or re-enrollment. Some may not be able to bounce back.

Still, correctional officials from most provinces regularly express opposition to intermittent sentences. This concern seems based on the added administrative and security costs generated by receiving and accommodating prisoners in an ordinary jail facility even though their stay will only be a few days. Perhaps the answer lies not in abolishing intermittent sentences but in providing appropriate facilities so that the problems associated with injecting prisoners into a secure jail to mix with the ordinary population would be diminished. Alternatively, perhaps we should be questioning the utility of short jail terms, whether intermittent or not. For now, the utility of intermittent sentences seems clear as do the inequities of abolishing them.

There are some technical problems that need to be considered. *R v Middleton*, below, considers the interpretation of s 732(3) as applied to a series of sentences imposed on an estranged domestic partner who used violence as a tool to respond to separation.

R v Middleton
2009 SCC 21, [2009] 1 SCR 674

FISH J (McLachlin CJ, LeBel, Charron, and Rothstein JJ concurring):

[1] The appellant, Timothy Middleton, was convicted at trial for having committed an assault causing bodily harm to his partner at the time, Lisa Dubreuil. For that offence, he was sentenced to 90 days' imprisonment, to be served intermittently. Mr. Middleton was convicted as well for having uttered a death threat and for pointing a firearm some five months after the assault. And for those offences, he received 18-month conditional

sentences of imprisonment, to be served concurrently, followed by probation for the ensuing three years.

[2] It is conceded that all three sentences were legal in themselves. It is conceded as well that they were carefully crafted by the trial judge in compliance with the sentencing principles and the correctional objectives applicable in the circumstances of this case. Neither the appellant nor the respondent has drawn to our attention a single provision of the *Criminal Code*, R.S.C. 1985, c. C-46, that prohibited either the intermittent sentence or the concurrent conditional sentences when each was imposed. Nor has our attention been drawn to a single judgment by any Canadian court precluding the combination of sentences imposed by the trial judge in this case.

[3] Justice Cromwell nonetheless finds that the intermittent sentence was rendered illegal by the conditional sentences in light of a sentence calculation provision set out in a different statute for purposes that, as we shall presently see, *have no application here*.

[4] My colleague's reasons may be briefly summarized this way. Intermittent sentences are governed by s. 732 of the *Criminal Code*. In virtue of s. 732(1), the court may order that a sentence of imprisonment be served intermittently where the term imposed does not exceed 90 days. Conditional sentences are sentences of imprisonment. Section 139 of the *Corrections and Conditional Release Act*, S.C. 1992, c. 20 ("*CCRA*"), requires that the 90-day intermittent sentence and the 18-month conditional sentences imposed in this case be "merged"—or amalgamated—to form a single sentence of 18 months' duration. Since this merged sentence exceeds the 90-day maximum permitted by s. 732(1), the intermittent sentence imposed by the trial judge was retrospectively rendered illegal by the subsequent imposition of the conditional sentences, though the conditional sentences were themselves both legal and fit.

[5] It will immediately be recognized that the result proposed by Justice Cromwell would only be warranted if both of its essential premises are correct: first, that a conditional sentence is a sentence of imprisonment within the meaning of s. 732(1); and second, that s. 139 of the *CCRA* requires that the intermittent and conditional sentences imposed by the trial judge be treated, for the purposes of s. 732(1), as a single sentence of imprisonment.

[6] In my respectful view, neither proposition withstands scrutiny. To hold that a conditional sentence is a sentence of imprisonment within the meaning of s. 732(1) of the *Criminal Code* and s. 139 of the *CCRA* is to disregard the plain wording of the provisions, their legislative purposes, and the nature and object of conditional sentences. It would disregard as well the valid sentencing objectives of the trial judge in this case and would unnecessarily, in the future, deprive judges of their ability to render similarly fit sentences where they conclude that a custodial sentence is required.

[7] For the reasons that follow, I have concluded that conditional sentences are not contemplated by either s. 732(1) of the *Code* or s. 139 of the *CCRA*, and that s. 139 has no application to the intermittent sentence imposed in this case.

II

. . .

[10] It is apparent from the words "confinement" and "prison" that s. 732(1) contemplates custodial sentences of imprisonment and not conditional sentences of imprisonment, which are served in the community. In my view, this textual consideration is alone sufficient

to warrant the conclusion that conditional sentences are not "sentences of imprisonment" within the meaning of s. 732(1).

[11] In arriving at an opposite conclusion, Justice Cromwell relies on the principle of statutory interpretation which favours giving a word or phrase "the same interpretation or meaning whenever it appears in an Act," unless "the contrary is clearly indicated by the context" (*Thomson v. Canada (Deputy Minister of Agriculture)*, [1992] 1 S.C.R. 385, at p. 400). Applying this same rule of interpretation, it seems to me plain that a conditional sentence is *not* a "sentence of imprisonment" within the meaning of s. 732(1). As mentioned at the outset, s. 732(1)(b) contemplates sentences that are served "in confinement" and probation orders "on release from prison after completing the intermittent sentence." Conditional sentences are, by definition, meant to be served in the community and not in prisons. To conclude that they are sentences of imprisonment within the meaning of s. 732(1) is thus inconsistent with a purposive and contextual interpretation of the provision, and also the express terms adopted by Parliament in providing for intermittent sentences.

[12] In my respectful view, we cannot reasonably hold that a conditional sentence is a sentence of imprisonment *for some purposes* under s. 732(1) (such as determining an offender's eligibility for an intermittent sentence), *but not for others* (such as permitting the intermittent service of a conditional sentence). And without straining the plain language of s. 732(1), we cannot reasonably find that a conditional sentence is a sentence of imprisonment for all purposes of s. 732, as urged by the appellant.

[13] To conclude that conditional sentences are sentences of imprisonment within the meaning of s. 732(1) is inconsistent as well with the distinct and different purposes of conditional sentences on the one hand, and intermittent sentences on the other. Justice Cromwell has explained this well in relating why the trial judge was moved by different reasons and different sentencing objectives to impose conditional sentences for two offences and an intermittent sentence for the other (notably at paras. 68, 69 and 111). It is thus hardly surprising that no intermittent conditional sentences of imprisonment—an anomalous notion at best—have been brought to our attention.

[14] Moreover, contrary to the appellant's submission, "imprisonment" in the phrases "sentence of imprisonment" and "term of imprisonment" does not bear a uniform meaning for all purposes of the *Criminal Code*. In several instances, these terms necessarily contemplate incarceration. Section 718.2(e), mentioned by the parties, is hardly the sole example. Section 732(1) must itself be taken as another since, as we have already seen, s. 732(1) refers explicitly to "confinement during the period that the sentence is being served" and "release from prison after completing the intermittent sentence."

[15] Likewise, s. 719(4) provides that "a term of imprisonment ... commences ... on the day on which the convicted person is arrested and taken into custody under the sentence." Section 719(5) is framed in analogous terms. Manifestly, conditional sentences of imprisonment are not terms of imprisonment within the meaning of either provision. The same is true of s. 743.3, which provides that "[a] sentence of imprisonment shall be served in accordance with the enactments and rules that govern the institution to which the prisoner is sentenced." Here again, a conditional sentence can hardly be characterized as a "sentence of imprisonment" within the meaning of the provision.

[16] Section 742.7(1) is yet another instance where the *Criminal Code* speaks of imprisonment in a manner that can hardly include conditional sentences. A finding that

it does would mean that a conditional sentence of imprisonment is suspended if, while it is being served, the offender receives a second conditional sentence of imprisonment. This can hardly be what Parliament intended.

[17]   On the contrary, reading s. 742.7 as a whole, I think it obvious that Parliament has drawn a clear and sharp distinction in that section between a conditional sentence being served in the community, and a custodial period served for breach of a conditional sentence order. Where an offender is ordered under s. 742.6 of the *Code* to serve all or part of an unexpired conditional sentence in custody, this custodial period is explicitly treated in s. 742.7(3) as imprisonment for the purposes of s. 139 of the *CCRA*; the rest of the conditional sentence, served in the community, is not. If s. 139 were intended to apply to conditional sentences, s. 742.7(3) would be entirely superfluous. At the very least, it is clear in this light that s. 139 applies to conditional sentences only if they result in incarceration—and, even then, only to the custodial period. The conditional sentences in this case involve no custody at all.

[18]   I am of course aware that the Court, in holding that "imprisonment" in s. 718.2(e) signifies "incarceration," referred to the difference between the English and French versions of the *Code*: see *R. v. Proulx*, 2000 SCC 5, [2000] 1 S.C.R. 61, at para. 95. As pointed out at the hearing of this appeal, however, a purposive and contextual reading of s. 718.2(e) would necessarily have arrived at the same result in the absence of the mentioned linguistic inconsistency. As Justice Cromwell recognizes at para. 87 of his reasons, "reading the term 'imprisonment' in s. 718.2(e) as including a conditional sentence was exactly contrary to the obvious legislative intent" of Parliament in creating conditional sentences as an alternative to incarceration.

[19]   And there is no conflict *at all* between the English and French versions in *any* of the other examples I have identified. Yet in every instance mentioned, "imprisonment" necessarily refers to "incarceration"—and not to conditional sentences served in the community.

• • •

[38]   Justice Cromwell concludes that the Court of Appeal erred in finding that the trial judge did not "otherwise order," within the meaning of s. 732(3). Not only were the intermittent and conditional sentences handed down by the same judge on the same day in a single set of reasons, but the trial judge also made clear his intention that the intermittent sentence be served intermittently, notwithstanding the conditional sentences imposed on the other counts. The reasons of the trial judge would thus satisfy the requirement of s. 732(3) to "otherwise order"—*if s. 732(3) applied, as a matter of law, to conditional sentences.*

[39]   I agree with the Crown that it does not. A purposive and contextual reading of "sentence of imprisonment" in s. 732(3) makes clear that it does not contemplate conditional sentences at all. As Sinclair J. observed in *R. v. Vajdl*, 2004 MBQB 167, 186 Man. R. (2d) 149, at para. 11:

> Clearly, it must have been the intention of Parliament that an intermittent sentence should not be converted to straight time upon the imposition of a conditional sentence. The intent of an intermittent sentence and a conditional sentence are the same—to allow the accused to serve his sentence in the community to the fullest extent possible.

In short, a conditional sentence is not a "sentence of imprisonment" within the meaning of s. 732(1), (2) or (3).

[40] As a matter of principle, I agree with Justice Cromwell that nothing in this appeal should turn on the order in which the sentences were pronounced. But this hardly favours the appellant's case. On the appellant's view, a 90-day intermittent sentence can be rendered illegal by the imposition in its final hours of another sentence of imprisonment (conditional or otherwise) of more than a single day. The intermittent sentence, legal when imposed and final for all legal purposes (never having been set aside on appeal), would in this example be almost entirely served, yet retroactively invalidated by a subsequent sentence for a different offence. Any different sequence of sentences leading to the same result would produce equally absurd effects, contrary to the "well established principle of statutory interpretation that the legislature does not intend to produce absurd consequences" (*Rizzo & Rizzo Shoes Ltd. (Re)*, [1998] 1 S.C.R. 27, at para. 27).

• • •

CROMWELL J (dissenting in part):

• • •

[84] An intermittent sentence is a "sentence of imprisonment." The manner in which it is served is by the offender being in custody at specified times rather than on consecutive days. It is therefore necessary to provide directions as to when the offender will be in custody and when he or she will not. The words relating to confinement and prison in s. 732(1)(b) are used in connection with the manner in which the sentence of imprisonment is to be served. These sorts of directions as to how an intermittent sentence of imprisonment is to be served have no bearing on whether a conditional sentence of imprisonment is a sentence of imprisonment within the opening words of s. 732(1).

[85] Including a conditional sentence of imprisonment within the words "sentence of imprisonment" in s. 732 does not permit an order that a conditional sentence be served intermittently. As I have said earlier, the intermittent sentence order and the conditional sentence order direct different ways of serving a sentence of imprisonment. They must be understood as being alternative ways of serving a sentence of imprisonment. There is no authority in the *Code* for combining (and no reason that I can think of for wanting to combine) these two different ways of serving a sentence of imprisonment.

• • •

[89] The appellant's interpretation of s. 732, with which I agree, is supported by s. 731(1)(b) of the *Code*. That section authorizes a judge to impose a period of probation "in addition to ... sentencing the offender to imprisonment for a term not exceeding two years." The Crown concedes that a period of probation may be added to a conditional sentence and that this flows from the fact that the imposition of the probation order is authorized by s. 731(1)(b). (This was the basis on which the judge in this case could impose the probationary term to follow the conditional sentences.) It follows that the sentence of imprisonment contemplated by s. 731(1)(b) must include a conditional sentence of imprisonment. Otherwise (and contrary to the Crown's concession), a sentencing judge would not be authorized to impose a period of probation in addition to a conditional sentence.

[90] If we were to accept the Crown's position on this appeal, we would have to decide that a conditional sentence *is* included in the phrase "sentencing the offender to imprisonment" for the purposes of s. 731(1)(b) (as the Crown concedes), but that a conditional sentence *is not* a sentence of imprisonment for the purposes of the very next sentencing

option in the *Code*, s. 732. I see no reason to conclude that Parliament intended such similar expressions—"sentence of imprisonment" and "sentencing ... to imprisonment"—to have different meanings in these consecutive sentencing options in the *Code*. The provisions are even more similar in French: "*... le tribunal peut ... en plus ... de le condamner à un emprisonnement maximal de deux ans ...*" in s. 731(1)(b) and "*[l]e tribunal qui ... le condamne à un emprisonnement maximal de quatre-vingt-dix jours ...*" in s. 732(1).

V. MAXIMUM SENTENCES

Generally, the maximum sentence is intended for the worst offence committed by the worst offender. Of course, this is an overly simplistic statement, given the infinite ways that offenders from various backgrounds commit offences. But it does indicate the necessarily high threshold for a maximum sentence. In Chapter 15, Preventive Detention and Preventive Supervision, we look at the indeterminate sentence that flows from a finding that an offender is a dangerous offender pursuant to s 753 of the *Criminal Code*. A number of appellate courts have held that a life sentence, as a maximum sentence, should not be imposed on the ground of dangerousness simply to circumvent the dangerous-offender procedures: see e.g. *R v Pontello* (1977), 38 CCC (2d) 262 (Ont CA), a case of rape. In an earlier rape case, a life sentence was upheld, given the planning, the brutality, and the dangerousness of the offender, who suffered from a personality disorder: see *R v Hill* (1974), 15 CCC (2d) 145 (Ont CA). Since the 1970s, there is a recognition that a dangerous-offender finding will likely result in a longer period of incarceration than a life sentence. In situations where there are patterns of behaviour involving violent sexual offences, there has been a substantial expansion in prosecutorial willingness to pursue dangerous-offender applications: see Chapter 15.

Courts have resorted to maximum sentences, especially life sentences, as a method of responding to perceived gravity as a result of particularly horrendous consequences to victims or an exceptionally egregious record for prior convictions. The following decisions reflect the view that a sentence at the maximum, while available, ought to be uncommon.

R v Klair
(2004), 186 CCC (3d) 285 (Ont CA)

SHARPE JA (McCombs J concurring):

[1] The appellant pleaded guilty to one count of arson causing bodily harm and was sentenced to life imprisonment. He seeks leave to appeal, and if leave is granted, appeals his sentence to this court.

Facts

1. Circumstances of the Offence

[2] In the early afternoon of September 20, 2000, the appellant, at the time seventy years old, was at his son's home babysitting Rajvir Klair, his four-year old grandson. Some of the downstairs tenants were at home although it is not clear whether the appellant was aware of their presence. Shortly after 2 p.m., the appellant started three fires in the

bedrooms of his son's house using gasoline as an accelerant. After setting the fires, he walked away from the house. One of the tenants heard smoke alarms and the cries of Rajvir and came upstairs. She could not enter the house to rescue Rajvir because of the intensity of the fire. Rajvir was screaming "monster, monster." After putting her own child in a safe place, the tenant managed to coax Rajvir outside and to douse the flames that covered him.

[3] The appellant returned to the house the next day. He was highly intoxicated. He asked if Rajvir had been saved and, when told that Rajvir was alive, said "Thank God." He stated that he had tried to hang himself with his turban. There were no physical signs of any such attempt, but the appellant was not wearing his turban when he was arrested.

[4] Rajvir suffered horrendous and devastating injuries as a result of the fire. He suffered excruciating pain from second and third degree burns to about sixty percent of his body. He has already undergone approximately twenty operations and further surgery is expected. Rajvir has almost no use of his right arm and limited movement of his left arm. He lost his left ear, all digits on his left hand, two fingers on his right hand and two toes. He has significant scarring and at the time of sentencing was in poor mental condition.

2. Circumstances of the Appellant

[5] The appellant came to Canada from India in 1982. He remains in Canada as a landed immigrant. He worked as a labourer until he retired about ten years ago. He was married in India over forty years ago and has four children. The appellant has no prior criminal record and was an active member in the local Sikh community. He offered letters on the sentencing hearing to the effect that he was well-regarded and respected in his community as a hardworking person of high morals and good character.

[6] The appellant has accepted responsibility for the offence. However, he offered no explanation whatsoever for his conduct. At the sentencing hearing, he denied that he intended to harm his grandson and expressed his remorse.

• • •

[11] In my view, the trial judge erred by placing undue emphasis upon the consequences of the offence and insufficient attention to the actual circumstances of the offence and the blameworthiness of the appellant. To be more precise, in my view, the trial judge erred by sentencing the appellant to life imprisonment primarily because of the horrific consequences to Rajvir. The appellant intentionally started the fire. However, on the basis of the charge to which he pleaded guilty, and on the facts upon which the Crown relied in the sentencing proceedings, he did not deliberately cause Rajvir to suffer his devastating injuries. Indeed, the defence position that he did not intend to harm Rajvir was not challenged at trial. The appellant pleaded guilty to an indictment alleging that he "unlawfully did intentionally or recklessly cause damage by fire to property ... and did thereby cause bodily harm to Rajvir Klair." He did not plead guilty to attempted murder. The offence to which he pleaded guilty did not include the element of intentional infliction of bodily harm. On the facts admitted by the appellant and relied upon by the Crown, he was plainly guilty of manifest disregard for the safety of the victim, but he was neither charged with, nor did he admit to intentionally causing the horrific harm suffered by Rajvir.

[12] After the trial judge delivered his reasons, and indeed after the oral argument of this appeal, the Supreme Court of Canada released its decision in *R v. Cheddesingh*, [2004]

SCJ No. 15 (March 19, 2004). We have received written submissions with respect to this judgment where McLachlin CJC stated, for a unanimous court:

> ... [T]erms such as "stark horror," "worst offence" and "worst offender" add nothing to the analysis and should be avoided. All relevant factors under the *Criminal Code*, RSC 1985, c. C-46, must be considered. A maximum penalty of any kind will by its very nature be imposed only rarely (see A. Manson, *Law of Sentencing* (2001), at p. 106) and is only appropriate if the offence is of sufficient gravity and the offender displays sufficient blameworthiness.

[13] I will return to the facts of *Cheddesingh* below, but I note here that the Supreme Court affirmed the life sentence that had been imposed by the trial judge on the basis of the "stark horror" category.

[14] In the case at bar, the trial judge relied exclusively on the "stark horror" category to justify the life sentence and there was no suggestion that apart from the "stark horror" principle, there was any other basis to justify a life sentence. While the term "stark horror" must now be avoided as unhelpful, the term was used to delineate factors common to a particular type of case for which the maximum life sentence is appropriate. The trial judge based his decision upon those cases and it is still useful to consider them to gauge the gravity of the offence and the blameworthiness of the offender required to justify the maximum sentence of life imprisonment.

[15] While I do not suggest that there is a fixed or inflexible set of factors, cases of this kind that have been found to justify the imposition of the maximum sentence of life imprisonment (formerly the "stark horror" cases) have presented one or more of the following features:

- cruelty, brutality, unusual violence
- terrorizing and torturing victim over a period of time
- intentional, prolonged, repeated violence against victim
- acts needlessly repeated or lack of feeling suggesting sadistic intent to cause terror or even torture
- intentional infliction of pain, fright, panic that is tantamount to torture solely for gratification or other perverse reason
- cruelty and callousness not frequently encountered
- deliberate infliction of brutal, disfiguring, life threatening injuries

[16] It is significant that *Cheddesingh* requires both an offence of "sufficient gravity" and an offender "who displays sufficient blameworthiness." The severe consequences to Rajvir were certainly very grave, but those severe consequences were not accompanied by conduct that rose to a level of blameworthiness sufficient to justify a sentence of life imprisonment. Counsel for the respondent was unable to point us to any case in which a life sentence has been imposed upon a first offender for unintended consequences, even where those consequences were caused recklessly. To do so would, in my view, amount to a significant and unwarranted shift in the law of sentencing and invite life sentences in a significant number of cases involving dire but unintended consequences and where the sentence could not be justified on the basis of the blameworthiness of the accused. As I do not consider the circumstances of the present case to warrant such a change, and as I do not consider it possible to justify a sentence of life imprisonment for this offender

for this offence, I would allow the appeal, set aside the sentence of life imprisonment, and in its place substitute a substantial custodial sentence.

[17] The seminal judgment in this area is that of Martin JA in *R v. Horvath* (1982), 2 CCC (3d) 196 (Ont. CA). The accused had subjected his female victim to a prolonged and sadistic attack. He gained access to her apartment on the pretext of wanting to rent it, then bound, gagged, choked, and stabbed her before finally slitting her throat. Martin JA observed that there were two broad categories in which the maximum life sentence was available: first, offences of stark horror, and second, pattern-of-violent-behaviour cases. This must now be read in the light of *Cheddesingh* and the principle that as "sentencing is an inherently individualized process" that cannot be achieved on the basis of solely fixed or pre-determined categories: *R v. M. (C.A.)*, [[1996] 1 SCR 500], at p. 567; *R v. Varga* (2001), 159 CCC (3d) 502 (Ont. CA) at p. 527; *R v. McArthur*, [2004] OJ No. 721 (CA).

• • •

[21] *Horvath* has been followed in many cases, several of which I review below. The startling feature of these cases attracting the maximum penalty of life imprisonment has been the brutality and cruelty of the actions of the accused. Considered in light of the *Cheddesingh* decision and the dual requirements of an offence of sufficient gravity and an offender of sufficient blameworthiness, the facts of these cases continue to warrant the imposition of a life sentence. In each case, the actions of the accused are exceedingly brutal and cruel, rendering them "sufficiently grave" on their face. Moreover, in each case the accused intended these consequences, thereby becoming "sufficiently blameworthy" for them. In no case do the consequences alone, unaccompanied by brutal or cruel conduct intentionally inflicting the consequences, convert the offence to one for which a life sentence is appropriate.

• • •

[25] Finally, in *Cheddesingh* itself the accused broke into two apartments before breaking into the victim's apartment in a senior citizen's residence. He announced his intention to rape the seventy-six-year old female occupant and then entered into a discussion about whether he would follow through. He told her that he had a razor and tried to suffocate her. He then sexually assaulted the victim, digitally penetrating her, performing cunnilingus, and violently raping her. The victim suffered severe lacerations to her vagina, requiring a blood transfusion. She died one month later from cirrhosis associated with vaginal trauma. The trial judge categorized the offence as one of stark horror. He based his finding on Cheddesingh's torturous discussion of whether or not he would rape the victim; the brutal violation of the victim's fundamental rights of privacy and security; the victim's membership in a vulnerable class of persons; the fact that the offences continued over a period of two to three hours; and the fact that the offence debased the victim's life. The life sentence was upheld on appeal by this court ((2002), 60 OR (3d) 721, 168 CCC (3d) 310) and, as I have noted, on appeal to the Supreme Court of Canada.

[26] In my view, the conduct of the appellant in the present case, while entirely deplorable, simply cannot be equated to the type of senseless brutality and cruelty found in *Horvath*, *Cheddesingh* and the other cases to which I have referred. In each of these cases, the justification for the imposition of the maximum penalty of life imprisonment was that severe and horrific harm had been deliberately inflicted upon the victim. In the present case, the appellant exposed his victim to the risk of similar harm, and for that he must be

severely punished. However, I cannot agree that it would be justifiable to sentence him on the same basis as if he had deliberately and callously inflicted the harm.

• • •

[36] This was a serious crime with disastrous consequences and the objectives of denunciation, deterrence, separating the offender from society and acknowledging the harm done to the victim and to society clearly call for a significant penitentiary sentence. The appellant intentionally set the fires and he exposed his victim to a startling risk of physical harm and death. As noted by the trial judge, the appellant's breach of trust as the victim's grandfather and babysitter is an aggravating factor. However, as stated by Prof. Manson in the passage from *The Law of Sentencing*, referred to in *Cheddesingh, supra*: "… the imposition of a maximum sentence is, and ought to be, rare. Few situations arise where a lesser term will not adequately protect society and also reflect an appropriate degree of denunciation."

[37] Factors weighing in the appellant's favour are his age and previously unblemished record, his plea of guilty and his acceptance of responsibility for the harm he has caused.

[38] In my view a fit sentence for this offender and this offence is twelve years. The appellant is entitled to credit for two-years of pre-trial custody. At trial, the Crown argued against the usual two for one credit as the appellant had delayed the proceedings while he tried to arrange financial restitution for the loss of his son's home. As the trial judge imposed a life sentence, he did not deal with this submission. I agree with the appellant's submission that in the circumstances of this case, he should not be denied the usual credit for pre-trial custody. Accordingly, the sentence I would impose after taking pre-trial custody into account is eight years.

FELDMAN JA (dissenting):

• • •

[52] Based on the circumstances of the crime itself, together with the appellant's failure to give any explanation for his actions, Watt J was satisfied, without expert evidence, that the appellant did have some mental problem that required treatment. Without this treatment, the court could not be assured that he did not represent an ongoing danger to the public or to a segment of it.

[53] My colleague disputes the trial judge's inference of mental disorder. In my view, the trial judge was entitled to draw the inference on the bases that he described. The drawing of inferences is the province of the trial judge: *Housen v. Nikolaisen*, [2002] 2 SCR 235. I also agree with Watt J that in circumstances where the accused elects not to participate in a psychiatric assessment, it would be problematic if the court were precluded from drawing inferences from the circumstances that would allow it to impose the appropriate sentence.

Conclusion

[54] This was a most difficult sentencing decision. The horrific aspects of the crime were not limited to its nature as a deliberate arson. The relationship of the young boy and his grandfather had previously been one of love and trust. The father of the boy was betrayed by his own father. The actions of the appellant were completely unexplained, leaving all involved with continuing unease, as well as despair. The ongoing pain and

suffering of the boy is unspeakable. The emotional and financial hardship on the parents is unfathomable. On the other hand, the appellant is an elderly man with no criminal record and a previously good reputation in the community.

[55] The experienced and learned trial judge gave reasons that are lucid and deal with each issue, balancing all of the statutory factors in the context of the relevant case law and the factual circumstances. It is clear that he recognized that the penalty of life imprisonment is to be imposed only rarely. In my view, he made no errors of law or principle and his decision that this was one of those rare cases deserves the deference of this court.

R v Dennis
(2005), 202 OAC 146 (CA)

BLAIR JA:

[1] Douglas Edward Dennis is a seventy-year old bank robber and career criminal. He is an addicted gambler and has an extensive criminal record for crimes of dishonesty, gambling-oriented offences, breach of release conditions and, of course, robbery.

[2] In June 2004, he was convicted of the offence of robbery for a fourth time—this time in connection with a bank in Niagara Falls. When he pleaded guilty to that offence, he was sentenced to life imprisonment by Justice D.J. Wallace of the Ontario Court of Justice. The trial judge imposed the sentence primarily because he was persuaded that a life sentence provided the parole authorities with more flexibility in terms of determining whether Mr. Dennis remained a danger to the public and therefore should or should not be released back into society.

· · ·

[5] The crime was committed in the following fashion. Mr. Dennis made an appointment to meet a small loans officer at the bank. When he arrived, he was carrying a bag and a TV remote device. He told the loans officer that he had a bomb in the bag, that there was another bomb located at the door of the bank, and that the device he held in his hand, if activated, would set off the explosives. He handed the bank officials a note with this message on it and saying that the strength of the bombs was sufficient to destroy the building. It also said that he was dying of cancer, had less than a year to live, and had nothing to lose if the bombs were detonated. He demanded that the bank officials open the bank vault.

[6] The demand was not met, as the bank officials in question professed not to know the combination to the vault. Mr. Dennis was therefore left to canvas a series of four tellers at various stations in the bank, as a result of which he obtained the $6,725 mentioned above. He then left the bank, but not before the bank's security camera took what the trial judge referred to as an "excellent" photograph that "[depicted] the offender clearly."

[7] Mr. Dennis did not have a bomb, or bombs, at the bank, but the bank personnel could not have known this and had to take the threat seriously. They were afraid to notify the police until the robber had left and, as directed, gave him time to make good his escape, after which the police were contacted. The area was evacuated and the Niagara Regional Police Service Explosive Disposal Unit was dispatched to the scene. The bag was determined to contain a non-explosive substance (a four-litre plastic jug of plumbing

antifreeze wrapped in paper). Mr. Dennis was identified from the surveillance tape and, as mentioned above, subsequently arrested.

[8] The appellant was seventy years of age at the time of his conviction and sentence. He is now seventy-one. He has one family member, a niece, who is supportive of him and who visits him and looks after his finances on the rare occasions when he is "on the street."

[9] In 1976, Mr. Dennis was sentenced to one year in prison for robbery; in 1983, to a total of seven years imprisonment on two counts of robbery; and in 1990, to thirteen years imprisonment for an armed robbery (in conjunction with a charge of unlawful imprisonment) after he held up a bank armed with a gun and took the bank manager hostage. For these, and the other crimes, Mr. Dennis has been sentenced to approximately thirty years in jail over the past forty years of his life. He is a career criminal and likely to re-offend as long as he is physically and mentally capable of doing so.

• • •

[11] While I am not persuaded that the trial judge erred in law by taking into account the particular parole considerations in the fashion he did, it is not necessary to determine that issue for purposes of this appeal. Respectfully—and leaving that issue aside—the trial judge made two errors in principle which, in combination, require us to re-open the question of his sentence, in my view. First, he approached the subject as if his options were to choose between the sentence proposed by the Crown and that suggested by counsel for Mr. Dennis. Secondly, he gave inadequate consideration to the practical realities arising from the age of the offender in the circumstances of this case. As a result, he failed to recognize that he could have accomplished the very goals he sought to achieve without imposing a sentence of life imprisonment.

[12] The jurisprudence is clear that maximum sentences of any kind are, by their very nature, to be imposed only rarely: see, for example, *R v. Cheddesingh*, [2004] 1 SCR 433 at para. 1; *R v. Klair* (2004), 71 OR (3d) 336 (CA) at para. 12. Here, the trial judge did not find that a life sentence would be otherwise appropriate, apart from his concern to ensure that the parole board had flexibility in determining whether, and when, Mr. Dennis should be released back into society.

[13] Mr. Dennis has a lengthy criminal record, as outlined above, including four prior convictions for robbery. He was sentenced to thirteen years imprisonment for his last robbery offence. Although that crime had been characterized by considerably more violence than the present case, and notwithstanding the submissions of defence counsel at trial, the trial judge was justified in imposing a more lengthy term of imprisonment on this occasion. He was also quite correct in treating the protection of the public as a primary consideration in sentencing. The record fully supports his view that Mr. Dennis is a risk to re-offend—and to re-offend in a violent manner—if he is released. But the goal could have been accomplished for all practical purposes, and in the circumstances of this case, by imposing a fixed term of imprisonment for a period of time between the life sentence sought by the Crown and the ten years suggested by the defence. The trial judge does not seem to have considered this option.

[14] The trial judge could have sentenced Mr. Dennis to a fixed term of fifteen to eighteen years' imprisonment, for example, and exercised his discretion under s. 743.6(1) of the *Criminal Code*—which, in the circumstances, it would have been open for him to do. In that event, Mr. Dennis would not have been eligible for parole for seven and one-half to nine years, and would not have been entitled to statutory parole for ten to twelve

years. Given his record, and prior history of release violations, it is unlikely that he would be released before his mandatory statutory release date. At that time, Mr. Dennis, if still alive, would be eighty or eighty-two years of age and subject to whatever conditions the parole board might see fit to require for another five or eight years. It seems to me that the likelihood of Mr. Dennis committing further violent crimes and continuing as a danger to the community at those ages, while not non-existent, is remote at best.

[15] There may be cases where the criminal history and incorrigibility of an offender may justify a maximum sentence in order to deter the offender and protect the public: *R v. Stairs*, [1994] OJ No. 1326 (CA). Here, however, both the paramount factors of specific deterrence and the protection of the public could have been equally well accommodated in reality without the imposition of a life sentence. That being the case, a sentence of life imprisonment ought not to have been ordered, as the trial judge did not find that such a sentence was otherwise warranted.

[16] Having regard to all of the circumstances, I would grant leave to appeal, allow the appeal, setting aside the sentence of life imprisonment and substituting a sentence of 16 years imprisonment with no eligibility for parole before the expiration of seven years of that sentence.

VI. MINIMUM SENTENCES

Minimum sentences have been challenged on Charter grounds. Essentially, the courts have held that the idea of a minimum sentence is not unconstitutional, but a specific example may violate s 12 of the *Canadian Charter of Rights and Freedoms*, Part I of the *Constitution Act, 1982*, being Schedule B to the *Canada Act 1982* (UK), 1982, c 11, if it imposes a sentence that is grossly disproportionate to the offence and the circumstances of the offender: see *R v Smith*, [1987] 1 SCR 1045; and *R v Goltz*, [1991] 3 SCR 485. However, these cases have adopted a methodology that permits a challenge based on either the facts presented by the offender's case or a "reasonable hypothetical." The use of the reasonable hypothetical approach produced a dilemma for the courts, as can be seen in the dissent of Arbour J in *R v Morrisey*, 2000 SCC 39, [2000] 2 SCR 90 at paras 68-90. Subsequently, the Supreme Court rejected constitutional exemptions in *R v Ferguson*, 2008 SCC 6, [2008] 1 SCR 96 and refined the "reasonable hypothetical" approach in *R v Nur*, 2015 SCC 15, [2015] 1 SCR 773. Both these cases, as well as *Smith*, are included in our new Chapter 17, The Charter and Sentencing.

VII. CREDIT FOR PRE-SENTENCE CUSTODY

Section 719(3) of the Code permits a sentencing judge to give credit for pre-sentence custody. Although there was some dispute among sentencing judges about the amount of credit and when it might be denied, s 719(3) received little judicial attention. This changed after the 1995 addition to the *Criminal Code* of ten mandatory minimum sentences for offences committed with firearms. Necessarily, this situation raised a significant legal question—that is, how does s 719(3) interact with a mandated minimum sentence? Imagine a situation where two offenders are accused of robbery, and it is alleged that a firearm was used. Section 344(a) imposes a mandatory sentence of four years. One offender is released on bail, while the other serves 12 months in custody before the trial. Both are convicted. Does fairness not require some credit for the pre-sentence custody? How can the judge give effect to both ss 719(3) and 344(a)? See the decision of Rosenberg JA for the Ontario Court of Appeal in *R v McDonald* (1998), 127 CCC (3d) 57 (Ont CA); *cf R v Lapierre* (1998), 123 CCC (3d) 332 (Qc CA). This issue has now been resolved by the Supreme Court of Canada in *R v Wust*, below. The decision in *Wust* also authoritatively explained considerations and norms that ought to apply to the application of s 719(3) generally. As you will see, this led to the notion of "enhanced credit," which, in turn, provoked legislative reaction and more litigation.

R v Wust

2000 SCC 18, [2000] 1 SCR 455

ARBOUR J (for the court):

. . .

[18] Mandatory minimum sentences are not the norm in this country, and they depart from the general principles of sentencing expressed in the Code, in the case law, and in the literature on sentencing. In particular, they often detract from what Parliament has expressed as the fundamental principle of sentencing in s. 718.1 of the Code: the principle of proportionality. Several mandatory minimum sentences have been challenged under s. 12 of the Charter, as constituting cruel and unusual punishment: see, for example, *R v. Smith*, [1987] 1 SCR 1045, 34 CCC (3d) 97, 40 DLR (4th) 435, *R v. Goltz*, [1991] 3 SCR 485, 67 CCC (3d) 481, and *Morrisey* ... .

[19] On some occasions, a mandatory minimum sentence has been struck down under s. 12, on the basis that the minimum prescribed by law was, or could be, on a reasonable hypothetical basis, grossly disproportionate to what the circumstances called for. See for example *Smith*, striking down s. 5(2) of the *Narcotic Control Act*; *R v. Bill* (1998), 13 CR (5th) 125 (BCSC), striking down the four-year minimum sentence for manslaughter with a firearm under s. 236(a) of the Code; *R v. Leimanis*, [1992] BCJ No. 2280 (QL) (Prov. Ct.), in which the s. 88(1)(c) minimum sentence of the BC *Motor Vehicle Act* for driving under a s. 85(a) prohibition was invalidated; and *R v. Pasacreta*, [1995] BCJ No. 2823 (QL) (Prov. Ct.), where the same penalty as in *Leimanis* for driving under a s. 84 prohibition was also struck down.

[20] In other cases, courts have fashioned the remedy of a constitutional exemption from a mandatory minimum sentence, thereby upholding the enactment as valid while exempting the accused from its application: see *R v. Chief* (1989), 51 CCC (3d) 265 (YTCA), and *R v. McGillivary* (1991), 62 CCC (3d) 407 (Sask. CA). Finally, in some of the cases where the courts have upheld a minimum sentence as constitutionally valid, it has been noted that the mandatory minimum sentence was demonstrably unfit or harsh in the case before the court. See, for example, *McDonald*, at p. 85, per Rosenberg JA, and *R v. Hainnu*, [1998] NWTJ No. 101 (QL) (SC) at para. 71.

[21] Even if it can be argued that harsh, unfit sentences may prove to be a powerful deterrent, and therefore still serve a valid purpose, it seems to me that sentences that are unjustly severe are more likely to inspire contempt and resentment than to foster compliance with the law. It is a well-established principle of the criminal justice system that judges must strive to impose a sentence tailored to the individual case: *R v. M. (C.A.)*,

[1996] 1 SCR 500 at para. 92, 105 CCC (3d) 327, per Lamer CJ; *R v. Gladue*, [1999] 1 SCR 688 at para. 93, 133 CCC (3d) 385, 171 DLR (4th) 385, per Cory and Iacobucci JJ.

[22] Consequently, it is important to interpret legislation which deals, directly and indirectly, with mandatory minimum sentences, in a manner that is consistent with general principles of sentencing, and that does not offend the integrity of the criminal justice system. This is entirely possible in this case, and, in my view, such an approach reflects the intention of Parliament that all sentences be administered consistently, except to the limited extent required to give effect to a mandatory minimum.

• • •

[28] In addition, and in contrast to statutory remission or parole, pre-sentence custody is time actually served in detention, and often in harsher circumstances than the punishment will ultimately call for. In *R v. Rezaie* (1996), 112 CCC (3d) 97 (Ont. CA), to which several lower courts have referred in their consideration of pre-sentencing custody, Laskin JA succinctly summarizes the particular features of pre-trial custody that result in its frequent characterization as "dead time" at p. 104:

> … [I]n two respects, pre-trial custody is even more onerous than post-sentencing custody. First, other than for a sentence of life imprisonment, legislative provisions for parole eligibility and statutory release do not take into account time spent in custody before trial (or before sentencing). Second, local detention centres ordinarily do not provide educational, retraining or rehabilitation programs to an accused in custody waiting trial.

[29] As this quotation from *Rezaie* demonstrates, pre-sentencing custody, pre-trial custody, pre-disposition custody and "dead time" are all used to refer to the time spent by an accused person in detention prior to conviction and sentencing. For the purposes of this decision, I consider all these terms to refer to the same thing; however, I prefer "pre-sentencing custody" as it most accurately captures all the time an offender may have spent in custody prior to the imposition of sentence.

[30] Several years ago, Professor Martin L. Friedland published an important study of pre-sentencing custody in which he referred to Professor Caleb Foote's Comment on the New York Bail Study project, noting that "accused persons … are confined pending trial under conditions which are more oppressive and restrictive than those applied to convicted and sentenced felons": "Detention Before Trial: A Study of Criminal Cases Tried in the Toronto Magistrates' Courts" (1965), at p. 104. As Rosenberg JA noted in *McDonald* at p. 72: "There has been little change in the conditions under which remand prisoners are held in this province in the almost forty years since Professor Friedland did his study." Considering the severe nature of pre-sentencing custody, and that the accused person is in fact deprived of his or her liberty, credit for pre-sentencing custody is arguably less offensive to the concept of a minimum period of incarceration than would be the granting of statutory remission or parole. It is therefore ironic that the applicability of s. 719(3) has encountered such difficulties in the case of minimum sentences, simply because the "interference" with the minimum is at the initial sentence determination stage and thus more readily apparent.

[31] As was pointed out by Rosenberg JA in *McDonald* at p. 73, Parliament enacted the forerunner to s. 719(3) of the *Criminal Code* as part of the *Bail Reform Act*, RSC 1970, c. 2 (2nd Supp.), for the very specific purpose of ensuring that the well-established practice of sentencing judges to give credit for time served while computing a sentence would be

available even to reduce a sentence below the minimum fixed by law. During the second reading of what was then Bill C-218, *Amendment of Provisions of the Criminal Code* relating to Arrest and Bail, Justice Minister John Turner described Parliament's intention regarding what is now s. 719(3):

> Generally speaking, the courts in deciding what sentence to impose on a person convicted of an offence take into account the time he has spent in custody awaiting trial. However, under the present *Criminal Code*, a sentence commences only when it is imposed, and the court's hands are tied in those cases where a minimum term of imprisonment must be imposed. In such cases, therefore, the court is bound to impose not less than the minimum sentence even though the convicted person may have been in custody awaiting trial for a period in excess of the minimum sentence. The new version of the bill would permit the court, in a proper case, to take this time into account in imposing sentence. [House of Commons Debates, February 5, 1971, at p. 3118.]

> • • •

[33] All of the above suggests that if indeed s. 719(3) had to be interpreted such as to prevent credit being given for time served in detention prior to sentencing under a mandatory minimum offence, the result would be offensive both to rationality and to justice. Fortunately, as was admirably explained by Rosenberg JA in *McDonald*, this result is avoided through the application of sound principles of statutory interpretation.

[34] In his judgment, Rosenberg JA employed several well-established rules of statutory interpretation to conclude as he did, at p. 69, that s. 719(3) provides sentencing judges with a "substantive power to count pre-sentence custody in fixing the length of the sentence." I agree with his analysis. In particular, I approve of his reference to the principle that provisions in penal statutes, when ambiguous, should be interpreted in a manner favourable to the accused (see *R v. McIntosh*, [1995] 1 SCR 686 at para. 29, 95 CCC (3d) 481, per Lamer CJ); to the need to interpret legislation so as to avoid conflict between its internal provisions, to avoid absurd results by searching for internal coherence and consistency in the statute; and finally, where a provision is capable of more than one interpretation, to choose the interpretation which is consistent with the Charter: *Slaight Communications Inc. v. Davidson*, [1989] 1 SCR 1038 at p. 1078, 59 DLR (4th) 416, per Lamer J (as he then was). Without repeating Rosenberg JA's analysis here, I wish to make a few observations.

B. The Distinction Between Punishment and Sentence

[35] Rosenberg JA relied on the distinction between the meaning of the words "punishment" and "sentence," the former being used in s. 344(a) and the latter in s. 719(3). I set out the relevant provisions again, for ease of reference:

> 344. Every person who commits robbery is guilty of an indictable offence and liable
> (a) where a firearm is used in the commission of the offence, to imprisonment for life and to a minimum punishment of imprisonment for a term of four years ...
> 719(3) In determining the sentence to be imposed on a person convicted of an offence, a court may take into account any time spent in custody by the person as a result of the offence.

[36] The distinction between "sentence" and "punishment" was developed by the Canadian Sentencing Reform Commission in its 1987 report, "Sentencing Reform: A Canadian

Approach," at pp. 110 et seq. In summary, Rosenberg JA emphasized at pp. 76-78 that "sentencing" is a judicial determination of a legal sanction, in contrast to "punishment" which is the actual infliction of the legal sanction. While this distinction is helpful, I do not think that it is fundamental to sustain the conclusion that s. 719(3) may be applied to s. 344(a). The French version does not employ a similar distinction in the language of the two sections. In French, the expression "la peine" is used interchangeably for "punishment" (s. 344(a)), for "sentencing" (title to s. 718.2) and for "sentence" (i.e., ss. 718.2 and 719). However, the expression "punishment" which is used twice in s. 718.3(1), is referred to in French first as "la peine" and the second time, in the same sentence, as "la punition." What is fundamental is less the words chosen, in the French or English version, but the concepts that they carry. Again, for ease of reference, I set out some of these provisions:

> 344. Quiconque commet un vol qualifié est coupable d'un acte criminel passible:
> (a) s'il y a usage d'une arme à feu lors de la perpétration de l'infraction, de l'emprisonnement à perpétuité, la peine minimale étant de quatre ans. ...
> 718.3(1) Lorsqu'une disposition prescrit différents degrés ou genres de peine à l'égard d'une infraction, la punition à infliger est, sous réserve des restrictions contenues dans la disposition, à la discrétion du tribunal qui condamne l'auteur de l'infraction. ...
> 719(3) Pour fixer la peine à infliger à une personne déclarée coupable d'une infraction, le tribunal peut prendre en compte toute période que la personne a passée sous garde par suite de l'infraction.

[37] Overall, both versions lead to the same conclusion, since the French phrase in s. 719(3), "pour fixer la peine" places the emphasis on the sentencing judge's role of calculating the appropriate sentence, and in doing so, provides the discretion for considering the amount of time already spent in custody by the convicted offender in relation to the offence. Since these sections refer to "la peine," it seems logical to conclude that in determining "la peine minimale" it is acceptable to apply s. 719(3), since "la peine minimale" is merely a subset of "la peine" generally, and has not been excluded expressly from the operation of s. 719(3). No violence is done to the language of the Code when the sections are read together, in French or in English, and are understood to mean, as Parliament intended, that an offender will receive a minimum sentence of four years, to commence when it is imposed, and calculated with credit given for time served.

C. The Effect of Pre-Sentencing Custody on the Legally Detained Accused

[38] I have already commented on the usually harsh nature of pre-sentencing custody and referred to the frequent characterization of this detention as "dead time." Some further comments are required.

[39] Counsel for the respondent urged this Court to consider the apparent fallacy of recognizing pre-sentencing custody as punishment, since it is commonly recognized that Canadian law does not punish innocent citizens. Rosenberg JA in *McDonald*, at p. 77, noted that "accused persons are not denied bail to punish them before their guilt has been determined." He referred to this Court's decision in *R v. Pearson*, [1992] 3 SCR 665 at pp. 687-88, 77 CCC (3d) 124, where Lamer CJ held that the presumption of innocence as guaranteed by s. 11(d) of the Charter has "no application at the bail stage of the criminal process, where the guilt or innocence of the accused is not determined and where punishment is not imposed."

[40] Counsel for the respondent also referred to this passage from Pearson to support the contention that pre-trial custody may not be considered as part of the offender's punishment. With respect, it is important to consider the broader context of Lamer CJ's comments. At that point in the Pearson judgment (at pp. 687-88), Lamer CJ was elaborating on the specific understanding of the s. 11(d) presumption of innocence in the trial context:

> Thus the effect of s. 11(d) is to create a procedural and evidentiary rule at trial that the prosecution must prove guilt beyond a reasonable doubt. This procedural and evidentiary rule has no application at the bail stage of the criminal process, where the guilt or innocence of the accused is not determined and where punishment is not imposed. Accordingly, s. 515(6)(d) does not violate s. 11(d).

Looking at this larger context, one cannot conclude that Lamer CJ was proposing that pre-sentencing custody could never be viewed as punishment or that it could not retroactively be treated as part of the punishment, as provided for by s. 719(3).

[41] To maintain that pre-sentencing custody can never be deemed punishment following conviction because the legal system does not punish innocent people is an exercise in semantics that does not acknowledge the reality of pre-sentencing custody so carefully delineated by Laskin JA, in *Rezaie, supra*, and by Gary Trotter in his text, *The Law of Bail in Canada* (1992), at p. 28:

> Remand prisoners, as they are sometimes called, often spend their time awaiting trial in detention centres or local jails that are ill-suited to lengthy stays. As the Ouimet Report stressed, such institutions may restrict liberty more than many institutions which house the convicted. Due to overcrowding, inmate turnover and the problems of effectively implementing programs and recreation activities, serving time in such institutions can be quite onerous.

Therefore, while pre-trial detention is not intended as punishment when it is imposed, it is, in effect, deemed part of the punishment following the offender's conviction, by the operation of s. 719(3). The effect of deeming such detention punishment is not unlike the determination, discussed earlier in these reasons, that time spent lawfully at large while on parole is considered nonetheless a continuation of the offender's sentence of incarceration.

[42] If this Court were to conclude that the discretion provided by s. 719(3) to consider pre-sentencing custody was not applicable to the mandatory minimum sentence of s. 344(a), it is certain that unjust sentences would result. First, courts would be placed in the difficult situation of delivering unequal treatment to similarly situated offenders: for examples, see *McDonald*, at pp. 80-81. Secondly, because of the gravity of the offence and the concern for public safety, many persons charged under s. 344(a), even first time offenders, would often be remanded in custody while awaiting trial. Consequently, discrepancies in sentencing between least and worst offenders would increase, since the worst offender, whose sentence exceeded the minimum would benefit from pre-sentencing credit, while the first time offender whose sentence would be set at the minimum, would not receive credit for his or her pre-sentencing detention. An interpretation of s. 719(3) and s. 344(a) that would reward the worst offender and penalize the least offender is surely to be avoided.

[43] These examples of the absurd results we could expect from an exclusion of the application of s. 719(3) to mandatory minimum sentences, such as that provided by

s. 344(a), are further indication that Parliament intended these two sections to be interpreted harmoniously and consistently within the overall context of the criminal justice system's sentencing regime.

D. Calculating the Amount of Credit for Pre-Sentence Custody

[44] I see no advantage in detracting from the well-entrenched judicial discretion provided in s. 719(3) by endorsing a mechanical formula for crediting pre-sentencing custody. As we have re-affirmed in this decision, the goal of sentencing is to impose a just and fit sentence, responsive to the facts of the individual offender and the particular circumstances of the commission of the offence. I adopt the reasoning of Laskin JA in *Rezaie*, at p. 105, where he noted that:

> ... provincial appellate courts have rejected a mathematical formula for crediting pre-trial custody, instead insisting that the amount of time to be credited should be determined on a case by case basis. ... Although a fixed multiplier may be unwise, absent justification, sentencing judges should give some credit for time spent in custody before trial (and before sentencing). [Citations omitted]

[45] In the past, many judges have given more or less two months credit for each month spent in pre-sentencing detention. This is entirely appropriate even though a different ratio could also be applied, for example if the accused has been detained prior to trial in an institution where he or she has had full access to educational, vocational and rehabilitation programs. The often applied ratio of 2:1 reflects not only the harshness of the detention due to the absence of programs, which may be more severe in some cases than in others, but reflects also the fact that none of the remission mechanisms contained in the *Corrections and Conditional Release Act* apply to that period of detention. "Dead time" is "real" time. The credit cannot and need not be determined by a rigid formula and is thus best left to the sentencing judge, who remains in the best position to carefully weigh all the factors which go toward the determination of the appropriate sentence, including the decision to credit the offender for any time spent in pre-sentencing custody.

. . .

Appeal allowed.

NOTES

1. After *Wust*, the following three points could be made:

    1. in part, pre-sentence custody was punishment;
    2. the pre-sentence custody credit was premised on both compensation for lost remission and parole eligibility and on the usual harshness of remand incarceration; and
    3. normally, credit should be given at a rate of two months' credit to one month served in pre-sentencing detention.

2. Another aspect of pre-sentence custody was the development of the "enhanced credit" (more than two months for one) in situations where judges have considered the conditions of confinement to have been especially egregious—for example, during a jail

guard strike: see e.g. *R v Kravchov* (2002), 4 CR (6th) 137 (Ont Ct J); *R v GR*, [2002] OJ No 4361 (QL) (Sup Ct J); and *R v Critton*, [2002] OJ No 2594 (QL) (Sup Ct J).

In *R v Downes* (2006), 79 OR (3d) 321, 205 CCC (3d) 488 (CA), the Ontario Court of Appeal recognized that the concept of credit for pre-sentence custody could apply to cases where there were stringent bail conditions like house arrest. The court eventually gave 5 months' credit for 18 months on bail.

Subsequently, cases of enhanced credit, the unsubstantiated lore that prisoners were "gaming the system" to increase pre-sentence custody credits, and the claim that pre-sentence custody credits undermined the public expression of a fit sentence attracted media attention. As a result, the Harper government brought forward the curiously named *Truth in Sentencing Act*, SC 2009, c 29, which amended s 719(3) as follows:

> 719(3) In determining the sentence to be imposed on a person convicted of an offence, a court may take into account any time spent in custody by the person as a result of the offence but the court shall limit any credit for that time to a maximum of one day for each day spent in custody.
>
> (3.1) Despite subsection (3), if the circumstances justify it, the maximum is one and one-half days for each day spent in custody unless the reason for detaining the person in custody was stated in the record under subsection 515(9.1) or the person was detained in custody under subsection 524(4) or (8).
>
> (3.2) The court shall give reasons for any credit granted and shall cause those reasons to be stated in the record.
>
> (3.3) The court shall cause to be stated in the record and on the warrant of committal the offence, the amount of time spent in custody, the term of imprisonment that would have been imposed before any credit was granted, the amount of time credited, if any, and the sentence imposed.
>
> (3.4) Failure to comply with subsection (3.2) or (3.3) does not affect the validity of the sentence imposed by the court.

These new provisions led to substantial litigation on a number of issues, initially about s 719(3.1) and which "circumstances" might justify a credit of 1.5 days for each day spent in pre-sentence custody. Ultimately, this issue reached the Supreme Court of Canada.

R v Summers
2014 SCC 26, [2014] 1 SCR 575 (footnotes omitted)

KARAKATSANIS J (McLachlin CJ and LeBel, Abella, Rothstein, Cromwell, and Wagner JJ concurring):

[1] When an accused person is not granted bail, and must be remanded in jail awaiting trial, the *Criminal Code*, R.S.C. 1985, c. C-46, allows time served to be credited towards a resulting sentence of imprisonment. A day in jail should count as a day in jail.

[2] However, crediting a single day for every day spent in a remand centre is often insufficient to account for the full impact of that detention, both quantitatively and qualitatively. Time in a remand centre does not count for the purposes of eligibility for parole, earned remission or statutory release, and this can result in a longer term of actual incarceration for offenders who were denied bail. Moreover, conditions in remand centres

tend to be particularly harsh; they are often overcrowded and dangerous, and do not provide rehabilitative programs.

[3] As a result, for many years courts frequently granted "enhanced" credit: 2 days for each day spent in pre-sentence custody. This practice was endorsed by this Court in *R. v. Wust*, 2000 SCC 18, [2000] 1 S.C.R. 455. When conditions were exceptionally harsh, judges granted credit at a rate of 3 to 1 or more.

[4] The *Truth in Sentencing Act*, S.C. 2009, c. 29 (*TISA*), passed in 2009, amended the *Criminal Code* to cap pre-sentence credit at a maximum of 1.5 days for every day in custody. The purpose was to remove any incentive for an accused to drag out time in remand custody, and to provide transparency so that the public would know what the fit sentence was, how much credit had been given, and why.

[5] In this case, the Court is called upon to interpret these amendments. There is no dispute that Parliament imposed a cap on enhanced credit at a rate of 1.5 to 1. However, there are conflicting lower court decisions on when "enhanced" credit at a rate higher than 1 to 1 is available.

[6] The statute does not definitively address the issue, providing simply that enhanced credit is available when "the circumstances justify it" (s. 719(3.1)). The legislative history is contradictory and inconclusive. We must interpret the provisions to determine what "circumstances" justify enhanced credit of up to a rate of 1.5 to 1. The appellant, the Attorney General of Ontario, argues that the loss of eligibility for parole and statutory release cannot be a "circumstance" justifying enhanced credit under the new s. 719(3.1) of the *Criminal Code*. The Ontario Court of Appeal in this case and the Nova Scotia Court of Appeal in the companion case, *R. v. Carvery*, 2012 NSCA 107, 321 N.S.R. (2d) 321, came to the opposite conclusion, and held that the loss of eligibility for parole and statutory release is a "circumstance" that can justify enhanced credit.

· · ·

[20] Prior to the enactment of the *TISA* in 2009, s. 719(3) of the *Criminal Code* simply provided that a sentencing court "may take into account any time spent in custody by the person as a result of the offence." The *Code* imposed no restrictions on the reasons for giving credit, nor the rate at which credit was granted. In *R. v. Rezaie* (1996), 31 O.R. (3d) 713, Laskin J.A. of the Ontario Court of Appeal explained the rationale for granting credit. He noted that

> a judge should not deny credit without good reason. To do so offends one's sense of fairness. Incarceration at any stage of the criminal process is a denial of an accused's liberty. [p. 721]

[21] This recognized that it would be unfair if a day spent in custody, prior to sentencing, were not counted towards an offender's ultimate sentence. Otherwise, an offender who spent time in pre-sentence custody would serve longer in jail than an identical offender who committed an identical offence, but was granted bail. Thus, a day of incarceration requires at least a credit of one day towards the sentence.

[22] Courts generally gave enhanced credit in recognition of the fact that "in two respects, pre-trial custody is even more onerous than post-sentencing custody" (*Rezaie*, at p. 721). As Laskin J.A. explained:

> First, other than for a sentence of life imprisonment, legislative provisions for parole eligibility and statutory release do not take into account time spent in custody before trial (or before

sentencing). Second, local detention centres ordinarily do not provide educational, retraining or rehabilitation programs to an accused in custody awaiting trial. [*ibid.*]

[23]   First, the *quantitative* rationale for the practice of granting enhanced credit is to ensure that the offender does not spend more time behind bars than if he had been released on bail.

. . .

[32]   In 2009, Parliament changed the statutory regime governing credit for pre-sentence detention. As noted above, the *TISA* amended s. 719 of the *Criminal Code* in two relevant ways. First, Parliament modified s. 719(3) to limit credit for pre-trial custody "to a maximum of one day for each day spent in custody." Second, Parliament provided in s. 719(3.1) that despite that limit, "if the circumstances justify it, the maximum is one and one-half days for each day spent in custody" unless the accused was detained pending trial for specific reasons such as breach of bail conditions.

[33]   Our task in this case is to interpret these provisions. Specifically, we must determine the meaning of "circumstances" in s. 719(3.1), and whether the lost opportunity for early release and parole in pre-sentence detention can be such a circumstance, capable of justifying enhanced credit at a rate of 1.5:1.

[34]   I conclude that loss of access to parole and early release constitutes a "circumstance" capable of justifying enhanced credit. In reaching this conclusion, I am in substantial agreement with the exemplary reasons of both Cronk J.A. in this case, and Beveridge J.A. in the companion case *Carvery.*

. . .

[37]   As Beveridge J.A. and Cronk J.A. noted, this provision is free of any language limiting the scope of what may constitute "circumstances." The legislature could easily have provided that only "exceptional circumstances" or "circumstances other than the loss of eligibility for early release and parole" justify enhanced credit.

[38]   As Cronk J.A. observed, language limiting the scope of the word "circumstances" is used elsewhere in the *Criminal Code.* For example, reference is made to "exceptional circumstances" or "compelling circumstances" in ss. 672.14(3) (fitness assessments last no longer than 30 days, except they may last for 60 if "compelling circumstances" so warrant), 672.47(2) (when an accused is found unfit to stand trial, a disposition must be made within 45 days but, in "exceptional circumstances" may be made within 90 days) and 742.6(16) (when an offender breaches a conditional sentence order, in "exceptional cases," some of the suspended sentence may be deemed to be time served).

[39]   The absence of qualifications on "circumstances" in ss. 719(3.1) is telling since Parliament *did* restrict enhanced credit, withholding it from offenders who have been denied bail primarily as a result of a previous conviction (s. 515(9.1)), those who contravened their bail conditions (ss. 524(4)(a) and 524(8)(a)), and those who committed an indictable offence while on bail (ss. 524(4)(b) and 524(8)(b)). Parliament clearly turned its attention to the circumstances under which s. 719(3.1) should *not* apply, but did not include any limitations on the scope of "circumstances" justifying its application.

[40]   Consequently, at the hearing before this Court, the Crown conceded that the circumstances referred to in s. 719(3.1) need not be exceptional. Instead, the Crown took the position that "circumstances" resulting from operation of law, and specifically lost

eligibility for early release and parole, could not justify enhanced credit. The Crown argues that "circumstances" suggest facts that are particular to the offender and do not include those consequences that are universal and inherent to the statutory regime.

[41]   However, the provision is devoid of any limiting language supporting this interpretation. Moreover, the *impact* of the legal regime is a circumstance that is particular to each offender because the law affects offenders differently. For example, the loss of parole or early release eligibility will not make a difference to offenders who would not have received early release or parole in any event. Moreover, the legislation can change over time such that its impact on offenders becomes less uniform.

[42]   The Crown submits that s. 719(3) creates a general rule of credit at a rate of 1:1, to which s. 719(3.1) is an exception. If lost eligibility for early release or parole, while in pre-sentence custody, is a "circumstance" justifying enhanced credit of 1.5:1, then almost every remand offender will qualify. This would transform the "exception" into the new "general rule" and render s. 719(3) irrelevant, an absurd result.

[43]   I agree that s. 719(3.1) is structured as an exception to s. 719(3). Section 719(3.1) begins with the words "[d]espite subsection (3)" and applies only when "circumstances justify it," which tends to indicate that it is an exception to the general rule. While marginal notes are not part of the enactment and are of limited value in statutory interpretation (*Interpretation Act*, R.S.C. 1985, c. I-21, s. 14), the fact that the subsection has the marginal note "[e]xception" is consistent with this conclusion.

[44]   I also agree with the Crown that it is somewhat inelegant to create an exception that applies in more cases than the general rule. However, the strength of this argument is limited for three reasons.

[45]   First, there is no general rule of statutory interpretation that the circumstances falling under an exception must be numerically fewer than those falling under the general rule. If the criteria that permit departure from a general proposition are satisfied, the numerical relationship is not relevant.

[46]   For example, s. 457(1) makes it an offence to make, publish, print, execute, issue, distribute or circulate anything in the likeness of a current bank-note. However s. 457(2) provides exceptions, including for the Bank of Canada, its employees carrying out their duties and its contractors. Presumably, the overwhelming majority of bank-notes are produced by the Bank of Canada, its employees, and its contractors, and therefore fall under the exception.

[47]   Indeed, Crown counsel accepts that the lack of programs in detention facilities and overcrowding are common problems, and could result in exceptions under s. 719(3.1) that are numerically greater than those limited by s. 719(3).

[48]   Second, an interpretation of "circumstances" that includes loss of eligibility for parole and early release does not render subsection 3 redundant. Where an accused falls under an explicit exception to s. 719(3.1) (for instance, because she has been detained for breach of bail conditions), the one-for-one cap set by s. 719(3) will apply. Moreover, enhanced credit need not be granted in every case. For example, when long periods of pre-sentence detention are attributable to the wrongful conduct of the offender, enhanced credit will often be inappropriate. Section 719(3) continues to exist for such cases.

[49]   Third, the structure of s. 719 is consistent with the rationales for the existence of pre-sentence credit. Section 719(3) reflects the general rationale for giving credit. As

Laskin J.A. wrote in *Rezaie*, at p. 721, "[i]ncarceration at any stage of the criminal process is a denial of an accused's liberty"—any time in jail should generally be credited day for day. On the other hand, s. 719(3.1) reflects the rationale for *enhanced* credit. Crediting a day in pre-sentence custody as a day served is insufficient to account for the full prejudicial circumstances of remand custody; enhanced credit accounts for both loss of eligibility for parole and early release (circumstances with quantitative impact) and the harshness of the conditions (circumstances with qualitative impact). Thus, the division between the subsections reflects the different theoretical underpinnings of credit and enhanced credit.

[50] Further, this structure builds resilience into the statutory scheme. For example, if Parliament were to amend the *Corrections and Conditional Release Act*, so that pre-sentence custody counted for the purposes of parole eligibility and early release, s. 719(3.1) would only be called upon to account for situations of *qualitative* harshness, and an increased number of cases would fall solely under s. 719(3). The structure of the provision logically mirrors the rationales for credit and enhanced credit.

• • •

[52] Parliament clearly intended to restrict the amount of pre-sentence credit. This is plain from the cap of 1.5 days credit for every day spent in detention. It is also consistent with statements made by the then Justice Minister, before the House of Common Standing Committee on Justice and Human Rights, on May 6, 2009:

> The practice of awarding overly generous credit can put the administration of justice into disrepute because it creates the impression that offenders are getting more lenient sentences than they deserve. The public does not understand how the final sentence reflects the seriousness of the crime. For these reasons, the current practice of routinely awarding two-for-one credit must be curtailed.

(*Evidence*, No. 20, 2nd Sess., 40th Parl., at p. 11.) This objective is achieved regardless of what circumstances may justify the use of enhanced credit in s. 719(3.1).

[53] Parliament also intended that the process of granting credit under s. 719 should be more transparent and easily understood by the public. It achieved this end through the insertion of ss. 719(3.2) and 719(3.3), which provide that judges should give reasons for granting credit and state both the fit sentence and the amount of credit granted.

[54] However, I agree with Beveridge J.A. and Cronk J.A. that the intention of Parliament with respect to what "circumstances" may justify enhanced credit under s. 719(3.1) is far less clear and even contradictory (*Carvery*, at paras. 79-82; *Summers*, at paras. 82-88). Therefore, the legislative history is of no assistance in answering this question.

• • •

[56] Parliament does, of course, have the power to exclude these circumstances from consideration (barring a constitutional challenge). However, it strikes me as inconceivable that Parliament intended to overturn a principled and long-standing sentencing practice, without using explicit language, by instead relying on inferences that could possibly be drawn from the order of certain provisions in the *Criminal Code*.

[57] Rather, it seems more likely that Parliament intended to do what it did explicitly. The amendments clearly impose a *cap* on the rate at which credit can be awarded, at 1.5:1. This is a substantial and clear departure from pre-*TISA* practice. Having made its intention so clear on that point, Parliament gave no indication it intended to alter the reasons for which enhanced credit can be granted.

[58] In my view, neither the language of the provision nor the external evidence demonstrates a clear intention to abolish one of the principled rationales for enhanced credit.

• • •

[60] As Beveridge J.A. and Cronk J.A. recognized, an interpretation of s. 719(3.1) that does not account for loss of eligibility for early release and parole during remand custody means that offenders who do not receive bail will serve longer sentences than otherwise identical offenders who are granted bail.

[61] This result is incompatible with the parity principle. A rule that results in longer sentences for offenders who do not obtain bail, compared to otherwise identical offenders, does not result in "similar … sentences imposed on similar offenders for similar offences committed in similar circumstances": s. 718.2(b).

[62] The Crown says that parity does not require absolute equality and that in any event, enhanced credit is an ineffective tool to achieve equality between offenders, since it is premised on both being released on their statutory release date (after two thirds of their sentence). In practice, some offenders will be released on parole after one third of their sentences; others will never be released during their sentence.

[63] Obviously, the scope of the disparity will vary, depending on if and when offenders are ultimately released. Nonetheless, a rule that creates structural differences in sentences, based on criteria irrelevant to sentencing, is inconsistent with the principle of parity.

[64] The Crown also says that the Court of Appeal's reliance on the sentencing principle of proportionality was misplaced. Proportionality is simply concerned with the imposition of a just sanction in a particular case; any comparison with similar offenders is irrelevant.

[65] However, it is difficult to see how sentences can reliably be "proportionate to the gravity of the offence and the degree of responsibility of the offender" (s. 718.1) when the length of incarceration is also a product of the offender's ability to obtain bail, which is frequently dependent on totally different criteria.

[66] Judicial interim release requires the judge to be confident that, amongst other things, the accused will neither flee nor reoffend while on bail. When an accused is able to deposit money, or be released to family and friends acting as sureties (who often pledge money themselves), this can help provide the court with such assurance. Unfortunately, those without either a support network of family and friends or financial means cannot provide these assurances. Consequently, as the intervener the John Howard Society submitted, this means that vulnerable and impoverished offenders are less able to access bail.

[67] For example, Aboriginal people are more likely to be denied bail, and make up a disproportionate share of the population in remand custody. A system that results in consistently longer, harsher sentences for vulnerable members of society, not based on the wrongfulness of their conduct but because of their isolation and inability to pay, can hardly be said to be assigning sentences in line with the principles of parity and proportionality. Accounting for loss of early release eligibility through enhanced credit responds to this concern.

• • •

[70] In determining credit for pre-sentence custody, judges may credit at most 1.5 days for every day served where circumstances warrant. While there is now a statutory maximum, the analytical approach endorsed in *Wust* otherwise remains unchanged. Judges should continue to assign credit on the basis of the quantitative rationale, to

account for lost eligibility for early release and parole during pre-sentence custody, and the qualitative rationale, to account for the relative harshness of the conditions in detention centres.

[71] The loss of early release, taken alone, will generally be a sufficient basis to award credit at the rate of 1.5 to 1, even if the conditions of detention are not particularly harsh, and parole is unlikely. Of course, a lower rate may be appropriate when detention was a result of the offender's bad conduct, or the offender is likely to obtain neither early release nor parole. When the statutory exceptions within s. 719(3.1) are engaged, credit may only be given at a rate of 1 to 1. Moreover, s. 719 is engaged only where the pre-sentence detention is a result of the offence for which the offender is being sentenced.

[72] This means that two offenders, one of whom lost the opportunity for early release and parole, and a second who, in addition to losing those opportunities, was also subject to extremely harsh conditions, will likely both have credit assigned at a rate of 1.5 to 1. The unavoidable consequence of capping pre-sentence credit at this rate is that it is insufficient to compensate for the harshness of pre-sentence detention in *all* cases. However, this does not mean that credit should be scaled back in order to "leave room at the top" of the scale for the most egregious cases. A cap is a cut-off and means simply that the upper limit will be reached in more cases. It should not lead judges to deny or restrict credit when it is warranted.

NOTE

The decision in *Summers* was reached through statutory interpretation. Although it was not based on the Charter, it did include an important statement about the principles of sentencing:

> [67] … A system that results in consistently longer, harsher sentences for vulnerable members of society, not based on the wrongfulness of their conduct but because of their isolation and inability to pay, can hardly be said to be assigning sentences in line with the principles of parity and proportionality.

Has the principle of proportionality risen to the level of principles of fundamental justice? There are some references to this possibility in judicial commentary: see LeBel J in *R v Ipeelee*, 2012 SCC 13 at para 36, [2012] 1 SCR 433 and *R v Anderson*, 2014 SCC 41 at para 21, [2014] 2 SCR 167. For the purpose of determining the constitutionality of a sentence, this role for proportionality was expressly rejected by the Supreme Court of Canada in *R v Lloyd*, 2016 SCC 13 and *R v Safarzadeh-Markhali*, 2016 SCC 14, discussed in Chapter 17, below.

However, relying on overbreadth, in *R v Safarzadeh-Markhali* the Supreme Court concluded that the words "the reason for detaining the person in custody was stated in the record under subsection 515(9.1)" in s 719(3.1) of the Code violate s 7 of the Charter and are not saved by s 1.

FURTHER READING

British Academy. *A Presumption Against Imprisonment* (London: British Academy, 2014).

Doob, Anthony N. "Principled Sentencing, Politics, and Restraint in the Use of Imprison-ment: Canada's Break with Its History" (2012) IX Champ Pénal/Penal Field, online: <http://champpenal.revues.org/8335>.

Doob, Anthony N & Cheryl Marie Webster. "Back to the Future? Policy Development in Pre-Trial Detention in Canada" in Karim Ismaili, Jane Sprott & Kimberly Varma, eds, *Canadian Criminal Justice Policy* (Toronto: Oxford University Press, 2012) 30.

Doob, Anthony & Cheryl Webster. "Countering Punitiveness: Understanding Stability in Can-ada's Imprisonment Rate" (2006) 40:2 Law & Soc'y Rev 325.

Doob, Anthony & Cheryl Webster. "The 'Truth in Sentencing' Act: The Triumph of Form over Substance" (2013) 17 Can Crim L Rev 365.

Ewald, A & Christopher Uggen. "The Collateral Effects of Imprisonment on Prisoners, Their Families, and Communities" in Joan Petersilia & Kevin Reitz, eds, *The Oxford Handbook of Sentencing and Corrections* (New York: Oxford University Press, 2012).

Gottschalk, Marie. *Caught: The Prison State and the Lockdown of American Politics* (Princeton, NJ: Princeton University Press, 2014).

Haney, Craig. "The Psychological Effects of Imprisonment" in Joan Petersilia & Kevin Reitz, eds, *The Oxford Handbook of Sentencing and Corrections* (New York: Oxford University Press, 2012).

Paciocco, David M. "The Law of Minimum Sentences: Judicial Responses and Responsibility" (2015) 19 Can Crim L Rev 173.

Parole Board of Canada. "History of Parole in Canada" (2015), online: <http://pbc-clcc.gc.ca/about/hist-eng.shtml>.

Pomerance, Renee M. "The New Approach to Sentencing in Canada: Reflections of a Trial Judge" (2013) 17 Can Crim L Rev 305.

Roberts, Julian. *Mandatory Sentences of Imprisonment in Common Law Jurisdictions: Some Representative Models* (Ottawa: Department of Justice Canada, Research Division, 2006).

Sherrin, Christopher. "Pre-Sentence Custody: Not Giving Credit When Credit Is Due" (2013) 17 Can Crim L Rev 155.

CHAPTER TWELVE

Conditional Sentence
of Imprisonment

I. INTRODUCTION

The conditional sentence was created in 1995 (SC 1995, c 22), coming into force in 1996 with the new Part XXIII of the *Criminal Code*, RSC 1985, c C-46 (as amended). Its purpose was to reduce the use of imprisonment as a sanction. A conditional sentence is a term of imprisonment that is served in the community. When the court concludes that an appropriate sentence is a jail term of less than two years, it may order that the sentence be served in the community, subject to conditions. Although this is the first such sanction in Canada, most common law jurisdictions have some mechanism that allows offenders to discharge a custodial sentence at home.

The conditional sentence has proven to be the most significant and controversial aspect of the reforms of 1996. There is no doubt, however, that the disposition is well established among sentencing options. Although some guidelines have been developed by the courts, controversy has continued about the proper scope of conditional sentences. Are there offences, or classes of offences, for which the conditional sentence should not be an available option? In 2007 (SC 2007, c 12), Parliament amended the Code to restrict the ambit of conditional sentences by excluding the conditional sentence as an option for any offence that can be characterized as a "serious personal injury offence," a terrorism offence, or a criminal-organization offence. This restrictive approach was replaced by another with a further amendment in 2012 (SC 2012, c 1, s 34), which is reproduced below in Section IV.B (s 742.1).

II. BACKGROUND OF THE CONDITIONAL SENTENCE

The idea of suspending dispositions for fixed periods of time can be traced to the Report of the Canadian Committee on Corrections, *Toward Unity: Criminal Justice and Corrections* (Ottawa: Queen's Printer, 1969) ("the Ouimet Report") and the English suspended sentence. Both examples are distinguishable from the traditional Canadian suspended sentence, where the imposition of sentence is suspended but not its execution. In 1984, a bill was tabled that contained proposals for sentencing reform based on *The Criminal Law in Canadian Society* (Ottawa: Department of Justice, 1982), a statement of government policy concerning the criminal law. The bill included a new option, entitled the "conditional sentence," which was to be defined in the following form:

> Where an offender other than a corporation is convicted of an offence, except an offence for which a minimum punishment is prescribed by law, the court may suspend the imposition of any other sanction and direct that the offender enter into a recognizance in Form 28 without sureties to keep the peace and be of good behaviour for such period, not exceeding two years, as the court thinks fit.

This proposal would have permitted the suspension of any kind of sentence without conditions, except to avoid further offences. It was essentially the Ouimet model, but it died on the order paper.

The government of Canada issued a green paper on sentencing and corrections in 1990. This led in 1992 to another sentencing reform bill, C-90. Neither the term "conditional sentence" nor any mechanism that might fit that name appeared in these documents. However, that was not the end of the idea. A major criticism of the green paper was the absence of new non-custodial options for sentencing judges. Around the same time as the release of that document came the publication of Norval Morris & Michael Tonry, *Between Prison and Probation: Intermediate Punishments in a Rational Sentencing System* (New York: Oxford University Press, 1991). Within this category of intermediate sanction would be non-custodial alternatives such as intensive supervision, house arrest, electronic monitoring, day-reporting centres, and community service. The Department of Justice circulated a series of discussion papers that canvassed some of the "intermediate sanction" alternatives. One paper, dated December 9, 1991, returned to the subject of a conditional sentence but defined it as "an alternative to the suspended sentence." In other words, rather than suspending the imposition of a sentence, as has been Canada's approach, the proposal would have suspended the execution of the sentence and amended the consequential breach procedure so that failures to comply would no longer be an offence but rather trigger court intervention. In essence, this would be a revision of the probation scheme. This proposal was ultimately rejected.

The background to s 742.1 demonstrates a recurring concern with three factors:

1. overuse of imprisonment,
2. greater use of community sentences, and
3. intermediate sanctions.

Apart from responding to the overuse of imprisonment, the manner in which the conditional sentence evolved is also important. It was clearly not a revision of probation. The probation provisions and the suspended sentence were continued with only minor amendments. Nor is the conditional sentence a free-standing, discrete sentencing option; it is available as an alternative mode of serving a sentence of imprisonment.

III. GENERAL PRINCIPLES

After the reform of 1996, trial and appellate courts in the provinces and territories grappled with the proper interpretation of the provisions concerning conditional sentences. Although discrepancies eventually diminished, there remained considerable variations in approach and results. Guidance was clearly needed from the Supreme Court of Canada. As seen in Chapter 2, Judicial Methodology and the Legislative Context, the Supreme Court does not often hear sentencing cases, and its practice in this regard is quite deliberate. In 1999, the Supreme Court heard five cases relating to conditional sentences and judgment was pronounced in all of them on the same day: *R v Proulx*, 2000 SCC 5, [2000] 1 SCR 61; *R v LFW*, 2000 SCC 6, [2000] 1 SCR 132; *R v RNS*, 2000 SCC 7, [2000] 1 SCR 149; *R v RAR*, 2000 SCC 8, [2000] 1 SCR 163; and *R v Bunn*, 2000 SCC 9, [2000] 1 SCR 183. The principal opinion was given by Lamer CJ for a unanimous court in *Proulx*, and it is still the leading statement on the subject. It is also appropriate to look at the other four cases, if only to consider whether the principles in *Proulx* are demonstrably at work in those decisions.

Proulx is lengthy and much of it is reproduced here. The relevant provisions of the Code concerned with conditional sentences are included in the opinion of Lamer CJ, although also bear in mind the amendments of s 742.1 in 2007 and 2012, noted above.

R v Proulx
2000 SCC 5, [2000] 1 SCR 61

LAMER CJ (L'Heureux-Dubé, Gonthier, McLachlin, Iacobucci, Major, Bastarache, and Binnie JJ concurring):

[1] By passing *An Act to amend the Criminal Code (sentencing) and other Acts in consequence thereof*, SC 1995, c. 22 ("Bill C-41"), Parliament has sent a clear message to all Canadian judges that too many people are being sent to prison. In an attempt to remedy the problem of overincarceration, Parliament has introduced a new form of sentence, the conditional sentence of imprisonment.

[2] As a matter of established practice and sound policy, this Court rarely hears appeals relating to sentences: see *R v. Gardiner*, [1982] 2 SCR 368, at 404; *R v. Chaisson*, [1995] 2 SCR 1118, at 1123; and *R v. M. (C.A.)*, [1996] 1 SCR 500, at para. 33. However, we have decided to hear this case and four related cases because they afford the Court the opportunity to set out for the first time the principles that govern the new and innovative conditional sentencing regime. Given the inevitable length of these reasons, I have summarized the essentials at para. 127.

I. Factual Background

[3] On the morning of November 1, 1995, after a night of partying involving consumption of some alcohol, the respondent decided to drive his friends home even though he knew that his vehicle was not mechanically sound. For a period of 10 to 20 minutes, the respondent, who had only seven weeks of experience as a licensed driver, drove erratically, weaving in and out of traffic, tailgating and trying to pass other vehicles without signalling, despite steady oncoming traffic and slippery roads. As the respondent was trying to pass

another vehicle, he drove his car into an oncoming lane of traffic, side-swiped a first car and crashed into a second one. The driver of the second vehicle was seriously injured. The accident also claimed the life of a passenger in the respondent's car. The respondent was in a near-death coma for some time, but ultimately recovered from his injuries. The respondent entered guilty pleas to one count of dangerous driving causing death and one count of dangerous driving causing bodily harm.

· · ·

III. Relevant Statutory Provisions

[10] Criminal Code, RSC, 1985, c. C-46

· · ·

742.1. Where a person is convicted of an offence, except an offence that is punishable by a minimum term of imprisonment, and the court

(a) imposes a sentence of imprisonment of less than two years, and

(b) is satisfied that serving the sentence in the community would not endanger the safety of the community and would be consistent with the fundamental purpose and principles of sentencing set out in sections 718 to 718.2,

the court may, for the purpose of supervising the offender's behaviour in the community, order that the offender serve the sentence in the community, subject to the offender's complying with the conditions of a conditional sentence order made under section 742.3.

· · ·

742.3(1) The court shall prescribe, as conditions of a conditional sentence order, that the offender do all of the following:

(a) keep the peace and be of good behaviour;

(b) appear before the court when required to do so by the court;

(c) report to a supervisor

(i) within two working days, or such longer period as the court directs, after the making of the conditional sentence order, and

(ii) thereafter, when required by the supervisor and in the manner directed by the supervisor;

(d) remain within the jurisdiction of the court unless written permission to go outside that jurisdiction is obtained from the court or the supervisor; and

(e) notify the court or the supervisor in advance of any change of name or address, and promptly notify the court or the supervisor of any change of employment or occupation.

(2) The court may prescribe, as additional conditions of a conditional sentence order, that the offender do one or more of the following:

(a) abstain from

(i) the consumption of alcohol or other intoxicating substances, or

(ii) the consumption of drugs except in accordance with a medical prescription;

(b) abstain from owning, possessing or carrying a weapon;

(c) provide for the support or care of dependants;

(d) perform up to 240 hours of community service over a period not exceeding eighteen months;

(e) attend a treatment program approved by the province; and

(f) comply with such other reasonable conditions as the court considers desirable, subject to any regulations made under subsection 738(2), for securing the good conduct of the offender and for preventing a repetition by the offender of the same offence or the commission of other offences.

$\bullet \bullet \bullet$

742.6. …

(9) Where the court is satisfied, on a balance of probabilities, that the offender has without reasonable excuse, the proof of which lies on the offender, breached a condition of the conditional sentence order, the court may

    (a) take no action;

    (b) change the optional conditions;

    (c) suspend the conditional sentence order and direct

        (i) that the offender serve in custody a portion of the unexpired sentence, and

        (ii) that the conditional sentence order resume on the offender's release from custody, either with or without changes to the optional conditions; or

    (d) terminate the conditional sentence order and direct that the offender be committed to custody until the expiration of the sentence.

$\bullet \bullet \bullet$

V. Analysis

A. The 1996 Sentencing Reforms (Bill C-41)

[14] In September 1996, Bill C-41 came into effect. It substantially reformed Part XXIII of the *Criminal Code*, and introduced, *inter alia*, an express statement of the purposes and principles of sentencing, provisions for alternative measures for adult offenders and a new type of sanction, the conditional sentence of imprisonment.

[15] As my colleagues Cory and Iacobucci JJ explained in *R v. Gladue*, [1999] 1 SCR 688, at para. 39, "[t]he enactment of the new Part XXIII was a watershed, marking the first codification and significant reform of sentencing principles in the history of Canadian criminal law." They noted two of Parliament's principal objectives in enacting this new legislation: (i) reducing the use of prison as a sanction, and (ii) expanding the use of restorative justice principles in sentencing (at para. 48).

(1) Reducing the Use of Prison as a Sanction

[16] Bill C-41 is in large part a response to the problem of over-incarceration in Canada. It was noted in *Gladue*, at para. 52, that Canada's incarceration rate of approximately 130 inmates per 100,000 population places it second or third highest among industrialized democracies. In their reasons, Cory and Iacobucci JJ reviewed numerous studies that uniformly concluded that incarceration is costly, frequently unduly harsh and "ineffective, not only in relation to its purported rehabilitative goals, but also in relation to its broader public goals" (para. 54). See also Report of the Canadian Committee on Corrections, *Toward Unity: Criminal Justice and Corrections* (1969); *Canadian Sentencing Commission, Sentencing Reform: A Canadian Approach* (1987), at pp. xxiii-xxiv; Standing Committee on Justice and Solicitor General, *Taking Responsibility* (1988), at p. 75. Prison has been characterized by some as a finishing school for criminals and as ill-preparing them for reintegration into society: see generally Canadian Committee on Corrections, *supra*, at p. 314; Correctional Service of Canada, *A Summary of Analysis of Some Major Inquiries on Corrections—1938 to 1977* (1982), at p. iv. At para. 57, Cory and Iacobucci JJ held:

Thus, it may be seen that although imprisonment is intended to serve the traditional sentencing goals of separation, deterrence, denunciation, and rehabilitation, there is widespread
consensus that imprisonment has not been successful in achieving some of these goals.
Overincarceration is a long-standing problem that has been many times publicly acknowledged but never addressed in a systematic manner by Parliament. In recent years, compared
to other countries, sentences of imprisonment in Canada have increased at an alarming rate.
*The 1996 sentencing reforms embodied in Part XXIII, and s. 718.2(e) in particular, must be
understood as a reaction to the overuse of prison as a sanction, and must accordingly be given
appropriate force as remedial provisions.* [Emphasis in original.]

[17]   Parliament has sought to give increased prominence to the principle of restraint
in the use of prison as a sanction through the enactment of s. 718.2(a) and (e). Section
718.2(d) provides that "an offender should not be deprived of liberty, if less restrictive
sanctions may be appropriate in the circumstances," while s. 718.2(e) provides that "all
available sanctions other than imprisonment that are reasonable in the circumstances
should be considered for all offenders, with particular attention to the circumstances of
aboriginal offenders." Further evidence of Parliament's desire to lower the rate of incarceration comes from other provisions of Bill C-41: s. 718(c) qualifies the sentencing
objective of separating offenders from society with the words "where necessary," thereby
indicating that caution be exercised in sentencing offenders to prison; s. 734(2) imposes
a duty on judges to undertake a means inquiry before imposing a fine, so as to decrease
the number of offenders who are incarcerated for defaulting on payment of their fines;
and of course, s. 742.1, which introduces the conditional sentence. In *Gladue*, at para. 40,
the Court held that "the creation of the conditional sentence suggests, on its face, a desire
to lessen the use of incarceration."

(2)   Expanding the Use of Restorative Justice Principles in Sentencing

[18]   Restorative justice is concerned with the restoration of the parties that are affected
by the commission of an offence. Crime generally affects at least three parties: the victim,
the community, and the offender. A restorative justice approach seeks to remedy the
adverse effects of crime in a manner that addresses the needs of all parties involved. This
is accomplished, in part, through the rehabilitation of the offender, reparations to the victim
and to the community, and the promotion of a sense of responsibility in the offender and
acknowledgment of the harm done to victims and to the community.

[19]   Canadian sentencing jurisprudence has traditionally focussed on the aims of
denunciation, deterrence, separation, and rehabilitation, with rehabilitation a relative
late-comer to the sentencing analysis: see *Gladue*, at para. 42. With the introduction of
Bill C-41, however, Parliament has placed new emphasis upon the goals of restorative
justice. Section 718 sets out the fundamental purpose of sentencing, as well as the various
sentencing objectives that should be vindicated when sanctions are imposed. In *Gladue*,
supra, Cory and Iacobucci JJ stated (at para. 43):

Clearly, s. 718 is, in part, a restatement of the basic sentencing aims, which are listed in paras.
(a) through (d). What are new, though, are paras. (e) and (f), which along with para. (d)
focus upon the restorative goals of repairing the harms suffered by individual victims and by
the community as a whole, promoting a sense of responsibility and an acknowledgment of the

harm caused on the part of the offender, and attempting to rehabilitate or heal the offender. The concept of restorative justice which underpins paras. (a), (e), and (f) is briefly discussed below, *but as a general matter restorative justice involves some form of restitution and reintegration into the community. The need for offenders to take responsibility for their actions is central to the sentencing process … . Restorative sentencing goals do not usually correlate with the use of prison as a sanction. In our view, Parliament's choice to include (e) and (f) alongside the traditional sentencing goals must be understood as evidencing an intention to expand the parameters of the sentencing analysis for all offenders.* [Emphasis added; citation omitted.]

[20] Parliament has mandated that expanded use be made of restorative principles in sentencing as a result of the general failure of incarceration to rehabilitate offenders and reintegrate them into society. By placing a new emphasis on restorative principles, Parliament expects both to reduce the rate of incarceration and improve the effectiveness of sentencing. During the second reading of Bill C-41 on September 20, 1994 (*House of Commons Debates*, vol. IV, 1st Sess., 35th Parl., at p. 5873), Minister of Justice Allan Rock made the following statements:

A general principle that runs throughout Bill C-41 is that jails should be reserved for those who should be there. Alternatives should be put in place for those who commit offences but who do not need or merit incarceration.

• • •

Jails and prisons will be there for those who need them, for those who should be punished in that way or separated from society. … [T]his bill creates an environment which encourages community sanctions and the rehabilitation of offenders together with reparation to victims and promoting in criminals a sense of accountability for what they have done.

It is not simply by being more harsh that we will achieve more effective criminal justice. We must use our scarce resources wisely.

B. The Nature of the Conditional Sentence

[21] The conditional sentence was specifically enacted as a new sanction designed to achieve both of Parliament's objectives. The conditional sentence is a meaningful alternative to incarceration for less serious and non-dangerous offenders. The offenders who meet the criteria of s. 742.1 will serve a sentence under strict surveillance in the community instead of going to prison. These offenders' liberty will be constrained by conditions to be attached to the sentence, as set out in s. 742.3 of the Criminal Code. In case of breach of conditions, the offender will be brought back before a judge, pursuant to s. 742.6. If an offender cannot provide a reasonable excuse for breaching the conditions of his or her sentence, the judge may order him or her to serve the remainder of the sentence in jail, as it was intended by Parliament that there be a real threat of incarceration to increase compliance with the conditions of the sentence.

[22] The conditional sentence incorporates some elements of non-custodial measures and some others of incarceration. Because it is served in the community, it will generally be more effective than incarceration at achieving the restorative objectives of rehabilitation, reparations to the victim and community, and the promotion of a sense of responsibility in the offender. However, *it is also a punitive sanction capable of achieving the*

objectives of denunciation and deterrence. It is this punitive aspect that distinguishes the conditional sentence from probation, and it is to this issue that I now turn.

(1) Comparing Conditional Sentences with Probation

[23] There has been some confusion among members of the judiciary and the public alike about the difference between a conditional sentence and a suspended sentence with probation. This confusion is understandable, as the statutory provisions regarding conditions to be attached to conditional sentences (s. 742.3) and probation orders (s. 732.1) are very similar. Notwithstanding these similarities, there is an important distinction between the two. While a suspended sentence with probation is primarily a rehabilitative sentencing tool, the evidence suggests that Parliament intended a conditional sentence to address both punitive and rehabilitative objectives.

(a) A Comparative Reading of the Provisions

[24] A comparative reading of the provisions governing conditional sentences and probation orders reveals three differences. First, a probation order includes only three compulsory conditions—to keep the peace and be of good behaviour, appear before the court when required, and notify the court or probation officer of any change in employment or address—whereas there are five such conditions in the case of a conditional sentence. The two additional compulsory conditions of a conditional sentence—to report to a supervisor and remain within the jurisdiction unless permission is granted to leave— are listed as optional conditions under a probation order.

[25] The second difference concerns the power of the judge to order the offender to undergo treatment. Under a conditional sentence, the sentencing judge can order the offender to attend a treatment program, regardless of whether the offender consents. Under a probation order, the judge can only impose a treatment order with the consent of the offender (with the exception of drug or alcohol addiction programs since the 1999 amendment to s. 732.1 (SC 1999, c. 32, s. 6)). In practice, however, this difference is not very significant, since it is unlikely that an offender faced with the choice between imprisonment and a suspended sentence with treatment as a condition of probation would refuse to consent to treatment.

[26] The third difference is in the wording of the residual clauses of the provisions governing the imposition of optional conditions. In the case of a conditional sentence, s. 742.3(2)(f) provides that the court may order that the offender comply with such other reasonable conditions as the court considers desirable "for securing the good conduct of the offender and for preventing a repetition by the offender of the same offence or the commission of other offences." By contrast, s. 732.1(3)(h) provides that the court may impose such other reasonable conditions of probation "for protecting society and for facilitating the offender's successful reintegration into the community."

[27] On their face, these three differences do not suggest that a conditional sentence is more punitive than a suspended sentence with probation. Moreover, the penalty for breach of probation is potentially more severe than that for breach of a conditional sentence. Pursuant to s. 733.1(1), breach of probation constitutes a new offence, punishable by up to two years imprisonment, while a breach of condition does not constitute a new offence *per se.* The maximum penalties are also different. In the case of a breach of

probation, the offender is subject to the revocation of the probation order and can be sentenced for the original offence (in cases where a suspended sentence was rendered): see s. 732.2(5). By contrast in the case of breaches of conditional sentences, the maximum punishment available is incarceration for the time remaining of the original sentence (s. 742.6(9)). Presumably, if a conditional sentence is more onerous than probation, the consequences of breaching a condition should be more onerous as well.

(b) Conditional Sentences Must Be More Punitive Than Probation

[28] Despite the similarities between the provisions and the fact that the penalty for breach of probation is potentially more severe than for breach of a conditional sentence, there are strong indications that Parliament intended the conditional sentence to be more punitive than probation. It is a well accepted principle of statutory interpretation that no legislative provision should be interpreted so as to render it mere surplusage. It would be absurd if Parliament intended conditional sentences to amount merely to probation under a different name. While this argument is clearly not dispositive, it suggests that Parliament intended there to be a meaningful distinction between the two sanctions. I will now consider more specific arguments in support of this position.

[29] The conditional sentence is defined in the Code as a sentence of imprisonment. The heading of s. 742 reads "Conditional Sentence of Imprisonment." Furthermore, s. 742.1(a) requires the court to impose a sentence of imprisonment of less than two years before considering whether the sentence can be served in the community subject to the appropriate conditions. Parliament intended imprisonment, in the form of incarceration, to be more punitive than probation, as it is far more restrictive of the offender's liberty. Since a conditional sentence is, at least notionally, a sentence of imprisonment, it follows that it too should be interpreted as more punitive than probation.

[30] On a related note, with the enactment of s. 742.1, Parliament has mandated that certain non-dangerous offenders who would otherwise have gone to jail for up to two years now serve their sentences in the community. If a conditional sentence is not distinguished from probation, then these offenders will receive what are effectively considerably less onerous probation orders instead of jail terms. Such lenient sentences would not provide sufficient denunciation and deterrence, nor would they be accepted by the public. Section 718 provides that the fundamental purpose of sentencing is "to contribute ... to respect for the law and the maintenance of a just, peaceful and safe society." Inadequate sanctions undermine respect for the law. Accordingly, it is important to distinguish a conditional sentence from probation by way of the use of punitive conditions.

[31] Earlier I drew attention to a subtle difference between the residual clauses in the provisions governing the imposition of optional conditions of probation orders and conditional sentences. While the difference between the two residual clauses is subtle, it is also significant. In order to appreciate this difference, it is necessary to consider the case law and practice that has developed with respect to probation.

[32] Probation has traditionally been viewed as a rehabilitative sentencing tool. Recently, the rehabilitative nature of the probation order was explained by the Saskatchewan Court of Appeal in *R v. Taylor* (1997), 122 CCC (3d) 376. Bayda CJS wrote, at p. 394:

> Apart from the wording of the provision, the innate character of a probation order is such that it seeks to influence the future behaviour of the offender. More specifically, it seeks to

secure "the good conduct" of the offender and to deter him from committing the same or other offences. *It does not particularly seek to reflect the seriousness of the offence or the offender's degree of culpability. Nor does it particularly seek to fill the need for denunciation of the offence or the general deterrence of others to commit the same or other offences. Depending upon the specific conditions of the order there may well be a punitive aspect to a probation order but punishment is not the dominant or an inherent purpose. It is perhaps not even a secondary purpose but is more in the nature of a consequence of an offender's compliance with one or more of the specific conditions with which he or she may find it hard to comply.* [Emphasis added.]

[33] Many appellate courts have struck out conditions of probation that were imposed to punish rather than rehabilitate the offender: see *R v. Ziatas* (1973), 13 CCC (2d) 287 (Ont. CA), at p. 288; *R v. Caja* (1977), 36 CCC (2d) 401 (Ont. CA), at pp. 402-3; *R v. Lavender* (1981), 59 CCC (2d) 551 (BC CA), at pp. 552-53; and *R v. L.* (1986), 50 CR (3d) 398 (Alta. CA), at pp. 399-400. The impugned terms of probation in these cases were imposed pursuant to a residual clause in force at the time whose wording was virtually identical to that presently used in s. 742.3(2)(f).

[34] Despite the virtual identity in the wording of s. 742.3(2)(f) and the old residual clause applicable to probation orders, it would be a mistake to conclude that punitive conditions cannot now be imposed under s. 742.3(2)(f). Parliament amended the residual clause for probation, s. 732.1(3)(h), to read "for protecting society and for *facilitating the offender's successful reintegration into the community*" (emphasis added). It did so to make clear the rehabilitative purpose of probation and to distinguish s. 742.3(2)(f) from s. 732.1(3)(h). The wording used in s. 742.3(2)(f) does not focus principally on the rehabilitation and reintegration of the offender. If s. 742.3(2)(f) were interpreted as precluding punitive conditions, it would frustrate Parliament's intention in distinguishing the two forms of sentence. Parliament would not have distinguished them if it intended both clauses to serve the same purpose.

[35] In light of the foregoing, it is clear that Parliament intended a conditional sentence to be more punitive than a suspended sentence with probation, notwithstanding the similarities between the two sanctions in respect of their rehabilitative purposes. I agree wholeheartedly with Vancise JA, who, dissenting in *R v. McDonald* (1997), 113 CCC (3d) 418 (Sask. CA), stated, at p. 443, that conditional sentences were designed to "permit the accused to avoid imprisonment but not to avoid punishment."

[36] Accordingly, conditional sentences should generally include punitive conditions that are restrictive of the offender's liberty. Conditions such as house arrest or strict curfews should be the norm, not the exception. As the Minister of Justice said during the second reading of Bill C-41 (*House of Commons Debates, supra,* at p. 5873), "[t]his sanction is obviously aimed at offenders who would otherwise be in jail but who could be in the community under *tight* controls" (emphasis added).

[37] There must be a reason for failing to impose punitive conditions when a conditional sentence order is made. Sentencing judges should always be mindful of the fact that conditional sentences are only to be imposed on offenders who would otherwise have been sent to jail. If the judge is of the opinion that punitive conditions are unnecessary, then probation, rather than a conditional sentence, is most likely the appropriate disposition.

[38] The punitive nature of the conditional sentence should also inform the treatment of breaches of conditions. As I have already discussed, the maximum penalty for breach

of probation is potentially more severe than that for breach of a conditional sentence. In practice, however, breaches of conditional sentences may be punished more severely than breaches of probation. Without commenting on the constitutionality of these provisions, I note that breaches of conditional sentence need only be proved on a balance of probabilities, pursuant to s. 742.6(9), whereas breaches of probation must be proved beyond a reasonable doubt.

[39] More importantly, where an offender breaches a condition without reasonable excuse, there should be a presumption that the offender serve the remainder of his or her sentence in jail. This constant threat of incarceration will help to ensure that the offender complies with the conditions imposed: see *R v. Brady* (1998), 121 CCC (3d) 504 (Alta. CA); J.V. Roberts, "Conditional Sentencing: Sword of Damocles or Pandora's Box?" (1997), 2 *Can. Crim. L Rev.* 183. It also assists in distinguishing the conditional sentence from probation by making the consequences of a breach of condition more severe.

• • •

C. Application of Section 742.1 of the Criminal Code

• • •

[46] [Section 742.1] lists four criteria that a court must consider before deciding to impose a conditional sentence:

(1) the offender must be convicted of an offence that is not punishable by a minimum term of imprisonment;
(2) the court must impose a term of imprisonment of less than two years;
(3) the safety of the community would not be endangered by the offender serving the sentence in the community; and
(4) a conditional sentence would be consistent with the fundamental purpose and principles of sentencing set out in ss. 718 to 718.2.

[47] In my view, the first three criteria are prerequisites to any conditional sentence. These prerequisites answer the question of whether or not a conditional sentence is possible in the circumstances. Once they are met, the next question is whether a conditional sentence is appropriate. This decision turns upon a consideration of the fundamental purpose and principles of sentencing set out in ss. 718 to 718.2. I will discuss each of these elements in turn.

(1) The Offender Must Be Convicted of an Offence That Is Not Punishable by a Minimum Term of Imprisonment

[48] This prerequisite is straightforward. The offence for which the offender was convicted must not be punishable by a minimum term of imprisonment. Offences with a minimum term of imprisonment are the only statutory exclusions from the conditional sentencing regime.

(2) The Court Must Impose a Term of Imprisonment of Less Than Two Years

[49] Parliament intended that a conditional sentence be considered only for those offenders who would have otherwise received a sentence of imprisonment of less than

two years. There is some controversy as to whether this means that the judge must actually impose a term of imprisonment of a *fixed* duration before considering the possibility of a conditional sentence. Far from addressing purely methodological concerns, this question carries implications as to the role of ss. 718 to 718.2 in the determination of the appropriate sentence, the duration of the sentence, its venue and other modalities.

[50] A literal reading of s. 742.1(a) suggests that the decision to impose a conditional sentence should be made in two distinct stages. In the first stage, the judge would have to decide the appropriate sentence according to the general purposes and principles of sentencing (now set out in ss. 718 to 718.2). Having found that a term of imprisonment of less than two years is warranted, the judge would then, in a second stage, decide whether this same term should be served in the community pursuant to s. 742.1. At first sight since Parliament said: "and the court (a) imposes a sentence of imprisonment of less than two years," it seems that the sentencing judge must first impose a term of imprisonment of a *fixed* duration before contemplating the possibility that this term be served in the community.

[51] This two-step approach was endorsed by the Manitoba Court of Appeal in the present appeal. However, this literal reading of s. 742.1 and the two-step approach it implies introduce a rigidity which is both unworkable and undesirable in practice.

(a) Duration and Venue Cannot Be Separated

[52] This two-step process does not correspond to the reality of sentencing. In practice, the determination of a term of imprisonment is necessarily intertwined with the decision of where the offender will serve the sentence. A judge does not impose a fixed sentence of "x months" in the abstract, without having in mind where that sentence will be served (see *Brady*, *supra*, at para. 86; *R v. Pierce* (1997), 114 CCC (3d) 23 (Ont. CA), at p. 39; *R v. Ursel* (1997), 96 BCAC 241, at p. 284 (*per* Ryan JA) and pp. 291-92 (*per* Rowles JA)). Furthermore, when a conditional sentence is chosen, its duration will depend on the type of conditions imposed. Therefore, the duration of the sentence should not be determined separately from the determination of its venue.

(b) "Penological Paradox"

[53] There is a contradiction embedded in this rigid two-step process. After having applied ss. 718 to 718.2 in the first stage to conclude that the appropriate sentence is a term of imprisonment of a fixed duration (in all cases less than two years), the judge would then have to decide if serving *the same sentence* in the community is still consistent with the fundamental purpose and principles of sentencing set out in ss. 718 to 718.2, as required by s. 742.1(b). It is unrealistic to believe that a judge would consider the objectives and principles twice or make a clear distinction in his or her mind between the application of ss. 718 to 718.2 in the first stage and in the second stage. Even if this could be done, it could lead to a "penological paradox," as described by J. Gemmell in "The New Conditional Sentencing Regime" (1997), 39 *Crim. LQ* 334, at p. 337:

> ... the judge must first determine that imprisonment is the only reasonable sanction in the circumstances, then decide whether the offender should nevertheless serve that sentence in

the community. The decision to impose a conditional sentence is almost a kind of *reductio ad absurdum* of the original decision that called for imprisonment. [Footnote omitted.]

[54] This second step of the analytical process would effectively compromise the principles of sentencing that led to the imposition of a sentence of imprisonment in the first place. For instance, the principle of proportionality, set out in s. 718.1 as the fundamental principle of sentencing, directs that all sentences must be proportional to the gravity of the offence and the degree of responsibility of the offender. When a judge—in the first stage decides—that a term of imprisonment of "x months" is appropriate, it means that *this* sentence is proportional. If the sentencing judge decides—in the second stage—that *the same term* can be served in the community, it is possible that the sentence is no longer proportional to the gravity of the offence and the responsibility of the offender, since a conditional sentence will generally be more lenient than a jail term of equivalent duration. Thus, such a two-step approach introduces a rigidity in the sentencing process that could lead to an unfit sentence.

(c) A Purposive Interpretation of Section 742.1(a)

[55] These problems can be addressed by a purposive interpretation of s. 742.1. For the reasons discussed above, the requirement that the court "imposes a sentence of imprisonment of less than two years" could not have been intended to impose on judges a rigid two-step process. Rather, it was included to identify the type of offenders who could be entitled to a conditional sentence. At one end of the range, Parliament denied the possibility of a conditional sentence for offenders who should receive a penitentiary term. At the other end, Parliament intended to ensure that offenders who were entitled to a more lenient community measure—such as a suspended sentence with probation—did not receive a conditional sentence, a harsher sanction in this legislative scheme.

[56] Section 742.1(a), when read in conjunction with ss. 718.2(d) and 718.2(e), cautions sentencing judges against "widening the net" of the conditional sentencing regime by imposing conditional sentences on offenders who would otherwise have received a non-custodial disposition (*Gagnon*, ... at p. 2645; *Mcdonald, supra*, at pp. 437-39). As Rosenberg JA puts it in *Wismayer* ... , at p. 42:

> Parliament's goal of reducing the prison population of nonviolent offenders and increased use of community sanctions will be frustrated if the courts refuse to use the conditional sentence order for offences that normally attract a jail sentence and resort to the conditional sentence only for offences that previously would have attracted non-custodial dispositions.

Erroneously imposing conditional sentences could undermine Parliament's objective of reducing incarceration for less serious offenders.

[57] These concerns are illustrated by the English experience with a similar sentence called a "suspended sentence." As Parker LCJ explained, writing for the Court of Appeal (Criminal Division) in *R v. O'Keefe* (1968), 53 Cr. App. R 91, at pp. 94-95:

> This Court would like to say as emphatically as they can that suspended sentences should not be given when, but for the power to give a suspended sentence, a probation order was the proper order to make. After all, a suspended sentence is a sentence of imprisonment. ...

> Therefore, it seems to the Court that before one gets to a suspended sentence at all, a court must go through the process of eliminating other possible courses such as absolute discharge, conditional discharge, probation order, fine, and then say to itself ... this is a case for imprisonment, and the final question, it being a case for imprisonment: is immediate imprisonment required, or can I give a suspended sentence?

[58] A similar approach should be used by Canadian courts. Hence, a purposive interpretation of s. 742.1(a) does not dictate a rigid two-step approach in which the judge would first have to impose a term of imprisonment of a *fixed* duration and then decide if that fixed term of imprisonment can be served in the community. In my view, the requirement that the court must impose a sentence of imprisonment of less than two years can be fulfilled by a preliminary determination of the appropriate range of available sentences. Thus, the approach I suggest still requires the judge to proceed in two stages. However, the judge need not impose a term of imprisonment of a *fixed* duration at the first stage of the analysis. Rather, at this stage, the judge simply has to exclude two possibilities: (a) probationary measures; and (b) a penitentiary term. If either of these sentences is appropriate, then a conditional sentence should not be imposed.

[59] In making this preliminary determination, the judge need only consider the fundamental purpose and principles of sentencing set out in ss. 718 to 718.2 to the extent necessary to narrow the range of sentence for the offender. The submissions of the parties, although not binding, may prove helpful in this regard. For example, both parties may agree that the appropriate range of sentence is a term of imprisonment of less than two years.

[60] Once that preliminary determination is made, and assuming the other statutory prerequisites are met, the judge should then proceed to the second stage of the analysis: determining whether a conditional sentence would be consistent with the fundamental purpose and principles of sentencing set out in ss. 718 to 718.2. Unlike the first stage, the principles of sentencing are now considered comprehensively. Further, it is at the second stage that the duration and venue of the sentence should be determined, and, if a conditional sentence, the conditions to be imposed.

[61] This purposive interpretation of s. 742.1(a) avoids the pitfalls of the literal interpretation discussed above, while at all times taking into account the principles and objectives of sentencing. As I stressed in *M. (C.A.)*, *supra*, at para. 82,

> In the final analysis, the overarching duty of a sentencing judge is to draw upon all the legitimate principles of sentencing to determine a "just and appropriate" sentence which reflects the gravity of the offence committed and the moral blameworthiness of the offender.

(3) The Safety of the Community Would Not Be Endangered by the Offender Serving the Sentence in the Community

[62] This criterion, set out in s. 742.1(b), has generated wide discussion in courts and among authors. I intend to discuss the following issues:

(a) Is safety of the community a prerequisite to any conditional sentence?
(b) Does "safety of the community" refer only to the threat posed by the specific offender?

(c)   How should courts evaluate danger to the community?

(d)   Is risk of economic prejudice to be considered in assessing danger to the community?

(a) A Prerequisite to Any Conditional Sentence

[63] As a prerequisite to any conditional sentence, the sentencing judge must be satisfied that having the offender serve the sentence in the community would not endanger its safety: see *Brady, supra,* at para. 58; *R v. Maheu,* [1997] RJQ 410, 116 CCC (3d) 361 (CA), at p. 368 CCC; *Gagnon, supra,* at p. 2641; *Pierce, supra,* at p. 39; *Ursel, supra,* at pp. 284-86 (*per* Ryan JA). *If the sentencing judge is not satisfied that the safety of the community can be preserved, a conditional sentence must never be imposed.*

[64] With respect, the Manitoba Court of Appeal in the case before us erred in concluding that safety of the community was the primary consideration in the decision to impose a conditional sentence. As the Alberta Court of Appeal in *Brady, supra,* at para. 58, stated:

> So to suggest that danger is the primary consideration is tendentious. It wrongly implies that absence of danger trumps or has paramountcy over other sentencing principles. Either the offender meets the no-danger threshold, or he does not. If he does, this consideration is spent and the focus must then properly be on the other sentencing principles and objectives.

[65] I agree. It is only once the judge is satisfied that the safety of the community would not be endangered, in the sense explained in paragraphs 66 to 76 below, that he or she can examine whether a conditional sentence "would be consistent with the fundamental purpose and principles of sentencing set out in sections 718 to 718.2." In other words, rather than being an overarching consideration in the process of determining whether a conditional sentence is appropriate, the criterion of safety of the community should be viewed as a condition precedent to the assessment of whether a conditional sentence would be a fit and proper sanction in the circumstances.

(b) "Safety of the Community" Refers to the Threat Posed by the Specific Offender

[66] The issue here is whether "safety of the community" refers only to the threat posed by the specific offender or whether it also extends to the broader risk of undermining respect for the law. The proponents of the broader interpretation argue that, in certain cases where a conditional sentence could be imposed, it would be perceived that wrongdoers are receiving lenient sentences, thereby insufficiently deterring those who may be inclined to engage in similar acts of wrongdoing, and, in turn, endangering the safety of the community.

[67] Leaving aside the fact that a properly crafted conditional sentence can also achieve the objectives of general deterrence and denunciation, I think the debate has been rendered largely academic in light of an amendment to s. 742.1(b) (SC 1997, c. 18, s. 107.1) which clarified that courts must take into consideration the fundamental purpose and principles of sentencing set out in ss. 718 to 718.2 in deciding whether to impose a conditional sentence. This ensures that objectives such as denunciation and deterrence will be dealt with in the decision to impose a conditional sentence. Since these factors will be

taken into account later in the analysis, there is no need to include them in the consideration of the safety of the community.

[68] In my view, the focus of the analysis at this point should clearly be on the risk posed by the individual offender while serving his sentence in the community. I would note that a majority of appellate courts have adopted an interpretation of the criterion referring only to the threat posed by the specific offender: see *Gagnon, supra*, at pp. 2640-41 (*per* Fish JA); *R v. Parker* (1997), 116 CCC (3d) 236 (NS CA), at pp. 247-48; *Ursel, supra*, at p. 260.1; *R v. Horvath*, [1997] 8 WWR 357 (Sask. CA), at p. 374; *Brady, supra*, at paras. 60-61; *Wismayer* ... , at p. 44.

(c) How Should Courts Evaluate Danger to the Community?

[69] In my opinion, to assess the danger to the community posed by the offender while serving his or her sentence in the community, two factors must be taken into account: (1) the risk of the offender re-offending; and (2) the gravity of the damage that could ensue in the event of re-offence. If the judge finds that there is a real risk of re-offence, incarceration should be imposed. Of course, there is always some risk that an offender may re-offend. If the judge thinks this risk is minimal, the gravity of the damage that could follow were the offender to re-offend should also be taken into consideration. In certain cases, the minimal risk of re-offending will be offset by the possibility of a great prejudice, thereby precluding a conditional sentence.

(I) RISK OF RE-OFFENCE

[70] A variety of factors will be relevant in assessing the risk of re-offence. In *Brady, supra*, at paras. 117-27, Fraser CJA suggested that consideration be given to whether the offender has previously complied with court orders and, more generally, to whether the offender has a criminal record that suggests that the offender will not abide by the conditional sentence. Rousseau-Houle JA in *Maheu, supra*, at p. 374 CCC enumerated additional factors which may be of relevance:

> [TRANSLATION] ... 1) the nature of the offence, 2) the relevant circumstances of the offence, which can put in issue prior and subsequent incidents, 3) the degree of participation of the accused, 4) the relationship of the accused with the victim, 5) the profile of the accused, that is, his [or her] occupation, lifestyle, criminal record, family situation, mental state, 6) his [or her] conduct following the commission of the offence, 7) the danger which the interim release of the accused represents for the community, notably that part of the community affected by the matter.

[71] This list is instructive, but should not be considered exhaustive. The risk that a particular offender poses to the community must be assessed in each case, on its own facts. Moreover, the factors outlined above should not be applied mechanically. As Fraser CJA held in *Brady, supra*, at para. 124:

> Forgetting a court date once ten years ago does not automatically bar an offender from any future conditional sentence. Nor does turning up for his trial guarantee an offender a conditional sentence. The sentencing judge must of course look at all aspects of these previous disobediences of courts. That includes frequency, age, maturity, recency, seriousness of disobedience and surrounding circumstances.

[72] The risk of re-offence should also be assessed in light of the conditions attached to the sentence. Where an offender might pose some risk of endangering the safety of the community, it is possible that this risk can be reduced to a minimal one by the imposition of appropriate conditions to the sentence: see *Wismayer* ... , at p. 32; *Brady*, *supra*, at para. 62; *Maheu*, *supra*, at p. 374 CCC. Indeed, this is contemplated by s. 742.3(2)(f), which allows the court to include as optional conditions "such other reasonable conditions as the court considers desirable ... for securing the good conduct of the offender and for preventing a repetition by the offender of the same offence or the commission of other offences." For example, a judge may wish to impose a conditional sentence with a treatment order on an offender with a drug addiction, notwithstanding the fact that the offender has a lengthy criminal record linked to this addiction, provided the judge is confident that there is a good chance of rehabilitation and that the level of supervision will be sufficient to ensure that the offender complies with the sentence.

[73] This last point concerning the level of supervision in the community must be underscored. As the Alberta Court of Appeal stressed in *Brady*, *supra*, at para. 135:

> A conditional sentence drafted in the abstract without knowledge of what actual supervision and institutions and programs are available and suitable for this offender is often worse than tokenism: it is a sham.

Hence, the judge must know or be made aware of the supervision available in the community by the supervision officer or by counsel. If the level of supervision available in the community is not sufficient to ensure safety of the community, the judge should impose a sentence of incarceration.

(II) GRAVITY OF THE DAMAGE IN THE EVENT OF RE-OFFENCE

[74] Once the judge finds that the risk of recidivism is minimal, the second factor to consider is the gravity of the potential damage in case of re-offence. Particularly in the case of violent offenders, a small risk of very harmful future crime may well warrant a conclusion that the prerequisite is not met: see *Brady*, *supra*, at para. 63.

(d) Risk of Economic Harm Can Be Taken into Consideration

[75] The meaning of the phrase "would not endanger the safety of the community" should not be restricted to a consideration of the danger to physical or psychological safety of persons. In my view, this part of s. 742.1(b) cannot be given this narrow meaning. As Finch JA stated in *Ursel*, *supra*, at p. 264 (dissenting in part but endorsed by the majority on this issue, at p. 287):

> I would not give to this phrase the restricted meaning for which the defence contends. Members of our community have a reasonable expectation of safety not only in respect of their persons, but in respect as well of their property and financial resources. When homes are broken into, motor-vehicles are stolen, employers are defrauded of monies, or financial papers are forged, the safety of the community is, in my view, endangered. We go to considerable lengths to protect and secure ourselves against the losses that may result from these sorts of crimes, and I think most ordinary citizens would regard themselves as threatened or endangered where their property or financial resources are exposed to the risk of loss.

[76] I agree with this reasoning. The phrase "would not endanger the safety of the community" should be construed broadly, and include the risk of any criminal activity. Such a broad interpretation encompasses the risk of economic harm.

(4) Consistent with the Fundamental Purpose and Principles of Sentencing Set Out in Sections 718 to 718.2

[77] Once the sentencing judge has found the offender guilty of an offence for which there is no minimum term of imprisonment, has rejected both a probationary sentence and a penitentiary term as inappropriate, and is satisfied that the offender would not endanger the community, the judge must then consider whether a conditional sentence would be consistent with the fundamental purpose and principles of sentencing set out in ss. 718 to 718.2.

[78] A consideration of the principles set out in ss. 718 to 718.2 will determine whether the offender should serve his or her sentence in the community or in jail. The sentencing principles also inform the determination of the duration of these sentences and, if a conditional sentence, the nature of the conditions to be imposed.

• • •

(c) Principles Militating For and Against a Conditional Sentence

[90] First, a consideration of ss. 718.2(d) and 718.2(e) leads me to the conclusion that *serious consideration* should be given to the imposition of a conditional sentence in all cases where the first three statutory prerequisites are satisfied. Sections 718.2(d) and 718.2(e) codify the important principle of restraint in sentencing and were specifically enacted, along with s. 742.1, to help reduce the rate of incarceration in Canada. Accordingly, it would be an error in principle not to consider the possibility of a conditional sentence seriously when the statutory prerequisites are met. Failure to advert to the possibility of a conditional sentence in reasons for sentence where there are reasonable grounds for finding that the first three statutory prerequisites have been met may well constitute reversible error.

[91] I pause here to consider an interpretive difficulty posed by s. 718.2(e). By its terms, s. 718.2(e) requires judges to consider "all available sanctions *other than imprisonment* that are reasonable in the circumstances" (emphasis added). A conditional sentence, however, is defined as a sentence of imprisonment. As a sentence of imprisonment, it cannot be an alternative to imprisonment. It would therefore appear as though s. 718.2(e) has no bearing on the sentencing judge's decision as to whether a conditional sentence or a jail term should be imposed. Indeed, if interpreted in the technical sense ascribed to imprisonment in Part XXIII of the *Criminal Code*, s. 718.2(e) would only be relevant to the judge's preliminary determination as to whether a sentence of imprisonment, as opposed to a probationary measure, should be imposed. Once the sentencing judge rejects a probationary sentence as inappropriate, the legislative force of s. 718.2(e) is arguably spent.

[92] This interpretation seems to fly in the face of Parliament's intention in enacting s. 718.2(e)—reducing the rate of incarceration. As this Court held in *Gladue, supra,* at para. 40:

The availability of the conditional sentence of imprisonment, in particular, alters the sentencing landscape in a manner which gives an entirely new meaning to the principle that imprisonment should be resorted to only where no other sentencing option is reasonable in the circumstances. *The creation of the conditional sentence suggests, on its face, a desire to lessen the use of incarceration. The general principle expressed in s. 718.2(c) must be construed and applied in this light.* [Emphasis added.]

Moreover, if this interpretation of s. 718.2(c) were adopted, it could lead to absurd results in relation to aboriginal offenders. The particular circumstances of aboriginal offenders would only be relevant in deciding whether to impose probationary sentences, and not in deciding whether a conditional sentence should be preferred to incarceration. This would greatly diminish the remedial purpose animating Parliament's enactment of this provision, which contemplates the greater use of conditional sentences and other alternatives to incarceration in cases of aboriginal offenders.

[93] The language used in the French version avoids this difficulty. The French version reads as follows:

> 718.2 Le tribunal détermine la peine à infliger compte tenu également des principes suivants.
>
> e) *l'examen de toutes les sanctions substitutives applicables* qui sont justifiées dans les circonstances, plus particulièrement en ce qui concerne les délinquants autochtones. [Emphasis added.]

[94] The use of "*sanctions substitutives*" for "sanctions other than imprisonment" in the French version of this provision means that s. 718.2(e) plays a role not only in the decision as to whether imprisonment or probationary measures should be imposed (preliminary step of the analysis), but also in the decision as to whether to impose a conditional sentence of imprisonment since conditional sentences are clearly "*sanctions substitutives*" to incarceration.

[95] The French version and the English version of s. 718.2(e) are therefore in conflict. In conformity with a long-standing principle of interpretation, to resolve the conflict between the two official versions, we have to look for the meaning common to both: see for instance *Kwiatkowsky v. Minister of Employment and Immigration*, [1982] 2 SCR 856, at pp. 863-64; *Gravel v. City of St-Léonard*, [1978] 1 SCR 660, at p. 669; *Pfizer Co. v. Deputy Minister of National Revenue for Customs and Excise*, [1977] 1 SCR 456, at pp. 464-65; *Tupper v. The Queen*, [1967] SCR 589, at p. 593; *Goodyear Tire and Rubber Co. of Canada v. T. Eaton Co.*, [1956] SCR 610, at p. 614; P.-A. Côté, *Interprétation des lois* (3rd ed. 1999), at pp. 412-15. Accordingly, the word "imprisonment" in s. 718.2(c) should be interpreted as "incarceration" rather than in its technical sense of encompassing both incarceration and a conditional sentence. Read in this light, s. 718.2(e) clearly exerts an influence on the sentencing judge's determination as to whether to impose a conditional sentence as opposed to a jail term.

[96] Both ss. 718.2(d) and 718.2(e) seek to vindicate the important objective of restraint in the use of incarceration. However, neither seeks to do so at all costs. Section 718.2(d) provides that "an offender should not be deprived of liberty if less restrictive sanctions *may be inappropriate in the circumstances*" (emphasis added). Section 718.2(e) provides that "all available sanctions other than imprisonment *that are reasonable in the circumstances*

should be considered" (emphasis added). In my view, a determination of when less restrictive sanctions are "appropriate" and alternatives to incarceration "reasonable" in the circumstances requires a consideration of the other principles of sentencing set out in ss. 718 to 718.2.

[97] In determining which principles favour of a conditional sentence and which favour incarceration, it is necessary to consider again the nature and purpose of the conditional sentence. Through an appreciation of Parliament's intention in enacting this new sanction and the mischief it seeks to redress, trial judges will be better able to make appropriate use of this innovative tool.

[98] The conditional sentence, as I have already noted, was introduced in the amendments to Part XXIII of the Code. Two of the main objectives underlying the reform of Part XXIII were to reduce the use of incarceration as a sanction and to give greater prominence to the principles of restorative justice in sentencing—the objectives of rehabilitation, reparation to the victim and the community, and the promotion of a sense of responsibility in the offender.

[99] The conditional sentence facilitates the achievement of both of Parliament's objectives. It affords the sentencing judge the opportunity to craft a sentence with appropriate conditions that can lead to the rehabilitation of the offender, reparations to the community, and the promotion of a sense of responsibility in ways that jail cannot. However, it is also a punitive sanction. Indeed, it is the punitive aspect of a conditional sentence that distinguishes it from probation. As discussed above, it was not Parliament's intention that offenders who would otherwise have gone to jail for up to two years less a day now be given probation or some equivalent thereof.

[100] Thus, a conditional sentence can achieve both punitive and restorative objectives. To the extent that both punitive and restorative objectives can be achieved in a given case, a conditional sentence is likely a better sanction than incarceration. Where the need for punishment is particularly pressing, and there is little opportunity to achieve any restorative objectives, incarceration will likely be the more attractive sanction. However, even where restorative objectives cannot be readily satisfied, a conditional sentence will be preferable to incarceration in cases where a conditional sentence can achieve the objectives of denunciation and deterrence as effectively as incarceration. This follows from the principle of restraint in s. 718.2(d) and (e), which militates in favour of alternatives to incarceration where appropriate in the circumstances.

[101] I turn now to the question of when a conditional sentence may be appropriate having regard to the six sentencing objectives set out in s. 718.

(i) DENUNCIATION

[102] Denunciation is the communication of society's condemnation of the offender's conduct. In *M. (C.A.)*, *supra*, at para. 81, I wrote:

> In short, a sentence with a denunciatory element represents a symbolic, collective statement that the offender's conduct should be punished for encroaching on our society's basic code of values as enshrined within our substantive criminal law. As Lord Justice Lawton stated in *R v. Sargeant* (1974), 60 Cr. App. R 74, at p. 77: "society, through the courts, must show its abhorrence of particular types of crime, and the only way in which the courts can show this is by the sentence they pass."

Incarceration will usually provide more denunciation than a conditional sentence, as a conditional sentence is generally a more lenient sentence than a jail term of equivalent duration. That said, a conditional sentence can still provide a significant amount of denunciation. This is particularly so when onerous conditions are imposed and the duration of the conditional sentence is extended beyond the duration of the jail sentence that would ordinarily have been imposed in the circumstances. I will discuss each point in turn.

[103] First, the conditions should have a punitive aspect. Indeed, the need for punitive conditions is the reason why a probationary sentence was rejected and a sentence of imprisonment of less than two years imposed. As stated above, conditions such as house arrest should be the norm, not the exception. This means that the offender should be confined to his or her home except when working, attending school, or fulfilling other conditions of his or her sentence, e.g. community service, meeting with the supervisor, or participating in treatment programs. Of course, there will need to be exceptions for medical emergencies, religious observance, and the like.

[104] Second, although a literal reading of s. 742.1 suggests that a conditional sentence must be of equivalent duration to the jail term that would otherwise have been imposed, I have explained earlier why such a literal interpretation of s. 742.1 should be eschewed. Instead, the preferred approach is to have the judge reject a probationary sentence and a penitentiary term as inappropriate in the circumstances, and then consider whether a conditional sentence of less than two years would be consistent with the fundamental purpose and principles of sentencing, provided the statutory prerequisites are met. This approach does not require that there be any equivalence between the duration of the conditional sentence and the jail term that would otherwise have been imposed. The sole requirement is that the duration and conditions of a conditional sentence make for a just and appropriate sentence: see *Brady, supra,* at para. 111; *Ursel, supra,* at pp. 284-86 and 291-92; *Pierce, supra,* at p. 39; J.V. Roberts, "The Hunt for the Paper Tiger: Conditional Sentencing after *Brady*" (1999), 42 *Crim. LQ* 38, at pp. 47-52.

[105] The stigma of a conditional sentence with house arrest should not be underestimated. Living in the community under strict conditions where fellow residents are well aware of the offender's criminal misconduct can provide ample denunciation in many cases. In certain circumstances, the shame of encountering members of the community may make it even more difficult for the offender to serve his or her sentence in the community than in prison.

[106] The amount of denunciation provided by a conditional sentence will be heavily dependent on the circumstances of the offender, the nature of the conditions imposed, and the community in which the sentence is to be served. As a general matter, the more serious the offence and the greater the need for denunciation, the longer and more onerous the conditional sentence should be. However, there may be certain circumstances in which the need for denunciation is so pressing that incarceration will be the only suitable way in which to express society's condemnation of the offender's conduct.

(ii) DETERRENCE

[107] Incarceration, which is ordinarily a harsher sanction, may provide more deterrence than a conditional sentence. Judges should be wary, however, of placing too much weight on deterrence when choosing between a conditional sentence and incarceration:

see *Wismayer* ... , at p. 36. The empirical evidence suggests that the deterrent effect of incarceration is uncertain: see generally *Sentencing Reform: A Canadian Approach: Report of the Canadian Sentencing Commission* (1987)], at pp. 136-37. Moreover, a conditional sentence can provide significant deterrence if sufficiently punitive conditions are imposed and the public is made aware of the severity of these sentences. There is also the possibility of deterrence through the use of community service orders, including those in which the offender may be obliged to speak to members of the community about the evils of the particular criminal conduct in which he or she engaged, assuming the offender were amenable to such a condition. Nevertheless, there may be circumstances in which the need for deterrence will warrant incarceration. This will depend in part on whether the offence is one in which the effects of incarceration are likely to have a real deterrent effect, as well as on the circumstances of the community in which the offences were committed.

(III) SEPARATION

[108] The objective of separation is not applicable in determining whether a conditional sentence would be consistent with the fundamental purpose and principles of sentencing because it is a prerequisite of a conditional sentence that the offender not pose a danger to the community. Accordingly, it is not necessary to completely separate the offender from society. To the extent that incarceration, which leads to the complete separation of offenders, is warranted in circumstances where the statutory prerequisites are met, it is as a result of the objectives of denunciation and deterrence, not the need for separation as such.

(IV) RESTORATIVE OBJECTIVES

[109] While incarceration may provide for more denunciation and deterrence than a conditional sentence, a conditional sentence is generally better suited to achieving the restorative objectives of rehabilitation, reparations, and promotion of a sense of responsibility in the offender. As this Court held in *Gladue, supra*, at para. 43, "[r]estorative sentencing goals do not usually correlate with the use of prison as a sanction." The importance of these goals is not to be underestimated, as they are primarily responsible for lowering the rate of recidivism. Consequently, when the objectives of rehabilitation, reparation, and promotion of a sense of responsibility may realistically be achieved in the case of a particular offender, a conditional sentence will likely be the appropriate sanction, subject to the denunciation and deterrence considerations outlined above.

[110] I will now consider examples of conditions that seek to vindicate these objectives. There are any number of conditions a judge may impose in order to rehabilitate an offender. Mandatory treatment orders may be imposed, such as psychological counseling and alcohol and drug rehabilitation. It is well known that sentencing an offender to a term of incarceration for an offence related to a drug addiction, without addressing the addiction, will probably not lead to the rehabilitation of the offender. *The Final Report of the Commission of Inquiry into the Non-Medical Use of Drugs* (1973) noted at p. 59 that

These adverse effects of imprisonment are particularly reflected in the treatment of drug offenders. Our investigations suggest that there is considerable circulation of drugs within penal institutions, that offenders are reinforced in their attachment to the drug culture, and that in many cases they are introduced to certain kinds of drug use by prison contacts. Thus imprisonment does not cut off all contact with drugs or the drug subculture, nor does it cut off contact with individual drug users. Actually, it increases exposure to the influence of chronic, harmful drug users.

[111] House arrest may also have a rehabilitative effect to a certain extent insofar as it prevents the offender from engaging in habitual anti-social associations and promotes pro-social behaviors such as attendance at work or educational institutions: see Roberts, "The Hunt for the Paper Tiger: Conditional Sentencing after *Brady*," *supra*, at p. 65.

[112] The objectives of reparations to the victim and the community, as well as the promotion of a sense of responsibility in offenders and acknowledgment of the harm done to victims and to the community, may also be well served by a conditional sentence. For example, in some cases, restitution orders to compensate the victim may be made a condition. Furthermore, the imposition of a condition of community service can assist the offender in making reparations to the community and in promoting a sense of responsibility. An interesting possibility in this regard would be an order that the offender speak in public about the unfortunate consequences of his or her conduct, assuming the offender were amenable to such a condition. Not only could such an order promote a sense of responsibility and an acknowledgment of the harm done by the offender, it could also further the objective of deterrence, as I discussed above. In my view, the use of community service orders should be encouraged, provided that there are suitable programs available for the offender in the community. By increasing the use of community service orders, offenders will be seen by members of the public as paying back their debt to society. This will assist in contributing to public respect for the law.

(v) SUMMARY

[113] In sum, in determining whether a conditional sentence would be consistent with the fundamental purpose and principles of sentencing, sentencing judges should consider which sentencing objectives figure most prominently in the factual circumstances of the particular case before them. Where a combination of both punitive and restorative objectives may be achieved, a conditional sentence will likely be more appropriate than incarceration. In determining whether restorative objectives can be satisfied in a particular case, the judge should consider the offender's prospects of rehabilitation, including whether the offender has proposed a particular plan of rehabilitation; the availability of appropriate community service and treatment programs, whether the offender has acknowledged his or her wrongdoing and expresses remorse; as well as the victim's wishes as revealed by the victim impact statement (consideration of which is now mandatory pursuant to s. 722 of the Code). This list is not exhaustive.

[114] Where punitive objectives such as denunciation and deterrence are particularly pressing, such as cases in which there are aggravating circumstances, incarceration will generally be the preferable sanction. This may be so notwithstanding the fact that restorative goals might be achieved by a conditional sentence. Conversely, a conditional sentence may provide sufficient denunciation and deterrence, even in cases in which restorative objectives are of diminished importance, depending on the nature of the conditions imposed, the duration of the conditional sentence, and the circumstances of the offender and the community in which the conditional sentence is to be served.

[115] Finally, it bears pointing out that a conditional sentence may be imposed even in circumstances where there are aggravating circumstances relating to the offence or the offender. Aggravating circumstances will obviously increase the need for denunciation and deterrence. However, it would be a mistake to rule out the possibility of a conditional sentence *ab initio* simply because aggravating factors are present. I repeat that each case must be considered individually.

[116] Sentencing judges will frequently be confronted with situations in which some objectives militate in favour of a conditional sentence, whereas others favour incarceration. in those cases, the trial judge will be called upon to weigh the various objectives in fashioning a fit sentence. As La Forest J stated in *R v. Lyons*, [1987] 2 SCR 309, at p. 329, "[i]n a rational system of sentencing, the respective importance of prevention, deterrence, retribution and rehabilitation will vary according to the nature of the crime and the circumstances of the offender." There is no easy test or formula that the judge can apply in weighing these factors. Much will depend on the good judgment and wisdom of sentencing judges, whom Parliament vested with considerable discretion in making these determinations pursuant to s. 718.3.

(d) Appropriate Conditions

[117] In the event that a judge chooses to impose a conditional sentence, there are five compulsory conditions listed in s. 742.3(1) that must be imposed. The judge also has considerable discretion in imposing optional conditions pursuant to s. 742.3(2). There are a number of principles that should guide the judge in exercising this discretion. First, the conditions must ensure the safety of the community. Second, conditions must be tailored to fit the particular circumstances of the offender and the offence. The type of conditions imposed will be a function of the sentencing judge's creativity. However, conditions will prove fruitless if the offender is incapable of abiding by them, and will increase the probability that the offender will be incarcerated as a result of breaching them. Third, punitive conditions such as house arrest should be the norm, not the exception. Fourth, the conditions must be realistically enforceable. This requires a consideration of the available resources in the community in which the sentence is to be served. I agree with Rosenberg JA, who, in "Recent Developments in Sentencing," a paper prepared for the National Judicial Institute's Supreme Court of Nova Scotia Education Seminar in Halifax, February 25-26, 1999, at p. 63, wrote that:

> ... the courts must be careful not to impose conditions that are purely cosmetic and are incapable of effective enforcement. For example, I would think that any condition that can only be effectively enforced through an intolerable intrusion into the privacy of innocent persons would be problematic. Conditions that impose an unacceptable burden on the supervisor might also be of dubious value. If the conditions that the court imposes are impractical, the justice system will be brought into disrepute.

D. Burden of Proof

[118] It is submitted by the intervener the Attorney General for Ontario that the offender has the burden of proving that a conditional sentence should be imposed pursuant to s. 742.1. According to the Attorney General:

[W]hen a sentencing court determines that a reformatory sentence of imprisonment is an appropriate sentence for an offender, there is, in effect, a *rebuttable presumption* that this custodial sentence will prevail unless the *offender* can convince the sentencing Court to make the sentence of imprisonment "conditional." [Emphasis in original]

[119] The Attorney General for Ontario's position seems to be premised on a rigid two-step approach, which I rejected for the reasons explained earlier. The Attorney General submits that the offender has to establish that: (a) he or she would not endanger the safety of the community by serving a conditional sentence; and (b) the imposition of a conditional sentence would be consistent with the fundamental purpose and principles set out in ss. 718 to 718.2.

[120] I disagree. The wording used in s. 742.1 does not attribute to either party the onus of establishing that the offender should or should not receive a conditional sentence. To inform his or her decision about the appropriate sentence, the judge can take into consideration all the evidence, no matter who adduces it (*Ursel, supra*, at pp. 264-65 and 287).

[121] In matters of sentencing, while each party is expected to establish elements in support of its position as to the appropriate sentence that should be imposed, the ultimate decision as to what constitutes the best disposition is left to the discretion of the sentencing judge. This message is explicit in ss. 718.3(1) and (2):

718.3(1) Where an enactment prescribes different degrees or kinds of punishment in respect of an offence, the punishment to be imposed is, subject to the limitations prescribed in the enactment, in the discretion of the court that convicts a person who commits the offence.

(2) Where an enactment prescribes a punishment in respect of an offence, the punishment to be imposed is, subject to the limitations prescribed in the enactment, in the discretion of the court that convicts a person who commits the offence, but no punishment is a minimum punishment unless it is declared to be a minimum punishment.

[122] The sentencing judge can take into account the submissions and evidence presented by counsel (s. 723), but is in no way bound by them in the decision as to the sentence. Having said this, in practice, it will generally be the offender who is best situated to convince the judge that a conditional sentence is indeed appropriate. Therefore, it would be in the offender's best interests to establish those elements militating in favour of a conditional sentence: see *Ursel, supra*, at pp. 264-65; *R v. Fleet* (1997), 120 CCC 457 (Ont. CA), at para. 26. For instance, the offender should inform the judge of his or her remorse, willingness to repair and acknowledgment of responsibility, and propose a plan of rehabilitation. The offender could also convince the judge that he or she would not endanger the safety of the community if appropriate conditions were imposed. It would be to the great benefit of the offender to make submissions in this regard. I would also note the importance of the role of the supervision officer in informing the judge on these issues.

E. *Deference Owed to Sentencing Judges*

[123] In recent years, this Court has repeatedly stated that the sentence imposed by a trial court is entitled to considerable deference from appellate courts: see *Shropshire*, [[1995] 4 SCR 227, 102 CCC (3d) 193], at paras. 46-50; M.(C.A.), *supra*, at paras. 89-94; *McDonnell, supra*, at paras. 15-17 (majority); *R v. W. (G.)*, [[1999] 3 SCR 597, 138 CCC (3d) 23], at paras. 18-19. In *M. (C.A.)*, at para. 90, I wrote:

Put simply, absent an error in principle, failure to consider a relevant factor, or an overemphasis of the appropriate factors, a court of appeal should only intervene to vary a sentence imposed at trial if the sentence is demonstrably unfit. Parliament explicitly vested sentencing judges with a *discretion* to determine the appropriate degree and kind of punishment under the *Criminal Code*. [Emphasis in original.]

[124] Several provisions of Part XXIII confirm that Parliament intended to confer a wide discretion upon the sentencing judge. As a general rule, ss. 718.3(1) and 718.3(2) provide that the degree and kind of punishment to be imposed is left to the discretion of the sentencing judge. Moreover, the opening words of s. 718 specify that the sentencing judge must seek to achieve the fundamental purpose of sentencing "by imposing just sanctions that have *one or more* of the following objectives" (emphasis added). In the context of the conditional sentence, s. 742.1 provides that the judge "may" impose a conditional sentence and enjoys a wide discretion in the drafting of the appropriate conditions, pursuant to s. 742.3(2).

[125] Although an appellate court might entertain a different opinion as to what objectives should be pursued and the best way to do so, that difference will generally not constitute an error of law justifying interference. Further, minor errors in the sequence of application of s. 742.1 may not warrant intervention by appellate courts. Again, I stress that appellate courts should not second-guess sentencing judges unless the sentence imposed is demonstrably unfit.

[126] As explained in *M. (C.A.), supra*, at para. 91:

This deferential standard of review has profound functional justifications. As Iacobucci J explained in *Shropshire*, at para. 46, where the sentencing judge has had the benefit of presiding over the trial of the offender, he or she will have had the comparative advantage of having seen and heard the witnesses to the crime. But in the absence of a full trial, where the offender has pleaded guilty to an offence and the sentencing judge has only enjoyed the benefit of oral and written sentencing submissions (as was the case in both *Shropshire* and this instance), the argument in favour of deference remains compelling. A sentencing judge still enjoys a position of advantage over an appellate judge in being able to directly assess the sentencing submissions of both the Crown and the offender. A sentencing judge also possesses the unique qualifications of experience and judgment from having served on the front lines of our criminal justice system. *Perhaps most importantly, the sentencing judge will normally preside near or within the community which has suffered the consequences of the offender's crime. As such, the sentencing judge will have a strong sense of the particular blend of sentencing goals that will be "just and appropriate" for the protection of that community. The determination of a just and appropriate sentence is a delicate art which attempts to balance carefully the societal goals of sentencing against the moral blameworthiness of the offender and the circumstances of the offence, while at all times taking into account the needs and current conditions of and in the community.* The discretion of a sentencing judge should thus not be interfered with lightly. [Emphasis added.]

This last justification is particularly relevant in the case of conditional sentences. Crafting appropriate conditions requires knowledge of both the needs and resources of the community.

VI. Summary

[127] At this point, a short summary of what has been said in these reasons might be useful:

1. Bill C-41 in general and the conditional sentence in particular were enacted both to reduce reliance on incarceration as a sanction and to increase the use of principles of restorative justice in sentencing.

2. A conditional sentence should be distinguished from probationary measures. Probation is primarily a rehabilitative sentencing tool. By contrast, Parliament intended conditional sentences to include both punitive and rehabilitative aspects. Therefore, conditional sentences should generally include punitive conditions that are restrictive of the offender's liberty. Conditions such as house arrest should be the norm, not the exception.

3. No offences are excluded from the conditional sentencing regime except those with a minimum term of imprisonment, nor should there be presumptions in favour of or against a conditional sentence for specific offences.

4. The requirement in s. 742.1(a) that the judge impose a sentence of imprisonment of less than two years does not require the judge to first impose a sentence of imprisonment of a fixed duration before considering whether that sentence can be served in the community. Although this approach is suggested by the text of s. 742.1(a), it is unrealistic and could lead to unfit sentences in some cases. Instead, a purposive interpretation of s. 742.1(a) should be adopted. In a preliminary determination, the sentencing judge should reject a penitentiary term and probationary measures as inappropriate. Having determined that the appropriate range of sentence is a term of imprisonment of less than two years, the judge should then consider whether it is appropriate for the offender to serve his or her sentence in the community.

5. As a corollary of the purposive interpretation of s. 742.1(a), a conditional sentence need not be of equivalent duration to the sentence of incarceration that would otherwise have been imposed. The sole requirement is that the duration and conditions of a conditional sentence make for a just and appropriate sentence.

6. The requirement in s. 742.1(h) that the judge be satisfied that the safety of the community would not be endangered by the offender serving his or her sentence in the community is a condition precedent to the imposition of a conditional sentence, and not the primary consideration in determining whether a conditional sentence is appropriate. In making this determination, the judge should consider the risk posed by the specific offender, not the broader risk of whether the imposition of a conditional sentence would endanger the safety of the community by providing insufficient general deterrence or undermining general respect for the law. Two factors should be taken into account: (1) the risk of the offender re-offending; and (2) the gravity of the damage that could ensue in the event of re-offence. A consideration of the risk posed by the offender should include the risk of any criminal activity, and not be limited solely to the risk of physical or psychological harm to individuals.

7. Once the prerequisites of s. 742.1 are satisfied, the judge should give serious consideration to the possibility of a conditional sentence in all cases by

examining whether a conditional sentence is consistent with the fundamental purpose and principles of sentencing set out in ss. 718 to 718.2. This follows from Parliament's clear message to the judiciary to reduce the use of incarceration as a sanction.

8. A conditional sentence can provide significant denunciation and deterrence. As a general matter, the more serious the offence, the longer and more onerous the conditional sentence should be. There may be some circumstances, however, where the need for denunciation or deterrence is so pressing that incarceration will be the only suitable way in which to express society's condemnation of the offender's conduct or to deter similar conduct in the future.

9. Generally, a conditional sentence will be better than incarceration at achieving the restorative objectives of rehabilitation, reparations to the victim and the community, and promotion of a sense of responsibility in the offender and acknowledgment of the harm done to the victim and the community.

10. Where a combination of both punitive and restorative objectives may be achieved, a conditional sentence will likely be more appropriate than incarceration. Where objectives such as denunciation and deterrence are particularly pressing, incarceration will generally be the preferable sanction. This may be so notwithstanding the fact that restorative goals might be achieved. However, a conditional sentence may provide sufficient denunciation and deterrence, even in cases in which restorative objectives are of lesser importance, depending on the nature of the conditions imposed, the duration of the sentence, and the circumstances of both the offender and the community in which the conditional sentence is to be served.

11. A conditional sentence may be imposed even where there are aggravating circumstances, although the need for denunciation and deterrence will increase in these circumstances.

12. No party is under a burden of proof to establish that a conditional sentence is either appropriate or inappropriate in the circumstances. The judge should consider all relevant evidence, no matter by whom it is adduced. However, it would be in the offender's best interests to establish elements militating in favour of a conditional sentence.

13. Sentencing judges have a wide discretion in the choice of the appropriate sentence. They are entitled to considerable deference from appellate courts. As explained in *M. (C.A.)*, *supra*, at para. 90: "Put simply, absent an error in principle, failure to consider a relevant factor, or an overemphasis of the appropriate factors, a court of appeal should only intervene to vary a sentence imposed at trial if the sentence is demonstrably unfit."

VII. Application to the Case at Hand

[128] In the case at hand, Keyser J considered that a term of imprisonment of 18 months was appropriate and declined to permit the respondent to serve his term in the community. She found that, while the respondent would not endanger the safety of the community by serving a conditional sentence, such a sentence would not be in conformity with the objectives of s. 718. In her view, even if incarceration was not necessary to deter the respondent from similar future conduct or necessary for his rehabilitation, incarceration

was necessary to denounce the conduct of the respondent and to deter others from engaging in similar conduct.

[129] While Keyser J seems to have proceeded according to a rigid two-step process, in deviation from the approach I have set out, I am not convinced that an 18-month sentence of incarceration was demonstrably unfit for these offences and this offender. I point out that the offences here were very serious, and that they had resulted in a death and in severe bodily harm. Moreover, dangerous driving and impaired driving may be offences for which harsh sentences plausibly provide general deterrence. These crimes are often committed by otherwise law-abiding persons, with good employment records and families. Arguably, such persons are the ones most likely to be deterred by the threat of severe penalties: see *R v. McVeigh* (1985), 22 CCC (3d) 145 (Ont. CA), at p. 150-51; *R v. Biancofiore* (1997), 119 CCC (3d) 344, at paras. 18-24; *R v. Blakely* (1998), 40 OR (3d) 541 (CA), at pp. 542-43.

[130] I hasten to add that these comments should not be taken as a directive that conditional sentences can never be imposed for offences such as dangerous driving or impaired driving. In fact, were I a trial judge, I might have found that a conditional sentence would have been appropriate in this case. The respondent is still very young, he had no prior record and no convictions since the accident, he seems completely rehabilitated, he wants to go back to school, he has already suffered a lot by causing the death of a friend and was himself in a coma for some time. To make sure that the objectives of denunciation and general deterrence would have been sufficiently addressed, I might have imposed conditions such as house arrest and a community service order requiring the offender to speak to designated groups about the consequences of dangerous driving, as was the case in *Parker, supra*, at p. 239, and *R v. Hollinsky* (1995), 103 CCC (3d) 472 (Ont. CA).

[131] However, trial judges are closer to their community and know better what would be acceptable to their community. Absent evidence that the sentence imposed by the trial judge was demonstrably unfit, the Court of Appeal should not have interfered to substitute its own opinion for that of the sentencing judge. The trial judge did not commit a reversible error in principle and she appropriately considered all the relevant factors. Although the Court of Appeal's decision is entitled to some deference (see the companion appeal *R v. R.A.R.*, 2000 SCC 8, at paras. 20-21), in my opinion it erred in holding that the sentencing judge had given undue weight to the objective of denunciation. I see no ground for the Court of Appeal's intervention.

VIII. Disposition

[132] I would allow the appeal. Accordingly, the 18-month sentence of incarceration imposed by the trial judge should be restored. However, given that the respondent has already served the conditional sentence imposed by the Court of Appeal in its entirety, and that the Crown stated in oral argument that it was not seeking any further punishment, I would stay the service of the sentence of incarceration.

NOTE

Proulx answered a number of questions arising from the creation of the conditional sentence. Note that on the spectrum of sentencing objectives the court plainly asserted that, in addition to restorative or rehabilitative objectives, a conditional sentence should include a punitive element. But *Proulx* did not make the judge's role easy. The difficulty in applying the principles set out to the hard cases that commonly come to court is illustrated in the companion cases released the same day as *Proulx*.

In *R v Bunn*, 2000 SCC 9, [2000] 1 SCR 183, a case of breach-of-trust theft by a lawyer, the Supreme Court upheld the conditional sentence five to three. The fact that the offender was the sole caregiver for a disabled spouse was a significant factor militating against a custodial term.

In *R v LFW*, 2000 SCC 6, [2000] 1 SCR 132, the judges split evenly on whether to uphold a conditional sentence for a man who, more than 25 years before, committed offences of indecent assault and gross indecency on a young girl between the ages of 6 and 12. The offender had apparently committed no other offences in the interim, had dealt successfully with an alcohol problem, and had a good work record.

In *R v RNS*, 2000 SCC 7, [2000] 1 SCR 149, the judges unanimously agreed that a nine-month sentence of imprisonment should be restored in a case of sexual assault and invitation to sexual touching committed on a stepdaughter who was between the ages of five and eight.

The case of *R v RAR*, 2000 SCC 8, [2000] 1 SCR 163 involved a sexual assault conviction and two convictions for common assault committed at a workplace by an employer on an employee in her early 20s. L'Heureux-Dubé J and five other judges allowed the appeal, restoring the one-year term of imprisonment. In dissent, Lamer CJ would have maintained the nine-month conditional sentence with house arrest and sex-offender treatment, although he remarked that a lengthier conditional sentence would have been preferable.

In the result, conditional sentences were maintained only in *Bunn* and *LFW*, but not without significant dissent. For the three other offenders, a sentence of imprisonment was substituted although stayed, because the conditional sentences had already been served and the Crown was not requesting additional punishments. Although *Proulx* remains the leading statement of the law relating to conditional sentences, it did not eliminate dispute about when the conditional sentence is an appropriate option or how conditions for such sentences should be structured.

IV. RESTRICTING THE CONDITIONAL SENTENCE

A. Judicial Action

Section 742.1 lists a number of statutory criteria that must be met before a sentencing court may impose a conditional sentence of imprisonment. One of these, s 742.1(a), restricts the imposition of a conditional sentence to terms of two years or less. In *R v Fice*, 2005 SCC 32, [2005] 1 SCR 742, the Supreme Court considered whether credit for time served could reduce a penitentiary term to bring the sentence below two years and thus make the offender eligible for a conditional sentence. A majority of the court concluded that the reduction might change the venue of imprisonment from the penitentiary to a provincial jail, but it could not result in a conditional sentence. To allow otherwise would disturb the approach to conditional sentences set out in *Proulx*. According to those principles, the judge must first determine whether an appropriate sentence would be a term of less than two years. Only then is the offender eligible for a conditional sentence. If credit for time served could make the offender eligible for a conditional sentence, it would indirectly transform that credit into a mitigating factor. Instead, according to the majority, the credit for time served should be considered as part of the total punishment. The minority took the view that s 719 allows the court to give credit for time served, and if this credit brings the term below two years, a sentencing court is entitled to impose a conditional sentence if the conditions for such a sentence are otherwise met. As between the two positions, the majority claims to be consistent with *Proulx* while the minority claims to be consistent with the Code. In dissent, Fish J concluded:

> [75] Where an offender has at the time of sentence already spent time in custody and a court would otherwise have imposed a sentence of more than two years, the deterrent and punitive purposes will in some instances have been satisfied by the time spent in custody.
>
> [76] A further custodial sentence may well frustrate *both* of Parliament's main objectives in reforming Part XXIII of the *Criminal Code*. The first, it will be recalled, was to reduce the use of incarceration as a sanction; the second, to give greater prominence to the principles of restorative justice, including rehabilitation.
>
> [77] A conditional sentence of imprisonment, on the other hand, will in some circumstances promote both of Parliament's objectives without overlooking the need for punishment or denunciation. Where this is the case, I see no reason of principle, policy or precedent to limit the sentencing court to a choice between a probationary sentence that is too lenient and a custodial sentence that is too severe.
>
> [78] Conditional sentences were introduced by Parliament to afford judges greater flexibility in sentencing: Section 742.1 should not be interpreted so as to frustrate this evident purpose.
>
> [79] In my respectful view, nothing in *Proulx* was meant to prevent trial courts from imposing conditional sentences where, on account of the time already served, further institutional detention is not required and a term of imprisonment to be served in the community best responds to the principles and purposes of sentencing set out by Parliament in the *Criminal Code*. At its highest, from the Crown's perspective, *Proulx* is silent on that issue.

While this may seem to be both persuasive and good sentencing policy, it did not find favour with a majority of the Supreme Court, although it seems entirely consistent with both the Code and with *Proulx*. Is there any argument available that would allow the court to reopen this issue? For further discussion of the issues involved, see Julian V Roberts, "Pre-Trial Custody, Terms of Imprisonment, and the Conditional Sentence: Crediting 'Dead Time' to Effect 'Regime Change' in Sentencing" (2005) 9 Can Crim L Rev 191; Patrick Healy, "The Effect of Pre-Sentence Custody in Eligibility for a Conditional Sentence" (2005) 9 Can Crim L Rev 261.

B. Legislative Action

A recurring question is whether conditional sentences should not be an option for certain offences or classes of offences. This question arises not only in individual cases but as a general issue of policy. *Proulx* confirmed that a conditional sentence is in principle a viable sentencing option, provided that it conforms to the statutory criteria and the guidelines developed in the courts. In 2006, the government introduced a bill that would have precluded conditional sentences or excluded from conditional-sentence consideration all indictable offences punishable by imprisonment by ten years or more. This was amended in Committee and, in 2007, Parliament passed an amendment that reflected continuing concern about the scope of conditional sentences. The purpose of the amendment was to restrict the availability of conditional offences for three categories of offences in which the maximum punishment is more than ten years. The section as then amended read as follows:

> 742.1 If a person is convicted of an offence, other than a serious personal injury offence as defined in section 752, a terrorism offence or a criminal organization offence prosecuted by way of indictment for which the maximum term of imprisonment is ten years or more or an offence punishable by a minimum term of imprisonment, and the court imposes a sentence of imprisonment of less than two years and is satisfied that the service of the sentence in the community would not endanger the safety of the community and would be consistent with the fundamental purpose and principles of sentencing set out in sections 718 to 718.2, the court may, for the purpose of supervising the offender's behaviour in the community, order that the offender serve the sentence in the community, subject to the offender's compliance with the conditions imposed under section 742.3.

Of these three classes of offences, the widest was the serious personal injury offence. Thus, conditional sentences would no longer be an option in respect of any indictable offence involving the use of violence, endangerment, or the infliction of severe psychological damage, provided that the maximum punishment is ten years or more. This classification also included sexual assault as defined in ss 271, 272, and 273. The amendment did not compel a sentence of imprisonment for the three classes of offences, but that would be its effect in most instances. Recall that prior to imposing a conditional sentence of imprisonment the court must have decided to impose a term of imprisonment. It would be anomalous if a court were to impose a non-custodial sentence—for example, probation—for an offence in the classes covered by the amendment of s 742.1.

The amendments of 2007 restricted the scope of conditional sentences, but they were problematic. There was a definitional problem in determining the meaning of a "serious personal injury offence." For example, did this phrase encompass an offence that involves risk, such as dangerous driving, or was it limited to offences of actual harm? There was also a more substantive problem in attempting to distinguish degrees of seriousness where personal injury is involved. There was also the continuing debate in more general terms about the appropriateness of the conditional sentence as a sentencing option.

As a result, a further amendment was enacted in 2012 (SC 2012, c 1, s 34). Section 742.1 now defines the scope of the conditional sentence as follows:

Imposing of conditional sentence

> 742.1 If a person is convicted of an offence and the court imposes a sentence of imprisonment of less than two years, the court may, for the purpose of supervising the offender's behaviour in the community, order that the offender serve the sentence in the community, subject to the conditions imposed under section 742.3, if
>
> > (a) the court is satisfied that the service of the sentence in the community would not endanger the safety of the community and would be consistent with the fundamental purpose and principles of sentencing set out in sections 718 to 718.2;
> >
> > (b) the offence is not an offence punishable by a minimum term of imprisonment;
> >
> > (c) the offence is not an offence, prosecuted by way of indictment, for which the maximum term of imprisonment is 14 years or life;
> >
> > (d) the offence is not a terrorism offence, or a criminal organization offence, prosecuted by way of indictment, for which the maximum term of imprisonment is 10 years or more;
> >
> > (e) the offence is not an offence, prosecuted by way of indictment, for which the maximum term of imprisonment is 10 years, that
> >
> > > (i) resulted in bodily harm,
> > >
> > > (ii) involved the import, export, trafficking or production of drugs, or
> > >
> > > (iii) involved the use of a weapon; and

(f) the offence is not an offence, prosecuted by way of indictment, under any of the following provisions:

   (i) section 144 (prison breach),

   (ii) section 264 (criminal harassment),

   (iii) section 271 (sexual assault),

   (iv) section 279 (kidnapping),

   (v) section 279.02 (trafficking in persons—material benefit),

   (vi) section 281 (abduction of person under fourteen),

   (vii) section 333.1 (motor vehicle theft),

   (viii) paragraph 334(a) (theft over $5000),

   (ix) paragraph 348(1)(e) (breaking and entering a place other than a dwelling-house),

   (x) section 349 (being unlawfully in a dwelling-house), and

   (xi) section 435 (arson for fraudulent purpose).

The amendment thus combines restrictions of a general nature with a list of specific offences. Where the conditional sentence is excluded as an option, there is in principle a broad choice between imprisonment for two years or less, or a suspended sentence. For practical purposes the effect is to increase the incidence of imprisonment, not least because the premise of the conditional sentence was that a fit sentence required imprisonment of two years or less. The amendment of 2012 was thus a partial repudiation of the original reform in 1995 and its development in the courts, notably in *Proulx*, by emphasizing that where the conditional sentence is not an option, sentences must underscore the objectives of denunciation and deterrence through imprisonment. The effect of this amendment is not only to exclude the conditional sentence as an option in objective terms by reference to the criteria listed in s 742.1; in practice, there has been a reduction in the use of a conditional sentence even in cases where it is a viable option.

The conditional sentence is excluded by three general criteria in s 742.1: (1) danger to the community: s 742.1(a), (2) inconsistency with general sentencing principles: s 742.1(a), and (3) mandatory minimum sentences of imprisonment: s 742.1(b). It is also excluded by more specific criteria—notably, the classification of the offence as indictable: ss 742.1(c), (d), (e), and (f); the maximum term of imprisonment: ss 742.1(c), (d), (e), and (f); aggravating circumstances: s 742.1(e); or designated offences: s 742.1(f). The conditional sentence is thus an option for summary conviction offences. It remains to be seen whether "prosecuted by indictment" refers generally to the classification of the offence in the statutory definition of the offence or to a requirement that the individual case proceed by indictment.

V. HARD CASES

The restrictions imposed by s 742.1 might exclude the conditional sentence as an option, but that exclusion does not necessarily imply that a custodial sentence is the only option, as demonstrated in *Voong*, below.

R v Voong
2015 BCCA 285

BENNETT JA (Garson and Stromberg-Stein JJA concurring):

[1] Those who embark in drug trafficking engage in serious criminal conduct. Absent exceptional circumstances, in British Columbia, they should expect to be sent to prison.

[2] Each of the four respondents pleaded guilty to trafficking drugs or possession of drugs for the purpose of trafficking in the context of a dial-a-dope operation.

[3] The maximum penalty for trafficking and possession for the purpose of trafficking in a Schedule I or II substance is life imprisonment (*Controlled Drugs and Substances Act*, S.C. 1996, c. 19, s. 5 [*CDSA*]). In 2012, the *Criminal Code*, R.S.C. 1985 c. C-46 was amended by the *Safe Streets and Communities Act*, S.C. 2012, c. 1, s. 34. As a result of this amendment, conditional sentence orders (CSOs) are no longer available where an offence has a maximum term of imprisonment of 14 years or life (*Criminal Code*, s. 742.1(c)) or where an offence involves the trafficking of drugs (*Criminal Code*, s. 742.1(e)(ii)). Therefore, a CSO is no longer available for the offences in the matter at bar.

[4] In these four appeals, sentencing judges imposed suspended sentences accompanied by probation orders. The Crown has appealed the sentences on the basis that the sentences do not sufficiently address the principles of deterrence and denunciation. The Crown says that in each case, except Voong, the judge used the suspended sentence as an unlawful substitute for a conditional sentence order.

[5] Three of the respondents, Charlton, Voong and Taylor, were selling drugs to support a drug habit and had criminal records. The fourth respondent, Galang, was a young, first offender who was selling drugs to help a friend avoid trouble as a result of a drug debt. I will address the details of each individual offender below, after I discuss the applicable legal principles.

. . .

[19] Where no minimum sentence is required, the *Criminal Code* permits a court to suspend the passing of a sentence, rather than impose a sentence (s. 731(1)(a)), and to place a person on probation for a maximum of three years (s. 732.2(2)(b)). If an offender who is on probation is convicted of an offence, the suspension of the sentence may be revoked and the offender may be brought back before the court for sentencing. At that point, the judge may impose any sentence that could have been imposed at the time the sentence was suspended (s. 732.2(5)(d)).

[20] If probation is ordered, the judge must impose certain mandatory conditions found in s. 732.1(2) and may also impose optional conditions (s. 732.1(3)(a)-(g.2)). Under s. 732.1(3)(h), the Court may also impose any other "reasonable condition ... for protecting society and for facilitating the offender's successful reintegration into the community."

[21] Suspended sentences were imposed in drug trafficking cases before CSOs became available in 1996 (introduced by the *Act to amend the Criminal Code (sentencing) and other Acts in consequences thereof*, S.C. 1995, c. 22). A suspended sentence is still a sentencing option in law in the cases at bar, as there is, at this time, no minimum sentence for the offences at issue.

[22] Where a suspended sentence was imposed in drug trafficking offences prior to the availability of a CSO, there was always an indication of exceptional mitigating circumstances. For example, in *R. v. Harding*, [1977] B.C.J. No. 839 (C.A.), this Court dismissed

a Crown appeal and upheld a suspended sentence with three years' probation with strict conditions, for a heroin addict who sold four caps of heroin. She had made significant steps towards overcoming her heroin addiction, and the majority concluded they should not interfere with the carefully reasoned sentence. The majority found that the trial judge had recognized that deterrence was of foremost importance but concluded that in the circumstances of the case before him, rehabilitation was worth the effort. The trial judge was alive to the fact that he could sentence her if his expectations of rehabilitation were not born out, and she breached the probation order.

[23] In *R. v. Huang*, [1993] B.C.J. No 1118 (C.A.), this Court dismissed a Crown appeal upholding a suspended sentence and three years' probation for an offender who pleaded guilty to possession of one ounce of 90 percent pure heroin for the purpose of trafficking. The offender was 18 years old at the time, attending community college and had no prior record. Although this Court and the sentencing judge expressed reservations about a sentence other than incarceration, this Court concluded that the sentence was carefully considered and declined to interfere with it. Similarly, see *R. v. Yamanaka*, [1994] B.C.J. 521 (B.C.C.A.).

Nature of the Conditional Sentence Order

[24] In *R. v. Proulx*, 2000 SCC 5 Chief Justice Lamer discussed the differences between CSOs and probation orders. He noted that in most respects, they appear very similar (para. 23). He also observed that the penalty for breach of a probation order could be more severe than a breach of a CSO (para. 27). In the case of a breach of probation, the suspended sentence can be revoked and the offender may be sentenced for the original offence. By contrast, in the case of a breach of conditional sentence, the maximum punishment available is incarceration for the time remaining in the original sentence.

[25] Lamer C.J.C. said, however, that there is one important distinction between the two: that the probation order is primarily rehabilitative in nature, while a CSO addresses both rehabilitative and punitive objectives of sentencing (para. 23). He came to this conclusion by comparing the "optional conditions" available for each order.

[26] The probation order and conditional sentence order provisions of the *Criminal Code* each prescribe mandatory conditions (three for probation orders and five for CSOs), conditions relating to treatment programs, and optional conditions (paras. 24–27).

[27] Prior to the *Act to amend the Criminal Code (sentencing) and other Acts in consequences thereof* coming into force on September 3, 1996, the optional condition provision for probation orders was as follows:

> 737(2) ... the court may prescribe as conditions in a probation order that the accused shall do any one or more of the following things as specified in the order, namely,
>
> (h) comply with such other reasonable conditions as the court considers desirable for securing the good conduct of the accused and for preventing a repetition by him of the same offence or the commission of other offences.

[28] This provision had been interpreted as meaning that terms of probation could not be imposed as "additional punishment." The conditions needed to be related to the offence and for the purposes set out in the section (see *R. v. Ziatas* (1973), 13 C.C.C. (2d) 287 (Ont. C.A.) and *R. v. Lavender* (1981), 59 C.C.C. (2d) 551 (B.C.C.A.)). In *Lavender*,

Lambert J.A., in concurring reasons held that a condition of probation could only be imposed for rehabilitative purposes. His reasons were approved in *R. v. D.E.S.M.* (1992), 80 C.C.C. (3d) 371 (B.C.C.A.) at p. 380 (a unanimous decision of a five-justice division). In that decision, the Court upholding a 45-day intermittent sentence and probation for historical sexual offences, affirmed that the maintenance of rehabilitation was a proper principle (the offender in that case having been completely rehabilitated long before the charge). The Court concluded that house arrest fell within the *Criminal Code* provisions, and that it was an appropriate sentence in the very special circumstances of that case where there were no factors that required punishment by conventional imprisonment.

[29] The 1996 amendments changed the nature of the optional conditions for probation orders. The language formerly found in s. 737 (the probation provision noted above) is now in found in the CSO provision, s. 742.3(2)(f):

> 742.3(2) The court may prescribe, as additional conditions of a conditional sentence order, that the offender do one or more of the following:
>
> • • •
>
> (f) comply with such other reasonable conditions as the court considers desirable, subject to any regulations made under subsection 738(2), for securing the good conduct of the offender and for preventing a repetition by the offender of the same offence or the commission of other offences.

[30] The optional condition provision for probation orders now reads:

> 732.1(3) The court may prescribe, as additional conditions of a probation order, that the offender do one or more of the following:
>
> • • •
>
> (h) comply with such other reasonable conditions as the court considers desirable, subject to any regulations made under subsection 738(2), for protecting society and for facilitating the offender's successful reintegration into the community.

[31] Lamer C.J.C. in *Proulx* interpreted this change as follows, at para. 34:

> Despite the virtual identity in the wording of s. 742.3(2)(f) and the old residual clause applicable to probation orders, it would be a mistake to conclude that punitive conditions cannot now be imposed under s. 742.3(2)(f). Parliament amended the residual clause for probation, s. 732.1(3)(h), to read "for protecting society and for *facilitating the offender's successful reintegration into the community.*" It did so to make clear the rehabilitative purpose of probation and to distinguish s. 742.3(2)(f) from s. 732.1(3)(h). The wording used in s. 742.3(2)(f) does not focus principally on the rehabilitation and reintegration of the offender. If s. 742.3(2)(f) were interpreted as precluding punitive conditions, it would frustrate Parliament's intention in distinguishing the two forms of sentence. Parliament would not have distinguished them if it intended both clauses to serve the same purpose. [Emphasis in original.]

[32] He discussed the type of terms that should be included in a CSO, and concluded that house arrest or strict curfews should be the norm (para. 36). I note that this is the type of condition that was imposed in *D.E.S.M.* under the same statutory language as now exists for the CSO.

[33] In essence, the CSO is a sentence that has a more punitive aspect to it than a probation order, whereas the focus of the probation order is rehabilitation. This is supported

when one examines the origins of a suspended sentence, and probation, between 1889 and 1955, which was initially available only for first offenders.

[34] The Court concluded that a CSO is, by statutory definition, a sentence of imprisonment (para. 40), and provides denunciatory and deterrent effect (para. 41). The CSO was introduced to relieve the high incarceration rates in this country, and to permit those who were sentenced to less than two years, and are no danger to the public, to serve the sentence in the community under "tight controls" (para. 36).

[35] Thus, despite the wording of the optional provisions being identical for probation orders pre-1996 and for the CSO, the Court found, that in the context of the entire amendment, the difference between the two provisions is that the CSO engaged the punishment principle of sentencing, and the suspended sentence with probation did not.

[36] The Crown says, as a result, it is an error in principle or law to equate the CSO with a suspended sentence and probation.

Deterrent Effect of Probation

[37] A probation order has primarily a rehabilitative objective; however, as the statutory terms refer to the purposes of "protecting society" and "reintegration into the community," it is not limited to this objective.

[38] What is required for the imposition of an optional condition in a probation order is a "nexus between the offender, the protection of the community and his reintegration into the community" (*R. v. Shoker*, 2006 SCC 44 at para. 13).

[39] A suspended sentence has been found to have a deterrent effect in some cases. Because a breach of the probation order can result in a revocation and sentencing on the original offence, it has been referred to as the "*Sword of Damocles*" hanging over the offender's head. For example, in *R. v. Saunders*, [1993] B.C.J. No. 2887 (C.A.) at para. 11, Southin J.A. said:

> Deterrence is an important part of the public interest but there are other ways of deterring some sorts of crime than putting someone in prison who has no criminal record as this appellant did not. The learned trial judge did not turn her mind to whether the deterrence which is important might be effected by certain terms of a discharge or a suspended sentence such as a lengthy period of community service.

[40] This Court, in *Oates*, recently confirmed that *Saunders* stands for the proposition that deterrence *might* be effected with a suspended sentence (*Oates* at para. 16).

[41] In *Shoker*, at para. 15, the Court concluded that supervised probation is a restraint on the probationer's freedom.

[42] Other Courts have confirmed the deterrent effect of a suspended sentence and a probation order in certain circumstances. See, for example, *R. v. George* (1992), 112 N.S.R. (2d) 183 (C.A.) at 187 (and a number of cases following, including *R. v. Martin*, 154 N.S.R. (2d) 268 (C.A.); *R. v. R.T.M.*, 151 N.S.R. (2d) 235 (C.A.)) and *R. c. Savenco* (1988), 26 Q.A.C. 291 (C.A.).

[43] The statutory phrase "protection of the public" now found in the *Criminal Code* gives a broad discretion to sentencing judges to impose conditions (see *Shoker* at para. 3). The public is protected when a former criminal is rehabilitated and deterred from committing more crimes (see *R. v. Grady* (1971), 5 N.S.R. (2d) 264 at 266). It is also protected

when other offenders are deterred by the sentence imposed. Thus, imposing conditions for the protection of the community may have a deterrent and denunciatory effect in addition to a rehabilitative effect. Put another way, a condition need not be punitive in nature in order to achieve deterrence or denunciation. In *D.E.S.M.* (and affirmed in *R. v. Sidhu* (1998), 129 C.C.C. (3d) 26 (B.C.C.A.)), this Court concluded that "home confinement" was an appropriate term of a probation order for the purpose of the maintenance of rehabilitation. The court concluded, at p. 381:

> It should not be thought that home confinement, if we may call it that, should readily be substituted for regular imprisonment. Such a disposition is suitable, in our judgment, only where *very special circumstances* are present such as where the accused demonstrates that he has rehabilitated himself prior to arrest, where he is not a danger to anyone, where others are dependent upon him, and where there are no factors that make it necessary in the public interest that punishment should be by conventional imprisonment. [Emphasis added.]

Range of Sentence

[44] What then is the range of sentence for dial-a-dope traffickers? We know the statutory range is from a suspended sentence to life imprisonment. We also know, from an abundance of cases decided by this Court, that the normal range of sentence for a first offence dial-a-dope drug trafficker is between six to nine months incarceration, and upwards to eighteen months in some cases, absent exceptional circumstances. A brief review of some of the cases will demonstrate this range.

[45] The exceptional circumstances must engage principles of sentencing to a degree sufficient to overcome the application of the main principles of deterrence and denunciation by way of a prison sentence.

[46] For example, in *R. v. Preston* (1990), 47 B.C.L.R. (2d) 273 a five-justice division of this Court examined the general principles of sentencing in the context of possession of heroin offences by a long-time heroin addict, with a lengthy criminal record. Ms. Preston had made substantial efforts at rehabilitation. Wood J.A., speaking for the Court, said, at 281:

> The object of the entire criminal justice system, of course, is the protection of society, and I say at once that if incarceration is the only way of protecting society from a particular offender, then transitory and expensive though it may be, that form of protection must be invoked. But where, as in this case, the danger to society results from the potential of an addict to commit offences to support her habit, and it appears to the court that there is a reasonable chance that she may succeed in an attempt to control her addiction, then it becomes necessary to consider the ultimate benefit to society if that chance becomes a reality.
>
> With respect, that benefit seems obvious. If the chance for rehabilitation becomes a reality, society will be permanently protected from the danger which the offender otherwise presents in the fashion described above. As well, the cost associated with her frequent incarceration will be avoided.

[47] This concept applies to all offences, not just drug offences. For example, in *R. v. Smith*, 2013 BCCA 173, a case of impaired driving causing death, this Court concluded that despite the extensive rehabilitative steps taken by Ms. Smith, the circumstances of the offence for which she was convicted and her circumstances did not outweigh the fundamental importance of deterrence and denunciation.

[48] A review of some of the many cases in the dial-a-dope context will demonstrate how this principle is applied.

[49] In *R. v. Ahmed*, 2001 BCCA 504, the Crown appealed a CSO of 18 months. The offender was 29 years old, and was convicted on six counts of trafficking cocaine. The first five transactions involved selling drugs from a store where he worked as a clerk, while the last transaction was a dial-a-dope sale. The total drugs were 7.2 grams of cocaine for $640. The Court affirmed that the "dial-a-dope" method of trafficking is an aggravating factor in sentencing. The other aggravating factors were that the offences were spread over several weeks, solely for profit and not to support an addiction, and were near a school in a neighbourhood where there had been a persistent drug problem. The sentencing judge also found that the accused had not taken responsibility for his actions. He was on judicial interim release for other offences, and therefore bound to "keep the peace and be of good behaviour" under that order. At para. 8, the Court concluded that there must be significant factors to justify a CSO:

> … In a case involving trafficking in hard drugs, there must be some significant factor or factors relating to the background of the offender, his underlying reasons for trafficking or his pre-sentence efforts at rehabilitation that would support the imposition of a conditional sentence.

[50] The Court substituted a sentence of 18 months in prison.

[51] In *R. v. Chang*, 2002 BCCA 644 a case of possession for the purpose of trafficking heroin and cocaine, this Court overturned a prison sentence of 9 months, and substituted a CSO of 9 months for a 22-year-old student, who was a first offender. Of interest are the observations of Esson J.A. commenting on the principles of deterrence, denunciation and rehabilitation, in response to the sentencing judge's view that a CSO would not serve the factors of general and specific deterrence:

> [13] As to general deterrence, that may be so, but each individual must be judged upon his own circumstances. Here we have a young man whose personal circumstances appear generally to be favourable. There was no real proof that he was engaged in a sophisticated operation. Having regard to those matters, I consider that the elements of specific deterrence and denunciation can adequately be met by a conditional sentence.
>
> [14] I consider that, in this particular case, such a sentence is more likely to serve the important end of rehabilitation. *It may be that this young man will learn his lesson from having been arrested, charged and convicted.* [Emphasis added.]

[52] In *R. v. Tran*, 2007 BCCA 613, the offender, a 28-year-old first offender was convicted of possession of heroin and cocaine for the purpose of trafficking in a dial-a-dope operation. He received a sentence of nine months incarceration, which was upheld on appeal. This Court said at para. 14:

> … Mr. Tran was not a drug user. He involved himself in the drug trade for financial gain. His behaviour was part of a "dial-a-dope" drug trafficking scheme—a mode of trafficking which this Court has observed in the past plays on the addiction and weakness of habitual drug users, and the degradation of the community. The drugs in question are hard drugs and are known to be highly addictive. In the circumstances, I see no error which would permit this Court to interfere with the sentence imposed.

[53] On the other hand, in *R. v. Charlie*, 2008 BCCA 44, the Crown appealed an 18 month CSO imposed on an Aboriginal offender, after a guilty plea, for possession for the purpose of trafficking cocaine. At the time of the offence, Mr. Charlie was bound by a CSO for a similar offence. However, the Crown appeal was not heard until two years after the offence occurred. In that time, Mr. Charlie had taken exceptional steps towards his rehabilitation, which were supported in a pre-sentence report. In dismissing the Crown appeal, Frankel J.A. said, at para. 35:

> The concern expressed in [*R. v. Morphy* (1974), 21 C.C.C. (2d) 62 (B.C.C.A.)] and [*R. v. Nelson*, [1992] Y.J. No. 171 (C.A.)] applies here. It would be unjust, and counterproductive not only to Mr. Charlie's interests, but those of society at large, to interfere with his successful efforts at rehabilitation by sentencing him a period of incarceration at this time. It is on this basis alone that I would dismiss this appeal.

[54] Similarly, in *R. v. Amhaz*, 2013 BCCA 348, the offender appealed a six-month incarceration sentence imposed after a guilty plea for one count of trafficking in cocaine, involving a continuing dial-a-dope operation. He was 25 years old and had no criminal record. He was selling drugs to pay off debts. Mr. Amhaz was not arrested until five months after the offences occurred. Shortly after the offences, Mr. Amhaz's family performed an "intervention," and as a result, by the time he was charged and sentenced, he had made profound changes in his life.

[55] Saunders J.A. discussed the need for some "out of the ordinary" circumstances that would permit a non-custodial sentence to be imposed. In allowing the appeal, and substituting a CSO, Saunders J.A. said this, at para. 19:

> While Mr. Ahmaz's involvement in the illegal business is to be deplored, and must be reflected in the sentence imposed, the fact he left this criminal lifestyle before engagement with the criminal justice system, reinforced by his assumption of an appropriate employment role and his move towards stable family life, is a feature that should have been reflected in the sentence imposed, in my respectful view. This feature demonstrates self-directed rehabilitation before contact with the criminal justice system, and distinguishes the case from those to which I have referred. In my view it comes within the descriptions "particularly positive" and "out of the ordinary."

[56] Of significance is the recent decision of this Court in *R. v. Cisneros*, 2014 BCCA 154. This case was decided after the CSO became unavailable for drug trafficking. The sentencing judge imposed a $2,000 fine and one-year probation for an offence of possession for the purpose of trafficking cocaine in a dial-a-dope operation.

[57] The offender was working a "shift" in a dial-a-dope operation between midnight and 6:30 a.m. He had 25 rocks of cocaine and 29 baggies of heroin. Each rock and bag contained less than 0.5 grams of the drug. He was 27 years old, had no criminal record and was selling the drugs for about ten years, for profit.

[58] In allowing the Crown appeal, and substituting a sentence of six months, Groberman J.A. said, at paras. 13-14:

> The case before us is a straightforward case in which the offender was involved in a busy dial-a-dope operation. While he had no criminal record, this was not an isolated event, as he conceded in his sentencing submissions. There were no extraordinary circumstances that would take this case out of the ordinary sentencing range.

I agree with the Crown's assessment that the ordinary sentencing range for a first offender in a crime of the nature involved in this case is approximately 6-9 months' imprisonment. Even before the option of giving a conditional sentence of imprisonment for such offences was removed by amendment to the *Criminal Code*, such sentences were very much the exception.

[59] In summary, absent exceptional circumstances, the sentence for a first offence or with a minimal criminal record, dial-a-dope drug seller will be in the range of six to eighteen months imprisonment, depending on the aggravating circumstances. Exceptional circumstances may include a combination of no criminal record, significant and object-ively identifiable steps towards rehabilitation for the drug addict, gainful employment, remorse and acknowledgement of the harm done to society as a result of the offences, as opposed to harm done to the offender as a result of being caught. This is a non-exhaustive list, but at the end of the day, there must be circumstances that are above and beyond the norm to justify a non-custodial sentence. There must be something that would lead a sentencing judge to conclude that the offender had truly turned his or her life around, and that the protection of the public was subsequently better served by a non-custodial sentence. However, Parliament, while not removing a non-custodial sentence for this type of offence, has concluded that CSO sentences are not available. Thus, it will be the rare case where the standard of exceptional circumstances is met.

[60] A CSO was considered a sentence of imprisonment because of the strict *and punitive* conditions that could be imposed. As we have seen above, a suspended sentence can attract similar strict conditions, but only if they are aimed at protection of the public and reintegration of the offender into society. Rehabilitation clearly plays a significant role in both of those conditions.

[61] A suspended sentence can achieve a deterrent effect, as noted above, as well as a denunciatory effect. And, as Esson J.A. stated in *Chang*, the fact of being arrested, tried and convicted, can also address these principles. In other words, the stigma of being a convicted drug trafficker and the consequences of that conviction—for example, restricted ability to travel outside of Canada and exclusion from many forms of employment—may also play a deterrent effect.

[62] Thus, while it is an error to simply substitute a suspended sentence for a CSO, as they are not governed by the same principles, that does not end the inquiry into whether these non-custodial sentences are fit.

[63] The issue then for each of these appeals becomes whether there were sufficient exceptional circumstances to justify going outside the normal range of sentence and imposing a non-custodial sentence. In each case, the sentencing judge concluded that there were exceptional circumstances.

Application to Cases at Bar

Dau Man Voong

[64] Mr. Voong was caught selling drugs on January 24, 2013. He pleaded guilty to one offence, possession for the purpose of trafficking cocaine (contrary to s. 5(2) of the *CDSA*), on June 30, 2014. He was sentenced on July 10, 2014 to a suspended sentence and 30 months' probation with strict conditions.

[65] The police had Mr. Voong under observation, and he was suspected of committing over 16 transactions before he was arrested. Upon his arrest, he was found in possession

of score sheets, 6.6 grams of cocaine and a small amount of heroin, and $680 in cash. The offence took place in the context of a dial-a-dope operation.

[66] Mr. Voong had a criminal record: in 1994, he was convicted of two counts of possession for the purpose of trafficking a narcotic and received a $500 fine for the first count and a suspended sentence with probation for one year for the second count. In 1996, he was convicted of breaking and entering and theft, and in 2002, he was convicted of breaking and entering. He has had no convictions since 2002.

[67] He was 40 years old at the time of sentencing. He has a long history of drug use and attempts at treatment. He was selling the drugs to support his drug habit. He is single, and lives with his mother. He has anxiety and panic disorders.

[68] After he was charged with this offence, he attended a drug treatment program at the Pender Community Health Centre. As a result, he has been free of illicit drugs since May 2013. He is tested regularly at the treatment program he is continuing.

[69] The sentencing judge referred to the proper principles and legal parameters. The Crown is not alleging that he made the error of simply substituting a suspended sentence for a CSO.

[70] The sentencing judge said the following at paras. 37-41:

> In the Court of Appeal decision authored by Chief Justice Finch [*R. v. Tucker,* [2011] B.C.J. No. 2212], it was noted that Tucker was on a methadone maintenance program and he had not committed any breaches of the terms of his probation order or committed any other offence. The Court of Appeal noted the sentence [a suspended sentence] was an unusual disposition, but the Court was not persuaded that it should intervene. Appellate courts, the Chief Justice said, are reluctant to substitute a custodial sentence for a non-custodial sentence when doing so would be detrimental to the offender's success and continued rehabilitation.
>
> No one can suggest that a suspended sentence is the usual sentence for people involved in dial-a-dope trafficking cases. The question is whether it is appropriate in the circumstances, whether it can meet the principles of sentencing, and whether jail is necessary in order to achieve those goals. I really cannot conclude that jail is necessary in order to meet those goals with respect to Mr. Voong.
>
> Mr. Voong has by the people who are dealing with him at the Pender Community Health Centre so consolidated a path of rehabilitation that in my mind it would not serve society or the public at all to take him off that path and to send him to jail for a period of time, notwithstanding that these are very serious offences, and they deserve a serious response by the courts.
>
> Every case is different; every case involves the personal circumstances of an accused and here we have Mr. Voong who was obviously suffering from multiple concurrent disorders. He has an anxiety panic disorder combined with a drug addiction that he was dealing with at the time. He was dealing in drugs in order to receive a discount on drugs and that was his involvement.
>
> Mr. Voong has left that business. He is on a path that is different from that; he is on a path that society would want to support and help him to consolidate further instead of imposing a sentence that would take him off that path.

[71] He suspended sentence, and placed Mr. Voong on probation for 30 months, with strict terms including house arrest for the first six months of his sentence, and 80 hours of community service.

[72] The high end of the custodial range, twelve months or more, would normally be appropriate for an offender with Mr. Voong's history. The question in this case is whether a prison sentence is necessary in order to satisfy the principles of denunciation and deterrence. The relevant circumstances include the fact that he was not selling drugs for profit (but rather to support a long-standing drug habit), and importantly, that he has apparently turned a corner in his drug addiction, which is supported by objective evidence from the Pender Community Health Centre. He has served almost one year of his sentence.

[73] In my view, given all of the circumstances, and taking into account all of the principles noted above, this offender does present an exceptional circumstance by his commitment to rehabilitation and his apparent success to date. I would not interfere with this sentence.

John Galang

[74] On December 11, 2013, Mr. Galang sold 1.04 grams of cocaine to an undercover police officer for $100, as part of a dial-a-dope operation. He was arrested shortly afterwards, and found to have $190 on his person, including the $100 from the sale. He had no other drugs in his possession.

[75] He pleaded guilty to the offence at an early opportunity. Mr. Galang had no prior criminal record. He had a steady work history, and at the time of sentencing, was running a legitimate business with two others. He was 22 years old at the time of sentencing.

[76] He said he became involved in the drug operation to help a friend who had found himself owing money to his superiors in the drug trafficking operation. The sentencing judge accepted this explanation, and concluded that Mr. Galang was "at a very low end of the drug trafficking business" (para. 35).

[77] During his careful analysis, the sentencing judge reviewed some historical features of sentencing. He referred to this under the heading "Re-emergence of Suspended Sentences in Drug Trafficking Cases" (paras. 27-30). He expressed the view that after the CSO became a sentencing option in 1996, judges tended to opt for this type of order instead of a suspended sentence. He opined that this may be because the two types of sentences were, in practice, very similar. This view, I note, is confirmed by Lamer C.J.C. in *Proulx*. On the other hand, he observed that a breach of a CSO can be enforced "swiftly and significant consequences can be imposed promptly" (para. 30) while the process for revoking a suspended sentence was procedurally more complicated.

[78] The Crown says that the error here was equating the suspended sentence with a conditional sentence order. It submits that in *Proulx*, the Court clearly distinguished between the two, and that the sentencing judge erred in considering them to be similar.

[79] In my view, the sentencing judge in this case did not equate the two and misunderstand that the CSO was a "jail term" (*Proulx*). He looked back in time, before a CSO was available, to see if a suspended sentence was an appropriate sentence for drug trafficking. He referred to one decision, *Harding*, which I have referred to above, to demonstrate that a suspended sentence could, in exceptional circumstances, be imposed for a serious offence. The judge said the same—he looked for "exceptional circumstances" and he was alive to the fact that a suspended sentence would be a very unusual sentence to impose.

[80] In sentencing Mr. Galang, the sentencing judge said, at paras. 37-38:

The accused's prospects for rehabilitation are good. Mr. Galang is young, has a good employment record, and is now engaged in the difficult task of running a business. He has no criminal record. He has taken responsibility for his offence by pleading guilty' at a relatively early stage in the process. There is no evidence that he lives an antisocial lifestyle. That is, this offence represents an isolated act in an otherwise law-abiding life. On the evidence that I have heard, I conclude that it is unlikely that he will reoffend.

Conclusion

A suspended sentence is one of the sentencing options available in this case. Is it a fit sentence in the circumstances? In my view it is. The accused's moral culpability is at the lower end of the spectrum of those who engage in drug trafficking. Even so, there is no question that a deterrent sentence must be imposed in such cases. However, the courts have found that in some circumstances a suspended sentence will accomplish that goal. In my view, the goals of rehabilitation and reintegration into the community outweigh the goals of deterrence and denunciation in these particular circumstances.

[81] He suspended the passing of sentence, and imposed a probation order for one-year. Mr. Galang is a young person with no criminal record, and who is of otherwise good character, running his own business. He was found to be at the low end of the drug trafficking chain. I would not interfere with the sentencing judge's weighing of the circumstances and the principles of sentencing, except to the following degree. In my view, one year probation does not satisfy the deterrence or denunciatory aspect of sentencing. The proverbial "*Sword of Damocles*" plays a significant role in satisfying both of these principles, and one year is not sufficient. I would increase the probation order to three years' probation. I would also impose a curfew. I would add the term that Mr. Galang be in his home between the hours of 10 p.m. and 6 a.m. seven days a week, except when he is at work or travelling to and from work, or for a medical emergency. He will present himself at his door upon request of either his probation officer or a peace officer.

[82] This condition will remain in place for 18 months from the commencement of the probation order, dated October 15, 2014.

Krystal Charlton

[83] Ms. Charlton pleaded guilty to one count of possession for the purpose of trafficking cocaine, one count for the purpose of trafficking heroin and one count of breach of a probation order, which required her not to possess illegal drugs.

[84] She was a courier for a dial-a-dope operation, and when arrested she possessed 5.7 grams of cocaine, 1.51 grams of powdered cocaine, 1.75 grams of heroin and $156. She has a lengthy criminal record, including four convictions for possessing illicit drugs. She was on probation for drug offences when she committed the additional offences. She is a drug addict.

[85] She was 28 years old at the time of sentencing, and was sharing custody of her five-year-old daughter with her mother under the auspices of the Ministry of Children and Families. Ms. Charlton has been on judicial interim release since March 8, 2014. She has had mental health issues in the past, and since her release is obtaining counselling from the local health authority. She has been prescribed a new medication that her counsellor says has caused major positive changes for her.

[86] Her counsellor provided a very positive report on her progress. Of significance, she obtained certification to be a nutritional coach, and has been hired by a local fitness club. Her employer, who was aware of her circumstances, provided a very positive reference and attended court and spoke at her sentencing hearing. Her employer said that if Ms. Charlton is sentenced to prison, her job would be waiting for her upon her release.

[87] In discussing the applicable principles, the sentencing judge acknowledged that generally, a suspended sentence would "fail to provide the measure of general deterrence appropriate in a dial-a-dope case, particularly for an offender with a record which includes previous drug offences" (para. 10). The Crown submits that the trial judge acknowledged that the sentence would not satisfy the principles of sentencing and thereby erred by imposing a suspended sentence. It is necessary to read the statement in context:

> [10] It must be conceded that a suspended sentence will fail to provide the measure of general deterrence appropriate in a dial-a-dope case, particularly for an offender with a record which includes previous drug offences. The question is whether, in this case, that factor is outweighed by the sentencing objective of rehabilitation and the statutory instruction that I am to consider all reasonable alternatives to incarceration; *Criminal Code*, section 718.2(e). In my view, it is. It is clear that, since her arrest, Ms. Charlton has taken meaningful, practical and successful steps to leave her life of crime and to become a useful and contributing member of society.

[88] The sentencing judge suspended the passing of sentence and imposed three years' probation with terms, as she had established, in his view, exceptional circumstances.

[89] Ms. Charlton was a drug addict, who had been six years' clean before she "fell off the wagon" in 2013. Her arrest was clearly a wake-up call for her. She has taken significant steps towards her rehabilitation. She has employment and a very supportive employer, which is not usual for drug addicts. At the time of sentencing she had accessed Mental Health and Addictions Services, and has new medication that seems to be helping her cope much better than she was before. The road to sobriety for drug addicts is long and difficult. She appears to be doing whatever is necessary to maintain her sobriety, and eventually obtain custody of her child.

[90] As noted in *Preston*, the public is best protected if Ms. Charlton is not committing offences.

[91] The sentencing judge recognized that he was obliged to sentence Ms. Charlton to imprisonment unless the circumstances were "so compelling as to justify a sentence outside the normal range" (para. 3).

[92] Without these significant steps towards rehabilitation, Ms. Charlton would be looking at the higher end of the range, 12 months or more. However, I agree with the conclusion of the sentencing judge that this is a case of exceptional circumstances that justifies a non-custodial sentence. I would not interfere with this sentence.

Thomas Taylor

[93] Mr. Taylor pleaded guilty to one count of possession for the purpose of trafficking in cocaine, one count of breach of a recognizance for possessing a cell phone, and one count of breach of a recognizance for failing to present himself for a curfew check. He was sentenced on November 21, 2014.

[94] On August 6, 2013, the police arranged to buy 3.5 grams of cocaine from Mr. Taylor in a dial-a-dope operation. When he was arrested he had 9 grams of cocaine packaged in two dozen small packets. He also had a $110 dollars. He has a minor criminal record for mischief and two breaches of an undertaking.

[95] He was 25 years old at the time of sentencing and worked for his father as a landscaper, and also found employment as a barber. Mr. Taylor was selling drugs for a period of time to fund his own addiction.

[96] The pre-sentence report indicates that he is making some efforts at rehabilitation and tackling his drug addiction. He is apparently doing well in his employment; however, this observation had no independent verification.

[97] He is on a methadone program, and medical records indicated that he last tested positive for cocaine in May 2014. The date of the pre-sentence report was July 21, 2014. Thus, post-offence, he was still using illicit drugs. He advised the probation officer that he found the selling of drugs stressful and did not want to return to that lifestyle.

[98] The sentencing judge was aware of the principles of sentencing, and said this at para. 30:

> In this case, where I am dealing with a young man who sold drugs to finance his own addiction, I am satisfied that all of the principles of sentencing can be met by suspending the passing of sentence and placing him on probation for a period of two years. I have not come to this decision easily. I am well aware of the comments of the Court of Appeal with respect to the appropriate range of sentencing, but given the conditions I am going to impose, this is still a significant sentence and can meet the principles of deterrence and denunciation while at the same time supporting Mr. Taylor's efforts at rehabilitation which, in my view, must be given the appropriate effect.

[99] She then suspended sentence and imposed a period of probation for two years.

[100] An examination of the reasons for sentence demonstrates that the sentencing judge did not give sufficient consideration to deterrence and denunciation. The steps taken by Mr. Taylor, while commendable, do not reach the level of "exceptional circumstances" that is described in the multitude of cases that address the issue.

[101] Much of the evidence supporting his progress came from his mother, who no doubt wishes to see the best for her son. There is, however, little independent evidence of progress, and he was clearly using drugs approximately ten months *after* the offence date in this case, which was August 2013.

[102] Mr. Taylor has not demonstrated the degree of "exceptional circumstances" in terms of rehabilitation that would justify a non-custodial sentence. In my view, the sentencing judge erred in overemphasizing rehabilitation over denunciation and deterrence, and that error led her to impose a sentence that was unfit.

[103] I would interfere with this sentence. Mr. Taylor has been on strict terms of probation since November, including house arrest. Therefore, I would impose a sentence at the lower end of the range, and substitute a sentence of six months imprisonment to be followed by one-year probation. The terms of the probation are the statutory terms, to report as directed by his probation officer and to attend and participate in any addiction counselling program as directed by the probation officer.

Summary

[104] I would grant leave to appeal with respect to Mr. Voong, but dismiss the appeal.

[105] I would grant leave to appeal with respect to Mr. Galang, and allow the appeal to the extent of increasing the probation order to three years, with a house arrest term. Mr. Galang has three days to present himself at the Court of Appeal Registry and enter into the new probation order.

[106] I would grant leave to appeal with respect to Ms. Charlton, but dismiss the appeal.

[107] I would grant leave to appeal with respect to Mr. Taylor, allow the appeal, set aside the suspended sentence and probation and substitute a sentence of six months' incarceration to be followed by one-year probation with the terms as set out above. Mr. Taylor will surrender to the Court of Appeal Registry in Victoria, B.C. within 72 hours of the issuance of these reasons or a warrant of committal will issue.

R v Wallis
2007 BCCA 377

LEVINE JA (Kirkpatrick JA concurring):

Introduction

[1] The appellant, Keith Gordon Wallis, applies for leave to appeal, and if leave is granted, appeals the sentence of fifteen months in jail and one year probation imposed after he was convicted of unlawful production of marihuana contrary to s. 7(1) of the *Controlled Drugs and Substances Act*. He claims the sentencing judge erred in not imposing a conditional sentence.

Circumstances of the Appellant

[2] The appellant ran a grow operation of 638 plants in his house, powered by stolen electricity. He co-owned the house with his parents. After his conviction, he sold the house, realizing a financial loss because of the damage to the house from the grow operation.

[3] The appellant was 28 years old when he committed the offence, and 32 at the time of sentencing. He had no prior criminal record. He is a high school graduate, and completed a pre-apprenticeship program in auto mechanics at BCIT. The appellant was steadily employed until he quit his job in 2002 to develop and manage the grow operation full time. He has been employed since his arrest for this offence. He paid his parents for the losses they suffered on the sale of the house.

[4] The appellant has the support of his parents and friends. He financially supports and has a close relationship with his twelve-year-old daughter, who lives with her mother and step-father.

Positions of Counsel at Sentencing

[5] At the sentencing hearing, Crown counsel suggested a jail sentence of one year. He took no position on whether the sentence should be served in custody or by a

conditional sentence. Defence counsel submitted that a one year conditional sentence was appropriate.

Reasons for Sentence

[6] In lengthy reasons, the sentencing judge reviewed the circumstances of the offence and the offender.

• • •

[9] He then reviewed (at paras. 48 and 49) the mitigating and aggravating factors. The mitigating factors were the appellant's lack of a prior criminal record, his relationship with and support of his child, parents, and friends, and his steady employment. The aggravating factors focused on the circumstances of the offence: the appellant left his secure, well-paid employment to undertake a criminal enterprise; he was motivated solely by greed; the grow operation was large and sophisticated; the appellant stood to profit greatly from his enterprise; he was the sole operating mind of the enterprise; and he created a serious risk to his neighbours by setting up an electrical by-pass at his house. The sentencing judge noted (at para. 50) that the appellant was not a mere "gardener" or custodian of the enterprise.

[10] The sentencing judge concluded (at para. 59) that considering the appellant's motivation of greed and his deceit of family and friends in setting up and operating the grow operation, he was "not satisfied on a balance of probabilities that the safety of the community would not be endangered if this defendant was allowed to serve his sentence in the community."

[11] The sentencing judge then went on to consider the effect of marihuana grow operations on the community. He considered (at para. 60) as aggravating factors the prevalence of this criminal activity in the community, and its corrupting influence.

[12] In conclusion, the sentencing judge said (at para. 67):

> In my view, the sentence which I impose must satisfy both the need for denunciation of the high degree of moral culpability of the defendant and deterrence of others from engaging in a criminal behaviour which is, as stated earlier, causing harm in so many ways to the members of this community and to the social contract and respect for the rule of law. A conditional sentence would, in the circumstances of this offence and this offender, utterly fail to achieve these objectives.

• • •

[13] The appellant claims that the sentencing judge erred in finding that the appellant was a danger to the community; by placing too little emphasis on the appellant's personal circumstances; by overemphasizing the aggravating factors and placing too little weight on the mitigating factors; by overemphasizing the principles of deterrence and denunciation; and in characterizing the community as uniquely affected by marihuana grow operations and not allowing counsel to make submissions on this issue.

• • •

Danger to the Community

[17] The sentencing judge found the safety of the community would continue to be endangered if the appellant served his sentence in the community, because he was motivated by greed and proceeded in secret in committing the offence.

• • •

[20] In determining whether the appellant was a danger to the community, the sentencing judge gave no weight to the evidence of the personal characteristics of the appellant, concluding that none of those factors was predictive of the appellant's future conduct. Rather, he focused on the appellant's criminal conduct, motivated by greed and carried out in secrecy. Because the criminal conduct was not anticipated by those closest to him before he offended, the sentencing judge found that the facts that he had not previously offended, was steadily employed, had a positive relationship with his family and friends, and expressed remorse for the offence were not predictive of his future conduct.

[21] Motive and manner of carrying out an offence may be relevant factors, but if greed and secrecy were determinative, there would be few offenders who would not be found to be a continuing danger to the community.

[22] The sentencing judge was clearly offended by the appellant's criminal conduct, and for good reason. When otherwise law-abiding citizens turn to criminal enterprise, respect for societal norms, governed by law, is undermined.

[23] The sentencing judge was also concerned about the effect of the offence on the community, implicitly addressing the second factor that Lamer CJC in *Proulx* said must be taken into account in assessing the danger to the community: the gravity of the damage if the appellant re-offended.

[24] In my opinion, however, the sentencing judge underemphasized the appellant's personal characteristics in concluding he was at risk to re-offend, and overemphasized the gravity of the damage in the event of re-offence. In the result, his conclusion that the appellant remained a danger to the community was unreasonable.

Principles and Purposes of Sentencing

[25] The sentencing judge found (at paras. 66-67) that the overriding principles of sentencing in this case were denunciation and general deterrence, supporting his conclusion that "incarceration will be the only suitable way in which to express society's condemnation of the offender's conduct or to deter similar conduct in the future."

[26] The sentencing judge's rejection of a conditional sentence is consistent with what this Court has said on many occasions: the principles of deterrence and denunciation are of prime importance in cases of this kind: see, for example, *R v. Van Santvoord*, 2007 BCCA 23 (decided after this sentencing decision). In *Van Santvoord*, Ryan JA, for the Court, cited *R v. Su*, 2000 BCCA 480, and *R v. Vu*, 2003 BCCA 339, and said (at para. 38):

> *Su* remains a guideline and has been referred to in many subsequent decisions of this court for the principles that denunciation and deterrence are appropriate sentencing objectives where commercial marihuana operations are involved, for the proposition that a conditional sentence for the owner of the operation is generally unsuitable, and for a guideline range.

[27] See also Ryan JA's more recent comments in *R v. Craig*, 2007 BCCA 234 at para. 126, and *R v. Huynh and Ta*, 2007 BCCA 235 at para. 46.

[28] The factors the sentencing judge considered in this case, including the motive of greed, the planning and deliberation in setting up the operation, the size and potential profitability of the operation, and the appellant's ownership of the operation, were all factors that led this Court in *Van Santvoord* to set aside a fine of $20,000 and substitute a sentence of one year in jail.

[29] Concern for the effect on the community of grow operations is also reflected in *Van Santvoord* (at para. 42), where Ryan JA for the Court said:

> … [O]ver the years other cases of marihuana production have demonstrated that its illegal production creates the risk that it will attract other illegal activities and dangerous consequences to the community in which it takes place.

[30] See also *R v. Hill*, 2007 BCCA 309 at para. 25 where Smith JA, for the Court, held that it was appropriate for a sentencing judge to take judicial notice of the existence in this province of a significant and lucrative marihuana industry:

> That there is a significant and lucrative illegal marihuana industry in this province and that it has grown in scale and pervasiveness in recent years can hardly have escaped the notice of any informed citizen of the province. These aggravating facts are within the first class mentioned in *R v. Find* [2001 SCC 32 at para. 48] and the sentencing judge did not err in judicially noticing them. Indeed, this Court has taken judicial notice of the illegal drug trade in previous cases. For example, in *R v. Chang* (2002), 179 BCAC 72, 2002 BCCA 644, Esson JA referred, at ¶12, to "the serious social problems that have been and are being created by the great level of drug distribution going on in our community and throughout this province"; in *R v. Aitkens* (2004), 202 BCAC 167, 2004 BCCA 411, Newbury JA remarked at ¶7 that "[d]rug trafficking has become a blight in our society in general"; and in *R v. Van Santvoord*, 2007 BCCA 23, Ryan JA said at ¶42 that "over the years other cases of marihuana production have demonstrated that its illegal production creates the risk that it will attract other illegal activities and dangerous consequences to the community in which it takes place."

[31] The impact of crime on the community is a factor that local judges are in a position to be aware of and reflect in their sentencing decisions, and is one of the reasons appellate courts show deference to those decisions: see *R v. M. (C.A.)*, [1996] 1 SCR 500 at paras. 91-92.

[32] This Court has not precluded the imposition of a conditional sentence for production of marihuana where the circumstances of the offence or the offender demonstrate that principles of sentencing other than denunciation and deterrence should be given more consideration. These include rehabilitation and restorative objectives, including reparation for harm done and acknowledgment of responsibility. In every case, consideration of the fundamental principle that "[a] sentence must be proportionate to the gravity of the offence and the degree of responsibility of the offender," as set out in s. 718.2 of the Code, is of major importance, and may lead to the conclusion that a conditional sentence is appropriate in the particular circumstances.

[33] If that were not so, the Court would be violating the basic principles of sentencing set out in the Code, and the guidelines set out by the Supreme Court of Canada in *Proulx*. These are: that incarceration is a last resort for all offenders (Code s. 718.2(d) and (e), *Proulx*, at paras. 100, 127(7)); no offence (except one punishable by a minimum term of imprisonment) is excluded from the conditional sentencing regime, and there is no presumptive sentence for specific offences (*Proulx*, at para. 127(3)); sentencing is an individualized process (*Proulx*, at para. 82); and a conditional sentence can provide significant denunciation and deterrence (*Proulx*, at paras. 102, 107, 127(8)).

[34] Examples of cases where consideration of all of the principles of sentencing led to the conclusion that a conditional sentence was appropriate in the particular circumstances

are: *R v. Nguyen*, 2001 BCCA 461; *R v. Godwin*, 2005 BCCA 477, *R v. Gan*, 2007 BCCA 59, and *R v. Kreutziger*, 2005 BCCA 231.

[35] In *Nguyen*, this Court substituted a conditional sentence of 12 months for a jail sentence of nine months and one year probation for the mother of two young children, where the father of the children carried on a grow operation in her home. She knew little of the business and did not participate. In *Godwin*, this Court substituted a 12 months conditional sentence for a sentence of 12 months in jail for a 38 year old man diagnosed as a schizophrenic while serving a previous conditional sentence. The evidence was that he committed the marihuana production and related offences during the onset of the mental illness, and by the time of sentencing and the appeal, was managing his illness in the community with significant community support. In *Gan*, this Court substituted a 12 months conditional sentence for three months in jail to be served intermittently, for a 69 year old illiterate immigrant convicted of unlawful production of marihuana, who was unable to work at his former employment in a restaurant because of arthritis.

[36] None of these cases involved the principal operator and owner of a large grow operation, who had quit his regular and well-paid employment to carry out the operation.

[37] In *Kreutziger*, 2005 BCCA 231, the Court substituted a conditional sentence of two years less a day for a jail sentence of three years because of "a number of extenuating circumstances which must be considered, the most compelling of which is that it has now been seven years since the date of the offence" (para. 21).

[38] In *R v. Tran*, 2004 BCCA 430, the appellant cited *Kreutziger* in support of his argument that because three years had passed since the offence date it would be "counter productive" to send him to jail. The Court rejected that argument, saying (at para. 8):

> ... it is not for this Court to convert a sentence of imprisonment to a conditional sentence when there is no error in law or principle in the sentence when it was imposed, merely because of some delay in the proceedings.

[39] For the same reason, I would not accede to the appellant's argument that the time that has elapsed between his arrest and this appeal should result in a different sentence than that imposed by the sentencing judge.

[40] In the circumstances of this offence and this appellant, the sentencing judge properly emphasized the principles of denunciation and deterrence. The sentence of incarceration is proportionate to the gravity of the offence and the responsibility of the offender. The offence is driven by greed, and has obvious deleterious effects on the communities in which it appears to thrive. The appellant, for no reasons that would serve to mitigate the circumstances of the offence, turned his back on lawful society, and embarked on a criminal enterprise that endangered his community. I find no basis to interfere with the sentence imposed.

Conclusion

[41] I would grant leave to appeal, and dismiss the appeal.

THACKRAY JA (dissenting):

[42] I have had the opportunity to read and consider the reasons for judgment of my colleague Madam Justice Levine. I cannot agree with her decision that on the facts of this case a jail sentence is appropriate.

• • •

Pre-Sentence Report

[48] The judge had before him the pre-sentence report referred to by counsel in their submissions. The report is dated 8 April 2005 by which time Mr. Wallis had been on bail for nearly two years. The author of the report interviewed Mr. Wallis, his mother, the mother of his daughter and Mr. Wallis' employer. I will replicate parts of the report:

By all accounts subject has positive peer associations and spends his leisure time in constructive activities. His last intimate relationship, a 3 year common-law relationship with a single mother, ended approximately one year ago. He is currently single. He works out at the gym at least three times a week, jogs the seawall and enjoys riding his motorcycle. He is very involved in the life of his 10 year old daughter who is a gifted soccer player. Subject attends as many of her practices and games as possible and has week-end access every second week. He now has a very close relationship with her mother ... . [She] confirmed that subject has always been actively involved in co-parenting her and supporting their child, even during periods when their relationship was strained. She now considers him to be a close friend and confidant. She advises that he also has a positive relationship with her husband and her other child. They often participate in shared family activities on alternate Sundays when subject returns their daughter from her access visit.

EDUCATION, VOCATION, EMPLOYMENT, FINANCES
Subject graduated from secondary school in 1992 and in 1993 completed a 10 month pre-apprentice automotive mechanics program at BCIT. He did not pursue an apprenticeship in that field, choosing instead a higher paying job in a sawmill in order to better provide for his soon to be born child.

... After his arrest he worked for a concrete cutting/coring company in Langley for approximately 6 months before moving on to a decking company in the Aldergrove/Abbotsford area. He worked there for approximately 12 months up until he sold his house in August of last year. He then took some personal time before starting his current job.

Subject now works as an iron worker for [...]. He enjoys his work and feels there is the potential for growth on the job. He hopes to develop the skill level required to become a unionized iron worker. Subject's employer, [...], confirms that subject has worked for him since October 2004 and that he is a valued, hardworking and dedicated employee. [...] is aware of subject's upcoming Court appearance for sentencing in this matter.

Subject's current financial situation is stable. He advises that he is debt free and that he has saved a few thousand dollars for emergencies. In addition to monthly cost of living expenses he pays between $350 and $400 per month in child support. He earns $18.00 per hour.

BEHAVIOUR, EMOTIONAL STATUS
Subject does not have past or current behavioural, emotional, psychological or health issues. He appears to be an average, well-adjusted young man.

SUBSTANCE MISUSE
There is no history of substance misuse.

COURT HISTORY
Present offence.

ATTITUDE AND RECEPTIVENESS TO PREVIOUS AND PROPOSED INTERVENTIONS

Although this is the subject's first criminal conviction, he came to the attention of BC Corrections in August 1992 when he served a 7-day jail sentence re: a motor vehicle infraction through the electric monitoring program. That sentence was completed successfully.

Subject has demonstrated a positive attitude towards community supervision and a willingness to comply with the expectations of any order imposed by the Court.

ATTITUDE AND UNDERSTANDING REGARDING OFFENCE

Subject regrets his behaviour with regards to the present offence. He appears to have rationalized his involvement by conceiving of the operation as a victimless crime and a justifiable, though unconventional, means of earning an income. He now recognized that his thinking was erroneous and that his actions caused many individuals, including his family, to suffer.

[49] The judge noted at paragraph 14 of his reasons that the pre-sentence report "paints a generally positive picture of the defendant, his history and his present circumstances." That understates the positive and supportive nature of the report which was described by *Crown* counsel at the hearing as "more supportive of an accused" than any other he had seen "in recent history." However, apart from noting the author's concern as to the technical suitability of electronic monitoring, the judge made no reference to the report in his reasons for judgment. In this case where the circumstances of the offender had to be of great significance to the sentence, where there was a detailed and positive report and where the position of both counsel was based upon the information supplied in the report, the report deserved a careful analysis.

Supporting Letters

[50] The judge noted that there were eight letters of support. Five of the letters were lost from the Provincial Court file, but copies of three were located in defence counsel's file. The others, including what must be considered an important letter from Mr. Wallis' employer, have not been found. The letter from the employer was referred to in defence counsel's submissions to the judge and the indications are the employer said Mr. Wallis' employment was secure and the employer would accommodate any conditions contained in a conditional sentence order. Nevertheless, the judge said:

> [18] Each of the letter-writers, as might be expected, speaks glowingly of the defendant and most of them express their surprise at learning that he had been charged and convicted of this crime. The vast majority of them describe the defendant's criminal activity as entirely out-of-character for the person they believe him to be.
>
> • • •

And later in his reasons:

> [54] The fact that none of the persons who wrote letters of support for the defendant had any suspicion, let alone knowledge, of his criminal behaviour shows how deceitful he was in his dealings with them. I have borne their ignorance of the defendant's true character in mind in assessing the weight I can attach to their letters.

That latter comment is inappropriate, especially with respect to the message sent to the Court by Mr. Wallis' employer. The judge gave no positive weight to the letters. Rather, he turned the letters against Mr. Wallis on the unusual basis that the writers did not know or suspect his criminal activity. It cannot be an acceptable practice to reject the views of people speaking in support of an accused person and instead turn their support letters against the accused.

. . .

Circumstances of Mr. Wallis

[66] At paragraph 47 the judge set forth mitigating and aggravating factors in Mr. Wallis' case. He then said as follows:

[50] In many of the numerous marijuana grow-operation cases which appear before the courts in this community, the defendant is found to be a mere "gardener" or custodian of the enterprise who is paid a relative pittance for his or her labour. That is not the case here.

[51] Nor is this a case in which an otherwise law-abiding citizen faces severe financial difficulties and succumbs to temptation.

[52] In the present case, the defendant had secure, well-paid employment and was the owner, with his parents, of the house in which the grow-operation was discovered. Instead of being satisfied with his comfortable circumstances, he chose to establish a large, sophisticated and expensive criminal enterprise. It must have taken some considerable time and money to convert the house into a grow-operation and the defendant could have abandoned the enterprise at any time. But such was his *greed* that he pursued its creation without regard for his family members or the public at large.

[53] The defendant submits that his personal circumstances and in particular his relationship with his daughter should be given considerable weight by the court and ought to lead to the imposition of a conditional sentence. This submission, in my respectful opinion, is *breathtaking in its brazen boldness*. Each of the circumstances that counsel for the defendant has outlined existed before the defendant decided to engage in criminal activity. He *callously* put his own desire for illegal gain ahead of concern for his daughter, her mother, his parents and his brother. Now he is asking the court to give both weight and consideration to matters to which he gave neither.

[54] The fact that none of the persons who wrote letters of support for the defendant had any suspicion, let alone knowledge, of his criminal behaviour shows how *deceitful* he was in his dealings with them. I have borne their ignorance of *the defendant's true character* in mind in assessing the weight I can attach to their letters.

[55] The fact that the defendant set up an electrical by-pass in a house located in a residential area is a serious aggravating factor. Once again, it shows the *callousness* of his actions. In the pursuit of his criminal goal, he completely disregarded the safety of his neighbours.

[56] There is no evidence before me as to when the grow-operation was established but it seems self-evident that the defendant must have intended to make use of it for more than a single harvest. It defies logic to suggest that someone motivated by *greed* would incur the expense and risk involved in setting up such a sophisticated operation in order to enjoy the benefits of only one crop.

[57] One must also assume that the defendant had a plan for the distribution and sale of the marijuana produced by the grow-operation, activities that would have involved him in further criminality.

> [58] The foregoing illustrates both the careful and *secret planning* the defendant must have engaged in over some time and the degree of his culpability. These facts must be borne in mind and given appropriate weight in the determination of a fit sentence. [Emphasis added.]

[67] My colleague noted at paragraph 22 of her reasons that the judge "was clearly offended by the appellant's criminal conduct, and for good reason." I have highlighted words in the above quotations that show just how personally offended the judge was over Mr. Wallis' entry into crime and the fact that he kept his criminal activity secret.

[68] It is not the place of the judiciary to take personal offence and turn that into a factor in sentencing. In my opinion the judge being "clearly offended," as can be seen by the above-noted comments, and his use of the supportive letters, led him into error. Furthermore, the fact that Mr. Wallis left a lawful occupation for a criminal enterprise is but one circumstance in the many that should have been weighed and cannot be used, as it was, to overcome all of the mitigating factors.

Danger to the Community

[69] On the issue of danger to the community the judge continued to emphasize the greed of Mr. Wallis and the secretive manner in which he operated:

> [59] Counsel for the defendant submits that the latter no longer poses any danger to re-offend. However, given the secretive manner in which the defendant behaved in the present case and the fact that he was motivated solely by greed, this suggestion must be viewed with some degree of caution, if not scepticism, in my respectful opinion. For my part, I am not satisfied on a balance of probabilities that the safety of the community would not be endangered if this defendant was allowed to serve his sentence in the community.

[70] The judge was concerned that the safety of the community would continue to be endangered if the appellant served his sentence in the community because he was motivated by greed and proceeded in secret in committing the offence. He made no reference to nor explained why he declined to accept the Crown's position that "the safety of the community would not be endangered by the defendant serving his sentence in the community" nor to the Crown's agreement that "a conditional sentence would be consistent with the principles of sentencing set out in sections 718 to 718.2 of the *Criminal Code.*"

[71] The judge did not discuss the factors that must be taken into account in determining whether the appellant was a danger to the community. He focused almost entirely on Mr. Wallis' criminal conduct which he repeatedly said was motivated by greed and carried out in secrecy. My colleague said it correctly when she noted (at paragraph 21) that "motive and manner of carrying out an offence may be relevant factors, but if greed and secrecy were determinative there would be few offenders who would not be found to be a continuing danger to the community."

[72] The sentencing judge's strong disapproval of the appellant's conduct, in my opinion, supplanted an analysis of the proper legal principles. He underemphasized the appellant's personal characteristics in concluding he was at risk to re-offend. His opinion that Mr. Wallis posed a significant risk to re-offend did not have any foundation in the evidence, and thus the conclusion that he posed a risk to the community was not open to be found and he erred in principle in so finding.

[73] This is in keeping with the conclusion reached by Madam Justice Levine who held (at paragraph 24) that the judge's "conclusion that the appellant remained a danger to the community was unreasonable." Thus, as found by both my colleague and myself, the judge erred in his weighing of the evidence. This cannot be compartmentalized and treated as simply an error without a result. It *must* be taken into account by this Court in determining whether the judge had a proper basis for the sentence which he meted out. In that this Court is unanimous that he erred and the error was germane to the sentence, this Court is not bound by his decision as to what was a fit sentence.

• • •

In keeping with that standard, I have no hesitation in saying that the sentence imposed in the case at bar was not a fit sentence. It is a sentence that is detrimental to all directly affected parties and can only be supported on the basis of general deterrence. In this case that is not enough to justify the destabilization of a segment of society.

• • •

[76] The circumstances in *Copeland* were vastly different from those in the case at bar. Mr. Copeland had a significant criminal record and it was held that his previous sentence for another drug offence relating to a grow-operation "obviously had no deterrent effect." Furthermore, if the words of Lowry JA are correct that, since *Su*, custodial sentences have "generally been considered necessary," there are many exceptions to the general rule. The fact that *Su* expressed no more than a general rule was made clear in *R v. Tran*, [2001] BCJ No. 1983, 2001 BCCA 503 where Mackenzie JA said:

> [8] … The learned trial judge rightly, in my view, rejected the submission that *Su* stands for the proposition that a conditional sentence is never appropriate in cases of marihuana cultivation. The circumstances of the particular offender must be considered.

R v. Proulx

[77] While it is instructive to consider previous cases with similar circumstances, *R v. Proulx*, 2000 SCC 5, [2000] 1 SCR 61 remains the leading authority on the interpretation and application of the statutory framework for conditional sentences. As pointed out by my colleague, it provides that in assessing the danger to the community posed by the offender serving his or her sentence in the community, one of the two matters that must be taken into account is the risk of the offender re-offending. She noted that the Chief Justice discussed the relevant factors in assessing that risk including criminal record; compliance with court orders; the nature of the offence; the relevant circumstances of the offence; the offender's personal circumstances, including occupation, lifestyle, family situation, age, and mental state; and the offender's conduct following the commission of the offence.

[78] The judge had before him evidence on all of those factors, but ignored most of them. In determining specifically whether the appellant was a danger to the community he gave no weight to the evidence of the personal characteristics of the appellant, in effect concluding that because the criminal conduct was not predicted by those closest to Mr. Wallis before he offended, the fact that he had not previously offended, was steadily employed, had a positive relationship with his family and friends and expressed remorse for the offence were found of no consequence.

[79] One of the factors that *Proulx* says is to be taken into account is the offender's conduct since the commission of the offence. Separately, the Chief Justice spoke of "subsequent incidents" as an additional factor in assessing the nature of the offence. In the case at bar the crime was committed in 2002 and early 2003 and the charge was laid on 2 June 2003. Mr. Wallis has been on judicial interim release for over four years. There have been no "subsequent incidents" and, as testified to in the supporting letters and in the pre-sentence report, his conduct has been exemplary over that period of time.

Judicial Delay

[80] There is no suggestion that the excessive time from the laying of the charge until now can be laid at the feet of Mr. Wallis. At the oral hearing of this appeal Crown counsel was asked by the Court to explain the long period of time. He was unable to do so. This is not a case wherein it can be said that the offender created a time zone in which to portray himself as a reformed person. It is a case in which the judicial system has moved slowly and Mr. Wallis has demonstrated throughout his resolve to act honestly.

[81] Mr. Wallis has been under and abided by the conditions of the parole order for over four years. That order provides that he keep the peace and be of good behaviour, report to a bail supervisor when directed, remain within British Columbia, not change his address without permission and deposit his passport with the Court. He has done all of this and surrendered himself into custody at each hearing and when reasons for judgment were delivered by the various courts.

[82] In *R v. Tran*, [2005] BCJ No. 1898, 2005 BCCA 430 it was two years from the offence to sentencing. This Court said (at paragraph 8) "it is not for this Court to convert a sentence of imprisonment to a conditional sentence when there is no error in law or principle in the sentence when it was imposed, merely because of some delay in the proceedings." Mr. Tran had a criminal record and was on probation at the time of the offences; thus *R v. Kreutziger*, [2005] BCJ No. 850, 2005 BCCA 231 was distinguished.

[83] In *Kreutziger* the offender was sentenced in 2002 to a three-year term of imprisonment for an offence which occurred in 1998. The total delay between the offence and appeal was seven years. Oppal JA wrote the majority reasons in which he said:

> [21] … While the sentencing judge correctly addressed the principle of general deterrence, there are a number of extenuating circumstances which must be considered, the most compelling of which is that it has new been seven years since the date of the offence. It must be noted that the delay is no fault of the appellant. His counsel at trial is deceased. In my view, *it would now be counterproductive to sentence the appellant to an unconditional term of imprisonment.* [Emphasis added.]

[84] The prison term was set aside and a conditional sentence of two years less a day was imposed. Madam Justice Levine wrote concurring reasons in which she said:

> [25] In my opinion, a sentence of three years incarceration for a first offence of trafficking in a large amount of cocaine could not be said to be unfit *at the time the sentence was pronounced.* …
>
> [26] If it were not for the passage of seven years from the date the offence occurred to the resolution of this appeal, I would not interfere with the sentence that was imposed. *In*

the particular circumstances of this case, however, I agree that it would be counterproductive to send the appellant to prison. [Emphasis added.]

[85] That logic must be applied to the case at bar. No benefit to society can be made out in this case by now putting Mr. Wallis in jail. Indeed, to the contrary, the detriment to his child, her mother and Mr. Wallis' employer and employment are readily obvious. Paraphrasing Madam Justice Levine, it would be counter-productive to send Mr. Wallis to prison.

[86] It must be recognized, in deference to His Honour Judge Lenaghan, that when he delivered his reasons for sentence on 17 June 2005 he could not have predicted two further years would pass before the judicial process would conclude.

Where Imprisonment Would Be "Counter-Productive"

[87] The theme of "counter-productive" imprisonment was applied by this Court in *R v. Godwin*, [2005] BCJ No. 2070, 2005 BCCA 477. Mr. Godwin was sentenced to [a] one-year term of imprisonment for marijuana production, mischief and theft of electricity. This Court substituted that sentence with a conditional one even though the trial judge had relied upon *Su* and *Copeland*. The Court said:

> [21] To take the appellant out of the community and away from the Strathcona Mental Health Team with its co-ordinated resources for vocational rehabilitation, for offences best seen as part of a short period of criminality already significantly punished, seems counter-productive, as both counsel recognized in arriving at the proposed disposition, not only for the appellant, but also for the community. Since being diagnosed [for schizophrenia] the appellant has gained insight into both his chronic condition and his criminal behaviour. He accepts the need for medication and community assistance. Fortunately, in this case, the diagnosis has been made and the required community assistance has been made available, including the necessary medications. Mr. Godwin has been fully compliant. Not all who suffer this terrible illness are so fortunate.

> [22] In our view, counsel fashioned, with the appellant's consent, a punishment best suited to satisfy the principles of sentencing for this offender and this offence. This is precisely the type of case where the guideline set down at para. 13 in *Su, supra*, should not be applied.

[88] In *R v. Shaw*, (2005), 199 CCC (3d) 93, 2005 BCCA 380 this Court recognized the counter-productive result in a case wherein the trial judge had sentenced the offender to two years' imprisonment for the production of marijuana. The Court said:

> [14] … The appellant is working and supporting his spouse and two small infant children as well as caring for his ailing father. No useful purpose will be served by maintaining a custodial sentence.

The Court referred to *Su*, but set aside the custodial sentence in favour of a two year less a day conditional sentence.

Rehabilitation

[89] The issue of rehabilitation seems to have been overlooked by the sentencing judge. In *Proulx*, Lamer CJC, after noting that "offenders who meet the criteria of s. 742.1 will

serve a sentence under strict surveillance in the community instead of going to prison," said:

> [22] The conditional sentence incorporates some elements of non-custodial measures and some other of incarceration. Because it is served in the community, it will generally be more effective than incarceration at achieving the restorative objectives of rehabilitation, reparations to the victim and community, and the promotion of a sense of responsibility in the offender. *However, it is also a punitive sanction capable of achieving the objectives of denunciation and deterrence.* [Emphasis in original.]

[90] In concentrating on the criminal act and deterrence the judge lost sight of the fact that a conditional sentence is punitive and denunciatory and that rehabilitation is a vital factor in sentencing. The evidence would suggest that rehabilitation has already been achieved and in any event there can be no suggestion that it will be accomplished by now jailing Mr. Wallis. Indeed, I would see it as more likely to have the opposite result.

• • •

[96] If in the circumstances of this case Mr. Wallis is to be given a jail sentence it must be that every offender who is a major player in a marijuana grow operation must, regardless of his or her circumstances, go to jail. I say that because it is difficult to imagine any set of circumstances more favourable to an offender than in the case of Mr. Wallis. In *R v. Innes*, [2001] BCJ No. 1713, 2001 BCCA 478, the sentencing judge referred to *Su* and imposed a jail sentence. This Court dismissed the appeal, but the Court said:

> [8] Counsel for the appellant submitted that in saying this [that in cases where there is a large and sophisticated grow operation the Court must primarily address the issues of deterrence and denunciation] the sentencing judge said, in effect, that a conditional sentence is never available where the offence of production involves a high number of plants in a sophisticated grow operation. I agree with counsel that if this is what the sentencing judge meant, it would be wrong.

[97] My colleague, in paragraphs 32 and 33, acknowledges that the principles of sentencing do not preclude the imposition of a conditional sentence for the production of marijuana. Nevertheless, in spite of all of the positive matters weighing in favour of a conditional sentence, she would have him sent to jail based on the principles of denunciation and deterrence.

[98] I do not in any way suggest that those principles are to be undervalued or that there will be many cases where the principal of a significant grow operation will avoid a jail sentence. However, if in the circumstances of this case a jail sentence is found to be required, it would shut the door to conditional sentences for owners of grow operations regardless of all personal characteristics and regardless of all mitigating circumstances.

[99] This is not what was intended by *Proulx* wherein the Chief Justice said at paragraph 44:

> The particular circumstances of the offender and the offence must be considered in each case.

[100] I am of the opinion that the appropriate sentence for this offender in these circumstances is a conditional sentence of 15 months. For over four years Mr. Wallis has lived a lawful and productive life, returned to lawful employment, expressed regret for his sojourn into crime and lived up to his word. During that time he also restored his

parents' financial losses on the house he co-owned with them and in which he carried on the grow operation. All of these actions are reflective of the principles and purposes of sentencing set out in s. 718 of the Code and in *Proulx* and a conditional sentence would fulfill the requirements of both.

[101] I acknowledge the frustration experienced by sentencing judges in trying to discern consistent guidelines from the decisions of this Court and can only make reference again to *Proulx* where Lamer CJC at paragraph 82 emphasized the importance of an individualized approach to sentencing. Sentencing individual offenders for particular crimes requires a consideration of all the facts and circumstances of the particular case. The inevitable result of that process, as Lamer CJC acknowledged, is a variation in sentences imposed for particular crimes.

[102] I would grant leave to appeal, allow the appeal, set aside the sentence imposed by the sentencing judge and substitute a conditional sentence of 15 months.

NOTE

The decisions in *Voong* and *Wallis* are good examples of the observation that the rejection of conditional sentences in "hard cases" almost always results from a conclusion that the combined effect of "denunciation and deterrence" requires custody—that is, that a conditional sentence of imprisonment is inconsistent with the purposes and principles found in ss 718 to 718.2 for this reason. This analytical view requires closer scrutiny, as *Voong* demonstrates. First, although there continues to be some debate about the existence of a general deterrent effect, most sentencing scholars agree that any deterrent effect is a product of the certainty of being caught and the combined impact of arrest, prosecution, conviction, and sentence. There seems to be no evidence to suggest that an increase in sentence alone can produce more general deterrence: see Anthony N Doob & Cheryl Marie Webster, "Sentence Severity and Crime: Accepting the Null Hypothesis" in Michael Tonry, ed, *Crime and Justice* (Chicago: University of Chicago Press, 2003). Consequently, there should be no support for the claim that general deterrence can be enhanced by deciding that a sentence of imprisonment should be custodial rather than community-based on strict conditions, which is essentially what the Supreme Court endorsed in *Proulx*.

As far as denunciation is concerned, in *R v M (CA)*, [1996] 1 SCR 500, a case that antedates the conditional sentence regime, Chief Justice Lamer explained the denunciatory role of sentencing as follows:

> [81] ... Retribution requires that a judicial sentence properly reflect the moral blameworthiness of that particular offender. The objective of denunciation mandates that a sentence should also communicate society's condemnation of that particular offender's conduct. In short, a sentence with a denunciatory element represents a symbolic, collective statement that the offender's conduct should be punished for encroaching on our society's basic code of values as enshrined within our substantive criminal law. As Lord Justice Lawton stated in *R v. Sargeant* (1974), 60 Cr. App. R 74, at p. 77: "[S]ociety, through the courts, must show its abhorrence of particular types of crime, and the only way in which the courts can show this is by the sentences they pass." The relevance of both retribution and denunciation as goals of sentencing underscores that our criminal justice system is not simply a vast system of negative penalties designed to prevent objectively harmful conduct by increasing the cost the offender must bear in committing an enumerated offence. Our criminal law is also a system of values. A sentence

which expresses denunciation is simply the means by which these values are communicated. In short, in addition to attaching negative consequences to undesirable behaviour, judicial sentences should also be imposed in a manner which positively instills the basic set of communal values shared by all Canadians as expressed by the *Criminal Code*.

This recognizes that our criminal law is more than a system of negative sanctions; it is also a "system of values." While disapproval and abhorrence may be the values that need to be expressed in some cases, there are other values that cannot be excluded from the sentencing matrix. These include compassion, mercy, acknowledgment of hardship, maintaining the integrity of family, and encouraging hard work. These values can, in appropriate cases, present expressive needs that diminish what would otherwise be the required denunciatory element of a sentence.

The answer to "hard cases" requires more than simply an attempt to compare sympathetic personal factors with the need to express disapproval of an offence. The focus must be on whether the court, as the official spokesperson for the legal regime, needs to use this occasion to express its disapprobation of this conduct, or are there values that the court ought to be contemplating? Are there other principles or objectives of sentencing that might diminish the comparative significance of denunciation in this case?

The following is a framework that might be useful in dealing with hard cases and the elusive objective of denunciation:

1. *Gravity of the offence does not compel denunciation:* The facts of the offence, or the circumstances of the offender, may mean that a harsh, denunciatory sentence is unnecessary.

2. *Circumstances of offender make denunciatory objective unfair:* Here, the major issue is fairness as a reflection of the values of mercy and compassion. In other words, regardless of the claim for denunciation, is it unfair to make this offender the bearer of that message? The most common claim made is infirmity due to age, illness, or disability and the intrinsic hardship that custody would produce. A similar claim can arise from psychiatric disorders, including substance abuse, where the offender has sought treatment and participated co-operatively in treatment. A good example is the case of *R v Jacobson* (2006), 207 CCC (3d) 270 (Ont CA), a charge of producing and possession of marijuana for the purpose of trafficking. In this case, not only would custody have been "devastating" given the "fragile and precarious" mental state of the accused, but there was some reason to suspect that the depression and addiction had some bearing on the offence. This brings into play the "reduced gravity" claim raised above. A similar, albeit less compelling argument, can arise in the case of a youthful first offender. In *R v Kutsukake* (2006), 213 CCC (3d) 80, the Ontario Court of Appeal reduced a 12-month custodial sentence for criminal negligence causing death to an 18-month conditional sentence. Sharpe JA commented that

> [20] … the only purpose to be served by requiring the appellant to serve her sentence in an institution would be denunciation of the unlawful conduct. That factor does not, in the circumstances of this case, outweigh the other factors that point to a conditional sentence. Moreover, I am of the view that denunciation of the unlawful conduct can be achieved without the appellant returning to jail. She has seen the inside of a prison and has served 41 days in custody. I am persuaded that an additional sentence to be served in the community under the conditions described below will serve as a sufficient denunciation of her conduct, consistent with the principles established in *Proulx*.

3. *Hardship to third party makes denunciatory objective unfair:* Again the value reflected here is fairness, and one of the best examples is in *R v Bunn*, 2000 SCC 9, [2000] 1 SCR 183, one of the companion cases to *Proulx*. There, a conditional sentence was approved in the case of a "breach of trust" theft by a lawyer. The offender was the sole caregiver to a disabled spouse. Custody for him would have produced considerable hardship for her.

4. *Denunciatory message can be expressed without custody:* The classic example is *R v Hollinsky* (1995), 103 CCC (3d) 472, a case that antedates the conditional sentence regime and involved an offender convicted of a driving offence after causing the death of his close friend. The offender began lecturing to high school students about the human effects on him and other survivors of his conduct. This was approved in *Proulx* and popped up again recently in *Kutsukake* (2006), 213 CCC (3d) 80 (Ont CA). If the goal is to denounce, and perhaps even to deter others who are similarly situated, conveying the message directly is likely more effective than a judicial pronouncement within the walls of a courtroom. Counsel can be imaginative in attempting to replicate this process. The key is to identify the right audience and an appropriate method of reaching them that will demonstrate the offender's commitment to the message.

VI. SUPERVISION AND BREACH

Of central importance to the effectiveness of conditional sentencing are measures relating to supervision and breach.

The procedure and principles applicable in cases of alleged breach of conditions have proved problematic, and ss 742.6 and 742.7 of the Code were amended in an attempt to clarify some of the difficulties: see SC 1999, c 5 and SC 2004, c 12. This matter has not been considered by the Supreme Court to date. For further exposition of these issues, though written before the amendments of 1999, see the editorial "Breach of a Conditional Sentence by Allegedly Committing Another Offence" (1998) 3 Can Crim L Rev 1. Of course, a breach may occur for reasons other than commission of a new crime.

The general view now accepted is that an allegation of breach, even if allegedly by the commission of a new offence, leads to a renewal or revival of the original sentencing hearing. On this basis, it is preferable that the offender be brought before the original sentencing judge. If the Crown establishes a breach on a balance of probabilities, the offender may seek to establish a reasonable excuse. Section 742.6(4) requires that an allegation of a breach be supported by the supervisor's report and that "where appropriate" this report should have as attachments the "signed statements of witnesses." The jurisprudence recognizes that s 742.6(4) simplifies the presentation of evidence on this point: see *R v McIvor*, 2008 SCC 11, [2008] 1 SCR 285. But there remain some ambiguities.

R v Laporte (RD)
2011 MBCA 96

STEEL JA (Hamilton and MacInnes JJA concurring):

[1] This is a Crown appeal from the dismissal of an allegation of breaching a conditional sentence order. The issue is whether the motions judge erred when she held that

under s. 742.6(4) of the *Criminal Code* (the *Code*) the *only* permissible form of proof was by way of documentary evidence.

Relevant Legislation

[2] Section 742.6(4) of the *Code* states as follows:

> 742.6(4) An allegation of a breach of condition must be supported by a written report of the supervisor, which report must include, where appropriate, signed statements of witnesses.

[3] Other relevant sections are ss. 742.6(5) and (8), which state as follows:

> 742.6(5) The report is admissible in evidence if the party intending to produce it has, before the hearing, given the offender reasonable notice and a copy of the report.
>
> 742.6(8) The offender may, with leave of the court, require the attendance, for cross-examination, of the supervisor or of any witness whose signed statement is included in the report.

Background Facts

[4] On April 17, 2009, a two-year conditional sentence order (CSO) was imposed on Mr. Laporte (the accused) following conviction on one count of assault with a weapon. One of the mandatory conditions of the CSO, pursuant to s 742.3(1) of the *Code*, was to "keep the peace and be of good behaviour."

[5] On November 24, 2010, the accused was arrested as a result of a domestic violence complaint. It was therefore alleged that he had breached his CSO by failing to "keep the peace and be of good behaviour." The accused contested the alleged breach and was remanded into custody.

[6] An Allegation of Non-Compliance with a CSO form (the allegation form) was prepared by a police officer and forwarded to the accused's conditional sentence supervisor, who then prepared the supervisor's report required under s. 742.6(4). The supervisor attached to his report a copy of the CSO and the allegation form.

[7] The allegation form is a printed form and indicates that the allegation is "police initiated" as opposed to "supervisor initiated." It contains some basic information, such as the name and address of the accused, the date of arrest, and the police report number of the domestic violence complaint, after which there is then the typed statement:

> I allege that the offender has breached the following condition or conditions of the conditional sentence order:
>
> 1. Fail to keep the peace and be of good behavior—November 24th, 2010.

[8] The allegation form is not signed by the officer whose information is contained in that form, but by another officer for him. There are no facts or circumstances of the alleged breach contained in the supervisor's report, apart from the reference to a numbered police report. There is no dispute that the witnesses' statements were not attached to the supervisor's report and that the supervisor had no personal knowledge of the breach.

[9] However, the police report referenced in the allegation form does include the signed witness statements. The accused acknowledged that he had received the full police report with the signed statements that supported the allegation. The judge was informed

that dates for the hearing of the alleged CSO breach had been set and at that time the Crown would produce witnesses to give *viva voce* evidence as to the alleged breach.

[10] Before the date set for the hearing of the CSO breach, the accused filed a motion claiming that the supervisor's report was not properly before the court since the signed witness statements were not attached to it and therefore the allegation should be dismissed for lack of compliance with s. 742.6(4) of the *Code*.

[11] Agreeing with the accused, the motions judge held that *R. v. McIvor*, 2008 SCC 11, [2008] 1 S.C.R. 285, addressed the Crown's obligations in terms of the contents of the supervisor's report pursuant to s. 742.6(4). That section requires the attachment of signed witness statements "where appropriate." The Supreme Court in *McIvor* held that where a conditional sentence supervisor has no personal knowledge of the alleged breach, it is "appropriate" and therefore mandatory that signed witness statements be attached to the supervisor's report.

[12] However, the motions judge further determined, and this is the point at issue on appeal, that (at para. 40):

> ... Section 742.6 does not offer the Crown a choice of proving the breach either by the documentary evidence specified in s. 742.6(4) or by a hearing with oral evidence. The only route to proof of the breach is by the documentary evidence, unless defence counsel seeks leave to cross-examine on the documentary evidence (the supervisor's report and any signed attached witness statements) ... .

[13] Ultimately, because the motions judge found that the supervisor's report was insufficient and the Crown was precluded from calling *viva voce* evidence, the charge was dismissed.

[14] The Crown appeals, arguing that:

   (a) the motions judge erred in law in finding that the Crown could not present *viva voce* evidence at a breach hearing;

   (b) the motions judge erred in law by finding that the supervisor's report did not meet the requirements of s. 742.6(4) of the *Code*; and

   (c) the motions judge erred in law by dismissing the allegation of a breach of a CSO prior to hearing the evidence that the Crown intended to present to prove the breach.

[15] It is interesting to note that the focus of the arguments in front of the motions judge were quite different than the arguments in front of us. At the motion, the Crown argued that the report's reference to the police file incorporated that file by reference. Thus, at best, the Crown had complied with the section or, at worst, there was a technical deficiency. At the appeal hearing, as is not unusual, the focus of the arguments changed. The Crown argued that the deficiency was irrelevant because it intended to call *viva voce* evidence from the witnesses whose statements had formed the basis of the allegation. The accused's position was that the requirements of the section were mandatory and only documentary proof of the breach was acceptable.

· · ·

[20] Section 742.6 generally sets out the procedure for determining whether an offender has breached a condition of a CSO. The hearing must be commenced within 30 days, or as soon thereafter as is practicable, after the offender's arrest or the compelling

of his appearance. At the conditional sentence breach hearing, the Crown must show, on a balance of probabilities, that the offender has breached a condition of the CSO. The burden is then on the offender to establish a reasonable excuse. See *Carpentier*.

[21] Sections 742.6(4) and (5) provide a method that allows the Crown to prove the breach by way of an exception to the normal rules of evidence. The breach may be proven by the written report of the supervisor, which report must include, where appropriate, signed statements of witnesses. This method may be used subject to providing appropriate notice to the offender (s. 742.6(5)). Where leave of the court has been obtained, the offender may cross-examine the supervisor or any witness whose signed statement is included in the report (s. 742.6(8)).

[22] In *McIvor*, the Supreme Court had to decide when it was "appropriate" (s. 742.6(4)) for the supervisor's report to include the signed statements of the witnesses in order to prove the allegation of a breach of condition. In doing so they had to consider the conditional sentence hearing as a whole. The court held that it was the intention of Parliament that allegations of non-compliance with a CSO be dealt with in a simple, efficient and expedited manner while still maintaining procedural fairness (see para. 18).

[23] So, for example, the contents of documentary evidence submitted under the section are still subject to the usual common law evidentiary rules relating to hearsay as well as the possibility that the maker of the document may be required to provide *viva voce* evidence pursuant to s. 742.6(8). In this way, the court is assured of a certain level of reliability in the evidence produced at a conditional sentence breach hearing. See *McIvor* at paras. 24–26.

[24] What *McIvor* did not decide was whether the Crown *must* prove its case by way of documentary evidence, as argued by the accused, or whether the provision is an "evidentiary shortcut" (at para. 5) which simply allows the Crown to prove the breach by adducing in documentary form the evidence it would otherwise have had to present in the usual way by *viva voce* evidence.

[25] The accused argues that reading the provisions as a whole, it is clear that Parliament intended for this simplified procedure to be mandatory. The procedure chosen by Parliament was a balancing of its desire for swift adjudication with the need to be fair to the accused. Since the allegation of a breach suspends the running of the conditional sentence, there is a need for a quick resolution. This is accomplished by requiring the Crown to proceed, not only within a short period of time, but also by way of documentary evidence. It is only the person whose jeopardy is at stake who can consent to a lengthening of the process by requesting leave of the court to cross-examine the witnesses at a *viva voce* hearing.

[26] With respect to the accused's argument as to the need for fairness to the accused, I would point out that a decision on the nature of the proof required under this section does not affect the time requirement that the hearings be held within 30 days or as soon as practicable. Moreover, the section as a whole provides for several avenues of relief with respect to the suspension of the running of the sentence upon the allegation of a breach depending upon whether the accused is released or detained in custody while awaiting adjudication. See ss. 742.6(12), 742.6(14), 742.6(15) and 742.6(16).

[27] I agree with the Crown that s. 742.6(4) is an evidentiary shortcut that does not preclude proof by way of *viva voce* evidence. While *McIvor* did not authoritatively decide that issue, the tenor of the decision certainly supports the Crown's argument. Indeed, it

is Justice Charron (writing for the Court) in that decision who refers to the procedure in s. 742.6(4) as an evidentiary shortcut and an enabling provision. She states (at para. 23):

> In my view, the meaning of s. 742.6(4) is plain when considered against the default evidentiary rules … subject to leave being granted requiring the attendance of any of the witnesses, the legislative scheme simply allows the Crown to prove the breach by adducing in documentary form the evidence it would otherwise have been required to present in the usual way by *viva voce* evidence. As such, it is an enabling provision. …

[28] Section 742.6(4) of the *Code* does not prevent the Crown from proving a breach of a CSO according to the usual rules of evidence. The *Code* presumes the existence of a body of rules of evidence derived from the common law. When the *Code* modifies or abolishes those common law rules, it does so through explicit language (see *R. v. Hawkins*, [1996] 3 S.C.R. 1043 at para. 57). The language in the disputed section does not explicitly preclude the use of the ordinary rules of evidence.

[29] In the case of *R. v. Balaj*, 2010 BCSC 362, 252 C.C.C. (3d) 560, the Crown filed a report from the supervisor, but did not file a signed witness statement from the key witness who it wished to call to provide *viva voce* testimony at the breach hearing. There too the accused argued that s. 742.6(4) cannot be treated simply as an evidentiary shortcut, but as a condition precedent to a lawful breach hearing. The court in *Balaj* recognized that the word "must," as it is used in s. 742.6(4), does not indicate that compliance with the shortcut is a prerequisite to proof of the breach. Rather, it is a prerequisite to reliance on the shortcut (at para. 34):

> … In my view, it is apparent from a plain reading of the provision that s. 742.6(4) has to do with what must be provided at a hearing in the event that the Crown seeks to avail itself of the evidentiary "short cut" afforded to it to establish breaches on CSOs, rather than providing a bar to proceeding at all.

[30] I note that the court in *Balaj* distinguished cases coming to a contrary conclusion, such as *R. v. Barnes*, [2009] O.J. No. 2351 (S.C.J.) (QL), and *R. v. Cruz (J.)*, [2001] O.T.C. 702 (S.C.J.), on the basis that in those cases no reasonable notice was given to the offender of the nature of the anticipated evidence. That is not the case here, where the defence acknowledged that it received both the supervisor's report and the police report on the same day and that the police report contained copies of the signed witness statements.

[31] This interpretation is consistent with the approach previously taken in Manitoba. Although decided before *McIvor*, the decision in *Le* (which does not appear to have been provided to the motions judge in this case) is still relevant to the issue at hand.

[32] In that case, Chartier P.J. (as he then was) allowed the Crown to call *viva voce* evidence in a breach hearing where the supervisor's report did not include signed statements from those who witnessed the alleged breaches. The court concluded that an evidentiary shortcut does not deprive the Crown of recourse to the default rules of evidence (at para. 21):

> … Section 742.6 allows the Crown to make its case in a fashion that is normally not allowed. In my view, the fact that the Crown can proceed in that manner does not prevent it from doing it the old-fashioned way. … It can do so by using the documentary evidence method provided by 742.6(4) or … it can call viva voce evidence. Irrespective of whether the Crown

avails itself of the streamlined process found in s. 742.6, it is never precluded from calling viva voce evidence on a conditional sentence breach hearing.

[33] There are other legislative examples of evidentiary shortcuts which allow, but do not require or replace, proof of an alleged fact by way of *viva voce* evidence. For example, s. 254(4) of the *Code* requires proof that blood samples were taken by or under the direction of a qualified medical practitioner. This can be established by a certificate as is provided for under s. 258(1)(h)(i) or (ii). This can also be proven by reliable, admissible *viva voce* evidence. The Crown may prove its case by either method. See *R. v. Richardson (W.C.)* (1998), 199 N.B.R. (2d) 203 at para. 19 (Q.B.). For other examples see also the *Canada Evidence Act* at s. 30(1) and the *Competition Act* at s. 70(4).

Conclusion

[34] Section 742.6(4) does not create mandatory requirements for the prosecution of a breach. It simply provides an evidentiary shortcut. Absent a provision requiring the Crown to prove a CSO breach according to the evidentiary shortcut, the Crown is entitled to choose whether to rely on the enabling provision.

[35] The motions judge erred in law in finding that the Crown could not present *viva voce* evidence at a breach of conditional sentence hearing. As a result of this error in law, she prematurely dismissed the allegation prior to hearing the evidence that the Crown intended to present to prove the breach. I would allow the appeal.

[36] However, I would add a caution. In *McIvor*, Justice Charron commented that, "[i]n accordance with Parliament's intent to keep the process simple and expeditious, however, the supervisor and the witnesses should not routinely be required to attend the hearing" (at para. 5). The same caution should be applied here. While the Crown has the discretion to prove the alleged breach by way of *viva voce* evidence, it should whenever possible and appropriate use the more expeditious method provided for in the legislation. It should not use its discretion to defeat the intention of Parliament that the majority of breach hearings be proven by way of documentary evidence.

[37] Given my decision on this point, it is unnecessary to deal with any of the other grounds of appeal. In particular, I make no comment on whether, when the Crown does wish to rely on the evidentiary shortcut, the practice of incorporating the police file by reference rather than physically attaching the signed witness statements to the supervisor's report is sufficient compliance with the section and the dictates of the Supreme Court of Canada in *McIvor*. In addition, I make no comment as to whether filing such a report with the court complies with the time requirement that the hearing be commenced within 30 days or as soon thereafter as is practicable. Although those arguments were addressed at the provincial court level, the appeal hearing was focussed on the motions judge's refusal to allow the Crown to prove its case by way of *viva voce* evidence and her consequent premature dismissal of the breach allegation.

[38] In different circumstances, I would have quashed the order of the motions judge and remitted the matter to the Provincial Court for hearing, which was the remedy requested by the Crown. However, as all counsel agreed, the accused has served his conditional sentence. The breach alleged was one of a failure to be of good behaviour and keep the peace. It arose out of a domestic violence complaint, which is the subject of a separate charge. Given all of the facts, in my view, it would not be fit and just at this stage

to subject the accused to the possibility of further penalties in respect of the CSO when he has served that sentence. The importance of this decision lies in the guidance it offers for future situations, not for this particular accused and this particular alleged breach.

In the absence of a reasonable excuse, the Crown may seek to vary the original sentencing order in any of the ways set out in s 742.6(9). The nature of the variation sought will vary with the gravity (including the repetition) of the breach. The variation, however, modifies the original sentence and is not a new sentence.

R v Bailey
2012 ABCA 165

MARTIN JA (Hunt and McDonald JJA concurring):

[1] This is a Crown appeal from an intermittent sentence imposed in response to the respondent's repeated breaches of his conditional sentence order (CSO).

Background Information

[2] The necessary background information may be reduced to the following narrative. In 2007, the respondent pleaded guilty to two counts of trafficking in a controlled substance. He was sentenced to a CSO of two years less one day with numerous conditions relating to residency, reporting, etc. He absconded and breached most of these conditions, some more than once. However, we are told that he did not re-offend. As the respondent explained it, he experienced great difficulty holding a job because of the reporting conditions, so he decided to move away from the jurisdiction and start over elsewhere. He apparently succeeded in doing so, as he has been gainfully employed the entire time and involved in a steady relationship. We are advised he continues to enjoy the support of his partner and her family.

[3] The respondent was eventually found and charged with twelve violations of his CSO. He was brought back for sentencing before the same judge who had imposed the CSO. The Crown asked the judge to collapse the CSO and require the respondent to serve the remainder of that time in custody. The judge sentenced the respondent to 90 days imprisonment, to be served intermittently so that he could continue with his employment and rehabilitation.

[4] The Crown appeals, arguing that:

   (i)   an intermittent sentence is unavailable for the breach of a CSO, and

   (ii) in any event, the sentence is unfit because it is too low.

Analysis

[5] The respondent's counsel agrees with the former submission, and so do we; an intermittent sentence of imprisonment is not available in these circumstances. Specifically, s. 742.6(9) of the *Criminal Code* spells out the only sanctions available when sentencing for a breach of a conditional sentence order:

... the court may

    (a) take no action;

    (b) change the optional conditions;

    (c) suspend the conditional sentence order and direct

        (i) that the offender serve in custody a portion of the unexpired sentence, and

        (ii) that the conditional sentence order resume on the offender's release from custody, either with or without changes to the optional conditions; or

    (d) terminate the conditional sentence order and direct that the offender be committed to custody until the expiration of the sentence.

[6] As s. 742.6 makes clear, a breach of a CSO is not a *Criminal Code* offence like all others. Rather, proof of the breach may be established by a written report from the offender's supervisor, and proven on a balance of probabilities. Further, and most importantly for these purposes, a finding that the offender has breached the CSO can only result in a modification of the sentence already imposed, not the imposition of a new sentence. As was noted in *R v Casey* (2000), 128 OAC 185 at para 13, 141 CCC (3d) 506, leave to appeal to SCC refused, [2000] SCR vii:

> ... in the event of a breach of a conditional sentence order, s. 742.6(9) limits the powers of the court. The court cannot impose a second sentence for the breach itself (as occurs when an offender is charged with the offence of breach of probation); nor can the court increase the length of the sentence originally imposed. The court can only deal with the unexpired part of the conditional sentence within the limits prescribed in s. 742.6(9).

See also *R v McIvor*, 2006 BCCA 343 at para 52, 228 BCAC 300 (*per* Hall J.A. in dissent), aff'd on other grounds 2008 SCC 11, [2008] 1 SCR 285, and *R v LeBorgne*, 2005 NSCA 156, 238 NSR (2d) 355 at para 13.

[7] Section 732(1) of the *Criminal Code* dictates when an intermittent sentence may be imposed. Those terms require that the sentence must not exceed 90 days, and the offender be subject to a probation order when not in custody. Between these two provisions (s. 742.6 and s. 732(1)), there is no room for an intermittent sentence imposed in response to the breach of a CSO. More specifically, the imposition of an intermittent sentence is not among the four statutorily prescribed options of s. 742.6(9). And while it may be argued that the third option of s. 742.6(9) (which directs the offender to serve a portion of the unexpired sentence in custody) allows that portion of the sentence to be served intermittently, s. 732(1) stands in the way. As mentioned, that provision only allows a sentence to be served intermittently if it is of 90 days or less. Here the sentence was more than 90 days; it was two years less one day. Additionally, s. 742.6(9) requires the CSO, not a probation order, to govern the offender's conduct whenever he was not in custody.

[8] I agree with *R v Langmaier*, 2009 SKCA 57, 331 Sask R 14, and *R v Ng*, 2007 ONCA 183, that an intermittent sentence cannot be imposed in response to a breach of a CSO. Pursuant to the existing legislation, the judge could have sentenced the respondent to an actual term of imprisonment of 90 days or less for the breaches, but she could not direct that he be allowed to serve that time on an intermittent basis. I would therefore allow that part of the Crown's appeal.

[9] With regard to Crown's appeal from the quantum of the sentence, the sentencing judge made it clear that some jail time was required as people who found themselves in

the respondent's position should not be allowed to so blatantly ignore a court order. However, it is equally clear that the judge was reluctant to impose a sentence greater than necessary to convey that message, and particularly not one that would interfere with the respondent's rehabilitation, which the judge saw as virtually complete. These conclusions were supported by the record and are entitled to deference. We are advised that the respondent has now served 152 days in prison. I think in all of the circumstances, that is sufficient.

[10] In the result, I agree that the sentencing judge erred in law by imposing an intermittent sentence in response to these offences, but I do not agree the respondent should be sentenced to an additional term of imprisonment for these violations.

The situation with regard to appeals from decisions at breach hearings is not entirely clear but the cases support several observations. If the Crown fails to prove a breach, there is no appeal because there is no statutory basis for it: see *R v Cross*, 2004 NSCA 156, 192 CCC (3d). The offender may appeal against either the finding that there was a breach or the variation of sentence ordered by the court. The premise for this is that the breach hearing is a continuation of the original sentencing.

PROBLEMS

1. Smith and Jones were married in 2006. In January 2016, Jones told Smith that she had decided to leave the relationship. Although she planned to stay in the matrimonial home temporarily, Jones told Smith that she did not want to continue a sexual relationship. On February 15, 2016, an argument escalated and Smith struck Jones. Jones left the matrimonial home and Smith was charged with common assault. It was a term of release that he not communicate with Jones. Smith subsequently persisted in his efforts to contact Jones, notwithstanding his undertaking pursuant to s 515(2) not to communicate with her. On one occasion, he met her on the street, and grabbed her by the shoulders and pushed her. These events were part of an unsolicited and unwanted attempt at reconciliation and resulted in new criminal charges—two charges of breach of an undertaking plus assault and criminal harassment. Smith pleaded guilty to all charges.

Smith has no previous record. Aside from these offences, he could be considered a person of good character. In the year prior to the end of his marriage, five close relatives had died, including his grandparents, who had raised him. He was under a great deal of stress and had no one close to him to discuss his personal problems. Smith had spent a month in pre-trial custody prior to his sentencing. A psychiatrist called by Smith testified that the period of pre-trial custody had impressed Smith with the seriousness of his conduct and its impact on Jones. The psychiatrist offered the opinion that Smith represented no danger to Jones or anyone else and proposed a treatment plan that, in his view, could be implemented in the community through regular sessions with him but that would not be available, at least through someone with his expertise, inside an institution.

Defence counsel agrees that these offences usually call for a term of imprisonment, but argues for a conditional sentence of 18 months. Crown counsel agrees with the 18 months, but argues that the sentence should be served in custody. How would you sentence Smith?

2. Mary Blanchard is a 30-year-old Indigenous woman from a small northern Ontario community. She has been living in Thunder Bay for the past 10 years. On January 20, 2016, she was charged with two counts of trafficking, arising from the sale of small quantities of marijuana and cocaine to an undercover officer. On March 10, 2016, she entered guilty pleas to the two charges and the sentencing was adjourned until April 15 to allow for the preparation of a pre-sentence report.

The pre-sentence report indicates that Blanchard has a substantial record for property offences and drug possession. In 2010 and 2011, she was convicted of trafficking in small quantities of cocaine. She received short jail terms (30 and 60 days) for both offences. It is apparent that she has suffered from both alcohol and substance abuse for many years. During this time she has not been gainfully employed for any substantial period. On two occasions she entered a residential drug treatment program, but both times left prematurely. She is a talented artist but has produced very little work since leaving her community in 1998.

Blanchard's counsel is seeking a conditional sentence. She has advised the court that a bed is waiting for Blanchard in a residential drug treatment centre. She has also submitted that Blanchard has been reunited with her family, who want her to return home after she has completed the treatment program. Her community, although poor, has organized an after-care schedule that involves a number of community volunteers who will be available to Blanchard on a daily basis to assist her in avoiding a relapse. They have also arranged for her to teach art part time at the local school.

The Crown has argued that trafficking requires a punitive response. Moreover, no hard evidence has been adduced about Blanchard's home community that would support reliance on s 718.2(e).

Can the judge consider Blanchard's Aboriginal background? Since most trafficking cases lead to incarceration, would a conditional sentence produce unjustifiable disparity? Can a conditional sentence be crafted that would meet the principles articulated in *Proulx* and *R v Wells*, 2000 SCC 10, [2000] 1 SCR 207?

3. On April 2, 2016, Rankin was charged with "over 80" after being stopped in a holiday roadside check in London, Ontario. After consulting with his lawyer, he had agreed to a breathalyzer test and blew 130 mg alcohol/100 ml of blood. He appeared in court on April 20 and a trial date was set for August 12, 2016. In the meantime, his conditional sentence supervisor learned about this new charge on April 19 and commenced a breach application under s 742.6 on the basis that Rankin had "failed to keep the peace and be of good behaviour as evidenced by the commission of a new offence"—namely, "impaired driving/over 80." As a result, a warrant was issued for Rankin's arrest on April 21. On May 2, 2016, Rankin was arrested in Windsor at his home and subsequently released by the officer in charge pursuant to s 742.6(1)(e) on a promise to appear in court on May 20 to answer the breach allegation.

Assume that Rankin appears in court on May 20 without counsel and asks for time to retain one.

- If he has no counsel, can the matter be adjourned to June 15, even though this is more than 30 days from the date of his arrest?
- Can the court proceed to entertain the breach allegation on June 15, given that it is based on a criminal charge for which he has not been found guilty or pleaded guilty to the new charge?

- What happens to the conditional sentence pending the determination of the breach?
- At the hearing of the breach allegation, can the Crown make its case without *viva voce* evidence by filing the allegation, complete with the supervisor's report and any written statements in support plus proof of notice upon the offender?
- Assume that you ultimately hear the breach allegation on September 5, 2016. Does it matter whether Rankin was convicted or acquitted on the impaired charge?
- If you decide that the breach has been made out, what remedy under s 742.6(9) is appropriate?
- If you are considering some time in custody short of termination, what effect will this have on the conditional sentence?
- If you are concerned about the duration of the sanction, can you give any credit for the time between the breach allegation and the breach finding?

FURTHER READING

Armstrong, Sarah et al. *International Evidence Review of Conditional (Suspended) Sentences: Final Report* (Glasgow: Scottish Centre for Crime and Justice, 2013).

Johnson, Sarah. "Outcomes of Probation and Conditional Sentence Supervision: An Analysis of Newfoundland and Labrador, Nova Scotia, New Brunswick, Saskatchewan and Alberta, 2003/2004 to 2004/2005" (2006) 26 Juristat Service Bull 7.

Pomerance, Renee M. "The New Approach to Sentencing in Canada: Reflections of a Trial Judge" (2013) 17 Can Crim L Rev 305.

Roberts, Julian V. *The Virtual Prison: Community Custody and the Evolution of Imprisonment* (Cambridge: Cambridge University Press, 2004).

Sanders, Trevor & Julian V Roberts. "Public Attitudes Toward Conditional Sentencing: Results of a National Survey" (2000) 32 Can J Behav Sci 199.

Collateral Sentencing Orders

I. INTRODUCTION

The sentencing process is often largely consumed by questions about which of the sanctions discussed in the previous chapters—for example, imprisonment, monetary penalties, and probation—should be imposed on an offender; however, this is only part of the puzzle. Various provisions in the *Criminal Code*, RSC 1985, c C-46, as amended, either permit or require the imposition of other orders as part of a sentence, such as driving prohibitions, weapons and firearms prohibitions, orders to provide a DNA sample to the state, and orders to comply with the *Sex Offender Information Registration Act*, SC 2004, c 10. In each case, care should be taken to ensure that the applicable statutory requirements are met before any of these orders are sought or imposed. Moreover, it is essential to distinguish between those situations in which an order *may* be imposed at the discretion of the court and those situations where it *must* be imposed.

II. DRIVING PROHIBITIONS

One of the most common and long-standing collateral sentencing orders is the prohibition found in s 259(1) of the *Criminal Code*, which requires an order prohibiting the offender from operating a motor vehicle if he or she is convicted of impaired operation, driving "over 80"—that is, with a blood alcohol level over 80 mg of alcohol in 100 ml of blood—or refusing to provide a breath sample:

    (a) for a first offence, for not more than three years and not less than one year;
    (b) for a second offence, for not more than five years and not less than two years;
    (c) for each subsequent offence, not less than three years.

Although this section is applied primarily in the case of offences committed by persons operating motor vehicles, it also applies to those operating a vessel, aircraft, or railway equipment.

Section 259(2) of the Code permits, at the discretion of the court, a similar prohibition following a conviction under ss 220 (criminal negligence causing death); 221 (criminal negligence causing bodily harm); 236 (manslaughter); 249 (dangerous operation of a motor vehicle, vessel, aircraft, or railway equipment); 249.1 (flight from a law enforcement officer causing death or bodily harm); 250 (failure to keep watch of a person towed on the water); 251 (unseaworthy vessel and unsafe aircraft); 252 (failure to stop at the scene of an accident); or 255(2) and (3) (impaired driving or driving over 80 causing bodily harm or death) when the offence was committed by means of a motor vehicle, vessel, aircraft, or railway equipment.

Under s 259(2), the length of the prohibition depends on the maximum sentence for the underlying offence. The duration of the prohibition can be significant. If the offender is sentenced to life imprisonment (s 259(2)(a)) or is liable to be sentenced to life imprisonment (s 259(2)(a.1)), the prohibition may be for life. This potential arises regularly in cases of drunk driving where the offender is convicted of criminal negligence causing death (s 220), an offence that carries a maximum sentence of life imprisonment. This is not the case with dangerous driving causing death (s 249(4)), where the maximum sentence is 14 years' imprisonment. Lengthy prohibitions may have a dramatic impact on a person's life. Consequently, the issue is often seriously litigated, resulting in a considerable body of case law on the appropriate length of driving prohibitions in these circumstances.

Prohibition orders made under s 259 of the *Criminal Code* apply throughout Canada. In addition to this sanction, provincial and territorial legislation provides for contemporaneous licence suspensions, the length of which varies by jurisdiction. Recently, some provinces have passed legislation establishing alcohol ignition interlock device programs. These devices are affixed to motor vehicles and thwart attempts to operate the ignition if the driver cannot provide a breath sample that is free of alcohol (or within an acceptable limit). Typically, these programs are geared at drivers who have completed prohibitions and suspensions and are considered to be "reinstated" drivers: see e.g. *Highway Traffic Act*, RSO 1990, c H.8, s 41.2. Section 259 of the Code was recently amended to provide a discretion to the sentencing judge to permit a person subject to a prohibition to drive, after prescribed minimum periods, if he or she registers in an alcohol interlock device program established by a province: see ss 259(1.1) to (1.4).

It is often said that the harshest penalty faced by those convicted of drunk-driving-related offences is the inconvenience posed by the driving prohibition. Keep in mind that anyone who fails to comply with a driving prohibition faces a further criminal charge (s 259(4)), with a maximum penalty of five years' imprisonment when prosecuted by indictment. If it were not for the prohibition, many of those charged with this offence might well plead guilty. Of course, the inflexible approach of the *Criminal Code* would be difficult to dislodge from a political perspective. Do you think exceptions to driving prohibitions should be made for people who require their cars to maintain their employment or discharge important family obligations (such as child or elder care)? If such exemptions were made available, would they be undermined by the prohibitive cost of insurance in these circumstances? How could they be effectively enforced?

III. FIREARMS PROHIBITIONS

The following provisions form part of a comprehensive reform of firearms legislation enacted by SC 1995, c 39, s 139, which replaced Part III of the *Criminal Code* in its entirety. It contains a restructured mandatory prohibition (s 109) and a discretionary prohibition (s 110). The mandatory prohibition is broader in its application than were its predecessors. Beyond offences involving violence, it now applies to a number of weapons offences and to offences under ss 6 and 7 of the *Controlled Drugs and Substances Act*, SC 1996, c 19.

A. Criminal Code, Sections 109 to 110

Mandatory prohibition order

109(1) Where a person is convicted, or discharged under section 730, of

(a) an indictable offence in the commission of which violence against a person was used, threatened or attempted and for which the person may be sentenced to imprisonment for ten years or more,

(b) an offence under subsection 85(1) (using firearm in commission of offence), subsection 85(2) (using imitation firearm in commission of offence), 95(1) (possession of prohibited or restricted firearm with ammunition), 99(1) (weapons trafficking), 100(1) (possession for purpose of weapons trafficking), 102(1) (making automatic firearm), 103(1) (importing or exporting knowing it is unauthorized) or section 264 (criminal harassment),

(c) an offence relating to the contravention of subsection 5(1) or (2), 6(1) or (2) or 7(1) of the *Controlled Drugs and Substances Act*, or

(d) an offence that involves, or the subject-matter of which is, a firearm, a cross-bow, a prohibited weapon, a restricted weapon, a prohibited device, any ammunition, any prohibited ammunition or an explosive substance and, at the time of the offence, the person was prohibited by any order made under this Act or any other Act of Parliament from possessing any such thing,

the court that sentences the person or directs that the person be discharged, as the case may be, shall, in addition to any other punishment that may be imposed for that offence or any other condition prescribed in the order of discharge, make an order prohibiting the person from possessing any firearm, cross-bow, prohibited weapon, restricted weapon, prohibited device, ammunition, prohibited ammunition and explosive substance during the period specified in the order as determined in accordance with subsection (2) or (3), as the case may be.

(2) An order made under subsection (1) shall, in the case of a first conviction for or discharge from the offence to which the order relates, prohibit the person from possessing

(a) any firearm, other than a prohibited firearm or restricted firearm, and any cross-bow, restricted weapon, ammunition and explosive substance during the period that

(i) begins on the day on which the order is made, and

(ii) ends not earlier than ten years after the person's release from imprisonment after conviction for the offence or, if the person is not then imprisoned or subject to imprisonment, after the person's conviction for or discharge from the offence; and

(b) any prohibited firearm, restricted firearm, prohibited weapon, prohibited device and prohibited ammunition for life.

(3) An order made under subsection (1) shall, in any case other than a case described in subsection (2), prohibit the person from possessing any firearm, cross-bow, restricted weapon, ammunition and explosive substance for life.

(4) In subparagraph (2)(a)(ii), "release from imprisonment" means release from confinement by reason of expiration of sentence, commencement of statutory release or grant of parole.

(5) Sections 113 to 117 apply in respect of every order made under subsection (1).

Discretionary prohibition order

110(1) Where a person is convicted, or discharged under section 730, of

(a) an offence, other than an offence referred to in any of paragraphs 109(1)(a), (b) and (c), in the commission of which violence against a person was used, threatened or attempted, or

(b) an offence that involves, or the subject-matter of which is, a firearm, a cross-bow, a prohibited weapon, a restricted weapon, a prohibited device, ammunition, prohibited ammunition or an explosive substance and, at the time of the offence, the person was not prohibited by any order made under this Act or any other Act of Parliament from possessing any such thing,

the court that sentences the person or directs that the person be discharged, as the case may be, shall, in addition to any other punishment that may be imposed for that offence or any other condition prescribed in the order of discharge, consider whether it is desirable, in the interests of the safety of the person or of any other person, to make an order prohibiting the person from possessing any firearm, cross-bow, prohibited weapon, restricted weapon, prohibited device, ammunition, prohibited ammunition or explosive substance, or all such things, and where the court decides that it is so desirable, the court shall so order.

(2) An order made under subsection (1) against a person begins on the day on which the order is made and ends not later than ten years after the person's release from imprisonment after conviction for the offence to which the order relates or, if the person is not then imprisoned or subject to imprisonment, after the person's conviction for or discharge from the offence.

(3) Where the court does not make an order under subsection (1), or where the court does make such an order but does not prohibit the possession of everything referred to in that subsection, the court shall include in the record a statement of the court's reasons for not doing so.

(4) In subsection (2), "release from imprisonment" means release from confinement by reason of expiration of sentence, commencement of statutory release or grant of parole.

(5) Sections 113 to 117 apply in respect of every order made under subsection (1).

The following cases address a number of technical and conceptual issues that relate to the imposition of these provisions. These cases refer to the predecessor provisions of ss 109 and 110.

R v Keays
(1983), 10 CCC (3d) 229 (Ont CA)

DUBIN JA:

This appeal brought by the Crown raises issues with respect to the interpretation of s. 98(1) of the *Criminal Code*, which provides as follows:

98(2) Where a person is convicted of an indictable offence in the commission of which violence against a person is used, threatened or attempted and for which the offender may be sentenced to imprisonment for ten years or more or of an offence under section 83, the court shall, in addition to any other punishment that may be imposed for that offence, make an order prohibiting him from having in his possession any firearm or any ammunition or explosive substance for any period of time specified in the order that commences on the day the order is made and expires not earlier than

(a) in the case of a first conviction for such an offence, five years, and

(b) in any other case, ten years,

after the time of his release from imprisonment after conviction for the offence.

In this case the accused was convicted of possession of a weapon for a purpose dangerous to the public peace, and the evidence disclosed that during the commission of that offence, an act of violence occurred.

Following his conviction, the Crown introduced into evidence the criminal record of the respondent, which disclosed two prior convictions for robbery while armed. Both those convictions preceded the date of the proclamation of s. 98(1) of the *Criminal Code*.

The learned trial judge held that since the convictions for robbery while armed preceded the effective date of s. 98(1), they were irrelevant and thus treated the conviction for possession of a weapon for a purpose dangerous to the public peace as a first conviction and limited the prohibition period to that of five years.

In this respect we think that he erred. In our view, it is not a case of a first conviction under s. 98(1) if a person convicted for an offence described in s. 98(1) has been previously convicted of such an offence even though such an offence had been committed prior to the proclamation of s. 98(1) into law. To interpret the section in this manner is not giving it a retrospective effect. Retrospectivity does not occur by merely bringing into play facts which have preceded the enactment.

. . .

In responding to the appeal, counsel for the respondent supported the judgment on two alternative grounds. He first argued that s. 98(1) is only applicable if the offence for which the accused had been convicted is an offence for which a person could not be convicted without committing an act of violence. Obviously, a person who is convicted of the offence of possession of a weapon for a purpose dangerous to the public peace could do so without committing an act of violence or threatening violence. However, in this case the evidence clearly disclosed that an act of violence was committed. In our view, once it is shown that a person has been convicted of an indictable offence in the commission of which violence against the person is used, threatened or attempted and for which the offender may be sentenced to imprisonment for 10 years or more, s. 98(1) becomes applicable, notwithstanding that the offence for which the accused has been convicted could have been committed without violence. That matter has been fully resolved by the judgment of this court in *R v. Broome* (1981), 63 CCC (2d) 426, 24 CR (3d) 254, and on that ground also the respondent fails.

However, a further point was made by counsel for the respondent which was not canvassed before the trial judge in light of the ground relied on by him in disposing of this matter. As has been noted, the Crown adduced evidence that the respondent in this case had been previously convicted on two occasions for robbery while armed. If those armed robberies were accompanied by violence, then the order under s. 98(1) must be one for not less than 10 years. But to constitute a second offence under s. 98(1) the person must have been previously convicted of an indictable offence in the commission of which violence against the person was used, threatened or attempted and for which the offender could have been sentenced to imprisonment for 10 years or more. But, by definition, a person could commit robbery while armed without an act of violence. Section 302(d) provides:

302. Every one commits robbery who ...
      (d) steals from any person while armed with an offence weapon or imitation thereof.

Thus mere proof of a conviction for robbery while armed does not constitute proof that an act of violence was actually committed during the commission of the offence.

Since this matter was not canvassed before the learned trial judge, we think the Crown should be given the opportunity to prove whether, during the course of the commission of the two armed robberies upon which the Crown relies, the accused had committed any acts of violence.

In the result therefore, the appeal will be allowed, the order under appeal set aside and the matter remitted to the trial judge to afford the Crown the opportunity of adducing evidence with respect to the two prior convictions.

Appeal allowed.

R v Avery
(1986), 30 CCC (3d) 16 (NWTCA)

HARRADENCE JA (dissenting):

The respondent Frederick Allen Avery was convicted of an offence under s. 85 of the *Criminal Code*. Following this conviction, a firearms prohibition order was entered against Mr. Avery on June 18, 1985. The order prohibited the respondent from possessing firearms, ammunition or explosive substances for a period of five years.

On August 13, 1985, the respondent was charged with violating the firearms prohibition order, contrary to s. 98(12) of the *Criminal Code*, when in an apparent attempt to comply with the order, Mr. Avery sold a rifle to one Mr. Bourque. The rifle was impounded and the respondent charged.

The trial judge dismissed the charge on the ground that the firearms prohibition order, made pursuant to s. 98(1) of the *Criminal Code*, was defective in that it did not contain the mandatory provision required by s. 98(13) specifying a reasonable period of time within which the respondent could dispose of firearms already in his possession. The Crown appeals.

• • •

I deal first with the argument that a prosecution under s-s. (12) may be supported where the order fails to comply with s-s. (13). Such an interpretation is to construe the word "shall" as other than imperative.

Further, this construction continues to expose the person against whom the order is made to criminal prosecution, not because of wrongdoing on his part but because he has been denied the benefit of the protection Parliament has mandated he shall have. He has been denied this protection through no fault of his own but because the court failed to give effect to the mandatory provisos of s-s. (13) of the *Criminal Code* of Canada.

• • •

I am therefore of opinion that if the period required by s-s. (13) is not contained in the order, then the legal mechanism by which s-s. (12) can be brought to bear is not in place and the section is not available to create an offence for breach of the prohibition.

This in no way detracts from the validity of the order and the prohibition it contains is in full force and effect. An offence for its breach is created by another section of the *Criminal Code*. I have in mind s. 88 of the *Criminal Code* of Canada. However, a prosecution under that section would enjoy little chance of success if a firearm was in lawful possession prior to the making of the order and a reasonable time for its disposition had not expired at the time the charge was laid. The protection contained in s-s. (13) against the mischief created in the previous enactment would not be contravened.

• • •

There is one final point to illustrate the important nexus of the reasonable disposal period in s. 98(13) to the *actus reus* in s. 98(12). The prosecution must not only prove the wrongful deed; it is legally incumbent upon the Crown at some point in the proceedings and whether or not by a primary or secondary burden of proof, to show that the crime was committed without a legal excuse. By the addition of s. 98(13), and limited to the facts of *Avery*, Parliament has pre-empted this Crown argument. This proposition is consistent with the genesis of this unique *actus reus*. As Glanville Williams explains (*ibid.*, p. 19):

> A further step must now be taken. *Actus reus* includes, in the terminology here suggested, *not merely the whole objective situation that has to be proved by the prosecution, but also the absence of any ground of justification or excuse*, whether such justification or excuse be stated in any statute creating the crime or implied by the courts in accordance with general principles.

(Emphasis added.)

As the accused could not through his conduct have committed the wrong physical act which Parliament contemplated, dismissal of the charge under s. 98(12) was proper and the appeal will be dismissed.

KERANS JA (Laycraft CJ concurring):

This is a Crown appeal from an acquittal on a charge, under s. 98(12) of the *Criminal Code*, of possession of a weapon in violation of an earlier judge's order prohibiting possession as a consequence of a conviction for violent crime.

The fact was not denied that the accused was in possession of a gun in contravention of the terms of a prohibition order made March 20, 1985, and entered June 18, 1985, pursuant to s. 98. The earlier order (which by happenstance had been made by him) was "defective." This was correct in the sense that he had failed to make any order under s. 98(13) nor indeed to address his mind to the issue posed by that subsection, which provides:

> 98(13) An order made pursuant to subsection (1), (2), (6) or (7) shall specify therein a reasonable period of time within which the person against whom the order is made may surrender to a police officer or firearm officer or otherwise lawfully dispose of any firearm or any ammunition or explosive substance lawfully possessed by him prior to the making of the order, and subsection (12) does not apply to him during such period of time.

This provision is not without relevance in this case because the offence occurred within four months after the order and came to light because the accused was trying to sell his gun in an apparent attempt to rid himself of it in rough compliance with the prohibition. The learned trial judge, admirably aware of his own earlier failing, perceived that he had unfairly exposed the accused to this charge.

• • •

In this case the accused could have, and did not, seek relief from the original error by appeal if not writ. In the fact of his having failed to do so, he must obey the order which he chose to let stand. When he argues now that he should not be convicted for the breach of it because it is bad, he is saying he did not have to obey it. A collateral attack is nothing less than a request for an affirmation of defiance.

The reason for the rule is that the law must encourage respect for due process by itself respecting it. It is a rule of practical necessity. For example, in *R v. Adams* (1978), 45 CCC (2d) 459, 6 CR (3d) 257, [1979] 2 WWR 108 (BCCA), an accused appealed a conviction for escape from lawful custody on the ground that his original detention was illegal. Craig JA observes at p. 469:

> [i]f a trial Judge permitted an accused to go behind a warrant of committal ... the judge would be holding, in effect, that the jailer had no right to detain the accused, yet the jailer would have to detain the accused because the warrant was still subsisting.

Worse, can a jailer refuse to detain because he thinks the committal bad, and wait until he is charged before demonstrating it is bad? The rule is designed to avoid an invitation to anarchy.

The great difficulty with the rule is that it can work a harsh result on an unsophisticated accused who, like the accused before us, fails to appreciate the need to make a direct attack on a bad order. His relative lack of blameworthiness cannot avoid favourable contrast, in cases of this sort, with errors by judicial officers, as often as not compounded by other errors by governmental officials. The accused's situation in such a case obviously stirs sympathy. Very often, I suspect, the Crown does not proceed with charges *ex debito justitiae*. Sometimes, as here, the Crown is less sympathetic than are the courts. Unfortunately, perhaps, the Crown discretion is not directly reviewable. Fortunately, the power to grant a discharge permits Canadian courts in most cases to offer relief where the blameworthiness of the accused is minimal: see *R v. Campbell and Mlynarchuk* (1972), 10 CCC (2d) 26, 21 CRNS 273, [1973] 2 WWR 246.

• • •

I would allow the appeal and declare the accused guilty of a breach of the order which he indubitably breached. In the circumstances, however, I would invoke s. 662.1(1) and grant him an absolute discharge.

Appeal allowed.

NOTE

What about constitutionality? Does the mandatory prohibition offend s 12 of the Charter? For a number of years there has been a controversy over whether the remedy known as a constitutional exemption applied to mandatory prohibitions. In some cases, courts held that the effect of a sanction that is otherwise valid constitutionally might be so disproportionate in the circumstances of the particular offender that it supported a claim under s 12 of the Charter. As a result, some courts upheld the statutory provision, but granted an exemption to the offender: see e.g. *R v Chief* (1989), 51 CCC (3d) 265 (YCA), and *R v Netser* (1992), 70 CCC (3d) 477 (NWTCA), cases involving claims that the offender was a subsistence hunter. Other courts held either that the provision is valid and should be applied or that the provision should be struck down, without allowing for an intermediate remedy such as the constitutional exemption: see e.g. *R v Kelly* (1990), 59 CCC (3d) 497 (Ont CA), a case involving police officers who were convicted of assault causing bodily harm, arising from an incident when they were off duty.

Since this controversy first arose, there have been two important developments. First, the *Criminal Code* has been amended through the addition of s 113 to accommodate specific exemptions relating to subsistence hunting as well as to other situations that may amount to a "virtual prohibition against employment." Second, in *R v Ferguson*, 2008 SCC 6, [2008] 1 SCR 96, the Supreme Court held that a constitutional exemption is not an appropriate remedy for a mandatory sentence alleged to violate s 12: see the discussion in Chapter 17, The Charter and Sentencing.

Consider *R v Wiles*, below, in which the Supreme Court examined s 109 and the impact of s 12 of the Charter in the context of a marijuana production conviction.

R v Wiles
2005 SCC 84, [2005] 3 SCR 895

CHARRON J (McLachlin CJ and Major, Bastarache, Binnie, LeBel, Deschamps, Fish, and Abella JJ concurring):

[1] Does the mandatory weapons prohibition order under s. 109(1)(c) of the *Criminal Code*, RSC 1985, c. C-46, when imposed upon conviction of the offence of production of cannabis, violate the appellant's right "not to be subjected to any cruel and unusual treatment or punishment" guaranteed by s. 12 of the *Canadian Charter of Rights and Freedoms*? If so, is the infringement a reasonable limit prescribed by law as can be demonstrably justified in a free and democratic society under s. 1 of the *Charter*? These are the constitutional questions raised on this appeal.

[2] Mr. Wiles entered a plea of guilty on two charges of unlawfully producing cannabis, contrary to s. 7(1) of the *Controlled Drugs and Substances Act*, SC 1996, c. 19 ("*CDSA*"), the second offence having been committed while he was on release in respect of the first. The marihuana grow operation was discovered on the first occasion when the police responded to a 911 call made accidentally by one of Mr. Wiles' daughters. At this time, the police noted that Mr. Wiles possessed six firearms, all properly stored and licensed. The firearms were left in his possession. At sentencing, the Crown sought the mandatory prohibition orders under s. 109(1)(c) of the *Criminal Code* in addition to the sentence jointly agreed upon by counsel. Under the terms of s. 109, a 10-year minimum prohibition order is mandatory upon first conviction of any one of certain enumerated drug offences (s. 109(2)). Upon subsequent convictions, the prohibition order is for life (s. 109(3)). Mr. Wiles challenged the constitutionality of s. 109(1)(c), alleging that the imposition of the mandatory weapons prohibition orders constitutes "cruel and unusual punishment" in violation of s. 12 of the *Charter*. The relevant legislative and *Charter* provisions are annexed.

[3] The Crown concedes that a weapons prohibition order constitutes a "treatment or punishment" within the meaning of s. 12 of the *Charter*. In my view, this concession is well made. Although the purpose of the prohibition order is primarily preventative, in taking away the privilege to possess weapons, it may have some punitive effect on the offender. The question then is whether the loss of this privilege upon conviction of the offence of production is "cruel and unusual."

[4] This Court has dealt with s. 12 on many occasions and there is no controversy on the test that must be met. Treatment or punishment which is disproportionate or "merely excessive" is not "cruel and unusual": *R v. Smith*, [1987] 1 SCR 1045, at p. 1072. The treatment or punishment must be "so excessive as to outrage standards of decency": *Smith*, at p. 1072; *R v. Goltz*, [1991] 3 SCR 485, at p. 499; *R v. Luxton*, [1990] 2 SCR 711, at p. 724. The court must be satisfied that "the punishment imposed is *grossly* disproportionate for the offender, such that Canadians would find the punishment abhorrent or intolerable": *R v. Morrisey*, [2000] 2 SCR 90, 2000 SCC 39, at para. 26 (emphasis in original).

[5] The court must first determine whether the treatment or punishment is grossly disproportionate for the individual offender having regard to all contextual factors. Relevant factors may include: the gravity of the offence, the personal characteristics of the offender, the particular circumstances of the case, the actual effect of the treatment or punishment on the individual, relevant penological goals and sentencing principles, the existence of valid alternatives to the treatment or punishment imposed, and a comparison of punishments imposed for other crimes in the same jurisdiction: see *Morrisey*, at paras. 27-28. If the treatment or punishment is grossly disproportionate for the individual offender in light of all relevant contextual factors, the court proceeds to determine whether the infringement can be justified under s. 1 of the *Charter*. If it is not disproportionate for the individual offender, the court must still consider whether the treatment or punishment is disproportionate having regard to reasonable hypotheticals. In *Goltz*, it was made clear that reasonable hypotheticals cannot be "far-fetched or only marginally imaginable" (p. 515). They cannot be "remote or extreme examples" (p. 515). Rather they should consist of examples that "could commonly arise in day-to-day life" (p. 516).

[6] Mr. Wiles presented no evidence as to his need for the firearms found in his possession and made no argument that the prohibition orders had any particular impact upon him. He bases his constitutional argument, rather, on the general effect of the mandatory weapons prohibition, essentially raising two grounds. First, he contends that by virtue of its mandatory nature, s. 109(1)(c) does not permit a distinction between big marihuana grow operators and small ones. To make his point, he raises the hypothetical of a 75-year-old grandmother experimenting with growing a single marihuana plant on the kitchen windowsill who is caught and charged under s. 7(1) of the *CDSA*. This hypothetical offender would be subject to the same minimum weapons prohibition as the large commercial producer. On this point, Mr. Wiles asks this Court to draw on its analysis in *Smith* where the mandatory imposition of a minimum seven-year jail sentence for the offence of importing narcotics was held to be unconstitutional, essentially on the basis of its grossly disproportionate effect on hypothetical offenders. Second, Mr. Wiles submits that s. 109(1)(c) is grossly disproportionate because it does not require any consideration as to whether the underlying offence involved violence or whether the individual offender poses a future risk to public safety.

[7] At the sentencing hearing, Chief Judge Batiot found that the mandatory prohibition infringed s. 12 of the *Charter* because there was not necessarily a nexus between the purpose of the mandatory prohibition—the reduction of the risk of future violence—and the offence of production under s. 7 of the *CDSA* ((2004), 110 CRR (2d) 1, 2003 NSPC 14). With respect to this particular offender, he noted that "but for" s. 109, there would not be any mention of a firearms prohibition, as it would have been "irrelevant," given that the accused's firearms were legally stored, and not used to defend his grow operation (para. 16).

Therefore, the fact that the mandatory prohibition attached to all offences under s. 7(1) without regard to whether the individual accused posed a risk of future violence rendered it "grossly disproportionate" and a violation of the accused's right not to be subjected to cruel and unusual punishment. Similarly, because s. 109 did not provide for discretion not to impose the prohibition in cases, such as the one at hand, where the accused did not present "an actual or potential danger with [a] firearm" (para. 41), the accused's right was not minimally impaired, and the violation could not be upheld as a demonstrably justified limit under s. 1. The sentencing judge therefore read down the section to provide for a discretionary rather than mandatory order and declined to make the prohibition orders.

[8] Bateman JA for the Nova Scotia Court of Appeal, Oland and Hamilton JJA concurring, overturned the sentencing judge's decision, holding that the test for an infringement of s. 12 had not been met ((2004), 220 NSR (2d) 126, 2004 NSCA 3). The Court of Appeal found that there was a connection between the mandatory prohibition and s. 7 offences, based on evidence presented at the hearing as to the frequency with which firearms are used to protect grow-operations against theft, to the point, as noted by the sentencing judge (at para. 17), that in any raid, the police will assume guns are present and will take the necessary precautions for the officers' safety. The Court of Appeal also found that the sentencing judge failed to take into account the ameliorative effects of the exception provided for by s. 113 of the *Criminal Code* in cases where the prohibition would result in a deprivation of livelihood or sustenance. In Bateman JA's opinion, this provision eliminated those cases where the imposition of a mandatory prohibition might be found to be "grossly disproportionate."

[9] I agree with the Court of Appeal. Mr. Wiles has not established that the imposition of the mandatory weapons prohibition orders constitutes cruel and unusual punishment. As noted by the Court of Appeal, the prohibition has a legitimate connection to s. 7 offences. The mandatory prohibition relates to a recognized sentencing goal—the protection of the public, and in particular, the protection of police officers engaged in the enforcement of drug offences. The state interest in reducing the misuse of weapons is valid and important. The sentencing judge gave insufficient weight to the fact that possession and use of firearms is not a right or freedom guaranteed under the *Charter*, but a privilege. It is also a heavily regulated activity, requiring potential gun-owners to obtain a licence before they can legally purchase one. *In Reference re Firearms Act (Can.)*, [2000] 1 SCR 783, 2000 SCC 31, this Court held that requiring the licensing and registration of firearms was a valid exercise of the federal criminal law power. If Parliament can legitimately impose restrictions on the possession of firearms by general legislation that applies to all, it follows that it can prohibit their possession upon conviction of certain criminal offences where it deems it in the public interest to do so. It is sufficient that Mr. Wiles falls within a category of offenders targeted for the risk that they may pose. The sentencing judge's insistence upon specific violence, actual or apprehended, in relation to the particular offence and the individual offender takes too narrow a view of the rationale underlying the mandatory weapons prohibition orders.

[10] Insofar as the individual offender is concerned, there is no evidence as to any effect that the prohibition orders will have on Mr. Wiles, apart from the loss of the firearms already in his possession. Since he was legally in possession of the firearms, the sentencing judge inferred that he was a recreational hunter and shooter. Even assuming that to be the case, the loss of this privilege would not support the sentencing judge's finding of gross

disproportionality. As a twice convicted producer of a controlled substance, Mr. Wiles' loss of the privilege to possess firearms for recreational purposes falls far short of punishment "so excessive as to outrage our standards of decency." In addition, the mandatory provision does not have a grossly disproportionate effect having regard to any reasonable hypothetical. Again here, I agree with the Court of Appeal that the sentencing judge did not properly weigh the ameliorative effect of s. 113 of the *Criminal Code* which permits the court to lift the order for sustenance or employment reasons. As stated by Bateman JA, "[t]his is a key companion provision to s. 109(1)(c) which would eliminate, where appropriate, any unacceptable consequences of a firearms prohibition" (para. 57).

[11]   For these reasons, I would dismiss the appeal.

IV. DNA DATABANK ORDERS

In 1998, Parliament enacted the *DNA Identification Act*, SC 1998, c 37, a piece of legislation that amended the *Criminal Code* in two important ways. First, it created a specific power for the seizure, with a warrant, for bodily samples for investigative purposes. Second, it provided for the establishment of a DNA databank and provided judges with the power to order that, in certain circumstances, samples be taken from offenders for the purposes of creating a databank of information for investigative purposes. The legislation has undergone several amendments over the years, the most recent of which were made by the *Protection of Communities and Exploited Persons Act*, SC 2014, c 25. Note that the *Criminal Code* makes the distinction between "primary designated offences" (considered to be the more serious offences in the *Criminal Code*) and "secondary designated offences." Lists of both groups of offences are found in s 487.04.

Order—primary designated offences
    487.051(1) The court shall make an order in Form 5.03 authorizing the taking of the number of samples of bodily substances that is reasonably required for the purpose of forensic DNA analysis from a person who is convicted, discharged under section 730 or found guilty under the *Youth Criminal Justice Act* or the *Young Offenders Act*, of an offence committed at any time, including before June 30, 2000, if that offence is a primary designated offence within the meaning of paragraphs (a) and (c.02) of the definition *primary designated offence* in section 487.04 when the person is sentenced or discharged.

Order—primary designated offences
    (2) The court shall make such an order in Form 5.03 in relation to a person who is convicted, discharged under section 730 or found guilty under the *Youth Criminal Justice Act* or the *Young Offenders Act*, of an offence committed at any time, including before June 30, 2000, if that offence is a primary designated offence within the meaning of any of paragraphs (a.1) to (c.01) and (c.03) to (d) of the definition *primary designated offence* in section 487.04 when the person is sentenced or discharged. However, the court is not required to make the order if it is satisfied that the person has established that the impact of such an order on their privacy and security of the person would be grossly disproportionate to the public interest in the protection of society and the proper administration of justice, to be achieved through the early detection, arrest and conviction of offenders.

Order—persons found not criminally responsible and secondary designated offences
    (3) The court may, on application by the prosecutor and if it is satisfied that it is in the best interests of the administration of justice to do so, make such an order in Form 5.04 in relation to

(a) a person who is found not criminally responsible on account of mental disorder for an offence committed at any time, including before June 30, 2000, if that offence is a designated offence when the finding is made; or

(b) a person who is convicted, discharged under section 730 or found guilty under the *Youth Criminal Justice Act* or the *Young Offenders Act*, of an offence committed at any time, including before June 30, 2000, if that offence is a secondary designated offence when the person is sentenced or discharged.

In deciding whether to make the order, the court shall consider the person's criminal record, whether they were previously found not criminally responsible on account of mental disorder for a designated offence, the nature of the offence, the circumstances surrounding its commission and the impact such an order would have on the person's privacy and security of the person and shall give reasons for its decision.

The purposes and mechanics, as well as the impact of these provisions on individual privacy interests, are discussed in the two cases below. Note that these decisions interpret a previous version of the legislation, but they are still helpful. Under the current provisions, under s 487.051(2), in relation to primary designated offences, a sentencing judge may decline to make the order if the offender is able to satisfy the statutory criteria. Under s 487.051(3), in relation to secondary designated offences, the same concepts are in play, but the onus is on the prosecutor.

R v Hendry
(2001), 161 CCC (3d) 275 (Ont CA)

[This judgment addresses a number of cases in which judges failed to make orders concerning secondary designated offences.]

ROSENBERG JA (Doherty and Borins JJA concurring):

• • •

Statutory Provisions

[3] In summary, the legislative scheme provides that after an offender has been found guilty the judge may order that he or she provide samples for forensic DNA analysis. These samples are then sent to the DNA data bank for analysis. The DNA profile is stored in the data bank and is available for comparison with evidence obtained from other investigations. In these appeals, the offenders had committed a secondary designated offence after the scheme came into effect or a designated offence (primary or secondary) before the scheme came into effect. In either case, the judge has a discretion to make the order where it is in the best interests of the administration of justice to do so. That discretion is described in similar terms under s. 487.051(1)(b) (secondary designated offences) and s. 487.052 (designated offences committed before the scheme came into effect).

[4] Section 487.04 defines "primary designated offences" and "secondary designated offences." The former include sexual interference under s. 151. The latter include break and enter (s. 348) and assault (s. 266). The other relevant sections are the following:

487.051(1) Subject to section 487.053, if a person is convicted, discharged under section 730 or, in the case of a young person, found guilty under the *Young Offenders Act*, of a designated offence, the court (a) shall, subject to subsection (2), in the case of a primary designated offence, make an order in Form 5.03 authorizing the taking, from that person, for the purpose of forensic DNA analysis, of any number of samples of one or more bodily substances that is reasonably required for that purpose, by means of the investigative procedures described in subsection 487.06(1); or (b) may, in the case of a secondary designated offence, make an order in Form 5.04 authorizing the taking of such samples if the court is satisfied that it is in the best interests of the administration of justice to do so. (2) The court is not required to make an order under paragraph (1)(a) if it is satisfied that the person or young person has established that, were the order made, the impact on the person's or young person's privacy and security of the person would be grossly disproportionate to the public interest in the protection of society and the proper administration of justice, to be achieved through the early detection, arrest and conviction of offenders. (3) In deciding whether to make an order under paragraph (1)(b), the court shall consider the criminal record of the person or young person, the nature of the offence and the circumstances surrounding its commission and the impact such an order would have on the person's or young person's privacy and security of the person and shall give reasons for its decision. 487.052(1) Subject to section 487.053, if a person is convicted, discharged under section 730 or, in the case of a young person, found guilty under the *Young Offenders Act*, of a designated offence committed before the coming into force of subsection 5(1) of the *DNA Identification Act*, the court may, on application by the prosecutor, make an order in Form 5.04 authorizing the taking, from that person or young person, for the purpose of forensic DNA analysis, of any number of samples of one or more bodily substances that is reasonably required for that purpose, by means of the investigative procedures described in subsection 487.06(1), if the court is satisfied that it is in the best interests of the administration of justice to do so. (2) In deciding whether to make the order, the court shall consider the criminal record of the person or young person, the nature of the offence and the circumstances surrounding its commission and the impact such an order would have on the person's or young person's privacy and security of the person and shall give reasons for its decision. ... 487.054 The offender or the prosecutor may appeal from a decision of the court made under subsection 487.051(1) or 487.052(1).

• • •

Burden of Proof

[9] Under s. 487.051(1)(b) and s. 487.052, the trial judge is to make a DNA data bank order if "satisfied" that it is in the best interests of the administration of justice. The section does not place the persuasive burden on either the Crown or defence. Once again some assistance can be obtained from the sentencing regime in resolving the question of the burden of proof. In *R v. Proulx* (2000), 140 CCC (3d) 449 (SCC), at para. 121, Lamer CJC rejected a submission from the Crown that the offender bears the legal burden of proof where the offender is seeking a conditional sentence: In matters of sentencing, while each party is expected to establish elements in support of its position as to the appropriate sentence that should be imposed, the ultimate decision as to what constitutes the best disposition is left to the discretion of the sentencing judge.

[10] He pointed out, however, at para. 122, that the offender will ordinarily bear the tactical burden of coming forward with information to support imposition of a conditional sentence. Having said this, in practice, it will generally be the offender who is best

situated to convince the judge that a conditional sentence is indeed appropriate. Therefore, it would be in the offender's best interests to establish those elements militating in favour of a conditional sentence. ...

[11] In my view, similar considerations apply to the making of the DNA data bank order. Strictly speaking, there is no burden on either Crown or defence under s. 487.051(1)(b) or s. 487.052. However, under s. 487.052 the order is made "on application by the prosecutor" and as a practical matter it will be the Crown that asks the judge to exercise his or her discretion under s. 487.051(1)(b). Thus, in my view the Crown bears an evidential burden to produce sufficient information to raise the issue. The trial judge must then be satisfied, after weighing and balancing all the relevant considerations, that the order should be made.

· · ·

Best Interests of the Administration of Justice

[17] In *R v. Briggs*, Weiler JA dealt with many of the issues that may arise in interpreting s. 487.051(1)(b) and s. 487.052. In particular, she held as follows:

(1) Whether or not there is evidence at the scene of the crime of which the offender was convicted that would likely yield a DNA profile of the perpetrator is not necessarily a relevant consideration.

(2) The phrase "best interests of the administration of justice" does not import as a prerequisite to making the order that there be reasonable and probable grounds to believe a further offence will be committed.

(3) The state interest in obtaining a DNA profile from an offender is not simply law enforcement by making it possible to detect further crimes committed by this offender. Rather, the provisions have much broader purposes including the following:

　　1. Deter potential repeat offenders;
　　2. Promote the safety of the community;
　　3. Detect when a serial offender is at work;
　　4. Assist in the solving of "cold" crimes;
　　5. Streamline investigations; and
　　6. Most importantly, assist the innocent by early exclusion for investigative suspicion or in exonerating those who have been wrongfully convicted.

(4) Provisions in the *Criminal Code* and the *DNA Identification Act* restricting the use that can be made of the DNA profile and protecting against improper use of the information offer significant protection of the offender's privacy.

(5) The procedures for seizures of bodily substances authorized by the provisions are of short duration and involve no, or minimal, discomfort. There is a minimal intrusion with no unacceptable affront to human dignity.

(6) A person convicted of a crime has a lesser expectation of privacy.

(7) The trial judge is entitled to look at the offender's entire record, not just the crimes that may be designated offences.

[18] I would summarize the effect of these holdings as follows. In balancing the offender's right to privacy and security of the person against the state interests in obtaining the offender's DNA profile, the court must consider the following. The legislation offers

significant protections against misuse of the DNA profile information, thus minimizing an improper intrusion into the offender's privacy. Having been convicted of a designated offence, the offender already has a reduced expectation of privacy. In the ordinary case of an adult offender the procedures for taking the sample have no, or at worst, a minimal impact on the security of the person. Thus, in the case of an ordinary adult offender there are important state interests served by the DNA data bank and few reasons based on privacy and security of the person for refusing to make the order.

[19] I do, however, wish to highlight one aspect of the DNA data bank legislative scheme that is of some concern. As Weiler JA points out in *Briggs*, a purpose of the *DNA Identification Act* is to protect the privacy of individuals with respect to personal information. To that end, the legislation includes some safeguards against appropriation of the information collected by the data bank for purposes other than those set out in the Act. The main purpose of the legislation is to provide the mechanism for comparison of DNA profiles gathered in a criminal investigation with the DNA profiles in the data bank. If there is a match, the Commissioner of the RCMP may inform the law enforcement agency of that fact along with any information, other than the DNA profile itself, that is contained in the data bank in relation to that DNA profile. Unauthorized use is an offence under the Act.

[20] Thus, use of the DNA data bank information resembles the use of fingerprint information that law enforcement agencies collect and have collected for many years under the *Identification of Criminals Act*, RSC 1985, c. I-1, with this important difference. So far as I am aware, fingerprint information can only be used for comparison purposes. It does not provide any personal information about the offender. A DNA profile is different. It is capable of providing the most intimate details of the person because it can show the person's genetic makeup. The DNA sample can be analyzed to determine, for example, if the person carries certain genes that make the person more susceptible to disease. It is not beyond the realm of possibility that in the future scientists may claim to be able to isolate genes that make a person more prone to violence. To guard against abuse, it is the policy of the DNA data bank to only use "non-coding" or "junk" DNA, that is, only that part of the DNA that does not predict any medical, physical or mental characteristics. This policy or convention is not, however, written into the legislation.

[21] Further, subject to certain exceptions, as where the offender's conviction is quashed and a final acquittal entered, the DNA bank is permitted to keep the sample, even after the DNA profile has been obtained. There are good forensic reasons for this. As the technology improves it may be possible to obtain additional comparison information from the sample. However, if government policy changes in the future the present limitations on the use of the information and the conventions for analysis may also change. The risk that personal information about medical, physical or mental characteristics may be obtained and used for purposes other than forensic comparison cannot be entirely discounted. The issue does not arise in this case, but such use of the bodily sample might well have implications under the *Canadian Charter of Rights and Freedoms*.

[22] I agree with Weiler JA's analysis in *Briggs* and with the importance of collecting DNA profiles for the salutary purposes she identifies. The courts must nevertheless keep in mind the distinction between routine fingerprinting and DNA profiling. This distinction is highlighted by the fact that under s. 487.051(3) and s. 487.052(2) the court is required to give reasons for making the DNA order. That said, and leaving aside other

considerations, I would expect that in most cases the balance would be struck in favour of making the order under s. 487.051(1)(b) or s. 487.052, as the case may be.

[23] There are, of course, other considerations. Under both of these provisions, the court is instructed to take into account the criminal record of the offender, the nature of the offence and the circumstances surrounding its commission. I will consider the latter two factors first. As explained by Weiler JA, the legislation is not focused solely on the possibility that this offender will commit another offence in which DNA profile information may prove useful. Thus, as she said, the fact that the offence of which the accused was convicted is not ordinarily one where DNA evidence might be found is not necessarily relevant. The legislation has already struck a balance by limiting the reach of the DNA data bank orders to persons convicted of serious offences, being those designated as primary or secondary offences. However, the description of some of these offences can also embrace some relatively minor conduct. For example, assaulting a police officer is a secondary designated offence, but this could include merely pushing a police officer who was in the execution of his or her duty. The trivial circumstances of the particular offence may be a factor favouring not making the order.

[24] The court is also directed to consider the offender's record. If the offender has no prior record and the circumstances of the secondary designated offence are relatively minor, the court may be justified in not making the order. However, particularly if the offender has a record that includes offences described as primary designated offences, I would think it exceptional that the order not be made. In general, the more serious the record the less likely the court could exercise its discretion against making the order.

[25] On balance, I would expect that in the vast majority of cases it would be in the best interests of the administration of justice to make the order under s. 487.051(1)(b) and s. 487.052, as the case may be. This follows simply from the nature of the privacy and security of the person interests involved, the important purposes served by the legislation and, in general, the usefulness of DNA evidence in exonerating the innocent and solving crimes in a myriad of situations.

R v RC
2005 SCC 61, [2005] 3 SCR 99

FISH J (McLachlin CJ and Major, Binnie, and Deschamps JJ concurring):

[1] R.W.C. stabbed his mother in the foot with a pen that lay on the floor beside his bed—after his mother had dumped dirty laundry on him because he refused to rise, dress and go off to school. For this he was charged with "assault with a weapon" and breach of an undertaking. R.W.C. had no previous convictions of any kind and pleaded guilty to both offences. He was 13 years old at the time.

[2] Assault with a weapon is one of the offences for which the trial court must make an order permitting DNA samples to be taken from anyone found guilty unless the person found guilty establishes that the effect of doing so would be "grossly disproportionate to the public interest," within the meaning of s. 487.051(2) of the *Criminal Code*, RSC 1985, c. C-46.

[3] The issue in this case is whether Gass J, of the Supreme Court of Nova Scotia (Family Division), erred in concluding that the appellant had discharged that burden. This in turn depends on whether Gass J misinterpreted or misapplied the governing statutory provisions. The Nova Scotia Court of Appeal held, on three grounds, that she had. In my respectful view, the Court of Appeal erred with regard to all three grounds.

[4] I would therefore allow the appeal, set aside the judgment of the Court of Appeal and affirm the decision of Gass J.

II

[5] When he committed the offence that concerns us here, R.W.C., as I have already mentioned, was 13 years old and therefore a "young person" within the meaning of the *Youth Criminal Justice Act*, SC 2002, c. 1 ("*YCJA*").

. . .

III

[16] Since 1995, Parliament has enacted two complementary schemes regulating the collection and use of DNA in the criminal justice system: DNA search warrants and the DNA Data Bank.

[17] The constitutionality of DNA search warrants was considered and upheld by this Court in *R v. S.A.B.*, [2003] 2 SCR 678, 2003 SCC 60. At issue here is the second legislative scheme, the Data Bank contemplated by ss. 487.051 to 487.055 of the *Criminal Code* and the *DNA Identification Act*, SC 1998, c. 37 ("*DNA Act*"). The *Criminal Code* provisions allow a court to order the collection of bodily substances from certain convicted offenders for inclusion in the Data Bank. The *DNA Act*, on the other hand, regulates the use of those substances once collected.

[18] When a DNA order is made, a sample of one or more bodily substances—blood, hair or buccal cells—is taken and sent to the National DNA Data Bank of Canada, where it is assigned a bar code and separated from information identifying the offender. The biological sample is processed and a profile created from the non-coding portions of the DNA sequence. This profile is put in a database known as the Convicted Offenders Index. A separate index, the Crime Scene Index, contains DNA profiles from unsolved crime scenes. The two indices are routinely compared and, when a match is found, investigators are alerted to the discovery of a match.

[19] Orders for taking DNA samples are made under either s. 487.051 or s. 487.052 of the *Criminal Code*. Section 487.052 applies to offences committed before the *DNA Act* was in force ... .

. . .

[20] Parliament has thus drawn a sharp distinction between "primary" and "secondary" designated offences, which are defined in s. 487.04 of the *Criminal Code*. Where the offender is convicted of a secondary designated offence, the burden is on the Crown to show that an order would be in the best interests of the administration of justice. Where an offender is convicted of a primary designated offence, however, ss. 487.051(1)(a) and (2), read together, provide that a DNA order must be made unless the judge is satisfied that the offender has established that s. 487.051(2) should apply instead.

[21] Much like the provision at issue in *R v. Araujo*, [2000] 2 SCR 992, s. 487.051(2) can be described as a "constitutional compromise" that seeks to strike an appropriate balance between individual rights and societal interests. In applying this provision, courts must determine whether a DNA order would adversely affect the individual's privacy and security interests in a manner that is grossly disproportionate to the public interest. We are neither invited nor required in this case to decide whether s. 487.051(2) passes constitutional muster.

[22] By its very terms, s. 487.051(2) implies that the public interest in a DNA order lies in the protection of society through the early detection, arrest and conviction of offenders. Section 3 of the *DNA Act*, for example, states that the purpose of the legislation is to assist in the identification of persons alleged to have committed designated offences.

[23] Other objectives include deterring potential repeat offenders, detecting serial offenders, streamlining investigations, solving "cold cases," and protecting the innocent by eliminating suspects and exonerating the wrongly convicted: see *R v. Briggs* (2001), 157 CCC (3d) 38 (Ont. CA) at para. 22, leave to appeal dismissed [2001] 2 SCR xii; *R v. Jordan*, 2002 NSCA 11, at paras. 32-39; and *R v. T. (T.N.)*, 2004 ABCA 238, at para. 2.

[24] These objectives, however laudable, may be seen to conflict with privacy and security interests that warrant judicial protection. Although the public interest is presumed to outweigh privacy interests in the case of primary designated offences, the exception in s. 487.051(2) recognizes that this is a rebuttable presumption.

[25] The making of a DNA order clearly engages two aspects of privacy protected by the *Canadian Charter of Rights and Freedoms*. The first relates to the person, and the second arises in what has been called the "informational context": *S.A.B.*, at para. 40; *R v. Dyment*, [1988] 2 SCR 417, at pp. 428-30.

[26] The physical intrusion caused by the taking of a DNA sample is minimal. In this regard, the comments of Arbour J in *S.A.B.* are apposite:

> With regards to privacy related to the person, the taking of bodily samples under a DNA warrant clearly interferes with bodily integrity. However, under a properly issued DNA warrant, the degree of offence to the physical integrity of the person is relatively modest (*R v. F. (S.)* (2000), 141 CCC (3d) 225 (Ont. CA), at para. 27). A buccal swab is quick and not terribly intrusive. Blood samples are obtained by pricking the surface of the skin—a procedure that is, as conceded by the appellant (at para. 32 of his factum), not particularly invasive in the physical sense. With the exception of pubic hair, the plucking of hairs should not be a particularly serious affront to privacy or dignity.
>
> Importantly, s. 487.07(3) of the legislation requires that the person who is authorized to take samples do so in a manner that respects the offender's privacy and is "reasonable in the circumstances." Thus, as Weiler JA articulated in *R v. Briggs* ... at para. 35, "a person would not ordinarily be required to expose a part of the body that is not ordinarily exposed to view."
>
> • • •
>
> In my view, the statutory framework alleviates any concern that the collection of DNA samples pursuant to a search warrant under ss. 487.04 to 487.09 of the *Criminal Code* constitutes an intolerable affront to the physical integrity of the person. [paras. 44, 45 and 47]

The same is true of samples taken pursuant to an order under s. 487.051(1)(a).

[27] Of more concern, however, is the impact of an order on an individual's informational privacy interests. In *R v. Plant*, [1993] 3 SCR 281, at p. 293, the Court found that s. 8

of the *Charter* protected the "biographical core of personal information which individuals in a free and democratic society would wish to maintain and control from dissemination to the state." An individual's DNA contains the "highest level of personal and private information": *S.A.B.*, at para. 48. Unlike a fingerprint, it is capable of revealing the most intimate details of a person's biological makeup.

[28] Without constraints on the type of information that can be extracted from bodily substances, the potential intrusiveness of a DNA analysis is virtually infinite. Comprehensive safeguards have therefore been put in place to regulate the use of the bodily substances and of the information contained in a profile: see *S.A.B.*, at paras. 49-50; see also *Briggs*, at para. 39.

[29] The court must consider the impact of a DNA order on each of these interests to determine whether privacy and security of the person are affected in a grossly disproportionate manner. This inquiry is highly contextual, taking into account not only that the offence is a primary designated offence, but also the particular circumstances of the offence and the character and profile of the offender.

[30] Some of the factors that may be relevant to this inquiry are set out in s. 487.051(3): the criminal record of the offender, the nature of the offence and the circumstances surrounding its commission, and the impact such an order would have on the offender's privacy and security of the person (*Jordan*, at para. 62).

[31] This is by no means an exhaustive list. The inquiry is necessarily individualized and the trial judge must consider all the circumstances of the case. What is required is that the offender show that the public interest is clearly and substantially outweighed by the individual's privacy and security interests.

[32] The central controversy in this case is whether a youth court judge may, in contemplating a DNA order with respect to a young person, take into account the underlying principles and defining characteristics of criminal justice legislation adopted by Parliament specifically for dealing with young persons.

[33] Section 487.051(1)(a) applies expressly to a "person" or "young person." Accordingly, the question is not whether youth criminal justice legislation supersedes or displaces the DNA order provisions, or governs the making or rejection of DNA orders under their auspices. Rather, the question is whether legislation designed specifically and exclusively for dealing with young persons who commit criminal offences may be considered in applying to them the provisions of the *Criminal Code* that govern the making of DNA orders.

[34] There has been some dispute whether, in answering this question, we should look to the now-repealed *Young Offenders Act*, RSC 1985, c. Y-1 ("*YOA*"), or to the new *YCJA*. The latter came into force April 1, 2003, after R.W.C. had pleaded guilty to the offence. Its transitional provisions stipulate that, where proceedings are commenced under the *YOA*, the *YOA* applies (s. 159 of the *YCJA*), except for sentencing (s. 161). The Crown submits that the appeal in this case is governed by the *YOA*.

[35] In my view, the result in this case does not turn at all on whether the *YOA* or the *YCJA* is held to apply. In all relevant aspects, the two Acts share the same basic assumptions and governing principles: some are simply spelled out in greater detail in the *YCJA*.

[36] Most significantly, both the *YOA* and the *YCJA* extend to youth justice courts exclusive jurisdiction in respect of offences alleged to have been committed by young

persons, and stipulate that, notwithstanding any other Act of Parliament, the young person shall be dealt with according to their terms (s. 14 *YCJA*; s. 5(1) *YOA*). Both Acts incorporate the provisions of the *Criminal Code* with "any modifications that the circumstances require" (s. 140 *YCJA*; similar wording in s. 51 *YOA*). While no specific provision of either Act modifies s. 487.051(1)(a) or (2) of the *Code*, it is clear that Parliament intended their shared principles to be respected whenever young persons are brought within the Canadian system of criminal justice.

[37] In particular, Parliament has taken care to ensure that the consequences of conviction for young persons are imposed in a manner that advances the objectives of youth criminal justice legislation. This legislative policy is apparent in both Acts. To disregard it is to frustrate Parliament's will.

[38] The *YOA*, for example, declared in s. 3(1)(a.1) that "young persons should not in all instances be held accountable in the same manner or suffer the same consequences for their behaviour as adults," recognized in s. 3(1)(c) their "state of dependency and level of development and maturity," and held in s. 3(1)(f) that young persons have "a right to the least possible interference with freedom that is consistent with the protection of society." Likewise, the *YCJA*, states in s. 3 that the criminal justice system for young persons must be separate from that of adults and must "emphasize … enhanced procedural protection to ensure that young persons are treated fairly and that their rights, including their right to privacy, are protected."

[39] A DNA order, while it is not a sentence, is undoubtedly a serious consequence of conviction. This is evident from the comprehensive procedural protections that are woven into the scheme of the DNA Data Bank. The taking and retention of a DNA sample is not a trivial matter and, absent a compelling public interest, would inherently constitute a grave intrusion on the subject's right to personal and informational privacy.

[40] Both the *YOA* and the *YCJA* protect young persons from publication of their identities. Both emphasize rehabilitation rather than punishment. And both require the destruction of youth records after a finite time period.

[41] In creating a separate criminal justice system for young persons, Parliament has recognized the heightened vulnerability and reduced maturity of young persons. In keeping with its international obligations, Parliament has sought as well to extend to young offenders enhanced procedural protections, and to interfere with their personal freedom and privacy as little as possible: see the United Nations *Convention on the Rights of the Child*, Can. T.S. 1992 No. 3, incorporated by reference in the *YCJA*.

[42] In protecting the privacy interests of young persons convicted of criminal offences, Parliament has not seen itself as compromising, much less as sacrificing, the interests of the public. Rather, as Binnie J noted in *F.N. (Re)*, [2000] 1 SCR 880, 2000 SCC 35, protecting the privacy interests of young persons serves rehabilitative objectives and thereby contributes to the long-term protection of society … .

[43] Moreover, Parliament has recognized in enacting youth criminal justice legislation that "most young offenders are one-time offenders only and, the less harm brought upon them from their experience with the criminal justice system, the less likely they are to commit further criminal acts" (*Re Southam Inc. and The Queen* (1984), 48 OR (2d) 678 (HC), at p. 697, *per* J. Holland J, aff'd. (1986), 53 OR (2d) 663 (CA), leave to appeal refused, [1986] 1 SCR xiv).

[44] It is not surprising, then, that the Court of Appeal for Ontario has held that the balancing of factors under the discretionary prong of s. 487.051(1)(b) must take into account the age of the young person and the principles of youth criminal justice legislation. ...

[45] The same holds true for decisions made pursuant to s. 487.051(1)(a) and (2): In determining whether the young person has established that the public interest in the protection of society and the proper administration of justice is clearly and substantially inferior to his or her privacy and security interests, the sentencing judge must examine both sides of the equation through the lens of the applicable youth criminal justice legislation.

IV

[46] The Nova Scotia Court of Appeal held that it owed no deference to the decision of Gass J in this case because that decision was made pursuant to a mandatory provision of the *Criminal Code*.

[47] With respect, I prefer the view taken on this point by the Court of Appeal for Ontario in *Briggs*, where Weiler JA (Austin and Borins JJA concurring) recognized that "a judge has a discretion to make an order authorizing the taking of a sample of DNA with respect to both primary and secondary offences although that discretion would appear to be more limited with respect to primary offences" (para. 3).

[48] Subsection (1)(a) of s. 487.051 of the *Criminal Code*, which is framed in mandatory terms, cannot be read in isolation from subs. (2). Read together, these provisions make the issuance of a DNA order mandatory only where (1) a person or young person has been convicted of a primary designated offence and (2) the burden cast upon that person or young person by s. 487.051(2) has not been discharged. Put differently, the court is not required to make the order if it is satisfied that the person or young person has established gross disproportionality. Such is the language of discretion.

[49] Accordingly, absent an error in principle, failure to consider a relevant factor, or an overemphasis of the appropriate factors, a court of appeal should only intervene to vary a decision to either make or refuse to make a DNA Data Bank order if the decision was clearly unreasonable: see, in the sentencing context, *R v. M.(C.A.)*, [1996] 1 SCR 500.

V

[50] The Court of Appeal intervened in this instance on three grounds.

[51] First, it found that Gass J had erred in holding that "the principles and purposes of the [*YCJA*] inform or otherwise modify the application of s. 487.051(1)(a) and (2)" (para. 17). In my respectful view, Gass J did not err at all in this regard. In balancing the governing factors under s. 487.051(2) in cases involving young offenders, I have already explained why sentencing judges commit no error in taking into account the principles and objectives of youth criminal justice legislation, such as the *YOA* or the *YCJA*.

[52] Second, the Court of Appeal held that Gass J failed to deal with certain circumstances that ought to have informed the balancing of factors under s. 487.051(2). In dealing with this branch of the matter, it is essential to bear in mind that all of the relevant circumstances were canvassed by counsel and considered by the trial judge cumulatively at the DNA stage. That is to say, the hearing on sentence was incorporated by reference into the DNA hearing that followed immediately afterward. There was no confusion at all regarding the different legal considerations applicable to each of the two distinct decisions—one

relating to sentence, the other to the DNA order. But the facts were not in dispute and the predisposition report, relevant at both stages, was not challenged by either side.

[53] Quite properly, Crown counsel thus acknowledged in this Court that, at trial, the submissions on sentencing, the sentencing disposition, the DNA hearing, and the DNA order in this matter all proceeded more or less simultaneously, without objection.

[54] It must be borne in mind as well that the trial judge, when asked by defence counsel whether she required more facts for the purposes of the DNA hearing, replied:

> I'm certainly satisfied that the Court has ample facts before it based on the facts that were given prior to the disposition or the sentencing hearing and the information provided in the presentence report and the submissions of counsel.

[55] In this light, I am not prepared to hold that the trial judge failed to consider the facts to which she thus adverted compendiously. Nor am I prepared to fault the appellant's counsel taking the judge at her word.

[56] More specifically, the Court of Appeal reproached Gass J for relying only on the age of the offender, the absence of a criminal record and the nature of the offence in refusing the DNA order. In its view, she had failed to address this additional information in the record:

- at the time of the commission of this assault offence the young person was on an undertaking to keep the peace and be of good behaviour;
- the only evidence of the young offender's remorse came through his father's report on the PSR interview;
- his school attendance has been an ongoing problem and precipitated this assault;
- the young offender's latest academic school report was not good;
- the young offender had a history of using illicit drugs and alcohol, although he maintained such use was in his past;
- the young offender has an anger management problem with a tendency to lose control of his behaviour as evidenced by this offence;
- there is a history of violence in the young offender's family;
- the assault against the mother continued after the stabbing with the pen, until it was stopped by the intervention of the young offender's uncle. [para. 23]

[57] The Court of Appeal's finding that Gass J had failed to consider this "relevant information" cannot be reconciled with the record as we have it. The opposite is in fact true. Gass J mentioned specifically that R.W.C. was bound by an undertaking at the time of the offence. She specifically mentioned as well R.W.C.'s anger management issues in her reasons on the DNA order, and on at least three separate occasions in her reasons for sentence. She stated that she did not wish to minimize them, but found that they were being addressed appropriately through the conditions she had imposed as part of R.W.C.'s probation order. That conclusion has not been attacked by the Crown.

[58] Likewise, Gass J expressly considered R.W.C.'s history of family violence, both in her reasons on the DNA order and her reasons for sentence. And she mentioned at least twice that the assault was precipitated by a dispute regarding his attendance at school.

[59] The Court of Appeal erred as well in stating that the only evidence of R.W.C.'s remorse came from his father's interview for the predisposition report. As appears from the extract of the probation report reproduced above, R.W.C. had personally expressed

his remorse to the probation officer, who also noted R.W.C.'s willingness to accept the consequences imposed upon him for his actions. ...

[60] Again, the Court of Appeal reproached Gass J for failing to mention R.W.C.'s "ongoing problem" with "school attendance" and an academic report that was "not good." These purported omissions by the trial judge should cause no surprise: In her representations on sentence, Crown counsel had expressly adopted the probation officer's assessment that "[o]verall in the home and school, the offender's behaviour appears to be compliant" (emphasis added).

[61] Other omissions imputed to Gass J by the Court of Appeal were either included in the predisposition report, which Gass J said that she had considered, or had been drawn to her attention moments earlier during counsels' submissions, or referred to by Gass J herself in her judgment on sentence.

[62] With respect, I am satisfied for all of these reasons that the Court of Appeal erred in holding that Gass J had failed to consider relevant information in declining to make a DNA order. And I turn now to the third ground upon which the Court of Appeal set aside her decision at trial.

[63] The Court of Appeal held that Gass J had failed to particularize her decision: In its view, she had "apparently concluded that taking a DNA sample from a young offender was, prima facie, an impermissible violation of the young person's privacy and security interests" (para. 16), and had "lacked an evidentiary foundation upon which to base a denial of the presumptively mandatory order" (para. 13).

[64] With respect, I find this reproach as well to be unwarranted.

[65] Gass J instructed herself impeccably in law on several occasions. She noted that the young person had been found guilty of a primary designated offence and that a DNA order could therefore be refused only if the conditions of s. 487.051(2) were met by R.W.C. The Nova Scotia Court of Appeal in *S.A.B.*, she noted, had held that "cases where an order that is properly sought under [s 487.051(1)(a)] may be refused will be very rare indeed" (para. 5), and that "the young person ... bears the burden of persuading the court that he falls within that exception. That has to be established by evidence on the record" (para. 21).

[66] Gass J went on to deal in very specific terms with the circumstances of this case. She noted that R.W.C. was 13 years of age, had no criminal record, and was involved in a fight with his mother in which he stabbed her with a pen in the foot. Gass J did not conclude that taking a DNA sample from young persons constituted, prima facie, an impermissible violation of their rights, but took care to explain that she saw R.W.C.'s circumstances as "significantly different than the minimal infringement involved in the taking of a sample from a 35 year old individual with an extensive criminal record or even of the taking of a bodily sample from a 17 year old with an extensive criminal record" (para. 31).

[67] Gass J took into consideration the principles of the *YCJA*, the level of development of an early adolescent, and the young person's circumstances as they were described in the predisposition report. Though counsel for R.W.C. had offered to call the young person to testify on his own behalf, Gass J was satisfied that the court had ample facts before it. I am not prepared to say that she erred in this regard.

[68] In the circumstances, the offence committed by R.W.C. was clearly at the low end of the spectrum of primary designated offences. I should not be understood to be minimizing the gravity of his offence: R.W.C. committed a reprehensible assault on his mother. But it was committed in the course of dispute between a 13-year-old boy and his mother about

going to school and as a reflexive response to the humiliation of having his dirty laundry dumped on him in his bed. His need for anger management, evidenced by this unacceptable attack on his mother, was addressed appropriately by Gass J.

[69] R.W.C. was a first-time offender. Gass J weighed the public interest in ordering that a DNA sample be taken from him and retained in the DNA Data Bank against the impact of such an order on his privacy and security interests. She conducted this exercise in light of the principles and objects of youth criminal justice legislation, and found that the impact of the order would be grossly disproportionate.

[70] Her finding was reasonable in the circumstances and should not have been set aside by the Court of Appeal.

VI

[71] For the foregoing reasons, I would allow the appeal and restore the order of the Supreme Court of Nova Scotia (Family Division).

ABELLA J (LeBel and Charron JJ concurring) (dissenting):

[72] I have had the benefit of reading the reasons of Fish J. With respect, I do not agree with his conclusion that the trial judge appropriately declined to make the DNA data bank order anticipated by s. 487.051(1)(a) of the *Criminal Code*, RSC 1985, c. C-46.

[73] Section 487.051(1)(a) requires that a DNA order be made in the case of a primary designated offence, such as the one in this case, unless the offender has established a grossly disproportionate impact on his or her "privacy and security of the person." The statutory onus is on the offender to rebut the presumption that a DNA order should issue.

[74] The data bank provisions explicitly extend their grasp to young offenders found guilty of a designated offence under either the *Young Offenders Act*, RSC 1985, c. Y-1, or the *Youth Criminal Justice Act*, SC 2002, c. 1. While I agree with Fish J that the principles of the *Young Offenders Act* and the *Youth Criminal Justice Act* are theoretically relevant to this determination, I am unable to see how they can be applied, as they were by the trial judge, so as to neutralize the clear language of the *Code*.

• • •

Analysis

[84] As Fish J points out (at para. 20), s. 487.051 of the *Code* draws a "sharp distinction" between DNA orders made in respect of those who commit offences designated as primary, such as in this case, and those designated as secondary. …

• • •

[85] Sections 487.051(1)(a) and (2) provide that when someone is convicted of a primary designated offence, a DNA order must be made unless the judge is satisfied that the offender has established that the impact of the order on his or her privacy and security of the person would be grossly disproportionate to the public's interest in the early detection, arrest and conviction of offenders. Any refusal would, based on the language of the provision, be exceptional.

[86] Three points bear emphasis: the onus is on the offender to satisfy the court that the order should not be made; the threshold for discharging the onus is gross disproportionality; and both adult and young offenders are explicitly made subject to the provisions.

[87] Section 487.051(1)(b) of the Code deals with secondary designated offences. It too makes specific reference to young persons being embraced by the provision's scope. The test, however, is completely different. If the offence is designated as secondary, a DNA order is not presumptively required. A discretion is given to the trial judge, who may make the order if satisfied that it is in the best interests of the administration of justice to do so based on the factors set out in s. 487.051(3): the criminal record, the nature of the offence, the circumstances surrounding its commission, and the impact such an order would have on the person's privacy and security. In other words, the best interests of the administration of justice are determined by balancing these factors.

[88] The test for primary designated offences, on the other hand, makes no reference to these factors and there is significantly less scope for discretion. The test, moreover, is not what is in the best interests of the administration of justice, as it is in the case of secondary offences. Instead, in the case of more serious offences Parliament has already codified the public interest and proper administration of justice as requiring a DNA order to achieve the early detection, arrest, and conviction of offenders. That is the articulated basis for carving out those more serious offences from the scheme, making a DNA data bank order presumptively mandatory and making the hurdle for avoiding the order far more onerous. Only if an offender, youthful or adult, can demonstrate that the impact of such an order on his or her privacy and security is grossly disproportionate to the public interest in the protection of society, can a court refuse to make the order.

[89] And this, in turn, is a question of evidence. Factors such as the offender's age, record and personal circumstances may well be advanced as part of the offender's evidentiary package if they relate to the question of impact on the offender's privacy and security of the person, but, unlike the case of secondary offences, they are not the focus of the inquiry. What is being weighed, instead, is whether the offender has discharged his burden of showing that the impact on his or her privacy and security interests is so overwhelming as to grossly outweigh society's interest in its own protection.

[90] Is this burden different for young offenders? As previously indicated, not only is no distinction drawn in s. 487.051(1) between adult and young offenders, young persons are specifically included. By expanding the operation of the provision to include young persons without words of limitation, Parliament has signalled its view that DNA data banks orders can or should be made even where the offender is not an adult. In the case of less serious offences, it has formulated a balancing test and, in the case of serious offences, designed a highly stringent one. Both tests apply to both adult and young offenders.

[91] This is not to say that Parliament has failed to recognize the unique privacy and security needs of young persons. On the contrary, there are a number of provisions in both the *DNA Identification Act*, SC 1998, c. 37, and the *Code* that explicitly recognize them. For example, s. 9.1 of the *DNA Identification Act*, provides that "[a]ccess to information in the convicted offenders index" will be "permanently removed without delay" once the young offender's record is destroyed under the *Young Offenders Act*. Similarly, s. 10.1 of the *DNA Identification Act* provides for the destruction of bodily substances collected from a young offender "when the last part of the record in relation to the same offence is … required to be destroyed." Section 487.07(4) of the *Code* provides that a young person against whom a DNA warrant is executed has, in addition to any other rights arising from his or her detention under the warrant, the right to a reasonable opportunity

to consult with, and have the warrant executed in the presence of, counsel and a parent, adult relative or other appropriate adult.

[92] That means, as for adult offenders, that a court can only decline to make a DNA data bank order in respect of a primary designated offence where there is evidence that the impact on the young person's privacy and security interests is grossly disproportionate to the public interest in the early detection, arrest and conviction of offenders. The court cannot simply infer a disproportionate impact on the basis that the offender is a young person. Such an approach would effectively turn the presumption on its head.

[93] While young offender legislation contains principles and protections to which all young offenders are always entitled, I have difficulty seeing how those principles and protections assist in any meaningful way in this case. The question is whether there was evidence that the impact of the order on this particular young person's privacy and security was so overwhelming as to be grossly disproportionate to the public's interest in protecting itself from potentially violent offenders. The test is the same for adult and young persons because the crime solving and public protection concerns that motivated Parliament are the same for both—both can be victims of wrongful convictions, both can be wrongfully accused, and both risk re-offending.

[94] Counsel for R.W.C. conceded that no evidence had been adduced with respect to the impact on his client. Rather, he had urged the trial judge to take judicial notice of the probable and likely effect of a DNA data bank order on young people in general. His argument was that because of the offender's age, lack of a criminal record and the domestic nature of the crime, the impact of a DNA order would be grossly disproportionate to R.W.C.

[95] The trial judge concluded that the case of R.W.C. was "so far removed from the usual situations contemplated by the legislative scheme" (para. 40) that the taking of the sample could not reasonably be justified. There was no evidence to support this, or any other conclusion about the impact on R.W.C. of such an order.

[96] The trial judge wisely expressed concern for the possibility that a DNA order could have a disproportionate impact on a young person. This is the kind of reality a judge dealing with young offenders is required to be sensitive to. But it ignores the legislative reality that Parliament has deemed the privacy and security interests of a young person convicted of a primary designated offence to be outweighed by the public interest in the protection of society and the proper administration of justice.

[97] The trial judge's error, with respect, was in basing her conclusion on generic considerations about impact, rather than on evidence of how disproportionate the impact was on this particular young offender. She essentially melted the test for primary offences into the one for secondary offences, turning an order that Parliament directed to be presumptively mandatory, into one that was presumptively inapplicable in the case of young offenders, replacing the requirement for evidence of gross disproportionality with a presumption of gross proportionality.

[98] This was a violent domestic incident involving the use of a weapon. The fact that the weapon was a pen does not diminish the fact that this was an offence designated to be primary and therefore governed by s. 487.051(1)(a). The stabbing was part of an escalating conflict which culminated in R.W.C. striking repeatedly at his mother's head with closed fists. Were it not for the intervention of a relative, the injuries sustained by the mother might have been far more serious.

[99] The trial judge made an express finding of fact that there was the potential for future violence if not addressed by remedial means. The record amply supports this finding. It is this very potential that the DNA data bank order is meant to address in the case of primary designated offences.

[100] The denial of an otherwise mandatory order must have a factual underpinning. I agree with Bateman JA of the Court of Appeal that the youth court judge lacked such a foundation … ((2004), 222 NSR (2d) 41, 2004 NSCA 30, at paras. 40-41).

[101] For these reasons, I would dismiss the appeal.

[Bastarache J provided separate, dissenting reasons for judgment.]

NOTE

The DNA provisions have generated some controversy in their application to young offenders. In *R v SC* (2011), 269 CCC (3d) 431 (Ont CA), the court addressed the question of whether the provisions are constitutional when applied to persons who have been found guilty under the *Youth Criminal Justice Act* (YCJA) and the *Young Offenders Act*. The case involved a Crown appeal from several decisions of a Youth Justice Court judge who refused to make a collection order unless the Crown could establish that such an order was "in the best interests of the administration of justice" viewed through the lens of the principles that animate the YCJA. In an informative judgment on the operation of the entire statutory scheme, the Court of Appeal concluded that the provisions, as applied to youth, do not violate either s 7 or s 8 of the Charter.

The DNA databank legislation is highly technical and complicated. Other interpretive issues arise. For example, in *R v Rodgers*, 2006 SCC 15, [2006] 1 SCR 554, the court dealt with the situation of a prisoner still serving a sentence for sexual assault that antedated the provisions. Section 487.055 appears to permit an *ex parte* hearing in this circumstance. The Court of Appeal held that this provision must be interpreted as providing a presumptive hearing upon notice, not an *ex parte* one. A majority of the Supreme Court (Fish, Binnie, and Deschamps JJ dissenting) reversed and agreed with the judge of first instance that an *ex parte* hearing did not violate either s 7 or s 8 of the Charter. Fish J, for the dissenters, concluded:

> [96] In the present matter, we have been shown no cause or justification for proceeding *ex parte*, while the reasons for giving notice are both compelling ⟨nd self-evident. The judge retains discretion, in any event, to order an *ex parte* hearing when there is a reasonable basis for doing so in the particular circumstances of the case.

Will this decision encourage Parliament to use *ex parte* hearings in other situations? What does this decision say about the minimum requirements of fundamental justice?

V. SEX OFFENDER REGISTRIES

In 2005, Parliament enacted the *Sex Offender Information Registration Act*, SC 2004, c 10. This legislation, which amended the *Criminal Code*, is aimed at monitoring the movement and activities of offenders convicted of committing sexual offences against adults or children. As set out in the principal provisions of this amending legislation, below, orders made under these provisions obligate an offender to report and file information with the police for periods of 10 years, 20 years, or life. These provisions of the *Criminal Code* operate alongside various pieces of provincial legislation that oblige sex offenders to provide information and be accountable to the police, such as *Christopher's Law (Sex Offender Registry), 2000*, SO 2000, c 1: see Vanessa Amyot, "Sex Offender Registries: Labelling Folk Devils" (2009) 55 Crim LQ 188.

The provisions as originally enacted make a distinction between "designated" offences in ss 490.011(1)(a), (c), (d), and (e) and those in ss 490.011(1)(b) and (f). With offences in the first category, a DNA order was mandatory. With offences in the second category, an order could be made only if the prosecutor proved beyond a reasonable doubt that the person committed an offence in s 490.011(1)(b) or (f) with the intent of committing an offence in ss 490.011(1)(a), (c), (d), and (e). Section 490.012(4) provided an exception to making any order:

> (4) The court is not required to make an order under this section if it is satisfied that person has established that, if the order were made, the impact on them, including on their privacy or liberty, would be grossly disproportionate to the public interest in protecting society through the effective investigation of crimes of a sexual nature, to be achieved by registration of information relating to sex offenders under the *Sex Offender Information Registration Act*.

Originally enacted provisions also permitted a person who was the subject of an order to apply to terminate the order after specified periods of time (ss 490.015 and 490.016). The criteria for termination mirrored the general exception in s 490.012(4).

The legislation has been amended a number of times. The general exception to making an order in s 490.012(4) was removed by the *Protecting Victims from Sex Offenders Act*, SC 2010, c 17, s 5. The legislation was amended again by the *Protection of Communities and Exploited Persons Act*, SC 2014, c 25. The new provisions, reproduced below, preserve the distinction between the different types of "designated" offences, but in a slightly more elaborate (if not overcomplicated) manner. Moreover, under the present legislation, a person may still apply to terminate an order after prescribed time periods (s 490.015) based on the same criteria (s 490.016).

Order

490.012(1) When a court imposes a sentence on a person for an offence referred to in paragraph (a), (c), (c.1), (d) or (e) of the definition *designated offence* in subsection 490.011(1) or renders a verdict of not criminally responsible on account of mental disorder for such an offence, it shall make an order in Form 52 requiring the person to comply with the *Sex Offender Information Registration Act* for the applicable period specified in section 490.013.

Order—if intent established

(2) When a court imposes a sentence on a person for an offence referred to in paragraph (b) or (f) of the definition *designated offence* in subsection 490.011(1), it shall, on application of the prosecutor, make an order in Form 52 requiring the person to comply with the *Sex Offender Information Registration Act* for the applicable period specified in section 490.013 if the prosecutor establishes beyond a reasonable doubt that the person committed the offence with the intent to commit an offence referred to in paragraph (a), (c), (c.1), (d) or (e) of that definition.

Order—if previous offence established

(3) When a court imposes a sentence on a person for a designated offence in connection with which an order may be made under subsection (1) or (2) or renders a verdict of not criminally responsible on account of mental disorder for such an offence, it shall, on application of the prosecutor, make an order in Form 52 requiring the person to comply with the *Sex Offender Information Registration Act* for the applicable period specified in section 490.013 if the prosecutor establishes that

(a) the person was, before or after the coming into force of this paragraph, previously convicted of, or found not criminally responsible on account of mental disorder for, an offence referred to in paragraph (a), (c), (c.1), (d) or (e) of the definition *designated offence* in subsection 490.011(1) or in paragraph (a) or (c) of the definition "designated offence" in section 227 of the *National Defence Act*;

(b) the person was not served with a notice under section 490.021 or 490.02903 or under section 227.08 of the *National Defence Act* in connection with that offence; and

(c) no order was made under subsection (1) or under subsection 227.01(1) of the *National Defence Act* in connection with that offence.

Date order begins

490.013(1) An order made under section 490.012 begins on the day on which it is made.

Duration of order

(2) An order made under subsection 490.012(1) or (2)

(a) ends 10 years after it was made if the offence in connection with which it was made was prosecuted summarily or if the maximum term of imprisonment for the offence is two or five years;

(b) ends 20 years after it was made if the maximum term of imprisonment for the offence is 10 or 14 years; and

(c) applies for life if the maximum term of imprisonment for the offence is life.

Duration of order

(2.1) An order made under subsection 490.012(1) applies for life if the person is convicted of, or found not criminally responsible on account of mental disorder for, more than one offence referred to in paragraph (a), (c), (c.1), (d) or (e) of the definition *designated offence* in subsection 490.011(1).

Duration of order

(3) An order made under subsection 490.012(1) or (2) applies for life if the person is, or was at any time, subject to an obligation under section 490.019 or 490.02901, under section 227.06 of the *National Defence Act* or under section 36.1 of the *International Transfer of Offenders Act*.

Duration of order

(4) An order made under subsection 490.012(1) or (2) applies for life if the person is, or was at any time, subject to an order made previously under section 490.012 of this Act or section 227.01 of the *National Defence Act*.

Duration of order

(5) An order made under subsection 490.012(3) applies for life.

490.015(1) A person who is subject to an order may apply for a termination order

(a) if five years have elapsed since the order was made, in the case of an order referred to in paragraph 490.013(2)(a);

(b) if 10 years have elapsed since the order was made, in the case of an order referred to in paragraph 490.013(2)(b); or

(c) if 20 years have elapsed since the order was made, in the case of an order referred to in paragraph 490.013(2)(c) or subsection 490.013(2.1), (3) or (5).

Multiple orders

(2) A person who is subject to more than one order made under section 490.012 of this Act, or under that section and section 227.01 of the *National Defence Act*, may apply for a termination order if 20 years have elapsed since the most recent order was made.

Pardon

(3) Despite subsections (1) and (2), a person may apply for a termination order once they receive a pardon or once a record suspension is ordered.

• • •

(5) A person whose application is refused may re-apply if five years have elapsed since they made the previous application. They may also re-apply once they receive a pardon or once a record suspension is ordered. However, they may not re-apply under this subsection if an order is made with respect to them under section 490.012 of this Act or section 227.01 of the *National Defence Act* after the previous application was made.

Jurisdiction

(6) The application shall be made to

(a) a superior court of criminal jurisdiction if

(i) one or more of the orders to which it relates were made by such a court under section 490.012, or

(ii) one or more of the orders to which it relates were made under section 227.01 of the *National Defence Act* and the Chief Military Judge does not have jurisdiction to receive the application under subsection 227.03(6) of that Act; or

(b) a court of criminal jurisdiction, in any other case in which the application relates to one or more orders made under section 490.012.

Termination order

490.016(1) The court shall make a termination order if it is satisfied that the person has established that the impact on them of continuing an order or an obligation, including on their privacy or liberty, would be grossly disproportionate to the public interest in protecting society through the effective prevention or investigation of crimes of a sexual nature, to be achieved by the registration of information relating to sex offenders under the *Sex Offender Information Registration Act*.

(2) The court shall give reasons for its decision.

(3) If the court makes a termination order, it shall cause the Commissioner of the Royal Canadian Mounted Police and the Attorney General of the province, or the minister of justice of the territory, to be notified of the decision.

Like the DNA databank provisions, courts have held that orders under s 490.012 do not constitute "punishment" for the purposes of the Charter: *R v Cross*, 2006 NSCA 30, 205 CCC (3d) 289. Constitutionally, they have remained intact. In *R v Dyck*, 2008 ONCA 309, 232 CCC (3d) 450, the court held that *Christopher's Law* is valid provincial legislation that did not conflict with or frustrate the objectives of federal registry legislation. Moreover, the court held that there was nothing to prevent compliance with both pieces of legislation. Moreover, while the court found that the obligations created by *Christopher's Law* engage an offender's liberty interests, they are not compromised in a manner that offends s 7 of the Charter. Will this reasoning be persuasive in determining the constitutionality of the *Criminal Code* provisions? Consider Yeshe Laine, "The Interplay Between *Christopher's Law* and the *Sex Offender Information Registration Act*" (2007) 52 Crim LQ 470.

In *R v RL*, 2015 ONSC 4509, it was argued that s 490.013(2.1) of the Code, which requires a lifetime order when the offender has been convicted of more than one offence, violated s 7 because it is arbitrary, overbroad, and grossly disproportionate. In that case, the accused was convicted of 3 counts of sexual assault that occurred within the course of a couple of hours against the same victim. The offender submitted that he should have been subject to an order of 20 years duration, not life. The Charter claim was rejected. Is the Charter breached when the Crown separates a single transaction into separate counts on an information or indictment?

There are a number of decisions that address the issue of gross proportionality under the previous version of s 490.012(4). They are relevant to the test-for-termination issue under s 490.016.

R v Redhead
2006 ABCA 84, 206 CCC (3d) 315

THE COURT (Russell, Picard, and Costigan JJA):

[1] In each of these matters, the Crown appeals the trial judge's refusal to grant an order under s. 490.012 of the *Criminal Code*, RSC 1985, c. C-46 ("*CCC*"), compelling each respondent to register personal information pursuant to the *Sex Offender Information Registry Act*, SC 2004, c. 10 ("*SOIRA*"), and report to the nearest registration centre on an annual basis for 20 years.

Background

R v. Redhead

[2] The respondent Redhead sexually assaulted a 28 year old complainant, who has the mental capacity of a 7 year old, in the early morning hours. When the complainant tried to run away, the respondent caught her, bit her, and forced her to have sexual intercourse with him twice. He was intoxicated at the time of the assault.

[3] The respondent pled guilty to sexual assault, and the trial judge accepted a joint submission for a 30 month custodial sentence. However, the trial judge refused to grant an order under s. 490.012 of the *CCC* ("*SOIRA* order") because the respondent's judgment was clouded by alcohol at the time of the offence, he was not a pedophile, and he was not likely to re-offend.

· · ·

R v. McIntyre

[5] The respondent McIntyre picked up the complainant prostitute in his minivan and negotiated a price in exchange for oral sex and sexual intercourse. They drove a short distance and parked, whereupon the respondent held a screwdriver to the complainant's neck, and proceeded to have both oral sex and sexual intercourse with her. He then drove the complainant back to where he had picked her up.

[6] The respondent was convicted of sexual assault with a weapon, and sentenced to four years in custody. The trial judge refused to grant a *SOIRA* order because the victim was not a child and the respondent had no prior related record.

Issues

[7] In *R v. Redhead*, the Crown alleges the trial judge erred in:

  1. Applying the wrong standard in deciding whether to grant a *SOIRA* order;

2. Finding the respondent had established the criteria under s. 490.012(4) for refusal of the *SOIRA* order in the absence of any relevant evidence; and

3. Considering irrelevant factors in deciding to refuse the *SOIRA* order, namely: the respondent was intoxicated at the time of the offense, he had no related record, and the complainant was not a child.

[8] In *R v. McIntyre*, the Crown alleges the trial judge erred in:

1. Finding the respondent had established the criteria in s. 490.012(4) for refusal of the *SOIRA* order in the absence of any relevant evidence; and

2. Considering irrelevant factors in deciding to refuse the *SOIRA* order, namely: the respondent was a first offender, and the complainant was not a child.

[9] The respondent McIntyre also raises, for the first time on appeal, the issue of whether granting an order under s. 490.012(1) violates s. 11(i) of the *Canadian Charter of Rights and Freedoms*, Part I of the *Constitution Act, 1982*, being Schedule B to the *Canada Act 1982* (UK), 1982, c. 11 (the *"Charter"*). Although not raised by Redhead, the Court will also consider that issue in relation to his appeal.

· · ·

Standard of Review

[12] A *SOIRA* order does not constitute a sentence. Like a DNA order, a *SOIRA* order is a consequence of conviction, and thus the standard of review for sentencing does not apply. However, the standard of review applied to DNA orders is informative given the parallels between DNA orders and *SOIRA* orders: both are consequences of a conviction; both exist to assist the police in investigating future crimes; and both infringe upon the privacy and liberty rights of the offender.

[13] This Court can alter a DNA order decision only where there is an error of principle, failure to consider a relevant factor, an over emphasis of appropriate factors, or a clearly unreasonable decision: *R v. Christie* (2004), 2004 ABCA 287 at para. 16; *R v. Hendry* (2001), 161 CCC (3d) 275 at 284 (Ont. CA). That same standard is applicable to *SOIRA* orders.

Analysis

[14] Upon sentencing an offender convicted of a designated offence within the meaning of s. 490.011(1) of the *CCC*, a court is required by s. 490.012 to make an order compelling the offender to comply with the *SOIRA* for the period specified in ss. 490.013(2), (3) or (4).

[15] A person who is registered under the *SOIRA* is required to provide information concerning his or her identity and whereabouts, and to report to the registration centre closest to his or her main residence on an annual basis for the period specified in the legislation. The *SOIRA* allows the RCMP to maintain a national database of convicted sex offenders, which can only be used by police to assist in the investigation of crimes of a sexual nature.

[16] If the court is satisfied the offender has established that the impact of such an order on his or her privacy or liberty would be grossly disproportionate to the public interest in protecting society through the effective investigation of crimes of a sexual nature, the offender falls within the exception provided under s. 490.012(4).

[17]   Each of the offences in these appeals is a designated offence within the meaning of s. 409.011 of the *CCC*. Therefore, an order under s. 490.012(1) is mandatory unless the respondent falls within the s. 490.012(4) exception. In both cases under appeal, the respondents would be required to report annually for 20 years.

[18]   The court making an order under s. 490.012 is required to provide reasons: s. 490.012(5).

Ground 1: R v. Redhead

[19]   Did the trial judge err in applying the wrong standard in deciding whether to grant an order under s. 490.012?

[20]   The test to determine whether the exception in s. 490.012(4) applies is: whether the impact of a *SOIRA* order on the liberty and privacy interests of a convicted sex offender would be grossly disproportionate to the public interest of effectively investigating crimes of a sexual nature. Thus, the court must assess the impact of a *SOIRA* order on the offender, including the impact on his or her privacy and liberty interests and determine whether that impact is grossly disproportionate to the public interest: *R v. R.E.M.*, [2005] BCJ No. 1191 (SC) and *R v. A.G.N.*, [2005] BCJ No. 2781 (Prov. Ct.).

[21]   The trial judge in *R v. Redhead* considered whether the imposition of a *SOIRA* order would be disproportionate to the respondent's privacy interest. In reaching that conclusion, the trial judge relied upon the respondent's lack of a prior record of sexual assault, the influence of alcohol on him, and the lack of evidence that the respondent was a pedophile. However, as discussed below, those factors are not relevant to the impact of the order on the offender.

[22]   Moreover, there is no indication that the trial judge considered whether the impact of the registration and reporting requirements on the offender would be grossly disproportionate to the public interest. Thus, the trial judge in *R v. Redhead* erred in applying the incorrect standard in refusing to grant the *SOIRA* order.

[23]   This issue was not raised in *R v. McIntyre*.

Ground Two: R v. Redhead and R v. McIntyre

Did the Trial Judges Err in Finding the Respondents Had
Established the Criteria in Section 490.012(4) for Refusal of the
SOIRA Order in the Absence of Any Relevant Evidence?

Impact on Offender

[24]   The first part of the test for an exemption under s. 490.012(4) requires the court to assess the impact of a *SOIRA* order on the offender, including the impact on his or her privacy and liberty interests. The Crown maintains that neither respondent presented evidence relating to that impact, and therefore *SOIRA* orders should have been granted in each case.

[25]   The New Brunswick Court of Appeal held there is no legal basis for refusing a *SOIRA* order where the offender has not adduced evidence to refute the order: *R v. Hayes* (2005), 288 NBR (2d) 197 (CA); see also *R v. Woodburn*, 2005 ONCJ 30 at para. 14. However, failure to adduce evidence during the *SOIRA* application is not necessarily determinative.

The court may consider evidence at trial and in the pre-sentence report: *R v. L.S.*, [2005] BCJ No. 1801 (Prov. Ct.), or take judicial notice of relevant evidence.

[26] Under s. 490.012(4), the offender bears the evidentiary burden of establishing that the impact of a *SOIRA* order on him or her would outweigh the public interest in protecting society by investigating crimes of a sexual nature: *R v. L.S.*, *supra* at para. 16; *R v. Casaway*, 2005 NWTSC 37 at para. 12.

[27] Subsection 490.012(4) does not specify the criteria a court must consider in assessing the impact on an offender. In contrast, comparable provisions relating to the test for imposing a DNA order in s. 487.051(3) of the *CCC* expressly require the court to consider the criminal record of the offender and the circumstances of the offence, as well as the impact such an order would have on the person's privacy and security. The absence of reference to the record and the offence in s. 490.012(4) suggests that Parliament did not intend those factors to be determinative in deciding whether to impose a *SOIRA* order.

[28] The assessment of how reporting obligations might disproportionally impact an offender requires an evidentiary foundation. The focus of that inquiry must be on the offender's present and possible future circumstances, and not on the offence itself.

[29] Different evidence is required to assess the extent to which the offender will require monitoring, which will necessarily include an examination of the nature of the particular circumstances of the offence and record of the offender. But that evidence is irrelevant to the determination of the impact of the registration and reporting on the offender.

[30] Thus, the analysis under s. 490.012(4) is restricted to the impact of a *SOIRA* order on the offender. Nevertheless, that subsection clearly contemplates that factors other than the offender's privacy and liberty interests may be considered, as it requires the court to consider the impact on an offender, including any impact on the offender's privacy and security interests.

[31] Other factors might include unique individual circumstances such as a personal handicap, whereby the offender requires assistance to report: *R v. J.D.M.*, [2005] AJ No. 1258 (Prov. Ct.). Courts have also considered the intangible effects of the legislation, including stigma, even if only in the offender's mind; the undermining of rehabilitation and reintegration in the community; and whether such an order might result in police harassment as opposed to police tracking: *J.D.M.*, *ibid.*; *A.G.N.*, *supra* at para. 21; *R v. Have* (2005), 194 CCC (3d) 151 (Ont. CJ).

[32] Counsel for McIntyre argues the impact of a *SOIRA* order on an offender is self-evident given the onerous obligations imposed on a registrant under such an order. Courts have held the 10 to 20 year reporting requirement has a substantial impact on any offender's liberty, considering it is enforceable by imprisonment: *R v. Worm*, 2005 ABPC 92 at para. 53; *R v. Burke*, 2005 ONCJ 422 at para. 22. But in *Casaway*, *supra* at para. 19, the Court held that the burden of a 20 year order was lessened by flexibility in location and method of reporting. In *Have*, *supra*, the Court concluded the mandatory reporting obligation was a significant infringement on liberty, and the stigma attached to such an order might undermine treatment, rehabilitation, and re-integration into the community.

[33] However, given the onus on the offender to demonstrate why the impact of such an order would be disproportional to the public interest, it appears there is no presumption of impact in the legislation arising from the length of reporting obligations alone.

Patently, the impact on anyone who is subject to the reporting requirements of a *SOIRA* order is considerable. But absent disproportional impact, the legislation mandates that anyone convicted of a prescribed offence is subject to the prescribed reporting period.

[34] This Court has held that the failure of an offender to adduce evidence of the impact of a DNA order on his or her privacy and security mandates the issuance of the order: *R v. Isbister* (2002), 303 AR 22, 2002 ABCA 54. Similarly, an offender has the onus to adduce evidence of the impact of a *SOIRA* order on him or her when seeking an exemption.

[35] In both cases before this Court, the trial judges erred in overlooking the lack of evidence of the impact of a *SOIRA* on the offender.

Public Interest

[36] The purpose of the Sex Offender Registry is stated in s. 2 of the *SOIRA*: "to help police services investigate crimes of a sexual nature." Subsection 2(2) specifies, "in the interest of protecting society through the effective investigation of crimes of a sexual nature, police services must have rapid access to certain information relating to sex offenders." The underlying assumption is that a sex offender will re-offend: *Have, supra* at para. 16.

[37] In *Have*, the Court determined the purpose and value of the legislation is related to the investigation of predatory offenders with a propensity to commit similar offences in the future, particularly those involving child abduction, where time is of the essence. Counsel for McIntyre relies on that case, arguing that because McIntyre had no related criminal record and the nature of the offence was less severe, he was a low risk to re-offend and not the type of offender Parliament had intended to register under *SOIRA*.

[38] We do not agree. The language of s. 490.012 does not suggest its application is so limited. Rather, the absence of such limiting language reflects Parliament's recognition of predictable repetitive behaviour of sexual offenders, and the inordinate consequences of sexual offences for victims of any age.

[39] Courts in some jurisdictions have found that where the offender is a low risk to re-offend, his inclusion would dilute the registry and make it less effective, rather than serve the public interest: *A.G.N., supra* at para. 2; *J.D.M., supra* at para. 48. The test in these jurisdictions is: how would registering the offender forward the public interest through the effective investigation of sexual crimes?: *Burke, supra* at para. 9.

[40] The Court in *Burke* at para. 57, suggested three factors that reduce the public interest in registering the offender: that the offender knew the victim; the circumstances of the offence; and a lack of criminal history: see also *A.G.N.* at para. 25; *R.E.M., supra* at para. 74; see also *Casaway, supra* at para. 12.

[41] Courts have considered the severity of the offence: *Worm, supra* at para. 53, and the limited deterrent effect on both the offender and others: *J.D.M., supra* at para. 48. An offender's cooperation in the past, the ease of exposure of misbehavior, an acceptance of responsibility for the incident, and a willingness to undergo treatment, have all been considered as factors in determining whether inclusion on the registry would serve the public interest.

[42] However, had Parliament intended that courts should determine whether there exists a public interest in registering an offender on a case-by-case basis, factoring in all of the individual circumstances surrounding each offender and his or her offence, it could

have made that intention clear in the wording of the provision. Instead, Parliament has pronounced that there is a public interest in having those who commit the prescribed offences registered. The language of s. 490.012(4) presumes a "public interest in protecting society through the effective investigation of crimes of a sexual nature, to be achieved by the registration of information relating to sex offenders," but questions whether the impact on the offender would be grossly disproportionate to that public interest. Thus, the focus of the inquiry is not on whether there is a public interest in having the offender registered, but rather on whether the impact on the offender would be grossly disproportionate to the public interest.

Proportionality

[43] Courts agree that the standard for this aspect of the test is very high and the offender must establish more than a mere disproportionate impact: *L.S.*, *supra* at para. 35. Something more is required than the "mere imbalance in the competition between requirements of the *SOIRA* legislation and the privacy and security rights" of the offender: *J.D.M.*, *supra* at para. 53. The term grossly means a "marked and serious imbalance": *J.D.M.*, *ibid.*

[44] If the exception in s. 490.012(4) is so narrow that the *SOIRA* order is effectively mandatory, then the exception becomes meaningless: *Have*, *supra* at para. 17. However, in the absence of evidence of the impact of such an order on the offenders, it is impossible to assess whether such impact would be grossly disproportionate to the public interest.

[45] It follows that both trial judges erred in failing to address the proportionality aspect of the test under s. 490.012(4).

• • •

Conclusion

[48] Given that both trial judges erred in finding the respondents had established the criteria for refusal of the *SOIRA* orders in the absence of any evidence in that regard, the Crown appeals in both *R v. Redhead* and *R v. McIntyre* are allowed.

[49] Orders in Form 52 are made under s. 490.012(1) of the *CCC*, requiring that each respondent comply with the *SOIRA* for a period of twenty years.

VI. OTHER PROHIBITION ORDERS: CRIMINAL CODE, SECTIONS 161 AND 447.1

Section 161 of the *Criminal Code* allows a judge to include within the terms of a sentence for various sexual offences an order that prohibits the offender from being in public places, parks, and swimming pools where children under the age of 14 are, or might be, present. A related provision, which authorized the imposition of similar restrictions, s 179(1)(b), was found to be overly broad and in violation of s 7 of the Charter: see *R v Heywood*, [1994] 3 SCR 761, 94 CCC (3d) 481. The majority of the court held that the provision was invalid because it was overly broad in its geographical ambit, it applied for the life of the offender, and there was no mechanism in place for review. When the case was argued before the Supreme Court, s 161 had already been enacted. However, it has since been amended by the

Safe Streets and Communities Act, SC 2012, c 1, s 16, to capture Internet and digital communications and to prohibit communications with any person under the age of 16 years (as opposed to 14, as originally enacted). The amended text is set out below.

Order of prohibition

161(1) When an offender is convicted, or is discharged on the conditions prescribed in a probation order under section 730, of an offence referred to in subsection (1.1) in respect of a person who is under the age of fourteen years, the court that sentences the offender or directs that the accused be discharged, as the case may be, in addition to any other punishment that may be imposed for that offence or any other condition prescribed in the order of discharge, shall consider making and may make, subject to the conditions or exemptions that the court directs, an order prohibiting the offender from

(a) attending a public park or public swimming area where persons under the age of fourteen years are present or can reasonably be expected to be present, or a daycare centre, schoolground, playground or community centre;

(b) seeking, obtaining or continuing any employment, whether or not the employment is remunerated, or becoming or being a volunteer in a capacity, that involves being in a position of trust or authority towards persons under the age of fourteen years;

(c) having any contact—including communicating by any means—with a person who is under the age of 16 years, unless the offender does so under the supervision of a person whom the court considers appropriate; or

(d) using the Internet or other digital network, unless the offender does so in accordance with the conditions set by the court.

Offences

(1.1) The offences for the purpose of subsection (1) are

(a) an offence under section 151, 152, 155 or 159, subsection 160(2) or (3), section 163.1, 170, 171, 171.1, 172.1 or 172.2, subsection 173(2), 212(1), (2), (2.1) or (4) or section 271, 272, 273, 280 or 281;

(b) an offence under section 144 (rape), 145 (attempt to commit rape), 149 (indecent assault on female), 156 (indecent assault on male) or 245 (common assault) or subsection 246(1) (assault with intent) of the *Criminal Code*, chapter C-34 of the Revised Statutes of Canada, 1970, as it read immediately before January 4, 1983; or

(c) an offence under subsection 146(1) (sexual intercourse with a female under 14) or section 153 (sexual intercourse with step-daughter), 155 (buggery or bestiality), 157 (gross indecency), 166 (parent or guardian procuring defilement) or 167 (householder permitting defilement) of the *Criminal Code*, chapter C-34 of the Revised Statutes of Canada, 1970, as it read immediately before January 1, 1988.

Duration of prohibition

(2) The prohibition may be for life or for any shorter duration that the court considers desirable and, in the case of a prohibition that is not for life, the prohibition begins on the later of

(a) the date on which the order is made; and

(b) where the offender is sentenced to a term of imprisonment, the date on which the offender is released from imprisonment for the offence, including release on parole, mandatory supervision or statutory release.

Court may vary order

(3) A court that makes an order of prohibition or, where the court is for any reason unable to act, another court of equivalent jurisdiction in the same province, may, on application of the offender or the prosecutor, require the offender to appear before it at any time and, after hearing

the parties, that court may vary the conditions prescribed in the order if, in the opinion of the court, the variation is desirable because of changed circumstances after the conditions were prescribed.

Offence

(4) Every person who is bound by an order of prohibition and who does not comply with the order is guilty of

(a) an indictable offence and is liable to imprisonment for a term of not more than four years; or

(b) an offence punishable on summary conviction and is liable to imprisonment for a term of not more than 18 months.

There are few cases that interpret this new provision.

Section 447.1(1)(a) of the Code also provides for a specialized sentencing prohibition. Anyone convicted of cruelty to animals may be prohibited from "owning or having the custody or control of an animal or a bird during any period that the court considers appropriate but, in the case of a second or subsequent offence, for a minimum of five years." Under s 447.1(1)(b), a sentencing judge may order restitution to any person or organization that has taken care of an animal or bird injured as a result of an offence under s 446 (animal cruelty). Section 447.1(2) provides that anyone who contravenes an order made under s 447.1(1)(a) is guilty of an offence punishable on summary conviction.

FURTHER READING

Amyot, Vanessa. "Sex Offender Registries: Labelling Folk Devils" (2009-2010) 55 Crim LQ 188.

Benedet, Janine. "A Victim-Centred Evaluation of the Federal Sex Offender Registry" (2012) 37 Queen's LJ 437.

Davis, Kevin E. "The Effects of Forfeiture on Third Parties" (2003) 48 McGill LJ 183.

Manson, Allan. "Specific Prohibitions" in *The Law of Sentencing* (Toronto: Irwin Law, 2001) 255.

Sentencing for Murder

I. INTRODUCTION

Since the last edition of this casebook, we have observed two important changes to sentencing for murder. First, the repeal of s 745.6, commonly, and carelessly, known as the "faint hope clause," means that after December 2, 2011, no prisoners convicted of murder can use this route to seek a reduction of their parole ineligibility after 15 years: see *An Act to amend the Criminal Code and another Act*, SC 2011, c 2, s 2. Second, in the aftermath of *R v Shropshire*, [1995] 4 SCR 227, we have seen both a larger number of second-degree murder sentences with parole ineligibility periods beyond ten years and more periods of ineligibility at the higher end of the scale.

For the purposes of sentencing, murder is treated differently from all other offences under the *Criminal Code*, RSC 1985, c C-46, as amended. On a conviction for murder (first or second degree), the sentencing judge has no discretion; the offender must be sentenced to life imprisonment. With first-degree murder, the offender must serve 25 years' imprisonment before he or she becomes eligible for parole. There is more flexibility with second-degree murder. The trial judge may set the offender's parole ineligibility between 10 and 25 years. Because of this mandated severity, many murder trials are effectively about whether the offence was murder (with the mandatory sentencing regime) or manslaughter (with a maximum sentence of life imprisonment but no minimum sentence). As discussed below in Section II, "Murder in Canada: Empirical and Constitutional Considerations," the constitutionality of the sentencing provisions for murder have been challenged on the ground that the lack of flexibility can sometimes lead to an injustice; however, the challenges have been unsuccessful.

The sentencing scheme for murder is also unique because of its inclusion of jury input. As set out in ss 745 and 746 of the *Criminal Code*, on a conviction for second-degree murder, the trial judge must seek a recommendation from the jury on the appropriate length of parole ineligibility. Moreover, until 2011, after an offender has served 15 years of his or her sentence for either first- or second-degree murder (if the ineligibility period was set at more than 15 years), he or she may bring an application under s 746 of the Code to have the period of ineligibility shortened or terminated. This provision, known colloquially as the "faint hope clause," has proven controversial in recent years. Its repeal in 2011 has only prospective application so, with added obstacles, it still applies to those convicted prior to December 2, 2011.

II. MURDER IN CANADA: EMPIRICAL AND CONSTITUTIONAL CONSIDERATIONS

This section situates murder and the statutory murder provisions set out in Section III in a broader context by throwing some light on why murder continues to be treated differently for sentencing purposes. Is it because, as a group, those convicted of murder are indeed more dangerous than other types of offenders? Do they tend to reoffend at a greater rate, or do we hope that the stiff and relatively inflexible sentencing scheme does a good job of deterring would-be offenders? Does the retention of the current scheme really boil down to a moral judgment—that is, do we sentence those convicted of murder so harshly because we believe that the intentional killing of another human being deserves harsh punishment: retribution, pure and simple? The resolution of these issues is vital to the questions surrounding the constitutionality of this sentencing scheme.

These important questions are difficult to answer. The Canadian Centre for Justice Statistics records many features of homicides committed in Canada through the Homicide Survey. Data from the survey may be found in periodic reports and the CANSIM tables, which are updated annually. In 2014, Canada recorded 516 homicide victims, which converts to a rate of 1.45 per 100,000 population: see CANSIM Table 253-0001, available (as are all CANSIM tables) online: Statistics Canada <http://www5.statcan.gc.ca/cansim/>. This represented a 25 percent decline over the previous ten years.

In its most recent full report on homicide (2011), Statistics Canada notes that, although the rate has fluctuated over the years, the national homicide rate has been declining since the mid-1970s: see Statistics Canada, "Homicide in Canada, 2011," by Samuel Perreault, in *Juristat*, Catalogue No 85-002-X (Ottawa: Canadian Centre for Justice Statistics, 2012). Some provinces have experienced a significant decline in the homicide rate. The 2011 rate in Ontario was the lowest since 1966. Since 1961, when national homicide statistics were first collected, there have been two distinct trends. Following a period of stability between 1961 and 1966, the homicide rate more than doubled over the next ten years, reaching a peak of 3.03 homicide victims per 100,000 population in 1975. Since 1975, the rate has gradually declined, albeit with some year-to-year fluctuations. However, the 2011 rate remains higher than rates recorded in the early 1960s. As with most crime, the homicide rate is generally higher in the western provinces and territories. The highest rate was recorded in Nunavut (21 per 100,000), while Prince Edward Island and Newfoundland and Labrador recorded the lowest rates (0.69 and 0.78, respectively).

With respect to international comparisons of homicides, Canada's 2011 homicide rate of 1.73 is the lowest in the Americas, around one-third that of the United States. The rate in

Canada is comparable to that found in many western European countries: see United Nations Office on Drugs and Crime, *Global Study on Homicide* (Vienna: UNODC, 2013).

There are many other aspects of homicide explored in the 2011 Statistics Canada report, including use of firearms, homicide rates in the various provinces, youth homicide rates, gang-related homicides, relationships with victims, victim involvement in illegal activities, and gender of perpetrators. Some findings are of particular interest. For example, in 2011, the rate of homicides committed with firearms declined to the lowest number in almost 50 years. As far as gender is concerned, in 2011, 90 percent of persons accused of homicide were male and 71 percent of victims were male. There were 46 young persons (aged 12-17) accused of homicide, 33 fewer than in 2009. It is worth noting that the Homicide Survey also collects information on whether the accused was suffering from a recognized or suspected mental or developmental disorder at the time of the offence. Approximately one-fifth of all persons accused of murder fell into this category.

These comparisons involve rates of homicide in general, including murder, manslaughter, and infanticide. This chapter looks principally at first- and second-degree murder. Recent data on the breakdown of cases across legal categories is unavailable, but, in 1999, Statistics Canada provided the following information about the distribution of cases:

> First degree murder, as a proportion of all homicides, has generally been increasing since 1976, although it has declined from 58% in 1996 to 51% in 1998. Conversely, homicides classified by the police as second degree murder have generally been decreasing, and in 1998, represented a proportion of 39%. Despite annual fluctuations, around 9% of all homicides are classified as manslaughter each year, and the remaining 1% are infanticides.

Statistics Canada, "Homicide in Canada—1998," by Orest Fedorowycz, in *Juristat* 19:10, Catalogue No 85-002-XIE (Ottawa: Statistics Canada, 1999) at 6.

Statistics provide some interesting insights into the commission of murder offences in Canada, but they do not tell us a great deal about the offenders who commit these offences. The following study, although dated, addresses the issue of recidivism of those convicted of homicide.

"Recidivism Among Homicide Offenders"
(1992) 4:2 Forum on Corrections Research 7, online: Correctional Service Canada <http://www.csc-scc.gc.ca/research/forum/e042/e042c-eng.shtml>

How well do murder and manslaughter offenders perform when they are finally released from federal prisons? This article presents statistics that may shed some light on the question.

Offenders Originally Incarcerated for Murder

A recent study followed murder offenders released on full parole between 1975 and 1990 to determine whether their time spent in the community on parole was successful or not. The length of the follow-up period varied—from up to 15 years for those released in 1975, to only a few months for those released in 1990.

Between 1 January 1975 and 31 March 1990, 658 murder offenders were released on full parole. Some of these offenders were released more than once for a total of 752 full-parole releases. ... [M]ore than three quarters of released murder offenders (77.5%) were not reincarcerated while on parole. Of those who were reincarcerated, 13.3% had their release revoked for a technical violation of their parole conditions and 9.2% for an indictable offence.

Of the 69 indictable offences committed by the released murder offenders, 30.4% (21) were offences against the person, 18.8% (13) were narcotics offences, 17.5% (12) were property offences, 8.7% (6) were robbery and 24.6% (17) were other *Criminal Code* offences.

Five released murder offenders (of a total of 658) were convicted of having committed a second murder while they were on full parole. Three of these were convicted of first-degree murder and two of second-degree murder. All five offenders had originally been convicted of non-capital murder. Besides these, no released murderer has been convicted of attempted murder or any other offence causing death.

Recidivism among murder offenders can be considered another way—murder offender groups can be divided into specific categories. ... [T]he outcome of the full-parole releases, as of 31 July 1990, [can be] compared among those who were convicted of capital murder, non-capital murder, first-degree murder and second-degree murder.

About one in 10 offenders convicted of second-degree murder, none convicted of first-degree murder, about one in three convicted of capital murder and one in four convicted of non-capital murder had their full parole revoked. Furthermore, 0.6% of second-degree murderers, no first-degree murderers, 2.7% of capital murderers and 3.5% of non-capital murderers committed an offence against another person while on full parole. Comparisons should not be made between these groups based on these data, since the size of some groups (e.g., first-degree murderers) is very small and the follow-up period was very brief.

Offenders Originally Convicted of Manslaughter

Between 1 January 1975 and 31 March 1990, 2,242 offenders originally convicted of manslaughter were released, either on full parole or mandatory supervision. Some of these offenders were released more than once, for a total of 3,172 releases. Of these, 222 (7%) were released at warrant expiry (i.e., at the end of their sentence) and, therefore, were not released to community supervision.

Of the 93% of manslaughter offenders who were released to community supervision, 47.7% (1,407) were released on full parole and 52.3% (1,543) on mandatory supervision. These offenders were followed until 31 July 1990 to determine whether any had been reincarcerated while on release.

Of the full-parole releases, less than one quarter (21.7%) were revoked: 14.6% for a technical violation of the condition of a parole, 6.5% for an indictable offence and 0.5% for a summary offence. About twice the proportion (41.5%) of those released on mandatory supervision were revoked: 30.6% for a technical violation of the conditions of parole, 10% for an indictable offence and 0.9% for a summary offence ... .

Of the 92 (6.5%) full-parole releases of manslaughter offenders that were revoked for an indictable offence, 2.1% were revoked for offences against the person, 0.6% for robbery, 1.7% for property offences, 0.4% for narcotics offences and 1.7% for other *Criminal Code* offences.

Of the releases to mandatory supervision, 10% (154) were revoked for indictable offences: 3.2% were revoked for an offence against the person, 1.2% for robbery, 3.4% for property offences, 0.1% for narcotics offences and 2% for other *Criminal Code* offences.

• • •

Marital Status

Available data indicate that about half of incarcerated offenders reported their marital status as single. Sentence length appeared to have no bearing on this finding. However, long-term offenders appeared somewhat less likely than other offenders to be involved in common-law relationships.

The breakdown of marital status, in decreasing order of frequency, is:

- single—50.5% of long-term inmates versus 47.5% of short-term inmates;
- common-law—21.5% of long-term inmates versus 28.6% of short-term inmates;
- married— 13.5% of long-term inmates versus 11.9% of short-term inmates;
- separated or divorced—11.1% of long-term inmates versus 10.6% of short-term inmates; and
- other (including not specified)—3.4% of long-term inmates versus 1.4% of short-term inmates.

Summary

About one quarter of the total federal-offender population is serving a long-term sentence (i.e. 10 years or more). This is true of both male and female offender populations. Three out of five long-termers are incarcerated and two out of five are on some form of conditional release.

Quebec and the Pacific region have proportionately more long-term offenders, while the Atlantic and Prairie regions have proportionately fewer. Ontario has a more equitable proportion of long-termers.

During the past 10 years, the number of long-term offenders under federal jurisdiction increased by the same proportion as the number of federal offenders in general. During this same period, federal corrections admitted proportionately fewer long-termers, and released proportionately more long-termers, than offenders in general.

The vast majority of long-termers are Caucasian. About half of all long-term offenders are single, while about one in three is married (includes common-law). During the past 10 years, the average age of long-term offenders has increased by almost three years and is now about 38 years. Offenders serving life sentences for first-degree murder as a group, show the most dramatic increase in age.

Long- and short-term offenders have similar histories of federal incarceration, with the majority of both groups having no previous federal incarceration. After a five-year follow-up, only about one in five long-term offenders had been reconvicted of a criminal offence, while none of the 75 released offenders serving life sentences for murder had been subsequently reconvicted of murder.

In the late 1980s and early 1990s, the Supreme Court of Canada was busy shaping the contours of the constitutional requirements of fault. This was largely played out in the context of murder offences. In *R v Vaillancourt*, [1987] 2 SCR 636, 60 CR (3d) 289, a murder case, the court solidified the subjective fault requirement as a constitutional imperative. A subsequent wave of cases provided the court with an opportuntity to refine its approach. Among these cases were *Arkell* and *Luxton*, both extracted below. Although both cases were concerned with the constitutionality of offence-creating provisions (then s 213 of the *Criminal Code*), they raised questions relating to the constitutionality of the sentencing provisions for first-degree murder. Given the breadth of the court's approach to these issues, *Arkell* and *Luxton* also address the constitutionality of mandatory sentencing for second-degree murder. As the extract by Allan Manson, which follows these cases, suggests, these issues appear to have been litigated and decided on an inadequate factual record.

R v Arkell
[1990] 2 SCR 695, 79 CR (3d) 207

LAMER CJ (Dickson CJ and Wilson, Gonthier, and Cory JJ concurring):
Indeed, the appellant concedes that s. 214(5) [now s 231(5)] is a sentencing classification provision.

The argument of the appellant suggests that the sentencing scheme is flawed and in violation of s. 7 of the Charter because it results in the punishment of individuals that is not proportionate to the seriousness of the offences giving rise to the sentences. First, I must note that as a result of this court's decision in *Martineau*, released concurrently, it can no longer be said that s. 214(5) has the potential to classify unintentional killings as first degree murder. A conviction for murder requires proof beyond a reasonable doubt of subjective foresight of death. Therefore, when we reach the stage of classifying murders as either first or second degree, we are dealing with individuals who have committed the most serious crime in our *Criminal Code*, and who have been proven to have done so with the highest level of moral culpability, that of subjective foresight. Section 214(5) represents a decision by Parliament to impose a more serious punishment on those found guilty of murder while committing certain listed offences.

This leads me to a second point, namely, a consideration of the underlying rationale of s. 214(5). Again, I refer to the decision of this court in *Paré*, at pp. 632-33:

> All murders are serious crimes. Some murders, however, are so threatening to the public that Parliament has chosen to impose exceptional penalties on the perpetrators. One such class of murders is that found in s. 214(5), murders done while committing a hijacking, a kidnapping and forcible confinement, a rape, or an indecent assault. ...
>
> The offences listed in s. 214(5) are all offences involving the unlawful domination of people by other people. Thus an organizing principle for s. 214(5) can be found. This principle is that where a murder is committed by someone already abusing his power by illegally dominating another, the murder should be treated as an exceptionally serious crime. Parliament has chosen to treat these murders as murders in the first degree.

I can find no principle of fundamental justice that prevents Parliament, guided by the organizing principle identified by this court in *Paré*, from classifying murders done while committing certain underlying offences as more serious, and thereby attaching more serious penalties to them. In the case of the distinction between first and second degree murder, the difference is a maximum extra 15 years that must be served before one is eligible for parole. This distinction is neither arbitrary nor irrational. The section is based on an organizing principle that treats murders committed while the perpetrator is illegally dominating another person as more serious than other murders. Further, the relationship between the classification and the moral blameworthiness of the offender clearly exists.

Section 214 only comes into play when murder has been proven beyond a reasonable doubt. In light of *Martineau*, this means that the offender has been proven to have had subjective foresight of death. Parliament's decision to treat more seriously murders that have been committed while the offender is exploiting a position of power through illegal domination of the victim accords with the principle that there must be a proportionality between a sentence and the moral blameworthiness of the offender and other considerations such as deterrence and societal condemnation of the acts of the offender. Therefore, I conclude that in so far as s. 214(5) is neither arbitrary nor irrational, it does not infringe upon s. 7 of the Charter. I note that in this appeal there was no argument made as regards s. 12 of the Charter, although that issue was raised in a case heard and disposed of concurrently, *R v. Luxton*.

R v Luxton
[1990] 2 SCR 711, 79 CR (3d) 193

LAMER CJ (Dickson CJ and Wilson, Gonthier, and Cory JJ concurring):

The remaining questions require an examination of the combined effect of s. 214(5)(e) and s. 669 of the Code on the rights guaranteed by ss. 7, 9 and 12 of the Charter, and s. 2(e) of the *Canadian Bill of Rights*. The appellant combines his argument in respect of s. 7 of the Charter and s. 2(e) of the *Canadian Bill of Rights*. He submits that the principles of fundamental justice require that differing degrees of moral blameworthiness in different offences be reflected in differential sentences, and that sentencing be individualized. The appellant cites the following judgments as support for the view that the combined effect of s. 214(5)(e) and s. 669 offends the principles that a just sentencing system contains a gradation of punishments differentiated according to the malignity of offences and that sentencing be individualized: *Re BC Motor Vehicle Act*, [1982] 2 SCR 486, per Wilson J; *R v. Smith*, [1987] 1 SCR 1045, per Lamer J and per Wilson J; and *R v. Lyons*, [1987] 2 SCR 309, per La Forest J. In my view, assuming that s. 7 incorporates the propositions cited by the appellant as principles of fundamental justice, the combined effect of s. 214(5)(e) and s. 669 is in accordance with them. Section 214(5) of the *Criminal Code* isolates a particular group of murderers, namely, those who have murdered while committing certain offences involving the illegal domination of the victim, and classifies them for sentencing purposes as murderers in the first degree. As a result of s. 669 the murderer is sentenced to life imprisonment without parole eligibility for 25 years. It is of some note that even in cases of first degree murder, s. 672 [now s 745] of the Code provides that after serving 15 years the offender can apply to the Chief Justice in the province for a reduction in the number of years of imprisonment without eligibility for parole having regard for the character of the applicant, his conduct while serving the sentence, the nature of the offence for which he was convicted and any other matters that are relevant in the circumstances. This indicates that even in the cases of our most serious offenders, Parliament has provided for some sensitivity to the individual circumstances of each case when it comes to sentencing.

I must also reiterate that what we are speaking of here is a classification scheme for the purposes of sentencing. The distinction between first and second degree murder only comes into play when it has first been proven beyond a reasonable doubt that the offender is guilty of murder, that is, that he or she had subjective foresight of death: *R v. Martineau*, handed down this day. There is no doubt that a sentencing scheme must exhibit a proportionality to the seriousness of the offence, or to put it another way, there must be a gradation of punishments according to the malignity of the offences. However, a sentencing scheme also must take into account other factors that are of significance for the societal interest in punishing wrongdoers. In *Lyons, supra*, at pp. 328-29, La Forest J considered the dangerous offender designation in the Code and said the following in respect of the relationship between sentencing and its objectives:

> I accordingly agree with the respondent's submission that it cannot be considered a violation of fundamental justice for Parliament to identify those offenders who, in the interests of protecting the public, ought to be sentenced according to considerations which are not entirely reactive or based on a "just deserts" rationale. The imposition of a sentence which "is partly punitive but is mainly imposed for the protection of the public" … seems to me to accord with the fundamental purpose of the criminal law generally, and of sentencing in particular, namely, the protection of society. In a rational system of sentencing, the respective importance of prevention, deterrence, retribution and rehabilitation will vary according to the nature of the crime and the circumstances of the offender.

In my view the combination of s. 214(5)(e) and s. 669 clearly demonstrates a proportionality between the moral turpitude of the offender and the malignity of the offence, and moreover it is in accord with the other objectives of a system of sentencing identified by La Forest J in *Lyons*. As I have stated, we are dealing with individuals that have committed murder and have done so with the now constitutionally mandated *mens rea* of subjective foresight of death. Parliament has chosen, once it has been proven that an offender has committed murder, to classify certain of those murders as first degree. Murders that are done while committing offences which involve the illegal domination of the victim by the offender have been classified as first degree murder. Forcible confinement is one of those offences involving illegal domination. The added element of forcible confinement, in the context of the commission of a murder, markedly enhances the moral blameworthiness of an offender. Indeed, forcible confinement is punishable by up to 10 years in prison. The decision of Parliament to elevate murders done while the offender commits forcible confinement to the level of first degree murder is consonant with the principle of proportionality between the blameworthiness of the offender and the punishment. Further, it is consistent with the individualization of sentencing especially since only those who have killed with subjective foresight of death while also committing the offence of forcible confinement are subjected to that punishment. I, therefore, can find no principle of fundamental justice that has been violated by the combination of s. 215(5)(e) and s. 669

of the *Criminal Code*. Equally, for these same reasons I conclude that there is no violation of s. 2(e) of the *Canadian Bill of Rights*.

The appellant also submits in a separate argument that the combination of s. 214(5)(e) and s. 669 contravenes s. 9 of the Charter because of the imposition of a mandatory term of imprisonment by statute for an offence that encompasses a range of moral turpitude. This argument overlaps a great deal with the appellant's s. 7 argument and I would only add the following comments to those I have already made above. The combined effect of the impugned sections do not demonstrate arbitrariness on the part of Parliament. Indeed, as I noted above, Parliament has narrowly defined a class of murderers under an organizing principle of illegal domination and has specifically defined the conditions under which the offender can be found guilty of first degree murder. In order to be found guilty of first degree murder under s. 214(5)(e), the offender must have committed murder with subjective foresight of death and must have committed the murder "while committing or attempting to commit ... forcible confinement." Where the act causing death and the acts constituting the forcible confinement "all form part of one continuous sequence of events forming a single transaction," the death is caused "while committing" an offence for the purpose of s. 214(5); see *Paré, supra*, at p. 632. To commit the underlying offence of forcible confinement, the offender must use "physical restraint, contrary to the wishes of the person restrained, but to which the victim submits unwillingly, thereby depriving the person of his or her liberty to move from one place to another": quote from *R v. Dollan* (1980), 53 CCC (2d) 146 (Ont. HC), as cited with approval in *R v. Gratton* (1985), 18 CCC (3d) 462 (CA) [at 473]. It is true that the definition of forcible confinement adopted by the courts allows for varying circumstances in each individual case. But this alone is not a sign of arbitrariness. The offence of forcible confinement as defined falls clearly under the rubric of the organizing principle enunciated by Wilson J in *Paré*, namely, that of the illegal domination of no person by another. The decision of Parliament to attach a minimum 25-year sentence without eligibility for parole in cases of first degree murder, having regard to all these circumstances, cannot be said to be arbitrary within the meaning of s. 9 of the Charter. The incarceration is statutorily authorized, it narrowly defines a class of offenders with respect to whom the punishment will be invoked and it prescribes quite specifically the conditions under which an offender may be found guilty of first-degree murder. Further, the policy decision of Parliament to classify these murders as first degree murders accords with the broader objectives of a sentencing scheme. The elevation of murder while committing a forcible confinement to first degree reflects a societal denunciation of those offenders who choose to exploit their position of dominance and power to the point of murder.

The appellant's final argument is that the combined effect of s. 215(5)(e) and s. 669 contravenes s. 12 of the Charter. Section 12 of the Charter protects individuals against cruel and unusual punishment. The phrase "cruel and unusual punishment" has been considered by this court in *R v. Smith, supra*. That case held that the criterion to be applied in order to determine whether a punishment is cruel and unusual is whether the punishment is so excessive as to outrage standards of decency. At pp. 1072-73 stated that:

> The test for review under s. 12 of the Charter is one of gross disproportionality, because it is aimed at punishments that are more than merely excessive. We should be careful not to stigmatize every disproportionate or excessive sentence as being a constitutional violation,

and should leave to the usual sentencing appeal process the task of reviewing the fitness of a sentence. Section 12 will only be infringed where the sentence is so unfit having regard to the offence and the offender as to be grossly disproportionate.

In assessing whether a sentence is grossly disproportionate, the court must first consider the gravity of the offence, the personal characteristics of the offender and the particular circumstances of the case in order to determine what range of sentences would have been appropriate to punish, rehabilitate or deter this particular offender or to protect the public from this particular offender.

In *Lyons, supra*, La Forest J addressed the meaning of the word "grossly" at pp. 344-45:

> The word "grossly" [as in "grossly disproportionate"], it seems to me, reflects this Court's concern not to hold Parliament to a standard so exacting, at least in the context of s. 12, as to require punishments to be perfectly suited to accommodate the moral nuances of every crime and every offender.

In my view, the combination of s. 214(5)(e) and s. 669 does not constitute cruel and unusual punishment. These sections provide for punishment of the most serious crime in our criminal law, that of first degree murder. This is a crime that carries with it the most serious level of moral blameworthiness, namely, subjective foresight of death. The penalty is severe and deservedly so. The minimum 25 years to be served before eligibility for parole reflects society's condemnation of a person who has exploited a position of power and dominance to the gravest extent possible by murdering the person that he or she is forcibly confining. The punishment is not excessive and clearly does not outrage our standards of decency. In my view, it is within the purview of Parliament, in order to meet the objectives of a rational system of sentencing, to treat our most serious crime with an appropriate degree of certainty and severity. I reiterate that even in the case of first degree murder, Parliament has been sensitive to the particular circumstances of each offender through various provisions allowing for the Royal prerogative of mercy, the availability of escorted absences from custody for humanitarian and rehabilitative purposes and for early parole: see s. 672, s. 674 [now s 747] and s. 686 [now s 751] of the *Criminal Code*. In *Smith, supra*, at p. 1070, I quoted with approval the following statement by Borins DCJ in *R v. Guiller*, Ont. Dist. Ct. [48 CR (3d) 226]:

> It is not for the court to pass on the wisdom of Parliament with respect to the gravity of various offences and the range of penalties which may be imposed upon those found guilty of committing the offences. Parliament has broad discussion in proscribing conduct as criminal and in determining proper punishment. While the final judgment as to whether a punishment exceeds constitutional limits set by the Charter is properly a judicial function the court should be reluctant to interfere with the considered views of Parliament and then only in the clearest of cases where the punishment prescribed is so excessive when compared with the punishment prescribed for other offences as to outrage standards of decency.

Therefore, I conclude that in the case at bar the impugned provisions in combination do not represent cruel and unusual punishment within the meaning of s. 12 of the Charter.

Allan Manson, "The Easy Acceptance of Long-Term Confinement in Canada"
(1990), 79 CR (3d) 265 at 265-67, 269-72 (footnotes omitted)

The History of Section 742(a)

The creation of two categories of murder, first and second degree, and the current punishments for these offences evolved from the debate over capital punishment which occupied Parliament and the Canadian public for over twenty years. In 1956, a joint committee of the Senate and House of Commons recommended the retention of capital punishment but suggested that the offence of murder be divided into capital and non-capital categories. In 1961, the *Criminal Code* was amended to provide for capital murder which would be · punishable by hanging unless the person was under the age of 18 years: *An Act to Amend the Criminal Code* (Capital Murder), SC 1960-61, c. 44, s. 1. Capital murder consisted of a killing that was planned and deliberate, a killing resulting from the direct intervention or counselling by the accused in the course of certain stipulated crimes, or the killing of a police officer or prison guard. All other murder was characterized as non-capital and was punishable by life imprisonment. This régime continued in force until 28th December 1967, although as a result of reviews by the Cabinet for the purpose of advising the Governor-General on commutation, the last hangings in Canada took place on 11th December 1962 at the Don Jail in Toronto. In 1967 the Code was again amended, to limit capital murder to those cases where an accused, by his or her own act, caused or assisted in the causing of the death of a police officer or prison officer, or counselled or procured that death: *An Act to Amend the Criminal Code*, SC 1967-68, c. 15, s. 1. This limitation was intended to last for only five years (s. 4), but was continued for a further five years in 1972: *Criminal Law Amendment (Capital Punishment) Act*, SC 1973-74, c. 38, s. 10. During this semi-moratorium, persons who had been sentenced to death but whose sentences had been commuted could not be released from confinement without the approval of the Governor in Council. Persons who were sentenced to life imprisonment for murder could be released on parole after serving ten years, unless the trial judge increased the period of parole ineligibility. This was the statutory sentencing background against which Parliament resumed the debate on capital punishment in 1976.

The often passionate and partisan Parliamentary discussion in 1976 focused on the fundamental issue of the legitimacy of capital punishment, and little attention was paid to the elements of the proposed alternatives. In the Standing Committee on Justice and Legal Affairs, a clause-by-clause consideration of the new bill took place. In that committee, statistics were tabled to show the Canadian experience with life imprisonment, as well as the régimes which operated in other jurisdictions where capital punishment had been abolished. The following table indicates the average periods actually served in custody in Canada between 1961 and 1974.

	1961-68	1968-74
Capital Murder (commuted)	12.0	13.2
Non-Capital Murder	6.2	7.7

These figures are particularly interesting when put into a comparative context as discussed by the parliamentarians in committee at the time. A United Nations group of experts had only a few years earlier observed that, in countries which employed life imprisonment as an alternative to capital punishment, the most common median length of term served was between 10 and 15 years, and the average custodial term was about 14 years. ...

• • •

With all the data, both Canadian and comparative, pointing to a period of between 10 and 15 years, why did the proposed legislation include a minimum term for first degree of 25 years? The answer is simple: politics and expedience. Warren Allmand, the Solicitor General, who had been given the responsibility of steering the struggle to abolish capital punishment, had been told by the Canadian Association of Police Chiefs, who supported the death penalty, that only a minimum sentence as severe as 25 years could conceivably be an alternative to the rope: see the minutes of the standing committee, ante, note 3, pp. 72:60-61. In retrospect, Mr. Allmand was probably correct in responding to views of that sort in order to achieve the success of the abolition movement. ...

• • •

... In *Luxton*, the test of outraging decency becomes the single analytical tool used to validate the mandatory long term confinement for first degree murder.

In essence, the judgment in *Luxton* says that it is constitutionally acceptable to impose the most severe punishment for the most serious offence. No one would quarrel with the logic of this proposition. While it must be true, it nevertheless misses the point in two significant ways. First, although the reasoning justifies the imposition of a harsher sentence for first degree murder, it ignores the actual length of the term imposed. The same analysis could be applied to justify mandatory terms of 30, 40 or 50 years. Secondly, by truncating the s. 12 analysis into solely a question about societal outrage, the court either ignores the effects of the duration of the sentence or assumes that the community knows the real effects of 25-year minimum terms and accepts them as legitimate aspects of penal policy. The issue of duration and its impact is clearly part of a proper s. 12 analysis, yet no evidence was adduced about the human impact of long term confinement. Although the Supreme Court has reminded us on a number of occasions that legislation might fail to pass Charter muster by reason of either its purpose or its effects, no empirical or expert material was placed before the court to explain the effects of the punishment in question. The argument proceeded entirely on conceptual grounds, with reference primarily to the idea of a hierarchy of punishments. The actual punishment was not assessed in real, human terms.

It is not fair to suggest that Lamer CJC has ignored the question of 25 years of confinement and its relation to the personal circumstances of offenders. He observes at p. 203 that "Parliament has been sensitive to the particular circumstances of each offender through various provisions allowing for the Royal prerogative of mercy, the availability of escorted absences from custody for humanitarian and rehabilitative purposes, and for early parole." In an abstract sense, the possibility of these indulgences exists, but the reality is that they are very rarely used. Last spring, when a 70-year-old woman received a pardon after serving 11 years of a first degree murder term, the newspapers announced that it was the first pardon granted to a person convicted of first degree murder, and that only nine prisoners had received pardons in the past ten years. The Royal prerogative of mercy is available to ameliorate the harshness of sentences, but it is most often used in situations where it has been established that a person was wrongly convicted. The availability of escorted temporary absence passes is another example of the sardonic gap between statutory possibility and practical reality. Passes of this sort for a lifer require the approval of the institution where the prisoner is confined, the approval of the National Parole Board and the deployment of one or two staff persons to act as escorts. The board's own manual advises that this power should be used "very sparingly" in order not to "depreciate" the seriousness of the sentence. Consequently, escorted passes are awarded principally for funerals, visits to sick relatives and other related family events. The reference to early parole must mean the parole ineligibility review pursuant to s. 745 [am. RSC 1985, c. 27 (2nd Supp.), s. 10] of the code, which a prisoner can commence after serving 15 years in custody. This process only provides a new parole eligibility date. The issue of release is then delegated to the parole board for the application of its usual criteria, typically a process which takes a minimum of three years. Again it is important to recognize that the court had no material before it demonstrating how these extraordinary processes really work. Had the court found the mandatory punishment to be illegitimate, these factors, along with issues of legislative objective and real impact, would have been relevant to the s. 1 justificatory analysis.

Conclusion

The rulings in *Luxton* and *Arkell* do not preclude any individual convicted of first degree murder from attempting to challenge the application of the mandatory sentence as it relates to his or her particular circumstances. ...

The more important question is whether the Supreme Court will decide to reconsider the constitutionality of the mandatory sentence for first degree murder when it is provided with a full, empirical record. Certainly the court has the power to rethink an important issue of this sort, particularly if persuasive material is presented to it. The prospect, however, is doubtful, and one might wonder whether, in the wake of *Luxton* and *Arkell*, a lawyer would have the temerity to bring a new leave application on this issue. However, as discussed above, a s. 12 argument can be based on individual impact, and it may be that, in the context of an individual challenge to the application of the mandatory sentence, the Supreme Court might choose to rehear the general issue.

For the time being, *Arkell* and *Luxton* effectively preclude further challenges to the legislation that creates the mandatory sentencing scheme for murder. However, as Manson points out, this does not mean that individual litigants must necessarily be deprived of a remedy in exceptional cases.

R v Latimer
2001 SCC 1, [2001] 1 SCR 3

[In 1997, Robert Latimer was convicted (a second time) of second-degree murder in relation to the death of his 12-year-old daughter, who was a quadriplegic suffering from severe cerebral palsy and who was in constant pain. He argued that his actions were motivated by his concern to free his daughter from her pain. Latimer appealed his conviction to the Saskatchewan Court of Appeal. During the jury deliberations, the jury sent this note to the trial judge:

1. What is the procedure once the verdict has been reached?

2. Sergeant Conlon's testimony he advised R. Latimer to get a lawyer because he would be charged with first degree murder. Why is R. Latimer charged with second degree murder?

3. Is there any possible way we can have input into a recommendation for sentencing?

After returning a verdict of guilty, the jury was asked for its recommendation for a period of parole ineligibility according to s 745.2 of the *Criminal Code*. Although that section stipulates a period between 10 and 25 years, the jury recommended that Latimer be eligible for parole after serving one year in custody. Notwithstanding the mandatory life sentence, the trial judge sentenced Latimer to a term of imprisonment of one year to be followed by a period of probation of one year less a day. This was essentially a constitutional exemption from the mandatory penalty. The Saskatchewan Court of Appeal allowed a Crown appeal and imposed a sentence of life imprisonment with no eligibility for parole for at least 10 years. Along with the defence of necessity, whether the mandatory murder punishment ought to have applied to Latimer was one of the issues that ultimately confronted the Supreme Court of Canada. In a unanimous decision, the Supreme Court dismissed the appeal.]

[10] Tracy underwent numerous surgeries in her short lifetime. In 1990, surgery tried to balance the muscles around her pelvis. In 1992, it was used to reduce the abnormal curvature in her back.

[11] Like the majority of totally involved, quadriparetic children with cerebral palsy, Tracy had developed scoliosis, an abnormal curvature and rotation in the back, necessitating surgery to implant metal rods to support her spine. While it was a successful procedure, further problems developed in Tracy's right hip: it became dislocated and caused her considerable pain.

[12] Tracy was scheduled to undergo further surgery on November 19, 1993. This was to deal with her dislocated hip and, it was hoped, to lessen her constant pain. The procedure involved removing her upper thigh bone, which would leave her lower leg loose without any connecting bone; it would be held in place only by muscle and tissue. The anticipated recovery period for this surgery was one year.

[13] The Latimers were told that this procedure would cause pain, and the doctors involved suggested that further surgery would be required in the future to relieve the pain emanating from various joints in Tracy's body. According to the appellant's wife, Laura Latimer, further surgery was perceived as mutilation. As a result, Robert Latimer formed the view that his daughter's life was not worth living.

[14] In the weeks leading up to Tracy's death, the Latimers looked into the option of placing Tracy in a group home in North Battleford. She had lived there between July and October of 1993, just prior to her death, while her mother was pregnant. The Latimers applied to place Tracy in the home in October, but later concluded they were not interested in permanently placing her in that home at that time.

[15] On October 12, 1993, after learning that the doctors wished to perform this additional surgery, the appellant decided to take his daughter's life. On Sunday, October 24, 1993, while his wife and Tracy's siblings were at church, Robert Latimer carried Tracy to his pickup truck, seated her in the cab, and inserted a hose from the truck's exhaust pipe into the cab. She died from the carbon monoxide.

• • •

[79] As is reflected in the constitutional questions before the Court, this appeal is restricted to a consideration of the particularized inquiry. In substance, the appellant concedes the general constitutionality of ss. 235 and 745(c) as these sections are applied in combination. Mr. Latimer's challenge to their overall constitutionality was put forward in the alternative but was not pressed forcefully since no substantive argument on point was offered. Furthermore, no reasonable hypothetical situation was presented for the Court's consideration. In short, the appellant's arguments wholly centred on the effect of the sentence in this specific case on this specific offender. Consequently, only the individual remedy sought by the appellant, namely a constitutional exemption, is at issue.

. . .

[80] The first factor to consider is the gravity of the offence. Recently, Gonthier J, in *Morrisey* [*R v*, 2000 SCC 39, [2000] 2 SCR 90], provided important guidance for the proper assessment of the gravity of an offence for the purposes of a s. 12 analysis. Specifically, Gonthier J noted, at para. 35, that an assessment of the gravity of the offence requires an understanding of (i) the character of the offender's actions, and (ii) the consequences of those actions.

[81] Certainly, in this case one cannot escape the conclusion that Mr. Latimer's actions resulted in the most serious of all possible consequences, namely, the death of the victim, Tracy Latimer.

[82] In considering the character of Mr. Latimer's actions, we are directed to an assessment of the criminal fault requirement or *mens rea* element of the offence rather than the offender's motive or general state of mind (*Morrisey, supra*, at para. 36). We attach a greater degree of criminal responsibility or moral blameworthiness to conduct where the accused knowingly broke the law (*Morrisey, supra*, at para. 36; *R v. Martineau*, [1990] 2 SCR 633, at p. 645). In this case, the *mens rea* requirement for second degree murder is subjective foresight of death: the most serious level of moral blameworthiness (*Luxton, supra*, at p. 724).

[83] Parliament has classified murder offences into first and second degree based on its perception of relative levels of moral blameworthiness. Parliament has also provided for differential treatment between them in sentencing, but only in respect of parole eligibility. As noted by Lamer CJ in *Luxton, supra*, at pp. 720-21:

> I must also reiterate that what we are speaking of here is a classification scheme for the purposes of sentencing. The distinction between first and second degree murder only comes into play when it has first been proven beyond a reasonable doubt that the offender is guilty of murder, that is, that he or she had subjective foresight of death: *R v. Martineau*, handed down this day. *There is no doubt that a sentencing scheme must exhibit a proportionality to the seriousness of the offence, or to put it another way, there must be a gradation of punishments according to the malignity of the offences.* [Emphasis added.]

[84] However, even if the gravity of second degree murder is reduced in comparison to first degree murder, it cannot be denied that second degree murder is an offence accompanied by an extremely high degree of criminal culpability. In this case, therefore, the gravest possible consequences resulted from an act of the most serious and morally blameworthy intentionality. It is against this reality that we must weigh the other contextual factors, including and especially the particular circumstances of the offender and the offence.

[85] Turning to the characteristics of the offender and the particular circumstances of the offence we must consider the existence of any aggravating and mitigating circumstances (*Morrisey, supra*, at para. 38; *Goltz* [*R v*, [1991] 3 SCR 485], at pp. 512-13). Specifically, any aggravating circumstances must be weighed against any mitigating circumstances. In this regard, it is possible that prior to gauging the sentence's appropriateness in light of an appreciation of the particular circumstances weighed against the gravity of the offence, the mitigating and aggravating circumstances might well cancel out their ultimate impact (*Morrisey, supra*, at para. 40). Indeed, this is what occurs in this case. On the one hand, we must give due consideration to Mr. Latimer's initial attempts to conceal his actions, his lack of remorse, his position of trust, the significant degree of planning and premeditation, and Tracy's extreme vulnerability. On the other hand, we are mindful of Mr. Latimer's good character and standing in the community, his tortured anxiety about Tracy's well-being, and his laudable perseverance as a caring and involved parent. Considered together we cannot find that the personal characteristics and particular circumstances of this case displace the serious gravity of this offence.

[86] Finally, this sentence is consistent with a number of valid penological goals and sentencing principles. Although we would agree that in this case the sentencing principles of rehabilitation, specific deterrence and protection are not triggered for consideration, we are mindful of the important role that the mandatory minimum sentence plays in denouncing murder. Denunciation of unlawful conduct is one of the objectives of sentencing recognized in s. 718 of the *Criminal Code*. As noted by the Court in *R v. M.(C.A.)*, [1996] 1 SCR 500, at para. 81:

> The objective of denunciation mandates that a sentence should communicate society's condemnation of that particular offender's *conduct*. In short, a sentence with a denunciatory element represents a symbolic, collective statement that the offender's conduct should be punished for encroaching on our society's basic code of values as enshrined within our substantive criminal law. [Emphasis in original.]

Furthermore, denunciation becomes much more important in the consideration of sentencing in cases where there is a "high degree of planning and premeditation, and where the offence and its consequences are highly publicized, [so that] like-minded individuals may well be deterred by severe sentences": *R v. Mulvahill and Snelgrove* (1993), 21 BCAC 296, at p. 300. This is particularly so where the victim is a vulnerable person with respect to age, disability, or other similar factors.

[87] In summary, the minimum mandatory sentence is not grossly disproportionate in this case. We cannot find that any aspect of the particular circumstances of the case or the offender diminishes the degree of criminal responsibility borne by Mr. Latimer. In addition, although not free of debate, the sentence is not out of step with valid penological goals or sentencing principles. The legislative classification and treatment of this offender meets the requisite standard of proportionality (*Lyons* [*R v*, [1987] 2 SCR 309], at p. 339). Where there is no violation of Mr. Latimer's s. 12 right there is no basis for granting a constitutional exemption.

[88] Having said all this, we wish to point out that this appeal raises a number of issues that are worthy of emphasis. The sentencing provisions for second degree murder include both ss. 235 and 745(c). Applied in combination these provisions result in a sentence that

is hybrid in that it provides for both a mandatory life sentence and a minimum term of incarceration. The choice is Parliament's on the use of minimum sentences, though considerable difference of opinion continues on the wisdom of employing minimum sentences from a criminal law policy or penological point of view.

[89] It is also worth referring again to the royal prerogative of mercy that is found in s. 749 of the *Criminal Code*, which provides "[n]othing in this Act in any manner limits or affects Her Majesty's royal prerogative of mercy." As was pointed out by Sopinka J in *R v. Sarson*, [1996] 2 SCR 223, at para. 51, albeit in a different context:

> Where the courts are unable to provide an appropriate remedy in cases that the executive sees as unjust imprisonment, the executive is permitted to dispense "mercy," and order the release of the offender. The royal prerogative of mercy is the only potential remedy for persons who have exhausted their rights of appeal and are unable to show that their sentence fails to accord with the *Charter*.

[90] But the prerogative is a matter for the executive, not the courts. The executive will undoubtedly, if it chooses to consider the matter, examine all of the underlying circumstances surrounding the tragedy of Tracy Latimer that took place on October 24, 1993, some seven years ago. Since that time Mr. Latimer has undergone two trials and two appeals to the Court of Appeal for Saskatchewan and this Court, with attendant publicity and consequential agony for him and his family.

• • •

[91] Mr. Latimer's appeals against conviction and sentence are dismissed.

In the subsequent case of *R v Ferguson*, 2008 SCC 6, [2008] 1 SCR 96, a unanimous majority of the Supreme Court rejected the availability of a constitutional exemption as a response to a s 12 Charter claim.

The *Latimer* case spawned an interesting body of literature raising various dimensions of the difficult sentencing issues that it generates: see Kent Roach, "Crime and Punishment in the Latimer Case" (2001) 64 Sask L Rev 469; Barney Sneiderman, "Latimer in the Supreme Court: Necessity, Compassionate Homicide, and Mandatory Sentencing" (2001) 64 Sask L Rev 511; M David Lepofsky, "The Latimer Case: Murder Is Still Murder When the Victim Is a Child with a Disability" (2001) 27 Queen's LJ 315; FC De Coste, "Conditions of Clemency: Justice from the Offender" (2003) 66 Sask L Rev 1; for a critique of the earlier decision of the Saskatchewan Court of Appeal ((1995), 41 CR (4th) 1), see also Tim Quigley, "R v. Latimer: Hard Cases Make Interesting Law" (1995), 41 CR (4th) 89.

Eradicating the mandatory sentencing scheme for murder, whether in general or on a case-by-case basis, is no simple matter. If Parliament were to alter the present law and permit judges to sentence murderers constrained only by the maximum sentence of life imprisonment, the consequences could well be dramatic. It would have the effect of blurring the distinction between manslaughter and murder, for the purposes of sentencing. Still, this might have the effect of inducing more guilty pleas in homicide cases. But the basis on which we currently distinguish liability for murder and manslaughter—that is, the intention of the offender—will be relevant to the length of the sentence that is imposed. Collapsing the categories of homicide in order to achieve a more discretionary sentencing regime may merely result in shifting these sorts of decisions from the "trial phase" to the "sentencing phase" of the proceedings. What will this do to the right to trial by jury in this context? Is a better answer the creation of a new category—for example, "compassionate homicide"?

These issues were considered in the United Kingdom by the Select Committee on Murder and Life Imprisonment. After careful consideration of the evidence and views of many leading experts, the committee rejected a proposal that the mandatory sentence of life imprisonment for murder be changed: see House of Lords, *Report of the Select Committee on Murder and Life Imprisonment*, HL-78-I (London: HMSO, 1989). One of the most ardent and persistent critics of the life sentence for murder is the British scholar David Hennessy, 3rd Baron Windlesham: see in particular "The Penalty for Murder" in *Responses to Crime* (Oxford: Clarendon Press, 1987); "Life Imprisonment: A Sentence Nobody Can Understand?" in *Responses to Crime—Penal Policy in the Making*, vol 2 (Oxford: Clarendon Press, 1993); and "Life Sentences: The Defects of Duality" in *Responses to Crime: Legislating with the Tide* (Oxford: Clarendon Press, 1996).

III. CRIMINAL CODE, SECTIONS 745 TO 745.5

Imprisonment for Life

Information in respect of parole

745.01(1) Except where subsection 745.6(2) applies, at the time of sentencing under paragraph 745(a), (b) or (c), the judge who presided at the trial of the offender shall state the following, for the record:

> The offender has been found guilty of (*state offence*) and sentenced to imprisonment for life. The offender is not eligible for parole until (*state date*). However, after serving at least 15 years of the sentence, the offender may apply under section 745.6 of the *Criminal Code* for a reduction in the number of years of imprisonment without eligibility for parole. If the jury hearing the application reduces the period of parole ineligibility, the offender may then make an application for parole under the *Corrections and Conditional Release Act* at the end of that reduced period.

Exception

(2) Subsection (1) does not apply if the offender is convicted of an offence committed on or after the day on which this subsection comes into force.

Persons under eighteen

745.1 The sentence to be pronounced against a person who was under the age of eighteen at the time of the commission of the offence for which the person was convicted of first degree murder or second degree murder and who is to be sentenced to imprisonment for life shall be that the person be sentenced to imprisonment for life without eligibility for parole until the person has served

(a) such period between five and seven years of the sentence as is specified by the judge presiding at the trial, or if no period is specified by the judge presiding at the trial, five years, in the case of a person who was under the age of sixteen at the time of the commission of the offence;

(b) ten years, in the case of a person convicted of first degree murder who was sixteen or seventeen years of age at the time of the commission of the offence; and

(c) seven years, in the case of a person convicted of second degree murder who was sixteen or seventeen years of age at the time of the commission of the offence.

Recommendation by jury

745.2 Subject to section 745.3, where a jury finds an accused guilty of second degree murder, the judge presiding at the trial shall, before discharging the jury, put to them the following question:

> You have found the accused guilty of second degree murder and the law requires that I now pronounce a sentence of imprisonment for life against the accused. Do you wish to make any recommendation with respect to the number of years that the accused must serve before the accused is eligible for release on parole? You are not required to make any recommendation but if you do, your recommendation will be considered by me when I am determining whether I should substitute for the ten year period, which the law would otherwise require the accused to serve before the accused is eligible to be considered for release on parole, a number of years that is more than ten but not more than twenty-five.

Recommendation by jury—multiple murders

745.21(1) Where a jury finds an accused guilty of murder and that accused has previously been convicted of murder, the judge presiding at the trial shall, before discharging the jury, put to them the following question:

> You have found the accused guilty of murder. The law requires that I now pronounce a sentence of imprisonment for life against the accused. Do you wish to make any recommendation with respect to the period without eligibility for parole to be served for this murder consecutively to the period without eligibility for parole imposed for the previous murder? You are not required to make any recommendation, but if you do, your recommendation will be considered by me when I make my determination.

Application

(2) Subsection (1) applies to an offender who is convicted of murders committed on a day after the day on which this section comes into force and for which the offender is sentenced under this Act, the *National Defence Act* or the *Crimes Against Humanity and War Crimes Act*.

Persons under sixteen

745.3 Where a jury finds an accused guilty of first degree murder or second degree murder and the accused was under the age of sixteen at the time of the commission of the offence, the judge presiding at the trial shall, before discharging the jury, put to them the following question:

> You have found the accused guilty of first degree murder (or second degree murder) and the law requires that I now pronounce a sentence of imprisonment for life against the accused. Do you wish to make any recommendation with respect to the period of imprisonment that the accused must serve before the accused is eligible for release on parole? You are not required to make any recommendation but if you do, your recommendation will be considered by me when I am determining the period of imprisonment that is between five years and seven years that the law would require the accused to serve before the accused is eligible to be considered for release on parole.

Ineligibility for parole

745.4 Subject to section 745.5, at the time of the sentencing under section 745 of an offender who is convicted of second degree murder, the judge who presided at the trial of the offender or, if that judge is unable to do so, any judge of the same court may, having regard to the character of the offender, the nature of the offence and the circumstances surrounding its commission, and to the recommendation, if any, made pursuant to section 745.2, by order, substitute for ten years a number of years of imprisonment (being more than ten but not more than twenty-five) without eligibility for parole, as the judge deems fit in the circumstances.

Idem

745.5   At the time of the sentencing under section 745.1 of an offender who is convicted of first degree murder or second degree murder and who was under the age of sixteen at the time of the commission of the offence, the judge who presided at the trial of the offender or, if that judge is unable to do so, any judge of the same court, may, having regard to the age and character of the offender, the nature of the offence and the circumstances surrounding its commission, and to the recommendation, if any, made pursuant to section 745.3, by order, decide the period of imprisonment the offender is to serve that is between five years and seven years without eligibility for parole, as the judge deems fit in the circumstances.

In 2011, the *Criminal Code* was amended to permit a trial judge to order, in cases of multiple murders, that the periods of parole ineligibility be served consecutively:

Ineligibility for parole—multiple murders

745.51(1)   At the time of the sentencing under section 745 of an offender who is convicted of murder and who has already been convicted of one or more other murders, the judge who presided at the trial of the offender or, if that judge is unable to do so, any judge of the same court may, having regard to the character of the offender, the nature of the offence and the circumstances surrounding its commission, and the recommendation, if any, made pursuant to section 745.21, by order, decide that the periods without eligibility for parole for each murder conviction are to be served consecutively.

In 2014, a 24-year-old man, Justin Bourque, pleaded guilty in New Brunswick to three counts of first-degree murder and two counts of attempted murder arising from a shooting rampage in which three RCMP officers were killed and two wounded. He was sentenced to five terms of life imprisonment. On the murder counts, the judge applied s 745.51 and ordered that the 25-year eligibility periods be served consecutively. Accordingly, Bourque is required to serve 75 years before being eligible for parole. At that time, he will be 99 years old, if he lives that long: see "Justin Bourque gets 5 life sentences, no chance of parole for 75 years" (31 October 2014), online: CBC News <http://www.cbc.ca/news/canada/new-brunswick/justin -bourque-gets-5-life-sentences-no-chance-of-parole-for-75-years-1.2818516>.

R v Bourque, 2014 NBQB 237 brings to light the issue of "life without parole," a question not yet considered by Canadian courts. In 2013, in *Vinter and Others v United Kingdom* (Application Nos 66069/09, 130/10, and 3896/10) (9 July 2013), the European Court of Human Rights (ECHR) decided that an "irreducible" life sentence would violate the guarantee in art 3 of the *European Convention on Human Rights*, prohibiting torture and "inhuman or degrading treatment or punishment" unless there were legitimate penological grounds for incarceration. Accordingly, a life sentence could remain compatible with art 3 of the Convention only if there was both a prospect of release and a possibility of review. At the time, the ECHR found the possibility of a secretary-of-state review to be an inadequate process. Subsequently, the issue returned to the ECHR in *Hutchinson v United Kingdom* (Strasbourg, 3 February 2015). By that time, the English Court of Appeal had issued its judgment in *R v Newell; R v McLoughlin*, [2014] EWCA Crim 188, in which the secretary of state's review power was interpreted "to provide to an offender 'hope' or the 'possibility' of release in exceptional circumstances." On this basis, the *Hutchinson* court dismissed the claim of a violation of art 3.

In the United States, the Supreme Court has held that "life without parole" for juveniles sentenced for a non-homicide offence violates the 8th amendment guarantee against cruel and unusual punishment: see *Graham v Florida*, 130 S Ct 2011 (2010). Subsequently, it also held that a mandatory life sentence without parole imposed on a juvenile, even in murder cases, would also be cruel and unusual punishment: see *Miller v Alabama*, 132 S Ct 2455 (2012). This means that a judge must have the discretion to take into account mitigating circumstances when deciding whether to impose life without parole on a juvenile.

From time to time, amendments have been made to the murder provisions. For an account of this history, see Allan Manson, "A Trip from Thoughtful to Thoughtless: Murder Sentencing in Canada" in Karim Ismaili, Jane B Sprott & Kim Varma, eds, *Canadian Criminal Justice Policy* (Toronto: Oxford University Press, 2012) 58-78. Accordingly, after a legislative change, the question arises as to which regime applies. What determines whether changes apply to a particular accused? What if a more lenient regime is enacted after sentencing is complete? The Canadian legal position is explained in the case below.

R v Giesbrecht (EH)
2007 MBCA 112, [2007] 11 WWR 54

SCOTT CJM:

[8] In support of his application, the applicant relies on sec. 44(e) of the federal *Interpretation Act* and sec. 11(i) of the *Charter*, which read as follows:

> 44. Where an enactment, in this section called the "former enactment," is repealed and another enactment, in this section called the "new enactment," is substituted therefor,
>
> • • •
>
> (e) when any punishment, penalty or forfeiture is reduced or mitigated by the new enactment, the punishment, penalty or forfeiture if imposed or adjudged after the repeal shall be reduced or mitigated accordingly[.]
>
> 11. Any person charged with an offence has the right
>
> • • •
>
> (i) if found guilty of the offence and if the punishment for the offence has been varied between the time of commission and the time of sentencing, to the benefit of the lesser punishment.

[9] With respect to sec. 44(e) of the *Interpretation Act*, the applicant places strong reliance on the decision of the Supreme Court of Canada in *R v. Dunn*, [1995] 1 SCR 226, where Major J, for eight of the nine members of the Supreme Court, held (at para. 27):

> I conclude that s. 44(e) of the *Interpretation Act* resolves the question raised by this appeal. Where an amendment to a sentencing provision has been passed after conviction and sentence by the trial judge, but before the appeal has been "decided," the offender is entitled to the benefit of the lesser penalty or punishment. The court of appeal, in reviewing a trial decision on sentence, is "adjudging" that sentence, in that it considers it judicially. The respondent's contention that "adjudge" extends only to the options on penalty that may be ordered at trial is too narrow an approach to the interpretation of s. 44(e), and disregards the meaning of the word "adjudge."

[10] Therefore, prisoners who were "in the system" at the time the amendments to the *Code* took place were given the benefit of the new parole eligibility regime. See, for example, *R v. Tourangeau*, (1995), 137 Sask. R 277 (CA).

[The appellant in *Giesebrecht*, however, as might commonly occur in these situations, required an extension of time within which to appeal. The Manitoba Court of Appeal (in *R v DBR*, 2005 MBCA 21 at para 6) explained the relevant test:

> An order to extend time is a discretionary order, with the overriding objective that justice be done in the circumstances. The criteria that are normally considered on such an application are:
>
> 1. there was a continuous intention to appeal from a time within the period when the appeal should have been commenced;
> 2. there is a reasonable explanation for the delay; and
> 3. there are arguable grounds of appeal.

Hamilton JA went on to describe this last criterion as "a low threshold"; one which "is meant to ensure that the appeal is not frivolous."]

Ultitimately, the court dismissed the application finding (at para 29) that it was not "persuaded that the applicant had a continuous intention to appeal throughout the 11-year period following the affirmation of his conviction by the Supreme Court of Canada."

IV. APPLYING THE PROVISIONS

A. Determining Parole Eligibility for Second-Degree Murder

The sentencing provisions for second-degree murder have caused Canadian courts great difficulties. The courts have struggled to reach an appropriate interpretation of the provisions. Until recently, there was some controversy over the general approach to this sentencing function. Courts divided on the issue whether there was a general presumption in favour of imposing the 10-year minimum, leaving the question of dangerousness to the parole board. This view saw increases beyond the minimum only in "unusual circumstances": see *R v Gourgon* (1981), 58 CCC (2d) 193 (BCCA) and *R v Jordan* (1983), 7 CCC (3d) 143 (BCCA). Others favoured an approach that allowed the sentencing judge to fix the period of parole eligibility at a level that he or she thought was "fit," free from presumptions of restraint: see *R v Mitchell* (1987), 39 CCC (3d) 141 (NSSC (AD)) and *R v Wenarchuk* (1982), 67 CCC (2d) 169 (Sask CA). After many years of (sometimes sharp) judicial debate, the Supreme Court of Canada purported to settle the issue in *R v Shropshire*.

R v Shropshire
[1995] 4 SCR 227, 43 CR (4th) 269

IACOBUCCI J (Lamer CJ and La Forest, L'Heureux-Dubé, Sopinka, Gonthier, Cory, McLachlin, and Major JJ concurring):

[1] This appeal was allowed on June 15, 1995, with reasons to follow. These are those reasons.

[2] At issue in this appeal are the factors and principles that should guide a trial judge in determining whether to extend the period of parole ineligibility on a second degree murder conviction beyond the statutory minimum of 10 years. This appeal also touches on the appropriate standard of appellate review to be exercised when considering a trial judge's decision to postpone the period of parole eligibility. Both of these issues engage the broad theme of when the discretion of a sentencing judge ought to be altered.

I. Background

[3] The respondent, Michael Thomas Shropshire, pleaded guilty to the second degree murder of Timothy Buffam. The offence was committed at the respondent's home in Abbotsford, British Columbia, on May 26, 1992, during a marijuana transaction between the respondent, the deceased, and Lorne Lang, a third person accompanying the deceased. Lang is otherwise known as "Animal." The respondent was acquainted with Buffam and Lang as the trio had had prior narcotics dealings. Without any warning, the respondent shot Buffam three times in the chest as they were about to enter the garage to complete the marijuana deal. The respondent then chased Lang in his vehicle shouting "Hacksaw told me to do it!" Hacksaw is the nickname of another associate.

[4] Two days later, the respondent gave himself up to the police. After a preliminary hearing, the respondent pleaded guilty to second degree murder. He professed remorse for his actions but was unwilling or unable to explain them. No motive for the killing was ever ascertained. The respondent has a prior criminal record including two convictions in Youth Court for robbery, a conviction for impaired driving, and two narcotic offences as an adult.

[5] On June 17, 1993, McKinnon J of the Supreme Court of British Columbia sentenced the respondent to life imprisonment without eligibility for parole for 12 years. This period of non-eligibility for parole is two years more than the minimum (and most common) period of parole ineligibility for second degree murder, namely 10 years. Trial judges are permitted, by virtue of the discretionary power accorded to them by s. 744 of the *Criminal Code*, RSC 1985, c. C-46, to extend the period of parole ineligibility beyond the statutory minimum. The respondent challenged the discretionary s. 744 decision of the trial judge.

[6] On May 4, 1994, a majority of the Court of Appeal for British Columbia allowed the respondent's appeal against sentence, and reduced the period of parole ineligibility to 10 years: (1994) 90 CCC (3d) 234, 45 BCAC 252, 72 WAC 252. Goldie JA dissented and would have dismissed the appeal.

· · ·

IV. Issues on Appeal

[15] I would state the issues in the following manner:

1. What are the appropriate factors for a sentencing judge to consider in determining whether a period of parole ineligibility of longer than 10 years should be awarded for an individual convicted of second degree murder?

· · ·

V. Analysis

A. What are the appropriate factors for a sentencing judge to consider in determining whether a period of parole ineligibility of longer than 10 years should be awarded for an individual convicted of second degree murder?

[16] The majority of the British Columbia Court of Appeal held that there are only two factors to consider in justifying an enhanced period of parole ineligibility: (1) an assessment of future dangerousness, and (2) denunciation. With respect, I disagree. Although these factors are of relevance in justifying an extension of the period of parole ineligibility, they are by no means determinative or exclusive.

[17] Section 744 of the *Criminal Code* authorizes a trial judge to impose a period of parole ineligibility greater than the minimum 10-year period. This provision, which governs this appeal, reads as follows:

> 744. Subject to section 744.1, at the time of the sentencing under paragraph 742(b) of an offender who is convicted of second degree murder, the judge who presided at the trial of the offender ... may, *having regard to the character of the offender, the nature of the offence and the circumstances surrounding its commission* ... substitute for ten years a number of years of imprisonment (being more than ten but not more than twenty-five) without eligibility for parole, as the judge deems fit in the circumstances.

[18] The determination under s. 744 is thus a very fact-sensitive process. The factors to be considered in fixing an extended period of parole ineligibility are:

(1) the character of the offender;
(2) the nature of the offence; and
(3) the circumstances surrounding the commission of the offence;

all bearing in mind the discretionary power conferred on the trial judge.

[19] No reference is made to denunciation or assessments of future dangerousness in the statutory language. By elevating "denunciation" and "assessment of future dangerousness" as the only criteria by which extended periods of parole ineligibility can be determined, the majority of the British Columbia Court of Appeal has, in effect, judicially amended the clear statutory language. This is not to say, however, that these two criteria should not be part of the analysis. For example, "denunciation" can fall within the statutory criterion of the "nature of the offence." Similarly, "future dangerousness" can fall within the rubric of the "character of the offender."

[20] On the issue of denunciation, Lambert JA stated that it would not provide a valid basis for ordering a longer period of parole ineligibility unless it is "concluded that the extra denunciation is worth more than $50,000 a year to society" (p. 239). I cannot accept that position. It is entirely inappropriate to require a trial judge to engage in such a cost-benefit budgetary analysis. As submitted by the appellant before this Court:

> The question of how society allocates public resources is for Parliament to determine. By enacting s. 744, Parliament has determined that some of society's resources will be allocated to imprisoning convicted murderers beyond the ten year point. If Parliament determines that the fiscal cost of that incarceration is too high, then they can amend s. 744. It is not the

task of individual judges carrying out the sentencing process to engage in that kind of budgetary analysis.

Furthermore, this sort of fiscal analysis would yield undesirable results from a policy perspective.

[21] "Deterrence" is also a relevant criterion in justifying a s. 744 order. Parole eligibility informs the content of the "punishment" meted out to an offender: for example, there is a very significant difference between being behind bars and functioning within society while on conditional release. Consequently, I believe that lengthened periods of parole ineligibility could reasonably be expected to deter some persons from reoffending. Such is also the position of a variety of provincial appellate courts, from which the British Columbia Court of Appeal presently diverges: *R v. Wenarchuk* (1982), 67 CCC (2d) 169 (Sask. CA); *R v. Mitchell* (1987), 39 CCC (3d) 141 (NSCA); *R v. Young* (1993), 78 CCC (3d) 538 (NSCA); *R v. Able* (1993), 65 OAC 37 (CA); *R v. Ly* (1992), 72 CCC (3d) 57 (Man. CA), per Twaddle JA (Scott CJM concurring), at p. 61: "Parliament's purpose in adding a minimum period of parole ineligibility to a life sentence was, in my view, twofold. It was to deter and denounce the crime."

[22] More importantly, the British Columbia Court of Appeal's position is also irreconcilable with the view taken by this Court of the interplay between parole eligibility and deterrence. For example, in *R v. Arkell*, [1990] 2 SCR 695, at p. 704 it was stated:

> ... the distinction between first and second degree murder ... is a maximum extra fifteen years that must be served before one is eligible for parole. ... Parliament's decision to treat more seriously murders that have been committed while the offender is exploiting a position of power through illegal domination of the victim [i.e. first degree murder] *accords with the principle that there must be a proportionality between a sentence and the moral blameworthiness of the offender and other considerations such as deterrence and societal condemnation of the acts of the offender.*

[23] The only difference in terms of punishment between first and second degree murder is the duration of parole ineligibility. This clearly indicates that parole ineligibility is part of the "punishment" and thereby forms an important element of sentencing policy. As such, it must be concerned with deterrence, whether general or specific. The jurisprudence of this Court is clear that deterrence is a well-established objective of sentencing policy. In *R v. Lyons*, [1987] 2 SCR 309, La Forest J held at p. 329:

> In a rational system of sentencing, the respective importance of prevention, deterrence, retribution and rehabilitation will vary according to the nature of the crime and the circumstances of the offender. No one would suggest that any of these functional considerations should be excluded from the legitimate purview of legislative or judicial decisions regarding sentencing.

Section 744 must be concerned with all of the factors cited in *Lyons*. In *R v. Luxton*, [1990] 2 SCR 711, the importance of structuring sentences to take into account the individual accused and the particular crime was emphasized. This is also a factor that any order made pursuant to s. 744 ought to take into consideration.

[24] The exercise of a trial judge's discretion under s. 744 should not be more strictly circumscribed than the sentencing itself. The section does not embody any limiting

statutory language; rather it is quite the contrary. In its terms, it is very similar to s. 745, which permits an application to be made to reduce the parole ineligibility period after 15 years of incarceration. Section 745 has recently been given judicial scrutiny by this Court in *R v. Swietlinski*, [1994] 3 SCR 481. That case involved an assessment of the relevant considerations for a jury hearing a s. 745 application; Lamer CJ concluded at p. 500:

> It is true that deterrence is one of the functions of the penalty and that it is therefore legit-
> imate for the jury to take this factor into account when hearing an application under s. 745.

There is no reason why the functions of s. 744 should be given a more restrictive interpretation than those of s. 745.

[25] In any event, independent of the effect that parole ineligibility may empirically have on recidivism, Lambert JA's reasoning, in both this case as well as in *R v. Hogben* (1994), 40 BCAC 257, completely precludes the concept of "deterrence" from informing the decision of whether or not to extend the period of parole ineligibility. This in my view constitutes an unduly restrictive interpretation of s. 744 and erroneously contravenes the jurisprudence of this court as well as other appellate courts.

[26] I also find it necessary to deal with Lambert JA's conclusion that a period of parole ineligibility in excess of 10 years will not be justified unless there are "unusual circum-
stances." This conclusion resonates in the earlier decisions of the British Columbia Court of Appeal in *R v. Brown* (1993), 83 CCC (3d) 394, and *R v. Gourgon* (1981), 58 CCC (2d) 193. In my opinion, this is too high a standard and makes it overly difficult for trial judges to exercise the discretionary power to set extended periods of parole ineligibility. The language of s. 744 does not require "unusual circumstances." As a result, to so require by judicial pronouncement runs contrary to Parliamentary intent.

[27] In my opinion, a more appropriate standard, which would better reflect the intentions of Parliament, can be stated in this manner: as a general rule, the period of parole ineligibility shall be for 10 years, but this can be ousted by a determination of the trial judge that, according to the criteria enumerated in s. 744, the offender should wait a longer period before having his suitability to be released into the general public assessed. To this end, an extension of the period of parole ineligibility would not be "unusual," although it may well be that, in the median number of cases, a period of 10 years might still be awarded.

[28] I am supported in this conclusion by a review of the legislative history, academic commentary, and judicial interpretation of s. 744, and the sentencing scheme for second degree murder.

[29] Section 742(b) of the Code provides that a person sentenced to life imprisonment for second degree murder shall not be eligible for parole "until he has served at least ten years of his sentence or such greater number of years, not being more than twenty-five years, as has been substituted therefor pursuant to section 744." In permitting a sliding scale of parole ineligibility, Parliament intended to recognize that, within the category of second degree murder, there will be a broad range of seriousness reflecting varying degrees of moral culpability. As a result, the period of parole ineligibility for second degree murder will run anywhere between a minimum of 10 years and a maximum of 25, the latter being equal to that prescribed for first degree murder. The mere fact that the median period gravitates towards the 10-year minimum does not, ipso facto, mean that any other period of time is "unusual."

[30] I should pause to repeat that in the instant appeal we are concerned with a period of parole ineligibility for second degree murder of 12 years, this being only two years more than the minimum.

[31] If the objective of s. 744 is to give the trial judge an element of discretion in sentencing to reflect the fact that within second degree murder there is both a range of seriousness and varying degrees of moral culpability, then it is incorrect to start from the proposition that the sentence must be the statutory minimum unless there are unusual circumstances. As discussed *supra*, a preferable approach would be to view the 10-year period as a minimum contingent on what the "judge deems fit in the circumstances," the content of this "fitness" being informed by the criteria listed in s. 744. As held in other Canadian jurisdictions, the power to extend the period of parole ineligibility need not be sparingly used.

[32] For example, in *R v. Wenarchuk, supra*, the Saskatchewan Court of Appeal (per Bayda CJS for a five-judge panel) held at p. 173 that:

> [It is no longer appropriate] that the "order (increasing the parole non-eligibility period) should be sparingly made." *The order should be made whenever such an order is "fit in the circumstances."*

[33] I would equally affirm the following passage from the decision of the Nova Scotia Court of Appeal in *R v. Doyle* (1991), 108 NSR (2d) 1, at p. 5, leave to appeal to this Court refused, [1992] 2 SCR vi, which I find apposite to the present discussion:

> The Code does not fix the sentence for second degree murder as life imprisonment with no parole eligibility for ten years. The discretion conferred on the sentencing judge by s. 742(b) and s. 744 is *not whether to move from a prima facie period of ten years, but rather what is a fit sentence, applying the proper guidelines. Unusual circumstances are not the prerequisite for moving away from the ten year minimum, although as the cases illustrate, they certainly play a role in the proper exercise of the judicial discretion* ... .
>
> It is not the law that unusual circumstances, brutality, torture or a bad record must be demonstrated before the judge may exercise his discretion to move above the ten years minimum. Nor is there any burden on the Crown to demonstrate that the period should be more than the minimum.

[34] On another note, I do not find that permitting trial judges to extend the period of parole ineligibility usurps or impinges upon the function of the parole board. I am cognizant of the fact that, upon the expiry of the period of parole ineligibility, there is no guarantee of release into the public. At that point, it is incumbent upon the parole board to assess the suitability of such release, and in so doing it is guided by the legislative objectives of the parole system: see ss. 101 and 102 of the *Corrections and Conditional Release Act*, SC 1992, c. 20. However, it is clear that the parole board is not the only participant in the parole process. All it is designed to do is, within the parameters defined by the judiciary, decide whether an offender can be released. A key component of those parameters is the determination of when the period of parole eligibility (i.e. when the parole board can commence its administrative review function) starts to run. This is the manner in which the system is geared to function—with complementary yet distinct input from both the judiciary and the parole administrators. It is the role of the sentencing judge to circumscribe, in certain statutorily defined circumstances, the operation of the parole

board. The decision of McKinnon J in the case at bar neither skews this balance nor unduly trumps the function of the parole board. As noted by the Saskatchewan Court of Appeal in *Wenarchuk, supra*, at pp. 172-73:

> The object of the provision in s. 671 [now s. 744] is not to take away from the Parole Board, or in some way diminish, the Board's function to determine whether the accused is sufficiently rehabilitated (from the standpoint of risk to and the protection of society) to permit his release into society. ... The object, rather, is to give back to the judge some of the discretion he normally has in the matter of sentencing—discretion that the statute took away from him when it provided for a life sentence [for murder]—so that the judge may do justice, not retributive or punitive justice, but justice to reflect the accused's culpability and to better express society's repudiation for the particular crime committed by the particular accused (with that repudiation's attendant beneficial consequences for society, including its protection through individual and general deterrence and, where necessary, segregation from society). ...
>
> An order under s. 671 does not impinge upon the powers of the Board. At most, it has the effect of postponing the Board's exercise of its powers—its full powers.

[35] Applying these legal principles to the particular facts of this case, I do not see any error on the part of the trial judge. He adverted to the fact that the respondent had pleaded guilty and was only 23 years old. He recognized that the Crown was not seeking a period of parole ineligibility beyond the minimum. Nevertheless, in a legitimate exercise of his discretionary power, and after correctly reviewing the factors set out in s. 744, he imposed a 12-year period of parole ineligibility. He referred to the following factors as specifically justifying the 12-year period of parole ineligibility:

(a) the circumstances of the killing were strange in that they provided no real answer to why it took place, and the respondent was unwilling or unable to explain his actions;

(b) the murder was committed during the course of committing another offence, namely a drug transaction; and

(c) the respondent has a record for both narcotic offences and violence.

[36] Factors (b) and (c) clearly fall within the categories ("character," "nature" and "circumstances surrounding") established by s. 744. As to factor (b), I further note that the Manitoba Court of Appeal, in *R v. Ly, supra*, held that the period of parole ineligibility could be increased when the murder is committed in the course of another crime, particularly a crime of violence.

[37] Factor (a), however, presents some difficulty. The respondent raises the question whether the trial judge erred in interpreting the respondent's silence in such a manner as to justify extending the period of parole ineligibility.

[38] In response, I would affirm the analysis of Goldie JA in the court below (at pp. 241-42) and would hold that this silence is readily assimilable within the "circumstances surrounding the offence" criterion. The crux of Goldie JA's comments is that, in the absence of any explanation for a random and seemingly senseless killing, the trial judge was correct in sentencing the respondent in light of his refusal to offer an explanation. It was found that his refusal was deliberate and in and of itself unusual. After all, the respondent, a drug dealer with previous convictions for robbery and armed robbery, shot the victim Buffam in cold blood without provocation of any kind.

[39] It is not for the trial judge to speculate what the respondent might have said to mitigate the severity of the offence. I quite agree with Goldie JA that the right to silence, which is fully operative in the investigative and prosecutorial stages of the criminal process, wanes in importance in the post-conviction phase when sentencing is at issue. However, in so agreeing, I emphasize that the respondent pleaded guilty; I leave for future consideration the question of drawing a negative inference from the silence of the accused when he or she has pleaded not guilty and wishes to appeal the conviction. In the case at bar, the trial judge even went so far as to invite the accused to suggest why he may have committed the offence, but no response was forthcoming. As held by Goldie JA (at p. 242), the respondent "cannot expect to be rewarded for remaining silent in the circumstances." The court and the public clearly have an interest in knowing why a human life was taken by an offender.

[40] Goldie JA's comments and the decision of the trial judge on the "silence" issue are fully consonant with the position taken by the Ontario Court of Appeal. In *R v. Able*, *supra*, the Court of Appeal increased two co-accused's periods of parole ineligibility. At page 39 it was held:

> No explanation has been forthcoming from either of the appellants with respect to the reason for the killing ... [which] can be best described as a callous, brutal, pointless, execution-style killing of a helpless victim.

I conclude that in certain circumstances, such as those presented in this case, it is proper to take into account the absence of an explanation of attenuating factors.

[41] The respondent suggests that Goldie JA's comments and the decision of the trial judge contravene the pronouncements of this Court in *R v. Gardiner*, [1982] 2 SCR 368. I recognize that, in *Gardiner*, this Court extended certain procedural rights to sentencing proceedings. However, these were limited to the right to counsel, the right to call evidence, the right to cross-examine and the right to address the court. There is no mention made of the creation in its identical form of a substantive right such as the right to silence.

[42] At the sentencing stage, the Crown has already proved beyond a reasonable doubt that the accused has committed the crime for which he or she stood charged or, as in this appeal, the accused has pleaded guilty to the offence; if the accused then seeks to receive the least severe sentence commensurate with his or her conviction (i.e. for second degree murder, life imprisonment with eligibility for parole after 10 years have elapsed) it is incumbent upon the accused to play a somewhat active role in the process. I note that the right to silence is a manifestation of the presumption of innocence: *R v. Broyles*, [1991] 3 SCR 595; *R v. Hebert*, [1990] 2 SCR 151; *R v. Chambers*, [1990] 2 SCR 1293. The presumption of innocence flows to those "charged with an offence" or suspected of having committed one; once an individual has been convicted of an offence he or she is no longer simply "charged."

• • •

VI. *Conclusions and Disposition*

[54] The trial judge properly considered the relevant factors in exercising the discretionary jurisdiction given to him under s. 744. The Court of Appeal erred in postulating an unduly restrictive and narrow approach to s. 744 and by adopting a standard of appellate review that was tantamount to substituting its opinion for that of the trial judge.

Consequently, I would allow the appeal, set aside the decision of the British Columbia Court of Appeal, and restore the trial judge's s. 744 order of a period of parole ineligibility of 12 years.

For commentary on this case, see Allan Manson, "The Supreme Court Intervenes in Sentencing" (1995), 43 CR (4th) 306; Gary Trotter, "*R v. Shropshire*: Murder, Sentencing and the Supreme Court of Canada" (1995), 43 CR (4th) 288; and John Norris, "Sentencing for Second-Degree Murder: *R v. Shropshire*" (1996) 1 Can Crim LR 199.

Despite the authoritative pronouncement in *Shropshire*, the debate about parole eligibility for second-degree murder persists: see the judicial debate in *Ryan*, below.

After *Shropshire*, there has been a marked increase in the number of murder sentencing decisions in which parole ineligibility has been set at more than 10 years: see Nathan Gorham, "The Effects of Shropshire on Parole Ineligibility for Second Degree Murder" (2002), 1 CR (6th) 324, where, after an empirical inquiry, the author concludes that judges are "much more willing to increase parole ineligibility beyond the 10-year minimum" but that the courts have not attained the objective of a sliding scale.

The decision in *Ryan*, below, illustrates the complexity of determining the appropriate parole ineligibility period in second degree murder cases. The Crown appealed from a sentence of life imprisonment with no parole for 13 years. Two judges, Picard and Wakeling JJA, agreed that the judge erred but disagreed on what the appropriate period should be. O'Farrell JA would have dismissed the appeal. Ultimately, Wakeling JA concurred with Picard JA in order to produce a practicable resolution, and the parole ineligibility period was set at 17 years. When reading the following excerpts, note the various factors considered and the different ways in which the judges approached them.

R v Ryan
2015 ABCA 286 (footnotes omitted)

[Ryan, then 29 years old, was addicted to crack cocaine. He was supporting himself and his habit by selling drugs. Ryan lent his truck to Head and provided him with some cocaine to be sold. Head disappeared with the cocaine and the truck. Ryan learned afterward that Head was still in Fort McMurray and bragging about stealing the truck and drugs. Angered, Ryan arranged for Head to come to an apartment where he and a friend, Sheppard, were waiting. Sheppard said he had a scheme by which Head could extricate himself. The three got in a truck and drove to a trailer. Ryan entered the trailer and came out with a hunting rifle. He rejoined the other two in the truck and then shot the deceased Head in the head. Ryan dumped the body in the bush and tried to set fire to the truck. He was charged with first-degree murder, but the trial judge was not satisfied beyond a reasonable doubt that the decision to kill Head had been planned and deliberate. The trial judge accepted the evidence indicating that Ryan did go and fetch the gun before the shooting. However, the evidence also largely coincided with an inference, accepted by the trial judge, that Ryan did not decide to shoot Head until Head reacted sneeringly and made a sarcastic comment when Ryan got back to the truck.]

PICARD JA:

[9] The sentencing was set over to a later date. Ryan was then 35 years of age. The trial judge calculated that Ryan had been in pre-sentence custody for 44 months. Throughout the trial, Ryan had the support of his family.

[10] Ryan's criminal record commenced in Newfoundland on April 3, 1991 when he was 15. It involved a significant number of largely property offences and breach offences until 1992. Sometime after 1992, Ryan relocated to Fort McMurray and was convicted of assault in 1995. Apart from a conviction for driving over .08 in 1997, Ryan's focus appears to have been reasonably prosocial. He was employed as a heavy equipment operator. The trial judge found, however, that cocaine use wrecked that life situation:

> It is clear on the evidence that he fell into the grip of a crack cocaine addiction in 2005, a year or so before he killed Mr. Head. He appears to have suffered a fast fall in the manner of his life style and respect for the law. He fell quickly over 2005 from an employed heavy equipment operator to someone living essentially a nomadic existence, trying to make a livelihood selling drugs to largely support his own drug habit. (SARD 40/31-36)

[11] The trial judge went on to note Ryan's increasing criminal conduct as reflected in his convictions in 2007. These were mainly due to his drug involvement. The trial judge added that Ryan continued his criminal conduct even after killing Head. The trial judge turned to whether Ryan could be expected to restore his life back to what it was before 2005. The trial judge found that although Ryan bragged to the undercover officers about his gang involvement, much of this was exaggeration: SARD 41/26-42/2. Consequently, the trial judge determined that Ryan was not a dangerous person earlier in his life, but that under cocaine addiction, he acted out.

· · ·

[23] … This Court has ruled that pre-sentence custody is not deductible under s 719(3.1) of the *Code* (on any calculation ratio) from the period of parole ineligibility: see *R v Toews*, 2015 ABCA 167, [2015] A.J. No 538 (QL). That is because Parliament has provided that the entire time spent in custody since arrest is counted by the corrections authorities as part of the ineligibility period imposed after trial: s 746(a) of the *Code*; see also *R v White*, 2011 BCCA 328 at para 13, 309 BCAC 37; *R v Stephen*, 1999 ABCA 190 at para 5, 73 Alta LR (3d) 205; *R v Tsyganov (S.)* (1998), 172 NSR (2d) 43 at para 21 (CA). Ryan's counsel, however, urges this Court to infer that the trial judge was merely noting the fact of 44 months of detention as a general factor affecting the overall impact of punishment.

· · ·

[25] The trial judge's comments reveal he was of the opinion that he was entitled to reduce Ryan's parole ineligibility period by the amount of time Ryan spent in pre-trial custody. Indeed, the trial judge appears to have calculated the "credit" as between 44 months and perhaps some greater amount depending on the approach taken under s 719(3.1) of the *Code*. This reflects that the trial judge was working from a notional number around 17 years and the pre-sentence custody was deducted from that.

[26] The inference that the trial judge was evaluating the case's aggravating circumstances as justifying a sentence of around 17 years, then reduced by pre-sentence custody, is also supported by his further comments that he started at 15 years, with an increase to

reflect the disposal of the body. Disposal of a body in order to deflect investigation or as indicative of a callous attitude has been held to justify an increase in parole ineligibility: see eg *R v Hansen* (1989), 96 AR 276 (CA); *R v Faid* (1984), 52 AR 338 at paras 4, 6 (CA); *R v Peterffy*, 2001 BCCA 698, 162 BCAC 24; *R v Evans*, 2004 BCCA 318, 197 BCAC 52; *R v Wristen* (1999), 141 CCC (3d) 1 at para 73 (Ont CA); *McLeod* ... [(2003), 177 OAC 385].

[27] The trial judge's error in principle in crediting Ryan for his pre-sentence custody had a profound impact on the disposition made here. I will discuss the impact of this error after discussing the other grounds of appeal.

• • •

[28] The trial judge was also persuaded that there was some mitigation in Ryan's guilty plea offer made at the outset of the trial. When arraigned, Ryan said: "I'd like to plead not guilty to murder, and I'd like to offer a guilty plea to manslaughter": Transcript 2/16-17. The Crown did not consent to that plea under s 606(4) of the *Code* and the trial proceeded. An agreed statement of facts was read in shortly thereafter to the trial judge. But that agreement largely set out relatively technical and inevitable facts concerning the cause of death, the discovery of the body, continuity of exhibits, and that there was no illegality in the wiretap respecting the undercover operation. There does not appear to have been an express admission, either then or later in the trial, that Ryan killed the victim.

• • •

[36] Here, Ryan did not offer to accept responsibility for the crime for which he was ultimately convicted—second-degree murder. His offer to plead guilty to manslaughter may have been genuine, but there is no reason to characterize it as anything but self-interested. The extent of Ryan's acknowledgment of responsibility was of an *actus reus* that the Crown clearly could prove beyond a reasonable doubt. Ryan's aim was to avoid the life sentence which, on the evidence, was otherwise unavoidable. As for saving cost in the trial, the killing was what created the need for the investigation and the trial in the first place. That Ryan may have simplified his own trial by not forcing fully elaborate proof of the matters that he admitted or did not vigorously resist in evidence is not, in my respectful view, a matter which would justify a sentence reduced from a proportional one that fits the gravity of the offence and Ryan's degree of responsibility.

[37] Giving any credit to Ryan's offer to plead guilty to the lesser offence of manslaughter was an error in principle.

• • •

[38] The trial judge found no basis to conclude that Ryan was a dangerous person by nature or as evidenced by prior conduct. This is a fact finding that has some evidential support in this record and was based, at least in part, upon the trial judge's perception of Ryan during the trial. It is entitled to deference in the absence of palpable and overriding error. I find no such error. The trial judge also said: "That is not to say that a drug addiction excuses anything, but it may help to explain the context of the offence": SARD 41/16-17. This does not suggest error either.

[39] It is certainly true that where a person convicted of murder shows traits of dangerousness, parole ineligibility periods have tended to be increased in order to serve the objectives of public protection and denunciation. The injunctive nature of parole ineligibility is self-explanatory ... .

[40] As I read the reasons of the trial judge, he accepted that while under the influence of cocaine, Ryan became a criminalized addict with dangerous impulses when in his 20s

in Fort McMurray. However, the trial judge was not prepared to draw the inference that after years in prison, Ryan would still be dangerous. As for Ryan's drug addiction, I read the trial judge's reasons as essentially setting out Ryan's life narrative, and the damage done to it by drugs. In effect, the trial judge recognized that the parole authorities would have regard to both topics over time. The trial judge was not persuaded to lengthen the injunction against future parole based on a forecast that Ryan would not change his ways. I do not find error on this issue and reject the Crown's submission respecting it.

. . .

[43] Those observations appear to accede to the view that for the purposes of *individual* deterrence, the life sentence by itself carries great deterrent effect and consequently enhanced parole ineligibility would not much increase deterrence on an individual basis. I have difficulty following this thread of reasoning. That said, I see no utility in attempting to come to grips with it since I am not persuaded that this aspect of the trial judge's reasons had any real effect on his conclusion. Consequently, I would not interfere with his decision on this basis.

[44] As for denunciation, I agree with Ryan that, taken as a whole, the reasons of the trial judge indicate that he did regard denunciation as a relevant objective in calculating the period of parole ineligibility. It would have been a serious error for the trial judge not to recognize that a key objective of determining parole ineligibility is expression of denunciation. The consultation with the jury which occurs as part of this set of provisions is a manifest expression of Parliament's intention that the sentence must reflect a community assessment of the gravity of the crime. However, I do not find that the trial judge made this error. Therefore, I reject this ground of appeal.

. . .

[48] My colleague, Wakeling JA seeks to reform sentencing practice in this area. He proposes definitions for the three areas mentioned in s 745.4, which in his view would contribute to a desirable degree of order and predictability in determining the period of parole ineligibility. He also identifies what he sees as three separate categories within the total statutory range from 10 years to 25 years of parole ineligibility. I respectfully disagree with certain aspects of his interpretation of s 745.4. ...

. . .

[57] That said, consistent with s 745.4 of the *Code*, the patterns observed in the cases are largely associated with (a) the gravity of the specific crime; (b) the degree of culpability and the individual responsibility of the offender (both case specific and linked to the offender's "character" in the larger sense); and (c) with the surrounding circumstances (such as the individual circumstances of the offender and the impact of the particular crime on the victim and on broader social norms and values). For example, factors that might result in an increase in the period of parole ineligibility include:

  i)   gratuitous violence;
  ii) targeting/luring of the victim;
  iii) additional degradation of the victim;
  iv) murder committed while on bail or probation;
  v)   murder committed in the presence of an innocent bystander/non-party;
  vi) abuse of power;
  vii) abuse of trust;

viii)   gang attack;

ix)   circumstances of domination or control;

x)   circumstances of retaliation, revenge or enforcement;

xi)   murder motivated by hostility towards a minority/vulnerable group or members of it;

xii)   obstructing justice in service of the murder or cover-up;

xiii)   profit from the murder;

xiv)   murder motivated by race, religion or gender;

xv)   murder committed in the context of a criminal enterprise;

xvi)   preparatory steps leading to the murder; and

xvii)   murder committed in the course of committing other crimes.

[58]   I need not catalogue a list of decisions that support a general range for the type of murder that occurred in this case. Sadly, Canada now seems to be plagued by drug crime involving the use of firearms for enforcement or revenge, particularly but not exclusively in major cities. Ryan was young, but not so young that he didn't know exactly what he was doing. He had a prior criminal record. He had a measure of foresight, having calculated the possibility of killing the victim depending on the circumstances. He also armed himself with a gun, thereby facilitating the commission of the murder. Given the facts here, it is evident that the murder took place against the backdrop of a criminal enterprise involving Ryan and the victim. The culminating factor that led to the murder, Head's smirking, cannot possibly qualify as provocation. Ryan's shooting of Head occurred without prior warning. It is aggravating that Ryan also took steps to dispose of the body and other evidence, and then resumed his participation in the drug business which he now knew was deadly. On the other hand, the trial judge found he was not a hardened veteran criminal with an innately violent disposition.

[59]   The character of the offence has therefore both negatives and positives in its influence on the appropriate level of parole ineligibility. Ryan's character does not militate towards the low end of such range but does not place him at the top of it. The nature of the murder, namely a drug enforcement slaying, is also an escalating factor. As to circumstances, Canadian society must be resolute in its response to criminal reprisals. These events have been known to harm innocent people, quite apart from the contribution to a dangerous and war zone environment in some parts of our communities.

[60]   It is tragic to see the life of one young man ended ignominiously, and another young man's life largely squandered. But this Court has a declaratory duty to perform. I believe that had the trial judge not fallen into error, he would have found the appropriate period of parole ineligibility to be 17 years. I am satisfied that the appropriate parole ineligibility period in this case is 17 years.

WAKELING JA:

• • •

[65]   He is correct. The Supreme Court of Canada and provincial appeal courts have not constructed a general framework that provides analytical measures for selecting a fit period of parole ineligibility for second degree murderers. As a result, offenders who are similarly situated may be the recipients of vastly different sentences and those who are not alike may be the recipients of similar sentences. Not only is this result undesirable, it is a contravention of equality principles that account for Parliament's declaration that

"a sentence should be similar to sentences imposed on similar offenders for offences in similar circumstances." The administration of justice is brought into disrepute by grossly disparate sentences. A five-judge panel of the Supreme Court of New South Wales stated that "[i]nconsistency in [sentencing decisions] offends the principles of equality before the law [and is itself] a manifestation of injustice."

[66] There are different mechanisms that a community may employ to promote rationality, predictability and consistency in its sentencing regime.

[67] Most Australian states have statutory provisions that allow their highest state courts either at the request of the attorney general or on their own motion to issue guideline sentencing judgments. A guideline sentencing judgment considers appropriate sentences for offenders convicted of a specific offence grouped together by distinguishing features of the offence and other relevant traits. Chief Justice Spigelman of the New South Wales Court of Criminal Appeal strongly endorsed this strategy:

> In my opinion, guideline judgments should now be recognised in New South Wales as having a useful role to play in ensuring that an appropriate balance exists between the broad discretion that must be retained to ensure that justice is done in each individual case, on the one hand, and the desirability of consistency in sentencing and the maintenance of public confidence in sentences actually imposed, and in the judiciary, as a whole, on the other.
>
> • • •
>
> … Guideline judgments are a mechanism for structuring discretion, rather than restricting discretion.

[68] Professor Ashworth has also supported the expanded use of guideline judgments:

> Whereas most appellate decisions deal with the facts of the individual case without relating it to sentences for similar offences and offenders, a "guideline" judgment considers sentences for a whole category of offences. This format has three principal advantages: it forces the Court which formulated the guidelines to consider the interrelationship of sentences for the different forms of an offence, it provides sentences with a more or less integrated framework instead of scattered and unrelated decisions, and it brings the guidance into a single place. Guideline judgments … [are] to be welcomed as an important step towards more rational and consistent sentencing practices.

[69] The United Kingdom has undertaken a number of initiatives the goal of which is the promotion of consistency in sentencing.

[70] I will mention only one.

[71] On May 31, 2002 the Lord Chief Justice of England and Wales issued a practice statement relating to the fixing of the minimum term of imprisonment that a person convicted of murder must serve before the Parole Board may consider whether an offender may be released from prison. A minimum term of imprisonment is comparable to a period of parole ineligibility under Canadian law.

[72] The 2002 practice statement identified types of murder cases and assigned presumptive analytical starting points for each subset. There was a correlation between the duration of the term of imprisonment a murderer must serve and the blameworthiness of the offender. The practice statement outlined a methodology that would allow a sentencing court to either increase or decrease the minimum terms of imprisonment represented by the starting point in response to the presence of aggravating or mitigating factors.

[73] Shortly after the publication of the 2002 practice statement the United Kingdom Parliament passed the *Criminal Justice Act 2003* and adopted the general theme of the 2002 practice statement. The 2003 enactment created subsets characterized by the seriousness of the offence. The subset reserved for cases of "exceptionally high" seriousness has life as the starting point. The subset capturing cases the seriousness of which is "particularly high" has a starting point of thirty years. The starting points for the two least egregious categories of cases is fifteen and twenty-five years. After a sentencing court selects the proper starting point, it must consider whether there are any aggravating and mitigating factors. The presence of aggravating factors could result in the increase of the minimum term; mitigating factors could result in the decrease of the minimum term. "Detailed consideration of aggravating or mitigating factors may result in a minimum term of any length (whatever the starting point), or in the making of a whole life order."

[74] In the United States many jurisdictions direct sentencing commissions to produce numerical grids that serve as the starting point for the analytical process undertaken to determine a fit sentence. For example, Minnesota has a sentencing guidelines commission. Its mandate is to publish sentencing guidelines, the purpose of which is set out below:

> The purpose of the Sentencing Guidelines is to establish rational and consistent sentencing standards that reduce sentencing disparity and ensure that the sanctions imposed for felony convictions are proportional to the severity of the conviction offense and the offender's criminal history. Equity in sentencing requires that: (a) convicted felons with similar relevant sentencing criteria should receive similar sanctions; and (b) convicted felons with relevant sentencing criteria substantially different from a typical case should receive different sanctions.

[75] The Canadian Sentencing Commission, in its 1987 report was alive to the harm that inconsistent sentences caused and recommended the establishment of a permanent sentencing commission with a mandate to create sentencing range guidelines for consideration and approval by the House of Commons: "The need for such a commission to ensure uniformity and consistency of approach across the country cannot be overemphasized nor can the crucial role that Appeal Courts will play in providing direction for the application of the guidelines to particular cases and making needed modifications where warranted."

[76] While Parliament introduced some of the recommendations contained in the report of the Canadian Sentencing Commission, it did not act on the recommendation to create a permanent sentencing commission.

[77] By default, appeal courts have the primary responsibility for introducing rationality, predictability and consistency into the sentencing process. For practical reasons, it cannot be accomplished by a sentencing court consisting of a large number of judges located in several judicial centres with original jurisdiction. On a theoretical level there is also a problem. An original jurisdiction sentencing court does not occupy a position in the court structure which gives its judgments the precedential value needed to accomplish the task.

[78] To introduce rationality, predictability and consistency an appeal court must construct an analytical framework that will encourage sentencing courts to adopt a common methodology. The Supreme Court of Canada has endorsed the pursuit of these values: "The wide discretion granted to sentencing judges has limits. It is fettered in part by the case law that has set down, in some circumstances, general ranges of sentences for particular offences, to encourage greater consistency between sentencing decisions in

accordance with the principle of parity enshrined in the *Code*." Irrational distinctions between sentences imposed in like cases cannot be tolerated just because sentencing is an individualized process and the precise facts and circumstances surrounding each offence and each offender are never the same. "Like cases should be treated in like manner. The administration of criminal justice works as a system; not merely as a multiplicity of unconnected single instances. It should be systematically fair, and that involves, amongst other things, reasonable consistency." Neither Parliament nor the Supreme Court of Canada has approved disparate sentences in like cases.

[79] The absence of a uniform analytical framework, not surprisingly, adversely impacts the sentencing process. Sentencing judgments frequently feature modest, if any, analytical dimensions. Many sentencing decisions are nothing more than a conclusionary statement following the recital of sentencing purposes and principles. A reader never knows what impact the various principles had on the outcome. The same can safely be said for the sentencer. It is not satisfactory for a sentencing court to recite the purposes and principles of sentencing and then to announce the period of parole ineligibility for second degree murder.

· · ·

[87] First, it selected a parole ineligibility period that was demonstrably unfit. Thirteen years was clearly unfit. The appropriate parole ineligibility period is twenty-three years.

[88] The nature of the offence and the circumstances surrounding its commission—a drug dealer planning to even the score with another drug dealer—considered alone, warrant a parole ineligibility period of twenty-three years. Consideration of Mr. Ryan's character does not require any adjustment to this assessment. There are no mitigating factors. The fact that the offender offered in open court to plead guilty to manslaughter does not constitute a mitigating factor. A guilty plea to second degree murder would have been a mitigating factor.

[89] Second, the sentencing court, in assessing the appropriate parole ineligibility period, should not have taken into account the time the respondent spent in pre-sentence custody. This is not a relevant criterion. The answer to the first question makes it unnecessary to remedy this second error.

[90] Both Justice Picard and I, unlike Justice O'Ferrall, agree that this appeal should be allowed. But a problem arises because Justice Picard and I disagree on the appropriate duration of Mr. Ryan's parole ineligibility period. Justice Picard believes that a seventeen-year parole ineligibility period is fit. I hold the view that the appropriate period is twenty-three years. To allow this panel to resolve the appeal, I adopt Justice Picard's position.

· · ·

[105] The next task is to ascertain the meaning of each of the three criteria in s. 745.4: "the character of the offender, the nature of the offence and the circumstances surrounding its commission."

[106] I am not aware of any decision which has discussed what "character" means. It is not a defined term in the *Criminal Code*. Most judgments assume that it requires consideration of an offender's background. I accept that background information is helpful when considering the offender's "character." But I do not believe "background" and "character" are the same concepts.

[107] Webster's presents this definition of character: "the complex of accustomed mental and moral characteristics and habitual ethical traits marking a person." Oxford

provides a similar definition: "The sum of the moral and mental qualities which distinguish an individual ... ; the individuality impressed by nature and habit on man ... ; mental or moral constitution." In the context of a s. 745.4 analysis, "the character of the accused" directs a sentencing court to assess the choices an offender has made in his or her life and the impact they have made on his or her law abidingness. For this reason a person's criminal record is an important consideration. Reference to the past allows a court to make an informed assessment about whether the offender will choose to comply with the law in the future. In *The Queen v. Murphy*, I said this:

> An offender who has spent a long time in prison and has not altered his or her decision-making processes and continues to make poor choices should in most cases, receive a harsher sentence than an offender who has no prior criminal record. A court may safely assume that a less harsh sentence may be a sufficient stimulus to cause the offender [with no prior criminal record] to make better choices which take into account the interests of others.

[108] This last observation allows a court to consider the fact that a person has pled guilty. A guilty plea is evidence that an offender recognizes that his unlawful acts adversely affect others, including the victim and participants in the administration of justice.

[109] What is the meaning of "the nature of the offence"? Again, very few sentencing courts have specifically tackled this question. Chief Justice Bayda did:

> I am not entirely sure of the significance of considering the nature (as distinct from the circumstances) of the offence. The nature of every offence of second degree murder is a killing of a human being and that nature does not vary from one offence to the next. In short, a killing is a killing. What distinguishes one second degree murder from another and categorizes the offences according to the degree of seriousness is the circumstances of each offence.

[110] Justice Watson also considered the issue in his dissenting opinion in *The Queen v. Harrish*. He gave it more scope than Chief Justice Bayda did: "Indeed, since the basic 'nature of the offence' under s. 745.4 of the *Code* is always murder, Parliament must have recognized and intended that the nature and gravity to be addressed ... would sometimes involve such aggravating circumstances."

[111] Like Justice Watson, I prefer a definition that is less abstract and takes into account the specific facts of the offence. According to Webster's, "nature" may mean "the distinguishing qualities or properties of something < the ~ of mathematics > ... ."

[112] Elsewhere I have sketched in the main features of the nature of the offence:

> [O]ne studies the subject matter of the offence—the physical and mental elements of the offence—in order to assess its level of gravity or egregiousness. Generally speaking, this measures such criteria as the nature of the conduct which constitutes an offence and the foreseeable physical and mental harm which the conduct caused to the victim and the moral blameworthiness of the offender.
>
> The mental element of an offence may encompass varying degrees of blameworthiness. A crime which demonstrates a high degree of blameworthiness is more grave or egregious than one based on a lesser degree of blameworthiness.

[113] The third criterion—"the circumstances surrounding [the] ... commission [of the offence]"—allows a court to consider the reasons why the offender committed the

crime, the offender's relationship to the victim, the amount of deliberation which preceded the crime and other factors which may account for the commission of the crime.

[114] By studying the second and third criteria, a sentencing judge is able to assess the "gravity or egregiousness of an offence." There is no better measure of the egregiousness of an offence.

. . .

[119] The best data available today strongly supports the conclusion that the median for reported cases written in English in the period January 1, 1990 to December 31, 2012 is fifteen years. The median for reported Alberta cases in the period January 1, 1990 to December 31, 2014 is also fifteen years. This data does not track parole ineligibility dispositions contained in unreported decisions.

[120] It is more likely than not that a very large portion of unreported judgments are based on joint recommendations. Arguably, these are not the best measure of the judicial mindset. Dispositions that are the products of a contest and the careful assessment of the sentencing court are the gold standard.

[121] The data I have reviewed confirms Justice Iacobucci's prediction that "an extension of the parole ineligibility period would not be 'unusual.'" Indeed, it is usual.

[122] The fundamental message conveyed in *Shropshire* is that the ten-year parole ineligibility period in s. 744 of the *Criminal Code*, as it was before September 3, 1996, is a statutory minimum reserved for second degree murderers whose cases fall in the least egregious category.

[123] My review of s. 745.4 and Part XXIII of the *Criminal Code*, as it has been since September 3, 1996, leads to the conclusion that the ten-year parole ineligibility period is still the statutory minimum appropriate for the subset of second degree murderers whose cases are the least egregious.

[124] The most important consideration is the benchmarks which distinguish cases that are justly granted different periods of parole ineligibility.

. . .

[137] To summarize, s. 745.4 of the *Criminal Code* does not ask a sentencing judge to determine whether a second degree murderer may be a danger to the community after he or she becomes eligible and applies for parole and should be granted parole. That is the difficult job assigned to the Parole Board. It is not undertaken until an offender has served the portion of his or her sentence that s. 745.4 stipulates. Nor does s. 745.4 require a sentencing judge to fix the duration of a prison sentence. Parliament has enacted that the just sanction is life imprisonment. Section 745.4 directs a sentencing judge to select the appropriate period of parole ineligibility for second degree murderers.

[138] Now the answer to the question why Parliament has asked a sentencing court to select the parole ineligibility period.

[139] The Canadian Parliament imposes a consequence on an offender adjudged to have violated a *Criminal Code* provision in order "to contribute … to respect for the law and maintenance of a just, peaceful and safe society." Sanction provisions in the *Criminal Code* and other statutes constitute an unequivocal statement by Parliamentarians that they believe something more than a judicial declaration identifying a person as an offender is generally necessary to accomplish the fundamental purpose of instilling respect for the law in community members and creating peaceful and safe communities.

[140] Parliament has given sentencing courts the responsibility to determine how much time each offender convicted of second degree murder must serve in a penitentiary before he or she may apply for parole in order to express the community's denunciation of the offender's conduct, to deter the offender and others from committing homicides and to promote public safety. To this limited extent, Parliament directs sentencing judges to individualize the sentence an offender receives for his or her crime. It must be remembered that the primary sanction is mandatory life imprisonment.

• • •

[169] More often than not, the case law reserves the shortest period of parole ineligibility for offences in which the offender acted impulsively and killed someone who was not the offender's current or former domestic partner or child, as a result of an incident that occurred shortly before the homicide. This subset captures the least egregious offences committed by second degree murderers. A parole ineligibility period of ten to fifteen years inclusive is the appropriate range to commence the analysis for this subset of offences. And, if there are no aggravating or mitigating circumstances requiring an adjustment to this starting point, it will also be the appropriate period of parole ineligibility. A death which ensues from a bar fight is a typical example of the kind of second degree murder which falls in this subclass. The offender and the victim usually do not know each other and the event which caused the conflict preceded the victim's death by a relatively short period of time.

[170] The second subset captures those offences in which there is often a familial relationship between the offender and the victim. This is the case if the victim is the offender's spouse or common-law partner or offspring. This subset is more egregious than the first subset because of the nature of the relationship between the offender and the victim. The offender has a moral duty, at the very least, and, in many cases, a legal duty to protect his or her spouse or common-law partner or offspring. Section 718.2(a)(iii) of the *Criminal Code* expressly declares that this subset warrants special attention: "a sentence should be increased … [if there is] evidence that the offender, in committing the offence, abused the offender's spouse or common-law partner." Justice Greckol's statement in *The Queen v. Diep* accurately explains why these offenders are singled out for special attention: "[W]ife homicide is an extreme form of domestic violence and a reprehensible abuse of power and control by a man … ." The second subset also sweeps in second degree murderers whose victims were vulnerable either because of their age, disability, the nature of their occupation or they were good Samaritans.

[171] A parole ineligibility period of sixteen to twenty years inclusive is the appropriate range to commence the analysis if

(a) the offender was or had been the domestic partner or was a parent or grandparent of the victim and the homicide was directly attributable to this relationship;

(b) the offender betrayed the kindness extended by the victim; or

(c) the victim was a vulnerable member of the community.

[172] The subset of second degree murderers whose offences are the most egregious or grave consists, primarily, of offenders who contemplated killing their victims well in advance of doing so—it cannot be said that their acts were impulsive—or who killed someone to effect another criminal purpose. The victim may have been the occupant of

a home who died as a result of a confrontation with the intruder or whose death is otherwise directly attributable to a criminal undertaking of the offender.

[173] A parole ineligibility period of twenty-one to twenty-five years inclusive is the appropriate range to commence the analysis if

(a) the offender gave consideration to causing the death of the victim well in advance of the act causing the death of the victim;

(b) the offender would not have committed the offence but for the offender's engagement in other criminal activities; or

(c) the offender committed acts of extreme violence in causing the victim's death.

[174] The sentencing court should attempt to be as precise as possible when it places a case within a subset. The importance of this admonition increases in direct proportion to the size of the range of a subset. If a subset covers a parole ineligibility period from sixteen to twenty years—a five-year range—a conclusion to place a case in subset two is less helpful than a determination that the case should attract, at this stage of the analysis, a parole ineligibility period near the low, middle or high part of the subset range.

· · ·

[210] Both Justice Picard and I, unlike Justice O'Ferrall, agree that this appeal should be allowed. But we disagree on the duration of the parole ineligibility period that should be substituted for the thirteen-year period the sentencing court imposed. I am satisfied that a parole ineligibility period of twenty-three years is a fit sentence. Justice Picard has determined that a parole ineligibility period of seventeen years is appropriate. This difference of opinion presents a problem. Section 687(1) of the *Criminal Code* directs a court of appeal in an appeal against sentence to either vary the sentence or dismiss the appeal. A disagreement between the two judges as to the sentence that is appropriate prevents this Court from varying the sentence.

[211] There are two possible solutions to this problem. The panel could inform the Chief Justice of Alberta that it has been unable to resolve the appeal. This would result in the appeal being reheard, probably by a panel consisting of five judges. Rehearing is a time consuming process. Or I could adopt Justice Picard's proposed disposition. By doing so, I would opt for a more lenient sentence than I think appropriate. This would not be contrary to Mr. Ryan's interests. Mr. Ryan could hardly complain about a disposition that is the product of the judge who favours a harsher sentence agreeing to adopt a more lenient sentence. He could validly complain if the judge who favoured a lesser sentence agreed to a greater sentence to generate the consensus necessary to constitute a lawful disposition of the appeal. Such a consensus would not do justice.

[212] Neither side can legitimately complain that another panel may dispose of the appeal in a manner different from what either Justice Picard or I favour. They have no right to a rehearing before a new panel. This panel has been assigned responsibility for this appeal. It is the obligation of the members of this panel to search for common ground.

[213] This is not a case of an equal division—the same number of judges are in favour of allowing and disallowing the appeal—which means that the Crown's appeal must fail. Justice Picard and I agree that the appeal must succeed.

[214] To produce a clear disposition of this appeal, as required by s. 687(1) of the *Criminal Code*, I adopt Justice Picard's position and state that a seventeen-year period of

parole ineligibility must be substituted for the thirteen-year period the sentencing court imposed under s. 745.4 of the *Criminal Code*.

Justice Wakeling advocated three subcategories of second-degree murder for the purpose of determining the parole ineligibility period. Can this be maintained in light of the majority of the Supreme Court's apparent rejection of judicially created subcategories in its more recent decision in *Lacasse*, discussed in Chapter 2, Judicial Methodology and the Legislative Context.

B. The Role of the Jury

Another reason why sentencing for murder is unique is the role that is given to the jury upon a conviction for second-degree murder. The jury is permitted to make a "recommendation" on the issue of parole eligibility. Murder is the only offence in the *Criminal Code* that contemplates any formal role for the jury in the sentencing process. This procedure casts the jury in an unusual role. Unlike its task in deciding guilt or innocence, in the sentencing context, the jury need not be unanimous. Indeed, it is possible (although unlikely) that each juror could come to a different conclusion on this issue. More fundamentally, the section only calls for a "recommendation." The reality is that sentencing juries often do not provide unanimous recommendations, leaving the presiding judge with several views on the appropriate period of parole eligibility.

The cases below demonstrate that the courts are ambivalent about how to integrate a jury's recommendation into the ultimate decision. Indeed, the courts cannot even agree on the proper procedure that ought to be employed in eliciting the input of the jury on this issue. Some courts have held that the offender and the Crown may address the jury before it makes its recommendation: see *R v Atsiqtaq*, [1988] NWTR 315 (SC). Other courts have held that there is no right to be heard on this issue: see *R v Nepoose*, below; *R v Okkuatsiak* (1993), 80 CCC (3d) 251 (Nfld CA); *R v Challice* (1994), 20 CRR (2d) 319 (Ont Ct (Gen Div)); and *R v Cruz* (1998), 124 CCC (3d) 157 (BCCA). As we shall see in the next section, the jury has de facto decision-making power on a review of parole eligibility after 15 years.

R v Nepoose
1988 ABCA 382, 46 CCC (3d) 421

STRATTON JA (Shannon and Dea JJA concurring):

[1] The question raised by this appeal is the propriety of the parties adducing evidence and addressing a jury under s. 670 of the *Criminal Code* after a conviction and before the jury respond to the question of whether or not they wish to make a recommendation with respect to ineligibility for parole.

• • •

[8] The appellant now contends that the Trial Judge erred in allowing counsel to adduce facts and make submissions to the jury with regard to the period of parole ineligibility. The second ground of appeal was that the 15 years imposed by the trial judge was excessive under all the circumstances.

[9] On the first point, no cases directly on the issue were presented to us for our consideration. ...

• • •

[11] Defence counsel argued strenuously that the jury's recommendation under s. 670 should be based solely on the evidence leading to the conviction and that the jury should hear no further evidence or argument for the purposes of a s. 670 recommendation.

[12] We agree with that submission which we conclude is supported by the very words and structure of the relevant sections of the Code.

[13] Section 670 is uniquely framed. The precise question required to be put to the jury is set out in quotations and contains within its wording a complete explanation of the jury's responsibility. It is abundantly clear that the jury's decision under s. 670 is not final. No statement whatsoever of the factors to be considered by the jury in making or declining to make such recommendation is set out.

[14] That situation must be contrasted to s. 671, which authorizes the final sentencing decision of the judge and specifies the factors which the judge must have regard to in so doing.

[15] Section 670 may also be compared with s. 672 which allows a jury to be empanelled for the purpose of reviewing, in certain specified circumstances, an earlier decision relating to parole ineligibility. Section 672(2) expressly states what the jury must have regard to in reaching a s. 672 decision. It is significant that a jury's decision under s. 672 is final and not a mere recommendation as in s. 670. A s. 672 jury must have regard to the character of the applicant, his conduct while serving his sentence, the nature of the offence for which he was convicted and such other matters as the judge deems relevant in the circumstances.

[16] If Parliament had intended that a "recommending jury" under s. 670 consider factors other than the material leading to the conviction, I am satisfied it would have so specified as it did for "final" sentencing pronouncements authorized by ss. 671 and 672.

[17] It has been suggested that it is unfair, particularly to an accused, to ask a jury for a recommendation without the benefit of counsel's arguments and the accused's record. The injury which an accused may appear to suffer is really illusory as a s. 670 decision of the jury is not final.

[18] The person empowered to make the final parole ineligibility decision must hear full submissions and must have regard to the specifics set out in s. 671, including the jury's recommendation. With that recommendation before him, the parties may adduce additional evidence and present arguments to the trial judge with respect to the final disposition of the sentencing.

[19] In short, we are of the view that s. 670 is a code of sorts. It is a section which is complete on its own and says with exactitude what is to be presented to the jury on this issue. We conclude that it was the intention of Parliament that a jury, acting under s. 670, should have put to them the exact question set out in the section along with whatever further explanation of the section the trial judge deems necessary. The jury should respond to the question put to it on the basis of only the evidence and arguments of counsel presented prior to and resulting in the conviction and the trial judge's instructions. To allow the jury to hear at that stage of the proceedings the full record of the accused and argument based on that record is, in our view, an error of law. Thus, the recommendation which the trial judge received from the jury was flawed and, although the learned

trial judge did not follow that recommendation, we do not know the extent to which it affected his final decision.

. . .

[26] In the result, notwithstanding the faulty procedure and the consequent flawed jury recommendation, I agree that the trial judge's determination of 15 years' parole ineligibility was a fit disposition for this appellant under the circumstances of this case.

R v Ly
(1992), 72 CCC (3d) 57 (Man CA)

TWADDLE JA (Scott CJM concurring):

With the exception of Ky Duong's criminal activity subsequent to the murder, the jury was well aware of all the circumstances relevant to sentencing when it was asked, pursuant to the Code, whether it wished to make any recommendation with respect to the number of years each accused should serve before he became eligible for release on parole. The jury chose to make a recommendation which was in these terms: "We recommend no more than ten years."

Despite the jury's recommendation, the learned trial judge was of the view that the crime itself merited denunciation by the imposition on each accused of a longer period of parole ineligibility than the minimum. He was also of the view that an even longer period was required in the case of Ky Duong "to reflect the relative role and character of the offenders." He consequently increased the minimum period to 15 years for Phat Ly and to 20 years for Ky Duong. It is from these increased periods of parole ineglibility that the accused appeal.

. . .

The Jury's Recommendation

In conferring a role on the jury in the sentencing process, Parliament must surely have intended to provide the judge with one measure of the public's revulsion at the crime. The judge is not, of course, bound by what the jury recommends, but it is an indication to him of the need for denunciation beyond that inherent in the mandatory sentence.

R v. Joseph (1984), 15 CCC (3d) 314 (BCCA), was a case in which the jury recommended 20 years of parole ineligibility. The trial judge accepted the recommendation, but the British Columbia Court of Appeal reduced the period to 10 years. The Court of Appeal accepted that the circumstances of the offence did not merit additional denunciation.

It is entirely possible that there will be a case in which the opposite is true. A jury may recommend leniency where none is warranted. Ordinarily, however, a trial judge should be slow to disregard a jury's lenient recommendation where there is a mitigating feature such as the youth of the offender.

. . .

In the result, I would allow the sentence appeal of each offender, set aside the period of parole ineligibility imposed on each and substitute, in Phat Ly's case, a period of 12 years and, in Ky Duong's case, a period of 15 years.

LYON JA (dissenting):

I have had the advantage of reading the reasons for judgment of my colleague Twaddle JA in these sentence appeals. I must, with respect, disagree with the result he arrives at.

A review of a number of recent decisions on second degree murders committed in furtherance of serious crimes such as robbery and break, enter and theft, indicates sentences for parole ineligibility ranging from the minimum of 10 years to 20 years. However, the majority of the sentences for such murders are in excess of the minimum and tend to range between 14 and 20 years. That there is no uniform consistency in sentencing and that longer periods of ineligibility tend to be given for serious or aggravated murders is the main conclusion one can draw from such a review.

· · ·

Finally, the overriding by the trial judge of the jury's recommendation for minimum eligibility is commented upon by Twaddle JA as another reason for lowering the trial judge's sentences. He states: "Ordinarily, however, a trial judge should be slow to disregard a jury's lenient recommendation where there is a mitigating feature such as the youth of the offender." Again, with respect, I must disagree.

There is nothing sacrosanct about the jury's recommendation. Indeed, as I mention later, the jury's recommendation is made without their receiving any instruction on the general principles of sentencing and, additionally, it is often made without full knowledge of pertinent sentencing information. There is ample authority for the proposition that the trial judge is not bound by the jury's recommendation and that the jury's recommendation is only one of a number of equal factors which the trial judge must consider in passing sentence "as he deems fit in the circumstances" (s. 744, *supra*).

· · ·

Why must the jury's recommendation be only one factor in sentencing? Simply put, because in many, if not most cases, the jury is not in possession of all of the facts; more importantly, it is never instructed in the jurisprudence which surrounds the sentencing function of a judge; and its participation in the process in the limited manner provided by Code, ss. 744 and 745 represents the only occasions when Parliament has permitted jury involvement in what is otherwise a totally judicial function. …

For many of the reasons given herein, the Law Reform Commission of Canada has recommended that jury involvement in the sentencing process be abolished. See Law Reform Commission of Canada, *Homicide, Working Paper 33*, pp. 79 and 116, and excerpt from the Law Reform Commission of Canada, *The Jury*, Report 16 (1982), appended hereto as Appendix "B."

As patently manifested in the case at bar, the jury's only information concerning the accused and their backgrounds was limited to the evidence adduced at trial through the Crown witnesses who dealt, quite properly, solely with matters relevant to the charge in question. The characters of the accused were not raised nor did the co-accused give evidence. Immediately after rendering their verdicts convicting the two accused, the jury made their parole eligibility recommendation and were then discharged. The following day, the trial judge heard extended representations from Crown and defence counsel, all of which contained, as is customarily the case, background and other information to which the jury was not privy. It was only after considering the totality of evidence, the submissions by counsel on sentence, and then *applying s. 774 and the general principles of sentencing* that the trial judge made his determination.

The jury's recommendation, as previously noted, was made without any knowledge whatsoever of the serious criminal activity of Ky Duong subsequent to the murder for which he was to be sentenced. Nor did they know of Ky Duong's ongoing associations with criminal groups in both Winnipeg and Toronto, matters which had been under police surveillance. Nor did the jury have the additional information which crown and defence counsel later gave the court in speaking to sentence. They did not know Ky Duong was associated with one Bau Diu described by Crown counsel as a dangerous and violent criminal living in Toronto. Nor was the jury apprised of the details of the gangland-type stabbing and shooting which resulted in Ky Duong's plea of guilty to a charge of manslaughter in Toronto.

As the trial judge noted in passing sentence (p. 1540 of the transcript):

> He is presently serving six and a half years manslaughter in Toronto, an offence which occurred after the commission of the crime presently before the court. He also had a conviction for break, enter and theft on May 30th, 1988, this offence also having occurred after the commission of this offence.
>
> Mr. Duong did not make any statements to the police as to his role in the crime.
>
> The evidence of Mr. Tong indicates that Mr. Duong bought the firearm and loaded it with bullets while he was in the car and before setting off to the Dunn-Rite plant.
>
> There is no indication of any remorse by Mr. Duong for his actions in this crime.

This information, save the evidence of Mr. Tong, was unknown to the jury. Taken together with all of the circumstances surrounding the crime itself, it represented, in my opinion, more than adequate justification for the sentence imposed on Ky Duong and for altering the jury's recommendation. The justification for the increased period of parole ineligibility for Phat Ly has earlier been reviewed.

In the result, I would dismiss the appeals against sentence.

For an interesting analysis of the history and role of the jury recommendation, see Micah B Rankin, "The Origins, Evolution and Puzzling Irrelevance of Jury Recommendations in Second-Degree Murder Sentencing" (2015) 40 Queen's LJ 531. The author questions the continuing validity of this practice. Do you think we should maintain a role for the jury in second-degree murder cases? If so, would you change the process to make it more meaningful—that is, by allowing the prosecutor and the offender to make submissions?

V. JUDICIAL REVIEW AFTER FIFTEEN YEARS

As noted above, the potential avenue to review parole ineligibility periods greater than 15 years has now been repealed. This was a long-promised part of the Harper government's "law-and-order" crime agenda. There were some who argued for its repeal on the basis that reducing the 25-year minimum incarceration period undermines the gravity of first-degree murder sentencing. Others suggested that the high success rate of applicants in reducing their parole ineligibility periods indicates systemic manipulation. This was an ironic criticism given that the decision-maker is a jury from the jurisdiction where the killing took place.

Moreover, as you will see from the data below, the high success rate was misleading because only a small fraction of eligible prisoners actually applied. Judicial review after 15 years continues to apply, with some new obstacles, to offenders convicted of murder before December 2, 2011.

The judicial review procedure set out in s 745.6 has received little attention in case law and legal literature. It was enacted in 1976, when the penalty for murder was restructured. It was part of the legislated alternative to hanging, along with the first- and second-degree murder regime, and is commonly known as the "faint hope" clause. Given that a person convicted of first-degree murder must wait 15 years before pursuing an application for judicial review, the first applications were not heard until the late 1980s. The first two cases were *Québec (Procureur général) c Chartrand*, *Ottawa Citizen* (31 December 1986) A4 and *R v Vaillancourt* (1988), 66 CR (3d) 66 (Ont H Ct J). Both Chartrand and Vaillancourt had originally been sentenced to hang but their death sentences were commuted as a transitional part of the 1976 legislation. Both men had killed police officers. Consistent with the experience that would unfold over time, the Quebec case succeeded and the Ontario application was rejected. The legislation provides for no right of appeal to the provincial courts of appeal. Accordingly, it was some years before any appellate guidance was provided. The only case in which the Supreme Court has pronounced on these types of hearings is *Swietlinski*, below.

In 1997, a series of amendments to s 745.6 were passed with the goal of limiting access to its relief. These included the disqualification of multiple murderers, the requirement for pre-vetting by the chief justice of the province, and the requirement for jury unanimity on the issue of granting relief: see s 745.63(3).

The following data, recorded as of April 12, 2009, when the parliamentary debate over repeal began, show the situation over a period of more than 20 years:

Number of offenders serving life sentences with more than 15 years parole ineligibility	1,792
Number of prisoners eligible for s 745 application	991
Number of eligible prisoners who have had reviews	173 (17.38% of eligible prisoners)
Number of prisoners who received some reduction	143 (14.43% of eligible prisoners)

It was thus correct, as the relevant minister regularly reminded us, that almost 83 percent of review applications were successful. However, this was not the full story. Given the small proportion of eligible prisoners who applied (17.38 percent), in total only 14.43 percent of eligible prisoners received a reduction in parole eligibility as a result of the 15-year review process. Moreover, only a tiny number of prisoners were made immediately eligible, with the vast majority of successful applications receiving reductions to between 17 and 22 years of parole ineligibility. As well, a reduction in ineligibility does not mean release—that is in the hands of the Parole Board of Canada. By April 2009, 130 offenders had been released—101 were being actively supervised in the community, 14 had been returned to custody, 11 were deceased, 1 was on bail, and 3 had been deported.

One can only guess why there were so few applications. Obviously, a process of self-selection has influenced prisoners' decisions on whether to apply. There are some plausible reasons for opting out. First, 15-year reviews are usually conducted in the place where the offence occurred and often generate a great deal of contemporary media attention. Some prisoners might prefer to let their case lay dormant, out of the public eye. Second, there may be a concern that an unsuccessful application may prejudice a future parole application. A third reason is perhaps the recognition that, in order to succeed, one needs to show some good evidence of progress and positive change. Accordingly, prisoners may want to wait until they have received minimum security status, or at least medium security, before seriously considering an application. Whatever the reasons, most cases that have gone forward have proven to be good cases in the eyes of jurors. Still, despite evidence that the process was working, its repeal was passed and became law on December 2, 2011.

A. Criminal Code, Sections 745.6 to 746

For those convicted of first-degree murder, or second-degree murder with parole ineligibility periods greater than 15 years, a review is still available for those convicted before 2 December 2011. The new legislation added a major procedural hurdle. It imposed a time limit that requires a prisoner to apply within 90 days of reaching 15 years: see s 745.6(2.1). This can be extended to 180 days by the relevant chief justice if the prisoner faced "circumstances beyond their control." This means that a prisoner can no longer wait to make more progress and present a better case—for example, by being transferred to lower security.

B. Criminal Code, Sections 745.6 to 745.64

Application for Judicial Review

745.6(1) Subject to subsections (2) to (2.6), a person may apply, in writing, to the appropriate Chief Justice in the province in which their conviction took place for a reduction in the number of years of imprisonment without eligibility for parole if the person

(a) has been convicted of murder or high treason;

(a.1) committed the murder or high treason before the day on which this paragraph comes into force;

(b) has been sentenced to imprisonment for life without eligibility for parole until more than fifteen years of their sentence has been served; and

(c) has served at least fifteen years of their sentence.

Exception—multiple murderers

(2) A person who has been convicted of more than one murder may not make an application under subsection (1), whether or not proceedings were commenced in respect of any of the murders before another murder was committed.

Less than 15 years of sentence served

(2.1) A person who is convicted of murder or high treason and who has served less than 15 years of their sentence on the day on which this subsection comes into force may, within 90 days after the day on which they have served 15 years of their sentence, make an application under subsection (1).

At least 15 years of sentence served

(2.2) A person who is convicted of murder or high treason and who has served at least 15 years of their sentence on the day on which this subsection comes into force may make an application under subsection (1) within 90 days after

(a) the end of five years after the day on which the person was the subject of a determination made under subsection 745.61(4) or a determination or conclusion to which subsection 745.63(8) applies; or

(b) the day on which this subsection comes into force, if the person has not made an application under subsection (1).

Non-application of subsection (2.2)

(2.3) Subsection (2.2) has no effect on a determination or decision made under subsection 745.61(3) or (5) or 745.63(3), (5) or (6) as it read immediately before the day on which this subsection comes into force. A person in respect of whom a time is set under paragraph 745.61(3)(a) or 745.63(6)(a) as it read immediately before that day may make an application under subsection (1) within 90 days after the end of that time.

Further five-year period if no application made

(2.4) If the person does not make an application in accordance with subsection (2.1), (2.2) or (2.3), as the case may be, they may make an application within 90 days after the day on which they have served a further five years of their sentence following the 90-day period referred to in that subsection, as the case may be.

Subsequent applications

(2.5) A person who makes an application in accordance with subsection (2.1), (2.2) or (2.3), as the case may be, may make another application under subsection (1) within 90 days after

(a) the end of the time set under paragraph 745.61(3)(a) or 745.63(6)(a), if a time is set under that paragraph; or

(b) the end of five years after the day on which the person is the subject of a determination made under subsection 745.61(4) or a determination or conclusion to which subsection 745.63(8) applies, if the person is the subject of such a determination or conclusion.

Subsequent applications

(2.6) A person who had made an application under subsection (1) as it read immediately before the day on which this subsection comes into force, whose application was finally disposed of on or after that day and who has then made a subsequent application may make a further application in accordance with subsection (2.5), if either paragraph (2.5)(a) or (b) is applicable.

(2.7) The 90-day time limits for the making of any application referred to in subsections (2.1) to (2.5) may be extended by the appropriate Chief Justice, or his or her designate, to a maximum of 180 days if the person, due to circumstances beyond their control, is unable to make an application within the 90-day time limit.

(2.8) If a person convicted of murder does not make an application under subsection (1) within the maximum time period allowed by this section, the Commissioner of Correctional Service Canada, or his or her designate, shall immediately notify in writing a parent, child, spouse or common-law partner of the victim that the convicted person did not make an application. If it is not possible to notify one of the aforementioned relatives, then the notification shall be given to another relative of the victim. The notification shall specify the next date on which the convicted person will be eligible to make an application under subsection (1).

• • •

Judicial screening

745.61(1) On receipt of an application under subsection 745.6(1), the appropriate Chief Justice shall determine, or shall designate a judge of the superior court of criminal jurisdiction to determine, on the basis of the following written material, whether the applicant has shown, on a balance of probabilities, that there is a substantial likelihood that the application will succeed:

(a) the application;

(b) any report provided by the Correctional Service of Canada or other correctional authorities; and

(c) any other written evidence presented to the Chief Justice or judge by the applicant or the Attorney General.

Criteria

(2) In determining whether the applicant has shown that there is a substantial likelihood that the application will succeed, the Chief Justice or judge shall consider the criteria set out in paragraphs 745.63(1)(a) to (e), with any modifications that the circumstances require.

Decision re new application

(3) If the Chief Justice or judge determines that the applicant has not shown that there is a substantial likelihood that the application will succeed, the Chief Justice or judge may

(a) set a time, no earlier than five years after the date of the determination, at or after which the applicant may make another application under subsection 745.6(1); or

(b) decide that the applicant may not make another application under that subsection.

If no decision re new application

(4) If the Chief Justice or judge determines that the applicant has not shown that there is a substantial likelihood that the application will succeed but does not set a time for another application or decide that such an application may not be made, the applicant may make another application no earlier than five years after the date of the determination.

Designation of judge to empanel jury

(5) If the Chief Justice or judge determines that the applicant has shown that there is a substantial likelihood that the application will succeed, the Chief Justice shall designate a judge of the superior court of criminal jurisdiction to empanel a jury to hear the application.

Appeal

745.62(1) The applicant or the Attorney General may appeal to the Court of Appeal from a determination or a decision made under section 745.61 on any question of law or fact or mixed law and fact.

Documents to be considered

(2) The appeal shall be determined on the basis of the documents presented to the Chief Justice or judge who made the determination or decision, any reasons for the determination or decision and any other documents that the Court of Appeal requires.

Sections to apply

(3) Sections 673 to 696 apply, with such modifications as the circumstances require.

Hearing of application

745.63(1) The jury empanelled under subsection 745.61(5) to hear the application shall consider the following criteria and determine whether the applicant's number of years of imprisonment without eligibility for parole ought to be reduced:

(a) the character of the applicant;

(b) the applicant's conduct while serving the sentence;

(c) the nature of the offence for which the applicant was convicted;

(d) any information provided by a victim at the time of the imposition of the sentence or at the time of the hearing under this section; and

(e) any other matters that the judge considers relevant in the circumstances.

Information provided by victim

(1.1) Information provided by a victim referred to in paragraph (1)(d) may be provided either orally or in writing, at the discretion of the victim, or in any other manner that the judge considers appropriate.

(2) [Repealed, 2015, c. 13, s. 34]

Reduction

(3) The jury hearing an application under subsection (1) may determine that the applicant's number of years of imprisonment without eligibility for parole ought to be reduced. The determination to reduce the number of years must be by unanimous vote.

No reduction

(4) The applicant's number of years of imprisonment without eligibility for parole is not reduced if

(a) the jury hearing an application under subsection (1) determines that the number of years ought not to be reduced;

(b) the jury hearing an application under subsection (1) concludes that it cannot unanimously determine that the number of years ought to be reduced; or

(c) the presiding judge, after the jury has deliberated for a reasonable period, concludes that the jury is unable to unanimously determine that the number of years ought to be reduced.

Where determination to reduce number of years

(5) If the jury determines that the number of years of imprisonment without eligibility for parole ought to be reduced, the jury may, by a vote of not less than two thirds of the members of the jury,

(a) substitute a lesser number of years of imprisonment without eligibility for parole than that then applicable; or

(b) terminate the ineligibility for parole.

Decision re new application

(6) If the applicant's number of years of imprisonment without eligibility for parole is not reduced, the jury may

(a) set a time, no earlier than five years after the date of the determination or conclusion under subsection (4), at or after which the applicant may make another application under subsection 745.6(1); or

(b) decide that the applicant may not make another application under that subsection.

Two-thirds decision

(7) The decision of the jury under paragraph (6)(a) or (b) must be made by not less than two thirds of its members.

If no decision re new application

(8) If the jury does not set a date on or after which another application may be made or decide that such an application may not be made, the applicant may make another application no earlier than five years after the date of the determination or conclusion under subsection (4).

Rules

745.64(1) The appropriate Chief Justice in each province or territory may make such rules as are required for the purposes of sections 745.6 to 745.63.

C. Applying the Provisions

The following two decisions, *Vaillancourt* and *Swietlinski*, were decided under the original formulation of the 15-year review.

R v Vaillancourt
(1988), 66 CR (3d) 66 (Ont H Ct J)

CALLAGHAN ACJHC:

The applicant has applied pursuant to s. 672 of the *Criminal Code* ("the Code") for a reduction of the number of years of imprisonment he must serve without eligibility for parole. On 1st October 1973 he was convicted of capital murder and sentenced to hang. This sentence was commuted to a "sentence of imprisonment for life for first degree murder" by operation of s. 25(1) of the *Criminal Law Amendment Act* (No. 2), 1976, proclaimed in force effective 26th July 1976. This enactment provided that the applicant would serve a term of life imprisonment without eligibility for parole until 25 years had been served. It also provided for a review of the ineligibility period pursuant to s. 672 of the Code: see *Criminal Law Amendment Act* (No. 2), 1976. SC 1974-75-76, c. 105, ss. 25(1) and 28(2).

. . .

The applicant submits that the onus of proof in determining the number of years of imprisonment without eligibility for parole under s. 672(2) of the Code must rest with the Attorney General of Ontario and that, to the extent that the aforesaid rules place a persuasive burden of proof on the applicant, they are *ultra vires* s. 672(5) of the Code. Furthermore, it is submitted that the said rules are contrary to the principles of fundamental justice to the extent that they place an obligation on the applicant to define issues in controversy, adduce evidence and address the jury before the Attorney General of Ontario on the application for review.

. . .

The fundamental issue on this application is the characterization of the review procedures established in s. 672.

The applicant takes the position that the procedure established under s. 672 is part of the sentencing process and involves an assessment of blameworthiness in order to determine the appropriate degree of denunciation which, in the eyes of the representatives of the community, i.e., the jury, needs to be satisfied. The applicant submits that Parliament has, by virtue of s. 672, provided a range of 15 to 25 years within which the jury may assess the degree of blameworthiness that should attach to the applicant's conduct. When blameworthiness is in issue, the applicant submits, it is a fundamental principle of justice that the state must bear the burden of establishing all matters in controversy beyond a reasonable doubt. As s. 672 is silent with respect to the issues of onus and standard of proof, the *Canadian Charter of Rights and Freedoms*, through the guarantees of s. 7 and s. 12, requires that the procedural protections which are attendant upon other proceedings under the Code be applied to a review under s. 672. It is submitted that the rules alter this substantive law and accordingly are *ultra vires* and of no force and effect.

The respondents characterize the review under s. 672 as a process entirely distinct from that of the sentencing process at trial. It is submitted that the review provided under s. 672 is an enlightened review process which seeks to provide hope of earlier release to those serving the longest possible sentences. The respondents take the position that the issue of blameworthiness was fully and finally assessed at trial, conviction and sentence, and that the determination of guilt made at that time is not subject to review under s. 672. Accordingly, the section does not contemplate a reassessment of blameworthiness.

Therefore, the onus and burden of persuasion should rest with the applicant, as he is the one moving to set aside a valid judicial order and the impugned rules are not violative of any Charter rights.

. . .

In my view, the language of s. 669(a) is mandatory. From that I infer that Parliament has specified precisely the degree of denunciation consequent upon a conviction for first degree murder. Where a conviction is registered for second degree murder, a jury has the right to make a recommendation with reference to parole eligibility under s. 670 of the Code. In contrast, when the conviction is for first degree murder, no such recommendation is available. The requisite degree of denunciation is established by Parliament in very clear language.

Counsel on behalf of the applicant submitted that the Charter, through ss. 7 and 12, requires that there be a proportional relationship between blameworthiness and punishment, and in this regard referred to the decision in *R v. Smith*, [1987] 1 SCR 1045, where it was held that a punishment is unconstitutional if it is grossly disproportionate to the offence. Counsel for the applicant submitted, therefore, that, in order for the mandatory sentence for first degree murder to be upheld as constitutional, s. 672 of the Code ought to be interpreted as requiring a jury to assess the blameworthiness of the individual offender and offence in order to determine the proportional number of years of ineligibility for parole. With respect, however, I do not agree. In *Smith*, Lamer J, with whom Dickson CJC concurred, expressly stated that a minimum mandatory sentence is not in and of itself cruel and unusual. In my view, the sentence provided in s. 669 of the Code cannot be said to be grossly disproportionate to the offence of first degree murder. A planned and deliberate killing necessarily involves an offence of the most serious order. In such circumstances, a mandatory sentence of life imprisonment without eligibility for parole for 25 years cannot be characterized as being so excessive or grossly disproportionate as to outrage standards of decency.

It was submitted on behalf of the applicant that the jury's role in a review under s. 672 is to reflect the community's condemnation of the offence and repudiation of the offender. On the contrary, that role has already been performed by the trial jury in its finding of guilt and by Parliament in its determination of the mandatory sentence that must be imposed. The issue of blameworthiness was finally assessed at trial, conviction and sentence. The determination of guilt, made at trial beyond a reasonable doubt, concludes all questions of the applicant's blameworthiness in respect of that offence. Accordingly, s. 672 does not, in my view, contemplate a reassessment of blameworthiness. Instead, it strikes a balance between considerations of leniency for the well-behaved convict in the service of his sentence, which may serve to assist in his rehabilitation, and the community interest in repudiation and deterrence of the conduct that led to his incarceration.

The jury under s. 672(2) is undertaking a review process, in the course of which they must consider the applicant's good conduct, and are given specific criteria to be applied in coming to their decision. But that jury does not again determine the degree of denunciation. With reference to the character of the applicant, his conduct while incarcerated and the circumstances of the offence, the jury determines whether or not present circumstances justify leniency and an early consideration of the applicant's case by the parole board. The review contemplated under s. 672 is a process distinct and apart from the sentencing process that took place at the conclusion at the trial. It is to be noted that the jury has no power to increase the penalty imposed at trial, but has the power only to recommend a reduction in that penalty. Accordingly, I must conclude that the review process provided for in s. 672 does not contemplate a proceeding which is part of the sentencing process, nor does blameworthiness fall to be determined again in the course of that review.

• • •

An application under s. 672 of the Code is permissive, and it is the applicant who has the option of determining whether or not to bring the application. There is nothing compelling the applicant to bring the application. In such circumstances, to place a persuasive onus on the applicant is not in my view violative of s. 11 of the Charter. It is the applicant who is seeking to set aside an otherwise valid judicial order. Having discharged the burden of establishing the guilt of the accused at trial beyond a reasonable doubt, the state, in my view, should not again be forced to bear the high cost of the onus of proof in post-conviction review matters. Moreover, it would be highly anomalous for the persuasive burden to revert to the state in the case of a convict such as the applicant, who had years earlier unsuccessfully appealed against the parole ineligibility period determination. The protections afforded by s. 11 of the Charter are simply inapplicable on a review under s. 672.

<h2 style="text-align:center">R v Swietlinski</h2>
[1994] 3 SCR 481, 92 CCC (3d) 449

LAMER CJ (Gonthier and Cory JJ concurring):
This case provides an opportunity for this court to consider for the first time the interpretation of s. 745 of the *Criminal Code*, RSC 1985, c. C-46, which authorizes a reduction of the period during which persons convicted of murder are ineligible for parole.

I. Facts

The appellant Roman Swietlinski was convicted of first degree murder. His conviction was upheld by the Ontario Court of Appeal, 5 CR (3d) 324, and by this court, 55 CCC (2d) 481. Since the earlier judgment of this court sets out the facts in detail, I will only give a brief description of the murder. On the night of September 18 to 19, 1976, the appellant met the victim, Mary Frances McKenna, in a bar in Toronto. Apparently, the pair left the bar about midnight on their way to the victim's apartment. The attack which followed was one of unspeakable brutality. The appellant stabbed the victim 132 times using five different knives. The force used was such that some of the knives were broken at the time the police located them.

In the course of the first two years of his sentence the appellant committed various disciplinary offences connected with smuggling and an attempted escape. Apparently, when he was placed in punitive segregation for the latter offence he underwent a complete change of heart and became a "model prisoner." In 1983, he was transferred to a medium security institution and then in 1990, to a minimum security institution. During his confinement in these various penal institutions the appellant became involved in various charitable or religious groups. He participated in work programs in the institutions. Since 1988, he has received several permits for escorted temporary absences. At various times he took part in Alcoholics Anonymous activities. He also participated in some training sessions and requested the assistance of a psychologist.

• • •

III. Judgment of Ontario Court of Justice (General Division)

O'Driscoll J of the Ontario Court (General Division) was designated for empanelling a jury and hearing the case.

At the preliminary hearing provided for in s. 10 of the Ontario Rules of Practice Respecting Reduction in the Number of Years of Imprisonment Without Eligibility for Parole, SOR/88-582, in effect at that time, O'Driscoll J held that statements by members of the victim's family were not admissible as evidence. He based his decision on *R v. Vaillancourt* (1989), 49 CCC (3d) 544, 71 CR (3d) 43, 43 CRR 60 (Ont. CA), in which the Ontario Court of Appeal held that a s. 745 hearing did not form part of the sentencing process. Since s. 735(1.1) of the Code made such statements admissible in order only to facilitate the determination of the sentence, they should be excluded from a s. 745 hearing. Further, O'Driscoll J considered that the statements disclosed no information relevant to the assessment of the factors listed in s. 745(2).

The hearing itself was subsequently held and the jury refused to reduce the period of the appellant's ineligibility for parole. Further, it set November 6, 2001 as the date on which the appellant could again make a similar application. Since that date corresponds to the time when the appellant will have served 25 years of his sentence, the jury's decision amounts to prohibiting the appellant from filing another application under s. 745.

The appellant sought and obtained leave to appeal directly to this court. Section 40 of the *Supreme Court Act*, RSC 1985, c. S-26, authorizes a direct appeal since the Code makes no provision for any other avenue of appeal: *R v. Vaillancourt* (1992), 76 CCC (3d) 384n, [1990] 1 SCR xii, 57 OAC 320n (SCC).

IV. Issues

The appellant raised the following grounds of appeal, most of which relate to the judge's charge to the jury:

1. the judge should not have limited consideration of the appellant's character to his character at the time of the murder: he should also have mentioned the appellant's present character;
2. the judge should not have referred to the three factors mentioned in s. 745(2) as three independent factors, each to be proved on a balance of probabilities;
3. the judge should have reread all of the agreed statement of facts: he should not have omitted the second part, relating to "extenuating circumstances";
4. the judge did not make a fair summation of the psychiatric evidence;
5. in questioning certain witnesses and in his address to the jury, counsel for the Crown introduced inflammatory and highly prejudicial matters.

I feel that the fifth ground provides a sufficient basis for allowing this appeal. Furthermore, the first, second and fourth grounds raise legitimate concerns which only aggravate the inequity resulting from the Crown counsel's inflammatory remarks.

Additionally, since I believe that a new hearing should be ordered, I will deal with the question of the admissibility of statements by the victim's family.

V. Analysis

A. General Observations on Section 745

Section 745 of the Code was adopted in 1976 in connection with the abolition of the death penalty. The compromise arrived at between the supporters and opponents of the death penalty was its replacement by long-term imprisonment without parole. Accordingly, in the case of first degree murder the penalty is life imprisonment with no eligibility for parole for 25 years. In the case of second degree murder, this time period is 10 years, but it may be extended to 25 years by the trial judge on the jury's recommendation. In both cases, however, Parliament provided that after 15 years a jury could be empanelled to reassess the period of ineligibility.

Section 745 put in place a procedure that is original in several respects. However, we need not consider all its aspects in order to deal with the case at bar. What is important is to understand that the procedure is one for reassessing long-term imprisonment imposed by law (in the case of first degree murder) or by a judge (in the case of second degree murder). The purpose of a reassessment procedure, especially when it takes place 15 years after the initial decision, is necessarily to re-examine a decision in light of new information or factors which could not have been known initially. It follows that the primary purpose of a s. 745 hearing is to call attention to changes which have occurred in the applicant's situation and which might justify imposing a less harsh penalty upon the applicant. Accordingly, the jury's decision is not essentially different from the ordinary decision regarding length of a sentence. It is similar to that taken by a judge pursuant to s. 744 of the Code as to the period of ineligibility in cases of second degree murder.

It should also be noted, in the context of an appeal to this court, that s. 745 gives the jury a broad discretionary power. This is quite different from a trial, at which the jury must choose between two options, guilt or innocence, based on very specific rules of law. Moreover, the discretionary nature of the jury's decision is made quite clear by the fact that Parliament did not see fit to grant any right of appeal to the Court of Appeal, although as I mentioned earlier that does not prevent an appeal to this court with leave. Consequently, there is no need to analyze the judge's charge to the jury in the detail that would be appropriate in the case of a trial. This court's function is essentially to determine whether the appellant was given a fair hearing at trial.

The discretionary nature of the decision also compels the jury to adopt a different analytical approach from that used in a trial. At a trial, the jury must decide whether it has been proven beyond all reasonable doubt that the accused committed the crime with which he or she is charged. In such a proceeding, the offence is generally defined by a number of elements which must all be proven for the accused to be convicted. Each element of the offence is thus a necessary condition for a conviction. At a s. 745 hearing, on the other hand, the jury does not determine whether the applicant is guilty: another jury (or, in some cases, a judge) has already performed that task. Its duty rather is to make a discretionary decision as to the minimum length of the sentence that the applicant must serve. The concept of an element of an offence cannot be transposed onto a discretionary decision. When a person makes such a decision he or she does not apply rigid logic, requiring for example that if conditions A, B and C are met, then decision X must be the result. When legislation lists various factors that a decision-maker must take into consideration, a finding reached upon one or all of the factors does not necessarily mandate a conclusion leading to a specific decision. They are instead factors, some of which may work in favour of the applicant and some against him, and which must be assessed and weighed as a whole in arriving at a conclusion. This is quite different from a trial where very strong evidence of one aspect of an offence cannot offset the weakness of evidence of another aspect.

Accordingly, the concepts of burden of proof, proof on a balance of probabilities, or proof beyond a reasonable doubt are of very limited value in a hearing pursuant to s. 745, where the decision lies exclusively in the discretion of the jury. The jury must instead make what it, in its discretion, deems to be the best decision on the evidence: On this point see also *R v. M. (S.H.)* (1989), 50 CCC (3d) 503 at pp. 547-8, [1989] 2 SCR 446, 71 CR (3d) 257 (SCC).

B. Grounds of Appeal

1. Inappropriate Language by Counsel for the Crown

The appellant objected to certain irrelevant and prejudicial language used by counsel for the Crown. Before considering the disputed remarks in detail, it should be recalled that the function of counsel for the Crown in a s. 745 hearing is no different from the function in a criminal trial. Taschereau J described his function as follows in *Boucher v. The Queen* (1954), 110 CCC 263 at p. 267 (SCC) (translation):

> The position held by counsel for the Crown is not that of a lawyer in civil litigation. His functions are quasi-judicial. His duty is not so much to obtain a conviction as to assist the judge and the jury in ensuring that the fullest possible justice is done. His conduct before the court must always be characterized by moderation and impartiality. He will have properly performed his duty and will be beyond all reproach if, eschewing any appeal to passion, and employing a dignified manner suited to his function, he presents the evidence to the jury without going beyond what it discloses.

The first category of unacceptable language had the effect of discrediting the process of reviewing ineligibility established by s. 745. Counsel for the Crown sought, in some measure, to present the procedure as fundamentally inequitable, first, because the victim had no opportunity, as the applicant did, to have her suffering reduced, and secondly, because the 25-year ineligibility period was a bargain compared with the death penalty imposed prior to 1976 and further reducing this period of time would be an additional concession to the accused.

For example, counsel began his opening statement with the following passage:

> Ladies and gentlemen of the jury, in 1976 this country, our government abolished capital punishment. Mr. Swietlinski was convicted of the worst crime known to our criminal justice system. You will hear shortly about the facts of this offence. In 1976, the same year, Mary Frances McKenna, someone that you won't hear very much about in this proceeding—this is an application brought by Mr. Swietlinski—but you won't hear much about a person by the name of Mary Frances McKenna, who was 37 years of age at the time.

He went on to add:

> ... please don't forget the victim in this case, Mary Frances McKenna. She doesn't have a
> chance to come before a group of people to ask for a second chance.

He concluded his opening statement by reminding the jurors that, "... Mr. Swietlinski,
a few years earlier, would have been sentenced to death for this offence ... ." In his final
submission to the jury he returned to the same themes:

> Mary Frances McKenna doesn't get a chance to come before a jury and ask to have her parole
> eligibility reduced. Mary Frances McKenna is gone.
>   If we wanted revenge, we would have capital punishment. As I say, we don't. We have a
> compromise. It's a mandatory sentence, life with no eligibility for parole for 25 years, and
> that's the sentence that our society imposes for the taking of a human life in the manner that
> Mr. Swietlinski took it. To do otherwise, as Mr. Swietlinski suggested to you about the rules
> at Millhaven, would be anarchy.

Counsel also sought, in questioning certain witnesses, to draw attention to the fact
that the victim could not obtain the second chance the appellant was seeking and to the
fact that no assistance programs were available to the victim's family whereas the penitentiary system offered the appellant a vast range of services.

Counsel further sought to discredit the parole process in the following language:

> Normally, issues of parole, parole hearings, are held by, basically, a faceless group of people.
> They're held in secret, in private, and really all that the Parole Board hears from is the appli-
> cant and perhaps his counsel and the kind of people that you're about to hear from, the vari-
> ous corrections people.

Finally, in questioning certain witnesses counsel insinuated that the Beaver Creek
Institution, where the appellant had spent the last two years, was too comfortable to be
called a prison and that in fact some visitors confused the institution with a neighbouring
campground. In his final submission, he suggested that the transfer to this institution was
sufficient reward for the appellant's good conduct during his sentence.

The combined effect of these remarks was to imply that the s. 745 hearing was a proceeding unduly favourable to the applicant, even a subversion of Parliament's intent to
impose a definite 25-year penalty on first degree murderers. The conclusion that emerged
from these observations, and it was not a difficult one to draw, was that the jury should
deal more severely with the appellant.

Nevertheless, s. 745 is as much a part of the Code as the provisions providing for no
parole for 25 years in cases of first degree murder. The possible reduction of the ineligibility period after 15 years is a choice made by Parliament which the jury must accept.
Clearly, the prosecution may not call this choice into question by suggesting to the jury
that it is an abnormal procedure, excessively indulgent and contrary to what it argues was
Parliament's intent. That amounts to urging the jurors not to make a decision in accordance with the law if they feel that it is bad law. It is clearly unacceptable for a lawyer to
make such an observation to the jury: R v. Morgentaler (1988), 37 CCC (3d) 449 at pp.
481-3, 44 DLR (4th) 385 at pp. 417-9, [1988] 1 SCR 30 (SCC); R v. Finta (1994), 88 CCC
(3d) 417, 112 DLR (4th) 513, [1994] 1 SCR 701 (SCC).

In the same way, counsel may not constantly repeat that imprisonment for 25 years is a substitute for the death penalty. That is an invitation to offset the alleged excessive clemency of Parliament by a severity not justified by the wording of s. 745. The jury does not have to decide whether the penalties imposed by Parliament are too severe or not severe enough. It must simply apply the Code. The Code no longer contains the death penalty: on the contrary, s. 745 gives the appellant the right to seek a reduction in his ineligibility period. No one can be permitted to undermine the fairness of the proceeding in which the appellant may obtain such a reduction by constant references to the death penalty.

Additionally, counsel for the Crown sought to draw the jury's attention to other cases of murderers who had used their parole to commit other murders. ...

Similarly, in his opening statement he invited the jury to take into consideration cases of violence other than those of the appellant:

> We read the papers. We open the headlines today and we see concerns about violence in our society, and, in particular, we hear concerns about violence against women. I want you, when you listen to that evidence, to bear in mind that you are here representing the best interests of this community as it pertains not only to Mr. Swietlinski but the broader issues that an application, such as this, brings to bear.

In his final submission he added the following:

> Violence is, unfortunately, increasing in our community. Every time you turn on the news, read the headlines you hear either reports of or people worried about the issue of violence and, in particular, violence against women.
>
> A lot of times people come into contact or read in the paper and hear, read or see on TV something that shocks them, and the facts of this case no doubt shocked you. Well, they have concerns about things going on in our society, and they think to themselves, "Someone should do something about that," and always the someone is someone off in the distance. For the purpose of this case ... you are the they. Consider that when you retire to reach your determination.

It is completely improper to invite the jury to consider isolated cases in which prisoners committed murder after being paroled. Even though the rules applicable in the s. 745 hearing are not as strict as in a criminal trial, the fact remains that the jury must consider only the applicant's case. Although the temptation may sometimes be very strong, the jury must not try the cases of other inmates or determine whether the existing system of parole is doing its job. The appellant should not be punished for the weaknesses of the system.

Furthermore, the other observations I have just referred to may have suggested to the jury that its function was in some way to solve the problem of violence in society. It is true that deterrence is one of the functions of the penalty and that it is, therefore, legitimate for the jury to take this factor into account when hearing an application under s. 745. However, the approach taken by counsel for the Crown was unacceptable. The jury cannot simply be referred to headlines in newspapers, which generally concern themselves with the worst crimes. Such a course could produce a disproportionate reaction in the jury by making it believe it could solve the problem of crime at one stroke and by giving the appellant's case the odour of a general threat. Such a tactic smacks of the in terrorem arguments disapproved by the Quebec Court of Appeal in *R v. Vallieres*, [1970] 4 CCC

69. In my view, it is possible to invite the jury to take the deterrent aspect of the penalty into account, but this should be done in the context of a general submission on the various functions performed by the penalty.

In a trial by jury it is usual for the judge to indicate to the jurors that they must base their decision solely on the evidence and that they should not read the newspapers while the trial is in progress. Sometimes drastic methods such as sequestering the jury or banning publication may be used to keep the jury free from undue influence by the media. That being the case, it is astonishing that counsel for the Crown could have invited the jury to do precisely what any good judge would tell it not to do. It is still more surprising that the trial judge did not react and rectify these remarks.

To sum up, I consider that the remarks of counsel for the Crown seriously compromised the fairness of the hearing. The judge's failure to reprimand him and to tell the jury that such remarks should not be taken into account, only aggravates the lack of fairness. However, the respondent argued that this court should dismiss the appeal because counsel for the appellant did not object to these remarks at trial. I cannot accept that argument. It is true that the absence of an objection is a factor which an appellate court may take into account in deciding whether to dismiss an appeal. In the case at bar, however, the hearing was unfair. The trial judge had a duty to ensure that the hearing was fair: *R v. Potvin* (1989), 47 CCC (3d) 289 at pp. 314-5 (SCC); *R v. L. (D.O.)* (1993), 85 CCC (3d) 289 (SCC), at p. 318. Since he did not do so, this court must intervene, whether counsel for the appellant objected or not.

I would allow the appeal for this reason alone. This conclusion is made all the more necessary when we take into account the court's errors in compartmentalizing the burden of proof and in the review of the evidence, although those errors by themselves are not sufficiently serious to justify a rehearing.

2. Distinction Between Present and Past Character: Burden of Proof

The common error disclosed by the first two grounds of appeal is an excessive compartmentalization of the various factors listed in s. 745(2) that the jury must take into account in arriving at its decision.

The judge's first error was to limit his discussion of the appellant's character to matters prior to or contemporaneous with the murder. He made no reference to the changes in the appellant's character since his imprisonment. As I mentioned, however, the purpose of the s. 745 proceeding is to reassess the penalty imposed on the offender by reference to the way his or her situation has evolved in 15 years. The judge should, therefore, have mentioned both the appellant's past and present character.

The second error results from the following observation by the judge, made at the start of the part of his charge dealing with conduct while serving sentence:

> Ladies and gentlemen, it is for you to say, but it would seem that the evidence establishes for you, on the balance of probabilities, that Roman Swietlinski was a model prisoner after he emerged from the 25 days in "the hole" at Millhaven penitentiary back in 1979 or 1980.

The judge expressed no similar opinion as to the other two factors mentioned in s. 745(2).

It is true that a judge may always give his or her opinion on the facts, so long as he or she makes it clear to the jurors that the final decision is theirs. However, this comment could have led the jury to think that the three factors mentioned in s. 745(2) were separate and that each had to be "establishe[d] ... on the balance of probabilities." As I have shown, this is not a very suitable approach in the case of a discretionary decision. The jury could have thought, in reliance on this comment, that it had to arrive at a decision favourable to the appellant on each of the three criteria.

3. Summary of Psychiatric Evidence

The appellant's psychiatric condition was one of the major questions raised in the court below. The points especially in dispute were the possibility that the appellant suffers from sexual sadism and the possibility of successful psychiatric treatment. Simplifying somewhat, it can be said that Dr. Dickey's testimony was very unfavourable to the appellant while the testimony of Mr. Jean, Drs. Wood-Hill and Quirt was favourable.

The trial judge undertook a lengthy review of the psychiatric evidence. It was probably not necessary to do this in so much detail. The issues were relatively straightforward. The expert testimony was fresh in the minds of the jurors. Moreover, each juror had a copy of the written reports available to him or her. However, when the trial judge considers it necessary or desirable to make such a review, he or she should not unduly devote greater attention to the aspects of the evidence that favour one party, yet this is what the trial judge did here. The judge placed his emphasis on Dr. Dickey's testimony, noting his professional qualifications and repeating certain parts of his testimony word for word. On the other hand, the judge made no mention at all of the testimony of Mr. Jean or Drs. Wood-Hill and Quirt. He simply mentioned short extracts from the written reports of Drs. Wood-Hill and Quirt. Though I am sure it was not intentional, the judge did nevertheless favour the respondent in his summation of the evidence. As an illustration, it can be pointed out that the review of Dr. Dickey's testimony took up 15 pages of the transcript of the charge to the jury while the passage from Dr. Wood-Hill's report extended only for a page and a half.

C. Admissibility of Victim's Statements

As I feel that a rehearing should be ordered, I think it is worth dealing with the question of the admissibility of statements by members of the victim's family. The respondent will undoubtedly seek to introduce such statements at that hearing. Additionally, since there is no right of appeal to the Court of Appeal, the appeal to this court is the only opportunity to introduce uniformity into the rulings of the superior courts on this point.

In *R v. Gardiner*, [1982] 2 SCR 368 (SCC), this court set out the general rules governing evidence at a sentencing hearing. Dickson J (as he then was) noted that the rules which applied to evidence at trial had been made more flexible: now, for example, hearsay evidence can be admitted if it is credible and reliable.

A s. 745 hearing differs from an initial hearing in many respects. However, the purpose of both is to determine the length of sentence. Consequently, evidence should be governed by similar rules. It is well known that the victim's testimony is admissible at a hearing on sentencing: see, e.g., *R v. Landry* (1981), 61 CCC (2d) 317 (NSCA). Since s. 745(2) states that the nature of the offence is one of the criteria the jury must take into account, it is clear that the victim's testimony is relevant and admissible at such a hearing. Since the ordinary rules of evidence have been loosened, this testimony can be presented by means of a written statement. Of course, such a statement should only contain relevant information. Counsel for the Crown clearly cannot use it in an attempt to introduce the type of remarks which I earlier condemned.

I, therefore, consider that the trial judge made an error in refusing to admit statements by members of the victim's family.

VI. Judgment

The appellant did not get the fair hearing to which he was entitled. The appeal is, therefore, allowed and a rehearing ordered in accordance with these reasons.

NOTE

Notwithstanding the order for a rehearing by the Supreme Court, the prisoner did not apply again. This shows the rigours of a s 745.6 application and, perhaps, the impact of being back in the media limelight.

After the 1997 amendments to s 745.6, aside from making all victim impact evidence statutorily admissible, it also became necessary for the chief justice of the relevant province or her designate to assess a s 745.6 application to determine whether it has a reasonable prospect of success. Clearly, the intention of Parliament was to provide some avenue to ensure that a hopeless application does not encumber court resources. How the test plays out is illustrated by the next case.

R v Fosty
2002 MBQB 269

BEARD J:

[1] Mr. Fosty has applied under s. 745.6 of the Criminal Code for a reduction in the number of years of imprisonment that he must serve before he is eligible to apply for parole. The first step in this proceeding is a hearing before a judge, referred to as a judicial screening, to determine whether there is a reasonable prospect that the application will succeed. The matter before me is the judicial screening regarding Mr. Fosty's application.

• • •

[7] Some principles to be considered in an application under s. 745.6 are as follows:

- The purpose of a s. 745.6 proceeding to reduce the period of parole ineligibility is not to reconsider the community's condemnation of the offence or the repudiation of the prisoner. The section strikes a balance between considerations of leniency for the well-behaved convict which may assist in his rehabilitation and the community interest in repudiation and deterrence of the conduct that led to his incarceration. (See *R v. Vaillancourt* (1988), 43 CCC (3d) 238 (Ont. CA).)
- Put another way, the purpose of the procedure is to re-examine the sentence in light of new information or factors which could not have been known initially. It is to call attention to changes that have occurred in the applicant's situation and which might justify imposing a less harsh penalty upon the applicant. (See *R v. Swietlinski* (1994), 92 CCC (3d) 449 (SCC).)

- The role of the jury, whether in determining guilt or in an application under s. 745.6, is to represent the community and its conscience. (See *R v. Nichols* (1992), 71 CCC (3d) 385 (Alta. QB) and *R v. Sherratt* (1991), 63 CCC (3d) 193 (SCC).)
- The burden of proof lies with the applicant/accused to establish that he deserves to be treated with clemency on a balance of probabilities. (See *R v. Swietlinski, supra.*)
- The factors set out in s. 745.63(1)(a) to (e) do not have to be proved individually in the same manner as the elements of an offence relevant to a decision of guilt or innocence. The jury is to make a discretionary decision after considering all of the factors, some of which may work in favour of the applicant and others of which may work against the applicant, and all of which must be assessed and weighed as a whole in arriving at a conclusion. This is different from a trial, where each element of an offence must be proved beyond a reasonable doubt. (See *R v. Swietlinski, supra.*)
- The concepts of burden of proof, proof on a balance of probabilities, or proof beyond a reasonable doubt are of very limited value in a hearing pursuant to s. 745.6, where the decision lies exclusively in the discretion of the jury. The jury must make what, in its discretion, it deems to be the best decision on the evidence. (See *R v. Swietlinski, supra.*)
- Because the purpose of s. 745.6 is to reassess the penalty imposed on the offender by reference to the way his or her situation has evolved in the 15 years following his conviction, the offender's past and present character are both relevant to the decision. (See *R v. Swietlinski, supra.*)
- The test to be met at the screening stage before a judge is relatively low, being that the applicant must show on a balance of probabilities that there is a reasonable prospect of success before a jury. It is the jury, and not the judge, that should decide whether an offender should be given an opportunity to apply for early release in all cases except those where there is no reasonable prospect of success before a jury. For a judge to dismiss any application that is not hopeless is tantamount to usurping the function of the jury. (See *R v. Kent*, [2001] MJ No. 575.)
- A reasonable chance is defined as being in accordance with reason, not absurd, within the limits of reason, not greatly more or less than might be expected. (See *R v. Kent, supra.*)

IV. Analysis

[8] Mr. Fosty has now served 15 years of the life sentence that he received on October 23, 1987, for first degree murder, making him eligible to apply for a reduction in the mandatory minimum 25-year imprisonment to which he was sentenced. The issue to be determined at the screening stage is whether Mr. Fosty has shown, on a balance of probabilities, that there is a reasonable prospect that his application before the jury will succeed. This decision is to be based on a consideration of the criteria set out in s. 745.63(1)(a) to (e) of the Criminal Code. My analysis of those criteria as they relate to Mr. Fosty follows.

(a) The Character of the Applicant

[9] The accused had no criminal record at the time of the offence for which he is now serving a life sentence, and he has been a model prisoner who has caused no discipline problems while serving his sentence.

[10] Before his involvement in this matter, he had completed high school and taken some technical training. He had worked with his father, who was and still is a building contractor, and he had developed considerable work skills in the construction trades. He has maintained strong contact with his family and some of his friends, who have visited him in prison. If he is released, he can return to work with his father in the same business.

(b) The Applicant's Conduct While Serving the Sentence

[11] As noted above, Mr. Fosty has caused no problems whatsoever and has had no discipline infractions while serving his sentence. In fact, he has participated in a very positive way in the work and recreational programmes in the prison throughout his time there. Overall, he has received very positive reports from both the professional staff who have done assessments and undertaken his treatment during his incarceration and from the Corrections staff. An example of the high regard in which he is held by the staff includes the following quote from a report prepared several years ago in support of his application for a transfer to a minimum security facility attached to Stony Mountain Institution:

> … Jim has volunteered to help out in all departments when required. I can say without a doubt that he is the most trusted inmate in this institution.
>
> • • •
>
> … I would be more than willing to put my job on the line and say that if given the chance to be set free at the earliest possible moment, he will never commit another crime.

[12] In addition, Mr. Fosty has undergone regular counselling over a lengthy period of time and attended several group programmes to help provide insight into the cause of his offending behaviour and to develop strategies to avoid any re-offending upon his release.

(c) The Nature of the Offence for Which the Applicant Was Convicted

[13] Mr. Fosty was convicted of first degree murder regarding the bludgeoning to death of an elderly man who was then left in his car, which was driven into a snow bank in a ditch in rural Manitoba. Mr. Fosty and his co-accused then fabricated an alibi to cover up their involvement and avoid being caught. As with all first degree murders, the circumstances were terrible and inexcusable.

(d) Any Other Information Provided by the Victim at the Time of the Imposition of the Sentence or at the Time of the Hearing Under This Section

[14] The crown attorney has advised me that neither he nor the police were able to locate any next-of-kin or relatives of the deceased to provide a victim impact statement.

(e) Any Other Matters That the Judge Considers Relevant in the Circumstances

[15] While the crown attorney did not consent to an order being made to permit this matter to proceed to a jury, neither did he strenuously oppose this application. He was candid in acknowledging that "the Applicant could fairly be described as a 'model prisoner'

as far as prisoners are capable of being models." As the crown attorney noted, the applicant in *R v. Kent, supra*, had many more strikes against him than does Mr. Fosty. Given that Associate Chief Justice Oliphant found that Mr. Kent had met the threshold test of having a reasonable prospect that his application would succeed before a jury, it would be difficult to find that Mr. Fosty did not meet that test as well.

V. Decision

[16] For the above-noted reasons, I find, on a balance of probabilities, that there is a reasonable prospect that Mr. Fosty's application before a jury would succeed and he would be permitted to apply to the Parole Board for a reduction in his parole ineligibility. I am, therefore, granting his application to make that application to a jury.

Beard J in *Fosty*, above, notes and assesses the "criteria" in s 745.63(1). By any stretch, these are not criteria. They do not provide elements of a decision-making process. Instead, they are just factors that the court must consider. The Code does not provide any help in determining the basis on which a s 745.6 decision should be made. The following case, *Pitre*, shows some of the evidentiary issues that can arise during a s 745.6 application.

Pitre v Attorney General of the Province of British Columbia
2005 BCSC 1483

DAVIES J:

[1] This is a ruling made mid-hearing on an application by Mr. Pitre under s. 745.63(1) of the *Criminal Code* for a reduction of the years of his parole ineligibility arising as a consequence of his conviction for first degree murder in 1989.

[2] During cross-examination of the applicant's witness, Mr. Czoka, an experienced corrections officer and administrator with the Corrections Services of Canada, Crown counsel asked questions about the fallibility of corrections assessments. Mr. Czoka responded that, to his knowledge, he had made no errors. Crown counsel followed up with a general question concerning errors occurring in the parole system generally from time to time which Mr. Czoka acknowledged. Mr. Luchenko then referred to recent difficulties at a Vernon halfway house that had been shut down as a consequence of murders committed by parolees previously convicted of murder.

[3] Out of the presence of the jury, I sought to determine the purpose behind the line of questioning and specifically the use of the example of the Vernon halfway house. I was told by the Crown counsel that the evidence was elicited to explore the efficacy of the parole board's classification of offenders and was led in response to Mr. Czoka's evidence about assessment procedures at a minimum risk institution.

[4] I advised Mr. Luchenko I would not permit further questioning in the area pending the hearing of complete submissions the next morning so that the matter could be addressed in the fullness of time with the benefit of appropriate legal research.

[5] I have now heard those submissions and I am satisfied that the questioning in relation to failures in the parole system generally or in specific instances ought not to have occurred and that I must take corrective action.

[6] Before this hearing started the applicant brought an application to challenge potential jurors for cause based upon, amongst other things, possible prejudice against the parole system. My discussions with counsel resulted in that challenge application being abandoned, after counsel for the applicant received my assurance that I would advise the members of the jury panel in the strongest of terms that if any believed that they could not try this case impartially and free of prejudice because of publicity or personal beliefs held about sentences for murder or about parole, they should not sit on this jury.

[7] In *R v. Swietlinski* (1994), 92 CCC (3d) 449, Mr. Justice Lamer, as he then was, speaking for the majority of the Supreme Court of Canada, said at p. 462:

> It is completely improper to invite the jury to consider isolated cases in which prisoners committed murder after being paroled. Even though the rules applicable in the s. 745 hearing are not as strict as in a criminal trial, the fact remains that the jury must consider only the applicant's case. Although the temptation may sometimes be very strong, the jury must not try the cases of other inmates or determine whether the existing system of parole is doing its job. The [applicant] should not be punished for the weaknesses of the system.

[8] The line of questioning embarked upon by Crown counsel in his cross-examination of Mr. Czoka is, in my view, precluded by that statement.

[9] I reach that conclusion notwithstanding Mr. Luchenko's submission that the line of cross-examination undertaken by him is relevant in this case to the jury's ability to assess the weight to be given to the evidence of Mr. Czoka as a correctional officer. That submission was based upon the proposition that because the applicant lead evidence which had the purpose of showing that he has performed well within the correctional system, the Crown is allowed to cross-examine upon failures in the system so that the jury can consider the weight to be placed upon the evidence of the correctional officer.

[10] In my view, that is far too narrow an interpretation of the clear warning given by the Supreme Court of Canada in *Swietlinski*. I note that the minority in *Swietlinski* would have allowed the type of questioning which the Crown wishes to continue but that the majority ruled that such questioning was improper. I am bound by the majority decision and I do not see this case as being distinguishable from it.

[11] Questions concerning general failures in the corrections or parole systems should not be allowed. No matter how phrased, such questioning invites improper reasoning and is irrelevant to the jury's task on this hearing which concerns only the application of those factors set forth in s. 745.63 to Mr. Pitre's circumstances.

[12] Mr. Pitre seeks relief as a consequence of the impugned evidence elicited in cross-examination, and I have determined that some of the relief sought should be granted.

[13] Firstly, Mr. Pitre says that no further questioning by counsel for the Crown should be permitted on the issue of whether the parole system makes errors. I agree. To the extent that there is any evidence of failure it is already improperly before the court. To further examine in the area would run afoul of the rulings in *Swietlinski*.

[14] Secondly, Mr. Pitre asks that an immediate warning be given to the jury outlining the extent to which they should disregard the evidence elicited on cross-examination. I agree that such a warning must be given at this time in order to preclude prejudice to a fair hearing. I do not agree necessarily with all of the language suggested by Ms. Sears and I will deliver the warning that I consider to be appropriate and necessary.

[15] Thirdly, Mr. Pitre asks that the applicant be entitled to re-examine Mr. Czoka on the issue of whether most parolees commit offences while on parole. Ms. Sears says such questioning is necessary to correct the prejudicial evidence now before the jury. I do not agree. It seems to me that the remedy sought would result in doing exactly what this hearing must not do, that is "put the parole system on trial." What is at issue here is Mr. Pitre's application, not the success or failure of the system generally.

D. Statistics on Section 745 Applications

The latest statistics (all statistics discussed here are derived from Public Safety Canada, *Corrections and Conditional Release Statistical Overview, 2014* (Ottawa: Public Safety Canada, 2015), online: <https://www.publicsafety.gc.ca/cnt/rsrcs/pblctns/ccrso-2014/2014-ccrs-eng .pdf>) indicate that 813 current prisoners are now eligible or will become eligible in the future for a judicial review hearing. As of the end of the 2013-14 fiscal year, 207 court decisions had been recorded. Unsurprisingly, because they involve longer periods of parole ineligibility, prisoners convicted of first-degree murder account for the vast majority of hearings (88 percent). More surprising is the fact that the success rate is only slightly lower for the first-degree murder applications (87 percent versus 77 percent).

The statistics reveal that although only a minority of eligible life prisoners apply for a judicial review hearing under this provision, the majority of those who do apply benefit from a favourable decision from the jury. Fully 78 percent of the applicants had their period of parole ineligibility reduced and 22 percent were denied any reduction. This statistic has remained relatively constant since the hearings began approximately ten years ago. In 2002, the success rate of the first 105 hearings was 80 percent: Julian V Roberts, "Determining Parole Eligibility Dates for Life Prisoners: Lessons from Jury Hearings in Canada" (2002) 4 Punishment & Society 103; for discussion of the amendments to s 745.6, see Julian V Roberts & David P Cole, "Sentencing and Parole Arrangements for Cases of Murder" in Roberts & Cole, *Making Sense of Sentencing* (Toronto: University of Toronto Press, 1999). This positive response to applications from prisoners serving life for the most serious crimes suggests that juries are sensitive to the case characteristics of the application, and do not dismiss these applications out of hand. What the statistics do not reveal is the extent of the reductions in parole ineligibility. Some applications result in reductions of only a couple of years. Previous research demonstrated that the most frequent outcome if a reduction in parole eligibility was awarded was ten years. The *average* reduction awarded by juries across the first 105 hearings was seven years.

Applications are more likely to be successful in some provinces, but in all jurisdictions a reduction is more likely than a denial. That said, there was significant variation in the success rate of applications. In Quebec, fully 93 percent of all applications attracted some reduction in the parole ineligibility period, while in Ontario the rate was only 51 percent: see the table, below. Without more detailed information about the cases, it is hard to know why the outcomes of hearings are so different in the adjoining provinces. It may be that applicants in Ontario have been convicted of more serious murders, possibly involving multiple counts; or the variation may reflect different public attitudes to punishing murder in the two provinces, or the degree to which the applications are opposed by the state. Of all prisoners granted a reduction in their parole eligibility, 90 percent had been granted release on parole.

Outcomes of Judicial Review Applications to End of Fiscal Year 2013-14

Province	First-degree murder		Second-degree murder			All hearings
	Number	Percentage	Number	Percentage	Total	Percentage resulting in reduction in period of parole ineligibility
Quebec	69	94	17	88	86	93
Ontario	22	52	1	0	43	51
Manitoba	9	89	3	100	12	92
Saskatchewan	9	67	0	9	67	
Alberta	26	73	0	26	67	
British Columbia	26	77	1	100	27	77
Canada	184	77	23	87	207	78

Notes: Only jurisdictions with more than five hearings included.

Source: Public Safety Canada, *Corrections and Conditional Release Statistical Overview, 2014* (Ottawa: Public Safety Canada, 2015) at 104, online: <http://www.publicsafety.gc.ca/cnt/rsrcs/pblctns/ccrso-2014/index-en.aspx>.

FURTHER READING

Jones, Craig E & Micah B Rankin. "Justice as a Rounding Error?: Evidence of Subconscious Bias in Second-Degree Murder Sentences in Canada" (2015) 52:1 Osgoode Hall LJ 109.

Manson, Allan. "Murder and Manslaughter" in *The Law of Sentencing* (Toronto: Irwin Law, 2000) ch 10.

Manson, Allan. "A Trip from Thoughtful to Thoughtless: Murder Sentencing in Canada" in Karim Ismaili, Jane B Sprott & Kim Varma, eds, *Canadian Criminal Justice Policy* (Cambridge: Oxford University Press, 2012) 58-78.

Mitchell, Barry & Julian V Roberts. *Sentencing for Murder: Exploring the Mandatory Sentence of Life Imprisonment for Murder* (Oxford: Hart, 2012).

Rankin, Micah. "The Origins, Evolution and Puzzling Irrelevance of Jury Recommendations in Second-Degree Murder Sentencing" (2015) 40 Queen's LJ 531.

Roberts, Julian V & David Cole. "Sentencing and Parole Arrangements for Cases of Murder" in *Making Sense of Sentencing* (Toronto: University of Toronto Press, 1999).

Statistics Canada. "Homicide in Canada—2013," by Adam Cotter, in *Juristat* 34:1, Catalogue No 85-002-X (Ottawa: Statistics Canada, 2014).

CHAPTER FIFTEEN

Preventive Detention and Preventive Supervision

I. INTRODUCTION

This chapter addresses the ways in which the sentencing provisions approach the issue of dangerousness. Generally, sentencing that focuses on the detention of offenders on the basis of an assessment of future dangerousness is referred to as "preventive detention." The emphasis is on confinement and control based on a perception of risk or fear of future crimes. In addition to sentencing, the *Criminal Code*, RSC 1985, c C-46, as amended, addresses perceived dangerousness at a number of points in the criminal process. For instance, at the bail stage, s 515(10)(b) permits detention before trial when there is a "substantial likelihood" that the accused person will commit further offences while out on bail. As well, detention, when "necessary to maintain confidence in the administration of justice, having regard to all the circumstances" under s 510(10)(c), has now been given a broader interpretation by the Supreme Court, which may extend to issues of dangerousness: see the controversial decision in *R v St Cloud*, 2015 SCC 27, [2015] 2 SCR 328. Also, ss 810.01, 810.1, and 810.2 of the Code provide for a recognizance with preventive conditions when there are reasonable grounds to believe that an individual will commit a criminal offence. Although, technically speaking, these recognizances operate outside the customary charge–trial– conviction criminal justice paradigm, the recognizances provided for in ss 810.01, 810.1, and 810.2 have been used to achieve post-sentence control over certain individuals. Accordingly, they are considered in this chapter.

As discussed in Chapter 2, Judicial Methodology and the Legislative Context, it has long been a principle of Canadian sentencing law that the primary purpose of sentencing is the protection of society. Section 718(c) of the Code identifies the separation of the offenders from society where necessary as an objective of sentencing. Thus, operating within the framework of the various statutory *maxima* established by Parliament, a sentencing judge can impose a sanction with public protection as the primary goal. The discretionary life sentence—for offences like manslaughter and aggravated sexual assault—is sometimes used with preventive detention in mind: see *R v Pontello* (1977), 38 CCC (2d) 267 (Ont CA); and *R v Mesgun* (1997), 121 CCC (3d) 439 (Ont CA).

The majority of this chapter focuses on *Criminal Code* Part XXIV, Dangerous Offenders and Long-Term Offenders, which establishes a specialized procedure for sentencing those offenders who are feared to pose a serious risk of reoffending. As set out below, the danger-ous offender provisions create a special designation and provide for indeterminate detention for certain offenders. Long-term offenders, who are thought to be a lower risk for recidivism, are dealt with through imprisonment followed by extended supervision in the community. The revisions in 1997 led to substantial litigation involving questions of retrospective appli-cation and integration between the dangerous offender and long-term offender sanctions. This culminated in the important 2003 decision of the Supreme Court of Canada in *R v Johnson*, 2003 SCC 46, [2003] 2 SCR 357, which returned the issue of treatability into the adjudicative matrix. However, Parliament responded with additional amendments that have bearing on disposition and treatability: see SC 2008, c 6, s 41. Consequently, this chapter has been substantially revised since the last edition.

The last section of this chapter considers recognizances under ss 810.01, 810.1, and 810.2 of the Code. By and large, Canada has rejected the propriety of further detention following a determinate sentence—that is, post-sentence detention. At one time, certain criminal justice and mental health personnel attempted to circumvent the inevitable release of dan-gerous prisoners at warrant expiry by having them committed under mental health legisla-tion: see *Starnaman v Penetanguishine Mental Health Centre* (1995), 24 OR (3d) 701 (CA). With the advent of ss 810.1 and 810.2, this practice may be dying a natural death. Moreover, the authority of *Starnaman* is of doubtful value after the important Ontario Court of Appeal decision in *PS v Ontario*, 2014 ONCA 900.

II. DANGEROUS OFFENDERS

Canada first enacted preventive detention legislation in 1947, when the habitual offender provisions were enacted: SC 1947, c 55, s 18. A "habitual offender" was someone who had previously been convicted at least three times of an indictable offence punishable by more than five years' imprisonment. The following year, Parliament added the designation of "criminal sexual psychopath" to the Code: SC 1948, c 39, s 43, defined as anyone who "by a course of misconduct in sexual matters has evidenced a lack of power to control his sexual impulses and who as a result is likely to attack or otherwise inflict injury on any person." Later, in 1961, the "criminal sexual psychopath" label was dropped in favour of the "dangerous sexual offender": SC 1960-61, c 43, s 32.

These early preventive detention provisions attracted a good deal of attention in the influential Report of the Canadian Committee on Corrections, *Toward Unity: Criminal Justice and Corrections* (Ottawa: Queen's Printer, 1969), also known as the Ouimet report. After a study of a group of individuals designated habitual offenders, the report determined that a substantial proportion of this group did not pose a serious threat to the public. The legislation seemed to be catching persistent offenders who, although constituting a serious social nuisance, were not dangerous (at 253). The way it was applied also reflected a disturbing disparity among the provinces. A hugely disproportionate number of individuals were sentenced as habitual offenders in British Columbia, where prosecutorial authorities found these provisions to be a useful tool for getting rid of "undesirables" in the West and stemming the immigration of criminals from eastern Canada: see Michael Jackson, "The Sentencing of Dangerous and Habitual Offenders in Canada" (1997) 9 Fed Sentencing Reporter 257. The Ouimet committee recommended substantial amendments to the preventive detention provisions, aimed at ensuring that only those whose background and criminal record created a real apprehension of further violence would be imprisoned indefinitely.

In 1975, the Supreme Court of Canada also expressed concern about the operation of the habitual offender provisions in *Hatchwell v R*, [1976] 1 SCR 39. Hatchwell was declared to be a habitual offender after being convicted of break and enter and theft of car keys. In reversing his sentence as a habitual offender, Dickson J (as he then was) described a 44-year-old individual with many convictions, the overwhelming majority of which related to property, automobiles in particular. There were no violent offences. As Dickson J said for the majority:

> ... There can be no doubt the appellant satisfies the habitual criminal criteria (s. 688(2)(a)) in that he, since the age of 18 years, on at least three separate and independent occasions has been convicted of an indictable offence for which he was liable to imprisonment for five years or more and he is leading persistently a criminal life. That leaves, therefore, for determination only the question whether the Crown has established, beyond a reasonable doubt, that because the appellant is a habitual criminal it is expedient for the protection of the public to sentence him to preventive detention.

> • • •

> Is Hatchwell a menace to society or just a nuisance? Should he be confined to prison for the rest of his life, subject only to annual review of his case by the Parole Board and release from custody only in the absolute discretion of that Board? These are not easy matters of decision for one must balance the legitimate right of society to be protected from criminal depredations and the right of the man to freedom after serving the sentence imposed on him for the substantive offence which he committed. Habitual criminal legislation and preventive detention are primarily designed for the persistent dangerous criminal and not for those with a prolonged record of minor offences against property. The dominant purpose is to protect the public when the past conduct of the criminal demonstrates a propensity for crimes of violence against the person, and there is a real and present danger to life or limb. In those cases the way is clear and the word "menace" seems particularly apt and significant. That is not to say that crimes against property can never be cause for the invocation of preventive detention legislation, for the legislation contains no such exclusion and society is undoubtedly entitled to reasonable protection against crimes involving loss of or damage to property. It would seem to me, however, that

when one is dealing with crime of this type, seeking to distinguish between that which is menace and that which is nuisance, there is greater opportunity and indeed necessity to assess carefully the true nature and gravity of the potential threat. For it is manifest that some crimes affecting property are very serious and others are not.

Major changes to the preventive detention legislation were soon to follow *Hatchwell*. In 1977, the *Criminal Code* was amended to create the current "dangerous offender" regime: SC 1976-77, c 53, s 14. A number, but not all, of the changes recommended in the Ouimet report were incorporated into this new legislation. The general structure of the current provisions (set out below) is rooted in these amendments. However, a few major changes, some procedural and others substantive, have since been made to this legislative scheme.

Approximately 20 years after the enactment of the dangerous offender provisions, Parliament was prompted to recalibrate this part of the *Criminal Code* once again. This new interest in preventive detention was the result of a few highly publicized cases involving crimes of catastrophic violence. The most significant was the death of Christopher Stephenson, a 10-year-old boy who was killed by Joseph Fredericks, a sexual offender who had recently been released from prison on mandatory supervision. The inquest into this murder was wide-ranging and transcended the terrible facts of the case. The jury heard evidence that suggested that, had different decisions been taken in Fredericks's situation, both by the prosecutor at the outset of the prosecution and then by the Correctional Service of Canada when Fredericks's mandatory supervision date arrived, the tragedy might have been avoided. The jury also heard evidence that portrayed the existing dangerous offender provisions as being inadequate, unable to deal with "mistakes" at the front end of the system. The jury was presented with the evidence of a justice official from the state of Washington who extolled the virtues of a "sexual predator" statute that had been passed in that jurisdiction. This type of measure, being a hybrid of criminal and mental health legislative power, permits the state, during the currency of a determinate sentence, to apply to have an individual detained indefinitely after a determinate sentence expires. In its sweeping recommendations, the jury recommended that justice officials in Canada develop similar legislation and that a federal–provincial task force be struck to facilitate this recommendation: see Verdict of the Coroner's Jury into the Death of Christopher Stephenson, Brampton, Ontario (22 January 1993). A few years later, another coroner's jury made similar recommendations, even though the case had nothing to do with the release of dangerous offenders from prison. The case involved a murder committed by a psychiatric patient on temporary leave from a psychiatric hospital: see Verdict of the Coroner's Jury into the Death of Dennis Kerr, Brockville, Ontario (12 April 1994).

Shortly afterward, the federal government did create a federal/provincial/territorial task force on high-risk offenders: see Report of the Federal/Provincial/Territorial Task Force on High-Risk Violent Offenders, *Strategies for Managing High-Risk Offenders* (January 1995). The significant proposal that emerged was a recommendation that Parliament pass legislation that would allow an offender to be designated a "long-term offender, " who could be supervised in the community for up to 10 years. The task force also made recommendations to change certain features of the existing dangerous offender provisions. Parliament followed the recommendation to create the new category of "long-term offender": SC 1997, c 17, ss 4-8. In terms of the dangerous offender provisions, Parliament went much further than the task force recommendations and made a few highly significant changes to the process.

The enactment of the long-term offender regime led to a significant new interpretation of both regimes by the Supreme Court in *R v Johnson*, below.

Data as of the end of fiscal year 2013-14 show that since 1978 there have been 678 people designated as dangerous offenders. Of that group, 72 percent have been convicted at least once of sexual assault. There were 573 dangerous offenders still on the books—548 were in custody and 25 were on parole. Of this group of 573, 29.7 percent were of Aboriginal background. (Note that Aboriginal offenders make up 21 percent of the penitentiary population, a dramatically inordinate proportion compared with the percentage of Aboriginal Canadians in the country.) In the years 2011-12, 2012-13, and 2013-14 there were, respectively, 45, 44, and 41 successful dangerous offender applications, the highest annual numbers since 1978: see Public Safety Canada, *Corrections and Conditional Release Statistical Overview, 2014* (Ottawa: Public Safety Canada, 2015) at 107.

For more on the history and background of preventive detention in Canada, see "Preventive Detention" in Allan Manson, *The Law of Sentencing* (Toronto: Irwin Law, 2000) ch 10.

A. The Statutory Provisions

The provisions of Part XXIV relating to dangerous offenders are set out below. In these provisions, there is occasional reference to "long-term offenders." The provisions respecting the latter are set out separately further below, although some of the provisions immediately below apply to both types of offenders. It is fair to say that there is a significant degree of procedural integration between the two designations, especially in terms of the specified set of antecedent offences and the requirement of a psychiatric assessment.

B. Criminal Code, Sections 752, 753, 755, 756, 758, 759, 760, and 761

Definitions
752. In this Part,
court means the court by which an offender in relation to whom an application under this Part is made was convicted, or a superior court of criminal jurisdiction;

• • •

long-term supervision means long-term supervision ordered under subsection 753(4), 753.01(5) or (6) or 753.1(3) or subparagraph 759(3)(a)(i);

primary designated offence means
    (a) an offence under any of the following provisions:
        (i) section 151 (sexual interference),
        (ii) section 152 (invitation to sexual touching),
        (iii) section 153 (sexual exploitation),
        (iv) section 155 (incest),
        (v) section 239 (attempt to commit murder),
        (vi) section 244 (discharging firearm with intent),
        (vii) section 267 (assault with weapon or causing bodily harm),
        (viii) section 268 (aggravated assault),
        (ix) section 271 (sexual assault),
        (x) section 272 (sexual assault with weapon, threats to third party or causing bodily harm),
        (xi) section 273 (aggravated sexual assault), and
        (xii) subsection 279(1) (kidnapping),

(b) an offence under any of the following provisions of the *Criminal Code*, chapter C-34 of the Revised Statutes of Canada, 1970, as they read from time to time before January 4, 1983:

(i)   section 144 (rape),

(ii) section 145 (attempt to commit rape),

(iii) section 149 (indecent assault on female),

(iv) section 156 (indecent assault on male),

(v)   subsection 245(2) (assault causing bodily harm), and

(vi) subsection 246(1) (assault with intent) if the intent is to commit an offence referred to in any of subparagraphs (i) to (v) of this paragraph,

(c) an offence under any of the following provisions of the *Criminal Code*, chapter C-34 of the Revised Statutes of Canada, 1970, as enacted by section 19 of *An Act to amend the Criminal Code in relation to sexual offences and other offences against the person and to amend certain other Acts in relation thereto or in consequence thereof*, chapter 125 of the Statutes of Canada, 1980-81-82-83:

(i)   section 246.1 (sexual assault),

(ii) section 246.2 (sexual assault with weapon, threats to third party or causing bodily harm), and

(iii) section 246.3 (aggravated sexual assault),

(d) an offence under any of the following provisions of the *Criminal Code*, chapter C-34 of the Revised Statutes of Canada, 1970, as they read from time to time before January 1, 1988:

(i)   subsection 146(1) (sexual intercourse with female under age of 14), and

(ii) paragraph 153(1)(a) (sexual intercourse with step-daughter), or

(e) an attempt or conspiracy to commit an offence referred to in any of paragraphs (a) to (d);

serious personal injury offence means

(a) an indictable offence, other than high treason, treason, first degree murder or second degree murder, involving

(i)   the use or attempted use of violence against another person, or

(ii) conduct endangering or likely to endanger the life or safety of another person or inflicting or likely to inflict severe psychological damage on another person,

and for which the offender may be sentenced to imprisonment for ten years or more, or

(b) an offence or attempt to commit an offence mentioned in section 271 (sexual assault), 272 (sexual assault with a weapon, threats to a third party or causing bodily harm) or 273 (aggravated sexual assault).

Prosecutor's duty to advise court

752.01 If the prosecutor is of the opinion that an offence for which an offender is convicted is a serious personal injury offence that is a designated offence and that the offender was convicted previously at least twice of a designated offence and was sentenced to at least two years of imprisonment for each of those convictions, the prosecutor shall advise the court, as soon as feasible after the finding of guilt and in any event before sentence is imposed, whether the prosecutor intends to make an application under subsection 752.1(1).

Application for remand for assessment

752.1(1) On application by the prosecutor, if the court is of the opinion that there are reasonable grounds to believe that an offender who is convicted of a serious personal injury offence or an offence referred to in paragraph 753.1(2)(a) might be found to be a dangerous offender under section 753 or a long-term offender under section 753.1, the court shall, by order in writing, before sentence is imposed, remand the offender, for a period not exceeding 60 days, to the custody of a person designated by the court who can perform an assessment or have an assessment performed by experts for use as evidence in an application under section 753 or 753.1.

(2) The person to whom the offender is remanded shall file a report of the assessment with the court not later than 30 days after the end of the assessment period and make copies of it available to the prosecutor and counsel for the offender.

(3) On application by the prosecutor, the court may extend the period within which the report must be filed by a maximum of 30 days if the court is satisfied that there are reasonable grounds to do so.

Application for finding that an offender is a dangerous offender

753(1) On application made under this Part after an assessment report is filed under subsection 752.1(2), the court shall find the offender to be a dangerous offender if it is satisfied

(a) that the offence for which the offender has been convicted is a serious personal injury offence described in paragraph (a) of the definition of that expression in section 752 and the offender constitutes a threat to the life, safety or physical or mental well-being of other persons on the basis of evidence establishing

(i) a pattern of repetitive behaviour by the offender, of which the offence for which he or she has been convicted forms a part, showing a failure to restrain his or her behaviour and a likelihood of causing death or injury to other persons, or inflicting severe psychological damage on other persons, through failure in the future to restrain his or her behaviour,

(ii) a pattern of persistent aggressive behaviour by the offender, of which the offence for which he or she has been convicted forms a part, showing a substantial degree of indifference on the part of the offender respecting the reasonably foreseeable consequences to other persons of his or her behaviour, or

(iii) any behaviour by the offender, associated with the offence for which he or she has been convicted, that is of such a brutal nature as to compel the conclusion that the offender's behaviour in the future is unlikely to be inhibited by normal standards of behavioural restraint; or

(b) that the offence for which the offender has been convicted is a serious personal injury offence described in paragraph (b) of the definition of that expression in section 752 and the offender, by his or her conduct in any sexual matter including that involved in the commission of the offence for which he or she has been convicted, has shown a failure to control his or her sexual impulses and a likelihood of causing injury, pain or other evil to other persons through failure in the future to control his or her sexual impulses.

(1.1) If the court is satisfied that the offence for which the offender is convicted is a primary designated offence for which it would be appropriate to impose a sentence of imprisonment of two years or more and that the offender was convicted previously at least twice of a primary designated offence and was sentenced to at least two years of imprisonment for each of those convictions, the conditions in paragraph (1)(a) or (b), as the case may be, are presumed to have been met unless the contrary is proved on a balance of probabilities.

(2) An application under subsection (1) must be made before sentence is imposed on the offender unless

(a) before the imposition of sentence, the prosecutor gives notice to the offender of a possible intention to make an application under section 752.1 and an application under subsection (1) not later than six months after that imposition; and

(b) at the time of the application under subsection (1) that is not later than six months after the imposition of sentence, it is shown that relevant evidence that was not reasonably available to the prosecutor at the time of the imposition of sentence became available in the interim.

(3) Notwithstanding subsection 752.1(1), an application under that subsection may be made after the imposition of sentence or after an offender begins to serve the sentence in a case to which paragraphs (2)(a) and (b) apply.

(4) If the court finds an offender to be a dangerous offender, it shall

(a) impose a sentence of detention in a penitentiary for an indeterminate period;

(b) impose a sentence for the offence for which the offender has been convicted—which must be a minimum punishment of imprisonment for a term of two years—and order that the offender be subject to long-term supervision for a period that does not exceed 10 years; or

(c) impose a sentence for the offence for which the offender has been convicted.

(4.1) The court shall impose a sentence of detention in a penitentiary for an indeterminate period unless it is satisfied by the evidence adduced during the hearing of the application that there is a reasonable expectation that a lesser measure under paragraph (4)(b) or (c) will adequately protect the public against the commission by the offender of murder or a serious personal injury offence.

(4.2) If the application is made after the offender begins to serve the sentence in a case to which paragraphs (2)(a) and (b) apply, a sentence imposed under paragraph (4)(a), or a sentence imposed and an order made under paragraph 4(b), replaces the sentence that was imposed for the offence for which the offender was convicted.

(5) If the court does not find an offender to be a dangerous offender,

(a) the court may treat the application as an application to find the offender to be a long-term offender, section 753.1 applies to the application and the court may either find that the offender is a long-term offender or hold another hearing for that purpose; or

(b) the court may impose sentence for the offence for which the offender has been convicted.

(6) [Repealed, 2008, c. 6, s. 42]

Application for remand for assessment—later conviction

753.01(1) If an offender who is found to be a dangerous offender is later convicted of a serious personal injury offence or an offence under subsection 753.3(1), on application by the prosecutor, the court shall, by order in writing, before sentence is imposed, remand the offender, for a period not exceeding 60 days, to the custody of a person designated by the court who can perform an assessment or have an assessment performed by experts for use as evidence in an application under subsection (4).

(2) The person to whom the offender is remanded shall file a report of the assessment with the court not later than 30 days after the end of the assessment period and make copies of it available to the prosecutor and counsel for the offender.

(3) On application by the prosecutor, the court may extend the period within which the report must be filed by a maximum of 30 days if the court is satisfied that there are reasonable grounds to do so.

(4) After the report is filed, the prosecutor may apply for a sentence of detention in a penitentiary for an indeterminate period, or for an order that the offender be subject to a new period of long-term supervision in addition to any other sentence that may be imposed for the offence.

(5) If the application is for a sentence of detention in a penitentiary for an indeterminate period, the court shall impose that sentence unless it is satisfied by the evidence adduced during the hearing of the application that there is a reasonable expectation that a sentence for the offence for which the offender has been convicted—with or without a new period of long-term supervision—will adequately protect the public against the commission by the offender of murder or a serious personal injury offence.

(6) If the application is for a new period of long-term supervision, the court shall order that the offender be subject to a new period of long-term supervision in addition to a sentence for the offence for which they have been convicted unless it is satisfied by the evidence adduced during the hearing of the application that there is a reasonable expectation that the sentence

alone will adequately protect the public against the commission by the offender of murder or a serious personal injury offence.

Victim evidence

753.02 Any evidence given during the hearing of an application made under subsection 753(1) by a victim of an offence for which the offender was convicted is deemed also to have been given during any hearing held with respect to the offender under paragraph 753(5)(a) or subsection 753.01(5) or (6).

· · ·

Hearing of application

754(1) With the exception of an application for remand for assessment, the court may not hear an application made under this Part unless

(a) the Attorney General of the province in which the offender was tried has, either before or after the making of the application, consented to the application;

(b) at least seven days notice has been given to the offender by the prosecutor, following the making of the application, outlining the basis on which it is intended to found the application; and

(c) a copy of the notice has been filed with the clerk of the court or the provincial court judge, as the case may be.

(2) An application under this Part shall be heard and determined by the court without a jury.

(3) For the purposes of an application under this Part, where an offender admits any allegations contained in the notice referred to in paragraph (1)(b), no proof of those allegations is required.

· · ·

Evidence of character

757 Without prejudice to the right of the offender to tender evidence as to their character and repute, if the court thinks fit, evidence of character and repute may be admitted

(a) on the question of whether the offender is or is not a dangerous offender or a long-term offender; and

(b) in connection with a sentence to be imposed or an order to be made under this Part.

Presence of accused at hearing of application

758(1) The offender shall be present at the hearing of the application under this Part and if at the time the application is to be heard

(a) he is confined in a prison, the court may order, in writing, the person having the custody of the accused to bring him before the court; or

(b) he is not confined in a prison, the court shall issue a summons or a warrant to compel the accused to attend before the court and the provisions of Part XVI relating to summons and warrant are applicable with such modifications as the circumstances require.

(2) Notwithstanding subsection (1), the court may

(a) cause the offender to be removed and to be kept out of court, where he misconducts himself by interrupting the proceedings so that to continue the proceedings in his presence would not be feasible; or

(b) permit the offender to be out of court during the whole or any part of the hearing on such conditions as the court considers proper.

Appeal—offender

759(1) An offender who is found to be a dangerous offender or a long-term offender may appeal to the court of appeal from a decision made under this Part on any ground of law or fact or mixed law and fact.

(1.1) [Repealed, 2008, c. 6, s. 51]

(2) The Attorney General may appeal to the court of appeal from a decision made under this Part on any ground of law.

(3) The court of appeal may

    (a) allow the appeal and

        (i) find that an offender is or is not a dangerous offender or a long-term offender or impose a sentence that may be imposed or an order that may be made by the trial court under this Part, or

        (ii) order a new hearing, with any directions that the court considers appropriate; or

    (b) dismiss the appeal.

(3.1) and (3.2) [Repealed, 2008, c. 6, s. 51]

(4) A decision of the court of appeal has the same force and effect as if it were a decision of the trial court.

(4.1) to (5) [Repealed, 2008, c. 6, s. 51]

(6) Notwithstanding subsection 719(1), a sentence imposed on an offender by the court of appeal pursuant to this section shall be deemed to have commenced when the offender was sentenced by the court by which he was convicted.

(7) The provisions of Part XXI with respect to procedure on appeals apply, with such modifications as the circumstances require, to appeals under this section.

Disclosure to Correctional Service of Canada

760 Where a court finds an offender to be a dangerous offender or a long-term offender, the court shall order that a copy of all reports and testimony given by psychiatrists, psychologists, criminologists and other experts and any observations of the court with respect to the reasons for the finding, together with a transcript of the trial of the offender, be forwarded to the Correctional Service of Canada for information.

Review for parole

761(1) Subject to subsection (2), where a person is in custody under a sentence of detention in a penitentiary for an indeterminate period, the Parole Board of Canada shall, as soon as possible after the expiration of seven years from the day on which that person was taken into custody and not later than every two years after the previous review, review the condition, history and circumstances of that person for the purpose of determining whether he or she should be granted parole under Part II of the *Corrections and Conditional Release Act* and, if so, on what conditions.

(2) Where a person is in custody under a sentence of detention in a penitentiary for an indeterminate period that was imposed before October 15, 1977, the Parole Board of Canada shall, at least once in every year, review the condition, history and circumstances of that person for the purpose of determining whether he should be granted parole under Part II of the *Corrections and Conditional Release Act* and, if so, on what conditions.

C. The Constitutionality of the Dangerous Offender Regime

Not long after the *Canadian Charter of Rights and Freedoms*, Part I of the *Constitution Act, 1982*, being Schedule B to the *Canada Act 1982* (UK), 1982, c 11 came into force, challenges were made to the dangerous offender provisions. None of them was successful. The leading case on this point is the decision of the Supreme Court of Canada in *R v Lyons*, below. The arguments made in *Lyons* represent the typical complaints about preventive criminal justice measures: (1) Is it fair to punish someone for a crime he or she has not yet committed, instead of imposing punishment only for past wrongful acts? (2) Is indeterminate detention not a "cruel and unusual" sort of punishment? (3) Given that social science tells us that our ability to predict dangerousness is quite weak, is it not arbitrary to detain someone indefinitely on this basis?

Since *Lyons*, there have been major changes to the dangerous offender regime. Accordingly, while you read *Lyons*, keep in mind that some of the specific procedures under consideration may be out of date, although the general conceptual approach is roughly similar. The current regime is discussed below in this chapter. For now, note that amendments to the dangerous offender provisions altered the regime in the following ways: (1) s 752.1 no longer requires the assessment of two psychiatrists, substituting the requirement of just one report; (2) s 753(2) allows a dangerous offender application to be made six months after the original imposition of sentence if new information arises; and (3) s 761(1) delays the first parole review of dangerous offenders from three years to seven years. Moreover, we have also seen significant developments in Charter analysis since *Lyons*. Still, in 2016, the Supreme Court decision in *Lyons* remains the leading case on constitutionality, notwithstanding potential criticisms that it is now anachronistic.

R v Lyons
[1987] 2 SCR 309, 61 CR (3d) 1

LA FOREST J (Dickson CJ and Estey, McIntyre, and Le Dain JJ concurring):

[1] The broad issues raised in this appeal are whether the dangerous offenders provisions of the *Criminal Code*, RSC 1970, c. C-34, Part XXI, ss. 687 to 695, contravene the rights guaranteed by the *Canadian Charter of Rights and Freedoms* to "liberty" and "not to be deprived thereof except in accordance with the principles of fundamental justice" (s. 7), "not to be arbitrarily detained or imprisoned" (s. 9), "to the benefit of trial by jury" (s. 11), and "not to be subjected to any cruel and unusual treatment or punishment" (s. 12), and if so whether they can be justified under s. 1 of the Charter as being "such reasonable limits prescribed by law as can be demonstrably justified in a free and democratic society."

Facts and Procedural History

[2] On 23rd September 1983 the appellant, Thomas Patrick Lyons, was arraigned on an information containing four charges: unlawfully breaking and entering a dwelling-house contrary to s. 306(1)(b) of the *Criminal Code*; unlawfully using a weapon or imitation thereof in committing a sexual assault, contrary to s. 246.2(a) of the *Code*; unlawfully using a firearm while committing an indictable offence, contrary to s. 83(1)(a) of the *Code*; and unlawfully stealing property of a total value exceeding $200, contrary to s. 294(a) of the *Code*. These offences were alleged to have been committed approximately one month after the appellant's sixteenth birthday.

[3] The appellant elected trial by a judge without a jury on all four charges and waived his right to a preliminary inquiry. He subsequently entered pleas of guilty to all counts in the indictment. O'Hearn Co. Ct. J of the County Court Judge's Criminal Court for District 1, Nova Scotia, requested a pre-sentence report and adjourned the matter of sentence.

[4] Just before the sentence hearing on 4th November 1983, defence counsel was informed, for the first time, that the Crown might bring a dangerous offender application under Part XXI of the *Code*. At the commencement of the hearing, the Crown requested

and was granted an adjournment to permit it to consider bringing such an application. The application was subsequently made. On 8th November 1983 consent to the application was obtained from the Deputy Attorney General of Nova Scotia, as required by s. 689(a)(a) of the *Code*.

[5] At the commencement of the hearing of the application on 14th December 1983, an agreed-upon statement of facts was read into the record. Evidence, including expert psychiatric testimony, was tendered on behalf of both the Crown and the appellant.

[6] Though O'Hearn Co. Ct. J had at the outset warned the Crown attorney that he would have an "uphill fight" owing to the age of the appellant, the judge in the end found, on the basis of medical and other evidence presented to him, that it had been established beyond a reasonable doubt that the appellant qualified as a dangerous offender under the provisions of the *Code*. In his view, it had been shown that the appellant had a "sociopathic personality" and had so little conscience that it did not govern his actions. He concluded that it could be said with "a high degree of confidence" that it was "very likely" that the appellant would constitute a danger to the psychological or physical health and lives of others owing to "his in-built, perhaps congenital indifference to the consequences to others, his lack of affect, his lack of feeling for others." He belonged, the judge stated, to a class of people who, though mentally able to understand the law and to conform their conduct to its dictates, are so irresponsive to the law that they must be dealt with by extraordinary measures.

[7] O'Hearn Co. Ct. J also considered and rejected the appellant's contentions that Part XXI of the *Code* was constitutionally invalid as offending against the guarantees embodied in ss. 7, 9 and 12 of the Charter, and proceeded to sentence the appellant to an indeterminate period of detention in a penitentiary.

[8] The appellant's appeal to the Nova Scotia Supreme Court, Appeal Division, was unanimously dismissed for reasons given by Macdonald JA. On 31st January leave to appeal to this Court was granted.

[9] The following constitutional questions were stated by the court on 26th March 1985:

> 1. Whether the provisions of Part XXI of the *Criminal Code of Canada*, dealing with an application for finding and sentencing, an individual as a dangerous offender, in whole or in part, infringe or deny the rights guaranteed by sections 7, 9, 11, and/or 12 of the *Canadian Charter of Rights and Freedoms*?
>
> 2. If so, then are the provisions of Part XXI of the *Criminal Code*, in whole or in part, justified on the basis of s. 1 of the *Canadian Charter of Rights and Freedoms* and therefore not inconsistent with the *Constitution Act, 1982*?

[10] The appellant also argued that his rights under s. 7 of the Charter were violated by the Crown's failure to give him notice, before his election of a mode of trial and the entry of his plea, that it intended to bring, or contemplated bringing, a "dangerous offender" application under Part XXI of the *Code*.

• • •

History and Analysis of Part XXI

[12] Part XXI of the *Criminal Code* establishes a scheme for the designation of certain offenders as "dangerous offenders" and for sentencing such persons to a penitentiary for

an indeterminate period. It is the product of frequently-amended legislation that has existed in Canada, in one form or another, since 1947. It has its genesis in the *Prevention of Crime Act, 1908* (8 Edw. 7, c. 59), ss. 10 to 16, under which a person convicted of a crime was subject to a "further sentence" of not less than five or more than ten years as preventive detention if he or she was found to be an habitual criminal. During the debates in Parliament on that Act, its author, Lord Gladstone, "made it clear that it was intended to deal not with the generality of 'habituals' but only with that more limited body of 'professional criminals' or 'persistent dangerous criminals' engaged in the more serious forms of crime" (Fox, *The Modern English Prison* (London 1934), at p. 168).

• • •

[16] The present legislation, enacted in 1977, clearly pursues the historical purpose of protecting the public, but is now carefully tailored so as to be confined in its application to those habitual criminals who are dangerous to others. In brief, Part XXI provides that, where a person has been found guilty of a "serious personal injury offence," the court may, upon application, find the offender to be a dangerous offender and may thereupon impose a sentence of indeterminate detention in lieu of any other sentence that the offender might have received for the offence. ...

[17] To trigger the operation of this procedure, it is necessary by virtue of the opening words of subs. (a) and subs. (b) that the accused have been found guilty of a "serious personal injury offence" ... . Two of the crimes of which the appellant was convicted fall within this definition.

[18] In addition to having been convicted of a serious personal injury offence, s. 688(a) and (b) provides that for the offender to qualify as a dangerous offender it must also be established that he constitutes a threat to the life, safety or well-being of others on the basis of evidence of the dangerous and intractably persistent or brutal behaviour described in paras. (i) to (ii), or that the offender has shown an inability to control his sexual impulses and a likelihood that he will thereby cause injury, pain or other evil to other persons. The findings of the courts below that behaviour described in s. 688 existed was not contested here.

[19] Owing to the nature of the findings that must be made, provision is made for psychological, psychiatric and criminological evidence (s. 690) as well as character evidence (s. 694). Indeed, the evidence of at least two psychiatrists is obligatory. As well, the judge is empowered to make directions and to remand the offender for the purposes of observation (s. 691).

[20] Because of the serious implications of the procedure for the accused, a number of safeguards have been provided. Thus the consent of the provincial Attorney General is required and the offender must, following the application, be given at least seven days' notice of the basis on which it is made (s. 689). The offender is allowed to nominate one of the psychiatric witnesses (s. 690(2)) and failure to do so obliges the court to nominate one on his or her behalf (s. 690(3)). The offender also has a right to be present at the hearing (s. 693), and to appeal against sentence (s. 694(1)). As well, the Solicitor General of Canada is to be furnished with copies of the psychological, psychiatric and criminological evidence and of the observations of the court (s. 695). Finally, and importantly, provision is made for review of the sentence at the expiration of three years from its imposition and every two years thereafter (s. 695.1).

• • •

[22] As already mentioned the case raises issues concerning ss. 7, 9, 11 and 12 of the Charter. Indeed, several s. 7 issues are raised, the most fundamental of which, and hence the one with which I propose to begin, being whether the imposition of preventive detention for an indeterminate period offends against the principles of fundamental justice. The remaining s. 7 issues focus not on the punishment itself, but on the fairness of the process by which the deprivation of liberty is occasioned. ...

A. Does Part XXI by Imposing Indeterminate Detention Offend Against Fundamental Justice Under Section 7 of the Charter?

[23] In *Ref re Section 94(2) of the Motor Vehicle Act*, [1985] 2 SCR 486, this court held that the phrase "principles of fundamental justice" sets out the parameters of the right not to be deprived of life, liberty and security of the person. These principles were stated to inhere in the basic tenets and principles not only of the judicial system but also of the other components of our legal system (at p. 512, per Lamer J). Hence, to determine whether Part XXI violates the principles of fundamental justice by the deprivation of liberty suffered by the offender, it is necessary to examine Part XXI in light of the basic principles of penal policy that have animated legislative and judicial practice in Canada and other common law jurisdictions.

[24] The appellant submits that Part XXI results in a deprivation of liberty that is not in accordance with the principles of fundamental justice, in that it permits an individual to be sentenced for crimes which he or she has not committed or for crimes for which he or she has already been punished. If this statement correctly described what in fact occurs under Part XXI, it would indeed constitute a violation of s. 7. The reality, however, is quite different. What s. 688 does is to permit a judge to impose a sentence of indeterminate detention on an individual for having committed an offence, which sentence is "*in lieu of any other sentence that might be imposed for the offence for which the offender has been convicted.*" (Emphasis added.) The individual is clearly being sentenced for the "serious personal injury offence" he or she has been found guilty of committing, albeit in a different way than would ordinarily be done. It must be remembered that the appellant was not picked up off the street because of his past criminality (for which he has already been punished), or because of fears or suspicions about his criminal proclivities, and then subjected to a procedure in order to determine whether society would be better off if he were incarcerated indefinitely. Rather he was arrested and prosecuted for a very serious violent crime and subjected to a procedure aimed at determining the appropriate penalty that should be inflicted upon him in the circumstances.

[25] Thus the appellant's contention that he is being punished for what he might do rather than for what he has done, or, in more traditional terms, that he is being found guilty in the absence of a finding of the requisite *actus reus*, must be rejected. The punishment, as I noted, flows from the actual commission of a specific crime, the requisite elements of which have been proved to exist beyond a reasonable doubt.

[26] Nor do I find it objectionable that the offender's designation as dangerous or the subsequent indeterminate sentence is based, in part, on a conclusion that the past violent, antisocial behaviour of the offender will likely continue in the future. Such considerations play a role in a very significant number of sentences. I accordingly agree with the respondent's submission that it cannot be considered a violation of fundamental justice for

Parliament to identify those offenders who, in the interests of protecting the public, ought to be sentenced according to considerations which are not entirely reactive or based on a "just deserts" rationale. The imposition of a sentence which "is partly punitive but is mainly imposed for the protection of the public" (*Re Moore and R* (1984), 54 OR (2d) 3 (HC)) seems to me to accord with the fundamental purpose of the criminal law generally, and of sentencing in particular, namely, the protection of society. In a rational system of sentencing, the respective importance of prevention, deterrence, retribution and rehabilitation will vary according to the nature of the crime and the circumstances of the offender. No one would suggest that any of these functional considerations should be excluded from the legitimate purview of legislative or judicial decisions regarding sentencing.

[27] It is thus important to recognize the precise nature of the penological objectives embodied in Part XXI. It is clear that the indeterminate detention is intended to serve both punitive and preventive purposes. Both are legitimate aims of the criminal sanction. Indeed, when society incarcerates a robber for, say, ten years, it is clear that its goal is both to punish the person and to prevent the recurrence of such conduct during that period. Preventive detention in the context of Part XXI, however, simply represents a judgment that the relative importance of the objectives of rehabilitation, deterrence and retribution are greatly attenuated in the circumstances of the individual case, and that of prevention correspondingly increased. Part XXI merely enables the court to accommodate its sentence to the common sense reality that the *present* condition of the offender is such that he or she is not inhibited by normal standards of behavioural restraint, so that *future* violent acts can quite confidently be expected of that person. In such circumstances it would be folly not to tailor the sentence accordingly.

[28] It is noteworthy that numerous examples exist, both in Canada and abroad, of ways in which the need to protect the public from the risk of convicted persons reoffending has been taken into consideration by the judiciary and legislature alike.

[29] The case law criteria for imposing a life sentence closely parallel those embodied in Part XXI. Indeed, life sentences and Part XXI sentences are primarily imposed for the same purposes and on the same type of offender. In *R v. Hill* (1974), 15 CCC (2d) 145 (Ont. CA), Jessup JA stated, at pp. 147-48:

> When an accused has been convicted of a serious crime in itself calling for a substantial sentence and when he suffers from some mental or personality disorder rendering him a danger to the community but not subjecting him to confinement in a mental institution and when it is uncertain when, if ever, the accused will be cured of his affliction, in my opinion the appropriate sentence is one of life. Such a sentence in such circumstances amounts to an indefinite sentence under which the Parole Board can release him to the community when it is satisfied, upon adequate psychiatric examination, it is in the interests of the accused and of the community for him to return to society. The policy expressed in my opinion is that of the Criminal Division of the English court of Appeal: *cf.* Thomas, *Principles of Sentencing*, at pp. 272-9.

> • • •

[30] It is true that the *Hill* principle, which amounts to judge-made dangerous offender law, has clearly been limited by subsequent decisions. However, the basis of the retrenchment has not been a rejection of the principle of indeterminate detention for dangerous offenders. Rather, it has been the concern that the *Hill* principle not be used to circumvent

the provisions of Part XXI with its attendant safeguards for the offender. As Martin JA, for the Ontario Court of Appeal, observed in *R v. Crosby* (1982), 1 CCC (3d) 233 at 240:

> The Crown, in our view, properly invoked the dangerous offender legislation in this case. This court has said on more than one occasion that rather than sentence a person who has been convicted of a serious offence and who is a continuing danger to life imprisonment, the prosecution should proceed under the dangerous offender provisions, where the offender has greater protection.

· · ·

[36] From what I have said already, I do not think that it could seriously be argued that the penological objectives embodied in Part XXI themselves violate s. 7 of the Charter. However, it is clear that the present Charter inquiry is concerned also, if not primarily, with the *effects* of the legislation. This requires investigating the "treatment meted out," i.e., what is actually done to the offender and how that is accomplished. Whether this "treatment" violates constitutional precepts seems to me to be an issue more aptly discussed under ss. 9 and 12 of the Charter, because these provisions focus on specific manifestations of the principles of fundamental justice. For convenience, I shall begin with s. 12.

B. Does Part XXI Constitute Cruel and Unusual Punishment Under Section 12 of the Charter?

[37] The appellant contends that Part XXI violates s. 12 of the Charter in that it imposes a punishment that is unusually severe and serves no valid penological purpose more effectively than a less severe punishment (e.g. a determinate sentence).

[38] This issue was addressed in *Re Moore and R*, supra and *R v. Langevin* (1984), 39 CR (3d) 333 (Ont. CA). In *Re Moore*, Ewaschuk J appears to have been influenced by the fact that this court had, in *Ex parte Matticks*, [1973] SCR vi, 15 CCC (2d) 213 [Que], upheld the previous habitual offender legislation under s. 2(b) of the *Canadian Bill of Rights*, RSC 1970, App. III, which provides that no law of Canada shall be construed or applied so as to "impose or authorize the imposition of cruel and unusual treatment or punishment." If that more Draconian legislation was valid, he reasoned, so must the present legislation be valid. The reasons given by Ewaschuk J for sustaining the legislation may be summarized thus: the legislation would be acceptable to a large segment of the population; the specificity of the statutory requirements ensured their application on a rational basis; the protection of society is an important social purpose; the legislation is not an affront to public standards of decency given the procedural safeguards built into the process; and finally, the legislation is tailored so as not to be disproportionate to the crime and the offender's potential to harm others. Although all punishment is in some degree degrading to human dignity, he concluded, Part XXI is not impermissibly, or cruelly and unusually, degrading to human dignity.

[39] While I agree with much of this reasoning, it is unnecessary to examine it in any detail. For since that decision, this court, in *Smith v. R*, 25th June 1987, [now reported (sub nom *R v Smith*) [1987] 1 SCR 1045], has had the opportunity to review the scope and meaning of s. 12, and it is against the backdrop of that case that this issue must be decided. *Smith* dealt with whether s. 5(2) of the *Narcotic Control Act*, RSC 1970, c. N-1, in providing for a mandatory minimum sentence of seven years on all persons found guilty of importing a narcotic, offended the right of individuals not to be subjected to

cruel and unusual treatment or punishment. A majority of this court held that s. 5(2) did violate s. 12 and was not sustainable under s. 1 of the Charter.

[40] Lamer J, speaking for the majority, set out the parameters of the right not to be subjected to cruel and unusual treatment or punishment in the following terms:

> In my view, the protection afforded by s. 12 governs the quality of the punishment and is concerned with the effect that the punishment may have on the person on whom it is imposed. I would agree with Laskin CJC in *Miller*, ... where he defined the phrase "cruel and unusual" as a "compendious expression of a norm." The criterion which must be applied in order to determine whether a punishment is cruel and unusual within the meaning of s. 12 of the Charter is, to use the words of Laskin CJC in *Miller* at p. 688, "whether the punishment prescribed is so excessive as to outrage standards of decency." In other words, though the state may impose punishment, the effect of that punishment must not be grossly disproportionate to what would have been appropriate.
>
> In imposing a sentence of imprisonment, the judge will assess the circumstances of the case in order to arrive at an appropriate sentence. The test for review under s. 12 of the Charter is one of gross disproportionality, because it is aimed at punishments that are more than merely excessive. We should be careful not to stigmatize every disproportionate or excessive sentence as being a constitutional violation, and should leave to the usual sentencing appeal process the task of reviewing the fitness of a sentence. Section 12 will be infringed only where the sentence is so unfit having regard to the offence and the offender as to be grossly disproportionate.
>
> In assessing whether a sentence is grossly disproportionate, the court must first consider the gravity of the offence, the personal characteristics of the offender and the particular circumstances of the case in order to determine what range of sentences would have been appropriate to punish, rehabilitate or deter this particular offender or to protect the public from this particular offender. The other purposes which may be pursued by the imposition of punishment, in particular the deterrence of other potential offenders, are thus not relevant at this stage of the inquiry. This does not mean that the judge or the legislator can no longer consider general deterrence or other penological purposes that go beyond the particular offender in determining a sentence, but only that the resulting sentence must not be grossly disproportionate to what the offender deserves. If a grossly disproportionate sentence is "prescribed by law," then the purpose which it seeks to attain will fall to be assessed under s. 1. Section 12 ensures that individual offenders receive punishments that are appropriate, or at least not grossly disproportionate, to their particular circumstances, while s. 1 permits this right to be overridden to achieve some important societal objective.
>
> One must measure the effect of the sentence actually imposed. If it is grossly disproportionate to what would have been appropriate, then it infringes s. 12. The effect of the sentence is often a composite of many factors and is not limited to the quantum or duration of the sentence but includes its nature and the conditions under which it is applied. Sometimes by its length alone or by its very nature will the sentence be grossly disproportionate to the purpose sought. Sometimes it will be the result of the combination of factors which, when considered in isolation, would not in and of themselves amount to gross disproportionality. For example, 20 years for a first offence against property would be grossly disproportionate, but so would three months of imprisonment, if the prison authorities decide it should be served in solitary confinement. ...

The numerous criteria proposed pursuant to s. 2(b) of the *Canadian Bill of Rights* and the Eighth Amendment of the American Constitution are, in my opinion, useful as factors to determine whether a violation of s. 12 has occurred. Thus, to refer to the tests listed by Professor Tarnopolsky, the determination of whether the punishment is necessary to achieve a valid penal purpose, whether it is founded on recognized sentencing principles, and whether there exist valid alternatives to the punishment imposed, are all guidelines which, without being determinative in themselves, help to assess whether the punishment is grossly disproportionate.

[41] It is clear from the foregoing that s. 12 is concerned with the relation between the effects of, and reasons for, punishment. At the initial stage of the inquiry into proportionality, those effects are to be balanced against the particular circumstances of the offence, the characteristics of the offender and the particular purposes sought to be accomplished in sentencing that person in the manner challenged. If, in light of these considerations, the punishment is found to be grossly disproportionate, a remedy must be afforded the offender in the absence of social objectives that transcend the circumstances of the particular case and are capable of justifying the punishment under s. 1 of the Charter.

[42] Let us first consider the substantive ways in which the present legislation itself seeks to accommodate the conflicting interests, on the one hand, of society in seeking to protect itself from dangerous criminals and, on the other, of the offender in not being subjected to punishment grossly disproportionate to the offence and the circumstances of the individual case. It seems to me that the legislative criteria embodied in s. 688 for designating offenders as dangerous and for sentencing such persons tend, although not conclusively, to sustain the legislation as not constituting a violation of s. 12. I say "not conclusively" for, as will be seen, it is only when s. 688 is read in the context of the scheme as a whole that the legislation can be upheld.

[43] First, the legislation applies only to persons convicted of a "serious personal injury offence" as defined in s. 687. These offences all relate to conduct tending to cause severe physical danger or severe psychological injury to other persons. Significantly, the maximum penalty for all these offences must be at least ten years' imprisonment. Secondly, it must be established to the satisfaction of the court that the offence for which the person has been convicted is not an isolated occurrence, but part of a pattern of behaviour which has involved violence, aggressive or brutal conduct, or a failure to control sexual impulses. Thirdly, it must be established that the pattern of conduct is very likely to continue and to result in the kind of suffering against which the section seeks to protect, namely, conduct endangering the life, safety or physical well-being of others or, in the case of sexual offences, conduct causing injury, pain or other evil to other persons. Also explicit in one form or another in each subsection of s. 687 is the requirement that the court must be satisfied that the pattern of conduct is substantially or pathologically intractable. Finally, the court has the discretion not to designate the offender as dangerous or to impose an indeterminate sentence, even in circumstances where all of these criteria are met.

[44] It seems to me that, having concluded that the legislative objectives embodied in Part XXI are not only of substantial importance to society's well-being but, at least in theory, sufficiently important to warrant limiting certain rights and freedoms, one must equally conclude that the legislative classification of the target group of offenders meets

the highest standard of rationality (and I use the word not as a term of art) and proportionality that society could reasonably expect of Parliament. Not only has a diligent attempt been made to carefully define a very small group of offenders whose personal characteristics and particular circumstances militate strenuously in favour of preventive incarceration, but it would be difficult to imagine a better-tailored set of criteria that could effectively accomplish the purposes sought to be attained.

[45] However, the legislative classification of offenders as dangerous is only one aspect of the "means analysis" under s. 12. It is equally important to consider the constitutional validity, under s. 12, of the actual "treatment meted out." There can be no doubt that detention per se, and preventive detention in particular, is not cruel and unusual in the case of dangerous offenders, for the group to whom the legislation applies has been functionally defined so as to ensure that persons within the group evince the very characteristics that render such detention necessary.

[46] It is argued, however, that it is not the detention itself but its *indeterminate quality* that harbours the potential for cruel and unusual punishment. And it is difficult to deny that the effects of an indeterminate sentence on a dangerous offender must be profoundly devastating. It has, for instance, been argued before the court that the imposition of an indeterminate sentence, because of its uncertainty, saps the will of an offender, removing any incentive to rehabilitate himself or herself. However, this is equally true of a "determinate" life sentence such as is provided for by s. 306(1)(b). Indeed, in view of the provisions regarding parole, it is possible, at least theoretically, that a dangerous offender could be released consequent on his first review, three years after the detention was imposed and well in advance of the seven or so years an offender serving a life sentence must serve before his or her first such review. This is, however, rather unrealistic. Evidence before the court indicated that between 1980 and 1986 only six dangerous offenders were granted day parole, two of whom had served 10 to 15 years, three 15 to 20 years, and one more than 20 years.

[47] In truth, there is a significant difference between the effect of a Part XXI sentence and other, more typical sentences. When a person is imprisoned for an absolute and determinate period, there is at least the certainty that the incarceration will end at the termination of that period. The convicted person, during the term of sentence, can remain in a passive state, secure in the knowledge that he or she will be released thereafter. For the offender undergoing an indeterminate sentence, however, the sole hope of release is parole. The ordinary convict, it is true, can also choose to actively affect the length of his or her sentence by attempting to conform his or her behaviour to meet the expectations of the parole board. But, whatever the legal nature of the interest in the availability of parole may be in general, it seems to me that, as a *factual* matter, the availability of parole is not as important a factor in deciding whether a determinate sentence is cruel and unusual as it is in assessing the constitutionality of a Part XXI sentence.

[48] This is so because in the context of a determinate sentencing scheme the availability of parole represents an additional super-added protection of the liberty interests of the offender. In the present context, however, it is, subsequent to the actual imposition of the sentence itself, the sole protection of the dangerous offender's liberty interests. Indeed, from the point of view of the dangerous offender, his or her detention is never complete until it is factually complete. In this sense, each opportunity for parole will appear to the dangerous offender as the sole mechanism for terminating his or her

detention, for rendering it certain. Moreover, it is clear that an enlightened inquiry under s. 12 must concern itself first and foremost with the way in which the effects of punishment are likely to be experienced. Seen in this light, therefore, the parole process assumes the utmost significance, for it is that process alone that is capable of truly accommodating and tailoring the sentence to fit the circumstances of the individual offender.

[49] In my opinion, if the sentence imposed under Part XXI was indeterminate, simpliciter, it would be certain, at least occasionally, to result in sentences grossly dispro-portionate to what individual offenders deserved. However, I believe that the parole process saves the legislation from being successfully challenged under s. 12, for it ensures that incarceration is imposed for only as long as the circumstances of the individual case require.

[50] When an indeterminate sentence is imposed, Part XXI provides for periodic review, for the purposes of determining whether parole should be granted, of the "*condi-tion, history and circumstances of that person*," after the first three years of detention and every two years thereafter. ... The criteria in light of which an application for parole is considered are specified in s. 10(1)(a) of the *Parole Act*, RSC 1970, c. P-2:

> 10(1) the Board may
>> (a) grant parole to an inmate, subject to any terms or conditions it considers desirable, if the Board considers that
>>> (i) in the case of a grant of parole other than day parole, the inmate has derived the maximum benefit from imprisonment.
>>> (ii) the reform and rehabilitation of the inmate will be aided by the grant of parole, and
>>> (iii) the release of the inmate on parole would not constitute an undue risk to society;

[51] While the criteria embodied in s. 10(1)(a) do not purport to replicate the factual findings required to sentence the offender to an indeterminate term of imprisonment, they do afford a measure of tailoring adequate to save the legislation from violating s. 12. It must be remembered that the offender is being sentenced indeterminately because *at the time of sentencing* he was found to have a certain propensity. The sentence is imposed "in lieu of any other sentence" that might have been imposed and, like any other such sentence, must be served according to its tenor. *The offender is not being sentenced to a term of imprisonment until he is no longer a dangerous offender.* Indeed, s. 695.1 provides that the circumstances of the offender be reviewed for the purpose of determining whether *parole* should be granted and, if so, on what conditions; it does not provide that the label of dangerous offender be removed or altered. Finally, the very words of s. 695.1 of the *Code* and s. 10(1)(a) of the *Parole Act* establish an ongoing process for rendering the sentence meted out to a dangerous offender one that accords with his or her specific circumstances.

[52] It may be argued that the legislation could be better tailored. For example, it might have been argued that the review process should focus solely on whether the offender continued to possess the characteristics that defined him or her as a proper subject of indeterminate detention. Indeed, one might say that to ask, as the Parole Board does, whether the individual has been reformed or rehabilitated is to pose a question that ex hypothesi cannot be answered affirmatively, for it was implicit in the designation of

the offender as dangerous that he or she was not amenable to rehabilitation by usual means. However, this argument must be rejected for a number of reasons.

[53] To begin with, the criteria actually used serve to emphasize the point made earlier in this judgment that sentencing, even under Part XXI, embodies a complex of penological objectives. I do not think it can be argued, as a matter either of logic or of common sense, that, by virtue of a decision to sentence an offender according to considerations based *primarily* on prevention, other equally valid, subsisting penal goals cease to be relevant. To reiterate, protecting society from the dangerous offender never wholly supplants the other legitimate objectives embodied in a Part XXI sentence.

[54] Seen in this light, it would be preposterous to require of dangerous offenders only that they demonstrate to the parole board that they have ceased to be "dangerous" (in terms identical to those used in Part XXI), for this would require of them a lesser showing than is required of other convicts. It seems to me that, had s. 695.1 provided for a "dangerous offender review," rather than a parole review, but borrowed the identical criteria employed in the *Parole Act*, it would perhaps be more readily apparent that the review provided for does indeed accomplish the requisite tailoring sufficient to sustain the legislative scheme as a whole. Section 10(1)(a)(iii) requires the board to consider whether the release of the inmate would constitute an "undue risk" to society; if the accused continues to be dangerous, then by definition this criterion remains unsatisfied. Section 10(1)(a) also requires that the board be satisfied that the inmate has derived the maximum benefit from incarceration and that the inmate's reform and rehabilitation would be aided by release.

[55] These criteria seem to me to be no less pertinent reflections of society's concerns in releasing dangerous offenders than they are in releasing other offenders. The fact that dangerous offenders may be less likely to satisfy these requirements is primarily a function of their dangerousness, not of the punishment imposed. Of course, the imposition of an indeterminate sentence may, like all sentences, sap the will of the offender to rehabilitate himself or herself. However, I would have thought the incentive to reform is far greater, at least theoretically, in the case of a dangerous offender. In this regard, I note that the availability of parole has been seen to validate mandatory life sentences in the context of similarly-motivated legislation in the United States (see *Solem v. Helm*, [100 S Ct 3001 (1983)], *per* Powell J., for the majority).

[56] Furthermore, I am not sure that to inquire into the presence or absence of less restrictive means is wholly compatible with the insistence of this court in *Smith*, supra, that s. 12 redress only punishment that is *grossly disproportionate* to the circumstances of any given case. The word "grossly," it seems to me, reflects this court's concern not to hold Parliament to a standard so exacting at least in the context of s. 12, as to require punishments to be perfectly suited to accommodate the moral nuances of every crime and every offender.

[57] I would therefore conclude that Part XXI does not violate s. 12 of the *Charter*.

· · ·

C. Does Part XXI Violate Section 9 of the Charter by Authorizing Arbitrary Detention or Imprisonment?

[59] Counsel for the appellant contended that Part XXI violates the right of persons not to be arbitrarily detained or imprisoned, contrary to s. 9 of the Charter. He suggested

that Part XXI results in arbitrary detention in the following respects: the test of "likelihood" under Part XXI is unconstitutionally vague; the labelling of persons as dangerous offenders is arbitrary, since it is based on inherently unreliable psychiatric evidence; and there are no guidelines with respect to the invocation of Part XXI such that the prosecutor has unfettered discretion as to when to make a dangerous offender application.

[60] This court has not yet pronounced on the scope of s. 9 and the meaning of the words "arbitrarily detained or imprisoned," and I do not think this would be an appropriate case to do so. The issue was not strenuously argued by the parties or examined in depth in the courts below. More to the point, however, is that, in my view, even assuming that s. 9 were given the broadest possible interpretation, the appellant's submissions in this regard must fail.

[61] There has been considerable controversy in the lower courts as to whether the ambit of protection afforded by s. 9 extends to imprisonment or detention specifically authorized under existing law or whether s. 9 is ipso facto satisfied when imprisonment is imposed in accordance with legislative requirements (see the cases canvassed in *R v. Konechny*, 38 C.R. (3d) 69 (BCCA), per Lambert J.A., dissenting, at pp. 70-71). ...

[62] However, even giving the word "arbitrary" its broadest signification, it is readily apparent that, not only is the incarceration statutorily authorized, but that the legislation narrowly defines a class of offenders with respect to whom it may properly be invoked, and prescribes quite specifically the conditions under which an offender may be designated as dangerous. If these criteria are themselves unconstitutional, it is because they otherwise fail adequately to safeguard the liberty of the individual, not because they are arbitrary. Indeed, as Ewaschuk J observed in *Re Moore*, supra, at p. 314, "the legislative criteria for finding a person a dangerous offender is [sic] perhaps the most detailed and demanding in the *Criminal Code*." Moreover, implicit in my discussion of the s. 12 issue is the common sense conclusion that the criteria in Part XXI are anything but arbitrary in relation to the objectives sought to be attained; they are clearly designed to segregate a small group of highly dangerous criminals posing threats to the physical or mental well-being of their victims.

[63] As I see it, then, the sole issue left for consideration under s. 9 is whether the lack of uniformity in the treatment of dangerous persons that arises by virtue of the prosecutorial discretion to make an application under Part XXI constitutes unconstitutional arbitrariness. The appellant is not suggesting that prosecutors, in his case or generally, have exercised their discretion arbitrarily in this regard. Indeed, the affidavit evidence filed by the Crown in the companion case of *Milne v. R* [now reported post, p 55 (sub nom *R v Milne*), [1987] 2 SCR 512] indicates that from 1978 to 1986 an average of only seven persons per year were sentenced under Part XXI. On average, each offender committed 12.12 offences, 2.2 of which were violent and 3.53 of which were sexual in nature. This suggests that the legislation has in general not been abused. I have no doubt that, if and when it is alleged that a prosecutor in a particular case was motivated by improper or arbitrary reasons in making a Part XXI application, a s. 24 remedy would lie. However, I do not think there is any warrant for presuming that the executive will act unconstitutionally or for improper purposes.

[64] More important, however, is the fact that prosecutors always have a discretion in prosecuting criminals to the full extent of the law, an aspect of which involves making sentencing submissions. In this respect, I am in complete agreement with Crown counsel's

submission that "… it is the absence of discretion which would, in many cases, render arbitrary the law's application." As he notes, "the absence of any discretion with respect to Part XXI would necessarily require the Crown to always proceed under Part XXI if there was the barest *prima facie* and the Court, upon making a finding that the offender is a dangerous offender, would always be required to impose an indeterminate sentence."

[65] The foregoing also dispenses with the argument, not pursued here, that the judge ought not to have discretion with respect to whether he or she sentences an offender found to be dangerous to an indeterminate sentence. As Ewaschuk J stated in *Re Moore*, supra, at p. 310, the offender cannot be heard to complain of a discretion that can operate only to the offender's benefit. Indeed, it is apparent that one feature of s. 5(2) of the *Narcotic Control Act* that disturbed this court in *Smith*, supra, was the very fact that the imposition of sentence followed automatically upon conviction.

[66] The remaining argument is that the prosecutorial discretion results in a geographical lack of uniformity and that this constitutes impermissible arbitrariness. However, the appellant is not arguing, as the accused did in *Morgentaler v. The Queen*, that this lack of uniformity is mandated *by the terms of the legislation* (which may or may not be a meritorious argument). Rather, this argument appears to recast the prosecutorial discretion argument. Moreover, variation among provinces in this regard may be inevitable, and indeed desirable, in a country where a federal statute is administered by local authorities. In any event, it may be observed parenthetically that, while the affidavit evidence suggests that dangerous offender applications are made more frequently in British Columbia (25 % of all such applications), and, perhaps surprisingly, never in Quebec, Newfoundland, Manitoba or Prince Edward Island, no attempt has been made to explain the significance of this data, for example, by relating it to the relevant population of offenders potentially coming within the provisions of Part XXI.

[67] Having dealt with the broader issues, I now turn to the more specifically procedural issues raised by the appellant.

D. Are the Part XXI Procedures by Which This Deprivation of Liberty Is Occasioned and Reviewed Fundamentally Unfair?

(i) Does Section 11(f) of the Charter Require a Jury Hearing of a Part XXI Application?

[68] Section 689(2) of the *Code* provides that an application under Part XXI shall be heard and determined by the court without a jury. The appellant submits that the procedure for designating an offender as dangerous is unfair and contrary to ss. 7 and 11(f) of the Charter, in particular, by denying the offender the right to the benefit of a jury's determination of dangerousness. I shall deal with the s. 11(f) issue first.

[69] Section 11(f) of the Charter provides that:

> 11. Any person charged with an offence has the right
>
> . . .
>
> (f) … to the benefit of trial by jury where the maximum punishment for the offence is imprisonment for five years or a more severe punishment;

[70] The key issue, for s. 11 purposes, is whether the Crown application to declare the offender a dangerous offender is equivalent to "charging" the offender with "an offence,"

for it is obvious that such offenders are liable to detention for periods much longer than five years.

. . .

[74] There would seem to be no warrant for reconsidering the conclusion of this court that the "labelling" procedure does not constitute the charge of an offence. Nor do I think that a different conclusion can be justified for the purposes of s. 11 of the Charter. As I observed in *Schmidt v. R* (sub nom. *Can. v. Schmidt*), [1987] 1 SCR 500, the phrase "any person charged with an offence" in the opening words of the section must be given a constant meaning that harmonizes with the various paragraphs of the section. It seems clear to me that for the purposes of s. 11 it would be quite inappropriate to conclude that a convicted person is charged with an offence when confronted with a Part XXI application. How can it be said that the right to the presumption of innocence until proven *guilty* (s. 11(d)) and the right to bail (s. 11(e)), for example, could have any application in the context of the unique post-conviction proceeding mandated by Part XXI?

(ii) Does Section 7 of the Charter Require a Jury Hearing and Do the Part XXI Hearing and Review Procedures Otherwise Meet the Standard of Fairness Under That Section?

[75] The conclusion that the appellant is not entitled to the benefit of trial by jury under s. 11(f) does not, however, conclusively decide the question whether he is entitled to a determination by a jury of the question of his dangerousness, or, more generally, whether the procedural incidents of the proceeding are constitutionally adequate to safeguard his liberty. ...

. . .

[84] The cases to which I have referred dealt primarily with the use of hearsay evidence in such proceedings and with the question whether dangerousness could constitutionally be proved simply on a preponderance of evidence rather than beyond a reasonable doubt. Quite apart from the specific conclusions of the American courts respecting these matters, I would adopt the functional reasons given by those courts for viewing the "labelling" hearing to be the kind of hearing that attracts a high level of procedural protection for the offender. I find their approach to be more attuned to the distinctive nature of such inquiries, and more congruent with the reality of the very profound consequences that the labelling procedure harbours for the offender. Nevertheless, I would conclude that it is not required, as a constitutional matter, that the determination of dangerousness be made by a jury.

[85] It is clear that, at a minimum, the requirements of fundamental justice embrace the requirements of procedural fairness: see, e.g., the comments to this effect of Wilson J in *Singh v. Can. (Min. of Employment & Immigration); Thandi v. Can. (Min. of Employment & Immigration); Mann v. Can. (Min. of Employment & Immigration)*, [1985] 1 SCR 177. It is also clear that the requirements of fundamental justice are not immutable; rather, they vary according to the context in which they are invoked. Thus certain procedural protections might be constitutionally mandated in one context but not in another. Suffice it to say, however, that a jury determination is not mandated in the present context. The offender has already been found guilty of an offence in a trial at which he had the option of invoking his right to a jury. Moreover, the procedure to which he was subjected subsequent to the finding of guilt does not impact on his liberty to the same extent as that

initial determination. Indeed, this is made clear by the same considerations that led this court, in [*Brusch v The Queen* (1953), 105 CCC 340 (SCC)], to classify the proceedings as part of the sentencing process. While the legal classification of the proceeding as part of the sentencing process does not necessarily decide the question of the scope of the procedural protection to be afforded the offender, the functional, factual considerations animating that conclusion must be taken into account.

[86] Finally, it is not insignificant that, unlike the situation in [*US v Maroney*, 335 F2d 302 (1966)], the judge at such a hearing does retain a discretion whether or not to impose the designation or indeterminate sentence, or both.

[87] It is noteworthy, too, that Part XXI provides considerable procedural protection to the offender. Section 689(1)(a) requires that the consent of the Attorney General be obtained either before or after the application is made. Section 689(1)(b) requires that "at least seven days notice be given to the offender by the prosecution, following the making of the application, outlining the basis on which it is intended to found the application." Moreover, the offender has the right to attend, present evidence and cross-examine witnesses, in addition to a right of appeal in the broadest terms on questions of fact, law or mixed fact and law.

[88] It seems to me that s. 7 of the Charter entitles the appellant to a fair hearing; it does not entitle him to the most favourable procedures that could possibly be imagined. I do not think it can be argued that the procedure at a Part XXI application is unfair insofar as it denies to an offender the right to a jury's determination of his or her dangerousness.

• • •

(iii) Is the Standard of Proof Required Under Part XXI, or the Use of Psychiatric Evidence in a Part XXI Application, Fundamentally Unfair?

[91] The appellant submits that Part XXI is fundamentally unfair in two other respects. He contends, first, that s. 688, in requiring proof that the offender constitutes a *threat* to the life, safety or physical or mental well-being of other persons, or that there is a *likelihood* of the offender causing injury, pain or other evil to other persons through a failure in the future to control his or her sexual impulses, is fundamentally unfair, in that the standard of proof required of the Crown is lower than that traditionally required in the criminal law process. Secondly, he argues that s. 690, by requiring that psychiatric evidence be tendered on an application under Part XXI, is fundamentally unfair to the extent that such evidence is an unreliable predictor of future conduct.

[92] I do not believe that either of these submissions is valid. First, it is important to recognize exactly what is and what is not required to be proved on such an application. Subsection (a) and (b) of s. 688 both require proof that the offender represents a *threat* of some sort to society. It is nowhere required that it be proved that the offender *will* act in a certain way. Indeed, inherent in the notion of dangerousness is the risk, not the certainty, of harm.

[93] The appellant asserts that a "likelihood" is ipso facto not susceptible of proof beyond a reasonable doubt. He cites in support the following statement of Isabel Grant, in her article "Dangerous Offenders" (1985), 9 *Dalhousie LJ* 347, at p. 360:

How does one prove beyond a reasonable doubt that at some time in *some* setting, an individual is *likely* to endanger *some* person[?] Surely if we add "beyond a reasonable doubt" to a "future likelihood" the sum total can be no greater than a balance of probabilities, a standard we would never accept in a criminal trial.

However, as Holmes has reminded us, the life of the law has not been logic: it has been experience. The criminal law must operate in a world governed by practical considerations rather than abstract logic and, as a matter of practicality, the most that can be established in a future context is a likelihood of certain events occurring. To doubt this conclusion is, in actuality, to doubt the validity of the legislative objectives embodied in Part XXI, for to require certainty in such matters would be tantamount to rendering the entire process ineffective.

[94] Moreover, I am not convinced, even as a matter of logic, that the appellant's submission is sound. It seems to me that a "likelihood" of specified future conduct occurring is the finding of fact required to be established; it is not, at one and the same time, the means of proving that fact. Logically, it seems clear to me that an individual can be found to constitute a *threat* to society without insisting that this require the court to assert an ability to predict the future. I do not find it illogical for a court to assert that it is satisfied beyond a reasonable doubt that the test of dangerousness has been met, that there exists a *certain* potential for harm. That this is really only an apparent paradox is aptly captured by Morden J. in *R. v. Knight* (1975), 27 C.C.C. (2d) 343 (Ont. HC), at p. 356:

> I wish to make it clear that when I refer to the requisite standard of proof respecting likelihood I am not imposing on myself an obligation to find it proven beyond a reasonable doubt that certain events will happen in the future—this, in the nature of things would be impossible in practically every case—but I do refer to the quality and strength of the evidence of past and present facts together with the expert opinion thereon, as an existing basis for finding present likelihood of future conduct.

[95] Having said the foregoing, it seems to me that when the appellant asserts that proof of a likelihood beyond a reasonable doubt still amounts merely to proof of a likelihood, it becomes apparent that what he is challenging is not the standard of proof but the fact that certain persons found to be "dangerous" will in fact not have been dangerous. This is the problem of "false positives," which I will address below.

[96] I believe that the foregoing discussion also disposes of the contention that it is fundamentally unfair to the offender to require proof of dangerousness to be based in part on psychiatric evidence. Counsel for the appellant cited both academic and judicial authority recognizing the inability of psychiatrists, or anyone else, for that matter, to predict accurately future events. This is hardly a revelation. Indeed, the psychiatrists who testified at the hearing in the present case expressly disavowed any such claim.

[97] It seems to me that the answer to this argument can be briefly stated. The test for admissibility is relevance, not infallibility. Judges at Part XXI hearings do not assume that psychiatrists can accurately predict the future; however, psychiatric evidence is clearly relevant to the issue whether a person is likely to behave in a certain way, and indeed is probably relatively superior in this regard to the evidence of other clinicians and lay persons; see Menzies, Webster and Sepejak, "The Dimensions of Dangerousness" (1985), 9 *Law and Human Behaviour* 1:49.

• • •

[99] Finally, the unreliability of psychiatric evidence also raises the problem of "false positives" (a statistical term representing the erroneous overprediction of future violence), discussed by Tobriner J. for the majority of the California Supreme Court in *People v. Murtishaw*, 175 Cal. Rptr. 738 (1981), at pp. 758 59:

> Numerous studies have demonstrated the inaccuracy of attempts to forecast future violent behaviour. Two commentators summarized the results as follows: "Whatever may be said for the reliability and validity of psychiatric judgments in general, there is literally no evidence that psychiatrists reliably and accurately can predict dangerous behaviour. To the contrary, such predictions are wrong more often than they are right." (Ennis & Litwack, *Psychiatry and the Presumption of Expertise: Flipping Coins in the Courtroom* (1974), 62 Cal. L Rev. 693, 737.) Professor Dershowitz in 1969 pointed to the skewed results characteristic of psychiatric forecasts: "it seems that psychiatrists are particularly prone to one type of error—over-predictions … [F]or every correct psychiatric prediction of violence, there are numerous erroneous predictions." (Dershowitz, *The Psychiatrist's Power in Civil Commitment: A Knife That Cuts Both Ways* (Feb. 1969), Psych. Today, at p. 47.) Cocozza and Steadman in 1976 reviewed the various studies and reported that "Whether one examined the legal, behavioural science, or psychiatric literature on predictions of dangerousness, one constantly encounters conclusions similar to the one reached by Dershowitz that psychiatrists are generally inaccurate predictors." (Cocozza & Steadman, *op. cit.*, supra, 29 Rutgers L Rev. at p. 1085.) In 1978 Professor Monahan undertook a further review of studies of violence prediction and noted that the percentage of false positives (erroneous predictions that a subject would engage in violent behaviour) never fell below 54 percent and went as high as 99.7 percent. (Monahan, *The Prediction and Control of Violent Behavior* (1978), pp. 179-196, in Hearings Before the House Subcom. on Domestic and International Scientific Planning, 95th Cong., 2d Sess., pp. 175-252.)

[100] This problem does not appear to undermine the utility and fairness of the scheme so much as to fortify the conclusion that the procedural protections accorded the offender, especially on review, ought to be very rigorous. In its *Report of the Committee on Mentally Abnormal Offenders*, the Butler Commission recognized the difficulties in assessing dangerousness but nevertheless recommended that the British Parliament enact dangerous offender legislation with reviewable indeterminate sentences. It stated, at p. 60:

> … [T]he fact that we cannot quantify the probability of future dangerous behaviour with actuarial precision is often allowed to obscure the fact that we can point with some confidence to categories of people who are more likely than others of the same sex and age-group to act in this way. Some kinds of sexual offence seem to be very repetitive. … Men with several convictions of violence are considerably more likely than their peers to be convicted of violence in the future. Again, it is sometimes argued that even if there are good grounds— clinical or actuarial—for assigning the individual to a high risk group, he might be one of the minority in that group who in the event will not behave in accordance with probability. But this dilemma is inescapably involved in every decision which is based on probabilities. All that can be done is to weigh the unpleasantness of the consequences for the individual against the harm which he may do to others. If the harm is likely to be slight the decision should be in his favour: if great and highly probable—for example, if a sexual offence is

accompanied by serious violence—the best we can do is to make sure that the precautions are as humane as possible.

Similarly, Floud and Young reject the notion that in enacting dangerous offender legislation Parliament unfairly sacrifices innocent persons in favour of the public good (at pp. 48-49):

> This argument is misconceived. Errors of prediction do not represent determinable individuals. It is not that we have difficulty in identifying the subjects of predicted error with the methods available to us; it is that they are in principle indeterminable. There are no hidden individuals identifiable in principle, but not in practice, who certainly would or would not reoffend. In this sense there are no innocent or guilty subjects of predictive judgment.
>
> • • •
>
> The question is not "how many innocent persons are to sacrifice their liberty for the extra protection that special sentences for dangerous offenders will provide?" But "what is the moral choice between the alternative risks: the risk of harm to potential victims or the risk of unnecessarily detaining offenders judged to be dangerous?"
>
> *The essential nature of the problem of preventing wilful harm is misrepresented by talk of balancing individual and social costs. The problem is to make a just redistribution of risk in circumstances that do not permit of its being reduced.* There is a risk of harm to innocent persons at the hands of an offender who is judged likely to inflict it intentionally or recklessly—in any case culpably—in defiance or disregard of the usual constraints. His being in the wrong by virtue of the risk he represents is what entitles us to consider imposing on him the risk of unnecessary measures to save the risk of harm to innocent victims. [Emphasis added.]

[One of the areas in which there has been significant evolution in Charter jurisprudence is with respect to the content of the principles of fundamental justice central to the s 7 protections. In *Lyons*, Wilson J (dissenting) focused on the issue of permitting a dangerous offender application to go forward even though the offender was not notified until after he entered guilty pleas. She stated:

> [127] It is, in my view, a principle of fundamental justice under s. 7 of the *Charter* that an accused know the full extent of his jeopardy before he pleads guilty to a criminal offence for which a term of imprisonment may be imposed. Common sense impels me to the conclusion that the thought uppermost in an accused's mind in deciding whether to plead guilty or stand upon his right to be presumed innocent until proved otherwise beyond a reasonable doubt by the Crown is: what is the worst that can happen to me if I am convicted of this offence? I think we have to ask ourselves the following question: had this accused known at the time he pleaded guilty that the Crown would be seeking an order of preventive detention against him for an indeterminate period, would he have pleaded guilty? If the answer to that question is probably not, then I think the accused is entitled to the protection of s. 7 unless knowledge of his exposure to such an order under Part XXI of the Code can properly be attributed to him simply by virtue of its presence in the *Code*.
>
> [128] I have concluded that such knowledge cannot be attributed to the accused. The *Code* expressly contemplates that notice will be given to the accused of the Crown's intention to make a Part XXI application. True, it is only required to be given seven days following the making of the application (s. 689(1)(b)) which is itself to be made "following the conviction of a person for an offence but before the offender is sentenced therefor" (s. 688). But I find

this helpful rather than harmful in considering whether the appellant should have envisaged such an application at the time he made his plea. I would think also that the fact that such applications are rare and probably even rarer in the case of 16-year-olds would make it unrealistic to attribute such knowledge to appellant's counsel and, through him, to the appellant.]

D. Applying the Provisions

Prior to the 1997 amendments to Part XXIV, numerous decisions addressed the content of these provisions. The 1997 amendments, which included the long-term offender provisions and other changes, generated a new round of litigation, including the Supreme Court of Canada decision in *Johnson*, below. Parliament, apparently responding to *Johnson*, again reconfigured Part XXIV in 2008, especially with respect to available dispositions. Not surprisingly, this has led to more litigation.

1. Pre-1997 Cases

Over the years, courts have struggled in applying the criteria for dangerous offender designations, which on their face are quite broad. Many thoughtful decisions are less important, and mostly of historical interest only, given the various statutory changes. However, there are still two sets of basic criteria that can underpin a dangerous offender finding—ss 753(1)(a) and (b). The two branches correspond to the bifurcated definition of "serious personal injury offence" in s 752, and call for different tests. Section 753(1)(a) relates to convictions for violent indictable offences punishable by 10 years or more. The question is whether the offender "constitutes a threat to the life, safety or physical or mental well-being of other persons" based on the application of the criteria in s 753(1)(a). The second, alternative branch for finding an individual to be a dangerous offender is found in s 753(1)(b). This follows conviction for certain categories of sexual offences and requires the court to consider (1) whether the offender's conduct in any sexual matter shows a "failure to control his or her sexual impulses," and (2) whether there is a likelihood of "causing injury, pain or other evil to other persons through failure in the future to control his or her sexual impulses." These two sets of criteria are essentially the same as they were when the new regime was enacted in 1977: see SC 1976-77, c 53, s 14. As a result, some older cases still have relevance. Below are excerpts from *Langevin*, *Currie*, and *Neve*, all of which continue to have interpretative value.

R v Langevin
(1984), 11 CCC (3d) 336 (Ont CA)

LACOURCIÈRE JA (Martin and Goodman JJA concurring):
This appeal raises broad questions respecting the application of the dangerous offender provisions of Part XXI of the *Criminal Code* and their constitutional validity in the light of the fundamental rights now protected by the *Canadian Charter of Rights and Freedoms*.
On May 12, 1980, the appellant pleaded guilty to the offence of rape, contrary to s. 144 of the Code, before The Honourable Judge F.G. Carter in the County Court Judge's Criminal Court in the County of Huron. After the conviction, the Crown filed an application to have the appellant declared a dangerous offender pursuant to s. 688 of the Code.

Following remands for the nomination of a psychiatrist by the appellant and for psychiatric observation, Judge Carter heard the application on September 10, 1980. He found the appellant to be a dangerous offender and, following a remand, sentenced him to an indeterminate period of detention, in lieu of any other sentence that might be imposed for the offence of rape.

. . .

Pattern of Repetitive Behaviour: Section 688(a)(i)

Mr. Gold submitted that, with respect to s. 688(a)(i), the learned trial judge erred in concluding that there existed a "pattern of repetitive behaviour," there being an insufficient number of repeated offences by the appellant as displayed in the reported cases under that paragraph.

In my opinion, this element is not based solely on the number of offences but also on the elements of similarity of the offender's behaviour. The offences committed were remarkably similar. Two young girls were grabbed from behind by the appellant, a stranger, and both were taken to a secluded place and ordered to undress. Both were forced into anal as well as vaginal intercourse. The younger girl was forced to fellate the appellant. Both were threatened to assure their co-operation and were released only after assurances not to tell anyone were extracted from them. In the circumstances, these two offences were properly found to establish a pattern of repetitive behaviour.

As to the failure of the appellant to restrain his behaviour, the learned trial judge concluded as follows:

> Having considered the offender's past behaviour, having heard and analyzed the evidence of the expert witnesses, and the other evidence adduced, I am compelled to conclude that the Crown has established to my satisfaction that there is a likelihood of the offender "causing death or injury to other persons or inflicting severe psychological damage upon other persons, through failure in the future to restrain his behaviour," as required by s. 688(a)(i). Whether such failure to refrain his behaviour stems from an inability to maintain control, or a refusal to maintain control, and whether such loss of control is triggered by aggressiveness or sexual impulse, and whether with or without the aid of alcohol it leads, in considering s. 688(a)(i), to the same result.

. . .

Although the finding that the appellant is a dangerous offender can be supported on s. 688(a)(i) alone, it is necessary to deal briefly with the other arguments to the effect that the Crown has failed to prove the elements of dangerousness set out in s. 688(a)(iii) and s. 688(b), respectively.

Behaviour of a "Brutal Nature": Section 688(a)(iii)

Mr. Gold submitted that the learned trial judge erred in concluding the Guelph rape satisfied the requirement of behaviour of a "brutal nature" as required by subpara. (iii). The submission is, basically, that any rape by definition contains severe physical and psychological abuse, but that the "brutal nature" requirement of subpara. (iii) requires a greater element of savagery evidenced by sadism, torture or mutilation. The learned trial judge concluded that the appellant's conduct towards the 12-year-old victim was "coarse, savage and cruel" and, accordingly, so "brutal" as to compel the conclusion that the appellant's behaviour in the future was "unlikely to be inhibited by normal standards of behavioural restraint" in the words of the subparagraph. This conclusion was supported by the expert evidence. I am satisfied that the brutal nature of the conduct which must be established before the requirements of the subparagraph are satisfied does not necessarily demand a situation of "stark horror" as exemplified by *R v. Hill* (1974), 15 CCC (2d) 145, and *R v. Pontello* (1977), 38 CCC (2d) 262.

Conduct which is coarse, savage and cruel and which is capable of inflicting severe psychological damage on the victim is sufficiently "brutal" to meet the test.

Failure to Control Sexual Impulses: Section 688(b)

With respect to s. 688(b), it was submitted that there was insufficient evidence of the appellant's failure to control his sexual impulses in the rape of the [D.] girl or in the rape of the [G.] girl and that the appellant's problem, as characterized by Dr. Hill, was related to aggressiveness but not necessarily of a sexual nature. From the nature of the offences and on the evidence of Dr. Fleming and Dr. Arnold, the Crown properly established the likelihood of the appellant causing future injury, pain or other evil through failure in the future to control his sexual impulses. For these reasons, I would not interfere with the finding that the appellant is a dangerous offender.

The following case of *R v Currie* concerns the second branch of the test in s 753(1), which focuses on sexual offences. Currie had a long history of committing sexual offences. In terms of their seriousness, the antecedent offences for the more recent dangerous offender application were far less serious than the past offences. The Court of Appeal for Ontario quashed the trial judge's dangerous offender declaration on the basis that the trial judge should have considered the relative seriousness of the antecedent offences. The Supreme Court of Canada disagreed with this approach and restored the trial judge's decision.

R v Currie
[1997] 2 SCR 260, 115 CCC (3d) 205

LAMER CJ (La Forest, L'Heureux-Dubé, Sopinka, Gonthier, Cory, McLachlin, Iacobucci, and Major JJ concurring):

[1] This appeal is concerned with the propriety of a dangerous offender designation and the corresponding indeterminate sentence that was imposed by the trial judge after the respondent, Robert Currie, was convicted of sexually assaulting three young girls. At the conclusion of the hearing of this appeal, this Court held, without providing reasons at that time, that neither the designation nor the sentence should be overturned. Our reasons now follow.

I. Facts and Procedural Background

[2] The respondent, Robert Currie, was charged with three counts of sexual assault, for a series of related incidents in which he sexually touched a number of young girls on

November 5, 1988 in a Towers department store in Barrie, Ontario. During the first incident, the respondent approached a group of four girls in the Towers toy section, felt and squeezed the buttocks of three of them, and left the area. During the second, more invasive incident, the respondent followed a group of three sisters near the store's tobacco department. At first, he placed his hand on the eldest girl's breast. Immediately thereafter, he approached the girls from behind and, as the trial judge described, "swept his hand between the legs of two of them in an attempt to touch their genitals." The frightened girls notified store employees and security personnel who eventually apprehended the respondent outside the store and awaited the arrival of the police.

[3] The respondent was convicted of all charges on April 12, 1989 before Tobias J. Prior to sentencing, the Attorney General for Ontario initiated dangerous offender proceedings pursuant to s. 753(b) of the *Criminal Code*, RSC, 1985, c. C-46. Section 753(b) essentially provides that the Crown may apply to have an offender declared a "dangerous offender" and sentenced to an indefinite term of imprisonment if: (a) he has been convicted of a "serious personal injury offence"; and (b) his failure to control his sexual impulses reveals "a likelihood of his causing injury, pain or other evil to other persons" in the future. A "serious personal injury offence" is defined in s. 752 of the *Criminal Code* to include all forms of sexual assault.

[4] These sexual assaults were not isolated incidents. Part of the rationale for seeking to have the respondent declared a dangerous offender was his lengthy history of sexual offences that occurred in the Ottawa, Toronto and Hamilton regions between 1975-1988. As outlined in disturbing detail in the judgments below and in the pleadings filed before this Court, the respondent had been previously convicted of numerous sexual offences, some of which were extremely violent and highly degrading to the victims.

[5] Robert Currie's criminal sexual activity began in and around Ottawa between September and November 1975. In separate incidents, the respondent stalked and sexually attacked four women. All four of the incidents were serious and frightening for the victims, but two were comparatively more severe. On September 30, 1975, the respondent followed a teenage girl into a field. He caught her, undressed her and forced her to perform fellatio and engage in repeated acts of sexual intercourse. When she resisted he pulled her hair and struck her in the face. On November 29, 1975, later on the same night that he had indecently assaulted another victim, the respondent stalked a young woman in Nepean. After approaching her from behind and striking her to the ground, he forced her into the deep snow of a deserted field. He then undressed his victim completely, repeatedly struck her in the face, forced her to perform fellatio, and forced her to submit to multiple acts of anal and vaginal intercourse. He had a hunting knife in his possession during the rape with which he threatened the victim after the attack. She was bleeding heavily when he abandoned her naked in the snow.

[6] As a result of these attacks, on May 20, 1976, the respondent was convicted of indecent assault, rape, and possession of a weapon and sentenced to five years' imprisonment. Since that time, whenever he was at large, his sexually impulsive criminal behaviour continued. In 1979, while on parole in Toronto, the respondent stalked and attacked a woman. When she screamed in response to his attempt to touch her genitals, he jammed his fingers into her mouth, pushed her to the ground and kicked her. He fled the scene, but was immediately apprehended by police and subsequently convicted of indecent assault. In Hamilton in 1981 and 1982, while under intensive police surveillance, the

respondent was observed following and stalking a number of women through the city streets. In one case, the girl sensed she was being followed and sought shelter on the porch of a nearby home. In another case, the respondent indecently assaulted a woman he had been following by putting his hand under her clothing between her legs in an effort to touch her genitals. When arrested by police for the latter incident, the respondent stated:

> It was me I did it. I couldn't help myself. I asked for help before but they released me. I needed help but they let me go. I was going to play hockey and I picked this girl up hitchhiking. She was wearing a bathing suit. I got all turned on. It was like she was asking for it. Not this one but the other one. How do you guys do it? I mean when you see these girls wearing bathing suits all day. I need help. I am always stalking women, little kids, and people. I can't stop. … I can't help myself. … I'm always thinking about women. … I didn't mean to harm anybody. I guess I figure it's just a few seconds of being frightened and it's all over and nobody is hurt.

A. Psychiatric Evidence

[7] To substantiate its dangerous offender application, the Crown elicited the testimony of a psychiatrist, Dr. Angus McDonald, who participated in a two-month team assessment of the respondent after the commission of the recent Towers department store sexual assaults—the so-called "predicate offences." Dr. McDonald evaluated the respondent as an obsessed and extremely temperamental "sexual deviate" who had a "biological anomaly in the wiring of his brain." As such he was "a very dangerous person to society." In making these findings, Dr. McDonald was influenced by the admission the respondent made to a psychometrist at the Penetanguishene Mental Health Centre in 1989, in which he stated:

> [The] stuff I was doing in '79, I got rid of that. I don't bruise them now but don't get me wrong. They had better give me sex if I want it because I often have a knife and I always have my hands.

By way of conclusion, Dr. McDonald gave the prognosis that the respondent "was not open to treatment any longer and posed a risk to women and female children."

[8] The defence-appointed psychiatrist, Dr. Basil Orchard, acknowledged that the respondent suffered from an impulsive personality disorder and "a polymorphous sexual deviation" that includes "voyeurism, heterosexual pedophilia and hebephilia and impulsive sexual aggressiveness." Given this diagnosis, he admitted that there was a likelihood that the respondent would re-offend. Dr. Orchard did conclude, however, that the respondent was neither schizophrenic nor psychotic and that he had shown change toward less violent behaviour. He prognosticated that if there were future recurrences of the respondent's criminal behaviour, his conduct would tend toward "nuisance-type offences" rather than offences of a violent nature. In sum, he did not "find him particularly dangerous at the present time."

• • •

II. Issues

[16] The fundamental disagreement in the judgments below on the suitability of designating Robert Currie a dangerous offender and imposing an indeterminate sentence raises, in my opinion, the following three issues on appeal to this Court:

(1) Must a trial judge, when evaluating a dangerous offender application under s. 753(b) of the *Criminal Code*, focus on the seriousness of the specific predicate offences that have led to the Crown's dangerous offender application?

(2) Were the dangerous offender designation and the corresponding indeterminate sentence reasonably supported by the evidence?

(3) Were the dangerous offender designation and the corresponding indeterminate sentence premised on any errors of law?

· · ·

[17] It is the stated opinion of this Court that Robert Currie was properly designated a dangerous offender and correctly sentenced to an indeterminate period of incarceration. That opinion is grounded in two basic legal propositions both of which I develop and apply below. Those propositions are: first, given the nature and structure of s. 753(b) of the *Criminal Code*, a presiding trial judge need not focus on the objective seriousness of a predicate offence in order to conclude that a dangerous offender designation is warranted. Second, a finding of dangerousness by a trial judge is a finding of fact, frequently based upon the competing credibility of experts, and as long as it is reasonable, it is a finding which should not be lightly overturned.

A. Must a Trial Judge Focus on the Seriousness of the Predicate Offences?

[18] The Court of Appeal quashed the trial judge's designation of Robert Currie as a dangerous offender principally because it found the trial judge erred by failing to focus on the seriousness of the predicate offences. The respondent has relied upon that finding and insists that, when evaluating the likelihood of danger that an offender presents, the sentencing judge must consider the relative gravity of the predicate offences. Unless there is "some rational relationship between the predicate offences and the sentences," the respondent contends that the offender is being sentenced for his past criminality.

[19] It is true that, when viewed in isolation, the predicate offences appear less serious than much of the respondent's past conduct. Indeed the appellant has admitted that "[t]he predicate offences in this case are properly characterized as offences of a less serious nature than the offender's earlier offences, and thankfully do not approach the gravity of the very violent earlier offences." However, that observation does not necessarily translate into a conclusion that the designation of Robert Currie as a dangerous offender was misplaced. Rather, once an individual has committed an offence specifically defined in the *Criminal Code* as a "serious personal injury offence," he or she has made it possible for the Crown to invoke the *Criminal Code*'s dangerous offender application process. If that process is invoked, it is incumbent upon the trial judge to evaluate the offender's potential danger to the public and this may or may not depend upon the specific nature and objective gravity of the predicate offence.

[20] Section 753(b) of the *Criminal Code* makes this point abundantly clear. ... In short, there are two thresholds that the Crown must surpass in order for the dangerous offender application to be successful. The Crown must first establish that the offender has been convicted of a "serious personal injury offence." Then the focus of the inquiry shifts. The question then becomes whether there is a "likelihood" that the offender will cause "injury, pain or other evil to other persons through [his] failure in the future to control his sexual impulses."

[21] There is no question in this appeal that the predicate sexual assaults committed by the respondent against the young girls in the Towers department store constituted "serious personal injury offences." Section 752(b) of the *Criminal Code* defines "serious personal injury offence" to include "an offence or attempt to commit an offence mentioned in section 271 (sexual assault)." However, the parties fundamentally disagree over the manner in which the trial judge applied the second standard. The respondent alleges that the trial judge erred because he did not take proper notice of the relative gravity of the predicate offences. He submits that an indeterminate sentence is disproportionate to the seriousness of sexual touching.

[22] My problem with this argument is twofold. First, the language of s. 753(b) explicitly states that there is no requirement to focus on the specific nature of the predicate offence. Section 753(b) provides that the prospective dangerousness of the offender is measured by reference to *"his conduct in any sexual matter including that involved in the commission of the offence for which he has been convicted"* (emphasis added). "[A]ny sexual matter" can refer to the predicate offence, but it need not. As long as the offender's past conduct, whatever conduct that might be, demonstrates a present likelihood of inflicting future harm upon others, the designation is justified. Second, the respondent's position is inconsistent with the nature and structure of the dangerous offender statutory scheme created by Parliament. As I indicated above, a crucial element of s. 753(b) is the notion of the "serious personal injury offence." Parliament has said that there are certain types of offences, which are inherently serious, that can trigger a dangerous offender application. As this Court observed in *R v. McCraw*, [1991] 3 SCR 72, at p. 83, sexual assault, whatever form it may take, is one of them. Other offences, presumably less threatening to the personal safety of others, do not trigger s. 753.

[23] As such, I would find it contradictory, as well as callous, to categorize the impugned predicate assaults as "nuisance-type offences." These sexual assaults, while not as violent or grave as some of the respondent's earlier offences, were nevertheless within the category of violent and grave. The predicate offences involved repeated sexual touching of young girls in public and at least two of the victims of the assaults have experienced serious psychological trauma and other side effects. If these sexual assaults were not serious, sexual assault would not be enumerated as a s. 752 offence. Nor would Parliament have ever seen fit to eliminate the distinction between rape and indecent assault—indeed it would have ensured that such a distinction endured.

[24] By definition, therefore, arguments of proportionality do not withstand scrutiny. There may be, as the respondent asserts, an objective difference between the nighttime rape at knife point and the predicate offences, but this distinction is not reflected in s. 752 or 753 of the *Criminal Code*. Indeed the respondent is asking the Court to alter or even reduce the definition of "serious personal injury offence." This alteration would, as the appellant notes, effectively guarantee that an accused who has committed an arguably less serious sexual predicate offence would never be declared a dangerous offender. I cannot imagine that Parliament wanted the courts to wait for an obviously dangerous individual, regardless of the nature of his criminal record and notwithstanding the force of expert opinion as to his potential dangerousness, to commit a particularly violent and grievous offence before he or she can be declared a dangerous offender.

[25] Does it defy reality, as the respondent submits, to treat all "serious personal injury offences" the same in applying s. 753(b)? In my opinion, it does not. This might be

problematic if s. 753(b) were a one-stage test. Section 753(b) might not make sense if, for example, it were to provide, without qualification, that a trial judge may designate any person who commits a "serious personal injury offence" as a dangerous offender. But, it is crucial to recognize that the conviction for a "serious personal injury offence" merely triggers the s. 753(b) application process. There remains a second stage to s. 753(b), at which point the trial judge must be satisfied beyond a reasonable doubt of the likelihood of future danger that an offender presents to society before he or she can impose the dangerous offender designation and an indeterminate sentence.

[26] Parliament has thus created a standard of preventive detention that measures an accused's present condition according to past behaviour and patterns of conduct. Under this statutory arrangement, dangerous offenders who have committed "serious personal injury offences" can be properly sentenced without having to wait for them to strike out in a particularly egregious way. For example, suppose a known sexual deviate has been convicted of repeated offences for stalking and sexually assaulting young girls in playgrounds. He operates by offering them candy, touching their private parts, and if the children seem to comply or submit to his criminal advances, by taking them away where he violently sexually assaults them. Now suppose that individual is at large in society and caught by a parent at a playground after having offered a child candy and improperly touching her. In this example, like the present case, the predicate offence is objectively less serious than a violent and invasive rape, but the trial judge need not justify the dangerous offender designation and an indeterminate sentence as a just desert for the isolated act of sexual touching. On the theory of s. 753(b), the offender has committed an inherently "serious personal injury offence." On a dangerous offender application, a trial judge is then entitled to consider his "conduct in any sexual matter" to determine if he presents a future danger to society. Otherwise, we would be saying that an offender's present condition is defined by the precise degree of seriousness of the predicate offences. That is equivalent to assuming that a dangerous individual will always act out, or be caught for that matter, at the upper limits of his dangerous capabilities.

• • •

B. Were the Dangerous Offender Designation and the Corresponding Indeterminate Sentence Reasonably Supported by the Evidence?

[32] On the basis of the language of s. 753(b) of the *Criminal Code* and the principles I have articulated above, I am satisfied that there was enough evidence before Tobias J for him to find that the respondent was a dangerous offender. The respondent's pattern of criminal sexual behaviour and the psychiatric evidence of the Crown-nominated psychiatrist are certainly sufficient proof, if accepted by a trier of fact, to justify such a conclusion.

• • •

[38] In my opinion, therefore, it was entirely open to the trial judge to prefer the evidence of Dr. McDonald to that of Dr. Orchard. It was not, however, similarly open to the Court of Appeal to re-evaluate the psychiatric evidence and overturn the dangerous offender designation because of a mere difference of opinion. I cannot overemphasize the point that no appellate court should lightly disturb a finding of dangerousness which is so heavily dependent upon the relative credibility of expert witnesses. In saying this, I have not forgotten the broad language of s. 759. However, having observed both experts

and evaluated their reports, Tobias J simply found the opinion of Dr. McDonald to be more credible. It was a reasonable conclusion amply supported by the evidence. It should not have been disturbed by the Court of Appeal.

· · ·

[42] ... The Court cannot forget that s. 753(b) does not require proof beyond a reasonable doubt that the respondent will re-offend. Such a standard would be impossible to meet. Instead, s. 753(b) requires that the court be satisfied beyond a reasonable doubt that there is a "likelihood" that the respondent will inflict harm, and the trial judge took explicit notice of this, citing *R v. Knight* (1975), 27 CCC (2d) 343 (Ont. HC); *R v. Dwyer* (1977), 34 CCC (2d) 293 (Alta. CA); *R v. Carleton* (1981), 69 CCC (2d) 1 (Alta. CA) (aff'd [1983] 2 SCR 58). See also *Langevin*, supra. I am thus unwilling to conclude, on the basis of a few misplaced words, that the trial judge either misunderstood or misapplied the burden of proof on this dangerous offender application.

Finally, consider the following excerpt from *R v Neve*. Lisa Neve was the second woman in Canadian history to be designated a dangerous offender. The prosecutor applied to have her declared a dangerous offender following a conviction for robbery. Consequently, the first branch of s 753(1) of the Code was engaged. The trial judge found Neve to be a dangerous offender and sentenced her to an indeterminate period of detention. The Court of Appeal for Alberta dismissed Neve's appeal against conviction, but concluded that her designation as a dangerous offender could not stand. The excerpts from the reasons in the Court of Appeal highlight some important contextual considerations relating to the operation of the dangerous offender provisions as a whole. They also address the issue of risk of harm from both qualitative and quantitative perspectives.

R v Neve
1999 ABCA 206, 137 CCC (3d) 97

FRASER CJA (Conrad and Picard JJA concurring):

[3] We identify a number of errors in the course of our analysis of these issues. Without in any way minimizing the complexity of these issues or their cumulative effect, Neve's appeal from her designation as a dangerous offender can be summarized this simply. According to Crown records, since 1947 (the year in which predecessor dangerous offender legislation first came into effect in Canada) until July 31, 1997, 219 offenders were designated dangerous offenders in Canada, an average of approximately 4 per year. Other data indicates that between 1978 and 1986, that number increased to an average of 7 per year. In the end, the overarching question to be answered is whether the decision designating Neve a dangerous offender was reasonable. Or to put the matter another way: does Neve, having regard to all relevant circumstances, fall within that very small group of offenders whom Parliament intended be designated as dangerous offenders—and which has led, in all of Canada over a 50-year period, to an average of 4 to 7 criminals a year being detained as dangerous offenders? In our view, for reasons we explain in detail below, the answer to this question is no.

· · ·

[7] Before addressing each of these issues in turn, we propose to review the facts relating to the robbery. One cannot overemphasize the importance of context, and hence the facts, not only to the conviction appeal, but also to the dangerous offender appeal. Context weighs heavily at many stages of a dangerous offender proceeding. The dangerous offender legislation requires a court to focus on the person (and all relevant circumstances relating to what that person has done) and not simply on numbers of convictions. Parliament has not chosen to adopt a formulaic "three strikes and you are out" approach to dangerous offender designations in Canada. Instead, before imposing one of the most serious sanctions under Canadian criminal law, a court is required to conduct a contextual analysis, concentrating on the offender and on the qualitative, quantitative and relative dimensions of the crimes the offender has committed.

• • •

[9] When these events occurred, Neve was 18 years old. She had been a prostitute since she was 12. Neve and her friend, Kim, approached the complainant, another prostitute. Neve and Kim believed that the complainant had beaten one of their pregnant friends causing her to miscarry. They asked the complainant if she would like to go for a drink. The complainant agreed. It was about midnight. The complainant climbed into a truck with Neve and Kim. They questioned the complainant about the assault on their friend. She denied any involvement.

[10] Kim drove to a field by a greenhouse just outside northeast Edmonton near a major highway and parked the vehicle. The trial judge found that the complainant was told to take her clothes off. Neve threatened to cut off the complainant's hair. Kim threatened that she would break the complainant's arm if she did not take her clothes off. The complainant refused to do so. Neve and Kim then proceeded to tear the complainant's clothes off, using a knife to cut the clothing so that it could be more easily torn. The complainant, whose evidence was accepted by the trial judge, confirmed that her clothes were being held away from her when the knife was used. In the process, the complainant received what she variously conceded was a "little scratch," a "tiny nick" or a "small cut." The complainant expressly acknowledged that the knife was being used quite carefully to remove her clothing, so as not to hurt her. ...

[11] During examination-in-chief, the complainant testified that Kim struck her about five times in the face. Although the complainant mentioned in cross-examination that Neve also struck her, she could not remember any details whatever, including the effect on her. Even with respect to Kim, the complainant testified that she did not remember having any pain or injury as a result of what Kim did. ... In fact, the complainant testified:

Q Okay. Now, did you receive any—any injuries as a result of this incident, ma'am?
A Nothing other than just a small cut.

• • •

[14] Neve and Kim drove away after first circling in the parking lot. The complainant testified that she did not know what was done with her clothes when they were removed from her. She was left without them. It was May and the temperature was then about five degrees Centigrade. She wrapped herself in some fibreglass insulation which she found nearby and made her way to the main highway where, according to her testimony, she was picked up a little bit later by a passing motorist who testified that she was "very, very cold, and she looked somewhat confused."

• • •

[17] With the complainant's help, the police later apprehended Neve. At the time of her arrest, a knife was found in her jacket pocket. She was informed of her right to counsel, but declined to exercise it. Neve was apparently then under the influence of drugs. At no time was Neve informed of her right to remain silent. Nor was she cautioned about the consequences of choosing to make a statement.

[18] Later, while in a police holding cell, Neve cut her wrists. She was taken to hospital where she was treated. She was then returned to the cell. She told one of the constables that he better not leave because she was going to do the same thing again. A police constable watched over her until 7:30 a.m. While there, he asked Neve some questions about the events which led to her arrest. (It is Neve's answers to these questions which Neve contends were wrongly admitted into evidence at the trial.) The constable asked her the name of the other assailant. Neve replied that it was Kim. Neve then went on to explain the nature of the grievance she had with the complainant. Specifically, the constable testified:

> She—she also told me in reference to the—the alleged assault that she did it to get even because the complainant had beat up one of her—her friends who was pregnant at the time and also that the complainant was yelling—was the type that was yelling and getting out of hand, getting out of control. That was another reason for—for what they did.

[19] Neve later asked to speak to a lawyer. After she had used the phone, she told the constable that instead of calling counsel, she had phoned Kim to advise her to leave the City.

• • •

[59] … Not everyone who is a criminal or for that matter a danger to the public is a dangerous offender. In the spectrum of offenders, the dangerous offender legislation is designed to target—and capture—those clustered at or near the extreme end. Were this otherwise, constitutionality might stumble. In other words, the dangerous offender legislation is not intended to be a process of general application but rather of exacting selection.

• • •

[289] In all these circumstances, we have concluded that the decision to designate Neve a dangerous offender was not reasonable. It is only by taking the global perspective we have described that it is possible to assess whether Neve, in view of her record, and the circumstances and context of the offences she has committed, belongs in that relatively small group such that the most severe sentence that can be imposed under the Code, short of life imprisonment, is strenuously required: *Lyons*, supra, at 339.

[290] There is no doubt that Neve has a history of offending the law; and we cannot say that Neve will not reoffend. That risk exists and it is a real risk. Indeed, it would be naive to think otherwise. However, the question is not whether there is a possibility or even a probability of Neve's reoffending in the future. While this consideration certainly goes on the scale, the central question which must be addressed at this stage is whether, given her past record and the various factors that we have noted and assessed, Neve falls within the intended small group of dangerous offenders in Canada. In our view, she does not.

[291] Neve is a criminal but the totality of the circumstances here do not warrant a dangerous offender designation at this stage in her life. Neve's life found her moving from one set of extreme circumstances to another: prostitution from a very young age; abuse from her pimp; foster homes; placement centres; and drug and alcohol abuse. When her actual criminal record is parsed out from her thoughts and fantasies, what we have is a young woman with a relatively short criminal record for violence, disposed to telling

shocking stories of violence. Considering her within the population of criminals in Canada, it cannot be said at this time that she falls within that "very small group of offenders whose personal characteristics and particular circumstances militate strenuously in favour of preventative incarceration." *Lyons*, supra, at 339.

2. Post-1997 Cases

The following case was necessitated by the 1997 amendments to the Code and the introduction of the long-term offender sanction into the Code. Given that those amendments were in effect as of August 1, 1997, there were cases in the system that were based on predicate offences that occurred before that date. How do the principles that generally apply to retroactive application deal with whether the long-term offender option should be on the table for an offence that antedates those provisions? Moreover, more important, how should a judge interpret and apply the dangerous offender test now that the Code contains the long-term offender option? Is there any interrelationship and, if so, what is it? The Supreme Court addressed these questions in *Johnson*, below.

R v Johnson

2003 SCC 46, [2003] 2 SCR 357

IACOBUCCI and ARBOUR JJ (McLachlin CJ and Gonthier, Major, Bastarache, Binnie, LeBel, and Deschamps JJ concurring):

[1] This case was heard at the same time as *R v. Edgar*, [2003] 2 SCR 388, 2003 SCC 47, *R v. Smith*, [2003] 2 SCR 392, 2003 SCC 48, *R v. Mitchell*, [2003] 2 SCR 396, 2003 SCC 49, *R v. Kelly*, [2003] 2 SCR 400, 2003 SCC 50, released concurrently herewith. Each case involves an appeal against a sentencing judge's decision to declare an offender dangerous and sentence him to an indeterminate period of detention. In deciding these appeals, the British Columbia Court of Appeal conducted an extensive review of the dangerous offender provisions in light of amendments to Part XXIV of the *Criminal Code*, RSC 1985, c. C-46, which contains the provisions governing dangerous offenders.

[2] The amendments, which took effect August 1, 1997, brought a number of changes to Part XXIV of the *Criminal Code*. For instance, the period before a dangerous offender's first parole hearing was extended from three years under the pre-1997 legislation to seven years under the amended legislation. Another change was the addition of the new category of long-term offender to Part XXIV of the *Code*. While Canada has had legislation providing for the indeterminate incarceration of high risk offenders in one form or another since 1947, the 1997 amendments introduced, for the first time, a mechanism to allow for supervision in the community, for a limited period after the expiry of a determinate sentence, of certain offenders who pose a risk of re-offence. This case requires this Court to consider for the first time the interaction between the dangerous offender provisions and the new long-term offender provisions, both of which govern the sentencing of offenders who pose an ongoing public threat.

[3] This appeal raises two primary issues. The first issue is whether a sentencing judge must, under the current regime, take into account the possibility of a long-term offender designation when considering a dangerous offender application. The second issue is

whether the current provisions, particularly the long-term offender provisions which were absent in the pre-1997 legislation, are available in instances in which the predicate offence occurred prior to the 1997 amendments.

. . .

II. *Judicial History*

[7] At the sentencing hearing, Tysoe J of the Supreme Court of British Columbia did not consider the availability of the long-term offender provisions, on the basis that the offence for which Mr. Johnson was convicted was committed prior to the 1997 amendments. He held that Mr. Johnson was a dangerous offender as defined by s. 753(1)(b) of the *Criminal Code* and sentenced him to detention in a penitentiary for an indeterminate period: [1998] BCJ No. 3216 (QL).

[8] Ryan JA, for the majority of the British Columbia Court of Appeal ((2001), 158 CCC (3d) 155, 2001 BCCA 456), concluded that the matter ought to have been determined in accordance with the current regime. Under s. 11(i) of the *Canadian Charter of Rights and Freedoms*, any person charged with an offence has the right "if found guilty of the offence and if the punishment for the offence has been varied between the time of commission and the time of sentencing, to the benefit of the lesser punishment." Ryan JA found that under the current regime the long-term offender provisions narrow the scope of the dangerous offender provisions by providing the sentencing judge with the option of sentencing an offender who would previously have been declared dangerous to a lesser punishment. Ryan JA thus concluded that the sentencing judge should have sentenced Mr. Johnson under the current regime, and in so doing should have considered the suitability of the long-term offender provisions.

[9] In reaching this conclusion, Ryan JA considered the dangerous offender provisions prior to the amendments. In her view, implicit in one form or another in each of the criteria under s. 753 is the requirement that the pattern of conduct be substantially or pathologically intractable. If the pattern of conduct is substantially or pathologically intractable, the sentencing judge *must* declare the offender dangerous. The sentencing judge, however, retains the discretion to sentence a dangerous offender to a determinate sentence, but only if a cure for the offender's behaviour is probable within the parameters of the fixed sentence.

[10] Ryan JA then concluded that under the current regime a sentencing judge does not retain the discretion to sentence a dangerous offender to a determinate sentence. However, the sentencing judge must consider the prospects for treatment or cure in order to determine whether the pattern of conduct exhibited by the offender is sufficiently intractable to satisfy the statutory criteria set out in s. 753(1)(a) and (b). If there is a reasonable possibility that a cure will be found within the time-frame of a fixed sentence, or that the offender will be controllable under the long-term offender provisions, the sentencing judge cannot rightly conclude that the offender is a dangerous offender. According to Ryan JA, the primary distinction between the long-term offender provisions and the dangerous offender provisions, under the current regime, is the absence of a requirement under the long-term offender provisions that the pattern of conduct be substantially or pathologically intractable. An offender whose conduct is not pathologically intractable may now qualify for long-term offender status rather than dangerous offender status.

[11] Saunders JA dissented on the basis that she was unable to say with certainty, at the time that the hearing commenced, that the current sentencing regime would result in a lesser punishment than the prior regime. According to Saunders JA, it is possible that an offender who would have been declared dangerous and sentenced to a fixed term under the former regime would be declared a long-term offender and sentenced to a fixed term with a period of probation under the current regime, or that a person who would not have been declared dangerous under the former regime would be declared a long-term offender under the current regime. If the predicate offence was committed prior to the 1997 amendments, the offender should be sentenced under the former regime.

III. Issues

[12] This appeal raises two primary issues: (i) whether, under the current regime, a sentencing judge must take into account the long-term offender provisions prior to declaring an offender dangerous and imposing an indeterminate sentence; and (ii) whether a sentencing judge must take into account the long-term offender provisions in instances in which the predicate offence occurred prior to the enactment of the long-term offender provisions. If the sentencing judge's failure to consider the long-term offender provisions constituted an error of law, a third issue arises as to whether the appeals should be allowed on the basis that the error of law resulted in no substantial wrong or miscarriage of justice.

IV. Analysis

[13] Section 11(i) of the *Charter* guarantees that everyone has the right, "if found guilty of the offence and if the punishment for the offence has been varied between the time of commission and the time of sentencing, to the benefit of the lesser punishment." The question in this appeal is whether the new provisions offer any benefit to the respondent such that his sentencing must be governed retrospectively by the provisions as amended in 1997. In order to answer this question, it is necessary to interpret both the old and the new provisions, to determine which offers the prospect of a lesser punishment to an accused in the position of the respondent who is sentenced under them.

A. Dangerous Offender Applications Under the Current Regime

[14] The Crown submits that an offender who meets the criteria in s. 753(1)(a) or (b) must be declared a dangerous offender and must be given an indeterminate sentence, without regard to whether the offender might also meet the criteria for a long-term offender designation. There are two branches to this argument: first, that under 753(1), courts have no discretion to decline to declare an offender a dangerous offender once the statutory criteria have been satisfied; and second, that s. 753(5)(a) of the *Criminal Code* prevents a sentencing judge from considering the long-term offender provisions on a dangerous offender application until after the court has already found that an offender is not a dangerous offender. We consider each aspect of the argument in turn.

(1) The Sentencing Judge's Discretion

[15] Section 753(1) provides that "[t]he court may, on application made under this Part following the filing of an assessment report under subsection 752.1(2), find the offender

to be a dangerous offender" if it is satisfied that the statutory criteria set out in paras. (a) or (b) are met. The Crown submits that the word "may" in s. 753(1) does not create a true discretion, but rather grants a power that is contingent only upon proof of the statutory conditions. On this view, the word "may" in the phrase "[t]he court may … find the offender to be a dangerous offender" should be treated as imperative; a sentencing judge who finds that the dangerous offender criteria are met *must* make a dangerous offender designation. For the following reasons, it is our opinion that this submission must fail.

[16] The language of s. 753(1) indicates that a sentencing judge retains a discretion whether to declare an offender dangerous who meets the criteria for that designation. As mentioned above, s. 753(1) provides that the court *may* find an offender to be a dangerous offender if it is satisfied that the statutory criteria set out in paras. (a) or (b) are met. On its face, the word "may" denotes a discretion, while the word "shall" is commonly used to denote an obligation: see for example *R v. Potvin*, [1989] 1 SCR 525, at p. 549. Indeed, s. 11 of the *Interpretation Act*, RSC 1985, c. I-21, requires "shall" to be construed as imperative and "may" to be construed as permissive. If Parliament had intended that an offender *must* be designated dangerous if each of the statutory criteria have been satisfied, one would have expected Parliament to have used the word "shall" rather than "may."

[17] That said, cases do exist in which courts have found that the power conferred by "may" is coupled with a duty once all the conditions for the exercise of the power have been met: R. Sullivan, *Sullivan and Driedger on the Construction of Statutes* (4th ed. 2002), at p. 58. See for example, *Brown v. Metropolitan Authority* (1996), 150 NSR (2d) 43, in which the Nova Scotia Court of Appeal ruled that Sackville's Metropolitan Authority was obliged to pay the claimant pursuant to s. 8(1) of the *Community of Sackville Landfill Compensation Act*, SNS 1993, c. 71, despite the fact that the section provided that the Authority *may* pay an amount to a person who is a resident, or an owner or occupier of real or personal property in the municipality on account of damages arising out of the operation of the landfill. But as Sullivan observes, at pp. 59-60:

> In a case like *Brown*, it is wrong to say that "may" means "shall" or "may" is imperative. As Cotton LJ wrote in *Nichols v. Baker*,
>
> > I think that great misconception is caused by saying that in some cases "may" means "must." It can never mean "must," so long as the English language retains its meaning; but it gives a power, and then it may be a question in what cases, where a Judge has a power given him by the word "may," it becomes his duty to exercise it. (*In re Baker*; *Nichols v. Baker* (1890), 44 Ch. D 262, at 270.)
>
> *The duty, if it arises, is inferred from the purpose and scheme of the Act or from other contextual factors.* [Emphasis added.]

[18] In this case, there is no indication of a duty to find an offender dangerous once the statutory criteria have been met. As we will elaborate, neither the purpose of the dangerous offenders regime, nor the principles of sentencing, nor the principles of statutory interpretation suggest that a sentencing judge must designate an offender dangerous if the statutory criteria in s. 753(1)(a) or (b) have been met. On the contrary, each of these factors indicates that a sentencing judge retains the discretion not to declare an offender dangerous even if the statutory criteria are met. This is particularly true now that it is clear that offenders declared dangerous must be given an indeterminate sentence.

[19] In *R v. Lyons*, [1987] 2 SCR 309, this Court affirmed that the primary purpose of the dangerous offender regime is the protection of the public: see also *Re Moore and The Queen* (1984), 10 CCC (3d) 306 (Ont. HC), cited with approval in *Lyons, supra*, at p. 329. In *Lyons*, La Forest J explained that preventive detention under the dangerous offender regime goes beyond what is justified on a "just deserts" rationale based on the reasoning that in a given case, the nature of the crime and the circumstances of the offender call for the elevation of the goal of protection of the public over the other purposes of sentencing. La Forest J confirmed, at p. 339, that the legislation was designed "to carefully define a very small group of offenders whose personal characteristics and particular circumstances militate strenuously in favour of preventive incarceration."

[20] Indeterminate detention under the dangerous offender regime is warranted only insofar as it actually serves the purpose of protecting the public. As we discuss more thoroughly below, there may be circumstances in which an offender meets the statutory criteria for a dangerous offender designation but the goal of protecting the public can be achieved without indeterminate detention. An interpretation of the dangerous offender provisions that would require a sentencing judge to declare an offender dangerous and sentence him or her to an indeterminate period of detention in each instance in which the statutory criteria for a dangerous offender designation have been satisfied would introduce an unnecessary rigidity into the process and overshoot the public protection purpose of the dangerous offender regime.

[21] Nor is there anything in the purposes of the sentencing regime as a whole, as set out both in the decisions of this Court and in ss. 718 to 718.2 of the *Criminal Code*, which would indicate a duty to find an offender dangerous in each circumstance in which the statutory criteria are met. On the contrary, the underlying objectives of the sentencing regime, of which the dangerous offender provisions form a part, indicate a discretion to impose a just and fit sentence in the circumstances of the individual case.

[22] In *R v. Proulx*, [2000] 1 SCR 61, 2000 SCC 5, Lamer CJ, writing for the Court, emphasized, at para. 82, that "sentencing is an individualized process, in which the trial judge has considerable discretion in fashioning a fit sentence." The rationale flows from the principles of sentencing set out in the *Criminal Code*, including s. 718.1, which states that a sentence "must be proportionate to the gravity of the offence and the degree of responsibility of the offender," and s. 718.2(d), which states that an offender "should not be deprived of liberty, if less restrictive sanctions may be appropriate in the circumstances."

[23] This Court has previously confirmed that dangerous offender proceedings form part of the sentencing process: see for example *R v. Jones*, [1994] 2 SCR 229, at pp. 279-80 and 294-95, and *Lyons, supra*, at p. 350. As such, their interpretation must be guided by the fundamental purpose and principles of sentencing contained in ss. 718 to 718.2. The role played by the purpose and principles of sentencing in guiding the interpretation of the dangerous offender provisions is reflected in the comments of La Forest J, in *Lyons*, at p. 329, that preventive detention "simply represents a judgment that the relative importance of the objectives of rehabilitation, deterrence and retribution are greatly attenuated in the circumstances of the individual case, and that of prevention, correspondingly increased."

[24] The proposition that a court is under a duty to declare an offender dangerous in each circumstance in which the statutory criteria are satisfied is in direct conflict with the underlying principle that the sentence must be appropriate in the circumstances of the individual case. A rigid rule that each offender who satisfies the statutory criteria in

s. 753(1) must be declared dangerous and sentenced to an indeterminate period of detention undermines a sentencing judge's capacity to fashion a sentence that fits the individual circumstances of a given case. Thus, rather than suggesting that a sentencing judge is under an obligation to find an offender dangerous once the statutory criteria are met, the principles and purposes underlying the *Criminal Code*'s sentencing provisions actually *favour* a sentencing judge's discretion whether to declare an offender dangerous who has met the statutory criteria in s. 753(1).

[25] The Crown has pointed to a line of lower court judgments, beginning with *R v. Moore* (1985), 16 CCC (3d) 328 (Ont. CA), which say that a sentencing judge must designate an offender dangerous once the statutory criteria for the designation have been satisfied: see also *R v. Boutilier* (1995), 144 NSR (2d) 293 (CA); *R v. Dow* (1999), 120 BCAC 16, 1999 BCCA 177, decided under the previous legislation; *R v. J.T.H.* (2002), 209 NSR (2d) 302, 2002 NSCA 138; *R v. D.W.M.*, [2001] AJ No. 165 (QL), 2001 ABPC 5, decided under the current regime. There is also a contrary line of cases affirming the court's discretion to decline to make the designation which relies on *Lyons*: see for example *R v. N. (L.)* (1999), 71 Alta. LR (3d) 92, 1999 ABCA 206, decided under the current and previous legislation; *R v. Driver*, [2000] BCJ No. 63 (QL), 2000 BCSC 69, decided under the previous legislation; *R v. O.G.*, [2001] OJ No. 1964 (QL) (CJ); *R v. Tremblay* (2000), 87 Alta. LR (3d) 229, 2000 ABQB 551; and *R v. Roy*, [1999] QJ No. 5648 (QL) (Sup. Ct.), rev'd on a different issue (2002), 167 CCC (3d) 203 (Que. CA), decided under the current regime. Other courts have expressed uncertainty as to which line of cases to follow: see for example *R v. F.W.M.*, [2001] OJ No. 4591 (QL) (SCJ); *R v. Morin* (1998), 173 Sask. R. 101 (QB); *R v. R.C.* (1996), 145 Nfld. & PEIR 271 (Nfld. CA).

[26] However, this Court confirmed in *Lyons, supra*, that the phrase "the court may ... find the offender to be a dangerous offender" denotes a discretion. In support of the Court's conclusion that the dangerous offender regime did not violate the prohibition on cruel and unusual punishment, La Forest J stated, at p. 338, that "*the court has the discretion not to designate the offender as dangerous* or to impose an indeterminate sentence, *even in circumstances where all of these criteria are met*" (emphasis added). He reiterated the point at p. 362, stating that a sentencing judge "*does retain a discretion whether or not to impose the designation* or indeterminate sentence, or both" (emphasis added). Insofar as *Moore* and its progeny suggest that sentencing judges must declare an offender dangerous if the statutory criteria have been satisfied, they have been overruled by *Lyons*.

[27] Having determined that the phrase "[t]he court may ... find the offender to be a dangerous offender" denotes a discretion, the next issue that falls to be considered is the legal principles and factors that a sentencing judge must consider in the exercise of that discretion. For the reasons that follow, it is our conclusion that one factor that a sentencing judge must consider is the possibility that the sanctions available pursuant to the long-term offender provisions would be sufficient to achieve the objectives that the dangerous offender provisions seek to advance.

(2) The Exercise of Discretion

[28] Like all discretion exercised in the sentencing context, a judge's discretion whether to declare an offender dangerous must be guided by the relevant principles of sentencing contained in ss. 718 to 718.2 of the *Criminal Code*. As mentioned above, these

include the fundamental principle of proportionality contained in s. 718.1 and, most relevant to the central issue in the present appeal, the principle of restraint enunciated in paras. (d) and (e) of s. 718.2, which provide as follows:

> 718.2 A court that imposes a sentence shall also take into consideration the following principles:
>
> $\cdots$
>
> (d) an offender should not be deprived of liberty, if less restrictive sanctions may be appropriate in the circumstances; and
>
> (e) all available sanctions other than imprisonment that are reasonable in the circumstances should be considered for all offenders, with particular attention to the circumstances of aboriginal offenders.

The joint effect of these principles is that a sentencing judge must consider the possibility that a less restrictive sanction would attain the same sentencing objectives that a more restrictive sanction seeks to attain.

[29] In this case, the sentencing objective in question is public protection: see for example *Lyons*, *supra*, at p. 329, and *Hatchwell v. The Queen*, [1976] 1 SCR 39, in which Dickson J (as he then was) wrote, at p. 43, that the dominant purpose of preventive detention is "to protect the public when the past conduct of the criminal demonstrates a propensity for crimes of violence against the person, and there is a real and present danger to life or limb." Absent such a danger, there is no basis on which to sentence an offender otherwise than in accordance with the ordinary principles of sentencing. The principles of sentencing thus dictate that a judge ought to impose an indeterminate sentence only in those instances in which there does not exist less restrictive means by which to protect the public adequately from the threat of harm, i.e., where a definite sentence or long-term offender designation are insufficient. The essential question to be determined, then, is whether the sentencing sanctions available pursuant to the long-term offender provisions are sufficient to reduce this threat to an acceptable level, despite the fact that the statutory criteria in s. 753(1) have been met.

[30] In order for the sentencing sanctions available pursuant to the long-term offender provisions to reduce the threat associated with an offender who satisfies the dangerous offender criteria to an acceptable level, it must be possible for the same offender to satisfy both the dangerous offender criteria and the long-term offender criteria. To repeat, the three criteria that must be established on a long-term offender application are: (i) it must be appropriate to impose a sentence of imprisonment of two or more years in respect of the predicate offence; (ii) there must be a substantial risk that the offender will reoffend; and (iii) there must be a reasonable possibility of eventual control of the risk in the community. On a dangerous offender application, the sentencing judge must be satisfied that the offender constitutes a threat to the life, safety or physical or mental well-being of other persons, on the basis of a pattern of repetitive or persistent aggressive behaviour, brutal behaviour, or sexual misconduct described in s. 753(1)(a) and (b).

[31] Almost every offender who satisfies the dangerous offender criteria will satisfy the first two criteria in the long-term offender provisions. In virtually every instance in which an offender is declared dangerous, it would have been appropriate to impose a sentence of imprisonment of two or more years in respect of the predicate offence and there will be a substantial risk that the offender will reoffend. In a certain percentage of

those cases there will also be a reasonable possibility of eventual control of the risk in the community. In those instances in which the offender currently constitutes a threat to the life, safety or physical or mental well-being of other persons yet there is a reasonable possibility of eventual control of the risk in the community, an offender will satisfy the criteria in both the dangerous offender *and* long-term offender provisions.

[32] In those instances where both the dangerous and long-term offender provisions are satisfied, it may be that the sentencing sanctions available under the long-term offender provisions are capable of reducing the threat to the life, safety or physical or mental well-being of other persons to an acceptable level. Under s. 753.1(3), long-term offenders are sentenced to a definite term of imprisonment followed by a long-term community supervision order of a maximum of ten years in accordance with the *Corrections and Conditional Release Act*. Supervision conditions under s. 134.1(2) of the Act may include those that are "reasonable and necessary in order to protect society." The very purpose of a long-term supervision order, then, is to protect society from the threat that the offender currently poses—and to do so without resort to the blunt instrument of indeterminate detention. If the public threat can be reduced to an acceptable level through either a determinate period of detention or a determinate period of detention followed by a long-term supervision order, a sentencing judge cannot properly declare an offender dangerous and sentence him or her to an indeterminate period of detention.

[33] The Crown refutes the conclusion that the long-term offender provisions must be considered before a dangerous offender designation is made with reference to *R v. Carleton* (1981), 32 AR 181 (CA), affirmed by this Court in brief oral reasons, [1983] 2 SCR 58. In that case, the Court of Appeal considered whether, prior to the 1997 amendments, prospects of cure or treatment ought to be considered on a dangerous offender application and, if so, at which stage. McGillivray CJA for the majority, held that treatment prospects were irrelevant to the question of whether an offender is a dangerous offender, but that such prospects may be taken into account in determining whether to impose a determinate or indeterminate sentence. The Crown relies on *Carleton* in support of its proposition that it is improper to consider prospective factors, including the possibility of eventual control of the risk in the community, in determining whether an offender is a dangerous offender.

[34] However, there is some question as to whether *Carleton* correctly determined that prospective factors were irrelevant at the designation stage. The Court of Appeal's analysis was based on the assumption that once the statutory criteria were satisfied, the sentencing judge first had to consider whether to declare the offender dangerous, and then had to consider whether to impose an indeterminate sentence. But it is unclear that this two-step approach is the proper one. First, the purpose of the dangerous offender provisions is not to designate offenders as dangerous for the sake of designating offenders dangerous, but to protect the public. No sentencing objective is advanced by declaring an offender dangerous and then imposing a determinate sentence. Moreover, the two-stage approach is inconsistent with the French text, which provides that once the statutory criteria in s. 753 are satisfied, the court "*peut déclarer qu'il s'agit là d'un délinquant dangereux et lui imposer, au lieu de toute autre peine qui pourrait être imposée pour l'infraction dont il vient d'être déclaré coupable, une peine de détention dans un pénitencier pour une période indéterminée.*" This clearly suggests that Parliament intended that a sentencing judge would ask but one question: whether it would be appropriate, in the circumstances of the case, to declare the offender dangerous and thereby impose a period of indeterminate detention.

[35] *Carleton* thus provides little support for the proposition that a sentencing judge cannot consider treatment prospects at the designation stage. After all, the Court of Appeal was unanimous in *Carleton* that treatment prospects must be considered at some point prior to imposing an indeterminate sentence. If the court had recognized that following a determination that the statutory criteria have been satisfied there is but one question to be asked—whether to declare the offender dangerous and thereupon impose an indeterminate period of detention—it is far from clear that it would subsequently have reached the same conclusion in respect of the relevance of treatment prospects in determining whether to designate an offender dangerous. On the one-stage approach that we have proposed, the Court of Appeal's concurrent findings that the treatment prospects cannot be considered at the designation stage yet must be considered prior to imposing an indeterminate sentence are incompatible.

[36] But even if *Carleton* correctly concluded that under the pre-1997 provisions, prospective factors, including the reasonable possibility of eventual control of the risk in the community, could not properly be considered at the stage of designating an offender dangerous, this is no longer the case under the amended provisions. *Lyons* held, at pp. 337-38, that a sentencing judge's discretion not to impose an indeterminate sentence, even where all of the statutory criteria are met, helped ensure proportionality between the goal of protecting the public on the one hand and the serious effect of indeterminate detention on the accused on the other. Consequently, the discretion helped ensure the dangerous offender provisions' constitutionality. In other words, as we state elsewhere in these reasons, the imposition of an indeterminate sentence is justifiable only insofar as it actually serves the objective of protecting society. Now that it is clear that a sentencing judge has but one discretion to exercise, prospective factors, including the possibility of eventual control of the risk in the community, must be considered at some point leading up to a dangerous offender designation. This is necessary to ensure that an indeterminate sentence is imposed only in those circumstances in which the objective of public protection truly requires indeterminate detention. Consequently, under this analysis, *Carleton*, which was decided prior to the 1997 amendments, has no bearing on the above analysis.

· · ·

(4) Conclusion

[40] For the above reasons, the British Columbia Court of Appeal was correct to conclude that a sentencing judge must take into account the long-term offender provisions prior to declaring an offender dangerous and imposing an indeterminate sentence. If a sentencing judge is satisfied that the sentencing options available under the long-term offender provisions are sufficient to reduce the threat to the life, safety or physical or mental well-being of other persons to an acceptable level, the sentencing judge cannot properly declare an offender dangerous and thereupon impose an indeterminate sentence, even if all of the statutory criteria have been satisfied.

B. Predicate Offences Committed Prior to the 1997 Amendments

[41] As a general matter, persons accused of criminal conduct are to be charged and sentenced under the criminal law provisions in place at the time that the offence allegedly was committed. The *Charter* aside, the four respondents convicted of offences committed

prior to the 1997 amendments are properly sentenced under the former regime. However, s. 11(i) of the *Charter* provides that any person charged with an offence has the right "if found guilty of the offence and if the punishment for the offence has been varied between the time of commission and the time of sentencing, to the benefit of the lesser punishment."

[42] Under the former regime, a dangerous offender application results in one of two sentences: (i) a determinate sentence; or (ii) an indeterminate sentence. In those instances in which an offender would receive a determinate sentence, there is no lesser punishment that the offender might receive under the current regime. If the proper sentence under the former regime is a determinate sentence, the offender must receive a determinate sentence. But in each of the four cases where pre-1997 provisions were in issue, the sentencing judge concluded that the proper sentence was an indeterminate sentence. The question that this appeal raises is whether it is possible that an offender properly sentenced to an indeterminate period of detention under the prior regime would receive a lesser punishment under the current regime.

[43] As the Crown correctly observes, the statutory criteria that must be satisfied under the former s. 753 are precisely the same as the statutory criteria that must be satis-fied under the current s. 753(1). The logical inference is that each offender who satisfies the criteria set out in s. 753 must also satisfy the criteria set out in s. 753(1). But it does not thereby follow that every person declared a dangerous offender and sentenced to an indeterminate period of detention under the former regime would continue to be declared a dangerous offender and sentenced to an indeterminate period of detention under the current regime.

[44] As we have discussed, a sentencing judge should declare the offender dangerous and impose an indeterminate period of detention if, and only if, an indeterminate sentence is the least restrictive means by which to reduce the public threat posed by the offender to an acceptable level. The introduction of the long-term offender provisions expands the range of sentencing options available to a sentencing judge who is satisfied that the dangerous offender criteria have been met. Under the current regime, a sentencing judge is no longer faced with the stark choice between an indeterminate sentence and a deter-minate sentence. Rather, a sentencing judge may consider the additional possibility that a determinate sentence followed by a period of supervision in the community might adequately protect the public. The result is that some offenders who may have been declared dangerous under the former provisions could benefit from the long-term offender designation available under the current provisions.

[45] It thus follows that the Court of Appeal was correct to conclude that the sentenc-ing judges were required to consider the applicability of the long-term offender provisions. If the respondent satisfies the long-term offender criteria and there is a reasonable pos-sibility that the harm could be reduced to an acceptable level under the long-term offender provisions, the proper sentence, under the current regime, is not an indeterminate period of detention, but, rather, a determinate period of detention followed by a long-term supervision order. If this is the case, s. 11(i) of the *Charter* dictates that the respondent is entitled to be sentenced to a period of determinate detention followed by a long-term supervision order.

[46] Importantly, this does not mean that the respondent will, in the end, be sentenced in accordance with the current regime. Under the prior regime, the first parole hearing took place three years after the offender was taken into custody. Under the current regime,

an offender sentenced to an indeterminate term is not entitled to a first parole review until the expiration of seven years. If the sentencing judge is not satisfied that the long-term offender criteria have been met, or finds that a determinate sentence followed by a long-term supervision order would not reduce the threat of harm to an acceptable level, the respondent retains the benefit of the early parole hearing.

· · ·

V. Disposition

[52] In the result, the appeal is dismissed. We confirm the Court of Appeal's decision to order a new sentencing hearing in accordance with the foregoing principles.

NOTE

After *Johnson*, Parliament again addressed Part XXIV by amending s 753(1) to read, "the court *shall find the offender* to be a dangerous offender if it is satisfied that … ," thereby removing the discretion to make a dangerous designation if the statutory criteria are met. As well, the issue of treatability or tractability, which had been returned to the decision-making matrix by *Johnson*, was turned into solely a disposition issue by amendments that created the new ss 753(4) and (4.1):

> *Sentence for dangerous offender*
> 753(4) If the court finds an offender to be a dangerous offender, it shall
>   (a) impose a sentence of detention in a penitentiary for an indeterminate period;
>   (b) impose a sentence for the offence for which the offender has been convicted—which must be a minimum punishment of imprisonment for a term of two years—and order that the offender be subject to long-term supervision for a period that does not exceed 10 years; or
>   (c) impose a sentence for the offence for which the offender has been convicted.
>
> *Sentence of indeterminate detention*
> (4.1) The court shall impose a sentence of detention in a penitentiary for an indeterminate period unless it is satisfied by the evidence adduced during the hearing of the application that *there is a reasonable expectation that a lesser measure under paragraph (4)(b) or (c) will adequately protect the public against the commission by the offender of murder or a serious personal injury offence* [emphasis added].

In sum, these changes removed the discretion to designate an offender as a dangerous offender when the statutory criteria were met and moved any question of treatability into the disposition decision. As well, the tests in *Johnson* as to (1) "the possibility of eventual control of the risk in the community" and (2) whether the long-term offender provisions are "sufficient to reduce the threat to the life, safety or physical or mental well-being of other persons to an acceptable level" have been replaced by the higher threshold in s 753(4.1) of a "reasonable expectation that a lesser measure under paragraph (4)(b) or (c) will adequately protect the public against the commission by the offender of murder or a serious personal injury offence."

3. Post-2008 Cases

R v Szostak

2014 ONCA 15

ROSENBERG JA (Rouleau and Strathy JJA concurring):

[1] Philip Szostak appeals from his convictions by Lofchik J. for assault causing bodily harm, aggravated assault, assault with a weapon, possession of a weapon for a purpose dangerous to the public, uttering threats, obstruction of justice and seven counts of breach of probation. The Crown appeals from the decision of Lofchik J. refusing to declare Mr. Szostak a dangerous offender and imposing a conventional sentence of six years imprisonment. At the hearing of the appeal, the court dismissed the conviction appeal but reserved on the Crown sentence appeal. These reasons explain why the court dismissed the conviction appeal and why I would allow the Crown sentence appeal.

· · ·

[25] The appellant's behavioural problems began when he was only seven years old. He had episodes of uncontrolled anger and was diagnosed with Attention Deficit Disorder and Oppositional Defiance Disorder. He did not do well in school and changed schools several times. He was expelled from high school in 2000 for making several bomb threats. He has worked in construction and prior to his arrest on the predicate offences was operating a dry-wall/home improvement business.

[26] The appellant was convicted of robbery as a result of an incident in 2000 when he and an accomplice punched a boy and stole his bicycle. The appellant would have been approximately 17 years of age at the time. He was involved in two much more serious offences in 2005 and 2006, which the Crown relied upon to prove the pattern of behaviour that would bring the appellant within the definition of a dangerous offender.

[27] In July 2005, the appellant was waiting in line for the washroom in a bar. Another customer objected to the appellant's behaviour in trying to get ahead in the line. After a short shoving match, the appellant hit the customer over the head with a beer bottle, cutting the man's head and right cheek bone. At the time of this offence, the appellant was on bail for a drug offence. The appellant pleaded guilty to assault with a weapon and breach of recognizance and received one day in jail in addition to 146 days of pre-sentence custody and two years' probation.

[28] While on probation, the appellant became involved in an altercation on the evening of May 30, 2006. The appellant, who was described as being drunk and high on drugs, became involved in a fight with five other individuals. Another person, who was not one of the five individuals, left the bar around this time. The appellant came up to him and slashed him across the neck with a pair of scissors. The victim sustained a three inch laceration to his neck that narrowly missed the carotid. The appellant pleaded guilty to aggravated assault and breach of probation. He was sentenced to two years imprisonment and three years' probation. While serving this penitentiary sentence, the appellant was involved in fights and was found in possession of contraband on several occasions. His parole was revoked three times.

[29] On June 6, 2009, just a few months before the second incident involving the complainant, the appellant pleaded guilty to threatening death and being unlawfully in a dwelling house. He had entered the home of his employer and threatened him over

some money that he believed he was owed for some renovation work. The appellant left without harming anyone or taking anything.

[30]   A psychologist, Dr. Mamak, and a psychiatrist, Dr. Chaimowitz, testified at the dangerous offender hearing. Various tests showed the appellant to have an anti-social personality disorder. He was not, however, a psychopath. He was at a medium to high risk to re-offend within one year of release. He lacked insight into his actions and was given to impulsive behaviour. He did not suffer from a major mental disorder and was willing to accept treatment. Dr. Chaimowitz concluded as follows:

> Absent intervention he runs the risk of causing harm to others, posing a threat to their life, safety and physical as well as mental wellbeing. That likelihood will be a function of his ability to restrain his behaviour and avoid drugs and alcohol.
>
> Mr. Szostak has now attacked two people with sharp instruments, namely a knife and scissors. He also struck an individual with a beer bottle. There is thus a suggestion that there may very well be a pattern of repetitive behaviour based on these acts.
>
> Mr. Szostak has expressed remorse albeit superficial and has been able to reflect on his actions. He is quite clearly able to place his behaviours in the area of criminality. He is also smart enough to know that not expressing remorse would not be a wise thing. Nonetheless, I do not believe that there is sufficient evidence to suggest that any indifference he has would be substantial at this time.
>
> • • •
>
> The absence of prior treatment or attempts to control him in the community would suggest that one cannot say assertively that there is no likelihood of eventual control in the community. Should he receive psychological attention including anger management, substance abuse treatment, psychological oversight and monitoring, it is reasonable to expect that there may be an opportunity for substantial control of this man in the community.

[31]   Both experts were of the opinion that the appellant met the criteria for a dangerous offender under both s. 753(1)(a)(i) and (ii). They agreed, however, that with treatment there was a possibility that the risk posed by the appellant could be managed in the community. They noted that the appellant had not had the benefit of any treatment, other than anger management, and that programs offered in the federal system would be more effective. There was a reasonable expectation that a lesser measure than indeterminate detention would adequately protect the public, namely long-term supervision.

• • •

[44]   The leading case on the interpretation of the 1997 legislation is *R. v. Johnson*, 2003 SCC 46, [2003] 2 S.C.R. 357. Much of the decision turned on the application of the new long-term offender provisions but the court made some observations on the operation of the scheme generally. Importantly, the court held that the proper interpretation of the scheme was, as I have said above, to give the offender access to the benefit of the long-term offender designation by exercising the discretion not to find the person to be a dangerous offender although they met the dangerous offender definition. As the court explained at para. 24:

> The proposition that a court is under a duty to declare an offender dangerous in each circumstance in which the statutory criteria are satisfied is in direct conflict with the underlying principle that the sentence must be appropriate in the circumstances of the individual case.

A rigid rule that each offender who satisfies the statutory criteria in s. 753(1) must be declared dangerous and sentenced to an indeterminate period of detention undermines a sentencing judge's capacity to fashion a sentence that fits the individual circumstances of a given case. Thus, rather than suggesting that a sentencing judge is under an obligation to find an offender dangerous once the statutory criteria are met, the principles and purposes underlying the *Criminal Code*'s sentencing provisions actually *favour* a sentencing judge's discretion whether to declare an offender dangerous who has met the statutory criteria in s. 753(1).

[45] But, the availability of the new long-term offender penalty removed intractability as a necessary element of the dangerous offender definition. This was because under the 1997 scheme a person could be eligible for a long-term offender disposition notwithstanding the person met both definitions of dangerous offender and long-term offender.

[46] The court made clear in paras. 30-32 that a person who fit the dangerous offender definition could nevertheless be found to be a long-term offender. For example, at para. 30:

> In order for the sentencing sanctions available pursuant to the long-term offender provisions to reduce the threat associated with an offender who satisfies the dangerous offender criteria to an acceptable level, it must be possible for the same offender to satisfy both the dangerous offender criteria and the long-term offender criteria.

The court made a similar point at para. 44:

> As we have discussed, a sentencing judge should declare the offender dangerous and impose an indeterminate period of detention if, and only if, an indeterminate sentence is the least restrictive means by which to reduce the public threat posed by the offender to an acceptable level. *The introduction of the long-term offender provisions expands the range of sentencing options available to a sentencing judge who is satisfied that the dangerous offender criteria have been met.* Under the current regime, a sentencing judge is no longer faced with the stark choice between an indeterminate sentence and a determinate sentence. Rather, a sentencing judge may consider the additional possibility that a determinate sentence followed by a period of supervision in the community might adequately protect the public. [Emphasis added.]

[47] I point out in passing this sentence from para. 34 of *Johnson*: "No sentencing objective is advanced by declaring an offender dangerous and then imposing a determinate sentence." This principle has been unequivocally abandoned in the 2008 legislation to which this appellant is subject.

. . .

[52] In my view, any doubt that intractability is not a necessary element to find a person to be a dangerous offender has been removed by the 2008 amendments. This legislation removes the discretion that existed under the 1997 legislation not to find a person to be a dangerous offender even though the person came within the definition in s. 753(1). That discretion has been replaced by a highly structured discretion in s. 753(4) and (4.1). Those provisions are as follows:

> (4) If the court finds an offender to be a dangerous offender, it shall
>
>> (a) impose a sentence of detention in a penitentiary for an indeterminate period;
>>
>> (b) impose a sentence for the offence for which the offender has been convicted— which must be a minimum punishment of imprisonment for a term of two years—and

order that the offender be subject to long-term supervision for a period that does not exceed 10 years; or

(c) impose a sentence for the offence for which the offender has been convicted.

(4.1) The court shall impose a sentence of detention in a penitentiary for an indeterminate period unless it is satisfied by the evidence adduced during the hearing of the application that there is a reasonable expectation that a lesser measure under paragraph (4)(b) or (c) will adequately protect the public against the commission by the offender of murder or a serious personal injury offence.

[53] Thus, the legislation contemplates that a person could be declared a dangerous offender because they meet the definition but nevertheless be given a disposition including a long-term supervision order or a conventional sentence. However, these two options are only available if an indeterminate sentence is not required to protect the public from the commission of murder or a serious personal injury offence. If a person, to be declared a dangerous offender, had to not only meet the statutory definition but display a pattern of conduct that was pathologically intractable, that person could, it seems to me, rarely, if ever, be eligible for a long-term supervision order or a conventional sentence.

[54] Further, while I agree that the legislation must be interpreted in the spirit of *Lyons* and bearing in mind the sentencing principles and objectives in ss. 718, 718.1 and 718.2, it is apparent that Parliament intended a broader group of offenders be declared dangerous offenders than was envisaged in *Lyons* where the court spoke of "a very small group of offenders." While the legislation is still narrowly targeted to a small group of offenders, that Parliament intended to broaden the group of persons to be labelled as dangerous offenders is apparent from the legislative reversal of the principle in *Johnson* referred to earlier that no sentencing objective is advanced by declaring an offender dangerous and imposing a determinate sentence. I point out that there has been no constitutional challenge to the 2008 regime in this case.

[55] Accordingly, it is of no assistance in interpreting the legislation to go beyond the words of the definition in s. 753(1) and introduce principles of intractability or attempt to predict the number of offenders that Parliament intended to bring within the legislative scheme.

• • •

[58] In my view, the trial judge erred in law in finding that the pattern required by s. 753(1)(a)(i) or (ii) was not made out. For convenience, I repeat the definitions of those two paragraphs:

(i) a pattern of repetitive behaviour by the offender, of which the offence for which he or she has been convicted forms a part, showing a failure to restrain his or her behaviour and a likelihood of causing death or injury to other persons, or inflicting severe psychological damage on other persons, through failure in the future to restrain his or her behaviour,

(ii) a pattern of persistent aggressive behaviour by the offender, of which the offence for which he or she has been convicted forms a part, showing a substantial degree of indifference on the part of the offender respecting the reasonably foreseeable consequences to other persons of his or her behaviour

[59] In my view, the trial judge erred in law in finding that the pattern of behaviour was not made out because the incidents were spontaneous and did not demonstrate intractability. I refer to the following, paras. 68-69, from the trial judge's reasons:

In none of the cases did the offender pursue the victim for the purpose of inflicting violence on him, as all the incidents can be described as "spontaneous occurrences" and thus it cannot be said that they were serial offences as is the case in many dangerous offender applications.

None of the injuries inflicted on the victims were life threatening or intended to be so. The injuries in all cases were inflicted in a different manner.

[60] First, the trial judge erred in finding that since the offences were "spontaneous occurrences" they could not be said to be "serial offences." There is no requirement that the offences be serial offences. Indeed, the fact that the various offences were spontaneous strongly tells in favour of a pattern in the sense of both paras. (i) and (ii). Looking particularly at para. (i), that the appellant was capable of spontaneously acting with such great violence as exhibited in the four offences demonstrates a failure to restrain his behaviour and a likelihood of causing death or injury to other persons through failure in the future to restrain his or her behaviour.

[61] Second, for reasons set out above, the trial judge also erred in requiring that the Crown demonstrate a relatively high level of intractability. The trial judge referred to this requirement on two occasions, at paras. 70 and 74:

> I find that the conduct of Mr. Szostak in connection with the offences relied upon by the Crown does not demonstrate the relatively high level of intractability required to find that the behaviour constitutes a pattern of conduct contemplated by s. 753(1)(a)(i) and (ii).
>
> • • •
>
> Also explicit in one form or another in each subparagraph of s. 753 is the requirement that the court must be satisfied that the pattern of conduct is substantially or pathologically intractable (see R. v. Lyons supra para. 43 [p. 338]). That is why most convicted criminals are not at real risk of being designated as dangerous offenders even where they could be said to represent a danger to public safety. The legislation is intended to capture a small group of highly dangerous criminals rather than snare [a] large group of common recidivists (see R. v. Neve, supra at para. 79).

[62] As I have said, the present legislation does not require intractability as a necessary element for a finding of dangerous offender. Intractability will be an important consideration for the sentencing judge in deciding what disposition to impose under s. 753(4) and (4.1).

[63] In my view, but for these errors in law, the trial judge would have found the appellant to be a dangerous offender. The appellant's repeated resort to force that caused serious injuries shows the necessary pattern under either para. (i) or (ii). There were sufficient relevant similarities to demonstrate the pattern called for in these paragraphs. As the court said in Neve at para. 113: "Similarity … can be found not only in the types of offences but also in the degree of violence or aggression threatened or inflicted on the victims." Over a very short period, four years, the appellant seriously injured three different people. He resorted to weapons in three of the offences and inflicted serious injuries. The trial judge's statement, at para. 69 of his reasons, that "[n]one of the injuries inflicted on the victims were life threatening or intended to be so," places too high a burden on the Crown and fails to reflect the gravity of the offences. Breaking a beer bottle over a person in a bar because of a dispute about standing in line; slashing a person with a pair of scissors because the appellant mistakenly thought the victim had some time earlier been involved in an altercation with him; beating an acquaintance so badly that he needed to go to hospital; and a year later slashing that same person with a knife across the face causing

permanent injury demonstrate the very type of pattern intended to be captured by paras. (i) and (ii).

[64] I would set aside the sentence imposed by the trial judge and, pursuant to s. 759(3)(a)(i), find that the offender is a dangerous offender. The question of further disposition poses some difficulty. Crown counsel concedes that it would not be appropriate to impose a sentence of indeterminate detention. It is apparent from the dialogue between counsel and the trial judge that the trial judge mistakenly was of the view that a finding of long-term offender was not available, even if the appellant was not found to be a dangerous offender. The trial judge appears to have been of the view that s. 753.1 applied only to sexual offences. This is a misreading of the section. The long-term offender designation is mandatory for certain sex offenders in the circumstances set out in s. 753.1(2), but this does not take away from the ability to find a person to be a long-term offender under the general provision in s. 753.1(1):

> 753.1(1) The court may, on application made under this Part following the filing of an assessment report under subsection 752.1(2), find an offender to be a long-term offender if it is satisfied that
>> (a) it would be appropriate to impose a sentence of imprisonment of two years or more for the offence for which the offender has been convicted;
>> (b) there is a substantial risk that the offender will reoffend; and
>> (c) there is a reasonable possibility of eventual control of the risk in the community.

[65] In the result, the trial judge gave no consideration to the possibility of a long-term supervision disposition and went right to the question of the length of a conventional sentence. The findings of fact by the trial judge, based on his acceptance of the evidence of Dr. Chaimowitz and Dr. Mamak, strongly suggest that the appellant should be subject to a long-term supervision order:

- The appellant may be classed as a violent offender;
- If the necessary rehabilitation is not carried out the appellant is likely to reoffend in a violent manner;
- The appellant has spent a good part of his adulthood running into difficulties with the law with two prior serious assaults on his record;
- He can be quite impulsive and aggressive;
- While not a psychopath, he has a history of anti-social behaviours meeting the criteria for Anti-Social Personality Disorder;
- He has had some substance abuse issues in the past but has no active mental disorders such as psychotic disorders, major mood disorders or anxiety disorders;
- The appellant has lived in a prosocial world in the now distant past and is able to easily articulate a prosocial view of the world and a potential path for him that avoids the criminal activities he has engaged in over his last several years;
- The appellant has not completed treatment programs beside anger management courses at the Hamilton-Wentworth Detention Centre during his recent incarceration;
- Risk reduction strategies that would be useful would be to ensure that he is absolutely abstinent from drugs and alcohol as they are accelerants to violence;

- If he were to be released into the community it would be important that he stay abstinent from drugs and alcohol and should be closely monitored in the community to ensure the avoidance of anti-social peers or colleagues as well as providing sufficient oversight to reduce the likelihood of him acting out in anti-social fashion;
- Absent intervention the appellant runs the risk of causing harm to others and posing a threat to life, safety and physical as well as mental well-being;
- Should the appellant receive psychological attention, including anger management, substance abuse treatment, psychological oversight and monitoring, it is reasonable to expect that there may be an opportunity for substantial control of the risk in the community.

[66] These findings of fact are entitled to deference and while they show that a sentence of two years or more is required and that there is a substantial risk that the appellant will reoffend, these findings also support the view that there is a reasonable possibility of eventual control of the risk in the community.

[67] On the other hand, in my view, this is not a case for a conventional sentence. Such a sentence would not adequately protect the public and would therefore be inconsistent with s. 753(4.1). The expert and other evidence shows that the appellant requires a lengthy period of supervision and monitoring to protect the public. A conventional sentence, even one followed by strict parole supervision would, on the evidence, not be sufficient. In my view, after taking into account the pre-sentence custody, a sentence of an additional five years imprisonment followed by a ten-year supervision order would be appropriate.

Disposition

[68] Accordingly, I would allow the Crown appeal, set aside the conventional sentence imposed by the trial judge and impose a total sentence of five years imprisonment followed by a ten-year supervision order.

R v Toutsaint
2015 SKCA 117

CALDWELL JA (Richards and Whitmore JJA concurring):

I. Introduction

[1] The Crown appeals against a determinate sentence of three years imprisonment and subsequent five-year long-term supervision order imposed on Joey John Toutsaint following his designation as a dangerous offender pursuant to ss. 753(1)(a)(i) and (ii) of the *Criminal Code* (see *R v Toutsaint*, 2014 SKPC 172, 455 Sask R 117). The Crown says the sentencing judge committed errors of law and ignored the evidence in reaching his conclusion under s. 753(4.1) that there is a reasonable expectation a lesser measure than an indeterminate sentence will adequately protect the public against the commission by Mr. Toutsaint of murder or a serious personal injury offence [SPIO]. For the reasons that

follow, I would allow the appeal and, pursuant to s. 759(3)(a) of the *Criminal Code*, impose a sentence of detention in a penitentiary for an indeterminate period.

II. Background

[2] The predicate SPIO is robbery. Briefly, in July 2009, Mr. Toutsaint, then aged 22, robbed an individual of $20, threatening to gut him with a knife. When the police arrived, Mr. Toutsaint gave a false name, physically resisted his arrest and assaulted the arresting officer. By that time, Mr. Toutsaint had amassed a record of 57 criminal convictions. He has since been convicted of 17 additional criminal offences.

[3] Following his conviction on the predicate offence, the Crown applied for a danger-ous offender designation under s. 753(1) of the *Criminal Code*. In the course of his reasons for decision on that application, the sentencing judge—who had not presided over the trial—comprehensively reviewed Mr. Toutsaint's criminal history leading up to and includ-ing the predicate offence (at paras. 12-37) and his history of offending and other behaviour while incarcerated (at paras. 38-60). There is no reason to revisit this information as the Crown accepts the sentencing judge's recounting of it is accurate; however, the following synopsis of Mr. Toutsaint's involvement with the criminal justice system is useful:

(a) Although not yet 30 years old, Mr. Toutsaint has nearly 30 convictions for violent, sexual, threatening or weapons-related offences on his record, eight of which arose *after* he committed the predicate offence.

(b) Mr. Toutsaint has spent most of his adult life in prison and the majority of that time has been spent in segregation, whether on a voluntary or involuntary basis; he consistently refuses to leave segregation, seemingly because he would then have to take programming.

(c) Mr. Toutsaint has never completed any programming geared toward his rehabili-tation because he either refuses to participate or purposely sabotages his own participation; to paraphrase his probation officer, Mr. Toutsaint is not engaged to do anything to better himself; and his parole officer testified Mr. Toutsaint is unmotivated, has no interest in any programming that could reduce his risk factors and prefers segregation to any other proposal.

(d) Mr. Toutsaint is either stubbornly uncooperative or threateningly disruptive with his healthcare providers; he does not comply with treatment directions; and he has sold or given away medications prescribed to him.

(e) Mr. Toutsaint has denounced Aboriginal Elders as "pieces of shit and … liars" and refuses to avail himself of their assistance or advice.

(f) He has little to no family support and no one has ever visited or called him in prison.

(g) More than once, Mr. Toutsaint's fellow inmates have acted preventively to disarm him—for their own protection—when he has fashioned or acquired a shank while residing with the general prison population.

(h) Due to his intractable, violent behaviour, Correctional Services Canada has considered transferring Mr. Toutsaint to the special handling unit at Ste-Anne-des-Plaines Institution in Québec, which is reserved for the most unmanageable offenders in the federal corrections system.

(i)   The National Parole Board has held Mr. Toutsaint to the warrant expiry date of more than one sentence.

(j)   When he has been released from custody at warrant expiry, Mr. Toutsaint has been subjected to orders under s. 810.2 of the *Criminal Code* in the interests of public safety.

(k)   Mr. Toutsaint's criminal record evinces unrestrained contumacy; when released into the community, he violates or breaches his bail, probation or s. 810.2 orders, usually within weeks.

[4]   As to the nature and quality of his risk of reoffending, in the expert assessments of the psychologist and psychiatrist who testified before the sentencing judge, Mr. Toutsaint is and remains at high risk to reoffend violently.

[5]   Dr. Roger W. Holden, a clinical psychologist appointed by the court, interviewed Mr. Toutsaint in October of 2010 and 2013. In his assessment (summarized at paras. 62-68 of the sentencing judge's reasons), Mr. Toutsaint does not suffer from any major mental illness but likely suffers from fetal alcohol spectrum disorder; he has little or no insight into his violent behaviour; he either denies responsibility or blames his victims for his violence; his release plan is not feasible; he is highly impulsive, reactive and explosive; he is a high risk to reoffend violently and sexually; and he is entirely unresponsive to treatment. As the sentencing judge put it (at para. 67), Dr. Holden concluded in 2010 that "unless treated successfully, Mr. Toutsaint will continue to re-offend violently."

[6]   On the basis of his later 2013 interview, Dr. Holden reported Mr. Toutsaint had *no interest* in programming, treatment or in working with Elders and he said this was the chief obstacle to reducing Mr. Toutsaint's risk. He was concerned Mr. Toutsaint had decided to eschew all family support upon release. He described Mr. Toutsaint as "highly dominant and overly aggressive" and said Mr. Toutsaint had little sympathy or patience for anyone who stands in his way. Dr. Holden concluded Mr. Toutsaint's violent and threatening conduct while incarcerated was "quite purposive"—it was about getting what he wanted. He assessed Mr. Toutsaint's prognosis as poor and said Mr. Toutsaint's exhibited preference for segregation prevented him from participating in any treatment. While Dr. Holden was not at all confident Mr. Toutsaint would participate in programming, he was confident that, until Mr. Toutsaint did so, he would remain a high-risk violent offender. Even if he were released, Dr. Holden opined Mr. Toutsaint would have to be released into a highly-structured and supportive community program and would have to commit to sobriety and a crime-free lifestyle.

[7]   Mr. Toutsaint retained Dr. Mansfield Mela, a forensic psychiatrist, to assess him and prepare a report for the sentencing judge. In Dr. Mela's opinion (summarized at paras. 71-72 of the sentencing judge's reasons), Mr. Toutsaint is at high risk to reoffend violently and will likely reoffend unless he participates in programming. He thought Mr. Toutsaint's risk of reoffending *might* improve if he participated in and benefited from high-intensity anger management and violence prevention programming alongside continued access to anti-depressants, trauma therapy, drug therapy and substance abuse treatment. But, most notably, Dr. Mela reported that Mr. Toutsaint had told Dr. Mela that he would *not* participate in such programming. And, while Dr. Mela thought there had been some improvement in Mr. Toutsaint's behaviour by October 2013, it is clear from Dr. Mela's testimony that he formed this opinion on the basis of the less-than-truthful

information provided by Mr. Toutsaint. On the basis of these representations, Dr. Mela also largely misconstrued the nature of Mr. Toutsaint's imprisonment from 2011 to 2013 at the Edmonton maximum security facility; not understanding Mr. Toutsaint had spent almost the entirety of his time in the Edmonton Institution in segregation. Dr. Mela was also unaware Mr. Toutsaint had threatened to kill the chairperson of the segregation review board and a corrections officer in July 2013. Additionally, while Dr. Mela expressed some hope upon learning Mr. Toutsaint was taking anti-depressants, three weeks after Dr. Mela had interviewed him, Mr. Toutsaint sabotaged his own treatment by selling his medication to other inmates.

[8]   Even assuming Mr. Toutsaint were receptive to programming, received the programming he needs and benefited from it, Drs. Holden and Mela both observed the need for significant positive community support under an intensely-structured, gradual release into the community; whereas, the evidence before the sentencing judge was that Mr. Toutsaint has almost no family support and there is no programming of the highly-intensive nature required to address Mr. Toutsaint's risk available in his home community of Black Lake, Saskatchewan, and there was *no evidence* of such programming or any support system being available in Toronto, Ontario, where Mr. Toutsaint had alternatively proposed he be released. For this reason, the sentencing judge pointedly described Mr. Toutsaint's ill-conceived release plans as "unrealistic."

[9]   As the sentencing judge correctly concluded, the evidence adduced at Mr. Toutsaint's dangerous offender hearing had very clearly established that he meets the criteria set out under ss. 753(1)(a)(i) and (ii) for a dangerous offender designation. And, Mr. Toutsaint does not challenge this designation or the determinate sentence he received in consequence thereof. But, the Crown challenges the analysis, factual findings and legal conclusions of the sentencing judge as they relate to his decision to impose a determinate sentence on Mr. Toutsaint. I turn now to address the Crown's allegations of error in this regard.

• • •

[13]   Nonetheless, having found Mr. Toutsaint met the criteria for a dangerous offender designation, the sentencing judge still sought to determine whether Mr. Toutsaint instead might meet the criteria for a long-term offender designation, invoking *R v Casemore*, 2011 SKCA 14, 366 Sask R 149 and *R v Johnson*, 2003 SCC 46, [2003] 2 SCR 357. By doing so, the sentencing judge committed an error of law by relying on repealed provisions of the *Criminal Code* and case law setting out a process rendered nugatory by the 2008 amendments.

[14]   While he concedes the error, Mr. Toutsaint submits we should ignore it. He says what matters is the sentencing judge went on to properly analyse the matter on the basis of the current, applicable law. Setting aside—for the moment—the Crown's allegations of error in respect of that analysis, I am hard pressed to ignore the sentencing judge's finding under the analysis formerly called for by Part XXIV—*i.e.*, that Mr. Toutsaint did not meet the criteria for a long-term offender designation. I say this because that finding was predicated on the sentencing judge's conclusion that the evidence disclosed *no reasonable possibility* of eventual control of the substantial risk that Mr. Toutsaint will reoffend in the community (see s. 753.1(1)(c) and *R v Goforth*, 2007 SKCA 144, 302 Sask R 265).

[15]   To be clear as to what this means, the sentencing judge properly cited *R v Goforth* (at para. 54) for the proposition that a *reasonable possibility* of eventual control of the risk of reoffending in the community "must involve something more than hope or empty

conjecture." Furthermore, when he evaluated the relevant psychological evidence in the light of this explanation from *R v Goforth*, the sentencing judge said this:

> [106] With respect, Dr. Holden's conclusion that Mr. Toutsaint at the time of that examination met the criteria for Long-term Offender status was based on a misconstruction of the legal standard. The possibility of eventual risk control must be reasonable, and the standard of reasonableness in law invariably requires that a premise be objectively demonstrable through evidence. *The possibility that the accused is treatable, pointed to by Dr. Holden in his reports of both 2010 and 2013, is not demonstrable on the facts he found: it is speculative.* Dr. Holden believes that in order for the risk posed by Mr. Toutsaint to be managed, Mr. Toutsaint would have to engage with programming while incarcerated, be released into a highly structured and supportive community program, and commit himself to sobriety and a crime free lifestyle. *As Mr. Toutsaint has not taken any steps to demonstrate his commitment to fulfilling any of these conditions, the possibility of eventually controlling his risk cannot be objectively demonstrated.*
>
> [107] Similarly, Dr. Mela expresses the "guarded hope" that the risk Mr. Toutsaint poses could be controlled through intensive multi-pronged programming and a highly structured and supported gradual re-release into the community. Dr. Mela also offered the opinion that Mr. Toutsaint fit the criteria for Long-term Offender status. However, the cautious optimism expressed by Dr. Mela is contingent upon suitable programming being both available to and embraced by the accused. *As noted, the past and present behaviour of Mr. Toutsaint makes this possibility highly speculative at best. Without a realistic plan for Mr. Toutsaint's reintegration, and considering the extent to which Mr. Toutsaint has resisted programming in the past, the designation of Long-Term Offender is not appropriate.*

(*R v Toutsaint*; Emphasis added)

[16] Although by law these findings were not called for, they are nevertheless quite difficult to ignore because they are so entirely at odds with the sentencing judge's later finding:

> [114] I am satisfied by the vast amount of evidence adduced during the hearing of this application that *there is a "reasonable expectation"* that a lesser measure [than an indeterminate sentence] will adequately protect the public against the commission by the offender of murder or a serious personal injury offence.

(*R v Toutsaint*; Emphasis added)

[17] These two sets of findings are contradictory by reason of the nature of the legal standards upon which they are based. That is to say, s. 753(4.1) sets out a narrower standard—*i.e.*, whether there is a reasonable *expectation*—than the standard set out under s. 753.1(1)(*c*)—*i.e.*, whether there is a reasonable *possibility*—of controlling the risk posed by a dangerous offender. ... And, therefore, a finding by a court that the evidence does not satisfy the broader test under s. 753.1(1)(c) *necessarily precludes* satisfaction of the narrower test under s. 753(4.1). In this way, the sentencing judge's reasons contain a contradiction that cannot be reconciled by simply ignoring his finding under s. 753.1(1)(c); one of his findings must fall to appellate review as it must have been borne of a reversible error of law.

[18] In that regard, I conclude the sentencing judge's finding under s. 753(4.1)—and the determinate sentence he imposed in consequence thereof—must be set aside on the law and on the evidence before the Court. I will first explain the legal significance of the contradiction in the sentencing judge's findings. I will then address the factual grounds that lead to the conclusion that there was *no evidence* before the sentencing judge upon which he could have concluded a lesser measure than a sentence of detention in a penitentiary for an indeterminate period could reasonably be expected to adequately protect the public from the commission by Mr. Toutsaint of murder or an SPIO.

• • •

[21] Put into context, the sentencing judge incorrectly sought to determine whether an indeterminate sentence of imprisonment *was a fit sentence* for Mr. Toutsaint, and this led him to ask the wrong questions. For example, he asked whether Mr. Toutsaint belonged in a category with "the most dangerous violent offenders and sexual predators who have shown repeatedly a complete inability to control their impulses" (at para. 108). He asked whether the relative gravity of just three of the SPIOs Mr. Toutsaint had committed outside prison were "such as to justify an indeterminate sentence" (at para. 115). He asked whether any of the SPIOs Mr. Toutsaint had committed had resulted in a serious personal injury (at para. 115)—thereby minimising Mr. Toutsaint's offending history by improperly distinguishing between a serious personal injury offence and an offence that results in a serious personal injury (see *R v Steele*).

[22] In general terms, the sentencing judge's inquiries all largely overlook the fact the principle of proportionality is already built into Part XXIV of the *Criminal Code* by way of the prerequisite commission of an SPIO, which acts as "a gatekeeper to ensure that the sentence is not disproportionate to the offence" … .

• • •

[24] Put simply, inquiry into the relative seriousness or gravity of the predicate offence or of any other SPIO committed by a dangerous offender may lend to an assessment of the *risk* posed by an offender and whether it can be managed (see *R v Daniels*, 2011 SKCA 67 at para 61, 271 CCC (3d) 339), but the focus of the inquiry called for by s. 753(4.1) is properly the nature and quality of the offender's propensity for committing violent crimes in the future, not the proportionality of the sentence to the relative severity of violent crimes committed in the past.

[25] On this basis, I find the sentencing judge committed clear errors of law in the exercise of his discretion under s. 753(4.1) by conducting an inquiry into factors irrelevant to the determination called for by that subsection. For this reason, I would set aside the sentencing judge's determination under s. 753(4.1) that there is a reasonable expectation that a lesser measure than a sentence of detention in a penitentiary for an indeterminate period would adequately protect the public from the commission by Mr. Toutsaint of murder or an SPIO.

[26] This means I must conduct the analysis called for under s. 753(4.1) afresh. But, this does not mean all of the sentencing judge's evidentiary findings must be set aside. While the Crown can point to a number of problems with the findings of fact made by the sentencing judge, only one bears comment; because, it illustrates—from an evidentiary basis—the inevitable conclusion under s. 753(4.1) that the sentencing judge erred in imposing a determinate sentence in this case.

• • •

[29] However, when the sentencing judge turned to s. 753(4.1) and asked (erroneously) whether an indeterminate period of imprisonment was a fit sentence in the circumstances, he wholly recast the same expert evidence, saying "both experts agree that there is a reasonable amount of hope, given his age and antecedents" (at para. 115). This characterisation is not supported by the evidence as neither of two expert's reports or testimony—even in the most favourable light—may be taken to endorse that conclusion.

[30] Finally, the sentencing judge plainly concluded there was *no reasonable possibility* of controlling the risk posed by Mr. Toutsaint "[w]ithout a realistic plan for Mr. Toutsaint's reintegration" (at para. 107). He then later concluded Mr. Toutsaint's release plan was "unrealistic at this time" (at para. 137). These conclusions are undoubtedly supported by the evidence. Both experts agreed Mr. Toutsaint required highly-intensive programming to reduce his risk to a manageable level before release into the community under a highly-structured long-term supervision order. But, notwithstanding this, the sentencing judge ended his decision on these terms:

> [137] His release plan is unrealistic at this time. To be released in Toronto and to then find a job to support himself is not realistic given his lack of education and lack of community and family support. Similarly a release plan to reside in Black Lake, his community of origin, would also seem to be unrealistic given that his family connections there are tenuous and the overall lack of the programming that he will need to survive. That programming would however be available in Prince Albert.
>
> [138] But simply because he has no family members left to help him transition does not seem to me to be an adequate reason to lock up this young aboriginal offender for the rest of his life. Through no real fault of his own, his path in life was laid down many years ago with the death of his primary caregiver, his grandfather, and the subsequent and most tragic death of his mother.
>
> [139] He deserves another chance.

This too was misplaced on the law. In *R v Lyons* at p. 329, La Forest J. held that preventive detention under Part XXIV "represents a judgment that the relative importance of the objectives of rehabilitation, deterrence and retribution are greatly attenuated in the circumstances of the individual case, and that of prevention, correspondingly increased" (see also *R v Steele* at para. 35). And, bluntly, there was just *no evidence* before the sentencing judge capable of supporting his finding that a lesser measure than indeterminate imprisonment could adequately protect the public from the very real risk to the life, safety and physical or mental well-being of other persons that Mr. Toutsaint poses.

IV. Conclusion

[31] For these reasons, I would allow the Crown's appeal, set aside the three-year determinate sentence and five-year long-term supervision order and, pursuant to s. 759(3)(a) of the *Criminal Code*, impose upon Mr. Toutsaint a sentence of detention in a penitentiary for an indeterminate period. As no appeal was taken from the ancillary, DNA and firearms orders, they remain in place.

For an analysis and criticism of *Toutsaint*, see Tim Quigley, "*R. v. Toutsaint*: Dangerous Offender Proceedings in Saskatchewan" (2016), 27 CR (7th) 17. The author, noting that the Court of Appeal reversed the sentence of three years imprisonment followed by five years long-term supervision and replaced it with an indeterminate sentence, remarked that "although the sentencing judge was certainly alive to the requirements of section 718.2(e), *R. v. Gladue* and *R. v. Ipeelee*, the Court of Appeal made no mention of them in its decision."

E. The Presumption: Three Strikes You're Dangerous

With an ambitious name, the *Tackling Violent Crime Act*, SC 2008, c 6 (in force 2 July 2008) created a presumption that would satisfy the criteria set out in s 753(1)(a) or (b) "unless the contrary is proved on the balance of probabilities."

> *Presumption*
> 753(1.1) If the court is satisfied that the offence for which the offender is convicted is a primary designated offence for which it would be appropriate to impose a sentence of imprisonment of two years or more and that the offender was convicted previously at least twice of a primary designated offence and was sentenced to at least two years of imprisonment for each of those convictions, the conditions in paragraph (1)(a) or (b), as the case may be, are presumed to have been met unless the contrary is proved on the balance of probabilities.

A primary designated offence is defined in s 752 by a long list of sexual and violent offences. Given the impact of this presumption on the conduct of dangerous offender proceedings, it was subsequently challenged on Charter grounds in the case of *R v Hill*, below.

R v Hill

2012 ONSC 5050, 291 CCC (3d) 321 (footnotes omitted)

BRYANT J:

[1] Roland Hill was convicted on January 11, 2000 of a sexual assault and received a custodial sentence of two years and six months. On September 20, 2004, Mr. Hill was convicted of assault causing bodily harm. He was sentenced to two years less one day after receiving eleven months' credit for five and one-half months pre-trial custody on a two-for-one basis.

[2] On July 26, 2010, Mr. Roland Hill pled guilty before this Court to two serious personal injury offences, one of which is also classified as a primary designated offence under s. 752 of the *Criminal Code*.

[3] The Crown sought an order that Mr. Hill be designated a dangerous offender. The Crown relied, in part, upon the presumption set out in s. 753(1.1) (*Tackling Violent Crime Act*, S.C. 2008, c. 6, in force July 2, 2008). Section 753(1.1) provides that if an offender is convicted of a primary designated offence for which it would be appropriate to impose a sentence of imprisonment of two years or more and the offender was previously convicted at least twice of a primary designated offence and was sentenced to at least two years of imprisonment for each of those convictions, the dangerous offender criteria (s. 753(1)(a) or (b)) are presumed to have been satisfied unless the contrary is proven on a balance of probabilities.

[4] Mr. Hill seeks an Order declaring that s. 753(1.1) of the *Criminal Code* is invalid and of no force or effect pursuant to s. 52 of the *Constitution Act, 1982*. Counsel for Mr. Hill submits that s. 753(1.1) infringes s. 7, s. 11(d) and s. 12 of the *Canadian Charter of Rights and Freedoms*.

• • •

[13] Mr. Hill was "convicted previously at least twice of a primary designated offence." On January 11, 2000, Mr. Hill was convicted of sexual assault (s. 271) and was sentenced to two years and six months for that offence. On September 20, 2004, Mr. Hill was convicted of assault causing bodily harm (s. 267(b)) and was sentenced to two years less one day after receiving eleven months' credit for five and one-half months pre-trial custody on a two-for-one basis (*R. v. Hill*, 2004 CarswellOnt 6217, [2004] O.J. No. 6276 (O.C.J.), aff'd 2005 CanLII 6783, [2004] O.J. No. 604 (C.A.)).

[14] On December 21, 2011, the Court ruled that the sentence imposed on September 20, 2004 for assault causing bodily harm was the equivalent of a sentence of two years and eleven months after having regard for the pre-trial incarceration credited to Mr. Hill by the trial judge (*R. v. Hill*, 2011 ONSC 7623, [2011] O.J. No. 6183).

[15] Mr. Hill was hospitalized before the commencement of the hearing and again after the completion of the Crown's case. He was returned to the Elgin-Middlesex Detention Centre pending the continuation of the hearing. The proceeding was delayed to allow counsel for Mr. Hill an opportunity to obtain funding from Legal Aid Ontario to retain a defence expert. The Court further adjourned the proceeding to allow the defence expert to conduct an assessment of Mr. Hill.

• • •

[17] Counsel for Mr. Hill submitted that s. 753(1.1) violates the presumption of innocence because proof of the basic facts does not lead inexorably to the conclusion that core dangerous offender criteria are satisfied (*R. v. Lyons*, [1987] 2 S.C.R. 309, at 350-353, 362, 44 D.L.R. (4th) 193; *R. v. Oakes*, [1986] 1 S.C.R. 103, 24 C.C.C. (3d) 321; *R. v. Downey*, [1992] 2 S.C.R. 10, at 30, 72 C.C.C. (3d) 1).

[18] Counsel for Mr. Hill submits that the presumption set out in s. 753(1.1) presumes that Mr. Hill is a dangerous offender unless the offender proves to a balance of probabilities that he does not satisfy the criteria in ss. 753(1)(a) or (b). Counsel argues that the statutory criteria set out in ss. 753(1)(a) or (b) are aggravating sentencing factors which must be proven by the Crown beyond a reasonable doubt (*R. v. Gardiner*, [1982] 2 S.C.R. 368, 140 D.L.R. (3d) 612; *R. v. Pearson*, [1992] 3 S.C.R. 665, 77 C.C.C. (3d) 124; *R. v. D.B.*, 2008 SCC 25, [2008] 2 S.C.R. 3, at paras. 78-80, 231 C.C.C. (3d) 338; *R. v. Currie*, [1997] 2 S.C.R. 260, at para. 25, 42, 115 C.C.C. (3d) 205; *R. v. Jackson*, [1981] N.S.J. No. 406, (1981), 61 C.C.C. (2d) 540, at paras. 174 (N.S.C.A.); *R. v. Vanderwal*, 2010 ONSC 265, [2010] O.J. No. 246, at para. 21).

[19] Counsel submits that the reversal of the burden of proof for aggravating factors violates principles of fundamental justice contrary to s. 7 of the *Charter* (*R. v. D.B.*, 2008 SCC 25, [2008] 2 S.C.R. 3, at paras. 25-27, 37-39; *R. v. Pearson*, at 683, 686).

• • •

[22] Crown counsel submits that s. 11(d) of the *Charter* creates a procedural and evidentiary rule which operates at trial requiring the prosecution to prove the guilt of the accused beyond a reasonable doubt. Counsel argues that s. 753(1.1) does not contravene the presumption of innocence protected by s. 11(d) of the *Charter* because Mr. Hill pled

guilty to the two offences committed on January 9, 2010 and the presumption of innocence is no longer a live issue (*R. v. Morales*, [1992] 3 S.C.R. 711, at 735, 77 C.C.C. (3d) 91).

[23] Crown counsel acknowledges that the Crown must prove contested aggravating facts beyond a reasonable doubt (*R. v. Gardiner*, *supra*; *R. v. Pearson*, *supra*). Counsel submits that it must prove the basic "facts" that the offender has been previously convicted twice of primary designated offences for which a sentence of two years or more was imposed and that the index offence is a primary designated offence for which a sentence of two years or more is appropriate. Counsel argues that once these "facts" are proven beyond a reasonable doubt, it is presumed that the criteria set out in ss. 753(1)(a) and (b) have been met. Counsel argues that this determination is "a legal conclusion as opposed to an aggravating fact."

· · ·

[28] Section 753(1.1) is a rule of substantive law which prescribes a particular legal consequence upon proof of particularized basic facts (James B. Thayer, "Presumptions and the Law of Evidence" (1889) 3 Harvard L. Rev. 141 at 149). A statutory rebuttable presumption is a legal device mandating that, upon proof of a basic fact(s), another fact is presumed.

[29] The proponent of the s. 753(1.1) rebuttable presumption has the onus to prove the basic facts beyond a reasonable doubt (*R. v. Egger*, [1993] 2 S.C.R. 451, at 474-475, 103 D.L.R. (4th) 678). Once the Crown proves the basic facts beyond a reasonable doubt, Mr. Hill has the persuasive (legal) burden to overcome the legal consequence of the presumption. Accordingly, s. 753(1.1) assists the prosecutor to prove that Mr. Hill is a dangerous offender and it compels Mr. Hill to rebut the presumption by satisfying a persuasive (legal) burden of proof on a balance of probabilities standard.

[30] The presumption created by s. 753(1.1) requires the Crown to prove three basic facts beyond a reasonable doubt:

1. the index offence for which the offender is convicted is a primary designated offence for which it would be appropriate to impose a sentence of imprisonment of two years or more;
2. the offender was convicted previously at least twice of a primary designated offence; and,
3. the offender was sentenced to at least two years of imprisonment for each of those convictions.

· · ·

[43] The majority of the Supreme Court in *R. v. Malmo-Levine*, 2003 SCC 74, [2003] 3 S.C.R. 571, at para. 96, rejected the "striking the right balance test." The Court proposed a three-prong test to determine the substance of the principles of fundamental justice:

> In short, for a rule or principle to constitute a principle of fundamental justice for the purposes of s. 7, it must be a legal principle about which there is significant societal consensus that it is fundamental to the way in which the legal system ought fairly to operate, and it must be identified with sufficient precision to yield a manageable standard against which to measure deprivations of life, liberty or security of the person.

[44] The presumption of innocence is the golden thread running throughout the web of English criminal law (*Woolmington v. D.P.P.*, [1935] A.C. 462, at 481 (H.L.)). In

Woolmington, the Law Lords held that the Crown has the burden to prove the elements of an offence beyond a reasonable doubt. An examination of values reflected by the legal system and its core rules confirm that the standard of proof beyond a reasonable doubt is not confined to elements of an offence. That standard is imposed generally whenever the Crown seeks to prove a fact that might adversely affect the liberty of the accused, including during the sentencing process.

• • •

[50] In *R. v. Oakes* (at p. 119), Chief Justice Dickson described the presumption of innocence which encompasses the standard of proof beyond a reasonable doubt as a "hallowed principle lying at the very heart of criminal law." His comment in *Gardiner*, that "crime and punishment are inextricably linked," and his message that the standard required by the presumption of innocence is no less important when facts relevant to sentencing are being proved, affirms that this basic principle is fundamental to the administration of justice in the context of criminal law.

• • •

[52] I therefore find:
  (i) the common law and the statutory law governing the onus and standard of proof for aggravating facts are "basic tenets of the legal system" which have "general acceptance among reasonable people";
  (ii) the onus and standard of proof are legal principles which have significant societal consensus that are fundamental to the way in which the legal system in Canada ought fairly to operate;
  (iii) the Crown's onus and standard of proof are standards against which to measure deprivations of life, liberty or security of the person; and,
  (iv) the onus and standard of proof for aggravating factors are principles of fundamental justice under the *Malmo-Levine* test.

• • •

[56] Section 753(1.1) creates a new rule allocating the burden of proof to an offender. Where the Crown proves the basic facts set out in s. 753(1.1), the offender must prove on a balance of probabilities that he is not a dangerous offender within the meaning of s. 753(1)(a) or (b). Section 753(1.1) is therefore a "reverse onus provision" as found in *R. v. Oakes*, and reverse onus provisions are *prima facie* in violation of the *Charter*. This is because they operate to permit a finding adverse to the liberty interest of the offender to be made "despite the existence of a reasonable doubt" (*R. v. Oakes*, at p. 132). Consider, for example, a case where the Crown proves the basic facts required for by s. 753(1.1) beyond a reasonable doubt, and where the accused, in response, presented evidence that did not disprove on a balance of probabilities that the required criteria of a dangerous offender finding under s. 753(1) were met. Even if that offender had managed to present sufficient evidence to raise a reasonable doubt about whether he was a dangerous offender within the meaning of s. 753(1), a Court would still be obliged to find that he was a dangerous offender pursuant to s. 753(1.1). Section 753(1.1) is therefore in *prima facie* violation of the principles of fundamental justice as it purports to require a dangerous offender finding to be made, even in the face of a reasonable doubt.

[57] In *R. v. D.B.*, the Supreme Court considered the constitutionality of s. 72(1) of the *Youth Criminal Justice Act*, S.C. 2002, c. 1, which operated in a similar manner in the sentencing context. The presumption provided that a young person 14 years or older who

committed an index offence shall be sentenced as an adult unless the young person persuades the court that a youth sentence was of sufficient length to hold the young person accountable for his or her offending behaviour.

[58]   In *R. v. D.B.*, the Supreme Court held that shifting the onus of proof to the young person to justify a youth sentence contravened a principle of fundamental justice that the Crown must prove aggravating factors upon which it relies on the beyond reasonable doubt standard. Justice Abella for the majority stated (at paras. 78, 81-82):

> The onus on the young person of satisfying the court of the sufficiency of the factors in s. 72(1) so that a youth sentence can be imposed also *contravenes what the Crown concedes in its factum is another principle of fundamental justice, namely, that the Crown is obliged to prove, beyond a reasonable doubt, any aggravating factors in sentencing on which it relies.* [emphasis added]

. . .

[59]   Section 753(1.1) takes away the "procedural benefit afforded to a convicted adult on sentencing, namely, that the burden is on the Crown to demonstrate why a more severe sentence is necessary and appropriate" (*R. v. D.B*, para. 82). Since s. 753(1.1) reverses the onus on the Crown to prove aggravating factors beyond a reasonable doubt, it contravenes s. 7 of the *Charter.*

[60]   As a result of the Court's conclusion that s. 753(1.1) breaches s. 7, it is unnecessary to consider and determine counsels' submissions whether s. 753(1.1) breaches s. 12 of the *Charter.*

. . .

[65]   I do not accept the Crown counsel's submission that there is a pressing need to streamline the process for labeling a small class of individuals as dangerous offenders. Government statistics concerning dangerous offenders do not indicate an urgent need for streamlining dangerous offender applications. Between 1978 and April 2005, 384 persons were designated as dangerous offenders. The number of persons designated as dangerous offenders increased from 8 in 1978 to a yearly average of 22 in the years 1995 to 2004. No women were found to be dangerous offenders during this period. Mr. Hill is an aboriginal and his community is over-represented, accounting for 20.3% of the dangerous offender population. A breach of an individual's s. 7 rights cannot be justified or condoned in a free and democratic society because the class of affected individuals is small.

. . .

[69]   The Court does not accept Crown counsel's argument that the presumption limits the rights of offenders in the least restrictive manner. As found above, s. 753(1.1) makes a fundamental change in the dangerous offender process by reversing the onus of proof which results in a significant infringement of s. 7 of the *Charter.*

[70]   The Supreme Court's reasoning in *R. v. D.B.* responds to the constitutionality of the s. 753(1.1) presumption. Although there is a rational connection between the imposition of an indeterminate sentence and the legislative objection to protect the public, it is a different question whether the reverse onus is a rational means of achieving the legislative objective (*Laba*, at p. 1008). In my view, it is the availability of an indeterminate sentence which advances the objective of the protection of the public rather than the allocation of the onus of proof to the offender. Further, the legislative objective of protecting the public can properly be served by placing the onus on the Crown to prove the s. 753(1)(a) or (b)

criteria without infringing the s. 7 rights of an offender. I find that s. 753(1.1) does not satisfy either the rational connection test or the minimal impairment test.

• • •

[74] The burden of proof on the balance of probabilities resting on the offender is oncrous because there are four discrete basis for an offender to be classified a dangerous offender under s. 753(1)(a)(i) or (ii) or (iii) or (b). Section 753(a)(i) contains the following elements: (1) a pattern is revealed by repetitive behaviour; (2) an element of the pattern is that the dangerous behaviour has not been restrained in the past; and, (3) a likelihood that the same behaviour in the future will not be restrained and will cause death or injury (*R. v. Dow*, [1999] B.C.J. No. 569, paras. 19-22; leave to appeal refused (1999), [1999] S.C.C.A. No. 302, 137 C.C.C. (3d) v (S.C.C.)). Section 753(b) criteria contains different elements: (1) the offender was convicted of a "personal injury offence" as described in s. 752(b); and, (2) there is a likelihood that the offender will cause injury, pain or other evil to other persons through the failure in the future to control his sexual impulses (*R. v. Currie*). Thus, the offender must satisfy the presiding judge that every element of each of the s. 753(a) or (b) criteria have been met on a balance of probabilities standard.

[75] Even if the offender proves on a balance of probabilities that the s. 753(a)(i) or s. 753(b) criteria have not been met, he will be presumed a dangerous offender because he failed to also prove on a balance of probabilities that the s. 753(a)(ii) or (iii) criteria were met. In my view, s. 753(1.1) constitutes a significant intrusion of an offender's s. 7 rights.

• • •

[78] The proof of the presumed fact (convictions of three designated offences) does not lead inexorably to proof of the presumed fact (proof of the s. 753(a) or (b) criteria). In my view, the s. 753(1.1) presumption is not internally rational.

• • •

[82] I find that s. 753(1.1) infringes the principles of fundamental justice guaranteed by s. 7 of the *Charter* and it cannot be saved by s. 1 (*R. v. D.B.*, at paras. 91-95).

[Unfortunately, Mr. Hill died before any further proceedings, including an appeal from this decision, could be taken. Subsequent cases have mentioned or distinguished *Hill*, but there does not appear to be any decision that has either adopted or rejected Bryant J's analysis of the constitutionality of s 753(1.1).]

III. LONG-TERM OFFENDERS

A. Background

As discussed in the introduction to this chapter, the long-term offender provisions were enacted in 1997. They were created on the recommendation of the Federal/Provincial/Territorial Task Force on High-Risk Violent Offenders. The provisions were designed to catch the type of offender who, while not worthy of the dangerous offender designation, still requires some form of preventive detention. Like the dangerous offender amendments, this measure arose from the government's (and the task force's) concern with "sexual predators." Remember that probation can be attached only to a sentence of imprisonment that is no longer than two years. The answer to this limitation was the creation of the long-term offender designation, which permits up to 10 years of supervision to be added onto a penitentiary sentence if the offender meets the "substantial risk" to reoffend standard in s 753.1. Thus the long-term offender designation was intended to be a middle ground between an indeterminate sentence and an ordinary fixed-term sanction. Between 1997 and April 14, 2013, Canadian courts imposed 832 long-term supervision orders, of which 70.4 percent were for a period of 10 years.

B. The Provisions

Application for finding that an offender is a long-term offender

753.1(1) The court may, on application made under this Part following the filing of an assessment report under subsection 752.1(2), find an offender to be a long-term offender if it is satisfied that

(a) it would be appropriate to impose a sentence of imprisonment of two years or more for the offence for which the offender has been convicted;

(b) there is a substantial risk that the offender will reoffend; and

(c) there is a reasonable possibility of eventual control of the risk in the community.

(2) The court shall be satisfied that there is a substantial risk that the offender will reoffend if

(a) the offender has been convicted of an offence under section 151 (sexual interference), 152 (invitation to sexual touching) or 153 (sexual exploitation), subsection 163.1(2) (making child pornography), 163.1(3) (distribution, etc., of child pornography), 163.1(4) (possession of child pornography) or 163.1(4.1) (accessing child pornography), section 170 (parent or guardian procuring sexual activity), 171 (householder permitting sexual activity), 171.1 (making sexually explicit material available to child), 172.1 (luring a child) or 172.2 (agreement or arrangement—sexual offence against child), subsection 173(2) (exposure) or section 271 (sexual assault), 272 (sexual assault with a weapon) 273 (aggravated sexual assault) or 279.011 (trafficking—person under 18 years) or subsection 279.02(2) (material benefit—trafficking of person under 18 years), 279.03(2) (withholding or destroying documents—trafficking of person under 18 years), 286.1(2) (obtaining sexual services for consideration from person under 18 years), 286.2(2) (material benefit from sexual services provided by person under 18 years) or 286.3(2) (procuring—person under 18 years), or has engaged in serious conduct of a sexual nature in the commission of another offence of which the offender has been convicted; and

(b) the offender

(i) has shown a pattern of repetitive behaviour, of which the offence for which he or she has been convicted forms a part, that shows a likelihood of the offender's causing death or injury to other persons or inflicting severe psychological damage on other persons, or

(ii) by conduct in any sexual matter including that involved in the commission of the offence for which the offender has been convicted, has shown a likelihood of causing injury, pain or other evil to other persons in the future through similar offences.

(3) If the court finds an offender to be a long-term offender, it shall

(a) impose a sentence for the offence for which the offender has been convicted, which must be a minimum punishment of imprisonment for a term of two years; and

(b) order that the offender be subject to long-term supervision for a period that does not exceed 10 years.

(3.1) The court may not impose a sentence under paragraph (3)(a) and the sentence that was imposed for the offence for which the offender was convicted stands despite the offender's being found to be a long-term offender, if the application was one that

(a) was made after the offender begins to serve the sentence in a case to which paragraphs 753(2)(a) and (b) apply; and

(b) was treated as an application under this section further to the court deciding to do so under paragraph 753(5)(a).

(4) and (5) [Repealed, 2008, c. 6, s. 44]

(6) If the court does not find an offender to be a long-term offender, the court shall impose sentence for the offence for which the offender has been convicted.

Long-term supervision

753.2(1) Subject to subsection (2), an offender who is subject to long-term supervision shall be supervised in the community in accordance with the *Corrections and Conditional Release Act* when the offender has finished serving

(a) the sentence for the offence for which the offender has been convicted; and

(b) all other sentences for offences for which the offender is convicted and for which sentence of a term of imprisonment is imposed on the offender, either before or after the conviction for the offence referred to in paragraph (a).

(2) A sentence imposed on an offender referred to in subsection (1), other than a sentence that requires imprisonment, is to be served concurrently with the long-term supervision.

(3) An offender who is required to be supervised, a member of the Parole Board of Canada or, on approval of that Board, the offender's parole supervisor, as defined in subsection 99(1) of the *Corrections and Conditional Release Act*, may apply to a superior court of criminal jurisdiction for an order reducing the period of long-term supervision or terminating it on the ground that the offender no longer presents a substantial risk of reoffending and thereby being a danger to the community. The onus of proving that ground is on the applicant.

(4) The applicant must give notice of an application under subsection (3) to the Attorney General at the time the application is made.

Breach of long-term supervision

753.3(1) An offender who, without reasonable excuse, fails or refuses to comply with long-term supervision is guilty of an indictable offence and liable to imprisonment for a term not exceeding 10 years.

(2) An accused who is charged with an offence under subsection (1) may be tried and punished by any court having jurisdiction to try that offence in the place where the offence is alleged to have been committed or in the place where the accused is found, is arrested or is in custody, but if the place where the accused is found, is arrested or is in custody is outside the province in which the offence is alleged to have been committed, no proceedings in respect of that offence shall be instituted in that place without the consent of the Attorney General of that province.

New offence

753.4(1) If an offender who is subject to long-term supervision commits one or more offences under this or any other Act and a court imposes a sentence of imprisonment for the offence or offences, the long-term supervision is interrupted until the offender has finished serving all the sentences, unless the court orders its termination.

(2) A court that imposes a sentence of imprisonment under subsection (1) may order a reduction in the length of the period of the offender's long-term supervision.

C. Applying the Provisions

R v Ipeelee
2012 SCC 13, [2012] 1 SCR 433

LeBEL J (McLachlin CJ and Binnie, Deschamps, Fish, and Abella JJ concurring):

[The *Ipeelee* decision deals with the sentence for a breach of a long-term supervision order. It is an important part of Canadian jurisprudence dealing with Aboriginal offenders and s 718.2(e) of the Code. It is discussed in detail in Chapters 2 and 16. Here, we have included only the general discussion of the long-term offender regime.]

[43] The rationale for the dangerous offender designation can be contrasted with that of the long-term offender provisions, which were not introduced to the *Criminal Code* until 1997. That year, extensive amendments were made to Part XXIV of the *Criminal Code* by Bill C-55 (*An Act to amend the Criminal Code (high risk offenders), the Corrections and Conditional Release Act, the Criminal Records Act, the Prisons and Reformatories Act and the Department of the Solicitor General Act*, S.C. 1997, c. 17). These amendments, following the recommendations of the Federal/Provincial/Territorial Task Force on High-Risk Violent Offenders (the "Task Force"), introduced the long-term offender designation and the availability of LTSOs [long-term supervision orders]. The Task Force noted that a lacuna existed in the law whereby serious offenders were denied the support of extended community supervision, except through the parole process. LTSOs were designed to fill this gap and supplement the all-or-nothing alternatives of definite or indefinite detention (Report of the Federal/Provincial/Territorial Task Force on High-Risk Violent Offenders, *Strategies for Managing High-Risk Offenders* (1995)).

[44] Section 753.1(1) of the *Criminal Code* now directs when a court may designate an offender as a long-term offender. The section states:

> 753.1(1) The court may, on application made under this Part following the filing of an assessment report under subsection 752.1(2), find an offender to be a long-term offender if it is satisfied that
>> (a) it would be appropriate to impose a sentence of imprisonment of two years or more for the offence for which the offender has been convicted;
>> (b) there is a substantial risk that the offender will reoffend; and
>> (c) there is a reasonable possibility of eventual control of the risk in the community.

If the court finds an offender to be a long-term offender, it must impose a sentence of two years or more for the predicate offence and order that the offender be subject to long-term supervision for a period not exceeding ten years (*Criminal Code*, s. 753.1(3)).

[45] LTSOs are administered in accordance with the *Corrections and Conditional Release Act*, S.C. 1992, c. 20 ("*CCRA*"). LTSOs must include the conditions set out in s. 161(1) of the *Corrections and Conditional Release Regulations*, SOR/92-620. In addition, the National Parole Board ("NPB") may include any other condition "that it considers reasonable and necessary in order to protect society and to facilitate the successful reintegration into society of the offender" (*CCRA*, s. 134.1(2)). A member of the NPB may suspend an LTSO when an offender breaches any of the LTSO conditions, or where the

NPB is satisfied that suspension is necessary and reasonable to prevent such a breach or to protect society (*CCRA*, s. 135.1(1)). Offenders serve the duration of the period of suspension in a federal penitentiary. Failure or refusal to comply with an LTSO is also an indictable offence under s. 753.3(1) of the *Criminal Code*, punishable by up to ten years' imprisonment.

[46] According to the *CCRA*, "[t]he purpose of conditional release is to contribute to the maintenance of a just, peaceful and safe society by means of decisions on the timing and conditions of release that will best facilitate the rehabilitation of offenders and their reintegration into the community as law-abiding citizens" (*CCRA*, s. 100). The *CCRA* also sets out a number of principles that shall guide the NPB in achieving the purpose of conditional release. These include, *inter alia*, "that the protection of society be the paramount consideration in the determination of any case" and "that parole boards make the least restrictive determination consistent with the protection of society" (*CCRA*, ss. 101(a) and 101(d)). These principles are intended to guide the NPB in its decision making, whereas courts must adhere to the principles set out in the *Criminal Code* when sentencing for breach of an LTSO.

[47] The legislative purpose of an LTSO, a form of conditional release governed by the *CCRA*, is therefore to contribute to the maintenance of a just, peaceful and safe society by facilitating the rehabilitation and reintegration of long-term offenders. This direction is consistent with this Court's discussion at para. 42 of *R. v. L.M.*, 2008 SCC 31, [2008] 2 S.C.R. 163, on the distinction between the dangerous offender designation (which does not include a period of conditional release) and the long-term offender designation.

> Although they both contribute to assuring public safety, the dangerous offender and long-term offender designations have different objectives. Unlike a *dangerous* offender (s. 753 *Cr. C.*), who will continue to be deprived of liberty, since such offenders are kept in prison to separate them from society (s. 718.1), a *long-term* offender serves a sentence of imprisonment of two years or more and is then subject to an order of supervision in the community for a period not exceeding 10 years for the purpose of assisting in his or her rehabilitation (s. 753.1(3) *Cr. C.*). This measure, which is less restrictive than the indeterminate period of incarceration that applies to dangerous offenders, protects society and is at the same time consistent with [TRANSLATION] "the principles of proportionality and moderation in the recourse to sentences involving a deprivation of liberty" (Dadour, at p. 228). [Emphasis in original.]

[48] Reading the *Criminal Code*, the *CCRA* and the applicable jurisprudence together, we can therefore identify two specific objectives of long-term supervision as a form of conditional release: (1) protecting the public from the risk of re offence, and (2) rehabilitating the offender and reintegrating him or her into the community. The latter objective may properly be described as the ultimate purpose of an LTSO, as indicated by s. 100 of the *CCRA*, though it is inextricably entwined with the former. Unfortunately, provincial and appellate courts have tended to emphasize the protection of the public at the expense of the rehabilitation of offenders. This, in turn, has affected their determinations of what is a fit sentence for breaching a condition of an LTSO.

[49] *R. v. W. (H.P.)*, 2003 ABCA 131, 18 Alta. L.R. (4th) 20, is the leading appellate court decision to consider the matter. In that case, the Alberta Court of Appeal canvassed the purpose of the long-term offender regime and how it bears on the sentencing process for breach of an LTSO. Ritter J.A. summarized the view of the court, at para. 46, stating:

Because the protection of society is the paramount goal when sentencing an offender who has breached a condition of his long-term supervision order, sentencing principles respecting specific and general deterrence together with separation of the offender from the community · are called into play. Rehabilitation has a limited role to play as the status of long-term offender is such that rehabilitation has already been determined to be extremely difficult or impossible to achieve.

Subsequent provincial and appellate court cases have generally adhered to this approach. For example, in *R. v. Nelson*, [2007] O.J. No. 5704 (QL), Masse J. of the Ontario Court of Justice held, at paras. 14 and 21, that "[t]he main consideration in sentencing these offenders is the protection of the public" and that "significant sentences must be imposed even for slight breaches of a long-term supervision order."

[50] The foregoing characterization of the long-term offender regime is incorrect. The purpose of an LTSO is two-fold: to protect the public *and* to rehabilitate offenders and reintegrate them into the community. In fact, s. 100 of the *CCRA* singles out rehabilitation and reintegration as the purpose of community supervision including LTSOs. As this Court indicated in *L.M.*, rehabilitation is the key feature of the long-term offender regime that distinguishes it from the dangerous offender regime. To suggest, therefore, that rehabilitation has been determined to be impossible to achieve in the long-term offender context is simply wrong. Given this context, it would be contrary to reason to conclude that rehabilitation is not an appropriate sentencing objective and should therefore play "little or no role" (as stated in *W. (H.P.)*), in the sentencing process.

[51] This is not to say that rehabilitation will always be the foremost consideration when sentencing for breach of an LTSO. The duty of a sentencing judge is to apply all of the principles mandated by ss. 718.1 and 718.2 of the *Criminal Code* in order to devise a sentence that furthers the overall objectives of sentencing. The foregoing simply demonstrates that there is nothing in the provisions of the *Criminal Code* or the *CCRA* to suggest that any of those principles or objectives will not apply to the breach of an LTSO. As with any sentencing decision, the relative weight to be accorded to each sentencing principle or objective will vary depending on the circumstances of the particular offence. In all instances, the sentence must be proportionate to both the gravity of the offence and the degree of responsibility of the offender.

[52] It would be imprudent to attempt to determine in the abstract the gravity of the offence of breaching a condition of an LTSO. The severity of a given breach will ultimately depend on all of the circumstances, including the nature of the condition breached, how that condition is tied to managing the particular offender's risk of re-offence, and the circumstances of the breach. However, a few comments may be instructive.

[53] Breach of an LTSO is an indictable offence punishable by up to ten years' imprisonment. This can be contrasted with breach of probation which is a hybrid offence with a maximum sentence of either 18 months or two years' imprisonment. In each of the present appeals, the Crown places significant emphasis on this distinction, suggesting that the high maximum penalty indicates that breach of an LTSO is a particularly serious offence warranting a significant sentence. My colleague, Rothstein J., reiterates this point at para. 123 of his reasons, concluding that the "necessary implication is that Parliament viewed breaches of LTSOs as posing such risk to the protection of society that long-term offenders may have to be separated from society for a significant period of time."

[54] The lengthy maximum penalty certainly indicates that Parliament views the breach of an LTSO differently (and more seriously) than the breach of a probation order. However, it would be too much to suggest that the mere existence of a high statutory maximum penalty dictates that a significant period of imprisonment should be imposed for any breach of an LTSO. Breaches can occur in an infinite variety of circumstances. Parliament did not see fit to impose a mandatory minimum sentence. Where no minimum sentence is mandated by the *Criminal Code*, the entire range of sentencing options is open to a sentencing judge, including non-carceral sentences where appropriate. In its recommendations, the Task Force specifically stated that a key factor to the success of a long-term offender regime is "a speedy and flexible mechanism for enforcing the orders *which does not result in lengthy re-incarceration* in the absence of the commission of a new crime" (p. 19 (emphasis added)).

[55] It is the sentencing judge's duty to determine, within this open range of sentencing options, which sentence will be proportionate to both the gravity of the offence and the degree of responsibility of the offender. The severity of a particular breach of an LTSO will depend, in large part, on the circumstances of the breach, the nature of the condition breached, and the role that condition plays in managing the offender's risk of reoffence in the community. This requires a contextual analysis. As Smith J.A. states in *R. v. Deacon*, 2004 BCCA 78, 193 B.C.A.C. 228, at para. 51, "the gravity of an offence under s. 753.3 must be measured with reference not only to the conduct that gave rise to the offence, but also with regard to what it portends in light of the offender's entire history of criminal conduct." Breach of an LTSO is not subject to a distinct sentencing regime or system. In any given case, the best guides for determining a fit sentence are the well-established principles and objectives of sentencing set out in the *Criminal Code*.

Other than *Ipeelee*, judicial consideration of the long-term supervision provisions has been limited. One important issue is whether long-term offender status is limited to sexual offences. *R v McLeod*, 1999 BCCA 347 involved a man who had not been convicted of sexual offences, but was charged with aggravated assault, use of a weapon during an assault, possession of a weapon for a purpose dangerous to the public peace, and uttering a threat to cause death or bodily harm. McLeod pleaded guilty to one count of assault causing bodily harm and one count of possession of a weapon for a purpose dangerous to the public peace. Subsequently, at his sentencing, he was found to be a long-term offender and was sentenced to two years' imprisonment to be followed by seven years' supervision. In the BC Court of Appeal, it was argued that only the sexual offences set out in s 753.1(2)(a) can trigger a long-term offender designation. The court concluded:

> It is evident when reading the Report in conjunction with Part XXIV of the *Code*, that the recommendations of the Task Force with respect to the long-term offender proposals were, for the most part, adopted in Bill C-55, *An Act to amend the Criminal Code* (high risk offenders), the *Corrections and Conditional Release Act*, the *Criminal Records Act*, the *Prisons and Reformatories Act* and the *Department of the Solicitor General Act*, SC 1997, c. 17. The provisions with which we are here concerned came into force on August 1, 1997. Thus, while paedophiles and other sexual predators may well have been the primary targets of the new long-term offender provisions, I can find nothing in the background or legislative history confining their application to sexual offenders.

. . .

> On the basis of my conclusion that the long-term offender provisions of the *Code* are not restricted in their application to those convicted of the sexual offences set out in s. 753.1(2)(a) of the *Code*, I would dismiss the first ground of appeal.

Does this view of an antecedent offence unduly expand the legitimate reach of the long-term offender provisions? The same issue was addressed more recently by the Saskatchewan Court of Appeal in *Weasel*.

R v Weasel
2003 SKCA 131, 181 CCC (3d) 358 (footnotes omitted)

CAMERON JA (Bayda CJS and Sherstobitoff JA concurring):

[1] This appeal raises a question of law central to its disposition: Does section 753.1 of the *Criminal Code*, which makes special provision for sentencing long-term offenders, apply only to offenders who are convicted of a sex offence, or does it extend to others, including offenders who are convicted of a violent offence such as assault causing bodily harm?

[2] The appellant, Everett Riel Weasel, was convicted of assault causing bodily harm contrary to section 267(b) of the *Criminal Code*. He had been convicted of this and other offences many times in the past, so the prosecutor asked the trial judge to order an assessment, as permitted by section 752.1(1), for the purpose of determining whether the appellant should be sentenced as a long-term offender under section 753.1. The trial judge acted on the request (with the concurrence of counsel for the appellant) and upon receipt of the assessment found the appellant to be a long-term offender. He then sentenced him to a term of imprisonment of three years, to be followed by a period of community supervision of eight years.

· · ·

[6] Subsection (2) lies at the heart of the issue. Anyone familiar with the conventional cast of statutes will appreciate the unconventional terminology of this subsection: "The court shall be satisfied that there is a substantial risk that the offender will reoffend if" the requisites of paragraphs (a) and (b) exist. This terminology is tactless and grating, having regard for judicial independence, but that is not the point. The point is that it lacks clarity. Is the subsection intended to define the term "substantial risk," as it appears in subsection (1)? Or is it intended, instead, to create a presumption of "substantial risk" in those circumstances in which the requisites of paragraphs (a) and (b) exist, leaving the presence or absence of such risk in other circumstances to be assessed without the aid of the presumption?

[7] Depending on what was intended, the drafter might have used conventional language such as this: "A substantial risk that the offender will reoffend means ..."; or "A substantial risk that the offender will reoffend shall be presumed or deemed to exist if ..."; or "Without limiting the generality of paragraph 753.1(1)(b), a substantial risk that the offender will reoffend exists if ... ." This would better have identified the intent. As it is, the intent is obscure and the effect uncertain.

[8] If subsection (2) serves in effect to define the term "substantial risk," then section 753.1 would appear to be limited to an offender who has been convicted of a sex offence of the type referred to in the subsection. If, instead, subsection (2) serves in effect to raise

a presumption of "substantial risk" in the circumstances described in paragraphs (a) and (b) thereof, then section 753.1 may extend to an offender who has been convicted of an offence of another type and who proves, on independent assessment without the aid of the presumption, to pose a "substantial risk" to re-offend.

[9] The legislative history of section 753.1 is ambiguous but contains an indication the section was intended to apply only to sex offenders. So does some academic comment on the subject. But such case law as exists either holds or suggests otherwise. A better understanding of the issue may be gained through a brief recounting of these.

(i) The Legislative History of Section 753.1

[10] The government placed these long-term offender provisions before Parliament in 1996, and Parliament enacted them in 1997. The government placed them before Parliament as part of a package of amendments contained in Bill C-55. The Bill was introduced for the two-fold purpose of amending the existing dangerous offender provisions (found in section 753 of the *Criminal Code*) and of creating the long-term offender provisions (found in section 753.1).

[11] The Bill drew upon a task force report for its content: The Report of Federal/Provincial/Territorial Task Force on High Risk Offenders, *Strategies for Managing High-Risk [Violent] Offenders* (Victoria: The Task Force, 1995). The Report spoke of the need for more effective measures for dealing with some categories of offender, stressing sex offenders, who may not qualify as dangerous offenders but may still pose a considerable risk of harm to others by reason of chronic behaviours. Speaking to a proposed new category of offender—the long-term offender—the Report states:

> A sentencing option providing for long term supervision would be aimed at cases where an established offence cycle with observable cues is present, and where a long term relapse prevention approach might be indicted. The success of [a long term supervision] scheme based on the relapse prevention model rests on several key factors.
>
> a. The measure should be focused on particular classes of offender. The inclination to make long-term supervision widely available should be resisted as costly, unwarranted in most cases, and as contributing to "net widening." The target group, and thus the expectations of the scheme, should be well defined;
>
> b. The criteria should selectively target those offenders who have a high likelihood of committing further *violent* or *sexual* crimes but who would not likely be found to be a Dangerous Offender; [p. 19] [emphasis added].

[12] On introduction of Bill C-55, the Department of Justice and the Solicitor General of Canada issued a document entitled "Protecting Canadians and their families—Measures to Deal with High-Risk Violent Offenders" (August 1996). It stated in part:

> The government has announced new measures to deal with high-risk offenders. The following initiatives will toughen the sentencing and correctional regime for those who pose a high risk of committing another violent crime:
>
> • a new "Long-Term Offender" designation that targets sex-offenders and adds a period of long-term supervision of up to 10 years following release from prison;

• • •

> Under the proposed changes, a new sentencing category, to be called Long-Term Offenders, will be added to the *Criminal Code*. It will target sex offenders who are less violent and brutal than those designated as Dangerous Offenders but are found to pose a considerable risk of reoffending.
>
> • • •
>
> The Long-Term Offender procedure will apply to persons convicted of sexual assault, sexual interference, invitation to sexual touching, sexual exploitation, exposure, aggravated sexual assault, and sexual assault with a weapon or causing bodily harm. It could also be applied to a person who committed another offence that had a sexual component—for example, somebody who committed a break and enter with a clear intention of sexually assaulting the occupant.

[13] Later, when Bill C-55 was before the Standing Committee on Justice and Legal Affairs, the Minister of Justice commented upon it, saying this:

> The second element in Bill C-55 has to do with the creation of the category of long-term offender. ...
>
> Naturally and properly, the test for the dangerous offender category is high and exacting. The reality is that 90% of successful dangerous offender applications involve sex offenders. Repeat sex offenders are the most troublesome, high-risk category in the criminal law. The creation of the long-term offender category is intended to provide another mechanism for dealing with this risk. ...
>
> As proposed, the offences that can give rise to a long-term offender designation are all sex crimes and involve patterns of reoffending.

[14] So the Minister of Justice and the Solicitor General seem to have thought the long-term offender provisions were confined to sex crimes and sex offenders, though it might be recalled the Task Force Report had suggested that such provisions "should be focussed on particular classes of offender" and should "target those offenders who have a likelihood of committing further violent or sexual crimes but who would not likely be found to be a Dangerous Offender."

• • •

[20] What all of this comes down to, as it did in *R v. McLeod*, is what Parliament had in mind in enacting section 753.1 in the terms it did. This entails interpreting the section along the lines adopted by the Supreme Court of Canada in *Rizzo and Rizzo Shoes Ltd. (Re)*, [1998] 1 SCR 27.

(b) The Resolution of the Issue: Interpreting Section 713.1

[21] In *Re Rizzo & Rizzo Shoes Ltd.*, the Supreme Court of Canada adopted the so-called "modern approach" to statutory interpretation:

> Today there is only one principle or approach, namely, the words of an Act are to be read in their entire context and in their grammatical and ordinary sense harmoniously with the scheme of the Act, the object of the Act, and the intention of Parliament.

The context includes the legislative history of an enactment, though the Court observed that this is of limited assistance, given the frailties of Hansard evidence pertaining to the intent of Parliament.

[22] The principle embodied in the modern approach to statutory construction is accompanied by another when it comes to interpreting penal enactments, namely the subsidiary principle of strict construction: If the attempt to interpret a penal enactment in accordance with the modern approach leaves a reasonable doubt as to the meaning or scope of the text of the enactment, then the meaning most favourable to the accused is to be adopted as long as it is compatible with the intention and goal of Parliament: *R v. Hasselwander*, [1993] 2 SCR 398, per Cory J at pp. 412-413.

[23] What Parliament had in mind, then, in enacting section 753.1, is to be determined in the context of the whole of the enactment in which the section appears, namely Part XXIV of the *Criminal Code*, including the scheme of the enactment and its purpose. The tendency is to do otherwise—to take an isolated view of the language of the section, treating the section as though it stood alone in providing for the sentencing of long-term offenders. This is not true of the approach taken by the British Columbia Court of Appeal in *R v. McLeod*. The Court went beyond the section itself and considered its scope in the broader context of the provisions dealing with both dangerous offenders and long-term offenders. In our judgment this is essential, for the long-term offender provisions are woven into Part XXIV and form part of an integrated whole larger than the section itself.

[24] Section 753.1 forms part of an integrated sentencing scheme established by Part XXIV and entitled DANGEROUS OFFENDERS AND LONG-TERM OFFENDERS. The purpose of Part XXIV lies in enhancing the effectiveness of conventional sentencing in relation to the two classes of offender for which it makes provision. To that end, it allows for *preventive detention or control* beyond the reach of conventional sentencing. For Dangerous Offenders, it allows for an indeterminate period of detention (section 753). For Long-term Offenders, it allows for a fixed period of detention of at least two years, followed by a fixed period of control by means of community supervision of up to ten years (section 753.1).

[25] These are offenders who, to begin with, have been convicted of "a serious personal injury offence" or "an offence referred to in paragraph 753.1(2)(a)" and who, after that, are found to be a threat of one nature or another to the safety or well-being of others by reason of their historical behaviour and risk of re-offending.

[26] The term "serious personal injury offence" is defined in section 752 to mean:

> (a) an indictable offence, other than high treason, treason, first degree murder or second degree murder, involving
>> (i) the use or attempted use of violence against another person, or
>> (ii) conduct endangering or likely to endanger the life or safety of another person or inflicting or likely to inflict severe psychological damage upon another person,
> and for which the offender may be sentenced to imprisonment for ten years or more, or
> (b) an offence or attempt to commit an offence mentioned in section 271 (sexual assault), 272 (sexual assault with a weapon, threats to a third party or causing bodily harm) or 273 (aggravated sexual assault).

[27] The phrase "an offence referred to in paragraph 753.1(2)(a)" embraces an offence under section 151 (sexual interference), 152 (invitation to sexual touching), and 153 (sexual exploitation); one under subsection 173(2) (exposure); and one under section 271 (sexual assault), 272 (sexual assault with a weapon), and 273 (aggravated sexual assault).

[28] These, then, are the two classes of offender and offence with which the scheme is concerned.

[29] The scheme is designed to operate step by step toward achieving its sentencing objectives. Certain conditions or requirements must be fulfilled at each step before advancing to the next. The first step, initiated by the prosecution following conviction but before sentencing, is to gain access to the scheme's sentencing options by means of an application to obtain an assessment of the offender under section 752.1. This is an entry-like provision, and it applies to all such applications, irrespective of whether the application be aimed at having the offender sentenced as a dangerous offender, or as a dangerous or long-term offender, or as long-term offender only. Section 752.1, the only one of its kind in the scheme, reads thus:

Dangerous Offenders and Long-Term Offenders

752.1(1) Application for remand for assessment—Where an offender is convicted of a serious personal injury offence or an offence referred to in paragraph 753.1(2)(a) and, before sentence is imposed on the offender, on application by the prosecution, the court is of the opinion that there are reasonable grounds to believe that the offender might be found to be a dangerous offender under section 753 or a long-term offender under section 753.1, the court may, by order in writing, remand the offender, for a period not exceeding sixty days, to the custody of the person that the court directs and who can perform an assessment, or can have an assessment performed by experts. The assessment is to be used as evidence in an application under section 753 or 753.1.

(2) Report—The person to whom the offender is remanded shall file a report of the assessment with the court not later than fifteen days after the end of the assessment period and make copies of it available to the prosecutor and counsel for the offender.

[30] As a pre-condition to the operation of this section, the offender must have been convicted of "a serious personal injury offence or an offence referred to in paragraph 753.1(2)(a)." Otherwise, there is no access to the sentencing options of the scheme. If the condition is fulfilled, and if the requirements of the section are met, the court may requisition an assessment. Assuming it does so, the first step is complete.

[31] Upon receipt of the assessment, the scheme contemplates the taking of the next step: Determining if the offender constitutes a dangerous offender under section 753 or a long-term offender under section 753.1, depending on the circumstances, including the aim of the application and the opinion of the court at the first step.

[32] If the offender is determined to be a dangerous or long-term offender, the next step entails sentencing the offender as provided for either by section 753 or by 753.1.

[33] These sections bear close examination for the purpose of determining what Parliament had in mind in enacting section 753.1 in the terms it did.

• • •

[36] None of the steps envisioned by either section 753 or 753.1 can, of course, be taken without the first step having been taken under section 752. And the first step can only have been taken, according to the *pre-condition* appearing in subsection 752(1), "where [the] offender has been convicted of a serious personal injury offence or an offence referred to in paragraph 753.1(2)(a)." This pre-condition to the operation of section 752—and by extension to the operation of sections 753 and 753.1—might be read to different effect.

[37] It might be read as establishing discrete pre-conditions, one reserved exclusively for gaining access to the dangerous offender provisions of section 753 (conviction for "a serious personal injury offence") and the other reserved exclusively for gaining access to the long-term offender provisions of section 753.1 (conviction for "an offence referred to in paragraph 753.1(2)(a)"). Were it to be read thus, the effect would be to confine the scope of section 753.1 to offenders who have been convicted of a sex offence of the type listed in paragraph 753.1(2)(a), thus excluding offenders who have been convicted of "a serious personal injury offence."

[38] It might also be read as establishing a pre-condition having alternative elements, namely a conviction for "a serious personal injury offence" or "an offence referred to in paragraph 753.1(2)(a)," with either serving to engage section 752.1 and, if the requirements thereof be met, to then engage section 753 or 753.1, whichever is appropriate in the circumstances. Reading the pre-condition to this effect would widen the scope of section 753.1 to include offenders who have been convicted of "a serious personal injury offence."

[39] Of the two readings, the second is more grammatically appealing and more suited to an integrated scheme. Even so, these are rather weak indications of Parliamentary intent. There are stronger ones, found first in the text of these provisions and then in the purpose of the enactment. Let us consider them in turn.

(i) The Text of These Provisions

[40 There are two textual indications suggesting the long-term offender provisions were not meant to apply only to an offender who has been convicted of a sex offence listed in paragraph 753.1(2)(a). One of these is found in subsection 753(5), the other in subsection 753.1(1).

[41] Subsection 753(5) covers the situation where, on a dangerous offender application, the court is not satisfied the offender qualifies as a dangerous offender. Should that happen, the court is empowered to resort to section 753.1, find the offender to be a long-term offender, and sentence the offender accordingly. The effect is this: If an offender has been convicted of "a serious personal injury offence"—assault causing bodily harm let us say—but is not found to be a dangerous offender under section 753, then that person may be found [to] be a long-term offender under section 753.1. This would not be possible were the latter confined to the sex offences listed in paragraph 753.1(2)(a). Madam Justice Prowse took note of this in *R v. McLeod*, at p. 504, saying there was nothing in the text to suggest "the court can only go on to determine whether the offender meets the long-term offender criteria if the predicate offences are sexual offences." We agree.

[42] Turning, then, to subsection 753.1(1), it may be noted that it covers the situation where, following the filing of an assessment report under section 752.1, the court is called upon to determine if the offender is a long-term offender. The court is empowered by subsection 753.1(1) to find "an offender" (meaning the offender to whom the assessment relates) to be a long-term offender if the requirements of paragraphs 753.1(1) (a), (b), and (c) be met. The first of these is that it would be appropriate in the view of the court to impose a sentence of imprisonment of two years or more "for *the offence* for which the offender has been convicted." The words in emphasis appear to be a general reference to an offence of the type underlying Part XXIV, namely a "serious personal injury offence"

or "an offence referred to in paragraph 753.1(2)(a)." On what premise, it might be asked, would one construe the words *the offence* to exclude the first but include the second?

[43] Had the intention been to exclude the first, which is to say had Parliament intended to exclude offenders convicted of "a serious personal injury offence" from the purview of the long-term offender provisions, that intention could readily have been achieved by casting paragraph (a) in terms referring not merely to "the offence for which the offender has been convicted" but to "the offence, referred to in paragraph 753.1(2)(a), for which the offender has been convicted," or to "the offence for which the offender has been convicted, being an offence referred to [in] paragraph 753.1(2)(a)." That paragraph (a) is not cast in some such terms is reminiscent of the point made by Madam Justice Prowse, in *R v. McLeod*:

> If Parliament had intended to limit the designation of long-term offender to those convicted of sexual offences, it could have done so by simply adding that as a fourth condition to be satisfied under s. 753.1(1). Counsel … is, in effect, asking us to read a fourth condition into that subsection which does not otherwise exist. [pp. 502, 503]

[44] These two textual considerations suggest that section 753.1 was not meant to apply only to sex offenders. And that brings us to the purpose of the enactment, which is to say the purpose of Part XXIV, and to the object of section 753.1.

(ii) The Purpose of the Enactment

[45] As noted earlier, the purpose of Part XXIV lies in enhancing the effectiveness of conventional sentencing in relation to the two categories of offender for which it makes provision. To that end, it allows for preventive detention or control beyond the reach of conventional sentencing. This is an idea which is grounded less in punishment for injury already inflicted, as in conventional sentencing, and more in prevention of future injury when the risk of re-offence is substantial. The concern is to better protect members of society from the threat of harm at the hands of offenders who have committed serious crimes against the person and who, because of their demonstrated propensities, are at considerable risk of doing so again. So generally speaking, Part XXIV targets those offenders who, having been convicted of a personal injury offence of a violent or sexual nature, pose a sufficient risk of re-offending as to call for either an indeterminate period of preventive detention or else a fixed term of detention, followed by a fixed period of community supervision.

[46] Were the object of section 753.1 to be seen as allowing for a term of detention followed by a period of community supervision in relation to sex offenders only, it would be difficult to fit the object of the section to the purpose of the enactment. The object would then seem to fall short of the purpose.

[47] And why, it might be asked, would Parliament have intended these preventive detention or control measures, insofar as they extend to long-term offenders, to apply only to offenders who have been convicted of a sex offence of the kind referred to in paragraph 753.1(2)(a)?

[48] No doubt Parliament was intent on including such offenders—given the comparatively high incidence of repetition associated with such offences—and it was intent on doing so expressly. It was intent on doing so expressly for the reason, among others perhaps, that the sex offences referred to in paragraph 753.1(2)(a) do not necessarily come

within the definition of a "serious personal injury offence." Those referred to by reference to sections 271 (sexual assault), 272 (sexual assault with a weapon) and 273 (aggravated sexual assault) fall within the definition. But those referred to by reference to section 153 (sexual exploitation) and subsection 173(2) (sexual exposure) do not. They do not fall within the definition because they are not punishable by imprisonment of ten years or more. Nor do those referred to by reference to section 151 (sexual interference) and 152 (invitation to sexual touching) necessarily fall within the definition, for the use of violence is not necessarily associated with their commission. Nevertheless, Parliament was intent on including persons convicted of such offences.

[49] What this suggests is that the section was intended primarily, though not necessarily exhaustively, as an inclusive provision, given the frequency with which sex offenders re-offend and the limited extent to which sex offences fall within the definition of "serious personal injury offence."

[50] But why would Parliament have wanted to exclude offenders convicted of a "serious personal injury offence"—an offence such as aggravated assault, assault with a weapon, or assault causing bodily harm? Potentially, these offenders are also at substantial risk to re-offend and to inflict serious harm on others. That being so, and since the long-term offender provisions are essentially sentencing provisions aimed at preventive control beyond the reach of conventional sentencing, it is difficult to think of any reason why Parliament should have wanted to exclude such offenders from the scope of section 753.1.

[51] Indeed, excluding them appears senseless. Were section 753.1 to exclude them, then an offender who is convicted of sexual assault, for example, and answers to the description of a long-term offender, could be sentenced to terms of preventive detention and control, but an offender who is convicted of assault causing bodily harm, or aggravated assault, or assault with a weapon, could not, even though this offender may answer to that description as well. This seems at odds not only with the thrust and central purpose of Part XXIV but with common sense. ...

[52] This consideration of the purpose of Part XXIV, combined with these textual considerations of its provisions, lead us to conclude that section 753.1 was not intended to be restricted to an offender who has been convicted of an offence referred to in paragraph 753.1(2)(a), but was intended to extend to an offender who has been convicted of a serious personal injury offence as defined by section 752.

[53] This conclusion is buttressed by the recent decision of the Supreme Court of Canada in *R v. Smith* (2003), 230 DLR (4th) 333, which came down after the case before us was heard. In *R v. Smith*, the accused had been convicted of: (i) uttering a threat of death or bodily harm, contrary to section 264.1(a) of the *Criminal Code* and (ii) assault causing bodily harm, contrary to section 267(1)(b) of the *Code*. Neither featured any sexual conduct in its commission. At trial, the prosecution applied to have the accused sentenced as a dangerous offender. It did so in reliance on the second of these convictions—a conviction in relation to "a serious personal injury offence" within the definition of this phrase. The trial judge heard the application, declared the accused to be [a] dangerous offender, and sentenced him to an indeterminate period of detention.

[54] On appeal to the Supreme Court of Canada, the Court ordered a new hearing on the authority of its contemporaneous decision in *R v. Johnson* (2003), 230 DLR (4th) 296. It did so on the premise the sentencing judge was required to consider the possibility of declaring the accused a long-term offender before declaring him a dangerous offender ... .

[55] Obviously, the Court would not have ordered a re-hearing in this instance if the long-term offender provisions applied only to an offender convicted of a sex offence of the type referred to in paragraph 753.1(2)(a). In this instance the offender had been convicted of a serious personal injury offence that had nothing to do with sex.

(c) *Conclusion*

[56] Based on the foregoing, we are of the opinion section 753.1 extends to an offender convicted of either a serious personal injury offence, as defined in section 752, or an offence referred to in paragraph 753.1(2)(a). That being so, subsection (2) is … not to be seen as defining the term "substantial risk" appearing in subsection 753.1. Rather, it is to be seen as creating a conclusive presumption of "substantial risk" in those circumstances to which paragraphs (a) and (b) of the subsection are addressed, leaving the issue of such risk in other circumstances to be determined without the aid of the presumption.

The conclusion reached in *Weasel* has been followed by both the Quebec Court of Appeal: see *Guindon c R*, 2008 QCCA 1445, and the Nova Scotia Court of Appeal: see *R v McLean*, 2009 NSCA 1.

IV. PREVENTIVE RECOGNIZANCES

A. Background

Dangerous offender and long-term offender applications follow the conviction of an individual. Thus a condition precedent to the operation of those provisions is a conviction for a "serious personal injury offence." We now turn our attention to preventive measures that may be employed in the absence of a trial and conviction.

Building on the use of common law peace bonds and the statutory peace bonds in s 810 of the *Criminal Code*, Parliament has created five new post-sentence preventive vehicles. The impetus for enacting these provisions came, at least in part, from a desire to address concerns about perceived dangerousness once a sentence has been completed. These provisions may be used to impose post-sentence supervision on individuals who are perceived to be dangerous.

While there are differences among the five provisions, they are similar in structure and effect. Section 810.01 is triggered by fear that someone will commit a criminal organization offence. Section 810.011 deals with terrorism offences. Section 810.1 can be triggered when someone fears on reasonable grounds that a sexual offence against a child will be committed. Section 810.02 applies to fear of forced marriages of a person under 16. Section 810.2 addresses fear of a serious personal injury offence. All five of these mechanisms require applications to a court and may result in a recognizance lasting up to 12 months that includes specific conditions. Sections 810.01 and 810.2 require the consent of the provincial attorney general before an information may be received by a provincial court judge. Sections 810.01 and 810.1 require fear that a particular person or persons may be victimized; there is no such requirement in s 810.2. A breach of any of these recognizances is a hybrid offence, which is punishable by up to two years' imprisonment when prosecuted by indictment.

B. The Provisions

Fear of certain offences

810.01(1) A person who fears on reasonable grounds that another person will commit an offence under section 423.1 or a criminal organization offence may, with the Attorney General's consent, lay an information before a provincial court judge.

(2) A provincial court judge who receives an information under subsection (1) may cause the parties to appear before a provincial court judge.

(3) If the provincial court judge before whom the parties appear is satisfied by the evidence adduced that the informant has reasonable grounds for the fear, the judge may order that the defendant enter into a recognizance to keep the peace and be of good behaviour for a period of not more than 12 months.

(3.1) However, if the provincial court judge is also satisfied that the defendant was convicted previously of an offence referred to in subsection (1), the judge may order that the defendant enter into the recognizance for a period of not more than two years.

(4) The provincial court judge may commit the defendant to prison for a term not exceeding twelve months if the defendant fails or refuses to enter into the recognizance.

(4.1) The provincial court judge may add any reasonable conditions to the recognizance that the judge considers desirable for preventing the commission of an offence referred to in subsection (1), including conditions that require the defendant

(a) to participate in a treatment program;

(b) to wear an electronic monitoring device, if the Attorney General makes the request;

(c) to remain within a specified geographic area unless written permission to leave that area is obtained from the judge;

(d) to return to and remain at their place of residence at specified times;

(e) to abstain from the consumption of drugs, except in accordance with a medical prescription, of alcohol or of any other intoxicating substance;

(f) to provide, for the purpose of analysis, a sample of a bodily substance prescribed by regulation on the demand of a peace officer, a probation officer or someone designated under paragraph 810.3(2)(a) to make a demand, at the place and time and on the day specified by the person making the demand, if that person has reasonable grounds to believe that the defendant has breached a condition of the recognizance that requires them to abstain from the consumption of drugs, alcohol or any other intoxicating substance; or

(g) to provide, for the purpose of analysis, a sample of a bodily substance prescribed by regulation at regular intervals that are specified, in a notice in Form 51 served on the defendant, by a probation officer or a person designated under paragraph 810.3(2)(b) to specify them, if a condition of the recognizance requires the defendant to abstain from the consumption of drugs, alcohol or any other intoxicating substance.

(5) The provincial court judge shall consider whether it is desirable, in the interests of the defendant's safety or that of any other person, to prohibit the defendant from possessing any firearm, cross-bow, prohibited weapon, restricted weapon, prohibited device, ammunition, prohibited ammunition or explosive substance, or all of those things. If the judge decides that it is desirable to do so, the judge shall add that condition to the recognizance and specify the period during which the condition applies.

• • •

Fear of terrorism offence

810.011(1) A person who fears on reasonable grounds that another person may commit a terrorism offence may, with the Attorney General's consent, lay an information before a provincial court judge.

(2) The provincial court judge who receives an information under subsection (1) may cause the parties to appear before a provincial court judge.

(3) If the provincial court judge before whom the parties appear is satisfied by the evidence adduced that the informant has reasonable grounds for the fear, the judge may order that the defendant enter into a recognizance, with or without sureties, to keep the peace and be of good behaviour for a period of not more than 12 months.

(4) However, if the provincial court judge is also satisfied that the defendant was convicted previously of a terrorism offence, the judge may order that the defendant enter into the recognizance for a period of not more than five years.

(5) The provincial court judge may commit the defendant to prison for a term of not more than 12 months if the defendant fails or refuses to enter into the recognizance.

• • •

Fear of forced marriage or marriage under age of 16 years

810.02(1) A person who fears on reasonable grounds that another person will commit an offence under paragraph 273.3(1)(d) or section 293.1 or 293.2 may lay an information before a provincial court judge.

(2) The judge who receives the information may cause the parties to appear before a provincial court judge.

(3) If the provincial court judge before whom the parties appear is satisfied by the evidence adduced that the informant has reasonable grounds for the fear, the judge may order that the defendant enter into a recognizance to keep the peace and be of good behaviour for a period of not more than 12 months.

(4) However, if the provincial court judge is also satisfied that the defendant was convicted previously of an offence referred to in subsection (1), the judge may order that the defendant enter into the recognizance for a period of not more than two years.

(5) The provincial court judge may commit the defendant to prison for a term not exceeding 12 months if the defendant fails or refuses to enter into the recognizance.

• • •

Where fear of sexual offence

810.1(1) A person who fears on reasonable grounds that another person will commit an offence under section 151 or 152, subsection 153(1), section 155 or 159, subsection 160(2) or (3), section 163.1, 170, 171, 171.1, 172.1 or 172.2, subsection 173(2), section 271, 272, 273 or 279.011, subsection 279.02(2) or 279.03(2), section 280 or 281 or subsection 286.1(2), 286.2(2) or 286.3(2), in respect of one or more persons who are under the age of 16 years, may lay an information before a provincial court judge, whether or not the person or persons in respect of whom it is feared that the offence will be committed are named.

(2) A provincial court judge who receives an information under subsection (1) may cause the parties to appear before a provincial court judge.

(3) If the provincial court judge before whom the parties appear is satisfied by the evidence adduced that the informant has reasonable grounds for the fear, the judge may order that the defendant enter into a recognizance to keep the peace and be of good behaviour for a period that does not exceed 12 months.

(3.01) However, if the provincial court judge is also satisfied that the defendant was convicted previously of a sexual offence in respect of a person who is under the age of 16 years, the judge may order that the defendant enter into the recognizance for a period that does not exceed two years.

(3.02) The provincial court judge may add any reasonable conditions to the recognizance that the judge considers desirable to secure the good conduct of the defendant, including conditions that

(a) prohibit the defendant from having any contact — including communicating by any means — with a person under the age of 16 years, unless the defendant does so under the supervision of a person whom the judge considers appropriate;

(a.1) prohibit the defendant from using the Internet or other digital network, unless the defendant does so in accordance with conditions set by the judge;

(b) prohibit the defendant from attending a public park or public swimming area where persons under the age of 16 years are present or can reasonably be expected to be present, or a daycare centre, schoolground or playground;

(b.1) prohibit the defendant from communicating, directly or indirectly, with any person identified in the recognizance, or refrain from going to any place specified in the recognizance, except in accordance with the conditions specified in the recognizance that the judge considers necessary;

(c) require the defendant to participate in a treatment program;

(d) require the defendant to wear an electronic monitoring device, if the Attorney General makes the request;

(e) require the defendant to remain within a specified geographic area unless written permission to leave that area is obtained from the provincial court judge;

(f) require the defendant to return to and remain at his or her place of residence at specified times;

(g) require the defendant to abstain from the consumption of drugs except in accordance with a medical prescription, of alcohol or of any other intoxicating substance;

(h) require the defendant to provide, for the purpose of analysis, a sample of a bodily substance prescribed by regulation on the demand of a peace officer, a probation officer or someone designated under paragraph 810.3(2)(a) to make a demand, at the place and time and on the day specified by the person making the demand, if that person has reasonable grounds to believe that the defendant has breached a condition of the recognizance that requires them to abstain from the consumption of drugs, alcohol or any other intoxicating substance; or

(i) require the defendant to provide, for the purpose of analysis, a sample of a bodily substance prescribed by regulation at regular intervals that are specified, in a notice in Form 51 served on the defendant, by a probation officer or a person designated under paragraph 810.3(2)(b) to specify them, if a condition of the recognizance requires the defendant to abstain from the consumption of drugs, alcohol or any other intoxicating substance.

• • •

Where fear of serious personal injury offence

810.2(1) Any person who fears on reasonable grounds that another person will commit a serious personal injury offence, as that expression is defined in section 752, may, with the consent of the Attorney General, lay an information before a provincial court judge, whether or not the person or persons in respect of whom it is feared that the offence will be committed are named.

(2) A provincial court judge who receives an information under subsection (1) may cause the parties to appear before a provincial court judge.

(3) If the provincial court judge before whom the parties appear is satisfied by the evidence adduced that the informant has reasonable grounds for the fear, the judge may order that the defendant enter into a recognizance to keep the peace and be of good behaviour for a period that does not exceed 12 months.

(3.1) However, if the provincial court judge is also satisfied that the defendant was convicted previously of an offence referred to in subsection (1), the judge may order that the defendant enter into the recognizance for a period that does not exceed two years.

(4) The provincial court judge may commit the defendant to prison for a term not exceeding twelve months if the defendant fails or refuses to enter into the recognizance.

(4.1) The provincial court judge may add any reasonable conditions to the recognizance that the judge considers desirable to secure the good conduct of the defendant, including conditions that require the defendant

(a) to participate in a treatment program;

(b) to wear an electronic monitoring device, if the Attorney General makes the request;

(c) to remain within a specified geographic area unless written permission to leave that area is obtained from the provincial court judge;

(d) to return to and remain at his or her place of residence at specified times;

(e) to abstain from the consumption of drugs except in accordance with a medical prescription, of alcohol or of any other intoxicating substance;

(f) to provide, for the purpose of analysis, a sample of a bodily substance prescribed by regulation on the demand of a peace officer, a probation officer or someone designated under paragraph 810.3(2)(a) to make a demand, at the place and time and on the day specified by the person making the demand, if that person has reasonable grounds to believe that the defendant has breached a condition of the recognizance that requires them to abstain from the consumption of drugs, alcohol or any other intoxicating substance; or

(g) to provide, for the purpose of analysis, a sample of a bodily substance prescribed by regulation at regular intervals that are specified, in a notice in Form 51 served on the defendant, by a probation officer or a person designated under paragraph 810.3(2)(b) to specify them, if a condition of the recognizance requires the defendant to abstain from the consumption of drugs, alcohol or any other intoxicating substance.

(5) The provincial court judge shall consider whether it is desirable, in the interests of the defendant's safety or that of any other person, to prohibit the defendant from possessing any firearm, cross-bow, prohibited weapon, restricted weapon, prohibited device, ammunition, prohibited ammunition or explosive substance, or all of those things. If the judge decides that it is desirable to do so, the judge shall add that condition to the recognizance and specify the period during which the condition applies.

(5.1) If the provincial court judge adds a condition described in subsection (5) to a recognizance, the judge shall specify in the recognizance how the things referred to in that subsection that are in the defendant's possession should be surrendered, disposed of, detained, stored or dealt with and how the authorizations, licences and registration certificates that are held by the defendant should be surrendered.

(5.2) If the provincial court judge does not add a condition described in subsection (5) to a recognizance, the judge shall include in the record a statement of the reasons for not adding the condition.

(6) The provincial court judge shall consider whether it is desirable to require the defendant to report to the correctional authority of a province or to an appropriate police authority. If the judge decides that it is desirable to do so, the judge shall add that condition to the recognizance.

C. The Constitutionality of the Provisions

As noted above, the five types of preventive recognizances differ in some respects, but they are similar in a number of crucial ways. The following decision of the Court of Appeal for Ontario in *Budreo* addresses the constitutionality of s 810.1 (sexual offences) of the Code. It also confronts a number of interpretive issues that are easily applicable to the other recognizances.

R v Budreo
(2000), 46 OR (3d) 481 (CA)

LASKIN JA (Finlayson and Rosenberg JJA concurring):

Introduction

[1] Section 810.1 of the *Criminal Code*, RSC 1985, c. C-46, enacted by Parliament in 1993, permits the court to impose a recognizance on any person likely to commit any one of a number of listed sexual offences against a child under 14 years of age and to prohibit that person for up to one year from engaging in activities or attending places—a public park, public swimming area, daycare centre, schoolground or playground—where children under 14 are likely to be present. ... A recognizance may be imposed though the person has not committed an offence and has no previous criminal record. If an informant fears on reasonable grounds that the person will commit one of the listed offences and a provincial court judge, after a hearing, is satisfied that the informant has reasonable grounds for the fear, then the person may be ordered to enter into a recognizance. The issue on this appeal is the constitutionality of s. 810.1.

[2] The appellant Wray Budreo is a paedophile. He has a long record of sexual offences against young boys. In November 1994, he was released from prison after serving a sentence for three convictions for sexual assault. The Crown immediately sought a recognizance under s. 810.1. The appellant brought an application to prohibit the provincial court judge, His Honour Judge Kelly, from holding the s. 810.1 hearing and for a declaration that s. 810.1 was unconstitutional because it violated ss. 7, 9, 11 and 15 of the *Canadian Charter of Rights and Freedoms*.

[3] In a lengthy and well-reasoned decision, Then J concluded that s. 810.1 was constitutional except in two respects. First, he declared "community centre," one of the places a person could be prohibited from attending under s. 810.1(3), to be inoperative because it was overly broad contrary to s. 7 of the Charter and could not be justified under s. 1. Second, he found that s. 810.1(2), which required the provincial court judge to cause the parties to appear before the court, infringed ss. 7 and 9 of the Charter and could not be justified under s. 1. To remedy this violation, however, Then J read down the word "shall" in s. 810.1(2) to read "may."

[4] The appellant Budreo appealed and was supported in his appeal by the intervenor, the Canadian Civil Liberties Association. In oral argument the appellant narrowed the focus of his appeal to three main issues. First, he submitted that s. 810.1 violated s. 7 of the Charter. In his submission, s. 810.1 deprived him of his liberty contrary to the principles of fundamental justice in three ways: s. 810.1 creates a status offence; it is impermissibly broad; and it is impermissibly vague. Second, he submitted that Then J erred in reading down "shall" to "may" in s. 810.1(2) and that he should instead have declared the subsection inoperative. Third, he submitted that Then J erred in holding that a person subject to a s. 810.1 proceeding can be compelled to court by an arrest warrant under s. 507(4) of the Code and can be detained pending the hearing under s. 515. As part of this third submission the appellant asked us to reconsider this court's decision in *R v. Allen* (1985), 18 CCC (3d) 155, 8 OAC 16 (CA) in the light of the Charter.

[5] I would dismiss the appellant's appeal. Because I agree substantially with the reasons of Then J, I will limit my own reasons to summarizing the main points on which I rely, focusing on the specific arguments that were made before us.

Background Facts

[6] The appellant is 55 years old. He has been diagnosed as a paedophile. He has an extensive criminal record dating back to 1961, which includes many convictions for indecent assault and sexual assault committed against young boys. These convictions, in the main, have resulted from the "physical touching" of boys between five and 17 years of age. Of the appellant's 36 convictions, 26 have been for the physical touching of young males.

[7] On November 18, 1994, the appellant was released from the Kingston Penitentiary, after having served a six-year sentence for three counts of sexual assault. These sexual assault convictions concerned three incidents in which the appellant convinced the victims—young boys—to lay down in a park and then fondled their bare stomachs, and in two cases their genitals. In sentencing the appellant, Webber DCJ wrote, "Clearly, Mr. Budreo is a person who has a paedophiliac problem which has existed for many, many years and it appears that there is very little that has been done for him and there is very little that he has done for himself, except on a spasmodic and irregular basis."

[8] On his release, at the request of the Correctional Service of Canada, the appellant submitted to a psychiatric assessment under the *Mental Health Act*, RSO 1990, c. M.7 to determine whether he was certifiable. The psychiatrist with the Correctional Service who did the assessment declined to certify the appellant. The psychiatrist concluded that the appellant did not pose a sufficient risk of serious harm to himself or to members of the public, that he had made considerable gains toward rehabilitating himself, and that he was "well motivated." Doctors at the Clarke Institute of Psychiatry also concluded that the appellant did not pose a danger to himself or others and, thus, should not be admitted under the *Mental Health Act*.

[9] Since his release, the appellant has followed a treatment plan devised for him. The treatment plan consists of continued psychiatric counselling directed by a doctor at the Clarke Institute and monthly injections of the anti-androgen drug Luperon.

[10] Nonetheless, the appellant's release from prison sparked considerable publicity, most of it negative. The appellant had gone first to Peterborough and then to Toronto. He was under continuous police surveillance in both cities and press releases were issued to tell the public of his whereabouts.

[11] Within three days of his release, the Crown began proceedings under s. 810.1 of the *Criminal Code*. The Crown acknowledges that it sought a recognizance under s. 810.1, not because the appellant had done anything improper or illegal since his release from prison, but because of his criminal record and his diagnosis as a paedophile.

[12] On November 20, 1994, Detective Wendy Leaver of the Metropolitan Toronto Police Service asked the appellant to agree to enter into recognizance under s. 810.1. The appellant was apparently unwilling to do so. The s. 810.1 application was then scheduled for November 22, 1994 and the appellant was told to obtain counsel.

[13] Detective Leaver swore an information under s. 810.1 in which she said she feared, on reasonable grounds, that the appellant would commit any one of a number of

specified sexual offences against children under the age of 14. She said that her fear was based on the appellant's psychiatric reports between 1963 and 1993, his criminal record, numerous hospital and parole board reports and a conversation with the appellant's treating psychiatrist at the Clarke Institute, who considered the appellant a high-risk paedophile if he did not take Luperon.

[14] Detective Leaver attended before Judge Kelly on November 22, 1994. The appellant came to court voluntarily. Nonetheless, Detective Leaver asked the appellant to leave the courtroom, and once he had done so, arrested him under s. 507(4) of the *Criminal Code.*

[15] The appellant was then in custody. The Crown therefore proceeded with a show cause hearing before Judge Kelly to determine whether the appellant would be released on bail pending the s. 810.1 application. The appellant had met with a lawyer the evening before, but that lawyer had not been retained to conduct the show cause hearing. The lawyer did ask that the hearing be adjourned 48 hours and that, in the interim, the appellant be released from custody. The Crown opposed the adjournment. Judge Kelly refused the adjournment request, saying that he would grant it only if the appellant remained in custody. The lawyer then withdrew. The appellant, unrepresented, agreed to the conditions of his release on bail sought by the Crown.

[16] These conditions included that he not engage in any activity involving contact with persons under the age of 14 unless in the presence of and under the supervision of Reverend Hugh Kirkegaard and another adult; that he not be at or be within 50 metres of a public park, swimming area, daycare, school ground, playground, community centre or any other place where persons under 14 can reasonably be expected to be found, except in the presence of and under the supervision of Reverend Kirkegaard and another adult; that he continue to take Luperon (or Provera) at least once a month; and that he continue counselling or treatment at the Clarke Institute. The s. 810.1 hearing was adjourned to November 28, 1994.

[17] On November 28, 1994, Judge Kelly varied the appellant's bail conditions. At the same time, the appellant brought an application for prerogative relief to prevent Judge Kelly from proceeding with the s. 810.1 hearing and for a declaration that ss. 810.1 and 507(4) of the Code violated ss. 7, 9, 11 and 15 of the Charter. Pending the resolution of the constitutional issues, the s. 810.1 hearing has been adjourned.

[18] However, on December 13, 1994, the appellant's bail conditions were further varied by Hoilett J. Under the amended conditions, the appellant continues to be prohibited from activities involving contact with persons under 14 years of age unless in the presence of an adult who does not have a criminal record, he continues to be restricted in his movement in parks and community centres, and he continues to be required to take counselling. The material in the record shows that the appellant was continuing his counselling at the Clarke Institute and was continuing to take Luperon.

[19] Fresh evidence filed on appeal showed that the appellant brought a further application to vary the conditions of his bail, which was opposed by the Crown. In a decision dated October 1, 1998, Keenan J refused the application. In his reasons, he noted that the appellant's bail conditions were virtually identical to the recognizance conditions under s. 810.1; that but for a single breach of the condition not to consume alcohol, the appellant had complied with all the conditions of his bail for four years; that he had co-operated with a Circle of Support and Accountability organized by volunteers of the Mennonite faith;

and that, indeed, Detective Leaver had participated in the Circle to supervise the appellant and assist in his treatment. Nonetheless, Keenan J could find "no basis for varying the recognizance of bail." I turn now to the constitutional issues in this appeal.

Discussion

First Issue: Does Section 810.1 Violate Section 7 of the Charter?

· · ·

[22] To make out a violation of s. 7 the appellant must show first that s. 810.1 deprives him of his right to life, liberty or security of the person; and second, that this deprivation is contrary to the principles of fundamental justice.

[23] The Crown acknowledges that the appellant meets the first branch of the s. 7 test. Section 810.1 deprives the appellant of his liberty. The conditions in s. 810.1 prevent the appellant from going to many places that other Canadians can freely go to and thus prevent the appellant from participating fully in a community's activities. Although not as serious an intrusion on his freedom as detention or imprisonment, these conditions in s. 810.1 still restrict the appellant's "liberty" under s. 7 of the Charter. Whether these restrictions on the appellant's liberty are in accordance with the principles of fundamental justice is at the heart of this appeal. The appellant argues that s. 810.1 contravenes the principles of fundamental justice for three reasons: it creates an offence based on status; it is overbroad; and it is void for vagueness.

(i) Does Section 810.1 Create a Status Offence?

[24] The appellant submits that s. 810.1 creates an offence based on a person's status alone, that is based on a person's medical diagnosis or even on a person's past criminal record but without any current offending conduct. The appellant argues that s. 810.1 is punitive, that it punishes a person though that person may have done nothing wrong. An offence based on status alone, according to the appellant, is contrary to the principles of fundamental justice.

[25] Accepting that a status offence contravenes fundamental justice, there are two answers to the appellant's submission. The main answer is that s. 810.1 does not create an offence. It is a preventive provision, not a punitive provision. It aims not to punish past wrongdoing but to prevent future harm to young children, to prevent them from being victimized by sexual abusers. The second answer is that s. 810.1 is not about a person's status. It is about assessing the present risk of a person committing a sexual offence against young children.

[26] Whether s. 810.1 is punitive or preventive permeated the argument of this appeal. Indeed, characterizing s. 810.1 as punitive is central to the appellant's position. If s. 810.1 is punitive, if it creates an offence, then the appellant fairly argues that it contains inadequate constitutional safeguards. Then J, however, held that s. 810.1 was a preventive measure aimed at the protection of children, and I agree with him.

[27] The criminal justice system has two broad objectives: punish wrongdoers and prevent future harm. A law aimed at the prevention of crime is just as valid an exercise of the federal criminal law power under s. 91(27) of the *Constitution Act, 1867*, as a law aimed at punishing crime. Thus, the appellant has not argued, nor could he, that Parliament cannot validly pass a law to prevent future harm to children.

[28] What the appellant does argue is that the law Parliament did pass, s. 810.1, is more punitive than preventive, and thus creates an offence, based solely on a person's status. Some aspects of s. 810.1 are punitive or coercive: the availability of an arrest warrant; detention pending a hearing unless the defendant is released on bail; and jail on the defendant's refusal to enter into a recognizance. These coercive aspects, however, are necessary to preserve the integrity of the s. 810.1 proceedings. By themselves, they do not turn s. 810.1 into a punitive provision. Nor does the stigma that undoubtedly accompanies a s. 810.1 proceeding make the proceeding punitive. That stigma will attach whether the section is preventive or punitive.

[29] To characterize s. 810.1 as punitive, as creating an offence, the appellant would have to show that its purpose is "to mete out criminal punishment" or that it has a "true penal consequence." A true penal consequence, according to the Supreme Court of Canada in *R v. Wigglesworth*, [1987] 2 SCR 541 at p. 561, 52 CCC (3d) 385 is "imprisonment or a fine which by its magnitude would appear to be imposed for the purpose of redressing the wrong done to society at large."

[30] By these standards, s. 810.1 does not create an offence. Its purpose is not to punish crime but to prevent crime from happening. Its sanctions are not punitive, nor are they intended to redress a wrong; they are activity and geographic restrictions on a person's liberty intended to protect a vulnerable group in our society from future harm.

[31] As Then J observed, s. 810.1 is analogous to s. 810, the peace bond provision of the *Criminal Code*. Typically, s. 810 is used to protect an identified victim, a person already harmed, from further harm where evidence points to the likelihood of danger to the victim from continuing contact with another person. Courts have consistently held that s. 810 is a preventive measure, that it does not create an offence or mete out a criminal punishment. The appellant did not suggest otherwise. Nor indeed did the appellant suggest that s. 810 was unconstitutional. Instead, he sought to distinguish s. 810 by arguing that it is meant to address breaches of the peace between citizens, and thus it amounts to a private remedy to ensure that named individuals remain law abiding.

[32] I see nothing "private" in s. 810. It authorizes a recognizance order in the same way as does s. 810.1. Both are concerned with preventing victimization. The main differences between s. 810 and s. 810.1 are the group of likely victims and the breadth of restrictions that may be imposed. A recognizance order under s. 810 aims to prevent harm to named individuals and the restrictions are tailored to prevent contact between those persons and the likely perpetrator. A recognizance order under s. 810.1 aims to prevent harm to a large group of children, identified only by their age, and the restrictions must necessarily be more extensive to prevent contact between this large group of children and the likely perpetrator. Section 810.1 is therefore broader than s. 810. But the two sections are similar enough that if s. 810 does not create an offence, it is hard to see how s. 810.1 does either.

[33] Moreover, I do not regard s. 810.1 as authorizing court-ordered restrictions on a person's liberty because of that person's status. Section 810.1 looks not to a person's status but to a person's present risk of future dangerousness. That risk will have to be assessed by looking at all relevant factors in a person's life, factors that are not immutable but will change over time.

[34] Thus, I conclude that s. 810.1 does not create a status offence. It is a preventive measure. Indeed, if the preventive aspect of the federal criminal law power is going to be

used anywhere, I cannot think of a more important use than the protection of young children from likely sexual predators. However, although s. 810.1 is properly characterized as a preventive measure, to be constitutionally valid, it must be neither overbroad nor vague.

(ii) Is Section 810.1 Overbroad?

[35] The appellant submits that s. 810.1 is overbroad contrary to ss. 7 and 9 of the Charter. Because I do not think that s. 9 adds anything to the appellant's position, I will focus only on s. 7.

[36] That a law not be overbroad is now accepted as a principle of fundamental justice: [*R v. Heywood* (1994), 94 CCC (3d) 481 (SCC)]. "Overbreadth" looks at the means a legislature has chosen to achieve a legitimate objective. The means chosen must be sufficiently tailored or narrowly targeted to meet their objective. If the means chosen are too broad or too wide, if the law goes further than necessary to accomplish its purpose, the law becomes arbitrary or disproportionate. A person's rights will be limited without good reason. The principles of fundamental justice will be violated.

[37] I accept the legitimacy, and indeed the importance, of Parliament's objective in passing s. 810.1 of the *Criminal Code*. Children are among the most vulnerable groups in our society. The sexual abuse of young children is a serious societal problem, a statement that needs no elaboration. A sizeable percentage of the sexual offences against children— according to the record, approximately 30 per cent—occurs in public places, the very places specified in s. 810.1. The expert evidence shows that recidivism rates for sexual abusers of children are high and that keeping high-risk offenders away from children is a sound preventive strategy. Parliament thus cannot be faulted for its objective in enacting s. 810.1. The state should not be obliged to wait until children are victimized before it acts. The societal interest in protecting children from sexual abuse supports Parliament's use of the preventive part of its criminal law power.

[38] Even accepting the legitimacy of Parliament's purpose, the appellant submits that the means it has chosen in s. 810.1 to achieve that purpose are too broad. The appellant focuses on four aspects of s. 810.1: the extent of the restrictions on his liberty, the imposition of these restrictions without a requirement of any previous offending conduct, the pre-hearing arrest and detention provisions to which he was subjected, and the extent of the procedural protections he was afforded. I will deal with each of these. Overall, however, I am not persuaded that s. 810.1 is overbroad. Parliament might have chosen other means to achieve its objective but the means that it did choose are reasonable and in accordance with the principles of fundamental justice.

1. Extent of Restrictions Does Not Make Section 810.1 Overbroad

[39] If a recognizance is ordered, a defendant may be restricted from participating in any activities or from attending a public park or public swimming area where children under 14 may reasonably be expected to gather or a daycare centre, schoolground or playground. In my view, these restrictions, although limiting a defendant's liberty, are not overbroad. I say that for three reasons. First, the restrictions stop short of detention or imprisonment. I think it fair to conclude that detention or imprisonment under a provision that does not charge an offence would be an unacceptable restriction on a defendant's liberty and would be contrary to the principles of fundamental justice. But as Then J

observed, the restrictions contemplated by s. 810.1 permit a defendant to lead a reasonably normal life.

[40] Second, these restrictions on a defendant's liberty are proportional to the important societal interest in s. 810.1, the protection of young children. As McLachlin J observed in *R v. Seaboyer*, [1991] 2 SCR 577 at p. 603, 66 CCC (3d) 321, "the principles of fundamental justice reflect a spectrum of interests, from the rights of the accused to broader societal concerns. Section 7 must be construed having regard to those interests. ..." The defendant's right to liberty is not the only s. 7 interest at stake in s. 810.1. The societal interest in protecting young children from harm must also be taken into account. Section 810.1 attempts to balance these two interests: the interest of likely child sexual abusers in going where they please, including places where young children gather, and the interest of the state in ensuring that young children can go safely and securely to places typically associated with children's activities. In my view, s. 810.1 strikes a reasonable compromise between these two interests. It provides a measured intrusion into a defendant's liberty consistent with protecting young children from harm.

[41] Third, accepting Then J's deletion of community centres, the restrictions contemplated by s. 810.1 are narrowly targeted to meet Parliament's objective. The only places a defendant may be prohibited from going are where children under age 14 are or can reasonably be expected to be present; and the only activities a defendant may be prohibited from engaging in are those involving contact with children under 14. By limiting the scope of s. 810.1 in this way, I do not accept the submission of the provincial Crown that s. 810.1(3) authorizes the court to impose broader restrictions on a defendant's liberty than activities, areas or places where children are likely to be found. Section 810.1(3) provides that a judge may "order the defendant to enter into a recognizance and comply with the conditions fixed by the provincial court judge, including" the specified conditions. The specified conditions following the word "including" are examples of the kinds of conditions that can be imposed. The context of s. 810.1 and its overall purpose suggest that the word "including" is used to limit the scope of the general term "conditions" to those conditions similar to the specified examples. On this interpretation, a judge could prohibit a defendant from going to a recreation hall where young children were likely to be present but could not, for example, require a defendant to take the drug Luperon, however desirable that may be. This interpretation, in my view, not only appropriately reflects the context and purpose of s. 810.1, it also accords with Charter values. A broader interpretation, permitting the judge to order a defendant to take a course of treatment or to take a particular drug, under a provision that does not create an offence would raise serious Charter concerns. Under the narrower interpretation I have adopted, the restrictions contemplated by s. 810.1 are not overbroad.

2. Lack of a Requirement of a Previous Criminal Record Does Not Make Section 810.1 Overbroad

[42] A recognizance order may be imposed on a defendant who has no previous criminal record, who has committed no overt sexual act, who has seemingly done nothing wrong. All that is required is for the presiding judge to be satisfied the informant has reasonable grounds for the fear that the defendant will commit a sexual offence against a child under 14. The appellant submits that without a triggering requirement of some

previous offending conduct, s. 810.1 is overbroad because it applies to too many people. I do not accept this submission.

[43] What s. 810.1 is trying to measure is a defendant's present likelihood of future dangerousness or present risk of committing a sexual offence against children in the future. Predicting future dangerousness is not an exact science. However, the impossibility of making exact predictions does not render s. 810.1 overbroad and contrary to our principles of fundamental justice. La Forest J addressed this point in dealing with the dangerous offender legislation in *R v. Lyons*, [1987] 2 SCR 309 at pp. 364-65, 37 CCC (3d) 1:

> However, as Holmes has reminded us, the life of the law has not been logic: it has been experience. The criminal law must operate in a world governed by practical considerations rather than abstract logic and, as a matter of practicality, the most that can be established in a future context is a likelihood of certain events occurring. ...
>
> It seems to me that a "likelihood" of specified future conduct occurring is the finding of fact required to be established; it is not, at one and the same time, the means of proving that fact. Logically, it seems clear to me that an individual can be found to constitute a threat to society without insisting that this require the court to assert an ability to predict the future.
>
> • • •

[44] A previous criminal record for sexual assault against children will no doubt be relevant to predicting future dangerousness in many cases. But insisting on a previous record before a recognizance can be ordered would undermine the preventive purpose of s. 810.1. It would require a child to be victimized before the Crown could act, even if the Crown had highly reliable evidence of dangerousness. If some previous offending conduct were required before a recognizance could be ordered, then the Crown could not protect children from child sexual abusers known to medical authorities but not yet charged or from sexual abusers who could not be charged because the victim was too traumatized to testify or because the victim could not be found. Instead of requiring some previous offending conduct, s. 810.1 invites the presiding judge to consider all the relevant evidence on whether a defendant will commit a sexual offence against children. I agree with Then J's summary of the kinds of evidence likely to be led before the presiding judge (at p. 365):

> For instance, evidence may be led that the defendant has made a threat or sexual proposition to a specific child or a group of children. More common, no doubt, will be cases where evidence will be led at the hearing concerning the individual's general proclivity to abuse children sexually. This could be based on a relevant criminal record and past behaviour around children. Evidence of a diagnosed medical mental disorder that predisposes the defendant to be sexually attracted to children might weigh in favour of ordering a recognizance, just as evidence of continuing successful treatment will be in the defendant's favour. On the very wording of the section, no one factor can be determinative.

[45] This passage reflects a sensible approach to a proceeding under s. 810.1. Requiring a criminal record or some other offending conduct as a condition of a recognizance order under s. 810.1 is at odds with the preventive purpose of the section. I conclude that s. 810.1 is not overbroad because it fails to require any offending conduct before a recognizance can be ordered.

3. The Pre-Hearing Provisions for Arrest and Bail Do Not Make Section 810.1 Overbroad

[46] The provisions for pre-trial arrest and bail—which, as I will discuss later in these reasons, apply to a proceeding under s. 810.1—carry with them the possibility of a sanction more severe—custody or detention—than any sanction that may be imposed as a result of a hearing under s. 810.1. That possibility, however, does not make the section overbroad. Pre-trial arrest or even pre-hearing detention may be necessary to secure the defendant's attendance at the hearing or to prevent harm to children pending a hearing because of a defendant's unwillingness to comply with reasonable terms of release. In short, as I have already said, pre-trial arrest and detention may be needed in some cases to ensure the integrity and viability of the s. 810.1 proceedings themselves.

4. Procedural Safeguards Are Sufficient to Not Make Section 810.1 Overbroad

[47] The procedural safeguards in s. 810.1 are adequate. Anyone subjected to a s. 810.1 application receives notice of the hearing. The hearing must meet the procedural fairness requirements of a summary conviction trial. No order can be made until after the hearing is completed. The presiding provincial court judge has discretion to limit the restrictions imposed. Any order made is not a lifelong injunction; it can last no longer than a year and may be renewed only after an entirely new hearing. A person subjected to a s. 810.1 order may appeal the order and may, at any time, seek to vary the conditions.

[48] I therefore conclude that s. 810.1 is not overbroad. Instead, it strikes a reasonable balance between the liberty interest of the defendant and the state's interest in protecting young children from harm. A defendant's liberty interest may be restricted only after a hearing complying with the requirements of natural justice and only to the extent needed to avoid unreasonably jeopardizing the safety and security of young children.

(iii) Is Section 810.1 Void for Vagueness?

[49] Like the overbreadth principle, the void for vagueness principle is also concerned with whether the legislature has used precise enough means to achieve its objective. But whereas overbreadth is concerned with whether the legislation is targeted sufficiently narrowly, vagueness is concerned with whether the legislation is defined with sufficient clarity. The rationale for the void for vagueness principle is that, unless a law sufficiently delineates the area of risk of unlawful conduct, citizens will not have the fair notice of the law to which they are entitled, and police officers and others will have too much discretion in deciding how and when to enforce the law. Thus, a law must provide "an intelligible standard according to which the judiciary must do its work" and "an adequate basis for legal debate, that is for reaching a conclusion as to its meaning by reasoned analysis applying legal criteria." Otherwise, the law will be impermissibly vague contrary to the principles of fundamental justice.

[50] The appellant submits that s. 810.1 does not sufficiently delineate an area of risk of unlawful conduct, and thus does not provide fair substantive notice to a citizen, because it allows for restrictions on liberty on an informant's fear on reasonable grounds. The appellant argues that the word "fear" should be contrasted with the word "belief," which is used in *Criminal Code* provisions authorizing an arrest or a search. "Fear," according

to the appellant, can be irrational or emotional and is invariably subjective, while "belief" can be assessed objectively.

[51] I do not accept the appellant's argument. The word "fear" or "fears" should not be considered in isolation but together with the modifying words in s. 810.1(1) "on reasonable grounds." Fear alone connotes a state of belief or an apprehension that a future event, thought to be undesirable, may or will occur. But "on reasonable grounds" lends objectivity to the apprehension. In other words, the phrase "fears on reasonable grounds" in s. 810.1(1) connotes a reasonably based sense of apprehension about a future event, or as Then J put it, it "equates to a belief, objectively established, that the individual will commit an offence" (at p. 381).

[52] Moreover, although an informant's fear triggers an application under s. 810.1, under s-s. (3) a recognizance order can only be made if the presiding judge is satisfied by "evidence" that the fear is reasonably based. Section 810.1(3) therefore requires the judge to come to his or her own conclusion about the likelihood that the defendant will commit one of the offences listed in s-s. (1). Although the "evidence" the judge relies on might include hearsay, a recognizance could only be ordered on evidence that is credible and trustworthy.

[53] Despite the need for the informant's state of belief to be objectively assessed and for the presiding judge to come to an independent conclusion, I acknowledge some imprecision in the phrase "fears on reasonable grounds." But some imprecision is to be expected because s. 810.1 requires a prediction about future dangerousness. So too does s. 810, which uses the same phrase. The phrase is not so imprecise that it fails to delineate an area of risk or fails to provide an adequate basis for legal debate. Moreover, it is surrounded by requirements in s. 810.1—the information, the summons, the hearing itself—that give the defendant fair notice of the conduct sought to be prevented; and if a recognizance is ordered, the defendant will have fair notice of the conditions imposed and, thus, will know how to comply. The threshold for declaring a law void for vagueness is appropriately high. Section 810.1 does not pass this threshold. I would not give effect to this ground of appeal.

Second Issue: Did Then J Err in Reading Down "Shall" to "May" in Section 810.1(2) of the Code?

[54] Section 810.1(2) provided that "a provincial court judge who receives an information under s-s. (1) shall cause the parties to appear before the provincial court judge." Then J held that, in the context of a preventive provision like s. 810.1, making the issuance of process on a defendant mandatory violated ss. 7 and 9 of the Charter and could not be justified under s. 1. In his view, "an automatic issuance of process, with the potential arrest of the defendant, is excessive and unwarranted." It provides "no control on obviously unfounded informations under which a person may be summonsed or arrested" (at pp. 399-401). Thus, it subjects the ordinary citizen to capricious or unjustifiable detention. In Then J's view, and relying on the Supreme Court's decision in *Baron v. Canada*, [1993] 1 SCR 416, 78 CCC (3d) 510, "a residual discretion is a constitutional requirement." The Crown does not take issue with Then J's holding that "shall" in s. 810.1(2) is unconstitutional.

[55] The appellant, however, takes issue with Then J's remedy. Having found that a discretion was a constitutional requirement, Then J applied s. 52 of the *Constitution Act, 1982*, and read down "shall" to "may." The appellant submits that he should simply have declared the subsection inoperative.

[56] The Supreme Court refused to read down "shall" to "may" in *Baron* itself, and in *R v. Swain*, [1991] 1 SCR 933, 63 CCC (3d) 481. Then J distinguished *Baron* on the grounds that the Attorney General in that case had not asked for the remedy of reading down and that, unlike the provision challenged in *Baron*, s. 810.1(2) was not central to the legislative regime in s. 810.1. I think it fair to say, however, that when legislation expressly excludes a judicial discretion, courts have been reluctant to read one in as a constitutional remedy. Nonetheless, in my view, Then J was correct to read down "shall" to "may" in this case.

[57] In deciding on the appropriate remedy under s. 52 for a Charter breach, "the court must apply the measures which will best vindicate the values expressed in the Charter while refraining from intrusion into the legislative sphere beyond what is necessary." Before reading down or reading in, the court must ask "whether it is safe to assume that the legislature would have enacted the legislation in its altered form." Here, "may" in s. 810.1(2) appropriately vindicates Charter values. Giving the presiding judge a discretion whether to summons or arrest a defendant once an information is sworn is an important constitutional safeguard. Thus, the remedy of reading in "may," although explicitly altering the legislation, will "preserve statutory objectives within clear constitutional contours."

[58] Recent legislation shows that we can safely assume Parliament would have enacted s. 810.1(2) with the word "may." In 1997 Parliament added two new provisions to the *Criminal Code* similar to s. 810.1, and in each new provision used the word "may" instead of "shall." Section 810.01 authorizes a recognizance order against a person likely to commit "a criminal organization offence," and s. 810.2 authorizes a recognizance order against a person likely to commit "a serious personal injury offence." Sections 810.01 and 810.2 are worded similarly to s. 810.1 with necessary modifications for their context. Sections 810.01(2) and s. 810.2(2) are identical to s. 810.1(2) except that in place of "shall cause the parties to appear before the provincial court judge," in the two new provisions Parliament has used "may cause the parties to appear before the provincial court judge." Because Parliament itself has enacted s. 810.01 and s. 810.2 to conform to Then J's decision, we can safely assume that reading down "shall" to "may" does not unnecessarily intrude into the legislative domain. I would not give effect to this ground of appeal.

Third Issue: Do Sections 507(4) and 515 of the Criminal Code Apply to a Proceeding Under Section 810.1?

[59] In *R v. Allen*, this court held that what is now s. 507(4) of the Code, allowing for the issuance of a warrant for the arrest of the accused, applies to s. 810 of the Code. Section 507(4) provides:

> 507(4) Where a justice considers that a case is made out for compelling an accused to attend before him to answer to a charge of an offence, he shall issue a summons to the accused unless the allegations of the informant or the evidence of any witness or witnesses taken in accordance with subsection (3) discloses reasonable grounds to believe that it is necessary in the public interest to issue a warrant for the arrest of the accused.

[60] In *Allen*, the accused argued that s. 507(4) applied to "a charge of an offence" and thus could not apply to a proceeding under s. 810, which did not create an offence. Goodman JA, writing for the court, rejected this argument. Section 507(4) is in Part XVI of the Code; s. 810 is in Part XXVII dealing with summary convictions. Section 795 of the Code,

which is also in Part XXVII, states that the provisions of Part XVI "with respect to compelling the appearance of an accused before a justice ... in so far as they are not inconsistent with the Part, apply, with such modifications as the circumstances require, to proceedings under this Part." In Goodman JA's view, s. 795 made s. 507(4) applicable to a proceeding under s. 810 even though s. 810 "does not create an offence" (at p. 158).

[61]　Section 515, the provision permitting bail pending trial, also is in Part XVI of the Code; and s. 810.1 is in Part XXVII of the Code. Therefore, applying *Allen*, both ss. 507(4) and 515 apply to proceedings under s. 810.1.

[62]　The appellant asked us to reconsider *Allen* on its own terms or in the light of the Charter. In my view, *Allen* was correctly decided. ...

[63]　*Allen*, however, was decided without reference to the Charter. The appellant submits that applying ss. 507(4) and 515 to a s. 810.1 proceeding violates s. 7 of the Charter. The argument has two branches: both permitting pre-hearing arrest and detention because of a fear of future misconduct and permitting a more severe sanction pending the hearing than could be ordered at the conclusion of the s. 810.1 hearing violates the principles of fundamental justice. I disagree.

[64]　First, the presiding judge has a discretion whether to issue a warrant for the arrest of a defendant or to detain a defendant pending a hearing. If a defendant is released pending a hearing, the judge has discretion concerning the bail conditions to be imposed. The existence of this judicial discretion is, as I have already said, an important constitutional safeguard and procedural protection for the defendant. The presiding judge has ample authority to balance the interests of the defendant and the interests of the public pending a s. 810.1 hearing and to ensure that the hearing is held promptly. Second, and repeating what I said earlier, provision for pre-hearing arrest and detention is needed to preserve the integrity of the s. 810.1 proceedings. The court may need the power of arrest and detention to ensure the attendance of a defendant at the hearing or to protect children from the possibility of serious harm pending the hearing.

[65]　Moreover, s. 810.1 is not rendered unconstitutional because, in a particular case, an arrest warrant may have been improvidently issued or inappropriate bail conditions may have been imposed pending the hearing. ...

[66]　The same analysis applies to the arrest and release procedure imported into s. 810.1. Under s. 507(4), the justice is to compel the defendant's attendance by means of a summons only, unless the allegations of the informant or the evidence "discloses reasonable grounds to believe that it is necessary in the public interest to issue a warrant for the arrest of the accused." Because a hearing under s. 810.1 can only result in the defendant being required to enter into a recognizance, the circumstances in which it would be "necessary in the public interest" to issue an arrest warrant will be limited to cases where that process is necessary to preserve the integrity of the s. 810.1 proceedings. The justice will require the informant to make out a case that the defendant will not otherwise attend court or that the defendant poses an imminent risk to the safety of children, which s. 810.1 is designed to protect.

[67]　If the justice does issue an arrest warrant, s. 515 of the *Criminal Code* directs the justice to release the defendant on a simple undertaking without conditions, unless the prosecutor shows cause why some more intrusive order—such as a recognizance with conditions—is required. The discretion under s. 515 must be exercised judicially and

bearing in mind the limited conditions that can be imposed following a successful s. 810.1 application.

[68] Finally, although s. 515 provides that the justice may order the detention of the defendant pending the s. 810.1 hearing, that discretion is circumscribed by the provisions of s. 515(10), which authorize detention only where necessary to ensure the defendant's attendance at court, for the protection or safety of the public or "any other just cause," including the maintenance of confidence in the administration of justice. Again, in the light of the limited consequences of a successful s. 810.1 application, only in unusual circumstances will the justice be entitled to order the detention of the defendant pending the hearing. Indeed, it will be a rare case where it would enhance confidence in the administration of justice to detain a defendant who is not alleged to have committed any crime and who can only be required to enter into a recognizance at the conclusion of the proceedings.

[69] So interpreted, these various provisions of the Code strike the appropriate balance between the public interest in the protection of children and the liberty interest of the defendant.

[70] For these reasons, I view ss. 507(4) and 515 in their application to s. 810.1 as being in accordance with the principles of fundamental justice. Therefore, I would not give effect to this ground of appeal.

The reasoning of the lower court decision (by Then J) in *Budreo* was applied in *R v Baker* (1999), 64 CRR (2d) 126, [1999] BCJ No 681 (QL) (SC), to reject a constitutional challenge to s 810.2 (serious personal injury offence). This provision is somewhat wider than s 810.1 because it is not necessary that a specified victim be named in the information or the subsequent recognizance. This reasoning was also applied in the notorious case of Karla Homolka (Teale), below, which received enormous media attention due to the grisly killings that led to her incarceration. Although a s 810.2 order was originally made, it was set aside on appeal.

Teale v Noble
(2005), 36 CR (6th) 258, [2006] RJQ 181 (Sup Ct) (footnotes omitted)

BRUNTON JSC:

[1] For her role in the homicides of Kristen French and Leslie Mahaffy, Karla Teale was sentenced to 12 years of imprisonment. On the eve of her release, after having served her entire sentence, the Attorney General of Quebec gave his consent to Mr. Brian Noble, a peace officer, to lay an information seeking an order under s. 810.2 Cr. C. which targeted Ms. Teale.

[2] Section 810.2 Cr. C. permits a judge to order that a defendant enter into a recognizance for a maximum period of 12 months to keep the peace and be of good behaviour. In general terms, other reasonable conditions can also be included.

[3] The order will only issue if the informant establishes on a balance of probabilities that he or she has reasonable grounds to fear that the defendant will commit a serious personal injury offence as that expression is defined in section 752 Cr. C.

• • •

[4] After an evidentiary hearing was held, an Order directed against Ms. Teale was issued on June 3, 2005. She has appealed that decision.

• • •

[20] One need only look to the type of evidence which was presented in the *Budreo* case at first instance on the constitutional question.

> The evidence the parties submitted took the form of affidavits from experts in the field of sexual offences or criminology, cross-examination of those affiants and the submission of scholarly works. In addition to the affidavit evidence, a large amount of documentary evidence was filed in the form of articles and studies to assist the court in dealing with the larger constitutional questions.

[21] It is clear that that material provided great assistance both in first instance and before the Court of Appeal of Ontario. In the absence of that type of proof in the present case, I hold that it would be improper to entertain the constitutional challenge for the first time at the appellate level. The challenge raises complex issues which should be addressed only if a proper factual foundation is set. It has not been in this case.

[22] If I am in error in refusing to entertain the challenge, I would nonetheless hold that based upon the record before me, s. 810.2 Cr. C. is constitutional. No cogent reason has been advanced why the decision in *Budreo* should not be followed.

• • •

D. The Sufficiency of the Evidence

[42] In order to succeed, the informant had to establish on a balance of probabilities that he had reasonable grounds to fear that Ms. Teale would commit a personal injury offence. It was not enough to invoke Ms. Teale's participation in the sordid homicides of Ms. French and Ms. Mahaffy. Since s. 810.2 Cr. C. proceedings look to the future, the fear relates to the present portrait which is offered of the defendant by the informant.

[43] Nor is it sufficient to equate the fear with a *risk* that the defendant will commit a personal injury offence sometime in the future. There is a temporal component to s. 810.2 Cr. C. proceedings. The fear must reflect a risk of *serious and imminent* danger. This is reflected both in the construction of the section and its subsequent interpretation by the courts.

[44] The section itself imposes a twelve month limit on the duration of the recognizance order. If the section called only for the proof of a fear of specified action sometime in the future, why place a twelve month limit on the court's response? This time limit, combined with the fact that the fear that is to be established is that the defendant will commit a personal injury offence imports a component of imminency.

> Judges should take care before exercising their preventive jurisdiction. Both ss. 810 and 810.1 speak of a reasonably grounded fear that the defendant "will" commit an offence. To my mind, as a matter of legislative construction, this takes the appropriate threshold a notch above a simple demonstration that the defendant is more likely than not to commit an offence. *A reasonably grounded fear of a serious and imminent danger must be proved on a balance of probabilities.* (emphasis added)

• • •

[46] The hearing judge held that the informant had established on a balance of probabilities reasonable grounds for his fears of a real and imminent danger that Ms. Teale would commit a personal injury offence. As will be seen, I hold that the proof presented did not establish, on a balance of probabilities, a fear of imminent danger.

[47] The proof presented before the hearing judge consisted generally of the following material. All psychological reports dealing with Ms. Teale over the years were produced. None of the authors of these reports were called as witnesses.

[48] Mr. Noble testified. He directed the hearing judge to various excerpts of the documentary evidence which in his mind objectively established the reasonable grounds for his fear that Ms. Teale would commit a serious personal injury offence.

[49] Ms. Teale responded by producing the Galligan report which had been commissioned to examine the circumstances of the plea bargain involving the appellant and whether it would be appropriate to charge her with sexual assault as regards a victim referred to as Jane Doe. The other significant element of proof produced by Ms. Teale was the testimony of Dr. Louis Morissette. Dr. Morissette, a psychiatrist, had been engaged by counsel for Ms. Teale. He had met her for a period of three and one half hours, days before the hearing. His report was produced as exhibit I-8. Ms. Teale chose not to testify.

[50] After stating that he had considered all the evidence, the hearing judge found that the informant had reasonable grounds to fear that Ms. Teale would commit a personal injury offence. He relied principally upon two elements of proof. Those elements consisted of a report prepared by Madam France Aubut, a psychologist (exhibit R-1, tab 6). The second element referred to the fact that in the recent past, Ms. Teale had been corresponding with an inmate she had met who was serving a sentence for the homicide of his former girlfriend.

[51] As for Dr. Morissette's testimony and report, the hearing judge summarily accorded these elements of proof less weight as they were based upon hearsay in his estimation.

[52] Exercising an appellate jurisdiction, my powers are limited as regards the hearing judge's appreciation of the evidence.

> Appellate courts may not interfere with the findings of fact made and the factual inferences drawn by the trial judge, unless they are clearly wrong, unsupported by the evidence or otherwise unreasonable. The imputed error must, moreover, be plainly identified. And it must be shown to have affected the result. "Palpable and overriding error" is a resonant and compendious expression of this well established norm.

[53] The experienced hearing judge was confronted with a difficult and complex case. He was also confronted with the pressures of time as the appellant's release date loomed on the horizon. Bearing these factors in mind together with my limited powers on appeal, I respectfully find that the hearing judge erred in holding that the informant had met his evidentiary burden. The errors consist of a combination of the following factors:

- the summary dismissal of Dr. Morissette's evidence;
- the lack of explanation of why numerous elements in the proof favourable to the appellant could have no bearing on the ultimate decision which had to be made;
- the lack of a contextual analysis of the two elements which the hearing judge relied upon to render his decision;

- the unreasonable conclusion based upon all the evidence that the appellant represented a "real and imminent" danger to commit a personal injury offence.

• • •

[56]   While it is true that the trier of fact, in assessing the weight to be given to an expert's testimony examines what portion of the factors which lead to the expert's opinion have been proven, the situation in the present case was unique. Almost all of the proof presented was generated from assessments of Ms. Teale, which in turn were based upon information which she had provided. If the fact that Ms. Teale did not testify affected the weight given to Dr. Morissette's opinion, why did it not affect the weight given to the reports produced by all the interveners in the file, including Madam Aubut?

• • •

[58]   Furthermore, the testimony of Dr. Morissette was a challenge to Madam Aubut's report or, at the very least, an attempt to put Madam Aubut's report in context. By summarily putting aside the Morissette evidence, the hearing judge's analysis of the Aubut report was flawed.

ii. Lack of Reference to Elements Favourable to the Appellant

[59]   I recognize that the hearing judge did not have to refer to every item of evidence in his judgment. However, this was a complex case which called for the analysis of the development, or lack thereof, of Ms. Teale over a period of twelve years. The proof presented was not exclusively negative from Ms. Teale's point of view. Indeed, it could be said that there was a steady stream of opinion over the years contained in the evidence which, if accepted, clearly would show that the informant had not met his burden.

[60]   No specific reference was made to any of this proof. The only indirect reference was contained in the following catch-all phrase:

> ... *après analyse attentive de toute la preuve, tant orale que documentaire, alors, la réponse à cette question, suite à une analyse complète de la preuve, est oui. La crainte raisonnable est démontrée par prépondérance de preuve.*

[61]   As mentioned above, the complexity of the case and the presence of many elements of proof favourable to Ms. Teale called for a more in-depth analysis than that detailed in the phrase quoted above.

iii. Contextual Analysis of the Factors Retained

[62]   As I have already stated, the hearing judge based his decision primarily on the contents of a report prepared by Madam France Aubut (exhibit R-1, tab 6) and the fact that Ms. Teale had corresponded in the recent past with one Gerbet, an inmate convicted for the homicide of his former girlfriend.

• • •

[74]   Madam Aubut concluded that the appellant offered an adequate collaboration during the course of the program. However, she refused on more than one occasion to delve into certain subjects because it was too disagreeable. Madam Aubut gave the example of Ms. Teale refusing to profoundly describe her thoughts, behaviour and emotions when she was committing the offences. For Madam Aubut, this attitude was dangerous—on the

one hand it reflected an attitude which Ms. Teale herself identified as one of her risk factors, and on the other, was the complete opposite of the type of behaviour she identified in her prevention plan, i.e. not being secretive and seeking aid from her support group.

[75] Madam Aubut concluded, in part, on this note:

> *Il nous est apparu que Madame Teale est portée à utiliser de façon sélective ses stratégies d'adaptation aux facteurs de risque qu'elle a identifiés. Il faut donc se questionner sur le fait qu'elle pourrait également généraliser, i.e. appliquer ses acquis, de façon sélective lorsqu'elle se retrouvera à l'extérieur des murs. Cette éventualité l'exposerait de nouveau à des situations à risque susceptibles de la projeter dans une progression de son cycle comportemental criminel. Conséquemment, nous considérons que l'impact du programme sur la diminution du risque qu'elle représente est de portée limitée jusqu'à présent.*

[76] For the hearing judge, this conclusion was capital. …

[77] Turning to the second specific factor upon which the hearing judge based his decision, the proof revealed that Ms. Teale began a relationship with a male inmate in January 2002. She was surprised exchanging a kiss with him in the institution's library.

[78] Searches revealed that the two had exchanged undergarments and were engaged in correspondence. A photo of the male inmate was found in Ms. Teale's possession. Although both were advised to stop the correspondence, it continued.

[79] The male inmate, Gerbet, was serving time for having killed his former girlfriend.

[80] The hearing judge noted that during the 1993 sentence representations, much was made of the fact that Ms. Teale was a victim of battered woman's syndrome and this explained her participation in the sordid events which led to the homicides of the victims.

[81] Subsequent reports highlighted the fact that the single greatest risk for Ms. Teale to re-offend would arise if she found herself in an abusive relationship. Her relationship with Gerbet, which continued notwithstanding that she had been warned, did not bode well for the future.

[82] I have stated earlier that the hearing judge erred in not considering the two factors he relied upon, together or individually, in the context of all the proof which was presented. At best these factors established that there was a risk that Ms. Teale would re-offend. They did not establish that there was a real and imminent danger that she would re-offend as is required by s. 810.2 Cr. C.

[83] In commentating on Madam Aubut's report, Dr. Morissette acknowledged that the results of Ms. Teale's participation in the program were not perfect. He added however that one cannot expect perfection in this type of endeavour. If the final assessment notes that the participant did not accomplish her assigned work projects, missed sessions or was not serious in her approach, then one begins to develop warning signs that she is a bad risk. This was not the case for Ms. Teale.

• • •

[85] As for the evidence concerning the correspondence between Ms. Teale and Gerbet, the following points should be noted to fully understand the context of this factor.

[86] First, the nature of the contents of the correspondence was never entered into evidence although it appears that certain letters were seized as early as 2002. Second, no intervener in the correctional system thought the contents of the correspondence so grave for Ms. Teale's personal development as to impose a ban on the exchanges.

[87] Third, no proof was made of Gerbet's character. The parties agreed that he was serving a sentence for having killed his ex-girlfriend. While this is extremely grave, the personality and inherent dangerousness of such an offender is not constant. Was the crime he committed an aberration in an otherwise unblemished past or was he a chronic abuser of women, prone to violent acts? Perhaps it was the latter, but in the absence of evidence, a Court cannot base a decision on speculation or educated guesses.

[88] Fourth, it appears the parties agreed that Gerbet was to be the subject of an eventual deportation order when he would become eligible for parole as he was not a Canadian citizen. This fact would eliminate Ms. Teale being able to interact with him except by way of correspondence. If the various experts who examined her over the years agreed that her entering another abusive relationship would greatly increase the risk of her re-offending, none suggested that this risk could be triggered at a distance. None of these points appear to have been considered by the hearing judge.

iv. The Totality of the Evidence

[89] No one denies that Ms. Teale's involvement in the horrifying homicides of Ms. French and Ms. Mahaffy and her sister Tammy displayed unspeakable depravity. However, the recurring themes in the assessments of her actions on the weight of the evidence is that (1) her participation in the crimes was due principally to the abuse she suffered at the hands of her husband; (2) she has made progress over the years of her incarceration; (3) she will need psychological support for the better part of her life; (4) the possibility that she will re-offend exists; and (5) the possibility does not translate into an imminent risk of re-offending.

[90] At the sentencing hearing, experienced and respected Crown counsel had this to say:

> The Crown's assessment, based on a review of such psychiatric evidence, is that absent the influence and association of someone whose behaviour bears the characteristics of what truly may be one of this province's and the country's most feared individuals, she is unlikely to re-offend.

[91] The Crown added:

> In light of the specific psychiatric evaluation of this accused, it is apparent that continued treatment will be required. I would venture that that is a lifetime proposition.

[92] The Honourable Mr. Justice F.J. Kovacs, in sentencing Ms. Teale, made reference to three psychological assessments. Dr. A.I. Malcolm, a psychiatrist, stated in a May 28, 1993 report that Ms. Teale was "not a dangerous person … but she will require much assistance." Dr. H.J. Arnot, a psychiatrist, in a May 30, 1993 report stated:

> … I do not see her as being a danger now or ever again to society, particularly as long as she is not in contact with her estranged husband, Paul Bernardo or someone like him. In my opinion, Karla requires lengthy psychiatric care. …

[93] Dr. J.A. Long, a clinical psychologist, in a report dated June 3, 1993 stated:

> … she is not a danger to herself nor to anyone else and therefore may be placed in a low-security institution.

[94] The documentary evidence produced before the hearing judge follows Ms. Teale through the years of her incarceration.

. . .

[110] Numerous decisions of the National Parole Board were produced before the hearing judge. In all cases, Ms. Teale's supervised or early release was denied. Two points should be made about these reports. First, Ms. Teale had made the decision to serve her entire sentence. Thus, both she and the Parole Board were aware that no decision of the Parole Board would be subject to review.

[111] Second, the Parole Board appeared to be cognizant of the fact that Ms. Teale's supervised or early release would be extremely difficult to manage due to the negative public opinion directed to her case. The combination of these two factors, at the very least, would not have incited the Parole Board to take the decision, which it might have considered bold, to gradually re-integrate Ms. Teale into society.

[112] I have already had occasion to discuss at length Madam Aubut's report of November 17, 2004. There remains the testimony of Dr. Morissette.

. . .

[115] As I have mentioned earlier in this judgment, Dr. Morissette had the occasion to meet Ms. Teale for a total of three and one-half hours prior to producing his May 26, 2005 report. This short period of time of consultation calls for a certain amount of caution when assessing his conclusions. Having said this, Dr. Morissette's opinions do reflect those of the majority of the professionals who had occasion to assess Ms. Teale over the years.

[116] His conclusions can be summarized in the following general terms:

- There was no indication of a psychotic personality based upon the results of the H.A.R.E. test. Ms. Teale's results placed her at the extreme low end of the scale and well below the average of federal inmates.
- She scored low on the SVR (Sexual Violence Risk) test.
- The majority of inmates who represent a risk to re-offend have a record of disciplinary offences during their incarceration. Ms. Teale's record was unblemished.
- The results of Ms. Teale's therapy with Madam Aubut were to be expected. It is clear that while Ms. Teale had made progress, she would require on-going professional aid.
- There were no clinical, historical or current mental problems which could lead one to conclude that Ms. Teale was more at risk to re-offend than the average federal inmate.

[117] Dr. Morissette ends his report with this conclusion:

Pour toutes ces raisons, nous croyons que Mme Teale devrait être considérée comme étant à très faible risque de récidive en terme de violence contre les personnes, de violence sexuelle, d'activités criminelles, etc. Sur une échelle de 0 à 10 (0 étant une absolue certitude qu'elle ne commettrait jamais à nouveau de délit et 10 étant une absolue certitude qu'elle commettra à nouveau des délits violents), nous la placerions entre 1 et 3.

[118] I am of the opinion that this statement aptly summarizes the conclusion which should be reached when all the proof I have described is analyzed. The weight of the psychological assessments of Ms. Teale and her progress support this conclusion.

[119] The possibility that Ms. Teale might re-offend one day cannot be completely eliminated. However, her development over the last twelve years demonstrates, on a balance of probabilities, that this is unlikely to occur. She does not represent a real and imminent danger to commit a personal injury offence as is required by s. 810.2 Cr. C.

The appeal should be granted.

FURTHER READING

Thompson, Jordan. "Reconsidering the Burden of Proof in Dangerous Offender Law: Canadian Jurisprudence, Risk Assessment and Aboriginal Offenders" (2016) 79 Sask L Rev 49.

CHAPTER SIXTEEN

Aboriginal Offenders

I. INTRODUCTION

The materials in this chapter only scratch the surface of a complex issue—the suitability of invoking Anglo-Canadian criminal justice structures and precepts to deal with Aboriginal offenders. Certainly, one must question how fairly our criminal justice system has responded to Aboriginal offenders. Empirically, there is no doubt that Aboriginal persons are overrepresented in our penal structures. The history of Canada's relationship with its First Nations and the acknowledged constitutional status of Aboriginal rights create an obligation to explore the reasons for overrepresentation, to question the record of systemic unfairness, and to find new ways of applying criminal justice.

II. SENTENCING ABORIGINAL OFFENDERS: STATISTICAL TRENDS AND CONTEXT

In many respects, the high rate of Aboriginal incarceration, resulting in the significant overrepresentation of Aboriginal peoples in prison, is the most intractable problem confronting sentencing in Canada. Judicial initiatives and legislative remedies need to be seen in the light of the problem to which they are a response. First, however, it is important to note that ethnic overrepresentation in prison statistics—and, in particular, Aboriginal overrepresentation—is a problem for most Western nations. For international comparisons, see Michael Tonry, ed, *Ethnicity, Crime and Immigration: Comparative and Cross-National Perspectives*, Crime & Justice, vol 21 (Chicago: University of Chicago Press, 1996); see also Julian V Roberts & Anthony N Doob, "Race, Ethnicity, and Criminal Justice in Canada" in Tonry, ed, *Ethnicity, Crime and Immigration*. New Zealand and Australia are two other countries where indigenous people account for a disproportionate number of prisoners. Maoris in New Zealand and Aboriginals in Australia have long been overrepresented in criminal justice statistics and, in particular, prison admissions. This reality has given rise to remedial initiatives in both countries, albeit with limited success: see Samantha Jeffries & Philip Stenning, "Sentencing Aboriginal Offenders: Law, Policy, and Practice in Three Countries" (2014) 56:4 Can J Corr 447.

A. Current Trends in Aboriginal Incarceration

The overrepresentation problem in Canada appears more pressing than in other countries and is of a long-standing nature. The statistics on Aboriginal overincarceration tell a grim tale. They reveal substantial overrepresentation in prison admissions and prison populations, both at the federal level and in several provinces. Moreover, the overrepresentation has been apparent in prison statistics for decades.

B. Federal Correctional Statistics

The National Household Survey (NHS) reveals that, in 2011, 1,400,685 people had an Aboriginal identity—representing 4.3 percent of the total Canadian population: see "Aboriginal Peoples in Canada: First Nations People, Métis and Inuit," online: Statistics Canada <http://www12.statcan.gc.ca/nhs-enm/2011/as-sa/99-011-x/99-011-x2011001-eng.cfm>. At the federal level, Aboriginal Canadians (the category Aboriginal includes persons who are Inuit, Innu, Métis, and North American Indian; offenders themselves identify their category) represented over one-fifth (21 percent) of the offender population (this includes all offenders in a CSC facility, offenders on temporary release from a CSC facility, and offenders who are currently actively supervised in the community): see Public Safety Canada, *Corrections and Conditional Release Statistical Overview, 2015* (Ottawa: Public Works and Government Services Canada, 2016) [Public Safety Canada, *2015 Annual Report*]. Aboriginal offenders in the federal system are also more likely to be in custody, rather than in the community under supervision, than non-Aboriginal offenders (approximately three-quarters of Aboriginal federal offenders were in custody, the remainder in the community under supervision; only two-thirds of non-Aboriginal federal offenders were in custody, one-third on community supervision: see Public Safety Canada, *2015 Annual Report*, Table C11). Aboriginal prisoners were more likely than non-Aboriginal prisoners to be detained in maximum security (only 15 percent of federal Aboriginal offenders were in minimum security compared to 23 percent of non-Aboriginals; 16 percent of Aboriginal federal offenders were in maximum security compared to 13 percent of non-Aboriginal federal offenders: Public Safety Canada, *2015 Annual Report*, Table C-12). Finally, the problem of Aboriginal overincarceration has been getting worse in recent years. Nationally, in 2009-10, there were 2,919 Aboriginal offenders in the federal corrections population; this number has increased steadily since then, and reached 3,542 in 2013-14, the most recent year for which data are currently available: Public Safety Canada, *2015 Annual Report*, Table C-16. This represents an increase of 21 percent in only four years. Over a longer period, the increase is even more striking—from 2004-05 to 2013-14, the "in custody" Aboriginal offender population increased by 46 percent.

Statistics relating to release from prison also reveal differences between Aboriginal and non-Aboriginal prisoners. In terms of full parole grant rates, the Aboriginal rate has increased in recent years—from 12 percent in 2009-10 to 23 percent in 2013—but is still significantly lower than the grant rate for non-Aboriginal prisoners—31 percent: Public Safety Canada,

2015 Annual Report, Table D4. The consequence is that Aboriginal offenders serve a higher proportion of their sentences before being released on parole.

C. Provincial and Territorial Trends

Matters look little different at the provincial level, although there is greater variation in the extent of the problem. Looking back almost 50 years we can see that in 1978-79, Aboriginal Canadians represented 16 percent of all provincial/territorial admissions to custody. (Statistics pertaining to the period 1978-2001 are drawn from Julian V Roberts & R Melchers, "The Incarceration of Aboriginal Offenders: An Analysis of Trends, 1978-2001" (2003) 45:2 Can J Corr 211.) This statistic has proved remarkably stable over the decades—it was 18 percent ten years later (in 1998-99). Fast-forward to the present (at the time of writing, the most recent Statistics Canada data pertain to 2013-14), and we see that little has changed.

Table 16.1 compares the two years, separated by almost half a century. A number of conclusions may be drawn. First, in the most recent year (2013-14), Aboriginal offenders represent an even higher percentage of provincial admissions to custody than in 1978-79 (26 percent versus 16 percent). Second, there is considerable variation across the jurisdictions in both periods. In Saskatchewan and Manitoba, over three quarters of admissions in 2013-14 were Aboriginal; in Quebec and Prince Edward Island, the percentage was less than 5 percent. Third, the provinces with highest Aboriginal admissions rates in 1978 were also the ones with the highest rates in 2013-14.

**Table 16.1   Provincial Variation in Aboriginal Admissions to Custody,
1978-79 and 2013-14**

	Percent of total 1978-79	Percent of total 2013-14
Saskatchewan	61	79
Yukon	51	75
Manitoba	50	77
Alberta	26	n/a
British Columbia	15	33
Ontario	9	12
Nova Scotia	—	11
Newfoundland and Labrador	3	23
Quebec	1	3
Prince Edward Island	3	2
Total	16	26

Note: excludes Nunavut; New Brunswick, Northwest Territories, and Alberta data unavailable.
Source: Adapted from Statistics Canada, *Adult Correctional Services in Canada, 2013-14* (Ottawa: Statistics Canada, 2015) table 2.

Table 16.2 presents trends for 2013-14 in terms of both custodial and community admissions at the provincial/territorial level. This table reveals that Aboriginal offenders are equally overrepresented in terms of the community caseload, and that the provincial and territorial variation also exists for community-based corrections.

Table 16.2   Aboriginal Admissions to Adult Correctional Services, by Type of Supervision and Jurisdiction, 2013-14

Jurisdiction	Custodial admissions	Community admissions	Total correctional supervision caseload
	percentage		
Newfoundland and Labrador	23	22	22
Prince Edward Island	2	4	3
Nova Scotia	11	7	8
New Brunswick	9	8	9
Quebec	3	5	5
Ontario	12	10	11
Manitoba	77	56	64
Saskatchewan	79	71	74
British Columbia	33	25	27
Yukon	75	55	59
Northwest Territories	90	84	87
Nunavut	100	100	100
Total	26	23	24

Note: Figures may not add up due to rounding.

Source: Adapted from Canadian Centre for Justice Statistics (Statistics Canada), Adult Correctional Services Survey (ACS), 2013/2014.

This statistical overrepresentation has persisted, even though this period saw publication of the Report of the Canadian Sentencing Commission, *Sentencing Reform: A Canadian Approach* (February 1987) (the Archambault Commission) and David Daubney, Chairman, *Taking Responsibility: Report of the Standing Committee on Justice and Solicitor General on Its Review of Sentencing, Conditional Release and Related Aspects of Corrections* (August 1988). Both reports acknowledged the Aboriginal sentencing problem and proposed remedies. In 1996, Bill C-41 introduced s 718(2)(e), a legislative step toward reducing the use of custody. A number of other commissions of inquiry also addressed the issue and proposed various solutions, including the Report of the Royal Commission on Aboriginal Peoples (RCAP) (4 October 1999) and the Ipperwash Inquiry (31 May 2007). Finally, judgments from the Supreme Court have affirmed the significance of s 718(2)(e). At the end of the day, the over-representation problem continues to be substantial and the gap in parole granting between Aboriginal and non-Aboriginal offenders continues to exist.

D. The Failure to Date and Future Alternatives

Why have remedial initiatives failed to improve matters for Aboriginal offenders and their communities? Two explanations suggest themselves. First, there was anecdotal evidence that the transformation in the judicial response to Aboriginal sentencing that *R v Gladue*, [1999] 1 SCR 688, *R v Ipeelee*, 2012 SCC 13, [2012] 1 SCR 433, and the statutory provision were designed to effect has not been achieved because counsel were slow to raise these issues in their sentencing submissions. Second, the language of s 718(2)(e) represents a relatively mild injunction to courts, and it has been suggested that the provision could have been more robustly drafted.

What other remedies exist? The most radical approach would involve creation of a separate sentencing regime for Aboriginal offenders. This was recommended by RCAP and from time to time has been supported by a number of academics and advocates. The strength of this approach is that it would permit a *de nouveau*, comprehensive approach to Aboriginal sentencing, one which would return to first principles and would be conceived and developed in consultation with First Nations across Canada. At present, courts must grapple with applying sentencing objectives and principles designed for non-Aboriginal offenders.

A second, more modest approach would entail creation of a statute to regulate Aboriginal sentencing. The *Youth Criminal Justice Act* (YCJA) offers a useful model in this respect. One of the explicit aims of the YCJA was to reduce the use of custody as a sanction in youth courts, and hence the volume of juvenile admissions to custody. Research has clearly demonstrated that the YCJA achieved a significant decline in the use of custody in youth courts: see Nicholas Bala, Peter J Carrington & Julian V Roberts, "Implementing Youth Justice Reform: Effects of the *Youth Criminal Justice Act*" in John A Winterdyk & Russell Smandych, eds, *Youth Justice in Canada* (Toronto: Oxford University Press, 2012) 80. This reduction resulted from creation of different sentencing objectives, principles, and disposals, and a similar approach would likely prove successful in the Aboriginal context.

Finally, in the event that Canada one day adopts a guideline scheme (as recommended by the official reports from the 1980s and as implemented in a number of other jurisdictions), an Aboriginal sentencing guideline would represent another way of reducing the use of Aboriginal custody. Until one of these solutions or some other remedial steps are taken, it seems likely that that problem of Aboriginal overincarceration will persist.

In 2015, the Truth and Reconciliation Commission of Canada released its final report: see online: Truth and Reconciliation Commission of Canada <http://www.trc.ca/websites/trcinstitution/index.php?p=3>. The report's call for action included the following recommendations regarding Aboriginal overincarceration:

30. We call upon federal, provincial, and territorial governments to commit to eliminating the overrepresentation of Aboriginal people in custody over the next decade, and to issue detailed annual reports that monitor and evaluate progress in doing so.
31. We call upon the federal, provincial, and territorial governments to provide sufficient and stable funding to implement and evaluate community sanctions that will provide realistic alternatives to imprisonment for Aboriginal offenders and respond to the underlying causes of offending.
32. We call upon the federal government to amend the *Criminal Code* to allow trial judges, upon giving reasons, to depart from mandatory minimum sentences and restrictions on the use of conditional sentences.

Further context to the problem of Aboriginal Incarceration can be found in several earlier commissions of inquiry, including the seminal Royal Commission on Aboriginal Peoples, immediately below.

Royal Commission on Aboriginal Peoples, *Bridging the Cultural Divide:*
A Report on Aboriginal People and Criminal Justice in Canada
(Ottawa: Supply and Services Canada, 1996) (footnotes omitted)

From our reading of these reports and from what we learned through our research and our hearings, we drew two principal conclusions. The first is that there is a remarkable consensus on some fundamental issues and, in particular, how the Canadian justice system has failed Aboriginal people; the second conclusion is that notwithstanding the hundreds of recommendations from commissions and task forces, the reality for Aboriginal people in 1996 is that the justice system is still failing them.

• • •

Aboriginal over-representation in the country's prisons, while presenting the face of injustice in its most repressive form, is only part of the picture. The Aboriginal Justice Inquiry of Manitoba commissioned a great deal of research on the other parts of a system that from beginning to end treats Aboriginal people differently. The Inquiry reported that

> Aboriginal over-representation is the end point of a series of decisions made by those with decision-making power in the justice system. An examination of each of these decisions suggests that the way that decisions are made within the justice system discriminates against Aboriginal people at virtually every point. …
>
> - More than half of the inmates of Manitoba's jails are Aboriginal
> - Aboriginal accused are more likely to be denied bail
> - Aboriginal people spend more time in pre-trial detention than do non-Aboriginal people
> - Aboriginal accused are more likely to be charged with multiple offences than are non-Aboriginal accused
> - Lawyers spend less time with their Aboriginal clients than with non-Aboriginal clients
> - Aboriginal offenders are more than twice as likely as non-Aboriginal people to be incarcerated
>
> The over-representation of Aboriginal people occurs at virtually every step of the judicial process, from the charging of individuals to their sentencing.

In a society that places a high value on equality before the law, documenting the appalling figures of over-representation might seem to be enough, without any further analysis, to place resolution of this problem at the very top of the national human rights agenda. However, as compelling as the figures are, we believe that it is equally important to understand what lies behind these extraordinary figures, which are a primary index of the individual and social devastation that the criminal justice system has come to represent for Aboriginal people. Understanding the root causes is critical to understanding what it will take by way of a national commitment to bring about real change.

Systemic Discrimination and Aboriginal Crime Rates

Over-representation of the magnitude just described suggests either that Aboriginal peoples are committing disproportionately more crimes or that they are the victims of systemic discrimination. Recent justice studies and reports provide strong confirmatory evidence that both phenomena operate in combination.

The Royal Commission on the Donald Marshall, Jr., Prosecution concluded that

Donald Marshall, Jr.'s status as a Native contributed to the miscarriage of justice that has plagued him since 1971. We believe that certain persons within the system would have been more rigorous in their duties, more careful, or more conscious of fairness if Marshall had been white.

A research study prepared for that commission, The Mi'Kmaq and Criminal Justice in Nova Scotia, by Scott Clark, found that

Systemic factors in Nova Scotia's criminal justice system lead to adverse effects for Aboriginal people because they live in or come from Aboriginal communities. Policing that has been designed specifically for Aboriginal communities is relatively ineffective. Justice processing, including legal representation in courts … [is] often at considerable distance from Native people both physically and conceptually. By the same token, a lack of understanding by many justice system personnel of Mi'Kmaq social and economic conditions and aspirations leads to differential and often inappropriate treatment. Probation and parole services apply criteria that have built-in biases against Natives by failing to allow for their unique social and economic conditions. Indigenous processes are officially by-passed, if not consciously weakened.

The Cawsey report in Alberta also concluded that "systemic discrimination exists in the criminal justice system." The report dealt specifically with the assertion of the police that discrimination on the basis of race did not exist in Alberta.

In their briefs, policing services in Alberta generally express the same response: we do not treat or police people differently on the basis of race, or: race is not a fact in policing functions. On the surface, this may seem satisfactory. However, it does not address systemic discrimination. Systemic discrimination involves the concept that the application of uniform standards, common rules, and treatment of people who are not the same constitutes a form of discrimination. It means that in treating unlike people alike, adverse consequences, hardship or injustice may result. …

It is clear the operational policies applied uniformly to Aboriginal people sometimes have unjust or unduly harsh results. The reasons may be geographical, economic, or cultural. However, it must be acknowledged that the application of uniform policies can have a discriminatory effect.

Before describing some of the ways systemic discrimination contributes to overrepresentation of Aboriginal people in the criminal justice system, it is important to review the available evidence on the incidence and nature of Aboriginal crime. This is because there is a significant interrelationship between systemic discrimination and crime rates that has powerful implications for the appropriate directions for change.

The available evidence confirms that crime rates are higher in Aboriginal communities than non-Aboriginal communities. Based on 1985 figures, the task force report of the Indian Policing Policy Review concluded that

- crime rates for on-reserve Indians are significantly higher than for off-reserve Indians and the overall national crime rate; [and that] …
- the rate of on-reserve violent crimes per 1,000 is six times the national average, for property crimes the rate is two times the national average, and for other criminal code offences the rate is four times the national average.

In urban areas, where more than 40 per cent of Aboriginal people live, the available data suggest that Aboriginal people commit more crime and disorder offences than similar groups of non-Aboriginal people but proportionately fewer violent offences than Indians living on-reserve.

The Aboriginal Justice Inquiry of Manitoba (AJI), using 1989-1990 crime rate figures for areas of Manitoba policed by the RCMP, found that the crime rate on Indian reserves was 1.5 times the rate in non-reserve areas. The AJI also found, based on its study of provincial court data, that on the reserves surveyed, 35 per cent of crime fell into a group of four offences: common assault, break and enter, theft under $1,000, and public mischief. Aboriginal persons were charged with fewer property offences and more offences against the person and provincial statute violations than non-Aboriginal persons.

An extensive study conducted for the Grand Council of the Crees in 1991, based on information obtained from police daily reports, current files, youth and adult court files and community interviews, found a significantly higher crime rate in nine Cree communities compared to both the Quebec and the overall Canadian rate. The assault rate in the Cree communities was more than five times the Quebec average and more than three times the national average. There were, however, significant differences among the Cree communities and, as the study itself noted, there was some difficulty in interpreting these findings, owing to a lack of information about the nature and seriousness of the assaults and their degree of comparability. The Cree research also found that much of the interpersonal violence was directed against family members, often in alcohol abuse situations. The high levels of interpersonal violence, particularly family violence, and the close relationship to alcohol abuse, parallels the findings of other studies.

Having concluded that there was a higher rate of crime among Aboriginal people (but one that varied considerably from community to community), the AJI also concluded that systemic discrimination contributed greatly to this. This was also the conclusion drawn by the Cawsey task force in Alberta. Both reports identified over-policing as one of the sources of systemic discrimination. Tim Quigley has described the phenomenon of over-policing and its impact on higher Aboriginal crime rates.

> Police use race as an indicator for patrols, for arrests, detentions. ... For instance, police in cities tend to patrol bars and streets where Aboriginal people congregate, rather than the private clubs frequented by white business people. ... This does not necessarily indicate that the police are invariably racist (although some are) since there is some empirical basis for the police view that proportionately more Aboriginal people are involved in criminality. But to operate patrols or to allocate police on ... [this] basis ... can become a self-fulfilling prophecy: patrols in areas frequented by the groups that they believe are involved in crimes will undoubtedly discover some criminality; when more police are assigned to detachments where there is a high Aboriginal population, their added presence will most assuredly detect more criminal activity.
>
> Consider, for instance, the provincial offence of being intoxicated in a public place. The police rarely arrest whites for being intoxicated in public. No wonder there is resentment on the part of Aboriginal people arrested simply for being intoxicated. This situation very often results in an Aboriginal person being charged with obstruction, resisting arrest or assaulting a peace officer. An almost inevitable consequence is incarceration. ... Yet the whole sequence of events is, at least to some extent, a product of policing criteria that include race as a factor and selective enforcement of the law.

The Aboriginal Justice Inquiry of Manitoba also addressed the systemic effect of police perceptions of Aboriginal people.

> Differences in crime statistics between Aboriginal and non-Aboriginal people result, at least in part, from the manner in which the behaviour of Aboriginal people becomes categorized and stigmatized. This may happen because, to a certain extent, police tend to view the world in terms of "respectable" people and "criminal" types. Criminal types are thought to exhibit certain characteristics which provide cues to the officer to initiate action. Thus, the police may tend to stop a higher proportion of people who are visibly different from the dominant society, including Aboriginal people, for minor offences, simply because they believe that such people may tend to commit more serious crimes. Members of groups that are perceived to be a danger to the public order are given much less latitude in their behaviour before the police take action. An example might be a group of Aboriginal youth who gather in a park. Because it is believed that their presence may be a precursor to more deviant action, they are subjected to controlling activities by the police.

Over-policing is not unique to Canadian police forces. A similar point is made in a New Zealand report dealing with the effect on crime control strategies of police perceptions of the high rate of Maori crime.

> Individual police, both as officers and as members of society, are aware of the high rate of Maori offending. … Individual police officers, subject to those perceptions, become susceptible to beliefs that Maori men are more likely to be criminal, or that certain types of conduct are more likely to be associated with them. Such beliefs unavoidably, if often unconsciously, affect the exercise of discretionary powers. These individual perceptions and stereotypes are reinforced by the intrinsic attitudes of the police institution which is constantly aware of the wider society's concerns and values. Thus, for example, a social perception of increasing gang or street crime, apparently disproportionately committed by Maori offenders, will lead to an increased allocation of police resources to those areas of activity. Such a concentration leads to a greater number of arrests of mainly Maori people who in turn will maintain the perception of Maori criminality. The likelihood that this perception will bias future use of discretionary powers by the police is thereby increased as well. It is a cyclic process of "deviancy amplification" in which stereotypes and perceptions help stimulate policies in a self-fulfilling weave of unfairness.

Significantly, several of the studies we reviewed concluded that some Aboriginal communities experience the extremes of both over-policing and under-policing. Jean-Paul Brodeur, in his study for the Grand Council of the Crees, provided this review of the research:

> In a joint study for the Government of Canada, the Government of Saskatchewan and the Indian Nations, authors Prefontaine, Opekokew and Tyler found that Native communities complained of an excessively rigorous enforcement of the law in relation to minor or petty offences. In his study on RCMP policing of Aboriginals, Loree also concluded that when compared to non-Aboriginal communities, Aboriginal communities received proportionately greater law enforcement attention and proportionately less peace-keeping and other services. The situation is best described by Depew when he states that:
>
>> Despite some similarities in Native and non-Native offender profiles, the prevalence of minor and alcohol-related offences provides the basis for Native over-representation in the correctional system which in many areas of the country is disturbingly high. …

> Native people also appear to be subject to the extremes of over-policing and under-policing which can lead to disproportionate levels of Native arrests and charges, and under-utilization of policing services, respectively.

Under-policing is an issue identified by Pauktuutit, the Inuit Women's Association of Canada, in its report, *Inuit Women and Justice*, as one of special concern in some smaller Inuit communities where there are no community-based police services. In an appendix documenting the concerns of Inuit women in Labrador, the report demonstrates forcefully how this places women and children at particular risk.

> The RCMP has a responsibility to protect and serve our community. Women and elders are major consumers of police services. In order to serve all parts of the communities, the police have to know our communities, they must be a part of our communities. They must also understand what the life of a woman who has been beaten can be like in the community along the Labrador coast where there are no police, or where the police are not very supportive. Without this knowledge and understanding, the RCMP will not be able to respond to the needs of the victims of violence. Until we have the necessary resources in our communities to provide for protection to women on a permanent basis (for example, police based in the community) and to provide a safe place where women can receive counselling, support and protection, many women will not leave and can't leave the violent home. ...
>
> While we recognize that the realities of violence in the family translate into the need for added resources, it is not acceptable, on the one hand, to tell us that this is a funding problem and that there is not enough money provided by the province to provide adequate policing. Yet on the other hand, the federal government provides enough funds to hire two police officers for Labrador and eight in Newfoundland to respond to cigarette smuggling. The communities of Postville, Rigolet, and Makkovik, like other communities on the coast, require police based in the community. Women in these communities are in a dangerous position.

Brodeur points out that simultaneous under- and over-policing prevail not only in Canadian Aboriginal communities but also have characterized the style of policing in Australian Aboriginal settlements and in inner-city areas in England where there are significant black populations. We were struck by the relevance of the following statement, based on the findings of Lord Scarman, who conducted a public inquiry into the riots in Brixton, a predominately black suburb of London.

> The true nature of police–black relations in the inner-cities of Britain can only be understood in terms of this simultaneous over-policing and under-policing. There is too much policing against the community and not enough policing that answers the needs of the community.

Brodeur concludes that

> [i]n a Canadian context, Aboriginals are submitted to over-policing for minor or petty offences—e.g., drinking violations—and suffer from under-policing with regard to being protected from more serious offences, such as violent assaults against persons (particularly within the family).

The Root Causes of Over-Representation and Aboriginal Crime

Although over-policing and other forms of systemic discrimination undoubtedly play their part in higher crime rates, the evidence available to us leads us to conclude that for many Aboriginal communities, crime and social disorder play more havoc in personal and community well-being than they do in the lives of non-Aboriginal people and communities. Like the figures on over-representation, the statistics on higher crime rates demand further answers to hard questions directed to the root causes. Misunderstanding the roots of the problem can lead only to solutions that provide, at best, temporary alleviation and, at worst, aggravation of the pain reflected in the faces of Aboriginal victims of crimes—in many cases women and children—and in the faces of the Aboriginal men and women who receive their "just" deserts in the form of a prison sentence.

We are not the first commission to grapple with the question of explaining and understanding the causes of Aboriginal over-representation and high crime rates. As the Aboriginal Justice Inquiry of Manitoba observed, an entire sub-specialty of criminology is devoted to determining the causes of crime, and a great deal of academic attention has been directed to the specific issue of Aboriginal over-representation. From our review and analysis of the research, we have identified three primary explanatory theories; although they have significant points of overlap, they point in different directions regarding what must be changed to stem and turn the tide.

One powerfully persistent explanation for the problems facing Aboriginal people in the justice system is cultural difference between Aboriginal people and other Canadians. This was invoked most recently by Chief Justice McEachern in his judgement in the *Gitksan and Wet'suwet'en* case, where the following explanation is offered for Indian disadvantage:

> For reasons which can only be answered by anthropology, if at all, the Indians of the colony, while accepting many of the advantages of the European civilization, did not prosper proportionately with the white community as expected. … No-one can speak with much certainty or confidence about what really went wrong in the relations between the Indians and the colonists. … In my view the Indians' lack of cultural preparation for the new regime was indeed the probable cause of the debilitating dependence from which few Indians in North America have not yet escaped.
>
> Being of a culture where everyone looked after himself or perished, the Indians knew how to survive (in most years) but they were not as industrious in the new economic climate as was thought to be necessary by the new-comers in the Colony. In addition, the Indians were a gravely weakened people by reason of foreign diseases which took a fearful toll, and by the ravages of alcohol. They became a conquered people, not by force of arms, for that was not necessary, but by an invading culture and a relentless energy with which they would not, or could not, compete.

A cultural explanatory model has provided the basis for a number of initiatives, referred to generically as the "indigenization" of the criminal justice system. The intent of these initiatives is to close the culture gap by adding to the existing system elements that make it more culturally appropriate for Aboriginal people. Thus, on the assumption that one of the important cultural problems facing Aboriginal people is understanding the language and formal processes of Canadian law, the introduction of Aboriginal court workers is designed to provide a cultural bridge within the existing process. Using the same cultural model, we have seen in different parts of Canada the appointment of Aboriginal police officers, probation officers and justices of the peace. We describe some of these developments in more detail in the next chapter.

There is no doubt that cultural conflict explains much of the alienation that Aboriginal people experience in the justice system, and we return to some of the fundamental cultural differences between Aboriginal and non-Aboriginal understandings of justice later in this report. The difficulty, however, with this explanation and the uses to which it has been put is that it is often based on an underlying assumption that the problem lies with the limitations of Aboriginal culture to adapt to non-Aboriginal legal culture—an assumption of inferiority reflected in the passage from Chief Justice McEachern's judgement just quoted.

Associate Chief Judge Murray Sinclair, one of the commissioners of the Aboriginal Justice Inquiry of Manitoba, recently addressed the limitations of this approach. After reviewing some of the principal conclusions of the Manitoba inquiry—including findings that Aboriginal people are less likely than non-Aboriginal people to plea bargain or to benefit from a negotiated plea, that they are more likely than non-Aboriginal people to plead guilty, even when they are not or do not believe themselves to be guilty, and that they are more likely to leave the legal process without understanding, and therefore without respecting, what has occurred to them or why—he makes the following comments:

> Many times I have heard people ask: "What is it about Aboriginal people that causes them to behave like that?" Such a question suggests the problem lies within the Aboriginal person or with his or her community. That, almost inevitably, leads one to conclude that the answer lies in trying to change the Aboriginal person or his or her community. As a result, almost all our efforts at reform have centred on informing or educating Aboriginal people about the justice system, on finding ways to get them to "connect" with the system or on finding ways to make it easier for them to find their way through it.
>
> Establishing and funding more and better Aboriginal court worker or Aboriginal paralegal programs, printing more and better Aboriginally focused information kits, making more and better audio and video tapes in Aboriginal languages about how courts and laws work, establishing Aboriginal law student programs, hiring more Aboriginal court staff with the ability to speak Aboriginal languages and recruiting or appointing more Aboriginal judges, all find their justification in such thinking.
>
> Attempts, at reforming the system itself in ways that address other, more significant, issues have not been undertaken. The main reason, I believe, is because the non-Aboriginal people who control the system have not seen the problem as lying within "the system." It is time to question whether at least some of the problem lies in the way we do business within the justice system. Perhaps the question should be restated as "what is wrong with our justice system that Aboriginal people find it so alienating?"

We agree with Judge Sinclair that asking the question in this way allows us to address the fundamental differences that Aboriginal people bring to the meaning of justice as a concept and a process.

As Judge Sinclair argues, theories of culture conflict have been applied in the past in a way that locates the source of the problem within Aboriginal culture. There is, however, a further limitation on the exclusively cultural explanation of over-representation in the criminal justice system that takes us deeper into an understanding of Aboriginal crime. This limitation is that an exclusively cultural explanation obscures structural problems grounded in the economic and social inequalities experienced by Aboriginal people. As described by Carole La Prairie,

What the early task forces and studies failed to recognize or did not want to address, was that the disproportionate representation of Native people as offenders in the system, was not tied exclusively to culture conflict but was grounded primarily in socio-economic marginality and deprivation. …

Access to justice by way of indigenization has both strengths and weaknesses. It provides employment to a number of Aboriginal people and it may help to demystify the criminal justice process so that Aboriginal people feel less alienated and fearful. What indigenization fails to do, however, is to address in any fundamental way the criminal justice problems which result from the socio-economic marginality. The real danger of an exclusively indigenized approach is that the problems may appear to be "solved," little more will be attempted, partly because indigenization is a very visible activity.

Cast as a structural problem of social and economic marginality, the argument is that Aboriginal people are disproportionately impoverished and belong to a social underclass, and that their over-representation in the criminal justice system is a particular example of the established correlation between social and economic deprivation and criminality.

We observed in our special report on suicide that Aboriginal people are at the bottom of almost every available index of socio-economic well-being, whether they measure educational levels, employment opportunities, housing conditions, per capita incomes or any of the other conditions that give non-Aboriginal Canadians one of the highest standards of living in the world. There is no doubt in our minds that economic and social deprivation is a major underlying cause of disproportionately high rates of criminality among Aboriginal people.

We are also persuaded that some of the debilitating conditions facing Aboriginal communities daily are aggravated by the distinctive nature of Aboriginal societies. Thus, as Carole La Prairie points out in her study for the James Bay Cree, there is evidential support for a correlation between over-crowded housing conditions and interpersonal conflict and violence, which often takes place between close family members residing together. In the case of the James Bay Cree, traditional concepts of order and the cultural values placed on the way people relate to each other in a social context reflect the legacy of nomadic-hunting settlement patterns. People not only have their distinctive roles but have their distinctive places in relationship to each other. Over-crowded housing where these distinctions cannot be reflected or respected can and does exacerbate an already problematic sedentary existence in contemporary Cree communities. Thus, current housing conditions, not only in Cree but other Aboriginal people, contribute to tensions in kinship relationships that may in turn be linked to problems of interpersonal conflict, violence and crime.

Socio-economic deprivation not only has explanatory power in relation to high rates of Aboriginal crime, but it also contributes directly to the systemic discrimination that swells the ranks of Aboriginal people in prison. …

But imprisonment for fine default is only the most obvious example of systemic discrimination built upon socio-economic deprivation. As the Aboriginal Justice Inquiry of Manitoba found, Aboriginal people are more likely to be denied bail and therefore subject to pre-trial detention. While there is certainly no evidence to suggest that judges deliberately discriminate against Aboriginal people, the factors taken into account in determining whether to subject a person to pre-trial detention relate to whether the person is employed, has a fixed address, is involved in educational programs, or has strong links with the community; as a result, social and economic disadvantage can influence the decision in a particular direction, and that direction is toward the doors of remand centres.

Pre-trial detention, once imposed, has a number of effects. It creates additional pressure to plead guilty in order to get the matter over with, it limits the accused's ability to marshal resources, whether financial or community, to put before the court a community-based sentencing plan, and it therefore increases the likelihood of a sentence of imprisonment.

The way apparently neutral and legally relevant criteria applied at various stages of the criminal justice process compound or snowball to produce systemic discrimination against Aboriginal people is described well by Quigley.

> There are also some other factors that might bear on the disproportionate rate of imprison-
> ment and that are more directly related to the sentencing process. Some of these are presently
> seen as legally relevant criteria—prior criminal record, employment status, educational level,
> etc. … Prior criminal record as a factor can have an undue influence on the imprisonment
> rate for Aboriginal people due to the snowball effect of some of the factors listed above. If
> there are more young Aboriginal people, if they are disproportionately unemployed, idle and
> alienated, and if they are overly scrutinized by the police, it should not be surprising that
> frequently breaches of the law are detected and punished. Add to that the greater likelihood
> of being denied bail (which increases the chance of being jailed if convicted), the greater
> likelihood of fine default and the diminished likelihood of receiving probation, and there is
> a greater probability of imprisonment being imposed. Some of the same factors increase the
> chances of the same person re-offending and being detected once again. After that, every suc-
> ceeding conviction is much more apt to be punished by imprisonment, thus creating a snowball
> effect: jail becomes virtually the only option, regardless of the seriousness of the offence.
>
> Socio-economic factors such as employment status, level of education, family situation,
> etc. appear on the surface as neutral criteria. They are considered as such by the legal system.
> Yet they can conceal an extremely strong bias in the sentencing process. Convicted persons
> with steady employment and stability in their lives, or at least prospects of the same, are
> much less likely to be sent to jail for offences that are borderline imprisonment offences. The
> unemployed, transients, the poorly educated are all better candidates for imprisonment.
> Given the social, political and economic aspects of our society place Aboriginal people
> disproportionately within the ranks of the latter; our society literally sentences more of them
> to jail. This is systemic discrimination.

The Aboriginal Justice Inquiry of Manitoba came to the same conclusion. The commissioners wrote:

> Historically, the justice system has discriminated against Aboriginal people by providing
> legal sanction for their oppression. This oppression of previous generations forced Aboriginal
> people into their current state of social and economic distress. Now, a seemingly neutral
> justice system discriminates against current generations of Aboriginal people by applying
> laws which have an adverse impact on people of lower socio-economic status. This is no less
> racial discrimination; it is merely "laundered" racial discrimination. It is untenable to say
> that discrimination which builds upon the effects of racial discrimination is not racial dis-
> crimination itself. Past injustices cannot be ignored or built upon.

There is no doubt in our minds that economic and social deprivation is a significant contributor to the high incidence of Aboriginal crime and over-representation in the justice system. We believe, however, that a further level of understanding is required beyond acknowledgement of the role played by poverty and debilitating social conditions in the creation and perpetuation of Aboriginal crime. We are persuaded that this further understanding comes from integrating the cultural and socio-economic explanations for over-representation with a broader historical and political analysis. We have concluded that over-representation is linked directly to the particular and distinctive historical and political processes that have made Aboriginal people poor beyond poverty.

Our analysis and conclusions parallel those set out in our special report on suicide. In that report we identified some of the risk factors that explain, in part, the high rate of Aboriginal suicide. As we have just demonstrated with respect to the high rate of Aboriginal crime, these factors include culture stress and socio-economic deprivation. We concluded, however, that

> Aboriginal people experience [these] risk factors ... with greater frequency and intensity than do Canadians generally. The reasons are rooted in the relations between Aboriginal peoples and the rest of Canadian society—relations that were shaped in the colonial era and have never been thoroughly reshaped since that time.

The relationship of colonialism provides an overarching conceptual and historical link in understanding much of what has happened to Aboriginal peoples. Its relationship to issues of criminal justice was identified clearly by the Canadian Bar Association in its 1988 report, *Locking Up Natives in Canada.*

> What links these views of native criminality as caused by poverty or alcohol is the historical process which Native people have experienced in Canada, along with indigenous people in other parts of the world, the process of colonization. In the Canadian context that process, with the advance first of the agricultural and then the industrial frontier, has left Native people in most parts of the country dispossessed of all but the remnants of what was once their homelands; that process, superintended by missionaries and Indian agents armed with the power of the law, took such extreme forms as criminalizing central Indian institutions such as the Potlatch and Sundance, and systematically undermined the foundations of many Native communities. The Native people of Canada have, over the course of the last two centuries, been moved to the margins of their own territories and of our "just" society.
>
> This process of dispossession and marginalization has carried with it enormous costs of which crime and alcoholism are but two items on a long list. ... The relationship between these indices of disorganization and deprivation and Canada's historical relationship with Native people has been the subject of intense scrutiny in the last decade. In the mid-1970s the MacKenzie Valley Pipeline Inquiry focused national attention on the implications for the Native people of the North on a rapid escalation of a large scale industrial development. Mr. Justice Berger (as he then was), in assessing the causes for the alarming rise in the incidence of alcoholism, crime, violence and welfare dependence in the North, had this to say:
>
>> I am persuaded that the incidence of these disorders is closely bound up with the rapid expansion of the industrial system and with its persistent intrusion into every part of the Native people's lives. The process affects the complex links between Native

people and their past, their culturally preferred economic life, and their individual, familial and political respect. We should not be surprised to learn that the economic forces that have broken these vital links, and that are unresponsive to the distress of those who have been hurt, should lead to serious disorders. Crimes of violence can, to some extent, be seen as expressions of frustrations, confusion and indignation, but we can go beyond that interpretation to the obvious connection between crimes of violence and the change the South has, in recent years, brought to the Native people of the North. With that obvious connection, we can affirm one simple proposition: the more the industrial frontier displaces the homeland in the North, the worse the incidence of crime and violence will be.

Important implications flow from this analysis. The idea that new programs, more planning and an increase in social service personnel will solve these problems misconstrues their real nature and cause. The high rates of social and personal breakdown in the North are, in good measure, the responses of individual families who have suffered the loss of meaning in their lives and control over their destiny.

The principal recommendations which come from the MacKenzie Valley Pipeline Inquiry were that the Native people of the North must have their right to control that destiny—their right to self-determination—recognized and that there must be a settlement of Native claims in which that right is entrenched as a lodestar. Only then could Native people chart a future responding to their values and priorities rather than living under the shadow of ours.

E. Statutory Law and the Cases

The incongruity of applying the standard methodology of sentencing to Aboriginal offenders has been apparent for many years. The case of *R v Fireman*, below, is almost 50 years old. Similar examples can be found in many cases involving accused persons from remote communities: see *R v Naqitarvik* (1986), 26 CCC (3d) 193 (NWTCA) and *R v Curley, Nagmalik, and Issigaitok*, [1984] NWTR 281 (CA).

R v Fireman

[1971] 3 OR 380 (CA)

BROOKE JA (Kelly and Jessup JJA concurring):

This is an appeal by Gabriel Fireman from the sentence of 10 years' imprisonment in the penitentiary imposed upon him by Wright J, on November 19, 1969, upon the appellant's plea of guilty on his arraignment on a charge of manslaughter.

The facts are not in dispute. The appellant and his victim were cousins who lived on friendly terms in their settlement on the shores of Attawapiskat River which is on the west shore of James Bay and distant some 470 miles north-east from the Town of Sioux Lookout and 250 miles north from the Town of Moosonee. On July 30, 1969, a large shipment of liquor was delivered to the settlement at the order of two relatives of the deceased and the appellant. These two shipments were the first that size to have been received by the people of the settlement for private use, and the trial Judge was told that the 12 persons who consumed this liquor, began as the shipments were unloaded and ended some 12 hours later, when Eli Fireman was shot to death by the appellant. Both men were deeply intoxicated. There was no real reason for the shooting. All that can be said is that after a night long of drinking, petty differences spawned arguments which culminated in a fight that ended with the fatal shot being fired. For what little significance it may be, the appellant is not said to have been a cause of the fight, nor directly involved in it.

The settlement is remote. It cannot be reached by road and is visited only twice each year by ship. Recently, mail delivery by aircraft was instituted. However, uncertain weather renders this service doubtful most of the year. The only real communication between the settlement and the rest of the country is through intermittent radio-telephone communication, the control of which is not in the hands of the Indian people at the settlement. The people at the settlement are members of the Cree nation and are called the Swamp Cree. Their dialect is not widely known even amongst the people of their nation. Very few of the people of the settlement speak any English, and it is only in recent years that the children have been taken to the nearest schools which are at the railhead at Moosonee, and there they have been given the opportunity of studying English. It is clear these people have no real familiarity with our way of life.

The police visit the area rarely as there have been very few calls for their services. Heretofore, the people of the settlement have enjoyed an excellent reputation for the 30 years that the settlement's existence has been known, for there have been no previous instances of major crimes there. The affairs of the people are governed by a chief and band council who exert strong control, and who, according to the police witnesses, are respected and obeyed in the community.

The settlement, then, is a truly remote place, cut off from the rest of the country, inhabited by people who have really little contact with our way of life; although, the evidence is that some of our material things are finding their way there now.

The principal occupation of the men of the settlement is trapping. With the approach of winter the population of the settlement dwindles from 500 to 200 persons as the men (in some cases, families) go to the traplines in the wilderness, where they remain for up to six months, returning in the spring with their catch of furs which are disposed of by sale to the Hudson's Bay post at the settlement. A good trapper can net $2,500 for his furs.

At the time of his conviction Gabriel Fireman was 25 years old. He was a good trapper quite capable of carrying on his business which included scheduling arrangements with an aircraft to fly him and his skidoo in and out from the traplines along with his cargo of furs, and he was able to manage the sale of his furs. On the other hand, the appellant is almost completely without an education, having finished the equivalent of our grade five when he was 22 years old. But this is not unusual in his community. In addition, the appellant failed grade seven three times because he did not have enough English to comprehend the basic things which were a part of that course. Perhaps because of the differences in the cultures, the appellant's IQ tests were found to be below the average for our whole society, but they were average for his own community. Some indication of the basic differences may be gained from the fact that he lived in a community where time is told only by seasons, that his sentence of 10 years is something that he is not likely to fully understand for he is unfamiliar with the calendar measurement of time in terms of days, weeks, months or years.

When it was discovered that the appellant had killed his cousin, the people of the settlement, including the families of the appellant and the deceased, were shocked and they rejected the appellant. It is plain from the evidence of the police officers, that under the direction of the chief and the band council, what evidence there was of the event was gathered up and retained for the police and Gabriel Fireman was detained by the people and turned over to the police upon their arrival. He remained ostracized by the community and it was only after he had taken communion at their church that his family would look upon him. It is said that following the process of the preliminary inquiry the community was prepared to accept him.

After considering the appellant's background, some aspects of the values of the people of the settlement, including their apparent different value of death, the learned trial Judge rejected the contention that lesser punishment would suffice and, placing the emphasis on the deterrent aspect of the sentence, imposed the term of 10 years on the appellant.

The appellant's contention is that the learned trial Judge failed to give due consideration to the effect of such a sentence upon the appellant, having regard to his background and the probabilities of his rehabilitation, and that the principle of deterrence to the whole community would have been satisfied by a much shorter term.

In my opinion, one can only proceed to consider the fitness of the sentence meted out to this man upon a proper appreciation of his cultural background and of his character, as it is only then that the full effect of the sentence upon him will be clear. When one considers these things, it is my opinion that even a short term of imprisonment in the penitentiary is substantial punishment to him. In the appellant's case, despite the best efforts of those who must be responsible for his care, the effect of his removal from his environment and his imprisonment would no doubt dull every sense by which he has lived in the north.

He can speak no English. It is not the language that he will use in his daily life upon his return to his home. There is no necessity for his knowing English there. There is little likelihood that he will learn English in the institution when one considers the restrictions on his ability to learn. With the difficulty in communication it is improbable that useful instruction would be available to him and, of some importance, how frustrating his existence when all those around him do not speak his language nor he theirs. I would think his imprisonment would produce a loneliness that would be greater than that in isolation.

On the other hand, does his sentence of 10 years take into consideration the desirability of his rehabilitation? From what I have said, in my view, it follows that it does not. To borrow words from the Canadian Committee on Corrections, I think it is probable that such a term will greatly reduce the chance of this man assuming a normal tolerable role on returning to his society and may well result in the creation of a social cripple.

His sentence as a deterrent to others raises important considerations. Normally, the trial of an accused man takes place in the area where the crime is said to have been committed. Members of the community may witness the trial and some indeed participate in it, and so through witnessing the trial and by word of mouth of those who have been there, what happened is known throughout the community. In this case, while the appellant was arrested at the settlement, his trial took place a very great distance away by reasons of the provisions of the territorial divisions of this Province.

There is no indication in the record that any person from his community participated in or was present at his trial, and it seems unlikely that this was so for the record discloses that there was difficulty in obtaining interpreters who knew the dialect of the Swamp Cree. What knowledge would his community have of the reasons of the learned trial Judge in sentencing the appellant or, for that matter, of this Court in dealing with his appeal? To ask the question is to answer it.

To the appellant and to the people of the settlement the deterrent value of the disposition of this case lies in the fact that the appellant's conduct which the people of the settlement condemned, was condemned by the rest of our society. The people of the settlement participated in and witnessed the arrest of the appellant and they know that he has been segregated from them by proceedings in a distant place. To the rest of the community the deterrent lies in the fact that this unsophisticated man of previous good character was sent to prison for his crime and surely, it is not dependent on the magnitude of the sentence for its value. I do not think it adds greatly to the deterrent value of what has taken place that such a severe sentence be imposed. What is important in these circumstances is that to the whole community justice appears to have been done and that there will be respect for the law. This is best accomplished in the case of this first offender if he is returned to his society before time makes him a stranger and impairs his ability to live there with some dignity.

With the greatest deference to the learned trial Judge, for the above reasons in my view the sentence is too severe and the appeal must be allowed. The determination of the appropriate quantum of sentence is not easy. The crime for which the appellant was convicted is a very serious one and, yet, the appellant has not by his previous conduct indicated that he is a dangerous person from whom society must be protected. Frankly, I think it is doubtful that prison is the answer, but that is our way. However, regard can properly be had to the institutions in our system and their flexibility for some guidance in determining and arriving at a proper conclusion. In this case, as the dominant consideration is the reformation and rehabilitation of this man and of course the respect of the community for our system, I think the appropriate sentence would have been two years less one day.

However, having regard to the time that has transpired since the appellant's conviction and sentencing, there would be little benefit to him in the change required by such a sentence and accordingly the appeal is allowed and the sentence will be reduced to one of two years.

NOTE

The problems faced by Aboriginal offenders and the need to explore different sentencing approaches are not restricted to residents of remote communities. Below, we examine sentencing circles, which attempt to shift the procedural and substantive paradigm. In *R v Morin* (1995), 101 CCC (3d) 124, 42 CR (4th) 339 (Sask CA), a Métis with a long record of prior convictions pleaded guilty to a robbery in Saskatoon. With the support of the local Métis community, the judge agreed to conduct a sentencing circle. Although a sentence in the range of four years would have been the usual result, after hearing the recommendations of the circle, the judge sentenced the offender to 18 months' incarceration to be followed by 18 months' intensive probation. The Crown appealed. The majority of the five-member panel of the Saskatchewan Court of Appeal allowed the appeal principally on the ground that there was no basis to give pre-eminence to rehabilitation. However, the court observed (at 375):

> From the perspective of consequences we appear to have two systems of justice. Sentencing circles have a role to play in breaking down that apparent anomaly.

III. THE 1996 AMENDMENTS AND SUPREME COURT GUIDANCE

As seen in Chapter 2, Judicial Methodology and the Legislative Context, the 1996 amendments added to the *Criminal Code*, RSC 1985, c C-46, as amended, a statement of purpose and objectives for sentencing and some of the major substantive principles. Along with proportionality (s 718.1), the Code also mandates respect for the principle of restraint in ss 718(c), 718.2(d), and 718.2(e). The last provision makes specific reference to Aboriginal offenders:

> 718.2. A court that imposes a sentence shall also take into consideration the following principles: ...
>
> (e) all available sanctions other than imprisonment that are reasonable in the circumstances should be considered for all offenders, *with particular attention to the circumstances of aboriginal offenders.*

In *R v Gladue*, below, the Supreme Court addressed the intended purpose and application of this provision.

R v Gladue
[1999] 1 SCR 688, 23 CR (5th) 197

CORY and IACOBUCCI JJ (Lamer CJ and L'Heureux-Dubé, Gonthier, Bastarache, and Binnie JJ concurring):

[57] Thus, it may be seen that although imprisonment is intended to serve the traditional sentencing goals of separation, deterrence, denunciation, and rehabilitation, there is widespread consensus that imprisonment has not been successful in achieving some of these goals. Over-incarceration is a long-standing problem that has been many times publicly acknowledged but never addressed in a systematic manner by Parliament. In recent years, compared to other countries, sentences of imprisonment in Canada have increased at an alarming rate. The 1996 sentencing reforms embodied in Part XXIII, and s. 718.2(e) in particular, must be understood as a reaction to the overuse of prison as a sanction, and must accordingly be given appropriate force as remedial provisions.

(2) The Overrepresentation of Aboriginal Canadians in Penal Institutions

[58] If overreliance upon incarceration is a problem with the general population, it is of much greater concern in the sentencing of aboriginal Canadians. In the mid-1980s, aboriginal people were about 2 percent of the population of Canada, yet they made up 10 percent of the penitentiary population. In Manitoba and Saskatchewan, aboriginal people constituted something between 6 and 7 percent of the population, yet in Manitoba they represented 46 percent of the provincial admissions and in Saskatchewan 60 percent: see M. Jackson, "Locking Up Natives in Canada" (1988-89), 23 UBC L Rev. 215 (article originally prepared as a report of the Canadian Bar Association Committee on Imprisonment and Release in June 1988), at pp. 215-16. The situation has not improved in recent years. By 1997, aboriginal peoples constituted closer to 3 percent of the population of Canada and amounted to 12 percent of all federal inmates: Solicitor General of Canada,

Consolidated Report, Towards a Just, Peaceful and Safe Society: The Corrections and Conditional Release Act—Five Years Later (1998), at pp. 142-55. The situation continues to be particularly worrisome in Manitoba, where in 1995-96 they made up 55 percent of admissions to provincial correctional facilities, and in Saskatchewan, where they made up 72 percent of admissions. A similar, albeit less drastic situation prevails in Alberta and British Columbia: Canadian Centre for Justice Statistics, Adult Correctional Services in Canada, 1995-96 (1997), at p. 30. ...

. . .

[61] Not surprisingly, the excessive imprisonment of aboriginal people is only the tip of the iceberg insofar as the estrangement of the aboriginal peoples from the Canadian criminal justice system is concerned. Aboriginal people are overrepresented in virtually all aspects of the system. As this Court recently noted in *R v. Williams*, [1998] 1 SCR 1128, at para. 58, there is widespread bias against aboriginal people within Canada, and "[t]here is evidence that this widespread racism has translated into systemic discrimination in the criminal justice system."

[62] Statements regarding the extent and severity of this problem are disturbingly common. ...

. . .

[65] It is clear that sentencing innovation by itself cannot remove the causes of aboriginal offending and the greater problem of aboriginal alienation from the criminal justice system. The unbalanced ratio of imprisonment for aboriginal offenders flows from a number of sources, including poverty, substance abuse, lack of education, and the lack of employment opportunities for aboriginal people. It arises also from bias against aboriginal people and from an unfortunate institutional approach that is more inclined to refuse bail and to impose more and longer prison terms for aboriginal offenders. There are many aspects of this sad situation which cannot be addressed in these reasons. What can and must be addressed, though, is the limited role that sentencing judges will play in remedying injustice against aboriginal peoples in Canada. Sentencing judges are among those decision-makers who have the power to influence the treatment of aboriginal offenders in the justice system. They determine most directly whether an aboriginal offender will go to jail, or whether other sentencing options may be employed which will play perhaps a stronger role in restoring a sense of balance to the offender, victim, and community, and in preventing future crime.

E. A Framework of Analysis for the Sentencing Judge

(1) What Are the "Circumstances of Aboriginal Offenders"?

[66] How are sentencing judges to play their remedial role? The words of s. 718.2(e) instruct the sentencing judge to pay particular attention to the circumstances of aboriginal offenders, with the implication that those circumstances are significantly different from those of non-aboriginal offenders. The background considerations regarding the distinct situation of aboriginal peoples in Canada encompass a wide range of unique circumstances, including, most particularly:

(A) The unique systemic or background factors which may have played a part in bringing the particular aboriginal offender before the courts; and

(B)   The types of sentencing procedures and sanctions which may be appropriate in the circumstances for the offender because of his or her particular aboriginal heritage or connection.

(a) Systemic and Background Factors

[67] The background factors which figure prominently in the causation of crime by aboriginal offenders are by now well known. Years of dislocation and economic development have translated, for many aboriginal peoples, into low incomes, high unemployment, lack of opportunities and options, lack or irrelevance of education, substance abuse, loneliness, and community fragmentation. These and other factors contribute to a higher incidence of crime and incarceration. A disturbing account of these factors is set out by Professor Tim Quigley, "Some Issues in Sentencing of Aboriginal Offenders," in *Continuing Poundmaker and Riel's Quest* (1994), at pp. 269-300. Quigley ably describes the process whereby these various factors produce an overincarceration of aboriginal offenders, noting (at pp. 275-76) that "[t]he unemployed, transients, the poorly educated are all better candidates for imprisonment. When the social, political and economic aspects of our society place Aboriginal people disproportionately within the ranks of the latter, our society literally sentences more of them to jail."

[68] It is true that systemic and background factors explain in part the incidence of crime and recidivism for non-aboriginal offenders as well. However, it must be recognized that the circumstances of aboriginal offenders differ from those of the majority because many aboriginal people are victims of systemic and direct discrimination, many suffer the legacy of dislocation, and many are substantially affected by poor social and economic conditions. Moreover, as has been emphasized repeatedly in studies and commission reports, aboriginal offenders are, as a result of these unique systemic and background factors, more adversely affected by incarceration and less likely to be "rehabilitated" thereby, because the internment milieu is often culturally inappropriate and regrettably discrimination towards them is so often rampant in penal institutions.

[69] In this case, of course, we are dealing with factors that must be considered by a judge sentencing an aboriginal offender. While background and systemic factors will also be of importance for a judge in sentencing a non-aboriginal offender, the judge who is called upon to sentence an aboriginal offender must give attention to the unique background and systemic factors which may have played a part in bringing the particular offender before the courts. In cases where such factors have played a significant role, it is incumbent upon the sentencing judge to consider these factors in evaluating whether imprisonment would actually serve to deter, or to denounce crime in a sense that would be meaningful to the community of which the offender is a member. In many instances, more restorative sentencing principles will gain primary relevance precisely because the prevention of crime as well as individual and social healing cannot occur through other means.

(b) Appropriate Sentencing Procedures and Sanctions

[70] Closely related to the background and systemic factors which have contributed to an excessive aboriginal incarceration rate are the different conceptions of appropriate

sentencing procedures and sanctions held by aboriginal people. A significant problem experienced by aboriginal people who come into contact with the criminal justice system is that the traditional sentencing ideals of deterrence, separation, and denunciation are often far removed from the understanding of sentencing held by these offenders and their community. The aims of restorative justice as now expressed in paras. (d), (e), and (f) of s. 718 of the *Criminal Code* apply to all offenders, and not only aboriginal offenders. However, most traditional aboriginal conceptions of sentencing place a primary emphasis upon the ideals of restorative justice. This tradition is extremely important to the analysis under s. 718.2(e).

[71] The concept and principles of a restorative approach will necessarily have to be developed over time in the jurisprudence, as different issues and different conceptions of sentencing are addressed in their appropriate context. In general terms, restorative justice may be described as an approach to remedying crime in which it is understood that all things are interrelated and that crime disrupts the harmony which existed prior to its occurrence, or at least which it is felt should exist. The appropriateness of a particular sanction is largely determined by the needs of the victims, and the community, as well as the offender. ...

[72] The existing overemphasis on incarceration in Canada may be partly due to the perception that a restorative approach is a more lenient approach to crime and that imprisonment constitutes the ultimate punishment. Yet in our view a sentence focused on restorative justice is not necessarily a "lighter" punishment. Some proponents of restorative justice argue that when it is combined with probationary conditions it may in some circumstances impose a greater burden on the offender than a custodial sentence. ...

[73] In describing in general terms some of the basic tenets of traditional aboriginal sentencing approaches, we do not wish to imply that all aboriginal offenders, victims, and communities share an identical understanding of appropriate sentences for particular offences and offenders. Aboriginal communities stretch from coast to coast and from the border with the United States to the far north. Their customs and traditions and their concept of sentencing vary widely. What is important to recognize is that, for many if not most aboriginal offenders, the current concepts of sentencing are inappropriate because they have frequently not responded to the needs, experiences, and perspectives of aboriginal people or aboriginal communities.

[74] It is unnecessary to engage here in an extensive discussion of the relatively recent evolution of innovative sentencing practices, such as healing and sentencing circles, and aboriginal community council projects, which are available to aboriginal offenders. What is important to note is that the different conceptions of sentencing held by many aboriginal people share a common underlying principle: that is, the importance of community-based sanctions. Sentencing judges should not conclude that the absence of alternatives specific to an aboriginal community eliminates their ability to impose a sanction that takes into account principles of restorative justice and the needs of the parties involved. Rather, the point is that one of the unique circumstances of aboriginal offenders is that community-based sanctions coincide with the aboriginal concept of sentencing and the needs of aboriginal people and communities. It is often the case that neither aboriginal offenders nor their communities are well served by incarcerating offenders, particularly for less serious or non-violent offences. Where these sanctions are reasonable in the circumstances,

they should be implemented. In all instances, it is appropriate to attempt to craft the sentencing process and the sanctions imposed in accordance with the aboriginal perspective.

· · ·

[78] In describing the effect of s. 718.2(e) in this way, we do not mean to suggest that, as a general practice, aboriginal offenders must always be sentenced in a manner which gives greatest weight to the principles of restorative justice, and less weight to goals such as deterrence, denunciation, and separation. It is unreasonable to assume that aboriginal peoples themselves do not believe in the importance of these latter goals, and even if they do not, that such goals must not predominate in appropriate cases. Clearly there are some serious offences and some offenders for which and for whom separation, denunciation, and deterrence are fundamentally relevant.

[79] Yet, even where an offence is considered serious, the length of the term of imprisonment must be considered. In some circumstances the length of the sentence of an aboriginal offender may be less and in others the same as that of any other offender. Generally, the more violent and serious the offence the more likely it is as a practical reality that the terms of imprisonment for aboriginals and non-aboriginals will be close to each other or the same, even taking into account their different concepts of sentencing.

[80] As with all sentencing decisions, the sentencing of aboriginal offenders must proceed on an individual (or a case-by-case) basis: For *this* offence, committed by *this* offender, harming *this* victim, in *this* community, what is the appropriate sanction under the *Criminal Code*? What understanding of criminal sanctions is held by the community? What is the nature of the relationship between the offender and his or her community? What combination of systemic or background factors contributed to this particular offender coming before the courts for this particular offence? How has the offender who is being sentenced been affected by, for example, substance abuse in the community, or poverty, or overt racism, or family or community breakdown? Would imprisonment effectively serve to deter or denounce crime in a sense that would be significant to the offender and community, or are crime prevention and other goals better achieved through healing? What sentencing options present themselves in these circumstances?

· · ·

(3) The Duty of the Sentencing Judge

[82] The foregoing discussion of guidelines for the sentencing judge has spoken of that which a judge must do when sentencing an aboriginal offender. This element of duty is a critical component of s. 718.2(e). The provision expressly provides that a court that imposes a sentence *should* consider all available sanctions other than imprisonment that are reasonable in the circumstances, and *should* pay particular attention to the circumstances of aboriginal offenders. There is no discretion as to whether to consider the unique situation of the aboriginal offender; the only discretion concerns the determination of a just and appropriate sentence.

[83] How then is the consideration of s. 718.2(e) to proceed in the daily functioning of the courts? The manner in which the sentencing judge will carry out his or her statutory duty may vary from case to case. In all instances it will be necessary for the judge to take judicial notice of the systemic or background factors and the approach to sentencing which is relevant to aboriginal offenders. However, for each particular offence and offender it may

be that some evidence will be required in order to assist the sentencing judge in arriving at a fit sentence. Where a particular offender does not wish such evidence to be adduced, the right to have particular attention paid to his or her circumstances as an aboriginal offender may be waived. Where there is no such waiver, it will be extremely helpful to the sentencing judge for counsel on both sides to adduce relevant evidence. Indeed, it is to be expected that counsel will fulfil their role and assist the sentencing judge in this way.

[84] However, even where counsel do not adduce this evidence, where for example the offender is unrepresented, it is incumbent upon the sentencing judge to attempt to acquire information regarding the circumstances of the offender as an aboriginal person. Whether the offender resides in a rural area, on a reserve or in an urban centre the sentencing judge must be made aware of alternatives to incarceration that exist whether inside or outside the aboriginal community of the particular offender. The alternatives existing in metropolitan areas must, as a matter of course, also be explored. Clearly the presence of an aboriginal offender will require special attention in pre-sentence reports. Beyond the use of the pre-sentence report, the sentencing judge may and should in appropriate circumstances and where practicable request that witnesses be called who may testify as to reasonable alternatives.

[85] Similarly, where a sentencing judge at the trial level has not engaged in the duty imposed by s. 718.2(e) as fully as required, it is incumbent upon a court of appeal in considering an appeal against sentence on this basis to consider any fresh evidence which is relevant and admissible on sentencing. In the same vein, it should be noted that, although s. 718.2(e) does not impose a statutory duty upon the sentencing judge to provide reasons, it will be much easier for a reviewing court to determine whether and how attention was paid to the circumstances of the offender as an aboriginal person if at least brief reasons are given.

(4) The Issue of "Reverse Discrimination"

[86] Something must also be said as to the manner in which s. 718.2(e) should not be interpreted. The appellant and the respondent diverged significantly in their interpretation of the appropriate role to be played by s. 718.2(e). While the respondent saw the provision largely as a restatement of existing sentencing principles, the appellant advanced the position that s. 718.2(e) functions as an affirmative action provision justified under s. 15(2) of the Charter. The respondent cautioned that, in his view, the appellant's understanding of the provision would result in "reverse discrimination" so as to favour aboriginal offenders over other offenders.

[87] There is no constitutional challenge to s. 718.2(e) in these proceedings, and accordingly we do not address specifically the applicability of s. 15 of the Charter. We would note, though, that the aim of s. 718.2(e) is to reduce the tragic overrepresentation of aboriginal people in prisons. It seeks to ameliorate the present situation and to deal with the particular offence and offender and community. The fact that a court is called upon to take into consideration the unique circumstances surrounding these different parties is not unfair to non-aboriginal people. Rather, the fundamental purpose of s. 718.2(e) is to treat aboriginal offenders fairly by taking into account their difference.

[88] But s. 718.2(e) should not be taken as requiring an automatic reduction of a sentence, or a remission of a warranted period of incarceration, simply because the offender

is aboriginal. To the extent that the appellant's submission on affirmative action means that s. 718.2(e) requires an automatic reduction in sentence for an aboriginal offender, we reject that view. The provision is a direction to sentencing judges to consider certain unique circumstances pertaining to aboriginal offenders as a part of the task of weighing the multitude of factors which must be taken into account in striving to impose a fit sentence. It cannot be forgotten that s. 718.2(e) must be considered in the context of that section read as a whole and in the context of s. 718, s. 718.1, and the overall scheme of Part XXIII. It is one of the statutorily mandated considerations that a sentencing judge must take into account. It may not always mean a lower sentence for an aboriginal offender. The sentence imposed will depend upon all the factors which must be taken into account in each individual case. The weight to be given to these various factors will vary in each case. At the same time, it must in every case be recalled that the direction to consider these unique circumstances flows from the staggering injustice currently experienced by aboriginal peoples with the criminal justice system. The provision reflects the reality that many aboriginal people are alienated from this system which frequently does not reflect their needs or their understanding of an appropriate sentence.

· · ·

[90]   The class of aboriginal people who come within the purview of the specific reference to the circumstances of aboriginal offenders in s. 718.2(e) must be, at least, all who come within the scope of s. 25 of the Charter and s. 35 of the *Constitution Act, 1982*. The numbers involved are significant. National census figures from 1996 show that an estimated 799,010 people were identified as aboriginal in 1996. Of this number, 529,040 were Indians (registered or non-registered), 204,115 Métis and 40,220 Inuit.

[91]   Section 718.2(e) applies to all aboriginal offenders wherever they reside, whether on- or off-reserve, in a large city or a rural area. Indeed it has been observed that many aboriginals living in urban areas are closely attached to their culture. ...

[92]   Section 718.2(e) requires the sentencing judge to explore reasonable alternatives to incarceration in the case of all aboriginal offenders. Obviously, if an aboriginal community has a program or tradition of alternative sanctions, and support and supervision are available to the offender, it may be easier to find and impose an alternative sentence. However, even if community support is not available, every effort should be made in appropriate circumstances to find a sensitive and helpful alternative. For all purposes, the term "community" must be defined broadly so as to include any network of support and interaction that might be available in an urban centre. At the same time, the residence of the aboriginal offender in an urban centre that lacks any network of support does not relieve the sentencing judge of the obligation to try to find an alternative to imprisonment.

NOTE

The Supreme Court dismissed Ms. Gladue's appeal against the three-year sentence primarily because, by the time the decision was released, she was already in the community on day parole.

R v Ipeelee
2012 SCC 13, [2012] 1 SCR 433

[This decision involved two Aboriginal offenders with long criminal records who had been convicted, declared long-term offenders, and made subject to long-term supervision orders (LTSOs). Both had served their prison terms and were released subject to the LTSOs. One offender committed an offence while intoxicated, thereby breaching a condition of his LTSO. For the LTSO breach, he was sentenced to three years' imprisonment, less six months of pre-sentence custody. The Court of Appeal dismissed his sentence appeal. The other offender failed a urinalysis test, breaching a condition of his LTSO. For the breach, he was sentenced to three years' imprisonment, less five months of pre-sentence custody. A majority of the Court of Appeal allowed his appeal and reduced the sentence to one year.]

LeBEL J (McLachlin CJ, Binnie, Deschamps, Fish, and Abella JJ concurring):

I. Introduction

[1] These two appeals raise the issue of the principles governing the sentencing of Aboriginal offenders for breaches of long-term supervision orders ("LTSOs"). Both appeals concern Aboriginal offenders with long criminal records. They provide an opportunity to revisit and reaffirm the judgment of this Court in *R. v. Gladue*, [1999] 1 S.C.R. 688. I propose to allow the offender's appeal in *Ipeelee* and to dismiss the Crown's appeal in *Ladue*.

II. Manasie Ipeelee

A. Background and Criminal History

[2] Mr. Manasie Ipeelee is an Inuk man who was born and raised in Iqaluit, Nunavut. His life story is far removed from the experience of most Canadians. His mother was an alcoholic. She froze to death when Manasie Ipeelee was five years old. He was raised by his maternal grandmother and grandfather, both of whom are now deceased. Mr. Ipeelee began consuming alcohol when he was 11 years old and quickly developed a serious alcohol addiction. He dropped out of school shortly thereafter. His involvement with the criminal justice system began in 1985, when he was only 12 years old.

[3] Mr. Ipeelee is presently 39 years old. He has spent a significant proportion of his life in custody or under some form of community supervision. His youth record contains approximately three dozen convictions. The majority of those offences were property-related, including breaking and entering, theft, and taking a vehicle without consent (joyriding). There were also convictions for failure to comply with an undertaking, breach of probation, and being unlawfully at large. Mr. Ipeelee's adult record contains another 24 convictions, many of which are for similar types of offences. He has also committed violent crimes. His record includes two convictions for assault causing bodily harm and one conviction each for aggravated assault, sexual assault, and sexual assault causing bodily harm. I will describe these offences in greater detail, as they provided the basis for his eventual designation as a long-term offender.

[4]   In December 1992, Mr. Ipeelee pleaded guilty to assault causing bodily harm. He and a friend assaulted a man who was refusing them entry to his home. Mr. Ipeelee was intoxicated at the time. During the fight, he hit the victim over the head with an ashtray and with a chair. He was sentenced to 21 days' imprisonment and one year's probation.

[5]   In December 1993, Mr. Ipeelee again pleaded guilty to assault causing bodily harm. The incident took place outside a bar in Iqaluit and both Mr. Ipeelee and the victim were intoxicated. Witnesses saw Mr. Ipeelee kicking the victim in the face at least 10 times, and the assault continued after the victim lost consciousness. The victim was hospitalized for his injuries. At the time of the offence, Mr. Ipeelee was on probation. He received a sentence of five months' imprisonment.

[6]   In November 1994, Mr. Ipeelee pleaded guilty to aggravated assault. The incident involved another altercation outside the same bar in Iqaluit. Once more, both Mr. Ipeelee and the victim were intoxicated. During the fight, Mr. Ipeelee hit and kicked the victim. After the victim lost consciousness, Mr. Ipeelee continued to hit him and stomp on his face. The victim suffered a broken jaw and had to be sent to Montréal for treatment. Mr. Ipeelee was once again on probation at the time of the offence. He was sentenced to 14 months' imprisonment.

[7]   Mr. Ipeelee received an early release from that sentence in the fall of 1995. Approximately three weeks later, while still technically serving his sentence, he committed a sexual assault. The female victim had been drinking in her apartment in Iqaluit with Mr. Ipeelee and others, and was passed out from intoxication. Witnesses observed Mr. Ipeelee and another man carrying the victim into her room. Mr. Ipeelee was later seen having sex with the unconscious woman on her bed. Mr. Ipeelee was sentenced to two years' imprisonment. He remained in custody until his warrant expiry date in February 1999, as Corrections Canada officials deemed him to be a high risk to reoffend.

[8]   After serving his sentence, Mr. Ipeelee moved to Yellowknife. He began drinking within one half-hour of his arrival and was arrested for public intoxication that evening, and again 24 hours later. In the six months leading up to his next conviction, he was arrested at least nine more times for public intoxication.

[9]   On August 21, 1999, Mr. Ipeelee committed another sexual assault, this one causing bodily harm, which led to his designation as a long-term offender. Mr. Ipeelee, while intoxicated, entered an abandoned van that homeless persons frequented. Inside, a 50-year-old woman was sleeping. She awoke to find Mr. Ipeelee removing her pants. She struggled and Mr. Ipeelee began punching her in the face. When she called out for help, he told her to shut up or he would kill her. He then sexually assaulted her. The victim was finally able to escape when Mr. Ipeelee fell asleep. He was arrested and the victim was taken to the hospital to be treated for her injuries.

[10]   At the sentencing hearing for this offence, Richard J. of the Northwest Territories Supreme Court noted that Mr. Ipeelee's criminal record "shows a consistent pattern of Mr. Ipeelee administering gratuitous violence against vulnerable, helpless people while he is in a state of intoxication" (*R. v. Ipeelee*, 2001 NWTSC 33, [2001] N.W.T.J. No. 30 (QL), at para. 34). The expert evidence produced at the sentencing hearing indicated that Mr. Ipeelee did not suffer from any major mental illness and had average to above average intelligence. However, he was diagnosed as having both an antisocial personality disorder and a severe alcohol abuse disorder. The expert evidence also indicated that Mr. Ipeelee

presented a high-moderate to high risk for violent reoffence, and a high-moderate risk for sexual reoffence. After evaluating all of the evidence, Richard J. concluded that there was a substantial risk that Mr. Ipeelee would reoffend and designated him a long-term offender under s. 753.1(1) of the *Criminal Code*, R.S.C. 1985, c. C-46. Mr. Ipeelee was sentenced to six years' imprisonment for the sexual assault, to be followed by a 10-year LTSO.

B. The Current Offence

[11] Mr. Ipeelee was detained until his warrant expiry date for the 1999 sexual assault causing bodily harm. His LTSO came into effect on March 14, 2007, when he was released from Kingston Penitentiary to the Portsmouth Community Correctional Centre in Kingston. One of the conditions of Mr. Ipeelee's LTSO is that he abstain from using alcohol.

[12] Mr. Ipeelee's LTSO was suspended on four occasions: from June 13 to July 5, 2007, for deteriorating performance and behaviour, and attitude problems; from July 23 to September 14, 2007, for sleeping in the living room and the kitchen, contrary to house rules; from September 24 to October 24, 2007, for being agitated and noncompliant, and for refusing urinalysis; and from October 25, 2007, to May 20, 2008, as a result of a fraud charge being laid against him (the charge was subsequently withdrawn). Mr. Ipeelee served those periods of suspension at the Kingston Penitentiary.

[13] On August 20, 2008, the police found Mr. Ipeelee riding his bicycle erratically in downtown Kingston. He was obviously intoxicated and had two bottles of alcohol in his possession. He was charged with breaching a condition of his LTSO, contrary to s. 753.3(1) of the *Criminal Code*. Mr. Ipeelee pleaded guilty to that offence on November 14, 2008.

C. Judicial History

(1) Ontario Court of Justice, [2009] O.J. No. 6413 (QL)

[14] On February 24, 2009, Megginson J. of the Ontario Court of Justice sentenced Mr. Ipeelee to three years' imprisonment, less six months of pre-sentence custody at a 1:1 credit rate. He emphasized the serious nature of the offence, stating:

> On its facts, this was a serious and not at all trivial breach of a very fundamental condition of the offender's [LTSO]. It is a very central and essential condition, because alcohol abuse was involved, not only in the "predicate" offence, but also in most of the offences on the offender's criminal record. On his history, Mr. Ipeelee becomes violent when he abuses alcohol, and he was assessed as posing a significant risk of re-offending sexually. Defence counsel argued that the facts of the present breach disclose no movement toward committing another sexual offence, but I think that is beside the point. [para. 10]

[15] Megginson J. held that, when sentencing an offender for breach of an LTSO, the paramount consideration is the protection of the public and rehabilitation plays only a small role. With that in mind, he addressed the requirement imposed by s. 718.2(e) of the *Criminal Code* that he consider Mr. Ipeelee's unique circumstances as an Aboriginal offender. He began by noting that Mr. Ipeelee's Aboriginal status had already been considered during sentencing for the 1999 offence giving rise to the LTSO. He went on to conclude that, when protection of the public is the paramount concern, an offender's Aboriginal status is of "diminished importance" (para. 15).

(2) *Ontario Court of Appeal, 2009 ONCA 892, 99 O.R. (3d) 419*

[16] Mr. Ipeelee appealed his sentence on the grounds that it was demonstrably unfit, and that the sentencing judge did not give adequate consideration to his circumstances as an Aboriginal offender. The Court of Appeal dismissed the appeal.

[17] Sharpe J.A., writing for the court, was not convinced that the sentence was demonstrably unfit. He agreed with the sentencing judge's characterization of the offence as a serious breach of a vital condition of the LTSO. Sharpe J.A. found that, despite the sentencing judge's comments, Mr. Ipeelee's Aboriginal status had not factored into the sentencing decision. He did not, however, think this was an error:

> It is not at all clear to me, however, that in the circumstances of this case, consideration of his aboriginal status should lead to a reduction in his sentence for breach of the long-term offender condition. The appellant's commission of violent offences and the risk he poses for re-offending when under the influence of alcohol make the principles of denunciation, deterrence and protection of the public paramount. This is one of those cases where "the appropriate sentence will … not differ as between aboriginal and non-aboriginal offenders": *R. v. Carrière*, [2002] O.J. No. 1429, 164 C.C.C. (3d) 569 (C.A.), at para. 17. As the appellant has been declared a long-term offender, "consideration of restorative justice and other features of aboriginal offender sentencing … play little or no role": *R. v. W. (H.P.)*, [2003] A.J. No. 479, 327 A.R. 170 (C.A.), at para. 50. [para. 13]

[18] Sharpe J.A. did concede that Mr. Ipeelee's Aboriginal background and the disadvantages he had suffered provided some insight into his repeated involvement with the criminal justice system. He concluded, however, that these considerations should not affect the sentence. He ended his reasons with a plea to correctional authorities to make every effort to provide Mr. Ipeelee with appropriate Aboriginal-oriented assistance.

• • •

IV. *Issues*

[33] These two appeals raise issues concerning the application of the principles and objectives of sentencing set out in Part XXIII of the *Criminal Code*. Specifically, the Court must determine the principles governing the sentencing of Aboriginal offenders, including the proper interpretation and application of this Court's judgment in *Gladue*, and the application of those principles to the breach of an LTSO. Finally, given those principles, the Court must determine whether either of the decisions under appeal contains an error in principle or imposes an unfit sentence warranting appellate intervention.

V. *Analysis*

A. *The Principles of Sentencing*

[34] The central issue in these appeals is how to determine a fit sentence for a breach of an LTSO in the case of an Aboriginal offender. In particular, the Court must address whether, and how, the *Gladue* principles apply to these sentencing decisions. But first, it is important to review the principles that guide sentencing under Canadian law generally.

[35] In 1996, Parliament amended the *Criminal Code* to specifically codify the objectives and principles of sentencing (*An Act to amend the Criminal Code (sentencing) and*

other Acts in consequence thereof, S.C. 1995, c. 22 (Bill C-41)). According to s. 718, the fundamental purpose of sentencing is to contribute to "respect for the law and the maintenance of a just, peaceful and safe society." This is accomplished by imposing "just sanctions" that reflect one or more of the traditional sentencing objectives: denunciation, general and specific deterrence, separation of offenders, rehabilitation, reparation to victims, and promoting a sense of responsibility in offenders and acknowledgment of the harm done to victims and to the community.

[36] The *Criminal Code* goes on to list a number of principles to guide sentencing judges. The fundamental principle of sentencing is that the sentence must be proportionate to both the gravity of the offence and the degree of responsibility of the offender. As this Court has previously indicated, this principle was not borne out of the 1996 amendments to the *Code* but, instead, has long been a central tenet of the sentencing process (see, e.g., *R. v. Wilmott* (1966), 58 D.L.R. (2d) 33 (Ont. C.A.), and, more recently, *R. v. Solowan*, 2008 SCC 62, [2008] 3 S.C.R. 309, at para. 12, and *R. v. Nasogaluak*, 2010 SCC 6, [2010] 1 S.C.R. 206, at paras. 40-42). It also has a constitutional dimension, in that s. 12 of the *Canadian Charter of Rights and Freedoms* forbids the imposition of a grossly disproportionate sentence that would outrage society's standards of decency. In a similar vein, proportionality in sentencing could aptly be described as a principle of fundamental justice under s. 7 of the *Charter*.

[37] The fundamental principle of sentencing (i.e., proportionality) is intimately tied to the fundamental purpose of sentencing—the maintenance of a just, peaceful and safe society through the imposition of just sanctions. Whatever weight a judge may wish to accord to the various objectives and other principles listed in the *Code*, the resulting sentence must respect the fundamental principle of proportionality. Proportionality is the *sine qua non* of a just sanction. First, the principle ensures that a sentence reflects the gravity of the offence. This is closely tied to the objective of denunciation. It promotes justice for victims and ensures public confidence in the justice system. As Wilson J. expressed in her concurring judgment in *Re B.C. Motor Vehicle Act*, [1985] 2 S.C.R. 486, at p. 533:

> It is basic to any theory of punishment that the sentence imposed bear some relationship to the offence; it must be a "fit" sentence proportionate to the seriousness of the offence. Only if this is so can the public be satisfied that the offender "deserved" the punishment he received and feel a confidence in the fairness and rationality of the system.

Second, the principle of proportionality ensures that a sentence does not exceed what is appropriate, given the moral blameworthiness of the offender. In this sense, the principle serves a limiting or restraining function and ensures justice for the offender. In the Canadian criminal justice system, a just sanction is one that reflects both perspectives on proportionality and does not elevate one at the expense of the other.

[38] Despite the constraints imposed by the principle of proportionality, trial judges enjoy a broad discretion in the sentencing process. The determination of a fit sentence is, subject to any specific statutory rules that have survived *Charter* scrutiny, a highly individualized process. Sentencing judges must have sufficient manoeuvrability to tailor sentences to the circumstances of the particular offence and the particular offender. Appellate courts have recognized the scope of this discretion and granted considerable deference to a judge's choice of sentence. As Lamer C.J. stated in *R. v. M. (C.A.)*, [1996] 1 S.C.R. 500, at para. 90:

Put simply, absent an error in principle, failure to consider a relevant factor, or an overemphasis of the appropriate factors, a court of appeal should only intervene to vary a sentence imposed at trial if the sentence is demonstrably unfit. Parliament explicitly vested sentencing judges with a *discretion* to determine the appropriate degree and kind of punishment under the *Criminal Code*. [Emphasis in original.]

[39] There are limits, however, to the deference that will be afforded to a trial judge. Appellate courts have a duty to ensure that courts properly apply the legal principles governing sentencing. In every case, an appellate court must be satisfied that the sentence under review is proportionate to both the gravity of *the offence* and the degree of responsibility of *the offender*. I will now turn to an assessment of these factors as they pertain to the present appeals.

. . .

C. *The Offender: Sentencing Aboriginal Offenders*

[56] Section 718.2(e) of the *Criminal Code* directs that "all available sanctions other than imprisonment that are reasonable in the circumstances should be considered for all offenders, *with particular attention to the circumstances of aboriginal offenders.*" This provision was introduced into the *Code* as part of the 1996 Bill C-41 amendments to codify the purpose and principles of sentencing. According to the then-Minister of Justice, Allan Rock, "the reason we referred specifically there to aboriginal persons is that they are sadly overrepresented in the prison populations of Canada" (House of Commons, *Minutes of Proceedings and Evidence of the Standing Committee on Justice and Legal Affairs*, No. 62, 1st Sess., 35th Parl., November 17, 1994, at p. 15).

[57] Aboriginal persons were sadly overrepresented indeed. Government figures from 1988 indicated that Aboriginal persons accounted for 10 percent of federal prison inmates, while making up only 2 percent of the national population. The figures were even more stark in the Prairie provinces, where Aboriginal persons accounted for 32 percent of prison inmates compared to 5 percent of the population. The situation was generally worse in provincial institutions. For example, Aboriginal persons accounted for fully 60 percent of the inmates detained in provincial jails in Saskatchewan (M. Jackson, "Locking Up Natives in Canada" (1989), 23 *U.B.C. L. Rev.* 215, at pp. 215-16). There was also evidence to indicate that this overrepresentation was on the rise. At Stony Mountain penitentiary, the only federal prison in Manitoba, the Aboriginal inmate population had been climbing steadily from 22 percent in 1965 to 33 percent in 1984, and up to 46 percent just five years later in 1989 (Commissioners A.C. Hamilton and C.M. Sinclair, *Report of the Aboriginal Justice Inquiry of Manitoba*, vol. 1, *The Justice System and Aboriginal People* (1991), at p. 394). The foregoing statistics led the Royal Commission on Aboriginal Peoples ("RCAP") to conclude, at p. 309 of its Report, *Bridging the Cultural Divide: A Report on Aboriginal People and Criminal Justice in Canada* (1996):

> The Canadian criminal justice system has failed the Aboriginal peoples of Canada—First Nations, Inuit and Métis people, on-reserve and off-reserve, urban and rural—in all territorial and governmental jurisdictions. The principal reason for this crushing failure is the fundamentally different world views of Aboriginal and non-Aboriginal people with respect to such elemental issues as the substantive content of justice and the process of achieving justice.

[58] The overrepresentation of Aboriginal people in the Canadian criminal justice system was the impetus for including the specific reference to Aboriginal people in s. 718.2(e). It was not at all clear, however, what exactly the provision required or how it would affect the sentencing of Aboriginal offenders. In 1999, this Court had the opportunity to address these questions in *Gladue*. Cory and Iacobucci JJ., writing for the unanimous Court, reviewed the statistics and concluded, at para. 64:

> These findings cry out for recognition of the magnitude and gravity of the problem, and for responses to alleviate it. The figures are stark and reflect what may fairly be termed a crisis in the Canadian criminal justice system. The drastic overrepresentation of aboriginal peoples within both the Canadian prison population and the criminal justice system reveals a sad and pressing social problem. It is reasonable to assume that Parliament, in singling out aboriginal offenders for distinct sentencing treatment in s. 718.2(e), intended to attempt to redress this social problem to some degree. The provision may properly be seen as Parliament's direction to members of the judiciary to inquire into the causes of the problem and to endeavour to remedy it, to the extent that a remedy is possible through the sentencing process.

[59] The Court held, therefore, that s. 718.2(e) of the *Code* is a remedial provision designed to ameliorate the serious problem of overrepresentation of Aboriginal people in Canadian prisons, and to encourage sentencing judges to have recourse to a restorative approach to sentencing (*Gladue*, at para. 93). It does more than affirm existing principles of sentencing; it calls upon judges to use a different method of analysis in determining a fit sentence for Aboriginal offenders. Section 718.2(e) directs sentencing judges to pay particular attention to the circumstances of Aboriginal offenders because those circumstances are unique and different from those of non-Aboriginal offenders (*Gladue*, at para. 37). When sentencing an Aboriginal offender, a judge must consider: (a) the unique systemic or background factors which may have played a part in bringing the particular Aboriginal offender before the courts; and (b) the types of sentencing procedures and sanctions which may be appropriate in the circumstances for the offender because of his or her particular Aboriginal heritage or connection (*Gladue*, at para. 66). Judges may take judicial notice of the broad systemic and background factors affecting Aboriginal people generally, but additional case-specific information will have to come from counsel and from the pre-sentence report (*Gladue*, at paras. 83-84).

[60] Courts have, at times, been hesitant to take judicial notice of the systemic and background factors affecting Aboriginal people in Canadian society (see, e.g., *R. v. Laliberte*, 2000 SKCA 27, 189 Sask. R. 190). To be clear, courts must take judicial notice of such matters as the history of colonialism, displacement, and residential schools and how that history continues to translate into lower educational attainment, lower incomes, higher unemployment, higher rates of substance abuse and suicide, and of course higher levels of incarceration for Aboriginal peoples. These matters, on their own, do not necessarily justify a different sentence for Aboriginal offenders. Rather, they provide the necessary *context* for understanding and evaluating the case-specific information presented by counsel. Counsel have a duty to bring that individualized information before the court in every case, unless the offender expressly waives his right to have it considered. In current practice, it appears that case-specific information is often brought before the court by way of a *Gladue* report, which is a form of pre-sentence report tailored to the specific circumstances of Aboriginal offenders. Bringing such information to the attention of the

judge in a comprehensive and timely manner is helpful to all parties at a sentencing hearing for an Aboriginal offender, as it is indispensable to a judge in fulfilling his duties under s. 718.2(e) of the *Criminal Code*.

[61] It would have been naive to suggest that sentencing Aboriginal persons differently, without addressing the root causes of criminality, would eliminate their overrepresentation in the criminal justice system entirely. In *Gladue*, Cory and Iacobucci JJ. were mindful of this fact, yet retained a degree of optimism, stating, at para. 65:

> It is clear that sentencing innovation by itself cannot remove the causes of aboriginal offending and the greater problem of aboriginal alienation from the criminal justice system. The unbalanced ratio of imprisonment for aboriginal offenders flows from a number of sources, including poverty, substance abuse, lack of education, and the lack of employment opportunities for aboriginal people. It arises also from bias against aboriginal people and from an unfortunate institutional approach that is more inclined to refuse bail and to impose more and longer prison terms for aboriginal offenders. There are many aspects of this sad situation which cannot be addressed in these reasons. What can and must be addressed, though, is the limited role that sentencing judges will play in remedying injustice against aboriginal peoples in Canada. Sentencing judges are among those decision-makers who have the power to influence the treatment of aboriginal offenders in the justice system. They determine most directly whether an aboriginal offender will go to jail, or whether other sentencing options may be employed which will play perhaps a stronger role in restoring a sense of balance to the offender, victim, and community, and in preventing future crime.

[62] This cautious optimism has not been borne out. In fact, statistics indicate that the overrepresentation and alienation of Aboriginal peoples in the criminal justice system has only worsened. In the immediate aftermath of Bill C-41, from 1996 to 2001, Aboriginal admissions to custody increased by 3 percent while non-Aboriginal admissions declined by 22 percent (J.V. Roberts and R. Melchers, "The Incarceration of Aboriginal Offenders: Trends from 1978 to 2001" (2003), 45 *Can. J. Crim. & Crim. Just.* 211, at p. 226). From 2001 to 2006, there was an overall decline in prison admissions of 9 percent. During that same time period, Aboriginal admissions to custody increased by 4 percent (J. Rudin, "Addressing Aboriginal Overrepresentation Post-*Gladue*: A Realistic Assessment of How Social Change Occurs" (2009), 54 *Crim. L.Q.* 447, at p. 452). As a result, the overrepresentation of Aboriginal people in the criminal justice system is worse than ever. Whereas Aboriginal persons made up 12 percent of all federal inmates in 1999 when *Gladue* was decided, they accounted for 17 percent of federal admissions in 2005 (J. Rudin, "Aboriginal Over-representation and *R. v. Gladue*: Where We Were, Where We Are and Where We Might Be Going," in J. Cameron and J. Stribopoulos, eds., *The Charter and Criminal Justice: Twenty-Five Years Later* (2008), 687, at p. 701). As Professor Rudin asks: "If Aboriginal overrepresentation was a crisis in 1999, what term can be applied to the situation today?" ("Addressing Aboriginal Overrepresentation Post-*Gladue*," at p. 452).

[63] Over a decade has passed since this Court issued its judgment in *Gladue*. As the statistics indicate, s. 718.2(e) of the *Criminal Code* has not had a discernible impact on the overrepresentation of Aboriginal people in the criminal justice system. Granted, the *Gladue* principles were never expected to provide a panacea. There is some indication, however, from both the academic commentary and the jurisprudence, that the failure can be attributed to some extent to a fundamental misunderstanding and misapplication of

both s. 718.2(e) and this Court's decision in *Gladue*. The following is an attempt to resolve these misunderstandings, clarify certain ambiguities, and provide additional guidance so that courts can properly implement this sentencing provision.

(1) Making Sense of Aboriginal Sentencing

[64] Section 718.2(e) of the *Criminal Code* and this Court's decision in *Gladue* were not universally well received. Three interrelated criticisms have been advanced: (1) sentencing is not an appropriate means of addressing overrepresentation; (2) the *Gladue* principles provide what is essentially a race-based discount for Aboriginal offenders; and (3) providing special treatment and lesser sentences to Aboriginal offenders is inherently unfair as it creates unjustified distinctions between offenders who are similarly situated, thus violating the principle of sentence parity. In my view, these criticisms are based on a fundamental misunderstanding of the operation of s. 718.2(e) of the *Criminal Code*.

[65] Professors Stenning and Roberts describe the sentencing provision as an "empty promise" to Aboriginal peoples because it is unlikely to have any significant impact on levels of overrepresentation (P. Stenning and J.V. Roberts, "Empty Promises: Parliament, The Supreme Court, and the Sentencing of Aboriginal Offenders" (2001), 64 *Sask. L. Rev.* 137, at p. 167). As we have seen, the direction to pay particular attention to the circumstances of Aboriginal offenders was included in light of evidence of their overrepresentation in Canada's prisons and jails. This overrepresentation led the Aboriginal Justice Inquiry of Manitoba to ask in its Report: "Why, in a society where justice is supposed to be blind, are the inmates of our prisons selected so overwhelmingly from a single ethnic group? Two answers suggest themselves immediately: either Aboriginal people commit a disproportionate number of crimes, or they are the victims of a discriminatory justice system" (p. 85; see also RCAP, at p. 33). The available evidence indicates that both phenomena are contributing to the problem (RCAP). Contrary to Professors Stenning and Roberts, addressing these matters does not lie beyond the purview of the sentencing judge.

[66] First, sentencing judges can endeavour to reduce crime rates in Aboriginal communities by imposing sentences that effectively deter criminality and rehabilitate offenders. These are codified objectives of sentencing. To the extent that current sentencing practices do not further these objectives, those practices must change so as to meet the needs of Aboriginal offenders and their communities. As Professors Rudin and Roach ask, "[if an innovative] sentence can serve to actually assist a person in taking responsibility for his or her actions and lead to a reduction in the probability of subsequent re-offending, why should such a sentence be precluded just because other people who commit the same offence go to jail?" (J. Rudin and K. Roach, "Broken Promises: A Response to Stenning and Roberts' 'Empty Promises'" (2002), 65 *Sask. L. Rev.* 3, at p. 20).

[67] Second, judges can ensure that systemic factors do not lead inadvertently to discrimination in sentencing. Professor Quigley aptly describes how this occurs:

> Socioeconomic factors such as employment status, level of education, family situation, etc., appear on the surface as neutral criteria. They are considered as such by the legal system. Yet they can conceal an extremely strong bias in the sentencing process. Convicted persons with steady employment and stability in their lives, or at least prospects of the same, are much less likely to be sent to jail for offences that are borderline imprisonment offences. The unemployed, transients, the poorly educated are all better candidates for imprisonment.

When the social, political and economic aspects of our society place Aboriginal people disproportionately within the ranks of the latter, our society literally sentences more of them to jail. This is systemic discrimination.

(T. Quigley, "Some Issues in Sentencing of Aboriginal Offenders," in R. Gosse, J.Y. Henderson and R. Carter, eds., *Continuing Poundmaker and Riel's Quest: Presentations Made at a Conference on Aboriginal Peoples and Justice* (1994), 269, at pp. 275-76)

Sentencing judges, as front-line workers in the criminal justice system, are in the best position to re-evaluate these criteria to ensure that they are not contributing to ongoing systemic racial discrimination.

[68] Section 718.2(e) is therefore properly seen as a "direction to members of the judiciary to inquire into the causes of the problem and to endeavour to remedy it, *to the extent that a remedy is possible through the sentencing process*" (*Gladue*, at para. 64 (emphasis added)). Applying the provision does not amount to "hijacking the sentencing process in the pursuit of other goals" (Stenning and Roberts, at p. 160). The purpose of sentencing is to promote a just, peaceful and safe society through the imposition of just sanctions that, among other things, deter criminality and rehabilitate offenders, all in accordance with the fundamental principle of proportionality. Just sanctions are those that do not operate in a discriminatory manner. Parliament, in enacting s. 718.2(e), evidently concluded that nothing short of a specific direction to pay particular attention to the circumstances of Aboriginal offenders would suffice to ensure that judges undertook their duties properly.

[69] Certainly sentencing will not be the sole—or even the primary—means of addressing Aboriginal overrepresentation in penal institutions. But that does not detract from a judge's fundamental duty to fashion a sentence that is fit and proper in the circumstances of the offence, the offender, and the victim. Nor does it turn s. 718.2(e) into an empty promise. The sentencing judge has an admittedly limited, yet important role to play. As the Aboriginal Justice Inquiry of Manitoba put it, at pp. 110-11:

To change this situation will require a real commitment to ending social inequality in Canadian society, something to which no government in Canada has committed itself to date. This will be a far-reaching endeavour and involve much more than the justice system as it is understood currently. ...

Despite the magnitude of the problems, there is much the justice system can do to assist in reducing the degree to which Aboriginal people come into conflict with the law. It can reduce the ways in which it discriminates against Aboriginal people and the ways in which it adds to Aboriginal alienation.

Cory and Iacobucci JJ. were equally cognizant of the limits of the sentencing judge's power to effect change. Paragraph 65 of *Gladue* bears repeating here:

It is clear that sentencing innovation by itself cannot remove the causes of aboriginal offending and the greater problem of aboriginal alienation from the criminal justice system. ... What can and must be addressed, though, is the limited role that sentencing judges will play in remedying injustice against aboriginal peoples in Canada. Sentencing judges are among those decision-makers who have the power to influence the treatment of aboriginal offenders in the justice system. They determine most directly whether an aboriginal offender will go to jail, or whether other sentencing options may be employed which will play perhaps a stronger role in restoring a sense of balance to the offender, victim, and community, and in preventing future crime.

[70] The sentencing process is therefore an appropriate forum for addressing Aborig inal overrepresentation in Canada's prisons. Despite being theoretically sound, critics still insist that, in practice, the direction to pay particular attention to the circumstances of Aboriginal offenders invites sentencing judges to impose more lenient sentences simply because an offender is Aboriginal. In short, s. 718.2(e) is seen as a race-based discount on sentencing, devoid of any legitimate tie to traditional principles of sentencing. A par ticularly stark example of this view was expressed by Bloc Québécois M.P. Pierrette Venne at the second reading for Bill C-41 when she asked: "Why should an Aboriginal convicted of murder, rape, assault or of uttering threats not be liable to imprisonment like any other citizen of this country? Can we replace all this with a parallel justice, an ethnic justice, a cultural justice? Where would it stop? Where does this horror come from?" (*House of Commons Debates*, vol. 133, 1st Sess., 35th Parl., September 20, 1994, at p. 5876).

[71] In *Gladue*, this Court rejected Ms. Gladue's argument that s. 718.2(e) was an affirmative action provision or, as the Crown described it, an invitation to engage in "reverse discrimination" (para. 86). Cory and Iacobucci JJ. were very clear in stating that "s. 718.2(e) should not be taken as requiring an *automatic* reduction of a sentence, or a remission of a *warranted* period of incarceration, simply because the offender is aborig inal" (para. 88 (emphasis added)). This point was reiterated in *R. v. Wells*, 2000 SCC 10, [2000] 1 S.C.R. 207, at para. 30. There is nothing to suggest that subsequent decisions of provincial and appellate courts have departed from this principle. In fact, it is usually stated explicitly. For example, in *R. v. Vermette*, 2001 MBCA 64, 156 Man. R. (2d) 120, the Manitoba Court of Appeal stated, at para. 39:

> The section does not mandate better treatment for aboriginal offenders than non-aboriginal offenders. It is simply a recognition that the sentence must be individualized and that there are serious social problems with respect to aboriginals that require more creative and innov ative solutions. This is not reverse discrimination. It is an acknowledgment that to achieve real equality, sometimes different people must be treated differently.

[72] While the *purpose* of s. 718.2(e) may not be to provide "a remission of a warranted period of incarceration," critics argue that the *methodology* set out in *Gladue* will inevitably have this effect. As Professors Stenning and Roberts state: "… the practical effect of this alternate methodology is predictable: the sentencing of an Aboriginal offender is less likely to result in a term of custody and, if custody is imposed, it is likely to be shorter in some cases than it would have been had the offender been non-Aboriginal" (p. 162). These criticisms are unwarranted. The methodology set out by this Court in *Gladue* is designed to focus on those unique circumstances of an Aboriginal offender which could reasonably and justifiably impact on the sentence imposed. *Gladue* directs sentencing judges to consider: (1) the unique systemic and background factors which may have played a part in bringing the particular Aboriginal offender before the courts; and (2) the types of sentencing procedures and sanctions which may be appropriate in the circumstances for the offender because of his or her particular Aboriginal heritage or connection. Both sets of circumstances bear on the ultimate question of what is a fit and proper sentence.

[73] First, systemic and background factors may bear on the culpability of the offender, to the extent that they shed light on his or her level of moral blameworthiness. This is perhaps more evident in *Wells* where Iacobucci J. described these circumstances as "the unique systemic or background factors *that are mitigating in nature* in that they may have played a part in the aboriginal offender's conduct" (para. 38 (emphasis added)). Canadian criminal law is based on the premise that criminal liability only follows from voluntary conduct. Many Aboriginal offenders find themselves in situations of social and economic deprivation with a lack of opportunities and limited options for positive development. While this rarely—if ever—attains a level where one could properly say that their actions were not *voluntary* and therefore not deserving of criminal sanction, the reality is that their constrained circumstances may diminish their moral culpability. As Greckol J. of the Alberta Court of Queen's Bench stated, at para. 60 of *R. v. Skani*, 2002 ABQB 1097, 331 A.R. 50, after describing the background factors that lead to Mr. Skani coming before the court, "[f]ew mortals could withstand such a childhood and youth without becoming seriously troubled." Failing to take these circumstances into account would violate the fundamental principle of sentencing—that the sentence must be proportionate to the gravity of the offence *and the degree of responsibility of the offender*. The existence of such circumstances may also indicate that a sanction that takes account of the underlying causes of the criminal conduct may be more appropriate than one only aimed at punishment *per se*. As Cory and Iacobucci JJ. state in *Gladue*, at para. 69:

> In cases where such factors have played a significant role, it is incumbent upon the sentencing judge to consider these factors in evaluating whether imprisonment would actually serve to deter, or to denounce crime in a sense that would be meaningful to the community of which the offender is a member. In many instances, more restorative sentencing principles will gain primary relevance precisely because the prevention of crime as well as individual and social healing cannot occur through other means.

[74] The second set of circumstances—the types of sanctions which may be appropriate—bears not on the degree of culpability of the offender, but on the effectiveness of the sentence itself. As Cory and Iacobucci JJ. point out, at para. 73 of *Gladue*: "What is important to recognize is that, for many if not most aboriginal offenders, the current concepts of sentencing are inappropriate because they have frequently not responded to the needs, experiences, and perspectives of aboriginal people or aboriginal communities." As the RCAP indicates, at p. 309, the "crushing failure" of the Canadian criminal justice system *vis-à-vis* Aboriginal peoples is due to "the fundamentally different world views of Aboriginal and non-Aboriginal people with respect to such elemental issues as the substantive content of justice and the process of achieving justice." The *Gladue* principles direct sentencing judges to abandon the presumption that all offenders and all communities share the same values when it comes to sentencing and to recognize that, given these fundamentally different world views, different or alternative sanctions may more effectively achieve the objectives of sentencing in a particular community.

[75] Section 718.2(e) does not create a race-based discount on sentencing. The provision does not ask courts to remedy the overrepresentation of Aboriginal people in prisons by artificially reducing incarceration rates. Rather, sentencing judges are required to pay particular attention to the circumstances of Aboriginal offenders in order to endeavour to achieve a truly fit and proper sentence in any particular case. This has been,

and continues to be, the fundamental duty of a sentencing judge. *Gladue* is entirely consistent with the requirement that sentencing judges engage in an individualized assessment of all of the relevant factors and circumstances, including the status and life experiences, of the person standing before them. *Gladue* affirms this requirement and recognizes that, up to this point, Canadian courts have failed to take into account the unique circumstances of Aboriginal offenders that bear on the sentencing process. Section 718.2(e) is intended to remedy this failure by directing judges to craft sentences in a manner that is meaningful to Aboriginal peoples. Neglecting this duty would not be faithful to the core requirement of the sentencing process.

[76] A third criticism, intimately related to the last, is that the Court's direction to utilize a method of analysis when sentencing Aboriginal offenders is inherently unfair as it creates unjustified distinctions between offenders who are otherwise similarly situated. This, in turn, violates the principle of sentence parity. This criticism is premised on the argument that the circumstances of Aboriginal offenders are not, in fact, unique. As Professors Stenning and Roberts put it, at p. 158:

> If the kinds of factors that place many Aboriginal people at a disadvantage *vis-à-vis* the criminal justice system also affect many members of other minority or similarly marginalized non-Aboriginal offender groups, how can it be fair to give such factors more particular attention in sentencing Aboriginal offenders than in sentencing offenders from those other groups who share a similar disadvantage?

[77] This critique ignores the distinct history of Aboriginal peoples in Canada. The overwhelming message emanating from the various reports and commissions on Aboriginal peoples' involvement in the criminal justice system is that current levels of criminality are intimately tied to the legacy of colonialism (see, e.g., RCAP, at p. 309). As Professor Carter puts it, "poverty and other incidents of social marginalization may not be unique, but how people get there is. No one's history in this country compares to Aboriginal people's" (M. Carter, "Of Fairness and Faulkner" (2002), 65 *Sask. L. Rev.* 63, at p. 71). Furthermore, there is nothing in the *Gladue* decision which would indicate that background and systemic factors should not also be taken into account for other, non-Aboriginal offenders. Quite the opposite. Cory and Iacobucci JJ. specifically state, at para. 69, in *Gladue*, that "background and systemic factors will also be of importance for a judge in sentencing a non-aboriginal offender."

[78] The interaction between ss. 718.2(e) and 718.2(b)—the parity principle—merits specific attention. Section 718.2(b) states that "a sentence should be similar to sentences imposed on similar offenders for similar offences committed in similar circumstances." Similarity, however, is sometimes an elusory concept. As Professor Brodeur describes ("On the Sentencing of Aboriginal Offenders: A Reaction to Stenning and Roberts" (2002), 65 *Sask. L. Rev.* 45, at p. 49):

> … "high unemployment" has a different meaning in the context of an Aboriginal reservation where there are simply no job opportunities and in an urban context where the White majority exclude Blacks from segments of the labour-market; "substance abuse" is not the same when it refers to young men smoking crack cocaine and to kids committing suicide by sniffing gasoline; "loneliness" is not experienced in a similar way in bush reservations and urban ghettoes.

[79] In practice, similarity is a matter of degree. No two offenders will come before the courts with the same background and experiences, having committed the same crime in the exact same circumstances. Section 718.2(b) simply requires that any disparity between sanctions for different offenders be justified. To the extent that *Gladue* will lead to different sanctions for Aboriginal offenders, those sanctions will be justified based on their unique circumstances—circumstances which are rationally related to the sentencing process. Courts must ensure that a formalistic approach to parity in sentencing does not undermine the remedial purpose of s. 718.2(e). As Professor Quigley cautions, at p. 286:

> Uniformity hides inequity, impedes innovation and locks the system into its mindset of jail. It also prevents us from re-evaluating the value of our aims of sentencing and their efficacy.
>
> It is true that on the surface imposing the same penalty for the nearly identical offence is only fair. That might be closer to the truth in a society that is more equitable, more homogenous and more cohesive than ours. But in an ethnically and culturally diverse society, there is a differential impact from the same treatment. Indeed, that has been recognized in the jurisprudence on equality rights under the Charter. Thus, there is a constitutional imperative to avoiding excessive concern about sentence disparity.

(2) *Evaluating Aboriginal Sentencing Post-Gladue*

[80] An examination of the post-*Gladue* jurisprudence applying s. 718.2(e) reveals several issues with the implementation of the provision. These errors have significantly curtailed the scope and potential remedial impact of the provision, thwarting what was originally envisioned by *Gladue*.

[81] First, some cases erroneously suggest that an offender must establish a causal link between background factors and the commission of the current offence before being entitled to have those matters considered by the sentencing judge. The decision of the Alberta Court of Appeal in *R. v. Poucette*, 1999 ABCA 305, 250 A.R. 55, provides one example. In that case, the court concluded, at para. 14:

> It is not clear how Poucette, a 19 year old, may have been affected by the historical policies of assimilation, colonialism, residential schools and religious persecution that were mentioned by the sentencing judge. While it may be argued that all aboriginal persons have been affected by systemic and background factors, *Gladue* requires that their influences be traced to the particular offender. Failure to link the two is an error in principle.

> (See also *R. v. Gladue*, 1999 ABCA 279, 46 M.V.R. (3d) 183; *R. v. Andres*, 2002 SKCA 98, 223 Sask. R. 121.)

[82] This judgment displays an inadequate understanding of the devastating intergenerational effects of the collective experiences of Aboriginal peoples. It also imposes an evidentiary burden on offenders that was not intended by *Gladue*. As the Ontario Court of Appeal states in *R. v. Collins*, 2011 ONCA 182, 277 O.A.C. 88, at paras. 32-33:

> There is nothing in the governing authorities that places the burden of persuasion on an Aboriginal accused to establish a causal link between the systemic and background factors and commission of the offence. ...
>
> As expressed in *Gladue*, *Wells* and *Kakekagamick*, s. 718.2(e) requires the sentencing judge to "give attention to the unique background and systemic factors which may have played a

part in bringing the particular offender before the courts": *Gladue* at para. 69. This is a much more modest requirement than the causal link suggested by the trial judge.

(See also *R. v. Jack*, 2008 BCCA 437, 261 B.C.A.C. 245.)

[83]   As the Ontario Court of Appeal goes on to note in *Collins*, it would be extremely difficult for an Aboriginal offender to ever establish a direct causal link between his circumstances and his offending. The interconnections are simply too complex. The Aboriginal Justice Inquiry of Manitoba describes the issue, at p. 86:

> Cultural oppression, social inequality, the loss of self-government and systemic discrimination, which are the legacy of the Canadian government's treatment of Aboriginal people, are intertwined and interdependent factors, and in very few cases is it possible to draw a simple and direct correlation between any one of them and the events which lead an individual Aboriginal person to commit a crime or to become incarcerated.

Furthermore, the operation of s. 718.2(e) does not logically require such a connection. Systemic and background factors do not operate as an excuse or justification for the criminal conduct. Rather, they provide the necessary context to enable a judge to determine an appropriate sentence. This is not to say that those factors need not be tied in some way to the particular offender and offence. Unless the unique circumstances of the particular offender bear on his or her culpability for the offence or indicate which sentencing objectives can and should be actualized, they will not influence the ultimate sentence.

[84]   The second and perhaps most significant issue in the post-*Gladue* jurisprudence is the irregular and uncertain application of the *Gladue* principles to sentencing decisions for serious or violent offences. As Professor Roach has indicated, "appellate courts have attended disproportionately to just a few paragraphs in these two Supreme Court judgments—paragraphs that discuss the relevance of *Gladue* in serious cases and compare the sentencing of Aboriginal and non-Aboriginal offenders" (K. Roach, "One Step Forward, Two Steps Back: *Gladue* at Ten and in the Courts of Appeal" (2009), 54 *Crim. L.Q.* 470, at p. 472). The passage in *Gladue* that has received this unwarranted emphasis is the observation that "[g]enerally, the more violent and serious the offence the more likely it is as a practical reality that the terms of imprisonment for aboriginals and non-aboriginals will be close to each other or the same, even taking into account their different concepts of sentencing" (para. 79; see also *Wells*, at paras. 42-44). Numerous courts have erroneously interpreted this generalization as an indication that the *Gladue* principles do not apply to serious offences (see, e.g., *R. v. Carrière* (2002), 164 C.C.C. (3d) 569 (Ont. C.A.)).

[85]   Whatever criticisms may be directed at the decision of this Court for any ambiguity in this respect, the judgment ultimately makes it clear that sentencing judges have a *duty* to apply s. 718.2(e): "There is no discretion as to whether to consider the unique situation of the aboriginal offender; the only discretion concerns the determination of a just and appropriate sentence" (*Gladue*, at para. 82). Similarly, in *Wells*, Iacobucci J. reiterated, at para. 50, that

> [t]he generalization drawn in *Gladue* to the effect that the more violent and serious the offence, the more likely as a practical matter for similar terms of imprisonment to be imposed on aboriginal and non-aboriginal offenders, was not meant to be a principle of universal application. In each case, the sentencing judge must look to the circumstances of the aboriginal offender.

This element of duty has not completely escaped the attention of Canadian appellate courts (see, e.g., *R. v. Kakekagamick* (2006), 214 O.A.C. 127; *R. v. Jensen* (2005), 196 O.A.C. 119; *R. v. Abraham*, 2000 ABCA 159, 261 A.R. 192).

[86]   In addition to being contrary to this Court's direction in *Gladue*, a sentencing judge's failure to apply s. 718.2(e) in the context of serious offences raises several questions. First, what offences are to be considered "serious" for this purpose? As Ms. Pelletier points out: "Statutorily speaking, there is no such thing as a 'serious' offence. The *Code* does not make a distinction between serious and non-serious crimes. There is also no legal test for determining what should be considered 'serious' " (R. Pelletier, "The Nullification of Section 718.2(e): Aggravating Aboriginal Over-representation in Canadian Prisons" (2001), 39 *Osgoode Hall L.J.* 469, at p. 479). Trying to carve out an exception from *Gladue* for serious offences would inevitably lead to inconsistency in the jurisprudence due to "the relative ease with which a sentencing judge could deem any number of offences to be 'serious' " (Pelletier, at p. 479). It would also deprive s. 718.2(e) of much of its remedial power, given its focus on reducing overreliance on incarceration. A second question arises: Who are courts sentencing if not the offender standing in front of them? If the offender is Aboriginal, then courts must consider all of the circumstances of that offender, including the unique circumstances described in *Gladue*. There is no sense comparing the sentence that a particular Aboriginal offender would receive to the sentence that some hypothetical non-Aboriginal offender would receive, because there is only one offender standing before the court.

[87]   The sentencing judge has a statutory duty, imposed by s. 718.2(e) of the *Criminal Code*, to consider the unique circumstances of Aboriginal offenders. Failure to apply *Gladue* in any case involving an Aboriginal offender runs afoul of this statutory obligation. As these reasons have explained, such a failure would also result in a sentence that was not fit and was not consistent with the fundamental principle of proportionality. Therefore, application of the *Gladue* principles is required in every case involving an Aboriginal offender, including breach of an LTSO, and a failure to do so constitutes an error justifying appellate intervention.

VI. *Application*

A. *Manasie Ipeelee*

[88]   Megginson J. sentenced Mr. Ipeelee to three years' imprisonment, less credit for pre-sentence custody. The Court of Appeal upheld that sentence. Both courts emphasized the serious nature of the breach, given the documented link between Mr. Ipeelee's use of alcohol and his propensity to engage in violence. As a result, both courts emphasized the objectives of denunciation, deterrence, and protection of the public.

[89]   In my view, the courts below made several errors in principle warranting appellate intervention. First, the courts reached the erroneous conclusion that protection of the public is the paramount objective when sentencing for breach of an LTSO and that rehabilitation plays only a small role. As discussed, while protection of the public is important, the legislative purpose of an LTSO as a form of conditional release set out in s. 100 of the *CCRA* is to rehabilitate offenders and reintegrate them into society. The courts therefore erred in concluding that rehabilitation was not a relevant sentencing objective.

[90]   As a result of this error, the courts below gave only attenuated consideration to Mr. Ipeelee's circumstances as an Aboriginal offender. Relying on *Carrière*, the Court of

Appeal concluded that this was the kind of offence where the sentence will not differ as between Aboriginal and non-Aboriginal offenders, and relying on *W. (H.P.)*, held that features of Aboriginal sentencing play little or no role when sentencing long-term offenders. Given certain trends in the jurisprudence discussed above, it is easy to see how the court reached this conclusion. Nonetheless, they erred in doing so. These errors justify the Court's intervention.

[91] It is therefore necessary to consider what sentence is warranted in the circumstances. Mr. Ipeelee breached the alcohol abstention condition of his LTSO. His history indicates a strong correlation between alcohol use and violent offending. As a result, abstaining from alcohol is critical to managing his risk in the community. That being said, the conduct constituting the breach was becoming intoxicated, not becoming intoxicated and engaging in violence. The Court must focus on the actual incident giving rise to the breach. A fit sentence should seek to manage the risk of reoffence he continues to pose to the community in a manner that addresses his alcohol abuse, rather than punish him for what might have been. To engage in the latter would certainly run afoul of the principles of fundamental justice.

[92] At the time of the offence, Mr. Ipeelee was 18 months into his LTSO. He was living in Kingston, where there were few culturally relevant support systems in place. There is no evidence, other than one isolated instance of refusing urinalysis, that he consumed alcohol on any occasion prior to this breach. Mr. Ipeelee's history indicates that he has been drinking heavily since the age of 11. Relapse is to be expected as he continues to address his addiction.

[93] Taking into account the relevant sentencing principles, the fact that this is Mr. Ipeelee's first breach of his LTSO and that he pleaded guilty to the offence, I would substitute a sentence of one year's imprisonment. Given the circumstances of his previous convictions, abstaining from alcohol is crucial to Mr. Ipeelee's rehabilitation under the long-term offender regime. Consequently, this sentence is designed to denounce Mr. Ipeelee's conduct and deter him from consuming alcohol in the future. In addition, it provides a sufficient period of time without access to alcohol so that Mr. Ipeelee can get back on track with his alcohol treatment. Finally, the sentence is not so harsh as to suggest to Mr. Ipeelee that success under the long-term offender regime is simply not possible.

• • •

VII. *Conclusion*

[98] For the foregoing reasons, I would allow the offender's appeal in *Ipeelee* and substitute a sentence of one year's imprisonment.

IV. CHALLENGING THE TRADITIONAL PARADIGM: THE USE OF SENTENCING CIRCLES

The traditional adversarial manner in which sentencing hearings are conducted has attracted some criticism. As a result, even before the decision in *Gladue*, much attention had been paid to alternative sentencing processes and options that are more consistent with Aboriginal traditions and experience. The importance of exploring alternatives was recognized by the Law Reform Commission of Canada in 1992.

Law Reform Commission of Canada, Report #34,
Aboriginal Peoples and Criminal Justice
(Ottawa: Supply and Services Canada, 1991) (footnotes omitted)

One prevalent focus within the literature on solutions to the problem of over-representation has been on what are called "alternatives to incarceration." While even the most
recent of analyses continue to support the creative use of well-designed and adequately
funded alternatives to incarceration or community sanctions, we recognize that many
experiments with these alternatives in recent years have been severely criticized.

Theoretically, several alternatives to imprisonment exist at the sentencing stage, such
as conditional discharges, suspended sentences, community service orders, compensation,
restitution and fine option programs. In addition, options such as diversion, victim–
offender reconciliation programs and mediation are also alternatives to imprisonment in
the sense that they do not entail resort to the ordinary process of trial and sentencing.
Our Commission has long supported these alternatives, but they are underused.

Recommendation

13(1) Alternatives to imprisonment should be used whenever possible. The *Criminal
Code* provisions creating such alternatives should ensure that those alternatives are given
first consideration at sentencing. A judge imprisoning an Aboriginal person for an offence
amenable to the use of alternative dispositions should be required to set forth the reasons
for using imprisonment rather than a non-custodial option.

The case for the use of creative Aboriginal methods of dispute resolution is cogently
argued and described by Jackson in our commissioned study entitled *In Search of the
Pathways to Justice*. In our view, special alternative programs for Aboriginal persons are
important for several reasons. First, they possess the potential to reduce the number of
Aboriginal persons in prisons. Further, they could with very little adjustment incorporate
customary law, thus increasing their acceptability to the affected population. Finally, they
are organized around the concept of community-involvement and thus can promote social
peace and a sense of community control. Alternative programs are consistent with Aboriginal values in that they seek reconciliation between an offender and the community as a
whole, and pursue the goal of restoring harmony.

NOTE

In the context of criminal proceedings involving Aboriginal offenders, some judges have
complained that the free flow of information is hampered by the bipolar nature of adversarial proceedings. This has led to the development of the "sentencing circle," whereby the
usual trappings of our criminal courts are cast aside. Instead, the judge, counsel, the offender,
and significant members of his or her community form a circle and engage in a discussion
about the appropriate disposition for the offender. The link between the sentencing circle
and First Nations culture was discussed in *R v Morin* (1995), 101 CCC (3d) 124, 42 CR (4th) 339
(Sask CA), in which Bayda CJS (in dissent) made the following observations:

In addressing the sentencing circle question it behooves one to be mindful of the origin of the
sentencing circle and its underlying philosophy. The sentencing circle has its genesis in the

healing circle which from time immemorial has been a part of the culture of many First Nations of Canada and of the indigenous people of other countries. The healing circle originated and developed amongst the First Nations people at a time when they lived in small relatively isolated communities. ... When a member of the community committed a wrongful act against another member, the community resorted to a healing circle to resolve the problems created by the wrongful act. The circle was premised on two fundamental notions: first, the wrongful act was a breach of the relationship between the wrongdoer and the victim and a breach of the relationship between the wrongdoer and the community; and second, the well-being of the community and consequently the protection of its members and the society generally depended not upon retribution or punishment of the wrongdoer, but upon "healing" the breaches of the two relationships. The emphasis was primarily, if not entirely, upon a restorative or healing approach as distinct from a retributive or punitive approach.

In addition to locating the origin of the sentencing circle, this passage underscores the intimate link between the use of the sentencing circle and the restorative or rehabilitative approach to sentencing in the Aboriginal context. Although the sentencing circle is dealt with here—in a discussion of procedural and evidentiary sentencing matters—there is also a large "substantive" component to this issue.

The use of the sentencing circle has received wide acceptance in a number of provinces. However, there is some disagreement about when it is appropriate to construct a sentencing circle. Indeed, as McEachern CJYT held in *R v Johnson* (1994), 91 CCC (3d) 21 (YCA), the availability of this procedure, along with its precise contours, ought to be the subject of rules of court, pursuant to s 482(2) of the *Criminal Code*. This would allow all the parties to know what is expected of them.

R v Moses was the seminal decision in the expansion of sentencing circles beyond a few northern communities. This case explains the purposes of sentencing circles and the process as it was practised in the town of Mayo in the Yukon in 1992. While reading the case, consider how the process fits within the usual sentencing hearing process and whether it could be adapted in conditions other than small remote communities. Also, ask yourself what we learn about the usual sentencing process by examining the sentencing circle process.

R v Moses
(1992), 71 CCC (3d) 347 (Y Terr Ct) (footnotes omitted)

STUART TERR CT J:

The reasons for this sentence will take us on an unusual journey. Unusual, because the process was as influential in moulding the final decision as any substantive factors. Consequently, this judgment examines the process as well as the traditional stuffings of sentences, mitigating and aggravating circumstances.

• • •

In this case, by changing the process, the primary issues changed, and consequently, the decision was substantially different from what might have been decided had the usual process been followed.

The justice system rules and procedures provide a comfortable barrier for justice professionals from fully confronting the futility, destruction, and injustice left behind in the wake of circuit courts. For those who dared in this case to step outside this comfortable barrier, I hope these reasons capture their input and courage.

1. Process

(A) Overview

Rising crime rates, especially for violent offences, alarming recidivist rates and escalating costs in monetary and human terms have forced societies the world over to search for alternatives to their malfunctioning justice systems. In the western world much of the energy expended in this search has focused on sentencing. While the underlying problems of crime and the gross inadequacies of the justice system stem from much broader, deeper ills within society, significant immediate improvement within the court process can be achieved by changing the sentencing process.

Currently, the search for improving sentencing champions a greater role for victims of crime, reconciliation, restraint in the use of incarceration and a broadening of sentencing alternatives that calls upon less government expenditure and more community participation. As many studies expose the imprudence of excessive reliance upon punishment as the central objective in sentencing, rehabilitation and reconciliation are properly accorded greater emphasis. All these changes call upon communities to become more actively involved and to assume more responsibility for resolving conflict. To engage meaningful community participation, the sentence decision-making process must be altered to share power with the community, and where appropriate, communities must be empowered to resolve many conflicts now processed through criminal courts.

An important step towards constructive community involvement must involve significant changes to the sentencing process before, during and after sentencing.

• • •

(C) Sentencing Hearing

In any decision-making process, power, control, the over-all atmosphere and dynamics are significantly influenced by the physical setting, and especially by the places accorded to participants. Those who wish to create a particular atmosphere, or especially to manipulate a decision-making process to their advantage, have from time immemorial astutely controlled the physical setting of the decision-making forum. Among the great predator groups in the animal kingdom, often the place secured by each member in the site they rest or hunt, significantly influences their ability to control group decisions. In the criminal justice process (arguably one of contemporary society's great predators), the physical arrangement in a court-room profoundly affects who participates and how they participate. The organization of the court-room influences the content, scope and importance of information provided to the court. The rules governing the court hearing reinforce the allocation of power and influence fostered by the physical setting.

The combined effect of the rules and the court-room arrangements entrench the adversarial nature of the process. The judge, defence and Crown counsel, fortified by their prominent places in the court-room and by the rules, own and control the process and no one in a court-room can have any doubt about that.

For centuries, the basic organization of the court has not changed. Nothing has been done to encourage meaningful participation by the accused, the victim, or by the community; remarkable, considering how the location of a meeting, the design of the room, furniture arrangements, and the seating of participants are so meticulously considered in most decision-making processes to ensure the setting reinforce the objective of the process. If the objective of the sentencing process is now to enhance sentencing options, to afford greater concern to the impact on victims, to shift focus from punishment to rehabilitation, and to meaningfully engage communities in sharing responsibility for sentencing decisions, it may be advantageous for the justice system to examine how court procedures and the physical arrangements within court-rooms militate against these new objectives. It was in this case.

(D) Advantages of Circle

In this case, a change in the physical arrangement of the court-room produced a major change in the process.

(1) Physical Setting

For court, a circle to seat 30 people was arranged as tightly as numbers allowed. When all seats were occupied, additional seating was provided in an outer circle for persons arriving after the "hearing" had commenced.

Defence sat beside the accused and his family. The Crown sat immediately across the circle from defence counsel to the right of the judge. Officials and members from the First Nation, the RCMP officers, the probation officer and others were left to find their own "comfortable" place within the circle.

(2) Dynamics of the Circle

By arranging the court in a circle without desks or tables, with all participants facing each other, with equal access and equal exposure to each other, the dynamics of the decision-making process were profoundly changed.

Everyone around the circle introduced themselves. Everyone remained seated when speaking. After opening remarks from the judge and counsel, the formal process dissolved into an informal but intense discussion of what might best protect the community and extract Philip from the grip of alcohol and crime.

The tone was tempered by the close proximity of all participants. For the most part, participants referred to each other by name, not by title. While disagreements and arguments were provoked by most topics, posturing, pontification, and the well-worn platitudes, commonly characteristic of court-room speeches by counsel and judges, were gratefully absent.

The circle setting dramatically changed the roles of all participants, as well as the focus, tone, content and scope of discussions. The following observations denote the more obvious benefits generated by the circle setting.

(i) Challenges Monopoly of Professionals

The foreboding court-room setting discourages meaningful participation beyond lawyers and judges.

The judge presiding on high, robed to emphasize his authoritative dominance, armed with the power to control the process, is rarely challenged. Lawyers, by their deference, and by standing when addressing the judge, reinforce to the community the judge's pivotal importance. All of this combines to encourage the community to believe judges uniquely and exclusively possess the wisdom and resources to develop a just and viable result. They are so grievously wrong.

Counsel, due to the rules, and their prominent place in the court, control the input of information. Their ease with the rules, their facility with the peculiar legal language, exudes a confidence and skill that lay people commonly perceive as a prerequisite to participate.

The community relegated to the back of the room, is separated from counsel and the judge either by an actual bar or by placing their seats at a distinct distance behind counsel tables. The interplay between lawyers and the judge creates the perception of a ritualistic play. The set, as well as the performance, discourages anyone else from participating.

The circle significantly breaks down the dominance that traditional court-rooms accord lawyers and judges. In a circle, the ability to contribute, the importance and credibility of any input is not defined by seating arrangements. The audience is changed. All persons within the circle must be addressed. Equally, anyone in the circle may ask a direct question to anyone. Questions about the community and the accused force discussions into a level of detail usually avoided in the court-room by sweeping assumptions and boiler-plate platitudes. In the court-room, reliance upon technical legal language imbues the process with the air of resolutely addressing difficult issues. In fact, behind the facade of legalese, many crucial considerations are either ignored or superficially considered. The circle denies the comfort of evading difficult issues through the use of obtuse, complex technical language.

(ii) Encourages Lay Participation

The circle setting drew everyone into the discussion. Unlike the court-room, where the setting facilitates participation only by counsel and the judge, the circle prompted a natural rhythm of discussion.

The physical proximity of all participants, the ability to see the face of the person speaking, the conversational tone, the absence of incomprehensible rituals, and the intermingling of professionals and lay members of the community during breaks, all a consequence of the circle, broke down many barriers to participation.

The highly defined roles imposed upon professionals by the formal justice process creates barriers to communication. The circle drew out the person buried behind their role, and encouraged a more personal and less professional contribution. The circle, in revealing the person behind the professional facade fostered a greater sense of equality between lay and professional participants in the circle. This sense of equality and the discovery of significant common concerns and objectives is essential to sustain an effective partnership between the community and the justice system.

(iii) Enhances Information

The justice system rarely acquires adequate information to competently target the sentencing process on the underlying causes of criminal behaviour. Too often courts are forced to precariously rely upon bare-bones information, usually based on second or third-hand sources. Consequently, sentencing guided by very incomplete information places too much reliance upon mythological understandings about deterrence and punishment, and upon stereotypical categories used to describe the crime and the offender.

The rituals and specialized language of the sentencing process produce an aura of competence. Rising crime rates (especially rising recidivism) despite staggering increases in expenditures, debunk this illusory aura. Sentencing could be vastly improved by enhancing the quantity and quality of information.

The paucity and stagnancy of sentencing information severely handicaps any endeavour to purposefully employ sentencing remedies. Very little is known in sentencing about offenders, victims, the crucial underlying factors causing the criminal behaviour, or about the larger context of the home and community, and almost nothing is known about how the court process affects the conflict or upon the persons involved. Acting on a woefully incomplete understanding of either the larger circumstances or of the specific life circumstances of those directly affected by crime, the court rarely appreciates whether the sentence resolves or exacerbates the fundamental problems promoting crime.

Of course, all judges and counsel know these circumstances exist, but the court-room setting, and emphasis on getting through the docket, of processing cases as any good bureaucracy might process licence applications, encourages wilful blindness about many relevant circumstances in sentencing. The sentencing process, in searching for an effective sentence to fit the specific needs in each case, is analogous to a "fast forwarded" game of Pin the Tail on the Donkey.

Community involvement through the circle generates not only new information, but information not normally available to the court. Through the circle, participants can respond to concerns, fill in gaps, and ensure each new sentencing option is measured against a broader, more detailed base of information. In the circle, the flow of information is alive, flexible and more readily capable of assessing and responding to new ideas.

Despite psychiatric and alcohol assessments, and an extensive and exceptionally researched pre-sentence report, the circle in this case provided additional relevant and particularly valuable information to probe and assess each new creative option.

Documents, files, reports, and assessments help introduce the offender to the court, but often present a lifeless portrayal which can be easily misconstrued. The circle, by enabling Philip to speak for himself, and by enabling others who have known him all his life to share their knowledge, substantially improved the court's perception.

Court-room procedures and rules often preclude or discourage many sources from contributing crucial information. The circle removes or reduces many of the impediments blocking the flow of essential information into court.

(iv) Creative Search for New Options

Public censure often focuses on the differences in sentences meted out for the same crime. There should be more, not fewer differences in sentences. If the reasons for the differences stems from personal attitudes of judges, the inadequacy of information, an inability to appreciate the remedial impact of various sentencing options, an absence of commonly accepted objectives, or ignorance of the impact of crime on victims, then public concern is warranted. The reasons for the differences, not simply the differences themselves, determine whether the differences are laudable or condemnable.

In a multicultural society, where gross inequities in opportunities, social resources, and social conditions abound, just sentencing cannot be monolithic or measured against any standard national "typical sentence." If the predominate objectives in sentencing are protection of the community, rehabilitation of the offender, minimizing adverse impacts on victims, and particularly greater community involvement, then even greater differences in sentencing for the same crime should be expected and welcomed. In at least two significant ways, the circle will accentuate differences in sentences for the same crime. The circle, by enhancing community participation, generates a richer range of sentencing options. Secondly, the circle by improving the quality and quantity of information provides the ability to refine and focus the use of sentencing options to meet the particular needs in each case.

In this case the circle promoted among all participants a desire to find an appropriate sentence that best served all of the above objectives. Their creative search produced a sentence markedly different from customary sentences for such crimes, and radically departed from the pattern of sentences previously imposed upon Philip for similar offences. The circle forged a collective desire for something different, something unlike the sentences imposed in the past 10 years, something everyone could support, something they believed would work. Fuelled by the expanded and responsive flow of information, the circle participants worked towards a consensus, towards a unique response to a problem that had plagued the community for 10 years and had stolen 10 years of productive life from Philip.

I was surprised by the result, but the new information and the option provided by the community rendered the final sentence obvious and compelling. The combination of new information and an array of new sentencing options can dramatically change sentencing dispositions from those based on information normally available and dependant upon the limited range of conventional sentencing remedies.

· · ·

(vi) Encouraging the Offender's Participation

Philip Moses, as is typical of most offenders, had not significantly participated in any of the previous seven sentencing hearings which had instrumentally shaped his life. Most offenders, during formal court proceedings, sit with head bowed, sometimes in fear, more often in anger as incomprehensible discussions ramble on about their life, crimes, and about how communities must be protected from such hardened criminals.

Circuit lawyers, usually different each time, carry the primary responsibility to speak on behalf of offenders such as Philip. Their knowledge of the offender is derived from a few brief interviews, police reports, criminal records and sometimes from pre-sentence reports.

However well intentioned they might be, circuit counsel can never know Philip as well as his family or others within his community. Nor can any counsel fully reflect the offender's pain, suffering, or desperate search for help. Equally, the anger, resentment and hostility of many offenders is rarely expressed, as competent counsel manage to ensure a properly contrite, dutiful face masks any burning feelings which may, if revealed, provoke a harsher sentence. Consequently, the court sentences in blissful ignorance, missing the opportunity to constructively appreciate perceptions and feelings that may perpetually frustrate rehabilitative plans.

In the circle, the police, mother, brother, Chief of the First Nation, the probation officer, and other community members expressed constructive concern about Philip. They repeatedly spoke of the need to "reintegrate" Philip with his family and his First Nation.

This was the first time Philip heard anyone from his community, or from his First Nation offer support. He could no longer believe that the police and the community were solely interested in removing him from their midst.

These comments within the circle drew Philip into the discussion. His eloquence, passion, and pain riveted everyone's attention. His contribution moved the search for an effective sentence past several concerns shared around the circle. No, he did not convince everyone, nor did he ultimately secure what he sought, but his passion and candour significantly contributed to constructing the sentence.

(vii) Involving Victims in Sentencing

Many offenders perceive only the state as the aggrieved party. They fail to appreciate the very human pain and suffering they cause. Absent an appreciation of the victim's suffering, offenders fail to understand their sentence except as the intrusion of an insensitive, oppressive state bent on punishment. An offender's remorse is more likely to be prompted by a desire to seek mercy from the state or by a recognition that they have been "bad." Only when an offender's pain caused by the oppression of the criminal justice system is confronted by the pain that victims experience from crime, can most offenders gain a proper perspective of their behaviour. Without this perspective, the motivation to successfully pursue rehabilitation lacks an important and often essential ingredient.

Much work remains to find an appropriate means of including the victim, or in the very least, including the impact on the victim in the sentencing process. The circle affords an important opportunity to explore the potential of productively incorporating the impact upon victims in sentencing.

. . .

(xii) Merging Values: First Nation and Western Governments

Because aboriginal people use the same language, engage in similar play and work, western society assumes similar underlying values govern and motivate their conduct. Particularly within the justice system, this widely spread erroneous assumption has had a disastrous impact on aboriginal people and their communities.

Much of the systemic discrimination against aboriginal people within the justice system stems from a failure to recognize the fundamental differences between aboriginal and western cultures. Aboriginal culture does not place as high a premium on individual responsibility or approach conflict in the direct confrontational manner championed by our adversarial process. Aboriginal people see value in avoiding confrontation and in refraining from speaking publicly against each other. In dealing with conflict, emphasis is placed on reconciliation, the restoration of harmony and the removal of underlying pressures generating conflict.

After extensive exposure to the justice system, it has been assumed too readily that aboriginal people have adjusted to our adversarial process with its obsession on individual rights and individual responsibility, another tragically wrong assumption. Similarly, we have erroneously assumed by inviting their involvement in our system they will be willing and eager participants. If we generally seek their partnership in resolving crime, a process that fairly accommodates both value systems must emerge.

The circle has the potential to accord greater recognition to aboriginal values, and to create a less confrontational, less adversarial means of processing conflict. Yet the circle retains the primary principles and protections inherent to the justice system. The circle contributes the basis for developing a genuine partnership between aboriginal communities and the justice system by according the flexibility for both sets of values to influence the decision-making process in sentencing.

(3) Safeguards: Protecting Individual Rights in Merging the Community and Justice System in the Circle

Courage, patience, and tolerance must accompany all participants in the search for a productive partnership between communities and the justice system. The search need not be foolhardy. Many safeguards can be adapted to protect individual rights while opening the process to community involvement. In this experiment with the circle, the following safeguards were used to cushion any adverse impact on individual rights. Within the justice system, a critical assessment must be made about what is truly inviolable and what has by convention been presumed to be. Many conventions have survived long past the justification for their original creation.

(i) Open Court

The court-room remained the same, only the furniture was rearranged. The door was open, the public retained free access to the room.

The long-standing reasons for open court may not be as persuasive in some sentencing hearings where privacy may be essential to precipitate frank exchanges which reveal extremely sensitive family or personal information. Normally, such information, vital to competently employing any sentencing option, is rarely available as participants are understandably reluctant to share intimate circumstances of their life in an open public court-room, especially in small communities where anonymity is impossible.

In most cases there will be no need to limit access. However, where clear advantages flow from a closed session, the longstanding reasons for open court must be dusted off and re-examined in light of the advantages derived from acquiring extremely sensitive and personal information from offenders, victims or their families and friends.

(ii) Transcripts

The court reporter remained a part of the circle.

In some cases, there are good reasons to question why a transcript embracing all circle discussions is necessary. Some aspects of the discussion may be best excluded from the transcript, or where the circle is closed to the public, the transcript retained in a confidential manner, available only if required by a court of appeal.

To establish appropriate guidelines in assessing the competing values of an open versus a closed process on a case-by-case basis, some of the ancient icons of criminal procedures need an airing and reassessment.

The tradition of a circle—"what comes out in a circle, stays in a circle"—runs counter to the justice tradition requiring both an open court and transcripts. A more flexible set of rules for exceptions must be fashioned to establish a balance in emerging First Nation, community, and justice system values in the circle.

(iii) Upper Limits to Sentence

The circle is designed to explore and develop viable sentencing options drawing upon, whenever possible, community-based resources. The circle is not designed to extract reasons to increase the severity of punishment. Accordingly, at the outset of the circle process, Crown and defence counsel were called upon to make their customary sentencing submissions. Based on these submissions, I indicated the upper-limit sentence for the offence.

By stating at the outset an upper limit to the sentence based on conventional sentencing principles and remedies, the offender enters the circle without fearing a harsher jail sentence provoked by candour or anger within the circle. This constitutes an important basis to encourage offenders to participate.

The upper limit also provides a basis for the circle to appreciate what will happen in the absence of community alternatives. The utility of the upper-limit sentence can be measured against any new information shared in the circle. Any community-based alternative developed by the circle may be substituted for part or all of this sentence.

(iv) Opportunity for Offender to Speak

The *Criminal Code*, s. 668, ensures the offender has an opportunity to speak in his own words before a sentence is imposed. This opportunity is generally offered after all submissions have been made, and the court has all but formally concluded what the sentence will be. It is generally a perfunctory step in the process, rarely used and generally of little effect.

Defence counsel bears the primary and often exclusive responsibility to represent the offender's interest. How far we have come from the time when lawyers were banned and offenders left to make their own submissions. Somewhere on this journey from exclusive reliance upon the offender to essentially exclusive reliance upon defence counsel, we passed a more fitting balance in the participatory roles of counsel and offender. It may be too cute to suggest courts currently sentence defence counsel, not offenders, but the thought does highlight how much sentencing depends upon the work, competence, knowledge, and eloquence of defence counsel.

The inequities in proceeding without counsel are staggering. Similarly, the involvement of communities creates its own inequities within the circle. In a very unequal world, no justice system can create equality, or for that matter render perfect justice. The circle improves the offender's ability to participate, and thereby reduces the obvious inequities in a process that minimizes participation by the very person who is the primary focus of the process. More thought, or innovation must be invested to extract the best from the existing justice process and from the circle to create a viable balance between individual rights and community involvement.

(v) Crown and Defence Counsel

The traditional and essential functions of Crown and defence counsel are not excluded by the circle.

The Crown at the outset placed before the circle the interests of the state in sentencing the offender. The Crown's participation through questions and by engaging in the discussions retains the circle's awareness of the larger interests of the state. Aware of community-provided alternatives, having acquired first-hand knowledge of a broad spectrum of community concerns and armed with detailed information about the offender, the Crown at the end of the circle discussions can more competently assess how the interests of the state, and the interests of the community are best addressed in sentencing.

Especially on circuit, the Crown is forced to make assumptions about what sentences protect the community. Through the circle, these assumptions are examined by members of the very community Crown submissions are designed to protect.

Defence counsel, knowing that at worst the offender faces a conventional sentence presaged at the outset of the hearing, can constructively use the circle to develop a sentencing plan to advance the immediate and long-term interests of his client. Community support generated by the circle, as it did in this case, creates viable alternatives to jail.

(vi) Disputed Facts

Any disputed fact must be proven in the customary manner. Proof of a disputed fact can be carried out in the circle by the examination of witnesses under oath. Alternatively, during a break in the circle discussions, court can be resumed and all the traditional trappings of the court-room engaged to resolve a disputed fact.

The circle moves along a different road to consensus than the adversarial character of the formal court-room hearings. The process in a circle can either resolve disputes in a less adversarial manner, or render the disputed fact irrelevant or unimportant by evolving a sentencing disposition principally relevant upon community-based alternatives. However, the formal court process provides a "safeguard" to be called upon by either counsel at any time a matter in the circle necessitates formal proof.

NOTE

Although much of the development of sentencing circles has occurred in the Yukon and northern Saskatchewan, credit for their modern introduction as a way of responding to the circumstances of Aboriginal offenders should be given to Judge C.C. Barnett, formerly of the BC Provincial Court, who sat for many years in Williams Lake and the Queen Charlotte Islands.

In different communities, sentencing circles have evolved in different forms, but always with the common feature of broad-based community participation. A brief account of their development in Saskatchewan was given by Fafard Prov Ct J in *R v Joseyounen*, [1995] 6 WWR 438:

> The first sentencing circle to be held in Saskatchewan took place in Sandy Bay in July of 1992. I was the presiding judge. Since then many sentencing circles have been held in Northern Saskatchewan (I estimate that I have dealt with over 60 cases in that manner myself), and out of this experience by me and my colleagues on the Provincial Court in the north, there have emerged seven criteria that we apply in deciding if a case for sentencing should go to a circle. These criteria are not carved in stone, but they provide guidelines sufficiently simple for the lay public to understand, and also capable of application so that our decisions are not being made arbitrarily.

It is imperative that the public, aboriginal and others, be able to know and understand what is happening in the development of sentencing circles: the credibility of the administration of justice depends on it.

Fafard J's criteria are:

1. The accused must agree to be referred to the sentencing circle.
2. The accused must have deep roots in the community in which the circle is held and from which the participants are drawn.
3. There are elders or respected non-political community leaders willing to participate.
4. The victim is willing to participate and has been subjected to no coercion or pressure in so agreeing.
5. The court should try to determine beforehand, as best it can, if the victim is subject to battered spouse syndrome. If she is, then she should have counselling made available to her and be accompanied by a support team in the circle.
6. Disputed facts have been resolved in advance.
7. The case is one in which a court would be willing to take a calculated risk and depart from the usual range of sentencing.

These criteria were applied by the majority of the Saskatchewan Court of Appeal in *R v Morin* (1995), 101 CCC (3d) 124 (Sask CA) to reject the appropriateness of a sentencing circle following a conviction for robbery by an Aboriginal offender who lived in Saskatoon. On the facts, there was some doubt about the offender's sincerity in seeking help from the local Aboriginal community.

In the Yukon, the use of circles has evolved since the decision in *Moses*, above. In *R v Gingell* (1996), 50 CR (4th) 32 (Y Terr Ct), Lilles J described the process that has been developed by Kwanlin Dun, the Aboriginal community near Whitehorse. Other alternative forms of sentencing procedure are also in use: see e.g. the decision in *R v P (JA)* (1991), 6 CR (4th) 126 (Y Terr Ct), for a description of sentencing in Teslin, a community in the southern Yukon, where the clan leaders sit with the sentencing judge to offer advice on an appropriate sentence.

One of the most successful examples of a circle approach has been used in the community of Hollow Water in Manitoba. Its sentencing circle is described by Ross Gordon Green.

RG Green, *Justice in Aboriginal Communities: Sentencing Alternatives*
(Saskatoon: Purich, 1998) at 85-92 (footnotes omitted)

Hollow Water is located 190 kilometres (118 miles) northeast of Winnipeg on the east shore of Lake Winnipeg. It covers 1620 hectares (4,000 acres) of land within the Canadian Precambrian Shield. The band's native language is Ojibway. As of 1994, the on-reserve population was 490 and off-reserve was 512. This band is a signatory to Treaty 5, signed in 1875. Hollow Water is bordered by the Métis communities of Aghaming, Manigotogan, and Seymourville. The total resident population of Hollow Water and the surrounding communities is 1200. Resources at Hollow Water include a K–12 school, a convenience store, a gas bar, a community hall, a band office, and a water treatment plant. No regular court sittings are held at Hollow Water. Provincial Court for this community is held 100 kilometres (62 miles) to the south in Pine Falls. However, since December of 1993, the

Provincial Court of Manitoba has convened at Hollow Water to conduct sentencing circles that have dealt with offenders charged with sexual assault.

Hollow Water represents a unique example of a community-driven approach to dispute resolution and the healing and treatment of both offenders and victims. Rupert Ross described its development:

> In 1984, a group of social service providers got together, concerned about the future of their young people. As they looked into the issues of youth substance abuse, vandalism, truancy and suicide, their focus shifted to the home life of those children and to the substance abuse and family violence that often prevailed. Upon closer examination of those issues, the focus changed again, for inter-generational sexual abuse was identified as the root problem. Other dysfunctional behaviour came to be seen primarily as symptomatic. By 1987, they began to tackle sexual abuse head on, creating what they have called their Community Holistic Circle Healing Program [CHCH]. They presently estimate that 75 percent of the population of Hollow Water are victims of sexual abuse, and 35 percent are "victimizers."

CHCH co-ordinator Berma Bushie cited frustration with the prevailing criminal justice and child welfare systems as factors contributing to CHCH's development:

> We also studied the *Child Welfare Act*, the legal system and how it was dealing with these [child sexual abuse] cases, and we were horrified to find out that our children were further victimized. … Child Welfare's practice at the time, and probably still is, is when a child disclosed [he or she was] … removed from the family and, in a lot of situations, a child was removed from the community. And then there's absolutely no help offered to the offender. Everything was turned over to the legal system and charges laid, court would take place, and that's it. And the child would be expected to testify against the offender in criminal court, and to us that's not protecting our children. So based on the laws that continue to govern us, we feel that we have to ensure protection for our children. We have to have a say in what happens to them.

As of February 6, 1995, the assessment team comprised seven sexual abuse workers, the local child and family service supervisor, a support worker, a councillor from the band, two Native Alcohol (NADAP) workers, a public health nurse, a local band constable, an RCMP officer from Pine Falls, a person from the Roman Catholic church, two people from provincial Child and Family Services, and the local school principal. The procedure followed by CHCH's assessment team is complex and includes provision of support and treatment for victims and victimizers and their respective families.

After initial disclosure of sexual abuse by a child, a thirteen-step process is followed by the assessment team. These steps are: (1) effecting disclosure, (2) protecting the child/victim, (3) confronting the victimizer, (4) assisting the victimizer's spouse, (5) assisting the family or families directly affected and the community, (6) calling together the assessment team, (7) getting the victimizer to admit and accept responsibility, (8) preparing the victimizer, (9) preparing the victim, (10) preparing all family or families, (11) organizing a special gathering, (12) implementing the healing contract, and (13) conducting the cleansing ceremony.

The assessment team is divided into support teams for the victim, victimizer, and family. After ensuring the safety of the victim, the accused is confronted by a member of the assessment team, who encourages the accused to take responsibility for his or her actions and to participate in CHCH. Berma Bushie explained:

> We feel as a community it's our job to go and confront the offender and not to rely on the RCMP, because they haven't been very successful in getting people to take responsibility for what they've done. When people see the RCMP, they just clam up, won't speak, and so we feel as a community we have a better … track record of getting people to take responsibility for what they've done. … Nine times out of ten, the offender takes responsibility, and we inform the offender of the plan in place. We inform [him] of the community approach. We also inform him about the treatment expectations, the circles that … he's going to have to go through. We also tell the offender that he has to go plead guilty in court.

When criminal charges follow a disclosure, the CHCH approach promotes acceptance of responsibility by the offender through entry of an early guilty plea in court. This practice stands in sharp contrast to the presumption of innocence enjoyed by accused persons in Canadian law and their right to remain silent. In fairness, though, the goal of team members is to help both child complainants and adult accused. After entry of a guilty plea, members of the assessment team then ask the court to adjourn sentencing for at least four months to allow treatment with the offender to begin. Berma Bushie indicated that this period of time was requested so that the assessment team could be assured that the offender was committed to healing.

Offenders are expected to participate in four circles. In the first circle, the offender discloses details of his offence to the CHCH assessment team. In the second circle, the victim tells the offender how the abuse has affected his or her life. In the third circle, the offender describes his actions to his family. Finally, in the fourth circle, the offender faces his community in a sentencing circle. Prior to the introduction of circle sentencing at Hollow Water in December 1993, the assessment team prepared and presented recommendations on sentence to the court sitting in Pine Falls. This procedure was outlined in *R v. S. (H.M.).*

CHCH has actively opposed offender incarceration and has argued that jail cannot break the generational cycle of violence. Assessment team member Marcel Hardesty supported this analysis. He explained that he had asked a sexual offender, recently returned from jail, whether he would commit the offence again. The offender had responded that he would be sure not to get caught if he did it again. Hardesty questioned the lesson being taught by jail and suggested incarceration only reduces the chances of other victims and abusers coming forward.

CHCH focusses on restoring harmony between victims and offenders and the community-at-large through traditional holistic practices. In this process, a conjunctive relationship has developed between CHCH and the criminal justice system both prior to and after sentencing. A protocol between the Manitoba Department of Justice and CHCH was negotiated in 1991 in which the department recognized CHCH's program as an option for the treatment and supervision of sexual assault offenders and agreed to consider a non-custodial sentence if that was the recommendation of the assessment team. This protocol was negotiated by CHCH to give the assessment team input into sentencing and to avoid repeatedly educating Crown attorneys about the CHCH approach.

The first sentencing circle at Hollow Water occurred December 9, 1993. It involved serious sexual assaults perpetrated by two parents on their children. The assessment team foresaw dire consequences for the offenders if this case went through the conventional system. According to assessment team member Lorne Hagel, Judge Murray Sinclair of the Provincial Court of Manitoba had advised the team that, given the offences and circumstances involved, eight to ten years' incarceration would be a realistic sentence. Judge Sinclair advised me that the initial Crown position on sentence was five to six years' incarceration, while even defence counsel conceded that two-and-a-half to four years might be appropriate for one offender, with less jail time for the other. The CHCH assessment team made representations to the Provincial Court requesting formation of a sentencing circle and explaining the evolution of community participation in that community. The submission characterized circle sentencing as an extension of the community's role in holding offenders accountable for their actions and heating the pain they inflicted on their victims:

> Up until now the sentencing hearing has been the point at which all of the parties of the legal system (Crown, defence, judge) and the community have come together. Major differences of opinion as to how to proceed have often existed. As we see it, the legal system usually arrives with an outside agenda of punishment and deterrence of the "guilty" victimizer, and safety and protection of the victim and community; the community on the other hand, arrives with an agenda of accountability of the victimizer to the community, and restoration of balance to all parties of the victimization.
>
> As we see it, the differences in the agendas are seriously deterring the healing process of the community. We believe that the restoration of balance is more likely to occur if sentencing itself is more consistent in process and in content with the healing work of the community. Sentencing needs to become more of a step in the healing process, rather than a diversion from it. … The sentencing circle promotes the above rationale. … As we see it, the sentencing circle plays two primary purposes (1) it promotes the community healing process by providing a forum for the community to address the parties at the time of sentencing, and (2) it allows the court to hear directly from the people most directly affected by the pain of the victimization. In the past the Crown and defence, as well as ourselves, have attempted to portray this information. We believe that it is now time for the court to hear from the victim, the family of the victim, the victimizer, the family of the victimizer and the community-at-large.

This first sentencing circle commenced at seven o'clock in the morning with a sunrise and pipe ceremony and ended at nine o'clock that night. Winnipeg Free Press reporter Kevin Rollason described the atmosphere and process followed at this circle:

> While the smell of sweet grass filled the air, two circles were formed in the centre of the hall for the sentencing of a man and woman charged with incest. The inner circle of about 40 people held the key participants—including both offenders and victims—while the outer circle consisted of about 200 other relatives, friends and community members. … Just before court was called to order, a man holding a tray of burning sweet grass and buffalo grass went around the inner circle, allowing each participant to "wash" the smoke over their hair, faces and clothes. Passing an eagle feather from hand to hand, each person spoke in order around the circles. The discussion went around a total of four times. During the first circle, people spoke about why they were there. During the second, participants were able to speak to the victims. The third and fourth circles were designed to be separate—one centering on the effects

of the crime and the other on "restoring balance" to the offenders. However, when the proceedings threatened to extend well into the night, the last two circles had to be melded into one.

At the conclusion of the circle, all participants, with the exception of a cousin of one of the victims but including the Crown prosecutor, agreed jail would be counterproductive for these offenders. Judge Sinclair indicated to me that these offenders had progressed from a state of total denial to one of total acceptance and responsibility for their actions. In addition, the two had actively worked in convincing one hundred other sexual abusers from Hollow Water to come forward and admit their actions publicly. At the circle's conclusion, Judge Sinclair imposed a three-year suspended sentence on each offender with probation containing a condition that each offender follow the directions of the CHCH assessment team.

Despite the many disclosures of abuse heard at the initial Hollow Water sentencing circle, few subsequent sentencing circles were conducted and there was no increase in sexual assault charges laid against Hollow Water residents. This suggests that many incidents of abuse were being dealt with locally outside the conventional justice system or were not being dealt with at all. An article on Hollow Water published on April 8, 1995, in *The Globe and Mail* stated that, since 1986, only five offenders had been jailed instead of entering the CHCH program and forty-eight offenders had enrolled in the treatment program.

The limited number of offenders sentenced through sentencing circles or incarcerated outside the CHCH program suggest that many offenders in the program were not being charged. This highlights the interesting and often complex relationship between local dispute-resolution processes and the broader justice system. At one level, the community of Hollow Water was working conjunctively with the formal justice system, through the involvement of CHCH members in court assessments and circle sentencing. At another level, the community was apparently operating separately from the formal system, assuming complete control of dispute resolution. The reality across the criminal justice system in Canada is that the number of cases processed through the formal system represents only a small proportion of ongoing criminal activity. What may be different at Hollow Water is the availability of local resources to address the behaviour of offenders, while at the same time protecting victims within that community.

As part of their local system of social control, and in an effort to hold offenders responsible for their actions and encourage their active participation in treatment, a community review was held on the six-month anniversary of each sentencing circle. Berma Bushie explained:

> One of the things that the community does is, after sentencing, we tell the offenders "for the next three years, you are on probation and every six months we are bringing the case back to the community, for the community to review how you are doing in treatment. ..." [The community review] is one of the ways, besides probation, ... used to make sure that people are following the [sentencing circle's] recommendation.

The review process encourages community assistance in holding offenders accountable for their victimization and promotes active participation in their treatment. As Bushie explained:

> We found that after the first sentencing circle back in December 1993 ... that in the treatment area ... there was a regression on the part of the offenders. They were getting back into their

denial process. They were getting back to creating negative support for their case and stuff like that. ... [W]e felt that ... [our assessment] team was not strong enough to stop the regression and to get the people [offenders] back on track with their healing. And because the community came out to speak and give recommendations to the court for their sentencing [circle] ... we felt as a team ... we needed to go back to the community to report ... what was happening. ... And as a team we felt that, before we thought about going through [the process of charging the offenders with breach of probation and bringing this case back to court, ... we felt that we ... should go back through the community. First, give all the details ... and have the community help us decide where this case should go. ... And they [the community members in attendance at the review] felt that these people should be given a chance, and that, again, they repeated their support for these people. They repeated their expectations of the kinds of treatments they wanted the offenders to take, and the work that they wanted them to do. And we said, "Okay, we'll do that and six months down the line, we'll come back and we'll report to you and see how these people are doing.

A community sentencing review held at Hollow Water on February 22, 1995 for three sexual offenders who had been sentenced through a sentencing circle was attended by approximately thirty community members including one of the victims. The victim in attendance had been victimized by two of the offenders. She was apparently sitting in a circle with her abusers for the first time, although she did not speak. The other victim had moved to Winnipeg. The assessment team members assigned to each victim and offender were present and reported to the circle.

This review followed a similar format to the sentencing circles. During successive rounds of the circle, participants in the review learned of the treatment and progress of all victims and offenders and, in turn, addressed the three offenders and one victim in attendance. Participants also developed recommendations for continued offender treatment and victim support. Comments by participants made it clear there was strong community pressure on the offenders to continue treatment. Several women, while acknowledging the progress made by each offender, openly challenged the offenders not to regress in their treatment and to assist the assessment team by naming their other victims. Berma Bushie commented to the offenders that jail "would have been the easy way out for you." She thanked them for taking responsibility for their actions and for facing their community in the circle.

NOTE

Although sentencing circles provide a more appropriate forum for the sentencing of Aboriginal offenders, they raise a number of questions. Must the offender have pleaded guilty, or is it sufficient that he or she accepts guilt in the circle? Can circles be used for all cases? Can they be modified for use in non-Aboriginal communities? Have they produced constructive results without diminishing the interests of the victim? With respect to the efficacy of sentencing circles, see Julian Roberts & Carole La Prairie, "Sentencing Circles: Some Unanswered Questions" (1996-97) 39 Crim LQ 69.

More recently, we have seen an evolution of the use of sentencing circles in Aboriginal communities across Canada. There have even been some experimental efforts to construct sentencing circles in urban and non-Aboriginal settings. Of course, these efforts always raise questions about how to appreciate and implement the concept of "community," so integral to the sentencing-circle idea. Still, sentencing circles are most common in Saskatchewan and the Yukon.

The following two Saskatchewan cases involve serious offences—manslaughter and perjury during a murder trial. The decision in *R v Kahpeaysewat* provides an example of how a properly constructed circle can generate a context that encourages a truly restorative and reparative sentence from both the perspective of the community and the offender. The decision of the Saskatchewan Court of Appeal in *R v Desnomie* is an example of an appellate court disapproving of the use of the sentencing circle and the sentence that it produced.

R v Kahpeaysewat
[2006] SJ No 587 (QL) (Prov Ct)

HUCULAK PROV CT J:

[1] The accused plead guilty to manslaughter on September 26, 2005. In May 2006, a sentencing circle was held. Present were Valerie Kahpeaysewat, her cousin Bernadette Bear, sister Andrea Kahpeaysewat, Gloria Muswa, Elder Ernie Poundmaker, George Laliberte, Wayne Bitternose, Cst. Ernie Loutitt, probation officer Nancy Marrick, Valerie's daughter and daughter-in-law.

Circumstances of the Offence

[2] The circumstances were read in at the circle by the Crown, as follows:

[3] The accused had an on–off relationship with the victim, who she met in 2001. The offence took place on the 22nd day of July, 2004. At the time of the incident, the victim, Frank Nadary, had been drinking with Valerie and other individuals at the apartment of her brother, Leon Kahpeaysewat. The incident began as a result of the victim being asked to leave on several occasions and he refused. Indicating that he would sit quietly and leave Valerie alone, as a result he was permitted to stay. After some time of drinking and playing cards, Valerie stated she was attempting to get some sleep and asked Mr. Nadary to leave and he refused. He then attempted to engage in intimate physical contact despite her demands to be left alone. Mr. Nadary continued with this course of advances until the accused left the room where she had been trying to sleep and moved towards the entrance to the apartment. She then opened the main door to the apartment and repeatedly told the victim to leave the premises. The victim responded by attempting to smother the accused by wrapping his arms around her. He grabbed Valerie by the back of the neck, pulling her hair. Valerie was able to escape his grasp and began to throw various objects in his direction to deter him. When the victim continued to pursue Valerie, she grabbed a knife that was sitting on the kitchen counter. She swung at Mr. Nadary three times, with the second strike inflicting a mortal wound on the victim. Upon realizing the injury that had been sustained by the victim, Valerie called an ambulance.

[4] In her statement to the police she stated: "We were all drinking and I was trying to sleep. He wouldn't let me sleep, he just kept bugging me and bugging me. And my daughter was sleeping, trying to sleep on the couch and me on the floor with my grandson. And him, he was laying on the other side to my grandson there. But he kept bugging me and I told him, I'm trying to sleep, leave me alone. Leave me alone.' And I got to the point where I got pretty frustrated and angry with him, told him to get out, you know, and he wouldn't listen anyways. How many times I told him to leave, get out, leave me alone,' he just wouldn't listen.

[5] So I got pretty angry and told him to get out and I went and opened the door for him to get out. I tried to push him out, he wouldn't go, he kept trying to get out of the situation, like, come on, Val,' you know, don't be like that, come on Val,' stuff like that, come on babe.' And then I was like—it was like I couldn't breathe, like, you know.

[6] So that's when I grabbed that knife, I think from a sink, I'm not sure. I tried first, I threw cups at him and I kept missing him, I was trying to get him to get out and he wouldn't leave. He kept moving around so I wouldn't hit him with the cups. That's when I grabbed the knife. I was looking, first thing I seen like, I would take it and throw it at him, but those were the cups. And then all of a sudden I had this knife and I was missing him with that, and I didn't know I connected because it was fast. I was trying to scare him out of there but I didn't realize I'd connected and it became a major big thing."

[7] Valerie admitted responsibility for the death of the victim at the earliest possible opportunity and plead guilty to a charge of manslaughter. She expressed remorse for her actions.

[8] Valerie never had the intention of killing the victim. Rather Valerie stated she grabbed the knife in an attempt to keep the victim away from her and force him out of the premises. Despite the fact that Valerie was swinging the knife at Mr. Nadary, he continued to attempt to grab her. Valerie had intended to scare Mr. Nadary and the motion that the knife was swung was toward his arms.

[9] She then described how she went to get help to call an ambulance for Frank. And it was Valerie who contacted other people within the building to make the calls to the police and to get an ambulance.

[10] The officer went back on a couple of occasions to talk about how Frank had been bothering Valerie and in a later statement she said: "Frank wouldn't let me sleep, he kept trying to get me to go lay beside him."

[11] She also described that when they went to the kitchen she went to the door first and told him to get out, and opened the door. And that's when he was putting his arms, or trying to put his arms around her and she told him to go home, but he wouldn't go.

[12] She described her thinking at the time: "I was pretty frustrated. It's kind of hard to describe when you're frustrated and angry at the same time. Like you're having a panic attack or something. Like for me it was like that smothering feeling, anger plus it's kind of hard to breathe for me, you know, when I'm trying to get him away and I can't, it's pretty frustrating."

[13] The police officer asked her how he was bugging her. And she said, "He wanted me to lay beside him and like he was—well he was always perverted, I guess. I called him a pervert because of the way he wanted sex all the time, got sick of him too that way, constantly bugging me in that way. So he wanted me to sleep beside him, he wouldn't

sleep and I kept saying, leave me alone I'm trying to sleep,' and he'd be swearing and I'd be swearing at him, leave me alone,' getting angrier and angrier."

[14] Frank was saying things like, "Don't get mad," and trying to kiss up to her and saying "Don't be like this, I love you. Things like that."

[15] A couple of other things that I wanted to make reference to is the autopsy report which showed that Mr. Nadary had a wound, a stab wound, and the stab would have penetrated the heart and so it actually penetrated to a depth of approximately 10 centimeters, and it penetrated both the left and right ventricles of the heart, and that stab wound to the heart was what caused Frank's death. And as well, there was a superficial lacerated wound on Frank's back, on the lower right thorax region which hadn't penetrated the skin.

[16] And I believe that occurs in Valerie's statement—I'll just find the part where there was more than one attempt to strike Frank with the knife. And I believe it was the second blow that was described as the one that killed him.

[17] "She said, I swung at him three times, the second one I connected, the other ones I didn't. But I didn't mean to connect, I just tried to scare him, tried to get him out of the house, the apartment. But he wouldn't leave." She said, "After he went down and my son was coming out of the bedroom, he heard all the commotion, I guess, cause I kept shouting to Frank to get out, get out. I was pretty pissed off more than anything. So my son came out of the bedroom, 'what's going on?' you know, something like that. And my son was trying to give me shit for what had happened."

[18] Frank Nadray's blood alcohol was measured as part of the autopsy and the amount of alcohol in his urine was measured as 249 milligrams of alcohol in 100 milliliters of blood, but the amount of alcohol in his blood was at 191; an elevated reading. Two had a half hours after the police arrived Valerie consented to provide a sample of her breath and it measured 150 milligrams of alcohol in 100 milliliters of blood.

The Accused's Background

[19] The accused is 44 years of age and is an Aboriginal female. Her family life has been very unstable throughout the years. She has seven children and two grandchildren. Her youngest children were apprehended by Social Services and one of her daughters was murdered in 1995. The accused has been in two spousal relationships, which were both very abusive.

[20] The accused's endured a difficult childhood and her home life was marked by violence and abuse. She and her siblings were placed in various foster homes at a young age. From age ten onwards, the accused has been placed in four different foster homes. She lost her mother who was violently killed in 1995. She was sexually, physically and emotionally abused throughout her life and recalls experiencing racism as a child. She was sexually abused by her foster brother, and her grandmother emotionally abused her. She has experienced some psychological problems and has attempted suicide on two occasions. Her four past relationships involved physical violence. The deceased had been convicted of unlawful confinement and assault on the accused.

[21] The accused has little work experience and is just short of a Grade 11 education. She is currently on social assistance, but has previously worked as a housekeeper. She has

attended life skills programming on two occasions and was formerly enrolled in a computer course at Career Campus, which she did not complete. The accused completed the Pathways to Employment Program in 2005. She plans to enroll in the Adult Basic Education Program through the Saskatchewan Indian Institute of Technology.

[22]   The accused has been a user of alcohol and drugs for several years. She began drinking at the age of fourteen, and her primary problem relates to her use of alcohol. She had her children taken away by Social Services because of her substance abuse issues. The accused has attended two weeks at a twenty-eight day inpatient treatment program and has completed a six-week residential treatment program. Despite this treatment, her alcohol use increased when she entered into a common-law relationship with the victim. The accused's tumultuous relationship with the victim was marked by heavy bouts of drinking. She claims that she has been sober for approximately one year. Nevertheless, an addictions assessment completed in 2005 suggests that the accused has a high probability of being substance dependant."

[23]   Presently the accused is involved in a relationship, but she does not live with her partner. She has indicated that her partner uses drugs and alcohol. The accused remains in contact with two of her siblings and with some of her children and grandchildren.

[24]   According to the defence lawyer's sentencing submissions, the accused has made great strides in the past two years, although more needs to be done to address the issues of alcohol, her victimization (sexual, physical and emotional), and the loss of her young child and her mother. She has mental health concerns that continue to need addressing in terms of counselling and therapy.

[25]   The accused has been involved in Tamara's House (which provides resources for sexually abused girls). She is living on her own and is working toward a better relationship with her children. She has a twelve-year-old son who she is wishing to have returned to her. She has grandchildren she sees frequently. She attends Sweats and meets with Elders. She has not seen a therapist but does not object to counselling. The accused is in need of long-term and in-depth counselling. She met with Addictions Services, one on one, with Ruth White. Val was withdrawn in the circle, having difficulty expressing her feelings publically, and having difficulty expressing remorse.

[26]   The accused has been residing in the community on an undertaking, and has been electronically monitored since October, 2004. With the exception of one violation involving the use of alcohol (pills), the accused has complied with the terms of the undertaking. She has attended required programming and has reported weekly to the probation office. In addition, the accused has been attending individual counseling at Saskatoon Health Region, Community Addiction Services. She has become involved in cultural traditions, such as Sweats and Healing Circles. The PSR reports that the accused is a medium risk to re-offend, which is based on her substance abuse issues, her negative peer association, family and personal relationship issues, transience and lack of vocational skills.

[27]   Dr. Menzie's report dated April 6, 2006, sets out her history, including the circumstances of the offence, and her relationship with Frank Nadary. In his opinion, Valerie Kahpeaysewat is a battered woman.

• • •

[28]   The following are Dr. Menzie's conclusions and recommendations.

Conclusions and Recommendations

This 44 year old woman, by her own account, is the product of alcoholic parents and a deprived, unsettled and abusive childhood. Although she said she was not physically or sexually abused while at home, evidently, she was sexually assaulted during her first foster home placement around the age of 10 or 11. She left school when she was 17 with Grade 9 and since then has done little in terms of gainful employment. She has been involved in a number of relationships and has seven surviving children. She has no significant psychiatric history and apparently did not begin to abuse alcohol until 1995.

Kahpeaysewat reported that in 1995, her mother died and about six months later, her 3½ year old daughter was killed by a babysitter. These deaths led to alcohol abuse until 2004, when evidently she stopped drinking.

Kahpeaysewat had been involved with the victim for about three years and throughout the relationship was afraid of him because he was intimidating, controlling and violent. The victim's violent behaviour towards Kahpeaysewat is confirmed by the material I reviewed including police reports. Accordingly, I am of the opinion that she was a battered woman. In addition, she reported symptoms consistent with post-traumatic stress disorder, precipitated by the victim's behaviour during the relationship. These aspects suggest that at the time of the homicide, Kahpeaysewat was suffering from significant features of battered woman syndrome. Likely she was vulnerable to developing this syndrome as a result of abuse in childhood, previous abusive intimate relationships and the significant impact of the deaths of her mother and daughter which both occurred within months of each other.

This syndrome, *inter alia*, results in chronic fear and helplessness, both of which make it difficult to end the relationship. In this case, Kahpeaysewat had been threatened by the victim who had recently been convicted of assaulting her. It appears that at the time of the homicide, Kahpeaysewat did not intend to kill the victim. However, she was afraid of him at the time.

It would be reasonable to include the fact that Kahpeaysewat suffered a degree of battered woman syndrome at the homicide as a mitigating factor in terms of the sentence. It would also be helpful to include alcohol rehabilitation and psychotherapy/counseling to help her deal with the deaths of her mother and daughter as well as the aftermath of her relationship with the victim and his death.

[29] The accused in this case was charged with assault with a weapon in 1991 on her ex-spouse, Mr. Fox. He had abused her throughout their relationship. According to her lawyer, at the time of this offence Val was pregnant with her daughter. Mr. Fox had her by the hair and was hitting her, so she gouged him with a small screwdriver. She plead guilty right away.

Frank Nadray's Background

[30] This information was provided by the Crown at the sentencing circle. He was born June 8, 1967 in Fort Smith in the Northwest Territories. He died July 22, 2004 in Saskatoon, so he was only 37 years old at the time of death. One of the last entries in the police records before his death show that Frank was 5 feet 11 inches tall, 151 pounds. So that and the autopsy photos show me that Mr. Nadary was a tall and a slim man.

[31] About five months before he died Mr. Nadary had a conversation with his probation officer, a man by the name of Brian Jones, and he told Mr. Jones that he came from

a very dysfunctional family. That he had suffered physical and sexual abuse during his childhood, that he was exposed to solvents as a child. His father died when he was five years of age and by about the age of 12 he was placed in group homes.

[32] He first came into conflict with the law at a relatively young age. He was first sentenced at the age of 17 and by the age of 18 his offending had the effect of severing him from his home community, both because he went to jail and because he believed that his home community had banned him from being there.

[33] Information from George Laliberte led George to believe that Frank had a firm belief that he was not entitled to go home, that he had been banned from his community. It seems that even 15 years later when Frank was in Saskatoon and got to know George, that he still spoke longingly and lovingly of his home and of his mother, who continued to reside there, and it appears that it was a pain in his life that never went away, that he couldn't go home, or he believed he couldn't go home.

[34] His removal from his home in Fort Smith in the Northwest Territories also had the effect of thrusting Mr. Nadary into an English-speaking environment; for the first 18 years of his life he spoke Dene. And until his death his facility in the English language was limited, somewhat limited, despite the fact that he lived in predominantly English-speaking communities after that. And when I spoke with George, one of the messages I got was that some of Frank's frustration and his anger and his loneliness appeared to relate to his dislocation from his home community.

[35] It was in July of 2000 that Frank took up residence in Saskatchewan and January 21st of 2000 is the first record that the Saskatoon Police Service have of a report in which Frank and Valerie are indexed as parties, as both being involved. It was a complaint from Valerie that she wanted Frank removed from her residence. And at that time she identified Frank as being a renter or a roommate in her residence.

[36] But it appears that in the year 2001 the relationship became closer and at least at times it was an intimate spousal relationship. The Crown stated in the circle that "I think there will be agreement that it was not a healthy relationship at all times and for either of the parties who were involved in it."

[37] For the circle, efforts had been made to locate friends or family for Frank, but despite efforts, only two individuals were located. Two individuals in the circle also knew Frank Nadray; George Laliberte and Wayne Bitternose attended. Both provided information to the circle.

[38] According to George Laliberte, he had met Frank Nadray 4 years ago at the Correctional Centre. He pointed to a number of problems Frank had. He described Frank Nadray as a man who loved Valerie. He had a big heart. Mr. Laliberte's view was the two shouldn't have had a relationship and predicted something like this would happen. According to George Laliberte, it could have gone either way. According to George Laliberte, Frank needed help and George offered it to him but it did not happen.

[39] Wayne Bitternose met Frank Nadray at the Regional Psychiatric Centre in 1996 and considered him a good friend. He never saw Frank's violent side. He described Frank as loving Val. He heard the two couldn't stay away from each other. He saw Frank as a lost person. His view was that the violence went both ways, with Val being violent towards Frank. He expressed his anger toward Val for Frank's death. He saw him as a nice man who didn't deserve to be killed. Efforts had been made to locate friends or family for Frank, but despite efforts only two individuals were located.

Sentencing Considerations

[40] Sentencing is a complex process of balancing numerous factors and the principles of sentencing. The process is subjective. The sentencing judge must consider the appropriate sentencing principles to achieve a sentence that balances rehabilitation against the need to denounce and deter. It is an inherently individualized process. The search for parity is often a fruitless exercise of academic abstraction. The challenge in sentencing is harmonizing the traditional emphasis on sentencing with the remedial requirements.

Sentencing for Manslaughter

[41] The accused plead guilty to manslaughter contrary to section 236 of the *Criminal Code*. There is a wide range of circumstances in which the crime of manslaughter many be committed; therefore, there are various sentencing options available. As a result, all sentencing objectives must be addressed and consideration must be given to the type of offender that committed the crime, along with the particular circumstances of the offence. Although it is important to achieve parity among sentences, sentencing must be individualized.

[42] The sentence can be and is tailored to meet the degree of moral fault of the offender. *R v. Creighton* (1993), 83 CCC (3d) 346 p. 374 (McLachlin J). There is no minimum sentence for manslaughter. Manslaughter can occur in a wide variety of ways; therefore the penalties are flexible.

[43] Manslaughter encompasses a wide range of different factual scenarios. It is necessary that an unlawful act has caused death, but otherwise circumstances range from near accident to near murder. As evidenced by the many cases that have been referred to by counsel, for both the Crown and the defence, there is a vast range of sentences for the crime of manslaughter depending on the particular circumstances of a case. The various sentencing principles, which the law provides in regard to a sentence for manslaughter may call for a very substantial period of incarceration in the range of 12 to 15 years at the one extreme and on the other end, to a conditional sentence as is now provided for in section 742.1 of the *Criminal Code*.

. . .

[46] The Crown's position is that the appropriate sentence is 5 years, over the time in remand and bail supervision. The defence's position is for a conditional sentence.

. . .

Aboriginal Offender: Gladue Factors

[54] Section 718.2(e) requires a sentencing judge to determine whether the aboriginal offender should be incarcerated. The sentencing judge must examine the unique systemic background circumstances common to all aboriginal offenders and then consider the particular circumstances which result in the offender committing the offence for which he is before the court. Armed with that information he or she must determine whether the goals of restorative justice should be given more weight than the traditional objects of sentencing, such as denunciation and deterrence, in deciding whether the aboriginal offender should be incarcerated

. . .

[56] The *Gladue* factors comprehended the root socio-economic circumstances which play a part in bringing an offender into contact with the criminal justice system (*R v. Laliberte*, [2000] 4 WWR 491, at para. 69) ... .

• • •

[58] Each situation must be examined in light of *Gladue*. At the same time, judges are required to take into account all the principles and objectives of sentencing, including denunciation, deterrence and parity. In the *John* decision ([2004] SJ No. 61), it was established that in cases involving aboriginal offenders, s. 718.2(e) requires the court to determine whether the offender should be imprisoned. The court stated that consideration must be given to the systemic background and the surrounding circumstances of the offence, offender, victim and community. It then must be determined whether restorative justice should be emphasized.

[59] In this case, these socio-economic factors figure significantly into sentencing considerations, since Valerie Kahpeaysewat's tragic upbringing, the murder of her child, racism, victimization, abuse, addictions, family dislocation, poverty, fragmentation, lack of education and employment, family dysfunction, and her shattered life all contributed in a major way to her criminal record.

[60] On July 14, 2006, the newspaper had an article with the heading "Sask. Leads in Spousal Homicide." Saskatchewan spouses are twice as likely to die from domestic violence compared to elsewhere in Canada. From 1995 to 2004, the average homicide rate in Saskatchewan was 8.4 victims to one million spouses, according to the report *Family Violence in Canada: A Statistical Profile*, 2006. I have read this report from the Canadian Centre for Justice Statistics—Statistics Canada. Women were more likely than men to report being targets of ten or more violent spousal episodes (Mihorean, 2005). Most spousal violence incidents are committed by males. The difference is very significant statistically. Between 1995 and 2004, two-thirds (65%) of spousal homicides involved a history of domestic violence (p. 55). Females accused of spousal homicide were more likely than male accused to have experienced a history of family violence.

[61] Domestic violence in the aboriginal community is a serious issue. The factors contributing to this are complex. What sentence the accused receives will not change this. The *Gladue* factors play a prominent role in creating the conditions where violence is turned inward toward family, friends and self. The tragedy is that without significant resources and a change in the socio-economic conditions, little will change.

The Circle

[62] Since 1992, judges in the Provincial Court of Saskatchewan have utilized sentencing circles. The circle provided an opportunity to engage in a restorative process. In this case, the offender publically accounted for her criminal conduct and took responsibility for her actions. Information was provided that provided greater insight into the dynamic of the offence. Participants were given an opportunity to provide input into sentencing options. This was a difficult and emotional process for the participants.

[63] In the circle, Cst. Ernie Louttit referred to the numerous occasions that the police were involved in the life of the accused and the victim. He noted twelve occasions. His view was the death could have gone either way; that this result was predictable. This is a chilling statement. The prosecutor provided me with a summary of police occurrence

reports involving the accused and Mr. Nadary, starting in January 2001 and ending in January 2004. On a number of occasions the accused was the complainant, in particular, reporting breaches of Mr. Nadary's no contact order of probation.

[64] In August, 2001, Mr. Nadary was charged with break and enter, assault and unlawful confinement. Valerie was the victim. He was convicted and received a suspended sentence and probation of eighteen months. In March, 2002, Frank Nadary was convicted of breach of probation concerning the no contact with Valerie condition. He received a three-month conditional sentence. On March 14, 2003, the accused made a complaint that Frank assaulted her. The charge did not proceed as she was unsure whether she wanted to proceed. In August, 2003, Frank Nadary was charged with assault causing bodily harm on Valerie, among other charges. He was convicted of common assault and sentenced to six months jail, followed by two years probation.

[65] There were numerous breach charges against Frank Nadary. Many were in relation to the non-contact order with the accused and abstention of alcohol condition. In January, 2004, the accused complained to police that Frank Nadary is writing her from jail. No action was taken as the police were unable to locate the existing probation order. Frank Nadary would have still been on probation from February, 2004.

[66] In the circle, the accused's aunt, cousin and sister participated. Her daughters were present for part of the circle. They all described her dysfunctional childhood and her difficult, fractured life. Sadly, all of the victim's relatives had been victims of domestic violence. They described Frank Nadary's possessiveness and obsession with the victim. They described how he would follow her. The accused's family were prepared to assist and support her.

Case Law

[67] Both Crown and defence provided numerous cases to support their position. Many of the Crown's cases can be distinguished as they relate to pre-*Criminal Code* amendments, and many refer to "home invasion" types of circumstances. Many of these cases were summarized in *R v. Machiskinic*, Sask. QB 2004, which I will not repeat here.

[68] From my perspective, the most relevant cases are those in relation to domestic violence. There are some Saskatchewan cases I believe are relevant to consider: *R v. Machiskinic, supra, R v. W.L.Q.* (2005) [2005] SJ No. 13, and *R v. J.S.* (1998), [1998] SJ No. 247. In *R v. Machiskinic, supra*, the accused stabbed her common-law husband during a drunken altercation. Here it was held that a conditional sentence was not consistent with the fundamental principles of sentencing and would endanger the safety of the community. She had a lengthy record (14 convictions, including 1 assault). She was given credit of six months of remand time, and one year for the eighteen months' bail. This case referred to institutional sentences of imprisonment and conditional sentences at pp. 3, 9 and 10.

[69] Her case can be distinguished on her lengthy record and history of assaults on her spouse. Further, the judge was not satisfied that serving the sentence in the community would not endanger the safety of the community and concluded that a sentence of three and a half to four years was appropriate, reduced by the bail conditions and remand time, to two and a half years.

[70] In *R v. W.L.Q.* (2005), a similar set of circumstances exist with the stabbing of a common-law spouse. Alcohol was a factor. It can be distinguished in that she failed to

attend alcohol and drug rehabilitation programs which were imposed as a condition. She had twelve prior convictions, including assault causing bodily harm. She posed a high risk to re-offend. The judge found four years to be the appropriate sentence, minus credit of six months for three months' remand and three-quarter's time credit for electronic monitoring. Her sentence was three years. The judge also found she posed a danger to the community and a sentence of less than two years was inappropriate. She had threatened to kill the victim on the night of the offence.

[71] In *R v. J.S.* (1998) (Sask. Prov. Ct.), the stabbing was of the offender's mother. Alcohol was a factor. This was not a spousal situation. She was sentenced to two years but was also given credit for six months on remand. She was directed to serve at the healing lodge to address the root causes of her destructive behaviour. The defence did not argue for a conditional sentence but rather on having her sentenced to two years with a recommendation to transfer to the Okemaw Ohci Healing Lodge for Women to focus on treatment and healing. Alcohol was a major problem. She had previously breached conditions.

Appropriate Sentence

[72] I have considered the principles and objectives of sentencing. I have taken into account all the aggravating factors, such as her prior record, her son and daughter were in the apartment at the time of the offence, her consumption of alcohol, and the victim was a spouse. She is not a youthful offender. She used a weapon. The mitigating factors are her history of physical, sexual and emotional abuse, post-traumatic stress disorder, her participation in the circle, the *Gladue* factors, her suffering a form of battered spouse syndrome, she was victimized by Frank Nadary and the fact she was remorseful. I find that Valerie Kahpeaysewat's stabbing of Frank Nadary was a derivative crime borne of the unresolved effects of past conditions of abuse, indignities and profound grief. I have concluded that a community-based sentence is the appropriate sentence for this offender. In my opinion, a sentence of two years less a day served in the community in the form of a conditional sentence, followed by probation, is the appropriate sentence for this particular offender, for this offence and this community. I find that a penitentiary term is not appropriate, nor is probation alone.

[73] In determining the appropriate range and in finding that a community-based sentence is appropriate, I have considered the circumstances required by *Gladue*, the decisions of the Saskatchewan and other courts.

[74] This offender, by serving her sentence in the community, would not endanger the safety of the community. This individual does not pose a risk to society while serving in the community. I have taken into account her risk of re-offending and the gravity of the damage that could issue in the event of re-offending. I have considered whether she is likely to abide by the order, the nature of the offence, the circumstances of the offence, her degree of participation, her profile, including lifestyle, occupation, criminal record, conduct following the offence, and the danger the offender represents to the community offended by the offence.

[75] I have referred to the offender's personal circumstances and Dr. Menzie's report. I referred to comments made in the circle. She is remorseful and took responsibility for the offence. She has been on judicial interim release since October 2004 under electronic monitoring, with numerous conditions. She breached once by taking pills. She has been

working toward dealing with issues such as addictions. There is a significant likelihood she will abide by the court order. There is little risk to the community in the effect of a re-offence.

[76] Having decided that the three pre-requisites for a conditional sentence have been satisfied, I must determine whether the imposition of a conditional sentence of imprisonment is consistent with the principles of sentencing set out in ss. 718 to 718.2. If a conditional sentence can facilitate both a punitive and a restorative objective and both objectives can be achieved in a given case, a conditional sentence is likely the better sanction than imprisonment.

[77] The primary question here is whether the principles of denunciation and deterrence can be satisfied by the imposition of a community-based sentence. In my opinion, the principles of deterrence and denunciation can be satisfied by the imposition of strict conditions in a conditional sentence of imprisonment. ...

[78] Incarceration will usually provide more denunciation than a conditional sentence of imprisonment, but a conditional sentence which deprives or restricts an offender's liberty can effectively satisfy those principles. The Supreme Court of Canada made it clear in *Proulx* that severe restrictions on the offender's liberty are to be the norm and not the exception.

[79] The court can effectively denounce the offender's conduct by imposing sufficiently stringent conditions such as house arrest, which will make it clear to members of the community that the offender's conduct carries severe consequences. The sanction will be visible, restrictive, enforceable, and capable of attracting a severe sanction for failing to comply with the conditions.

[80] As Chief Justice Lamer noted in *Proulx*, judges should be wary of placing too much weight on deterrence. The public nature of the sentence in this community is a constant reminder of the offender's conduct and the consequences of such conduct, and in my opinion is a more effective deterrent than a prison sentence served in some distant community. Sanctions other than imprisonment may be at least as onerous as a prison sentence. A person who serves the sentence in the community still carries a societal stigma of being a convicted offender serving a criminal sentence. Deterrence, to the extent that it is effective, can be satisfied by the imposition of a community based sentence.

[81] After a full consideration of the seriousness of the offence, all the principles of sentencing, including rehabilitation and the principles of restorative justice, as well as the principles of deterrence and denunciation, I find that a sentence of two years less one day to be served in the community is a fit and appropriate sentence for this individual. I have taken into account the time she has been on bail supervision.

• • •

[83] The accused will comply with the following conditions for the full term of the conditional sentence:

(a) the accused shall reside at her residence and shall be confined to her residence for the first six months of the conditional sentence, leaving only at such times as the probation officer or the supervisor monitoring the conditional sentencing order shall permit, attend treatment, or perform other authorized activities, subject to medical emergencies. Thereafter, the accused shall be confined to her residence between the hours of 6:00 p.m. and 7:00 a.m. for the next six months, and for the remaining part between the hours of 7:00 p.m. and 7:00 a.m.

(b)   the accused must personally present herself to any peace officer or the probation officer or supervisor monitoring the conditions of this order, and shall follow the lawful instructions of the probation officer/supervisor as they pertain to treatment.

(c)   the accused shall perform 240 hours of community service over a period of two years less one day. The type of community service shall be determined, assigned and coordinated by the supervisor.

(d)   the accused shall abstain from the purchase, possession or consumption of alcohol and non-prescription (illicit) drugs, and must not enter any premises where the primary function is the sale or consumption of alcohol. She shall submit to alcohol and/or drug testing as arranged and directed by the probation officer;

(e)   the accused shall take such treatment and counselling as ordered by the Chief Probation Officer, including addictions, personal, grief, etc.

[84]   Her sentence will be followed by two years' probation with the standard terms, reporting, continued addictions treatment and personal counselling. There will be a DNA order and a ten-year weapons prohibition order. The sentence should not be considered lenient, nor should it be read to mean the life of Frank Nadary had no value. The tragedy reminds us of the need to intervene early in cases of domestic violence and provide support and resources to the victim, as well as the perpetrator. The socio-economic and environmental back-drop to domestic violence must also be addressed which is beyond the scope of this court.

R v Desnomie
(2005) 275 Sask R 167 (CA)

GERWING JA (Cameron and Vancise JJA concurring):

[1]   The Crown appeals a sentence of 18 months conditional, including six months of electronic monitoring, and $100 surcharge on a charge that the respondent, in a trial on second degree murder charge gave evidence which was contrary to the evidence she gave at the preliminary on the same matter, contrary to s. 136(1) of the *Criminal Code*.

[2]   The second degree murder preliminary and trial related to the death of a child, Antonio Kakakaway. The accused in that trial was the grandmother of the deceased and his primary caregiver. The accused Kakakaway called an ambulance for the child, suggesting that he had fallen from his crib. He died in hospital two days later. Medical experts reported that the injury was produced by greater force than a fall and testimony was led to this effect. Further, the child's body had numerous bruises, scrapes and lacerations which varied in age.

[3]   The respondent contacted police and offered information, as a former friend of the accused Kakakaway, including that the latter had told her she was guilty. She also told the investigating officers and subsequently the preliminary inquiry that on a second occasion the accused, Kakakaway, had told her she was tired and stressed out and that the child had been crying all day. She said she hit him and he fell to the floor unconscious.

[4]   The accused Kakakaway was committed for trial on second degree murder. During the course of that trial, the respondent denied the second conversation and testified that

she had lied at the preliminary inquiry about the admission that the accused Kakakaway had struck the victim.

[5] It is critical to note that the trial judge was satisfied that Antonio Kakakaway was the victim of a homicide, dying from "blunt force injury consistent with a blow from an adult person." The trial judge correctly instructed himself that the respondent's credibility as a witness was damaged by her admission that she had lied at the preliminary inquiry. The trial judge, in the circumstances, and because the accused Kakakaway did not have exclusive access to the victim over the time period when the injury could have occurred, acquitted her. It is clear that if the respondent had testified as she did at the preliminary inquiry her testimony would have been relevant and could have affected the outcome of the trial.

[6] The trial judge in this matter, for reasons which are not clear, convoked a sentencing circle which she said was for information purposes. Given the nature of this offence, it is highly doubtful a sentencing circle should have been called, but in any event, it is of no utility, having been attended almost exclusively by members of the respondent's family. At the sentencing circle, she admitted she lied at the trial. She said she knew Antonio had been injured by Kakakaway and that her testimony at the preliminary was the truth.

[7] The conditional sentence in no way reflects the gravity of the situation. To repeat, the respondent gave false testimony in the course of a trial for second degree murder of a child. The investigation of who caused a homicide is one of the most significant that a court can undertake and one that must be carried out with openness and with the greatest attention to seeking the truth in order to preserve society's respect for the judicial system. It is fundamental in any judicial proceeding that witnesses treat the process with respect and tell the truth, and that if they do not, the court deal with them appropriately to show not only other witnesses, who may potentially do the same, but society that it takes extremely seriously the process of ascertaining the truth. This can nowhere be more important, both for the system itself and for the respect society gives to the system as a means of resolving disputes in society, than in the case of a homicide. The courts must treat this process with utmost seriousness, not only for the parties involved in each case, but because society must be confident that these questions can be fully dealt with in an appropriate manner by the court system. Structure in society depends on this.

. . .

[10] Cases in other jurisdictions indicate that it is frequent for persons convicted of lying under oath in murder trials to be sentenced to federal custody. See for example, *R v. Gushue* [(1976), 32 CCC (2d) 189 (Ont CA)] and *R v. Glauser* [(1981), 25 CR (3d) 287 (Alta CA)].

[11] In this case, the Crown asked at the trial for two years less a day and in this Court says that it feels bound to ask for no more than that.

[12] In the circumstances of this case, the sentence imposed took no account of the above principles with respect to determining the gravity of the offence with respect to which the false evidence was given. It in no way is adequate for specific or general deterrence and undercuts the respect of society for the process of the Court and the Court's guardianship of that process.

[13] In the circumstances, the sentence is increased to two years less a day. In imposing this sentence, we are not to be taken to suggest that federal incarceration would not be appropriate. Were it not for the concession by the Crown and the way this matter unfolded

before the trial judge, it is probable that a substantial term of federal incarceration would be appropriate.

[14] The Crown noted that months served on the conditional sentence have imposed minimal inconvenience on the respondent. In light of this and in light of the lenient sentence being imposed because of the Crown concession, no credit is allowed for any time served under the conditional sentence. That is, there will be a sentence imposed of two years less a day to run from today's date. The Crown appeal is allowed to this extent.

QUESTIONS

1. What is the source of the Court of Appeal's concern that this was an inappropriate case for a sentencing circle? Was it the composition of the circle or the nature and severity of the offence?

2. What does this decision say about deference and the use of sentencing circles?

V. CONDITIONAL SENTENCES AND ABORIGINAL OFFENDERS

In Chapter 12, Conditional Sentence of Imprisonment, we discussed in detail the new sanction of a conditional sentence that was the subject of the Supreme Court's attention in *R v Proulx*, 2000 SCC 5. Although a number of conditional-sentence cases were argued at the same time as *Proulx*, one judgment that was not released until later was *R v Wells*, below. It dealt with the application of the conditional sentence regime to an Aboriginal offender.

R v Wells
2000 SCC 10, [2000] 1 SCR 207

[The offender was convicted of sexual assault involving an 18-year-old victim who was either asleep or unconsious by reason of intoxication. He was sentenced to 20 months' incarceration. Prior to the Supreme Court decision in *Gladue* dealing with s 718.2(e), his sentence appeal was heard and dismissed. Fresh evidence was filed indicating his involvement with the Aboriginal community and his efforts to deal with his alcohol abuse problem by attending an Aboriginal treatment centre. On appeal to the Supreme Court, the relationship between s 718.2(e) and conditional sentences was a central issue.]

IACOBUCCI J (L'Heureux-Dubé, Gonthier, McLachlin, Bastarache, and Binnie JJ concurring):

[36] In *Gladue, supra*, the Court concluded that, as a general principle, s. 718.2(e) indicates that a custodial sentence is the penal sanction of last resort for all offenders, to be used only where no other sanction is appropriate. As to the words "with particular attention to the circumstances of aboriginal offenders," the Court reasoned that sentencing judges should pay particular attention to the fact that the circumstances of aboriginal offenders are unique in comparison with those of non-aboriginal offenders. Section 718.2(e) has a remedial purpose for all offenders, focusing as it does on the concept of restorative justice, a sentencing approach which seeks to restore the harmony that existed

prior to the accused's actions. Again, the appropriateness of the sentence will take into account the needs of the victims, the offender, and the community as a whole.

[37]   While the objective of restorative justice, by virtue of s. 718.2(e), applies to all offenders, the requirement to pay "particular attention to the circumstances of aboriginal offenders" recognizes that most traditional aboriginal conceptions of sentencing hold restorative justice to be the primary objective. In addition, s. 718.2(e) has a particular remedial purpose for aboriginal peoples, as it was intended to address the serious problem of overincarceration of aboriginal offenders in Canadian penal institutions. In singling out aboriginal offenders for distinct sentencing treatment in s. 718.2(e), it is reasonable to assume that Parliament intended to address this social problem, to the extent that a remedy was possible through sentencing procedures.

[38]   In order to provide guidance to sentencing judges as to the manner in which the remedial purpose of s. 718.2(e) could be given effect, the reasons in *Gladue* set out a framework of analysis for the sentencing judge. In considering the circumstances of aboriginal offenders, the sentencing judge must take into account, at the very least, both the unique systemic or background factors that are mitigating in nature in that they may have played a part in the aboriginal offender's conduct, and the types of sentencing procedures and sanctions which may be appropriate in the circumstances for the offender because of his or her particular aboriginal heritage or connection (*Gladue*, at para. 66). In particular, given that most traditional aboriginal approaches place a primary emphasis on the goal of restorative justice, the alternative of community-based sanctions must be explored.

[39]   In the search for a fit sentence, therefore, the role of the sentencing judge is to conduct the sentencing process and impose sanctions taking into account the perspective of the aboriginal offender's community. As was noted in *Gladue*, it is often the case that imposing a custodial sentence on an aboriginal offender does not advance the remedial purpose of s. 718.2(e), neither for the offender nor for his community. This is particularly true for less serious or non-violent offences, where the goal of restorative justice will no doubt be given greater weight than principles of denunciation or deterrence.

[40]   However, the scope of s. 718.2(e), as it applies to all offenders, restricts the adoption of alternatives to incarceration to those sanctions that are "reasonable in the circumstances." Again, as was expressly stated in *Gladue*, the Court in no way intended to suggest that as a general rule, the greatest weight is to be given to principles of restorative justice, and less weight accorded to goals such as denunciation and deterrence. Indeed, such a general rule would contradict the individual or case-by-case nature of the sentencing process, which proceeds on the basis of inquiring whether, given the particular facts of the offence, the offender, the victim and the community, the sentence is fit in the circumstances.

. . .

(1) Significance of the Goal of Restorative Justice in Sentencing Aboriginal Offenders Convicted of Serious Crimes

[43]   The appellant submits that in according greater weight to the goals of denunciation and deterrence based on the nature of his offence, the sentencing judge did not take into account, as required by s. 718.2(e), the paramount significance of restorative justice within

aboriginal communities. The appellant also submits that on the same basis, the Court of Appeal was in error when it held that it would be unreasonable to conclude that a fit sentence for a non-aboriginal offender would not also be a fit sentence for an aboriginal offender. It is important to note, however, that consistent with the reasoning in Gladue, *supra*, the Court of Appeal was referring to "serious crimes," rather than offences in general, as follows (at p. 140):

> For *serious* crimes, it would not be reasonable to conclude that a fit sentence for a non-aboriginal person would not also be fit for an aboriginal person, and this point was made by Esson JA speaking for the majority in the British Columbia Court of Appeal decision of *R v. Gladue* (1997), 119 CCC (3d) 481 at p. 506, who stated, "To put it another way, the particular circumstances could not reasonably support a conclusion that the sentence, if a fit one for a non-aboriginal person, would not also be fit for an aboriginal person." [Emphasis added.]

[44] Let me emphasize that s. 718.2(e) requires a different *methodology* for assessing a fit sentence for an aboriginal offender; it does not mandate, necessarily, a different *result*. Section 718.2(e) does not alter the fundamental duty of the sentencing judge to impose a sentence that is fit for the offence and the offender. Furthermore, in *Gladue*, as mentioned the Court stressed that the application of s. 718.2(e) does not mean that aboriginal offenders must always be sentenced in a manner which gives greatest weight to the principles of restorative justice and less weight to goals such as deterrence, denunciation, and separation (at para. 78). As a result, it will generally be the case, *as a practical matter*, that particularly violent and serious offences will result in imprisonment for aboriginal offenders as often as for non-aboriginal offenders (*Gladue*, at para. 33). Accordingly, I conclude that it was open to the trial judge to give primacy to the principles of denunciation and deterrence in this case on the basis that the crime involved was a serious one.

[45] Whether a crime is indeed serious in the given circumstances is, in my opinion, a factual matter that can only be determined on a case-by-case basis. I am not suggesting that there are categories of offences which presumptively exclude the possibility of a non-custodial sentence. Indeed, Lamer CJ specifically rejected such an approach in relation to the conditional sentencing regime (*Proulx, supra*, at para. 79). ...

[48] I cannot conclude that the trial judge misconstrued the seriousness of the crime. In addition, the judge's use of the words "near major" or "major" instead of "serious" does not constitute a reversible error. I find no error in principle, no overemphasis of the appropriate factors, nor a failure to consider a relevant factor, and, accordingly, defer to the trial judge's assessment of the particular circumstances of the offence and offender (*M. (C.A.)* [[1996] 1 SCR 500]. Therefore, the trial judge made a reasonable determination as to the availability of a conditional sentence.

[49] I would like to add at this point that the reasons in *Gladue, supra*, do not foreclose the possibility that, in the appropriate circumstances, a sentencing judge may accord the greatest weight to the concept of restorative justice, notwithstanding that an aboriginal offender has committed a serious crime. As was concluded in *Gladue*, at para. 81, the remedial purpose of s. 718.2(e) directs the sentencing judge not only to take into account the unique circumstances of aboriginal offenders, but also to appreciate relevant cultural differences in terms of the objectives of the sentencing process:

• • •

[50] The generalization drawn in *Gladue* to the effect that the more violent and serious the offence, the more likely as a practical matter for similar terms of imprisonment to be imposed on aboriginal and non-aboriginal offenders, was not meant to be a principle of universal application. In each case, the sentencing judge must look to the circumstances of the aboriginal offender. In some cases, it may be that these circumstances include evidence of the community's decision to address criminal activity associated with social problems, such as sexual assault, in a manner that emphasizes the goal of restorative justice, notwithstanding the serious nature of the offences in question.

[51] As Lamer CJ noted in *M. (C.A.)*, *supra*, at para. 92, sentencing requires an individualized focus, not only of the offender, but also of the victim and community as well:

> It has been repeatedly stressed that there is no such thing as a uniform sentence for a particular crime. … Sentencing is an inherently individualized process, and the search for a single appropriate sentence for a similar offender and a similar crime will frequently be a fruitless exercise of academic abstraction. As well, sentences for a particular offence should be expected to vary to some degree across various communities and regions in this country, *as the "just and appropriate" mix of accepted sentencing goals will depend on the needs and current conditions of and in the particular community where the crime occurred.* [Emphasis added.]

[52] In this respect, I note that the appellant introduced evidence of the availability of an aboriginal-specific alcohol and drug abuse treatment program. There was, however, an indication that this program would be inappropriate for the appellant as a sexual offender. In addition, there was no evidence of the existence of, or the appellant's participation in, an anti-sexual-assault program.

(2) Extent of the Sentencing Judge's Obligation to Inquire into the Circumstances of an Aboriginal Offender

[53] As noted in *Gladue*, *supra*, at para. 83, it will be necessary in every case for the sentencing judge to take judicial notice of systemic or background factors that have contributed to the difficulties faced by aboriginal people in both the criminal justice system, and throughout society at large. In addition, the judge is obliged to inquire into the unique circumstances of aboriginal offenders.

[54] At times, it may be necessary to introduce evidence of this nature. It is to be expected in our adversarial system of criminal law that counsel for both the prosecution and the accused will adduce this evidence, but even where counsel do not provide the necessary information, s. 718.2(e) places an affirmative obligation upon the sentencing judge to inquire into the relevant circumstances. In most cases, the requirement of special attention to the circumstances of aboriginal offenders can be satisfied by the information contained in pre-sentence reports. Where this information is insufficient, s. 718.2(e) authorizes the sentencing judge on his or her own initiative to request that witnesses be called to testify as to reasonable alternatives to a custodial sentence.

[55] Having said that, it was never the Court's intention, in setting out the appropriate methodology for this assessment, to transform the role of the sentencing judge into that of a board of inquiry. It must be remembered that in the reasons in *Gladue*, this affirmative obligation to make inquiries beyond the information contained in the pre-sentence report

was limited to "appropriate circumstances," and where such inquiries were "practicable" (at para. 84). The application of s. 718.2(e) requires a practical inquiry, not an impractical one. As with any other factual finding made by a court of first instance, the sentencing judge's assessment of whether further inquiries are either appropriate or practicable is accorded deference at the appellate level.

[The appeal was dismissed.]

NOTE

For a discussion of *Wells*, *Proulx*, and *Gladue* in the context of an Aboriginal offender convicted of trafficking, see *R v Laliberte*, 2000 SKCA 27.

FURTHER READING

Balfour, Gillian. "Do Law Reforms Matter? Exploring the Victimization–Criminalization Continuum in the Sentencing of Aboriginal Women in Canada" (2012) 19:1 Intl Rev Victimology 85.

Gevikoglu, Jeanette. "*Ipeelee/Ladue* and the Conundrum of Indigenous Identity in Sentencing" (2013) 63 SCLR 205.

Jeffries, Samantha & Philip Stenning. "Sentencing Aboriginal Offenders: Law, Practice, and Policy in Three Countries" (2014) 56:4 Can J Corr 447.

Manikis, Marie. "The Recognition of Prosecutorial Obligations in an Era of Mandatory Minimum Sentences of Imprisonment and Over-Representation of Aboriginal People in Prisons" (2015) 71 SCLR 277.

Monchalin, Lisa. *The Colonial Problem: An Indigenous Perspective on Crime and Injustice in Canada* (Toronto: University of Toronto Press, 2016).

Roberts, Julian V & Ron Melchers. "The Incarceration of Aboriginal Offenders: An Analysis of Trends, 1978-2001" (2003) 45:2 Can J Corr 211.

Rudin, Jonathan. "Looking Backward, Looking Forward: The Supreme Court of Canada's Decision in *R. v. Ipeelee*" (2012) 57 SCLR (2d) 375.

Rudin, Jonathan. "There Must Be Some Kind of Way Out of Here: Aboriginal Over-Representation, Bill C-10, and the Charter of Rights" (2013) 17 Can Crim L Rev 349.

Statistics Canada. "The Incarceration of Aboriginal People in Adult Correctional Services," by Samuel Perreault, in *Juristat* 29:3, Catalogue No 85-002-X (Ottawa: Statistics Canada, 2009).

The Charter and Sentencing

I. INTRODUCTION

On April 17, 1982, the *Canadian Charter of Rights and Freedoms*, Part I of the *Constitution Act, 1982*, being Schedule B to the *Canada Act 1982* (UK), 1982, c 11, was entrenched in the Canadian Constitution (except for s 15, the equality provision, which was delayed for three years). Given the essential fact that sentencing and imprisonment necessarily involve state actors and liberty, it was not surprising that various Charter guarantees were raised, accepted, or rejected in response to myriad issues. One could write a book canvassing the numerous situations and cases—many have already been mentioned throughout this text. This chapter focuses on those major cases that best illustrate, both in theory and practice, the relationship between the Charter and aspects of sentencing and punishment.

II. SECTION 3: THE RIGHT TO VOTE

In Chapter 3, Aggravating and Mitigating Factors, we discussed the issue of collateral consequences that may be relevant to the sentencing decision. One of the most dramatic consequences was the denial to prisoners of the right to vote. Throughout Canada, electoral statutes both federal and provincial contained various prohibitions to this effect. Apparently, this was considered to be a self-evident consequence of imprisonment, reminiscent of the days of "civil death," which included the disabilities that flowed from the status of felon—outlawry, corruption of the blood, and attainder. Certainly, the felon was disenfranchised.

On its face, s 3 of the Charter appears to guarantee the right to vote to "everyone." However, governments continued to claim justification. Section 1 of the Charter permits the state to show that a law that limits guaranteed rights or freedoms can be "demonstrably justified in a free and democratic society." The federal legislation was all embracing in its efforts to deny all prisoners the right to vote in federal elections. The Supreme Court of Canada found this prohibition to be overbroad and struck it down in 1993: see the first *Sauvé* case, [1993] 2 SCR 438. However, Parliament responded by enacting a new prohibition that applied only to prisoners serving sentences of two years or more, which would exclude all penitentiary prisoners from the vote. This remained on the books for a decade before the basic conflict between s 3 and an ostensible justification under s 1 came before the Supreme Court of Canada in the second *Sauvé* case, immediately below. For the government, the justification was based primarily on the views of political philosophers who gave "expert" evidence arguing the legitimacy of disenfranchisement as an element of punishment. In a five-to-four majority decision written by Chief Justice McLachlin, this was rejected. In a carefully crafted judgment, the majority emphasized the need for precision in terms of offering a legislative objective for s 1 justificatory purposes beyond simply asserting claims of "moral unworthiness."

Sauvé v Canada (Chief Electoral Officer)
2002 SCC 68, [2002] 3 SCR 519

McLACHLIN CJ (Iacobucci, Major, Binnie, Arbour, and LeBel JJ concurring):

[1] The right of every citizen to vote, guaranteed by s. 3 of the *Canadian Charter of Rights and Freedoms*, lies at the heart of Canadian democracy. The law at stake in this appeal denies the right to vote to a certain class of people—those serving sentences of two years or more in a correctional institution. The question is whether the government has established that this denial of the right to vote is allowed under s. 1 of the *Charter* as a "reasonable limi[t] ... demonstrably justified in a free and democratic society." I conclude that it is not. The right to vote, which lies at the heart of Canadian democracy, can only be trammeled for good reason. Here, the reasons offered do not suffice

[2] The predecessor to s. 51(e) of the *Canada Elections Act*, R.S.C. 1985, c. E-2, prohibited all prison inmates from voting in federal elections, regardless of the length of their sentences. This section was held unconstitutional as an unjustified denial of the right to vote guaranteed by s. 3 of the *Charter: Sauvé v. Canada (Attorney General)*, [1993] 2 S.C.R. 438. Parliament responded to this litigation by replacing this section with a new s. 51(e) (S.C. 1993, c. 19, s. 23), which denies the right to vote to all inmates serving sentences of two years or more. ...

• • •

[7] To justify the infringement of a *Charter* right, the government must show that the infringement achieves a constitutionally valid purpose or objective, and that the chosen means are reasonable and demonstrably justified: *R. v. Oakes*, [1986] 1 S.C.R. 103. This two-part inquiry—the legitimacy of the objective and the proportionality of the means—ensures that a reviewing court examine rigorously all aspects of justification. Throughout the justification process, the government bears the burden of proving a valid objective and showing that the rights violation is warranted—that is, that it is rationally connected, causes minimal impairment, and is proportionate to the benefit achieved.

[8] My colleague Justice Gonthier proposes a deferential approach to infringement and justification. He argues that there is no reason to accord special importance to the right to vote, and that we should thus defer to Parliament's choice among a range of reasonable alternatives. He further argues that in justifying limits on the right to vote under s. 1, we owe deference to Parliament because we are dealing with "philosophical, political and social considerations," because of the abstract and symbolic nature of the government's stated goals, and because the law at issue represents a step in a dialogue between Parliament and the courts.

[9] I must, with respect, demur. The right to vote is fundamental to our democracy and the rule of law and cannot be lightly set aside. Limits on it require not deference, but careful examination. This is not a matter of substituting the Court's philosophical preference for that of the legislature, but of ensuring that the legislature's proffered justification is supported by logic and common sense.

[10] The *Charter* distinguishes between two separate issues: whether a right has been infringed, and whether the limitation is justified. The complainant bears the burden of showing the infringement of a right (the first step), at which point the burden shifts to the government to justify the limit as a reasonable limit under s. 1 (the second step). These are distinct processes with different burdens. ...

• • •

[13] The core democratic rights of Canadians do not fall within a "range of acceptable alternatives" among which Parliament may pick and choose at its discretion. Deference may be appropriate on a decision involving competing social and political policies. It is not appropriate, however, on a decision to limit fundamental rights. This case is not merely a competition between competing social philosophies. It represents a conflict between the right of citizens to vote—one of the most fundamental rights guaranteed by the *Charter*—and Parliament's denial of that right. Public debate on an issue does not transform it into a matter of "social philosophy," shielding it from full judicial scrutiny. It is for the courts, unaffected by the shifting winds of public opinion and electoral interests, to safeguard the right to vote guaranteed by s. 3 of the *Charter*.

[14] *Charter* rights are not a matter of privilege or merit, but a function of membership in the Canadian polity that cannot lightly be cast aside. This is manifestly true of the right to vote, the cornerstone of democracy, exempt from the incursion permitted on other rights through s. 33 override. Thus, courts considering denials of voting rights have applied a stringent justification standard: *Sauvé v. Canada (Attorney General)* (1992), 7 O.R. (3d) 481 (C.A.) ("*Sauvé No. 1*"), and *Belczowski v. Canada*, [1992] 2 F.C. 440 (C.A.).

• • •

[24] The rhetorical nature of the government objectives advanced in this case renders them suspect. The first objective, enhancing civic responsibility and respect for the law, could be asserted of virtually every criminal law and many non-criminal measures. Respect for law is undeniably important. But the simple statement of this value lacks the context necessary to assist us in determining whether the infringement at issue is demonstrably justifiable in a free and democratic society. To establish justification, one needs to know what problem the government is targeting, and why it is so pressing and important that it warrants limiting a *Charter* right. Without this, it is difficult if not impossible to weigh whether the infringement of the right is justifiable or proportionate.

[25] The second objective—to impose additional punishment on people serving penitentiary sentences—is less vague than the first. Still, problems with vagueness remain. The record does not disclose precisely why Parliament felt that more punishment was required for this particular class of prisoner, or what additional objectives Parliament hoped to achieve by this punishment that were not accomplished by the sentences already imposed. This makes it difficult to assess whether the objective is important enough to justify an additional rights infringement.

[26] Quite simply, the government has failed to identify particular problems that require denying the right to vote, making it hard to say that the denial is directed at a

pressing and substantial purpose. Nevertheless, despite the abstract nature of the government's objectives and the rather thin basis upon which they rest, prudence suggests that we proceed to the proportionality analysis, rather than dismissing the government's objectives outright. The proportionality inquiry allows us to determine whether the government's asserted objectives are in fact capable of justifying its denial of the right to vote. At that stage, as we shall see, the difficulties inherent in the government's stated objectives become manifest.

· · ·

[43] The idea that certain classes of people are not morally fit or morally worthy to vote and to participate in the law-making process is ancient and obsolete. Edward III pronounced that citizens who committed serious crimes suffered "civil death," by which a convicted felon was deemed to forfeit all civil rights. Until recently, large classes of people, prisoners among them, were excluded from the franchise. The assumption that they were not fit or "worthy" of voting—whether by reason of class, race, gender or conduct—played a large role in this exclusion. We should reject the retrograde notion that "worthiness" qualifications for voters may be logically viewed as enhancing the political process and respect for the rule of law. As Arbour J.A. stated in *Sauvé No. 1*, *supra*, at p. 487, since the adoption of s. 3 of the *Charter*, it is doubtful "that anyone could now be deprived of the vote on the basis ... that he or she was not decent or responsible."

[44] Denial of the right to vote on the basis of attributed moral unworthiness is inconsistent with the respect for the dignity of every person that lies at the heart of Canadian democracy and the *Charter*: compare *August*, *supra*. It also runs counter to the plain words of s. 3, its exclusion from the s. 33 override, and the idea that laws command obedience because they are made by those whose conduct they govern. For all these reasons, it must, at this stage of our history, be rejected.

[45] This brings us to the government's final argument for rational connection—that disenfranchisement is a legitimate weapon in the state's punitive arsenal against the individual lawbreaker. Again, the argument cannot succeed. The first reason is that using the denial of rights as punishment is suspect. The second reason is that denying the right to vote does not comply with the requirements for legitimate punishment established by our jurisprudence.

[46] The argument, stripped of rhetoric, proposes that it is open to Parliament to add a new tool to its arsenal of punitive implements—denial of constitutional rights. I find this notion problematic. I do not doubt that Parliament may limit constitutional rights in the name of punishment, provided that it can justify the limitation. But it is another thing to say that a particular class of people for a particular period of time will completely lose a particular constitutional right. This is tantamount to saying that the affected class is outside the full protection of the *Charter*. It is doubtful that such an unmodulated deprivation, particularly of a right as basic as the right to vote, is capable of justification under s. 1. Could Parliament justifiably pass a law removing the right of all penitentiary prisoners to be protected from cruel and unusual punishment? I think not. What of freedom of expression or religion? Why, one asks, is the right to vote different? The government offers no credible theory about why it should be allowed to deny this fundamental democratic right as a form of state punishment.

· · ·

[52] When the facade of rhetoric is stripped away, little is left of the government's claim about punishment other than that criminals are people who have broken society's norms and may therefore be denounced and punished as the government sees fit, even to the point of removing fundamental constitutional rights. Yet, the right to punish and to denounce, however important, is constitutionally constrained. It cannot be used to write entire rights out of the Constitution, it cannot be arbitrary, and it must serve the constitutionally recognized goals of sentencing. On all counts, the case that s. 51(e) furthers lawful punishment objectives fails.

• • •

D. The Guarantee of Equality under Section 15(1) of the Charter

[63] Having found that s. 51(e) unjustifiably infringes s. 3 of the *Charter*, it is unnecessary to consider the alternative argument that it infringes the equality guarantee of s. 15(1).

GONTHIER J (L'Heureux-Dubé, Major, and Bastarache JJ concurring) (dissenting):

• • •

[71] A further dimension of this qualitative difference is that serious criminal offenders are excluded from the vote for the reason that they are the *subjects of punishment*. The disenfranchisement only lasts as long as the period of incarceration. Thus, disenfranchisement, as a dimension of punishment, is attached to and mirrors the fact of incarceration. This fact makes the Canadian experience significantly different from the situation in some American states which disenfranchise ex-offenders for life, a situation addressed by many American academics: see, for example, L. H. Tribe, "The Disenfranchisement of Ex-Felons: Citizenship, Criminality, and 'The Purity of the Ballot Box'" (1989), 102 Harv. L. Rev. 1300.

[72] It is important to look at prisoner disenfranchisement from the perspective of each serious criminal offender rather than perceive it as a form of targeted group treatment. Disenfranchised prisoners can be characterized loosely as a group, but what is important to realize is that each of these prisoners has been convicted of a serious criminal offence and is therefore serving a personalized sentence which is proportionate to the act or acts committed. Punishment is guided by the goals of denunciation, deterrence, rehabilitation and retribution and is intended to be morally educative for incarcerated serious criminal offenders. Each prisoner's sentence is a temporary measure aimed at meeting these goals, while also being aimed at the long-term objective of reintegration into the community.

• • •

[75] The argument that the temporary disenfranchisement of serious criminal offenders undermines the inherent "worth" or "dignity" of prisoners presents a potentially problematic line of reasoning. Is it possible to "punish" serious criminals without undermining their "worth"? It must be so. This is inherently recognized in the *Charter* itself insofar that s. 12 only renders unconstitutional punishment that is "cruel and unusual." The *Criminal Code* and its provisions are declaratory of values, values on which Canadian society rests: see *R. v. Keegstra*, [1990] 3 S.C.R. 697, at pp. 769 and 787. Protecting and enhancing these values through the imposition of punishment for criminal activity is not an affront to dignity. On the contrary, the temporary disenfranchisement of serious criminal offenders

reiterates society's commitment to the basic moral values which underpin the *Criminal Code*; in this way it is morally educative for both prisoners and society as a whole.

[76] The punishment of serious criminal offenders is also aimed at protecting society and the "dignity" and "worth" of those members of society who have been or may become the victims of crime. Punishment is intended to act as a general deterrent to potential criminals and as a specific deterrent *vis-à-vis* incarcerated persons. *Charter* analysis is meant to consider the *Charter* rights of other members of society: see *R. v. Sharpe*, [2001] 1 S.C.R. 45, 2001 SCC 2, at para. 187; *Keegstra, supra*, at p. 756. Serious criminal activity is clearly often an affront to numerous *Charter* values.

III. SECTION 12: CRUEL AND UNUSUAL TREATMENT OR PUNISHMENT

The historical guarantee against "cruel and unusual" punishment is enshrined in s 12 of the Charter and it is central to the relationship between the state and punishment. The gravest and most egregious examples of punishment in Canada were repealed prior to the constitutional entrenchment of s 12—whipping in 1972, and capital punishment in 1976. The phrase "cruel and unusual" has been *interpreted* as a "compendious expression of a norm." You will have noted reference to it earlier in this book in the context of mandatory minimum sentences, the most common place for its application: see e.g. Chapter 4, Facts of the Offence for Sentencing; Chapter 11, Imprisonment. Although this issue has received much judicial attention, the scope of its application has been limited. The test for determining a s 12 violation was articulated in the seminal case of *Smith*, below, and has not been developed or refined since. It has been expressed as follows:

> The test for whether a particular sentence constitutes cruel and unusual punishment is whether the sentence is grossly disproportionate … . As this Court has repeatedly held, to be considered grossly disproportionate, the sentence must be more than merely excessive. The sentence must be "so excessive as to outrage standards of decency" and disproportionate to the extent that Canadians "would find the punishment abhorrent or intolerable."

See *R v Ferguson*, 2008 SCC 6 at para 14.

As a result of this threshold, few cases have succeeded. This is partly due to the distraction of the Supreme Court by methodological questions, discussed below.

R v Smith (Edward Dewey)
[1987] 1 SCR 1045, 34 CCC (3d) 97

LAMER J (Dickson CJ, Wilson, Le Dain, and La Forest JJ concurring):

In measuring the content of the legislation, the courts are to look to the purpose and effect of the legislation. Dickson J, as he then was, in *R v. Big M Drug Mart Ltd.* (1985), 18 CCC (3d) 385 at p. 414, 18 DLR (4th) 321 at p. 350, [1985] 1 SCR 295, at p. 331, speaking for the majority of this court, stated: "In my view, both purpose and effect are relevant in determining constitutionality; either an unconstitutional purpose or an unconstitutional effect can invalidate legislation." And further, at pp. 415-6 CCC, pp. 351-2 DLR, p. 334 SCR:

I agree with the respondent that the legislation's purpose is the initial test of constitutional validity and its effects are to be considered when the law under review has passed or, at least, has purportedly passed the purpose test. ...

Thus, if a law with a valid purpose interferes by its impact, with rights or freedoms, a litigant could still argue the effects of the legislation as a means to defeat its applicability and possibly its validity. In short, the effects test will only be necessary to defeat legislation with a valid purpose; effects can never be relied upon to save legislation with an invalid purpose.

Thus, even though the pursuit of a constitutionally invalid purpose will result in the invalidity of the impugned legislation irrespective of its effects, a valid purpose does not end the constitutional inquiry. The means chosen by Parliament to achieve that valid purpose may result in effects which deprive Canadians of their rights guaranteed under the Charter. In such a case it would then be incumbent upon the authorities to demonstrate under s. 1 that the importance of that valid purpose is such that, irrespective of the effect of the legislation, it is a reasonable limit in a free and democratic society.

The undisputed fact that the purpose of s. 5(2) of the *Narcotic Control Act* is constitutionally valid is not a bar to an analysis of s. 5(2) in order to determine if the minimum has the effect of obliging the judge in certain cases to impose a cruel and unusual punishment, and thereby is a prima facie violation of s. 12; and, if it is, to then reconsider under s. 1 that purpose and any other considerations relevant to determining whether the impugned legislation may be salvaged.

The Meaning of Section 12

It is generally accepted in a society such as ours that the State has the power to impose a "treatment or punishment" on an individual where it is necessary to do so to attain some legitimate end and where the requisite procedure has been followed. The Charter limits this power: s. 7 provides that everyone has the right not to be deprived of life, liberty and security of the person except in accordance with the principles of fundamental justice, s. 9 provides that everyone has the right not to be arbitrarily detained or imprisoned, and s. 12 guarantees the right not to be subjected to any cruel and unusual treatment or punishment.

The limitation at issue here is s. 12 of the Charter. In my view, the protection afforded by s. 12 governs the quality of the punishment and is concerned with the effect that the punishment may have on the person on whom it is imposed. I would agree with Laskin CJC in *Miller and Cockriell* [[1977] 2 SCR 680, 70 DLR (3d) 324, 31 CCC (2d) 177], where he defined the phrase "cruel and unusual" as a "compendious expression of a norm." The criterion which must be applied in order to determine whether a punishment is cruel and unusual within the meaning of s. 12 of the Charter is, to use the words of Laskin CJC in *Miller and Cockriell, supra*, at p. 183 CCC, p. 330 DLR, p. 688 SCR, "whether the punishment prescribed is so excessive as to outrage standards of decency." In other words, though the State may impose punishment, the effect of that punishment must not be grossly disproportionate to what would have been appropriate.

In imposing a sentence of imprisonment the judge will assess the circumstances of the case in order to arrive at an appropriate sentence. The test for review under s. 12 of the Charter is one of gross disproportionality, because it is aimed at punishments that are more than merely excessive. We should be careful not to stigmatize every disproportionate or excessive sentence as being a constitutional violation, and should leave to the usual sentencing appeal process the task of reviewing the fitness of a sentence. Section 12 will only be infringed where the sentence is so unfit having regard to the offence and the offender as to be grossly disproportionate.

In assessing whether a sentence is grossly disproportionate, the court must first consider the gravity of the offence, the personal characteristics of the offender and the particular circumstances of the case in order to determine what range of sentences would have been appropriate to punish, rehabilitate or deter this particular offender or to protect the public from this particular offender. The other purposes which may be pursued by the imposition of punishment, in particular the deterrence of other potential offenders, are thus not relevant at this stage of the inquiry. This does not mean that the judge or the legislator can no longer consider general deterrence or other penological purposes that go beyond the particular offender in determining a sentence, but only that the resulting sentence must not be grossly disproportionate to what the offender deserves. If a grossly disproportionate sentence is "prescribed by law," then the purpose which it seeks to attain will fall to be assessed under s. 1. Section 12 ensures that individual offenders receive punishments that are appropriate, or at least not grossly disproportionate, to their particular circumstances, while s. 1 permits this right to be overridden to achieve some important societal objective.

One must also measure the effect of the sentence actually imposed. If it is grossly disproportionate to what would have been appropriate, then it infringes s. 12. The effect of the sentence is often a composite of many factors and is not limited to the quantum or duration of the sentence but includes its nature and the conditions under which it is applied. Sometimes by its length alone or by its very nature will the sentence be grossly disproportionate to the purpose sought. Sometimes it will be the result of the combination of factors which, when considered in isolation, would not in and of themselves amount to gross disproportionality. For example, 20 years for a first offence against property would be grossly disproportionate, but so would three months of imprisonment if the prison authorities decide it should be served in solitary confinement. Finally, I should add that some punishments or treatments will always be grossly disproportionate and will always outrage our standards of decency: for example, the infliction of corporal punishment, such as the lash, irrespective of the number of lashes imposed, or, to give examples of treatment, the lobotomisation of certain dangerous offenders or the castration of sexual offenders.

The numerous criteria proposed pursuant to s. 2(b) of the *Canadian Bill of Rights* and the Eighth Amendment of the American Constitution are, in my opinion, useful as factors to determine whether a violation of s. 12 has occurred. Thus, to refer to tests listed by Professor Tarnopolsky, the determination of whether the punishment is necessary to achieve a valid penal purpose, whether it is founded on recognized sentencing principles, and whether there exist valid alternatives to the punishment imposed, are all guidelines which, without being determinative in themselves, help to assess whether the punishment is grossly disproportionate.

There is a further aspect of proportionality which has been considered on occasion by the American courts: a comparison with punishments imposed for other crimes in the same jurisdiction: see *Solem v. Helm* (1983), 463 US 277 at p. 291. Of course, the simple fact that penalties for similar offences are divergent does not necessarily mean that the greater penalty is grossly disproportionate and thus cruel and unusual. At most, the divergence in penalties is an indication that the greater penalty may be excessive, but it will remain necessary to assess the penalty in accordance with the factors discussed above. The notion that there must be a gradation of punishments according to the malignity of offences may be considered to be a principle of fundamental justice under s. 7, but, given my decision under s. 12, I do not find it necessary to deal with that issue here.

• • •

This is what offends s. 12, the certainty, not just the potential. Absent the minimum, the section still has the potential of operating so as to impose cruel and unusual punishment. But that would only occur if and when a judge chose to impose, let us say, seven years or more on the "small offender." Remedy will then flow from s. 24. It is the judge's sentence, but not the section, that is in violation of the Charter. However, the effect of the minimum is to insert the certainty that, in some cases, as of conviction the violation will occur. It is this aspect of certainty that makes the section itself a *prima facie* violation of s. 12, and the minimum must, subject to s. 1, be declared of no force or effect.

• • •

This then brings us to the next phase of the test, the proportionality of the means chosen to reach that "important" result. Of course, the means chosen do "achieve the objective in question." The certainty that all those who contravene the prohibition against importing will be sentenced to at least seven years in prison will surely deter people from importing narcotics. Therefore, rationality, the first prong of the proportionality test, has been met. But the Crown's justification fails the second prong, namely minimum impairment of the rights protected by s. 12. Clearly there is no need to be indiscriminate. We do not need to sentence the small offenders to seven years in prison in order to deter the serious offender. Indeed, the net cast by s. 5(2) for sentencing purposes need not be so wide as that cast by s. 5(1) for conviction purposes. The result sought could be achieved by limiting the imposition of a minimum sentence to the importing of certain quantities, to certain specific narcotics of the schedule, to repeat offenders, or even to a combination of these factors. But the wording of the section and the schedule is much broader. I should add that, in my view, the minimum sentence also creates some problems. In particular, it inserts into the system a reluctance to convict and thus results in acquittals for picayune reasons of accused who do not deserve a seven-year sentence, and it gives the Crown an unfair advantage in plea bargaining as an accused will be more likely to plead guilty to a lesser or included offence. For these reasons, the minimum imprisonment provided for by s. 5(2) breaches s. 12 of the Charter and this breach has not been justified under s. 1

NOTE

After *Smith*, the death penalty raised its head in *United States v Burns*, 2001 SCC 7, [2001] 1 SCR 283, in the context of an extradition application by an American jurisdiction in which two young Canadians would face the death penalty if convicted. In a unanimous judgment, relying on the combined effect of ss 7 and 12 of the Charter, the Supreme Court required the minister to seek an assurance prior to extradition that the accused would not face the death penalty if convicted. Coming a mere hair from declaring capital punishment "cruel and unusual," the court concluded that "such assurances are constitutionally required in all but exceptional cases." In the course of the judgment, the court considered the scope of s 12 and remarked:

[68] Use of the "shocks the conscience" terminology was intended to convey the exceptional weight of a factor such as the youth, insanity, mental retardation or pregnancy of a fugitive which, because of its paramount importance, may control the outcome of the *Kindler*
[*Kindler v Canada (Minister of Justice)*, [1991] 2 SCR 779] balancing test on the facts of a particular
case. The terminology should not be allowed to obscure the ultimate assessment that is
required: namely whether or not the extradition is in accordance with the principles of fundamental justice. The rule is not that departures from fundamental justice are to be tolerated
unless in a particular case it shocks the conscience. An extradition that violates the principles of
fundamental justice will *always* shock the conscience. The important inquiry is to determine
what constitutes the applicable principles of fundamental justice in the extradition context.

[69] The "shocks the conscience" language signals the possibility that even though the
rights of the fugitive are to be considered in the context of other applicable principles of fundamental justice, which are normally of sufficient importance to uphold the extradition, a particular treatment or punishment may sufficiently violate our sense of fundamental justice as to tilt
the balance against extradition. Examples might include stoning to death individuals taken in
adultery, or lopping off the hands of a thief. The punishment is so extreme that it becomes the
controlling issue in the extradition and overwhelms the rest of the analysis.

Looking back at *Smith*, we must note the dissent of McIntyre J, which argued that only the
circumstances of the offender and offence before the court should be evaluated for s 12
purposes. The judges in the majority, however, held that, just as nobody should be convicted under a penal provision that would be unconstitutional in another case, nobody
should be sentenced by a mandatory provision that would be unconstitutional in another
case. Lamer J (as he then was) focused on the "certainty" that a small offender would *be
caught by the offence and subjected to a minimum penalty*. This might be referred to as a
"scope of culpability" approach. McIntyre J, however, characterized it as a "reasonable hypothetical" approach.

Subsequently, s 12 cases did not build on the various *Smith* opinions, but concentrated
on methodological issues to the detriment of the potential richness of the "cruel and
unusual" standard. First, we saw the Supreme Court of Canada attempt to define the scope
of "reasonable hypotheticals." In *R v Goltz*, [1991] 3 SCR 485, Gonthier J, for the majority, held
that reasonable hypotheticals are " imaginable circumstances which could commonly arise
in day-to-day life." In *R v Morrisey*, 2000 SCC 39, [2000] 2 SCR 90, Gonthier J, again for the
majority, found that even reported cases might not qualify as sufficiently common. For a full
discussion of the methodological issue, see Allan Manson, "Arbitrary Disproportionality: A
New Charter Standard for Measuring the Constitutionality of Mandatory Minimum Sentences" (2012) 57 SCLR (2d) 173. This evolution may have reached a more useful end with the
analysis in *Nur*, immediately below.

R v Nur

2015 SCC 15, [2015] 1 SCR 773 (footnotes omitted)

[Two cases, *Nur* and *Charles*, came together to the Supreme Court. Both involved firearms conviction under s 95(1) of the Code and the mandatory sentencing scheme in s 95(2):

95(2) Every person who commits an offence under subsection (1)

   (a) is guilty of an indictable offence and liable to imprisonment for a term not exceeding 10 years and to a minimum punishment of imprisonment for a term of

      (i) in the case of a first offence, three years, and

      (ii) in the case of a second or subsequent offence, five years; or

   (b) is guilty of an offence punishable on summary conviction and liable to imprisonment for a term not exceeding one year.]

McLACHLIN CJ (LeBel, Abella, Cromwell, Karakatsanis, and Gascon JJ concurring):

[39] This Court has set a high bar for what constitutes "cruel and unusual ... punishment" under s. 12 of the *Charter*. A sentence attacked on this ground must be grossly disproportionate to the punishment that is appropriate, having regard to the nature of the offence and the circumstances of the offender: *R. v. Smith*, [1987] 1 S.C.R. 1045, at p. 1073. Lamer J. (as he then was) explained at p. 1072 that the test of gross disproportionality "is aimed at punishments that are more than merely excessive." He added, "[w]e should be careful not to stigmatize every disproportionate or excessive sentence as being a constitutional violation." A prescribed sentence may be grossly disproportionate as applied to the offender before the court or because it would have a grossly disproportionate impact on others, rendering the law unconstitutional.

• • •

[44] Mandatory minimum sentences, by their very nature, have the potential to depart from the principle of proportionality in sentencing. They emphasize denunciation, general deterrence and retribution at the expense of what is a fit sentence for the gravity of the offence, the blameworthiness of the offender, and the harm caused by the crime. They function as a blunt instrument that may deprive courts of the ability to tailor proportionate sentences at the lower end of a sentencing range. They may, in extreme cases, impose unjust sentences, because they shift the focus from the offender during the sentencing process in a way that violates the principle of proportionality. They modify the general process of sentencing which relies on the review of all relevant factors in order to reach a proportionate result. They affect the outcome of the sentence by changing the normal judicial process of sentencing.

[45] General deterrence—using sentencing to send a message to discourage others from offending—is relevant. But it cannot, without more, sanitize a sentence against gross disproportionality: "General deterrence can support a sentence which is more severe while still within the range of punishments that are not cruel and unusual" (*R. v. Morrisey*, 2000 SCC 39, [2000] 2 S.C.R. 90, at para. 45, per Gonthier J.). Put simply, a person cannot be made to suffer a grossly disproportionate punishment simply to send a message to discourage others from offending.

[46] To recap, a challenge to a mandatory minimum sentencing provision on the ground it constitutes cruel and unusual punishment under s. 12 of the *Charter* involves

two steps. First, the court must determine what constitutes a proportionate sentence for the offence having regard to the objectives and principles of sentencing in the *Criminal Code*. Then, the court must ask whether the mandatory minimum requires the judge to impose a sentence that is grossly disproportionate to the fit and proportionate sentence. If the answer is yes, the mandatory minimum provision is inconsistent with s. 12 and will fall unless justified under s. 1 of the *Charter*.

• • •

[49] For the reasons that follow, I conclude that excluding consideration of reasonably foreseeable applications of a mandatory minimum sentencing law would run counter to the settled authority of this Court and artificially constrain the inquiry into the law's constitutionality.

[50] To confine consideration to the offender's situation runs counter to the long and settled jurisprudence of this Court relating to *Charter* review generally, and to s. 12 review in particular.

• • •

[56] These are the only three cases to directly address the question of what cases, or "hypotheticals," the court should consider on a s. 12 challenge to a mandatory minimum sentencing provision. In my view, they do not establish that the jurisprudence is "irreconcilable." A single theme underlies *Goltz* and *Morrisey*—the only two cases to discuss the issue in detail—reasonable foreseeability. When Gonthier J. in *Goltz* speaks of the "reasonable hypothetical" he is speaking of *a situation that may reasonably be expected to arise*—not "marginally imaginable," not "far-fetched," but "reasonable." The early case of *Smith* is not inconsistent in words or result with the theme developed in *Goltz* and *Morrisey*—in determining whether mandatory minimum sentencing laws violate s. 12, it is appropriate to consider how the law may impact on third parties in reasonably foreseeable situations.

[57] Unfortunately, the word "hypothetical" has overwhelmed the word "reasonable" in the intervening years, leading to debate on how general or particular a hypothetical must be, and to the unfortunate suggestion that if a trial judge fails to assign a particular concatenation of characteristics to her hypothetical, the analysis is vitiated. With respect, this overcomplicates the matter. The question is simply whether it is reasonably foreseeable that the mandatory minimum sentence will impose sentences that are grossly disproportionate to some peoples' situations, resulting in a violation of s. 12. The terminology of "reasonable hypothetical" may be helpful in this regard, but the focus remains squarely on whether the sentence would be grossly disproportionate in reasonably foreseeable cases. At its core, the process is simply an application of well established principles of legal and constitutional interpretation.

[58] I conclude that the jurisprudence on general *Charter* review and on s. 12 review of mandatory minimum sentencing provisions supports the view that a court may look not only at the offender's situation, but at other reasonably foreseeable situations where the impugned law may apply. I see no reason to overrule this settled principle.

• • •

[63] Not only is looking at the law's impact on persons whom it is reasonably foreseeable the law may catch workable—it is essential to effective constitutional review. Refusing to consider reasonably foreseeable impacts of an impugned law would dramatically curtail the reach of the *Charter* and the ability of the courts to discharge their duty to scrutinize the constitutionality of legislation and maintain the integrity of the constitutional order.

The protection of individuals' rights demands constitutional review that looks not only to the situation of the offender before the court, but beyond that to the reasonably foreseeable reach of the law. Testing the law against reasonably foreseeable applications will prevent people from suffering cruel and unusual punishment in the interim until the mandatory minimum is found to be unconstitutional in a particular case.

[64] Refusing to consider an impugned law's impact on third parties would also undermine the prospect of bringing certainty to the constitutionality of legislation, condemning constitutional jurisprudence to a wilderness of single instances. Citizens, the police and government are entitled—and indeed obliged—to know what the criminal law is and whether it is constitutional. Looking at whether the mandatory minimum has an unconstitutional impact on others avoids the chilling effect of unconstitutional laws remaining on the statute books.

[65] I conclude that a mandatory minimum sentence may be challenged on the ground that it would impose a grossly disproportionate sentence either on the offender or on other persons in reasonably foreseeable situations. The constant jurisprudence of this Court and effective constitutional review demand no less. In the result, a mandatory minimum sentencing provision may be challenged on the basis that it imposes cruel and unusual punishment (i.e. a grossly disproportionate sentence) on the particular offender before the court, or failing this, on the basis that it is reasonably foreseeable that it will impose cruel and unusual punishment on other persons.

. . .

[68] The reasonable foreseeability test is not confined to situations that are likely to arise in the general day-to-day application of the law. Rather, it asks what situations may reasonably arise. It targets circumstances that are foreseeably captured by the minimum conduct caught by the offence. Only situations that are "remote" or "far-fetched" are excluded: *Goltz*, at p. 515. Contrary to what the Attorney General of Ontario suggests there is a difference between what is foreseeable although "unlikely to arise" and what is "remote [and] far-fetched" (A.F. (*Nur*), at para. 66). Moreover, adoption of the likelihood standard would constitute a new and radically narrower approach to constitutional review of legislation than that consistently adhered to since *Big M*. The Court has never asked itself whether a projected application of an impugned law is common or "likely" in deciding whether a law violates a provision of the *Charter*. To set the threshold for constitutional review at common or likely instances would be to allow bad laws to stay on the books.

. . .

[71] This brings us to the second ancillary question—the effect of a ruling that a particular mandatory minimum provision does not violate s. 12. Two questions arise. First, can a particular offender argue in a future case that the provision violates s. 12 because it imposes cruel and unusual punishment on him or her? The answer, all agree, must be yes. If the offender can establish new circumstances or evidence, including mitigating factors specific to the offender, it is open to a court to reconsider the constitutionality of the law. Second, can the offender in a future case argue that the provision as applied to others violates s. 12? The answer to this question is that it depends. Once a law is held not to violate s. 12, *stare decisis* prevents an offender in a later case from simply rearguing what constitutes a reasonably foreseeable range of the law. But *stare decisis* does not prevent a court from looking at different circumstances and new evidence that was not considered in the preceding case. A court's conclusion based on its review of the provision's reasonably

foreseeable applications does not foreclose consideration in future of different reasonable applications (*Morrisey*, at para. 89, per Arbour J.). That said, the threshold for revisiting the constitutionality of a mandatory minimum is high and requires a significant change in the reasonably foreseeable applications of the law. In a nutshell, the normal rules of *stare decisis* answer the concern raised by the Attorney General of Ontario that "each subsequent trial court [will be asked] to duplicate the analysis" (A.F. (*Nur*), at para. 39).

· · ·

[73]   A fourth ancillary question concerns the personal characteristics of hypothetical offenders that should be considered. Some have suggested that the consideration must be generalized to the point where all personal characteristics are excluded, while others assert that any and all characteristics should be included. This debate is largely the result of the reification of the notion of the reasonable hypothetical discussed earlier. It is answered by recognizing two aspects of the reasonably foreseeable application test.

[74]   First, what is reasonably foreseeable necessarily requires consideration of the sort of situations that may reasonably be expected to be caught by the mandatory minimum, based on experience and common sense. This means that personal characteristics cannot be entirely excluded. For example, as we will see in applying the test to this case, it may be relevant to look at the fact that an offender at the licensing end of the spectrum caught by the mandatory minimum might come into innocent possession of the prohibited or restricted firearm, or be mistaken as to the scope of the prohibition.

[75]   Second, cutting the other way, is the admonition of *Goltz* that far-fetched or remotely imaginable examples should be excluded from consideration. This excludes using personal features to construct the most innocent and sympathetic case imaginable—on that basis almost any mandatory minimum could be argued to violate s. 12 and lawyerly ingenuity would be the only limit to findings of unconstitutionality. To repeat, the inquiry must be grounded in common sense and experience.

[76]   Thus, the inquiry into reasonably foreseeable situations the law may capture may take into account personal characteristics relevant to people who may be caught by the mandatory minimum, but must avoid characteristics that would produce remote or far-fetched examples.

[77]   In summary, when a mandatory minimum sentencing provision is challenged, two questions arise. The first is whether the provision results in a grossly disproportionate sentence on the individual before the court. If the answer is no, the second question is whether the provision's reasonably foreseeable applications will impose grossly disproportionate sentences on others. This is consistent with the settled jurisprudence on constitutional review and rules of constitutional interpretation, which seek to determine the potential reach of a law; is workable; and provides sufficient certainty.

· · ·

[82]   Section 95(1) casts its net over a wide range of potential conduct. Most cases within the range may well merit a sentence of three years or more, but conduct at the far end of the range may not. At one end of the range, as Doherty J.A. observed, "stands the outlaw who carries a loaded prohibited or restricted firearm in public places as a tool of his or her criminal trade. … [T]his person is engaged in truly criminal conduct and poses a real and immediate danger to the public" (para. 51). At this end of the range—indeed for the vast majority of offences—a three-year sentence may be appropriate. A little further

along the spectrum stands the person whose conduct is less serious and poses less danger; for these offenders three years' imprisonment may be disproportionate, but not grossly so. At the far end of the range, stands the licensed and responsible gun owner who stores his unloaded firearm safely with ammunition nearby, but makes a mistake as to where it can be stored. For this offender, a three-year sentence is grossly disproportionate to the sentence the conduct would otherwise merit under the sentencing provisions of the *Criminal Code*.

[83] Given the minimal blameworthiness of the offender in this situation and the absence of any harm or real risk of harm flowing from the conduct (i.e. having the gun in one residence as opposed to another), a three-year sentence would be grossly disproportionate. Similar examples can be envisaged. A person inherits a firearm and before she can apprise herself of the licence requirements commits an offence. A spouse finds herself in possession of her husband's firearm and breaches the regulation. We need not focus on a particular hypothetical. The bottom line is that s. 95(1) foreseeably catches licensing offences which involve little or no moral fault and little or no danger to the public. For these offences three years' imprisonment is grossly disproportionate to a fit and fair sentence. Firearms are inherently dangerous and the state is entitled to use sanctions to signal its disapproval of careless practices and to discourage gun owners from making mistakes, to be sure. But a three-year term of imprisonment for a person who has essentially committed a licensing infraction is totally out of sync with the norms of criminal sentencing set out in the s. 718 of the *Criminal Code* and legitimate expectations in a free and democratic society. As the Court of Appeal concluded, there exists a "cavernous disconnect" between the severity of the licensing-type offence and the mandatory minimum three-year term of imprisonment (para. 176). Consequently, I conclude that s. 95(2)(a)(i) breaches s. 12 of the *Charter*.

• • •

[103] I agree that the Court of Appeal erred in concluding that it was reasonably foreseeable that a repeat offender could be a licensed owner of a prohibited or restricted firearm. This does not end the analysis, however. The court must test the reasonably foreseeable applications of s. 95(2)(a)(ii). Under the impugned mandatory minimum, a five-year term of imprisonment could be imposed on an individual who breached a prohibition order imposed while on bail and who, some years later, innocently came into possession of a restricted or prohibited firearm without an authorization or a licence together with usable ammunition that he stored nearby and which was readily accessible.

[104] A five-year minimum term of imprisonment for offenders such as these would be draconian. It goes far beyond what is necessary in order to protect the public, far beyond what is necessary to express moral condemnation of the offender, and far beyond what is necessary to discourage others from engaging in such conduct. In a phrase, such a sentence would be grossly disproportionate. An offender in these circumstances has not caused any harm, nor is there a real risk of harm to the public. Such an offender is not engaged in any criminal activity.

[105] There is little doubt that in many cases those who commit second or subsequent offences for the purpose of s. 95(2)(a)(ii) should be sentenced to terms of imprisonment, and some for lengthy terms of imprisonment. The seven-year term of imprisonment imposed on Charles is an example. But the five-year minimum term of imprisonment would be grossly disproportionate for less serious offenders captured by the provision.

[106] It follows that s. 95(2)(a)(ii) violates the guarantee against grossly disproportionate punishment in s. 12 of the *Charter*.

• • •

[119] I would dismiss the appeals. The mandatory minimum sentences imposed by s. 95(2)(a) are inconsistent with s. 12 of the *Charter* and are therefore declared of no force or effect under s. 52 of the *Constitution Act, 1982.*

[120] It remains appropriate for judges to continue to impose weighty sentences in other circumstances, such as those in the cases at bar. For this reason, I would decline to interfere with the sentences.

Although the majority refined "reasonable hypothetical" into a "reasonable foreseeable" standard, in essence it used a "scope of culpability" approach by recognizing that the offence encompassed a licensing mode that is almost a regulatory offence. In this respect, the gross disproportionality conclusion was, perhaps, easy. How this will play out in future mandatory minimum cases is difficult to predict.

Recently, two more difficult cases involving mandatory minimum sentences under the *Controlled Drugs and Substances Act*, SC 1996, c 19, as amended [CDSA] came before Canadian courts. In *R v Vu*, 2015 ONSC 7965, Justice Durno dealt with the constitutionality of the mandatory minimum for cultivation of marijuana in s 7(2)(b) of the CDSA, which is based on the number of plants found. Using the reasonable hypothetical of a culpable "gardener" who was mistaken as to the number of plants, Durno J found a violation of s 12.

In *R v Lloyd*, 2014 BCPC 8, Galati Prov Ct J found s 5(3)(a)(i) unconstitutional, using as a reasonable hypothetical the situation of a heroin addict who gives a small amount of heroin to his partner, also an addict. The Crown appeal to the BC Court of Appeal was allowed on the combined basis of standing and the inability of a provincial judge to issue a declaration of invalidity. On further appeal to the Supreme Court of Canada, the court applied a *Nur* analysis and affirmed the finding of unconstitutionality on s 12 grounds.

R v Lloyd
2016 SCC 13

McLACHLIN CJ (Abella, Cromwell, Moldaver, Karakatsanis, and Côté JJ concurring):

[1] Parliament has the power to proscribe conduct as criminal and determine the punishment for it, and judges have the duty to apply the laws Parliament adopts on punishment to offenders. But individuals are also entitled to receive, and judges have a duty to impose, sentences that are constitutional having regard to the circumstances of each case that comes before them. Sometimes a judge's duty to apply a mandatory minimum sentence provision conflicts with the judge's duty to impose a sentence that does not violate the guarantees of the *Canadian Charter of Rights and Freedoms*. In this appeal, the Court is once again confronted with the problem of how the imposition of a mandatory minimum sentence can be reconciled with the imperative that no person shall be punished in a manner than infringes the *Charter*.

[2] We are asked to decide the constitutionality of a one-year mandatory minimum sentence for a controlled substances offence. I conclude that this provision, while permitting

constitutional sentences in a broad array of cases, will sometimes mandate sentences that violate the constitutional guarantee against cruel and unusual punishment. Insofar as the law requires a one-year sentence of imprisonment, it violates the guarantee against cruel and unusual punishment in s. 12 of the *Charter* and is not justified under s. 1.

[3] As this Court's decision in *R. v. Nur*, 2015 SCC 15, [2015] 1 S.C.R. 773, illustrates, the reality is that mandatory minimum sentences for offences that can be committed in many ways and under many different circumstances by a wide range of people are constitutionally vulnerable because they will almost inevitably catch situations where the prescribed mandatory minimum would require an unconstitutional sentence. One solution is for such laws to narrow their reach, so that they catch only conduct that merits the mandatory minimum sentence. Another option to preserve the constitutionality of offences that cast a wide net is to provide for residual judicial discretion to impose a fit and constitutional sentence in exceptional cases. This approach, widely adopted in other countries, provides a way of resolving the tension between Parliament's right to choose the appropriate range of sentences for an offence, and the constitutional right to be free from cruel and unusual punishment.

• • •

[5] Section 5(3)(a)(i)(D) of the *Controlled Drugs and Substances Act*, S.C. 1996, c. 19 ("*CDSA*"), provides:

> 5(1) No person shall traffic in a substance included in Schedule I, II, III or IV or in any substance represented or held out by that person to be such a substance.
>
> (2) No person shall, for the purpose of trafficking, possess a substance included in Schedule I, II, III or IV.
>
> (3) Every person who contravenes subsection (1) or (2)
>
> (a) subject to paragraph (a.1), if the subject matter of the offence is a substance included in Schedule I or II, is guilty of an indictable offence and liable to imprisonment for life, and
>
> (i) to a minimum punishment of imprisonment for a term of one year if
>
> • • •
>
> (D) the person was convicted of a designated substance offence, or had served a term of imprisonment for a designated substance offence, within the previous 10 years, or

[6] To be subject to the mandatory minimum sentence of one year of imprisonment, an offender must be convicted of trafficking, or of possession for the purpose of trafficking, of either any quantity of a Schedule I substance, such as cocaine, heroin or methamphetamine, or three kilograms or more of a Schedule II substance, namely cannabis: s. 5(3)(a) and (a.1), *CDSA*. The offender must also have been convicted within the previous 10 years of a "designated substance offence," which is defined at s. 2(1) of the *CDSA* as any offence under Part I of the *CDSA* other than simple possession.

• • •

[7] The appellant, Joseph Ryan Lloyd, was a drug addict and dealer in Vancouver's Downtown Eastside. He was addicted to cocaine, methamphetamine and heroin, and sold drugs to support his addiction. He had been convicted of a number of drug-related offences.

[8] On February 8, 2013, Mr. Lloyd was convicted of possession of a Schedule I substance, methamphetamine, for the purpose of trafficking, and sentenced to jail. A

month after his release, he was again arrested and charged with three counts of possession for the purpose of trafficking of a Schedule I drug, namely crack cocaine, methamphetamine, and heroin. The presiding judge, Galati Prov. Ct. J., convicted him on all three counts.

[9] At the sentencing hearing, Mr. Lloyd told the provincial court judge that he trafficked in drugs to support his drug addiction, but that he was taking steps to get help. He acknowledged that the drugs he trafficked in were dangerous and addictive, and that until recently he had given no thought to their effect on the people who purchased them. Because he had been convicted of a similar drug offence shortly before, he was subject to a mandatory minimum sentence of one year of imprisonment, pursuant to s. 5(3)(a)(i)(D) of the *CDSA*. Mr. Lloyd therefore asked for a declaration under s. 24(1) of the *Charter* that the mandatory minimum provision is unconstitutional and of no force or effect because it violates ss. 7, 9 and 12 of the *Charter*.

[10] Galati Prov. Ct. J. acknowledged that lower sentences have occasionally been imposed on repeat offender, addicted traffickers (2014 BCPC 8). In this case, however, he found—without considering the mandatory minimum provision—that the appropriate sentencing range for Mr. Lloyd's offences was 12 to 18 months, and that the appropriate sentence for him was 12 months. He noted that, in spite of this conclusion, Mr. Lloyd had standing to challenge the constitutional validity of the mandatory minimum because of its potential inflationary effect on the appropriate sentencing range. Turning to that issue, Galati Prov. Ct. J. found that the mandatory minimum violates s. 12 of the *Charter* because it would impose cruel and unusual punishment in cases where, for example, an addict possesses a small amount of a Schedule I drug to share with a spouse or a friend. A one-year sentence for such an offender, he held, would be grossly disproportionate to what is justified by the legitimate penological goals and sentencing principles of the *CDSA*, and would be considered abhorrent or intolerable by most Canadians. Galati Prov. Ct. J. rejected the claim that the mandatory minimum sentence also violates ss. 7 and 9 of the *Charter*. He found that the violation of s. 12 was not justified under s. 1 of the *Charter* (2014 BCPC 11), and sentenced Mr. Lloyd to one year of imprisonment.

• • •

[13] Three issues are raised on appeal: (1) Did the provincial court judge have the power to decide the constitutionality of the mandatory minimum sentence? (2) Is the mandatory minimum sentence law at issue unconstitutional? (3) Did the Court of Appeal err in increasing Mr. Lloyd's sentence from 12 months to 18 months?

• • •

[15] The law on this matter is clear. Provincial court judges are not empowered to make formal declarations that a law is of no force or effect under s. 52(1) of the *Constitution Act, 1982*; only superior court judges of inherent jurisdiction and courts with statutory authority possess this power. However, provincial court judges do have the power to determine the constitutionality of a law where it is properly before them. As this Court stated in *R. v. Big M Drug Mart Ltd.*, [1985] 1 S.C.R. 295, at p. 316, "it has always been open to provincial courts to declare legislation invalid in criminal cases. No one may be convicted of an offence under an invalid statute." See also *Cuddy Chicks Ltd. v. Ontario (Labour Relations Board)*, [1991] 2 S.C.R. 5, at pp. 14-17; *Douglas/Kwantlen Faculty Assn. v. Douglas College*, [1990] 3 S.C.R. 570, at p. 592; *Re Shewchuk and Ricard* (1986), 28 D.L.R. (4th) 429 (B.C.C.A.), at pp. 439-40; K. Roach, *Constitutional Remedies in Canada* (2nd ed. (loose-leaf)), at p. 6-25.

[16] Just as no one may be convicted of an offence under an invalid statute, so too may no one be sentenced under an invalid statute. Provincial court judges must have the power to determine the constitutional validity of mandatory minimum provisions when the issue arises in a case they are hearing. This power flows directly from their statutory power to decide the cases before them. The rule of law demands no less.

[17] In my view, the provincial court judge in this case did no more than this. Mr. Lloyd challenged the mandatory minimum that formed part of the sentencing regime that applied to him. As the Court of Appeal found, he was entitled to do so. The provincial court judge was entitled to consider the constitutionality of the mandatory minimum provision. He ultimately concluded that the mandatory minimum sentence was not grossly disproportionate as to Mr. Lloyd. The fact that he used the word "declare" does not convert his conclusion to a formal declaration that the law is of no force or effect under s. 52(1) of the *Constitution Act, 1982*.

[18] To be sure, it does not follow that a provincial court judge is obligated to consider the constitutionality of a mandatory minimum provision where it can have no impact on the sentence in the case at issue. Judicial economy dictates that judges should not squander time and resources on matters they need not decide. But a formalistic approach should be avoided. Thus, once the judge in this case determined that the mandatory minimum did not materially exceed the bottom of the sentencing range applicable to Mr. Lloyd, he could have declined to consider its constitutionality. To put it in legal terms, the doctrine of mootness should be flexibly applied. If an issue arises as to the validity of the law, the provincial court judge has the power to determine it as part of the decision-making process in the case. To compel provincial court judges to conduct an analysis of whether the law could have any impact on an offender's sentence, as a condition precedent to considering the law's constitutional validity, would place artificial constraints on the trial and decision-making process.

[19] The effect of a finding by a provincial court judge that a law does not conform to the Constitution is to permit the judge to refuse to apply it in the case at bar. The finding does not render the law of no force or effect under s. 52(1) of the *Constitution Act, 1982*. It is open to provincial court judges in subsequent cases to decline to apply the law, for reasons already given or for their own; however, the law remains in full force or effect, absent a formal declaration of invalidity by a court of inherent jurisdiction.

[20] I conclude that the provincial court judge in this case had the power to consider the constitutional validity of the challenged sentencing provision in the course of making his decision on the case before him.

. . .

[22] The analytical framework to determine whether a sentence constitutes a "cruel and unusual" punishment under s. 12 of the *Charter* was recently clarified by this Court in *Nur*. A sentence will infringe s. 12 if it is "grossly disproportionate" to the punishment that is appropriate, having regard to the nature of the offence and the circumstances of the offender: *Nur*, at para. 39; *R. v. Smith*, [1987] 1 S.C.R. 1045, at p. 1073. A law will violate s. 12 if it imposes a grossly disproportionate sentence on the individual before the court, or if the law's reasonably foreseeable applications will impose grossly disproportionate sentences on others: *Nur*, at para. 77.

. . .

[24] This Court has established a high bar for finding that a sentence represents a cruel and unusual punishment. To be "grossly disproportionate" a sentence must be more than merely excessive. It must be "so excessive as to outrage standards of decency" and "abhorrent or intolerable" to society: *Smith*, at p. 1072, citing *Miller v. The Queen*, [1977] 2 S.C.R. 680, at p. 688; *Morrisey*, at para. 26; *R. v. Ferguson*, 2008 SCC 6, [2008] 1 S.C.R. 96, at para. 14. The wider the range of conduct and circumstances captured by the mandatory minimum, the more likely it is that the mandatory minimum will apply to offenders for whom the sentence would be grossly disproportionate.

[25] This brings us to the law challenged in this case. Mr. Lloyd concedes that the one-year minimum jail term is not a sentence that is grossly disproportionate as applied to him but only in relation to reasonably foreseeable applications of the law to others. The question before us is therefore: Could a one-year sentence of imprisonment be grossly disproportionate to the offence of possession for the purpose of trafficking a Schedule I substance in reasonably foreseeable cases?

· · ·

[27] The problem with the mandatory minimum sentence provision in this case is that it "casts its net over a wide range of potential conduct": *Nur*, at para. 82. As a result, it catches not only the serious drug trafficking that is its proper aim, but conduct that is much less blameworthy. This renders it constitutionally vulnerable.

[28] Three features of the law make it applicable in a large number of situations, varying greatly in an offender's blameworthiness.

[29] First, it applies to any amount of Schedule I substances. As such, it applies indiscriminately to professional drug dealers who sell dangerous substances for profit and to drug addicts who possess small quantities of drugs that they intend to share with a friend, a spouse, or other addicts.

[30] Second, the definition of "traffic" in the *CDSA* captures a very broad range of conduct. It targets not only people selling drugs, but all who "administer, give, transfer, transport, send or deliver the substance" (s. 2(1)), irrespective of the reason for doing so and regardless of the intent to make a profit. As such, it would catch someone who gives a small amount of a drug to a friend, or someone who is only trafficking to support his own habit.

[31] Third, the minimum sentence applies when there is a prior conviction for any "designated substance offence" within the previous 10 years, which captures any of the offences in ss. 4 to 10 of the *CDSA*, except the offence of simple possession. In addition, the prior conviction can be for any substance, in any amount—even, for example, a small amount of marihuana.

[32] At one end of the range of conduct caught by the mandatory minimum sentence provision stands a professional drug dealer who engages in the business of dangerous drugs for profit, who is in possession of a large amount of Schedule I substances, and who has been convicted many times for similar offences. At the other end of the range stands the addict who is charged for sharing a small amount of a Schedule I drug with a friend or spouse, and finds herself sentenced to a year in prison because of a single conviction for sharing marihuana in a social occasion nine years before. I agree with the provincial court judge that most Canadians would be shocked to find that such a person could be sent to prison for one year.

[33] Another foreseeable situation caught by the law is the following. A drug addict with a prior conviction for trafficking is convicted of a second offence. In both cases, he

was only trafficking in order to support his own addiction. Between conviction and the sentencing he goes to a rehabilitation centre and conquers his addiction. He comes to the sentencing court asking for a short sentence that will allow him to resume a healthy and productive life. Under the law the judge has no choice but to sentence him to a year in prison. Such a sentence would also be grossly disproportionate to what is fit in the circumstances and would shock the conscience of Canadians.

[34] It is argued that the exception to the mandatory minimum sentence provisions at issue in this case cures its constitutional infirmity. The law does not require the court to impose the one-year minimum jail term if, prior to the imposition of sentence, the offender successfully completes an approved drug treatment court program or a treatment program under s. 720(2) of the *Criminal Code*: s. 10(5), *CDSA*. This exception is a step in the right direction. However, it is too narrow to cure the constitutional infirmity. First, it is confined to particular programs, which a particular offender may or may not be able to access. At the time of Mr. Lloyd's sentencing, there was only one approved drug treatment program in Vancouver. Second, to be admissible to these programs, the offender must usually plead guilty and forfeit his right to a trial. One constitutional deprivation cannot cure another. Third, the requirement that the offender successfully complete the program may not be realistic for heavily addicted offenders whose conduct does not merit a year in jail. Finally, in most programs, the Crown has the discretion to disqualify an applicant. As stated in *Nur*, exemptions from minimum sentences based on Crown discretion provide only "illusory" protection against grossly disproportionate punishment: para. 94.

[35] As I have already said, in light of *Nur*, the reality is this: mandatory minimum sentences that, as here, apply to offences that can be committed in various ways, under a broad array of circumstances and by a wide range of people are vulnerable to constitutional challenge. This is because such laws will almost inevitably include an acceptable reasonable hypothetical for which the mandatory minimum will be found unconstitutional. If Parliament hopes to sustain mandatory minimum penalties for offences that cast a wide net, it should consider narrowing their reach so that they only catch offenders that merit the mandatory minimum sentences.

[36] Another solution would be for Parliament to build a safety valve that would allow judges to exempt outliers for whom the mandatory minimum will constitute cruel and unusual punishment. Residual judicial discretion for exceptional cases is a technique widely used to avoid injustice and constitutional infirmity in other countries ... . There is no precise formula and only one requirement—that the residual discretion allow for a lesser sentence where application of the mandatory minimum would result in a sentence that is grossly disproportionate to what is fit and appropriate and would constitute cruel and unusual punishment.

[37] I conclude that the challenged mandatory minimum sentence of one year of imprisonment violates s. 12 of the *Charter*.

(2) Does the Law Violate Section 7 of the Charter?

[38] In view of my conclusion that the law violates s. 12 of the *Charter*, the question of whether it also violates the s. 7 guarantee of liberty need not be addressed. However, it may be useful to comment on the issue, since it has arisen in this and other cases.

[39] Section 7 of the *Charter* provides that no person may be deprived of liberty except in accordance with the principles of fundamental justice. Mr. Lloyd argues that the

principle of proportionality in sentencing—that the judge should impose a fit sentence having regard to all relevant factors—is a principle of fundamental justice under s. 7. The challenged mandatory minimum sentence prevents trial judges from considering all relevant circumstances in sentencing. Therefore, Mr. Lloyd asserts, it violates s. 7.

[40] I am unable to accept the submission that the principle of proportionality in sentencing is a principle of fundamental justice under s. 7 of the *Charter*. My starting point is the observation that principles of fundamental justice in s. 7 must be defined in a way that promotes coherence within the *Charter* and conformity to the respective roles of Parliament and the courts.

[41] I turn first to coherence within the *Charter*. It is necessary to read s. 7 in a way that is consistent with s. 12. Mr. Lloyd's proposal would set a new constitutional standard for sentencing laws—a standard that is lower than the cruel and unusual punishment standard prescribed by s. 12. As McIntyre J. (dissenting on another issue) stated in *Smith*, at p. 1107:

> While section 7 sets out broad and general rights which often extend over the same ground as other rights set out in the *Charter*, it cannot be read so broadly as to render other rights nugatory. If section 7 were found to impose greater restrictions on punishment than s. 12—for example by prohibiting punishments which were merely excessive—it would entirely subsume s. 12 and render it otiose. For this reason, I cannot find that s. 7 raises any rights or issues not already considered under s. 12.

[42] This Court again held that ss. 7 and 12 could not impose a different standard with respect to the proportionality of punishment in *R. v. Malmo-Levine*, 2003 SCC 74, [2003] 3 S.C.R. 571, at para. 160, per Gonthier and Binnie JJ.:

> Is there then a principle of fundamental justice embedded in s. 7 that would give rise to a constitutional remedy against a punishment that does not infringe s. 12? We do not think so. To find that gross and excessive disproportionality of punishment is required under s. 12 but a lesser degree of proportionality suffices under s. 7 would render incoherent the scheme of interconnected "legal rights" set out in ss. 7 to 14 of the *Charter* by attributing contradictory standards to ss. 12 and 7 in relation to the same subject matter. Such a result, in our view, would be unacceptable.

[43] Recognition of the principle of proportionality in sentencing as a principle of fundamental justice under s. 7 would also have implications for the respective roles of Parliament and the courts. The principle of proportionality is an admirable guide for judges seeking to impose fit sentences within the legal parameters established by Parliament. But it is not an overarching constitutional principle that allows judges to subvert the norms of punishment enacted by Parliament. Those norms are judged only by the standard of s. 12.

[44] It has been said that "proportionality in sentencing could aptly be described as a principle of fundamental justice": *R. v. Ipeelee*, 2012 SCC 13, [2012] 1 S.C.R. 433, at para. 36. However, this does not mean that proportionality constitutes a new principle of fundamental justice distinct from the well-established principle of gross disproportionality under s. 7 of the *Charter*.

[45] Parliament has the power to make policy choices with respect to the imposition of punishment for criminal activities and the crafting of sentences that it deems

appropriate to balance the objectives of deterrence, denunciation, rehabilitation and protection of society.

[46] Similarly, in *Lyons*, at pp. 344-45, La Forest J. stressed the importance of the high threshold of s. 12, explaining that the word "grossly" "reflect[ed] this Court's concern not to hold Parliament to a standard so exacting ... as to require punishments to be perfectly suited to accommodate the moral nuances of every crime and every offender."

[47] I conclude that proportionality is not a principle of fundamental justice, and that the challenged mandatory minimum does not violate s. 7 of the *Charter*.

(3) Is the Violation of Section 12 Saved by Section 1 of the Charter?

[48] In my view, the Crown has not made the case that the challenged law's imposition of grossly disproportionate punishment on some people is justified by an overarching objective. It is therefore not a reasonable limit on the s. 12 right.

[49] Parliament's objective—to combat the distribution of illicit drugs—is unquestionably an important objective: *R. v. Oakes*, [1986] 1 S.C.R. 103, at p. 141. This objective is rationally connected to the imposition of a one-year mandatory minimum sentence for the offence of possession for the purpose of trafficking of Schedule I drugs. However, the law does not minimally impair the s. 12 right. As discussed above, the law covers a wide array of situations of varying moral blameworthiness, without differentiation or exemption, save for the single exception in s. 10(5) of the *CDSA*. The Crown has not established that less harmful means to achieve Parliament's objective of combatting the distribution of illicit drugs, whether by narrowing the reach of the law or by providing for judicial discretion in exceptional cases, were not available. Nor has it shown that the impact of the limit on offenders deprived of their rights is proportionate to the good flowing from their inclusion in the law.

[50] I conclude that the violation of the s. 12 right is not justified under s. 1 of the *Charter*.

· · ·

V. Conclusion

[56] The appeal is allowed. Section 5(3)(a)(i)(D) of the *CDSA* is declared to be inconsistent with s. 12 of the *Charter* and not justified under s. 1. It is therefore of no force or effect under s. 52(1) of the *Constitution Act, 1982*. The sentence of the Court of Appeal is set aside and the sentence of one year of imprisonment imposed by the provincial court judge is restored.

NOTE

The decision in *Lloyd* puts to rest any notion that the use of "proportionality" in earlier discussions of s 7 can have any implications for the constitutionality of a sentence. While overbreadth is also an aspect of s 7 analysis, for minimum sentences this is encompassed to a great extent within the scope of the culpability dimension of *Nur*. That is, as applied in *Lloyd*, when an offence "casts its net over a wide range of potential conduct," a mandatory sentence for the lower range of culpability may meet the s 12 test. However, the scope of s 7 also includes issues of arbitrariness. This is another area that may warrant sentencing consideration, especially when there is an argument that no legitimate penological purpose is advanced by a mandatory sentence. For another consideration of s 7, see *R v Safarzadeh-Markhali*, 2014 ONCA 627, below, which was issued the same day as *Lloyd*.

Another methodological issue that developed in the face of the high threshold for s 12 challenges was the use of a constitutional exemption. This was a judicially developed tool, applied only in some provinces, that permitted a sentencing judge to conclude that, although valid, in the vast majority of situations would produce an anomalous "cruel and unusual" impact on the offender before the court. This approach came to the Supreme Court of Canada in *R v Ferguson*, below, and was rejected.

R v Ferguson
2008 SCC 6, [2008] 1 SCR 96

McLACHLIN CJ (Bastarache, Binnie, LeBel, Deschamps, Fish, Abella, Charron, and Rothstein JJ concurring):

[1] This appeal raises two questions. First, does imposition of the four-year mandatory minimum sentence for manslaughter with a firearm constitute cruel and unusual punishment contrary to s. 12 of the *Canadian Charter of Rights and Freedoms* in the circumstances of this case? Second, can an offender who demonstrates that a mandatory minimum sentence would constitute cruel and unusual punishment in his case obtain a stand-alone constitutional exemption from the application of that minimum sentence?

[2] I conclude that the answer to both questions is no. On the facts of this case, the minimum sentence imposed by s. 236(a) of the *Criminal Code*, RSC 1985, c. C-46, is not grossly disproportionate and so does not constitute cruel and unusual punishment in violation of s. 12 of the *Charter*. In any event, a constitutional exemption is not an appropriate remedy for a s. 12 violation. If a minimum sentence is found to be unconstitutional on the facts of a particular case, the law imposing the sentence is inconsistent with the *Charter* and therefore falls under s. 52 of the *Constitution Act, 1982*.

• • •

[12] Constable Ferguson relies instead on Arbour J's concurring remarks in *Morrisey* to the effect that, given the wide range of circumstances under which the offences of unlawful act manslaughter and criminal negligence causing death can be committed, it is not possible to conclude on the basis of a reasonable hypotheticals analysis that the mandatory minimum sentence will be constitutional in every possible application. He argues that *Morrisey* should be read as having held that s. 220(a) and s. 236(a) are constitutional only in most of their applications, and that a constitutional exemption should be granted in those rare cases where applying the sentence would lead to an unconstitutional result.

• • •

2. If the Imposition of the Four-Year Mandatory Minimum Sentence Violated Section 12 of the Charter in the Circumstances of This Case, Was the Trial Judge Entitled to Grant a Constitutional Exemption from the Four-Year Minimum and to Impose a Lesser Sentence?

[33] Having found that the four-year minimum sentence of imprisonment required by s. 236(a) does not violate Constable Ferguson's right not to suffer cruel and unusual punishment contrary to s. 12 of the *Charter*, it is not necessary to consider whether a

constitutional exemption would have been available had we found a violation of s. 12. As the Court of Appeal recognized, however, there has been considerable debate and disagreement in the lower courts as to whether the remedy of a constitutional exemption is available. The matter having been fully argued, it is appropriate to settle the question of whether a constitutional exemption would have been available to Constable Ferguson, had the minimum sentence violated s. 12 of the *Charter*.

[34] I note at the outset that the issue is not *whether* a remedy lies to prevent the imposition of cruel and unusual punishment contrary to the *Charter*, but *which* remedies are available. The imposition of cruel and unusual punishment contrary to ss. 12 and 1 of the *Charter* cannot be countenanced. A court which has found a violation of a *Charter* right has a duty to provide an effective remedy. The only issue is whether a law imposing such punishment can be permitted to stand subject to constitutional exemptions in particular cases, or whether the only remedy is a declaration that the law is inconsistent with the *Charter* and hence falls under s. 52 of the *Constitution Act, 1982*.

[35] Two remedial provisions govern remedies for *Charter* violations: ss. 24(1) of the *Charter* and s. 52(1) of the *Constitution Act, 1982*. Section 24(1) confers on judges a wide discretion to grant appropriate remedies in response to *Charter* violations:

> 24(1) Anyone whose rights or freedoms, as guaranteed by this Charter, have been infringed or denied may apply to a court of competent jurisdiction to obtain such remedy as the court considers appropriate and just in the circumstances.

Section 24(1) has generally been seen—at least until now—as providing a case-by-case remedy for unconstitutional acts of government agents operating under lawful schemes whose constitutionality is not challenged. The other remedy section, s. 52(1) of the *Constitution Act, 1982*, confers no discretion on judges. It simply provides that laws that are inconsistent with the *Charter* are of no force and effect to the extent of the inconsistency:

> 52(1) The Constitution of Canada is the supreme law of Canada, and any law that is inconsistent with the provisions of the Constitution is, to the extent of the inconsistency, of no force or effect.

When a litigant claims that a law violates the *Charter*, and a court rules or "declares" that it does, the effect of s. 52(1) is to render the law null and void. It is common to describe this as the court "striking down" the law. In fact, when a court "strikes down" a law, the law has failed by operation of s. 52 of the *Constitution Act, 1982*.

[36] The usual remedy for a mandatory sentencing provision that imposes cruel and unusual punishment contrary to s. 12 of the *Charter* is a declaration that the law is of no force and effect under s. 52 of the *Constitution Act, 1982*. This was the remedy sought in *Goltz, Morrisey*, and *R v. Luxton*, [1990] 2 SCR 711. The mandatory minimum sentence provisions in these cases were held to be constitutional. But it was argued that had the provisions been held to be unconstitutional, the appropriate remedy was the s. 52 remedy of striking down.

[37] In this case, despite the allegation of a constitutional violation, Constable Ferguson does not request that the law that caused the alleged violation, s. 236(a) of the *Criminal Code*, be struck down. Instead, Constable Ferguson argues that if the four-year mandatory sentence is found to violate the *Charter*, a constitutional exemption under s. 24(1) should be granted. The argument for a constitutional exemption proposes that the law remain

in force, but that it not be applied in cases where its application results in a *Charter* violation. The judge would thus be free to impose a sentence below the minimum set by law, which would nevertheless continue to stand.

[38] The argument in favour of recognizing constitutional exemptions is simply put. The first prong of the argument is that where a mandatory minimum sentence that is constitutional in most of its applications generates an unconstitutional result in a small number of cases, it is better to grant a constitutional exemption in these cases than to strike down the law as a whole. The s. 52(1) remedy of declaring invalid a law that produces a result inconsistent with the *Charter* is a blunt tool. A law that may be constitutional in many of its applications—and indeed ruled constitutional on a reasonable hypothetical analysis—is struck down because in one particular case, or in a few cases, it produces an unconstitutional result. Would it not be better, the argument goes, to allow the law to stand, while providing an individual remedy in those cases—arguably rare—where its application offends the *Charter*?

[39] The second and complementary prong of the argument asserts that the remedy is available on the wording of the *Charter* and the jurisprudence. Section 24(1), it is argued, grants courts a wide discretion to grant such constitutional remedies as are "appropriate and just." Granting a constitutional exemption and substituting a constitutional sentence removes the law's inconsistency with the *Charter*, making s. 52(1) inapplicable. The cases that have considered the matter, while inconclusive, do not rule constitutional exemptions out as a remedy for unconstitutional sentences flowing from mandatory minimum sentence laws. More generally, granting constitutional exemptions for unconstitutional effects of mandatory minimum sentence laws fits well with the Court's practices of severance, reading in and reading out in order to preserve the law to the maximum extent possible: see *Schachter v. Canada*, [1992] 2 SCR 679.

[40] Attractive as they are, the arguments for constitutional exemptions in a case such as this are, on consideration, outweighed and undermined by counter-considerations. I reach this conclusion on the basis of four considerations: (1) the jurisprudence; (2) the need to avoid intruding on the role of Parliament; (3) the remedial scheme of the *Charter*; and (4) the impact of granting constitutional exemptions in mandatory sentence cases on the values underlying the rule of law.

(1) The Jurisprudence

[41] This Court has not definitively ruled whether constitutional exemptions are available as a remedy for mandatory minimum sentences that produce unconstitutional sentences. In concurring opinions, judges of this Court have expressed both positive and negative evaluations of constitutional exemptions as remedies for unconstitutional minimum sentences.

• • •

[47] In summary, the majority of this Court in *Seaboyer* has commented critically on the use of constitutional exemptions as a stand-alone remedy in the case of mandatory laws generally, a view supported by Wilson J in *Osborne* and consistent with the majority's reasoning in *Corbiere*. In *Smith*, Le Dain J rejected their use in the context here at issue, mandatory minimum sentence laws. On the other side of the issue are the remarks of L'Heureux-Dubé and Arbour JJ in their respective concurring opinions in *Rose* and *Morrisey*.

[48] I conclude that while the availability of constitutional exemptions for mandatory minimum sentencing laws has not been conclusively decided, the weight of authority thus far is against them and sounds a cautionary note.

(2) Intrusion on the Role of Parliament

[49] Section 52(1) grants courts the jurisdiction to declare laws of no force and effect only "to the extent of the inconsistency" with the Constitution. It follows that if the constitutional defect of a law can be remedied without striking down the law as a whole, then a court must consider alternatives to striking down. Examples of alternative remedies under s. 52 include severance, reading in and reading down. Constable Ferguson is proposing a constitutional exemption under s. 24(1) as an additional tool for minimizing interference with Parliament's legislative role when a court must grant a remedy for a constitutionally defective provision.

[50] On the other hand, it has long been recognized that in applying alternative remedies such as severance and reading in, courts are at risk of making inappropriate intrusions into the legislative sphere. An alternative to striking down that initially appears to be less intrusive on the legislative role may in fact represent an inappropriate intrusion on the legislature's role. This Court has thus emphasized that in considering alternatives to striking down, courts must carefully consider whether the alternative being considered represents a lesser intrusion on Parliament's legislative role than striking down. Courts must thus be guided by respect for the role of Parliament, as well as respect for the purposes of the *Charter*: *Schachter*; *Vriend v. Alberta*, [1998] 1 SCR 493; *R v. Sharpe*, [2001] 1 SCR 45, 2001 SCC 2. These principles apply with equal force to the proposed alternative remedy of the constitutional exemption. In this case, the effect of granting a constitutional exemption would be to so change the legislation as to create something different in nature from what Parliament intended. It follows that a constitutional exemption should not be granted.

[51] When a court opts for severance or reading in as an alternative to striking down a provision, it does so on the assumption that had Parliament been aware of the provision's constitutional defect, it would likely have passed it with the alterations now being made by the court by means of severance or reading in. For instance, as this Court noted in *Schachter*, the test for severance "recognizes that the seemingly laudable purpose of retaining the parts of the legislative scheme which do not offend the Constitution rests on an assumption that the legislature would have passed the constitutionally sound part of the scheme without the unsound part" (p. 697). If it is not clear that Parliament would have passed the scheme with the modifications being considered by the court—or if it is probable that Parliament would *not* have passed the scheme with these modifications—then for the court to make these modifications would represent an inappropriate intrusion into the legislative sphere. In such cases, the least intrusive remedy is to strike down the constitutionally defective legislation under s. 52. It is then left up to Parliament to decide what legislative response, if any, is appropriate.

[52] It follows that we must ask whether granting a constitutional exemption for a mandatory minimum sentence would represent a lesser intrusion on Parliament's legislative role than striking it down. In my view, the answer to this question is no, because allowing courts to grant constitutional exemptions for mandatory minimum sentences directly contradicts Parliament's intent in passing mandatory minimum sentence legislation.

[53] A constitutional exemption has the effect of conferring on judges a discretion to reject the mandatory minimum sentence prescribed by Parliament. The mandatory minimum applies, unless the judge concludes that its application constitutes unjustifiable cruel and unusual punishment and that it therefore should not apply.

[54] The intention of Parliament in passing mandatory minimum sentence laws, on the other hand, is to remove judicial discretion to impose a sentence below the stipulated minimum. Parliament must be taken to have specifically chosen to exclude judicial discretion in imposing mandatory minimum sentences, just as it was taken to have done in enacting the rape shield provisions struck down in *Seaboyer*. Parliament made no provision for the exercise of judicial discretion in drafting s. 236(a), nor did it authorize any exceptions to the mandatory minimum. There is no provision permitting judges to depart from the mandatory minimum, even in exceptional cases where it would result in grossly disproportionate punishment. Parliament has cast the prescription for the minimum four-year prison sentence here at issue in clear unambiguous terms. Parliament must be taken to have intended what it stated: that all convictions for manslaughter with a firearm would be subject to a mandatory minimum sentence of four years imprisonment. The law mandates a floor below which judges cannot go. To permit judges to go below this floor on a case-by-case basis runs counter to the clear wording of the section and the intent that it evinces.

[55] In granting a constitutional exemption, a judge would be undermining Parliament's purpose in passing the legislation: to remove judicial discretion and to send a clear and unequivocal message to potential offenders that if they commit a certain offence, or commit it in a certain way, they will receive a sentence equal to or exceeding the mandatory minimum specified by Parliament. The discretion that a constitutional exemption would confer on judges would violate the letter of the law and undermine the message that animates it.

[56] It is thus clear that granting a constitutional exemption from a mandatory minimum sentence law that results in an unconstitutional sentence goes directly against Parliament's intention. To allow constitutional exemptions for mandatory minimum sentences is, in effect, to read in a discretion to a provision where Parliament clearly intended to exclude discretion. If it would be inappropriate to read in such a discretion under s. 52, then necessarily it would be inappropriate to allow judges to grant constitutional exemptions having the same effect under s. 24(1). It cannot be assumed that Parliament would have enacted the mandatory minimum sentencing scheme with the discretion that allowing constitutional exemptions would create. For the Court to introduce such a discretion would thus represent an inappropriate intrusion into the legislative sphere.

[57] I conclude that these considerations are sufficient to exclude constitutional exemptions as an appropriate remedy for unconstitutional mandatory minimum sentences. In the absence of any provision providing for discretion, a court that concludes that a mandatory minimum sentence imposes cruel and unusual punishment in an exceptional case before it is compelled to declare the provision invalid.

(3) The Remedial Scheme of the Charter

[58] As I noted at the outset, remedies for breaches of the *Charter* are governed by s. 24(1) of the *Charter* and s. 52(1) of the *Constitution Act, 1982*.

[59] When a law produces an unconstitutional effect, the usual remedy lies under s. 52(1), which provides that the law is of no force or effect to the extent that it is inconsistent with the *Charter*. A law may be inconsistent with the *Charter* either because of its purpose or its effect: *R v. Big M Drug Mart Ltd.*, [1985]1 SCR 295; *R v. Edwards Books and Art Ltd.*, [1986] 2 SCR 713. Section 52 does not create a personal remedy. A claimant who otherwise has standing can generally seek a declaration of invalidity under s. 52 on the grounds that a law has unconstitutional effects either in his own case or on third parties: *Big M*; see also Peter Sankoff, "Constitutional Exemptions: Myth or Reality?" (1999-2000), 11 *NJCL* 411, at pp. 432-34; Morris Rosenberg and Stéphane Perrault, "Ifs and Buts in Charter Adjudication: The Unruly Emergence of Constitutional Exemptions in Canada" (2002), 16 *SCLR* (2d) 375, at pp. 380-82. The jurisprudence affirming s. 52(1) as the appropriate remedy for laws that produce unconstitutional effects is based on the language chosen by the framers of the *Charter*: see Sankoff, at p. 438.

[60] Section 24(1), by contrast, is generally used as a remedy, not for unconstitutional laws, but for unconstitutional government acts committed under the authority of legal regimes which are accepted as fully constitutional: see *Eldridge v. British Columbia (Attorney General)*, [1997] 3 SCR 624; *Multani v. Commission scolaire Marguerite-Bourgeoys*, [2006] 1 SCR 256, 2006 SCC 6. The acts of government agents acting under such regimes are not the necessary result or "effect" of the law, but of the government agent's applying a discretion conferred by the law in an unconstitutional manner. Section 52(1) is thus not applicable. The appropriate remedy lies under s. 24(1).

[61] It thus becomes apparent that ss. 52(1) and 24(1) serve different remedial purposes. Section 52(1) provides a remedy for *laws* that violate *Charter* rights either in purpose or in effect. Section 24(1), by contrast, provides a remedy for *government acts* that violate *Charter* rights. It provides a personal remedy against unconstitutional government action and so, unlike s. 52(1), can be invoked only by a party alleging a violation of that party's own constitutional rights: *Big M*; *R v. Edwards*, [1996] 1 SCR 128. Thus this Court has repeatedly affirmed that the validity of laws is determined by s. 52 of the *Constitution Act, 1982*, while the validity of government action falls to be determined under s. 24 of the *Charter*: *Schachter*; *R v. 974649 Ontario Inc.*, [2001] 3 SCR 575, 2001 SCC 81. We are here concerned with a *law* that is alleged to violate a *Charter* right. This suggests that s. 52(1) provides the proper remedy.

[62] It is argued that s. 24(1), while normally applicable to government acts, can also be used to provide a stand-alone remedy for the unconstitutional effects of mandatory minimum sentence laws. The wording of s. 24(1) is generous enough to permit this, it is argued, conferring a discretion on judges to grant "such remedy as the court considers appropriate and just in the circumstances."

[63] The jurisprudence of this Court allows a s. 24(1) remedy in connection with a s. 52(1) declaration of invalidity in unusual cases where additional s. 24(1) relief is necessary to provide the claimant with an effective remedy: *R v. Demers*, [2004] 2 SCR 489, 2004 SCC 46. However, the argument that s. 24(1) can provide a stand-alone remedy for laws with unconstitutional effects depends on reading s. 24(1) in isolation, rather than in conjunction with the scheme of the *Charter* as a whole, as required by principles of statutory and constitutional interpretation. When s. 24(1) is read in context, it becomes apparent that the intent of the framers of the Constitution was that it function primarily as a remedy for unconstitutional government acts.

[64] The highly discretionary language in s. 24(1), "such remedy as the court considers appropriate and just in the circumstances," is appropriate for control of unconstitutional acts. By contrast, s. 52(1) targets the unconstitutionality of laws in a direct non-discretionary way: laws are of no force or effect to the extent that they are unconstitutional.

[65] The presence of s. 52(1) with its mandatory wording suggests an intention of the framers of the *Charter* that unconstitutional laws are deprived of effect to the extent of their inconsistency, not left on the books subject to discretionary case-by-case remedies: see *Osborne*, *per* Wilson J In cases where the requirements for severance or reading in are met, it may be possible to remedy the inconsistency judicially instead of striking down the impugned legislation as a whole: *Vriend*; *Sharpe*. Where this is not possible—as in the case of an unconstitutional mandatory minimum sentence—the unconstitutional provision must be struck down. The ball is thrown back into Parliament's court, to revise the law, should it choose to do so, so that it no longer produces unconstitutional effects. In either case, the remedy is a s. 52 remedy that renders the unconstitutional provision of no force or effect to the extent of its inconsistency. To the extent that the law is unconstitutional, it is not merely inapplicable for the purposes of the case at hand. It is null and void, and is effectively removed from the statute books.

. . .

(4) The Rule of Law

[67] Constable Ferguson's principal argument for constitutional exemptions, as we have seen, is an appeal to flexibility. Yet this flexibility comes at a cost: constitutional exemptions buy flexibility at the cost of undermining the rule of law.

[68] The principles of constitutionalism and the rule of law lie at the root of democratic governance: *Reference re Secession of Quebec*, [1998] 2 SCR 217. It is fundamental to the rule of law that "the law must be accessible and so far as possible intelligible, clear and predictable": Lord Bingham, "The Rule of Law," (2007), 66 *Cambridge LJ* 67, at p. 69. Generality, promulgation, and clarity are among the essential elements of the "morality that makes law possible": Lon L. Fuller, *The Morality of Law*, (2nd ed. 1969), at pp. 33-39.

[69] Constitutional exemptions for mandatory minimum sentence laws raise concerns related to the rule of law and the values that underpin it: certainty, accessibility, intelligibility, clarity and predictability.

[70] As noted in the last section, a constitutional exemption under s. 24(1) is a personal remedy. The remedy proposed by Constable Ferguson is thus distinct from a s. 52 remedy that reads in an exception for a well-defined class of situations—as, for instance, the remedy in *Sharpe*. When a constitutional exemption is granted, the successful claimant receives a personal remedy under s. 24(1), but the law remains on the books, intact. As Wilson J put it in *Osborne*, the legislation remains as enacted "in its pristine over-inclusive form" (p. 77). The mere possibility of such a remedy thus necessarily generates uncertainty: the law is on the books, but in practice, it may not apply. As constitutional exemptions are actually granted, the law in the statute books will in fact increasingly diverge from the law as applied.

[71] Constitutional exemptions from mandatory minimum sentences leave the law uncertain and unpredictable, as Le Dain J pointed out in *Smith*. It is up to judges on a case-by-case basis to decide when to strike down a minimum sentence that is inconsistent

with the *Charter*, and when to grant an individual exemption under s. 24(1). But the *Charter* is silent on how a judge should make this decision—the decision, literally, of whether the law stands or falls. In theory, all violations could be remedied under s. 24(1), leaving no role for s. 52(1). The only option would be to introduce a meta-rule as to when a s. 24(1) exemption is available and when a declaration of invalidity should be made under s. 52(1). How such a rule should be fashioned—where the line should be drawn—is far from clear. Constitutional exemptions, it is suggested, should be confined to laws that usually operate constitutionally and only occasionally result in constitutional violations. But how is the judge to decide whether the case before her is rare? The bright line required for constitutional certainty is elusive.

[72] The divergence between the law on the books and the law as applied—and the uncertainty and unpredictability that result—exacts a price paid in the coin of injustice. First, it impairs the right of citizens to know what the law is in advance and govern their conduct accordingly—a fundamental tenet of the rule of law. Second, it risks over-application of the law; as Le Dain J noted in *Smith*, the assumed validity of the law may prejudice convicted persons when judges must decide whether to apply it in particular cases. Third, it invites duplication of effort. The matter of constitutionality would not be resolved once and for all as under s. 52(1); in every case where a violation is suspected, the accused would be obliged to seek a constitutional exemption. In so doing, it creates an unnecessary barrier to the effective exercise of the convicted offender's constitutional rights, thereby encouraging uneven and unequal application of the law.

[73] A final cost of constitutional exemptions from mandatory minimum sentence laws is to the institutional value of effective law making and the proper roles of Parliament and the courts. Allowing unconstitutional laws to remain on the books deprives Parliament of certainty as to the constitutionality of the law in question and thus of the opportunity to remedy it. Legislatures need clear guidance from the courts as to what is constitutionally permissible and what must be done to remedy legislation that is found to be constitutionally infirm. In granting constitutional exemptions, courts would be altering the state of the law on constitutional grounds without giving clear guidance to Parliament as to what the Constitution requires in the circumstances: Rosenberg and Perrault, at p. 391. Bad law, fixed up on a case-by-case basis by the courts, does not accord with the role and responsibility of Parliament to enact constitutional laws for the people of Canada.

V. *Conclusion*

[74] I conclude that constitutional exemptions should not be recognized as a remedy for cruel and unusual punishment imposed by a law prescribing a minimum sentence. If a law providing for a mandatory minimum sentence is found to violate the *Charter*, it should be declared inconsistent with the *Charter* and hence of no force and effect under s. 52 of the *Constitution Act, 1982*.

IV. SECTION 7: THE PRINCIPLES OF FUNDAMENTAL JUSTICE

It has always been clear that sentencing issues implicate the right to liberty protected by s 7 of the Charter. However, only with the evolution of jurisprudence dealing with the meaning and scope of the principles of fundamental justice, often in non-criminal contexts, have we seen serious attempts to develop s 7 challenges to sentencing. In *R v Safarzadeh-Markhali*, immediately below, a convicted person challenged the role of s 719(3.1), which would limit his pre-sentence custody credit to one day for every day of pre-sentence custody. The Ontario Court of Appeal found a violation of s 7 that could not be justified under s 1: see *R v Safarzadeh-Markhali*, 2014 ONCA 627. On appeal to the Supreme Court, that conclusion was upheld, but on different grounds.

R v Safarzadeh-Markhali
2016 SCC 14

McLACHLIN CJ (Abella, Cromwell, Moldaver, Karakatsanis, Wagner, Gascon, Côté, and Brown JJ concurring):

[1] A person charged with a crime is held in custody pending trial unless released on bail. If found guilty at trial, an issue arises: In calculating the sentence, how much credit should the person receive for the time already spent in custody? A credit of one day for every day of pre-sentence custody will almost never put the person on equal footing with offenders released on bail, because the time spent in pre-sentence custody does not count for purposes of parole eligibility, earned remission and statutory release: *R. v. Summers*, 2014 SCC 26, [2014] 1 S.C.R. 575, at para. 26. A one-for-one credit, in other words, results in longer incarceration for offenders detained in pre-sentence custody than for offenders released on bail. On account of this discrepancy and the reality that pre-sentence custody is generally more onerous than post-sentence custody, sentencing courts have historically given "enhanced" credit for time spent in pre-sentence custody.

[2] Parliament revised this regime in 2009. It did not do away with enhanced credit, but it capped that credit at one and a half days for each day of pre-sentence custody. Parliament also—which brings us to the issue in this case—removed a sentencing court's discretion to give any enhanced credit to offenders for pre-sentence custody, if they were denied bail primarily on the basis of their criminal record. The question is whether this law violates the right to liberty guaranteed by s. 7 of the *Canadian Charter of Rights and Freedoms*.

[3] For the reasons that follow, I conclude that the provision infringes s. 7 of the *Charter*, and is not justified under s. 1 of the *Charter*.

• • •

[21] The Court of Appeal based its analysis on the principle of proportionality in the sentencing process, which it found to be a principle of fundamental justice. The Crown argues that, while proportionality is an important principle of sentencing, it should not be treated as a principle of fundamental justice under s. 7. I agree with the Crown. Proportionality in the sentencing process, as distinct from the well-accepted principle of gross disproportionality under s. 7, is not a principle of fundamental justice.

[22] However, I conclude that the portion of the *Truth in Sentencing Act* challenged in this appeal—the denial of any enhanced credit for pre-sentence custody to persons to

whom bail is denied primarily because of a prior conviction—violates s. 7 of the *Charter* for another reason: it is overbroad. Laws that curtail liberty in a way that is arbitrary, overbroad or grossly disproportionate do not conform to the principles of fundamental justice: *Canada (Attorney General) v. Bedford*, 2013 SCC 72, [2013] 3 S.C.R. 1101, at para. 105. Mr. Safarzadeh-Markhali contends that the challenged provision violates all three of these principles. For the reasons that follow, I conclude that the challenged law is unconstitutionally overbroad, because its effect is to deprive some persons of liberty for reasons unrelated to its purpose. This conclusion makes it unnecessary to address whether the law is arbitrary or grossly disproportionate.

· · ·

[24] Whether a law is overbroad within the meaning of s. 7 turns on the relationship between the law's purpose and its effect: *R. v. Moriarity*, 2015 SCC 55, [2015] 3 S.C.R. 485, at para. 24. It is critically important, therefore, to identify the purpose of the challenged law at the outset of the s. 7 inquiry.

[25] *Moriarity* summarizes the considerations that guide the task of properly characterizing Parliament's purpose in a s. 7 analysis into overbreadth.

[26] First, the law's purpose is distinct from the means used to achieve that purpose: *Moriarity*, at para. 27. A law's means may be helpful in determining its objective, but the two must be treated separately.

[27] Second, the law's purpose should be characterized at the appropriate level of generality, which "resides between the statement of an 'animating social value'—which is too general—and a narrow articulation" that amounts to a virtual repetition of the challenged provision, divorced from its context: *Moriarity*, at para. 28.

[28] Third, the statement of purpose should be both precise and succinct: *Moriarity*, at para. 29. Precision requires that courts focus on the purpose of the particular statutory provision subject to constitutional challenge: *ibid.*; see also *RJR-MacDonald Inc. v. Canada (Attorney General)*, [1995] 3 S.C.R. 199, at para. 144.

[29] Fourth, the analysis is not concerned with the appropriateness of the legislative purpose. The court must take the legislative objective "at face value" and assume that it is appropriate and lawful: *Moriarity*, at para. 30. The appropriateness of a legislative objective may be relevant to its constitutionality under other *Charter* provisions. But it has no place in the s. 7 analysis of overbreadth.

[30] With these propositions in mind, I turn to the task at hand: to formulate a statement of purpose for s. 719(3.1)'s denial of enhanced credit to persons denied bail primarily because of a prior conviction.

[31] To determine a law's purpose for a s. 7 overbreadth analysis, courts look to: (1) statements of purpose in the legislation, if any; (2) the text, context, and scheme of the legislation; and (3) extrinsic evidence such as legislative history and evolution: *Moriarity*, at para. 31.

· · ·

[45] In summary, examined in the light of *Moriarity*, the text, context and scheme of the legislation, coupled with the Minister's statements of purpose, lead me to the following conclusions.

[46] First, the *animating social value* behind the denial of enhanced credit for pre-sentence custody in s. 719(3.1) is enhancing public confidence in the justice system.

[47] Second, the *legislative purpose* of the total denial of enhanced credit for pre-sentence custody to offenders who are denied bail because of a prior conviction is *to enhance public safety and security by increasing violent and chronic offenders' access to rehabilitation programs.* To be sure, the Minister referred to other legislative purposes—providing adequate punishment, increasing transparency in the pre-sentence credit system, and reducing manipulation. But these are peripheral, for the reasons discussed above.

[48] Third, the *means* for achieving the purpose of enhancing public safety and security is the challenged provision itself—the denial of enhanced credit for pre-sentence custody to persons refused bail primarily on the basis of their existing criminal record.

[49] Finally, the *effect* of the provision is to impose longer periods of custody on all persons who receive an endorsement indicating they were denied bail primarily on the basis of a previous conviction.

. . .

[52] The denial of enhanced credit for pre-sentence custody to offenders who are denied bail primarily because of a prior conviction is overbroad because it catches people in ways that have nothing to do with enhancing public safety and security.

[53] First, the provision's ambit captures people it was not intended to capture: offenders who do not pose a threat to public safety or security. Section 515(9.1) is broadly worded. It catches any person denied bail primarily for a criminal record, without specifying or even broadly identifying the nature or number of offences that would warrant a s. 515(9.1) endorsement. The section may therefore ensnare persons whose imprisonment does not advance the purpose of the law. For example, a person with two or three convictions for failing to appear in court might be subject to a s. 515(9.1) endorsement, even though he or she did not pose any real threat to public safety or security. And even if such a person receives greater access to rehabilitative programming and benefits from it, the consequence is not necessarily to improve public safety and security. In short, a s. 515(9.1) endorsement is an inexact proxy for the danger that an offender poses to public safety and security. The Crown says the law casts the net broadly because targeting all offenders with a criminal record is a more practical option than attempting to identify only offenders who pose a risk to public safety and security. But practicality is no answer to a charge of overbreadth under s. 7: *Bedford*, at para. 113.

[54] Second, regardless of the types of offenders the challenged provision was meant to capture, the provision suffers from overbreadth because, as the intervener the Criminal Lawyers' Association (Ontario) notes, the limited availability of judicial review means that persons wrongly tagged with an endorsement will be without recourse to have the error remedied. There is dispute about precisely when if ever review for an endorsement is available. But the Crown concedes that if the reviewing judge finds that the detention order was properly made, he or she is powerless to vacate an endorsement and that the sentencing judge has no choice under the challenged provision but to give effect to an endorsement in computing an offender's sentence. This absence of review and discretion renders the challenged provision overbroad for at least two categories of individuals: (1) persons who erroneously received the endorsement because their detention is not warranted primarily because of their criminal record, and (2) persons who, during the period between the bail hearing and sentencing, successfully appeal the conviction that drew the endorsement. In both cases, the effect of the provision is to strip persons of liberty even though their detention does not obviously advance public safety and security.

[55] I conclude that the challenged provision seeks to advance the objective of enhancing public safety and security in a manner that is overbroad.

C. Is the Infringement Justified Under Section 1 of the Charter?

• • •

[60] The real issue is whether the means chosen here are proportionate to this objective. For reasons much the same as those discussed in the overbreadth analysis, I conclude that this has not been established.

[61] The challenged provision is rationally connected to its purpose of enhancing public safety and security. The denial of enhanced credit gives rise to longer periods of custody. It is therefore likely to increase the opportunities of some offenders to access rehabilitative programs.

[62] However, the law is neither minimally impairing nor proportionate in the balance it achieves between salutary and deleterious effects.

[63] To establish minimal impairment, the Crown must show the absence of less drastic means of achieving the objective in a "real and substantial manner": *Carter*, at para. 102. The Crown has not discharged that burden. Alternative and more reasonable means of achieving its purposes were open to Parliament. Strathy J.A. provided one example—a law requiring the sentencing judge to consider whether to grant enhanced credit for pre-sentence custody based on (i) the offender's criminal record, (ii) the availability of rehabilitative programs and the desirability of giving the offender access to those programs, and (iii) whether the offender was responsible for prolonging his or her time in pre-sentence custody. Such a regime would achieve the goal of promoting public safety and security through rehabilitation, without catching chronic or other offenders who pose no risk to public safety.

[64] The Crown argues that the provision is reasonably tailored to its objective because it "applies to a relatively narrow class of offenders, focusing on the most serious recidivists": A.F., at para. 62. But the law plainly does the opposite: it makes any person with a criminal record, even for missed court dates, a potential target for restriction of enhanced credit. In my view, the challenged provision is not minimally impairing of the right to liberty.

[65] Finally, I agree with Court of Appeal that the Crown has failed to establish benefits that outweigh the detrimental effect of the challenged provision on the right to liberty. The benefit to public safety by increasing access to rehabilitation programs is not trivial. But the law's overbreadth means that offenders who have neither committed violent offences nor present a risk to public safety will be unnecessarily deprived of liberty. The Crown has failed to meet that high bar required to justify such a deprivation.

[66] I conclude that the challenged provision is not saved under s. 1.

V. SECTION 24(1): CHARTER REMEDIES

Within the criminal process, claims of Charter violations can be directed to situations that arise during investigations, on arrest, or during the trial itself. For the most part, these relate to ss 8, 9, 10, and 11. The accused must establish the violation on a balance of probabilities. If established, the issue then moves to remedy. There might be a stay of proceedings or an exclusion of evidence under s 24(2). In these cases, a conviction will usually be avoided. However, there will be other instances where a lesser remedy or even no remedy will be granted. On numerous occasions, the question has been raised whether the proven Charter violation can be the basis for sentence mitigation through s 24(1) of the Charter. In *R v Carpenter*, 2002 BCCA 301, the BC Court of Appeal was faced with an appellant arguing that by reason of the breaches of ss 8 and 10(b) of the Charter, he should have his sentence reduced as a "remedy" for those breaches. Newbury JA, with Smith JA concurring, rejected the argument and concluded:

> [27] In the case at bar, for example, if Mr. Carpenter were to have his sentence materially reduced in recognition of the *Charter* breaches found by the Court of Appeal, the sentence would not be similar to that imposed on his co-accused and might well not be proportionate to the gravity of the offence and the degree of the appellant's responsibility. The focus would be shifted from this offence and this offender, where it should be, to the *Charter* violations committed by Customs officials. Those violations were found *not* to be of a serious nature and not to have arisen from any bad faith on their part. The sentencing judge was seeking to send a message to the offender and to society about the seriousness of the appellant's crime, but that message would be substantially blunted by the sending of a competing message to those officials in respect of a "non-serious" infringement of the appellant's *Charter* rights. In cases where the offender is a danger to society, the mixing of the messages would have even more serious implications.

Donald JA dissented, finding that:

> [50] In the present case, the *Charter* breaches resulted in strip searches and other indignities. These were, in effect, a hardship or penalty suffered by the appellant. The trial judge, however, did not "credit" the appellant with this penalty—determining the appropriate sentence to be six years. I am of the view that while the *Charter* breaches do not warrant an exclusion of evidence, their effect must be factored into the overall punishment that the appellant receives. Therefore, if the trial judge concluded that the appropriate penalty, with no reduction for *Charter* breaches, is six years, that term must be reduced so that the total penalty, including the hardships suffered as a result of the breach of the appellant's rights, does not exceed six years. Reducing the length of the appellant's jail sentence does not indicate that the appellant is less culpable, rather it merely balances the punishments so as not to create an overall punishment that would indicate greater culpability.

However, Donald JA expressed (at para 51) reservations about whether "24(1) could be used to sanction police misconduct because that comes close to reversing the s. 24(2) analysis on seriousness of the breach." Leave to appeal to the Supreme Court of Canada was denied, so the issue remained to a great extent unresolved, although the weight of appellate opinion seemed to be against this role for s 24(1). More recently, the issue seemed to be in front of the Supreme Court in the case of *R v Nasogaluak*, immediately below. In that case, the offender was punched and kicked during an arrest for impaired driving, resulting in broken ribs, which subsequently punctured one of his lungs. The trial judge found that the police actions warranted a conditional discharge on both counts. The Alberta Court of Appeal agreed with the finding of excessive force and also that a sentence could be reduced pursuant to s 24(1) of the Charter, but not below the statutorily mandated minimum. On appeal to the Supreme Court, it seemed that, at least in the context of egregious state misconduct, a decision would be produced about sentencing and Charter violations.

R v Nasogaluak
2010 SCC 6, [2010] 1 SCR 206

LeBEL J (McLachlin CJ, Binnie, Deschamps, Fish, Abella, Charron, Rothstein, and Cromwell JJ concurring):

[1] This is a sentencing appeal from the Court of Appeal of Alberta that raises important issues in respect of constitutional remedies. The respondent, Mr. Lyle Marcellus Nasogaluak, had his sentences for the offences of impaired driving and flight from police reduced to conditional discharges as a remedy for the breaches of the *Canadian Charter of Rights and Freedoms* that he endured at the time of his arrest and detention. The main issue is whether his sentences were lawfully reduced as a remedy for the excessive force used by police.

[2] The parties have focussed their submissions on the question of whether a court may grant a sentence reduction under s. 24(1) of the *Charter* to remedy a *Charter* breach by state actors. Framing the issue in those terms presupposes that *Charter* breaches can only be effectively remedied in the context of a separate and distinct *Charter* application. However, that is clearly not so. As all statutes and the common law must be *Charter* compliant, it should come as no surprise that an effective remedy for a proven wrong, which also happens to be a *Charter* breach, may well be crafted within the confines of a statutory or common law regime. The statutory sentencing regime under ss. 718 to 718.2 of the *Criminal Code*, R.S.C. 1985, c. C-46, is one example.

[3] As we shall see, the sentencing regime provides some scope for sentencing judges to consider not only the actions of the offender, but also those of state actors. Where the state misconduct in question relates to the circumstances of the offence or the offender, the sentencing judge may properly take the relevant facts into account in crafting a fit sentence, without having to resort to s. 24(1) of the *Charter*. Indeed, state misconduct which does not amount to a *Charter* breach but which impacts the offender may also be a relevant factor in crafting a fit sentence.

[4] Where the state misconduct does not relate to the circumstances of the offence or the offender, however, the accused must seek his or her remedy in another forum. Any inquiry into such unrelated circumstances falls outside the scope of the statutory sentencing regime and has no place in the sentence hearing. Likewise, a reduction of sentence could hardly constitute an "appropriate" remedy within the meaning of s. 24(1) of the *Charter* where the facts underlying the breach bear no connection to the circumstances of the offence or the offender.

[5] As a general rule, therefore, it is neither necessary nor useful to invoke s. 24(1) of the *Charter* to effect an appropriate reduction of sentence to account for any harm flowing from unconstitutional acts of state agents consequent to the offence charged. When acting within the boundaries of the statutory sentencing regime, of course, the sentencing judge must exercise his or her discretion within the parameters of the *Criminal Code*. The judge must impose sentences complying with statutory minimums and other provisions which prohibit certain forms of sentence in respect of the offence.

[6] Save in exceptional cases, these constraints also apply where the remedial power of the court under the *Charter* is invoked. A sentence reduction outside statutory limits does not generally constitute an "appropriate" remedy within the meaning of s. 24(1), unless the constitutionality of the statutory limit itself is challenged. However, the

remedial power of the court under s. 24(1) is broad. I therefore do not foreclose the possibility that, in some exceptional cases, a sentence reduction outside statutory limits may be the sole effective remedy for some particularly egregious form of misconduct by state agents in relation to the offence and the offender. However, this is not such a case.

[7] On the facts of this case, the Court of Appeal did not err in upholding the trial judge's finding of excessive force by police in arresting Mr. Nasogaluak. The police officers' excessive use of force amounted to a violation of the respondent's right to life, liberty and security of the person under s. 7 of the *Charter*. The sentencing judge committed no error of law or principle in choosing to take this conduct into account as a factor tending toward a reduced sentence. However, he erred in ordering a sentence that fell below the statutory minimum in the *Code*. The Court of Appeal correctly substituted the order of a conditional discharge on the offence of impaired driving with the statutorily mandated minimum fine.

· · ·

[43] The language in ss. 718 to 718.2 of the *Code* is sufficiently general to ensure that sentencing judges enjoy a broad discretion to craft a sentence that is tailored to the nature of the offence and the circumstances of the offender. The determination of a "fit" sentence is, subject to some specific statutory rules, an individualized process that requires the judge to weigh the objectives of sentencing in a manner that best reflects the circumstances of the case (*R. v. Lyons*, [1987] 2 S.C.R. 309; *M. (C.A.)*; *R. v. Hamilton* (2004), 72 O.R. (3d) 1 (C.A.)). No one sentencing objective trumps the others and it falls to the sentencing judge to determine which objective or objectives merit the greatest weight, given the particulars of the case. The relative importance of any mitigating or aggravating factors will then push the sentence up or down the scale of appropriate sentences for similar offences. The judge's discretion to decide on the particular blend of sentencing goals and the relevant aggravating or mitigating factors ensures that each case is decided on its facts, subject to the overarching guidelines and principles in the *Code* and in the case law.

[44] The wide discretion granted to sentencing judges has limits. It is fettered in part by the case law that has set down, in some circumstances, general ranges of sentences for particular offences, to encourage greater consistency between sentencing decisions in accordance with the principle of parity enshrined in the *Code*. But it must be remembered that, while courts should pay heed to these ranges, they are guidelines rather than hard and fast rules. A judge can order a sentence outside that range as long as it is in accordance with the principles and objectives of sentencing. Thus, a sentence falling outside the regular range of appropriate sentences is not necessarily unfit. Regard must be had to all the circumstances of the offence and the offender, and to the needs of the community in which the offence occurred.

[45] The discretion of a sentencing judge is also constrained by statute, not only through the general sentencing principles and objectives enshrined in ss. 718 to 718.2 articulated above but also through the restricted availability of certain sanctions in the *Code*. For instance, s. 732 prohibits a court from ordering that a sentence of imprisonment exceeding 90 days be served intermittently. Similar restrictions exist for sanctions such as discharges (s. 730), fines (s. 734), conditional sentences (s. 742.1) and probationary terms (s. 731). Parliament has also seen fit to reduce the scope of available sanctions for certain offences through the enactment of mandatory minimum sentences. A relatively new phenomenon in Canadian law, the minimum sentence is a forceful expression of

governmental policy in the area of criminal law. Certain minimum sentences have been successfully challenged under s. 12 of the *Charter* on the basis that they constituted grossly disproportionate punishment in the circumstances of the case (*R. v. Smith*, [1987] 1 S.C.R. 1045; *R. v. Bill* (1998), 13 C.R. (5th) 125 (B.C.S.C.)), while others have been upheld (*R. v. Morrisey*, 2000 SCC 39, [2000] 2 S.C.R. 90). Absent a declaration of unconstitutionality, minimum sentences must be ordered where so provided in the *Code*. A judge's discretion does not extend so far as to override this clear statement of legislative intent.

• • •

[47] The sentencing principles described above must be understood and applied within the overarching framework of our Constitution. Thus it may, at times, be appropriate for a court to address a *Charter* breach when passing sentence. This may be accomplished without resort to s. 24(1) of the *Charter*, given the court's broad discretion under ss. 718 to 718.2 of the *Code* to craft a fit sentence that reflects all the factual minutiae of the case. If the facts alleged to constitute a *Charter* breach are related to one or more of the relevant principles of sentencing, then the sentencing judge can properly take those facts into account in arriving at a fit sentence. Section 718.2(a) of the *Code* provides that a court should reduce a sentence "to account for *any* relevant ... mitigating circumstances relating to the offence or the offender." It would be absurd to suggest that simply because some facts also tend to suggest a violation of the offender's *Charter* rights, they could no longer be considered relevant mitigating factors in the determination of a fit sentence.

[48] Indeed, the sentencing regime under Canadian law must be implemented within, and not apart from, the framework of the *Charter*. Sentencing decisions are always subject to constitutional scrutiny. A sentence cannot be "fit" if it does not respect the fundamental values enshrined in the *Charter*. Thus, incidents alleged to constitute a *Charter* violation can be considered in sentencing, provided that they bear the necessary connection to the sentencing exercise. As mitigating factors, the circumstances of the breach would have to align with the circumstances of the offence or the offender, as required by s. 718.2 of the *Code*. Naturally, the more egregious the breach, the more attention the court will likely pay to it in determining a fit sentence.

[49] This is consistent with the communicative function of sentencing. A proportionate sentence is one that expresses, to some extent, society's legitimate shared values and concerns. As Lamer C.J. stated in *M. (C.A.)*:

> Our criminal law is also a system of values. A sentence which expresses denunciation is simply the means by which these values are communicated. In short, in addition to attaching negative consequences to undesirable behaviour, judicial sentences should also be imposed in a manner which positively instills the basic set of communal values shared by all Canadians as expressed by the *Criminal Code*. [para. 81]

A sentence that takes account of a *Charter* violation is therefore able to communicate respect for the shared set of values expressed in the *Charter*. In the words of Professor Allan Manson:

> The communicative function of sentencing is all about conveying messages. The messages are directed to the community. They are about the values which ought to be important to the community.

("*Charter* Violations in Mitigation of Sentence" (1995), 41 C.R. (4th) 318, at p. 323)

Indeed, s. 718 of the *Criminal Code* describes the fundamental purpose of sentencing as that of contributing to "respect for the law and the maintenance of a just, peaceful and safe society." This function must be understood as providing scope for sentencing judges to consider not only the actions of the offender, but also those of state actors. Provided that the impugned conduct relates to the individual offender and the circumstances of his or her offence, the sentencing process includes consideration of society's collective interest in ensuring that law enforcement agents respect the rule of law and the shared values of our society.

[50] The conclusion that the circumstances of alleged *Charter* breaches can be considered during sentencing, when they are relevant to the offender and to the offence, is consistent with much of the sentencing jurisprudence. In several cases, courts have reduced a sentence to reflect the prejudice caused to the accused by the incident giving rise to a *Charter* violation, without invoking s. 24(1). For instance, in *R. v. Munoz*, 2006 ABQB 901, 69 Alta. L.R. (4th) 231, an offender's overall sentence was reduced to take account of the breach of his s. 7 and s. 12 rights by police guards. While awaiting trial for serious offences including robbery and aggravated assault, the accused was subject to acts of physical violence by the guards and was forced to wear a degrading prisoner uniform called a "baby doll." Writing for the court, Wilkins J. described the accused's treatment at the hands of the police as "grossly disproportionate to the punishment that was appropriate" (para. 77). He held that a fit sentence, notwithstanding the *Charter* breaches, would have been seven years' imprisonment, on the high end of the scale for those particular offences. Taking the breaches into account, and after ordering an enhanced credit of 33 months for time served in the remand facility, he ordered a sentence of two years less a day in jail. The court did not cite s. 24(1) of the *Charter* as authority for the sentence reduction.

. . .

[53] It is important to note that a sentence can be reduced in light of state misconduct even when the incidents complained of do not rise to the level of a *Charter* breach. In *Pigeon*, the court did not need to determine whether the accused's s. 7 rights had been violated, as there was sufficient scope within the regular sentencing process to address the impropriety of the police officers' actions. Likewise, the Ontario Court of Appeal held in *R. v. Bosley* (1992), 18 C.R. (4th) 347, that the trial judge had properly considered excessive but not unconstitutional delay as a mitigating factor in his determination of a fit sentence (see also *R. v. Leaver* (1996), 3 C.R. (5th) 138 (Ont. C.A.)). And in *R. v. Panousis*, 2002 ABQB 1109, 329 A.R. 47, the Alberta Court of Queen's Bench treated the delay in the proceedings as a relevant mitigating factor that led to a reduced sentence for the offence of trafficking in cocaine. Although the delay did not amount to a s. 11(b) violation, the court held that it had caused prejudice to the accused that was relevant and probative to the sentencing process. The majority of the Alberta Court of Appeal, in brief oral reasons (2004 ABCA 211 (CanLII)), reversed the trial judge's decision and imposed a sentence of incarceration of two years less a day and a heavy fine. The majority did not state whether it disagreed with the trial judge's finding that delay was a relevant mitigating circumstance, but it is notable that its final sentence went below the trial judge's appreciation of the usual sentences for serious drug offences.

. . .

[55] Thus, a sentencing judge may take into account police violence or other state misconduct while crafting a fit and proportionate sentence, without requiring the offender to prove that the incidents complained of amount to a *Charter* breach. Provided the interests at stake can properly be considered by the court while acting within the sentencing regime in the *Criminal Code*, there is simply no need to turn to the *Charter* for a remedy. However, if a *Charter* breach has already been alleged and established, a trial judge should not be prevented from reducing the sentence accordingly, so long as the incidents giving rise to the breach are relevant to the usual sentencing regime. Of course, as we shall see, as a general rule, a court cannot reduce a sentence below a mandatory minimum or order a reduced sentence that is not provided for by statute. That said, circumstances of a *Charter* breach or other instances of state misconduct, in exceptional circumstances, do allow a court to derogate from the usual rules to which its decisions are subject.

[56] Much of the discussion in this appeal turned on the reduction of sentences for acts that might also be *Charter* breaches. But this intense debate reflects a misapprehension of the flexibility and contextual nature of the sentencing process in Canada. It is true that a substantial strand of jurisprudence, emanating from several provinces, has granted reductions of sentences under s. 24(1) as *Charter* remedies, in order to impose a just and appropriate punishment in specific cases. This jurisprudence may not have been completely mindful that events which justify findings of *Charter* breaches may also be circumstances which can legitimately form part of the analytical process leading to a fit sentence under the provisions of the *Criminal Code*. On their own, without the need to fall back upon the *Charter*, these provisions can generally provide remedial protection to individuals whose rights have been infringed. With this in mind, I will now briefly review these cases.

[57] In the early days of the *Charter*, La Forest J. recognized sentence reduction as falling along the range of potential s. 24(1) remedies in *Mills v. The Queen*, [1986] 1 S.C.R. 863, at p. 974. Since then, the disagreements in the jurisprudence about whether sentence reduction is *prima facie* available as a *Charter* remedy have centred more on the types of limits that should constrain a court's resort to this remedy than on the availability of such a remedy.

· · ·

[61] Other courts have approached the use of sentence reduction as a *Charter* remedy with greater hesitation. In *Glykis*, the Ontario Court of Appeal held that the trial judge should not have compensated for improper police action by reducing the offenders' sentences. The two accused were apprehended at Pearson airport when they admitted to smuggling drugs into the country under their clothing. They were informed of their right to counsel but were denied the right to consult with a lawyer until after they had been searched. As a result, their consultation was delayed by approximately two hours. Writing for the court, Dubin C.J.O. upheld the trial judge's finding of a s. 10(b) breach but concluded that sentence reduction should only be afforded as a *Charter* remedy if the breach somehow mitigates the seriousness of the offence, or if it constitutes a form of additional punishment or hardship for the accused. Despite his concerns with the trial judge's reasoning, Dubin C.J.O. upheld the 12-month concurrent sentences ordered at trial.

[62] These two limits on the use of sentence reduction to remedy a *Charter* breach from *Glykis* were mentioned by the B.C. Court of Appeal in *R. v. Carpenter*, 2002 BCCA

301, 168 B.C.A.C. 137. In that case, the court delivered a fairly scathing criticism of sentence reduction as a s. 24(1) remedy. The accused in *Carpenter* was convicted for importing heroin into Canada and appealed his conviction and his sentence based on the ss. 8 and 10(b) breaches he suffered at the time of his arrest. Newbury J.A., for the majority, held that sentence reduction under s. 24(1) was problematic in that it would offend the principles and objectives of sentencing in ss. 718 to 718.2 of the *Criminal Code*, it would impermissibly shift the focus of the inquiry from the offender and the offence to the conduct of state officials, and it would stretch "judicial resources to their limit" (para. 28). Her ruling essentially foreclosed the possibility of ever reducing a sentence to remedy a *Charter* violation. In dissenting reasons, Donald J.A. relied on *Glykis* and concluded that the *Charter* breaches imposed hardship on the offender that was relevant to his punishment. To "credit" the offender for the penalty of the breaches, Donald J.A. would have reduced the sentence from six to five years' imprisonment.

[63] The judgments relying on s. 24(1) appear to have been concerned about instances of abuse of process or misconduct by state agents in the course of the events leading to an arrest, to charges or to other criminal procedures. But, inasmuch as they relate to the offender and the offence, those facts become relevant circumstances within the meaning of the sentencing provisions of the *Criminal Code*. As such, they become part of the factors that sentencing judges will take into consideration in order to determine the proper punishment of the offender, without a need to turn to s. 24(1). Factors unrelated to the offence and to the offender will remain irrelevant to the sentencing process and will have to be addressed elsewhere. In addition, the discretion of the sentencing judge will have to be exercised within the parameters of the *Criminal Code*. The judge must impose sentences respecting statutory minimums and other provisions which prohibit certain forms of sentence in the case of specific offences.

[64] A few final comments about the position of the *Charter* in relation to the sentencing process are in order. Like other legal processes, the sentencing system remains subject to the scrutiny of the *Charter* and its overarching values and principles. Although, as we have seen above, the proper interpretation and application of the sentencing process will allow courts to effectively address most of the situations where *Charter* breaches are alleged, there may be exceptions to this general rule. I do not foreclose, but do not need to address in this case, the possibility that, in some exceptional cases, sentence reduction outside statutory limits, under s. 24(1) of the *Charter*, may be the sole effective remedy for some particularly egregious form of misconduct by state agents in relation to the offence and to the offender. In that case, the validity of the law would not be at stake, the sole concern being the specific conduct of those state agents.

[65] In the present case, I agree that the acts of the police officers are serious. Although the Court of Appeal did not need to rely on s. 24(1) of the *Charter*, it crafted a fit and appropriate sentence which addressed the circumstances of the accused, while remaining within the statutory parameters of the *Criminal Code*.

NOTE

After *Nasogaluak*, in cases of egregious state misconduct, a sentencing judge can consider whether to mitigate the sentence without resort to s 24(1). However, not all Charter violations constitute egregious state misconduct, but *still, the accused's constitutional rights have been violated.* As far as a potential role for s 24(1) in the face of a mandatory penalty, LeBel J said (*Nasogaluak* at para 55), without amplification:

> Of course, as we shall see, as a general rule, a court cannot reduce a sentence below a mandatory minimum or order a reduced sentence that is not provided for by statute. That said, circumstances of a *Charter* breach or other instances of state misconduct, *in exceptional circumstances, do allow a court to derogate from the usual rules to which its decisions are subject.* [Emphasis added.]

FURTHER READING

Cairns Way, Rosemary. "A Disappointing Silence: Mandatory Minimums and Substantive Equality" (2015), 18 CR (7th) 297.

Dufraimont, Lisa. "*R. v. Ferguson* and the Search for a Coherent Approach to Mandatory Minimum Sentences Under Section 12" (2008) 42 SCLR (2d) 459.

Manson, Allan. "Arbitrary Disproportionality: A New Charter Standard for Measuring the Constitutionality of Mandatory Minimum Sentences" (2012) 57 SCLR (2d) 173.

Paciocco, Palma. "Proportionality, Discretion, and the Roles of Judges and Prosecutors at Sentencing" (2014) 18 Can Crim L Rev 241.

Parkes, Debra. "From *Smith* to *Smickle*: The Charter's Minimal Impact on Mandatory Sentences" (2012) 57 SCLR (2d) 149.

Roach, Kent. "Searching for *Smith*: The Constitutionality of Mandatory Sentences" (2001) 39 Osgoode Hall LJ 367.

Appeals

I. INTRODUCTION

In sentencing, as in all other matters, there is no right of appeal unless it is specifically provided by statute. The *Criminal Code* makes provision in Part XXI for appeals against sentence in indictable cases and in Part XXVII for appeals in summary conviction matters.

The first part of this chapter, Section II, "General Principles," reviews basic principles relating to appeals against sentence as set out in the Code and in the jurisprudence of the Supreme Court of Canada. This review is somewhat skeletal, not least because as "a matter of established practice and sound policy" (*R v Proulx*, 2000 SCC 5 at para 2, [2000] 1 SCR 61) the Supreme Court infrequently hears appeals in sentencing matters, although, since the reform of 1995, there have been many more than was previously the case. Thus the first part of this chapter presents a formal sketch of the framework for sentencing appeals. The second part, Section III, "Practical Considerations," examines some practical considerations that arise in these matters.

The function of appellate courts is to correct error and provide guidance for lower courts. In theory, a sentence appeal is not simply an opportunity to reargue the case on the basis that the court below should have imposed a different sentence. There must be some identifiable error that warrants intervention on appeal. The fact that an appellate court would have imposed a different sentence is not a sufficient ground for appellate intervention. As in other matters, however, this general proposition allows for different perspectives. A judge or a court that takes a wide view of error or the need for guidance will intervene more frequently to disturb in some way the judgment of the lower court. Proponents of this view believe that the ultimate function of the appellate court is to ensure that justice is done in the case, and thus the threshold of appellate intervention is flexible. Another judge or court might take a narrower view of the role of appellate intervention. From this perspective, deference to the conclusion of the trial court is an important principle of restraint that justifies appellate intervention only where that conclusion is conspicuously anomalous. When these differing perspectives are coupled with the purposes, principles, and objectives of sentencing in any given case, and where they might conflict, it can be difficult to predict whether and why an appellate court will intervene. It's possible that a court will profess adherence to one view in principle and demonstrate another in practice.

These two perspectives are caricatures to some extent. They do not describe categories that can be easily contrasted—for example, as between liberal activism and conservative restraint. The jurisprudence is replete with examples that run in both directions, and with examples that seem to run in both directions at once. An important theme that runs through this chapter is the threshold for appellate intervention in sentencing matters and the extent to which appellate courts should substitute a different order for that imposed at first instance.

On a sentencing appeal there is ultimately only one question at issue—was the sentence fit? If it is not fit, it calls for correction. Current jurisprudence frames this question somewhat differently—does the sentencing decision require deference from an appellate court?

II. GENERAL PRINCIPLES

A. The Role of Appellate Courts

Typically, at the beginning of a considered judgment in a sentencing matter, it is common-place to find a paragraph such as this:

> An appellate court should not interfere with a sentence unless it is demonstrably unfit, there has been an error in principle, a failure to consider a relevant factor, consideration of improper factors, or an overemphasis of appropriate factors: R v M (CA) [1996] 1 SCR 500 at para 90; R v McDonnell, [1997] 1 SCR 948 at para 46. A sentence will be demonstra-bly unfit if it is clearly unreasonable, or is a substantial and marked departure from the sentences customarily imposed for similar offenders committing similar crimes: R v Shropshire, [1995] 4 SCR 227 at para 46; R v M (CA), supra at para 92. An error in principle, a failure to consider a relevant factor, consideration of improper factors, or an overempha-sis of appropriate factors are grounds that give rise to appellate review for reasons of inconsistency.

As will be seen below, there are other grounds that will attract appellate review, but a passage such as this restates basic points about the substantive reasons for appellate inter-vention with the terms of a sentence. The appellate court should be reluctant to intervene and the appellant, correspondingly, must persuade the court that there is a good reason to intervene. In McDonnell, below, the Supreme Court reviewed the approach to follow. Con-sider closely what the court said about this deferential standard of appellate review.

R v McDonnell
[1997] 1 SCR 948

SOPINKA J (Lamer CJ, Cory, Iacobucci, and Major JJ concurring):
    [15] Two recent cases, R v. Shropshire, [1995] 4 SCR 227, and R v. M. (C.A.), [1996] 1 SCR 500, set out the applicable standard of review of sentencing decisions. Iacobucci J, writing for the Court, stated in Shropshire at paras. 45-50:

Section 687(1) reads as follows:

> 687(1) Where an appeal is taken against sentence, the court of appeal shall, unless the sentence is one fixed by law, consider the *fitness* of the sentence appealed against, and may on such evidence, if any, as it thinks fit to require or to receive,
>
> (a) vary the sentence within the limits prescribed by law for the offence of which the accused was convicted; or
>
> (b) dismiss the appeal.

The question, then, is whether a consideration of the "fitness" of a sentence incorporates the very interventionist appellate review propounded by Lambert JA. With respect, I find that it does not. An appellate court should not be given free reign to modify a sentencing order simply because it feels that a different order ought to have been made. The formulation of a sentencing order is a profoundly subjective process; the trial judge has the advantage of having seen and heard all of the witnesses whereas the appellate court can only base itself upon a written record. A variation in the sentence should only be made if the court of appeal is convinced it is not fit. That is to say, that it has found the sentence to be clearly unreasonable.

I would adopt the approach taken by the Nova Scotia Court of Appeal in the cases of *R v. Pepin* (1990), 98 NSR (2d) 238, and *R v. Muise* (1994), 94 CCC (3d) 119. In *Pepin*, at p. 251, it was held that:

> … in considering whether a sentence should be altered, the test is not whether we would have imposed a different sentence; we must determine if the sentencing judge applied wrong principles or (if) the sentence is clearly or manifestly excessive.

Further, in *Muise* it was held at pp. 123-24 that:

> In considering the fitness of a sentence imposed by a trial judge, this court has consistently held that it will not interfere unless the sentence imposed is clearly excessive or inadequate. …

> • • •

> The law on sentence appeals is not complex. If a sentence imposed is not clearly excessive or inadequate it is a fit sentence assuming the trial judge applied the correct principles and considered all relevant facts. … My view is premised on the reality that sentencing is not an exact science; it is anything but. It is the exercise of judgment taking into consideration relevant legal principles, the circumstances of the offence and the offender. The most that can be expected of a sentencing judge is to arrive at a sentence that is within an acceptable range. In my opinion, that is the true basis upon which Courts of Appeal review sentences when the only issue is whether the sentence is inadequate or excessive.

> • • •

> Unreasonableness in the sentencing process involves the sentencing order falling outside the "acceptable range" of orders; this clearly does not arise in the present appeal. An error of law involves a situation such as that found in *R v. Chaisson*, [1995] 2 SCR 1118, in which a sentencing judge, while calculating the total time period of incarceration for the purposes of a "half-time" parole ineligibility order under s. 741.2 of the *Code*, erroneously included two offences in the calculations notwithstanding the fact that these specific offences were not listed in the schedule of offences to which the s. 741.2 orders apply. [Emphasis in original.]

[16] The deferential approach set out in *Shropshire* was confirmed and refined in *M. (C.A.)*. In that case, Lamer CJ, on behalf of the Court, stated at paras. 90-92:

> Put simply, absent an error in principle, failure to consider a relevant factor, or an overemphasis of the appropriate factors, a court of appeal should only intervene to vary a sentence imposed at trial if the sentence is demonstrably unfit. Parliament explicitly vested sentencing judges with a *discretion* to determine the appropriate degree and kind of punishment under the *Criminal Code*. As s. 717(1) reads:
>
> > 717(1) Where an enactment prescribes different degrees or kinds of punishment in respect of an offence, the punishment to be imposed is, subject to the limitations prescribed in the enactment, in the *discretion* of the court that convicts the person who commits the offence.
>
> This deferential standard of review has profound functional justifications. As Iacobucci J explained in *Shropshire*, at para. 46, where the sentencing judge has had the benefit of presiding over the trial of the offender, he or she will have had the comparative advantage of having seen and heard the witnesses to the crime. But in the absence of a full trial, where the offender has pleaded guilty to an offence and the sentencing judge has only enjoyed the benefit of oral and written sentencing submissions (as was the case in both *Shropshire* and this instance), the argument in favour of deference remains compelling. A sentencing judge still enjoys a position of advantage over an appellate judge in being able to directly assess the sentencing submissions of both the Crown and the offender. A sentencing judge also possesses the unique qualifications of experience and judgment from having served on the front lines of our criminal justice system. Perhaps most importantly, the sentencing judge will normally preside near or within the community which has suffered the consequences of the offender's crime. As such, the sentencing judge will have a strong sense of the particular blend of sentencing goals that will be "just and appropriate" for the protection of that community. The determination of a just and appropriate sentence is a delicate art which attempts to balance carefully the societal goals of sentencing against the moral blameworthiness of the offender and the circumstances of the offence, while at all times taking into account the needs and current conditions of and in the community. The discretion of a sentencing judge should thus not be interfered with lightly.
>
> Appellate courts, of course, serve an important function in reviewing and minimizing the disparity of sentences imposed by sentencing judges for similar offenders and similar offences committed throughout Canada. ... But in exercising this role, courts of appeal must still exercise a margin of deference before intervening in the specialized discretion that Parliament has explicitly vested in sentencing judges. It has been repeatedly stressed that there is no such thing as a uniform sentence for a particular crime. ... Sentencing is an inherently individualized process, and the search for a single appropriate sentence for a similar offender and a similar crime will frequently be a fruitless exercise of academic abstraction. As well, sentences for a particular offence should be expected to vary to some degree across various communities and regions in this country, as the "just and appropriate" mix of accepted sentencing goals will depend on the needs and current conditions of and in the particular community where the crime occurred. For these reasons, consistent with the general standard of review we articulated in *Shropshire*, I believe that a court of appeal should only intervene to minimize the disparity of sentences where the sentence imposed by the trial judge is in

substantial and marked departure from the sentences customarily imposed for similar offenders committing similar crimes. [Emphasis in original.]

[17] I have included extensive references to these cases because in my view they are highly significant to the case at bar. *M. (C.A.)* set out that, in the absence of an error of principle, failure to consider a relevant factor, or overemphasis of the appropriate factors, a sentence should only be overturned if the sentence is demonstrably unfit. The respondent submitted that the sentencing judge in the present case failed to consider relevant factors and that the sentence was demonstrably unfit. Moreover, both the respondent and the Court of Appeal appear to have treated the failure of the sentencing judge to characterize the offence as a major sexual assault as an error in principle. I will discuss these contentions in turn.

. . .

[46] In my opinion, the decision to order concurrent or consecutive sentences should be treated with the same deference owed by appellate courts to sentencing judges concerning the length of sentences ordered. The rationale for deference with respect to the length of sentence, clearly stated in both *Shropshire* and *M. (C.A.)*, applies equally to the decision to order concurrent or consecutive sentences. In both setting duration and the type of sentence, the sentencing judge exercises his or her discretion based on his or her first-hand knowledge of the case; it is not for an appellate court to intervene absent an error in principle, unless the sentencing judge ignored factors or imposed a sentence which, considered in its entirety, is demonstrably unfit. The Court of Appeal in the present case failed to raise a legitimate reason to alter the order of concurrent sentences made by the sentencing judge; the court simply disagreed with the result of the sentencing judge's exercise of discretion, which is insufficient to interfere.

Layered over, under, and all around the settled policy of deference are the challenging and Byzantine principles relating to standards of appellate review, which apply in theory with the same vigour and coherence in sentencing appeals as in any other area. These principles, distilled to their essential elements, are as follows: Appellate intervention is justified if the court finds palpable and overriding error on a question of fact, but on a question of law the standard is correctness. On a question of mixed fact and law, it depends—correctness if there is some extricable question that is chiefly a question of law, and palpable and overriding error if it is chiefly a question of fact. In short, appellate intervention is justified either to set the instant case right because of a serious error of fact or to set the law right for the instant case and future cases because of an error of law—or both.

Since *Shropshire*, [1995] 4 SCR 227, *M (CA)*, [1996] 1 SCR 500, and *McDonnell*, above, the restrictive and deferential approach approved by the Supreme Court remains settled law. As suggested above, this trilogy of cases is routinely cited by appellate courts. Despite this consistency in the law, it must be recalled that the line between the margin for deference and the margin of reversible error is not always consistently drawn. In *Lacasse*, immediately below, the Supreme Court of Canada again considered the approach to appellate review. There is an important division between the majority and the minority concerning the grounds for appellate intervention.

R v Lacasse
2015 SCC 64, [2015] 3 SCR 1089

[The Court of Appeal reduced a sentence of six-and-a-half years to four years for two counts of impaired driving causing death.]

WAGNER J (Abella, Moldaver, Karakatsanis, and Côté JJ concurring):

[10] This appeal affords this Court, first of all, an occasion to clarify the standard on the basis of which an appellate court may intervene and vary a sentence imposed by a trial judge. The Court must determine, *inter alia*, the extent to which a deviation from a sentencing range that is otherwise established and adhered to may justify appellate intervention.

[11] This Court has on many occasions noted the importance of giving wide latitude to sentencing judges. Since they have, *inter alia*, the advantage of having heard and seen the witnesses, sentencing judges are in the best position to determine, having regard to the circumstances, a just and appropriate sentence that is consistent with the objectives and principles set out in the *Criminal Code* in this regard. The fact that a judge deviates from the proper sentencing range does not in itself justify appellate intervention. Ultimately, except where a sentencing judge makes an error of law or an error in principle that has an impact on the sentence, an appellate court may not vary the sentence unless it is demonstrably unfit.

• • •

[36] Appellate courts generally play a dual role in ensuring the consistency, stability and permanence of the case law in both the criminal and civil law contexts. First, they act as a safeguard against errors made by trial courts and are thus required to rectify errors of law and review the reasonableness of the exercise of discretion. They must ensure that trial courts state the law correctly and apply it uniformly.

[37] Second, appellate courts must ensure the coherent development of the law while formulating guiding principles to ensure that it is applied consistently in a given jurisdiction. They must therefore clarify the law where clarification is necessary or where conflicting decisions have been rendered: T. Desjardins, *L'appel en droit criminel et pénal* (2nd ed. 2012), at p. 1. In Quebec, the Court of Appeal has an additional responsibility in civil cases, since it ensures the harmonious interpretation of the distinctive rules of Quebec civil law.

[38] In the criminal law context, appellate courts play this dual role in appeals from both verdicts and sentences. In the case of an appeal from a sentence, the power of an appellate court to substitute a sentence for the one imposed by the trial judge is provided for in s. 687 of the *Criminal Code*:

> 687(1) Where an appeal is taken against sentence, the court of appeal shall, unless the sentence is one fixed by law, consider the fitness of the sentence appealed against, and may on such evidence, if any, as it thinks fit to require or to receive,
>
> (a) vary the sentence within the limits prescribed by law for the offence of which the accused was convicted; or
>
> (b) dismiss the appeal.
>
> (2) A judgment of a court of appeal that varies the sentence of an accused who was convicted has the same force and effect as if it were a sentence passed by the trial court.

[39] This Court has reiterated on many occasions that appellate courts may not intervene lightly, as trial judges have a broad discretion to impose the sentence they consider appropriate within the limits established by law: s. 718.3(1) of the *Criminal Code*; see also *R. v. Shropshire*, [1995] 4 S.C.R. 227, at para. 46; *R. v. L.M.*, [2008] 2 S.C.R. 163, at para. 14; *R. v. L.F.W.*, [2000] 1 S.C.R. 132, at para. 25; *R. v. Nasogaluak*, [2010] 1 S.C.R. 206, at paras. 43-46.

[40] In this regard, Iacobucci J. explained in *Shropshire* that consideration of the fitness of a sentence does not justify an appellate court taking an interventionist approach on appeal:

> An appellate court should not be given free rein to modify a sentencing order simply because it feels that a different order ought to have been made. The formulation of a sentencing order is a profoundly subjective process; the trial judge has the advantage of having seen and heard all of the witnesses whereas the appellate court can only base itself upon a written record. A variation in the sentence should only be made if the court of appeal is convinced it is not fit. That is to say, that it has found the sentence to be clearly unreasonable. [para. 46]

[41] In *Proulx*, this Court, per Lamer C.J., discussed these same principles, which continue to be relevant:

> In recent years, this Court has repeatedly stated that the sentence imposed by a trial court is entitled to considerable deference from appellate courts: see *Shropshire* ... , at paras. 46-50; *M. (C.A.)* ... , at paras. 89-94; *McDonnell* ... , at paras. 15-17 (majority); *R. v. W. (G.)*, [1999] 3 S.C.R. 597, at paras. 18-19. In *M. (C.A.)*, at para. 90, I wrote:

> > *Put simply, absent an error in principle, failure to consider a relevant factor, or an overemphasis of the appropriate factors, a court of appeal should only intervene to vary a sentence imposed at trial if the sentence is demonstrably unfit.* Parliament explicitly vested sentencing judges with a *discretion* to determine the appropriate degree and kind of punishment under the *Criminal Code*. [First emphasis added; second emphasis in original]

> • • •

> Although an appellate court might entertain a different opinion as to what objectives should be pursued and the best way to do so, that difference will generally not constitute an error of law justifying interference. Further, minor errors in the sequence of application of s. 742.1 may not warrant intervention by appellate courts. Again, I stress that appellate courts should not second-guess sentencing judges unless the sentence imposed is demonstrably unfit. [paras. 123 and 125]

These principles have since been reiterated in *L.M.* and *Nasogaluak*.

[42] My colleague states that a sentence may be unfit if there is a reviewable error in the thought process or reasoning on which it is based (para. 140). For this reason, in his view, where there is a reviewable error in the trial judge's reasoning, for example where the judge has characterized an element of the offence as an aggravating factor (para. 146), it is always open to an appellate court to intervene to assess the fitness of the sentence imposed by the trial judge. Having done so, the court can then affirm that sentence if it considers the sentence to be fit, or impose the sentence it considers appropriate without having to show deference (paras. 139 and 142). In other words, any error of law or error

in principle in a trial judge's analysis will open the door to intervention by an appellate court, which can then substitute its own opinion for that of the trial judge.

[43] With all due respect for my colleague, I am of the view that his comments on this point need to be qualified. I agree that an error in principle, the failure to consider a relevant factor or the erroneous consideration of an aggravating or mitigating factor can justify the intervention of an appellate court and permit that court to inquire into the fitness of the sentence and replace it with the sentence it considers appropriate. However, in my opinion, every such error will not necessarily justify appellate intervention regardless of its impact on the trial judge's reasoning. If the rule were that strict, its application could undermine the discretion conferred on sentencing judges. It is therefore necessary to avoid a situation in which [TRANSLATION] "the term 'error in principle' is trivialized": *R. v. Lévesque-Chaput*, 2010 QCCA 640, at para. 31 (CanLII).

[44] In my view, an error in principle, the failure to consider a relevant factor or the erroneous consideration of an aggravating or mitigating factor will justify appellate intervention only where it appears from the trial judge's decision that such an error had an impact on the sentence.

[45] For example, in *R. v. Gavin*, 2009 QCCA 1, the Quebec Court of Appeal found, first, that the trial judge had erred in considering a lack of remorse and the manner in which the defence had been conducted as aggravating circumstances (para. 29 (CanLII)). However, it then considered the impact of that error on the sentence and stated the following, at para. 35 :

> [TRANSLATION] I find that the lack of remorse was a secondary factor in the trial judge's assessment. This is apparent in the wording of the judgment. The judge referred to and considered all of the relevant sentencing factors, and the issue of lack of remorse was nothing more than incidental. … Consequently, unless the Court finds that the sentence imposed was harsher because the judge erroneously determined that the defence's conduct (as in *R. v. Beauchamp* …) and the lack of remorse were aggravating circumstances, this error in principle had no real effect on the sentence. Essentially, therefore, our task now is to ensure that the sentence is not clearly unreasonable … .

Thus, the Court of Appeal, finding that the error in principle made by the trial judge was not determinative and had had no effect on the sentence, rightly concluded that the error in question could not on its own justify the court's intervention. This ultimately led the court to inquire into whether the sentence was clearly unreasonable having regard to the circumstances.

[46] The Quebec Court of Appeal also adopted this reasoning in *R. v. Sidhu*, 2009 QCCA 2441. As in *Gavin*, the trial judge had considered lack of remorse as an aggravating factor (para. 23 (CanLII)), but the Court of Appeal found that this error was not determinative and had had no effect on the sentence (para. 24). Since the sentence the judge imposed would not have been different had there been no mistake in that respect (para. 26), the error was not reviewable (para. 55). Thus, rather than simply substituting its opinion for that of the trial judge because he had made an error in principle, the Court of Appeal limited itself to considering whether, independently of that error, the sentence was unreasonable or demonstrably unfit. On finding that that was not the case, it decided not to intervene (para. 55).

[47] On this issue, the impact of two decisions cited by my colleague in support of his opinion that any error of law or error in principle justifies the intervention of a court of appeal needs to be clarified and qualified. In *R. v. Flight*, 2014 ABCA 380, 584 A.R. 392, the Alberta Court of Appeal found that the trial judge had erred in considering the consumption of alcohol and the death of a victim as aggravating circumstances where the accused was charged with impaired driving causing death (para. 4). The Court of Appeal therefore intervened to substitute its own opinion for that of the trial judge on the ground that the judge had erred in principle. However, the court explained that it was difficult to determine what weight the trial judge had given to the aggravating factors at issue in his judgment (para. 5). And in *Stimson*, the Alberta Court of Appeal identified at least four errors in principle in the trial judge's reasons, and there was no doubt that they had affected his analysis (paras. 20-27). The Court of Appeal's intervention was therefore clearly warranted.

[48] The reminder given by this Court about showing deference to a trial judge's exercise of discretion is readily understandable. First, the trial judge has the advantage of having observed the witnesses in the course of the trial and having heard the parties' sentencing submissions. Second, the sentencing judge is usually familiar with the circumstances in the district where he or she sits and therefore with the particular needs of the community in which the crime was committed: *R. v. M. (C.A.)*, [1996] 1 S.C.R. 500, at para. 91. Finally, as Doherty J.A. noted in *R. v. Ramage* (2010), 2010 ONCA 488, 257 C.C.C. (3d) 261, the appropriate use of judicial resources is a consideration that must never be overlooked:

> Appellate repetition of the exercise of judicial discretion by the trial judge, without any reason to think that the second effort will improve upon the results of the first, is a misuse of judicial resources. The exercise also delays the final resolution of the criminal process, without any countervailing benefit to the process. [para. 70]

[49] For the same reasons, an appellate court may not intervene simply because it would have weighed the relevant factors differently. In *Nasogaluak*, LeBel J. referred to *R. v. McKnight* (1999), 135 C.C.C. (3d) 41 (Ont. C.A.), at para. 35, in this regard:

> To suggest that a trial judge commits an error in principle because in an appellate court's opinion the trial judge gave too much weight to one relevant factor or not enough weight to another is to abandon deference altogether. The weighing of relevant factors, the balancing process is what the exercise of discretion is all about. To maintain deference to the trial judge's exercise of discretion, the weighing or balancing of relevant factors must be assessed against the reasonableness standard of review. Only if by emphasizing one factor or by not giving enough weight to another, the trial judge exercises his or her discretion unreasonably should an appellate court interfere with the sentence on the ground the trial judge erred in principle. [para. 46]

[50] The Quebec Court of Appeal commented to the same effect in *Lévesque-Chaput*, at para. 31:

> [TRANSLATION] There is no doubt that he focused on the mitigating circumstances, over-emphasizing them in the appellant's opinion, but that balancing exercise was within his jurisdiction and the reasons he gave make it easy to follow his reasoning.

[51] Furthermore, the choice of sentencing range or of a category within a range falls within the trial judge's discretion and cannot in itself constitute a reviewable error. An appellate court may not therefore intervene on the ground that it would have put the sentence in a different range or category. It may intervene only if the sentence the trial judge imposed is demonstrably unfit.

[52] It is possible for a sentence to be demonstrably unfit even if the judge has made no error in imposing it. As Laskin J.A. mentioned, writing for the Ontario Court of Appeal, the courts have used a variety of expressions to describe a sentence that is "demonstrably unfit": "clearly unreasonable," "clearly or manifestly excessive," "clearly excessive or inadequate," or representing a "substantial and marked departure": *R. v. Rezaie*, (1996), 31 O.R. (3d) 713 (C.A.), at p. 720. All these expressions reflect the very high threshold that applies to appellate courts when determining whether they should intervene after reviewing the fitness of a sentence.

[53] This inquiry must be focused on the fundamental principle of proportionality stated in s. 718.1 of the *Criminal Code*, which provides that a sentence must be "proportionate to the gravity of the offence and the degree of responsibility of the offender." A sentence will therefore be demonstrably unfit if it constitutes an unreasonable departure from this principle. Proportionality is determined both on an individual basis, that is, in relation to the accused him or herself and to the offence committed by the accused, and by comparison with sentences imposed for similar offences committed in similar circumstances. Individualization and parity of sentences must be reconciled for a sentence to be proportionate: s. 718.2(a) and (b) of the *Criminal Code*.

[54] The determination of whether a sentence is fit also requires that the sentencing objectives set out in s. 718 of the *Criminal Code* and the other sentencing principles set out in s. 718.2 be taken into account. Once again, however, it is up to the trial judge to properly weigh these various principles and objectives, whose relative importance will necessarily vary with the nature of the crime and the circumstances in which it was committed. The principle of parity of sentences, on which the Court of Appeal relied, is secondary to the fundamental principle of proportionality. This Court explained this as follows in *M. (C.A.)*:

> It has been repeatedly stressed that there is no such thing as a uniform sentence for a particular crime. ... Sentencing is an inherently individualized process, and the search for a single appropriate sentence for a similar offender and a similar crime will frequently be a fruitless exercise of academic abstraction. [para. 92]

[55] This principle of parity of sentences also means that the deference owed to the sentencing judge must be shown except in the circumstances mentioned above. The Court said the following in this regard in *L.M.*:

> This exercise of ensuring that sentences are similar could not be given priority over the principle of deference to the trial judge's exercise of discretion, since the sentence was not vitiated by an error in principle and the trial judge had not imposed a sentence that was clearly unreasonable by failing to give adequate consideration to certain factors or by improperly assessing the evidence (*M. (C.A.)*, at para. 92, quoted in *McDonnell*, at para. 16; *W. (G.)*, at para. 19; see also Ferris, at p. 149, and Manson, at p. 93). [para. 35]

• • •

[68] My colleague finds that the Court of Appeal's reasons, read as a whole, show that it did not intervene solely because of a deviation from the sentencing range (para. 144). With respect, I cannot agree with this interpretation. As can be seen from the Court of Appeal's reasons, it justified its intervention on the basis that it was not open to the trial judge to impose a sentence falling into the third category of the sentencing range, because personal factors unfavourable to the respondent, which would normally support such a sentence rather than one from the second category, were almost non-existent in this case. It is clear from the Court of Appeal's reasons that it based its intervention primarily on an erroneous determination of the applicable sentencing category by the trial judge.

[69] I believe that the Court of Appeal was wrong to apply the sentencing range rigidly. By saying that the sentence should have been in the second category rather than at the lower end of the sentences in the third category, the Court of Appeal substituted its own assessment for that of the trial judge without first determining that the sentence in question was demonstrably unfit. In doing so, the Court of Appeal erred in applying the sentencing range mechanism as if it were a straitjacket. The sentencing ranges must in all cases remain only one tool among others that are intended to aid trial judges in their work.

[70] In this case, even though the sentence fell outside one of the categories of sentences that have been established since *Comeau*, this did not mean that it was manifestly excessive. Terms of imprisonment of six years or more have in fact been imposed on people without criminal records who were convicted of impaired driving causing death. For example, in *Kummer*, the Ontario Court of Appeal upheld an eight-year prison sentence imposed on a driver with no criminal record who had caused the deaths of three people while driving under the influence of alcohol. In *R. v. Wood* (2005), 196 C.C.C. (3d) 155, the Ontario Court of Appeal upheld a nine-year sentence imposed on a person who had no criminal record for impaired driving but had caused the deaths of three people and caused permanent injuries to another. In *Morneau*, the Quebec Court of Appeal upheld a six-year term of imprisonment on a charge of impaired driving causing the death of one person. Although the offender in that case already had a criminal record consisting of three convictions, the convictions all dated back more than ten years. In light of the foregoing, therefore, the sentence of six and a half years imposed in the instant case on an offender who caused the deaths of two young girls was not disproportionate.

[71] Moreover, by justifying its intervention on the basis of the trial judge's failure to adhere to the categories of sentences, the Court of Appeal was acknowledging that a six-year sentence was one of the possible results in this case. The six-month difference between the sentence imposed by the trial judge and the one the Court of Appeal believed should have been imposed on the basis of the category of sentences it chose does not constitute a marked departure that would have authorized it to intervene. In addition, although the sentence imposed at trial departs somewhat from the sentences applicable to the category the Court of Appeal considered the most appropriate, it falls within the overall range established by the Quebec courts, and lies clearly within the range of sentences imposed elsewhere in the country for similar offences.

[72] In sum, the sentence imposed by Judge Couture is consistent with the sentencing objectives and principles set out in the *Criminal Code*. Judge Couture properly emphasized the importance of deterrence and denunciation in this case, but he did not overlook the objective of rehabilitation (para. 92). Indeed, the Court of Appeal acknowledged that [TRANSLATION] "[t]he trial judge gave extensive reasons for the judgment to which the

motion relates, and it is clear that he very carefully weighed the sentencing objectives and principles set out in sections 718 to 718.2 of the *Criminal Code*" (para. 5 (CanLII)). Because Judge Couture did not make a reviewable error in his judgment, and because the sentence he imposed was not demonstrably unfit, it was not open to the Court of Appeal to intervene and substitute its own assessment for his. The Court of Appeal nevertheless reduced the sentence imposed at trial, which was indeed severe, without taking account of the principle that deterrence and denunciation must be emphasized in such cases. In reducing the sentence imposed by Judge Couture on the basis that it departed from the principle of proportionality, the Court of Appeal also disregarded the local reality, thereby itself departing from the objectives of deterrence and denunciation.

GASCON J (McLachlin CJ concurring) (dissenting):

• • •

[135] My colleague states that this appeal affords the Court an opportunity to clarify the standard on the basis of which an appellate court may intervene in sentencing decisions (para. 10). In my opinion, there is no reason to believe that this is necessary. The applicable standard is well known, and when all is said and done, the appeal before us concerns only how it should be applied in the circumstances of this case.

[136] In *Nasogaluak*, this Court summarized the applicable law as follows: "... a sentence [can] only be interfered with if it [is] 'demonstrably unfit' *or* if it reflect[s] an error in principle, the failure to consider a relevant factor, or the over-emphasis of a relevant factor" (para. 46, citing *M. (C.A.)*, at para. 90 (emphasis added)). In *Paré*, a case that was referred to in the decisions of the courts below, the Quebec Court of Appeal reiterated the principles established in those cases and wrote the following:

> [TRANSLATION] ... *a court of appeal may intervene only* in circumstances indicating an error in principle, an overemphasis of an appropriate factor, or a failure to consider a relevant factor, *unless* the sentence is quite simply demonstrably unfit or, in other words, clearly unreasonable. Thus, appellate courts retain the power to ensure that sentences are consistent with those imposed "for similar offences committed in similar circumstances"; indeed, this is set out in subsection 718.2(b) *Cr. C.* [Emphasis added; para. 38 (CanLII).]

[137] If a party shows that the trial judge made an error in principle, failed to consider a relevant factor or overemphasized appropriate factors, I do not think it can be said that the judge acted within the limits of his or her discretion in sentencing matters. In such cases, the relevant decisions of this Court do not require that the sentence also be shown to be demonstrably unfit before an appellate court can intervene. The effect of such a requirement would be to raise the recognized standard of intervention.

[138] In my opinion, the current approach is neither incongruous nor unfair. The highly deferential standard of appellate review must be adhered to as long as the trial judge did not err in principle, fail to consider a relevant factor or overemphasize appropriate factors: *R. v. Stone*, [1999] 2 S.C.R. 290, at para. 230. Even if none of these three situations exists, however, intervention may be necessary if the sentence is demonstrably unfit. This other ground for intervention has been described in several ways: a court of appeal can still vary a sentence if it is convinced that the sentence is "not fit" or "clearly unreasonable" (*R. v. Shropshire*, [1995] 4 S.C.R. 227, at para. 46), that it is "unreasonabl[e]"

or "fall[s] outside the 'acceptable range'" (*Shropshire*, at para. 50), or that it is "demonstrably unfit" (*R. v. McDonnell*, [1997] 1 S.C.R. 948, at para. 17; *M. (C.A.)*, at para. 90).

[139] Therefore, where a reviewable error is shown in the reasoning on which a sentence is based, it is appropriate for an appellate court to be able to intervene and assess the fitness of the sentence. This does not necessarily mean that the court will automatically vary the sentence. As the passage from *Paré* quoted above indicates, the court's role in ensuring consistency in sentencing requires it before intervening to ascertain, among other things, that the sentence represents a "substantial and marked departure from the sentences customarily imposed for similar offenders committing similar crimes": *M. (C.A.)*, at para. 92; see also *Stone*, at para. 230. An error merely opens the door to intervention and permits an appellate court to reopen the sentencing analysis. Only by correctly repeating the analytical exercise can the court determine whether the sanction imposed on the offender is just and appropriate or whether it should be varied. In other words, the court can then impose the sentence it considers appropriate without having to show deference: T. Desjardins, *L'appel en droit criminel et pénal* (2nd ed. 2012), at p. 217, citing, *inter alia*, *R. v. Gallon*, 2006 NBCA 31, 247 N.B.R. (2d) 317; *R. v. Biancofiore* (1997), 35 O.R. (3d) 782 (C.A.), at p. 789; and *R. v. Gagnon* (1998), 130 C.C.C. (3d) 194 (Que. C.A.), at para. 6.

[140] In this regard, it seems to me that this Court's decisions reflect a careful reading of s. 687 *Cr. C.* What emerges from the Court's remarks is that the fitness of a sentence is not assessed in the abstract. There is no such thing as a uniform sentence for a particular crime, and sentencing is an inherently individualized process: *M. (C.A.)*, at para. 92. A sentence must reflect a consideration of all the relevant factors, and it is in this sense that the "process" of sentencing is important. In the words of Dickson J. in *R. v. Gardiner*, [1982] 2 S.C.R. 368, "[i]f policy considerations are to enter the picture, as they often do, there would appear to me to be every reason why this Court should remain available to adjudicate upon difficult and important questions of law in the sentencing process": p. 404. The fitness of a sentence is determined on the basis of several relevant principles, objectives and factors, and a sanction may be unfit if there is a reviewable error in the thought process or reasoning on which it is based. However, it is only by assessing that process or reasoning that an appellate court can determine whether the identified errors make the sentence unfit.

[141] I note that my colleague seems to detect a certain absoluteness in my words that is quite simply not there (paras. 42-43). I am not saying that a sentence cannot be fit if there is a reviewable error in the reasoning process on which it is based. Rather, I am saying that a sanction *may be unfit* in such a case, which is very different. The first of these wordings would be absolute. The second depends on the appellate court's assessment of the sanction in question, which is in fact made in accordance with the principles set out in my reasons.

[142] Therefore, although I agree that, as Hall J.A. stated in *R. v. Orr*, 2008 BCCA 76, 228 C.C.C. (3d) 432, at para. 7, an appellate court should not vary a sentence that is fit, I consider it imperative that that court retain its ability to rule on the trial court's analysis and to intervene where there is an error warranting its intervention.

[143] Finally, I agree with my colleague that it is accepted that the ranges established by appellate courts are in fact only guidelines, and not hard and fast rules (para. 60). A judge can therefore order a sentence outside the established range as long as it is in accordance

with the principles and objectives of sentencing. Regard must be had not only to the circumstances of the offence and the needs of the community in which the offence occurred, but also to the circumstances of the offender: *Nasogaluak*, at para. 44. As a corollary, the mere fact that a sentence falls within the range applicable to a certain type of crime does not necessarily make it fit, since the judge may, in determining the sentence, have failed to take account of the particular circumstances of the offender. It is by analyzing the trial judge's reasoning or thought process that an appellate court can determine whether a sentence that falls within the proper range is tailored to fit the circumstances of the offender and is therefore individualized and proportionate.

(3) Intervention of the Court of Appeal

[144] In light of the above, I find that the Court of Appeal properly justified its intervention in this case. Although the comments it made in para. 15 of its reasons might at first glance suggest that it took an inflexible view of the sentencing ranges, I believe that the substance of the court's reasoning can instead be found at paras. 16-17. I do not agree with my colleague that the Court of Appeal intervened solely because the trial judge had deviated from the proper sentencing range (para. 11) or because the sentence fell outside the accepted sentencing range (para. 16), or that it essentially focused its analysis on the application of the sentencing range (para. 30) or applied that range mechanically (para. 69). Rather, its reasons, read as a whole, show that its analysis went much further than that. I think it will be helpful to reproduce the entirety of paras. 15-17, which I find to be enlightening in this regard:

> [TRANSLATION] By imposing a sentence of 77 months' imprisonment (six years and six months minus one month because of the time spent by the applicant in pre-trial custody), the trial judge unquestionably placed the sentence at the lower end of the third category of sentences, the most severe ones. The respondent argued at the hearing that the sentence was actually in the second category, increased slightly because of the serious consequences of the offence, which had claimed two victims. *But that argument must be rejected, because "personal factors of the accused" that are unfavourable to the accused are normally what justify a move from the second to the third category.* This can be seen from the breakdown of sentences in recent cases.
>
> *However, such factors are almost non-existent in this case, as is clear from the report prepared by a probation officer for sentencing purposes and from the testimony given by the psychologist and the social worker who attended the applicant following the accident. The applicant has strong support from his family. There is virtually no possibility of him reoffending. It is likely that, once he has served his sentence, he will be able to find a job in an autobody repair business* owned by his mother. *There is no doubt that he is aware of the extreme seriousness of the consequences of his wrongdoing: he was and still is tortured by remorse,* so much so that the professionals around him became concerned about possible suicidal tendencies and took preventive action accordingly.
>
> *In light of the foregoing, the sentence imposed on October 4, 2013 is excessive because it departs from the principle of proportionality.* In individualizing the sentence in this case, *the judge should have given greater consideration to the applicant's potential for rehabilitation, which is substantial, and reduced the emphasis he placed on exemplarity.* A sentence that is severe without being draconian will be more than sufficient for the purposes of this last factor

in the case of *individuals who, like the applicant, have no record* (despite a few *Highway Safety Code* offences in his case), *are law-abiding and are capable of understanding the magnitude, for all those close to the victims,* of a tragedy like the one that occurred on June 17, 2011. [Emphasis added; footnote omitted.]

[2014 QCCA 1061, at paras 15-17 (CanLII).]

B. Jurisdiction

With respect to indictable offences, the rights of appeal for the accused and the Crown are set out in ss 675 and 676, respectively. In those sections, the Code refers specifically to a "sentence." In addition to orders relating to the more conspicuous sentencing options, s 673 defines a "sentence" to include various other orders and dispositions. Rights of appeal against sentence in summary conviction matters are provided in s 813 and, although there is no analogue to s 673 in Part XXVII, that definition is applicable *mutatis mutandis*. Where an indictable offence is tried with a summary conviction offence, an appeal against sentence on the latter may be taken under Part XXI.

Summary conviction appeals may be taken as of right to the "appeal court," which is defined by the Code as the superior court of the province or territory. In indictable matters, all appeals against sentence require leave of the Court of Appeal or a judge of that court. In several jurisdictions it is standard practice for the leave application and the appeal to be heard together. In others, the application is presented to a single judge who decides whether the case should be heard by a panel of the court.

The Supreme Court of Canada may hear sentencing appeals on a question of law or on a question of general importance. Although it has said in *Gardiner* and *Proulx* that it will rarely hear such cases, the language of s 40(1) of the *Supreme Court Act* gives the court a broad discretion to consider sentencing appeals.

Appellate review is essential to ensure the fitness of sentences, but an appellate court cannot interfere with a sentence unless it is properly seized of an appeal against sentence. On an appeal against conviction, for example, the court cannot open a question about the fitness of sentence: see *R v W (G)*, [1999] 3 SCR 597. It remains to be seen whether this principle applies with equal force in cases where the accused represents herself before the appellate court. To take an extreme example, suppose that the accused acts for herself on appeal against conviction, but it is transparently clear to the appellate court that the sentence was not only wrong in principle but also illegal. Would it not be appropriate for the court to suggest that the appellant be granted an extension of time in which to consider filing an appeal against sentence?

C. Powers

The most important power affecting the conduct of sentencing appeals is the discretion to admit fresh evidence, which is found in ss 683 and 687. As a general rule on appeals of any kind, fresh evidence refers to relevant information that was not available to be produced at first instance through the exercise of due diligence. The admissibility of such evidence is governed by the principles stated by the Supreme Court in *Palmer v R*, [1980] 1 SCR 759. The same principles apply in sentencing appeals.

R v Lévesque

2000 SCC 47, [2000] 2 SCR 487

GONTHIER J (McLachlin CJ, L'Heureux-Dubé, Iacobucci, Bastarache, and Binnie JJ concurring):

I. Issue

[1] This appeal concerns the rule that applies to the admission of fresh evidence on appeal from a sentence. In *Palmer v. The Queen*, [1980] 1 SCR 759, this Court set out the principles governing the admission of fresh evidence on appeal from a verdict. In the case at bar, it must be determined whether the criteria that apply are the same for both types of appeal, and whether the majority of the Court of Appeal erred by admitting in evidence the two expert reports tendered by the respondent, despite the objections of the appellant.

II. Facts

[2] On June 22, 1996, the respondent and his two accomplices went to the home of the Fortier family intending to make off with large amounts of money that he believed were kept in a safe. While these three individuals were in the shed located behind the house, they were surprised by David Fortier, aged thirteen. After grabbing him and tying him up, the respondent questioned him about the location of the safe and the people who were in the house. He put a shotgun cartridge in his mouth, which he then taped shut, and threatened him several times, both verbally and with his gun. The respondent then left the shed, taking David, with his gun pointed at the boy's head, and escorted him towards the house. The two accomplices followed. Once the respondent was inside the house, he attacked Bertrand Fortier, David's father, as he sat watching television with his wife. A fight broke out and a shot was fired in the fray. While this was going on, the two accomplices fled and one of the Fortier boys called the police. Mr. Fortier ultimately wrestled the respondent to the ground and the police arrived shortly afterward.

[3] On December 18, 1996, the respondent pleaded guilty to fifteen counts arising from the events of June 22, 1996. In appealing his sentence, the respondent is seeking to have three new reports admitted in evidence. The first, dated April 3, 1997, is entitled [TRANSLATION] "Psychological/psychiatric assessment report." This report was prepared by Marc Daigle, a psychologist, for Correctional Service Canada. The second report was written by Louis Morissette, a psychiatrist, at the respondent's request. It is dated March 17, 1998. The appellant objects to the admission of these two reports in evidence, but consents to the admission of the third report, which is by Jacques Bigras, a psychologist. That report is dated March 31, 1998, and was prepared for Correctional Service Canada at the end of a course taken by the respondent during his incarceration.

III. Relevant Legislation

[4] The relevant provisions of the *Criminal Code*, RSC, 1985, c. C-46, are as follows:

> 683(1) For the purposes of an appeal under this Part, the court of appeal may, where it considers it in the interests of justice,

(a) order the production of any writing, exhibit or other thing connected with the proceedings;

(b) order any witness who would have been a compellable witness at the trial, whether or not he was called at the trial,

(i) to attend and be examined before the court of appeal, or,

(ii) to be examined in the manner provided by rules of court before a judge of the court of appeal, or before any officer of the court of appeal or justice of the peace or other person appointed by the court of appeal for the purpose;

(c) admit, as evidence, an examination that is taken under subparagraph (b)(ii);

(d) receive the evidence, if tendered, of any witness, including the appellant, who is a competent but not compellable witness;

687(1) Where an appeal is taken against sentence, the court of appeal shall, unless the sentence is one fixed by law, consider the fitness of the sentence appealed against, and may on such evidence, if any, as it thinks fit to require or to receive,

(a) vary the sentence within the limits prescribed by law for the offence of which the accused was convicted; or

(b) dismiss the appeal.

IV. Proceedings

A. Court of Québec, Criminal and Penal Division, No. 505-01-008036-960, February 19, 1997

[5] On December 18, 1996, the respondent pleaded guilty to charges of kidnapping, confinement, assault with a weapon, uttering threats, disguise with intent, pointing a firearm, possession of an unregistered restricted weapon, robbery, breaking and entering a dwelling-house, and conspiracy to commit robbery. After the guilty pleas were entered, Judge Yves Lagacé ordered that a pre-sentence report be prepared pursuant to s. 721 of the *Criminal Code*. On February 19, 1997, after hearing submissions from both counsel and the testimony of Bernard Fortier, the accused's brother, the probation officer Philippe David, and the respondent himself, Judge Yves Lagacé sentenced the respondent to several terms of imprisonment to be served concurrently. The longest sentence was imprisonment for a term of ten years and six months on the kidnapping charge.

B. Quebec Court of Appeal, [1998] QJ No. 2680 (QL)

[6] On appeal, the respondent filed two motions seeking leave to adduce fresh evidence, in the form of the reports by Marc Daigle, a psychologist, and Louis Morissette, a psychiatrist. On April 6, 1998, a panel of three judges of the Court of Appeal (Beauregard, Gendreau and Baudouin JJA) referred that request to the panel that would determine the application to appeal the sentence.

[7] These motions were heard by Deschamps, Chamberland and Nuss JJA on July 8, 1998. They unanimously allowed the application for leave to appeal, since in their view the trial judge had erred by comparing this case with cases involving hostage-taking for ransom in determining the appropriate sentence. That finding is not in issue in this appeal. The majority of the Court of Appeal also allowed the motions to adduce fresh evidence, Chamberland JA. dissenting.

1. Deschamps JA (Nuss JA concurring)

[8] After stating that the principles laid down in *Palmer, supra,* are to be applied more flexibly in criminal cases than in civil cases, and that the provisions governing the admission of fresh evidence on appeal are different, depending on whether the Court is ruling in respect of a verdict (s. 683 of the *Criminal Code*) or a sentence (s. 687 of the *Criminal Code*), Deschamps JA said that a liberal approach must be taken on an appeal from a sentence when the admissibility of fresh evidence is in dispute. At para. 12, she concluded: [TRANSLATION] "while the two sections [ss. 683 and 687 of the *Criminal Code*] do not establish different rules, it is my view that at the very least the wording of s. 687 prescribes a flexible and liberal approach."

[9] Deschamps JA was of the opinion that the report prepared by the psychologist, Marc Daigle, met the requirements for admissibility. She noted that the appellant did not ask to have this assessment done and that the report was written less than two months after the probation officer's report, which was submitted to the trial judge. In addition, the report could not have been tendered at trial, since the psychological assessment takes place after sentencing. She says at para. 15:

> [TRANSLATION] While it is true that the appellant could have requested a separate expert opinion following receipt of the pre-sentence report, I cannot criticize him for failing to do so since, first, the appellant could not have foreseen that Mr. Daigle would have had an opinion diametrically opposed to that of Mr. David and, second, that would amount to encouraging competing expert opinions in cases where accused persons are dissatisfied with pre-sentence reports.

Ultimately, Deschamps JA felt that it was in the interests of justice to admit the psychologist's report by Mr. Daigle in evidence, since [TRANSLATION] "it explains the appellant's past in greater detail and shows his personality from a perspective that was not evident in the trial record. Whereas the pre-sentence report refers to a significant probability of reoffending, the psychologist's report by Mr. Daigle states the opposite" (para. 16).

[10] According to Deschamps JA, the admissibility of the report prepared by the psychiatrist, Dr. Morissette, was more debatable. She commented that the report was prepared at the respondent's request and that thirteen months had intervened between sentencing and the preparation of the report. She also stated that the portion of the report in which Dr. Morissette responded to the probation officer's report did not carry much weight. Nonetheless, she determined that the report was admissible, since it shed additional light on Mr. Daigle's report.

[11] In view of the error committed by the trial judge and in light of the fresh evidence, Deschamps JA substituted a sentence of five and a half years for the sentence of ten and a half years imposed by Judge Lagacé.

2. Chamberland JA (dissenting)

[12] In the view of Chamberland JA, the reports by Mr. Daigle and Dr. Morissette should not be admitted in evidence. It was his opinion that the respondent, by exercising minimal diligence, could have sought other opinions for the purpose of countering the probation officer's opinion concerning his personality and submitted them to the trial judge. At para. 31 he stated:

[TRANSLATION] I appreciate that the provisions governing fresh evidence differ depending whether the Court is being asked to rule as to guilt (section 683 Cr. C.) or the sentence (section 687 Cr. C.) but not, in my view, to the point that the Court must, unless there are completely exceptional circumstances (which are not found in the case at bar) or unless, of course, the other party consents, admit evidence that was readily available at trial (*R v. Stolar*, [1988] 1 SCR 480; *Palmer and Palmer v. R.*, [1980] 1 SCR 759). In short, it is my view that the present adversarial debate concerning the appellant's personality should have been conducted at trial rather than on appeal.

[13] In view of the error committed by the trial judge in sentencing, Chamberland JA would have substituted a sentence of imprisonment for eight years and six months for the sentence imposed by Judge Lagacé. He allowed the motion to submit fresh evidence for the sole purpose of admitting in evidence the report by Jacques Bigras, the psychologist.

V. Analysis

A. The Criteria Laid Down in Palmer

[14] In *Palmer, supra*, this Court considered the discretion of a court of appeal to admit fresh evidence pursuant to s. 610 of the *Criminal Code*, the predecessor of s. 683. After emphasizing that, in accordance with the wording of s. 610, the overriding consideration must be "the interests of justice," McIntyre J set out the applicable principles, at p. 775:

(1) The evidence should generally not be admitted if, by due diligence, it could have been adduced at trial provided that this general principle will not be applied as strictly in a criminal case as in civil cases: see *McMartin v. The Queen.*

(2) The evidence must be relevant in the sense that it bears upon a decisive or potentially decisive issue in the trial.

(3) The evidence must be credible in the sense that it is reasonably capable of belief, and

(4) It must be such that if believed it could reasonably, when taken with the other evidence adduced at trial, be expected to have affected the result.

In *R v. M. (P.S.)* (1992), 77 CCC (3d) 402 (Ont. CA), at p. 410, Doherty JA wrote the following concerning these principles:

The last three criteria are conditions precedent to the admission of evidence on appeal. Indeed, the second and third form part of the broader qualitative analysis required by the fourth consideration. The first criterion, due diligence, is not a condition precedent to the admissibility of "fresh" evidence in criminal appeals, but is a factor to be considered in deciding whether the interests of justice warrant the admission of the evidence: *McMartin v. The Queen*, [[1964] SCR 484], at pp. 148-50; *R v. Palmer, supra*, at p. 205.

In my view this is a good description of the way in which ... the principles set out in *Palmer* interact.

[15] This court was recently asked to apply these criteria in *R v. Warsing*, [1998] 3 SCR 579. In that case, the British Columbia Court of Appeal determined that the accused had not satisfied the due diligence criterion and refused to admit fresh evidence. At para. 51, Major J, for the majority, pointed out that due diligence is only one factor and its absence,

particularly in criminal cases, should be assessed in light of other circumstances. In other words, failure to meet the due diligence criterion should not be used to deny admission of fresh evidence on appeal if that evidence is compelling and it is in the interests of justice to admit it.

B. Criteria Applicable to Appeals Against Sentence

[16] Relying on the different wording of ss. 683 and 687 of the *Criminal Code* and the fact that the words used in s. 687, in her view, convey [TRANSLATION] "a much more discretionary connotation" (para. 10), Deschamps JA expressed the view that the rules set out in *Palmer* are to be applied more flexibly in an appeal from a sentence. With respect, I do not share that view. Although the rules concerning sources and types of evidence are more flexible in respect of sentence, the criteria for admitting fresh evidence on appeal are the same, regardless of whether the appeal relates to a verdict or a sentence.

[17] For purposes of comparison, I will reproduce again the relevant passages of ss. 683 and 687 of the *Criminal Code*:

> 683(1) For the purposes of an appeal under this Part, the court of appeal may, *where it considers it in the interests of justice*, ...
>
> 687(1) Where an appeal is taken against sentence, the court of appeal shall, unless the sentence is one fixed by law, consider the fitness of the sentence appealed against, and may on such evidence, if any, *as it thinks fit to require or to receive*, ... [Emphasis added.]

At first glance, it seems to me that the applicable criterion is not different: see *R v. Hogan* (1979), 50 CCC (2d) 439 (NSCA), at p. 449; and *R v. Edwards* (1996), 105 CCC (3d) 21 (Ont. CA), at p. 27. If a court of appeal thinks *fit* to admit fresh evidence, it will do so because it is *in the interests of justice* to admit it. Furthermore, I do not see how the discretion conferred on courts of appeal by s. 687 could be broader than the discretion conferred by s. 683 since, if such were the case, courts of appeal could exercise their discretion in a manner contrary to the interests of justice. However, it is assumed that the legislator did not intend statutes to apply in a way contrary to justice: P.-A. Côté, *The Interpretation of Legislation in Canada* (2nd ed. 1991), at p. 373. Like McIntyre J in *Palmer, supra*, at p. 775, I believe that the overriding consideration must be the interests of justice, regardless of whether the appeal is from a verdict or a sentence.

[18] In any case, it is my belief that the criteria stated by this Court in *Palmer* already call for a relaxed and flexible application and could hardly be relaxed any further. In accordance with the last three criteria, a court of appeal may admit only evidence that is relevant and credible, and could reasonably, when taken with the other evidence adduced at trial, be expected to have affected the result. If these criteria were made more flexible, it would be open to a court of appeal to accept evidence that was not relevant or credible, and that could not reasonably, when taken with the other evidence adduced at trial, be expected to have affected the result to which they led at trial. In my view, it would serve no purpose and be contrary to the interests of justice to introduce this kind of flexibility.

[19] Failure to satisfy the first criterion, due diligence, is not always fatal. As Major J said in *Warsing, supra*, at para. 51:

> It is desirable that due diligence remain only one factor and its absence, particularly in criminal cases, should be assessed in light of other circumstances. If the evidence is compelling

and the interests of justice require that it be admitted then the failure to meet the test should yield to permit its admission.

This passage clearly shows that the due diligence criterion must be applied flexibly. In my view, it is not necessary to make it more flexible in the context of appeals from sentence. While due diligence is not a necessary prerequisite for the admission of fresh evidence on appeal, it is an important factor that must be taken into account in determining whether it is in the interests of justice to admit or exclude fresh evidence. As Doherty JA said in *M. (P.S.)*, *supra*, at p. 411:

> While the failure to exercise due diligence is not determinative, it cannot be ignored in deciding whether to admit "fresh" evidence. The interests of justice referred to in s. 683 of the *Criminal Code* encompass not only an accused's interest in having his or her guilt determined upon all of the available evidence, but also the integrity of the criminal process. Finality and order are essential to that integrity. The criminal justice system is arranged so that the trial will provide the opportunity to the parties to present their respective cases and the appeal will provide the opportunity to challenge the correctness of what happened at the trial. Section 683(1)(d) of the *Code* recognizes that the appellate function can be expanded in exceptional cases, but it cannot be that the appellate process should be used routinely to augment the trial record. Were it otherwise, the finality of the trial process would be lost and cases would be retried on appeal whenever more evidence was secured by a party prior to the hearing of the appeal. For this reason, the exceptional nature of the admission of "fresh" evidence on appeal has been stressed: *McMartin v. The Queen*, *supra*, at p. 148.
>
> The due diligence criterion is designed to preserve the integrity of the process and it must be accorded due weight in assessing the admissibility of "fresh" evidence on appeal.

In my view, these considerations are equally relevant in the context of an appeal from sentence. Accordingly, due diligence in producing fresh evidence is a factor that must be taken into account in an appeal from sentence, on the same basis as the other three criteria set out in *Palmer*.

[20] While the admission of fresh evidence in an appeal from a sentence cannot lead to a new trial, unlike admission of fresh evidence in an appeal from a verdict (see the wording of ss. 687 and 683 of the *Criminal Code*), I do not believe that this difference justifies the application of different tests. The integrity of the criminal process and the role of appeal courts could be jeopardized by the routine admission of fresh evidence on appeal, since this would create a two-tier sentencing system. That kind of system would be incompatible with the high standard of review applicable to appeals from sentences and the underlying "profound functional justifications": see *R v. M. (C.A.)*, [1996] 1 SCR 500, at para. 91. Despite the fresh evidence, the sentencing judge, unlike the appeal judge, has the benefit of being able to directly assess the other evidence, the testimony and the submissions of the parties, as well as being familiar with the needs and current conditions of and in the community where the crime was committed: see *M. (C.A.)*, *supra*, at para. 91. Furthermore, appeal courts are not the appropriate forum in which to determine questions of fact, and they should do so only when the fresh evidence presents certain characteristics such as would justify expanding their traditional role. This Court has already identified those characteristics, in *Palmer*. In my view, whether the appeal relates to a verdict or a sentence, the criteria laid down by this Court in *Palmer* are the criteria that are to be applied where a court of appeal is determining whether to admit fresh evidence.

[21] In addition to citing the different wording of ss. 683 and 687 of the *Criminal Code*, Deschamps JA refers to cases decided in other provinces. A number of courts of appeal have considered the issue of admission of fresh evidence on an appeal from a sentence: see *R v. Lockwood* (1971), 5 CCC (2d) 438 (Ont. CA); *Hogan, supra*; *R v. Irwin* (1979), 48 CCC (2d) 423 (Alta. CA); *R v. Langille*, (1987), 77 NSR (2d) 224 (CA); *R v. Archibald* (1992), 15 BCAC 301; *R v. Lemay* (1998), 127 CCC 528 (3d) (Que. CA); *R v. Gauthier*, [1996] QJ No. 952 (QL) (CA); *R v. McDow* (1996), 147 NSR (2d) 343 (CA); *Edwards, supra*; *R v. Riley* (1996), 107 CCC (3d) 278 (NSCA); and *R v. Mesgun* (1997), 121 CCC (3d) 439 (Ont. CA). Some courts of appeal have maintained that the criteria to be applied are the same, whether the appeal relates to a verdict or a sentence: see *Hogan, supra*, at p. 449, and *Edwards, supra*, at p. 27. Others have stated that the rules relating to the admission of fresh evidence were applied more flexibly or informally in the context of an appeal from a sentence: see *Hogan, supra*, at p. 453; *Langille, supra*; *Edwards, supra*, at p. 28; and *Riley, supra*, at p. 283. However, a careful review of the jurisprudence reveals that, far from applying different criteria, courts of appeal have invariably applied the criteria set out in *Palmer*, whether expressly or by implication (for examples of the application of the due diligence criterion, see *Lockwood, Hogan, Irwin, Langille, Edwards* and *Mesgun*; for examples of the application of the relevance criterion, see *Edwards* and *Lemay*; and for an example of the application of the criteria relating to credibility and effect on the result, see *Langille*). In addition, as I have already explained, it is neither desirable nor really possible to relax the rule laid down in *Palmer*, in view of its inherent flexibility and the requirements associated with the interests of justice.

[22] I therefore find that the criteria set out in *Palmer* are applicable to applications to tender fresh evidence in an appeal from a sentence. Before applying these criteria to the two reports in the case at bar, I believe it is worthwhile to briefly discuss the concepts of admissibility and probative value in the context of the admission of fresh evidence on appeal, as well as certain specific characteristics of the sentencing process.

• • •

[28] To summarize, the probative value of fresh evidence must be considered in order to determine whether it is admissible on appeal. To facilitate determination of the probative value of fresh evidence, it is desirable that it be tested by the party challenging it. For this purpose, that party should make a formal motion to the court of appeal and explain how it wishes to test the fresh evidence. Failure by a party to test fresh evidence does not relieve a court of appeal from applying the criteria established in *Palmer*.

[29] The application of those criteria in the context of an appeal from a sentence will inevitably be influenced by the specific characteristics of the sentencing process, even though the criteria for the admission of fresh evidence remain fundamentally the same. I will now briefly consider some of these specific characteristics and their interaction with the *Palmer* criteria.

D. Application of the Criteria in the Context of an Appeal Against Sentence

[30] As pointed out by Macdonald JA in *Langille, supra*, the strict rules of a trial do not apply to a sentencing hearing. For example, hearsay evidence may be accepted at the sentencing stage *where found to be credible and trustworthy*: see *R v. Gardiner*, [1982] 2 SCR 368, at p. 414. This relaxation of the rules is explained by the fact that the judge must determine the appropriate sentence for the accused, and to do so must have as much

information as possible about him. In my view, the *Palmer* criteria do not compromise the more flexible nature of the rules relating to the sources and types of evidence on which judges may base their sentences. The criteria concerning the admission of fresh evidence on appeal do not relate to the sources and types of evidence and do not demand that the strict rules of a trial apply to fresh evidence proffered on an appeal from a sentence. To be admissible, the fresh evidence need only be relevant and credible and, when taken with the other evidence adduced at trial, be expected to have affected the result. The purpose of the due diligence criterion is to protect the interests and the administration of justice and to preserve the role of appeal courts: see: *M. (P.S.)*, *supra*.

[31] Another specific characteristic of the sentencing process that should be emphasized is the importance of opinion evidence. At the sentencing stage, judges must often consider reports prepared by probation officers, correctional service officers, psychologists or psychiatrists reporting their opinions concerning the personality of the accused, and his or her chances of rehabilitation and risk of reoffending. As I have already noted, the probative value to be assigned to an expert opinion is directly related to the amount and quality of admissible evidence on which it relies: *Lavallee* [[1990] 1 SCR 852], at p. 897. Accordingly, before admitting new opinion evidence on appeal, it may be necessary to determine the basis of that opinion (for example, the version of events relied on by the expert, the documents he or she consulted, and so forth) and to establish whether the facts on which the opinion is based have been proven and are credible.

[32] Quite often, fresh evidence submitted to an appeal court in the context of an appeal from a sentence relates to events subsequent to the sentence, or consists of information from the penitentiary administration relating to an accused's progress in terms of adjustment and rehabilitation: see, for example, *Archibald, Lemay, Gauthier, McDow, Riley* and *Mesgun*. It is frequently the case that the Crown consents to the introduction of this fresh evidence, since the facts reported are seldom controversial: see *Edwards, supra*, at p. 28; *Gauthier, supra*, at para. 14; *McDow, supra*, at para. 18; *Mesgun, supra*, at para. 8; and C. Ruby, *Sentencing* (5th ed. 1999), at p. 607. In the case at bar, the appellant consented to the production of the report by Jacques Bigras, the psychologist. It is important to bear in mind that whether or not consent is given, the production of fresh evidence on appeal is possible only with the leave of the court of appeal: *Hogan, supra*, at p. 448. Evidence relating to events subsequent to the sentence or an accused's rehabilitation process normally meet the due diligence criterion, since by their very nature they were not available at the time of sentencing. However, in order to be found to be admissible, the evidence must also satisfy the other criteria, particularly the criterion relating to the likelihood that the result would be affected. The court of appeal may properly take into account the fact that the Crown has consented or that admission is uncontested particularly when assessing the relevance, credibility and probative value of fresh evidence.

[33] Having completed my review of the concepts of admissibility and probative value and of the specific characteristics of the sentencing process, I now turn to the application of the *Palmer* criteria to the two reports in question in the instant case.

E. Application to the Case at Bar

[34] In this case, the majority of the Court of Appeal found (at para. 16) that the report by the psychologist, Mr. Daigle, was admissible because it explained the respondent's past in greater detail and showed his personality from a perspective that was not evident in

the trial record. The report by the psychiatrist, Dr. Morissette, was admitted in evidence because it shed additional light on Mr. Daigle's report (para. 17). In my opinion, these grounds are inadequate to justify the admission of those two reports, since they could justify the admission of a very broad range of additional evidence on appeal. Furthermore, the admission of any evidence on appeal which merely adds certain details to or clarifies the evidence adduced at trial would be contrary to the *Palmer* criteria and the limited role of appellate courts in respect of sentencing.

[35]   In my view, neither of these two reports should have been admitted in evidence. It is worthwhile to reproduce the applicable criteria again, that is, the criteria set out in *Palmer*:

(1)   The evidence should generally not be admitted if, by due diligence, it could have been adduced at trial provided that this general principle will not be applied as strictly in a criminal case as in civil cases.

(2)   The evidence must be relevant in the sense that it bears upon a decisive or potentially decisive issue relating to the sentence.

(3)   The evidence must be credible in the sense that it is reasonably capable of belief.

(4)   The evidence must be such that if believed it could reasonably, when taken with the other evidence adduced at trial, be expected to have affected the result.

1. Report by the Psychologist, Mr. Daigle

[36]   The report by Mr. Daigle, a psychologist, is relevant in that it expresses opinions regarding the respondent's personality, dangerousness and risk of reoffending. In addition, this report is reasonably capable of belief, particularly in that it was prepared independently and not at the request of the respondent. In addition, it can be concluded that this report satisfies the due diligence criterion. Although Mr. Daigle relied on facts prior to sentencing and the respondent could have sought the opinion of another psychologist concerning his personality and dangerousness, this particular report was not available at the time of sentencing and the respondent could not have obtained it before sentencing. This report was prepared for classification purposes for Correctional Service Canada, while the respondent was at the Regional Reception Centre in Québec.

[37]   Despite the foregoing, I find that Mr. Daigle's report should not have been admitted in evidence by the Court of Appeal, since its probative value is not such that if it had been presented to the trial judge it might have affected the result. I note, first, that Mr. Daigle did not look into the proceedings at trial, did not read the testimony and did not consult the court documents (p. 1 of the report). While he did not prepare his report at the respondent's request, he relied only on his version of the facts. That version portrays the respondent as a victim who did not wish to commit the robbery and was allegedly acting in response to threats by his accomplices (pp. 1-2 of the report). This account makes no mention of the violence and the threats against the child. In addition, according to the report, Bertrand Fortier attacked the respondent rather than the reverse (p. 2 of the report). As well, the respondent told Mr. Daigle that he wanted to commit the robbery in order to win back his former girlfriend (p. 7 of the report).

[38]   The version of the facts set out in Mr. Daigle's report differs in quite a few respects from the version given by the respondent under oath at trial. I will point out only the most obvious contradictions: the respondent stated during his testimony that he wanted

to commit the robbery to repay a drug debt; that he planned the crime with one of his accomplices; and that he grabbed Bertrand Fortier while he was sitting in the living room.

[39] It is true that the version of the facts set out in Mr. Daigle's report is not wholly inconsistent with the respondent's testimony at trial. In that testimony, the respondent also sought to portray himself as a victim by claiming that he did not want to commit the robbery; that he would have run away if the opportunity had presented itself; and that he was only following the orders of his accomplices when he tied up the Fortier boy, put a cartridge in his mouth and took him hostage. However, the respondent's testimony is confused and full of contradictions, and is also inconsistent with the account given by the Fortier family. The trial judge clearly rejected the respondent's version of the facts. He found that the crime was planned (pp. 4-6 of the reasons) and that the respondent scratched the face of the Fortier boy with his weapon (p. 6 of the reasons) and threatened to kill him several times (p. 4 of the reasons). He also stated, at p. 7 of his reasons:

> [TRANSLATION] Your submissions at the beginning of the sentencing submissions dealt a lot with how you were in fact a victim, I was talking about bad luck just now, we choose our friends, we choose our girlfriends. When something goes wrong, you can't always blame other people.
>
> It is quite clear from an exchange between the trial judge and counsel for the respondent just before sentencing that the judge did not assign much weight to the defence theory that the respondent was a victim in this case.

[40] Mr. Daigle therefore relied on a version of the facts that was not accepted by the trial judge, or on facts that were not established in evidence. Since the probative value of an expert opinion depends on the *amount* and *quality* of admissible evidence on which it relies (*Lavallee, supra*, at p. 897), I find that little probative value can be assigned to the psychologist's report prepared by Mr. Daigle. Having regard to that low probative value and the fact that the trial judge, on passing sentence, stressed the seriousness of the offences committed by the respondent rather than his personality, I am of the view that Mr. Daigle's report would not have affected the result if it had been introduced at trial with the other evidence. Accordingly, the Court of Appeal should not have admitted it in evidence, since it does not meet the *Palmer* criteria.

2. Report by the Psychiatrist, Dr. Morissette

[41] The report prepared by Dr. Morissette, a psychiatrist, does not meet the due diligence criterion. It is dated March 17, 1998, that is, more than a year after sentencing. Unlike the report by the psychologist, Mr. Daigle, Dr. Morissette's opinion was solicited by the respondent. I agree with Chamberland JA that the respondent, by exercising minimal diligence, could have sought this opinion before sentence was passed and submitted Dr. Morissette's report to the trial judge for the purpose of countering the probation officer's opinion concerning his personality (see *Mesgun, supra*, at para. 8).

[42] Nonetheless, failure to meet the due diligence criterion is not always fatal: *Warsing, supra*, at para. 51. It is therefore necessary to consider the other three criteria set out in *Palmer* in order to determine whether their strength is such that failure to satisfy the due diligence requirement is overborne: *R v. McAnespie*, [1993] 4 SCR 501, at pp. 502-3.

[43] Like the psychologist's report prepared by Mr. Daigle, the psychiatrist's report written by Dr. Morissette is relevant, since it communicates an opinion concerning the respondent's personality, danger to others and risk of reoffending. Furthermore, there is nothing to indicate that it is not reasonably capable of belief, even though it was prepared at the respondent's request. However, its probative value is low. Like the psychologist, Mr. Daigle, Dr. Morissette based his opinion on a version of the facts that was not established or adopted at trial. Although he reviewed the report prepared by the probation officer, he does not seem to have read the testimony or consulted the trial transcript. His description of the events of June 22, 1996, is very brief and does not reflect the seriousness of the offences committed or the violence employed. Furthermore, the respondent gave Dr. Morissette an explanation that was completely different from the explanation he gave under oath in respect of his participation in the events. At p. 15 of the report we read:

> [TRANSLATION] Mr. Lévesque now explains that at the time of his arrest and when he arrived at the penitentiary, he did not to want to say that he had committed a robbery for a woman ... , he did not want to say that he was so dependent on a woman that he would commit a robbery ... . He felt that it would look "better" if he explained the reason for his robbery in terms of a drug debt. He is now telling us that he never had a drug debt, that he never cheated a drug dealer. According to his explanation, the only purpose of the robbery was financial gain in order to impress Francine, since Mr. Lévesque felt that if he had more money she might come back to him.

In addition, none of the details of the respondent's love life referred to by Dr. Morissette were established in evidence at trial. Thus, for the reasons I stated concerning the psychologist's report by Mr. Daigle, I find that the psychiatrist's report by Dr. Morissette is of little probative value and would not have affected the result if it had been adduced at trial with the other evidence.

[44] In my view, as in *McAnespie*, *supra*, at pp. 502-3, "the strength of the other factors is *not* such that failure to satisfy the due diligence requirement in this case is overborne by the other factors" (emphasis in original). Accordingly, the report by the psychiatrist, Dr. Morissette, should not have been admitted in evidence on appeal.

VI. Disposition

[45] For the foregoing reasons, I would allow the appeal, set aside the judgment of the Court of Appeal of Quebec and, for the reasons stated by Chamberland JA, substitute a sentence of imprisonment for eight years and six months for the sentence imposed by the trial judge.

ARBOUR J (dissenting):

[46] I have had the benefit of the reasons of my colleague, Justice Gonthier, on this appeal. With respect, on the very particular facts of this case, I believe that the majority of the Court of Appeal was entitled to admit the reports prepared respectively by Marc Daigle and Dr. Louis Morissette. Here, the trial judge fundamentally mischaracterized the principal crime, of which the respondent had been convicted, in determining the just and appropriate sentence, with the result that the Court of Appeal was, for all intents and purposes, required to sentence afresh. In these specific circumstances, it was for the Court

of Appeal to equip itself, pursuant to its broad statutory discretion under s. 683(1) of the *Criminal Code*, RSC, 1985, c. C-46, with whatever evidence it deemed fit and necessary to decide the question of sentence. Accordingly, I would dismiss the appeal.

[47] I am in general agreement with the statement of the law governing the admission of fresh evidence in appeals against sentence, provided by my colleague at paras. 16-22 of his opinion. However, in view of the fundamental error committed by the trial judge, I do not believe that the principles articulated by Gonthier J are germane to the disposition of this appeal. I must also emphatically disagree with Gonthier J that *R v. Lavallee*, [1990] 1 SCR 852 (*per* Wilson J), applies as stringently as he suggests in the sentencing context.

[48] The Court of Appeal was unanimous that the trial judge erred in concluding that kidnapping for ransom was the dominant offence committed by the respondent. There is no challenge before us to the unanimous conclusion of the Court of Appeal that robbery was the central, predominant offence, the hostage-taking being merely [TRANSLATION] "ancillary to the main criminal operation carried out by the [respondent] and his cohorts" ([1998] QJ No. 2680 (QL), at para. 35).

[49] The trial judge's initial error in identifying kidnapping as the [TRANSLATION] "central matter alleged" against the respondent, which he described as [TRANSLATION] "one of the most serious crimes in the *Criminal Code* ... right after murder" (see CQ, No. 505-01-008036-960, February 19, 1997, at p. 2), tainted his entire analysis, and produced a sentence that did not accurately reflect the circumstances of the offence. The Court of Appeal's task was thus not simply to assess the fitness of the sentence imposed at first instance, and, to this end, to determine the admissibility of the reports tendered by the respondent as fresh evidence on appeal. Instead, having set aside the sentence, the Court of Appeal was required to intervene essentially for the purpose of sentencing the respondent anew. In these circumstances, I believe that the Court of Appeal was entitled to consider what it deemed to be evidence relevant to the exercise of determining a just and appropriate sentence. Like a sentencing judge, a court of appeal, in circumstances such as these, must

> ha[ve] wide latitude as to the sources and types of evidence upon which to base [its] sentence. [It] must have the fullest possible information concerning the background of the accused if [it] is to fit the sentence to the offender rather than to the crime.

> (*R v. Gardiner*, [1982] 2 SCR 368, *per* Dickson J (as he then was), at p. 414.)

[50] This "wide latitude" reflects the legal environment of a sentencing hearing—described in *R v. M. (C.A.)*, [1996] 1 SCR 500, at para. 92, as an "inherently individualized process"—wherein the sentencing judge's task is to develop a composite picture or understanding of the offender, including his past and present circumstances as well as his prospects for rehabilitation and the danger that he will re-offend, with a view to crafting a just and appropriate sentence. In this environment, as was recognized in *Gardiner, supra*, at p. 414:

> ... it is manifest that the judge should not be denied an opportunity to obtain relevant information by the imposition of all the restrictive evidential rules common to a trial. ...
>
> It is commonplace that the strict rules which govern at trial do not apply at a sentencing hearing and it would be undesirable to have the formalities and technicalities characteristic

of the normal adversary proceeding prevail. The hearsay rule does not govern the sentencing hearing. Hearsay evidence may be accepted where found to be credible and trustworthy.

[51] The holding in *Lavallee, supra*, that the weight properly attributable to expert opinion is a direct function of the amount and quality of admissible evidence on which it is based, is a product of the general rule governing the inadmissibility of hearsay evidence at trial, where considerations of probative value are critical to the presumption of innocence and the fundamental fairness of the trial process. The sentencing environment is entirely different and permits, indeed encourages, recourse to evidentiary materials that would not be appropriate in the determination of guilt or innocence. Hearsay evidence is admissible in sentencing proceedings (see s. 723(5) of the *Code*). For example, probation officers' reports, produced pursuant to s. 721 of the *Code*, will inevitably contain opinions and hearsay of the type that would not be admissible at trial. Similarly, victim impact statements, prepared in accordance with s. 722(2) of the *Code*, must be considered by the sentencing judge, and may be given whatever weight the sentencing judge sees fit, regardless of the fact that they often contain non-expert opinions and hearsay information that would have no probative value, even if relevant, in the trial proper. Finally, s. 724(1) of the *Code* explicitly provides that "[i]n determining a sentence, a court may accept as proved any information disclosed at the trial or at the sentencing proceedings. ..."

[52] In my opinion, the nature of the sentencing process, and of the statutory rules that govern it, contemplate that the sentencing court should have the benefit of "the fullest possible information concerning the background of the [offender]," from the widest array of sources. It is therefore inappropriate to tie the probative value of evidence tendered under these rules to the probative value of evidence proffered at trial, and thus, more specifically, to assess the weight of an expert opinion on the basis of the quantity and quality of non-hearsay evidence introduced to support that opinion. Indeed, such a requirement would largely rob the permissive use of hearsay, recognized and endorsed by this Court in *Gardiner, supra*, of all its utility. A sentencing court must be entitled to receive and rely on any credible and trustworthy evidence which assists it in obtaining as complete an understanding of the offender as possible. The extent to which evidence presented on sentencing conflicts with the facts upon which the conviction was founded is a matter for the sentencing court to take into consideration, but is not, as such, a matter for exclusion of the evidence in question. A sentencing court is entitled to discount any part of an expert opinion that may be based on a misapprehension of the circumstances of the offence as found by the trial judge, while making use of any insight that the opinion may properly provide into the personality of the accused, his personal and emotional life, as well as his dangerousness and risk of recidivism.

[53] In the case at bar, while I accept that the Daigle and Morissette reports each contain an account of the events surrounding the offences committed by the respondent that differ from facts accepted by the trial judge, I cannot agree that they are of little probative value.

[54] In my opinion, it was open to the Court of Appeal to find both reports sufficiently credible and trustworthy to assist in the development of a fuller picture of the respondent, based as they were on the experts' face-to-face psychological assessment and evaluation of the former. As such, I believe that the Court of Appeal was entitled to consider and rely on all or part of the opinions offered therein in sentencing the respondent. Even

though the Daigle and Morissette reports were tendered as fresh evidence on appeal, they were not tendered simply to demonstrate that the sentence imposed by the trial judge was unfit, in light of the subsequent opinions offered by these experts. As indicated above, the sentence imposed by the trial judge was unfit because of his misunderstanding of the central offence of which the respondent was convicted. Having set aside that sentence, the Court of Appeal was free to admit any evidence that it deemed to be of assistance in discharging its sentencing function.

[55] For these reasons, I believe that the Court of Appeal's decision to admit the reports by Marc Daigle and Dr. Morissette was correct and should be upheld. I would therefore dismiss the appeal.

R v Angelillo
2006 SCC 55, [2006] 2 SCR 728

CHARRON J (McLachlin CJ, Bastarache, LeBel, and Deschamps JJ concurring):

1. Introduction

[1] During sentencing, is it appropriate for the court to consider evidence of facts tending to establish the commission of another offence in respect of which the offender has been charged but not convicted? If such evidence is admissible in principle, is it in the interests of justice in the instant case to allow the Crown to introduce this fresh evidence on appeal?

[2] After pleading guilty to a charge of theft, Gennaro Angelillo was sentenced to a term of imprisonment of two years less a day to be served in the community, subject to his complying with certain conditions that are not in issue in this appeal. At the time of sentencing, Crown counsel was unaware that Mr. Angelillo was under police investigation once again for incidents that had occurred after his guilty plea and that later led to new charges. Relying on that evidence, the Crown introduced three motions in the Quebec Court of Appeal in which it sought leave to introduce fresh evidence, leave to appeal the sentence and a stay of sentence. The Court of Appeal dismissed the motion to introduce fresh evidence, because in its view [TRANSLATION] "[t]his evidence is not relevant" and because "[t]o accept what the prosecution is proposing would mean accepting that the respondent can be punished more severely for committing an offence of which he might be found not guilty" ([2004] QJ No. 11670 (QL), at paras. 6 and 14). The court also dismissed the other two motions. The Crown has appealed to this Court.

[3] As was the case in the Court of Appeal, the main issue in this appeal relates to the admissibility of the fresh evidence. The rules governing admissibility are the same in this Court, and they are well known. The Court of Appeal had to determine pursuant to s. 687(1) of the *Criminal Code*, RSC 1985, c. C-46 ("*Cr. C.*"), whether it was appropriate to require or receive additional evidence. According to the rules laid down in *Palmer v. The Queen*, [1980] 1 SCR 759, and applied in *R v. Lévesque*, [2000] 2 SCR 487, 2000 SCC 47, an appellate court should not generally admit evidence if, by due diligence, it could have been adduced at trial—although this general principle is not to be applied as strictly in a criminal case as in civil cases—and should only admit evidence that is relevant and

credible and that could reasonably be expected to have affected the result had it been adduced at trial together with the other evidence.

[4] The Crown submits that the Court of Appeal erred in holding that evidence of facts tending to establish the commission of another offence is irrelevant to the determination of the appropriate sentence, regardless of the purpose being pursued, unless the offence in question resulted in a conviction. The Crown wishes to produce this fresh evidence not to prove that the other offence was committed, but for the sole purpose of establishing Mr. Angelillo's character—a distinction that was accepted by the Ontario Court of Appeal in *R v. Edwards* (2001), 155 CCC (3d) 473, but rejected by the Court of Appeal in the case at bar. In light of the sentencing submissions, and more particularly of the pre-sentence report, according to which Mr. Angelillo [TRANSLATION] "has done some soul-searching, which seems to be sincere, about his inappropriate behaviour" and his "time in court [has] had a major deterrent effect," the Crown contends that the fresh evidence easily meets the requirement of relevance.

[5] Although I have concluded that the fresh evidence is relevant and I recognize that, in principle, evidence of facts tending to establish the commission of another offence of which the offender has not been convicted can in certain cases be admitted to enable the court to determine a just and appropriate sentence, I would, for the reasons that follow, dismiss the appeal. Since the fresh evidence constitutes the basis for outstanding charges against Mr. Angelillo for which he has not yet stood trial, it can be admitted only in the context of the procedure provided for in s. 725(1)(b) or (b.1) *Cr. C.* The conditions for that procedure include a requirement that the offender's consent be obtained. Furthermore, I feel that the Crown has not shown due diligence. Accordingly, the Court of Appeal's decision not to admit the fresh evidence is affirmed and the appeal is dismissed.

2. Facts and Judgments Below

2.1 Court of Québec

[6] On January 13, 2003, Mr. Angelillo pleaded guilty in the Court of Québec to a charge of theft over $5,000, contrary to s. 334(a) *Cr. C.* More than 37 times over a period of about a month and a half, Mr. Angelillo, who was employed as a security guard, failed to make deposits his employer had instructed him to make and instead took the money for his own use, thus misappropriating more than $425,000. He used a large part of that amount to pay debts he had incurred to persons associated with organized crime, who were threatening him and his family. The police also seized $150,000 during a search of his home.

[7] For reasons that are not apparent from the record, the sentencing hearing was not completed until April 21, 2004, more than 15 months after the guilty plea. At that time, Judge Corte sentenced Mr. Angelillo to a term of imprisonment of two years less a day to be served in the community followed by two years' probation, and ordered him to pay $268,430 as restitution under s. 738 *Cr. C.* In imposing this sentence, the court accepted the submissions of the defence rather than those of Crown counsel, who had asked for an unconditional three-year term of imprisonment.

[8] Judge Corte noted that the offender had no criminal record, had pleaded guilty at the start of the proceedings and had expressed remorse, and that the pre-sentence report was favourable to him. She also noted that Mr. Angelillo had three jobs at the time and

was the sole source of support for his wife and for his three children, who were respectively 15 months, four years and seven years old. Referring to the pre-sentence report dated May 15, 2003, the judge added that the offender [TRANSLATION] "has done some sincere soul-searching about his inappropriate behaviour [and] has undertaken a rehabilitation process … and also counselling," and that "his time in court has had a major deterrent effect on him." The report also stated that Mr. Angelillo was not dangerous and that his risk of re-offending was low. Judge Corte noted that there was a special circumstance in Mr. Angelillo's case, namely that he had stolen because his life and the lives of his family were being threatened by creditors who had ties to organized crime. There was physical evidence confirming that Mr. Angelillo had been threatened, and this fact was not disputed by the Crown. Judge Corte therefore concluded that, in this instance, the penological objectives of deterrence and denunciation could be achieved by imposing a conditional sentence with certain conditions restricting Mr. Angelillo's freedom.

2.2 Fresh Evidence

[9] Following that decision, the Crown introduced motions in the Court of Appeal for leave to appeal, for a stay of sentence and for leave to introduce fresh evidence. Through the last of these motions, the Crown intended to file evidence showing: (1) that, on August 20, 2003, Mr. Angelillo was arrested at an Insta-Chèque counter while attempting to cash a forged certified cheque from the National Bank of Canada made payable to him in the amount of $12,000; and (2) that, on January 21, 2004, during a search of Mr. Angelillo's home, police officers found a National Bank stamp with the words [TRANSLATION] "certified cheque" on it and a starter kit containing a set of non-personalized cheques, which came from a National Bank branch where Mr. Angelillo worked as a cleaner. These allegations were the basis for the new charges against Mr. Angelillo.

[10] The Crown argues that this evidence was not available at trial and that it acted diligently to produce all the relevant evidence before Judge Corte. In support of this argument, the Crown has submitted an affidavit from the prosecutor responsible for the case at trial. The affidavit states that, in early June 2003, after the detective sergeant responsible for the case had committed an indiscretion by telling Mr. Angelillo the sentence the Crown intended to seek, Crown counsel told the detective sergeant that her presence at the sentencing hearing would no longer be required and that from then on counsel would be in contact only with the detective sergeant's supervisor. Before the hearing, counsel checked the *plumitif*, in which there was nothing about Mr. Angelillo, but did not contact either the detective sergeant or her supervisor. On April 21, 2004, shortly after Judge Corte handed down her sentence, the detective sergeant ran into counsel at the courthouse by chance and told her the facts that the Crown is now seeking to introduce as fresh evidence. According to the affidavit of the police officer responsible for the new investigation, the detective sergeant had been aware of this investigation since January 19, 2004.

2.3 Court of Appeal

[11] The Quebec Court of Appeal (Beauregard, Mailhot and Doyon JJA) dismissed the three motions filed by the Crown because, in the court's view, the evidence was not relevant. The court began by stating that, because of the presumption of innocence, the

fact that Mr. Angelillo had been charged proved nothing. It added that, in the present case, what the Crown wished to prove was not that he had been charged with another crime, but that the charge was substantiated. The court rejected the Crown's submission that the fresh evidence was admissible as character evidence under the principles stated by Rosenberg JA in *Edwards*. In the court's view, it is contrary to the presumption of innocence to consider, in sentencing an accused, facts that could constitute the basis for a separate criminal charge that has not resulted in conviction (para. 11). The court concluded that taking into account evidence of facts tending to establish that an accused has committed another offence of which he or she has not been convicted amounts to punishing the accused more severely for having committed an act in respect of which he or she might ultimately be found not guilty (para. 14).

3. Analysis

3.1 Admissibility of Fresh Evidence

[12] As mentioned above, an appellate court considering a motion to admit fresh evidence must decide, under s. 687(1) *Cr. C.*, whether it thinks fit to require or receive additional evidence. What must guide the court of appeal in assessing the admissibility of fresh evidence is therefore a concern to serve the interests of justice.

[13] In *Lévesque*, at para. 35, this Court adapted to an appeal against sentence the four criteria set out in *Palmer* for determining whether it is in the interests of justice to admit fresh evidence on an appeal from a verdict:

(1)   The evidence should generally not be admitted if, by due diligence, it could have been adduced at trial provided that this general principle will not be applied as strictly in a criminal case as in civil cases.

(2)   The evidence must be relevant in the sense that it bears upon a decisive or potentially decisive issue relating to the sentence.

(3)   The evidence must be credible in the sense that it is reasonably capable of belief.

(4)   The evidence must be such that if believed it could reasonably, when taken with the other evidence adduced at trial, be expected to have affected the result.

[14] In *Lévesque*, the Court recognized that the strict rules of a trial do not apply to a sentencing hearing, because in order to determine the appropriate sentence the judge must have as much information as possible about the accused (para. 30). The Court held that the *Palmer* criteria do not compromise this more flexible application of the rules and noted that those criteria are just as important where the appeal relates to the sentence. It will be helpful for the purposes of the case at bar to recall why this is true:

The integrity of the criminal process and the role of appeal courts could be jeopardized by the routine admission of fresh evidence on appeal, since this would create a two-tier sentencing system. That kind of system would be incompatible with the high standard of review applicable to appeals from sentences and the underlying "profound functional justifications": see *R v. M. (C.A.)*, [1996] 1 SCR 500, at para. 91. Despite the fresh evidence, the sentencing judge, unlike the appeal judge, has the benefit of being able to directly assess the other evidence, the testimony and the submissions of the parties, as well as being familiar with the needs and current conditions of and in the community where the crime was committed: see *M. (C.A.)*, *supra*, at para. 91. Furthermore, appeal courts are not the appropriate forum in which to determine questions of fact, and they should do so only when the fresh evidence presents certain characteristics such as would justify expanding their traditional role. This Court has already identified those characteristics, in *Palmer*. In my view, whether the appeal relates to a verdict or a sentence, the criteria laid down by this Court in *Palmer* are the criteria that are to be applied where a court of appeal is determining whether to admit fresh evidence. [para. 20]

[15] In accordance with the last three of the *Palmer* criteria, an appellate court can therefore admit evidence only if it is relevant and credible and if it could reasonably be expected to have affected the result had it been adduced at trial together with the other evidence. With respect to the first criterion, this Court has stated a number of times that failure to meet the due diligence criterion should not be used to refuse to admit fresh evidence on appeal if the evidence is compelling and if it is in the interests of justice to admit it (*Lévesque*, at para. 15; *R v. Warsing*, [1998] 3 SCR 579, at para. 51). The fact remains that this criterion is an important one whose specific purpose is to protect the interests and the administration of justice and to preserve the role of the appellate court (*Lévesque*, at para. 30, citing *R v. M. (P.S.)* (1992), 77 CCC (3d) 402 (Ont. CA), at p. 410).

[16] In the present case, I am of the view that the Crown did not act with due diligence and that, in the interests of the administration of justice, the failure to do so is determinative. The conflict between Crown counsel and the detective sergeant may explain why the evidence that the Crown now seeks to introduce by motion was not adduced during the sentencing hearing, but this circumstance does not constitute evidence of due diligence. The record shows unequivocally that the Crown could have submitted the evidence in question to the trial judge were it not for that breakdown in communication. It cannot be in the interests of the administration of justice to condone such a lack of co-ordination and co-operation between the Crown and the police.

[17] Since I consider the lack of due diligence to be determinative in the case at bar, it is not necessary to make a final determination as to the decisiveness of the fresh evidence or to decide whether that evidence—which Mr. Angelillo contests vigorously—is sufficiently credible. However, I feel that it may be helpful to make a few general comments regarding the relevance of evidence of acts that have resulted neither in charges nor in convictions, since the Court of Appeal seems to have rejected out of hand the reasoning of Rosenberg JA of the Ontario Court of Appeal in *Edwards*. The court stated in particular that it did not see the distinction Rosenberg JA had drawn in saying that evidence of such acts cannot be adduced for the purpose of obtaining a disproportionate sentence against the offender for the offence in question or of punishing the offender for an offence of which he or she has not been convicted, but that such evidence can be adduced to shed light on the offender's background and character. In my view, Rosenberg JA was correct in drawing that distinction, and it is an important one. I will therefore begin by discussing certain general principles relating to the admissibility of extrinsic evidence for sentencing purposes before commenting on the relevance of the evidence the Crown wished to adduce in the case at bar.

Fish J delivered a concurring opinion in which he agreed with the foregoing.

A recurring concern in sentence appeals is the extent to which an appeal may be taken and a decision rendered on the basis of a change in circumstances since the sentence was originally imposed. This concern is not a free-standing ground of appeal, but arises as an incident in the course of a sentencing appeal that is otherwise properly framed. It almost always arises on appeals by the offender. For example, suppose an offender has been given a lengthy suspended sentence for a sequence of property offences. A significant feature of the case is that the offender committed the offences to support his drug addiction. Since the sentence was imposed the offender has successfully followed a rigorous program of rehabilitation. A plausible argument can be made that the profile of the offender, and particularly the risk of reoffending, should be viewed differently. This does not raise a question of evidence that could have been produced at first instance, but it is new evidence about the offender. Section 687 of the Code allows the appellate court to receive any evidence that it considers appropriate. But if it admits and considers evidence of developments since the sentence was originally imposed, the court is, in effect, considering a case that is different from the case before the sentencing judge. Should the appellate court be entitled to take this information into account?

D. Orders

If a court allows an appeal from sentence it is entitled to make any order that could have been made by the sentencing judge. Indeed, it must make an order that it considers a fit sentence in the matter because there is no power for an appellate court to remit a case to the sentencing judge for reconsideration: see e.g. *R c Pelletier* (1989), 52 CCC (3d) 340 (Qc CA). Because the function of the appellate court is to ensure a fit sentence, and because the court is empowered to receive any evidence it considers appropriate, the absence of a power to remit might be considered a factor that weighs in favour of a more interventionist approach.

The Supreme Court affirmed in *Hill v R*, [1977] 1 SCR 827 that when an appellate court varies a sentence it can reduce or increase it.

III. PRACTICAL CONSIDERATIONS

Sentence appeals in indictable cases require leave, but not in summary conviction matters. In either case, as we have seen previously, appellate courts will not intervene to review or vary a sentence unless there is a good reason to do so. That, at any rate, is the prevailing statement of principle, but there are many instances that might seem to contradict it.

In all instances, the underlying theme of sentence appeals is a claim that the sentence is unfit and should be varied. Although this is a claim in any sentence appeal, there are also many instances in which the reason advanced for reviewing a sentence is somewhat more formal. For example, if a judge fails to provide an opportunity for submissions to be made on sentence, this may be considered a defect that calls the fitness of the sentence into question and may justify not only appellate review but modification of the sentence. Similarly, if the reasons for sentence are deficient, an appellate court might well find in this a sufficient basis to review the sentence and modify it.

Appellate intervention typically occurs in two situations. Either the court at first instance has imposed a sentence that is out of line in some material aspect with other cases of a similar nature or there is some particular aspect of the individual case that calls for attention in the sentence. These two situations are not mutually inconsistent and might arise in a single case. In the first case, the emphasis is placed on the general norm, while, in the second, it is focused on the particular features of the individual case.

It is inevitable that appellate judges will have varying views of what is a case for deference and what is a case for intervention. Where one might see a question of principle, another might see none. Where one might see a case of manifest unfitness in a sentence, another might see a difference of opinion that does not merit interference. There are discrepancies in sentence appeals as surely as there are discrepancies at first instance. This is a necessary corollary of a system that insists, rightly, on individualized sentencing.

In the following case, the Court of Appeal for Quebec altered the sentence imposed. At the time that sentence was pronounced, penitentiary time was the norm for importing heroin and cocaine in large quantities and the range was typically around ten years. The accused pleaded guilty, and substantial submissions, well supported by evidence, were made on the sentencing hearing. The trial judge clearly went out of her way to temper the length of the sentence, based on favourable and sympathetic facts, and she reached a conclusion of eight years for each offender after giving credit for time served. Both the Crown and the offenders appealed. The latter succeeded. Consider carefully the basis on which the Court of Appeal intervened and the significance of the result.

Fortin c R
2005 QCCA 735, 34 CR (6th) 360, [2005] RJQ 2177 (footnotes omitted)

[This is an unofficial translation posted by CanLII.]

[2] Annie Fortin was born on January 28, 1979 and is 26 years old. Sébastien Renaud was born on August 9, 1977 and is 28 years old.

[3] On May 6, 2002, on their way back from Costa Rica, they were arrested at Toronto's Pearson Airport. They were hiding 4,170 grams of heroin (70% pure) and 1,468 grams of cocaine (56% pure) in their luggage.

[4] In the spring of 2002, Annie Fortin was going through a difficult time. She was depressed and in debt. At one point she became close to Sébastien Renaud's sister, Noémie, who introduced her to a certain Rosie. Rosie asked Ms. Fortin if she would be interested in taking a trip to Costa Rica to bring drugs back to Canada.

[5] Ms. Fortin was interested in the proposal. Rosie insisted that she find herself a travelling companion, however. Ms. Fortin therefore approached two friends, who refused, before speaking to Sébastien Renaud, who agreed.

[6] At that time, the plan involved going to Costa Rica and bringing back a few pairs of shoes filled with ecstasy. In payment, they each would receive $3000, their trip to and accommodation in Costa Rica would be paid for, and they would be given $250 in pocket money.

[7] There was never any question of heroin or cocaine; they did know, however, that bringing back ecstasy constitutes an illegal transaction.

[8] The trial judge found that they had [TRANSLATION] "agreed to import a small quantity of ecstasy" and that [TRANSLATION] "it was only once they were in Costa Rica

that they agreed to import a larger quantity of drugs. ... [T]hey agreed to bring back to Canada what they knew at that time to be a significant quantity of an illegal substance."

[9] The appellants met with Rosie several times in preparation for the trip. When she told them that the departure date was set and the tickets had been purchased, they hesitated. Annie Fortin felt threatened; Rosie told her that she would have to reimburse the cost of the plane tickets if she and her friend reneged. She was afraid. Sébastien Renaud was also worried, and when he voiced his concerns to Rosie, she answered that she knew where his mother and sister lived.

[10] The trial judge was satisfied on a balance of probabilities of the existence of threats from Rosie, but she added that these threats *do not constitute* [TRANSLATION] "the event that triggered their agreement to commit the crime."

[11] The appellants left on April 29, 2002.

[12] In Costa Rica, two men were waiting for them. The appellants say that they were Colombian. The men took their luggage, brought them to San Jose, and then gave them the bags that they were to bring back to Canada. It was clear to the appellants that they did not contain shoes. When they expressed their concerns to the two men about this change in plans, they were told not to ask questions.

[13] The trial judge was satisfied on a balance of probabilities of the existence of threats from the two men in Costa Rica.

[14] The appellants felt caught in a trap.

[15] Apprehensive, they telephoned Rosie, who told them not to worry and to do what they were told.

[16] They considered leaving the bags there, but quickly rejected this option, convinced that members of the organization were waiting for them in Canada.

[17] They did not seriously consider going to the police in Costa Rica, fearing they were corrupt.

[18] They left Costa Rica on May 6, 2002.

[19] At no time did they consider turning themselves in to authorities once they arrived on Canadian soil.

[20] They both claim they were relieved that their adventure was over when customs officials stopped them and found the narcotics in their bags.

[21] They did not know exactly what their luggage contained, but they were aware that it was not ecstasy. The trial judge found that [TRANSLATION] "they realized they had imported cocaine when they were arrested at the airport" and that they [TRANSLATION] "learned only several weeks after their arrest" that the bags also contained heroin.

[22] Three experts—a psychologist, a psychiatrist and a criminologist—testified. They all agreed that the risk of re-offending was nil or practically nil in the case of both appellants.

[23] The appellants are remorseful and regret what happened. Both reaffirm their intention to lead productive lives.

[24] The nearly three-year period between the offences and the sentencing confirms that they are on the right path. Sébastien Renaud is working. Annie Fortin has gone back to university after having worked and is studying anthropology and psychology.

[25] Both have partners with whom they share their lives and make plans for the future.

[26] Both receive very strong support from their families.

• • •

[27] The appellants raise five grounds of appeal:

- the trial judge erred in her interpretation and application of the principles to be considered, specifically with respect to the objective of social deterrence;
- the trial judge erred in not according exceptional treatment to this case, which can only be considered exceptional;
- the trial judge erred in applying what she perceived to be a kind of "sentence threshold" established in the case law, even though she had raised several factors that favour greater clemency;
- in applying this "sentence threshold," the trial judge erred in treating the weak, vulnerable, gullible and naïve couriers, who had been recruited despite themselves, as severely as the traffickers, who have made crime a way of life;
- the sentences are clearly unreasonable having regard to all the circumstances of the case and all the more so in light of the trial judge's finding that the appellants deserved to be treated with clemency.

• • •

[28] In *R v. Proulx*, 2005 SCC 5 (CanLII), [2000] 1 SCR 61, the Supreme Court of Canada affirmed the broad discretionary power of a trial judge in sentencing matters. Chief Justice Lamer notes, at para. 123, that sentences imposed by trial judges are entitled to considerable deference from appellate courts, and that "absent an error in principle, failure to consider a relevant factor, or an overemphasis of the appropriate factors, a court of appeal should only intervene to vary a sentence imposed at trial if the sentence is demonstrably unfit" (at para. 123).

[29] How does this apply to the present case?

[30] The trial judge's analysis is complete and detailed. All the objectives, principles and factors relevant to sentencing are dealt with exhaustively.

[31] The case law from Quebec and elsewhere in Canada is replete with decisions reaffirming that denunciation and deterrence are the primary factors to consider in cases involving the importation of heroin and cocaine, although sentencing is not so rigid an exercise as to require reliance on only those two factors in all cases.

[32] Heroin is the most harmful drug on the market, while cocaine is a close second.

[33] These drugs are produced in other countries, hence the importance of attaching a harsh penalty to their importation into Canada.

[34] Consumption of these drugs is a social evil and a tragedy for all victims, both direct and indirect.

[35] The severity of punishment in such cases is justified by the hope that it will make it more difficult for criminal organizations to recruit drug couriers and that it will discourage people who are tempted by something that they see as nothing more than a simple adventure.

[36] In *R v. Smith*, [1987] 1 SCR 1045, Justice Lamer (as he then was) wrote the following, at 1053:

Those who import and market hard drugs for lucre are responsible for the gradual but inexorable degeneration of many of their fellow human beings as a result of their becoming drug addicts. The direct cause of the hardship cast upon their victims and their families, these importers must also be made to bear their fair share of the guilt for the innumerable serious crimes of all sorts committed by addicts in order to feed their demand for drugs. Such persons, with few exceptions (as an example, the guilt of addicts who import not only to meet but also to finance their needs is not necessarily the same in degree as that of cold-blooded non-users), should, upon conviction, in my respectful view, be sentenced to and actually serve long periods of penal servitude.

[37] In our view, these comments are as relevant today as they were twenty years ago.

[38] Despite the seriousness of the crime, the case law does recognize those "few exceptions" where long periods of imprisonment are not appropriate. In *Smith*, *supra*, Justice Lamer provides one example. There are others in the case law; see, for instance, *R v. Marshall*, [1988] BCJ No. 2367, where the British Columbia Court of Appeal reduced the sentence imposed on a writer with no criminal record to 5 years for importing 4 ounces of heroin into Canada. See also *R v. Borges*, [2000] JQ No. 4732, where this Court reduced the 30-month prison sentence of a 21-year-old man with no criminal record to a suspended sentence of two years less one day for importing 1,214 grams of cocaine.

[39] In our view, the situation of the appellants warrants exceptional treatment. Indeed, the trial judge implicitly recognized this fact when she wrote the following at paragraph 97: [TRANSLATION] "the particular circumstances of the accused, taken as a whole, favour the leniency of the Court" and when she stated that she accepted that the appellants believed that they were importing ecstasy (and not heroin or cocaine) [TRANS-LATION] "in terms of their premeditation and their state of mind." Her error consists of not having translated this clemency into a lenient sentence. In fact, in light of the circumstances as a whole, the punishment is harsh. As such, it is "demonstrably unfit" and warrants our intervention.

[40] At trial, the Crown sought a 15-year prison sentence, and its position has not changed on appeal. For its part, the defence suggested a suspended sentence of 2 years less one day. On appeal, however, in light of the trial judge's findings of fact, it seeks a sentence of 4 or 5 years in prison.

[41] In our view, the objectives, principles and factors relevant to sentencing, in the very particular circumstances of the present case, justify imposing a sentence of 5 years of imprisonment.

[42] A number of factors weigh against imposing a lighter sentence:

- the appellants have been convicted of a serious crime, which attracts a maximum sentence of life in prison;
- the drugs imported (heroin and cocaine) are the most harmful on the market;
- the quantity of drugs imported is significant;
- the appellants do not use drugs; they consciously agreed to smuggle the drugs for lucre and as a way to fulfil their wish to travel;
- although they initially believed they would be smuggling ecstasy, they were aware that this was an illegal transaction;
- after realizing that they were being asked to smuggle something other than ecstasy and in a larger quantity than originally planned, they nevertheless decided to continue the transaction and to try to import the drug into Canada instead of turning themselves in to Canadian customs officials. It should also be noted that they do not seem to have made any real effort to find out the exact nature of the drug they had been asked to smuggle;

- contrary to what the appellants submit, they were not drawn in "despite themselves"; both are intelligent young people who knew what they were doing when they told Rosie that they were interested in the proposed trip to Costa Rica. The threats they received do not entirely excuse their actions since, as the trial judge found, they were not [TRANSLATION] "the event that triggered the commission of the crime."

[43] At the same time, certain factors make this case an exceptional one and, as the trial judge determined, justify a more lenient sentence than what is usually imposed in this type of case:

- the psychological and economic vulnerability of the appellants when they were recruited;
- their age and complete lack of criminal record;
- the practically non-existent risk of re-offending in the case of both appellants;
- the strong support they both receive from family and friends;
- the mitigating circumstances surrounding the perpetration of the crime, notably:
  - the threats they received in Montréal and Costa Rica when they wanted to back out of the agreement;
  - the fact that they were recruited to smuggle a small amount of ecstasy;
  - the fact that at all times, even once they arrived in Canada, they were unaware of the type of drug they were carrying;
- their immediate collaboration with authorities as soon as customs officials became suspicious;
- their sincere remorse and regret;
- the fact that they are, for all intents and purposes, rehabilitated.

[44] In our opinion, it is important to emphasize the psychological vulnerability of the appellants when they were recruited. The psychiatrist Morissette wrote that the decisions Ms. Fortin made in the spring of 2002 can be explained not by any lack of intellectual capacity but rather by [TRANSLATION] "her emotional and interpersonal naïveté, a certain developmental immaturity, a selective vulnerability ... ." He added that Rosie [TRANSLATION] "deceived Ms. Fortin, but Ms. Fortin was also easily manipulated for the purpose of getting the plan underway."

[45] The psychologist Gadoua is in full agreement. He writes that Ms. Fortin's motives for accepting Rosie's offer [TRANSLATION] "express confusion and lack of judgment: aware of threats and manipulation, she became paralyzed and passive, her judgment and behaviour altered. She no longer had the capacity to stop the process ... ." A little later, he adds that [TRANSLATION] "[she] hesitated for a good period of time, during which she became confused. She was especially sensitive to threats and manipulation, which stirred up remnants of trauma that were still within her" and finally, "without realizing it, she adopted survival modes linked to her still unresolved internal confusion and distress (victim of a criminal act) in order to avoid even further personal disintegration."

[46] The psychiatrist Morissette wrote that the decision made by Mr. Renaud during the same period is [TRANSLATION] "the result of a decision made too quickly, the result of the attraction of easy money and finally, the result of a (relative) sense of responsibility in that he did not want to involve his mother in his problems."

[47] The psychologist Gadoua wrote that Mr. Renaud's motivation for accepting the proposed job was [TRANSLATION] "staying physically and psychologically safe since he was a child and adolescent when he was a victim of physical abuse giving rise to sequelae related to post-traumatic stress syndrome." He added that the threats he received made it so that [TRANSLATION] "he was unable to exercise his practical judgment dispassionately" and spoke of [TRANSLATION] "internal distress significantly [impairing] his social functioning as well as his judgment."

[48] The psychiatrist Morissette wrote the following regarding the two appellants:

> [TRANSLATION] In a certain way, the two protagonists were "perfect" recruits, as they were generally inexperienced and completely lacking in criminal experience. In addition, they each (for their own reasons) had trouble trusting or opening up to others and, despite their youth, had over a number of years developed very good social functioning (resourcefulness, financial autonomy, etc.).

[49] In summary, in view of their respective weaknesses, the appellants fed off each other's fears.

[50] After a careful consideration of all the factors, we find that a 5-year prison sentence is just in the circumstances.

[51] In the case of the appellant Renaud, it is appropriate to take into account and give double credit for the time served in interim detention (4 months) and to subtract 8 months from the sentence.

[52] FOR THESE REASONS, THE COURT:

[53] allows the appeal;

[54] overturns the sentence for the sole purpose of *substituting* for the sentences previously imposed the following:

- In the case of the appellant Annie Fortin, a sentence of 5 years' imprisonment;
- In the case of the appellant Sébastien Renaud, a sentence of 4 years and 4 months' imprisonment.

The other elements of the sentence remain unchanged.

QUESTION

How would you explain this decision in view of the principles of appellate review examined earlier in this chapter; in particular, how would you assess it after *Lacasse*?

FURTHER READING

Trotter, Gary. "Appellate Review of Sentencing Decisions" in Julian V Roberts & David Cole, eds, *Making Sense of Sentencing* (Toronto: University of Toronto Press, 1999).

CHAPTER NINETEEN

Post-Appeal Sentence Issues

I. PAROLE AND EARLY RELEASE: BACKGROUND

This section provides an overview of parole and early release in Canada. From a procedural perspective, these issues can be technical and complex. Rather than addressing the many issues in detail, we sketch the framework of early release and set out some aspects of the substantive discussions about its legitimacy and efficacy. We deal only with the federal context and the Parole Board of Canada (PBC), formerly the National Parole Board (NPB). Provinces and territories have their own correctional statutes that govern temporary absences and release from sentences of less than two years. Ontario and Quebec have their own provincial parole boards. For the most part, the elements are similar and sometimes identical. In the other provinces and territories, parole is dealt with by the PBC. A few years ago, British Columbia disbanded its provincial board in favour of the federal one. When concerned about a non-federal prisoner, particularly one from Ontario, or Quebec, one should consult the relevant provincial or territorial legislation. (For a discussion of the history of parole in Canada, see David P Cole & Allan Manson, *Release from Imprisonment: The Law of Sentencing, Parole, and Judicial Review* (Toronto: Carswell, 1990) [Cole & Manson] at 159-89.)

The following excerpt will give you the flavour of the modern parole context and controversies, as well as a good sense of its current limited use.

Anthony N Doob, Cheryl Marie Webster & Allan Manson,
"Zombie Parole: The Withering of Conditional Release in Canada"
(2014) 61 Crim LQ 301 at 301-02, 303-06, 312-13, 316-18, 324-25, 327
(footnotes omitted)

1. Introduction

In 1956, with the best of intentions, and based on considerable consultation and the best data available at the time, the Fauteux Committee recommended the "establishment of a national parole board" to provide fair, uniform and flexible decisions about the release of offenders into the community. The Committee was impressed with the need to re-integrate prisoners at the appropriate time with supervision and after-care geared to the situation and needs of the prisoner. Recognizing that not all prisoners would obtain a favourable response from the proposed board, it also recommended a form of "statutory parole" to ensure the "beneficial result of providing a degree of supervision and control for all persons released from penal institutions." In its structural form, the current system of early release in Canada would appear to the casual observer to be exactly what Fauteux envisaged.

But appearances are notoriously deceptive. After more than fifty years since the establishment of the National Parole Board, now the Parole Board of Canada, there has been very little examination of how our system of early release actually works. For a number of reasons, it occurred to us that it was time to have a serious look. From various sources there seems to be a popular conception that most prisoners are released on parole and probably at, or shortly after, they reach their eligibility dates. Is this an accurate assessment of how parole works in Canada? At the same time, one finds the inevitable critical commentary any time a prisoner on parole or statutory release commits an offence. These are deemed to be systemic failures. While sometimes sensational, how often does this occur and how much does this subset contribute to crime in Canada?

• • •

2. Brief Description of the Current System

For Canadian purposes, we must distinguish between federal prisoners and those sentenced to provincial or territorial prisons. Federal prisoners fall into two categories: those serving determinate or fixed sentences of two years or more, and those serving indeterminate sentences. The latter category consists of life sentences for murder and indeterminate sentences for dangerous offenders. All provincial and territorial prisoners are serving sentences of less than two years. In the federal sphere, all early release on parole or day parole is determined by the Parole Board of Canada upon application by the prisoner after reaching the statutory eligibility date. In the provinces and territories, only Ontario and Quebec have their own parole authorities operating models essentially the same as the federal model. In the rest of Canada, the Parole Board of Canada exercises parole jurisdiction. All prisoners on parole, regardless of its source, are subject to conditions imposed by the parole board and supervision until their warrant expiry date. Supervision includes the potential for suspension, revocation, and return to imprisonment.

Parole eligibility is a creature of statute. For federal prisoners serving fixed sentences, the *Corrections and Conditional Release Act* provides that normally one-third of the sentence be served before a prisoner is eligible for full parole. This is replicated in provincial and territorial statutes for that group of prisoners. For prisoners serving a life sentence imposed as a maximum punishment, the parole ineligibility period is seven years. For many offences, these ineligibility periods are now subject to the discretion of the sentencing judge pursuant to s. 743.6 of the *Criminal Code* to increase parole ineligibility to one-half of the sentence or ten years, whichever is less, if satisfied that, in the circumstances of the offence and the offender, the "expression of society's denunciation" or the "objective of specific or general deterrence" requires it. For murder, the *Criminal Code* stipulates that life imprisonment is a minimum punishment, and parole ineligibility is 25 years for first degree and, for second degree, a period between 10 and 25 years as determined by the trial judge.

As well as the possibility of early release as a result of the discretion of the paroling authority, federal prisoners serving fixed sentences are, for the most part, released on statutory release at two-thirds of their sentence. This is to some extent mitigated by the power of the Board to detain a prisoner until warrant expiry on grounds that there is a substantial risk of serious re-offending. In the provincial and territorial systems, an artifact of earlier times continues to exist, a remission-based form of release provided by the *Prisons and Reformatories Act*, for prisoners who either do not apply for, or are not granted, parole. Here, an important systemic distinction occurs. Federal prisoners on statutory release are subject to the same supervision and revocation regime as parolees. However, a provincial or territorial prisoner released by reason of remission is released free and clear. It is generally accepted that the lengths of the remaining sentences are too short to warrant any supervisory regime.

3. Conceptual Controversies and the Current System

Although conditional release has been a long-standing tradition in Canadian corrections, it has not been without controversy. On the one hand, proponents argue that this correctional procedure is fundamental in ensuring the long-term protection of the public. As most incarcerated offenders will eventually return to free society, the gradual, supervised release mechanisms associated with this procedure provide support and controls while offenders transition from prison back into the community. As criminological research has consistently shown, conditional release is more effective in promoting a prisoner's successful reintegration into society as a law-abiding citizen than would be his/her sudden freedom—at sentence expiry—without any assistance or supervision.

On the other hand, opponents of conditional release argue that it conflicts with the principles of proportionality by rendering prison sentences less predictable. Indeed, three years in penitentiary means—in actuality—different things for different prisoners as one may be released into the community sooner than another. ...

The fact that offenders may serve part of their custodial sentences outside of the prison is frequently viewed by the general public as unmerited leniency. This perception risks diminishing public confidence in the ability of the justice system to impose—and enforce—fair and just sanctions. At the same time, punishment decisions are transferred from judges to an extra-judiciary agency, further reducing the transparency of the criminal process.

This controversy becomes particularly acute when one considers parole. Day parole is a discretionary release by the parole board requiring nightly return to an institution or a halfway house. It allows offenders to participate in community-based activities during the day. Day parole can be granted six months before an inmate's full parole eligibility date. Although this form of conditional release is for a maximum period of six months, it can be repeated (*Corrections and Conditional Release Act*, s. 122(5)). In contrast, full parole—also a discretionary release by the parole board—allows offenders to serve the rest of their custodial sentences in the community under supervision. Most inmates are eligible for full parole at the one-third point in their sentence.

Perhaps the only broad consensus currently on the issue of parole in Canada is the belief that this form of conditional release continues to be alive and well in the correctional system. Indeed, the continuing debate about the merits of parole suggests that it is still a common reality in Canadian corrections.

· · ·

6. A New Methodology to Examine the Reality of Parole

Clearly, a more systematic and comprehensive approach is needed to capture the use of parole in Canada. As our principal measure, we have chosen to examine the effect of parole on imprisonment rates. This measure has several advantages. On the one hand, it takes into account both the overall prisoner population as well as the proportion of it that actually applies for parole. On the other hand, it constitutes a composite measure in that it takes into consideration not only the number of prisoners who are granted parole but also—and importantly—at what point in their sentence they are paroled. As for our methodology, we have opted to compare the effect of the current use of parole on imprisonment rates with the effect of the complete absence of any recourse to parole on imprisonment rates. Large differences between these two measures would indicate a sizable impact of parole, suggesting that this form of conditional release continues to be alive and well in Canadian corrections. Small differences in the imprisonment rates would indicate a negligible impact of parole, suggesting that this form of conditional release has withered away.

While arguably a more comprehensive strategy to examine the current recourse to parole, we signal one important caveat to our proposed methodology. Our calculations are, by necessity, *estimates* of the effect of parole releases on imprisonment rates. First, there are occasional minor inconsistencies in the data that are used because the ideal data were not—at times—available or the data varied in minor ways across sources. These issues may reflect problems such as the use of calendar years in one source and fiscal years in another, or "census day" figures in some sources (*e.g.*, for prison populations) and "average counts" across a year for other sources. In other cases, figures are routinely updated as minor errors or missing cases are discovered. In order to minimize the problem of variation in definitions (and dates), most of our findings come from a single source: Public Safety Canada's *Corrections and Conditional Release Statistical Overview*, 2013 and some earlier years.

Second, the calculations described in this paper were carried out with data that may not take into account the full impact of the end of accelerated parole review. Normally, prisoners in federal penitentiaries (those serving sentences of two years or more) are eligible for parole after serving one third of their sentences and are presumptively released (under statutory release) at the two-thirds point in their sentences. Under accelerated parole review, non-violent first time penitentiary prisoners were presumptively released at the one-third point in their sentences without necessarily having an in-person hearing. And finally, our calculations also assume no compensatory changes (*e.g.*, that sentences might change if full parole were abolished) and they assume that correctional authorities would not change the use of other forms of release such as unescorted temporary absences (*Corrections and Conditional Release Act*, ss. 115-118) if full and/or day parole were abolished.

(a) Estimating the Effect of Full Parole Release on Prison Populations

. . .

(iii) Overall Estimated Impact of the Abolition of Full Parole

If correct, these estimates suggest that in the case that all full parole were abolished for fixed sentence prisoners, there would be an additional 664 federal prisoners and 395 more provincial/territorial prisoners or roughly 1,059 more prisoners on an average day than the 39,567 currently imprisoned in Canada. In terms of rate, our estimate (using the most recent data) is that Canada's current imprisonment rate is 113.1. In the case that parole had already been officially abolished, it would have been 116.1 or about 2.7% higher. One shouldn't minimize these possible shifts in terms of their impact on an estimated 1,059 Canadians who would be in prison on an average day rather than in the community in the case that parole were to be abolished for those serving determinate sentences. Our point is only that, relatively speaking, the effect would not be large. But looking at these estimates from the perspective of the institution of full parole in Canadian prisons and penitentiaries, it is quite clear that parole has, in effect, withered away. Said differently, if the purpose of parole is to facilitate the safe and peaceful reintegration of prisoners into society, it is failing.

(b) Estimating the Effect of Day Parole Release on Prison Populations

The abolition of day parole is quite a different issue. Even in the case that full parole were abolished, one could easily imagine that day parole would be maintained. Indeed, the advantage of some form of gradual re-integration into society (whereby the offender spends the night in a community-based residential facility) would make sense. Day parole is now a precursor to full parole or statutory release. It is not available to provincial or territorial prisoners.

In 2013, an average of 966 federal offenders were on day parole. One can see that, on average, they are on day parole for a relatively short period of time by the fact that there were, during that year, 3,080 day paroles completed (mostly successfully). Those prisoners who are released on day parole have served, on average, 38.3% of their penitentiary sentences. Our presumption is that these offenders would have completed their day parole before their statutory release date. Assuming that *all* of the time on day parole is "saved" time, a reasonable estimate would be that if day parole were simply abolished, there would be an additional 966 prisoners in federal institutions.

(c) Estimating the Effect of Full and Day Parole Release on Prison Populations

The combination of the day parole figure (966 offenders) with the "savings" from full parole (664 offenders) means that the abolition of full and day parole would result in 1,630 more penitentiary prisoners. It is interesting to note that the abolition of day parole would—it seems—bring about a larger increase in the penitentiary population than the abolition of full parole. The combined abolition of full and day parole would result in a federal imprisonment rate of 46.6 prisoners per 100,000 Canadian residents—an 11.1% increase.

As we have already seen, the abolition of full parole in provincial/territorial institutions would signify an additional 395 provincial/territorial prisoners. Therefore, the combined (estimated) impact of the abolition of full and day parole from both federal and provincial/territorial institutions would result in a total of 2,025 prisoners (an additional 1,630 federal prisoners and 395 provincial/territorial prisoners) in addition to the 39,567 currently being incarcerated. The cumulative effect on the overall rate of imprisonment in Canada would be an increase of roughly 5.1% (or from about 113.1 to about 118.9 prisoners per 100,000 Canadian residents).

In sum, it would appear that the impact of parole (as an institution) on imprisonment rates was minimal by 2013 and that much of the "savings" comes from day parole. Essentially, we are suggesting that in recent years, the likelihood for those serving determinant sentences of being released on parole—particularly full parole—is so low and the actual "savings" of prison time so small that parole exists more in theory, legislation and the imagination of its critics than it does in the everyday reality of release from Canadian correctional institutions. In fact, those believing that a sentence of imprisonment includes any real likelihood of parole would be well advised to revise their thinking. Indeed, the notion of asking for a longer sentence, suggesting that a client will be released early from prison or inflaming public opinion about excessive leniency in the justice system based on the belief in the frequent recourse to parole would appear largely unfounded.

• • •

8. *Implications*

Using a more comprehensive measure of the current recourse to parole, we hope to have convincingly demonstrated that belief in this form of conditional release as being alive and well in Canadian corrections is seriously flawed. A comparison of the effect of the present use of parole on imprisonment rates with the effect of the complete absence of any recourse to parole on imprisonment rates showed only small differences, indicating a negligible use of parole in Canadian corrections today. For all intents and purposes, this form of conditional release has withered away.

Illustratively, it is hard to see why a "parole board" *per se* is even necessary in Ontario. The Ontario Parole Board's decisions on parole do not seem to be a very important determinant of Ontario's prison population. In 2010-11, 31,307 people entered Ontario's prisons as sentenced offenders. About 7% of these prisoners (or about 2,191 people) were handed down custodial sentences of 6 months or more (and hence were eligible to appear before the parole board for release on parole). The Ontario Parole Board 2012-13 Annual Report indicates that it considered 1,021 parole applications that year, and 302 offenders were granted parole. In other words, for every 100 sentenced prisoners entering Ontario's prisons, an average of about 1 will leave prison on parole.

Clearly, a continuing belief that parole is alive and well in Canada stands in stark contrast with the current reality in the Canadian correctional system. The concern—we argue—is that this perception of the continuing recourse to parole has both immediate as well as broader implications. From a practical perspective, all decisions being made on the assumption that parole continues to be used with some frequency need to be reassessed. Most obviously, it would not seem implausible to think that criminal justice professionals might take the likelihood of parole into account when thinking about fit sentences or advising clients of their options. Similarly, clamour for harsher sentences from the general public is likely directly linked to a belief that many or most offenders generally leave prison on parole at or near the $1/3$ point in their sentences. Even from a legislative perspective, the continuing belief in the recourse to parole could have unforeseen consequences.

• • •

9. Conclusion

The continuing belief in the frequent use of parole may mean that we currently have the worst of all possible worlds. On the one hand, we have none of the advantages of parole. With so few prisoners being granted parole today, successful reintegration is rendered even more difficult for many ex-inmates, further enhancing the "revolving door" phenomenon and diminishing the long-term protection of the public. On the other hand, we continue to have all of the challenges of parole. As the Conservative Minister of Justice (A. Kim Campbell) and the Conservative Solicitor General of Canada (Pierre H. Cadieux) noted in their 1990 *Framework for Sentencing, Corrections and Conditional Release,*

> Canadians do not feel that the criminal justice system punished criminals severely enough …
> At the same time, Canadians … overestimate the ease with which parole is granted, under-
> estimate the length of time served by most offenders before parole is given, and overestimate
> the number of offenders on parole who commit new crimes.

These challenges are just as relevant today as they were in 1990. The difference, of course, is that the underlying controversy surrounding parole of which these challenges constitute one side of the debate has—for all intents and purposes—been rendered moot by the current withering of this form of conditional release.

In 1992, the passage of the *Corrections and Conditional Release Act*, SC 1992, c 20 [CCRA] replaced both the *Penitentiary* and *Parole Acts*. This new statute changed many aspects of the former regime. Among other important provisions, it replaced the remission-based release on mandatory supervision with statutory release after two-thirds of a sentence is served. As well, for the first time, the CCRA included a general statement of purpose and applicable principles:

> 100 The purpose of conditional release is to contribute to the maintenance of a just, peaceful and safe society by means of decisions on the timing and conditions of release that will best facilitate the rehabilitation of offenders and their reintegration into the community as law-abiding citizens.
> 100.1 The protection of society is the paramount consideration for the Board and the provincial parole boards in the determination of all cases.
> 101 The principles that guide the Board and the provincial parole boards in achieving the purpose of conditional release are as follows:
>   (a) parole boards take into consideration all relevant available information, including the stated reasons and recommendations of the sentencing judge, the nature and gravity of the

offence, the degree of responsibility of the offender, information from the trial or sentencing process and information obtained from victims, offenders and other components of the criminal justice system, including assessments provided by correctional authorities;

(b) parole boards enhance their effectiveness and openness through the timely exchange of relevant information with victims, offenders and other components of the criminal justice system and through communication about their policies and programs to victims, offenders and the general public;

(c) parole boards make decisions that are consistent with the protection of society and that are limited to only what is necessary and proportionate to the purpose of conditional release;

(d) parole boards adopt and are guided by appropriate policies and their members are provided with the training necessary to implement those policies; and

(e) offenders are provided with relevant information, reasons for decisions and access to the review of decisions in order to ensure a fair and understandable conditional release process.

Prior to 2012, s 101 contained the provision that "parole boards make the least restrictive determination consistent with the protection of society." Now, s 101(c) has been changed to read that parole boards "are limited to only what is necessary and proportionate to the purpose of conditional release": see SC 2012, c 1, s 71. What might the impact of this change be for parole litigation?

A. Conditional Release Glossary

In order to help you understand the technical aspects of parole law, we have prepared a short glossary of some of the basic terms that apply to the different kinds of releases, and the various consequential processes that can occur. We have listed them in sequential, not alphabetical, order.

Full parole. This is defined by s 99 simply as the "authority granted to an offender to be at large during the offender's sentence." Parole and its applicable conditions continue until warrant expiry unless parole is suspended, cancelled, terminated, or revoked.

Day parole. Section 99 defines this as the authority granted by the PBC to an offender "to be at large during the offender's sentence in order to prepare the offender for full parole or statutory release, the conditions of which require the offender to return to a penitentiary, a community-based residential facility or a provincial correctional facility each night, unless otherwise authorized in writing."

Temporary absence. There are two types of temporary absence—escorted (ETA) and unescorted (UTA). For prisoners serving a life sentence for murder and for dangerous offenders, the jurisdiction over UTAs is vested in the PBC. For most other prisoners, UTAs can be granted by the institution head: see CCRA s 116(2). Again, with the exception of murderers, ETAs are granted by the institutional head for limited periods (usually less than 5 days, but up to 15 days, with the approval of the commissioner), or for an unlimited period for medical reasons: see CCRA s 17. Assuming that the prisoner does not present an undue risk, the statutory reasons for an ETA include "medical, administrative, community service, family contact, personal development for rehabilitative purposes, or compassionate reasons, including parental responsibilities." A common reason for an ETA, besides a medical reason, is to attend a family funeral.

Statutory release. This is the point, usually after serving two-thirds of a sentence, at which a prisoner is entitled to be released pursuant to s 127, unless the prisoner is subject to detention, discussed below.

Detention. Prisoners who have committed offences within stipulated categories (see Schedules I and II, which list sexual offences, offences of violence, and serious drug offences) can be referred to the board to consider whether they should be detained instead of released on statutory release. Either the Correctional Service Canada (CSC) or the commissioner can refer a case to the board if there are reasonable grounds to believe that the offender, before the expiration of sentence, is likely to commit an offence causing death or serious harm, a sexual offence involving a child, or a serious drug offence. The board can then conduct a hearing to decide whether it should deny release because of any of these likelihoods. The detention process is governed by ss 129 to 132.

Suspension. The parole or statutory release of an offender is subject to suspension under s 135(1) by decision of a member of the PBC or a designate when that person is satisfied that the offender has breached a condition or that it is "necessary and reasonable to suspend the parole or statutory release in order to prevent a breach of any condition thereof or to protect society." The suspension decision is accompanied by a warrant of apprehension and the recommitment to custody of the offender. Unless the suspension is cancelled, the board must conduct a post-suspension hearing.

Revocation. At a post-suspension hearing, if the board is satisfied that the offender does not present an "undue risk," the suspension is cancelled and the offender can continue in the community subject to conditions. However, if the board is not satisfied, then it ends the parole of statutory release by revocation or termination. A revocation means that the prisoner is returned to custody to serve the unexpired portion of the sentence. The prisoner can apply again for parole subject to the eligibility provisions, but is not entitled to statutory release until two-thirds of the unexpired portion of the sentence has been served.

Termination. This option is available at a post-suspension hearing if the board concludes that there is undue risk that is "due to circumstances beyond the offender's control": see ss 135(5)(b) and (7). Upon termination, the prisoner is returned to custody and can apply again for parole. However, the original statutory release date, based on two-thirds of the original sentence, is maintained.

As you can see from the glossary above, the elements of conditional release are complicated. They are prescribed by Part II of the CCRA and its regulations, which are often amended in technical ways. The framework has been interpreted and applied in a body of case law, mostly emanating from judicial review in the Federal Court. The statute and the cases are far too complex to deal with here. We will look in detail only at eligibility.

B. Eligibility

The law in effect on the date of sentencing determines the prisoner's eligibility for all forms of statutory release. For murder, this has usually been stipulated in the *Criminal Code*. For all other offences, eligibility has been established by the parole legislation in force at the time of the offence. Currently, the CCRA establishes the day parole eligibility date (DPED) and the full parole eligibility date (PED) as follows:

119(1) Subject to section 746.1 of the *Criminal Code*, subsection 140.3(2) of the *National Defence Act* and subsection 15(2) of the *Crimes Against Humanity and War Crimes Act*, the portion of a sentence that must be served before an offender may be released on day parole is

(a) one year, where the offender was, before October 15, 1977, sentenced to preventive detention;

(b) where the offender is an offender, other than an offender referred to in paragraph (b.1), who was sentenced to detention in a penitentiary for an indeterminate period, the longer of

(i) the period required to be served by the offender to reach the offender's full parole eligibility date, determined in accordance with section 761 of the *Criminal Code*, less three years, and

(ii) the period required to be served by the offender to reach the offender's full parole eligibility date, determined in accordance with subsection 120.2(2), less three years;

(b.1) where the offender was sentenced to detention in a penitentiary for an indeterminate period as of the date on which this paragraph comes into force, the longer of

(i) three years, and

(ii) the period required to be served by the offender to reach the offender's full parole eligibility date, determined in accordance with subsection 120.2(2), less three years;

(c) where the offender is serving a sentence of two years or more, other than a sentence referred to in paragraph (a) or (b), the greater of

(i) the portion ending six months before the date on which full parole may be granted, and

(ii) six months; or

(d) one half of the portion of the sentence that must be served before full parole may be granted, where the offender is serving a sentence of less than two years.

• • •

120(1) Subject to sections 746.1 and 761 of the *Criminal Code* and to any order made under section 743.6 of that Act, to subsection 140.3(2) of the *National Defence Act* and to any order made under section 140.4 of that Act, and to subsection 15(2) of the *Crimes Against Humanity and War Crimes Act*, an offender is not eligible for full parole until the day on which the offender has served a period of ineligibility of the lesser of one third of the sentence and seven years.

Life sentence

(2) Subject to any order made under section 743.6 of the *Criminal Code* or section 140.4 of the *National Defence Act*, an offender who is serving a life sentence, imposed otherwise than as a minimum punishment, is not eligible for full parole until the day on which the offender has served a period of ineligibility of seven years less any time spent in custody between the day on which the offender was arrested and taken into custody, in respect of the offence for which the sentence was imposed, and the day on which the sentence was imposed.

Essentially, this scheme provides for full parole eligibility after serving one-third of a sentence and day parole eligibility six months before that date. Before 1992, the day parole eligibility date was one-sixth of the sentence. The prolongation to six months before full parole eligibility diminished the use of long periods of successive day paroles. The PBC also has authority over UTAs for lifers and prisoners serving a sentence for a schedule I or II offence: see ss 116(1) and 107(1)(e). Generally, eligibility for a UTA occurs at one-half of the parole eligibility period: see s 115(1)(c). No maximum security prisoners can qualify for a UTA: see s 115(3).

A person sentenced to imprisonment for life as a maximum sentence—that is, for an offence other than murder—is eligible for parole after serving seven years. For all life sentences, credit toward eligiblity begins when the prisoner is arrested for the offence, and includes any days in custody after that time. For all other offences, credit toward parole eligibility accumulates only after the sentence is imposed.

C. Increasing Parole Eligibility

Amendments to the *Criminal Code* in 1992 permit a trial judge, in certain circumstances, to increase the period of parole ineligibility up to one-half of the sentence. The *Criminal Code* now provides

> 743.6(1) Notwithstanding subsection 120(1) of the *Corrections and Conditional Release Act*, where an offender receives, on or after November 1, 1992, a sentence of imprisonment of two years or more, including a sentence of imprisonment for life imposed otherwise than as a minimum punishment, on conviction for an offence set out in Schedule I or II to that Act that was prosecuted by way of indictment, the court may, if satisfied, having regard to the circumstances of the commission of the offence and the character and circumstances of the offender, that the expression of society's denunciation of the offence or the objective of specific or general deterrence so requires, order that the portion of the sentence that must be served before the offender may be released on full parole is one half of the sentence or ten years, whichever is less.
>
> $\cdots$
>
> (2) For greater certainty, the paramount principles which are to guide the court under this section are denunciation and specific or general deterrence, with rehabilitation of the offender, in all cases, being subordinate to these paramount principles.

More recently, Parliament added ss 743.6(1.1) and (1.2) to include organized crime and terrorism offences within this regime.

After a variety of approaches by appellate courts, the Supreme Court addressed this issue in *R v Zinck*, immediately below, and discussed the relevant factors that a judge should consider before making an order under s 743.6 of the Code (formerly s 741.2).

R v Zinck

2003 SCC 6, [2003] 1 SCR 41

I. Introduction

LeBEL J (McLachlin CJ, Gonthier, Iacobucci, Major, Bastarache, Binnie, Arbour, and Deschamps JJ concurring):

[1] On November 20, 1996, the appellant Thomas Zinck shot and killed his 19-year-old neighbour, Stéphane Caissie. He was charged with second degree murder. He pleaded guilty to manslaughter. The trial judge sentenced him to a 12-year term of imprisonment and ordered that his parole eligibility be delayed for six years under s. 743.6 of the *Criminal Code*, RSC 1985, c. C-46. The appellant challenged this part of his sentence in the New Brunswick Court of Appeal and now in this Court, where it is the sole issue remaining on appeal. In his view, the order to delay parole eligibility was made without evidence of the exceptional circumstances which would justify it, without sufficient reasons being given by the trial judge, and after a hearing conducted in breach of procedural fairness. None of these grounds has been established. For the reasons which follow, I would dismiss this appeal.

II. Background

[2] At the time of his trial, Zinck was 56 years old. He had a long history of run-ins with the law. His extensive criminal record speaks for itself. It goes back some 30 years. It includes a conviction for robbery, for which he received a 10-year jail sentence, together with a string of thefts and other property crimes. A number of alcohol and gun offences, as well as breaches of parole or probation, are also listed in this record.

[3] The victim was a neighbour of the accused. Based on the evidence, it seems that they got along well. At the time, Zinck drank heavily. He was also fond of firearms and kept a number of them in his house. Before the shooting, three successive break-ins had occurred at the Caissie house. It appears that Zinck took it on himself to watch for burglars. This plan led to Caissie's tragic death. On the day of the shooting, Zinck had been drinking heavily. It seems that he thought he had noticed burglars. So he went to Caissie's house, where the victim was in bed. Zinck was carrying a loaded gun. He started banging on the door. Stéphane Caissie went to the door to check what was going on. He opened the door. The gun went off. Caissie was killed instantly.

[4] Zinck was never able to explain what happened. As the trial judge found, he was heavily intoxicated at the time of the shooting, he was fascinated with guns especially when he was drunk, and he had said, shortly after the shooting, that he had "got one" (a burglar). As mentioned above, he was charged with murder, but agreed to plead guilty to the reduced and included offence of manslaughter.

[5] On November 17, 1997, following the guilty plea, Godin J adjourned the sentencing hearing to December 22. Zinck had legal representation throughout. During the hearing, Crown counsel reviewed the circumstances of the crime and the record of the accused. He asked the court to consider a 15-year term of imprisonment as a fit punishment for the offence. Then, close to the end of his submissions, the Crown prosecutor raised the issue of delayed parole and of the application of s. 743.6 of the *Code*. He asked the trial judge to consider applying this provision and delaying parole. His argument on the issue was very brief. Counsel stated only that he was asking for delayed parole because Zinck had violated parole before.

[6] After a break of a few hours, defence counsel made representations on behalf of his client. His argument addressed the issues pertaining to what should be the appropriate punishment. Despite the application for delayed parole made by the Crown, the lawyer who was then acting for the appellant never mentioned the issue during his argument.

• • •

[8] The judge noted that the Crown had applied for delayed parole. He agreed that the case was a proper one for the application of s. 743.6. His specific reasons on the question remained faithful to the virtue of conciseness:

> In addition, having regards to Section 743.6 of the *Criminal Code*, I am satisfied, having regards to the circumstances of the commission of the offence and the character and the circumstances of the offender, that the expression of society's denunciation of the offence requires an order that the portion of the sentence that must be served before the offender may be released on full parole is at least one-half of the sentence.

• • •

V. Analysis

A. The Issue

[14] This appeal is concerned solely with the question of delayed parole under s. 743.6 of the *Criminal Code* (formerly s. 741.2). The fitness of the 12-year jail term was not questioned in our Court. No issues of inadequate representation by trial counsel in connection with the Crown's application for delayed parole eligibility were raised in the Court of Appeal or in our Court.

[15] The appeal raises closely connected procedural and substantive issues. First, Zinck challenges the procedural fairness of the process which led to the order delaying his eligibility for parole. He submits that the prosecution should give notice in advance of its intention to apply for delayed parole, in order to allow the accused to respond effectively to such an application. Following both parties' submissions, the reasons of the trial judge should address the issue with clarity and precision. Second, the appellant raises the argument that a proper interpretation of s. 743.6 requires that it be applied only in limited cases, upon evidence of extraordinary or exceptional circumstances.

• • •

B. The Nature of Orders for Delayed Parole

[18] The delayed parole scheme under s. 743.6 reflects a relatively recent change in legislative policy on sentencing. It is true that a related provision, which is now found in s. 745.4, had provided for a number of years that a sentencing judge must fix the period of parole ineligibility of an accused convicted of second degree murder. This exception aside, the principles of sentencing drew a clear distinction between the functions of courts, which determined the proper punishment for an offence, and the role of agencies which ran the jails and oversaw the execution of sentences. Eligibility for parole fell within the mandate of the National Parole Board. Considerations relating to parole eligibility normally remained irrelevant to the determination of the fitness of the sentence: *R v. M. (C.A.)*, [1996] 1 SCR 500, at para. 62, *per* Lamer CJ. While some courts may have increased the length of a jail term to manipulate the term of parole ineligibility, such a practice is quite improper. (See H. Dumont, *Pénologie: Le droit canadien relatif aux peines et aux sentences* (1993), at p. 151; see also A. Manson, "Judges and Parole Eligibility: Section 741.2" (1995), 37 CR (4th) 381.)

[19] Determining the date and conditions of parole eligibility is usually the prerogative of an administrative body, the Parole Board, in the discharge of its supervisory functions over the execution of sentences. Over time, however, the focus of legislation has shifted. The *Corrections and Conditional Release Act* (the "Act") now puts more emphasis than before on the protection of the public and less on pure rehabilitation objectives and concerns. (See, for example, ss. 4, 102 and 126 of the Act; also, Dumont, *supra*, at p. 299.) Nevertheless, the decision-making process under the Act remains much different from the judicial determination of a fit sentence. It is largely based on the ongoing observation and assessment of the personality and behaviour of the offender during his or her incarceration, which focuses on dangerousness and the offender's ability to re-enter the community (Dumont, *supra*, at p. 333). Such a process may extend over several years and lead

to decisions that are highly attentive to context and based, at least in part, on what actually happened during the incarceration of the offender.

[20] At the end of this process of observation and review, full parole may be granted. The granting of full parole does not amount to a reduction of the jail sentence. The offender is still serving his or her sentence until the end of the term. Our Court has defined such a decision as an alteration of the conditions under which the sentence is being served (*Cunningham v. Canada*, [1993] 2 SCR 143, at pp. 150-51, *per* McLachlin J (as she then was); *M. (C.A.)*, *supra*, at para. 61). At the same time, under s. 128 of the Act, the offender on full parole is entitled to remain at large and is not obliged to live within the four walls of the correctional institution. Although the sentence is not over and measures of supervision remain in place, full parole grants an offender a very substantial degree of personal freedom. As mentioned above, this process generally used to fall outside the functions of the sentencing courts, which did not have to concern themselves about parole eligibility, its conditions and its supervision.

[21] In respect of second degree murder, s. 745.4 created a first exception to this principle when it brought initial access to parole within the province of the sentencing judge (*R v. Shropshire*, [1995] 4 SCR 227). This power was granted in the case of one class of crimes, where delaying parole beyond the statutory minimum of 10 years had become the sole discretion the judge could exercise at the time of sentencing.

[22] The adoption of s. 743.6 altered more significantly the nature and scope of sentencing decisions in Canadian criminal law. Section 743.6 applies to a wide spectrum of offences. Some of them carry minimum sentences. In many cases, punishment may range from conditional discharge to life imprisonment. The sentencing judge already had to exercise a broad discretion in determining the appropriate punishment for the specific crime committed by a particular offender. Now, whenever s. 743.6 applies, judges may have to factor in parole ineligibility as an additional variable.

[23] It is now well established that the power to delay parole eligibility is part of the sentencing process. Deferred access to parole has now become a part of the punishment, in the case of criminal offences falling within the scope of s. 743.6. ...

[24] Delaying parole can be a significant component of a sentence. It may almost entirely extinguish any hope of early freedom from the confines of a penal institution with its attendant rights or advantages. In this manner, it brings a new element of truth, but also of harshness, to sentencing. The time served in a penitentiary will be closer to the sentence imposed, although, under the Act, the sentence is not over. Given its potential impact, it would have been preferable to be clear about when and why this new sentencing tool is to be used. Regrettably, the drafting of s. 743.6 left many substantive and procedural questions unanswered. As Fish JA of the Quebec Court of Appeal pointed out in one of the earliest cases on the interpretation of this provision, which was decided, like the *Goulet* case, before the enactment of s. 743.6(2), its conceptual basis remains "elusive." It concerns offences in respect of which the sentencing judge must first apply the normal principles of sentencing to the facts in order to determine a fit punishment for the crime. Then, the court must use the same principles all over again, in respect of the same facts—although now with a priority to deterrence and denunciation pursuant to s. 743.6(2)—in order to decide whether parole should be delayed (*R v. Dankyi* (1993), 86 CCC (3d) 368, at p. 376). The nature of the analytical process required in order to apply this provision remains far from clear. This degree of uncertainty goes a long way towards explaining the problems

courts have encountered in their search for a workable and consistent interpretation of s. 743.6, as well as the development of apparently conflicting jurisprudential currents in provincial appellate courts. It remains to be seen whether this conflict amounts to more than a question of semantics, given that Canadian courts have tried to ascertain what the provision really means and how it should work. I will now turn to this problem.

C. *The Interpretation of Section 743.6*

. . .

[26] Many judgments have referred in some way to delayed parole as an exceptional measure. Until now, our Court has had no opportunity to consider this issue, which was not raised in *Chaisson*. In *Shropshire*, we reviewed the criteria and procedures governing delayed parole eligibility, but only in the context of a second degree murder, under what is now s. 745.4. Our Court held in that case that the prosecution need not demonstrate unusual circumstances, and that the law did not require that the power to delay parole be used sparingly (*Shropshire*, at para. 31, *per* Iacobucci J). As mentioned above, the provision at issue in *Shropshire* applied to a particular crime. The problems of the exercise of judicial discretion, the interplay of the sentencing factors, and their respective importance, arise in a different manner under s. 743.6. A method of interpretation and application, coordinating the application of this provision with the classical principles of sentencing and defining its sphere of application, remains to be developed.

[27] The theme of the exceptional character of the measure has been much stressed in an important strand of Canadian appellate jurisprudence. Many judgments express the view that the order to delay parole should be considered an exceptional one. ...

[28] Other appellate decisions adopted what appears to be a significantly different and broader approach to the interpretation and application of s. 743.6. According to these decisions, a sentencing judge does not have to look for unusual circumstances before ordering delayed parole. The judge has been granted discretionary power to be used in the appropriate circumstances, where consideration of the relevant sentencing factors justifies its exercise. ...

VI. *The Function of Section 743.6*

[29] The extent of this jurisprudential conflict has been overplayed. It does not reflect a basic disagreement between courts in Canada as to the nature of this provision and its place in the sentencing process. On the contrary, both views address the same difficulty and adopt ultimately consistent solutions to the integration of delayed parole into the process of sentencing. Under both approaches, the same method must be used. That method accepts that delayed parole is a decision that remains out of the ordinary and must be used in a manner that is fair to the offender. Both jurisprudential approaches to the application of s. 743.6 appear to require that the sentencing judge use a two-step intellectual process when deciding whether to delay parole. The addition of this section has not abolished the first duty of the sentencing judge. He or she must first determine what would be the appropriate punishment for the crime. The issue of parole eligibility is not considered at this stage. Courts consider all relevant factors and weigh them, in the circumstances of the case and taking into account the character of the offender. On the

basis of this analysis, the judge determines the duration of the jail sentence, if imprisonment is required by law or appears necessary.

[30]   At this point, the analysis may shift to the exercise of the power to delay parole. The position of s. 743.6 in the *Criminal Code* signals that it should not be applied in a routine manner. The power should not be exercised in a mechanical or automatic way, nor invoked in connection with every jail term imposed for an offence covered by s. 743.6. The judge must once again apply the sentencing factors. In this part of the process, however, the addition of s. 743.6(2) requires that, in the course of this second balancing, priority be given to the factors of general and specific deterrence, and of denunciation. The other factors remain relevant, but, to the extent of any conflict, subordinated to those identified by Parliament. It is worth noting that Parliament has not given priority to these specific factors in the application of s. 745.4.

[31]   At this stage, having given priority to the factors of deterrence and denunciation as required by law, and having duly considered all the criteria and principles relevant to sentencing, based on the evidence at the sentencing hearing and at trial, the court must arrive at its conclusion as to whether this additional punishment is required. The prosecution has the burden of demonstrating that it is. The judge must satisfy himself or herself that the order is needed to reflect the objectives of sentencing, with awareness of the special weight ascribed by Parliament to the social imperatives of denunciation and deterrence. Nevertheless, at the end of this intellectual process, the sentencing decision must remain alive to the nature and position of delayed parole in criminal law as a special, additional form of punishment. Hence it should not be ordered without necessity, in a routine way. This idea is acknowledged by Griffiths JA of the Ontario Court of Appeal in *Goulet* (p. 65). It is this aspect of s. 743.6 that explains the development of the jurisprudential current emphasizing its exceptional nature. The other stream of jurisprudence, which shies away from using the vocabulary of an "exceptional measure," does not seem, in practice, to have applied s. 743.6 in a different manner. None of these judgments has suggested that a delayed parole order should be considered an ordinary measure, to be applied in the normal course; they agree that it should be invoked only on the basis of demonstrated need.

[32]   The application of s. 743.6 will probably never be an easy task for judges. Sentencing remains a heavy responsibility for trial and appellate judges throughout Canada. The exercise of the power to delay parole adds to the difficulties of this task. With a proper understanding of the nature of the measure, it is to be hoped that its application will be less problematic.

[33]   As mentioned above, courts must perform a double weighing exercise. First, they must evaluate the facts of the case, in light of the factors set out in s. 718 of the *Code*, in order to impose an appropriate sentence. Then, they must review the same facts primarily in the perspective of the requirements of deterrence and denunciation, which are given priority at this stage, under s. 743.6(2). The decision to delay parole remains out of the ordinary, but may and should be taken if, after the proper weighing of all factors, it appears to be required in order to impose a form of punishment which is completely appropriate in the circumstances of the case. This decision may be made, for example, if, after due consideration of all the relevant facts, principles and factors at the first stage, it appears at the second stage that the length of the jail term would not satisfy the imperatives of denunciation and deterrence. This two-stage process, however, does not require a special

and distinct hearing. It should be viewed as one sentencing process, where issues of procedural fairness will have to be carefully considered.

VII. Procedural Issues and Fairness

[34] Acknowledging that delayed parole should not be a routine part of every sentencing decision under s. 743.6 does not imply that there should be a special and distinct hearing on the issue, where evidence of unusual or extraordinary circumstances must be introduced. Section 743.6 does not require the creation of such an additional procedure. A two-step intellectual process does not turn the sentencing hearing into two separate procedures. It should be enough that the issue be raised in a fair and timely manner so as to allow the offender to respond effectively. A breach of this basic obligation would justify quashing the order, as courts have done on occasion. (See *Corneau v. La Reine*, [2001] RJQ 2509 (CA), at p. 2515.) Beyond this, the sentencing hearing should not be overburdened with formalistic and unnecessary procedural requirements.

[35] The need for fairness does not impose any obligation to give written notice to the offender before the hearing that delayed parole will be applied for. Such an obligation would often be impractical, especially since sentencing hearings frequently take place immediately after the conviction or guilty plea. In addition, the *Criminal Code* does not expressly require written notice any more than did s. 745.4, which was considered in *Shropshire, supra*.

[36] The obligation to assure fairness in the process is of critical importance, but it may be discharged in different and equally valid ways. When possible, the Crown may give notice in writing or verbally before the hearing. The application may be made at the sentencing hearing itself. The issue may also be raised by the judge in the course of the hearing. Whenever and however the question is brought up, the offender must be informed clearly that he is at risk in this respect. The offender must be allowed to make submissions and to introduce additional evidence, if needed, in response to the request for delayed parole. Courts should be generous if adjournments are requested for this purpose. Fairness must be preserved, but in a flexible manner, taking into account the specifics of each case, without pointless procedural constraints.

[37] At the end of the process, the offender is entitled to reasons. The judgment must state with sufficient clarity the reasons why the delayed parole order is made. It must remain consistent with the principles set out in *R v. Sheppard*, [2002] 1 SCR 869, 2002 SCC 26. The reasons need not be elaborate. The basis of the decision must be at least ascertainable from the record; precision and clarity remain advisable in the drafting of such judgments. Deficiencies in reasons may sometimes require quashing an order for the sake of the perceived fairness and the transparency of the criminal process.

VIII. Application of Principles

[38] A review of the judgment and proceedings in this case confirms that none of the grounds of appeal have been established. The trial judge did not err in his application of s. 743.6. The order was justified on the basis of the record and was made after a hearing that did not breach the rules of procedural fairness.

[39] I concede that the part of the reasons dealing expressly with the issue of delayed parole is somewhat imprecise. A more detailed analysis should have been attempted. The

reasons, though, must be viewed as a whole and read in connection with the evidence and the submissions made at the hearing. Although not extensive, the reasons permit an appellate court to ascertain and review the basis of the order made by the trial judge. Thus, they do not breach the *Sheppard* standard. Godin J carefully reviewed all relevant facts, particularly the gratuitousness of the crime and the need to protect the public. They confirm his conclusion that the objectives of deterrence and denunciation could not be satisfied without delaying parole eligibility.

[40]　Procedural fairness was observed. In its submissions, the Crown asked for delayed parole. The accused, through his counsel, could have made his own submissions or presented evidence to oppose the Crown's request. He could have requested an adjournment, if the Crown's move took him by surprise. None of this was attempted. It was never suggested that this was a case of inadequate representation. The accused was given a sufficient opportunity to respond to the Crown's request. He failed to use it. He cannot fault the judge for this.

[41]　The Court of Appeal took the appropriate approach to the review of a sentencing decision. In the absence of an error of principle, a breach of the principles of procedural fairness or a clearly erroneous and material finding of fact, it decided that it should not intervene. Its decision was well founded. It can be upheld under both the narrow and the broad interpretations of s. 743.6, which can be reconciled, as indicated above.

IX. *Disposition*

[42]　For these reasons, I would dismiss the appeal.

D. Parole by Exception

Although it rarely occurs, it is possible for some prisoners to be considered for parole before their eligibility date. This has become known as parole by exception.

> 121(1)　Subject to section 102 and notwithstanding section 119 or 120 or any order made under section 741.2 of the *Criminal Code*, parole may be granted at any time to an offender
>> (a)　who is terminally ill;
>> (b)　whose physical or mental health is likely to suffer serious damage if the offender continues to be held in confinement;
>> (c)　for whom continued confinement would constitute an excessive hardship that was not reasonably foreseeable at the time the offender was sentenced; or
>> (d)　who is the subject of an order to be surrendered under the *Extradition Act* or the *Fugitive Offenders Act* and to be detained until surrendered.
>
> (2)　Subsection (1) does not apply to any offender who is
>> (a)　serving a sentence of life imprisonment imposed as a minimum punishment or commuted from a sentence of death; or
>> (b)　serving, in a penitentiary, a sentence of detention for an indeterminate period.

This provision does not apply to prisoners serving life sentences or indeterminate sentences. In May 2000, a subcommittee of the House of Commons Standing Committee on Justice and Human Rights released a review of the CCRA five years after its enactment ("the five-year review"). With respect to parole by exception, the subcommittee recommended that "offenders serving life sentences or indeterminate sentences who are terminally ill and who present, in the opinion of the NPB, no undue risk" should also be eligible for extraordinary consideration. However, any such decisions must be approved by the chair of the NPB (see Sub-committee on Corrections and Conditional Release Act of the Standing Committee on Justice and Human Rights, *A Work in Progress: The Corrections and Conditional Release Act* (Ottawa: Public Works Canada, 2000) [*A Work in Progress*] at 39-40. This recommendation has not been adopted.

E. Accelerated Parole

This mechanism, intended to fast-track non-violent offenders, was first introduced in 1992 with the CCRA. Section 125 of the CCRA and its related regulations provide that cases of first-time penitentiary prisoners who are not serving a sentence for murder, a life sentence, or an offence from the list that would qualify for detention, shall be sent to the board prior to day parole eligibility. For this category of offender, eligibility for day parole was "six months, or one sixth of the sentence, whichever is longer." The file was then reviewed without a hearing by the board. If the NPB was "satisfied that there are no reasonable grounds to believe that the offender, if released, is likely to commit an offence involving violence before the expiration of the offender's sentence," it ordered that the offender be released on day parole: see ss 126(2) and 126.1. A successful day parole usually led to full parole. If the board did not order release, the prisoner must get reasons and is subsequently entitled to a hearing on reaching full parole eligibility.

This mechanism received substantial consideration by the House of Commons subcommittee, which conducted the five-year review of the CCRA. *A Work in Progress* at 33-35 ultimately recommended its retention with the addition of two amendments:

> 4.30 Although the Sub-committee considers it important to retain accelerated parole review, so first time federal offenders considered non-violent need not be subjected to the negative influence of some repeat offenders, it also considers two amendments to the accelerated parole review procedure essential. The Sub-committee believes offenders incarcerated for Schedule I or Schedule II offences should not be eligible. As well, the recidivism criterion taken into account by the National Parole Board in reviewing these cases should specify general recidivism, not violent recidivism. It is the Sub-committee's view that the Parole Board should grant parole only if it is convinced there are no reasonable grounds to believe that any offence will be committed before the expiry of the warrant of committal.

Nonetheless, during the era of the Harper government, it was eliminated: see *Abolition of Early Parole Act*, SC 2011, c 11, in force 28 March 2011. This spawned litigation over the issue of eligibility and retrospectivity that finally reached the Supreme Court of Canada in the case of *Whaling*, below.

Canada (Attorney General) v Whaling
2014 SCC 20, [2014] SCR 392

WAGNER J (McLachlin CJ, LeBel, Abella, Rothstein, Cromwell, Moldaver, and Karakatsanis JJ concurring):

[1] In this appeal, the Court revisits the definition of the term "punishment" in the context of s. 11(h) of the *Canadian Charter of Rights and Freedoms*. The criminal law distinguishes between the sentence imposed on an offender and the conditions of the sentence. Changes to the conditions of a sentence, such as eligibility for parole, do not

alter the sentence itself. This Court must decide whether retrospective changes to the conditions of a sentence may in some circumstances constitute "punishment" in violation of the s. 11(h) right not to be punished twice for the same offence.

[2] This appeal results from Parliament's conclusion that accelerated parole review, or APR, was not working. Established by legislation enacted in November 1992, APR was a simplified process that allowed first-time non-violent offenders to be considered for parole on the basis of a single question: Are there no reasonable grounds to believe that the offender, if released, is likely to commit a violent offence? (See the *Corrections and Conditional Release Act*, S.C. 1992, c. 20 ("*CCRA*").)

• • •

[8] The question before this Court is whether the retrospective application of the delayed eligibility for day parole to incarcerated offenders who had been sentenced before the APR provisions were repealed violated the respondents' right, guaranteed by s. 11(h) of the *Charter*, not to be punished anew for their offences.

[9] This appeal affords the Court the opportunity to revisit the purpose of s. 11(h) and to define its scope. For the reasons that follow, I find that s. 11(h) applies to the respondents' claim. The retrospective application of delayed day parole eligibility violated the respondents' s. 11(h) right not to be "punished ... again," and that violation was not justified under s. 1 of the *Charter*.

• • •

[15] With the coming into force of the *AEPA*, APR (including early day parole eligibility), was abolished. Sections 3 and 5 of the *AEPA* repealed the *CCRA*'s APR provisions (ss. 119.1, 125, 126 and 126.1, cited above), while s. 10(1) of the *AEPA* made the abolition of APR apply retrospectively to offenders already serving their sentences. Section 10(1) reads:

> 10(1) Subject to subsection (2), the accelerated parole review process set out in sections 125 to 126.1 of the *Corrections and Conditional Release Act*, as those sections read on the day before the day on which section 5 comes into force, does not apply, as of that day, to offenders who were sentenced, committed or transferred to penitentiary, *whether the sentencing, committal or transfer occurs before, on or after the day of that coming into force.*

[16] In other words, APR, which the *AEPA* abolished, "does not apply" even if the offender was sentenced before the *AEPA* came into force. Instead of APR, the normal parole provisions of the *CCRA* would now apply. This changed the timing of eligibility for day parole: eligibility after the offender had served one sixth of the sentence or six months (repealed s. 119.1) was replaced with eligibility six months before the full parole eligibility date (s. 119). It also changed the review process for both day and full parole: automatic referral to the Board (repealed ss. 126(4) and 126.1) was eliminated, which meant that the offender would have to submit an application (s. 122), and the review on paper without a hearing (repealed s. 126(1)) was replaced with the hearing and personal appearance by the offender required in the normal review process (s. 140). In addition, the repeal changed the test for granting parole: the lower, presumptive standard of violent recidivism, which left the Board no discretion to deny parole if the test was met (repealed s. 126(2)), reverted to the more onerous one of "undue risk to society," which does leave it with such a discretion (s. 102).

[17] The immediate effect of the repeal was to delay the day parole eligibility dates of all three respondents: Mr. Whaling's by three months, Ms. Slobbe's by nine months, and Mr. Maidana's by twenty-one months.

. . .

[32] Section 11(h) of the *Charter* reads as follows:

> 11. Any person charged with an offence has the right
>
> . . .
>
> (h) if finally acquitted of the offence, not to be tried for it again and, if finally found guilty and punished for the offence, not to be tried or punished for it again;

[33] Parliament's purpose in enacting s. 11(h) was to protect against double jeopardy. Section 11(h) mirrors the language and purpose of art. 14.7 of the *International Covenant on Civil and Political Rights*, 999 U.N.T.S. 171, which reads:

> 7. No one shall be liable to be tried or punished again for an offence for which he has already been finally convicted or acquitted in accordance with the law and penal procedure of each country.

[34] But equating s. 11(h) with double jeopardy does not conclude the discussion of its purpose, since the very definition of "double jeopardy" is contested. Don Stuart says the following in this regard in *Charter Justice in Canadian Criminal Law* (5th ed. 2010):

> Under existing Canadian law there is certainly no one rule on double jeopardy. The subject is one of the utmost complexity and subtlety and is certainly in need of clarification. The law provides protection against harassment of multiple trials for the same act but also protection against multiple punishment. The concern to do something about double punishment stems from a distinct consideration based far more squarely on the fairness of proportionate punishment. [p. 464]

[35] As several authors have noted, the scope of s. 11(h) is narrow (see M.L. Friedland, "Legal Rights Under The Charter" (1982), 24 *Crim. L.Q.* 430, at pp. 435 and 449; Stuart, at p. 467). Stuart states that s. 11(h) has had "little impact on the protection of the accused against double jeopardy and double punishment," in part because of this narrow scope (*ibid.*). Both Friedland and Stuart suggest that broader interpretations of double jeopardy may fit more easily into s. 7 of the *Charter* (Friedland, at p. 435; Stuart, at p. 468). This view may seem especially compelling in this case, which concerns alleged punishment arising from retrospective legislation, given that there are two provisions that deal explicitly with retrospectivity: s. 11(g), which protects against retroactive criminal legislation, and s. 11(i), which protects against the imposition of a harsher punishment where the punishment for the offence has been varied between the time of commission of the crime and the time of sentencing.

[36] In my view, it is not necessary to resort to a different *Charter* provision. The language of s. 11(h), the academic literature and this Court's jurisprudence support a reading of s. 11(h) according to which the right not to be "punished ... again" applies where an offender has been sentenced, even if no separate proceeding has taken place.

[37] Let me begin by addressing the plain meaning of s. 11(h). The introductory words to s. 11 indicate that the subject of the entire section is a "person charged with an offence."

Paragraph (h) then provides that this person has the right, "if finally found guilty and punished for the offence, not to be tried or punished for it again." The disjunctive language of the words "tried *or* punished" clearly indicates that s. 11(h)'s protection against additional punishment is independent of its protection against being tried again. In other words, as Stuart notes in respect of double jeopardy more generally, the protection applies to both the harassment of multiple trials and the harassment of additional punishment (p. 464). The conjunctive language of the words "found guilty *and* punished" further accentuates the disjunctive language of "tried *or* punished." It is thus clear from the plain meaning of the words that either being tried again *or* being punished again is sufficient to engage s. 11(h).

[38] The plain meaning of s. 11(h) is supported by common sense. It would be far more questionable to punish someone without a proceeding than to punish him or her with a proceeding. The purpose of s. 11(h) cannot be to protect against punishment imposed following a trial in which due process has been observed, but not against punishment imposed without the protections afforded by a trial.

• • •

[48] In my view, the case at bar once again pushes the limits of the "punishment" concept, requiring us to revisit the principles that define the scope of s. 11(h). Whereas in *Wigglesworth* the Court established that non-criminal proceedings may engage s. 11(h) if they result in true penal consequences, and in *Rodgers* it articulated a test for determining whether a given consequence or sanction constitutes punishment, the question in the instant case eludes both tests.

[49] Rather than requiring us to determine whether a discrete sanction is punitive in nature, this case requires us to determine whether retrospective changes to parole eligibility, which modify the manner in which an existing sanction is carried out, constitute punishment. The alleged punishment is neither a second proceeding nor a "sanction" in the sense contemplated in *Rodgers*. Rather, the offender's expectations about the original punishment or sanction have been frustrated and this is said to constitute new punishment.

[50] The following makes clear that the two-part *Rodgers* test cannot apply to determine whether retrospective changes to parole eligibility constitute punishment. In the first branch of the *Rodgers* test, "punishment" is defined by referring to the traditional forms of punishment provided for in the *Criminal Code*, in which "[t]he words 'sentence' and 'sanction' are ... used interchangeably" (para. 62). The function of this branch of the test is to enable courts to determine whether other types of sanctions—such as a DNA order or a driving prohibition—share the characteristics of punitive sanctions and thus constitute "punishment." Since "a grant of parole represents a change in the conditions under which a judicial sentence must be served, rather than a reduction of the judicial sentence itself" (*R. v. M. (C.A.)*, [1996] 1 S.C.R. 500, at para. 62 (emphasis deleted)), changes to the parole system do not generally form part of the "arsenal of sanctions" contemplated in *Rodgers*.

[51] On the other hand, a retrospective change to parole eligibility may have the effect of extending an offender's term of incarceration. Incarceration is "the most severe deprivation of liberty known to our law" (*Wigglesworth*, at p. 562), and the most obvious example of punishment in the "arsenal of sanctions" available under the *Criminal Code*. It and heavy fines are the benchmark sanctions against which other, less severe sanctions are

assessed under the *Rodgers* test. That incarceration constitutes "punishment" is a core underlying assumption of the *Rodgers* test.

[52] In short, when applied in this context, the *Rodgers* test is overly formalistic, as the "arsenal of sanctions" test would exclude most changes to parole eligibility, whereas even marginal increases in the likelihood of additional incarceration easily meet the test. The problem is that the *Rodgers* test does not assist in identifying situations in which, from a functional rather than a formalistic perspective, the harshness of punishment has been increased. The *Rodgers* test was designed for a different purpose, namely to determine whether a discrete sanction—one that does not modify the original sanction—has the characteristics of a criminal sanction, and thus constitutes "punishment."

• • •

[57] Generally speaking, offenders have constitutionally protected expectations as to the duration, but not the conditions, of their sentences. Various changes in the management of an offender's parole are not punitive, even though they may engage the offender's liberty interest by marginally increasing the likelihood of additional incarceration. McLachlin J. (as she then was) held as follows in *Cunningham*:

> The *Charter* does not protect against insignificant or "trivial" limitations of rights ... . It follows that qualification of a prisoner's expectation of liberty does not necessarily bring the matter within the purview of s. 7 of the *Charter*. The qualification must be significant enough to warrant constitutional protection. To require that all changes to the manner in which a sentence is served be in accordance with the principles of fundamental justice would trivialize the protections under the *Charter*. To quote Lamer J. in *Dumas* [*v Leclerc Institute*, [1986] 2 SCR 459], at p. 464, there must be a "substantial change in conditions amounting to a further deprivation of liberty." [p. 151]

[58] The requirement of a "substantial change in conditions amounting to a further deprivation of liberty" was articulated in the context of s. 7, and I will not import it into that of s. 11(h), the purpose of which is distinct. Retrospective changes to the parole system that engage a liberty interest under s. 7 will not necessarily constitute punishment for the purposes of s. 11(h). However, certain of the conclusions reached in *Cunningham* do apply to my analysis under s. 11(h). First of all, the Court recognized that an offender has an expectation of liberty that is based on the parole system in place at the time of his or her sentencing, and that thwarting that expectation may engage a constitutionally protected liberty interest. Changes to the parole system that add retrospectively to the offender's incarceration may violate s. 7 even if they do not affect the sentence itself. As McLachlin J. put it in *Cunningham*: "One has 'more' liberty, or a better quality of liberty, when one is serving time on mandatory supervision than when one is serving time in prison" (p. 150).

[59] This being said, the Court recognized in *Cunningham* that not all expectations of liberty in the parole context are constitutionally protected. Even where a change to the conditions of a sentence engages a liberty interest under s. 7, it may nonetheless be consistent with the principles of fundamental justice. Some line drawing becomes necessary. In my view, this same basic point applies to a retrospective change that constitutes double punishment in the s. 11(h) context. Some retrospective changes to the parole system affect the expectation of liberty of an offender who has already been sentenced to such an extent

that they amount to new punishment, while other changes have a more limited impact and do not trigger *Charter* protection.

[60] I will not articulate a formula that would apply to every case, because such a formula is not needed to resolve this appeal and the effect of every retrospective change will be context-specific. That said, the dominant consideration in each case will in my view be the extent to which an offender's settled expectation of liberty has been thwarted by retrospective legislative action. It is the retrospective frustration of an expectation of liberty that constitutes punishment. At one extreme, a retrospective change to the rules governing parole eligibility that has the effect of automatically lengthening the offender's period of incarceration constitutes additional punishment contrary to s. 11(h) of the *Charter*. A change that so categorically thwarts the expectation of liberty of an offender who has already been sentenced qualifies as one of the clearest of cases of a retrospective change that constitutes double punishment in the context of s. 11(h).

[61] I reach this conclusion on the basis of many of the reasons cited by the courts below and advanced by the respondents. Although a sentencing judge is not to consider parole eligibility in assessing the fitness of the sentence (*Zinck*, at para. 18), the punitive effect of delayed parole eligibility is expressly recognized in the *Criminal Code*, which empowers a sentencing judge to consider delayed parole eligibility to be part of the sentence in certain circumstances. For example, s. 743.6(1) empowers a court to impose delayed parole eligibility for the purpose of denunciation or of specific or general deterrence. Furthermore, a sentencing judge may increase the parole ineligibility period of an offender convicted of second degree murder: *Chaisson*, at para. 12. The Court said the following in this regard in *R. v. Wust*, 2000 SCC 18, [2000] 1 S.C.R. 455, at para. 24:

> Rarely is the sentencing court concerned with what happens after the sentence is imposed, that is, in the administration of the sentence. Sometimes it is required to do so by addressing, by way of recommendation, or in mandatory terms, a particular form of treatment for the offender. *For instance in murder cases, the sentencing court will determine a fixed term of parole ineligibility: s. 745.4 of the Code.* [Emphasis added.]

In *Shropshire*, Iacobucci J. noted that the duration of parole ineligibility is the only difference in terms of punishment between first and second degree murder, which "clearly indicates that parole ineligibility is part of the 'punishment' and thereby forms an important element of sentencing policy" (para. 23).

[62] The fact that delayed parole eligibility can be imposed in the sentencing process confirms my view that retrospectively imposing delayed parole eligibility on offenders who have already been sentenced constitutes punishment. Where Parliament imposes through retrospective legislation a consequence that sentencing judges may themselves impose for the purpose of punishment, the s. 11(h) protection against double punishment applies.

[63] Whether less drastic retrospective changes to parole constitute double punishment will depend on the circumstances of the particular case. Generally speaking, a retrospective change to the conditions of a sentence will not be considered punitive if it does not substantially increase the risk of additional incarceration. Indicators of a lower risk of additional incarceration include a process in which individualized decision making focused on the offender's circumstances continues to prevail and procedural rights continue to be guaranteed in the determination of parole eligibility. Though I caution against directly importing principles drawn from the s. 7 jurisprudence into this context, the

replacement of an automatic release system with a discretionary release system was found to be constitutional in *Cunningham* owing in part to various procedural safeguards, including a hearing and the entitlement to counsel. While s. 11(h) is not directly concerned with procedural safeguards, the presence or absence of such safeguards is relevant in considering the likelihood of the punishment's severity being increased. As I mentioned above, the dominant consideration will be the extent to which the offender's settled expectation of liberty has been thwarted. A change that directly results in an extension of the period of incarceration without regard to the offender's individual circumstances and without procedural safeguards in the assessment process will clearly violate s. 11(h).

• • •

[70] The effect of the retrospective application provision, s. 10(1) of the *AEPA*, was to deprive the three respondents of the possibility of being considered for early day parole, which was an expectation they had had at the time they were sentenced. This amounts to a lengthening of the minimum period of incarceration for persons—like the respondents— who would have qualified for early day parole under the APR system.

[71] In my view, s. 10(1) had the effect of punishing the respondents again. It retrospectively imposed a delay in day parole eligibility in relation to offences for which they had already been tried and punished. The effect—extended incarceration—was automatic and without regard to individual circumstances.

[72] This situation is one of the "clearest of cases" discussed above. The imposition of a delay in parole eligibility in this case is analogous to the imposition of delayed parole eligibility by a judge under the *Criminal Code* as part of the sentence. As I mentioned above, Iacobucci J. noted in *Shropshire* that the imposition of such a delay "clearly indicates that parole ineligibility is part of the 'punishment'" (para. 23). Imposing this same consequence by means of retrospective legislation triggers the protection against double punishment set out in s. 11(h).

[73] My conclusion is not altered by the fact that the extension of parole ineligibility was imposed by means of legislation in the context of the *CCRA*, which concerns, *inter alia*, sentence administration, as opposed to being judicially imposed under the *Criminal Code*. This formal distinction does not change the basic point that, from a functional perspective, the new period of parole ineligibility thwarted the expectations of liberty of offenders who had already been "tried or punished" for their offences and resulted in harsher penalties than they would have received under the legislation that was in force at the time of their sentencing. Nor does the fact that the legislation extending their parole ineligibility was passed in the context of the *CCRA* rather than that of the *Criminal Code* shield Parliament's measure from the scrutiny under s. 11(h) of the *Charter* that would otherwise apply. If that were the case, Parliament could enact punitive laws resulting in double punishment simply by choosing to amend the *CCRA* rather than the *Criminal Code*.

• • •

[77] The trial judge held, and the Court of Appeal agreed, that the objectives of s. 10(1) of the *AEPA* are pressing and substantial, but they both found that the provision failed at the minimal impairment stage. I agree with this result.

[78] As I mentioned above, Parliament based its decision to abolish APR on considerable evidence, presented by the Crown in this case, that the system was not working effectively. It was within Parliament's prerogative to pass legislation it thought necessary to improve the system. The trial judge found that the objective of ensuring that sentences

as administered are consistent with the sentences courts impose, which, by extension, includes maintaining or restoring public confidence in the administration of justice, is pressing and substantial (para. 121). Parliament's decision to apply these same objectives to all offenders, including those who had already been sentenced, reflects its legitimate concern to ensure uniformity of parole administration and maintain confidence in the justice system. Having agreed that these objectives are pressing and substantial, I also find that the legislative measure—the *AEPA*—chosen by Parliament, including the retrospective application of its provisions, is rationally connected to the objectives.

[79] However, the Crown has not discharged its burden of proving that there was no less intrusive alternative to retrospective application of the *AEPA*'s provisions. Uniformity of parole administration may be a worthy objective, but the Crown has failed to provide compelling evidence that that uniformity would be impaired if the APR system continued to apply to offenders who were sentenced under it. I adopt the Court of Appeal's conclusion in this regard:

> Sentence management objectives in general, and the objectives of the *AEPA* in particular, are recognizably important, but they do not rise to such significance that justifies implementing them in a manner that deprives the respondents of their constitutional rights. The corrections authorities have for twenty years administered different parole regimes for different offenders, including APR. [para. 65]

[80] In my view, having the repeal apply only prospectively was an alternative means available to Parliament that would have enabled it to attain the objectives of reforming parole administration and maintaining confidence in the justice system without violating the s. 11(h) rights of offenders who had already been sentenced. Regarding the Crown's argument that retrospective application is necessary to maintain confidence in the justice system, I would point out that the enactment of *Charter*-infringing legislation does great damage to that confidence. The Crown has produced no evidence to show why the alternative of a prospective repeal, which would have been compatible with the respondents' constitutional rights, would have significantly undermined its objectives.

• • •

[89] I would dismiss the appeal and uphold the remedy ordered by the trial judge. Section 10(1) of the *AEPA* violates s. 11(h) of the *Charter* and is accordingly of no force or effect. Sections 125, 126, 126.1 and, by implication, 119.1 of the *CCRA* therefore continue to apply to offenders who were sentenced prior to the coming into force on March 28, 2011, of the *AEPA*.

NOTE

Whaling dealt with prisoners who had been convicted and sentenced prior to the enactment of the statute that repealed the availability of accelerated parole. What about prisoners who committed offences prior to that date but were convicted and sentenced after the date of enactment of the AEPA? In these situations, eligibility for accelerated parole was challenged by the government of Canada in a series of post-*Whaling* cases that reached appellate courts: see *Liang v Canada (Attorney General)*, 2014 BCCA 190, 311 CCC (3d) 159, leave to appeal to SCC refused, [2014] SCCA No 298 (QL); *Lewis v Canada (Attorney General)*, [2015] OJ

No 2734 (QL), leave to appeal to SCC refused. One might have thought that this was simply a question about the applicability of the Supreme Court decision in *R v Gamble*, [1988] 2 SCR 595, in which Wilson J stated, "it is fundamental to any legal system which recognizes the rule of law that an accused must be tried and punished under the law in force at the time the offenses were committed." However, influenced by *Whaling*, appellate courts resorted to s 11(h) of the Charter to conclude that the AEPA could not apply retrospectively to prisoners when the relevant offences were committed prior to the coming into force of the AEPA. In *Liang*, Mackenzie JA concluded:

> [15] It is difficult to avoid a straightforward application of the logic of *Whaling* to this case, along the following lines. The offences at issue here were committed in 2009 and 2010; the APR system was abolished in 2011; the offenders were sentenced in 2012 and 2013. Thus, at the time of the commission of the offences in question, the law permitted offenders the benefit of the APR system; at the time of sentencing, the APR system was no longer available. If the abolition of APR constitutes "punishment," then the punishment for the offence has been "varied between the time of commission and the time of sentencing," so the offenders are constitution-ally entitled to the "benefit of the lesser punishment" (i.e., the parole system in place before the changes, including APR). The Supreme Court of Canada in *Whaling* found the abolition of the APR system constituted "punishment" because it substantially increased the risk of additional incarceration. The same legislation would have the same effect in this case. Therefore, the offenders are entitled to the "lesser" punishment; that is, to APR.

Liang was followed by the Ontario Court of Appeal in *Lewis*, and in both cases leave to appeal to the Supreme Court was denied.

F. Other Elements of Conditional Release

As you will have noted from Section I.A, "Conditional Release Glossary," there are a number of other integral elements of the existing conditional release system. Parole and statutory release can be suspended and subsequently revoked. Designated officers can suspend a release and return an offender to custody if satisfied that it is "necessary and reasonable ... in order to prevent a breach of condition or to protect society." Once the offender has been returned to custody, the case is reviewed and the suspension can be cancelled or the case can be referred to the PBC to determine whether the release should be terminated or revoked. Both result in return to confinement under s 138(1), but there are some differences in consequences that arise from the fact that termination is usually a result of "circumstances beyond the offender's control" (see s 135(5)(b)).

Also, a prisoner can be denied statutory release pursuant to the detention process. First, there is a referral by the Correctional Service or commissioner and then a detention hearing before the PBC. The standard for detention is whether the PBC is satisfied that the offender is likely to commit an offence causing death or serious harm, a sexual offence involving a child, or a serious drug offence if released. When first introduced, the government argued that there were 50 dangerous prisoners in penitentiary at the time who ought not to be released prior to warrant expiry. As you can see from the data below, the number of deten-tion orders and reviews annually has proven to be far more than the original estimate of only 50 in total.

Outcome of Initial Detention Reviews

	Detained				Statutory release		
Year	Aboriginal	Non-Aboriginal	Total	%	Aboriginal	Non-Aboriginal	Total
2009-10	96	165	261	93.9	2	15	17
2010-11	111	128	239	94.5	4	10	14
2011-12	88	119	207	96.7	3	4	7
2012-13	89	143	232	98.3	4	0	4

Source: Public Safety Canada, *Corrections and Conditional Release Statistical Overview, 2014* (Ottawa: Public Safety Canada, 2015) at 104, online: <http://www.publicsafety.gc.ca/cnt/rsrcs/pblctns/ccrso-2014/index-en.aspx>.

The mechanisms of suspension, revocation, and detention have attracted some judicial attention. Much of the case law involves administrative law principles; statutory interpretation; and, occasionally, the Charter. The issues raised can be technical and complex, especially because the relevant statutory provisions are detailed.

II. CHALLENGING PAROLE AND PENITENTIARY DECISIONS: JUDICIAL REMEDIES

At common law, the convicted offender suffered "civil death." This included the disabilities that flowed from the status of felon, which included outlawry, corruption of the blood, and attainder. Certainly, the felon was disenfranchised. This particular disability survives to this day in many jurisdictions. Second, there is the issue of judicial remedies. It is trite to say that a right without a remedy is hardly a real right. For many years, Canadian courts seemed to follow their American counterparts in adopting a hands-off approach to prison and parole issues. This meant that most legal grievances remained beyond the scope of judicial scrutiny. Even the historic remedy of *habeas corpus* acquired some peculiar characteristics that, until recently, created impediments to its development and use. (For a detailed account of prisoners' efforts to obtain remedies, see the chapter entitled "The Prisoner Before the Courts" in Cole & Manson at 39-108.)

A. Judicial Review and Relief in the Nature of Certiorari

The supervisory jurisdiction over federal decision-makers was moved to the Federal Court when it was established in 1972. At the time, it was anticipated that the new s 28 remedy in the *Federal Courts Act* would apply to federal prisoners. This provision included a broad "review and set aside" power that applied to any decision required by law to be made on a judicial or quasi-judicial basis. However, any expectation that this would provide a remedy for prisoners was dashed in *Martineau v Matsqui Institution Inmate Disciplinary Board*, [1978] 1 SCR 118, where the majority held that neither the commissioner's directives nor the incipient duty to act fairly placed penitentiary discipline decisions in this category of decisions required "by law" to be made on a judicial or quasi-judicial basis. In dissent, Laskin CJ was critical of the majority's conception of "law," and described it as "too nihilistic" for him to accept. Shortly afterward, the issue returned to the Supreme Court as a *certiorari* application under s 18 of the *Federal Courts Act* in what has been commonly called *Martineau (No 2)* (*Martineau v Matsqui Disciplinary Bd*, [1980] 1 SCR 602). In the interim, the Supreme Court had firmly rejected the traditional classification approach to judicial review and adopted the general duty to act fairly as the standard for procedural obligation owed by public and statutory decision-makers (see *Re Nicholson and Haldimand-Norfolk Regional Board of Police Commissioners*, [1979] 1 SCR 311).

In *Martineau*, the defendant had been charged with the serious disciplinary offences of having two persons in a cell and committing an indecent act. He was convicted of an apparently included offence that was recorded as "being in an indecent position." He was convicted and sentenced to 15 days' dissociation. At his hearing, he was absent when some of the evidence against him was heard. The commissioner's directive dealing with disciplinary hearing procedures expressly stated that no finding should be made against an inmate for a serious or flagrant offence unless he or she has appeared at the hearing so that the evidence can be given in his or her presence. Martineau sought *certiorari* in the Federal Court (Trial Division). The Correctional Service disputed the court's jurisdiction to grant such relief. Although the court of first instance agreed that it had jurisdiction, on appeal to the Federal Court of Appeal, the arguments against remedial jurisdiction prevailed. Jackett CJ was content that disgruntled prisoners could satisfy their grievances by writing to their member of parliament. On appeal to the Supreme Court, shortly after its acceptance of the duty to act fairly, the argument in favour of a remedy received a more welcome reception. The court allowed the prisoner's appeal unanimously. For the majority, Pigeon J accepted that *certiorari* was available to challenge disciplinary decisions on procedural grounds, but that its use should be restricted to "cases of serious injustice." The opinion of Dickson J has, in subsequent years, been accepted as more accurately explaining the proper scope of *certiorari* as an evolving remedy.

Martineau v Matsqui Disciplinary Bd
[1980] 1 SCR 602, 50 CCC (2d) 1

DICKSON J (Laskin CJ and McIntyre JJ concurring):

The appeal raises in general terms the question of the supervisory role, if any, of the Federal Court, Trial Division, in respect of disciplinary boards within Canadian penitentiaries. It also calls for consideration of three related issues of importance in Canadian administrative law.

First, it compels resolution of the continuing debate concerning the review jurisdiction of the Trial Division and Court of Appeal under, respectively, ss. 18 and 28 of the *Federal Court Act*, RSC 1970, c. 10 (2nd Supp.), an issue left open by this Court in earlier judgments. If the Court of Appeal lacks jurisdiction under s. 28 to entertain an application to review and set aside, then the question which must be asked, and to which this case must give the answer, is whether the impugned decision or order can be challenged by application for *certiorari* under s. 18 of the Act.

Second, the case calls for closer analysis of the duty to act fairly—the English "fairness doctrine"—than has hitherto been necessary.

Third, the appeal raises the question of the potential breadth of the common law remedy of *certiorari* in Canada.

. . .

It has been argued that s. 18 purports to transfer jurisdiction from provincial Courts to the Trial Division of the Federal Court and clothes the latter with exclusive jurisdiction to grant relief by way of *certiorari* against federal boards, commissions or other tribunals, but that s. 28 removes that jurisdiction from the Trial Division in respect of *certiorari*, despite the express words of s. 18. In other words, the terms of s. 28 completely exclude what s. 18 apparently granted. If that view be correct, and s. 18 is indeed sterile and without independent life, then a narrow reading of s. 28 will virtually deny Canadians recourse against federal tribunals. It is not disputed that the Inmate Disciplinary Board of Matsqui Institution is a federal board, commission or other tribunal.

• • •

Thus, *Howarth, supra*, distinguishes between ss. 18 and 28 review jurisdiction in the Federal Court, the new remedy under s. 28 not being exhaustive of Federal Court jurisdiction to review federal Government action. The consequence, as Mr. Justice Pigeon puts it, is that under the *Federal Court Act* "a distinction is made between two classes of orders of federal boards."

• • •

Restrictive reading of s. 28 of the *Federal Court Act* need not, of necessity, lead to a reduction in the ambit for judicial review of federal Government action. Section 18 is available. Section 28 has caused difficulties, not only because of the language in which it is cast but, equally, because it tended to crystallize the law of judicial review at a time when significant changes were occurring in other countries with respect to the scope and grounds for review. Sections 18 and 28 of the *Federal Court Act* were obviously intended to concentrate judicial review of federal tribunals in a single federal Court. As I read the Act, Parliament envisaged an extended scope for review. I am therefore averse to giving the Act a reading which would defeat that intention and posit a diminished scope for relief from the actions of federal tribunals. I simply cannot accept the view that Parliament intended to remove the old common law remedies, including *certiorari*, from the provincial superior Courts, and vest them in the Trial Division of the Federal Court, only to have those remedies rendered barren through the interaction of ss. 18 and 28 of the Act. I would apply the principle laid down by Brett LJ in *R v. Local Government Board* (1882), 10 QBD 309 at p. 321, that the jurisdiction of a Court ought to be exercised widely when dealing with matters perhaps not strictly judicial, but in which the rights or interests of citizens are affected.

VI

The dominant characteristic of recent developments in English administrative law has been expansion of judicial review jurisdiction to supervise administrative action by public authorities. *Certiorari* evolved as a flexible remedy, affording access to judicial supervision in new and changing situations. In 1689 Chief Justice Holt could say, in *Re Cardiffe Bridge* (1689), 1 Salk. 146, 91 ER 135 "wherever any new jurisdiction is erected, be it by private or public Act of Parliament, they are subject to the inspections of this Court by writ of error, or by *certiorari* and *mandamus*." And in *Groenwelt v. Burwell et al.* (1694), 1 LD Raym. 454 at pp. 467-9, 91 ER 1202, Holt CJ, held again, in the context of the censors of the College of Physicians of London, that it is plain, that the censors have judicial power ... where a man has power to inflict imprisonment upon another for punishment of his offence, there he hath judicial authority ... for it is a consequence of all jurisdictions, to have their proceedings returned here by *certiorari*, to be examined here. ... Where any Court is erected by statute, a *certiorari* lies to it. ...

Nor has perception of *certiorari* as an adaptable remedy been in any way modified. The amplitude of the writ has been affirmed time and again: see, for example, the judgment of Lord Parker LJ in *R v. Criminal Injuries Compensation Board, Ex. p. Lain*, [1967] 2 QB 864 at p. 882:

> The position as I see it is that the exact limits of the ancient remedy by way of *certiorari* have never been and ought not to be specifically defined. They have varied from time to time being extended to meet changing conditions. At one time the writ only went to an inferior court. Later its ambit was extended to statutory tribunals determining a *lis inter partes*. Later again it extended to cases where there was no *lis* in the strict sense of the word but where immediate or subsequent rights of a citizen were affected. The only constant limits throughout were that it was performing a public duty.

Roskill LJ, in *Re Liverpool Taxi Owners' Ass'n*, [1972] 2 All ER 589 at p. 596 expressed the thought in these words:

> The long legal history of the former prerogative writs and of their modern counterparts, the orders of prohibition, *mandamus* and *certiorari* shows that their application has always been flexible as the need for their use in differing social conditions down the centuries had changed.

The principles of natural justice and fairness have matured in recent years. And the writ of *certiorari*, in like measure, has developed apace. The speeches in *Ridge v. Baldwin et al.*, [1964] AC 40, show the evolutionary state of administrative law.

Does *certiorari* lie to the Inmate Disciplinary Board? The usual starting point in a discussion of this nature is the "Electricity Commissioners" formula, found at p. 205 of *R v. Electricity Com'rs, Ex p. London Electricity Joint Committee Co. (1920), Ltd., et al.*, [1924] 1 KB 171 (CA), where Atkin LJ had this to say:

> Wherever any body of persons having legal authority to determine questions affecting the rights of subjects, and having the duty to act judicially, act in excess of their legal authority they are subject to the controlling jurisdiction of the King's Bench Division exercised in these writs.

Difficulty has arisen from the statement of Atkin LJ in part from the fact that his words have been treated as if they had been engraved in stone, and in part because it is not clear what Atkin LJ meant. How far, if at all, did he mean to limit the use of orders for *certiorari* and prohibition by the phrase "and having the duty to act judicially"? What did he mean by "judicially" in the context? It will be recalled that in the *Electricity Com'rs* case itself *certiorari* and prohibition issued to a group of administrators who were acting far more as part of the legislative than of the judicial process.

Rights of Subjects

The term "rights of subjects" has given concern, often being treated by Courts as the *sine qua non* of jurisdiction to permit review. There has been an unfortunate tendency to treat "rights" in the narrow sense of rights to which correlative legal duties attach. In this sense, "rights" are frequently contrasted with "privileges," in the mistaken belief that only the former can ground judicial review of the decision-maker's actions. *Lain, supra*, is invaluable on this branch of Lord Atkin's test. There the absence of any legal right on the part of the claimants to *ex gratia* payments from the criminal injuries compensation board would seem to pose an insuperable obstacle, but Ashworth J disposed of this impediment without trouble and in broadest language (p. 892):

> For my part I doubt whether Atkin LJ was propounding an all-embracing definition of the circumstances in which relief by way of *certiorari* would lie. In my judgment the words in question read in the context of what precedes and follows them, would be of no less value if they were altered by omitting "the rights of" so as to become "affecting subjects."

Lord Denning aptly summarized the state of the law on this aspect in *Schmidt v. Secretary of State for Home Affairs*, [1969] 2 Ch. 149 (CA). There, the Master of the Rolls stated [p. 170]:

> The speeches in *Ridge v. Baldwin* ... show that an administrative body may, in a proper case, be bound to give a person who is affected by their decision an opportunity of making representations. It all depends on whether he has some right or interest, or, I would add, some legitimate expectation, of which it would not be fair to deprive him without hearing what he has to say.

• • •

When concerned with individual cases and aggrieved persons, there is the tendency to forget that one is dealing with public law remedies, which, when granted by the Courts, not only set aright individual injustice, but also ensure that public bodies exercising powers affecting citizens heed the jurisdiction granted them. *Certiorari* stems from the assumption by the Courts of supervisory powers over certain tribunals in order to assure the proper functioning of the machinery of Government. To give a narrow or technical interpretation to "rights" in an individual sense is to misconceive the broader purpose of judicial review of administrative action. One should, I suggest, begin with the premise that any public body exercising power over subjects may be amenable to judicial supervision, the individual interest involved being but one factor to be considered in resolving the broad policy question of the nature of review appropriate for the particular administrative body.

Duty to Act Judicially

Prior to the decision in *Ridge v. Baldwin, supra*, it was generally accepted that *certiorari* would only be granted when the nature of the process by which the decision was arrived at was a judicial process or a process analogous to the judicial process: *Nakkuda Ali v. Jayaratne*, [1951] AC 66, [1950] 2 WWR 927 (PC). This notion of a "super-added duty to act judicially," as a separate and independent precondition to the availability of natural justice, and inferentially, to recourse to *certiorari*, was unequivocally rejected by Lord Reid in *Ridge, supra* (p. 75):

> If Lord Hewart meant that it is never enough that a body simply has a duty to determine what the rights of an individual should be, but that there must always be something more to

impose on it a duty to act judicially before it can be found to observe the principles of natural justice, then that appears to me impossible to reconcile with the earlier authorities.

In the *Electricity Commissioners* case itself, *supra*, Lord Reid observed, the judicial element was inferred from the nature of the power.

Perhaps the best expression of the significance of the decision in *Ridge v. Baldwin*, *supra*, is found in the reasons of Lord Widgery CJ in *R v. London Borough of Hillingdon, Ex p. Royco Homes Ltd.*, [1974] 2 All ER 643 at p. 649 (QBD), wherein he considered the availability of *certiorari* to review the grant of a planning permission by a local authority:

> Accordingly it may be that previous efforts to use *certiorari* in this field have been deterred by Atkin LJ's reference to it being necessary for the body affected to have the duty to act judicially. If that is so, that reason for reticence on the part of applicants was, I think, put an end to in the House of Lords in *Ridge v. Baldwin* … in the course of his speech Lord Reid made reference to that oft-quoted dictum of Atkin LJ and pointed out that the additional requirement of the body being under a duty to act judicially was not supported by authority. Accordingly it seems to me now that that obstacle, if obstacle it were, has been cleared away and I can see no reason for this court holding otherwise than that there is power in appropriate cases for the use of the prerogative orders to control the activity of a local planning authority.

A flexible attitude toward the potential application of *certiorari* was furthered in another recent English case, this one in the Court of Appeal, in *R v. Barnsley Metropolitan Borough Council, Ex p. Hook*, [1976] 3 All ER 452.

In a *habeas corpus* case, *Re H.K. (An Infant)*, [1967] 2 QB 617, Lord Parker was of the opinion that the immigration officers who refused to admit a boy into the United Kingdom were acting in an administrative and not in a judicial or quasi-judicial capacity: nevertheless, he held they must act honestly and fairly, otherwise their decision could be questioned by *certiorari*. And in the *Liverpool Taxi Owners* case, *supra*, Roskill LJ spoke of the power of the Courts to intervene in a suitable case when the function was administrative and not judicial or quasi-judicial (p. 596):

> The power of the court to intervene is not limited, as once was thought, to those cases where the function in question is judicial or quasi-judicial. The modern cases show that this court will intervene more widely than in the past. Even where the function is said to be administrative, the court will not hesitate to intervene in a suitable case if it is necessary in order to secure fairness.

Then there is the well-known passage in the speech of Lord Morris of Borth-y-Gest in *Furnell v. Whangarei High Schools Board*, [1973] AC 660 at p. 679 (PC), speaking for a Privy Council majority of three: "[n]atural justice is but fairness writ large and juridically. It has been described as 'fair play in action.' Nor is it a leaven to be associated only with judicial or quasi-judicial occasions." In the same case, the penultimate paragraph from the speech of Viscount Dilhorne and Lord Reid, dissenting, reads (p. 691):

> It is not in this case necessary to decide whether the function of the subcommittee is to be described as judicial, quasi-judicial or administrative. I am inclined to think that it is at least quasi-judicial, but if it be administrative, it was the duty of the sub-committee before they condemned or criticised Mr. Furnell "to give him a fair opportunity of commenting or contradicting what is said against him." That they did not do.

Professor John Evans, writing in 23 *McGill LJ* 132 at pp. 134-5 (1977), has noted:

> Recent English decisions have severed the availability of *certiorari* and prohibition from the
> requirement that the body must act "judicially" in the sense that it is bound by the rules of
> natural justice. It may be concluded, therefore, that there is nothing in the judgment of
> Pigeon J [in *Howarth*] to prevent the Trial Division from quashing decisions of a "purely
> administrative" nature or from developing procedural requirements derived from the "duty
> to act fairly."

In the view of another commentator, Professor Jones 21 *McGill LJ* 434 at p. 438 (1975):

> Certainly in England and in most other parts of the Commonwealth, the requirement for
> judicial review that the exercise of a statutory power must not only affect the rights of a
> subject, but also be subject to a superadded duty to act judicially, is now thoroughly discred-
> ited. In other words, the ratio of *Nakkuda Ali v. Jayaratne* in the Privy Council—and hence,
> one would have thought, of *Calgary Power v. Copithorne* in the Supreme Court of Canada—is
> no longer good law.

The authorities to which I have referred indicate that the application of a duty of fairness with procedural content does not depend upon proof of a judicial or quasi-judicial
function. Even though the function is analytically administrative, Courts may intervene
in a suitable case.

In the case at bar, the Disciplinary Board was not under either an express or implied
duty to follow a judicial type of procedure, but the board was obliged to find facts affecting
a subject and to exercise a form of discretion in pronouncing judgment and penalty.
Moreover, the board's decision had the effect of depriving an individual of his liberty by
committing him to a "prison within a prison." In these circumstances, elementary justice
requires some procedural protection. The rule of law must run within penitentiary walls.

In my opinion, *certiorari* avails as a remedy wherever a public body has power to decide
any matter affecting the rights, interests, property, privileges, or liberties of any person.

VIII

Fairness

The approach taken to the "fairness" doctrine by the Court in *Re Nicholson and Haldimand-Norfolk Regional Board of Com'rs of Police* (1978), 88 DLR (3d) 671, [1979] 1 SCR
311, 23 NR 410, notably its differentiation from traditional natural justice, permits one
to dispense with classification as a precondition to the availability of *certiorari*. Conceptually, there is much to be said against such a differentiation between traditional natural
justice and procedural fairness, but if one is forced to cast judicial review in traditional
classification terms, as is the case under the *Federal Court Act*, here can be no doubt that
procedural fairness extends well beyond the realm of the judicial and quasi-judicial, as
commonly understood.

Once one moves from the strictures of s. 28 of the *Federal Court Act*, the judgment in
Nicholson, *supra*, permits departure from the rigidity of classification of functions for the
purposes of procedural safeguards. In finding that a duty of fairness rested upon the Police
Commissioners in a dismissal case, Chief Justice Laskin, speaking for a majority of the
Court, employed the English fairness cases to import that duty. While the cases were there

used to establish minimal protection for the constable under the *Judicial Review Procedure Act, 1971* (Ont.), c. 48, the same cases have been employed in England to extend the reach of *certiorari* to decisions not strictly judicial or quasi-judicial. After referring to the emergence of a notion of fairness "involving something less than the procedural protection of traditional natural justice," the Chief Justice had this to say (p. 681 DLR, p. 325 SCR):

> What rightly lies behind this emergence is the realization that the classification of statutory functions as judicial, quasi-judicial or administrative is often very difficult, to say the least; and to endow some with procedural protection while denying others any at all would work injustice when the results of statutory decisions raise the same serious consequences for those adversely affected, regardless of the classification of the function in question: see, generally, Mullan, "Fairness: The New Natural Justice," 25 *Univ. of Tor. LJ* 281 (1975).

The Chief Justice also quoted a passage from Lord Denning's judgment in *Selvarajan v. Race Relations Board*, [1976] 1 All ER 12 (CA), in which the Master of the Rolls summed up his earlier decisions and formulated the "fundamental rule" (p. 19):

> that, if a person may be subjected to pains or penalties, or be exposed to prosecution or proceedings, or deprived of remedies or redress, or in some such way adversely affected by the investigation and report, then he should be told the case made against him and be afforded a fair opportunity of answering it.

Of particular interest in the passage is the absence of reference to "rights." The imprecise "rights/privileges" dichotomy is utterly ignored.

IX

One matter remains—the so-called "disciplinary exception." There are authorities (see *R v. Army Council, Ex p. Ravenscroft*, [1917] 2 KB 504; *Dawkins v. Lord Rokeby* (1871), 8 QB 255; *Re Armstrong and Whitehead* (1973), 11 CCC (2d) 327, [1973] 2 OR 495) which hold that review by way of *certiorari* does not go to a body such as the armed services, police, or firemen, with its own form of private discipline and its own rules. Relying on this analogy, it is contended that disciplinary powers are beyond judicial control and that this extends to prison discipline. I do not agree.

In *Fraser v. Mudge et al.*, [1975] 3 All ER 78 (CA), it was held that the *English Prison Act, 1952*, requiring the Home Secretary to give an inmate charged with an offence a proper opportunity of presenting his case, did not entitle the inmate to legal representation at the hearing, but Lord Denning MR observed that those who heard the case had the duty to act fairly. Judicial review was not precluded.

There is the more recent case of *R v. Board of Visitors of Hull Prison, Ex. p. St. Germain et al.*, [1979] 1 All ER 701. The central issue in that case was whether *certiorari* would go to quash a disciplinary decision of a board of visitors, the duties of which embraced inquiry into charges against inmates. The Divisional Court found that disciplinary procedures within the prison were judicial, but invoked the "disciplinary exception," and held that the actions of the board of visitors were not amenable to the review by way of *certiorari*. A unanimous Court of Appeal disagreed, however, holding that adjudication by boards of visitors in prisons were, indeed, amenable to *certiorari*. The Court rejected the submission that prisoners have no legally enforceable rights. Megaw LJ concluded that the observance of procedural fairness in prisons is properly a subject for review. Shaw LJ held that despite deprivation of his general liberty a prisoner remains invested with residuary rights appertaining to the nature and conduct of his incarceration. Waller LJ accepted the proposition of Lord Reid in *Ridge v. Baldwin et al.*, [1964] AC 40, that deprivation of rights or privileges are equally important and applied that proposition to the context of prison discipline.

* * *

The Supreme Court of the United States in *Wolff v. McDonnell* (1978), 418 US 539, was called upon to consider what "due process," assured by the Fourteenth Amendment of the *American Constitution*, required in a prison setting. The Court, speaking through Mr. Justice White, held that where the prisoner was in peril of losing good time, or being placed in solitary confinement, he was entitled to written notice of the charge and a statement of fact findings and to call witnesses and present documentary evidence where it would not be unduly hazardous to institutional safety or correctional jails. However, there was no constitutional right to confront and cross-examine witnesses or to counsel.

It seems clear that although the Courts will not readily interfere in the exercise of disciplinary powers, whether within the armed services, the police force or the penitentiary, there is no rule of law which necessarily exempts the exercise of such disciplinary powers from review by *certiorari*.

The authorities, in my view, support the following conclusions:

1. *Certiorari* is available as a general remedy for supervision of the machinery of Government decision-making. The order may go to any public body with power to decide any matter affecting the rights, interests, property, privileges, or liberty of any person. The basis for the broad reach of this remedy is the general duty of fairness resting on all public decision-makers.

2. A purely ministerial decision, on broad grounds of public policy, will typically afford the individual no procedural protection, and any attack upon such a decision will have to be founded upon abuse of discretion. Similarly, public bodies exercising legislative functions may not be amenable to judicial supervision. On the other hand, a function that approaches the judicial end of the spectrum will entail substantial procedural safeguards. Between the judicial decisions and those which are discretionary and policy-oriented will be found a myriad decision-making processes with a flexible gradation of procedural fairness through the administrative spectrum. That is what emerges from the decision of this Court in *Nicholson, supra*. In these cases, an applicant may obtain *certiorari* to enforce a breach of the duty of procedural fairness.

3. Section 28 of the *Federal Court Act*, that statutory right of review compels continuance of the classification process in the Federal Court of Appeal, with clear outer limits imposed on the notion of "judicial or quasi-judicial." No such limitation is imported in the language of s. 18, which simply refers to *certiorari*, and is therefore capable of expansion consistent with the movement of the common law away from rigidity in respect of the prerogative writs. The fact that a decision-maker does not have a duty to act judicially, with observance of formal procedure which that characterization entails, does not mean that there may not be a duty to act fairly which involves importing something less than the full panoply of

conventional natural justice rules. In general, Courts ought not to seek to distinguish between the two concepts, for the drawing of a distinction between a duty to act fairly, and a duty to act in accordance with the rules of natural justice, yields an unwieldy conceptual framework. The *Federal Court Act*, however, compels classification for review of federal decision-makers.

4. An inmate disciplinary board is not a Court. It is a tribunal which has to decide rights after hearing evidence. Even though the board is not obliged, in discharging what is essentially an administrative task, to conduct a judicial proceeding, observing the procedural and evidential rules of a Court of law, it is, none the less, subject to a duty of fairness and a person aggrieved through breach of that duty is entitled to seek relief from the Federal Court, Trial Division, on an application for *certiorari*.

5. It should be emphasized that it is not every breach of prison rules of procedure which will bring intervention by the Courts. The very nature of a prison institution requires officers to make "on the spot" disciplinary decisions and the power of judicial review must be exercised with restraint. Interference will not be justified in the case of trivial or merely technical incidents. The question is not whether there has been a breach of the prison rules, but whether there has been a breach of the duty to act fairly in all the circumstances. The rules are of some importance in determining this latter question, as an indication of the views of prison authorities as to the degree of procedural protection to be extended to inmates.

6. A widening of the ambit of *certiorari* beyond that of a s. 28 application will, undoubtedly, at times, present a problem in determining whether to commence proceedings in the Court of Appeal or in the Trial Division. However, the quandary of two possible forums is not less regrettable than complete lack of access to the Federal Court.

7. It is wrong, in my view, to regard natural justice and fairness as distinct and separate standards and to seek to define the procedural content of each. In *Nicholson, supra*, the Chief Justice spoke of a "notion of fairness involving something less than the procedural protection of the traditional natural justice." Fairness involves compliance with only some of the principles of natural justice. Professor de Smith, *Judicial Review of Administrative Action* (1973), 3rd ed. p. 208, expressed lucidly the concept of a duty to act fairly:

> In general it means a duty to observe the rudiments of natural justice for a limited purpose in the exercise of functions that are not analytically judicial but administrative.
>
> The content of the principles of natural justice and fairness in application to the individual cases will vary according to the circumstances of each case, as recognized by Tucker LJ, in *Russell v. Duke of Norfolk et al.*, [1949] 1 All ER 109 at p. 118.

8. In the final analysis, the simple question to be answered is this: Did the tribunal on the facts of the particular case act fairly toward the person claiming to be aggrieved? It seems to me that this is the underlying question which the Courts have sought to answer in all the cases dealing with natural justice and with fairness.

XI

I would allow the appeal, set aside the judgment of the Federal Court of Appeal, and restore the judgment of Mr. Justice Mahoney of the Federal Court, Trial Division. There should be no costs in this Court nor in the Federal Court of Appeal.

Appeal allowed.

B. Habeas Corpus: Jurisdiction and Scope of Review

At least since the *Magna Carta*, forms of *habeas corpus* have been available to enforce liberty and free illegally detained prisoners. Blackstone described *habeas corpus* as applicable to "all manner of illegal confinement." By virtue of this remedy, superior courts became the repository of the liberty rights of all prisoners. Yet, in the mid-20th century in Canada, *habeas corpus* started to lose its vigour as a remedy to protect liberty.

In parole cases, where the loss of parole was clearly a loss of liberty, *habeas corpus* was available, but only in a limited number of situations. First, the issue had to engage an arguable jurisdictional defect or illegality such that success meant release from custody. Second, the illegality had to be apparent without going behind the warrant: see *Mitchell v R*, [1976] 2 SCR 570. In *Mitchell*, the majority held that a court could not go behind a warrant of suspension or revocation to find a jurisdictional defect or illegality. This was a case where a parolee attempted to argue that his committal breached the due process guarantee of the *Canadian Bill of Rights* because he was given no reasons for his suspension and no opportunity to respond to any allegations against him before he was revoked and recommitted to custody. An earlier decision had held that the usual practice of seeking *certiorari* in aid of *habeas corpus* to enable a court to examine affidavit material was no longer available because *certiorari* jurisdiction had been transferred to the Federal Court. Accordingly, it was argued in *Mitchell*, one could not obtain *certiorari* in aid from a superior court. In dissent, Laskin CJ pointed out the distinction between *certiorari* to quash and *certiorari* to bring up the record that had been missed by some of his colleagues. Although the *Mitchell* decision was a blow to *habeas corpus*, it came just before the Supreme Court adopted the duty to act fairly. How could a parolee ever raise a fairness argument if he or she could not use an affidavit or transcript to go behind a warrant of committal?

Looking at penitentiary issues, a narrow conception of the scope of *certiorari* (and prohibition, its temporal flip-side) was used to deny remedies to prisoners. In retrospect, actions for declaratory relief were likely available to prisoners, but these were not attempted. The probable reason was cost and delay. *McCann v R*, [1976] 1 FC 570 (TD), a successful action for a declaration under the *Canadian Bill of Rights* that long-term confinement in segregation at the BC penitentiary constituted cruel and unusual punishment, demonstrates both the potential role and the enormous amount of time and money involved in such actions.

Another issue that arose related to involuntary transfers to a higher security institution. If made unfairly or without jurisdiction, the decision would seem to be open to challenge, but the question was how? Was *habeas corpus* an available vehicle for this purpose, or was it necessary to seek *certiorari* in the Federal Court? Certainly, *habeas corpus* was a less expensive and more expeditious remedy. Aside from the issue of extrinsic material, it was also argued that an involuntary transfer was not the proper subject matter of *habeas corpus* because it would not result in complete liberty, but merely a transfer back to the original place of confinement.

These issues came together in a trilogy of cases decided by the Supreme Court in the mid-1980s: *Cardinal v Kent Institution*, [1985] 2 SCR 643; *Morin v National Special Handling Unit Review Committee*, [1985] 2 SCR 662; and *R v Miller*, [1985] 2 SCR 613. The lead decision on the role of *habeas corpus* was *Miller*, which dealt with an inmate's transfer from Matsqui Institution in British Columbia to the special handling unit, located then at Millhaven Institution in Ontario. Although initially denied *habeas corpus* relief, the Ontario Court of Appeal reversed and supported a modern approach to the remedy. The Crown appealed to the Supreme Court.

R v Miller
[1985] 2 SCR 613

Le DAIN J (Dickson CJ, Beetz, Estey, McIntyre, Lamer, and Wilson JJ concurring):

[3] According to the respondent's affidavit in support of his application for *habeas corpus* with *certiorari* in aid, he was an inmate in Matsqui penitentiary on June 2, 1981, when a "disturbance" occurred in the dining area where he was employed. He claimed that he was not in the dining area at the time and that he was not responsible in any way for the disturbance. He was, nevertheless, placed in administrative segregation in Matsqui on June 5th and in segregation in Kent Institution and Millhaven, to which he was subsequently transferred, on July 11th and July 23rd respectively. On July 29, 1981, he was placed in the special handling unit at Millhaven.

[4] Confinement in a special handling unit is reserved for particularly dangerous inmates, as indicated by s. 5 of Commissioner's Directive 274 of December 1, 1980, which defines "Special Handling Unit" as follows:

> "Special Handling Unit" (SHU) is a facility established to deal exclusively with inmates who, in addition to requiring maximum security, have been identified as being particularly dangerous.

According to the directive, a special handling unit programme of confinement consists of four phases, the first of which is a period of assessment in administrative segregation. According to the respondent's affidavit, which describes the nature of the confinement in the various phases in considerable detail, in the first phase consisting of administrative segregation the inmate is cut off from all association with other inmates and is confined to his cell for all but one hour of the day. In subsequent phases of the programme limited association with other inmates and somewhat longer periods outside the cell are permitted, but speaking generally, it may be said that confinement in a special handling unit is a significantly more restrictive form of detention than the normal one in a penitentiary, involving the loss or denial of several privileges or amenities enjoyed by the general inmate population.

[5] According to the respondent's affidavit, he was advised by letter about two weeks after he was placed in the special handling unit that he had been put there because of his involvement in the disturbance at Matsqui and specifically because he had broken windows in the kitchen and had manufactured an explosive device. The respondent states that he was never given an opportunity to confront the evidence, if any, of his involvement

in the incident at Matsqui on which the decision to confine him in the special handling unit was based. He was never charged with a disciplinary offence arising out of that incident nor was any criminal charge laid against him. He was not given a psychological examination, and there was nothing in his background or in the nature of the offences of which he was convicted to suggest that he was a particularly dangerous inmate. In October, 1981, he attended a hearing of the National Special Handling Unit Review Committee, but he was not informed of the evidence against him nor given any opportunity to meet it. He was told that he could only secure his release from the special handling unit into normal association with the general population of the penitentiary by good behaviour. In the respondent's submission there was no basis nor justification whatever for placing him in the special handling unit.

[6]   In his application for *habeas corpus* with *certiorari* in aid the respondent contended that confinement in the special handling unit at Millhaven is not authorized by statute or regulation and is therefore unlawful, and further or alternatively, that his confinement in the special handling unit was carried out in a manner that denied him procedural fairness. The respondent conceded that he was lawfully required to be detained in a penitentiary. His mandatory supervision release date was July 3, 1983, and we were informed at the hearing of the appeal that he had been released.

• • •

[9]   The question whether a provincial superior court has jurisdiction to issue *certiorari* in aid of *habeas corpus* to review the validity of a detention imposed by federal authority arises, as has been indicated, because of the terms of s. 18 of the *Federal Court Act*, which confers on the Trial Division of the Federal Court of Canada an exclusive original jurisdiction to issue *certiorari* against any federal board, commission or other tribunal.

• • •

[13]   On the question of jurisdiction to issue *certiorari* in aid of *habeas corpus* I am in respectful agreement with the conclusion of Laskin CJ in *Mitchell*, essentially for the reasons given by him, which I understand to be the importance of making the *habeas corpus* jurisdiction of the provincial superior courts an effective one and the distinction between *certiorari* to quash and *certiorari* in aid, regarded as a procedural or evidentiary device to make *habeas corpus* more effective. With reference to this distinction Laskin CJ said at pp. 246-7 CCC, p. 83 DLR, p. 578 SCR:

> It is quite clear to me that there is a marked difference between *certiorari*, used to quash a conviction or an order by its own strength, and *certiorari* in aid of *habeas corpus* to make the latter remedy more effective by requiring production of the record of proceedings for that purpose.

[14]   One must approach this issue, I think, from the same point of departure as was adopted by Laskin CJ that the provisions of the *Federal Court Act* indicate a clear intention on the part of Parliament to leave the jurisdiction by way of *habeas corpus* to review the validity of a detention imposed by federal authority with the provincial superior courts. While s. 18 of the *Federal Court Act* confers an exclusive and very general review jurisdiction over federal authorities by the prerogative and extraordinary remedies, to which specific reference is made, it deliberately omits reference to *habeas corpus*. That this was not an oversight but a well-considered decision is indicated by s. 17(5) of the Act, which expressly confers exclusive jurisdiction on the Federal Court with respect to an application

for *habeas corpus* by a member of the Canadian Forces serving outside Canada. I agree with Laskin CJ that because of its importance as a safeguard of the liberty of the subject *habeas corpus* jurisdiction can only be affected by express words. One may think of reasons why it was thought advisable to leave the *habeas corpus* jurisdiction with respect to federal authorities with the provincial superior courts, including the importance of the local accessibility of this remedy. The important thing, as I see it, is that the decision to create this exception to the exclusive review jurisdiction of the Federal Court, with whatever problems arising from concurrent or overlapping jurisdiction it might cause, is really determinative of the question of jurisdiction to issue *certiorari* in aid. There can be no doubt that *certiorari* in aid is important, if not essential, to the effectiveness of *habeas corpus*. This was emphasized by both Anderson JA, with whom the other members of the British Columbia Court of Appeal agreed on this issue in *Cardinal* and *Oswald*, and by Cory JA in the case at bar. In many cases it may not be possible for a court to determine whether there has been an absence or excess of jurisdiction if the record of the tribunal which imposed or authorized the detention is not brought before it. The importance of *habeas corpus* itself, and by implication the importance of maintaining it as a fully effective remedy is, as Laskin CJ observed, given particular emphasis by its inclusion as a guaranteed right in s. 2(c)(iii) of the *Canadian Bill of Rights*. To this recognition may now be added the constitutional guarantee of the right to *habeas corpus* in s. 10(c) of the *Canadian Charter of Rights and Freedoms*. Because of the clear intention to leave the *habeas corpus* jurisdiction over federal authorities with the provincial superior courts and the importance of *certiorari* in aid to the effectiveness of *habeas corpus*, it cannot, in my opinion, have been intended that the reference to *certiorari* in s. 18 of the *Federal Court Act* should have the effect of undermining or weakening the *habeas corpus* jurisdiction of the provincial superior courts by the exclusion or denial of *certiorari* in aid. Certainly such a construction is to be avoided if at all possible. It can be avoided by application of the distinction emphasized by Laskin CJ between *certiorari* as an independent and separate mode of review having as its object to quash the decision of an inferior tribunal and *certiorari* as an ancillary procedure used to serve an essentially evidentiary purpose. A very full discussion of this distinction, with reference to many of the decisions in which it has been noted and applied, is to be found in Cromwell, "*Habeas Corpus* and Correctional Law," 3 *Queen's LJ* 295 at pp. 320-3 (1977). Applying the distinction to the reference to *certiorari* in s. 18 of the *Federal Court Act*, it is reasonable to conclude, because of the association in that section of *certiorari* with the other prerogative and extraordinary remedies, that the reference is to the independent remedy of *certiorari* to quash. It is unlikely that Parliament intended to confer an exclusive jurisdiction to issue *certiorari* in aid when it had clearly withheld the jurisdiction to issue *habeas corpus*. For these reasons I conclude that a provincial superior court has jurisdiction to issue *certiorari* in aid of *habeas corpus* to review the validity of a detention authorized or imposed by a federal board, commission or other tribunal as defined by s. 2 of the *Federal Court Act*, and that accordingly the Ontario Court of Appeal did not err in concluding as it did on this issue.

III

[15] In view of this conclusion on the question of jurisdiction to issue *certiorari* in aid of *habeas corpus* it may not be strictly necessary to deal with the question which was

treated as an alternative issue by the British Columbia Court of Appeal in *Cardinal* and *Oswald* and by the Ontario Court of Appeal in the case at bar—whether on *habeas corpus* without *certiorari* in aid a court may consider affidavit or other extrinsic evidence to determine whether there has been an absence or excess of jurisdiction. It is well established that affidavit evidence is admissible on *certiorari* to show jurisdictional error. Both Courts of Appeal were led, however, by their analysis of this question to reach a conclusion on it at variance with that of Ritchie J in *Mitchell*, without much explicit consideration of the jurisprudence of this Court on which the opinion of Ritchie J purported to be based. Moreover, this question may well be an issue in the *Morin* appeal. For these reasons it is probably desirable that it be dealt with here in order to remove the uncertainty which now necessarily exists concerning it.

* * *

[17]   In *Re Shumiatcher*, [1962] SCR 38, the relevant issue was whether the court could look at certain solemn declarations which the applicant for *habeas corpus* was charged with having induced a person to make, knowing them to be false, and thereby being a party, by virtue of s. 22(1) of the *Criminal Code*, to the offence defined by s. 114 (now s. 122). The application for *habeas corpus* challenged the validity of the committal for trial on the ground that the person making the solemn declarations was not a person permitted, authorized or required by law to make them, within the meaning of s. 114. The solemn declarations made reference to a statement of claim. Judson J framed the issue as follows, at p. 45:

> This brings me to the question of what use may be made of this material on a motion for *habeas corpus* before a Judge of this Court.
>
> The Crown's submission is that I am limited to looking at the warrant of committal and that I cannot look at these declarations and the statement of claim any more than I can look at the evidence—seven or eight volumes of it—given on the preliminary hearing.

[18]   After quoting from the judgments of this Court in *Re Trepanier* (1885), 12 SCR 111; *Ex parte Macdonald* (1896), 27 SCR 683, and *Goldhar v. The Queen*, [1960] SCR 431, with reference to *habeas corpus* against a warrant of committal after conviction, and observing that this Court did not have jurisdiction to issue *certiorari* in aid of *habeas corpus*, Judson J concluded on this issue as follows, at p. 47:

> In my opinion the jurisdiction of this Court is similarly limited in an inquiry into a committal for trial. In the absence of power to issue a writ of *certiorari* in aid of *habeas corpus*, a Judge of this Court has no power to look at the evidence at the preliminary hearing or to receive affidavit evidence relating to it.
>
> My jurisdiction is limited to a consideration of the warrant of committal and the other material that I have referred to—the recognizances and the order of Judge Hogarth. I cannot look at evidence, whether a transcript of the evidence at the preliminary hearing or evidence sought to be introduced by way of affidavit identifying a portion of such evidence.
>
> I am founding my reasons on this branch of the case entirely on that principle and I am expressing no opinion on the point on which I heard full argument—whether there does exist, by virtue of provincial legislation, permission to take a declaration of this kind.

[19]   In *Goldhar*, the issues raised on the application for *habeas corpus* were the regularity on its face of a calendar of sentences as a certificate of the appellant's conviction and

the applicable maximum penalty, having regard to a change that had taken place in the law. Fauteux J (as he then was), with whom Taschereau, Abbott and Judson JJ concurred, expressed the rationale for the exclusion of extrinsic evidence on an application for *habeas corpus* as follows, at p. 439:

> The question, which counsel for the appellant admittedly sought to be determined by way of *habeas corpus* proceedings, is stated in the reasons for judgment of other members of the Court. In my view, it is one which would require the consideration of the evidence at trial and which, in this particular case, extends beyond the scope of matters to be inquired under a similar process. To hold otherwise would be tantamount to convert the writ of *habeas corpus* into a writ of error or an appeal and to confer, upon every one having authority to issue the writ of *habeas corpus*, an appellate jurisdiction over the orders and judgments of even the highest Courts. It is well settled that the functions of such a writ do not extend beyond an inquiry into the jurisdiction of the Court by which process the subject is held in custody and into the validity of the process upon its face.
>
> I agree with the view that the appellant has been convicted and sentenced by a Court of competent jurisdiction, that the calendar is a certificate regular on its face that the appellant has been so convicted and sentenced and that, with the material before him, Martland J rightly dismissed the application for a writ of *habeas corpus*.

[20] The above passage, in my respectful opinion, reflects the true distinction or criterion respecting the consideration of extrinsic evidence on an application for *habeas corpus*—the distinction between issues going to the merits and issues going to jurisdiction. The issues in both *Shumiatcher* and *Goldhar* were clearly issues going to the merits. The same is true of *Re Trepanier*, where the applicant alleged that the convicting magistrate erred on the facts in convicting him. He sought a writ of *habeas corpus* with *certiorari* in aid to bring up the record of the proceedings to ascertain whether there was sufficient evidence to convict. This was clearly an attempt to employ *habeas corpus* to review the merits of a conviction. Ritchie CJ said at p. 113:

> The jurisdiction of the magistrate being unquestionable over the subject-matter of complaint and the person of the prisoner, and there being no ground for alleging that the magistrate acted irregularly or beyond his jurisdiction, and the conviction and warrant being admitted to be regular, the only objection being that the magistrate erred on the facts and that the evidence did not justify the conclusion as to the guilt of the prisoner arrived at by the magistrate, I have not the slightest hesitation in saying that we cannot go behind the conviction and inquire into the merits of the case by the use of the writ of *habeas corpus*.

[21] In the subsequent case of *Re Sproule* (1886), 12 SCR 140, the issues were jurisdictional but the Court held that extrinsic evidence could not be considered on *habeas corpus* to contradict the record of a superior court that is regular on its face. The conviction and sentence by the court of *oyer* and *terminer* and general jail delivery had been confirmed by the Supreme Court of British Columbia and Ritchie CJ spoke in terms of the conclusive character of the record of a superior court as follows at p. 191:

> I venture to propound without fear of successful contradiction, that by the law of England and of this Dominion, where the principles of the common law prevail, that if the record of a superior court contains the recital of facts requisite to confer jurisdiction, which the records

in this case did, it is conclusive and cannot be contradicted by extrinsic evidence; and if the superior courts have jurisdiction over the subject-matter and the person, as the court of *oyer* and *terminer* and general gaol delivery and the Supreme Court of British Columbia had in this case, the records of their judgments and sentences are final and conclusive, unerring verity, and the law will not, in such a case, allow the record to be contradicted.

[A]nd he emphasized the distinction in this respect between the records of inferior courts and those of superior courts as follows at p. 193:

And I venture humbly, and with all respect, to suggest that the difficulty in this case has arisen from a misapprehension of what can, and what cannot, be done under a writ of *habeas corpus*, but more especially from not duly appreciating the distinction between the validity and force of records of courts of inferior, and of courts of superior, jurisdiction, but treating records of superior and inferior courts as being of the same force and effect.

[22] *Re Sproule* was applied by this Court in *Ex parte Macdonald, supra*, and *Re Henderson*, [1930] SCR 45, where there were jurisdictional issues involved, in support of the more general or unqualified proposition that the court was limited on *habeas corpus* to an examination of the warrant of committal in determining whether there had been an absence or excess of jurisdiction.

[23] Thus the true basis of this Court's jurisprudence with respect to the admission or consideration of extrinsic evidence on an application for *habeas corpus* consists of two principles: the principle that extrinsic evidence must not be permitted to convert an application for *habeas corpus* into an appeal on the merits, and the principle that the record of a superior court is conclusive as to the facts on which the court's jurisdiction depends and cannot be contradicted by extrinsic evidence. It has been suggested that the court was particularly concerned about the first principle when it was exercising an original jurisdiction in respect of *habeas corpus*, and that this may have led to the broad and unqualified expression of the rule respecting the consideration of extrinsic evidence on *habeas corpus* that is to be found in some of its decisions: see Sharpe, *The Law of Habeas Corpus* (1976), p. 51, note 2. With respect to the second principle, I agree with the suggestion in Sharpe, "*Habeas Corpus* in Canada," 2 *Dal. LJ* 241 at p. 261 (1975), that it should apply only to the records of superior courts or courts of general common law jurisdiction. In *Mitchell v. The Queen* (1975), 24 CCC (2d) 241, 61 DLR (3d) 77, [1976] 2 SCR 570, neither of these principles was applicable. As I have indicated, the grounds of attack were clearly jurisdictional, and the record, dependent as it was on the proceedings and decisions of an inferior tribunal, was not of the character entitled to be treated as conclusive of the facts of jurisdiction. In my respectful opinion, the view expressed in *Mitchell* that the affidavit evidence could not be considered went beyond the true basis of the court's jurisprudence on this question. In fact, two members of the majority in the result (Martland and de Grandpré JJ), as well as the minority (Laskin CJ, Spence and Dickson JJ), did consider the affidavit evidence in deciding whether there had been an absence or excess of jurisdiction in ordering the detention.

[24] As the British Columbia and Ontario Courts of Appeal pointed out in *Cardinal* and *Oswald* and in the case at bar, it may only be possible to establish jurisdictional error on *habeas corpus* by affidavit evidence, even where the record is brought up by *certiorari* in aid. This is particularly true of a violation of natural justice or a denial of procedural fairness.

This is a compelling reason, in my opinion, for confining the rule against consideration of extrinsic evidence on an application for *habeas corpus* within its proper boundaries.

[25] Support for a broader approach to the admission or consideration of extrinsic evidence on *habeas corpus* to determine issues of jurisdiction may be found in the decision of the House of Lords in *Schtraks v. Government of Israel et al.*, [1964] AC 556, which was relied on by the Courts of Appeal in *Cardinal* and *Oswald* and the case at bar. There it was held that fresh evidence was admissible on an application for *habeas corpus* to show that the magistrate lacked jurisdiction to make the committal order in an extradition case because the offence was of a political character. Lord Hodson appears to have held in effect that the rule concerning the admission of affidavit evidence on *habeas corpus* is the same as it is on *certiorari*, as suggested by the following passage at pp. 605-6:

> Proceeding by *habeas corpus* is analogous to that by *certiorari* to remove a conviction, see Short and Mellor's *Crown Practice* (1908), p. 319. Affidavits are not admissible to controvert facts found by the judgment of a court of competent jurisdiction, though they may be received to show some extrinsic collateral matter essential to jurisdiction or to show total want or excess of jurisdiction.

[26] I am therefore of the opinion that, subject to the limitation arising from the conclusive character of the records of courts of superior or general common law jurisdiction, a court may on an application for *habeas corpus* without *certiorari* in aid consider affidavit or other extrinsic evidence to determine whether there has been an absence or excess of jurisdiction.

IV

[27] I turn to the question whether *habeas corpus* will lie to determine the validity of the confinement of an inmate of a penitentiary in a special handling unit and to obtain his release from such confinement, if it is found to be unlawful, into normal association with the general population of the penitentiary.

[28] This issue turns on the view that one takes of the proper role of *habeas corpus* and the extent to which it should be adapted to the reality of the various forms of confinement or detention within penal institutions. An important policy consideration, in the context of the exclusive review jurisdiction of the Federal Court, is the extent to which the use of *habeas corpus* to determine the validity of a particular form of detention amounts to an indirect assumption of the Federal Court's review jurisdiction with respect to the administrative decisions of federal correctional authorities.

[29] Those who oppose the resort to *habeas corpus* to challenge the validity of a particular form of confinement or detention in a penal institution contend that it fails to meet two essential conditions of the traditional availability of this remedy: (a) that there be a deprivation of liberty, and (b) that what is sought is the complete liberty of the applicant and not merely his or her transfer to another form of detention or restraint of liberty. This view of the traditional role of *habeas corpus* is reflected in the decisions in *Ex parte Rogers* (1843), 7 Jur. 992, and *R v. Governor of Wandsworth Prison, Ex parte Silverman* (1952), 96 Sol. J 853. In *Rogers* a prisoner applied for *habeas corpus* to obtain his release from a part of a prison "where the confinement was stricter and the food more scanty" to the place in the prison where he had been confined before the transfer. In

dismissing the application Denman CJ, with whom Williams, Coleridge and Wightman JJ concurred, said:

> It is quite clear that we cannot entertain this application. The object of the writ of *habeas corpus* is, generally, to restore a person to his liberty, not to pronounce a judgment as to the room or part of a prison in which a prisoner ought to be confined.

In *Silverman*, a prisoner in preventive detention complained that he was not receiving the special treatment which the applicable statute required to be provided, and he sought by an application for *habeas corpus* to be transferred to a place where such treatment was provided. In dismissing the application for *habeas corpus* Hilberry J is reported to have held that if a writ of *habeas corpus* were issued,

> the only question would be whether the applicant should be released or not; and the prison governor's return would state that he was being detained under a sentence of preventive detention, which would be a perfectly good answer.

[30] These cases were relied on by Hugessen ACJ, as he then was, in *Berrouard v. The Queen*, an unreported judgment of November 30, 1981, and related unreported decisions (referred to by the Quebec Court of Appeal in *Morin*) in dismissing applications for *habeas corpus* to challenge the validity of confinement in what appears from the expressions used to have been a special handling unit. I quote from an English version of what he said, as reported in *Re Morin and Yeomans et al.* (1982), 1 CCC (3d) 438 at p. 441:

> [TRANSLATION] These six motions for *habeas corpus* each raise the same point of law. In each case, the applicant alleges that he is at present serving a sentence and that he has been unjustifiably transferred into a special detention unit, or a special segregation unit.
>
> An essential pre-condition to the granting of the remedy of *habeas corpus* is the privation of the subject's liberty: *Massella v. Langlais* (1955), 112 CCC 1, [1975] 4 DLR 346, [1955] SCR 263. Similarly, in a motion for *habeas corpus*, the principal object of this remedy is the obtaining of liberty for the subject: *R v. Governor of Wandsworth Prison; Ex p. Silverman* (1952), 96 Sol. Jo. 853 (Queen's Bench Div. Ct., Hilberry, Streatfeild and McNair JJ); *Ex parte Rodgers* (1843), 7 Jur. 992 (Court of Queen's Bench, Denman CJ, Williams, Coleridge and Wightman JJ). I have read with much interest the judgment of my colleague Chief Justice McEachern, of the Supreme Court of British Columbia, in *Cardinal* and *Oswald v. Attorney-General*, an unreported judgment delivered on December 30, 1980. With all respect which I have for my colleague, I am not in agreement with his position that the writ of *habeas corpus* can be used to modify the conditions of detention since, even if the writ is granted, the prisoner's detention will continue after the final judgment is delivered. This is also our case.
>
> It accordingly follows that I am in agreement with the decision of my colleague Mr. Justice Jean-Paul Bergeron in the *Morin v. Yeomans* case, an unreported judgment delivered on November 18, 1981.

[31] In *Morin*, which, as I have said, was a case of *habeas corpus* without *certiorari* in aid, Bergeron J referred to the conclusion of McEachern CJSC in *Cardinal* and *Oswald* that *habeas corpus* would lie to determine the validity of a particular form of detention in a penitentiary and said he could not agree with it. He held that judicial review of the administrative decisions of the federal correctional authorities fell within the exclusive jurisdiction of the Federal Court by way of *certiorari*. In his view, the conditions of

detention of a person who was otherwise lawfully imprisoned under a valid warrant of committal could not give rise to *habeas corpus*. In dismissing the appeal from the judgment of Bergeron J, the Quebec Court of Appeal noted that the appellant had taken proceedings by way of *certiorari* in the Federal Court to challenge the validity of his confinement in the special handling unit and that there would therefore be the danger of conflicting judgments if it were held that the Superior Court had jurisdiction to issue *habeas corpus* to determine the same issue. The Court of Appeal concluded that proceedings to challenge administrative action within federal penitentiaries was within the exclusive jurisdiction of the Federal Court. Thus it would appear that the Superior Court and the Court of Appeal in *Morin* were influenced in the view which they took of the proper application of *habeas corpus* by the implications of a concurrent or overlapping review jurisdiction with respect to the administrative decisions of the federal correctional authorities.

[32] The British Columbia courts in *Cardinal* and *Oswald* and the Ontario Court of Appeal in the case at bar applied the notion of a "prison within a prison" in holding that *habeas corpus* would lie to determine the validity of confinement in administrative segregation or a special handling unit, and if such confinement be found unlawful, to order the release of the inmate into the general population of the penitentiary. The concept of a "prison within a prison" is referred to by Sharpe, *The Law of Habeas Corpus*, p. 149, where he speaks in favour of such an application of *habeas corpus*, and by Dickson J, as he then was, in *Martineau* [*v Matsqui Institution Disciplinary Board (No 2)*, [1980] 1 SCR 602], where, with reference to the decision of the disciplinary board which sentenced the inmate for a disciplinary offence to 15 days in the penitentiary's special corrections unit, he said at p. 622:

> Moreover, the board's decision had the effect of depriving an individual of his liberty by committing him to a "prison within a prison." In these circumstances, elementary justice requires some procedural protection. The rule of law must run within penitentiary walls.

This statement reflects the perception that a prisoner is not without some rights or residual liberty (see also *Solosky v. The Queen*, [1980] 1 SCR 821 at p. 839) and that there may be significant degrees of deprivation of liberty within a penal institution. The same perception is reflected in the reasons for judgment of McEachern CJSC and Anderson JA in *Cardinal* and *Oswald* and Cory JA in the case at bar on this issue. In effect, a prisoner has the right not to be deprived unlawfully of the relative or residual liberty permitted to the general inmate population of an institution. Any significant deprivation of that liberty, such as that effected by confinement in a special handling unit, meets the first of the traditional requirements for *habeas corpus*, that it must be directed against a deprivation of liberty.

[33] Moreover, the principle that *habeas corpus* will lie only to secure the complete liberty of the subject is not invariably reflected in its application. There are applications of *habeas corpus* in Canadian case-law which illustrate its use to release a person from a particular form of detention although the person will lawfully remain under some other restraint of liberty. Examples are the use of *habeas corpus* to recover the custody of children (*Stevenson v. Florant*, [1927] AC 211; aff'g [1925] SCR 532; *Dugal v. Lefebvre*, [1934] SCR 501); to release a person on parole where the parole has been unlawfully revoked (*Re Cadeddu and The Queen* (1982), 4 CCC (3d) 97; *Swan v. Attorney General of British*

Columbia (1983), 35 CR (3d) 135); and to transfer an inmate from an institution in which he has been unlawfully confined to another institution (*Re Bell and Director of Springhill Medium Security Institution et al.* (1977), 34 CCC (2d) 303; *R v. Frejd* (1910), 18 CCC 10, 22 OLR 566). In all of these cases the effect of *habeas corpus* is to release a person from an unlawful detention, which is the object of the remedy. The use of *habeas corpus* to release a prisoner from an unlawful form of detention within a penitentiary into normal association with the general inmate population of the penitentiary is consistent with these applications of the remedy.

[34] An enlarged approach to the concept of custody for purposes of *habeas corpus* is reflected in American case-law. Formerly American courts took the view that *habeas corpus* would only lie where a favourable judgment would result in immediate release from all forms of detention: *McNally v. Hill* (1934), 293 US 131. Since then the concept of custody has been greatly expanded to permit a wider use of *habeas corpus* for the protection of prisoners' rights. In *Jones v. Cunningham* (1963), 371 US 236, where *habeas corpus* was held to be available to an applicant who was not in physical custody but on parole, the Court said at p. 243 that *habeas corpus* is "not now and never has been a static, narrow, formalistic remedy; its scope has grown to achieve its grand purpose—the protection of individuals against erosion of their right to be free from wrongful restraints upon their liberty." In *Peyton v. Rowe* (1968), 391 US 54, *habeas corpus* was allowed to challenge the validity of a sentence yet to be served. In *Johnson v. Avery* (1969), 393 US 483, *habeas corpus* was allowed to challenge the validity of a condition of confinement in the form of a prison regulation which limited the access of illiterate inmates to the courts by forbidding their fellow prisoners from serving as jailhouse lawyers. It was held that the unlawful regulations made the custody unlawful. In *Wilwording v. Swenson* (1971), 404 US 249, the United States Supreme Court reversed the Missouri courts which had held that *habeas corpus* would not lie where the object was not to secure the release of the petitioners from the penitentiary altogether but to challenge their living conditions and disciplinary measures. The Supreme Court affirmed the approach it had adopted in *Johnson v. Avery*. It should be noted, however, that in *Preiser v. Rodriguez* (1973), 411 US 475, Stewart J, speaking for the majority, expressed himself in terms which might suggest that the question was regarded as still being open. He said at p. 499: "This is not to say that *habeas corpus* may not also be available to challenge such prison conditions. See *Johnson v. Avery*, 393 US 483 (1969); *Wilwording v. Swenson, supra*, at 251. When a prisoner is put under additional and unconstitutional restraints during his lawful custody, it is arguable that *habeas corpus* will lie to remove the restraints making the custody illegal. See Note, Developments in the Law—*Habeas Corpus*, 83 *Harv. L Rev.* 1038, 1084 (1970)." The note to which Stewart J referred approved the approach adopted in the leading case of *Coffin v. Reichard* (1944), 143 F2d 443 (6th Cir.), where it was said at p. 445: "A prisoner is entitled to the writ of *habeas corpus* when, though lawfully in custody, he is deprived of some right to which he is lawfully entitled even in his confinement, the deprivation of which serves to make his imprisonment more burdensome than the law allows or curtails his liberty to a greater extent than the law permits." After referring to *Coffin* the note states at pp. 1085-6:

> No other circuit purports to follow *Coffin*. Most courts instead believe that *habeas* jurisdiction is lacking when the petitioner is not asking for the invalidation of a custody imposed

by sentence, on the theory that the petitioner is not seeking a present or future release. But this fails to recognize that the lawfulness of a custody depends, not merely upon the legal basis for some kind of custody, but upon the lawfulness of the specific type and manner of confinement in question. Where the specific detention abridges federally protected interests—by placing petitioner in the wrong prison, denying him treatment, imposing cruel and unusual punishment, impeding his access to the courts, and so on—it is an unlawful detention and *habeas* lies to release the petitioner therefrom. It is immaterial that the petitioner might then be placed in a different, lawful custody or that his being sentenced to a term of confinement might itself be lawful. The custody requirement, and the corresponding insistence on discharge from custody, do not prevent *habeas corpus* from being an appropriate remedy for the review of unlawful prison administration.

Since that note was written the point of view expressed in it has been adopted by federal courts of appeal. See, for example, the following cases recognizing the availability of *habeas corpus* to challenge the validity of various forms of segregated confinement in a prison on the ground of a violation of due process: *McCollum v. Miller* (1982), 695 F2d 1044 (7th Cir.); *Krist v. Ricketts* (1974), 504 F2d 887 (5th Cir.); *Bryant v. Harris* (1972), 465 F2d 365 (7th Cir.); *Dawson v. Smith* (1983), 719 F2d 896 (7th Cir.), and *Streeter v. Hopper* (1980), 618 F2d 1178 (5th Cir.).

[35] After giving consideration to the two approaches to this issue, I am of the opinion that the better view is that *habeas corpus* should lie to determine the validity of a particular form of confinement in a penitentiary notwithstanding that the same issue may be determined upon *certiorari* in the Federal Court. The proper scope of the availability of *habeas corpus* must be considered first on its own merits, apart from possible problems arising from concurrent or overlapping jurisdiction. The general importance of this remedy as the traditional means of challenging deprivations of liberty is such that its proper development and adaptation to the modern realities of confinement in a prison setting should not be compromised by concerns about conflicting jurisdiction. As I have said in connection with the question of jurisdiction to issue *certiorari* in aid of *habeas corpus*, these concerns have their origin in the legislative judgment to leave the *habeas corpus* jurisdiction against federal authorities with the provincial superior courts. There cannot be one definition of the reach of *habeas corpus* in relation to federal authorities and a different one for other authorities. Confinement in a special handling unit, or in administrative segregation as in *Cardinal* and *Oswald* is a form of detention that is distinct and separate from that imposed on the general inmate population. It involves a significant reduction in the residual liberty of the inmate. It is in fact a new detention of the inmate, purporting to rest on its own foundation of legal authority. It is that particular form of detention or deprivation of liberty which is the object of the challenge by *habeas corpus*. It is release from that form of detention that is sought. For the reasons indicated above, I can see no sound reason in principle, having to do with the nature and role of *habeas corpus*, why *habeas corpus* should not be available for that purpose. I do not say that *habeas corpus* should lie to challenge any and all conditions of confinement in a penitentiary or prison, including the loss of any privilege enjoyed by the general inmate population. But it should lie in my opinion to challenge the validity of a distinct form of confinement or detention in which the actual physical constraint or deprivation of liberty, as distinct from the mere loss of certain privileges, is more restrictive or severe than the normal one in an institution.

Steele v Mountain Institution, [1990] 2 SCR 1385, a unanimous judgment written by Cory J, confirmed *habeas corpus* relief for a prisoner who had been imprisoned for almost 37 years as a "criminal sexual psychopath," a predecessor to the modern dangerous offender desig-nation. Steele was 18 years old when he was given that designation after his conviction for attempted rape. His counsel argued that, in the absence of any indicia of dangerousness, it was cruel and unusual punishment in violation of s 12 of the *Canadian Charter of Rights and Freedoms*, Part I of the *Constitution Act, 1982*, being Schedule B to the *Canada Act 1982* (UK), c 11, to continue his confinement. Over the years, Steele had been released on parole, but parole privileges had been revoked for breach of conditions. Instead of returning to the National Parole Board, he brought his case to court.

Steele v Mountain Institution
[1990] 2 SCR 1385

CORY J (Dickson CJ, Lamer CJ, La Forest, L'Heureux?Dubé, Gonthier, and McLachlin JJ concurring):

Theodore Steele, the respondent, has attained the age of 55. For almost 37 of those years he has been detained in an institution. In my view the issue raised on this appeal is whether the Parole Board erred in refusing to release him on parole with the result that his continuing imprisonment constitutes cruel and unusual punishment.

The period of incarceration has been long indeed. When the respondent entered prison, Mr. St. Laurent was Prime Minister and General Eisenhower was President. He remained incarcerated through the Cuban missile crisis, the assassination of President Kennedy, the Vietnam War, the FLQ crisis, the Watergate scandal, the Iran/Iraq War, the easing of tension between the Soviet Union and the United States, and the enactment of the *Canadian Charter of Rights and Freedoms*. An era has passed.

· · ·

It will be remembered that it was determined by Paris J, and upheld by the Court of Appeal, that although the indeterminate continuing detention of a dangerous offender had been held in *Lyons, supra*, to be constitutional, nevertheless, in certain rare cases such as this one, the continuing detention of an offender would constitute cruel and unusual punishment in violation of s. 12 of the Charter. If this position is correct it would mean that while the parole review process would work effectively in the vast majority of cases, there would be the occasional case in which even the most responsible and careful applica-tion of the parole review process could not prevent a continuing detention from becoming cruel and unusual punishment.

I must, with respect, differ from that conclusion. It seems to me to fly in the face of the decision of this Court in *Lyons, supra*, where this Court observed at p. 363 that "the fair-ness of certain procedural aspects of a parole hearing may well be the subject of consti-tutional challenge, at least when the review is of the continued incarceration of a dangerous offender." In my view the unlawful incarceration of Steele was caused, not by any structural flaw in the dangerous offender provisions, but rather by errors committed by the National Parole Board. These errors are apparent upon a review of the record of Steele's treatment by the Board over the long years of his detention.

In 1948, provisions for the indeterminate sentencing of "criminal sexual psychopaths" were enacted. The same group of amendments to the Code provided for a review of the condition, history and circumstances of the offender's detention once every three years by the Minister of Justice. In 1958, the National Parole Board was created by the *Parole Act*, SC 1958, c. 38. At this time the authority for conducting the review of the sentences of criminal sexual psychopaths was transferred to the Parole Board. Section 8(a) of the *Parole Act* established the following criteria for granting parole:

> 8. The Board may
>
> (a) grant parole to an inmate if the Board considers that the inmate has derived the maximum benefit from imprisonment and that the reform and rehabilitation of the inmate will be aided by the grant of parole;

These criteria remained in effect until 1968 when they were replaced by the provisions of s. 16(1) cited above. These provisions require the Board to grant parole where: (i) the inmate has derived the maximum benefit from imprisonment; (ii) the inmate's reform and rehabilitation will be aided by the grant of parole; and (iii) the inmate's release would not constitute an undue risk to society.

In reviewing the indeterminate sentences of dangerous offenders, it is fundamentally important that the Board consider these criteria. As La Forest J stated in *Lyons* at pp. 340-41:

> ... in the context of a determinate sentencing scheme the availability of parole represents an additional, superadded protection of the liberty interests of the offender. In the present context, however, it is, subsequent to the actual imposition of the sentence itself, the sole protection of the dangerous offender's liberty interests. ...
>
> Seen in this light, therefore, the parole process assumes the utmost significance for it is that process alone that is capable of truly accommodating and tailoring the sentence to fit the circumstances of the individual offender.

It is only by a careful consideration and application of these criteria that the indeterminate sentence can be made to fit the circumstances of the individual offender. Doing this will ensure that the dangerous offender sentencing provisions do not violate s. 12 of the Charter. If it is clear on the face of the record that the Board has misapplied or disregarded those criteria over a period of years with the result that an offender remains incarcerated far beyond the time he or she should have been properly paroled, then the Board's decision to keep the offender incarcerated may well violate s. 12. In my opinion, this is such a case.

First, Steele's imprisonment had long ago reached the point at which he had derived "the maximum benefit from imprisonment." During his incarceration governments have changed, wars have begun and ended and a generation has grown to maturity. He has been in prison longer than the vast majority of the most cruel and callous murderers. Indeed, it is uncertain whether imprisonment provided Steele with any benefit at all. During the first 20 years of his detention there were no facilities in British Columbia that could provide the psychiatric treatment Steele needed. By the time it was available, Steele was a middle-aged institutionalized offender who, not surprisingly, viewed the treatment program as a means of gaining his release rather than as an opportunity for rehabilitation.

Throughout the period of his imprisonment, numerous observers expressly stated not only that Steele had received the maximum benefit from imprisonment, but also that continued detention would cause him to deteriorate. As early as 1960, Dr. P. Middleton warned that any treatment facilities available in the penitentiary would not offset "the pernicious effects of association" with other inmates. Others who made this same point include: Dr. D.C. MacDonald, Deputy Warden W.H. Collins and Field Representative P.D. Redecopp in 1964; Dr. J.C. Bryce in 1968; Mr. Lee Pulos in 1970; Field Parole Officer William F. Foster and Mr. Pulos, again, in 1972; Dr. Milton H. Miller and Dr. A. Saad in 1974; and Dr. W.J. Ross in 1981. Even Dr. Noone, who testified for the Crown in this application, acknowledged the detrimental effects of indeterminate sentencing for dangerous offenders. While some observers expressed the opinion that Steele should not be released, not one of them appears to have argued that continued incarceration had been or would be beneficial for Steele.

The second criterion has also long been satisfied. Steele has deteriorated in the prison environment. Many, indeed the great majority of those psychiatrists and psychologists who assessed him, expressed the opinion that his rehabilitation could only be facilitated and attained by his gradual, supervised release into the community. It appears that the Parole Board acknowledged this in its decisions to grant Steele limited freedom between 1968 and 1970 and between 1980 and 1987. During both of these periods the Board permitted Steele to undertake a programme of escorted passes that resulted in brief stays in a half-way house environment. These periods of relative freedom were terminated when Steele infringed his parole conditions by drinking alcohol and breaking curfew. Unfortunately, despite assessments by observers suggesting that these parole violations were merely adjustment problems, the Board seems to have presumed that Steele was incapable of benefitting from an association with the community outside the prison.

There remains then the third and most important criterion, namely whether the offender constitutes an undue risk to society. If an inmate's release continues to constitute an undue risk to the public, then his or her detention can be justifiably maintained for a lifetime. There can be no doubt that in the ordinary course of events the assessment as to whether or not an inmate's release would pose an undue risk to the community is best left in the discretion of the experts who participate in the Parole Board review decisions. However, in light of the inordinate length of Steele's period of incarceration, it is appropriate to consider whether the Board erred in its evaluation that Steele did in fact constitute a danger to the community.

Of the psychiatrists and psychologists who interviewed Steele and whose reports were provided to the Parole Board, sixteen expressed a recommendation as to whether or not he should be paroled. Thirteen of the sixteen recommended that he should be released on some form of supervised parole. Two stated that he should not be released. One psychologist changed his mind over the course of several years from a position which cautioned against parole to one of arguing in favour of parole. Those recommending release were: Dr. MacDonald in 1956 and 1964; Dr. Middleton in 1960; Dr. Bryce in 1968; Dr. Lipinski in 1970 and 1972; Dr. Bulmer in 1970; Mr. Pulos in 1970 and 1972; Mr. P. DesLauriers in 1972; Dr. Robert Halliday in 1973; Dr. Miller, Dr. Saad, Mr. F.M. Van Fleet and Mr. K.S. Oey in 1974; and Dr. Tyhurst in 1979 and 1985. Those counselling against release were: Dr. Eaves in 1979 and 1980; and Dr. Noone in 1985 and 1988. Dr. W.J. Ross considered that Steele was not "a good risk" when he first assessed him in 1978; however, by 1981 he was recommending that Steele be released on gradual parole.

On the application, Paris J heard testimony from three psychiatric experts. Of those, Dr. Marcus and Dr. Koopman testified that Steele was not dangerous and should be released. Dr. Noone stated that Steele remained an untreated sexual psychopath who should not be released. After carefully reviewing the evidence in extensive detail, Paris J concluded that Steele's release would not endanger the public.

Upon the evidence presented to this Court, the careful reasons and conclusion of Paris J on this issue are in my view preferable to those of the Parole Board which as will be demonstrated did not properly exercise its jurisdiction.

It is difficult to find any evidence of acts committed by Steele during the past two decades that would suggest that he remained an undue risk to society. His parole violations resulted not from a tendency to repeatedly engage in violent or sexually deviant behaviour, but from the difficulties he had in abiding by parole curfew restrictions and abstaining from drinking alcohol. The nature of these problems was described by Dr. Marcus in these words:

> He finds it very hard to adhere to inflexible rules such as those that are imposed when he is on parole. … His personality style is always to stretch the clock. … It is a similar attitude which has led Mr. Steele into situations where he has been in breach of parole conditions relating to meeting curfews. Here again Mr. Steele holds the view that he is now 53 years old and after a lifetime in prison he should not be held to requirements which treat him in a somewhat childlike [manner]. It is precisely this attitude which has made him a bad parole prospect in terms of meeting all the expectations and rules imposed by his Parole Officer. Yet, in my opinion, what must be kept firmly in mind in the context of assessing the degree of risk of harm to others that Mr. Steele poses at the present time, is that Mr. Steele in the course of these recent infractions did not repeat the pattern either of his original offence nor of his re-offending while on parole in 1962.

The problems inherent in requiring chronic alcoholics to meet rigid drinking restrictions have been well documented in the *Report of the Inquiry into Habitual Criminals in Canada*, vol. 1 (1984), where Judge Leggett wrote at p. 83:

> Many of the habitual criminals are alcoholic. This disease has been a significant factor in the "revolving-door syndrome" of these individuals. When released on parole, a condition to abstain from alcohol is frequently included as a condition to such release. While some of the habitual criminals have been able to abide by this condition and successfully complete parole, many others have not. Those who have failed to abide by such conditions have found themselves, sooner or later, re-incarcerated as a result of the revocation of their parole.

Steele may have a problem with alcohol and in dealing with rigid discipline. But those factors in themselves cannot justify his continued detention. If breaches of a domestic curfew and the consumption of alcohol were the sole criteria for liberty then a significant proportion of our society should be incarcerated for an indefinite period. That is not to say that breaches of the conditions of parole should not be seriously considered. However, all the circumstances of the breach and any explanations as to the reasons for its occurrence should also be taken into account.

The statutory criteria should be applied to the individual inmate and considered in light of all the relevant circumstances. One of those circumstances will be length of the term served. The passage of several decades in prison may not in itself justify parole. However, it may well serve as an indication that the inmate is no longer dangerous. Surely with the passage of very long periods of time sexual appetite might reasonably be expected to decline to an extent that it may at least be controlled, if not extinguished. As well, a lengthy incarceration with the concomitant institutionalizing effect upon the inmate may serve to explain and perhaps to some extent excuse certain breaches of discipline.

In my view the evidence presented demonstrates that the National Parole Board has erred in its application of the criteria set out in s. 16(1)(a) of the *Parole Act*. The Board appears to have based its decision to deny parole upon relatively minor and apparently explicable breaches of discipline committed by Steele, rather than focussing upon the crucial issue of whether granting him parole would constitute an undue risk to society. As a result of these errors, the parole review process has failed to ensure that Steele's sentence has been tailored to fit his circumstances. The inordinate length of his incarceration has long since become grossly disproportionate to the circumstances of this case.

It will only be on rare and unique occasions that a court will find a sentence so grossly disproportionate that it violates the provisions of s. 12 of the Charter. The test for determining whether a sentence is disproportionately long is very properly stringent and demanding. A lesser test would tend to trivialize the Charter.

As well, it should not be forgotten that there is in place a method whereby appellate courts can review sentences to ensure that they are appropriate. In *R v. Smith*, [1987] 1 SCR 1045, Lamer J set out the strict test for reviewing a sentence under s. 12 of the Charter. At page 1072 he wrote:

> The test for review under s. 12 of the Charter is one of gross disproportionality, because it is aimed at punishments that are more than merely excessive. We should be careful not to stigmatize every disproportionate or excessive sentence as being a constitutional violation, and should leave to the usual sentencing appeal process the task of reviewing the fitness of a sentence. Section 12 will only be infringed where the sentence is so unfit having regard to the offence and the offender as to be grossly disproportionate.

The history of the offence and the offender which I have set out makes it apparent that the sentence is now "so unfit having regard to the offence and the offender as to be grossly disproportionate." This is one of those rare cases where the sentence continuing Steele's detention after 37 years in prison violates s. 12 of the Charter.

It is necessary to make a further comment. As I have made clear above, the continuing detention of a dangerous offender sentenced pursuant to the constitutionally valid provisions of the *Criminal Code* will only violate s. 12 of the Charter when the National Parole Board errs in the execution of its vital duties of tailoring the indeterminate sentence to the circumstances of the offender. This tailoring is performed by applying the criteria set out in s. 16(1) of the *Parole Act*. Since any error that may be committed occurs in the parole review process itself, an application challenging the decision should be made by means of judicial review from the National Parole Board decision, not by means of an application for *habeas corpus*. It would be wrong to sanction the establishment of a costly and unwieldly parallel system for challenging a Parole Board decision. As well, it is important that the release of a long term inmate should be supervised by those who are experts in this field. I agree with the comments of Locke JA:

> In the case of persons subject to an indeterminate sentence who have spent many years in prison, it is highly desirable that their release, if and when it occurs, should be conditional, should be subject to supervision by those experienced in the parole or probation fields, and

should be accompanied by the sort of assistance which will increase their likelihood of adjusting to the change in environment and, if possible, becoming self-sufficient and useful members of society. Under the present statutory and administrative arrangements, it seems that this can be achieved only in association with release by the parole board, in the exercise of its discretion under s. 761 of the *Criminal Code*.

However, in view of Steele's age and the length of his detention, it would be unfair to require him to commence new proceedings by way of judicial review from the National Parole Board decision. In these highly unusual circumstances, I would confirm Steele's release on the basis of the application for *habeas corpus*. I further agree with the position taken by the Court of Appeal that since his release cannot be regulated through normal parole procedures, it is appropriate, in the interest of public safety, to maintain the conditions placed by the Court of Appeal upon his release.

NOTE

In total, 13 judges examined Steele's case and all agreed that he was entitled to be released as a result of a breach of s 12 of the Charter. This serves as an important example of the potential use of *habeas corpus* to bring forward a Charter claim. However, it is important to note that the s 12 violation was not grounded in the length of confinement, but rather in the error of the National Parole Board "in the execution of its vital duties of tailoring the indeterminate sentence to the circumstances of the offender." Along with cases like *R v Gamble*, [1988] 2 SCR 595, which dealt with s 7 and parole ineligibility for first-degree murder after a conviction under the wrong law, there appeared to be a renaissance in the use of *habeas corpus* as an accessible and effectual remedy.

However, the final three paragraphs in the judgment of Cory J in *Steele* blunted this progress. His admonition about establishing a "costly and unwieldy parallel system for challenging a Parole Board decision" was made in the context of a lifetime indeterminate sentence. This was a case where it was legitimate to ask whether there was any need to supervise Steele in the community. This is the key to Cory J's comments. Clearly, a court does not have supervisory resources. However, given that the relief is sought under s 24(1) of the Charter, the court is empowered to do what is "appropriate and just." In *Steele*, that meant imposing conditions on his release. Although there may be some preventive detention cases that raise a procedural fairness argument that might better be dealt with by way of judicial review that returns the matter to the National Parole Board, cases that engage fundamental questions about the legality of confinement, like *Steele*, should not be barred from access to *habeas corpus*.

Regrettably, some superior courts were persuaded that the final paragraph in *Steele* meant that no parole issue should be dealt with by way of *habeas corpus* and that all issues should be raised by judicial review in the Federal Court. This elevated Cory J's comment in *Steele* from a caution raised in the context of indeterminate sentences to a complete denial of *habeas corpus* relief in a much larger class of cases. Moreover, deference to Federal Court jurisdiction quickly moved from just parole cases to other penitentiary issues, primarily transfers to higher security. While this raised questions of consistency with the role of *habeas corpus* as explained in *Miller*, it was not long before Courts of Appeal started to reach the same conclusion based on a fuzzy notion that jurisdiction was discretionary and could be declined. By 2004, the doors of *habeas corpus*, that "great and efficacious writ" were almost completely closed to penitentiary prisoners who wanted to challenge the legality of deprivations of their residual liberty. The Supreme Court of Canada unanimously opened the doors by rejecting any discretionary jurisdiction and recognizing the prisoner's right to select her remedy regardless of concurrent jurisdiction in the Federal Court. When you read the case below, note how Justices Lebel and Fish deal with the issue of burden of proof on a *habeas corpus* application. This part of the judgment represents the first time in Canada that this issue has been authoritatively considered.

May v Ferndale Institution
2005 SCC 82, [2005] 3 SCR 809

LeBEL and FISH JJ (McLachlin CJ, Binnie, Deschamps, and Abella JJ concurring):

I. Introduction

[1] These cases involve the overlap and potential conflict of jurisdiction between provincial superior courts and the Federal Court. At stake is the right of federal prisoners to challenge the legality of their detention by way of *habeas corpus* in provincial superior courts. The question to be resolved in these cases is whether the Supreme Court of British Columbia should have declined *habeas corpus* jurisdiction in favour of Federal Court jurisdiction on judicial review. If the court properly exercised its jurisdiction, we will also have to assess whether the appellants have been unlawfully deprived of their liberty.

[2] In our view, the Supreme Court of British Columbia has properly exercised its *habeas corpus* jurisdiction. This is not one of the limited circumstances pursuant to which a superior court should decline to exercise its jurisdiction: first, these cases do not involve a statute that confers jurisdiction on a court of appeal to correct the errors of a lower court and release the applicant if need be; and second, Parliament has not put in place a complete, comprehensive and expert procedure for review of an administrative decision.

[3] Moreover, we believe that the appellants have been unlawfully deprived of their liberty. The respondents did not comply with their statutory duty to provide all the information or a summary of the information considered in making the transfer decisions. The appeal should therefore be allowed.

II. Facts and Judicial History

[4] Each of the appellants are prisoners serving life sentences for murder and/or manslaughter. Terry Lee May was convicted of first-degree murder for killing one adolescent boy so that he could sexually assault another without interference. David Edward Owen was convicted of second-degree murder for beating his ex-wife to death. Maurice Yvon Roy was convicted of second-degree murder for killing his common law wife. Gareth Wayne Robinson was convicted on two counts of manslaughter after he stabbed his girlfriend, and then, three years later, struck his wife on the head with a hammer. Segen Uther Speer-Senner was convicted of second-degree murder in circumstances unspecified in the record before us. After varying periods of incarceration, the appellants became residents of Ferndale Institution, a minimum security federal penitentiary located in British Columbia.

[5] Between November 2000 and February 2001, all five appellants were involuntarily transferred from Ferndale Institution to medium-security institutions. Mr. May, Mr. Roy, Mr. Robinson and Mr. Speer-Senner were transferred to Mission Institution and Mr. Owen, to Matsqui Institution. It is not in issue that a transfer from a minimum- to a medium-security institution involves a significant deprivation of liberty for inmates. Consequently, the appellants filed grievances and also applied for *habeas corpus* relief with *certiorari* in aid directing the responsible correction officials to transfer them back to Ferndale Institution. Their applications were not joined, but the arguments before the British Columbia Court of Appeal were adopted by all five appellants.

[6] The transfers were the result of a direction from the Correctional Service of Canada ("CSC") to review the security classifications of all inmates serving life sentences in minimum-security institutions who had not completed their violent offender programming in the aftermath of a sensational crime committed by a former inmate in another province. CSC used computer applications to assist the classification review process. Mr. Roy, Mr. Robinson, Mr. Speer-Senner and Mr. Owen were advised that their transfers were based on a computerized reclassification scale which yielded a medium-security rating. Mr. May was told that his security rating had been adjusted because the security classification tool could not rate him as minimum-security because he had not completed violent offender programming. There were no allegations of fault or misconduct.

[7] The appellants attacked the decision-making process leading to their transfers. They submitted that a change in general policy, embodied in a direction to review the security classification of offenders serving a life sentence at Ferndale Institution using certain classification tools, was the sole factor prompting their transfers. They said that the transfers were arbitrary, made without any "fresh" misconduct on their parts, and made without considering the merits of each case. The appellants also claimed that their right to procedural fairness was breached by the failure to disclose the scoring matrix for one of the classification tools, leaving them unable to challenge the usefulness of that tool in the decision-making process.

[8] The Supreme Court of British Columbia dismissed the *habeas corpus* application: [2001] BCJ No. 1939 (QL), 2001 BCSC 1335. Bauman J first considered whether a provincial superior court had jurisdiction to review a federal prisoner's involuntary transfer on an application for *habeas corpus* (with *certiorari* in aid) and, in the affirmative, whether it should decline to exercise it. The issue arose because the Federal Court is granted exclusive jurisdiction in respect of *certiorari* proceedings involving the decisions of federal tribunals by its constituent statute.

[9] Bauman J found that he had jurisdiction to hear the application. He relied on *R v. Miller*, [1985] 2 SCR 613, which held that provincial superior courts have retained concurrent jurisdiction with the Federal Court to issue *certiorari* in aid of *habeas corpus* to review the validity of a detention authorized or imposed by a federal board, commission or other tribunal as defined by s. 2 of the *Federal Court Act*, RSC 1985, c. F-7 (formerly RSC 1970 (2nd Supp.), c. 10) ("*FCA*").

[10] Bauman J then dealt with the substantive issues, which he agreed to examine under his *habeas corpus* jurisdiction. He found against the appellants. He held that they had not made out their allegations of failure to disclose relevant information, the computer matrix not being available, and that the transfers had not been arbitrary. In his opinion, although the transfers had been prompted by a general instruction issued to CSC, the

decisions had been made after an individualized assessment of all relevant factors. He concluded that they had not been made in the absence or in excess of jurisdiction. The applications for *habeas corpus* and *certiorari* in aid were then dismissed.

[11] The British Columbia Court of Appeal dismissed the appeal: (2003), 188 BCAC 23, 2003 BCCA 536. On the jurisdiction issue, the Court of Appeal had asked for and received written submissions from counsel on the issue raised in *Spindler v. Millhaven Institution* (2003), 15 CR (6th) 183 (Ont. CA).

[12] In *Spindler*, prisoners had been placed in a maximum-security prison as a result of a new policy applicable to convicted murderers. They raised arguments which were similar to the submissions of the appellants in the present appeals. The Ontario Court of Appeal had held that, where a remedy is available in the Federal Court on the exercise of a statutory power granted under a federal statute to a federally appointed individual or tribunal, the provincial superior court should decline to hear an application for *habeas corpus* if no reasonable explanation for the failure to pursue judicial review in the Federal Court was offered by the petitioner. In doing so, the Ontario Court of Appeal agreed with the British Columbia Court of Appeal's decision in *Hickey v. Kent Institution*, [2003] BCJ No. 61 (QL), 2003 BCCA 23.

[13] Ryan JA felt that those comments were particularly apt in the case at bar. Although the issues raised in these cases were not identical to those raised in *Spindler*, they all involved policies and procedures adopted by the Commissioner of Corrections in determining the security classifications of the appellants. In her view, these cases should have been heard by the "specialized" Federal Court. The appellants had offered no reasonable explanation for failing to pursue judicial review in the Federal Court, so Ryan JA was of the opinion that Bauman J ought to have declined to hear the applications in these cases, though it is implicit from her reasons that he had jurisdiction to do so. Nevertheless, Ryan JA decided to examine the substantive issue, but she found no error in Bauman J's conclusion that there were no procedural flaws which would entitle the appellants to an order for *habeas corpus*.

[14] Since the Supreme Court of British Columbia heard the application, the record indicates that the situation of most of the appellants has changed. On June 30, 2002, Mr. May was transferred from medium- to minimum-security confinement at Ferndale Institution. On February 6, 2003, Mr. Speer-Senner was also transferred back to Ferndale Institution. On January 30, 2005, Mr. Owen was released on full parole. The record is silent with respect to the updated situation of Mr. Roy; however, at the hearing, Ms. Pollack, one of the counsel for the appellants, informed us that only Mr. Robinson is still incarcerated in a medium-security institution.

III. Issues and Position of the Parties

[15] These cases revolve around two core issues. First, whether the Supreme Court of British Columbia should have declined *habeas corpus* jurisdiction and, second, whether the appellants have been unlawfully deprived of their liberty.

[16] The appellants argue that the jurisdiction of provincial superior courts to grant *habeas corpus* is not affected by the fact that the unlawful detention results from a breach of relevant statutory and regulatory rules and of principles of natural justice by a federal authority. The applicant is entitled to choose the forum in which to challenge unlawful

restrictions of liberty in the prison context. In addition, the appellants contend that the decisions to transfer them from a minimum-security institution to medium-security institutions were arbitrary and unfair.

[17] On the other hand, the respondents submit that the Court of Appeal did not err in holding that the lower court should have declined *habeas corpus* jurisdiction in the instant case. *Habeas corpus* jurisdiction should be assessed purposively, in view of the comprehensive statutory schemes that provide effective comparable remedies. In any event, the respondents contend that the transfer decisions were lawfully made.

IV. Analysis

A. Did the Superior Court of British Columbia Properly Exercise Its Habeas Corpus Jurisdiction?

[18] Should the Supreme Court of British Columbia have declined *habeas corpus* jurisdiction in favour of Federal Court jurisdiction on judicial review? This issue is particularly important in the context of recent jurisprudential and legal developments and to ensure that the rule of law applies inside Canadian prisons. The continuing relevance of *habeas corpus* is also at stake in a changing social and legal environment. In the case of prisons, access to relief in the nature of *habeas corpus* is critical in order to ensure that prisoners' rights are respected. Accordingly, we will review and discuss five subjects: (1) the nature of *habeas corpus*; (2) the *Miller, Cardinal* and *Morin* trilogy (*R v. Miller*, [1985] 2 SCR 613; *Cardinal v. Director of Kent Institution*, [1985] 2 SCR 643; *Morin v. National Special Handling Review Committee*, [1985] 2 SCR 662) and the concurrent jurisdiction of the superior courts and of the Federal Court; (3) the rise of a limited discretion of superior courts to decline to exercise their *habeas corpus* jurisdiction; (4) the expansion of the limited discretion to decline *habeas corpus* jurisdiction in the prison context by provincial courts of appeal; and (5) the need for and protection of federal prisoners' access to *habeas corpus*.

(1) The Nature of Habeas Corpus

[19] The writ of *habeas corpus* is also known as the "Great Writ of Liberty." As early as 1215, the *Magna Carta* entrenched the principle that "[n]o free man shall be seized or imprisoned except by the lawful judgement of his equals or by the law of the land." In the 14th century, the writ of *habeas corpus* was used to compel the production of a prisoner and the cause of his or her detention: W.F. Duker, *A Constitutional History of Habeas Corpus* (1980), at p. 25.

[20] From the 17th to the 20th century, the writ was codified in various *habeas corpus* acts in order to bring clarity and uniformity to its principles and application. The first codification is found in the *Habeas Corpus Act*, 1679 (Engl.), 31 Cha. 2, c. 2. Essentially, the Act ensured that prisoners entitled to relief "would not be thwarted by procedural inadequacy": R.J. Sharpe, *The Law of Habeas Corpus* (2nd ed. 1989), at p. 19.

[21] According to Black J of the United States Supreme Court, *habeas corpus* is "not now and never has been a static, narrow, formalistic remedy; its scope has grown to achieve its grand purpose—the protection of individuals against erosion of their right to be free from wrongful restraints upon their liberty": *Jones v. Cunningham*, 371 US 236

(1962), at p. 243. In his book, Sharpe, at p. 23, describes the traditional form of review available on *habeas corpus* as follows:

> The writ is directed to the gaoler or person having custody or control of the applicant. *It requires that person to return to the court, on the day specified, the body of the applicant and the cause of his detention.* The process focuses upon the cause returned. If the return discloses a lawful cause, the prisoner is remanded; *if the cause returned is insufficient or unlawful, the prisoner is released.* The matter directly at issue is simply the excuse or reason given by the party who is exercising restraint over the applicant. [Emphasis added.]

[22]   *Habeas corpus* is a crucial remedy in the pursuit of two fundamental rights protected by the *Canadian Charter of Rights and Freedoms*: (1) the right to liberty of the person and the right not to be deprived thereof except in accordance with the principles of fundamental justice (s. 7 of the *Charter*); and (2) the right not to be arbitrarily detained or imprisoned (s. 9 of the *Charter*). Accordingly, the *Charter* guarantees the right to *habeas corpus*:

> 10. Everyone has the right on arrest or detention …
>   (c) to have the validity of the detention determined by way of *habeas corpus* and to be released if the detention is not lawful.

[23]   However, the right to seek relief in the nature of *habeas corpus* has not always been given to prisoners challenging internal disciplinary decisions. At common law, for a long time, a person convicted of a felony and sentenced to prison was regarded as being devoid of rights. Convicts lost all civil and proprietary rights. The law regarded them as dead. On that basis, courts had traditionally refused to review the internal decision-making process of prison officials: M. Jackson, *Justice Behind the Walls: Human Rights in Canadian Prisons* (2002), at pp. 47-50. By the end of the 19th century, although the concept of civil death had largely disappeared, the prisoner continued to be viewed in law as a person without rights: M. Jackson, *Prisoners of Isolation: Solitary Confinement in Canada* (1983), at p. 82.

[24]   It was this view that provided the original rationale for Canadian courts' refusal to review the internal decisions of prison officials. The "effect of this hands-off approach was to immunize the prison from public scrutiny through the judicial process and to place prison officials in a position of virtual invulnerability and absolute power over the persons committed to their institutions": Jackson, *Prisoners of Isolation*, at p. 82.

[25]   Shortly after certain serious incidents in federal penitentiaries occurred in the 1970s and reviews of their management took place, this Court abandoned the "hands-off" doctrine and extended judicial review to the decision-making process of prison officials by which prisoners were deprived of their residual liberty. In *Martineau v. Matsqui Institution Disciplinary Board*, [1980] 1 SCR 602, Dickson J (as he then was) laid the cornerstone for the modern theory and practice of judicial review of correctional decisions:

> In the case at bar, the disciplinary board was not under either an express or implied duty to follow a judicial type of procedure, but the board was obliged to find facts affecting a subject and to exercise a form of discretion in pronouncing judgment and penalty. Moreover, the board's decision had the effect of depriving an individual of his liberty by committing him to a "*prison within a prison.*" In these circumstances, elementary justice requires some procedural protection. *The rule of law must run within penitentiary walls.* [Emphasis added; p. 622]

[26] Dickson J made it clear that "*certiorari* avails as a remedy wherever a *public body* has power to decide any matter affecting the rights, interest, property, privileges, or *liberties* of *any person*," including prisoners (pp. 622-23). However, he did not specifically examine whether provincial superior courts have jurisdiction to issue *certiorari* in aid of *habeas corpus* to review the validity of a detention imposed by federal authority. The question would certainly arise in the present case because s. 18 of the *FCA* confers on the Federal Court exclusive jurisdiction to issue *certiorari* against any "federal board, commission or other tribunal." A few years later, a trilogy of cases dealt with this important issue.

(2) The Miller, Cardinal and Morin Trilogy and the Concurrent Jurisdiction of the Superior Courts and the Federal Court

[27] In 1985, in the trilogy of *Miller*, *Cardinal*, and *Morin*, the Court expanded the scope of *habeas corpus* by making the writ available to free inmates from restrictive forms of custody within an institution, without releasing the inmate. *Habeas corpus* could thus free inmates from a "prison within a prison." Each case involved challenges by prisoners of their confinement in administrative segregation and their transfer to a special handling unit. This unit was reserved for particularly dangerous inmates and was characterized by more restrictive confinement.

[28] In *Miller*, Le Dain J., writing for the Court, recognized that confinement in a special handling unit or in administrative segregation is a form of detention that is distinct and separate from that imposed on the general inmate population because it involves a significant reduction in the residual liberty of the inmate. In his view, *habeas corpus* should lie "to challenge the validity of a distinct form of confinement or detention in which the actual physical constraint or deprivation of liberty, as distinct from the mere loss of certain privileges, is more restrictive or severe than the normal one in an institution" (p. 641).

[29] The issue remained, however, whether the remedy should be sought in a provincial superior court or the Federal Court. Le Dain J pointed out that Parliament had made a conscious decision not to include *habeas corpus* in the list of prerogative remedies over which the Federal Court has exclusive jurisdiction. *Habeas corpus* jurisdiction, as an essential safeguard of the liberty interest, could only be affected by express words, which were not present in s. 18(1) of the *FCA* (pp. 624-25). Therefore, *habeas corpus* remained within the long standing inherent jurisdiction conferred to provincial superior court judges appointed under s. 96 of the *Constitution Act, 1867*. To remove that jurisdiction from the provincial superior courts would require clear and direct statutory language such as that used in s. 18(2) of the *FCA* referring to members of the Canadian Forces stationed overseas.

[30] Le Dain J specifically addressed the issue, which arises in these cases, of whether jurisdiction for judicial review of federal boards by the Federal Court under s. 18 of the *FCA* trumped the provincial superior courts' *habeas corpus* jurisdiction. He concluded, without any ambiguity, "that a *provincial superior court has jurisdiction* to issue *certiorari in aid* of *habeas corpus* to review the validity of a detention authorized or imposed by a *federal board, commission or other tribunal* as defined by s. 2 of the Federal Court Act" (p. 626 (emphasis added)).

[31] Throughout his analysis, Le Dain J carefully examined which forum was the most appropriate to review the legality of federal prisoners' detention, with reference to s. 18

of the *FCA*, the importance of local accessibility of the *habeas corpus* remedy, and the problems arising out of concurrent jurisdiction. Dealing with the issue of concurrent jurisdiction, he stated:

> After giving consideration to the two approaches to this issue, I am of the opinion that the better view is that *habeas corpus* should lie to determine the validity of a particular form of confinement in a penitentiary notwithstanding that the same issue may be determined upon *certiorari* in the Federal Court. The proper scope of the availability of *habeas corpus* must be considered first on its own merits, apart from possible problems arising from concurrent or overlapping jurisdiction. *The general importance of this remedy as the traditional means of challenging deprivations of liberty is such that its proper development and adaptation to the modern realities of confinement in a prison setting should not be compromised by concerns about conflicting jurisdiction.* [Emphasis added; pp. 640-41]

[32]   The same reasoning was also applied by this Court in *Cardinal* and *Morin*, the companion cases to *Miller*. In our view, the trilogy supports two distinct propositions. First and foremost, provincial superior courts have jurisdiction to issue *certiorari* in aid of *habeas corpus* in respect of detention in federal penitentiaries in order to protect residual liberty interests. This principle is crucial in these cases. In the prison context, the applicant is thus entitled to choose the forum in which to challenge an allegedly unlawful restriction of liberty. Under *Miller*, if the applicant chooses *habeas corpus*, his or her claim should be dealt with on its merits, without regard to other potential remedies in the Federal Court. The second proposition, which does not arise in these cases, is that *habeas corpus* will lie to determine the validity of the confinement of an inmate in administrative segregation, and if such confinement is found unlawful, to order his or her release into the general inmate population of the institution.

(3) The Emergence of a Limited Discretion to Decline Jurisdiction

[33]   As we have seen, the starting point is that a prisoner is free to choose whether to challenge an unlawful restriction of liberty by way of *habeas corpus* in a provincial superior court or by way of judicial review in the Federal Court. Historically, the writ of *habeas corpus* has never been a discretionary remedy. It is issued as of right, where the applicant successfully challenges the legality of the detention:

> *In principle, habeas corpus is not a discretionary remedy: it issues ex debito justitiae on proper grounds being shown.* It is, however, a writ of right rather than a writ of course, and there is a long-established practice of having a preliminary proceeding to determine whether there is sufficient merit in the application to warrant bringing in the other parties.
>
> This means, simply, that it is not a writ which can be had for the asking upon payment of a court fee, but one which will only be issued where it is made to appear that there are proper grounds. While the court has no discretion to refuse relief, it is still for the court to decide whether proper grounds have been made out to support the application. *The rule that the writ issues ex debito justitiae means simply that the court may only properly refuse relief on the grounds that there is no legal basis for the application and that habeas corpus should never be refused on discretionary ground such as inconvenience.* [Emphasis added.]

(Sharpe, at p. 58)

[34] Thus, as a matter of general principle, *habeas corpus* jurisdiction should not be declined merely because of the existence of an alternative remedy. Whether the other remedy is still available or whether the applicant has foregone the right to use it, its existence should not preclude or affect the right to apply for *habeas corpus* to the Superior Court of the province: Sharpe, at p. 59.

[35] However, given that alternative remedies to *habeas corpus* are often available and in consideration of the development of various forms of judicial review and of rights of appeal in the law of civil and criminal procedure, questions have arisen as to the proper scope of the traditional writ of *habeas corpus* and about the existence of a discretion of superior courts to decline jurisdiction. Courts have sometimes refused to grant relief in the form of *habeas corpus* because an appeal or another statutory route to a court was thought to be more appropriate. The obvious policy reason behind this exception is the need to restrict the growth of collateral methods of attacking convictions or other deprivations of liberty: Sharpe, at pp. 59-60. So far, these situations have primarily arisen in two different contexts.

[36] Strictly speaking, in the criminal context, *habeas corpus* cannot be used to challenge the legality of a conviction. The remedy of *habeas corpus* is not a substitute for the exercise by prisoners of their right of appeal: see *In re Trepanier* (1885), 12 SCR 111; *Re Sproule* (1886), 12 SCR 140, at p. 204; *Goldhar v. The Queen*, [1960] SCR 431, at p. 439; *Morrison v. The Queen*, [1966] SCR 356; *Karchesky v. The Queen*, [1967] SCR 547, at p. 551; *Korponay v. Kulik*, [1980] 2 SCR 265.

[37] Our Court reaffirmed this in *R v. Gamble*, [1988] 2 SCR 595. In *Gamble*, the Court considered *inter alia* whether a superior court judge should have declined to exercise his *habeas corpus* jurisdiction. The appellant had been denied parole eligibility because of a pre-*Charter* law, the continued application of which was alleged to violate the *Charter*.

[38] Wilson J, writing for the majority, found that while superior courts do have the discretion not to exercise their *habeas corpus* jurisdiction, this discretion should "be exercised with due regard to the constitutionally mandated need to provide prompt and effective enforcement of *Charter* rights" (p. 634). Considering the argument that *habeas corpus* jurisdiction should not be asserted because a parallel mechanism already exists in the Federal Court, she held that the assertion of *Charter* rights by way of *habeas corpus* does not create a parallel system and that those who argued that jurisdiction should be declined on this basis did "no credit to that existing system by attempting to place procedural roadblocks in the way of someone like the appellant who is seeking to vindicate one of the citizens' most fundamental rights in the traditional and appropriate forum" (p. 635). However, referring to the criminal process, she ultimately confirmed that:

> Under section 24(1) of the Charter courts should not allow habeas corpus *applications to be*
> *used to circumvent the appropriate appeal process,* but neither should they bind themselves
> by overly rigid rules about the availability of *habeas corpus* which may have the effect of
> denying applicants access to courts to obtain *Charter* relief. [Emphasis added; p. 642.]

[39] A second limitation to the scope of *habeas corpus* has gradually developed in the field of immigration law. It is now well established that courts have a limited discretion to refuse to entertain applications for prerogative relief in immigration matters: *Pringle v. Fraser*, [1972] SCR 821; *Peiroo v. Canada (Minister of Employment and Immigration)*

(1989), 69 OR (2d) 253 (CA) (leave to appeal denied, [1989] 2 SCR x). In the words of Catzman JA in *Peiroo*:

> Parliament has established in the [*Immigration Act*], particularly in the recent amendments which specifically address the disposition of claims of persons in the position of the appellant, a *comprehensive scheme* to regulate the determination of such claims and to provide for review and appeal in the Federal Court of Canada of decisions and orders made under the Act, the ambit of which review and appeal *is as broad as or broader than* the traditional scope of review by way of *habeas corpus* with *certiorari* in aid. In the absence of any showing that the available review and appeal process established by Parliament is *inapprop riate or less advantageous* than the *habeas corpus* jurisdiction of the Supreme Court of Ontario, it is my view that this court should, in the exercise of its discretion, decline to grant relief upon the application for *habeas corpus* in the present case, which clearly falls within the purview of that *statutory review and appeal process*. [Emphasis added; pp. 261-62]

[40]   In *Reza v. Canada*, [1994] 2 SCR 394, the trial judge refused to hear a constitutional challenge to the *Immigration Act* brought in provincial superior court. The Court confirmed once again that the trial judge "properly exercised his discretion on the basis that Parliament had created a *comprehensive scheme of review of immigration matters* and the Federal Court was an effective and appropriate forum" (p. 405). Thus, it can be seen from these cases that, in matters of immigration law, because Parliament has put in place a complete, comprehensive and expert statutory scheme which provides for a review at least as broad as that available by way of *habeas corpus* and no less advantageous, *habeas corpus* is precluded.

[41]   From the two recognized exceptions to the availability of *habeas corpus*—criminal appeals and the "*Peiroo* exception," adopted in *Reza*—we turn now to the decision of this Court in *Steele v. Mountain Institution*, [1990] 2 SCR 1385. *Steele* has on occasion been thought, mistakenly in our view, to have established a rule of general application barring access to *habeas corpus* whenever an alternative remedy is available. In light of the unusual circumstances of that case, we think it important to consider more closely its true significance.

[42]   The issue here is not whether the result in *Steele* was justified in the circumstances—we believe that it was—but whether *Steele* created a fresh and independent exception to the availability of *habeas corpus*. In our view, it did not. *Steele* was the product of a convergent set of unusual facts and can only be understood in that light. Without any discussion of the principles governing access to *habeas corpus*, the Court in *Steele* granted that remedy while questioning its availability. No judicial barrier to the venerable right to *habeas corpus*, now constitutionalized in Canada, can be made to rest on so fragile a jurisprudential foundation.

[43]   Nor should this Court's decision in *Idziak v. Canada (Minister of Justice)*, [1992] 3 SCR 631, be thought to have decided otherwise: the Court did not in that case elevate the result in *Steele* into a principled rule barring access to *habeas corpus* in matters not caught by the two recognized exceptions set out above. The decisive issue in *Idziak* was whether Parliament had created with respect to extradition a comprehensive statutory scheme similar to the scheme created by Parliament for immigration matters. The Court held that it had not. Accordingly, there was no reason for provincial superior courts to decline to exercise their *habeas corpus* jurisdiction where the impugned detention resulted from proceedings in extradition.

[44] To sum up therefore, the jurisprudence of this Court establishes that prisoners may choose to challenge the legality of a decision affecting their residual liberty either in a provincial superior court by way of *habeas corpus* or in the Federal Court by way of judicial review. As a matter of principle, a provincial superior court should exercise its jurisdiction when it is requested to do so. *Habeas corpus* jurisdiction should not be declined merely because another alternative remedy exists and would appear as or more convenient in the eyes of the court. The option belongs to the applicant. Only in limited circumstances will it be appropriate for a provincial superior court to decline to exercise its *habeas corpus* jurisdiction. For instance, in criminal law, where a statute confers jurisdiction on a court of appeal to correct the errors of a lower court and release the applicant if need be, *habeas corpus* will not be available (i.e. *Gamble*). Jurisdiction should also be declined where there is in place a complete, comprehensive and expert procedure for review of an administrative decision (i.e. *Pringle* and *Peiroo*).

(4) The Expansion of the Limited Discretion to Decline Habeas Corpus Jurisdiction in the Prison Context by Provincial Courts of Appeal

[45] The British Columbia Court of Appeal, in these cases and in *Hickey*, and the Ontario Court of Appeal in *Spindler*, each discussed earlier, have recently restricted access to relief in the form of *habeas corpus* in the provincial superior courts. The respondents rely heavily on this line of decisions to support the position that superior courts should generally decline jurisdiction in favour of statutory judicial review when it is available. If such an approach were to be accepted by our Court, the *habeas corpus* jurisdiction of superior courts might be significantly curtailed. It might evolve into a discretionary residual jurisdiction, available only when everything else has failed. Such a result would be inconsistent with this Court's jurisprudence. Given their importance in the courts below, we will now review and comment on *Hickey* and *Spindler*.

[46] In *Hickey*, an inmate who was serving a life sentence was ordered to be transferred to a special handling unit. The inmate opposed the transfer by way of *habeas corpus* instead of using the internal grievance procedures or applying by way of judicial review to the Federal Court. Ryan JA, for the British Columbia Court of Appeal, ultimately held that the trial judge had jurisdiction. However, referring to *Steele*, she further stated:

> It is trite that the court has a discretion to refuse to entertain an application for *habeas corpus* if there exists a viable alternative to the writ. *In the context of prison law the fact that there is in place a complete, comprehensive and expert procedure for review of a decision affecting the prisoner's confinement is a factor which militates against hearing a petition for habeas corpus.* But there will be exceptions. ...
>
> *In the case at bar the appellant provided the Supreme Court with no explanation as to why he had not pursued either the grievance procedures or judicial review to the Federal Court.* Without any information setting out why these procedures were inadequate to deal with Mr. Hickey's situation, the Chambers judge ought not to have heard the application for *habeas corpus*. [Emphasis added; paras. 50 and 53]

> (See also the companion case to *Hickey, Bernard v. Kent Institution*, [2003] BCJ No. 62 (QL), 2003 BCCA 24, at paras. 6-7.)

[47] In *Spindler*, the inmates were serving life sentences for murder and were incarcerated in a maximum-security penitentiary. They applied for *habeas corpus* claiming that

their detention was illegal and seeking an order directing that they be moved to "a penitentiary of a lower security level." The motions judge stated that he had jurisdiction to consider the *habeas corpus* application but declined to do so holding that the Federal Court was the more appropriate forum. Doherty JA dismissed the appeal. Relying on *Steele* and agreeing with *Hickey*, he said:

> As I read Steele, supra, except in exceptional circumstances, a provincial superior court should decline to exercise its habeas corpus jurisdiction where the application is in essence, a challenge to the exercise of a statutory power granted under a federal statute to a federally appointed individual or tribunal. Those challenges are specifically assigned to the Federal Court under the Federal Court Act RSC 1985 c. F-7 s. 18, s. 28. By directing such challenges to the Federal Court, Parliament has recognized that individuals or tribunals exercising statutory powers under federal authority must exercise those powers across the country. It is important that judicial interpretations as to the nature and scope of those powers be as uniform and consistent as possible. *By giving the Federal Court jurisdiction over these challenges, Parliament has provided the means by which uniformity and consistency can be achieved while at the same time, facilitating the development of an expertise over these matters in the Federal Court.* [Emphasis added; para. 19]

[48]   Finally, in the case at bar, Ryan JA, for the British Columbia Court of Appeal, relied on *Hickey* and *Spindler* to support her conclusion that the Chambers judge ought to have refused to hear the application for *habeas corpus*. She further explained:

> In my view the observations of Doherty JA, with regard to the importance of pursuing remedies in the Federal Court are particularly apt in the case at bar. While the issues raised in the cases at bar may not be identical to those raised in *Spindler, supra*, all, like *Spindler*, involve policy and procedure adopted by the Commissioner in determining the security classifications of the appellants. *In my view these cases ought to have been heard by that specialized court.*
>
> *The appellants have offered no reasonable explanation for failing to pursue judicial review in the Federal Court.* In my view, the Chambers judge in this case ought to have refused to hear the applications in this case. [Emphasis added; paras. 21-22]

[49]   The position adopted by the British Columbia Court of Appeal and the Ontario Court of Appeal can be summarized as follows. First, the court has a discretion to refuse to entertain an application for *habeas corpus* if there exists a viable alternative to the writ. Second, in the context of prison law, the existence of a complete, comprehensive and expert procedure for review of a decision affecting the prisoner's confinement is a factor which militates against hearing a petition for *habeas corpus*. Third, by giving the Federal Court jurisdiction over these challenges, Parliament has provided the means by which uniformity and consistency can be achieved while at the same time facilitating the development of an expertise over these matters in the Federal Court. Fourth, except in exceptional circumstances, a provincial superior court should decline to exercise its *habeas corpus* jurisdiction where the application is, in essence, a challenge to the exercise of a statutory power granted under a federal statute to a federally appointed tribunal. And fifth, the applicant has to provide a reasonable explanation as to why he or she has not pursued either the grievance procedures or judicial review to the Federal Court.

[50]   Given the historical importance of *habeas corpus* in the protection of various liberty interests, jurisprudential developments limiting *habeas corpus* jurisdiction should

be carefully evaluated and should not be allowed to expand unchecked. The exceptions to *habeas corpus* jurisdiction and the circumstances under which a superior court may decline jurisdiction should be well defined and limited. In our view, the propositions articulated by the Court of Appeal in these cases, as in *Hickey* and *Spindler*, unduly limit the scope and availability of *habeas corpus* review and are incompatible with this Court's jurisprudence. With respect, we are unable to reconcile this narrow view of superior court jurisdiction with the broad approach adopted by the *Miller* trilogy and confirmed in subsequent cases. In principle, the governing rule is that provincial superior courts should exercise their jurisdiction. However, in accordance with this Court's decisions, provincial superior courts should decline *habeas corpus* jurisdiction only where (1) a statute such as the *Criminal Code*, RSC 1985, c. C-46, confers jurisdiction on a court of appeal to correct the errors of a lower court and release the applicant if need be or (2) the legislator has put in place complete, comprehensive and expert procedure for review of an administrative decision.

(5) Confirming Federal Prisoners' Access to Habeas Corpus

[51] The British Columbia Court of Appeal erred in barring access to *habeas corpus* in these cases. Neither of the two recognized exceptions to the general rule that the superior courts should exercise *habeas corpus* jurisdiction are applicable here. The first exception has no application in these cases because they do not involve a criminal conviction, but rather administrative decisions in the prison context. The second exception does not apply since, for the reasons explained below, Parliament has not enacted a complete, comprehensive and expert procedure for review of a decision affecting the confinement of prisoners. Moreover, as will be shown below, a purposive approach to the issues that arise here also clearly favours a concurrency of jurisdiction.

[52] The respondents argue that the same reasoning that applies to immigration cases should apply to prison law. In their view, Parliament has created a comprehensive statutory scheme, in the *Corrections and Conditional Release Act*, SC 1992, c. 20 ("*CCRA*"), and its regulations, for the resolution of inmate grievances, including those relating to decisions to transfer, segregate or otherwise restrict liberty.

[53] The respondents contend that the scheme dovetails with Parliament's intention that review of such matters generally occurs in the Federal Court. The scheme is specifically tailored to individuals who are incarcerated and provides internal grievances or appeals for decisions that have an impact upon the liberty of inmates. Many of the decisions made by correction officers require the application of policy developed in the specialized circumstances of the federal prison system. According to the respondents, the Federal Court has acquired considerable expertise in reviewing the decisions of grievance boards.

[54] We must therefore examine the legal and regulatory framework of inmate classification in the federal penitentiary system in order to determine whether Parliament has put in place a complete statutory code for the administration and review of inmates' grievances. The starting point is the administrative decision by which inmates are classified for security purposes. By virtue of s. 30(1) of the *CCRA*, CSC "shall assign a security classification of maximum, medium or minimum to each inmate." Security classifications are made pursuant to the statutory factors provided for in ss. 17 and 18 of the *Corrections and Conditional Release Regulations*, SOR/92-620 ("*Regulations*").

[55] As a matter of principle, CSC must use the "least restrictive measures consistent with the protection of the public, staff members and offenders": s. 4(d) of the *CCRA*. Where a person is to be confined in a penitentiary, CSC must provide the "least restrictive environment for that person" taking into account specific criteria: s. 28 of the *CCRA*. Section 30(2) of the *CCRA* further provides that CSC "shall give each inmate reasons, in writing, for assigning a particular security classification or for changing that classification." Of course, correctional decisions, including security classifications, must "be made in a forthright and fair manner, with access by the offender to an effective grievance procedure": s. 4(g) of the *CCRA*.

[56] Inmates who are dissatisfied with transfer decisions can grieve the decisions through the correction system. Sections 90 and 91 of the *CCRA* establish the general framework for the inmate grievance procedure. The *CCRA* requires that inmates have access to a fair and expeditious grievance procedure, to be prescribed by regulation and Commissioner's Directives: ss. 96(u), 97 and 98. The nuts and bolts of the procedure are found in ss. 74 to 82 of the *Regulations*. The process allows inmates to pursue any complaint up the successive administrative rungs of CSC so that supervisors are reviewing the actions of their subordinates. Pursuant to s. 74(1) of the *Regulations*, when an inmate is unhappy with an action or a decision of a staff member, the inmate may submit a complaint to the staff member's supervisor. Written complaints by offenders are to be resolved informally if at all possible. If complaints are not resolved to the satisfaction of the inmate, he or she has access to the grievance procedure.

[57] The grievance procedure has essentially three levels. At the first level, if the inmate is dissatisfied with the resolution of a complaint by the staff member's supervisor, the inmate can grieve to the Warden of the institution: s. 75(a) of the *Regulations*. At the second level, if the inmate is dissatisfied with the Warden's decision, or if the Warden is the origin of the complaint, the inmate may bring a grievance to the Regional Head: s. 75(b) and 80(1) of the *Regulations*. At the third level, if the inmate is dissatisfied with the Regional Head's response, the inmate may grieve directly to the Commissioner of Corrections: s. 80(2) of the *Regulations*. The Commissioner has delegated his or her authority as the final decision-maker with respect to grievances to the Assistant Commissioner: ss. 18 and 19 of the *Commissioner's Directive 081*, "Offender Complaints and Grievances," 2002-03-04 ("*CD 081*"). Ultimately, by virtue of ss. 2 and 18 of the *FCA*, the inmate may challenge the fairness and *Charter* compliance of the decision at the third level by way of judicial review before the Federal Court.

[58] As mentioned earlier, the law requires that inmates have access to an effective, fair and expeditious grievance procedure. As a result, the inmate is entitled to written reasons at all levels of the grievance procedure: ss. 74(3), 74(5), 77(3), 79(3) and 80(3) of the *Regulations*. Naturally, the inmate is required to participate in the resolution process and *CD 081* requires that confidentiality of complaints and grievances be preserved "to the greatest possible extent" (ss. 6(c) and 6(e)). The *Regulations* also prescribe that decisions on complaints and grievances must be issued "as soon as practicable": ss. 74(3), 74(5), 77(3), 79(3) and 80(3); see also ss. 6(d), 7 and 8 of *CD 081* for a more precise timetable. Finally, the institution must show that corrective action is taken when a grievance is upheld: s. 10 of *CD 081*.

[59] The question before us is whether the grievance procedure is a complete, comprehensive and expert procedure for review of an inmate's security classification. In *Pringle*, Laskin J (as he then was), writing for the Court, held:

> *I am satisfied that in the context of the overall scheme for the administration of immigration policy the words in s. 22 ("sole and exclusive jurisdiction to hear and determine all questions of fact or law, including questions of jurisdiction") are adequate not only to endow the Board with the stated authority but to exclude any other court or tribunal from entertaining any type of proceedings*, be they by way of *certiorari* or otherwise, in relation to the matters so confided exclusively to the Board. [Emphasis added; p. 826]

[60] The decisive issue for Laskin J therefore was the intention of the legislature to grant exclusive jurisdiction to the Board. However, there is no such language in the *CCRA* or in the *Regulations*. In fact, it is clear that it was not the intention of the Governor-in-Council, the regulator, to grant paramountcy to the grievance procedure over the superior courts' *habeas corpus* jurisdiction. Section 81(1) of the *Regulations* provides:

> 81(1) Where an offender decides to pursue a *legal remedy* for the offender's complaint or grievance in addition to the complaint and grievance procedure referred to in these Regulations, *the review of the complaint or grievance pursuant to these Regulations shall be deferred until a decision on the alternate remedy is rendered* or the offender decides to abandon the alternate remedy.

[61] Section 81(1) makes it clear that the regulator contemplated the possibility that an inmate may choose to pursue a legal remedy, such as an application for *habeas corpus*, in addition to filing an administrative grievance under the *Regulations*. The legal remedy supersedes the grievance procedure. The regulator did not intend to bar federal prisoners' access to *habeas corpus*. But there is more.

[62] In our view, the grievance procedure can and should be distinguished from the immigration context for several other reasons. The scheme of review which militated against the exercise of *habeas corpus* jurisdiction in *Pringle* and *Peiroo* is substantially different than the grievance procedure provided in the *CCRA*. The *Immigration Act* in force at the time of *Peiroo* provided for an appeal from decisions of immigration authorities to an independent administrative tribunal, the Immigration Appeal Division, vested with all the powers of a superior court of record including jurisdiction to issue summons, administer oaths and enforce its orders: s. 71.4(2). It was a process wherein the impartiality of the adjudicator was statutorily assured, the grounds for review were articulated, and the process for review was clearly laid out: ss. 63, 64 and 71.4-78. A detailed procedure was also provided for the manner in which applications and appeals were to be brought before the Federal Court: ss. 83.1-85.2.

[63] In contrast, the internal grievance process set out in the *CCRA* prescribes the review of decisions made by *prison authorities by other prison authorities*. Thus, in a case where the legality of a Commissioner's policy is contested, it cannot be reasonably expected that the decision-maker, who is subordinate to the Commissioner, could fairly and impartially decide the issue. It is also noteworthy that there are no remedies set out in the *CCRA* and its regulations and no articulated grounds upon which grievances may be reviewed. Lastly, the decisions with respect to grievances are not legally enforceable. In *Peiroo*, the

Ontario Court of Appeal emphasized that Parliament had put in place a complete, comprehensive and expert statutory scheme that provided for a review at least as broad as *habeas corpus* and no less advantageous. That is clearly not the case in this appeal.

[64]   Therefore, in view of the structural weaknesses of the grievance procedure, there is no justification for importing the line of reasoning adopted in the immigration law context. In the prison context, Parliament has not yet enacted a comprehensive scheme of review and appeal similar to the immigration scheme. The same conclusion was previously reached in *Idziak* with regard to extradition (pp. 652-53).

[65]   As we have seen, these cases do not fall within the recognized exceptions where a provincial superior court should decline to exercise its *habeas corpus* jurisdiction. The respondents submit that this Court should assess the *habeas corpus* jurisdiction of the superior courts purposively by acknowledging that the statutory scheme provides for effective and comparable remedies. A purposive approach, however, also requires that we look at the entire context. In our view, the following five factors militate in favour of concurrent jurisdiction and provide additional support for the position that a provincial superior court should hear *habeas corpus* applications from federal prisoners: (1) the choice of remedies and forum; (2) the expertise of provincial superior courts; (3) the timeliness of the remedy; (4) local access to the remedy; and (5) the nature of the remedy and the burden of proof.

[66]   First, in the prison context, the applicant may choose either to seek relief in the provincial superior courts or in the Federal Court. In *Idziak*, this Court noted that the applicants in the *Miller*, *Cardinal* and *Morin* trilogy each had a choice of whether to seek a remedy in the provincial superior courts or in Federal Court. The applicants' decision to resort to the provincial superior courts for their remedy was accepted (pp. 651-52).

[67]   Furthermore and as noted previously, this Court recognized in *Miller* that the availability of *habeas corpus* "must be considered first on its own merits, apart from possible problems arising from concurrent or overlapping jurisdiction. The general importance of this remedy as the traditional means of challenging deprivations of liberty is such that its proper development and adaptation to the modern realities of confinement in a prison setting should not be compromised by concerns about conflicting jurisdiction" (p. 641).

[68]   Second, the greater expertise of the Federal Court in correctional matters is not conclusively established. The Federal Court has considerable familiarity in federal administrative law and procedure and deservedly enjoys a strong reputation in these parts of the law as in other federal matters. On the other hand, prison law revolves around the application of *Charter* principles in respect of which provincial superior courts are equally well versed. Moreover, prison law and life in the penal institution remain closely connected with the administration of criminal justice, in which the superior courts play a critical role on a daily basis. In this context, we find no strong grounds for the adoption of a policy of deference in favour of judicial review in the Federal Court.

[69]   Third, a hearing on a *habeas corpus* application in the Supreme Court of British Columbia can be obtained more rapidly than a hearing on a judicial review application in the Federal Court. Rule 4 of the *Criminal Rules of the Supreme Court of British Columbia*, SI/97-140, provides for a hearing of a *habeas corpus* application on six days notice. In contrast, the request for hearing a judicial review application in the Federal Court is filed at day 160 following the impugned decision, if all time limits have run completely: s. 18.1(2) of the *FCA* and Rules 301-314 of the Federal Court Rules, 1998, SOR/98-106.

This is a matter of great significance for prisoners unlawfully deprived of their liberty. It is also relevant if counsel is acting *pro bono* or on limited legal aid funding or if the prisoner is representing himself. The importance of the interests at stake militates in favour of a quick resolution of the issues.

[70] Fourth, relief in the form of *habeas corpus* is locally accessible to prisoners in provincial superior courts. Access to justice is closely linked to timeliness of relief. Moreover, it would be unfair if federal prisoners did not have the same access to *habeas corpus* as do provincial prisoners. Section 10(c) of the *Charter* does not support such a distinction. In *Gamble*, Wilson J recognized the importance of access by federal prisoners to the superior courts of the province where they are incarcerated:

> This Court has previously recognized "*the importance of the local accessibility of this remedy*" of *habeas corpus* because of the traditional role of the court as "a safeguard of the liberty of the subject": *R v. Miller*, [1985] 2 SCR 613, at pp. 624-25. *Relief in the form of habeas corpus should not be withheld for reasons of mere convenience.* [Emphasis added; p. 635]

[71] Finally, a writ of *habeas corpus* is issued as of right where the applicant shows that there is cause to doubt the legality of his detention: Sharpe, at p. 58. In contrast, on judicial review, the Federal Court can deny relief on discretionary grounds: D.J. Mullan, *Administrative Law* (2001), at p. 481. Also, on *habeas corpus*, so long as the prisoner has raised a legitimate ground upon which to question the legality of the deprivation of liberty, the onus is on the respondent to justify the lawfulness of the detention: Sharpe, at pp. 86-88. However, on judicial review, the onus is on the applicant to demonstrate that the "federal board, commission or other tribunal" has made an error: s. 18.1(4) of the *FCA*.

[72] Our review of the relevant factors favours the concurrent jurisdiction approach. This approach properly recognizes the importance of affording prisoners a meaningful and significant access to justice in order to protect their liberty rights, a *Charter* value. Timely judicial oversight, in which provincial superior courts must play a concurrent if not predominant role, is still necessary to safeguard the human rights and civil liberties of prisoners, and to ensure that the rule of law applies within penitentiary walls.

B. Have the Appellants Been Unlawfully Deprived of Their Liberty?

[73] Having concluded that the British Columbia Court of Appeal erred in finding that the Chambers judge should have declined to exercise his *habeas corpus* jurisdiction, we must now consider whether the Chambers judge erred in denying the appellants' *habeas corpus* application on its merit.

[74] A successful application for *habeas corpus* requires two elements: (1) a deprivation of liberty and (2) that the deprivation be unlawful. The onus of making out a deprivation of liberty rests on the applicant. The onus of establishing the lawfulness of that deprivation rests on the detaining authority.

[75] With respect to the first element of *habeas corpus*, the appellants claim that transfer to a more restrictive institutional setting deprives them of their residual liberty. With respect to the second element of *habeas corpus*, the appellants contend that the deprivation of their residual liberty was unlawful because it was arbitrary and violated CSC's statutory duty to disclose entrenched in s. 27(1) of the *CCRA*.

(1) Deprivation of Liberty

[76] The decision to transfer an inmate to a more restrictive institutional setting constitutes a deprivation of his or her residual liberty: *Miller*, at p. 637; *Dumas v. Leclerc Institute*, [1986] 2 SCR 459, at p. 464. As a result, there is no question that the appellants have discharged their burden of making out a deprivation of liberty. We must therefore go on to consider whether that deprivation was lawful.

(2) Lawfulness of the Deprivation of Liberty

[77] A deprivation of liberty will only be lawful where it is within the jurisdiction of the decision-maker. Absent express provision to the contrary, administrative decisions must be made in accordance with the *Charter*. Administrative decisions that violate the *Charter* are null and void for lack of jurisdiction: *Slaight Communications Inc. v. Davidson*, [1989] 1 SCR 1038, at p. 1078. Section 7 of the *Charter* provides that an individual's liberty cannot be impinged upon except in accordance with the principles of fundamental justice. Administrative decisions must also be made in accordance with the common law duty of procedural fairness and requisite statutory duties. Transfer decisions engaging inmates' liberty interest must therefore respect those requirements.

[78] The appellants raise two arguments with respect to the lawfulness of the deprivation in these cases. First, they argue that the transfer decisions were arbitrary because they were solely based on a change in policy, in the absence of any "fresh" misconduct on their part. Second, they submit that the respondents did not comply with their duty of disclosure by withholding a relevant scoring matrix. We will consider each argument in turn.

[LeBel and Fish JJ then proceeded to examine the reclassification and transfer decisions and whether the processes under the new policy complied with the duty to act fairly. The significant issue was the failure of the CSC to disclose the scoring matrix used to weight the various factors used in the Security Reclassification Scale to produce a score. This score led to the transfer of the prisoners to higher security.]

[110] In our view, the information provided by the respondents to the courts below as to the nature and role of the matrix was misleading. At the hearing before this Court, counsel for the respondents indicated that, at the time of the reclassifications, the scoring matrix was not available because it was the practice not to produce it. Counsel explained that it was thought to be a duplication of information already disclosed.

[111] The new evidence clearly provides information on the numerical values to be assigned to each factor and to the manner in which a final score is generated by the computerized tool. Given that the appellants had repeatedly requested this information—and not solely the factors used to establish their security classification—it is disingenuous to suggest that the information was believed to be duplicative. This behaviour is highly objectionable. The Chambers judge was falsely led to believe that the scoring matrix was not available when, in fact, it was.

[112] The new evidence confirmed that the scoring matrix existed. The duty to disclose information used in making transfer decisions is substantial. Therefore, if the scores generated by the computerized tool played a role in the transfer decisions, its scoring matrix

should have been disclosed. In fact, it does appear that the scores generated by the computerized tool played an important role. As a result, the transfer decisions were unlawful.

[113]   An analysis of SOP directives reveals that inmates were presumptively reclassified through the use of the SRS. SOP 700-14 states that security reclassification shall be determined primarily by using the SRS (paras. 1-18). The SRS classification is only subject to variation in limited situations. Discretion is provided when the score in within 5 per cent of the sanctioned cut-off values: SRSFS, at pp. 9-10. In other cases, no discretion is allowed. The SRS classification may not be modified unless an override security classification is relied upon.

[114]   The procedure applicable to the override classification confirms the presumptive nature of the SRS rather than invalidating it. SOP 700-14 makes it clear that the override is not normally relied upon and requires a detailed justification for bypassing the SRS score:

> Normally, there will be no overrides above or below the rating produced by the Custody Rating Scale or the Security Reclassification Scale. Where the caseworker believes that it is necessary to override or underride the results of the Custody Rating Scale or the Security Reclassification Scale, he/she shall include a detailed justification in the *Assessment for Decision* in conformity with section 18 of the *Corrections and Conditional Release Regulations*, by setting out the analysis under the three headings of institutional adjustment, escape risk and risk to public safety. [para. 23]

[115]   The override must also be approved by a supervisor or, in some cases, by the Assistant Commissioner, Correctional Operations and Programs (para. 25). It is noteworthy that the override function was not used in the instant cases. This suggests that the computer application ultimately fixed the security classification of each appellant.

[116]   Based on the evidence, we cannot accept the respondents' argument that the SRS was only a preliminary assessment tool. Although it is true that an individual assessment of each inmate's security classification is made subsequently to the SRS assessment, in our view, the SRS presumptively classifies inmates and constitutes an important aspect of the classification process.

[117]   Considering the nature of the scoring matrix and its role in the SRS, its non-disclosure constituted a major breach of the duty to disclose inherent in the requirement of procedural fairness. The appellants were deprived of information essential to understanding the computerized system which generated their scores. The appellants were not given the formula used to weigh the factors or the documents used for scoring questions and answers. The appellants knew what the factors were, but did not know how values were assigned to them or how those values factored into the generation of the final score.

[118]   How can there be a meaningful response to a reclassification decision without information explaining how the security rating is determined? As a matter of logic and common sense, the scoring tabulation and methodology associated with the SRS classification score should have been made available. The importance of making that information available stems from the fact that inmates may want to rebut the evidence relied upon for the calculation of the SRS score and security classification. This information may be critical in circumstances where a security classification depends on the weight attributed to one specific factor.

[119]   Hence, given the importance of the information contained in the scoring matrix, the presumptive validity of the score and its potential effect on the determination of

security classification, it should have been disclosed. The respondents had a duty to do so under s. 27(1) of the *CCRA*.

[120] In conclusion, the respondents failed to disclose all the relevant information or a summary of the information used in making the transfer decisions despite several requests by the appellants. The respondents concealed crucial information. In doing so, they violated their statutory duty. The transfer decisions were made improperly and, therefore, they are null and void for want of jurisdiction. It follows that the appellants were unlawfully deprived of their liberty.

V. Conclusion

[121] For the foregoing reasons, the appeal should be allowed. The applications for *habeas corpus* and the motion to adduce new evidence are granted. The transfer decisions are declared null and void for want of jurisdiction. The appellant still incarcerated in a medium-security institution pursuant to the impugned decision is thus to be returned to minimum-security institutions.

[Although the court was unanimous on the *habeas corpus* issue, it split on the breach-of-fairness question and the appellants' entitlement to a remedy.]

CHARRON J (Major and Bastarache JJ concurring) (dissenting):

[122] I have considered the reasons of LeBel and Fish JJ and agree that the Supreme Court of British Columbia has properly exercised its *habeas corpus* jurisdiction in this matter. I also agree with their analysis on the limited circumstances in which a superior court should decline to exercise its jurisdiction in *habeas corpus* matters. However, I do not agree with their conclusion that the appellants have been unlawfully deprived of their liberty and therefore I would not interfere with the Chambers judge's dismissal of their applications for *habeas corpus*.

• • •

[125] On the procedural fairness issue, my colleagues aptly reject the appellants' contention that *Stinchcombe* disclosure requirements apply (*R v. Stinchcombe*, [1991] 3 SCR 326). They describe the applicable statutory duty of disclosure in this administrative context. I agree with this analysis. I also agree in the circumstances of these cases that the "scoring matrix," utilized to compute the SRS score, should have been disclosed to the appellants. However, I respectfully disagree with my colleagues' conclusion that the failure to provide this information constituted a breach of statutory duty rendering the transfer decisions null and void for want of jurisdiction. It is not every instance of non-disclosure that deprives the decision-maker of its jurisdiction. As I will explain, in these cases, each appellant was provided with sufficient information to know the case he had to meet.

NOTE

There is a curious aspect to this reversal by the Supreme Court of what had quickly become a national trend to encourage, or at least condone, decisions by Superior Court judges not to hear *habeas corpus* applications brought by penitentiary prisoners. In *May v Ferndale*, the underlying decision of the BC Court of Appeal favouring a deferral to the Federal Court relied heavily on the judgment of the Ontario Court of Appeal in *Spindler v Warden of Millhaven Institution* (2003), 15 CR (6th) 183 (Ont CA). If you look at the ruling in *Spindler*, you will see that Justice Charron, while a member of the Ontario Court of Appeal, concurred in that decision. To her credit, she brought an open mind to the issue when both she and it reached Ottawa.

Following the important decision in *May v Ferndale*, the scope of review on *habeas corpus* returned to the Supreme Court of Canada in *Mission v Khela*, below. It raised the question of whether reasonableness, as explained in *Dunsmuir v New Brunswick*, 2008 SCC 9, applied to *habeas corpus*.

Mission Institution v Khela
2014 SCC 24, [2014] SCR 502

LeBEL J (McLachlin CJ, Abella, Rothstein, Cromwell, Moldaver, Karakatsanis, and Wagner JJ concurring):

[1] This case arises from a decision of correctional authorities to transfer a federal inmate from a medium security institution to a maximum security institution on an emergency and involuntary basis. In response to the transfer decision, the inmate filed an application for relief in the form of *habeas corpus* on the grounds that the decision taken was unreasonable and that it was procedurally unfair.

[2] At issue in this case is the state of the law with respect to the writ of *habeas corpus*. In particular, this Court must clarify the scope of a provincial superior court's review power on an application for *habeas corpus* made by a prison inmate. The first question before the Court is whether on such an application a provincial superior court may rule on the reasonableness of an administrative decision to transfer an inmate to a higher security institution or whether the reasonableness of the decision must be dealt with by the Federal Court on an application for judicial review. The second question concerns the information that must be disclosed to ensure that a transfer decision is procedurally fair.

[3] In my view, superior courts are entitled to review an inmate transfer decision for reasonableness on an application for *habeas corpus* with *certiorari* in aid. If a decision is unreasonable, it will be unlawful. Support for this conclusion can be found in the nature of the writ, in past court decisions regarding the writ, and in the importance of swift access to justice for those who have been unlawfully deprived of their liberty.

[4] Moreover, it is well established that a superior court hearing a *habeas corpus* application may also review a transfer decision for procedural fairness. The statute at issue in this case, the *Corrections and Conditional Release Act*, S.C. 1992, c. 20 ("*CCRA*"), outlines the disclosure that is required for a reviewing court to find such a decision fair, and therefore lawful.

[5] In this case, the correctional authorities did not comply with the statutory disclosure requirements. The breach of the statutory requirements rendered the decision procedurally unfair, and therefore unlawful. Given this finding, I would dismiss the appeal. The judgments of both the British Columbia Supreme Court and the British Columbia Court of Appeal are well founded.

· · ·

[23] With regard to the first issue, the appellants argue that on an application for *habeas corpus* in this context, the scope of a provincial superior court's review is limited to an

assessment of whether the decision was "lawful." In the appellants' view, the merits of the underlying decision are irrelevant to that assessment. Only the Federal Court can assess the reasonableness of federal administrative decisions. The respondent argues, on the contrary, that it is open to a superior court on an application for *habeas corpus* to review the reasonableness of a correctional decision which resulted in a deprivation of liberty.

[24] The interveners largely support Mr. Khela on this issue. The British Columbia Civil Liberties Association ("BCCLA") argues that to determine whether a decision was "lawful," a provincial superior court hearing a *habeas corpus* application must be able to conduct a robust review. It nevertheless cautions against allowing a superior court to conduct a "wholesale review for 'reasonableness.'" According to the Canadian Civil Liberties Association ("CCLA"), *habeas corpus*, as a *Canadian Charter of Rights and Freedoms* remedy, should be interpreted in a manner that is responsive to the particular needs of an individual who has been unlawfully deprived of his or her liberty. For this purpose, a superior court must be able to consider the merits of the underlying decision. Finally, the John Howard Society of Canada and the Canadian Association of Elizabeth Fry Societies submit that the appellants' interpretation of the scope of *habeas corpus* is too restrictive, but that "*Dunsmuir* reasonableness" cannot apply as a standard of review on a *habeas corpus* application ... .

• • •

A. Habeas Corpus: The History and Nature of the Remedy

[27] W. Blackstone, in his *Commentaries on the Laws of England* (1768), vol. III, c. 8, at p. 131, asserted that *habeas corpus* is "the great and efficacious writ in all manner of illegal confinement" (cited by D. Parkes, "The 'Great Writ' Reinvigorated? *Habeas Corpus* in Contemporary Canada" (2012), 36 Man. L.J. 351, at p. 352); *May* at para. 19; W.F. Duker, *A Constitutional History of Habeas Corpus* (1980), at p. 3). In an earlier incarnation, *habeas corpus* was a means to ensure that the defendant in an action was brought physically before the Court. (Duker, at p. 4; J. Farbey, R.J. Sharpe and S. Atrill, *The Law of Habeas Corpus* (3rd ed. 2011), at p. 16; P.D. Halliday, *Habeas Corpus: From England to Empire* (2010), at p. 2). Over time, however, the writ was transformed into a vehicle for reviewing the justification for a person's imprisonment (Duker, at p. 4). Indeed, by the late 17th century, Vaughan C.J. of the Court of Common Pleas stated that "[t]he Writ of *habeas corpus* is now the most usual remedy by which a man is restored again to his liberty, if he have been against law deprived of it" (Duker, at p. 54, citing *Bushell's Case* (1670), Vaughan 135, 124 E.R. 1006, at p. 1007).

[28] The first legislation respecting *habeas corpus* was enacted in 1641. The remedy was subsequently codified a second time in the *Habeas Corpus Act* of 1679 (Engl.), 31 Cha. 2, c. 2 (T. Cromwell, "Habeas Corpus and Correctional Law—An Introduction" (1997), 3 Queen's L.J. 295, at p. 298), the many purposes of which included addressing problematic delays in obtaining the writ, ensuring that prisoners were provided with copies of their warrants so that they would know the grounds for their detention, and ensuring that prisoners "would not be taken to places beyond the reach of the writ" (Farbey, Sharpe and Atrill, at p. 16; Halliday, at pp. 239-40).

[29] Through both the *Charter* and the common law, Canada has attempted to maintain and uphold many of the goals of the *Habeas Corpus Act*, which embodied the evolving

purposes and principles of the writ. *Habeas corpus* has become an essential remedy in Canadian law. In *May*, this Court emphasized the importance of *habeas corpus* in the protection of two of our fundamental rights:

> (1) the right to liberty of the person and the right not to be deprived thereof except in accordance with the principles of fundamental justice (s. 7 of the *Charter*); and (2) the right not to be arbitrarily detained or imprisoned (s. 9 of the *Charter*). [para. 22]

These rights belong to everyone in Canada, including those serving prison sentences (*May*, at paras. 23-25). *Habeas corpus* is in fact the strongest tool a prisoner has to ensure that the deprivation of his or her liberty is not unlawful. In articulating the scope of the writ both in the *Miller* trilogy and in *May*, the Court has ensured that the rule of law continues to run within penitentiary walls (*Martineau v. Matsqui Institution Disciplinary Board*, [1980] 1 S.C.R. 602, at p. 622) and that any deprivation of a prisoner's liberty is justified.

[30] To be successful, an application for *habeas corpus* must satisfy the following criteria. First, the applicant must establish that he or she has been deprived of liberty. Once a deprivation of liberty is proven, the applicant must raise a legitimate ground upon which to question its legality. If the applicant has raised such a ground, the onus shifts to the respondent authorities to show that the deprivation of liberty was lawful (Farbey, Sharpe and Atrill, at pp. 84-85; *May*, at paras. 71 and 74).

B. Court Oversight of Penal Institutions

[31] Both the Federal Court and provincial superior courts are tasked with reviewing decisions made within federal prison walls. Section 18 of the *Federal Courts Act*, R.S.C. 1985, c. F-7 ("*FCA*"), confers exclusive original jurisdiction on the Federal Court to issue an injunction, writ of *certiorari*, writ of prohibition, writ of *mandamus* or writ of *quo warranto*, or grant declaratory relief against any federal board, commission or other tribunal. In *Martineau* this Court held that the writ of *certiorari* is available if an administrative decision was unfair, regardless of whether the decision was "judicial or quasi-judicial" (at pp. 628-29 and 634). Dickson J. (as he then was) stated, in minority concurring reasons, that under s. 18, *certiorari* is available in the Federal Court whenever "a public body has power to decide any matter affecting the rights, interests, property, privileges, or liberties of any person" (pp. 622-23).

[32] However, *habeas corpus* was "deliberately omit[ted]" from the list of writs set out in s. 18 of the *FCA*. This means that although the Federal Court has a general review jurisdiction, it cannot issue the writ of *habeas corpus* (*Miller*, at pp. 624-26). Jurisdiction to grant *habeas corpus* with regard to inmates remains with the provincial superior courts.

[33] The jurisdiction of the provincial superior courts over prisoners in federal institutions was explained by this Court in the 1985 *Miller* trilogy and confirmed more recently in *May*. In the trilogy, Le Dain J. held that a provincial superior court has jurisdiction to hear an application for *habeas corpus* in order to review the validity of a detention authorized by a federal decision maker, despite the fact that alternative remedies are available in the Federal Court (*Miller*, at pp. 626 and 640-41). Le Dain J. concluded in *Miller*:

> [H]abeas corpus should lie to determine the validity of a particular form of confinement in a penitentiary *notwithstanding that the same issue may be determined upon certiorari in the Federal Court*. The proper scope of the availability of *habeas corpus* must be considered first

on its own merits, apart from the possible problems arising from concurrent or overlapping jurisdiction. *The general importance of [*habeas corpus*] as the traditional means of challenging deprivations of liberty is such that its proper development and adaptation to the modern realities of confinement in a prison setting should not be compromised by concerns about conflicting jurisdiction.* [Emphasis added; pp. 640-41.]

Thus, the availability of the writ is more important than the possibility of hypothetical issues arising as a result of concurrent jurisdiction.

[34] Le Dain J. also held in *Miller* that relief in the form of *habeas corpus* is available in a provincial superior court to an inmate whose "residual liberty" has been reduced by a decision of the prison authorities, and that this relief is distinct from a possible decision to release the inmate entirely from the correctional system (*Miller*, at p. 641). Decisions which might affect an offender's residual liberty include, but are not limited to, administrative segregation, confinement in a special handling unit and, as in the case at bar, a transfer to a higher security institution.

[35] Finally, *Miller* enhanced the effectiveness of *habeas corpus* by confirming that inmates may apply for *certiorari* in aid of *habeas corpus*. Without *certiorari* in aid, a court hearing a *habeas corpus* application would consider only the "facts as they appear[ed] on the face of [the] return" or on the "face" of the decision, as the case may be, in determining whether the deprivation of liberty was lawful (D.A.C. Harvey, *The Law of Habeas Corpus in Canada* (1974), at p. 103). But *certiorari* in aid brings the record before the reviewing judge so that he or she may examine it to determine whether the challenged decision was lawful (*Mooring v. Canada (National Parole Board)*, [1996] 1 S.C.R. 75, at para. 117). *Certiorari* in aid therefore operates to make *habeas corpus* more effective by requiring production of the record of the proceedings that resulted in the decision in question (*Miller*, at p. 624; Chief Justice Laskin in *Mitchell v. The Queen*, [1976] 2 S.C.R. 570, at p. 578).

[36] It should be noted that *certiorari* applied for in aid of *habeas* corpus is different from *certiorari* applied for on its own. The latter is often used to quash an order, and it is only available in the Federal Court to an applicant challenging a federal administrative decision. In the context of a *habeas corpus* application, what is in issue is only the writ of *certiorari* employed to "inform the [c]ourt" and assist it in making the correct determination in a specific case, and not the writ of *certiorari* used to bring the record before the decision maker in order to "have it quashed" as would be done on an application for judicial review in the Federal Court (Cromwell, at p. 321).

[37] This being said, there are, from a functional standpoint, many similarities between a proceeding for *habeas corpus* with *certiorari* in aid and a judicial review proceeding in the Federal Court. After all, "judicial review," "[i]n its broadest sense," simply refers to the supervisory role played by the courts to ensure that executive power is exercised in a manner consistent with the rule of law (Farbey, Sharpe and Atrill, at pp. 18 and 56). This is also the purpose of *habeas corpus*, if distilled to its essence (see generally, Farbey, Sharpe and Atrill, at pp. 18 and 52-56).

[38] Despite the functional similarities between *certiorari* applied for in aid of *habeas corpus* in a provincial superior court and *certiorari* applied for on its own under the *FCA*, however, there are major remedial and procedural differences between them. These differences include (a) the remedies available in each forum, (b) the burden of proof and (c) the non-discretionary nature of *habeas corpus*.

[39] In the Federal Court, a wide array of relief can be sought in an application for judicial review of a CSC decision (see s. 18.1(3)(b) of the *FCA*). But all a provincial superior court can do is determine that the detention is unlawful and then rule on a motion for discharge.

[40] Further, on an application for judicial review, it is the applicant who must show that the federal decision maker made an error (*May*, at para. 71, citing to s. 18.1(4) of the *FCA*), whereas, on an application for *habeas corpus*, the legal burden rests with the detaining authorities once the prisoner has established a deprivation of liberty and raised a legitimate ground upon which to challenge its legality (*May*, at para. 71; Farbey, Sharpe and Atrill, at pp. 84-86). This particular shift in onus is unique to the writ of *habeas corpus*. Shifting the legal burden onto the detaining authorities is compatible with the very foundation of the law of *habeas corpus*, namely that a deprivation of liberty is permissible only if the party effecting the deprivation can demonstrate that it is justified. The shift is particularly understandable in the context of an emergency or involuntary inmate transfer, as an individual who has been deprived of liberty in such a context will not have the requisite resources or the ability to discover why the deprivation has occurred or to build a case that it was unlawful. On an application for judicial review, on the other hand, the onus remains on the individual challenging the impugned decision to show that the decision was unreasonable.

[41] Finally, judicial review is an inherently discretionary remedy (C. Ford, "Dogs and Tails: Remedies in Administrative Law," in C.M. Flood and L. Sossin, eds., *Administrative Law in Context* (2nd ed. 2013), 85, at pp. 107-9). On an application for judicial review, the court has the authority to determine at the beginning of the hearing whether the case should proceed (D.J. Mullan, *Administrative Law* (2001), at p. 481). In contrast, a writ of *habeas corpus* issues as of right if the applicant proves a deprivation of liberty and raises a legitimate ground upon which to question the legality of the deprivation. In other words, the matter *must* proceed to a hearing if the inmate shows some basis for concluding that the detention is unlawful (*May*, at paras. 33 and 71; Farbey, Sharpe and Atrill, at pp. 52-54).

[42] Twenty years after the *Miller* trilogy, in *May*, this Court stressed the importance of having superior courts hear *habeas corpus* applications. The majority in *May* unambiguously upheld the *ratio* of *Miller*: "[h]*abeas corpus* jurisdiction should not be declined merely because of the existence of an alternative remedy" (para. 34). In *May*, the Court established that, in light of the historical purposes of the writ, provincial superior courts should decline jurisdiction to hear *habeas corpus* applications in only two very limited circumstances:

> ... where (1) a statute such as the *Criminal Code*, R.S.C. 1985 c. C-46, confers jurisdiction on a court of appeal to correct the errors of a lower court and release the applicant if need be or (2) the legislator has put in place complete, comprehensive and expert procedure for review of an administrative decision. [para. 50]

As was true in *May*, the first exception does not apply to the instant case. As for the second exception, the appellants have offered no argument to suggest that the transfer and review process of CSC has, since *May*, become "a complete, comprehensive and expert procedure" (paras. 50-51).

[43] The majority in *May* set out five factors that provided further support for the position that provincial superior courts should hear *habeas corpus* applications from federal prisoners regardless of whether relief is available in the Federal Court.

[44] First, given their vulnerability and the realities of confinement in prisons, inmates should, despite concerns about conflicting jurisdiction, have the ability to choose between the forums and remedies available to them, (*May*, at paras. 66-67). As this Court very succinctly put it in *May*, "[t]he [remedial] option belongs to the applicant" (para. 44).

[45] Second, there is no reason to suppose that the Federal Court is more expert than the provincial superior courts when it comes to inmates' fundamental rights. The Federal Court is of course well acquainted with administrative decisions and administrative procedure. The superior courts, on the other hand, are eminently familiar with the application of *Charter* principles and values, which are directly in issue when an inmate claims to have been unlawfully deprived of liberty (*May*, at para. 68).

[46] Third, a hearing of a *habeas corpus* application in a superior court can be obtained more rapidly than a hearing of a judicial review application in the Federal Court. For example, according to Rule 4 of the *Criminal Rules of the Supreme Court of British Columbia*, SI 97/140, a hearing of a *habeas corpus* application requires only six days' notice. This is minimal in comparison with the timeline for having a judicial review application heard in the Federal Court. In that court, if the parties take the full time allotted to them at each step of the procedure, the request that a date be set for the hearing of the application will be filed 160 days after the challenged decision (s. 18.1(2) of the *FCA* and Rules 301 to 314 of the *Federal Court Rules, 1998*, SOR/98-106, cited at para. 69 of *May*).

[47] Fourth, inmates have greater local access to a provincial superior court. This Court recognized the importance of local access in both *Miller* (at pp. 624-26) and *R. v. Gamble*, [1988] 2 S.C.R. 595 (at pp. 634-35), as well as in *May* (para. 70).

[48] Fifth, as I mentioned above, the non-discretionary nature of *habeas corpus* and the burden of proof on an application for this remedy both favour the applicant.

[49] These factors all weigh against acceptance of a bifurcated jurisdiction. The history and nature of the remedy, combined with what this Court has said on this issue in the past, unequivocally support a finding that favours access to justice for prisoners, namely that of concurrent jurisdiction. As the majority stated in *May*, "[t]imely judicial oversight, in which provincial superior courts must play a concurrent if not predominant role, is still necessary to safeguard the human rights and civil liberties of prisoners" (para. 72).

[50] The cases discussed above form the basis for the approach the Court must take to the first issue.

C. Scope of the Review

[51] In essence, the effect of the *Miller* trilogy and *May* is that an inmate who has been deprived of his or her liberty as a result of an unlawful decision of a federal board, commission, or tribunal can apply to a provincial superior court for relief in the form of *habeas corpus*. What must now be done is to establish the scope of that court's review power.

[52] As I mentioned above, on an application for *habeas corpus*, the basic question before the court is whether or not the decision was lawful. Thus far, it is clear that a decision will not be lawful if the detention is not lawful, if the decision maker lacks jurisdiction to order the deprivation of liberty (see, for example, *R. v. J.P.G.* (2000), 130 O.A.C. 343), or if there has been a breach of procedural fairness (see *May*, *Miller* and *Cardinal*). However, given the flexibility and the importance of the writ, as well as the underlying reasons why the jurisdiction of the provincial superior courts is concurrent with that of the Federal

Court, it is clear that a review for lawfulness will sometimes require an assessment of the decision's reasonableness.

[53] Including a reasonableness assessment in the scope of the review is consistent with this Court's case law. In particular, allowing provincial superior courts to assess reasonableness in the review follows logically from how this Court has framed the remedy and from the limits the courts have placed on the avenues through which the remedy can be obtained.

[54] This Court has recognized in its decisions that *habeas corpus* should develop over time to ensure that the law remains consistent with the remedy's underlying goals: no one should be deprived of their liberty without lawful authority. The significance of *habeas corpus* to those who have been deprived of their liberty means that it must be developed in a meaningful way (*Miller*, at pp. 640-41). In *May*, the Court quoted with approval the statement by Black J. of United States Supreme Court that *habeas corpus* is "not now and never has been a static, narrow, formalistic remedy; its scope has grown to achieve its grand purpose—the protection of individuals against erosion of their right to be free from wrongful restraints upon their liberty" (*May*, at para. 21; *Jones v. Cunningham*, 371 U.S. 236 (1962), at p. 243; see also the preface to R.J. Sharpe's *The Law of Habeas Corpus* (2nd ed. 1989)). This remedy is crucial to those whose residual liberty has been taken from them by the state, and this alone suffices to ensure that it is rarely subject to restrictions.

[55] This Court has been reluctant to place limits on the avenues through which an individual may apply for the remedy. As I mentioned above, the Court confirmed in *Miller* that *habeas corpus* will remain available to federal inmates in the superior courts regardless of the existence of other avenues for redress (pp. 640-41). Similarly, Wilson J. stated in *Gamble* that courts have not bound themselves, nor should they do so, to limited categories or definitions of review where the review concerns the subject's liberty (pp. 639-40). In *May*, the Court confirmed that there are in fact only two instances in which a provincial superior court should decline to hear a *habeas corpus* application: (1) where the *Peiroo* exception applies (that is, where the legislature has put in place a complete, comprehensive and expert procedure) (*Peiroo v. Canada (Minister of Employment and Immigration)* (1989), 69 O.R. (2d) 253), and (2) where a statute such as the *Criminal Code*, R.S.C. 1985, c. C-46, confers jurisdiction on a court of appeal to correct errors of a lower court and release the applicant if need be (*May*, at paras. 44 and 50). Reviews of decisions of correctional authorities for reasonableness do not fall into either of these exceptions, and in accordance with *May*, they therefore can and should be considered by a provincial superior court.

[56] Many of the same principles which weighed in favour of concurrent jurisdiction in *May* apply to the determination of the scope of a provincial superior court's review power. First, each applicant should be entitled to choose his or her avenue of relief. If a court hearing a *habeas corpus* application cannot review the reasonableness of the underlying decision, then a prisoner who has been deprived of his or her liberty as a result of an unreasonable decision does not have a choice of avenues through which to obtain redress but must apply to the Federal Court.

[57] Second, there is no reason to assume that the Federal Court is more expert than the superior courts in determining whether a deprivation of liberty is lawful. While it is true that the Federal Court may regularly be asked to determine whether decisions regarding a "mere loss of privileges" are reasonable, when a loss of liberty is involved, the

superior courts are well versed in the *Charter* rights that apply when an inmate is transferred to a higher security facility (s. 7 and s. 9).

[58] Third, if inmates are not able to obtain review of their potentially unreasonable loss of liberty under an application for *habeas corpus*, they will have to wade through the lengthy grievance procedure available under the statute in order to have their concerns heard. If, for example, an inmate has lost his or her liberty as a result of a decision that was made on the basis of irrelevant evidence or was completely unsupported by the evidence, he or she is entitled to apply for and obtain a speedy remedy.

[59] In the instant case, the appellants have filed an affidavit suggesting that *habeas corpus* proceedings are becoming increasingly time-consuming as superior court judges review the records of prison decision makers. There is a difficulty, however, with accepting this affidavit as convincing evidence that a *habeas corpus* application in a superior court no longer provides quicker relief than an application for judicial review in the Federal Court. Although the affidavit outlines how long it has taken to obtain decisions on *habeas corpus* applications in *certain* circumstances, it does not compare this with the length of time it takes to obtain decisions from the Federal Court on applications for judicial review in similar circumstances.

[60] The case at bar itself provides compelling evidence against the proposition advanced in the appellants' affidavit. Mr. Khela, after receiving the final decision with respect to his transfer on March 15, 2010, filed a notice of application in the British Columbia Supreme Court on April 27, 2010. The notice stated that the application would be made on May 11, 2010. A decision was rendered only ten days later by Bruce J. of that court.

[61] Moreover, the affidavit failed to take into account the structure of the grievance procedure provided for in the *Corrections and Conditional Release Regulations*, SOR/92-620 ("*CCRR*"). Mr. Khela could not have challenged the decision in the Federal Court for want of procedural fairness and for unreasonableness without first going through an internal review process required by the statutory scheme. According to the statutory scheme, Mr. Khela would have had to submit a complaint. According to *Commissioner's Directive 081*, "Offender Complaints and Grievances," such complaints have multiple levels. The Directive indicates that grievors who are dissatisfied with the "decision rendered at the *final* level ... may seek judicial review of the decision at the Federal Court" (s. 15 (emphasis added)). However, even if an inmate's complaint is designated as a high priority, it can take as long as 90 days after the complaint was made before the inmate receives the final decision. Mr. Khela would not have been able to apply for judicial review until after he had received a decision at that level. Given the structure of this grievance procedure, an application for *habeas corpus* in a provincial superior court remains the more timely remedy.

[62] The appellants argue to allow the provincial superior courts to review CSC transfer decisions for reasonableness would lengthen the duration of applications, increase their cost and cause a shift in the allocation of judicial resources. However, as Wilson J. stated in *Gamble*, "[r]elief in the form of *habeas corpus* should not be withheld for reasons of mere convenience" (p. 635).

[63] Fourth, the fact that inmates have local access to relief in the form of *habeas corpus* also weighs in favour of including a review for reasonableness. In *May*, this Court noted that "it would be unfair if federal prisoners did not have the same access to *habeas corpus* as do provincial prisoners" (*May*, at para. 70). If the appellants' position were

accepted, whereas provincial prisoners can apply to their provincial superior court for *habeas corpus* on procedural or jurisdictional grounds while also having that same court review the decision which resulted in their loss of liberty for reasonableness on an application for judicial review (see, for example, *Libo-on v. Alberta (Fort Saskatchewan Correctional Centre)*, 2004 ABQB 416, 32 Alta. L.R. (4th) 128, at para. 1), federal inmates would be required to apply to two different courts for redress flowing from a single impugned decision with the exact same record. It seems inconsistent to force the latter to do so solely because they are in federal prisons.

[64] Fifth, the non-discretionary nature of *habeas corpus* and the traditional onus on an application for that remedy favour an inmate who claims to have been unlawfully deprived of his or her liberty. If the inmate were forced to apply to the Federal Court to determine whether the deprivation was unreasonable, the remedy would be a discretionary one. Further, on an application for judicial review, the onus would be on the applicant to show that the transfer decision was unreasonable. As Farbey, Sharpe and Atrill state, "[i]t would be wrong ... to deny [the benefits of the writ] by forcing the applicant to pursue some alternative remedy (p. 54).

[65] Ultimately, weighing these factors together leads to the conclusion that allowing a provincial superior court to conduct a review for reasonableness in deciding an application for *habeas corpus* would lead to greater access to a more effective remedy. Reasonableness should therefore be regarded as one element of lawfulness.

[66] Whether a decision is "lawful" cannot relate to jurisdiction alone. The appellants suggest that a review on a *habeas corpus* application is "limited to an analysis of whether there is jurisdiction to make a decision," as opposed to a review of the reasonableness of the underlying decision. For this proposition, the appellants rely on Le Dain J.'s conclusions in *Miller* (1) that *certiorari* in aid cannot be employed to convert an application for *habeas corpus* into an appeal on the merits (p. 632), and (2) that an application for *habeas corpus* addresses issues going to jurisdiction rather than issues going to the merits (p. 630). However, the appellants misread the context of Le Dain J.'s comments, which were made in reference to the earlier cases of *Goldhar v. The Queen*, [1960] S.C.R. 431, *Re Sproule* (1886), 12 S.C.R. 140, and *Re Trepanier* (1885), 12 S.C.R. 111. Le Dain J. was simply echoing earlier decisions in which this Court had held that *habeas corpus* is not to be used to appeal a *conviction*. Thus, he was saying in that case what the Court subsequently clarified in *May*, namely that "provincial superior courts should decline *habeas corpus* jurisdiction ... where ... a statute such as the *Criminal Code* ... confers jurisdiction on a court of appeal to correct the errors of a lower court and release the applicant if need be" (para. 50). This cannot be interpreted as a statement that a provincial superior court may not rule on the reasonableness of an administrative decision in the context of an application for *habeas corpus* with *certiorari* in aid.

[67] Nor does *May* prohibit a provincial superior court from examining the reasonableness of an underlying transfer decision in the context of an application for *habeas corpus* with *certiorari* in aid. In *May*, this Court confirmed that "[a] deprivation of liberty will only be lawful where it is within the jurisdiction of the decision maker" (para. 77). This cannot be read as a signal that *only* decisions outside the decision maker's jurisdiction will be unlawful. On the contrary, it simply means that jurisdiction is one requirement to be met for a decision to be lawful. On its own, however, this requirement is not sufficient to make a decision lawful. A decision that is within the decision maker's jurisdiction

but that lacks the safeguards of procedural fairness will not be lawful. Likewise, a decision that lacks an evidentiary foundation or that is arbitrary or unreasonable cannot be lawful, regardless of whether the decision maker had jurisdiction to make it.

• • •

[70] Finally, requiring inmates to challenge the reasonableness of a CSC transfer decision in the Federal Court could also result in a waste of judicial resources. For example, an inmate may take issue with both the process and the reasonableness of such a decision. Were we to accept the appellants' position, it would be possible for the inmate to first challenge that decision for want of procedural fairness by applying for *habeas corpus* with *certiorari* in aid in a provincial superior court and then, should that application fail, challenge the reasonableness of the same decision by seeking *certiorari* in the Federal Court. This bifurcation makes little sense given that *certiorari* in aid is available, and it would undoubtedly lead to a duplication of proceedings and have a negative impact on judicial economy.

[71] In an earlier article, Robert Sharpe had written that "the scope of review on *habeas corpus* depends upon the material which may be looked at by the court" (R.J. Sharpe, "Habeas Corpus in Canada" (1976), 2 Dal. L.J. 241, at p. 262; Chiasson J.A., at para. 72). If this is correct, which I believe it is, and the scope of the review is inextricably related to the material before the reviewing court, it is only logical on an application for *habeas corpus* to include an assessment of reasonableness in a review for lawfulness. Given that it is now well settled that on an application for *habeas corpus* with *certiorari* in aid the court will have before it "the complete record of inferior proceedings," the court has the power to review that record to ensure that the record supports the decision (Farbey, Sharpe and Atrill, at pp. 45-46). This will also aid in the conservation of scarce judicial resources.

[72] The above reasoning leads to the conclusion that an inmate may challenge the reasonableness of his or her deprivation of liberty by means of an application for *habeas corpus*. Ultimately, then, where a deprivation of liberty results from a federal administrative decision, that decision can be subject to either of two forms of review, and the inmate may choose the forum he or she prefers. An inmate can choose either to challenge the reasonableness of the decision by applying for judicial review under s. 18 of the *FCA* or to have the decision reviewed for reasonableness by means of an application for *habeas corpus*. "Reasonableness" is therefore a "legitimate ground" upon which to question the legality of a deprivation of liberty in an application for *habeas corpus*.

[73] A transfer decision that does not fall within the "range of possible, acceptable outcomes which are defensible in respect of the facts and law" will be unlawful (*Dunsmuir*, at para. 47). Similarly, a decision that lacks "justification, transparency and intelligibility" will be unlawful (*ibid.*). For it to be lawful, the reasons for and record of the decision must "in fact or in principle support the conclusion reached" (*Newfoundland and Labrador Nurses' Union v. Newfoundland and Labrador (Treasury Board)*, 2011 SCC 62, [2011] 3 S.C.R. 708, at para. 12, quoting with approval D. Dyzenhaus, "The Politics of Deference: Judicial Review and Democracy," in M. Taggart, ed., *The Province of Administrative Law* (1997), 279, at p. 304).

[74] As things stand, a decision will be unreasonable, and therefore unlawful, if an inmate's liberty interests are sacrificed absent any evidence or on the basis of unreliable or irrelevant evidence, or evidence that cannot support the conclusion, although I do not foreclose the possibility that it may also be unreasonable on other grounds. Deference

will be shown to a determination that evidence is reliable, but the authorities will nonetheless have to explain that determination.

[75] A review to determine whether a decision was reasonable, and therefore lawful, necessarily requires deference (*Dunsmuir*, at para. 47; *Canada (Citizenship and Immigration) v. Khosa*, 2009 SCC 12, [2009] 1 S.C.R. 339, at para. 59; *Newfoundland and Labrador Nurses' Union*, at paras. 11-12). An involuntary transfer decision is nonetheless an administrative decision made by a decision maker with expertise in the environment of a particular penitentiary. To apply any standard other than reasonableness in reviewing such a decision could well lead to the micromanagement of prisons by the courts.

[76] Like the decision at issue in *Lake*, a transfer decision requires a "fact-driven inquiry involving the weighing of various factors and possessing a 'negligible legal dimension'" (*Lake v. Canada (Minister of Justice)*, 2008 SCC 23, [2008] 1 S.C.R. 761, at paras. 38 and 41). The statute outlines a number of factors to which a warden must adhere when transferring an inmate: the inmate must be placed in the least restrictive environment that will still assure the safety of the public, penitentiary staff and other inmates, should have access to his or her home community, and should be transferred to a compatible cultural and linguistic environment (s. 28 CCRA). Determining whether an inmate poses a threat to the security of the penitentiary or of the individuals who live and work in it requires intimate knowledge of that penitentiary's culture and of the behaviour of the individuals inside its walls. Wardens and the Commissioner possess this knowledge, and related practical experience, to a greater degree than a provincial superior court judge.

[77] The intervener the BCCLA argues that the application of a standard of review of reasonableness should not change the basic structure or benefits of the writ. I agree. First, the traditional onuses associated with the writ will remain unchanged. Once the inmate has demonstrated that there was a deprivation of liberty and casts doubt on the reasonableness of the deprivation, the onus shifts to the respondent authorities to prove that the transfer was reasonable in light of all the circumstances.

[78] Second, the writ remains non-discretionary as far as the decision to review the case is concerned. If the applicant raises a legitimate doubt as to the reasonableness of the detention, the provincial superior court judge is required to examine the substance of the decision and determine whether the evidence presented by the detaining authorities is reliable and supports their decision. Unlike the Federal Court in the context of an application for judicial review, a provincial superior court hearing a *habeas corpus* application has no inherent discretion to refuse to review the case (see Farbey, Sharpe and Atrill, at pp. 52-56). However, a residual discretion will come into play at the second stage of the *habeas corpus* proceeding, at which the judge, after reviewing the record, must decide whether to discharge the applicant.

[79] Third, the ability to challenge a decision on the basis that it is unreasonable does not necessarily change the standard of review that applies to other flaws in the decision or in the decision-making process. For instance, the standard for determining whether the decision maker complied with the duty of procedural fairness will continue to be "correctness."

[80] It will not be necessary to determine whether the decision made by the Warden in the instant case was unlawful on the basis of unreasonableness. As I will explain below, the decision was unlawful because it was procedurally unfair.

· · ·

[87] Where, pursuant to s. 27(3), the correctional authorities do not disclose to the inmate *all* the information considered in their transfer decision or a summary thereof, they should generally, if challenged on an application for *habeas corpus*, submit to the judge of the reviewing court a sealed affidavit that contains both the information that has been withheld from the inmate compared with the information that was disclosed and the reasons why disclosure of that information might jeopardize the security of the penitentiary, the safety of any person or the conduct of a lawful investigation.

[88] When the prison authorities rely on kites or anonymous tips to justify a transfer, they should also explain in the sealed affidavit why those tips are considered to be reliable. When liberty interests are at stake, procedural fairness also includes measures to verify the evidence being relied upon. If an individual is to suffer a form of deprivation of liberty, "procedural fairness includes a procedure for verifying the evidence adduced against him or her" (*Charkaoui v. Canada (Citizenship and Immigration)*, 2008 SCC 38, [2008] 2 S.C.R. 326, at para. 56).

[89] Section 27(3) authorizes the withholding of information when the Commissioner has "reasonable grounds to believe" that should the information be released, it might threaten the security of the prison, the safety of any person or the conduct of an investigation. The Commissioner, or his or her representative, is in the best position to determine whether such a risk could in fact materialize. As a result, the Commissioner, or the warden, is entitled to a margin of deference on this point. Similarly, the warden and the Commissioner are in the best position to determine whether a given source or informant is reliable. Some deference is accordingly owed on this point as well. If, however, certain information is withheld without invoking s. 27(3), deference will not be warranted, and the decision will be procedurally unfair and therefore unlawful.

[90] I should point out that not all breaches of the *CCRA* or the *CCRR* will be unfair. It will be up to the reviewing judge to determine whether a given breach has resulted in procedural unfairness. For instance, if s. 27(3) has been invoked erroneously or if there was a strictly technical breach of the statute, the reviewing judge must determine whether that error or that technicality rendered the decision procedurally unfair.

E. Lawfulness of the Deprivation of Liberty

[91] As I mentioned above, the writ of *habeas corpus* will issue if (1) the applicant has been deprived of his or her liberty and (2) that deprivation was unlawful. No one has contested the fact that the transfer of Mr. Khela to Kent Institution was a deprivation of his liberty. However, the parties disagree on whether that deprivation was lawful.

[92] It is clear from the record that the Warden, in making the transfer decision, considered information that she did not disclose to Mr. Khela. Nor did she give him an adequate summary of the missing information. The withholding of this information was not justified under s. 27(3). As a result, the Warden's decision did not meet the statutory requirements related to the duty of procedural fairness.

NOTE

In *Khela*, the Supreme Court goes to lengths to ensure that "*[h]abeas corpus* is in fact the strongest tool a prisoner has to ensure that the deprivation of his or her liberty is not unlawful." However, in pragmatic terms, some concern has been expressed about the importation of deference into *habeas corpus* review through the vehicle of reasonableness.

FURTHER READING

Kerr, Lisa. "The Chronic Failure of Control Prisoner Isolation in US and Canadian Law" (2015) 40:2 Queen's LJ 483.

Kerr, Lisa. "Contesting Expertise in Prison Law" (2014) 60:1 McGill LJ 43.

Kerr, Lisa. "The Origins of Unlawful Prison Policies" (2015) 4:1 Can J Human Rights 91.

O'Connor, Fergus J. *Halsbury's Laws of Canada: Penitentiaries, Jails and Prisoners* (Markham, Ont: LexisNexis Canada, 2014).

Zinger, Ivan. "Conditional Release and Human Rights in Canada: A Commentary" (2012) 54 Can J Corr 117.